ENVIRONMENTAL SCIENCE

A Framework for Decision Making

ENVIRONMENTAL SCIENCE
A Framework for Decision Making

DANIEL D. CHIRAS

University of Colorado at Denver

THE BENJAMIN/CUMMINGS PUBLISHING COMPANY, INC.
Menlo Park, California • Reading, Massachusetts • Don Mills, Ontario
Wokingham, U.K. • Amsterdam • Sydney • Singapore
Tokyo • Mexico City • Bogota • Santiago • San Juan

To My Mother and Father

Sponsoring Editor: Andrew Crowley
Developmental Editor: Bonnie Garmus
Production Editor: Julie Kranhold/Ex Libris
Copy Editor: William Waller
Designer: Gary Head
Art Coordinator: Sara Hunsaker
Photo Researcher: Jo Andrews
Artists: Wayne Clark, Parry Clark, Barbara Haynes
Cover photo by Dan Morrill Photography
Photo and text credits appear after the Glossary.

Library of Congress Cataloging in Publication Data

Chiras, Daniel D.
  Environmental science.

  Includes bibliographies and index.
  1. Environmental policy.   2. Environmental protection.
3. Natural resources. I. Title.
HC79.E5C485 1985   363.7   84-24269

abcdefghij—MU—8987654

ISBN 0-8053-2255-8

The Benjamin/Cummings Publishing Company, Inc.
2727 Sand Hill Road
Menlo Park, Ca 94025

Preface

My primary goal in writing *Environmental Science: A Framework for Decision Making* was to create a current, comprehensive, and holistic overview of critical environmental issues useful to readers with little or no background in science. The subjects and controversies explored in this book are essential to every one of us—because they are the issues that must be decided today. My hope is that this book will serve as a valuable and solid foundation for its readers who will make the decisions that shape the future of our world.

Because environmental problems are so broad in scope, such decisions require knowledge and understanding from many seemingly unrelated disciplines. Thus, I have chosen an eclectic approach for this text, employing areas of ecology, geology, atmospheric science, biology, chemistry, law, economics, ethics, and others to examine the world around us. The melding of these many disciplines results in new ways of looking at and interpreting our environment and the vital role we play in determining its destiny.

Themes

The central theme of this book is that the time for action is running short; overpopulation, resource depletion, pollution, neglect, and indifference are rapidly catching up with us. Long-term survival on this planet means developing a sustainable society—one that conserves natural resources, controls population growth, explores alternative sources of clean energy, and relies whenever possible on renewable resources. Such a society may seem foreign or even unattainable, but it remains our only realistic hope for continued prosperity. Careful planning and implementation now will usher in our sustainable future.

The second major theme is that complex environmental problems require complex solutions, not simply ameliorative steps that address only the symptoms. Political, technological, economic, and indeed even ethical changes all come into play in solving the world's environmental dilemmas. I have therefore employed simple analytical and conceptual models that will help the student see environmental issues more clearly. Proper use of these models will allow the reader to focus on the interrelationships inherent in these intricate issues and thereby reach appropriate solutions.

Finally, and most importantly, this book stresses that we are all part of the problem, and must therefore be part of the solution. There is no "them" to blame; the blame rests equally on all our shoulders. Air pollution is not just a problem of inadequate laws, but also the result of our burning wood, consuming electricity produced at coal-fired power plants, and driving cars with inefficient internal combustion engines. Solving these problems need not mean reverting to old-fashioned ways, or even making tremendous sacrifices. It does mean using energy and resources wisely, conserving energy whenever possible, recycling all that we can, and utilizing renewable resources.

The future belongs to each of us. We can remain apathetic and permit it to become dirty, limited, and dreary; or we can make it clean, full of opportunity, and richly rewarding. The choice is ours.

Organization of This Book

This book is divided into five parts and organized around three central issues: population, resources, and pollution. Part I provides the necessary base of knowledge in ecology and human social development. In essence, it concentrates on the big picture and its interrelationships—a view sorely needed in this age of specialization. Part II deals with population growth, the impact of population, and population control. Part III treats a variety of resources and outlines plans for attaining a sustainable society. Part IV presents the enigma of pollution, and the legal, technical, and personal solutions for it. Part V is the capstone of the book and places the environmental crisis against a social backdrop by examining ethics, economics, and politics. It specifically concentrates on the steps necessary in making the transition to a sustainable society.

Special Features

In order to make this text more useful as a teaching and learning tool and to increase student interest and involvement, the following special features have been included:

Models

Perhaps the greatest distinguishing feature of this book is the simple conceptual models presented in theory in Chapters 2 and 17, and then applied where appropriate throughout the text. These simple diagrams are easy to understand and teach, and are designed to encourage holistic thinking. For the mathematically inclined, they can even be adapted to the computer. Below is a brief description of each model and its importance:

- *Population, Resource, and Pollution Model:* presents a fuller view of the human niche, and examines the interdependence among humans, resources, and pollution.

- *Multiple Cause-and-Effect Model:* helps students to analyze the causes of many of our current environmental dilemmas by exhibiting the tangled web of cause and effect.

- *Impact Analysis:* shows the various impacts humans can have on the environment and the ways we are affected by our own actions.

- *Risk Analysis Model:* examines the risks and benefits associated with today's new and existing hazards.

- *Ethical Analysis Model:* looks at some key ethical factors involved in making critically important environmental decisions.

To give the students more familiarity with the conceptual models, eight applied exercises are included in various chapters.

Point/Counterpoints and Viewpoints

As might be expected, the complexity involved in solving environmental problems oftentimes results in hotly contested debates:

- Is outerspace the answer to our population and resource problems?

- Does hunger exist in America?

- Should smoking be allowed in public places?

- What are our obligations to future generations?

- What impact do illegal aliens have on our economy?

- How do we control human population growth?

These and many other important and timely issues are debated in point/counterpoints written specifically for this book by such luminaries as Ben Bova, Garrett Hardin, Julian Simon, Nancy Amidei, Richard Lamm, Robert Rodale, and many others. The purpose of including these point/counterpoints is to present both sides of complex issues and to spur classroom discussions. Individual editorials present additional viewpoints on environmental issues.

Chapter Supplements

In order to provide more flexibility to the instructor, I've included Chapter Supplements at the end of appropriate chapters. Some topics of current interest include acid rain, stratospheric ozone depletion, radiation pollution, and nuclear war. These supplements are designed to be complementary, and may be omitted without any loss in continuity.

Unique Coverage

In addition to the traditional environmental science topics, I have included chapters on some new and particularly important topics such as hazardous wastes, personal and occupational pollutants, toxicology and environmental health, and risk assessment. Once again, my goals are to provide an up-to-date and flexible text to meet the needs of a wide variety of course outlines.

Illustration Program

The text is punctuated with over 400 photos, illustrations, graphs, and maps. In addition, there are four full-color galleries on biomes, endangered species, Landsat images, and resource misuse.

Acknowledgments

This book is the offspring of a great many people, for whom a simple thanks seems terribly inadequate. First and foremost are the thousands of scholars in all scientific disciplines. Their ideas, their research, indeed their lives, form the foundation upon which this book rests. To them a world of thanks and an enormous debt of gratitude.

A special note of appreciation to Bill Waller and Andrew Alden who expertly and carefully smoothed out the manuscript's rough spots; to research assistants Dave Shugarts, Cynthia Stuart, Diane Short, and Ann Beckenhauer, who worked with me in finding references and updating statistics; to Julie Kranhold and Sara Hunsaker of Ex Libris for their truly excellent production work; and to Wayne and Parry Clark and Barbara Haynes, who let their creativity run wild and produced superior artwork.

A gracious debt of gratitude to the hardworking, dedicated staff at Benjamin/Cummings who labored over this book as if it were their own. A special thanks to Jim Behnke, who kept a watchful eye throughout the project; to biology editor Andrew Crowley, who read and commented on the manuscript throughout, who infused the project with enthusiasm, and whose high standards helped produce a fine textbook; to Jo Andrews for her diligence and expertise in selecting appropriate photographs; to Lisa Stanziano, a conscientious editorial assistant; and to friend, compatriate, and developmental editor, Bonnie Garmus, who worked closely with me from the outset, who helped interpret reviewer's comments, who injected creativity and humor into the project, and who worked hard to improve the manuscript at each and every stage.

Many manuscript reviewers (listed below) provided very helpful and constructive criticism:

David M. Armstrong, *University of Colorado, Boulder*

Robert Auckerman, *Colorado State University*

Bayard H. Brattstrom, *California State University, Fullerton*

Lester Brown, *Worldwatch Institute*

Richard Haas, *California State University, Fresno*

John P. Harley, *Eastern Kentucky University*

Gary James, *Orange Coast College*

Alan R.P. Journet, *Southeast Missouri State University*

David Lovejoy, *Westfield State College*

Glenn P. Moffat, *Foothill College*

Charles Mohler, *Cornell University*

Brian C. Myres, *Cypress College*

John Peck, *St. Cloud State University*

Michael Priano, *Westchester Community College*

Joseph Priest, *Miami University*

Robert J. Robel, *Kansas State University*

Roger E. Thibault, *Bowling Green State University*

Leland Van Fossen, *DeAnza College*

Bruce Webb, *Animal Protection Institute*

Ross W. Westover, *Canada College*

Stephen W. Wilson, *Central Missouri State University*

Susan Wilson, *Miami Dade Community College*

I am very thankful for their caring and guidance. This book is so much better because of their insights, thoughts, and evaluations.

DANIEL D. CHIRAS

Brief Contents

Detailed Contents

I

PRINCIPLES OF THE ENVIRONMENT

1

Environmental Science: Reshaping Society

The ability of our minds to imagine, coupled with the ability of our hands to devise our images, brings us a power almost beyond our control.

JOAN MCINTYRE

Environmental science is a new name for an activity our species has been engaged in throughout time: learning how to live on this planet without damaging it or threatening our own existence in the process.

Today, environmental science is practiced by many thousands of specialists, ranging from researchers testing new metals to naturalists searching for new plants, to astronauts in space learning how to better monitor the earth's activities (Figure 1-1).

Defining Environmental Science

The word *environmental* broadly refers to everything around us: the air, the oceans, and the continents as well as the plants, animals, and microorganisms that inhabit them. *Science,* of course, refers to the deliberate and painstaking search for facts and natural laws. It seeks exactness through mathematics, insight through close observation, and foresight through theories.

Figure 1-1
The earth from space.

Mastering the Environment—and Ourselves

In early human history, environmental science did not exist as a recognized endeavor. Nonetheless, our earliest ancestors were avid students of the environment, observing plants and animals and learning to protect themselves from harmful ones and make use of others. When our ancestors turned to farming and began to settle in towns, they learned to make better use of animals and plants, and how to follow the movements of the stars to time annual planting and harvesting. As modern industries and nations arose, humans turned to resources such as coal and mineral ores—learning where they could be found, how they could be extracted efficiently, and how they could be made to serve our needs. In the process, we learned to master many forms of energy and matter, ultimately becoming manipulators of the environment with an awesome power to change the destiny of our planet.

Today, environmental science has come into being as an identifiable science in response to enormous environmental problems. These problems, the stuff of the daily headlines, include the many signs of overpopulation, the pains in the world economy as natural resources begin to grow scarce, pollution of all kinds, and the symptoms of societal despair and political instability.

At the root of these problems is a development never known before: we humans have now reached numbers that many experts believe threaten our own existence. For many reasons, the "out of sight, out of mind" philosophy so prevalent in past times is no longer acceptable. When we smelt metals or plow up prairies to plant corn and wheat, more often than not we find that some harm accompanies the short-term benefits we gain.

Modern environmental science is aimed at helping us master our own actions in the natural world to avoid irreparable damage; in this sense, environmental science means learning to improve self-mastery.

A New Kind of Science

Solving the highly complex problems mentioned above—overpopulation, resource depletion, pollution, and social unrest—requires a knowledge of many scientific fields, including chemistry, biology, sociology, geology, climatology, anthropology, forestry, agriculture, and other traditional disciplines. This wide range of knowledge requires a new discipline, one that spans the traditional fields and offers new insights. Thus environmental science emerges as the study of the complex and interrelated issues of population, resources, and pollution.

The new science takes on the colossal task of understanding environmental issues in their entirety. As such, it is an often awkward melding of science, engineering, and liberal arts that requires broadly educated men and women in an age of specialization. More and more, though, human survival depends on the lessons we can learn from this science.

At a time like today, when men and women float freely in space and robots work in factories, a knowledge of science and its tools has become essential. As voters, consumers, and homeowners, we consider scientific evidence in all our decisions. In our jobs and in our homes we work and play amid the products of science. Chapter Supplement 1-1 covers how science works in more detail.

A knowledge of science is necessary not only to understand environmental issues but also to solve these problems. In that respect, environmental science is a new kind of science, different from the traditional "pure," or objective, science, which seeks knowledge for its own sake. Instead, environmental science offers a great deal of urgent advice and reaches many conclusions that challenge beliefs and practices held dear by us. In contrast to the astronomer in a mountaintop observatory or the mathematician at the blackboard, the environmental scientist is in the thick of things, at the heart of today's hottest debates.

With these facts in mind, it is time to define this discipline more carefully. **Environmental science** is the study of the environment, its biological and nonbiological components, and especially the interactions of these components. It focuses its attention on the ways in which human societies fit into the complex network of connections. It seeks to learn how we affect the environment and, in turn, how we are affected by it. This sketchy definition will take on more substance as we survey some of the more pressing issues with which this science concerns itself.

Outlines of Crisis

The previous section mentioned four main environmental problems; the first three can be labeled overpopulation, depletion, and pollution. Entwined throughout these three is a more subtle problem of values and feelings, which will be discussed under the heading of desperation.

This book takes its form around these four headings. After Part I, which describes the principles and practices of environmental science, Part II discusses population; Part III deals with resources; Part IV covers pollution; and Part V, in many ways the capstone of this book, looks into the question of values, economics, and politics, which must all be part of a better, more environmentally sound way of living.

Overpopulation

In 1984 the world's population reached 4.8 billion, and despite several decades of agricultural research aimed at increasing the food supply, one of every three persons living in the poor, developing nations was unable to find enough to eat. In areas hardest hit by hunger, the population doubled every 35 years!

This explosion of population was an outgrowth of the industrial age. Increased food output, disease control, and better sanitation all played a big part in increasing the survival of newborns, resulting in an increase in people's average life span that swelled populations. This great change occurred without any adjustment in the number of children people had. Until family size is decreased throughout the world, especially in the poorer nations, population will continue to soar, and resource depletion and pollution will worsen.

Depletion

As world population continues to increase, many things we need will come into short supply. Consider the example of firewood. A citizen of rural India needs only a few pieces of wood each day to cook. Throughout the countryside, though, millions of these rural people scour the land in search of wood; and those sticks add up to an alarming total. Forests around many villages have been stripped bare, and many people now spend most of their waking hours in search of wood. Because of the shortages, many people burn dried cow dung, which is easier to find.

All resources can become scarce if their use by populations exceeds their supply. Water, petroleum, silver, and lumber are familiar examples. Species of plants and animals are being depleted, too, as their habitat is altered or as they are killed for food and sport (see Essay 1-1). Prime agricultural land is being used up by farming practices that result in soil erosion or nutrient depletion; in some cases this land has been converted into barren desert. Finally, wilderness is fast disappearing on every continent; even Antarctica is being coveted for its mineral potential.

Pure population pressure lies behind much of this resource depletion. But another important factor is wasteful industrial processes, which squander resources and produce excessive pollution for short-term profits.

Pollution

Air, water, and land pollution are probably more familiar to people than other environmental problems. But pollution plagues more than just the cities or regions we live in; it is pervasive.

In the spring of 1983 atmospheric scientists flying over the Arctic made the first measurements of a thick, orange-brown layer of industrial pollution that covered an area the size of North America and extended more than 8500 meters (28,000 feet) into the atmosphere. That same year, U.S. astronauts returning from a space shuttle flight deplored the filthy blanket of air visible around the earth.

As for water pollution, perhaps the most vivid cases occurred in the 1950s and 1960s in Cleveland. The Cuyahoga River, which cuts through the industrial sections of the city, caught fire and burned because levels of inflammable pollutants were so high (Figure 1-2).

One of 1983's most dramatic news stories originated in Times Beach, Missouri. This sleepy town southwest of St. Louis was contaminated when a contractor sprinkled waste oil on its streets for dust control. Unknown to him, the

Figure 1-2
Cuyahoga River in Cleveland, Ohio, on fire from inflammable pollutants.

oil contained dangerous levels of dioxin. Because this poisonous by-product of the chemical industry could not be removed, and because it would not break down in the soil, the whole town had to be purchased by the federal government for $32 million and abandoned.

Desperation

These are only a few of the many problems plaguing the world's people. Together, the problems of overpopulation, depletion, and pollution have created an *ecological crisis*—a threat to the integrity of natural systems of which humans are a part, and therefore a threat to the survival of human life.

It is common knowledge that as we solve environmental problems, we often make additional ones. These unanticipated, adverse effects, or *ecological backlashes,* are many. One of the most obvious ones resulted from the eradication of some infectious diseases, which are caused by viruses and bacteria and transmitted from one person to the next. Although successful in lowering the death rate worldwide, this campaign has created a worldwide population explosion.

Pesticides and fertilizers, used to increase agricultural output to feed the more than 80 million new world residents each year, are released into the environment where they can destroy wildlife and pollute our drinking water. In some cases these chemical substances cause birth defects in human babies, miscarriages in pregnant women, and cancer in adults. An epidemic of cancer in fish is now evident in polluted waters of the Great Lakes.

Another visible example of an ecological backlash can be found on the edge of most cities. There, farmers clear forests, drain swamps, and plow up open fields to make room for new farms to meet the demand for food in the growing cities. In time, our cities will expand into the countryside and engulf the farmland.

The ecological crisis is the sum of the interconnected problems of population, depletion, and pollution. However, a crisis of the human spirit is also evident. As many psychologists point out, it is easy for people to escape into materialistic life-styles. With equal ease, many among us view ourselves as apart from nature and immune to its laws. Technological advancement and economic growth, which have brought great prosperity and improved living conditions, have become the primary goals of society. Little thought is given to future generations and the long-term health and well-being of the planet.

This "crisis of the spirit" is responsible for much of the damage that occurs in the name of progress. Part V of this book, "Environment and Society," will examine this topic of values and ethics and show how it is manifested in

The Forgotten People

The term *endangered species* suggests the problem of plants and animals destroyed or threatened by habitat alteration, hunting, and pollution. But certain human populations—tribal peoples—are also threatened with extinction. About one out of every 25 humans alive today is an Eskimo, Pygmy, Bushman, Indian, aborigine, or some other tribal member. These people live the way their ancestors did thousands of years ago, as hunters and gatherers or subsistence-level farmers.

Tribal peoples have been uprooted in the name of progress to develop farms, mineral deposits, timber, dams, and reservoirs. Often driven from their homeland, they are forced into an area unlike that in which they have lived for centuries. In Paraguay, for example, the remnants of the Toba-Maskoy tribe have been moved to an arid region where their survival is in doubt.

Those who are allowed to stay are susceptible to new diseases brought by the developer. Brazil's Indian population has shrunk from 6 million to 200,000 since the first Portuguese explorers arrived in the early 1500s. Although war was responsible for some of the deaths, diseases brought from foreign lands were, and still are, the greatest killers. The director of Survival International (an organization dedicated to the protection of tribal people), Barbara Bentley, says, "The

Bushwoman from the Kalahari (N.E. Namibia) resting on her digging stick.

easiest way to dispose of these isolated tribal people is by sneezing."

Some tribes have been "assimilated" into the invading culture with disastrous results. Having suddenly been catapulted two or three centuries in time, they become lost, frightened, and confused by modern technology. Often, they return to their homeland only to find it destroyed. Loss of homeland and traditional values can lead to fatal psychic trauma: from Brazil to Australia, alcoholism, severe depression, and destitution take their toll. Once-skilled hunters are often reduced to begging.

The stories go on: copper mining in Panama threatens thousands of Guaymi Indians; Kalinga tribes in the Philippines fight the construction of hydroelectric dams that would flood their rice terraces; 300,000 Chilean Mapuche Indians have recently been told that their land will be opened for timber cutting; in Peru, the long-isolated Amuesha Indians are threatened by a new highway that would link them to civilization.

The elimination of these cultures will mean not only the end of age-old languages, myths, and social customs but also the irreversible loss of knowledge, including information on medicinal plants, dyes, and diet. Tribal peoples are responsible for discovering more than 3000 plant species with antifertility properties, a boon for birth control research. Some of their plant materials give promising clues to cancer prevention and cure.

The question of whether we can afford to allow these tribal people a continued existence is changing. Now the question is, Can we afford to live without them?

Figure 1-3
Small solar home community made up of 10 "zome" units. The outside surface of a zome unit is covered with insulated aluminum. Solar panels on the roof heat water, which is stored inside the unit in a drum, which provides hot water and maintains heat at night. Other features include the unique shape of the structures and wind power generators on the roof.

today's economic and political practices. The solutions to the environmental crisis lie not only in new scientific discoveries and new technologies but also in the way we view ourselves and the world around us.

Many optimistic observers believe that our problems can be solved without devastating ecological backlashes. In fact, the ecological crisis to them represents an opportunity for unprecedented change. This view is expressed in the Chinese word for crisis, *wei-chi,* the first part of which means "beware of danger," and the second part, "opportunity for change." In short, the dangers posed by overpopulation, pollution, and resource depletion provide an opportunity to strike out in new directions—to change. Such an optimistic view is not meant to minimize the severity of our predicament but rather to give us a refreshingly new outlook.

In a study of societal attitudes toward the future, the Dutch futurist Fred Polak showed that people's image of the future can radically shape a society. Their view of the future is a barometer that foretells not only the potential success or failure of a society, but also whether it will survive at all. Polak concluded that "bold visionary thinking is in itself the prerequisite for effective social change." When pessimism abounds, the future will be gloomy, but with a positive outlook the future of a society will be brighter.

The challenge before us is immense: to create a society that can operate and thrive within the limits of a finite planet. To do so we must redirect technology, economics, industry, and government for the betterment of all human beings and the survival of this planet. The goal is to achieve a sustainable future that robs neither the earth of its beauty and strength nor its inhabitants of their chance for survival (Figure 1-3).

The Evolution of Our Crisis

The answers to our problems will not always be clear-cut. As H. L. Mencken once noted, "There's always an easy solution to every human problem—neat, plausible, and wrong." With that warning in mind, let us trace the story of our origins as science has deciphered it. Much of what is self-contradictory in our civilization makes more sense when seen from this viewpoint. How have we changed in our 3 million years or so on earth? What is different about the world today that makes our choice of values, economic systems, technology, government, and life-style so important? This historical survey will help show what kind of arena the environmental scientist acts in today.

Beginnings of Culture

Many millions of years ago our ancestors—a species of the primates, which today includes apes and monkeys—lived a simple existence in the great forests of the Old

World. About 15 million years ago the forests began to diminish, and our apelike ancestors left the trees. This shift to life on the ground brought about many changes. The foot became specialized for walking. An upright stance was adopted, freeing the hands to grip and manipulate tools, a skill made possible by an opposable thumb. Most important, the brain began to enlarge.

The earliest known cultures probably had three main characteristics that are still present in every culture today: the use of language, the use of edged tools, and the use of fire. The exact times when these were adopted are not known. Language grew out of vocal communication, essential for tree-dwelling creatures. The use of tools, present in rudimentary form in many primates, came to have great importance to early humans for hunting and protection. Fire provided warmth and later became the basis of the modern pyrotechnological society.

The first humans, more than 3 million years ago, had roughly the form we have today. Although we know nothing of their skin, hair, or facial expressions, they could probably pass for human on today's streets. The most drastic changes in our evolution occurred millions of years ago; the physical refinements since then have been relatively slight. Thus, the changes that brought us to the industrial age come through *cultural evolution*—through learned behavior.

Culture and Human Impact

Ecology is the study of living organisms and how they interact with one another as well as their environment. **Human ecology** specifically looks at the ways in which we interact with other organisms and the nonliving components of our environment.

Figure 1-4 shows a highly simplified view of the ways in which societies interact with their environment. This diagram is a qualitative flow network, a nonnumerical representation of how materials pass from the environment to society and back again. To study these interactions more carefully, we will look at hunting-and-gathering, agricultural, and industrial societies. A study of the three social systems shows basic shifts that have occurred during our cultural development (Table 1-1).

The division of human societies into three categories gives the impression that there are sharp lines between them, but in truth, social development has taken place over thousands of years; one type of society has gradually evolved into the next. The dates and sequence of various advances are a matter of debate among paleoanthropologists, so it is best to steer clear of such details here.

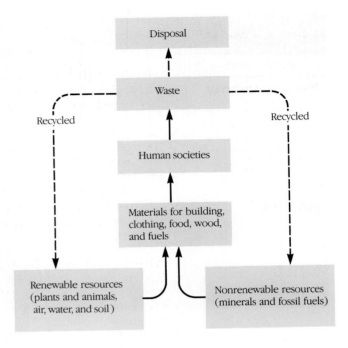

Figure 1-4
Environmental economy. Human societies use many renewable and nonrenewable resources from the environment. Waste products constitute the chief environmental output. Wastes can be recycled to lengthen the life span of nonrenewable resources and help sustain renewable resources.

It is important to note that the chronological listing of social systems does not mean that the earlier forms have vanished. It only points out a major trend in the way human society formed. Today, more than 200 million people live as hunters and gatherers or in early agricultural societies. In the Amazonian jungles, for instance, primitive agricultural societies live in relative harmony with the environment, clearing away small plots to grow the food they need. In Australia, hunters and gatherers roam the Outback in search of food and water. These remnant cultures provide an exciting glimpse of ancient societies.

Hunting-and-Gathering Societies

Hunting-and-gathering societies have been the dominant form of human organization throughout most of human history. Characteristics of hunting-and-gathering societies are summarized in Table 1-1. During most of the last 3 million years, such cultures appear to have been restricted to the tropics and subtropics of Asia and Africa. During the latter years of the Paleolithic period (Old Stone Age),

Table 1-1 Classification of Human Social Systems

Social System	Features
Hunting and gathering	1. The people were nomadic or semipermanent. 2. They benefited from their intelligence and ability to manipulate tools and weapons. 3. They were knowledgeable about the environment, and skilled at finding food and water. 4. On the whole, they were generally exploitive of their resources. 5. The environmental impact was generally small because of low population density and lack of advanced technology. 6. They lived healthy lives, were well fed and experienced low disease rates. 7. Their widespread use of fire may have caused significant environmental damage.
Agriculture	1. Farmers were generally either subsistence level or urban based. 2. They benefited from new technologies to enhance crops and resource acquisition needed for their survival. 3. They were knowledgeable about domestic crops and animals. 4. They were highly exploitive of their resources. 5. The impact of subsistence-level farming was significant, but because population size was small, damage was minimized. The impact of urban-based agriculture was much larger because of new technologies, trade in food products, increasing population, and lack of good land-management practices. 6. Disease was more common among city dwellers because of increased population density. 7. Poor agriculture, overgrazing, excessive timber cutting caused widespread environmental damage.
Industry	1. Industry includes early and advanced forms. 2. It relies on new technologies, energy, new forms of transportation, tremendous input of materials, and reduced number of workers. 3. Mass production and modern technology were transferred to the farm. 4. Industry is highly exploitive, more so than earlier societies; devoted to maximum material output and consumption. 5. Impact is enormous and includes pollution, species extinction, waste production, dehumanization. 6. Humans become subject to infectious disease and new industrial-age diseases including ulcers, heart disease, and mental illness. 7. Widespread environmental damage results from industry, agriculture and population growth.

these people began to spread into new regions, slowly populating the world. From tropical regions of Asia and Africa they migrated into Europe and the rest of Asia and along the island chains to Australia. Eventually, they migrated into North America across the Bering land bridge that once connected Siberia and Alaska. From here, they moved southward and spread throughout the New World.

Much of what we know about the hunting-and-gathering societies comes from archeological findings and the study of remnant cultures in Australia, South America, and Africa. From these studies we have found that our ancient ancestors lived in a rich and competitive world, closely tied to the environment and its bounty. Though slow and weak in comparison with other animals, the early humans managed quite well, thanks to their intelligence, tools, and weapons. Social organization aided these early people in achieving relative security and acquiring the resources they needed. The use of fire also made their lives easier.

Ancient hunters and gatherers knew a great deal about their surroundings. Experts in survival, they knew where to find water, edible plants, and animals; how to predict the weather; and what plants had medicinal properties. This profound ecological knowledge is evident today in existing hunting-and-gathering societies. For example, the Bushmen of southern Africa can find water in the desert where most of us would not be able to. The Australian aborigines can locate and catch a variety of lizards, insects, and grubs far better than a trained biologist (Figure 1-5).

(a) *(b)*

Figure 1-5
Hunting-and-gathering societies wander the land in search of food and water. *(a)*
The men hunt. *(b)* The women are the primary food gatherers, foraging for roots,
berries, bark, and other plant products.

Studies of present-day hunters and gatherers also suggest that, contrary to the popular conception, our earlier ancestors did not live with the constant threat of starvation and did not spend the greater part of their lives in search of food. Instead, they worked less than we do and had more free time. Studies also suggest that they were healthy and well nourished and suffered from few diseases.

Hunters and gatherers were nomads—wanderers—who foraged for plants and captured a variety of animals using only primitive weapons. Because their technology did not give them a great advantage over other species, their populations never grew very large.

Later hunters and gatherers discovered areas rich in wildlife and edible plants and formed semipermanent villages where they could reap the benefits of their environment. The Indian tribes of North America's Pacific Northwest exemplify this type of existence. Living along fishing streams, they feasted on salmon and learned new skills such as boat building and smoking fish to preserve them over the winter.

At first glance it may seem that hunting-and-gathering societies were environmentally benign. However, the evidence shows that they exploited the environment to meet their needs, just as all other organisms do. As Bertrand

Russell once noted, "Every living thing is a sort of imperialist, seeking to transform as much as possible of the environment into itself and its seed." The hunters and gatherers were no exception. Deliberately or accidentally, early humans altered the landscape.

They killed animals with sharp-edged tools, cut down trees with hand axes, and cleared brush with stone blades mounted on sticks. Spears enabled them to kill dangerous animals such as the cave bear or saber-toothed tiger while staying out of reach. Many scientists believe that humans were responsible for killing off many species of large animals in prehistoric times, most notably the cave bear, giant sloth, mammoth, giant bison, mastodon, giant beaver, sabertoothed tiger, and Irish elk (Figure 1-6). They killed these animals directly, drove them out of their preferred habitat, and may have wiped them out by killing their prey.

Far greater changes resulted from the use of fire. The Plains tribes of Canada, for instance, were sophisticated users of fire. They burned clearings regularly to keep

Figure 1-6
Artist's recreation of three species that became extinct approximately 10,000 years ago. Human populations may have played a major role in their extinction. Climatic changes may also have been a factor.

them open, thus maintaining the preferred habitat of deer and useful shrubs. Today, Canada is dotted with large open meadows, but without the fires of native tribes it would be covered with unbroken coniferous forest. The tribes to the south set prairie fires to drive herds of bison into traps or over cliffs, killing thousands at once—many more than they could possibly use. Such a wasteful action does not exactly fit the image of the hunter and gatherer as a wise steward of the land.

On the whole, the transient nature of early hunters and gatherers kept the impact of most of their activities to a minimum. What damage they created from trampling or cutting vegetation and the wastes they left behind could easily be repaired by the environment. As hunters and gatherers began to establish semipermanent settlements in areas of natural abundance, their populations grew, and they began to have an ever-increasing impact on their surroundings.

Agricultural Societies

Agricultural societies slowly took shape during the Neolithic period (New Stone Age) about 10,000 B.C. Gradually, over many thousands of years, humans became increasingly dependent on cultivated crops and less and less dependent on wild varieties. In the Old World, wheat, barley, rye, peas, lentils, and other seed crops rose into widespread use. In the New World, potatoes, corn, squash, and tomatoes were developed. Along with this shift toward agriculture came the domestication of animals.

The Beginnings of Agriculture Anthropologists believe that agriculture got its start in the monsoon lands of eastern India, Burma, and Thailand (Figure 1-7). The early agriculturalists in these areas practiced **swidden**, or **slash-and-burn**, agriculture, still in use today in some regions such as the Amazon. Swidden agriculture starts

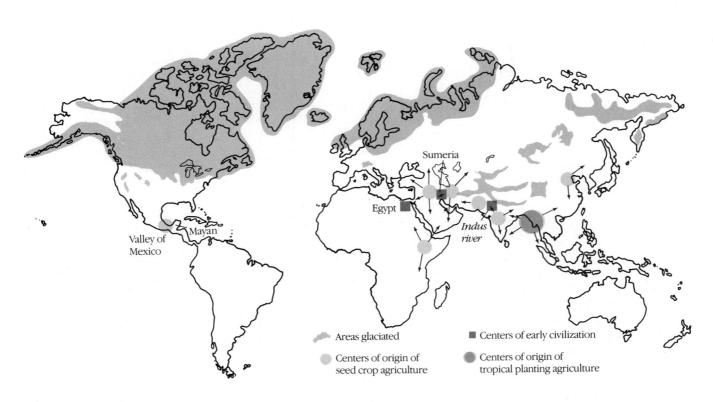

Figure 1-7
The areas where tropical planting and seed crop agriculture originated.

Figure 1-8
Swidden agriculture in the Amazon Basin, where tropical forest is cut and burned.

with the clearing of small plots in tropical forests by cutting and burning the vegetation (Figure 1-8). Seeds and root crops are then planted in the clearings. The ashes from burning provide nutrients to the nutrient-poor soil. Crops grow well for a few years, until the soil becomes depleted or the forest invades the clearing, both of which force farmers to move on to other nearby areas to start the process anew. This cycle can be repeated roughly every 25 years at any one location.

The early agricultural societies of Southeast Asia also domesticated many animals such as the pig and fowl. These became vital food sources, greatly supplementing the crops (Figure 1-9).

Seed crops originated in the drier regions extending from India to eastern Africa, Turkey, and China (Figure 1-7). Cereal grains such as wheat and barley were first planted in cleared woodlands, because forest soils had fewer roots than the rich grassland soils and thus were much easier to cultivate with primitive stick tools. The people of these regions also domesticated a variety of animals to supplement their plant diet; most notable were the goat, sheep, ass, cow, and horse. The cat became an important member of the household, because it kept the grain free of mice.

The domestication of animals (animal husbandry) and plants (agriculture) gave agricultural societies the means to greatly increase the productivity (output) of the land. As a result, they achieved a greater degree of control over their subsistence. This marks an important shift in the human–environment interaction. For the first time human populations could expand beyond the limits previously set by the natural food supply.

Agriculture and animal husbandry altered human lifestyles, too. It was no longer necessary to wander from one location to another with the seasons in search of food. People could set up permanent villages and abandon their nomadic ways. Their concern shifted from the naturally occurring plants and animals they could use for food to those few species that could be raised near their villages. The need to establish exact times for planting and harvesting led to the earliest science, astronomy.

The earliest agriculturalists practiced *subsistence-level farming*, which provides food for the farmer's family. Crops were small, and fields were barely cleared of stumps and obstructions. The people lived close to the land, using crude tools fashioned from stone or sticks. But because each farmer provided for only a few people, the first villages and their human populations were small.

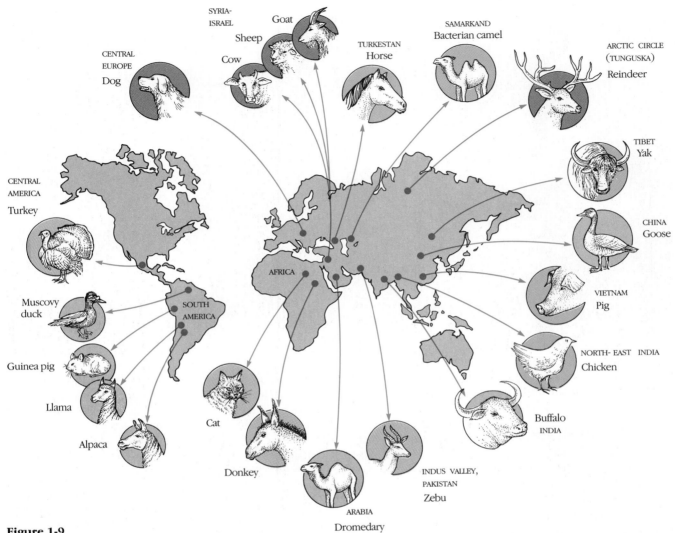

Figure 1-9
Probable areas of origin of the major domesticated animals.

The Emergence of Cities Subsistence-level farming gave way to a more advanced form of agriculture with the development of the plow and other metal tools. The plow allowed farmers to cultivate the rich grassland soils, in which larger crops could be grown with much less effort (Figure 1-10). Other advances, such as irrigation and the use of animals to cultivate fields, also greatly expanded productivity. Because of increasing crop yield, farmers could grow enough food that some could be set aside to prevent hardship in bad times.

In the wake of these advances a significant social change came about: Because a few farmers could produce enough food for everyone, many farm workers moved to villages and branched into new areas such as pottery, toolmaking, and weaving (Figure 1-11). These displaced workers traded their goods for food, but as time went on, they began to do business with neighboring cities. The human population began to grow more interconnected.

With each improvement in agricultural technology crop production grew, and agricultural trade became more widespread. Eventually, villages grew into cities. These became major trade centers. Agricultural societies began to emphasize economics, and the link with the natural environment, so visible in hunting-and-gathering societies and early agricultural societies, was weakened.

Figure 1-10
The advent of the plow allowed early agriculturalists to cultivate rich grasslands, such as these in Pakistan.

Figure 1-11
As food became abundant through farming, people developed crafts and traded their goods for food and other items. Pictured here is a Navajo weaver. Today, the Navajos are renowned for their weaving skills.

Trade in both food and manufactured goods created the need for more sophisticated political systems. Governing bodies formed to regulate the production and distribution of goods. During these changing times land ownership became prevalent, and landowners began to look upon the land not so much as a means of providing food for survival but more as an economic resource.

Severing the Ties The growth of cities put increasing demands on the surrounding countryside. Growing urban populations needed food; wood for fuel; metals for plows, weapons, and tools; and timber and stone for buildings. The flow of materials into the cities and villages was stepped up. Forests were cleared, and ores were extracted from open-pit mines.

By 8000 years ago the inhabitants of the large cities, who were dependent on the surrounding countryside for food and materials, formed an *agriculture-based urban society*. Although the cities had become centers of manufacturing and trade, industry was limited to small shops producing hand-crafted items in small quantities. The cities brought imported goods to the farmer, governed transactions between farmers and consumers, produced new technologies, provided protection from invaders, and became centers for religion.

The transportation of timber, grain, and vegetables to the cities drained nutrients from the soils of the surrounding countryside. Because each of these products incorporates soil nutrients, their exportation to cities created a net loss of nutrients (nutrient drain) from the countryside. Agricultural societies, like hunting-and-gathering societies, created wastes, but now the wastes were piled in dumps near the cities and no longer returned to the soil.

The environmental impact of the agriculture-based urban societies was enormous. Archeological and historical records show us that overgrazing, widespread destruction of the forests, and poor farming practices changed fruitful regions into barren, arid landscapes (Figure 1-12). Ancient civilizations perished as a result, either directly as their crops failed or indirectly as other displaced peoples invaded.

This decline was especially evident in the Middle East, North Africa, and the Mediterranean from 5000 B.C. to A.D. 200. As an example, the Babylonian Empire once occupied most of what is now Iran and Iraq. At the outset this land was covered with productive forest and grasslands. Huge herds of cattle, goats, and sheep overgrazed the grasslands, however, and eventually destroyed the natural

Figure 1-12
This ancient city was once surrounded by rich forests and grasslands. Deforestation, overgrazing, and poor agricultural practices denuded the land, turning it into desert.

vegetation. Forests were cut to provide timber and create more pasture. The loss of grassland and forest vegetation decreased rainfall and eventually parched the land, and sediment that washed from the barren soils robbed the land of essential plant nutrients and filled irrigation canals, making them useless. These changes and a succession of invading armies eventually destroyed this once-great empire.

This story has been repeated all around the Mediterranean Sea. Throughout Saharan Africa in what are now dry and uninhabitable regions, for example, remnants of once wealthy cities can be found buried in the sand.

The agriculturalists' attitudes toward nature were much like those of hunters and gatherers. Both cultures respected natural events. Things out of their control were made sacred, personified as gods. The hunter apologized to the spirit of a slain animal; the farmer paid respect to the gods that regulated the weather and crops.

This paganistic view of nature gave way to a more scientific view during the Middle Ages. In the early 1600s Francis Bacon, an influential English scientist, proposed a new method of learning based on the scientific method, an approach providing "objective knowledge." René Descartes, who followed in Bacon's footsteps, argued that the key to understanding the world lay in mathematics. All physical and biological phenomena could be explained in mathematical terms. Consequently, natural phenomena became better understood and were gradually made less sacred, a process philosophers call desacralization.

Knowledge and control over nature, philosophers tell us, result in a gradual decline in respect for nature. With growing control, human societies came to view themselves as independent and superior to the natural world. Chapter 23, "Environmental Ethics," takes a closer look at these changes in attitude.

The new view of the world that originated with Bacon and Descartes, called a *mechanistic view,* sought greater control over the environment to put nature to human use. Advances in science brought about many new technologies that ushered in the industrial age and further weakened the link between humans and the environment.

Table 1-2   Characteristics of Modern Technology
1. Is complex
2. Often provides meaningless and boring work (assembly lines)
3. Is capital intensive
4. Uses expensive machinery
5. Often depends on imported materials for production
6. Often produces materials for export
7. Requires centralized production in urban areas
8. Produces multiple copies of the same thing, designed for mass marketing and short life span
9. Often uses of synthetic materials
10. Requires large amounts of energy and materials
11. Creates large amounts of pollution
12. Often relies on nonrenewable energy resources
13. Is efficient only on a large scale
14. Can overwhelm the environment

Source: Modified from Miller, G. T. (1982). *Living in the Environment.* Belmont, Calif.: Wadsworth.

Industrial Societies

The agricultural society was transformed into an industrial society as a result of the Industrial Revolution. Beginning in England about 1760 and in the United States in the early 1800s, the **Industrial Revolution** brought about a dramatic change in the social and economic organization of society as large-scale machine manufacturing replaced hand manufacturing (Table 1-2). On the whole, it was a movement away from human and animal labor toward mechanical labor, primarily the steam engine fueled by coal. With the increase in machine labor came a dramatic escalation in energy demand and a need for new modes of transportation to move goods to and from the city. As industries grew, the influx of materials—fuel, food, minerals, and timber—into the city rose sharply.

The shift to machine production changed the working environment, the city, and the surrounding countryside that supplied the resources. The new manufacturing technologies were the fruit of scientific and engineering advances. They were complex, often paradoxically making work tasks meaningless and boring; they displaced manual labor; and they produced large quantities of smoke, ash, and other wastes (Figure 1-13).

Agriculture, too, was ushered into the industrial age. Technological advances such as Jethro Wood's cast-iron plow with interchangeable parts or Cyrus McCormick's reaper brought on a rapid increase in agricultural production. Perhaps one of the most significant advances was the invention of the internal combustion engine, which made horse-drawn implements obsolete. Other significant advances include the development of fertilizers, which allowed an increase in agricultural productivity without increasing the amount of land cultivated, and plant breeding, which produced higher-yield crops that were drought- and disease-resistant.

New medicines and better control of infectious disease through insecticides and improved sanitation also grew out of the Industrial Revolution. These important new developments enhanced human survival; people began to live longer. Population began a rapid ascent.

Impact on the Environment   Population growth, the agricultural transformation, the rise of industry, and the rising demand for resources had tremendous environmental repercussions. Pollution became more widespread. Increased agricultural output destroyed wildlife habitat, depleted soil fertility, and caused severe soil erosion and subsequent pollution of waterways. Dredging new harbors destroyed productive fishing grounds and shellfish beds. Mine waste, city sewage, and industrial discharges polluted waters and wiped out native fish populations, such as the Atlantic salmon.

Throughout the industrial age our control over the environment escalated. Consequently, we have come to

Figure 1-13
The Industrial Revolution marked a new day for human societies. Populations grew, resource demands skyrocketed, and pollution became widespread.

view ourselves more and more apart from nature and superior to it. The prevailing attitude today can be traced back to the English philosopher John Locke, who argued that the purpose of government was to allow people the freedom to exercise their power over nature to produce wealth. "The negation of nature," Locke stated, "is the way toward happiness." People must become "emancipated from the bonds of nature." These notions of subjugation and disassociation from nature have been passed from generation to generation throughout the industrial age. Locke also preached unlimited economic growth and expansion, with the belief that individual wealth was socially important for a harmonious society, an idea that has also been passed down through the generations.

Advanced Industrial Societies After World War II, production in industrial societies underwent a huge leap, peaking in the late 1960s and early 1970s. The high-production society, the **advanced industrial society,** is characterized by high per capita consumption of food and energy and high waste production. Manufacturing in these societies has become more energy- and capital-intensive

and less labor-intensive. That is, advanced industrial societies require more energy and capital to buy machines than early industrial societies, and they employ fewer workers to produce the same product. In essence, energy and machines have replaced human labor.

Advanced industrial societies also shifted in a large way to synthetics. Synthetics are manufactured substances such as plastics, nylon, and polyester produced from inorganic substances such as petroleum and minerals. Some important synthetic materials are listed in Table 1-3 along with the natural products they have replaced.

Synthetics can create problems in nature, because the bacteria in soil and water, which normally decompose organic materials, are frequently unable to break them down. Thus, synthetics may persist in the environment for decades. If they are biologically harmful, they can have significant environmental effects. The persistent insecticide DDT, for example, can accumulate in fatty tissues in birds and disrupt reproduction (see Chapter 18 for a discussion of this phenomenon). Finally, synthetics are usually derived from nonrenewable resources—resources that are not regenerated or replaced by natural processes;

Table 1-3 Shift from Natural Products to Synthetics in the Advanced Industrial Age

Natural Product	Synthetic Substitute
Natural fibers (cotton, silk, hemp, wool)	Synthetic fibers (nylon, polyester, acrylic)
Wood	Plastics, metals
Soap	Detergent
Natural foods (whipped cream)	Synthetic food (synthetic toppings)
Manure, organic wastes	Inorganic fertilizer
Natural predators	Pesticides
Natural rubber	Synthetic rubber
Dyes from plants	Synthetic dyes

Source: Modified from Miller, G. T. (1981). *Living in the Environment.* Belmont, Calif.: Wadsworth, p. 12.

Figure 1-14
Modern agriculture depends heavily on machinery, energy, and additional resources. Large fields are worked to achieve maximum output.

for instance, plastics are derived from nonrenewable petroleum; metals are made from nonrenewable ores.

Farming has also become more mechanized and more dependent on scarce fossil fuels such as oil and natural gas formed from once-living plants and animals. Between 1940 and 1970 the energy input required to produce food in the United States increased more than 300%, whereas the population increased by only 53%. Massive infusions of fertilizer and pesticides have also been used to increase production. Both of these products are derived from nonrenewable fossil fuels. Today, the amount of energy used to produce, process, and transport food far exceeds the energy in the foods produced (Figure 1-14).

Like modern industry, agriculture has become increasingly less labor-intensive. In fact, the human labor used on U.S. farms is six times lower than that used in primitive agricultural societies. Now, only 3% of the U.S. population works on farms; in 1800, 90% of the people were farmers and farm workers.

Twentieth-century industry has brought us to the present environmental crisis for three main reasons: its technological advances have unleashed our enormous reproductive potential, resulting in rapid population growth; a good many of its waste products are of a new and unnatural form and persist in the environment; its heavy reliance on nonrenewable resources slowly erodes our resource supply. Each of these contributes to a sense of desperation. The details of these problems are the subject of Parts II, III, and IV of this book.

Our Future Society

All this paints an unflattering picture of the modern world: an energy glutton; a flagrant polluter of land, water, and air; a greedy exploiter bent on economic gain and unconcerned with the environment. Modern society and its underlying beliefs have come under attack from all sides.

One thing that this book will make clear is that modern industrial society as we know it cannot continue. Part II will show that the curve of population growth, growing steeper every year, must eventually stop rising. Part III will document how the resources we rely on—oil, metals, land, and water—are reaching their limits or, in some cases, are already at them. Part IV will describe the facts about pollution and its effects. Part V will outline the attitudes and practices of both economics and politics that are fast becoming outdated, even dangerous, in a finite world.

Sustaining Gaia

If human society is to endure, not just for another century but for thousands and thousands of years, we need to learn a way of life that can be sustained. Human society must learn to control population size and develop more efficient technologies that produce as little harmful waste as possible. Wherever plausible, we must learn to rely on resources that are renewable. A society based on these ideas is called a *sustainable society.* Developing this new

Is Outer Space the Answer to Our Population and Resource Problems?

No Escape from the Population Bomb

Daniel Deudney

The author is a senior researcher at the Worldwatch Institute in Washington, D.C., where he studies and writes on space, the "global commons" (the oceans, the atmosphere, and Antarctica), and resource issues. He is the author of several papers on space resources and coauthor of Renewable Energy: The Power to Choose *(Norton, 1983).*

Much of the recent writing about humanity's future in space has been dominated by outlandish proposals for large-scale space operations that aim to bypass the earth's resource limits, either by exporting people from the planet or by importing energy and materials from space. These include space colonies, solar power satellites in space, and asteroid mining operations. At first glance, these massive undertakings have a logical appeal: the earth is limited, space is infinite.

Even though space contains vastly more "living" room, energy, and materials than the earth, this abundance cannot be brought to bear meaningfully on the earth's problems. Whatever the long-term prospect for human colonies in space, the earth's population and resource problems will have to be solved on earth in the near term.

Long a staple of science fiction writers, space colonies were among the many visionary ideas proposed by the pioneers of rocket technology in the early years of this century. In recent years space colonies have been advanced as a near-term solution to the earth's population and environmental problems by Professor Gerard O'Neill, a Princeton University physicist. In his writings he details plans to build colonies with first 10,000 inhabitants, and later a million. Manufactured out of materials from the earth, and then the moon and asteroids, the colonies would be made completely self-sufficient by harnessing the sun for all sources of energy. Such colonies would float freely in space, circumventing the need to tame the harsh environments of other planets. Space colonization is specifically promoted as a solution to overcrowding and environmental degradation on earth. By exporting ever greater numbers of people into these orbiting cities, the wildlife and wilderness qualities of earth could be protected, or perhaps even expanded.

Life in space is envisioned as pastoral, pollution-free, and pluralistic—like floating garden cities. Yet in reality, space habitation would probably be bleak. Thick metal shielding would be necessary to block the lethal cosmic and solar radiation. Life would be like that in a submarine—cramped, isolated, and uneventful. For at least the next several decades people will go into space to perform various specialized missions—or perhaps briefly as tourists—but they will not live there in significant numbers.

No scientific laws forbid large space colonies, but the technology to build and maintain such structures remains conjecture. Structures of the size envisioned are thousands of times larger than anything yet built for space; no doubt there will be unforeseen and even insurmountable technical problems. The ecologist Paul Ehrlich points out that scientists have no idea how to create large, stable ecosystems of the sort that would be needed to make space colonies self-sufficient. The key to such knowledge is, of course, much more study of the ecosystems on earth, many of which are becoming less diverse and less stable. It could be many decades before scientists know enough to understand—let alone re-create—ecosystems as complex as those now being degraded. There are also unanswered questions of human biology: Can babies be born and grow up in a weightless environment? Would the various forms of cosmic and solar radiation make the mutation and cancer rate unacceptably high?

Space colonies are not even a partial answer to the population and environmental problems of earth. At a time when 800 million people live in "absolute poverty" on earth, it makes little sense to think about building fabulously expensive habitats in space. Simply transporting the world's daily increase of about 200,000 people into space would consume the annual gross national product of the United States. Each launch of the space shuttle costs a quarter of a billion dollars, and that doesn't even include the $25 billion in research and other initial costs. Maintaining the complex life-support systems in orbit costs thousands of dollars an hour.

Population stabilization is a difficult social challenge, but it is certainly less complex than the organizational and political skills needed for large-scale colonization of space.

Solar power satellites, or Sunsats, are often seen as complements of large-scale space colonization and as a source of energy for earthlings. The Sunsat's principal appeal is its ability to collect virtually unlimited amounts of solar energy day and night without polluting the earth's atmosphere. The construction of Sunsat, however, would be an undertaking of unprecedented size and cost. A 1980 NASA and U.S. Department of Energy study estimated that 60 satellites, each as big as Manhattan island, would be needed to produce the current U.S. electrical usage. The cost estimates ranged from an optimistic $1.5 trillion to a more probable $3 trillion. If two Sunsats were built each year, one heavy-life rocket—seven times the largest rocket ever built—would have to be launched each day for 30 years to build and service them.

More troubling are planetary-scale environmental risks. Beaming trillions of watts of microwaves through the atmosphere for extended periods is almost certain to alter the composition of gases in unpredictable ways. Launching millions of tons of material into orbit would also release large quantities of exhaust gases into the upper atmosphere, perhaps disrupting the ozone layer which screens out ultraviolet light. An operational Sunsat system big enough to make a difference in the terrestrial energy equation would be a shot-in-the-dark experiment with our atmosphere.

The other mirage of abundance in space that has recently received attention is asteroids. These irregularly shaped rocks, which orbit the sun, range in size from as small as a grain of sand to as big as the state of Texas. Although there is probably enough metal in the asteroid belt to meet world needs for many centuries, getting them to the earth's surface would be costly and energy-intensive, and would risk an accidental collision and ecological disruption on a colossal scale. Long before it becomes feasible or economical to bring rare metals from space, scientists should be able to turn the abundant clay, silicon, alumina, hydrocarbons, and iron in the earth's crust into materials which can be used to meet global needs.

In summary, large-scale space colonization and industrialization is an unworkable attempt to escape from the problems of the earth. In the struggle to protect the earth from overpopulation, ecological degradation, and resource depletion, outer space has a great, largely unfulfilled role to play. It can be valuable not as a source of energy or materials or as a place to house the world's growing population, but rather as a tool both for learning more about our planet and to assist problem solving here on earth.

Toward a New World

Ben Bova

The author is past editor of Omni *magazine and a distinguished science and science fiction writer who has published numerous nonfiction works, short stories, and novels. His most recent book,* The High Road *(Pocket Books, 1983), deals specifically with energy and mineral acquisition from space.*

We live in a solar system that is incredibly rich in energy and raw materials. More wealth than any emperor could dream of is available for every human being alive, in interplanetary space. Instead of thinking of our world as a finite pie that must be sliced thinner and thinner as population swells, we must go out into space and create a larger pie so that everyone can have bigger and bigger slices of wealth.

What can we gain from the New World that begins a couple of hundred miles above our heads? Of immediate concern, there is energy in space—enormous energy from unfiltered sunlight. The sun radiates an incomprehensible flood of energy into space—the equivalent of 10 billion megatons of H-bomb explosions every second. The earth intercepts only a tiny fraction of this energy, less than two 10-millionths of a percent.

For the purposes of our generation, a few dozen solar-power satellites in geostationary orbit above the equator may be sufficient. Each would beam 5 billion watts of energy to us, making a substantial contribution to our energy supplies.

Natural resources are also there in superabundance. Thanks to the Apollo explorations of the moon, we know that lunar rocks and soil contain many valuable elements such as aluminum, magnesium, titanium, and silicon.

Looking further afield, there are asteroids which sail through the solar system, especially in a region between Mars and Jupiter called the Asteroid Belt. To a miner or an industrialist they are a bonanza. An MIT astronomer, Tom McCord, estimates that there are hundreds of millions of billions of tons of nickel–iron asteroids in the belt. The economic potential of these resources is incalculably large. And mixed in with these are many other valuable metals and minerals.

This "mother lode" of riches is a long way from earth—hundreds of millions of miles—but in space, distance is not so important as the amount of energy you must expend to get where you want to go. Like sailing ships, spacecraft do not burn fuel for most of their flight; they simply coast after achieving sufficient speed to reach their destination. Space is not a barrier, it is a highway. The biggest and most difficult step in space flight is getting off the earth's surface.

The opportunity offered by space is not to export people from earth, but to import valuable resources to earth.

We will move outward into space because it is biologically necessary for us to do so. Like children driven by forces beyond our understanding, we head into space citing all the good and practical and necessary reasons for going. But in actuality we go because we are driven.

The rocket pioneer Krafft Ehricke has likened our situation on earth today to the situation in a mother's womb after nine months of gestation. The baby has been living a sweet life, without exertion, nurtured and fed by the environment in which it has been enclosed. But the baby gets too big for that environment, and the baby's own waste products are polluting that environment to the point where it becomes unlivable. Time to come out into the real world.

Our biological heritage, our historical legacy, our real and pressing economic and social needs are all pointing toward the same conclusion: It's time to come out into the real world. Time to expand into the new world of space.

society is the theme of this book, and is promoted by many scientists and world leaders today.

In some ways, the sustainable society is so profoundly different from the way we live that it cannot be imagined without a strenuous exercise of the mind. But there are some simple ways to approach this concept.

One of these, discussed in more detail in Chapter 23, is an explanation of the natural world called the *Gaia* (pronounced GAY-a) *hypothesis.* It was developed by the British scientist James Lovelock, and it holds that the earth has all the characteristics of an organism; that is, this planet can be regarded as a living thing.

Like a human body, the earth has its "organs" that adjust to changes—in climate, nutrient levels, and other aspects of the environment—to maintain its stability. And just as the human organism is made of trillions of cells, so is the world organism: each of us is a cell of Gaia (Greek for "earth mother"). Building a sustainable society, in terms of this hypothesis, means preserving the functions of Gaia that maintain constancy and adjust to change.

Changing Our Ways

Taking this analogy further, human society can be likened to a nervous system of the earth superorganism—Gaia. We extract information from the environment, consider

what it means, and make decisions that respond to it. To change human society to a sustainable society, we can become the global brain. As the brain manages one's body, so human society must learn to manage the earth for the good of all its inhabitants, no one part hurting another, and all operating together.

The first order of business is to learn to manage human society as it affects the world. This is where environmental science fits in. It has played an active part in dealing with overpopulation and in establishing population control. It has already done much for our understanding of resources and their depletion and our knowledge of ways to treat and prevent pollution. Transforming values and institutions is already under way, and environmental science will have a lot to contribute to future changes.

This last task is in its infant stages, but some of the new attitudes we need are clear. To counter the attitude that "there is always more"—labeled the *frontier mentality* in this book and by many ecologists today—will come the knowledge that this world is limited: "There is not always more." Limits are all around us, set by the availability of fossil fuel energy, minerals, and land. A closely related concept, brought into sharp focus by the discipline of ecology, is that every living thing on this planet is connected with all other forms of life. In a scientific as well as a philosophical sense, we are all one.

The Role of Environmental Science

Changing our ways will be a colossal task, a process that will take generations to complete. It will involve arduous work in many fields. The moon landing was a weekend home-improvement chore compared with the job ahead. The study of environmental science is a cornerstone of change.

But what has science to say to a philosopher, a public policymaker, a social leader, or a religious thinker? Aren't these people outside the sphere of science? As we shall see, the boundaries between the world of science and the rest of society are being erased by the problems we face.

Science enters into all environmental issues. Legislatures and citizens must make laws on the basis of scientific facts gleaned from government reports, expert testimony, and the news media. How can we understand the issues surrounding energy economics, for example, without a knowledge of the basic scientific rules that govern energy? Environmental problems affect every aspect of life; thus, environmental science is truly a science of all purposes.

Pessimistic thinkers believe that the human species is already doomed—that wars over resources, poisonous pollutants, radiation, and changes in global climate that we have induced, alone or together, will slowly wipe our species out. At the least, they say, things will get worse: we could lose centuries of technological and economic progress in the next few decades if trends continue.

Many other people see a glimmer of hope among the debris of a cluttered, polluted world. They hold that the technology that got us into this mess can also get us out of it. Technological responses to current problems, or *technological fixes,* are the answer. But "technological optimists", a popular term for people who paint an unrealistic picture of the future and do not always distinguish what is technologically possible from what is feasible and economical, they see outer space as a source of new minerals, free energy, and more living space for the crowded citizenry of the world (see the Point/Counterpoint, "Is Outer Space the Answer to Our Population and Resource Problems?"). They propose new technologies such as nuclear fission and nuclear fusion to solve the energy crisis. They view new pollution-control technologies as the answer to our polluted waters and skies.

Beyond the incompatible visions of these two groups, a few things remain certain. First, time is short. Indeed, shortage of time may be the greatest shortage of our time. Another certainty is that during your lifetime, vast and unforeseeable changes will take place; some will be bad, others good. What is also certain is that humans have grown into a force rivaling nature itself; as Walt Whitman wrote, "Here at last is something in the doings of men that corresponds with the broadcast doings of the day and night."

To build a sustainable society, we must learn ways we can better treat our earth. We must learn not to rival nature but to cooperate with it and live in harmony. For that great task, environmental science is our single most important tool.

Life can only be understood backwards; but it must be lived forwards.

KIERKEGAARD

Summary

Environmental science is the study of the nonliving (air, land, and water) and living (plants, animals, and microorganisms) things that make up the environment. Environmental science is now a recognized scientific discipline, but it has existed for thousands of years on a less formal basis to aid human survival. It is so important today because it helps us understand and solve a growing number of environmental problems: pollution, resource shortages, and overpopulation.

Ecology is the science that deals with the interconnections of living organisms and their environment. *Human ecology* specifically looks at the interactions between humans and their environment. An ecological view of history helps us determine how our role in the environment has changed over time.

There are three social systems recognized by anthropologists: hunting-and-gathering, agricultural, and industrial societies. *Hunting-and-gathering societies* emerged more than 3 million years ago. Their members had a profound knowledge of the environment and lived a relatively good life with plenty of leisure time and good health. Contrary to popular opinion, hunters and gatherers were not environmentally benign but exploited the environment. Their use of fire shaped the ecosystems around them. Nonetheless, they created much less damage than later peoples because of their nomadic way of life, small population size, and relatively primitive technology.

Agricultural societies developed between 10,000 and 6000 B.C. Agriculture originated in Southeast Asia, where *swidden, or slash-and-burn, farming* was practiced. Swidden agriculture involves the planting of crops in small jungle clearings until soil nutrients are used up, at which time plots are abandoned.

Seed crops originated in a wide region extending from India to eastern Africa and in China. At first, woodlands were cleared and planted, but with the development of plows, farmers were able to plant in grassland soils. As a result, productivity increased, populations grew, and fewer people were needed to provide food. People left the farms and moved to villages and cities, where they took up crafts and small-scale manufacturing. The growth of population and small-scale industry placed more demands on the environment for food and other resources. The city became a center of trade, commerce, government, and religion. Heightened exploitation accompanied by poor land management resulted in widespread destruction of the natural environment. Many once-prosperous areas were destroyed by overgrazing, excessive timber cutting, and poor agricultural practices.

The *industrial society* is a recent phenomenon in human history brought on by the *Industrial Revolution,* a drastic change in manufacturing marked by a shift from small-scale manufacturing by hand to large-scale manufacturing by machine. Manufacturing became more capital- and energy-intensive and less labor-intensive; mechanization also occurred on the farms, displacing more farm workers and swelling the populations of cities.

The shift from an agricultural to an industrial society drastically changed human–environment interactions. Environmental damage became more widespread and took on many additional forms. Air pollution, water pollution, and destruction of wildlife habitat were the predominant signs of the increasing demand placed by industrial societies on the environment.

Advanced industrial societies arose in the period following World War II. They are characterized by a marked rise in production and consumption, a shift toward synthetics such as plastics and nonrenewable resources such as oil, and a huge increase in energy demand.

This view of history shows the shifting role of humans in the environment and the increasing demands placed on air, water, and natural resources. It also shows that as society gained control over the environment, the perceived link between human society and the natural world weakened. Humans began to see themselves as apart from and superior to nature.

Discussion Questions

1. Define environmental science. What does it attempt to study, and what are its practical applications? How is it helpful to you?

2. In your opinion, should we be optimistic about the future, or pessimistic? Why?

3. Describe the social classification system presented in this chapter.

4. List the major features of hunting-and-gathering societies. Overall, why was their impact so much less than that of agricultural and industrial societies?

5. What role did tools play in the life of the hunter and gatherer?

6. How did hunters and gatherers use fire? What were the effects of their use of fire?

7. Debate the assertion that hunters and gatherers lived a life of hard work and dire necessity.

8. When and where did agriculture start? Why were the early farming activities restricted to forest soils?

9. Define swidden and subsistence-level farming and their impacts on the environment.

10. In general, what advantages did agriculture and animal husbandry give the early agricultural societies?

11. What changes did the plow bring to early agricultural societies? What changes came about in crop production, farm labor, and city size?

12. What were the functions of the early cities?

13. Describe the impact of the overgrazing, excessive timber cutting, and poor farming practices of the agricultural societies.

14. What was the Industrial Revolution? Describe the changes that took place as a result of it. What happened to cities, human population size, agricultural output, and the environment?

15. What is meant by energy-intensity, labor-intensity and capital-intensity? How have industrial societies evolved in regard to these?

16. In what ways has modern agriculture kept pace with modern industry?

17. Discuss the major changes that have occurred during the transition from hunting-and-gathering societies to industrial societies in each of these categories: population, agriculture, use of tools and machines, use of resources, and environmental damage.

Suggested Readings

Brown, L. R., Chandler, W., Flavin, C., Postel, S., Starke, L., and Wolf, E. (1984). *State of the World*. New York: Norton. Comprehensive study of progress toward a sustainable society.

Capra, F. (1982). *The Turning Point: Science, Society, and the Rising Culture*. New York: Bantam. Insightful look at the past, present, and future.

Carter, V. G., and Dale, T. (1974). *Topsoil and Civilization*. Norman: University of Oklahoma Press. An in-depth account of the impacts of early societies on the soil.

Clapham, W. B. (1981). *Human Ecosystems*. New York: Macmillan. Lengthy account of the stages of cultural development and the impact of society on the environment.

Commoner, B. (1976). *The Poverty of Power: Energy and the Economic Crisis*. New York: Bantam. Insightful coverage of economic and energy problems of industrial societies.

Dasmann, R. F. (1976). *Environmental Conservation* (4th ed.). New York: Wiley. Detailed sections on early societies and their impact on the environment.

Isaacs, J. (1980). *Australian Dreaming: 40,000 Years of Aboriginal History*. Sydney, Australia: Lansdowne Press. A wonderfully illustrated book on the aborigines of Australia.

Lovelock, J. E. (1979). *Gaia: A New Look at Life*. Oxford: Oxford University Press. In-depth account of the Gaia hypothesis.

Murphy, E. M. (1983). *The Environment to Come: A Global Survey*. Washington, D.C.: Population Reference Bureau. Survey of major environmental trends.

Pinney, R. (1968). *Vanishing Tribes*. New York: Crowell. Beautifully written account of existing hunting-and-gathering and agricultural societies.

Rifkin, J., and Howard, T. (1980). *Entropy: A New World View*. New York: Viking. See the first 30 pages for a superb analysis of changing world views.

Russel, P. (1983). *The Global Brain*. Los Angeles: Tarcher. Well-written view of possible evolutionary changes that could radically reshape society.

Smith, R. L. (1976). *The Ecology of Man: An Ecosystem Approach* (2nd ed.). New York: Harper and Row. Elegantly written accounts of the impacts of society on the environment.

Science and Scientific Method

In this day of rapid change and scientific advancement, a knowledge of science is essential to our well-being and to wise governance. Our society makes numerous public policy decisions on complex issues such as energy, pollution, wildlife, and population. We cannot make wise decisions without a knowledge of the science behind the issues. Throughout this book we will learn some fundamental principles of science and many of the scientific facts behind the headlines.

To be effective, solutions to our complex problems must be sound from a scientific standpoint. They must obey the laws of chemistry, biology, and physics to have a lasting and useful effect. Unsound solutions will only make matters worse in the long run.

We tend to think of science and ethics as separate entities. Values, according to the common conception, are a subjective code of behavior, whereas science is objective and free of value. Science, in this view, does not prescribe our behavior but is simply a way of studying the world around us and describing how it works.

A study of the history of science and society, however, suggests that this view is not very accurate. Our value systems have long been affected by science. The scientific truths we glean from nature are applied to our everyday life. For example, in the England of the early 1800s, while the industrial age was coming into being, the concept of evolution was integrated into the value system of everyday life. Evolution was popularly viewed as a process of change that inevitably led to superior forms of life. Thus, some life forms were better than others. For example, it became socially acceptable (ethically proper) for some people to prosper in the new industrial age while others (the workers) suffered in the dangerous factories. This disparity was affirmed by the notion of evolution. The application of Darwin's theory of evolution to social ethics is called *social Darwinism*.

Our values can come from science. In other words, what is right or wrong in society can be judged from the laws of science. Values that do not take into account the scientific principles that govern life can be destructive to human society and the environment.

Throughout this book we will examine the principles of science in an effort to establish a new ethic, a new view of what is right and wrong in regard to our life-sustaining environment and all the living organisms that call the earth their home. In this supplement we will look more closely at scientific method to answer the question, "How does science operate?"

Scientific Method

The study of science is generally orderly and precise. Most scientists start with observations and measurements of things they want to study (Figure S1-1). From these observations they develop generalizations, or *hypotheses,* which are tentative explanations of the observed phenomena. The development of hypotheses from observation and measurement is called *inductive reasoning.* We all reason inductively every day. For example, suppose you were driving your car at night and, each time you hit a bump, one of the headlights flickered. When you were driving on smooth sections, however, the lights worked fine. From these observations you might hypothesize that the bumps were rattling the filament in the headlight, causing it to flicker. You arrived at this hypothesis by inductive reasoning.

Once a hypothesis is made, it is up to the scientist to determine how valid it is. The scientist tests the validity of hypotheses by performing experiments. In the example discussed above, you might test to see if the road bumps were actually affecting the headlight by replacing it. If the headlight continued to flicker when you hit bumps, then you would conclude that your hypothesis was invalid.

Experiments either support or refute our hypotheses. If a hypothesis is refuted, a new theory may be created. For example, after determining that the filament in your headlight was not faulty, you might propose a new hypothesis—that the electrical wiring was faulty. You could easily test this hypothesis by rattling the electrical wires connected to the headlight. If the light flickered during the new experiment, you could conclude that your

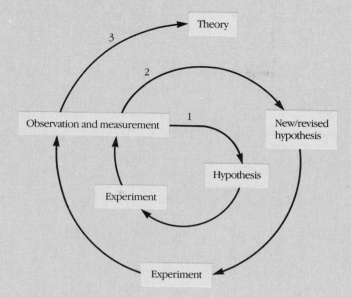

Figure S1-1
The scientific method starts with observation and measurement, from which scientists develop hypothesis, or tentative explanations. The scientist next tests his/her hypothesis by experimentation. If the results of the experiment do not support the hypothesis, a new or modified hypothesis is created, which can then be retested and refined until a theory is formed.

new hypothesis was valid. To be certain, though, you might experiment by tightening the connections. If the problem was fixed, you would be certain of your hypothesis.

Good scientific experiments are carefully conducted, using control and experimental groups whenever possible (these are described below). Let's take a look at an example to see how a good experiment might be set up and run. Sewage treatment plants frequently treat wastewater with chlorine to kill bacteria and viruses before the water is released into streams and lakes. At the site where this chlorinated waste is released, scientists have often found that fish are absent, leading one to suspect (hypothesize) that the chlorinated effluents are killing fish. To ensure a fair and objective test of this hypothesis, the scientist would re-create the conditions of the stream in the laboratory by filling fish tanks with fish and water taken from the stream. Two separate groups would be established—the experimental and the control. The *experimental group* would be treated with chlorinated wastewater, and the *control group* would not be. The two groups would be the same in all respects except for one variable, the *experimental (independent) variable*.

Suppose in this example that the experimental fish died shortly after the introduction of chlorinated wastewater. We could conclude that our hypothesis appeared to be valid. As researchers, we might want to find out what chemicals in the treated sewage

had killed our fish. Measurements of the treated sewage might have shown us that there were extraordinarily high concentrations of chlorinated organic compounds. Thus, we might reformulate our original hypothesis, stating that the chlorinated organic compounds were the agents responsible for the fish deaths. To test this, we would design another experiment with a control and an experimental group. They would be identical except that the experimental group would be treated with chlorinated organics in the same concentration as in the stream. If the fish did not die, we would conclude that our hypothesis was invalid and would have to develop and test an alternative hypothesis. If the fish died, we would conclude that our revised hypothesis was valid.

Other researchers might test our hypothesis by setting up the same experiment. If enough scientists came up with the same results, then the hypothesis would be elevated to a level where many people could be more certain of its validity. We call a hypothesis supported by substantial evidence a *theory*.

Changing Theories

Hypotheses and theories are subject to change and modification. As new results come in, new interpretations may be possible. It may become necessary to alter basic hypotheses. For example, many years ago scientists found that people who consumed large amounts of table sugar (sucrose) had a higher incidence of lung cancer than people who ate less sugar. It was, therefore, hypothesized that sucrose caused lung cancer. When scientists tested this hypothesis, however, they found that their data did not support it. Instead, they found that smokers generally ate more sugar than nonsmokers, and that smoking, not sugar, was probably the cause for the higher levels of lung cancer.

The development of new research techniques also results in the revision of existing hypotheses. New techniques create new facts that cannot be interpreted on the basis of existing hypothesis and theory.

Perhaps the best known example of changing theory is the Copernican revolution of astronomy. The Greek astronomer Ptolemy hypothesized in A.D. 140 that the earth was the center of the universe (geocentric view). The moon, the stars, and the sun were all thought to revolve around the earth. This notion held sway for hundreds of years. In the early 16th century, however, Nicolaus Copernicus showed that the observations were better explained by assuming that the sun was the center of the universe (heliocentric view). Copernicus was not the first to put forth the heliocentric view. Early Greek astronomers had suggested the idea, but it gained little attention until Copernicus's time.

The new view of the solar system was condemned as heretical by the Roman Catholic Church. When Copernicus published his theory, it was placed on the Papal Index of forbidden books. Eighty years later the German astronomer Johannes Kepler presented findings that further supported the heliocentric view of our solar system. Gradually the old geocentric theory became obsolete and was replaced by an entirely new theory.

The dominant theoretical framework, or set of assumptions, that underlies any branch of science is called a *paradigm*. A paradigm is likened to a "supertheory," a basic model of reality in any science.

Paradigms govern the way scientists think, form theories, and interpret the results of experiments. They govern the way non-scientists think, too. In the example above, the geocentric view was the central paradigm of astronomy for over a thousand years.

Once a paradigm is accepted, it is rarely questioned. New observations are interpreted according to the paradigm; those that are inconsistent with it are rejected or ignored. However, phenomena that fail to fit conventional wisdom often amass to the point at which they can no longer be ignored. They may cause the central paradigm to be changed. Such a change is called a *paradigm shift*.

Paradigms are found in all areas of human endeavor. These central ideas of biology, ecology, chemistry, philosophy, health, and education are all paradigms that are subject to radical change as new observations are made and new theories are developed. Paradigm shifts are important to all fields of study because they change the way we view reality. Part V of this book will show how shifts in our attitudes toward nature (philosophical paradigms) affect the human–environment interaction.

Scientists Shouldn't Disagree—Or Should They?

"Air pollution causes lung cancer," says one medical scientist. "There is no substantial evidence to support this claim," argues another of equal reputation. How can scientists disagree? Aren't they trained to find the objective truth? How does controversy exist in something as precise as science?

Room for disagreement among scientists is great. Paradigm shifts, discussed above, create an environment sometimes overflowing with disagreement. Disagreement among scientists may also occur early in the stages of hypothesis formation, when information itself is simply too contradictory to form lasting hypotheses. For instance, many studies have been performed to determine whether urban air pollution causes lung cancer; even today, however, the results are still too contradictory for us to draw firm conclusions. Some studies show a clear relationship between lung cancer and urban air pollution; others don't.

But why should contradictory results arise from experiments on the same phenomenon? With all the controls built into a scientific experiment, wouldn't it be likely that the results would be the same? The answer is that no two experiments are the same. Even slight differences can affect the outcome. In our example, the major difference between two contradictory studies may be that in one case the subjects are urban residents who have been exposed to high levels of pollution on the job. In the second, the subjects may be urban residents who are office workers and therefore have not been exposed to pollution in the work place. Without looking carefully at the experimental design, we might have been confused about why two similar studies had markedly different outcomes.

Disagreement among scientists also results from biases entering into the design of experiments and the interpretation of results. As many scientific historians note, scientific theory is greatly influenced by social conditions. Thomas Aquinas, for instance, formulated a widely accepted view of nature that was a mirror image of the feudal system of medieval Europe. He simply projected onto nature the traits of his society. Some scientific historians argue that the development of Charles Darwin's theory of evolution was greatly influenced by the social, political, and economic conditions of England as it entered the industrial age. They contend that his theory represents nature as we want it to be, not as it really is.

Bias is an inescapable human trait, coloring even the scientist's perceptions. As a result, scientists are acutely aware of bias and attempt to design their experiments to avoid it.

Disagreement among scientists also stems from the fact that some hypotheses are extremely difficult to test. For instance, the effect of chemicals on cancer in humans is extraordinarily difficult to study. It is neither feasible nor ethical to subject humans to potential cancer-causing agents in a controlled experiment. Therefore, we must often rely on statistical studies that attempt to correlate cancer in human populations with exposure to certain chemicals. This type of study is crude and imprecise and shows only a correlation, not causation. In other words, even though a statistical link may be found between cancer and exposure to a certain chemical, the link cannot be absolutely confirmed.

Scientists will always disagree because of shifts in paradigms, personal bias, conflicting data, and difficulty in testing some hypotheses. Regardless, we will constantly seek to find scientific truth. This quest is essential because the rules of science are so important to a good understanding of the world and especially of its environmental problems.

Suggested Readings

Kuhn, T. (1970). *The Structure of Scientific Revolutions.* Chicago: University of Chicago Press. The original description of paradigms and paradigm shifts.

Rifkin, J. (1983). *Algeny.* New York: Viking. Interesting view of the influence of society on science (see Parts 2 and 3).

Framework for Understanding Environmental Problems

In a world where events and ideas are analyzed to the point of lifelessness, where complexity grows by quantum leaps, where the information din is so high we must shriek to be heard above it, we are hungry for structure. With a simple framework we can begin to make sense of the world.

JOHN NAISBITT

Environmental problems such as those described in Chapter 1 grow in number every day. Such problems are a legacy of many years of carelessness and disrespect for the environment and are a result of the sudden upsurge in human population in the last two centuries.

Many people find environmental issues complex and confusing; they feel as if there is no hope for a solution. Even experts disagree on what is causing our problems and how to solve them. How can there be a solution with so many conflicting views or confusing facts?

Others find environmental problems clear-cut. "Politics is to blame," one person proclaims. "It's our attitudes toward nature," another argues. Still a third argues, "Technology and energy waste are the roots of our troubles." Such people often support narrow solutions: political reform, a new system of values, or new technologies. Their solutions often fall short of the mark, however, and may

Figure 2-1
Population segment of a world computer model, showing how the many factors are interrelated. Each factor is assigned numerical values, and the computer calculates how changes in one or more factors affect others.

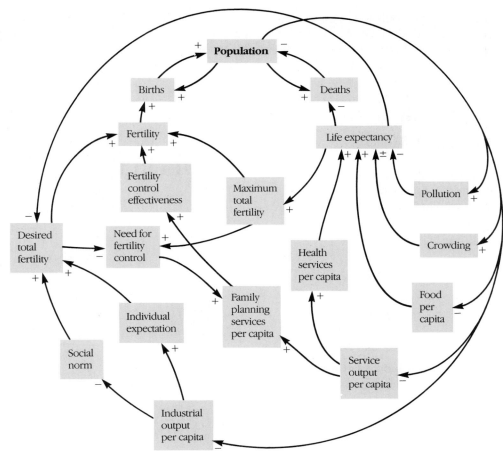

even create ecological backlashes, whose solutions place additional financial burdens on society.

Those puzzled by the complexity of current environmental issues need something to help bring order to the facts. In contrast, those with simplistic views need some way to expand their understanding. This chapter presents a number of diagrams, or "conceptual models," to satisfy these two needs. Careful study of the models will be rewarded many times over, for they present ways to analyze complex environmental issues that will appear throughout this book. To make these models more meaningful, many chapters feature special exercises, encouraging "hands-on" experience with the models.

Models are one of the most powerful tools of the working environmental scientist. They can be adapted to computers and used to study complex issues such as the world food supply, industrial production, or the interactions of populations, resources, and pollution. The computer study of complex systems is called *system dynamics.*

System-dynamics computer models in environmental science are mathematical programs designed to deal with many environmental problems on different levels. The first global model, introduced in 1970 by J. W. Forrester, was used to study the future of human civilization by looking at global population growth, industrialization, agriculture, pollution, and the depletion of natural resources. Figure 2-1 depicts just one part (population) of an updated version of the model, showing how complex it is. To study urban and regional problems such as air pollution, water supply, and traffic, less complex models are used.

Perhaps you have worked with a computer to manage your budget. These budget programs, like all computer programs, are developed from simple conceptual models (called algorithms), much like those presented in this chapter. On a home computer, budget programs can forecast how changing your living expenses will affect your savings or spending money. This program is very similar to many of the models that scientists use (see Essay 2-1 for more details). Even though we will examine only the simplest models here, each of them will deepen your understanding of environmental science, giving you a glimpse into human ecology.

Population, Resource, and Pollution Model

The first model, shown in Figure 2-2, seems general at first glance. It shows in the most basic terms how humans interact with their environment. Don't be deceived by its

simplicity. Upon careful analysis you will see that it contains a wealth of useful information.

Vital Links: Humans and the Environment

The **Population, Resource, and Pollution model** shows that human populations acquire resources from the environment to survive. Hunting-and-gathering societies, for example, collect plant materials such as roots, berries, and bark. They also hunt animals for food. Agricultural societies cultivate their own crops and raise their own animals, but they still depend on the soil to grow their crops

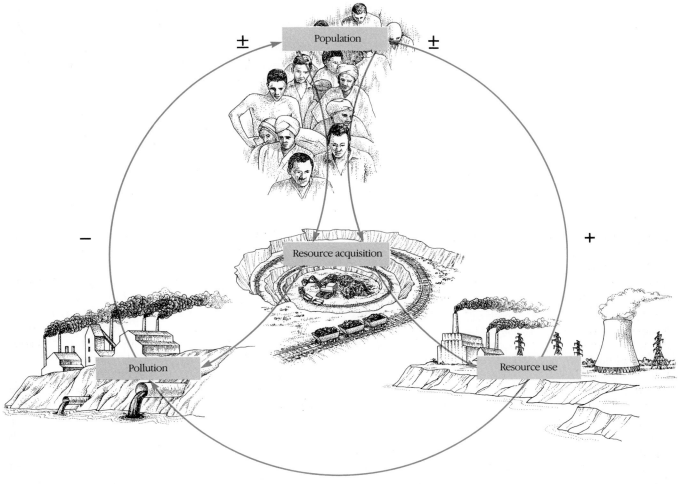

Figure 2-2
Population, Resource, and Pollution model. Arrows with plus marks indicate positive feedback loops, and arrows with minus signs indicate negative feedback loops.

The Computerized Farm Report

Farmers in Kern County, California, consult the computer to judge how much water will be available to them in the year 2070. This arid agricultural county, which rarely receives more than 10 to 12.5 centimeters (4 to 5 inches) of rainfall a year, is entirely dependent on irrigation water from three sources: the Kern River, wells, and diversion canals. But the supply of irrigation water is increasingly threatened by the growth of population and new industries.

The computer analysis shown in the flowchart was devised to determine whether there would be enough water available for agriculture from now until the year 2070, taking into account population growth, increases in land under irrigation, industrial water consumption, and other factors. The results of the computer study showed farmers that unless some changes were made, the region would soon run out of water. County officials and farmers have come up with several solutions to avoid catastrophe: curtailing population and industrial growth, importing more water, and conserving water.

Computers have changed our lives in many ways. They are helping us save energy, reduce our consumption of resources, and reduce pollution and production of hazardous wastes. They are also helping us store vast amounts of information produced at a record rate. They have helped create a global economic system and more unity among the world's people.

Computers are also helping us take some of the guesswork out of long-range planning. Even though computer models bring precision to environmental analysis they are still often only imperfect simulations of real social systems. They are based on many assumptions that may not be accurate. Unless we are aware of the basic assumptions, we can easily be led astray.

Adapted from Boughey, A.S. (1976). *Strategy for Survival. Menlo Park, CA: W.A. Benjamin.*

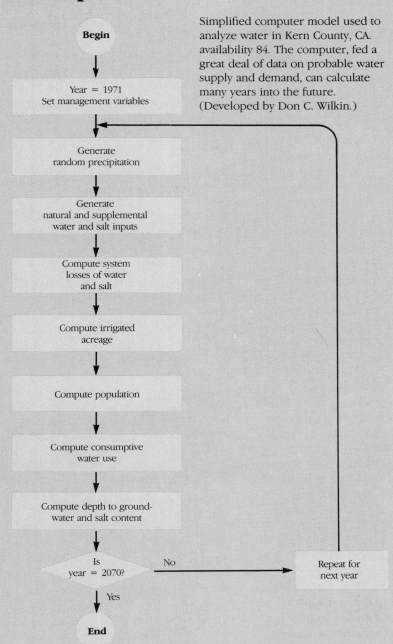

Simplified computer model used to analyze water in Kern County, CA. availability 84. The computer, fed a great deal of data on probable water supply and demand, can calculate many years into the future. (Developed by Don C. Wilkin.)

and the grasslands to provide food for domestic animals. Modern societies, too, exploit resources but in a much accelerated fashion. Oil and coal from the depths of the earth, metals from open-pit and underground mines, fish from the sea—all flow into the cities, where they are processed and distributed to the earth's growing population.

The acquisition and use of resources by human populations create **pollution,** any alteration in the physical, chemical, or biological components of air, water, or soil that threatens life. Pollution affects a variety of environmental components. For example, water pollution may kill fish or water birds that feed on fish. Destruction of land by mining or poor agricultural practices ruins the homes of many animals. Pollution may also cause serious illness and death in humans. Understanding how we acquire and use resources can help our species find new ways of minimizing pollution and protecting the air, water, and soil and the other organisms that share this planet with us.

Resource acquisition and use are not always harmful to all other organisms. Harvesting trees in forests, for example, destroys the habitat of squirrels but creates openings where grasses and small shrubs can grow, promoting deer and elk populations. On the whole, the acquisition and use of various resources has been a tremendous boon to human society, allowing our population to prosper and spread throughout the planet.

The Population, Resource, and Pollution model says that human populations acquire and use resources (water, air, minerals, plant products, and other organisms) from the environment. In most cases these resources enhance our survival and promote population growth; this is indicated in the model by arrows leading from resources to population. This response is an example of a *positive feedback loop,* in which one factor leads to the growth of another. In some cases, though, acquisition (coal mining) and use (coal burning) may deplete resources or pollute the environment with serious effects on population. These are examples of *negative feedback loops,* in which one factor causes another to decrease.

This model takes on a greater significance when we expand its three key factors: population, resources, and pollution. Table 2-1 lists some additional factors discussed in more detail throughout this book. For now, though, it is too confusing to break up the major elements of the model. Nonetheless, it should be clear that there is much to be studied before you can thoroughly understand the interaction of population, pollution, and resources. Let's look at a technique that can help you understand how these factors interact.

Table 2-1 Breakdown of Factors of the Population, Resource, and Pollution Model

Population	Resources	Pollution
Size	Acquisition	Water
Distribution	Use	Land
Density	Supply	Air
Growth rate	Demand	
	Character	

Studying the Interactions: Cross-Impact Analysis

The three elements of the PRP model interact with one another in so many ways that only a computer could keep track of them. We can get a glimpse of how they affect one another by using a technique called **cross-impact analysis.** "Cross-impact" refers to the ways one thing affects something else, and "analysis" literally means to break things apart. This technique, then, helps you break down complex interactions into simpler ones that are more easily understood.

Figure 2-3 is a simplified cross-impact analysis chart. In this chart the three elements of the PRP model are lined up twice, in two perpendicular columns. Column A is for factors that do the affecting, and Column B is for the affected factors. In box 1 you can describe how population factors affect resource factors, such as supply, demands, acquisition, and use. In box 2 you can describe how population factors affect pollution (see Table 2-2). Using this technique, you can compare each of the three elements with the others, sorting out the interactions in an organized and understandable way. This will give you a deeper appreciation of the complexity of modern society. As your knowledge of the three factors of the PRP model expands,

Column A			
Population	X	1	2
Resources	3	X	4
Pollution	5	6	X
Column B	Population	Resources	Pollution

Figure 2-3
Cross-impact analysis chart used to compare the interactions between the three factors in the Population, Resource, and Pollution model.

Table 2-2 Completed Cross-Impact Analysis

Box	Summary of Interactions
1	**Effects of Population on Resources**

The size of a population determines, in part, the resource demand, how resources are acquired, and how much is used. Social, economic, and technological development of a country (all considered population factors) affect the demand for resources as well as the manner of acquiring them and how they are used. More-developed countries tend to have more-complex resource needs and tend to use resources that are nonrecyclable and nonrenewable. Growth rate affects resource allocation and use. Resource demand in rapidly growing populations may result in less concern for the consequences of resource allocation and use and, thus, more damage than in populations with slower growth. Population distribution affects resource supply, allocation, and use.

2 **Effects of Population on Pollution**

Populations create pollution through resource allocation and use. Pollution may result from using a resource as a depository for human and industrial waste. In addition, allocation of resources (coal, oil, gas) may result in environmental degradation. The amount of resources and manner in which these resources are acquired and used determine the amount of pollution.

3 **Effects of Resources on Population**

Positive Effect. Discovery and use of new resources (oil, coal) can increase the population size, growth rate, and distribution, as well as social, economic, and technological development. Resources allow humans to move to new habitats and extract and utilize resources not previously available. In addition, resource development allows habitation in inimical environments.

Negative Effect. Depletion of resources can limit population growth, size, and distribution, as well as social, economic, and technological development. Degradation of resources (air pollution) by misuse can theoretically reduce population size or eliminate populations.

4 **Effects of Resources on Pollution**

The amount and manner of resource allocation and use can affect pollution. The more resources are allocated and used, the more pollution, although methods of use and allocation greatly affect pollution. Resource depletion can reduce pollution.

5 **Effects of Pollution on Population**

Pollution can limit population size, growth rate, and distribution and social, economic, and technological development. Pollution can increase mortality and morbidity, thus having a social and economic impact. Pollution has an aesthetic impact. Pollution can change attitudes, which serve to change laws and the ways resources are allocated and used.

6 **Effects of Pollution on Resources**

Pollution of one medium (air) can contribute to the destruction of another. New laws designed to reduce pollution could shift resource demand, supply, acquisition, and use.

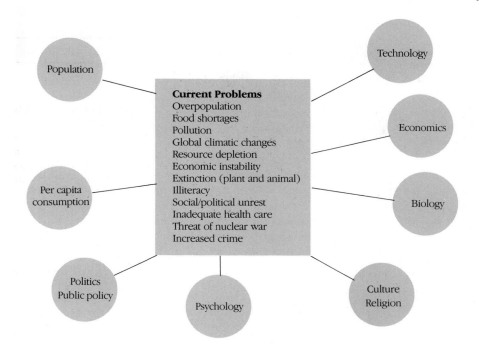

Figure 2-4
Multiple Cause and Effect model for analyzing specific environmental issues. The circled factors contribute in many ways to the problems facing the world.

you can make more-complex and more-sophisticated cross-impact analyses.

Multiple Cause and Effect Model

The PRP model is not an end-all; it merely is a way of looking at the big picture—the human–environment interaction. To dissect individual issues, we can use the **Multiple Cause and Effect model** (Figure 2-4).

In the late 1960s and early 1970s, when environmental issues came to the forefront of attention, two noted scientists stimulated a debate over the underlying causes. Paul Ehrlich, a Stanford University biologist, argued that the root of all our pollution and resource problems was overpopulation—too many people. His argument was hotly contested by another biologist, Barry Commoner, who argued that technology was primarily to blame. Their debate engaged but misled the scientific community and the public for years. Upon closer examination, it becomes clear that both scientists were wrong. The complex problems of poverty, resource depletion, pollution, wildlife extinction, and food shortages are not the result of technology

or overpopulation alone but rather are caused by a variety of factors, as shown in Figure 2-4.

To illustrate the multiple etiology of environmental problems, we will look at wildlife extinction, for which commercial and sport hunting and habitat destruction are often blamed. As we will see, this view—like Ehrlich's and Commoner's—gives us a simplified picture of a problem that has many hidden causes. To see why this is so, and to see how the model is used, let us examine each element of the model individually.

Population

The human population destroys wildlife habitat in many ways. We build roads through forests once occupied by bear; we build airports and housing tracts on land that once provided food and shelter for birds and other animals; we pollute streams once the home of fish and otter; we strip-mine for coal and gravel, in the process destroying vegetation once the food of deer. These activities enhance human survival and prosperity but decrease the amount of wildlife habitat (Figure 2-5). The extent of the environmental damage depends on numerous population factors such as population size, growth rate, and geographical distribution. For example, the larger our pop-

Figure 2-5
The activities of modern society destroy the habitat of numerous species. Development along the San Franciso Bay has reduced the habitat of many birds and marine animals.

ulation, the greater its impact. Likewise, the faster our population grows, the more impact we have. But population is only one of many underlying causes of extinction.

Per Capita Consumption

The amount of resources used by each member of society, *per capita consumption,* also plays a key role in the destruction of wildlife habitat. For example, in the United States per capita consumption of water has increased 300% in the past 80 years. Electrical energy consumption has more than doubled in the past 20 years. This rapid increase in resource consumption strains the earth's available land and water resources. It also pollutes the planet. The cars we drive pollute the air animals breathe; the oil we use to make the gasoline that powers our automobiles can, if accidentally released, pollute the ocean and rivers. Thus, how much a society consumes also plays a significant role in wildlife extinction.

Politics and Public Policy

The legal system also has an important role in wildlife extinction. Laws can affect how much habitat is destroyed, how much hunting and poaching occurs, and which species will or will not be hunted. In addition, laws influence population growth, which, in turn, affects wildlife habitat. (For instance, tax laws give families deductions for each child, reducing the financial burden of rearing children and thus may promote population growth.) Laws also affect resource acquisition and use—for example, how much coal is mined, how it is mined, and how reclamation is carried out. Before 1977 there were few legal controls on surface mining. At that time more than 1 million acres of land had been surface-mined in the United States, and about two-thirds of this land (mostly in the East) had been left barren. New laws now require the revegetation of surface-mined land and create a fund for reclaiming abandoned, unreclaimed lands. Thus, laws must also be taken into account when discussing animal extinction.

Economics

Economics is a key element in animal extinction. It plays an important role in determining how resources are acquired and used. For example, surface mining of coal is preferred to underground mining worldwide because it is much cheaper. Because surface mining is more environmentally destructive, the decision to acquire coal this way, dictated by economics, affects wildlife habitat.

Economics affects many of our daily business decisions. On the surface, there is nothing wrong with this. However, economics often fails to account for *external costs*—pollution, habitat destruction, and other environmental impacts that are not entered into the cost of producing goods. Air pollution from factories, cars, and power plants, for example, may cause up to $16 billion worth of damage to crops, health, forests, and buildings in the United States each year. These external costs are borne by members of the public who suffer ill health, pay a higher price for food, or pay for repairing buildings. If companies invested in pollution control devices, the external costs would be greatly reduced, but consumers would pay a higher price for energy and goods. Thus, a system of economics in which the consumer pays for the external cost would diminish environmental pollution and its threat to wildlife habitat. But because economic thinking often ignores economic externalities, it too is a prime causative agent in the reduction of the world's wildlife.

Psychology, Culture, and Religion

How we behave toward the environment is a function of our attitudes, as shown in Chapter 23. Underlying all of our behavior is a psychology that tends to put immediate needs before the long-term good of the environment and future generations. Rather than thinking about the future, we tend to be concerned with things that affect us in the short term and ways we can make the present as comfortable as possible. Although this type of thinking is shortsighted, it is very much a biological characteristic. Survival in the animal world is generally the result of animals' satisfying immediate needs by using environmental resources. Being animals ourselves, we tend to think and act with an eye to the immediate. Because our population is so large and our technologies are so well developed, however, short-term thinking leads to many problems, such as wildlife extinction.

Another crucial psychological element is the way we perceive our place in the environment. Do we see ourselves as superior to nature and at odds with the natural world? Or are we a part of nature, willing to live in harmony in accordance with important ecological laws? An attitude of being superior and somehow separated from nature predominates today. It gives many license to run roughshod over wildlife and plants, contributing to the extinction of many species.

Social, cultural, and religious factors determine to a large extent our psychological makeup. Cultural and religious attitudes in which humans are viewed as supreme and apart from nature, as we have seen, can have devastating effects on wildlife. If, however, animals are revered for cultural or religious reasons, extinction from hunting and habitat destruction may be curbed.

Technology

Technology, like population, is only one of a complex of factors contributing to wildlife extinction. We typically think of technology as instruments or tools to make better use of the world's resources in meeting our needs for food, shelter, clothing, water, and so on. Technology offers us many advantages in the struggle for survival. As a result of technological developments, we travel freely around the world and through space, inhabit new regions, and acquire resources from distant sites. Technology allows us to prosper in environments where survival might otherwise be impossible.

Our travels, new settlements, and resource acquisitions all contribute to the shrinking supply of wildlife habitat. This happens partly because technology enhances population growth. The more people there are, the more resources are needed and the greater the conflict over living space.

Technological advances have spelled trouble for wildlife for other reasons, too. For instance, improvements in guns used for whaling have allowed humans to severely deplete the populations of many whales. New drugs have eradicated diseases, thereby reducing infant mortality; in the process, though, they have contributed to rapid population growth. New chemical pesticides have increased agricultural productivity but have also devastated populations of birds and other animals. Therefore, although technology has been a boon to society, it has exacted a price, too.

Biology

Numerous biological features play a role in wildlife extinction, adding to the growing list of contributing factors. Some of the most important ones are adaptability, number of offspring, and sensitivity to environmental pollutants. Highly specialized species, like the California condor, are generally unable to adapt to changes brought about by human beings and are more vulnerable than less specialized animals like the coyote, which seems immune to human presence. The number of offspring a species produces also affects the resistance of the species to human pressures such as hunting, habitat alteration, and pesticide use. Sensitivity to environmental pollutants varies considerably among plants and animals, making some much more susceptible than others.

This brief example of the use of the Multiple Cause and Effect model shows that wildlife extinction, like all environmental issues, is a complex matter. This model enlarges our focus and contributes to a more organized, scientific view of the world around us. It will help us avoid the oversimplified diagnosis and treatment of contemporary problems.

Impact Analysis Model

In Chapter 1 we saw how human life-styles and needs have changed over the years. In particular, we looked at the changing impact of human populations—how humans have become a major molding force in the environment

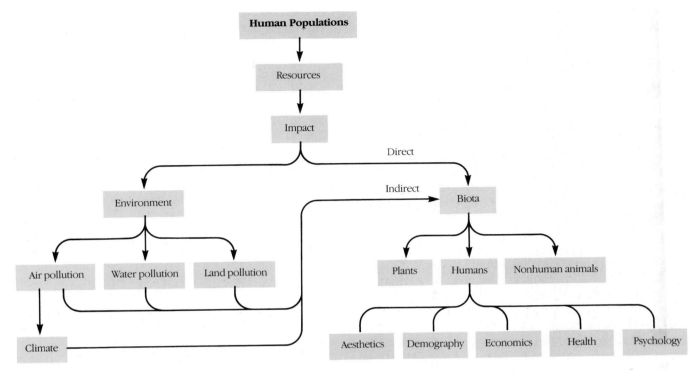

Figure 2-6
Impact Analysis model, showing the range of impacts caused by human activities.

and how increasing technological development and increasing population size have affected the environment.

To develop a deeper understanding of human impact, let us briefly examine a third model, illustrated in Figure 2-6. This simplified version of the **Impact Analysis model** shows that humans have an impact on the environment—the air, water, and land—as well as the *biota,* the plant, animal, and microbial inhabitants of the environment. Impact analysis is far more than an intellectual exercise; it is the basis of *environmental impact statements* that must be prepared for almost all major construction projects (see Chapter Supplement 25-1).

Pollution

To illustrate the Impact Analysis model, let us take a brief look at the mining and combustion of coal in the United States. Environmental impacts include air, water, and land pollution (Figure 2-6). Air pollution may result from mining or related activities such as trucks traveling on dirt roads near mines. Combustion of coal to generate electricity creates a much larger air pollution problem. A sin-

gle 1000-megawatt coal-fired power plant, which serves roughly 1 million people, emits approximately 1500 to 30,000 metric tons (1650 to 33,000 tons) of particulates (smoke and ash) and 11,000 to 110,000 metric tons (12,000 to 121,000 tons) of sulfur dioxide gas each year.

Water pollution can also be caused by coal mining. In abandoned underground coal mines in the eastern United States, for example, certain sulfur-bearing minerals (iron pyrite) react with oxygen and water to produce highly caustic sulfuric acid. This acid drains from the mine and pollutes rivers and lakes downstream (Chapter 13).

Land pollution occurs from the actual mining of coal. In the West huge surface mines are used to reach the thick beds of coal. Large draglines rip up the surface to dig down to the coal, in the process destroying the vegetation (Figure 2-7).

Indirect Effects of Human Activities   All forms of pollution described above affect organisms. For example, the sulfur dioxide produced by coal-fired power plants is converted to sulfuric acid in the atmosphere; carried as small droplets in the air, this acid may be washed from

Figure 2-7
A dragline used to remove coal disturbs the normal soil structure. If the land is not carefully reclaimed, it could be permanently ruined.

the sky by rain or snow. This phenomenon, *acid precipitation,* occurs widely in the eastern half of the United States and in Canada. In particularly susceptible regions such as southern Canada and the Adirondack Mountains of New York, acids have destroyed several hundred lakes. Lakes once known for sport fishing have turned acidic, and virtually all life has been destroyed in them. (For more on acid precipitation see Chapter Supplement 19- 2.)

Water pollutants affect a variety of organisms. Acid draining from coal mines in the East kills fish and aquatic plants. It corrodes bridges, locks, barges, pumps, and other metallic structures, costing millions of dollars a year for repair and replacement.

These examples illustrate a few of the many impacts of coal mining and combustion on the environment (for additional examples, see Chapter 13), showing us the indirect ways in which the environmental pollutants affect biological organisms, including humans.

Direct Effects of Human Activities Human activities may also have direct impacts on the biota. Surface mining in the West, for example, destroys the habitat of elk, pronghorn antelope, and prairie dogs. In the Yellowstone River basin, an area richly endowed with thick coal seams, about 36,440 hectares (90,000 acres) of land will be mined between 1977 and 2000. The impacts on native wildlife populations will be severe. Disturbance of land will also affect underground water supplies, requiring landowners to redrill wells that supply water for livestock and human uses.

A large increase in coal mining may result in changes in populations in nearby towns. These are called *demographic changes.* The town of Craig in northwestern Colorado, for example, experienced a rapid influx of miners and their families between 1970 and 1980. With this came a tripling in the crime rate. Many other towns in the United States, like Craig, were hit hard by the sudden upturn in coal production in the late 1970s. In most cases they did not have enough housing for newcomers. Schools, hospitals, sewage systems, water supply systems, stores, and recreational facilities were inadequate for their swelling populations and had to be upgraded at considerable expense. As a consequence of the influx of miners, the whole social fabric of communities has changed almost overnight. Quaint agricultural towns have become noisy and crowded.

Why Study Impacts?

The Impact Analysis model is helpful when studying the effects of a particular technology, such as coal or oil shale development. It shows the areas that should be examined when making an impact analysis.

We study impact before we build roads, dams, power plants, gravel pits, and other projects to better understand how we will affect the environment. Commonly, too little is known about the impact of human activities to make predictions concerning overall damage. As a result, we must often rely on educated guesswork or speculation.

One of the dangers of speculation is that it is imprecise. Estimates may be off by 100% or more; people forget that estimates are based on many assumptions that may not be accurate. Even though the uncertainties and assumptions are disclosed in scientific studies, people have a tendency to omit the qualifiers. Thus, what is a tentative judgment becomes an ironclad fact. The statement "Under certain weather conditions, the proposed coal-fired power plant may cause damage to neighboring crops" may be transformed into "Coal Plant Will Damage Crops." The dangers of this distortion are obvious.

Figure 2-8
Impact analysis chart is used for summarizing the positive and negative effects of a given technology or potential hazard. As an aid in decision making, impacts are listed according to the degree of probability of their occurrence.

Impacts		High Probability	Medium Probability	Low Probability	Unknown Probability
Air pollution	+				
	−				
Water pollution	+				
	−				
Land pollution	+				
	−				
Plants	+				
	−				
Humans	+				
	−				
Nonhuman animals	+				
	−				

Assessing the Probability of Impacts

One way of dealing with uncertainty is to carefully analyze impacts with respect to the *degree of probability* of their occurrence. Figure 2-8 illustrates how this analysis might be done. First, when analyzing a potential impact, determine the probability of its happening. For convenience, probability can be divided into four levels: high, medium, low, and unknown. High probability is indicated when the data supporting a given conclusion are strong and numerous. Medium probability is indicated when the impact is suspected, but there is some uncertainty. Low probability is assigned when the impact might theoretically happen, but the data do not support the contention. The fourth level of uncertainty—unknown probability— might also be added when there are no data at all showing either an impact or the absence of one.

Figure 2-8 also takes into account a much overlooked variable—the fact that not all impacts are deleterious. For example, as mentioned earlier, removing trees from forests in large numbers opens up meadows, which are used by elk for grazing. By indicating the positive as well as the negative impacts, a more balanced analysis of the impacts can be made.

In this chapter we have looked at models designed for improving the understanding of environmental problems. These are important tools that help us delineate our problems and their causes, allowing us to think creatively to find new solutions. Chapter 17 will present some models used to solve problems. Chapters 24–26 will present ethical, economic, and political issues that enter into our solutions.

A problem well stated is a problem half solved.
CHARLES KETTERING

Summary

Conceptual models help us understand complex systems and the problems that arise in these systems. The models presented in this chapter help people organize their thinking to come up with comprehensive solutions.

The *Population, Resource, and Pollution model* illustrates the fundamental working relationship between populations, resources, and pollution. It shows that all organisms acquire and use resources from the environment and that these activities create *pollution*. Resource acquisition and use affect both population and pollution. Pollution also affects the other factors in a complex fashion. To understand the impacts of one factor on another, a *cross-impact analysis* can be made.

The *Multiple Cause and Effect model* illustrates eight factors that play a large role in environmental problems. These are population, per capita consumption, politics and public policy, psychology, culture and religion, biology, economics, and technology. To thoroughly understand a problem, we must understand each of these causative elements.

The *Impact Analysis model* simply illustrates the major impacts of human actions. These are divided into effects on two general categories—environment and biota (organisms). The environmental impacts include air, water, and land pollution. The impacts on biota include effects on plants, humans, and nonhuman animals. Impacts on humans are often the most complex, because of the inherent complexity of human societies. They may include aesthetic, demographic, economic, health, and psychological (mental health) impacts.

Discussion Questions

1. Describe the Population, Resource, and Pollution model, defining the three factors that make up the model and illustrating their interaction.

2. Describe how human populations are different from nonhuman populations in terms of resource acquisition, resource use, and pollution. What is the significance of these differences in terms of environmental impact?

3. Describe how the factors in column A affect those in column B. Give examples.

A	B
Population	Resources
Resource allocation	Pollution
Resource use	Pollution
Pollution	Population

4. What factors can be altered to reduce resource demand and pollution? Which of your solutions is (are) practical? How would you go about implementing them?

5. The combustion of fossil fuels is a major source of air pollution in the world. What ways could reduce air pollution? Which of your solutions is (are) practical?

6. Choose an environmental issue with which you are familiar, and analyze it using the Multiple Cause and Effect model to the best of your ability.

7. Why are our views of current issues (social, political, and environmental) often so narrow?

9. What are the dangers of an oversimplified view of environmental issues?

Suggested Readings

Boughey, A. S. (1976). *Strategy for Survival: An Exploration of the Limits to Further Population and Industrial Growth*. Menlo Park, Calif.: W. A. Benjamin. Study of computer models used in environmental science.

Charlton, R. E. (1979). Futuristics in Biology: Some Techniques. *Amer. Biol. Teacher* 41: 136. A good analysis of techniques used to study the future.

Chiras, D. (1980). Models for Analyzing Environmental Issues in the Classroom. *Amer. Biol. Teacher* 42(8): 471. The author's original presentation of the models discussed in this chapter.

Meadows, D. H., Meadows, D. L., Randers, J., and Behrens, W. W. (1974). *The Limits to Growth*. New York: Universe Books. Controversial results of an extensive system-dynamics computer modeling study of the future of humankind.

Ripley, S. D. (1975). *The Paradox of the Human Condition*. New Delhi: Tata McGraw-Hill. An engaging essay on the environmental impact of human populations.

White, L. (1967). The Historical Roots of Our Ecologic Crisis. *Science* 1555: 1203. A classic that has sparked considerable controversy over the origin of our attitudes toward nature.

Principles of Ecology: Ecosystem Structure

Never does nature say one thing and wisdom another.

JUVENAL

An urban dweller awakens to the buzz of his alarm clock, eats a hurried breakfast, and heads toward the concrete, steel, and glass towers of Downtown, America. Bumper to bumper on the highway, encased in his shiny automobile, he listens to the radio while his tension grows. After half an hour on the freeway he parks his car and rides the elevator to a 15th-floor office already busy with the sounds of photocopiers, typewriters, and telephones.

Sitting back in his chair, looking out at the skyscrapers and the paved arteries bringing more office workers like him to the city, he entertains only vague notions of nature. To him, ecology may mean recycling cans or turning off the lights to save energy, activities that he hasn't the time or the inclination to do. His connection with the environment is obscured by business reports to prepare, bills to pay, faucets to fix, college educations to plan for, and a myriad of annoying chores to do. He does not think of himself as an organism in the environment, subject to the rules and constraints that govern all living organisms. Why should he? Everything around him—his office, the skyline, his home, even the carefully tended park across the street—bespeaks human mastery over nature.

Albert Camus once wrote, "Man is the only creature that refuses to be what he is." It is too tempting to think

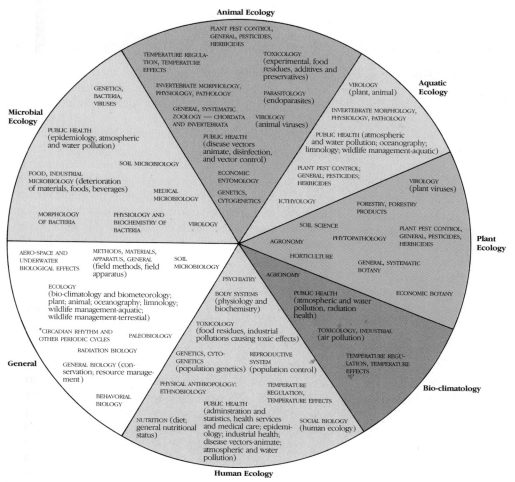

Figure 3-1
Major subdivisions within the immense realm of ecology are human, plant, aquatic, animal, microbial, bioclimatic, and general ecology.

of ourselves as apart from and even above nature. It is too easy to think that technology has made us immune to the rules that govern all living organisms. However, in the words of ecologist Raymond Dasmann, "A human apart from environment is an abstraction—in reality no such thing exists." Humans are very much a part of the environment. The ecological rules that govern the populations of earth's living organisms govern the human populations as well.

This book will show how our lives are rooted in the sun, soil, and air and how interdependent all life forms really are. It will also show that we break nature's rules at our own peril. The study of ecology, which we take up

in the next three chapters, helps us understand our part in nature and the danger of breaking its rules.

Ecology is a field of scientific study that is part of biology, the study of life. *Ecology* is the study of living organisms and their relationship to one another and to the environment. Ecology takes the entire living world as its domain, in an attempt to understand all organism–environment interactions. Given the large number of different plants, animals, and microorganisms in the world, the realm of ecology is immense. For convenience, it can be split into many subdivisions, as illustrated in Figure 3-1. In this chapter, we will first review some facts about life and then look at how life is organized and subdivided.

Some Principles of Life

Living organisms, on an individual or a population level, have five common features: (1) they can reproduce their own kind; (2) they are able to synthesize and degrade molecules, a process called *metabolism;* (3) they are able to respond to stimuli, a feature called *irritability;* (4) they are able to grow; and (5) they can adapt to changes. Of these five features, irritability and adaptability are of the utmost importance in the study of environmental science.

Irritability

Irritability is the ability to respond to various chemical and physical stimuli. It requires that an organism first perceive a stimulus through various sensory organs (eyes, ears, temperature receptors) and then react to it. Reactions to the stimuli may occur on several different levels. For example, we may respond consciously to cold weather by adding more clothes or turning up the heat. Or we may undergo certain involuntary physiological changes, such as shivering, which creates additional body heat through muscle contraction.

Responses to stimuli in organisms vary considerably. For example, a seedling orients itself to gravity: no matter what position it sprouts in, the stem grows upward, and the roots downward. Many single-celled organisms such as the amoeba move toward light; other aquatic organisms avoid light. The ability to change is essential to all living organisms, because the physical and chemical components of the environment are constantly changing. Survival would be impossible if organisms were unable to change in response to sudden environmental changes.

Adaptation and Evolution

Irritability allows an organism to adapt to changes in its environment. More permanent change may occur through evolution. **Evolution** is a process of anatomical, physiological, and even behavioral change that takes place in **populations**, groups, or organisms of the same species.

The theory of evolution is often linked to Charles Darwin, the 19th-century British naturalist. The truth is that Darwin did not invent the idea; evolution was already widely discussed in his time. In fact, Darwin's grandfather Erasmus had written about it in poems. What Darwin did was convince the scientific world that evolution had indeed occurred. More importantly, though, he proposed a theory to explain how evolution worked. This was his theory of natural selection. Darwin's ideas on natural selection were controversial, opposing the prevalent religious belief that God controlled the process of evolution. As a result, he delayed publishing his theory until 1859, more than 20 years after its development, and then only because Alfred Russell Wallace was about to publish a virtually identical theory. Like many great ideas, natural selection took a long time to catch on. It was not until the 1940s that the idea became widely accepted, nearly a hundred years after its publication.

Evolution, according to Darwin, requires both variation and natural selection. The process of evolution begins by random and spontaneous variations in the genetic material of the germ cells (sperm and ova) of individual members of a population. Such changes provide genetic variation in a population—that is, some slightly different genotypes (genetic types). The genetic material (DNA) of the germ cells is replicated after fertilization. Exact copies are produced, so that each body cell contains an exact replica of the parents' germ cells. In body cells the DNA controls cellular structure and function and ultimately determines anatomical, behavioral, and physiological features of organisms. In other words, the DNA determines what an organism looks like, how it behaves (at least in part), and how it functions. Random mutations of the DNA may have no effect, may be harmful, or may be beneficial to offspring. If a genetic mutation is deleterious, the affected organism will be less likely to mature and reproduce. If the genetic change is advantageous, however, it may give the organism a better chance of surviving and, subsequently, reproducing. In short, the mutation may give the organism an advantage over other members of the same species called a *selective advantage.* The *differential reproductive success* of the favored variant means that its offspring should make up a progressively larger portion of future generations. If the new trait truly offers an advantage in survival, in time the genetic composition of the population will shift.

Biologists call any genetically based characteristic that increases an organism's chances of passing on its genes an adaptation. More precisely, an **adaptation** is a genetically controlled anatomical, physiological, or behavioral characteristic that increases the probability that the genetic material of an organism will be passed to future generations. It does this by increasing an organism's ability to cope with its local environment.

Variation is the ever-present raw material of evolution. But what molds this raw material into new life forms? The molding or driving force of evolution is **natural selection**. Darwin described natural selection as the process in which

Figure 3-2
The white *(a)* and black *(b)* forms of the peppered moth rest on a soot-covered tree in England.

slight variations, if useful, are preserved. It is important to note that environment does nothing to the genetic material; it only picks and preserves by natural selection those organisms in a population with random variations that confer some selective advantage.

Evolution and natural selection are the ways that species change into forms that better fit into their environment. This does not mean that evolution continually builds more complex forms of life from simpler ones. Evolution simply enables species to fit their environment better; in some cases, that means abandoning an "advance" made in an ancestral species.

There are many interesting examples of evolution, but few are as graphic as the evolution of the peppered moth. This example illustrates natural selection that occurs as a result of human intervention in the environment.

The peppered moth was first described in 1845 in England (Figure 3-2). At that time 99% of the population was white, and 1% was black. By 1895, however, the black form of this species constituted 99%.

Why did the moth population evolve? The answer is quite simple. As the bark of trees became covered with soot from factories, the white moths stood out. As a result, insect-eating birds began to catch a higher proportion of the conspicuous white forms. Better camouflaged, the black moths were left behind to breed. Gradually, the dark moths made up a larger and larger part of the total population.

How did the black form originate in the first place? Was it a response to the darkened tree trunks? According to the theory of evolution, the black form originated as a random genetic variation in a population of white moths. This mutation was not in any way linked to pollution.

Because the mutation proved to be beneficial to the moth, it is called an adaptation. This adaptation gave the moth a better chance of surviving and reproducing its own kind. It gave the dark form a selective advantage over the white form. Now that soot and other industrial pollutants are decreasing in most major industrial cities, the balance of black and white may change again.

There are many interesting examples of adaptation among organisms. For instance, many insects have glands that release chemicals to repel predators. The bombardier beetle, for instance, emits a hot toxic spray to ward off spiders and other predators. The whip scorpion emits a spray of acetic acid when disturbed. Other organisms blend into their surroundings so well that they are difficult to see. Still others develop markings on their hind end that seem to confuse or frighten potential enemies. Brightly colored reptiles and insects often carry powerful toxins. One taste of the poison, and the predator will never forget that the bright colors are a polite reminder to "keep away."

How rapidly a species evolves is the subject of much debate. For many years evolutionists believed that evolutionary changes occurred gradually over many millions of years. If this were true, paleontologists reasoned, the fossil record should contain many intermediate forms of organisms, illustrating the gradual transformation. With a few exceptions, however, the fossil record shows few intermediate stages. This absence led the noted paleontologists Stephen Gould of Harvard and Niles Eldredge of the American Museum of Natural History to propose a slightly different theory: that the history of life was characterized by long, fairly quiet periods punctuated by times of fairly rapid change. This theory, called **punctuated**

Figure 3-3
An evolutionary classification of organisms. Monera the first life forms, gave rise to three branches of protista, which in turn gave rise to animals, plants, and fungi.

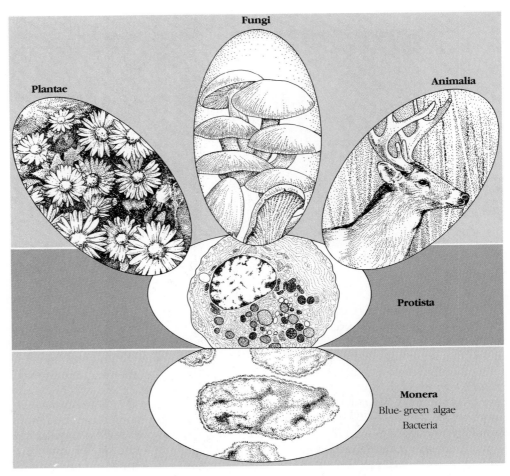

equilibrium, accounts for the lack of geological evidence to support gradualism. (For a discussion of the evolutionary timetable, see Essay 3-1.)

A further modification, not yet widely accepted, is the **temporal theory of evolution**. It states that organisms are selected according to their ability to anticipate and react favorably to change in the environment. Those that can sense environmental changes and respond appropriately will enjoy differential reproductive success, which provides the driving force of evolution.

Kingdoms: An Evolutionary Classification of Organisms

The millions of organisms can be grouped into a number of categories. At the most general level, scientists classify organisms into five **kingdoms** (Figure 3-3). This system of classification is one of many based primarily on similarities and differences in anatomy and physiology. It is an *evolutionary classification* which illustrates how the kingdoms developed. The five kingdoms are Monera, Protista (protists), Plantae (plants), Fungi, and Animalia (animals).

Monera The monera are believed to be the earliest inhabitants of the earth, having arisen more than 3 billion years ago. (The earth itself is generally believed to be about 4.6 billion years old.) Within this kindgom are many single-celled organisms, notably bacteria and blue-green algae (Figure 3-4). The common characteristic of these organisms is that they do not have distinct nuclei.

Bacteria play a vital role in nature, helping to decay animal and plant waste and thereby returning nutrients to the air, soil, and water, where they can be reused. Blue-green algae live mostly in freshwater ponds and pools,

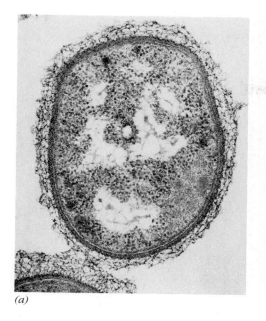

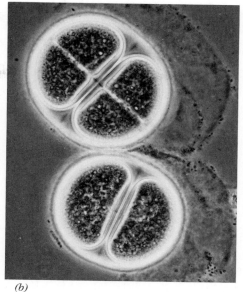

(a)

(b)

Figure 3-4
(a) A view of a bacterium taken with an electron microscope. The bacterium is a single-celled organism belonging to the kingdom Monera (53,000 ×). *(b)* A blue-green algae, also a member of the kingdom Monera. Here small groups of cells are enclosed within a gelatinous sheath (560 ×).

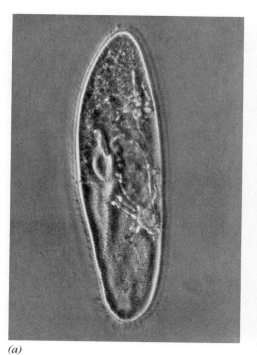

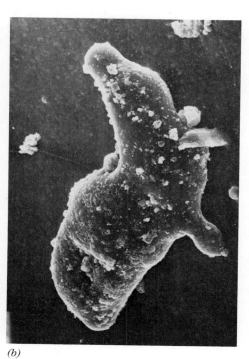

(a)

(b)

Figure 3-5
Two members of the kingdom Protista. *(a)* the *Paramecium* (400 ×). *(b)* An amoeba taken with a scanning electron micrograph (200 ×).

where they often unite with others, forming globular colonies or long filaments.

Protista Protists are single-celled organisms that evolved from monerans. They are larger and more complex than the monerans. It is believed that they gave rise to plants, fungi, and animals; thus, there are three distinct groupings within this kindgom. You may be familiar with some protists, such as *Paramecium* and *amoeba,* from a high school biology class (Figure 3-5).

The Accelerating Pace of Evolution

We commonly speak about how fast life seems to be getting; in fact, the pace of life has continually been accelerating from the beginning of the universe. What we are witnessing today is simply the culmination of a long-term acceleration process that began 15 billion years ago with the Big Bang—a gigantic explosion in space that gave rise to the universe. Let's look at the developments since then.

Our solar system developed from the hot gases in outer space following the Big Bang (see diagram). Slowly condensing as the temperature cooled, the earth was formed about 10 billion years after the Big Bang (about 4.6 billion years ago). The next major event was the evolution of simple organic molecules necessary for life. These were formed from inorganic molecules such as carbon dioxide, water, and ammonia found in the atmosphere of the early earth. Energy from sunlight and lightning combined these smaller molecules into the organic compounds that would eventually be the basis of all life on earth. About half a billion to a billion years later, simple cells called monera (bacteria and later blue-green algae) formed. After this, evolution slowed, and for nearly 2 billion years life on earth was a rather uninteresting mix of these bacteria and blue-green algae.

Following this respite, more-complex cells, called protists, arose. Formed about 1.2 to 1.5 billion years ago, the protists dominated the scene for about 600 million years, and were followed by mollusks and worms.

At this stage, in the Cambrian period, the evolutionary process really picked up. Thousands of new life forms emerged in what ecologists call the *Cambrian explosion*, which took 10 to 20 million years— a mere blink of the eye in geological time (1/450th of the earth's history). Evolution speeded up even further with the forma-

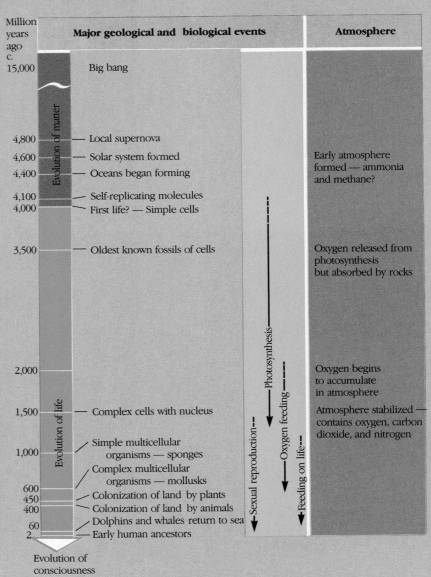

Major stages in the evolution of life.

tion of plants, following the Cambrian explosion. Fifty million years later, animals began to colonize the land. Humans evolved about 3.5 to 3.7 million years ago. In a period of 4.5 billion years the earth has been converted from a barren, volcanic landscape into a biological wonderland. If anyone had been around 4.5 billion years ago, would they have guessed that such an improbable and forbidding place could have changed so drastically and produced such wondrous and diverse creatures?

A sharp appreciation for the accelerating pace of evolution can be achieved by putting all these events on a film that lasts exactly one year. The film opens on January 1 with the Big Bang, which takes only a hundred-millionth of a second! Soon, though, the universe begins to cool. Stable atoms form from the hot gases of space in the first 25 minutes of the film. Throughout January, the hot gases formed during the Big Bang begin to expand, but it's not until February and March that they begin to cool enough to condense and form planets.

Throughout the spring and summer of our film very little happens. Not until September does our solar system develop. By the beginning of October, simple bacteria and blue-green algae are formed. The first multicellular organisms appear around the beginning of December. Dinosaurs rule the land for less than a week, from Christmas to midday December 30.

On the middle of the last day of the film, our apelike ancestors make their entry. At 11:00 P.M. that day they begin to walk upright. Human language begins to develop a minute and a half before midnight, and in the last 30 seconds agriculture is developed. The Industrial Revolution occurs in the last half-second, and World War II occurs one-tenth of a second before the film stops.

But the film is not over yet. We still have one frame left, or one inch of film in what was a 200,000-mile media extravaganza. Everything from World War II to now occurs in that last frame.

Adapted from Russell, P. (1983). *The Global Brain.* Los Angeles: J.P. Tarcher.

Fungi The fungi are a group of familiar organisms including molds, mushrooms, and yeasts (Figure 3-6). Commonly and incorrectly thought of as plants, because they are sedentary, fungi are a unique group that generally feed on dead organic matter. They play a vital role in the decay of organic matter and the return of nutrients to the environment for reuse.

Plantae The plants include a wide variety of species such as green algae, mosses, ferns, shrubs, trees, grasses, cacti, wildflowers, and herbs (Figure 3-7). Plants occupy a special place in nature as producers of the organic matter essential for all animal life.

Virtually all plants contain a green pigment called *chlorophyll,* which has the unique capability of capturing energy

Figure 3-6
The kingdom Fungi, represented here by mushrooms, consists of thousands of species, which feed off dead organic matter and are part of the decomposer food chain. Fungi do not contain chlorophyll and are, therefore, incapable of photosynthesis.

Figure 3-7
The kingdom Plantae consists of a wide fariety of species such as the cacti shown here. Plants have one feature in common—the presence of chlorophyll capable of absorbing sunlight, which the plant then uses to form organic molecules such as glucose.

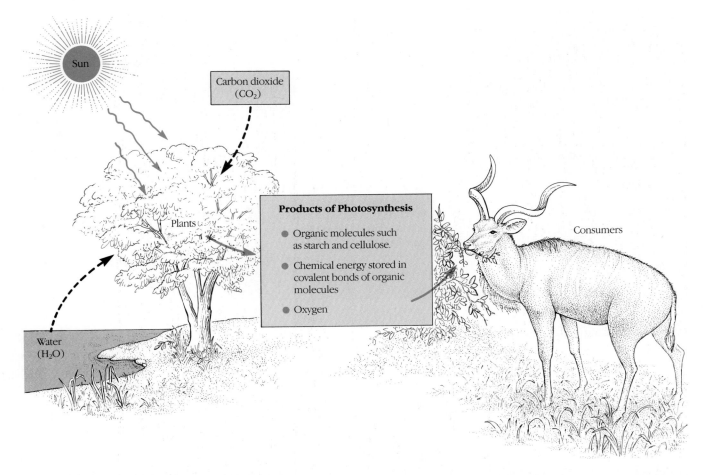

Figure 3-8
Simplified version of photosynthesis showing the flow of matter and energy. Energy
is supplied by sunlight, which the plant absorbs. Carbon dioxide and water are
converted to organic molecules in the chloroplast of plants. These materials then
are consumed by herbivores, which use the bond energy and organic building
blocks to build new protein and other essential organic chemicals.

from sunlight. The plant uses the energy to make organic
molecules (such as starch and glucose) from water and
carbon dioxide, both readily available from the environment (Figure 3-8). This process is called *photosynthesis*.
The organic molecules (carbohydrates) created during
photosynthesis store energy in the chemical (covalent)
bonds that link the individual atoms of the carbohydrates
together. Plants ultimately feed every other form of life.

Animalia   Whereas plants have the ability to make their
own organic molecules, animals must ingest organic sub-

stances to survive. As we shall see when we study food
chains, they acquire these organic molecules by consuming plants and other animals.

It is difficult to make generalizations about the animal
kingdom that will apply to all animals. The most common
feature is mobility, afforded by muscles. However, there
are exceptions such as sponges. The kingdom comprises
a remarkable diversity of creatures, from human beings
and other mammals to anatomically and physiologically
less complex organisms such as insects, jellyfish, coral
polyps, and worms (Figure 3-9).

(a)

(b)

(c)

Figure 3-9
Examples of the diverse animal kingdom: *(a)* Chinese farmer, *(b)* Monarch
butterflies, and *(c)* elephant seal pups.

The Biosphere, Biomes, and Aquatic Life Zones

We will continue our study of ecology by looking at the organization of life, starting on a large scale and gradually focusing in on smaller and smaller units.

The Biosphere

That part of the earth that supports life is commonly called the *biosphere*. If the earth were the size of an apple, the biosphere would be about as thick as its skin. As shown in Figure 3-10, the biosphere extends from the floor of

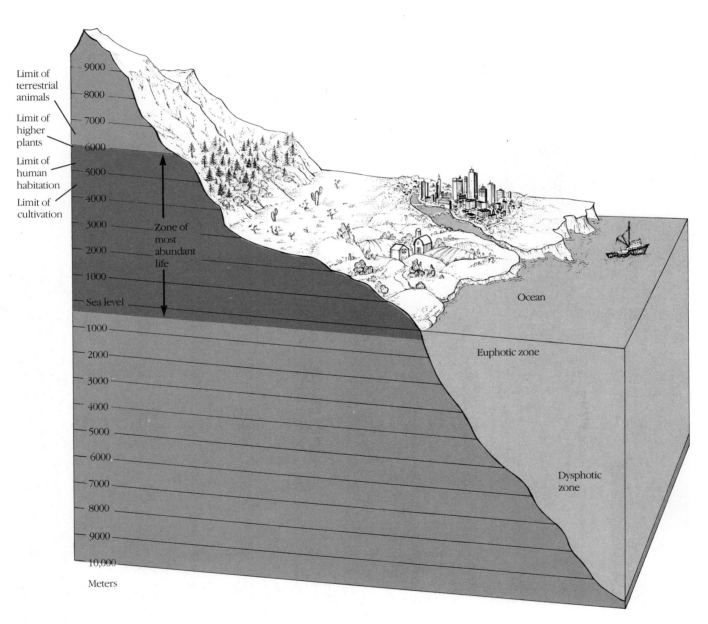

Figure 3-10

Vertical dimensions of the biosphere. Life exists in a broad band extending from the highest mountain peaks to the depths of the ocean. However, life at the extremes is rare, and most organisms are restricted to a narrow zone shown here.

the ocean, some 11,000 meters (36,000 feet) below the surface, to the tops of the highest mountains, or about 9000 meters (30,000 feet) above sea level. It includes three distinct parts: the *atmosphere* (air), the *hydrosphere* (water), and the *lithosphere* (land) (Figure 3-11).

Life is scarce at the extremes of the biosphere. On the tops of the highest mountains, only inert spores (reproductive cells) of bacteria and fungi can be found. Likewise, the deep ocean, with a few exceptions, is virtually lifeless. Life forms tend to concentrate in a much narrower zone

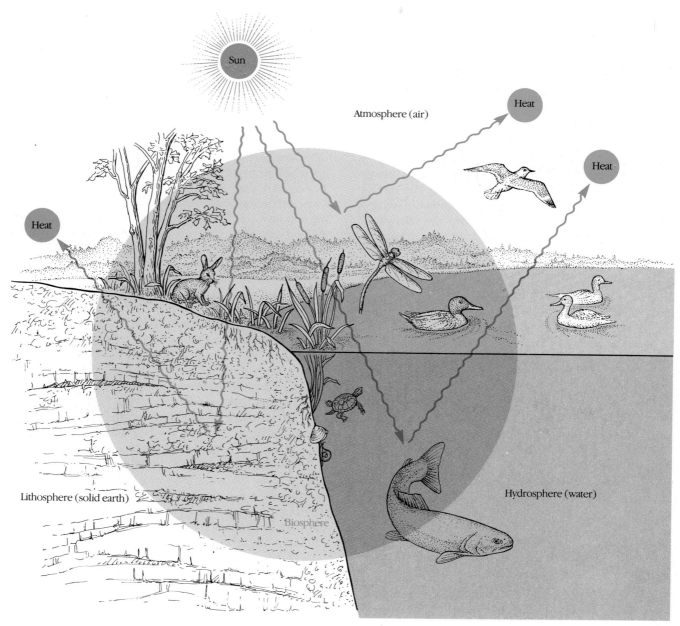

Figure 3-11
The biosphere exists at the intersection of land (lithosphere), air (atmosphere), and water (hydrosphere). As shown here, the biosphere is energized by sunlight.

extending less than 200 meters (660 feet) below the surface of the ocean and about 6000 meters (20,000 feet) above sea level.

The energy necessary for life within the biosphere comes from the sun. The chemicals that are the building blocks of all living organisms come from the air, water, and soil. Because matter does not come from outside, the biosphere is a **closed system**. Consequently, all the chemicals necessary for life must be contained within it, and they must be recycled over and over for life to continue as it has for billions of years. When an organism dies, chemicals it has ingested are returned to the land, air, or water and reused by subsequent generations. In this way, new generations are built upon those that went before them.

Biomes and Aquatic Life Zones

The terrestrial portion of the biosphere is divided into huge biomes, enormous regions characterized by climate, vegetation, animal life, and general soil type. The earth's dozen or more biomes spread over millions of square miles and span entire continents. No two are alike.

Climate, the average weather conditions in a given region, determines the boundaries of a biome and the abundance of plants and animals found in each one. The most important climatic factors are precipitation and temperature.

The sea is also divided into more or less distinct life zones, including coral reefs, estuaries, deep ocean, and continental shelf. These life zones are not generally called biomes but are very similar in that they are regions of relatively distinct plant and animal life. The major differences between them can be traced to levels of dissolved nutrients, water temperature, and depth of sunlight penetration. (For more detail on biomes see Chapter Supplement 3-1.)

Ecosystems

Biomes are much like the pieces of a huge puzzle fitting across the terrestrial portion of our planet (Figure 3-12). But each biome can be subdivided into smaller units. For example, the grassland biome of North America is characterized by grasses such as buffalo gramma and bluestem. Prairie voles, 13-lined ground squirrels, and coyotes are some of the major animals found there. However, groves of cottonwoods may grow along streams, supporting a whole different group of plants and animals. A subdivision of a biome, such as the cottonwood grove, is called an *ecological system,* or *ecosystem.*

An **ecosystem** is a complex network consisting of organisms, their environment, and all the interactions that could possibly arise. In short, it is an interdependent and dynamic biological, physical, and chemical system.

An ecosystem might be a pond, a cornfield, a river, a field, a terrarium, or a small clearing in the forest. Accordingly, ecosystems vary considerably in terms of their complexity. Some may be quite simple. For instance, a rock with lichens growing on it is a relatively simple ecosystem. Others, like tropical rain forests, are quite complex. They contain an abundance of living organisms and a wide variety of species as well.

Anyone who has walked through forests and neighboring fields knows that there is often a transition zone between adjacent ecosystems. These zones are called **ecotones**. Animals and plants of adjacent ecosystems intermingle in the ecotone. In addition, it supports many species not found in either of the adjacent ecosystems. Thus, the number of different species (*species diversity*) is usually higher in ecotones than in most ecosystems. In Colorado, for instance, the habitat with the highest species diversity is the cottonwood riparian ecosystem—cottonwood groves along rivers. Two ecotones are found here: the transition zone between neighboring grassland and cottonwood grove and the transition zone between cottonwood grove and river. Over 200 species of vertebrates (animals with backbones) can be found in this ecotone.

Ecologists recognize two major types of ecosystem. **Natural ecosystems** are those that are undisturbed or relatively undisturbed by humans. Few ecosystems today have not experienced some disturbance; thus, as long as the disturbance is relatively minor, the ecosystem is considered undisturbed. **Anthropogenic ecosystems** are those that humans have significantly altered through agriculture, forestry, livestock grazing, home construction, and other activities. Of course, the ecosystems most severely altered are those where our cities are built.

Dividing ecosystems in this way is somewhat misleading. By using the word *natural* to describe undisturbed ecosystems, we imply that humans are *unnatural* or not a part of the natural world. Nothing could be further from the truth; the distinction merely refers to the relative amount of human disturbance.

In general, there are two major components to any ecosystem: abiotic and biotic.

Abiotic Factors

The **abiotic factors** are physical and chemical factors. The physical factors include (1) precipitation (how much, how

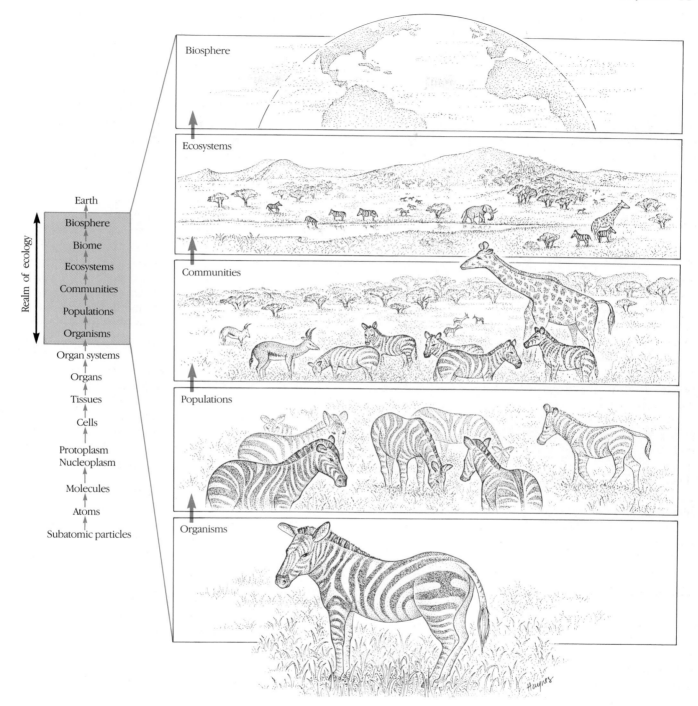

Earth
Biosphere
Biome
Ecosystems
Communities
Populations
Organisms
Organ systems
Organs
Tissues
Cells
Protoplasm
Nucleoplasm
Molecules
Atoms
Subatomic particles

Realm of ecology

Biosphere

Ecosystems

Communities

Populations

Organisms

Figure 3-12
The organization of living matter. Ecologists concern themselves with the study of individual organisms, populations, and communities as well as the ecosystem and biosphere.

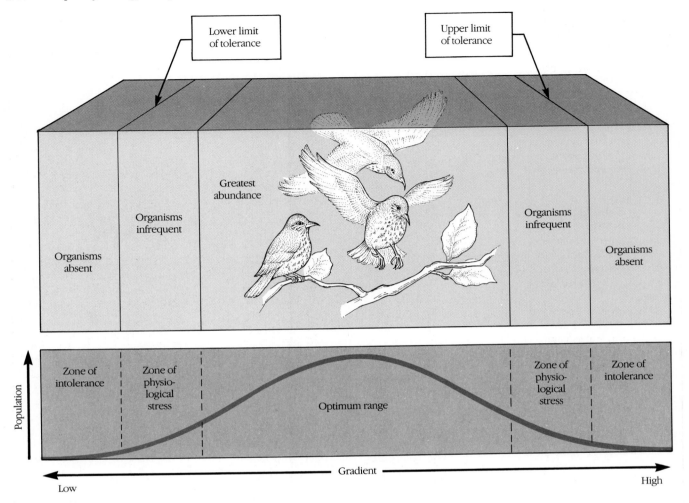

Figure 3-13
Each organism has a range of tolerance for abiotic factors. It survives within this range and can be killed by shifts below or above the range.

often, and when during the year); (2) temperature; (3) the amount of sunlight; and (4) humidity levels. The chemical factors include the availability of oxygen, carbon dioxide, phosphorus, and nitrogen.

As we shall see in later chapters, each organism in an ecosystem is finely tuned to its physical and chemical environment; if one or more of the abiotic factors is depleted, survival is threatened. Survival may also be endangered by an excess of one of the abiotic factors. Thus, all organisms operate within a range of chemical and physical factors called the **range of tolerance**. When the upper or lower limits of this range are exceeded, survival is impossible. For example, fish generally tolerate

a narrow range of water temperature (Figure 3-13). If the water cools below the range of tolerance, they may die or move to warmer water. During a cold snap in January 1981, for instance, the sudden drop in water temperature killed thousands of fish in the shallow coastal waters of southern Florida.

In all ecosystems one factor—usually abiotic—limits growth and is therefore called a **limiting factor**. The concept of limiting factors was introduced in 1840 by the chemist Justus von Liebig, who was studying the effects of chemical nutrients on plant growth. The limiting factor is the one factor that outweighs all of the others necessary for growth. It is the primary determinant of growth because

Ecology, the Subversive Science

William Tucker

The author, a journalist and critic of the environmental movement, has written numerous articles on environmental issues. His latest book, Progress and Privilege, *is a thought-provoking and controversial discussion of environmentalism.*

One of the key realizations of ecology is that the earth is a kind of living system governed by many self-regulating (homeostatic) mechanisms. The earth is in a state of equilibrium [see the Gaia hypothesis, Chapter 1]. If pushed too far in any one direction, the self-regulating mechanisms can become overloaded and break down, resulting in radical changes.

In its scientific aspects, ecology seems to offer an extraordinary broadening of our understanding of life on the planet. Yet with its transfer into the public domain, it has become little more than a sophisticated way of saying "we don't want any more progress." Somehow this exciting discipline has been translated into a very conservative social doctrine. People have often waved the flag of "ecology" as a new way of saying that nature must be preserved and human activity minimized. Ecology has sometimes been touted as being "subversive" to technological progress. It supposedly tells us that our ignorance of natural systems is too great for us to proceed any further with human enterprise. Just as nationalistic conservatives always try to throw a veil of reverence around such concepts as "patriotism" and "national tradition," so environmentalists try to maintain the same indefinable quality around ecosystems.

The lesson environmentalists drive home is that since we do not understand ecosystems in their entirety, and never will, we dare not touch them. Our knowledge is too limited, and nothing should be done until we understand more fully the implications of our actions.

To say that ecology is the science that does not yet grasp the complex interrelationships of organisms is like trying to define medicine as the science that does not yet know how to cure cancer. Environmentalists emphasize the negative parts of the discipline because it fits their concept that we have already had enough technological progress.

The lessons of ecology tell us many things. They tell us that organisms cannot go on reproducing uncontrollably. But they also tell us that many organisms have developed behavioral systems that keep their populations from exploding. The laws of ecology tell us that we cannot throw things away into the environment without having them come back to haunt us. But they also tell us that nature evolved intricate ways of recycling wastes long before human beings appeared, and ecosystems are not as fragile as they seem.

In fact, the whole notion of "fragile ecosystem" is somewhat contradictory. If these systems are so fragile, how could they have survived this long? If ecology teaches us anything, it enhances our appreciation of how resilient nature is, and how tenaciously creatures cling to life in the most severe circumstances. This, of course, should not serve as an invitation for us to see how efficiently we can wipe them out. But it does suggest that the rumors of our powers for destruction may be exaggerated.

The environmentalist interpretation of ecology has been that ecosystems have somehow perfectly evolved, and that human intervention always leads to degradation. It should be clear that even if a particular ecosystem did represent biological perfection, that is not reason in and of itself to preserve it at the expense of human utility. Our ethical position cannot be one of completely detached aesthetic appreciation. We must first be human beings in making our ethical judgments. We cannot be completely on the side of nature.

We are not a group of imbeciles aimlessly poking into the backs of watches or tossing rocks into the gears of Creation. There is purpose to what we do, and it is essentially the same as nature's. We are trying to rearrange the elements of nature for our own survival, comfort, and welfare. We can certainly act stupidly, but we can also act out of wisdom. It is foolish to argue that everything is already perfect and must be left alone. To portray humans as meddling outsiders in an already perfected world is nonsense. In going to this extreme to reaffirm nature, we only deny that we are a part of it.

Environmental writers suggest that we practice an "ecological ethic," extending our moral concerns to other animals, plants, ecosystems, and the entire biosphere. I would accept this proposal, with one important qualification: that is, that our ethical concerns still retain a hierarchy of interest. We should extend our moral concerns to plants, trees, and animals, but not at the expense of human beings. Our first obligation is to humanity. We should avoid actions that are destructive to the biosphere, but we must recognize that at some point our interests are going to impinge upon other living things.

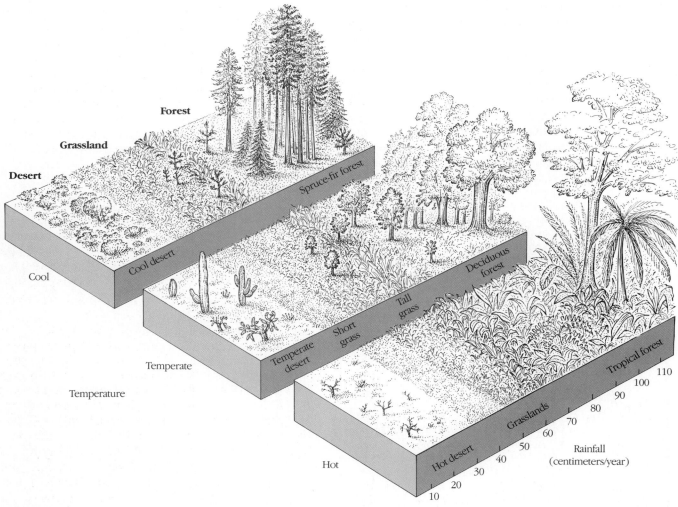

Figure 3-14
The relationship between rainfall, temperature, and vegetation. Rainfall determines
the basic type of vegetation and temperature is responsible for alterations in the
basic vegetative type.

it easily falls below the range of tolerance. In certain aquatic
ecosystems, for example, phosphorus is a limiting abiotic
factor. It is the first to be used up. When phosphorus is
reduced, the growth of algae is impaired. Nitrate can also
be a limiting abiotic factor in soil and water.

The limiting factor is analogous to the slowest camel in
a caravan. Just as the pace of an entire caravan is set by
the slowest camel, so the entire structure of an ecosystem
is determined by the limiting factor. Removal of the slowest camel would surely speed up the caravan, but a new
pace would be set by the second-slowest camel. This is
true in ecosystems as well. The presence of a limiting
factor at adequate levels does not ensure full develop-

ment, as other factors may now become limiting. For
example, precipitation is an obvious limiting factor for
plant growth. Adequate moisture, however, will not promote maximum plant growth and development if the soil
lacks nitrogen.

For most ecosystems, rainfall is *the* limiting factor. As
illustrated in Figure 3-14, rainfall determines whether land
is covered by forest, grassland, or desert. Although rainfall
determines the type of vegetation, temperature accounts
for variations on these three basic themes. For example,
when annual rainfall exceeds 70 to 80 centimeters (27 to
31 inches), forest ecosystems develop (Figure 3-14). In
warm climates the forests are tropical; in temperate cli-

mates deciduous forests predominate; but in cool climates spruce–fir forests are typical. Within each of these types of forest, differences in soil characteristics may cause more subtle changes in the type of vegetation.

As mentioned above, just as a shortage of an abiotic factor impairs the survival of organisms in an ecosystem, so can an excess. Excesses may eliminate living organisms either directly or indirectly. For example, hot water from a power plant may raise the temperature of the stream where it is disposed of by 10° to 30° C (50° to 86° F), killing fish and other aquatic organisms (Figure 3-15). This *thermal shock* is a direct effect of heat. An indirect effect is illustrated by overwatering of trees. Excess water saturates the soil and eliminates oxygen needed for plant growth. The roots suffocate and die.

Figure 3-15
Fish kill below a power plant. Hot water fused for cooling was released into the stream and suddenly raised the temperature. Fish unable to escape were killed by the rapid increase in temperature above the range of tolerance.

Living organisms also have tolerance limits for pollutants in air, water, and soil. Anytime the tolerance limit for a pollutant is exceeded, plants, animals, and microorganisms are affected in varying degrees, depending on how harmful the pollutant is. Animals, for example, may simply become ill and thus more susceptible to predators. Or the number of offspring they produce may be reduced, which threatens the species' survival. Pollutants may force animals to migrate to new environments, but if there is no suitable habitat or they can't migrate, they may die.

Biotic Factors

The **biotic (living) components** of an ecosystem are the organisms. A discrete group of organisms of the same kind incapable of breeding with others is called a **species**. Individual species occupying a specific region form a population (see Figure 3-12). Populations are dynamic groups, changing in size, age structure, and genetic composition in response to changes in the environment.

The boundaries of a population are arbitrary. For instance, we might talk about the population of great blue herons along a given stream, in a state, or in the entire United States. In nature, real boundaries may be formed by mountain ranges, deserts, lakes, oceans, and rivers. A single population may be split by the uplifting of a mountain range or the formation of a new lake or river. This splitting may result in the gradual evolution of the populations, thus creating two slightly different groups (subspecies) still capable of interbreeding. In other cases, the two populations may evolve in entirely different directions, forming two different species incapable of interbreeding.

Ecosystems are usually composed of several different populations. In the desert of southern Arizona, for instance, various plant populations such as saguaro cactus, prickly pear cactus, barrel cactus, and ocotillo coexist with populations of cactus wren, curve-billed thrasher, black-throated sparrow, burrowing owl, and ringtail.

The populations of plants, animals, and microorganisms in an ecosystem form a **biological community** (Figure 3-12). Just as the community you live in is made up of different species (humans, pets, birds, trees, and so on), so the biological community is a mix of different species interacting on many different levels. (See Chapter 5 for a discussion of species interactions.)

The biological community is bound together in an intricate web: Many species depend upon another. All species depend on the physical and chemical environment. The community takes essential nutrients from the environment but also modifies its immediate environment, at times changing it so much that the community itself is imperiled. (This change, called succession, is discussed in Chapter 5.)

Communities are generally named after the dominant plant species. In the eastern United States, for instance, oak and hickory trees dominate in many regions and form oak–hickory communities containing a variety of plants, animals, and microorganisms. In New Mexico, pinyon pine and juniper trees populate dry hillsides; these are called pinyon–juniper communities.

Niche and Habitat   Each organism within a community occupies a specific region, called its **habitat**. This term is often confused with another widely used term, the **ecological niche**, which describes where an organism fits in the ecosystem—what it consumes, what consumes it, where it lives, and how it interacts with the abiotic and biotic factors. In short, the habitat is the physical space an organism occupies; the niche is both its habitat and its role in the ecosystem—its relationship with abiotic and biotic components of the environment.

Certain organisms may live in the same habitat and have similar life-styles, but no two species occupy the same niche in a given ecosystem. For example, elk and deer live in the same habitat in the Rocky Mountains. However, elk feed primarily on grasses and herbaceous plants, whereas deer feed primarily on shrubs. Therefore, they occupy two different niches.

The implications of the rule that no two species occupy the same niche are important. Thus, similar species can coexist in a given habitat without threatening each other's survival. By occupying different niches, they minimize the level of **interspecific competition**—competition between species.

The closer the niches are, the more likely it is that interspecific competition will occur. For example, golden-mantled ground squirrels and chipmunks occupy similar habitats and niches in the Rocky Mountains (Figure 3-16). They both consume herbs, seeds, and berries and therefore compete with each other for food as well as habitat (nesting sites). If the competition becomes intense in periods when food supply is low, one species may be eliminated from the habitat—that is, made locally *extinct* (see Chapter 10). The reason is that one species will usually be better adapted to the environment; it may be better able to ward off predators or to hide when threatened. Any advantage that one species enjoys over the other can tip the ecosystem balance in their favor (see Chapter 5).

(a)   *(b)*

Figure 3-16
Ground squirrel and chipmunk have similar niches in the Rocky Mountains. As a result, they compete for shelter and food. *(a)* Golden-mantled squirrel. *(b)* Chipmunk.

Biomes

The biosphere is divided into geographically distinct land parts called biomes, each having its own specialized climate, plants, and animals. These diverse regions, made up of intricately balanced ecosystems, offer us a kaleidoscope of information on evolution and adaptation, which increases our understanding of the way the world works within the constraints of nature.

And yet, whenever we think we understand the workings of a biome (its climate, its topography, its predictability), we experience a Mt. St. Helens—a reminder from nature that life on earth is constantly in flux; changing, adjusting, adapting. Like nature, humans have altered biomes and ecosystems—but unlike nature, many of our changes have become irrevocable.

Through an understanding of the biomes we can learn about structure and function of the environment, which in turn will give us an awareness of how our world works—and, just as importantly, how it doesn't.

1 Atypical of the desert biome, the Great Sand Dunes National Monument in southern Colorado is lifeless and virtually barren.

2 The rim of the Grand Canyon in Arizona shows yet another face of the desert biome.

3 Cactus abound in the desert, blossoming briefly after the spring rains.

4 The tropical rain forest is perhaps the most diverse of all biomes. It is estimated that over 90% of the living organisms in these rain forests remain unclassified. Venezuela.

5 Rain forest in the Olympic Peninsula, Washington. Receiving over 200 inches of rain each year, this area maintains a lush growth of mosses, ferns, epiphytes, and trees.

6 The towering Alaska range overlooks the coniferous forests of the taiga, a biologically rich biome that extends across North America and much of Europe and Asia. Denali National Park, Alaska.

7 The taiga consists of large stands of one or two species of coniferous tree. Meadows occur naturally in mountain valleys, as shown here. Jasper Park, British Columbia.

8 An autumn view of the temperate deciduous forest biome.

9 Golden aspens herald autumn in the Maroon Bells-Snowmass Wilderness area, Colorado. High altitude yields a mix of coniferous and deciduous trees.

4

2

3

5

6

7

8

9

10 Alpine tundra is characterized by a short growing season, prohibiting the growth of trees or shrubs. Wildflowers, like the columbine shown here, grow densely in these areas.

11 Summery wildflowers and lichens add color to arctic tundra in the Soviet Union. Despite minimal precipitation, tundra areas remain damp from the presence of permafrost—permanently frozen soil that resists water absorption.

12 Flint Hills Preserve in Alena, Kansas, is one of the last remaining examples of the tall-grass prairie.

13 The African savannah is richly populated by grazing species that feed off trees, grass, and herbs. Kenya, Masai Mara Game Reserve.

10

11

12

13

(a)

(b)

Figure 3-17
Ecological equivalents are species with identical or very similar niches that live in different regions. The bison *(a)* and the zebra *(b)* feed on herbs and grasses. Placed in the same ecosystem, ecological equivalents would compete for food and other resources.

(a)

(b)

Figure 3-18
(a) The koala is a specialist, for it eats only the leaves of eucalyptus trees. A loss of this food source would result in its extinction. *(b)* The coyote is a generalist. Like humans, it is an opportunist, capable of eating a wide variety of foods from insects to field mice to carrion. It's existence is not so delicately balanced.

Organisms can occupy the same or very similar niches but only in geographically different locations. Such organisms are called **ecological equivalents**. For example, North America's bison are the ecological equivalent of the zebra that graze on the savannas of Africa (Figure 3-17). Both feed on grasses and herbs.

An organism's niche can be classified as specialized or generalized, depending primarily on its feeding relationships and the extent of its habitat. For example, the koala is a **specialist** that lives in Australia, where it feeds exclusively on eucalyptus leaves (Figure 3-18). Without the eucalyptus, the koala would perish. The coyote of North

America, on the other hand, is a **generalist**. It is very versatile and feeds on a wide variety of animals—mice, rabbits, chipmunks, ground-nesting birds, snakes, shrews, voles, woodrats, marmots, pocket gophers, and an occasional sheep (Figure 3-18). In the winter, coyotes may kill sick or elderly deer or elk and will feed on carrion (dead animals). The coyote occupies a wide range of habitats, too, unlike the koala.

Generalists are less subject to changes in the abiotic and biotic environment than specialists and, therefore, are less likely to become extinct. Specialists walk a tightrope. If the habitat changes faster than the species can adapt, the species will become extinct.

Humans are the ultimate generalists, thanks to our intelligence. We can make use of a wide variety of food sources and live in diverse habitats. Even though humans are generalists in terms of habitat and food, some societies have become highly specialized in some critical areas, such as energy. For example, technological societies are highly dependent on fossil fuel resources—oil, coal, and natural gas (see Chapter 13). This dependency, like the koala's dependency on eucalyptus, places technological societies in a vulnerable position.

Heterotrophs and Autotrophs   Living organisms can be categorized by the way they obtain their organic nutrients and energy. Accordingly, they fit into one of two categories: autotrophs and heterotrophs. The common root of these words, *troph,* means to feed or nourish.

Autotrophs, or "self-feeders," are organisms capable of making their own foodstuffs. Plants are the major autotrophic organisms in the biosphere, making their own food during photosynthesis.

Another interesting but minor group of autotrophs is the *chemotrophs,* or *chemosynthetic organisms.* These bacteria are capable of capturing energy from certain chemical reactions called oxidation reactions. In chemistry an **oxidation reaction** is one in which electrons are lost from an atom or molecule. Energy is released during these reactions. The chemotrophs capture energy from the oxidation of a number of chemicals such as sulfur, nitrite (NO_2^-), and ammonia (NH_4^+). Fascinating as these

organisms may be, they are of only minor significance in the flow of energy through ecosystems (discussed in Chapter 4).

All other organisms are called **heterotrophs** (*hetero = other*). Whereas plants acquire energy from the sun, heterotrophs get their energy by consuming organic matter (plants and animals). Heterotrophs—especially the animals—can be further categorized on the basis of the food source. For instance, heterotrophs that feed exclusively on plants are called **herbivores.** Deer, elk, and cattle are good examples (Figure 3-19). Heterotrophs such as the mountain lion that feed only on other animals are called **carnivores.** Those heterotrophs that feed on both plants and animals are called **omnivores.** We human beings are a classic example of omnivores. Heterotrophic organisms such as fungi that feed strictly on dead organic matter are called **saprobes,** or **saprophytes.**

Survival of the entire ecosystem ultimately depends on the autotrophs. Without them, herbivores, carnivores, omnivores, and saprobes would have nothing to eat. But autotrophs also depend on heterotrophs in many different ways. Autotrophs and heterotrophs are highly interdependent. Autotrophs capture solar energy and use it to make living tissue, in the process giving off oxygen as a waste product. Heterotrophs consume the plants and oxygen. The plant matter is broken down in a series of carefully controlled reactions that yield small amounts of energy. These reactions produce carbon dioxide and water, both needed by autotrophs to make organic materials. Thus, a full circle is made. The products of one type of organism are essential to the survival of the other.

Because autotrophs produce all the organic matter that exists in the biosphere, they are called *producers,* or *producer organisms.* In contrast, heterotrophs are called *consumers.* These are discussed in more detail in Chapters 4 and 5.

The definitions and concepts presented in this chapter give you a general idea of the structure of the ecosystem. With this necessary framework in place, we can begin to understand the intricate relationships between organisms. From here we can look more closely at important questions of ecology that involve us. And we can begin to look at how ecosystems function.

Man must go back to nature for information
THOMAS PAINE

Figure 3-19
(a) The bear is an omnivore; *(b)* the cheetah, a carnivore; *(c)* the giraffe, an herbivore.

Summary

All living organisms are characterized by five major features: reproduction, metabolism, irritability, growth, and adaptability. One of the most important is adaptability—the capacity to change to better fit the environment. This process of change is called *evolution.* Evolution occurs by random, spontaneous changes in the genetic material of organisms; if advantageous, these are preserved by *natural selection.* The population evolves as the new trait becomes widespread.

Biological organisms are divided into five major groups, called *kingdoms:* Monera, Protista, Fungi, Plantae, and Animalia. These organisms exist in a complex web of life found in the *biosphere.* The biosphere is a closed system, which means that all materials for life must come from within it or must be recycled. The biosphere is divided into major subregions, called *biomes,* each with a unique plant and animal life. The boundaries of a biome are determined by *climate,* the average of the weather conditions over long periods of time. Precipitation and temperature are the most important climatic factors. Biomes can be divided into smaller units, called *ecosystems.* These complex, living networks consist of organisms, their environment, and all the interactions that exist between them. Arbitrarily, *natural ecosystems* are those that are relatively undisturbed by humans. *Anthropogenic ecosystems* are those significantly altered by humans, such as cities and farmland.

Each ecosystem consists of *biotic* (living) and *abiotic* (nonliving) components. The abiotic components are physical and chemical factors that are needed for life. Each organism operates within a range of chemical and physical factors known as the *range of tolerance*. When the upper or lower limits of this range are exceeded, the organism cannot survive. In all ecosystems, one factor usually limits growth and is called a *limiting factor*.

The organisms are the *biotic* components of the ecosystem. A group of similar organisms incapable of breeding with others is called a *species*. An individual species occupying a specific region forms a *population*. Populations are dynamic groups that change in size, age structure, and genetic composition in response to the environment.

The populations of plants, animals, and microorganisms in an ecosystem form a *biological community*. Each organism within a community occupies a specific region, or *habitat*. It also occupies a specific niche, which includes its habitat but also all the relationships with abiotic and biotic components of the environment. No two species occupy the same niche in the same ecosystem, a fact that reduces *interspecific competition*.

Organisms occupying the same niche but in different ecosystems are called *ecological equivalents*. The bison and zebra are good examples. If they were placed in the same ecosystem, competition for food and other resources would most likely be intense.

Organisms may be generalists or specialists *Generalists* occupy many different habitats and feed off a wide variety of foods. *Specialists* generally live in one habitat and feed off one or only a few organisms, making them more susceptible to changes in the habitat and prone to extinction.

Organisms are also classified on the basis of where they derive their nutrients. Plants that make their own organic nutrients are called *autotrophs*, or self-feeders. All other organisms are *heterotrophs*, feeding on others. If heterotrophs feed exclusively on plants, they are called *herbivores*. If they feed on animals, they are called *carnivores*. And if they consume plants and animals, they are called *omnivores*. *Saprobes*, such as the fungi, feed on dead organic material.

Discussion Questions

1. What is ecology? What are some of the subdivisions of this vast scientific discipline?

2. List the characteristics of all living organisms, and describe the term *irritability*. Give some examples of irritability.

3. Describe the process of evolution. Be certain to include the following concepts in your discussion: natural selection and adaptation.

4. Genetic changes during evolution are random events. How could they result in the major changes that occur in evolution? What role does the environment play in evolution?

5. Define the term *biosphere*. Why is the biosphere considered a closed system? Can you name some other closed systems?

6. Define the term *biome*. What determines the type of vegetation in a biome?

7. Define the term *ecosystem*. What are the common features of all ecosystems?

8. Describe the abiotic components of the ecosystem. How do these factors affect plant and animal life?

9. Discuss the concept *range of tolerance*. Can you think of any examples in which the range of tolerance was exceeded in ecosystems you are familiar with? What happened during these incidents?

10. What is a limiting factor? What is the limiting factor in most terrestrial ecosystems?

11. Discuss the terms *niche* and *habitat*.

12. Discuss this statement: no two organisms can occupy the same niche in the same habitat.

13. What is an ecological equivalent? Give an example.

14. Why is the coyote a generalist? Why is the koala a specialist? Why are specialists more prone to extinction?

15. Define the following terms: *autotroph, heterotroph, herbivore, carnivore, omnivore,* and *saprobe*. Give examples.

Suggested Readings

Colinvaux, P. (1973). *Introduction to Ecology*. New York: Wiley. An excellent textbook of basic ecology.

Curtis, H. (1979). *Biology*. New York: Worth. A must for students who want to supplement their knowledge of ecology without having to read an entire ecology text.

Dasmann, R. F. (1975). *The Conservation Alternative*. New York: Wiley. A good general work on ecology.

———. (1976). *Environmental Conservation* (4th ed.). New York: Wiley. Contains a particularly good discussion of ecological principles.

Ehrlich, P. A.; Ehrlich, A. H.; and Holdren, J. P. (1977). *Ecoscience: Population, Resources, Environment*. San Francisco: Freeman. A higher-level text that covers ecology in detail. A superb reference book.

Gould, S. J. (1977). *Ever Since Darwin*. New York: Norton. Brilliant collection of essays on evolution and natural history.

———. (1980). *The Panda's Thumb*. New York: Norton. Brilliant and witty collection of essays on evolution.

Hitching, F. (1982). *The Neck of the Giraffe: Where Darwin Went Wrong*. New York: Ticknor and Fields. Popular account criticizing Darwinian theory of evolution.

Keeton, W. T. (1980). *Biological Science*. New York: Norton. A carefully written and well-illustrated book for students who want to expand their knowledge of ecology without tackling an ecology text.

Rifkin, J. (1983). *Algeny*. New York: Norton. Critique of Darwinian evolutionary theory. Contains controversial discussion on origin of theory of natural selection.

Rodgers, C. L., and Kerstetter, R. E. (1974). *The Ecosphere: Organisms, Habitats, and Disturbances*. New York: Harper and Row. An account on biomes and human disturbance of natural ecosystems.

Rosenzweig, M. L. (1974). *And Replenish the Earth*. New York: Harper and Row. A detailed and carefully written account of evolution and population ecology.

Smith, R. L. (1976). *The Ecology of Man: An Ecosystem Approach* (2nd ed.). New York: Harper and Row. Advanced readings on ecology and environmental problems.

———. (1980). *Ecology and Field Biology* (3rd ed.). New York: Harper and Row. A comprehensive textbook for students wishing to delve into this subject in more detail.

The Biomes

Ecologists divide the terrestrial portion of the biosphere into **biomes**, large regions each with its own distinctive flora, fauna, climate, and soil type. The dozen or more biomes spread over millions of square miles and span entire continents. In this supplement, we will look at some of the major world biomes. Gallery 1, World Biomes, vividly illustrates the earth's diverse topography (see first color insert).

Tundra

The **tundra** is a vast, virtually treeless region in the far northern parts of North America, Europe, and Asia (Figure S3-1). It lies between a region of perpetual ice and snow to the north and a band of coniferous forests (the taiga) to the south. One of the largest biomes, the tundra occupies approximately 20 million square miles, or about one-tenth of the earth's land surface.

The tundra receives very little precipitation (less than 25 centimeters [10 inches] a year), and most of this comes during the summer months; snowfall during the long winter is rare, and the mean monthly temperature is well below zero. The deeper layers of soil remain permanently frozen throughout the year and are called **permafrost**.

The tundra is usually a gently rolling landscape dominated by herbaceous plants (grasses, sedges, rushes, and heather), mosses, lichens, and dwarf willows. Trees and other deep-rooted plants cannot grow there because of the permafrost. Most of the rest of the plants are stunted because of the short growing season, the annual freeze–thaw cycle, which damages roots, and the strong winter winds, which carry abrasive snow and ice crystals that take their toll on the vegetation.

In the summer, the days are long and warm; the superficial layers of soil thaw. The ground becomes soggy because of a low

Figure S3-1
Rolligons are used in Alaska. These tires are designed to carry heavy equipment across the tundra with a minimal amount of damage to the delicate topsoil.

evaporation rate and because the permafrost prevents water from soaking into the ground. Consequently, the land becomes dotted with thousands of shallow lakes, ponds, and bogs, which support great colonies of birds that come north to nest and feed off the abundant insects.

In North America, musk oxen and caribou inhabit the tundra along with a variety of small rodents (including lemmings) and other mammals (white foxes and rabbits). They share their habitat with snowy owls and ptarmigans (ground-dwelling birds similar to grouse).

The tundra is a fragile biome. Where vegetation has been destroyed decades are required for it to grow back. Especially harmful are vehicles whose tires tear up the vegetation. New vehicles such as those shown in Figure S3-1 may help reduce this impact on the tundra.

Taiga

South of the tundra, also extending across North America, Europe, and Asia, is a broad band of coniferous (evergreen) forests known as the **taiga**. The average annual precipitation in the taiga is considerably higher than that of the tundra. Furthermore, the temperature is warmer, which makes the taiga a far more hospitable place for plant and animal life.

With a growing season of 150 days and a complete thawing of the subsoil, the taiga supports a higher diversity and abundance of vegetation and animal life than the tundra. The conifers are the dominant form of plant life. Black spruce, white spruce, balsam fir, and tamarack are common. Conifers are especially well adapted to the long, cold, snowy winters. Water loss is minimized by waxy coatings on their needles. During winter, when water transport from the roots is at a standstill, reduced evaporation is critical. The flexible branches of conifers can bend under the burden of snow.

Some deciduous trees (trees that shed their leaves each year) are found in the taiga in localized regions. These include the paper birch, larch, alder, quaking aspen, and white birch. They grow in areas that are recovering after fires or heavy timber cutting.

Bear, moose, wolves, lynx, wolverines, martens, porcupines, and numerous small rodents inhabit the forests, as do a variety of bird species such as the ruffed grouse, spruce grouse, common raven, hairy woodpecker, and great horned owl. Insects, such as mosquitoes, also thrive during the warm summer months. Over 50 species of insects that feed on conifers live in the taiga, including the spruce budworm, pine beetle, tussock moth, and pine sawfly. These can cause widespread damage to trees when populations increase as a result of warm winters or droughts, which weaken the ability of trees to resist them. Cold-blooded vertebrates such as reptiles and amphibians are rare.

Numerous lakes, ponds, and bogs highlight the landscape. In North America trappers once traveled by boat into the interior of the taiga on the interconnected waterways in search of beaver and other animals. The taiga has long been of interest to the logging industry. Loggers have stripped large sections of land in a process known as **clear cutting** (discussed further in Chapter 11). Until recently, little or no effort was made to replant denuded areas. The result has been severe soil erosion, which depletes the forests of topsoil, destroys wildlife habitat, and pollutes streams and lakes.

Temperate Deciduous Forest

The **temperate deciduous forest** biome is located in the eastern United States, Europe, and northeastern China. A region with a warm, mild growing season and abundant rainfall, the temperate deciduous forest supports a wide variety of plants and animals.

The climate in this biome varies considerably; for instance, on the North American continent the average temperature in January is $-12°$ C ($10°$ F) in the north and $15°$ C ($60°$ F) in the south. Thus, the growing season also varies from north to south—from five months in the northern sections of the biome up to ten months in the southern sections.

The dominant vegetation consists of broad-leafed deciduous trees such as maple, oak, and hickory. The dominant species may vary depending on temperature and precipitation.

Temperate deciduous forests support a variety of organisms, including white-tailed deer, opossum, raccoons, squirrels, chipmunks, foxes, rabbits, black bear, mice, shrews, nuthatches, wrens, downy woodpeckers, and owls. During the summer, warblers and other bird species migrate in and breed in the forests.

The soil is rich in organic matter and nutrients because of the leaves deposited on it each year. The gradual decay of leaves adds to the soil organic and inorganic nutrients, both important for further plant growth. The roots of deciduous trees act as "nutrient pumps," drawing nutrients up from the subsoil to the leaves, which are then deposited on the ground.

This biome has been extensively exploited. In North America it once extended from the Mississippi River to the Atlantic coast; now, however, only about 0.1% of the original forest remains, much having been cleared away for farms and orchards. The forests that remain are second and third growth. Early settlers often failed to practice good soil-conservation methods and allowed their land to erode away. Forced to move westward into virgin territory, farmers often continued to seek short-term benefits while disregarding the long-term effects of their actions. Today, agricultural practices have improved, but there is still need for great improvement. Over 3 million tons of topsoil are eroded from agricultural land each year in the United States. This would fill over 14 trains each extending around the equator! (For more on soil erosion, see Chapter 8 and Chapter Supplement 9-2.)

Grasslands

Grasslands exist in both temperate and tropical regions where rainfall is relatively low or uneven. As shown in Figure S3-1, the **temperate grasslands** are found in North America in an extensive region from the Rockies to the Mississippi River known as the Great Plains. In addition, moister regions of the Great Basin—lying between the Sierra Nevada and the Rockies—support grasslands. Other major regions of temperate grassland are found in South America, Australia, and Eurasia. **Tropical grassland** exists in Africa and South America (see Figure S3-1).

Temperate and tropical grasslands are similar in appearance (Figure S3-2). Both are characterized by periodic drought and flat, or slightly rolling, terrain. Large grazers feed off the lush grasses in this biome. In North America the pronghorn antelope

(a)

(b)

Figure S3-2
Grassland exists in both temperature and tropical regions. They are used worldwide for both *(a)* grazing and *(b)* agriculture.

and bison are the leading grazers. In Africa zebras and a variety of antelope species are predominant. In Australia the kangaroo fills this niche. A number of large predators live on the grasslands.

The temperate and tropical grasslands differ in respect to rainfall pattern. Tropical grasslands undergo long periods of drought, followed by abundant rain. In temperate grasslands, rainfall is usually more evenly distributed throughout the year.

The grasslands are sometimes considered to be transition zones between deciduous forests and desert. On the North American continent, the dominant grasses are little bluestem, big bluestem, grama grass, and buffalo grass. All of these species

are well adapted to periodic drought, for their deep root systems penetrate the subsoil, as deep as 10 meters (33 feet).

In North America the grasslands undergo a gradual transition from west to east. In the West, lower precipitation and poorer soil gave rise to a **short-grass prairie**, while in the eastern portions of this biome, where rainfall is more abundant and soil is richer, **tall-grass prairie** abounded. Today, only a few remnants of the original tall-grass prairie are left in the Midwest, for the soil is well suited for agriculture. The short-grass prairie has also been reduced because of agriculture, especially cattle grazing but also irrigated grain farming.

Figure S3-3
Result of 1930s duststorm.

Because their soils are so rich in nutrients and organic matter, grasslands throughout the world have been extensively utilized for agriculture. However, this soil can be easily damaged by poor farming practices (Chapter 8). Failure to practice erosion control on U.S. farms over the past 200 years has resulted in the erosion of about 30% of the topsoil.

The dust bowl era in the 1930s is a stark testament to the effects of poor soil management. During and after World War I, American farmers increased production to offset the loss of European farm production by planting 40 million acres of land. Huge fields of wheat sprang up, but increased wheat production produced a glut on the market, resulting in a drop in price. The farmers responded by increasing production even further; fields were plowed from fence post to fence post. More wheat produced an even larger glut, and the price fell more. Then came the devastating drought. Crops died. The winds came and swept the uncovered grassland soil away. Windstorms produced clouds of dust that blackened the sky. At times the dust was so thick that a bare lightbulb glowing in a room appeared only as a faint glow (Figure S3-3).

The dust bowl was a major ecological disaster. As we will see in Chapter 9, agriculture need not lead to such calamity if only efforts are made to protect the soil from erosion and to replenish soil nutrients.

Desert

Deserts are found throughout the world. The Sahara, the world's largest contiguous desert, stretches across the African continent and is nearly as large as the United States. In North America deserts are primarily located on the downwind side (leeward) of mountain ranges, for reasons discussed in Chapter 12. When it does rain in a desert, rainfall is often quite intense and frequently results in flash floods and severe soil erosion.

The desert air is dry. Evaporation from the land occurs at a rapid rate because of sparse vegetation and because of high average temperatures, which may reach 62° C (145° F) on the desert floor in the summer. The temperature drops rapidly at night to 10° C (50° F) because dry air allows a rapid loss of heat into the atmosphere.

Desert plants have developed a number of adaptations to cope with the dry conditions. These include (1) thick, waterproof outer layers, which reduce water loss; (2) no leaves or small ones, which reduce the surface area for evaporation of water; (3) hairs and thorns, which reflect sunlight and shade the plants; (4) the ability to drop leaves when moisture levels are low; (5) extensive, shallow root systems to absorb as much water as possible during the short cloudbursts; (6) deep taproots, which tap groundwater; (7) succulent water-retaining tissues to store water; (8) recessed pores (stomata), which reduce water loss; (9) wide spacing between plants, so that competition for available water is reduced; and (10) short life spans, which allow plants to develop to maturity quickly after intense rainfall.

A surprising variety of plants and animals have adapted to the intense heat and low precipitation. Plants include cacti, other succulents, and shrubs (mesquite, acacia, greasewood, and creosote bush). Small, fast-growing annual herbs are also found in the desert. Many of these are wild flowers that bloom only in the spring or after drenching rains, turning the desert into a colorful landscape almost overnight.

Like the plants, desert animals have evolved a number of strategies to survive in the harsh climate. Many animals such as the ring-tailed cat are active only at night (nocturnal) or during the early and late hours of the day (crepuscular) when the heat is less intense. Snakes have thick scales that prevent water loss. The kangaroo rat conserves body moisture by excreting a solid urine containing nitrogen wastes (in the form of uric acid). Some animals obtain water from vegetation they eat, and others get it from the blood and tissue fluids of their prey. To combat the heat, certain species such as the gila monster live underground during the day.

Large cities have sprung up in the American deserts, and farmers have plowed the poor soil to plant a variety of crops. But the desert soil contains little of the organic matter necessary to retain moisture; therefore, crops are successful only if nitrogen and water are provided. As discussed in Chapter 8, cities and farmers compete for the limited water available in the desert biome. With rising population and agriculture, water supplies have begun to decline, forcing many farms to shut down (Chapters 8 and 12).

Human populations have expanded the borders of the world's deserts through overgrazing of livestock, heavy foresting, and poor agricultural practices. For instance, the Sahara's southern boundaries are currently spreading into the Sahel region because of intense grazing in bordering grassland (Chapter 8).

Tropical Rain Forest

Tropical rain forests are located near the equator on all tropical continents and several islands. With an average annual temperature of approximately 18° C (64° F), and rainfall of 200 to 400 centimeters (80 to 160 inches) a year, the tropical rain forest is one of the richest and most complex biomes on earth. Because rainfall and temperature are fairly constant, they do not limit growth, as in other biomes.

The dominant vegetation consists of tall trees, which tower 50 to 60 meters (165 to 200 feet) above the forest floor. The tops of these trees interlace, forming a dense canopy that blocks out much of the sunlight. Smaller trees form a lower canopy, which also reduces light penetration; thus, 99% to 99.9% of the sunlight never reaches the forest floor. Because of this, only a few low-light plant varieties can grow on the ground. Except near clearings or river banks, the ground is practically bare.

Woody vines grow in the rain forest, and a large number of plants of the type called **epiphytes** live among the taller trees, where sunlight is abundant. These plants, like Spanish moss, which grows in the temperate deciduous forests of the southern United States, gather moisture and nutrients from the humid tropical air. They have no roots and no need for soil.

The tall trees of the tropical rain forest have shallow root systems because the abundant rainfall makes it unnecessary for roots to penetrate deep into the soil for water. Since their root systems are shallow, many trees develop wide bases (buttresses) to provide support.

The tropical rain forest is well known for its species diversity (discussed in Chapter 5). Over a hundred different species of trees may be found in a 1-hectare (2.5-acre) plot that in a temperate deciduous forest would have only two or three species. The rain forest supports a diverse array of insects, birds, and other animals, too. For example, there are as many species of butterfly (500 to 600) in tiny Costa Rica in a tropical rain forest as there are in the entire United States.

Because the ground is bare, many of the animals and insects live in the treetops, where there is food. Thus, the treetops are the most heavily and diversely populated regions of the tropical rain forest.

The soils of these forests are thin and extremely poor in nutrients. In fact, almost all of the inorganic and organic nutrients are tied up in the vegetation. Dead plants and animal wastes are rapidly and completely decomposed on the forest floor; therefore, organic matter does not build up as it does in deciduous forests and grasslands. Minerals returned during decomposition are rapidly taken up by the shallow roots of trees or are leached from the soil by rain and carried to the groundwater, where they are often unavailable to plants.

Because of the low level of nutrients, rain-forest soils are often poor for agriculture. In addition, many of the soils are **laterites**, composed of red clay. When vegetation is cleared from these soils, they are easily eroded away by rain. Where crops are successfully grown, the soil turns into an impenetrable crust after one or two seasons. Despite this, people today clear large sections of tropical rain forests for agriculture. Rain forests are also cleared to produce beef for export. Millions of pounds of beef sold in American fast-food outlets comes from pastures of Central and South America that were once lush rain forests. After seven to ten years of torrential rains and overgrazing, pastures are destroyed and then abandoned. New forests must be cut down. The government of Brazil has been particularly active in encouraging the development of the Amazon basin for beef production and agriculture.

Destruction of tropical rain forests for agriculture, beef production, and timber is so extensive that some ecologists project

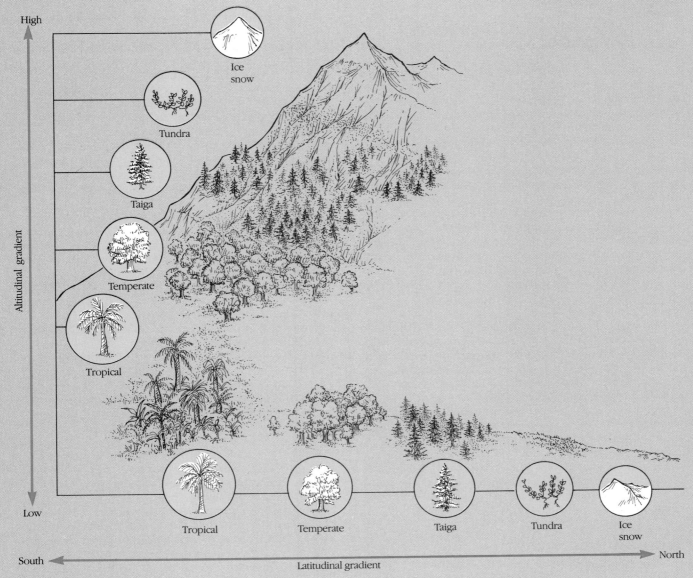

High

Low

Altitudinal gradient

Ice
snow

Tundra

Taiga

Temperate

Tropical

Tropical

Temperate

Taiga

Tundra

Ice
snow

South

North

Latitudinal gradient

Figure S3-4
Vegetation varies with altitude in any given region. Altitudinal gradients mirror
latitudinal gradients.

that those forests, which constitute about half the world's forest, will be gone by the year 2000. With them, they assert, will vanish thousands of animal species. (See the Point/Counterpoint in Chapter 11 for a debate over the extent of deforestation and the effects.)

In our survey of biomes, we have been looking at differences in ecosystem structure as they relate to latitude. If you have been in the mountains, you know that life zones also vary with altitude (Figure S3-4). The reason is that temperature and rainfall vary with altitude. Thus, in the Rockies and other great mountain ranges, climatic conditions high on the mountaintops are similar to those of the tundra, hence the name **alpine tundra**. As in the arctic tundra, the growing seasons are short and winters are cold even in mountains in the tropics. Vegetation and animal life are also similar to that of the far northern tundra. Below the tundra, taiga forests grow. Areas below that (but still well above sea level) resemble the temperate forests.

Principles of Ecology: Ecosystem Function

And this our life, exempt from public haunt, finds tongues in trees, books in running brooks, sermons in stones, and good in everything.

SHAKESPEARE

In this chapter we will turn our attention to how ecosystems function. You will see how producers and consumers are related in an ecosystem and how energy and chemical nutrients flow through the biosphere.

Food Chains and Food Webs

As described in Chapter 3, producers and consumers are interdependent. Through photosynthesis the producers create energy-rich organic compounds, which they use for a variety of purposes. These substances support the consumer organisms (Figure 4-1). For example, plants are eaten by a variety of herbivores (one type of consumer), such as cows, insects, rodents, and deer. These organisms, in turn, are eaten by omnivores, carnivores, and ultimately saprobes, reaffirming the biblical saying "All flesh is grass."

The interconnections between producers and consumers are visible all around us. Mice living in and around our homes, for example, eat the seeds of domestic and

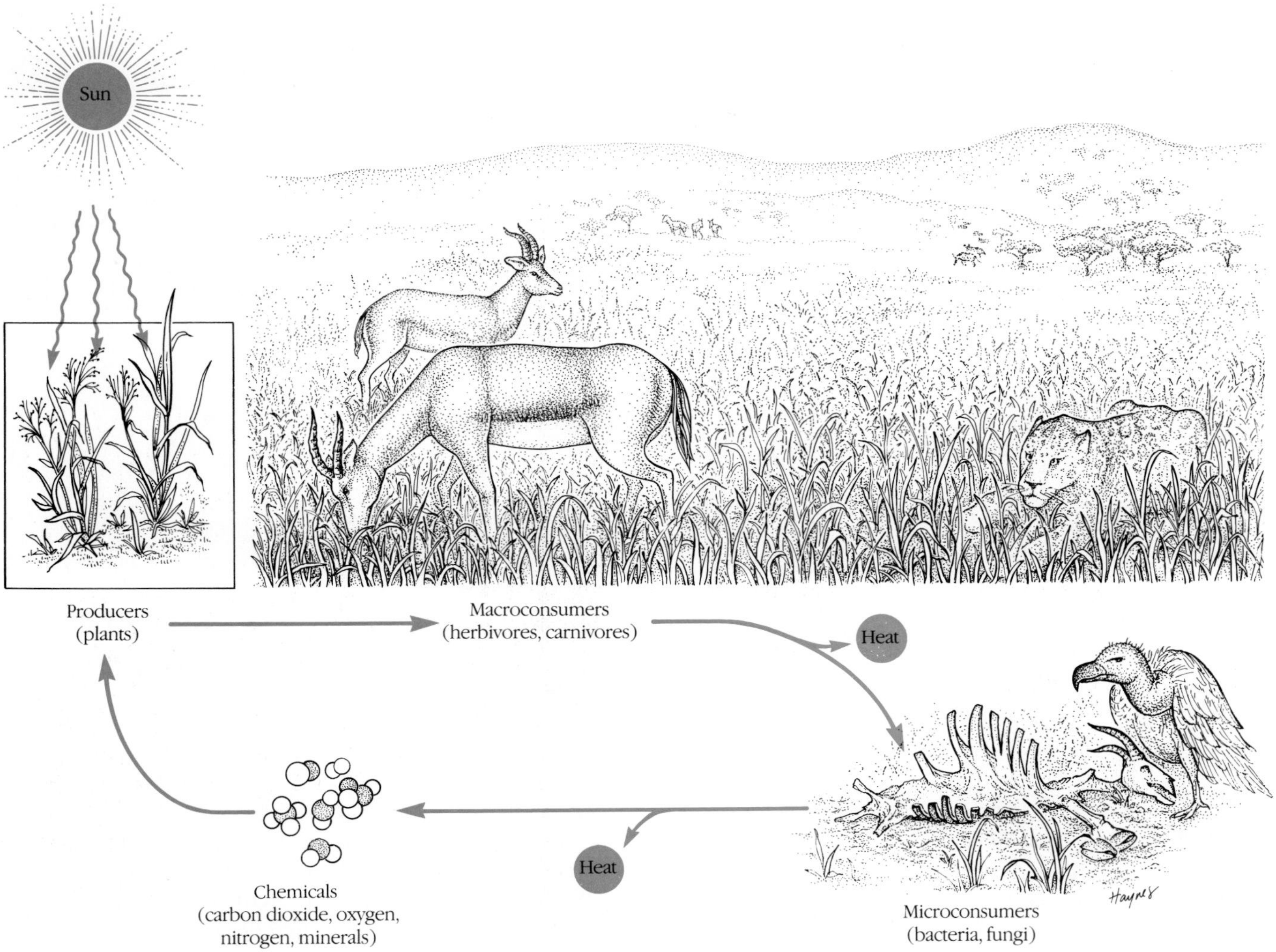

Figure 4-1
Relationship between producers and consumers, showing basic econsystem
structure and function. Nutrients flow from producers to consumers and are
eventually returned to the environment. Energy flows from producers to consumers
and is eventually lost as heat.

wild plants and, in turn, are preyed upon by cats and by
owls that venture forth from nearby fields and forests.
When the mice or owls die, they are consumed by bacteria. In every ecosystem each plant and animal is at some
point the dinner—or perhaps a snack—of another
organism.

A series of organisms, each feeding on the preceding
one, is called a **food chain** (Figure 4-2). A food chain
shows us the order in which organisms in an ecosystem

are consumed, thus defining the most basic relationship
between the biological components of the ecosystem.

There are two types of food chains: grazing and decomposer (detritus). Food chains like the one discussed above
involving seeds, mice, owls, and cats, are called **grazing
food chains** because they start with plants being consumed by grazers, a term broadly applied to organisms
that feed on plant life. Figure 4-2 illustrates familiar terrestrial and aquatic grazing food chains.

Hawk

Insect-eating
birds

Terrestrial

Grasshopper

Grass

Humans

Aquatic

Diatoms

Zooplankton

Small fish

Larger fish

Figure 4-2
Examples of grazer food chains occuring on land and in water.

Figure 4-3
(a) Decomposer food chain. Bacteria and other organisms feed on plant and animal remains. (b) Link between the grazer and the decomposer food chains.

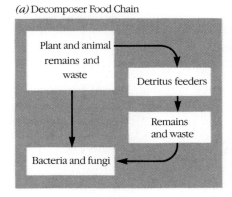

(a) Decomposer Food Chain

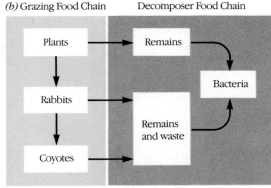

(b) Grazing Food Chain   Decomposer Food Chain

In a **decomposer**, or **detritus, food chain**, waste products and the remains of dead plants and animals are the major food source (Figure 4-3). This organic waste material is consumed on two levels. For instance, in the grasslands of Africa a gazelle that dies of old age is consumed by vultures, hyenas, and the larvae of various flies. These are called detritus feeders. Detritus is dead organic matter such as fallen leaves or animal wastes. The actual process of decomposition is carried out primarily by microscopic organisms, known as microconsumers. They consume all uneaten materials. All of these organisms, microscopic or not, derive energy and essential organic building blocks from detritus. In the process, they liberate carbon dioxide and water needed by plants to make more plant material and maintain the cycle.

The kingdom Fungi, which contains mainly detritus feeders, comprises tens of thousands of different species, including molds, puffballs, and mushrooms. These organisms have an extensive network of rootlike filaments, or rhizoids, that penetrate detritus and release enzymes, proteins that facilitate chemical reactions. These enzymes digest or break down the organic matter into smaller compounds that can be absorbed by the rhizoids and used by the fungus. Single-celled fungi do not have rhizoids but digest organic matter in the same way. Bacteria also release digestive enzymes extracellularly, as the fungi do.

The major difference between the decomposer and grazing food chains is that detritus feeders and microconsumers do not subsist on live plant material. The grazing and decomposer food chains, however, function as part of a great cycle. As illustrated in Figure 4-3, virtually all organic matter in the grazing food chain is ultimately consumed by decomposers.

Food chains can be regarded as conduits for the flow of energy and nutrients through ecosystems. The sun's energy is first captured by plants and stored in organic molecules. It then passes through the grazing and decomposer food chains. In addition, plants incorporate a variety of inorganic materials such as nitrogen, phosphorus, sulfur, and magnesium from the soil and water. These *chemical nutrients* become part of the plant's living matter. When the green plant is consumed, these nutrients enter the food chain. Like carbon, they are eventually returned to the environment through decomposition.

The cycling of nutrients is an essential function of all food chains, and it is an area of great interest to ecologists. The reason for this interest is that many human activities disrupt natural nutrient cycles. Because all life, including our own, depends on these cycles, alterations can have serious consequences for the ecological health of the planet.

Classifying Consumers

Within grazing and decomposer food chains, consumer organisms can be divided into a number of categories (Figure 4-4). In a grazing food chain, for example, herbivores are called **primary consumers**, because they are the first organisms to consume the plants. Thus, mice, elk, cows, bison, zebra, and grasshoppers are all primary consumers. Organisms that feed on primary consumers are called **secondary consumers**, and so on through tertiary consumers and quaternary consumers.

Let's look at an example. In arctic waters, phytoplankton, or free-floating photosynthetic microorganisms such as algae, are the producers. These are consumed by zooplankton such as copepods, which are small crustaceans.

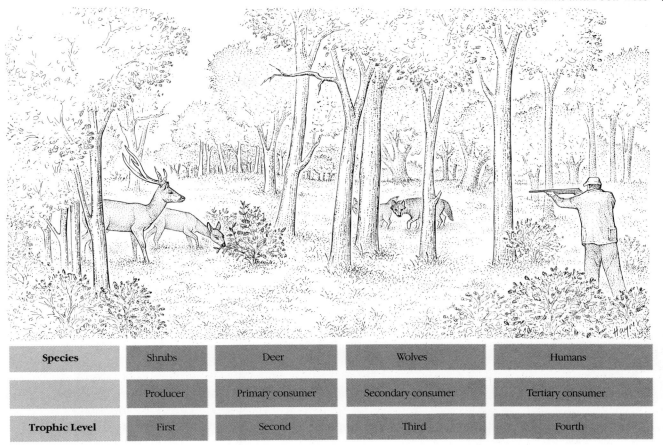

Species	Shrubs	Deer	Wolves	Humans
	Producer	Primary consumer	Secondary consumer	Tertiary consumer
Trophic Level	First	Second	Third	Fourth

Figure 4-4
Grazer food chain, showing feeding and trophic levels.

The zooplankton are the primary consumers. Copepods, in turn, are consumed by fish (secondary consumers), which are consumed by seals (tertiary consumers). Seals are killed and eaten by Eskimos and polar bears (quaternary consumers).

The feeding level an organism occupies in a food chain is called the **trophic level**. At the beginning of the food chain are the producers, which are on the first feeding level (self-feeding), or the **first trophic level**. Primary consumers occupy the **second trophic level**, and secondary, tertiary, and quaternary consumers occupy the third, fourth, and fifth trophic levels, respectively. Figure 4-4 shows a food chain broken down into four trophic levels.

The simple food chain exists only on the pages of ecology texts; in reality, organisms are usually involved in many interconnected chains which form a larger food web. The **food web** consists of all the feeding interactions in an ecosystem (Figure 4-5). It is a composite of all the food chains, giving us a more complete picture of who consumes whom.

Trophic levels can be assigned in food webs just as in food chains; in a food web, however, many species can occupy more than one trophic level. As illustrated in Figure 4-6, a grizzly bear feeding on berries and roots in alpine meadows of Yellowstone National Park is acting as a herbivore, or a primary consumer. It occupies the second trophic level. When feeding on marmots (an animal similar to the woodchuck), however, the grizzly is considered a secondary consumer and occupies the third trophic level. In other instances a grizzly may feed on chipmunks (which eat insects). It thus occupies the fourth trophic level.

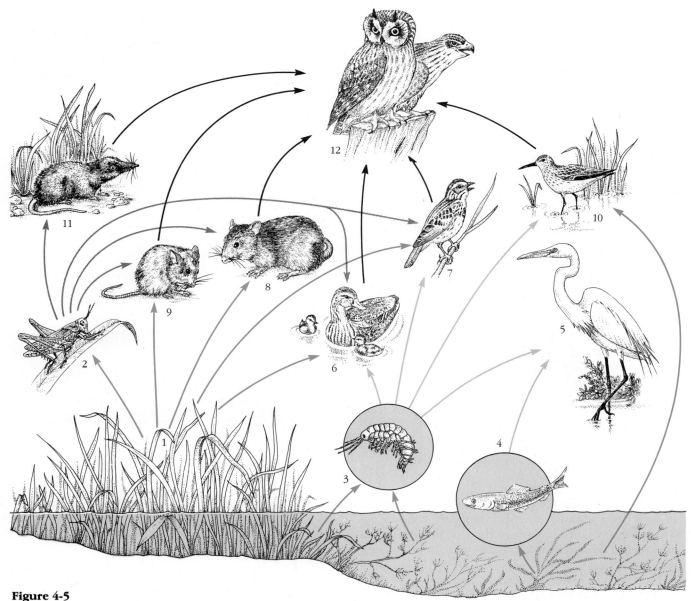

Figure 4-5

A simplified food web, showing the relationships between producers and consumers. In a *Salicornia* salt marsh (San Francisco Bay area) producer organisms (1), terrestrial and salt marsh plants, are consumed by herbivorous invertebrates, represented by the grasshopper and the snail (2). The marine plants are consumed by herbivorous marine and intertidal invertebrates (3). Fish, represented by smelt and anchovy (4) feed on vegetative matter from both terrestrial and marine environments. The fish in turn are eaten by first-level carnivores represented by the great blue heron and the common egret (5). Continuing through the food web, we have the following omnivores: clapper rail and mallard duck (6); savannah and song sparrows (7); Norway rat (8); California vole and salt marsh harvest mouse (9); east and western sandpipers (10). The vagrant shrew (11) is a first-level carnivore, while the top carnivores (second level) are the marsh hawk and the short-eared owl (12).

Grizzly

Elk

Grasses

Berries
Roots

Chipmunk

Insects

(a)

Marmot

Grass

Figure 4-6
The grizzly eats widely from
the food web, as shown in *(a)*.
When individual food chains
are drawn separately, as in *(b)*,
this becomes evident.

Trophic level

Fourth			Grizzly
Third		Grizzly	Chipmunk
Second	Grizzly	Elk Marmot	Insects
First	Berries and Roots Grasses	Grasses	Grasses

(b)

The Flow of Matter and Energy Through the Ecosystem

In the previous section we saw that plants form the starting point of all food chains, because they alone are capable of tapping the sun—the ultimate source of energy for all ecosystems. But plants capture very little of the energy that the sun transmits to the earth. In fact, only 1% or 2% of the incident (incoming) solar radiation is absorbed by photosynthesis (Figure 4-7). On this small fraction of the sunlight is built the entire living world. In this section we will study the flow of energy and matter through the ecosystem. But first, let's take a brief look at energy.

What Is Energy?

We are all familiar with the term *energy*. Despite our frequent use of this term, it is rather difficult to define. One of the reasons is that energy comes in many forms, such as heat, light, sound, electricity, coal, oil, gasoline, natural gas, steam, wind, water, and nuclear reactions (Figure 4-8). A lump of coal, a gallon of gasoline, a stone perched on a ledge, a moving bus—all are said to have energy, even though they are outwardly different from one another.

Figure 4-7
Distribution of incoming solar radiation. Note that plants absorb only a small fraction.

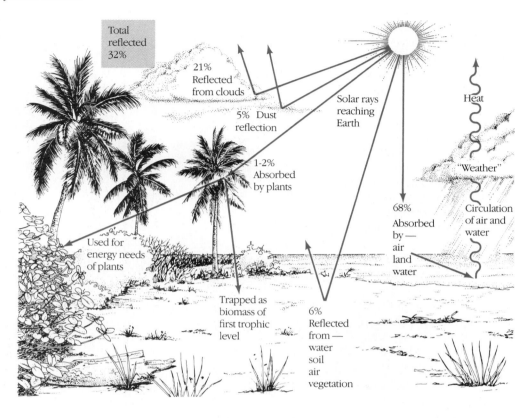

Total reflected 32%

21% Reflected from clouds

5% Dust reflection

1-2% Absorbed by plants

Solar rays reaching Earth

Heat

"Weather"

68% Absorbed by — air land water

Circulation of air and water

Used for energy needs of plants

Trapped as biomass of first trophic level

6% Reflected from — water soil air vegetation

(a)

(b)

Figure 4-8
Energy is the capacity to do work and comes in various forms. Here we have examples of *(a)* potential energy, and *(b)* kinetic energy.

The one commonality of these many forms of energy is that they all have the ability or capacity to do work. Therefore, **energy** is defined as the capacity to do work. To the physicist, *work* is performed when an object is forced to move. A box pushed along a hallway represents work being performed.

Why do we consider coal or oil, for example, to have energy? A lump of coal is not doing work, but it has the capacity to do work. When burned, it yields heat, which can be used to run steam engines. Thus, coal contains **potential energy**. When the chemical bonds within coal are broken down, this potential energy is released, and work can be performed.

Objects in motion, like a moving car or a jet plane or a train, also have the capacity to do work, and they are said to possess **kinetic energy**, or energy of motion. For instance, a sledgehammer in the middle of its swing has kinetic energy. When it strikes a railroad spike, it may drive the spike into the ground and perform work.

All forms of energy follow basic laws, called the **laws of thermodynamics**. A good understanding of these laws will help us understand ecology and also many of our environmental problems.

First Law The **first law of thermodynamics** is often called the law of *conservation of energy*. This law simply states that energy can be neither created nor destroyed but only transformed from one form to another.

Let's look at the first law more closely. First, it says that we cannot create energy; all energy that we use must come from existing sources. Plants, for instance, "make" energy, but they "make it" from sunlight. The law also says that energy cannot be destroyed. This seems to go against our own experience. What happens to the gasoline we burn in automobiles? Isn't it destroyed? No, it is simply converted into heat and mechanical energy (Figure 4-9). The heat is given off as a waste product, and the mechanical energy propels the car along the highway. Eventually, it too is converted to waste heat (by friction). Thus, the heat produced by a car is exactly equal to the amount of energy released from the fuel.

Second Law The **second law of thermodynamics** explains what happens to energy when it changes from one form to another. The law simply states that energy is "degraded" when it changes form (Figure 4-10). Another way of saying this is that energy goes from a concentrated to a less concentrated form during a transformation. In

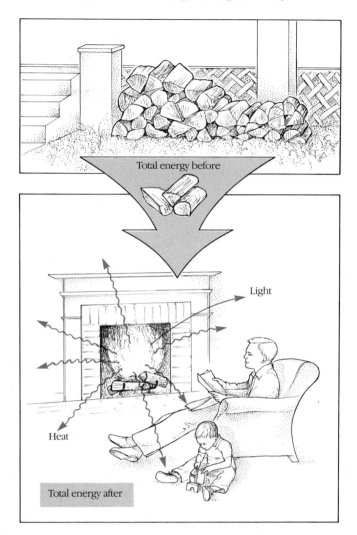

Figure 4-9
The first law of thermodynamics. In energy conversions, the total energy before and after the transformation is the same.

the example above, when gasoline is burned, it goes from a very concentrated form to much less concentrated heat. Concentrated energy forms are said to have a great deal of available work. Less concentrated forms have a lower work capacity and are said to have less available work.

The laws of thermodynamics have many implications in our lives, especially in terms of energy production and consumption. For now, we will concentrate on the flow of energy in the ecosystem and see how these laws apply to the ecosystem's functioning. We will begin by looking at biomass.

Figure 4-10
Second law of thermodynamics. During energy transformations the amount of useful work diminishes as we go from high-quality (concentrated) energy forms to low-quality (less concentrated) energy forms.

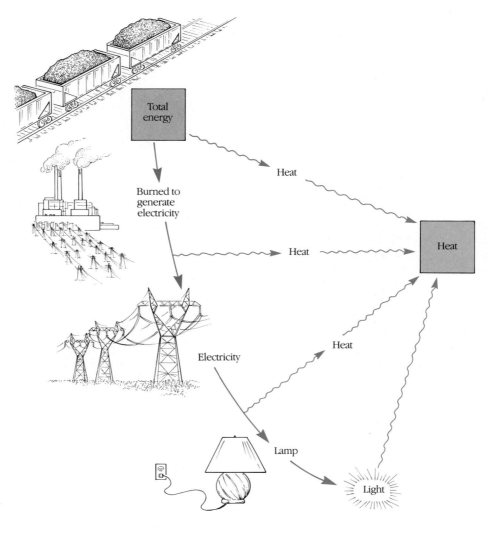

Biomass and Ecological Pyramids

Food webs are the route that matter and energy take through ecosystems. In a biological sense, energy and matter are one and the same (see Chemistry Appendix). To study this dynamic flow of energy and matter, we will first look at the transfer of organic matter from one trophic level to the next.

At the first trophic level, plants generate organic matter, called **biomass.** If we wanted to measure plant biomass in an ecosystem such as a grassland, we would dig up a given area of vegetation—one square meter is enough—then separate the dirt from the plant roots, dry the plant material, and weigh it. The dried weight of plant matter is its biomass. Biomass is a measure of the amount of

carbon dioxide converted into organic plant matter in any given biome. Biomass can also be determined for the rest of the trophic levels.

The biomass at the first trophic level in almost all ecosystems represents a large amount of potential (chemical) energy. Not all of the biomass at the first trophic level, however, is converted into biomass at the second trophic level (Figure 4-11). In other words, not all plant matter becomes animal matter, for several reasons. The first is obvious: only a small part of the plant matter in any given ecosystem is eaten by the primary consumers, as shown in Figure 4-11. Second, not all of the biomass eaten by the herbivores is digested—some passes through the gastrointestinal tract unchanged and is excreted. Third, most of what is digested is broken down into carbon dioxide

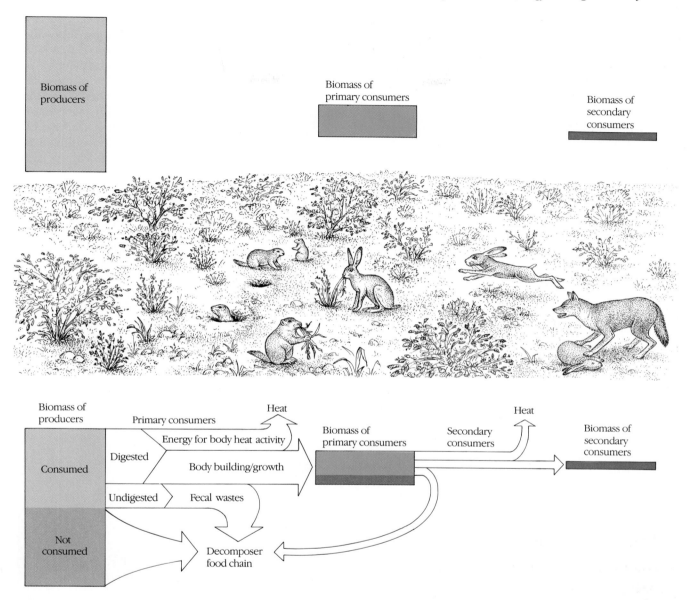

Figure 4-11
Energy and nutrient flow through the ecosystem. Note that a large fraction of the
first trophic level biomass is not consumed. Also note the losses from one trophic
level to the next.

and water and into the energy used to move about, to
breathe, and to maintain body temperature. This heat, the
consequence of the first law of thermodynamics, is dissipated into the environment and is eventually lost into
space. Body heat represents biomass from the first trophic
level that is not converted into biomass at the second
trophic level.

Because of these factors, biomass at the second trophic
level is greatly reduced from that at the first level. The
transfer of biomass from the second to the third trophic
level entails another significant "loss," for similar reasons:
not all of the herbivores are eaten by carnivores, some
flesh eaten by carnivores goes undigested, and much of
what is digested goes into cellular energy and body heat.
Thus, the biomass at the third trophic level is significantly
less than that at the second level.

Graphically represented, biomass at the different trophic levels forms a pyramid, the **pyramid of biomass** (Figure 4-12). Because biomass and energy are equivalent, as biomass decreases in the food chain, so does potential energy. Thus, energy forms a pyramid called the **pyramid of energy** (Figure 4-13). Both the energy and biomass pyramids are called *ecological pyramids*.

To illustrate the pyramid of energy, let's use some numbers to look at energy flow through the ecosystem, start-ing first with plants (Figure 4-13). For our unit of energy, we will use the kilocalorie. One kilocalorie raises the temperature of 1 kilogram (1 liter) of water 1° C. A kilo-calorie is the same as one calorie as used by dieters.

Plants are able to capture only about 1% of the solar radiation striking the earth; therefore, when 1 million kilocalories of solar energy strikes the earth, plants make about 10,000 kilocalories worth of biomass. Herbivores, in turn, are only 10% to 20% efficient in converting plant

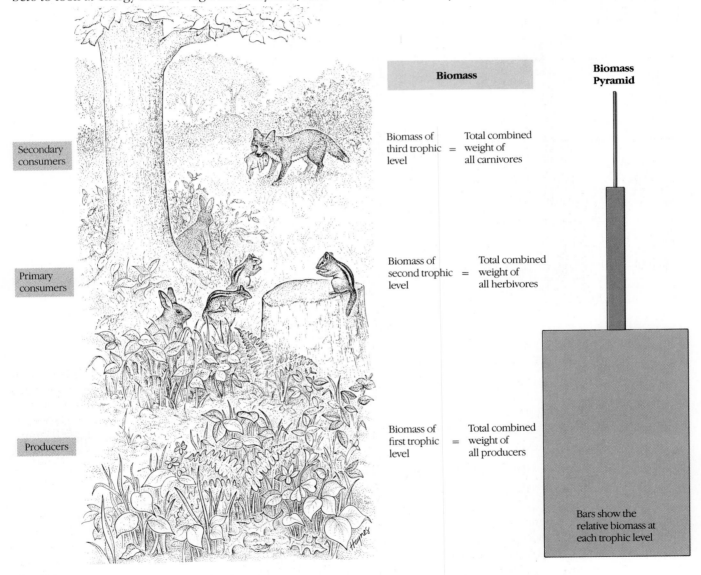

Biomass

Biomass of third trophic level	=	Total combined weight of all carnivores
Biomass of second trophic level	=	Total combined weight of all herbivores
Biomass of first trophic level	=	Total combined weight of all producers

Biomass Pyramid

Bars show the relative biomass at each trophic level

Secondary consumers

Primary consumers

Producers

Figure 4-12
Biomass pyramid. Note that the pyramid corresponds to a single food chain at successive trophic levels.

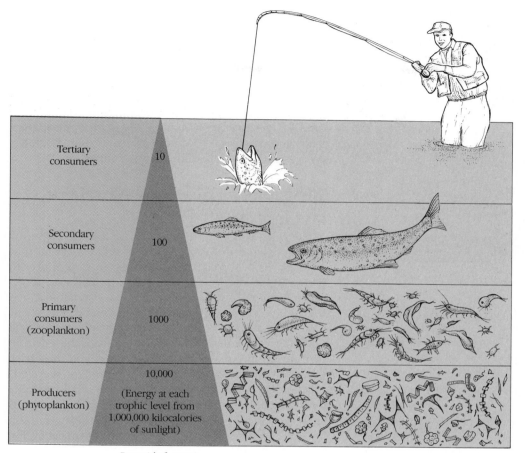

Figure 4-13
Pyramid of energy. Note the rapid decrease in potential energy as we ascend the food chain.

Tertiary consumers	10	
Secondary consumers	100	
Primary consumers (zooplankton)	1000	
Producers (phytoplankton)	10,000 (Energy at each trophic level from 1,000,000 kilocalories of sunlight)	

Pyramid of energy

matter into animal matter; therefore, 10,000 kilocalories of plant matter, consumed by herbivores, is converted to 1000 to 2000 kilocalories of animal biomass. Carnivores convert biomass with about 10% efficiency; accordingly, that 1000 to 2000 kilocalories is converted into about 100 to 200 kilocalories of carnivore biomass. Consumers at a fourth trophic level, operating with the same conversion efficiency, produce only 10 to 20 kilocalories of biomass.

What are the implications of decreasing energy and biomass? First, because biomass decreases and organisms tend to increase in size the higher they are in the food chain, fewer organisms can be supported at the higher trophic levels. Thus, the number of organisms decreases from one trophic level to the next, forming a **pyramid of numbers** (Figure 4-14). The second implication is a logical extension of the first: more organisms can be supported in an ecosystem if they can feed at lower trophic levels. As illustrated in Figure 4-14, more than twice as many herbivores (trophic level 2) can be supported in a grassland biome as carnivores (trophic levels 3 and 4).

For humans, this means that consuming meat is much more wasteful of solar energy than eating plants. If 20,000 kilocalories' worth of corn were fed to a steer, 2000 kilocalories of beef would be produced. This would feed only one person (assuming a person can survive on 2000 kilocalories per day). However, if the 20,000 calories of corn were eaten directly, it would feed ten persons for a day. This issue is discussed in more detail in Chapter 9.

The third implication is that the loss of biomass from one trophic level to the next seems to set limits on the length of the food chain. Food chains usually have no more than four or five (rarely, six) trophic levels, because the biomass at the top of the trophic structure is so small that it cannot adequately support another level.

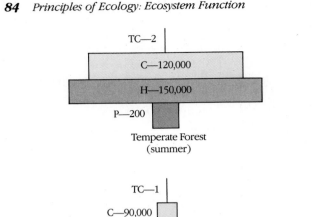

Figure 4-14
Pyramid of numbers for a grassland community in the summer. The numbers represent individuals per 1000 square meters. P = producers, H = herbivores, C = carnivores, TC = top carnivores (highest consumer in a food chain).

Productivity

The rate of conversion of sunlight to chemical bond energy is called **productivity**. Productivity is of great interest to scientists, because ecosystems with high productivity are often potential food sources for humans as well as other organisms. To examine productivity in an ecosystem, ecologists look at three variables: (1) gross primary productivity, (2) the rate of respiration by producers, and (3) the net primary productivity.

Gross primary productivity (GPP) is a measure of the rate at which sunlight is converted to chemical bond energy by producers; it is expressed as kilocalories per square meter per year. Part of the sun's energy that plants capture must be used to meet their own energy needs. By subtracting the energy used by plants during cellular respiration (R) from the gross primary productivity, we can determine the amount of energy stored in chemical bonds by producers. This measure is known as the **net primary productivity** (NPP). The simple mathematical equation for net primary productivity is NPP = GPP − R.

Table 4-1 shows the gross primary productivity for various ecosystems. From this information it is clear that estuaries and reefs, moist temperate forests, agricultural land, and wet tropical and subtropical forests have the highest gross primary productivity in the world (see col-

umn 2). They produce biomass at a higher rate than the other ecosystems. But how important each ecosystem is to total annual biomass production depends on its total land area. Estuaries and reefs, for example, have high gross primary productivity, but they constitute only a small portion of the earth's surface (column 1). Therefore, their percentage of the total world productivity is small (column 3). As shown in column 3, the open oceans, grasslands and pastures, and wet tropical and subtropical forests produce the bulk of the earth's biomass.

Biogeochemical, or Nutrient, Cycles

Organic matter, inorganic nutrients, and energy all flow simultaneously through the ecosystem from producer to consumer. However, energy flows in only one direction—from the sun to producer to consumer—and is eventually converted to heat and dissipated into space. Therefore, it cannot be recycled. Organic matter and nutrients, in contrast, flow in a cycle from the environment to the producers to the consumers and then back to the environment, where they are reused, or recycled.

There are many inorganic nutrients flowing cyclically through the ecosystem. The most important of this group are water, carbon, phosphorus, nitrogen, oxygen, and sulfur. The cycles they form are called **biogeochemical cycles**, or **nutrient cycles**.

As shown in Figure 4-15, the nutrient cycles involve two general phases: the **environmental phase**, in which the chemical nutrient is in the soil, water, or air, and the **organismic phase**, in which the nutrient becomes part of the living tissue of producers and consumers. These two phases are intimately linked and highly interdependent. As in any cycle, the disturbance of one part can severely alter another part.

Nutrient cycles are often classified as either *gaseous cycles* or *sedimentary cycles,* according to the location of the major environmental reservoir of the particular nutrient. The carbon and nitrogen cycles, for example, are considered gaseous cycles, and the phosphorus cycle is a sedimentary cycle.

Of the 92 naturally occurring elements, about 40 are essential to life. Six of these elements—carbon, oxygen, hydrogen, nitrogen, phosphorus, and sulfur—form 95% of the mass of all plants, animals, and microorganisms. These elements are called **macronutrients**. Others such as iron, zinc, molybdenum, and iodine, are also required, but only in small amounts, and are called **micronutrients**.

Table 4-1 Estimated Annual Gross Primary Productivity of the Biosphere and Major Ecosystems

Ecosystem	Area (10^6 km^2)	Gross Primary Productivity (kcal/m^2 year)	Worldwide Annual Gross Primary Production (10^{16} kcal)
Marine			
Open ocean	326.0	1,000	32.6
Coastal zones	34.0	2,000	6.8
Upwelling zones	0.4	6,000	0.2
Estuaries and reefs	2.0	20,000	4.0
Marine total	**362.4**		**43.6**
Terrestrial			
Deserts and tundras	40.0	200	0.8
Grasslands and pastures	42.0	2,500	10.5
Dry forests	9.4	2,500	2.4
Boreal coniferous forests	10.0	3,000	3.0
Cultivated lands with little or no energy subsidy	10.0	3,000	3.0
Moist temperate forests	4.9	8,000	3.9
Fuel-subsidized (mechanized) agriculture	4.0	12,000	4.8
Wet tropical and subtropical (broadleaved evergreen) forests	14.7	20,000	29.0
Terrestrial total	**135.0**		**57.4**
Biosphere total (round figures, not including ice caps)	**500.0**	**2,000**	**100.0**

Source: Odum, E. (1971). *Fundamentals of Ecology* (3rd ed.). Philadelphia: Saunders.

Figure 4-15
Nutrient (biogeochemical) cycles have two basic phases:
environmental and organismic.

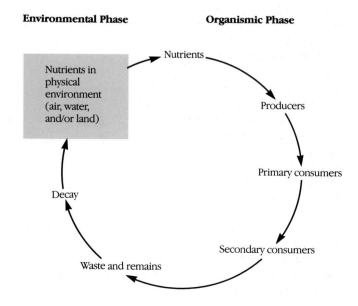

The importance of the micronutrients is far greater than many people realize. For example, cancer of the throat in China has been linked to low levels of molybdenum in the soil. Low molybdenum causes vegetable crops to concentrate nitrite in their leaves. In the stomachs of the Chinese people, the nitrites were converted into nitrosamines, potent cancer-causing agents. To treat the problem, seeds are soaked in a solution containing molybdenum before planting.

In this chapter we will examine three of the many nutrient cycles: carbon, nitrogen, and phosphorus. The water cycle is discussed in Chapter 12.

The Carbon Cycle

The carbon cycle is a gaseous nutrient cycle that describes the movement of carbon, an essential component of all organic molecules. Like many other elements, carbon cycles between the environment and its organisms, but it moves much more quickly than most nutrients.

A simplified version of the carbon cycle is shown in Figure 4-16. Atmospheric carbon dioxide enters terrestrial and aquatic ecosystems. On land, carbon dioxide is absorbed through small pores, or stomata, in the leaves of plants. Within the plant, carbon dioxide gas enters the cells, where it is combined with hydrogen (obtained from water molecules) during photosynthesis. Organic molecules are made in series of chemical reactions that are part of photosynthesis. The reaction is written as follows:

$$6\ CO_2 + 6\ H_2O + E \rightarrow C_6H_{12}O_6 + 6\ O_2$$

Carbon dioxide + Water + Energy→ Glucose + Oxygen

Driven by sunlight, the photosynthetic reactions link atoms of carbon, oxygen, and hydrogen to form larger organic molecules, a process called *carbon fixation*. These organic molecules are transferred to higher trophic levels as primary consumers eat plants and, in turn, are eaten by secondary consumers. Thus, carbon flows from the atmosphere into and through the organismic phase of the cycle. It returns to the atmosphere in two ways. First, within the plants and animals, some of the organic molecules are broken down (oxidized) to generate cellular energy. This process is called cellular respiration. It results in the production of usable energy, heat, carbon dioxide, and water. The breakdown reaction for glucose is written:

$$C_6H_{12}O_6 + 6\ O_2 \rightarrow 6\ CO_2 + 6\ H_2O + E$$

Glucose + Oxygen→Carbon dioxide + Water + Energy

The carbon released in cellular respiration reenters the environmental phase of the cycle.

Carbon also returns to the atmosphere through the decomposer food chain. Here, decomposer organisms consume detritus and convert it into living tissue and energy, liberating carbon dioxide.

Carbon also returns when plant materials are burned outright by natural causes such as lightning and forest fires or as a result of human activities such as combustion of wood and coal or deliberately set grass fires.

The oceans contain about 50 times more carbon dioxide than the atmosphere. An equilibrium exists between the oceans and the atmosphere. Carbon dioxide escapes from its oceanic reservoir to compensate for any depletion in the atmosphere.

The carbon cycle also has some dead ends—places where carbon is taken out of the cycle. For example, many aquatic organisms manufacture shells out of carbonate ($CaCO_3$). Trillions of small shells left by generations of these creatures collect on the ocean floor. Over millions of years, they are compacted and converted into limestone, locking up the carbon. However, water may dissolve some of the limestone, thus allowing carbon to return

Figure 4-16
The carbon cycle.

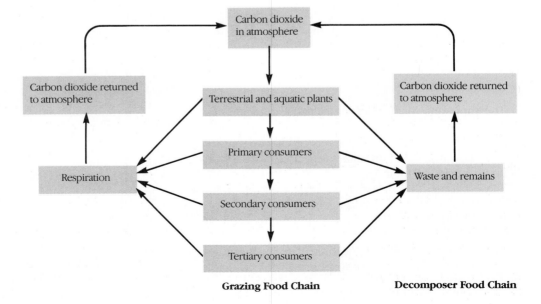

Grazing Food Chain   Decomposer Food Chain

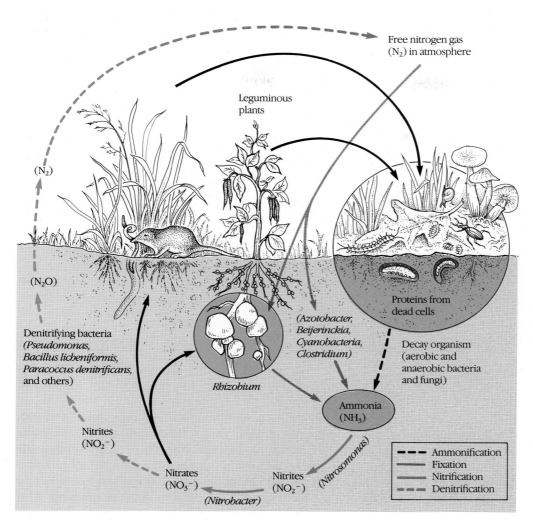

Figure 4-17
The nitrogen cycle.

to the atmosphere. Volcanic eruptions may also release carbon (as CO_2) as lava heats up underground limestone and converts it into carbon dioxide and calcium oxide (CaO).

In another dead end, plant material is deposited in swampy areas like the Everglades. Quickly buried by sediment, it escapes decomposition and gradually is converted into coal. Combustion of coal in power plants returns much of this carbon to the atmosphere.

Oil, natural gas, and oil shale are also produced from undecayed organic matter that becomes buried by sediments but under slightly different conditions. Their formation also represents a dead end in the global carbon cycle that can be opened up by combustion.

Humans intervene in the global carbon cycle in two major ways: (1) by removing forests and vegetation that fix atmospheric carbon dioxide and (2) by liberating carbon dioxide during the combustion of coal, oil, and natural gas. Combustion of fossil fuel and removal of vegetation have increased global carbon dioxide concentrations by at least 11% since 1870. Further increases could have a devastating effect on global temperature and climate and, ultimately, on the multitude of the earth's organisms. (For more detail see Chapter 19.)

The Nitrogen Cycle

Nitrogen forms part of many essential organic molecules—notably, amino acids, the building blocks of proteins; and the genetic materials RNA and DNA. Approximately 79% of the air we breathe is nitrogen gas (N_2). Plants and animals cannot use nitrogen in this form. To be usable it must first be converted into ammonia (NH_3) or nitrate (NO_3) (Figure 4-17).

Essay 4-1

Benign Neglect in Texas: An Ecological Solution to a Perennial Problem

Texas highway officials and taxpayers have found that "benign neglect" is both economically and ecologically the best way to conduct roadside maintenance along the state's 71,000 miles of highways.

Fifty years ago, the Lone Star state began sowing wild flower seeds along its nearly 800,000 acres of roadside, encouraging the brightly colored blossoms of the state's 5000 native wild flowers.

Texas is the leader in this ecological solution to roadside maintenance, which has typically involved the planting of delicate grasses, regular mowing, irrigation, fertilization, and spraying with insecticides and herbicides—all for roadside lawns as well-groomed as a golf course. In Texas road crews mow a few times a year to help spread the flower seeds, but that's about the extent of roadside maintenance.

Besides beautifying the landscape, the hardy flowers reduce erosion and provide habitat for native species. More importantly, native wildflowers require only the water that falls naturally from the sky, and they need little if any fertilizer and care. They resist drought, insects, and freezing weather, because they inhabit the land they have evolved over millions of years to live in.

Benign neglect makes good sense and reminds us of the words of Montaigne: "Let us permit nature to have her way; she understands her business better than we do."

Adapted from McCommon, M. (1983). "A Blooming Boom in Texas." *National Wildlife* 21 (5): pp. 4-5.

The conversion of atmospheric nitrogen into usable forms occurs in small amounts in the atmosphere and in certain organisms found in the soil and water. Once these compounds are produced, plants can absorb them through their roots and use them to make amino acids, proteins, DNA, and RNA. Animals get the nitrogen they need by consuming plants.

The conversion of atmospheric nitrogen into inorganic molecules is called *nitrogen fixation* and is carried out naturally (1) in aquatic ecosystems by blue-green algae; (2) in terrestrial ecosystems by nitrogen-fixing bacteria found in the soil and in small swellings (called root nodules) on the roots of the legumes (peas, alfalfa, beans, and clover) and possibly even other plants; and (3) in the atmosphere as a result of lightning.

Nitrogen is returned to the soil by the breakdown of detritus (Figure 4-17). Ammonifying bacteria and certain fungi in the soil digest the nitrogen-rich detritus and convert organic nitrogen into ammonia and ammonium salts. The ammonium salts can be incorporated by the roots of plants. Ammonia can evaporate and enter the atmosphere. It is also converted to nitrite by soil bacteria. Nitrite can, in turn, be converted to nitrate, which is taken up by plant roots. Finally, nitrite, nitrate, and ammonia may be converted into nitrogen gas by denitrifying bacteria in the soil. Nitrogen escapes into the air and completes the cycle.

In various forms, nitrogen travels from air to soil to plant to animal and then back to soil and atmosphere in a never-ending cycle. Human farming practices allow nitrogen, especially the nitrates, to be washed from the soil, where it enters lakes, streams, and the ocean. Excessive nitrate losses result in serious water pollution problems (Chapter 20) and in soil depletion, which decreases agricultural productivity (Chapter 8).

The Phosphorus Cycle

Phosphorus is essential to life. It is found in living organisms as phosphates (PO_4), important parts of RNA and DNA. They are also found in fats (phospholipids) in cell membranes. Unlike the nitrogen and carbon cycles the phosphorus cycle is a sedimentary cycle, because the major environmental reservoir for phosphorus is in the rocks (Figure 4-18).

Phosphate is slowly dissolved (leached) from rocks by rain and melting snow and is carried to lakes, streams,

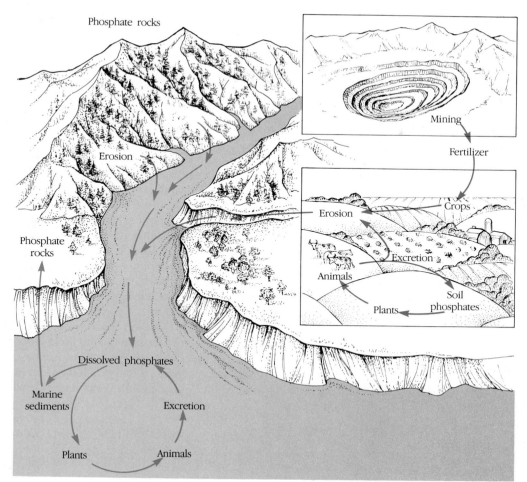

Figure 4-18
The phosphorus cycle.

ponds, and oceans. Dissolved phosphate is used by plants, which pass it to animals in the food web. It reenters the environment in several ways: (1) Some is excreted directly by animals. (2) When plants and animals die, phosphate is liberated from the organic compounds by bacteria. Each year large quantities of phosphate are washed into the oceans, where much of it settles to the bottom and is incorporated into the marine sediments. These may release some of the phosphate for use by aquatic organisms. The rest may become buried in time and hence be taken out of circulation.

Phosphate is a major component of fertilizer. By applying excess fertilizer, humans may alter the phosphorus cycle. Because phosphorus is a limiting factor in aquatic ecosystems, excesses entering from farmland may cause rapid growth in algae and other aquatic plants. This problem is discussed in more detail in Chapter 20.

Interactions of Organisms

This chapter has primarily been concerned with the flow of energy and matter in ecosystems. On an organismic level there are many different interactions between organisms of different species. In this section we will take a brief look at the major interactions to help us better understand the interconnections.

Predation occurs when an organism of one species (predator) kills an individual of another species (prey) for food—for instance, when a robin catches a worm or a wolf attacks and kills a caribou. This interaction is obviously beneficial to the predator, but predation also benefits prey populations, for predators often kill weakened, sick, and aged members of society. This culling of the prey population reduces the population size and ensures that the remaining members have a larger share of the available food supply, a benefit that is especially important in the winter and at other times when resources are low.

Commensalism is an interaction between two species that is of benefit to one but neutral (neither good nor bad) to the other. For example, humans house numerous bacteria in their intestinal tract that are neither harmful nor beneficial. The bacteria benefit from this association by having a relatively consistent food supply.

Mutualism is a relationship that is beneficial to both organisms. A classic example is the small organism called the lichen. Lichens inhabit barren rock, where they capture water from rainfall and get nutrients by eroding the surface of the rock. Lichens are fungi with algae living inside, a relationship termed *endosymbiosis*. The algae produce carbohydrates that the fungi need to survive, and the fungi provide the algae with moisture and a place to grow; thus, both organisms benefit from this living arrangement.

In some examples of mutualism one of the organisms may be so dependent on the other that survival without its partner is impossible.

Competition, as expressed in the last chapter, describes species that occupy similar niches often competing for food, water, and other environmental resources. When interspecific competition is severe, one species may dis-

place the other; in other cases, extreme competition may deplete a resource so severely that the populations of both species are eliminated or greatly reduced.

Parasitism denotes one species (the parasite) living in or on another organism, the host. In this relationship the parasite obtains its food by slowly eating away at the host. A parasite may be a temporary resident, such as a wood tick, or it may set up a long-term relationship, as tapeworms do. These long-term relationships can, but rarely do, debilitate a host and cause death.

Neutralism, as the name implies, is of no consequence to either organism. One organism lives in close proximity to another, but they do not affect each another in any substantial manner. As an example, chickadees live with mule deer in the Rocky Mountain forest, but they do not interact in any direct or observable fashion.

The ecosystem is a dynamic entity kept in operation by the constant flow of matter and energy through the food web and the interaction of living things. We are a part of many ecosystems and can affect the flow of energy and matter profoundly. With this background in ecosystem function, let us examine how ecosystems stay in balance, paying particular attention to the forces that help achieve balance. From that discussion we will begin to see how ecosystems change through natural events and human intervention.

Nothing can survive on the planet unless it is a cooperative part of larger global life.

Barry Commoner

Summary

Producers and consumers are interdependent organisms that form food chains. A *food chain* is a series of organisms, each feeding on the preceding one, showing the major relationships between organisms in an ecosystem. *Grazing food chains* are nutrient and energy pathways that start with plants, which are consumed first by grazers, or herbivores. *Decomposer food chains* are nutrient and energy pathways that start with *detritus*—dead organic matter such as leaves and animal waste—which is eaten by a variety of organisms, including insects, bacteria, and fungi.

Organisms are classified by their position in a food chain. The terms *primary, secondary, tertiary,* and *quaternary* are applied

to consumers. *Primary consumers* are the first level of consumers; they feed directly on plants in the grazer food chain and on detritus in the decomposer food chain. *Secondary consumers* feed on primary consumers (herbivores).

The feeding level an organism occupies in a food chain is called the *trophic level*. Producers form the *first trophic level;* they are self-feeders. Primary consumers form the *second trophic level,* and secondary, tertiary, and quaternary consumers occupy the third, fourth, and fifth levels, respectively.

In reality, food chains fit into a complex *food web,* which gives a more accurate picture of the feeding relationships in an ecosystem. Organisms may also occupy several different trophic levels.

Energy is defined as the capacity to do work. Organic matter in living organisms contains *potential energy*. Energy of motion is called *kinetic energy*. Energy is governed by the *laws of thermodynamics*. The *first law* states that energy is neither created nor destroyed but only converted from one form to another. The *second law* states that when energy is converted from one form to another, there is a loss of available work—thus, energy has been degraded or converted from a more concentrated to a less concentrated form. The laws of thermodynamics have many implications in ecology and everyday life.

Dried organic matter is called *biomass*. It is a form of potential energy that is passed from one trophic level to the next. Graphically represented, biomass at the different trophic levels forms a *pyramid of biomass*. Since biomass contains energy, the amount of potential energy at subsequently higher trophic levels also decreases and forms a *pyramid of energy*. Finally, the number of organisms decreases from one trophic level to the next higher one; this forms a *pyramid of numbers*.

Productivity is the measure of biomass production. The *gross primary productivity* is the total biomass production. If we subtract the amount of biomass a producer uses itself from the gross primary productivity, we can determine the *net primary productivity*. Regions with high net primary productivity such as tropical rain forests are important to humans, because they supply many valuable resources such as timber.

Organic and inorganic matter cycle within the ecosystem in *biogeochemical,* or *nutrient, cycles*. Those substances needed in large amounts are called *macronutrients*. Those needed in smaller amounts are *micronutrients*. The movement of carbon, nitrogen, and phosphorus in the ecosystem is described by the carbon, nitrogen, and phosphorus cycles. These cycles are essential for life and may be altered by human activities.

Discussion Questions

1. What is a food chain? What are the two major types of food chain? How are they different? How are they similar?

2. Sketch several simple food chains, and indicate all producers and consumers. Also indicate the trophic level of each organism. Can one organism occupy several trophic levels? Give an example.

3. What are microconsumers? Why are they important?

4. Define the following terms: *consumer, producer, trophic level,* and *food web.*

5. What is biomass? How is it measured?

6. Why does biomass decrease as we ascend the food chain?

7. What is cellular respiration? Why is carbon dioxide released during respiration in producers and consumers?

8. What are the implications of decreasing biomass in the food chain? How does this affect the number of higher-level consumers?

9. Define *pyramid of energy, pyramid of biomass,* and *pyramid of numbers,* and describe why each exists.

10. Is it good or bad advice to instruct an overpopulated country to feed its people beef to supply them with necessary protein? Why?

11. Define the terms *gross primary productivity* and *net primary productivity.* What are the most productive regions of the earth? Can we tap these for food? Why or why not?

12. Draw a detailed picture of the carbon cycle, and describe what happens during the various parts of the cycle. How does carbon reenter the environmental phase? How does it enter the organismic phase?

13. What organisms fix atmospheric nitrogen? Why is this critical to the operation of the nitrogen cycle? How does nitrogen reenter the environmental phase? How does nitrogen enter the organismic phase of the nitrogen cycle?

14. Describe the phosphorus cycle.

15. Define the following terms: *predation, commensalism, mutualism, neutralism,* and *competition.* Compare them for similarities and differences.

Suggested Readings

Colinvaux, P. (1973). *Introduction to Ecology.* New York: Wiley. An excellent textbook of basic ecology; good treatment of history of ecological concepts.

Curtis, H. (1979). *Biology.* New York: Worth. A must for students who want to supplement their knowledge of ecology without having to read an entire ecology text.

Dasmann, R. F. (1975). *The Conservation Alternative.* New York: Wiley. A good general work on ecology.

——— (1976). *Environmental Conservation* (4th ed.). New York: Wiley. Contains a particularly good discussion of ecological principles.

Ehrlich, P. A.; Ehrlich, A. H.; and Holdren, J. P. (1977). *Ecoscience: Population, Resources, Environment.* San Francisco: Freeman. A higher level text that covers ecology in detail. A superb reference book.

Gould, S. J. (1977). *Ever Since Darwin.* New York: Norton. Brilliant collection of essays on evolution and natural history.

——— (1980). *The Panda's Thumb.* New York: Norton. Brilliant and witty collection of essays on evolution.

Hitching, F. (1982). *The Neck of the Giraffe: Where Darwin Went Wrong.* New York: Ticknor and Fields. Popular account criticizing Darwinian theory of evolution.

Keeton, W. T. (1980). *Biological Science*. New York: Norton. A carefully written and well-illustrated book for students who want to expand their knowledge of ecology without tackling an ecology text.

Rifkin, J. (1983). *Algeny*. New York: Norton. Critique of Darwinian evolutionary theory. Contains controversial discussion on origin of theory of natural selection.

Rodgers, C. L., and Kerstetter, R. E. (1974). *The Ecosphere: Organisms, Habitats, and Disturbances*. New York: Harper and Row. A nicely written account on biomes and human disturbance of natural ecosystems.

Rosenzweig, M. L. (1974). *And Replenish the Earth*. New York: Harper and Row. A detailed and carefully written account of evolution and population ecology.

Smith, R. L. (1976). *The Ecology of Man: An Ecosystem Approach* (2nd ed.). New York: Harper and Row. Advanced readings on ecology and environmental problems.

———. (1980). *Ecology and Field Biology* (3rd ed.). New York: Harper and Row. A comprehensive textbook for students wishing to delve into this subject in more detail.

Principles of Ecology: Ecosystem Balance and Imbalance

The danger is not what nature will do with man, but what man will do with nature.

EVAN ESAR

Knowing how an ecosystem is structured (Chapter 3) and the way the energy and matter flow within it (Chapter 4) does not give us a complete picture of it. Some questions have not yet been answered; for instance, how can an ecosystem be altered, and in what ways can it recover from damage? How far can we push a natural community before permanently changing it?

These questions all bear upon ecosystem stability and instability. If we understand the roots of ecosystem stability, we can judge which actions will affect the environment and how, and we can tell what might be needed to promote recovery from past abuses.

Ecosystem Stability

Stability is commonly defined as a state in which change does not occur. But stable ecosystems change constantly; for example, population levels increase and decrease from day to day, season to season, and year to year. As Ralph Waldo Emerson wrote in his essay "Nature," "To the attentive eye, each moment of the year has its own beauty, and in the same field, it beholds, every hour, a picture which was never seen before."

Only fully developed, or mature, ecosystems (described later) are stable. They are considered stable because their structure and function remain more or less the same over long periods. They are in a state of **dynamic equilibrium (steady state)**, in which things change but remain more or less the same. For example, if we examined a mature ecosystem each spring for an extended period—say, 20 years—we would find that (1) the total number of species was fairly constant from year to year, (2) the same species were present each year, and (3) the population size of each species was approximately the same from year to year. As a tightrope walker moves along the high wire, tilting right, then left, but always staying on the wire, so a mature ecosystem undergoes small-scale fluctuations as it remains on its main course.

Stability is also the ability of a disturbed ecosystem to return to its original condition (**resilience**). After minor changes induced by natural and human causes, a stable ecosystem can "bounce back" to its previous condition. Stability is also a property of an ecosystem that causes it to resist being changed by natural events or by human interference (**inertia**). Resilience and inertia will be described in more detail later.

What Keeps Ecosystems Stable?

Population Growth and Environmental Resistance

The forces that affect an ecosystem's stability are the factors that control the size of its populations. These forces can be broken down into two groups: those factors that tend to increase population size, or **growth factors**, and those that tend to decrease population size, or **reduction factors**. As illustrated in Figure 5-1, growth and reduction factors can be biotic or abiotic. At any given moment population size is determined by the balance of these and other factors; and because the ecosystem contains many species, the entire ecosystem balance can be crudely related to the sum of the population balances.

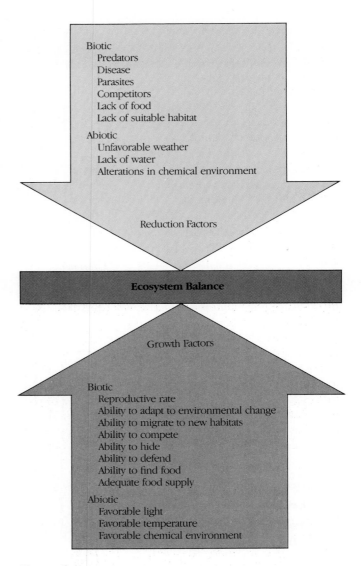

Figure 5-1
Ecosystem balance is affected by forces that tend to increase population size and forces that tend to decrease it. Growth and reduction factors consist of abiotic and biotic components.

The biotic factors that enhance population growth include an organism's ability to produce many offspring, to adapt to new environments and to environmental change, to migrate into new territories, to compete with other species, to blend into the environment, to defend itself against enemies, and to find food (Figure 5-1). Certain favorable abiotic conditions also tend to increase population size. Favorable light, temperature, and rainfall, for example, all promote maximum plant growth, and because animals depend on plants, these conditions often promote increases in many animal populations.

Opposing these positive influences are the abiotic and biotic reduction factors, which ecologists collectively describe as **environmental resistance**. For example, predators, disease, parasites, and competition by other species all effectively reduce population size, as do unfavorable weather and lack of food and water.

An example will help illustrate this concept. On the Great Plains of North America lives a small, mouselike rodent called the prairie vole. Its population size is dependent on a variety of factors such as light, rainfall, available food supply, predation by coyotes and hawks, temperature, and disease. The size of the vole population affects the size of other populations; thus, it becomes a biotic factor affecting the balance of populations such as the coyote and red-tailed hawk.

The prairie vole has a high reproductive capacity. When raised in the laboratory under optimum conditions, a pair of voles can produce a litter of six or seven pups every three weeks. The optimum conditions are low temperature (slightly above freezing), long days (14 hours of sunlight a day), and plenty of water and food. If voles reproduced at their maximum rate in the wild, the prairies of Kansas and Oklahoma would be overrun with them.

In the wild, all the optimum conditions are not met simultaneously. For example, when food, water, and day length are optimum (in the summer), the temperature is too warm. But when the temperature is just right for breeding (in the winter), the days are short and the food supply is less plentiful. Thus, environmental resistance counteracts the growth factors. If the growth and reduction factors are in balance, the population will be in balance.

This example shows us how population balance is maintained for one species, but how is balance maintained in an entire ecosystem? As mentioned above, the entire ecosystem balance can be crudely determined by the sum of the individual population balances. Put another way, if all the populations are in balance, you can expect the entire ecosystem to be in balance, too.

The ability of an ecosystem to resist change (inertia) and to return to a balanced state if disturbed (resilience) is primarily a function of the biotic growth factors shown in Figure 5-1, for these are the factors that tend to increase

population size and to keep it constant when something attempts to shift the balance. If we examine Figure 5-1, this statement becomes clearer. Change in an ecosystem is caused by a shift in growth and reduction factors, both biotic and abiotic. For instance, the introduction of new predators, a shortage of food, and unfavorable rainfall or temperature all tend to decrease population size and may throw the ecosystem out of balance. Conversely, certain factors, such as an abundance of food, may cause populations to increase. The balance is maintained by counteracting increases or decreases in population. Organisms may increase their reproductive rate, find new food sources, migrate into new territory, and so on. When wolf populations increase, the new adults may move away in search of new territory, keeping the local balance from being disturbed. If territory is not available, they may remain with the pack but do not reproduce. The dominant pair keeps all other sexually mature animals from breeding; this prevents the local wolf population from sky rocketing.

Species Diversity and Ecosystem Stability

Ecosystem stability may also be affected by species diversity. **Species diversity** is a measure of the number of different species in a biotic community, or a measure of variety in an ecosystem. Species diversity is related to at least three variables: the number of different species in an ecosystem, the number of individuals in each species, and the total number of individuals of all species in a community.

Species diversity is high in *mature,* or *climax, communities*—those that have reached a definitive stage of development and will remain at this stage barring natural disaster or serious human intervention. A high level of diversity is believed to confer a high degree of stability. In support of this idea are observations that extremely complex ecosystems, such as tropical rain forests, remain unchanged almost indefinitely if undisturbed. Simple ecosystems such as the tundra are more volatile, experiencing sudden and immense shifts in population size. Other simplified ecosystems such as fields of wheat and corn also show extreme vulnerability to change, and may collapse if abiotic or biotic factors shift too much. From this it appears that complexity, or species diversity, results in stability.

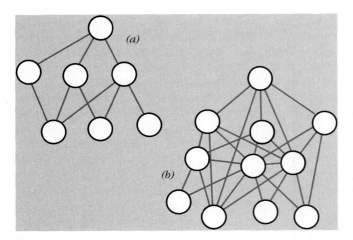

Figure 5-2
(a) Simplified food web. Circles represent organisms. Note the lack of links in the simplified web. *(b)* Complex food chain. Some ecologists believe that complex ecosystems are more stable because of the increased number of links.

To support this idea, we might look at the differences in food webs in simple and complex ecosystems. As illustrated in Figure 5-2, the number of different species in a food web in a mature ecosystem is large, as is the number of interactions between these organisms. Some ecologists contend that in a complex ecosystem the elimination of one species would have little effect on ecosystem balance. In sharp contrast, the number of species in the food web of a simple ecosystem is small, so eliminating one species could have repercussions for all others.

Although some experimental evidence indicates a link between species diversity and ecosystem stability, some ecologists believe that this link has not been adequately tested. Thus, the reason that tropical rain forests are stable may be that the climate is relatively uniform throughout the year. On the tundra, a relatively simple and somewhat unstable ecosystem, the climate shifts dramatically from season to season. Thus, the stability of the tropical rain forest may not result from species diversity but from a constant climate.

What is the upshot of this debate? Although it is not known for certain whether diversity creates stability, we can say that simplifying ecosystems may have deleterious effects. Intentional simplification of ecosystems (removing species) can cause irreparable damage. The removal of a species upon which many others feed, for example, will have a noticeable impact, especially if an alternative

food supply is not available. In the food web shown in Figure 5-3, the loss of water plants would have a noticeable impact, because many species feed on them. Since these plants are the sole source of food for some primary consumers, their loss would undoubtedly jeopardize those consumers. As we will see later, human populations have a tendency to reduce species diversity, in the process making ecosystems more vulnerable to change.

Imbalance in Ecosystems

Stability is a useful concept to apply to ecosystems. It helps us understand imbalances that occur naturally or from human activities. This section will examine imbalance brought about by shifts in the growth and reduction factors discussed earlier.

Small-Scale Changes

An ecosystem's balance can be tilted temporarily by natural shifts in the abiotic and biotic growth and reduction factors shown in Figure 5-1. For instance, an increase in rainfall on the grasslands of Texas would increase ground cover and food supply for mice, resulting in a sharp increase in reproduction and population size. Coyotes, which prey on mice, would increase in response. In time, the increase in coyotes would reduce the rodent population; that decrease would cause the coyote population to decline.

Human activities may bring about similar events. For example, sewage accidentally dumped into a stream adds organic and inorganic chemicals to the water (Figure 5-4). The organic molecules are consumed by bacteria and cause the number of bacteria to increase. Because bacteria use up oxygen as they consume organic materials, the level of dissolved oxygen in the stream usually drops. This can kill fish and other organisms or cause them to migrate to new areas.

In time, the stream will return to normal. The bacteria will die if the level of organic matter falls off, and the dissolved oxygen will return to normal, thus allowing fish to return. Chapter 20 treats this topic in detail.

Small shifts in the growth and reduction factors in an ecosystem, whether brought about by natural causes or by humans, are fairly common. Ecosystems respond to these changes in a way that ensures the survival of the community. However, drastic shifts can seriously, sometimes irreversibly, upset ecosystem balance.

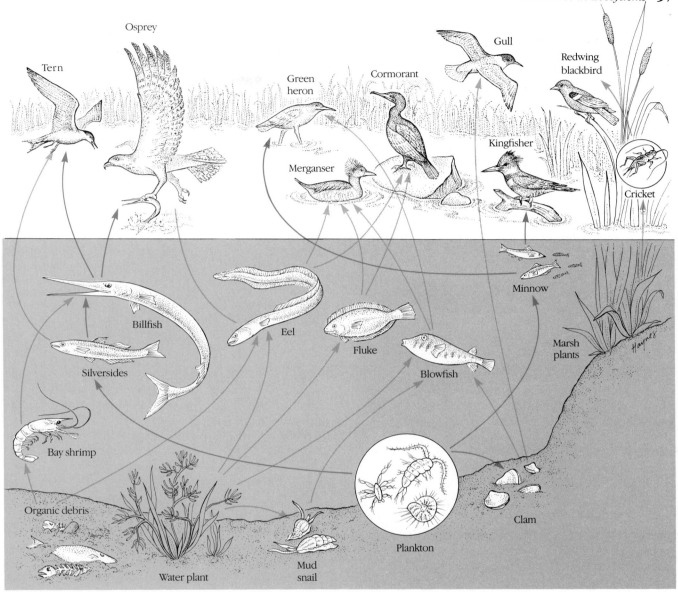

Figure 5-3
Food web in a Long Island estuary, showing the numerous interconnections.

Large-Scale Changes: Succession

Major ecosystem perturbations may be caused by natural events (shifts in climate, floods, volcanic eruptions, fires, and drought) or human intervention (mining and logging). In either case, damage to the ecosystem may be so severe that it takes years or decades for the original community to be restored.

A biotic community destroyed by natural or human causes is gradually replaced in a series of changes until a mature or climax community is reached. The replacement of one biotic community by another is called **succession**. There are two types of succession, primary and secondary.

Primary Succession Primary **succession** is the sequential development of biotic communities where none

Figure 5-4
The events that follow the dumping of organic wastes into a stream.

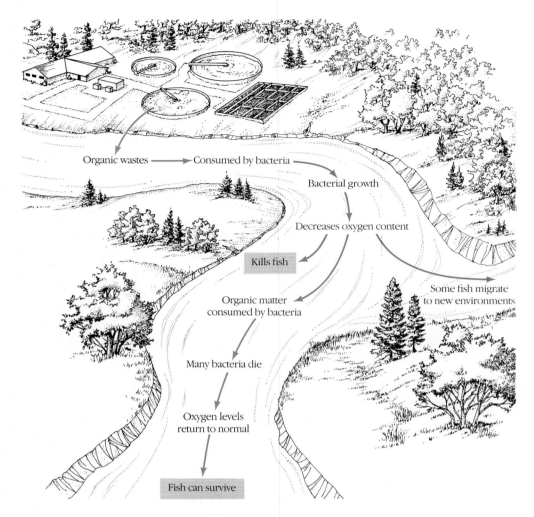

Organic wastes → Consumed by bacteria

Bacterial growth

Decreases oxygen content

Kills fish

Some fish migrate to new environments

Organic matter consumed by bacteria

Many bacteria die

Oxygen levels return to normal

Fish can survive

previously existed. For instance, when the great glaciers began to retreat 15,000 years ago, large tracts of land and rock were exposed. The exposed rock gradually became populated with lichens (Figure 5-5). These plantlike organisms cling to rock and live off moisture from rain. By secreting a weak acid called carbonic acid, lichens slowly dissolve the rock, making soil. Lichens thrive there, but they are gradually replaced by mosses. The mosses are eventually replaced by ferns, grasses, and larger plants, which eventually give way to shrubs and trees. Why does this succession of plant life take place?

The answer is that each biotic community alters its habitat so much that it can no longer survive. The lichens live off the rock and spread over its surface. Tiny insects may become part of the community. Together, the first inhabitants form the **pioneer community**—that is, the first community to become established in a once-barren environment. The lichens and insects gradually change their environment. Capturing windblown dirt particles, for example, the lichens promote the development of soil. Dead lichens crumble, and insect wastes and remains also contribute to soil formation. Over time, soil develops sufficiently for mosses to grow there. The mosses shade the lichens and eventually kill them. Mosses, fungi, bacteria, and insects form a new biotic community. But the new biological community also brings about deleterious changes, which result in its replacement by an altogether new community.

A classic example of primary succession occurs on newly formed volcanic islands like the Hawaiian Islands. Seeds borne on the wind and seas or carried by birds first inhabit the barren volcanic rock. After a number of intermediate

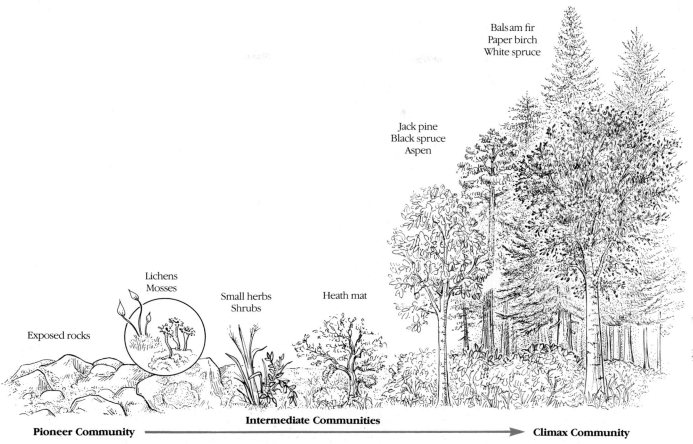

Balsam fir
Paper birch
White spruce

Jack pine
Black spruce
Aspen

Lichens
Mosses

Small herbs
Shrubs

Heath mat

Exposed rocks

Intermediate Communities

Pioneer Community ⟶ **Climax Community**

Figure 5-5
Primary succession. Here, exposed rock goes through a series of changes as one
biotic community replaces another until a mature community is formed. During
succession the plants of each community alter their habitat so drastically that
conditions become more suitable for other species.

communities have come and gone, a climax community
is established. The succession of a lake to a forest ecosystem is also a type of primary succession (Figure 5-6).

Secondary Succession **Secondary succession** is the
sequential development of biotic communities after the
complete or partial destruction of an existing community.
Usually the long, slow development of soil is unnecessary.
A mature or intermediate community may be destroyed
by natural events such as volcanic eruptions, floods,
droughts, fires, or storms or by human intervention such
as agriculture, intentional flooding, fire, or mining.

Let us look briefly at an example of secondary succession occurring on an abandoned eastern farm that had
previously supported a natural biotic community (Figure
5-7). Abandoned farmland is first invaded by crabgrass, a
hardy species well adapted to survive in bare, sun-baked
soil. Crabgrass, insects, and mice form the pioneer community. However, crabgrass is soon joined by tall grasses
and herbaceous plants. The shade these newcomers create eventually eliminates the sun-loving crabgrass. The tall
grasses and herbaceous plants dominate the ecosystem
for few years along with mice, rabbits, insects, and seed-
eating birds.

Figure 5-6
Primary succession. In this
example, a pond is gradually
converted to a forest
ecosystem. Sediment begins to
accumulate, and a series of
biotic communities develops
until the mature ecosystem is
reached.

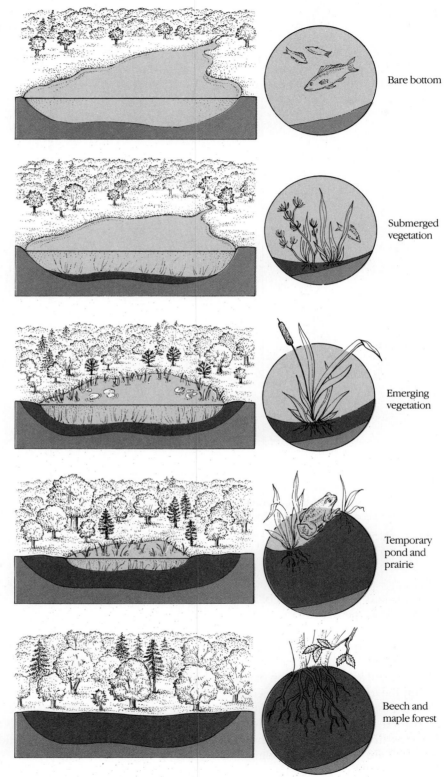

**Pioneer
Community**

Bare bottom

Submerged
vegetation

Emerging
vegetation

Temporary
pond and
prairie

Beech and
maple forest

**Climax
Community**

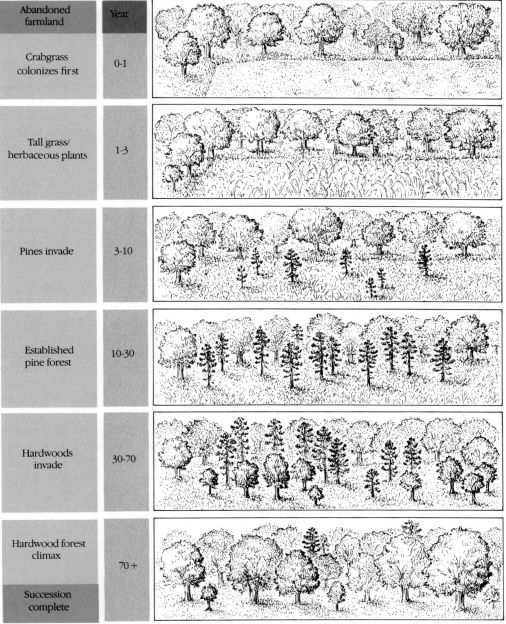

Abandoned farmland	Year
Crabgrass colonizes first	0-1
Tall grass/ herbaceous plants	1-3
Pines invade	3-10
Established pine forest	10-30
Hardwoods invade	30-70
Hardwood forest climax / Succession complete	70+

Figure 5-7
Secondary succession. Here, abandoned farmland is gradually replaced by crabrass, which in turn gives way to herbaceous plants. Trees move in, and over time a mature hardwood ecosystem is formed.

In time, pine seeds settle in the area. Young pine trees begin to pop up in the open field. The pine thrives in the sunny, hot, dry fields. Over the next three decades pines predominate in the ecosystem, slowly shading out grasses and herbs. Animals such as woodchucks, which feed on herbs (forbs) and grasses, move on to more hospitable environments. Squirrels and chipmunks, which prefer a wooded habitat, invade the new ecosystem.

The shade the pines create gradually creates an inhospitable environment for pine seedlings and a favorable environment for the growth of shade-tolerant hardwood trees. As the hardwoods grow, they begin to tower over the pines; their shade gradually kills the pines that had invaded 60 years earlier.

During the transition from one biotic community to another in both primary and secondary succession, the

Table 5-1   Characteristics of Mature and Immature Ecosystems

Characteristic	Immature Ecosystem	Mature Ecosystem
Food chains	Linear, predominantly grazer	Weblike, predominantly detritus
Net productivity	High	Low
Species diversity	Low	High
Niche specialization	Broad	Narrow
Nutrient cycles	Open	Closed
Nutrient conservation	Poor	Good
Stability	Low	Higher

Source: Modified from Odum, E. (1969). The Strategy of Ecosystem Development. *Science* 164: 262–270. Copyright 1969 by the American Association for the Advancement of Science.

plants create conditions that result in the development of a new biotic community. As new plants dominate the land, the animal populations also shift.

The early stages in succession are characterized by high levels of productivity—that is, high levels of photosynthesis (see Table 5-1). In addition, early communities typically have a low species diversity but contain rapidly growing populations, which are expanding to exploit the resources of the untapped ecosystem. Because there are fewer species in the early stages of succession, food webs tend to be simple, and populations tend to be susceptible to change. Mature biotic communities, in contrast, are characterized by high species diversity and stable populations (Table 5-1). Food webs are intricate, and, therefore, stability is assured if changes are not too drastic.

Biomass is at the maximum level supportable by the environment.

As ecosystems become increasingly complex, the food chains become woven into more complex food webs. The grazing food chain accounts for the bulk of the biomass flow in immature or developing ecosystems. In mature ecosystems, however, most of the biomass flows through the detritus food chain. In fact, in a mature forest less than 10% of the net productivity is consumed by grazers. In mature ecosystems the nutrient cycles tend to become closed as mature ecosystems have a great capacity to entrap and hold nutrients. In contrast, immature or developing ecosystems tend to lose a considerable amount of their nutrients because of erosion and other factors.

From the standpoint of ecosystem stability, pioneer and

Figure 5-8
A simplified graphical representation of changing population size and environmental resistance as a community develops during succession. Note that environmental resistance increases the establishment before the new community does. Environmental resistance is caused by unfavorable conditions created by the community itself.

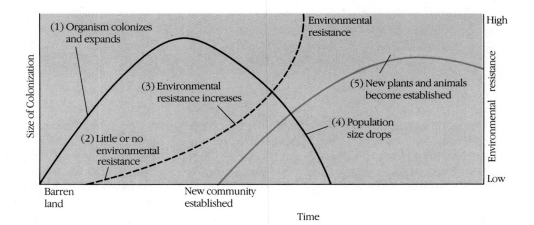

intermediate communities are in a state of imbalance. The abiotic and biotic factors that regulate population size and give the ecosystem stability are not well balanced. There is little environmental resistance (such as predators), so there are few limitations to growth. Thus, growth factors such as the availability of food, favorable light, and suitable temperature outweigh the environmental resistance. As a result, populations expand. During succession, however, each community goes through a phase of increasing environmental resistance as competitors increase in number and as abiotic conditions shift (Figure 5-8). When environmental resistance peaks a new community becomes established.

Human Impact on Ecosystems

In this section we will examine the general ways in which humans alter the biosphere. This topic is worth close study, because what we do to the biosphere, we also do to ourselves. Keep this section in mind when studying Part II, "Population."

Table 5-2 briefly summarizes the various levels of human impact brought about by disturbing abiotic and biotic factors in the environment.

Altering Biotic Factors

Introducing Competitors   Over and over, humans have introduced foreign species into new regions only to face serious problems caused by excessive growth of the introduced species. For example, 12 pairs of European rabbits were introduced on Thomas Austin's ranch in Australia in 1859. In the next few years the rabbits proliferated wildly and began eating grass intended for sheep, creating a major national environmental problem (Figures 5-9a and 5-9b). Five rabbits eat as much grass as one sheep. Despite a major campaign to remove rabbits from Australia, by 1953 more than 1 billion rabbits inhabited nearly 3 million square kilometers (1.2 million square miles).

Plants introduced to new environments can also compete with existing species. For instance, in 1884 the water hyacinth was introduced into Florida from South America as an ornamental flower. The plant accidentally spread into the waterways of Florida, where it proliferated at a remarkable rate. Ten plants can multiply to 600,000 in just eight months. Outcompeting many native plants, the

Table 5-2   Human Impact on Ecosystems

Organism Level

Death
Physiological and biochemical changes
Reduction in number of offspring
Behavioral changes
Psychological disorders
Death of offspring
Genetic defects (mutagenic effects)
Birth defects (teratogenic effects)
Cancer (carcinogenic effects)

Population Level

Population increase or decrease
Change in age structure
Alteration of genetic structure
Loss of genetic diversity
Survival of strains resistant to pesticides
Extinction

Community–Ecosystem Level

Distruption of energy flow
  Decreases in input of solar energy
  Changes in heat output and input
  Changes in trophic structure

Disruption of nutrient cycles
  Depletion of nutrients
  Addition of nutrients
  Alteration of nutrient flow patterns by
  eliminating species

Simplification
  Reduction in species diversity
  Reduction in habitat
  Reduction in filled niches
  Possibility of lowered stability
  Possibility of ecosystem collapse

Source: Modified from Miller, G. T. (1982). *Living in the Environment.* Wadsworth, Belmont, CA.

hyacinth clogs waterways and makes navigation impossible (Figure 5-10). Today, approximately 800,000 hectares (2 million acres) of rivers and lakes from Florida to California are plagued with thick surface mats of hyacinth. In Florida, Louisiana, and Texas, where the problem is most severe, approximately $11 million is spent to clear waterways each year. (As discussed in Essay 5-1, however, the water hyacinth can be put to good use in pollution control.)

Figure 5-9
(a) Rabbits introduced in small numbers to Australia increased dramatically in a few years, posing a major environmental problem. They ate vegatiation intended for sheep and cost the government and ranchers millions of dollars.
(b) Widespread destruction caused by rabbits in Australia. Range on the right was protected by rabbit-proof fencing.

(a)

(b)

Figure 5-10
The water hyacinth was introduced accidentally into Florida waters. It has proliferated at a tremendous rate, choking canals and streams and outcompeting many native species.

Putting a Pest to Work: An Ecological Solution to Water Pollution

It's not often a pest makes good, but such is the case of the water hyacinth. Long infamous for clogging canals, rivers, and ponds and costing state governments millions for cleanup, the water hyacinth has been put to work as a water purifier in sewage treatment plants.

Unlike many other plants, water hyacinths need no soil. Their roots simply dangle below the surface and absorb the nutrients the plant needs to grow. The nutrients these plants need are, coincidentally, also major water pollutants—nitrates, phosphates, and potassium. Thus, the water hyacinth acts as a biological filter, removing these harmful pollutants from the water.

Grown in special ponds in which wastes from sewage plants are dumped, the hyacinths provide an inexpensive alternative to conventional wastewater treatment (see Chapter 20 for more detail on this subject). As an added benefit, the water hyacinth also absorbs certain toxic wastes, pesticides, and heavy metals.

At Disney World near Orlando, Florida, officials have constructed five ponds, each roughly the size of a football field. Wastewater from the park is pumped into these ponds, purified by the water hyacinths, and then returned for reuse. San Diego is spending $3.5 million to develop a similar wastewater treatment facility.

The advantages of this approach are several. Conventional wastewater treatment is costly, requiring large amounts of electricity and numerous maintenance workers. Hyacinth treatment, in contrast, may cost about half as much because of the low energy requirements and the lack of personnel. It also allows for recycling of water, a boon to water-short regions. Also, periodic harvesting of the hyacinths yields food for livestock or fertilizer for fields. The water hyacinth provides an important ecological solution to help us build a sustainable society.

Eliminating or Introducing Predators   Humans have a tendency to eliminate predators such as bear, eagles, and wolves from their habitat. For example, on the north rim of the Grand Canyon on the Kaibab Plateau, mountain lions, wolves, coyotes, and deer lived in balance for many years. In the early 1900s, however, the state of Arizona put a bounty on wolves, coyotes, and mountain lions, which triggered their wholesale slaughter. Within 15 years virtually all of these predators had been eliminated. This intervention unleashed growth factors, which sent the population of deer skyrocketing. Before the establishment of the bounties there were approximately 4000 deer on the Kaibab Plateau, but by 1924, the deer population had reached about 100,000. The deer overgrazed the plateau, and approximately 60,000 died from starvation in the following winters. The vegetation has still not completely recovered.

Occasionally, predators are introduced into areas. The mosquito fish, for example, is a native of the southeastern United States that has been introduced into many subtropical regions throughout the world because it feeds

on the larvae of mosquitoes and thus helps control malaria. Unfortunately, the mosquito fish also feeds heavily on zooplankton, small floating protists that consume algae. Depleting the zooplankton, the fish removes environmental resistance to algal populations; this causes algae to proliferate and form thick mats that reduce light penetration and plant growth in aquatic ecosystems.

From these examples it should be evident that altering the trophic structure by introducing or eliminating predators has a direct impact on the ecosystem and also on humans.

Introducing Disease Organisms   Pathogenic (disease-producing) organisms are as much a part of the ecosystem as any other; as illustrated in Figure 5-1, they are a part of environmental resistance. However, humans have unknowingly introduced pathogens into new environments where there are no natural controls. There, they reproduce at a high rate and cause serious damage. For example, in the late 1800s a fungus that infects Chinese chestnuts was introduced accidentally into the United States

Ecology or Egology?

Peter Russell

The author has been closely involved with the development of the Learning Methods Group, an international organization that helps people make fuller use of their mental potential. His books include The TM Technique, The Brain Book, Meditation, *and* The Global Brain, *which presents an optimistic vision of our long-term future.*

The environmental sciences usually focus on understanding the many intricate relationships and interdependencies that have evolved between the millions of living systems inhabiting the earth. Rather than looking further into the many facets of these sciences, I wish here to explore this question: "Why are such studies necessary in the first place? Why is it that one species out of millions can disrupt the natural balance in so many ways and with such dire consequences?"

The rapid and liberal development of technology is clearly part of the problem. *Homo sapiens* has always been a manipulative species. A million years ago, long before civilization appeared, our opposable thumbs and large brain would have singled us out as the creature most capable of modifying its environment. In more recent history technology has amplified this capacity, and to such an extent that today one person's decision may have global repercussions.

Yet it is also clear that technological might is not the sole cause of environmental mismanagement. It is ultimately human beings who choose how to use technology, and they initiate the actions that result in ecological disturbances. In some cases the disturbance is totally unforeseen. In other cases we may already realize that a certain approach could lead to trouble. But somehow those concerned are able to ignore the warning or, worse, seek evidence to the contrary, displaying an apparent lack of care for other species, the biosystem as a whole, and, paradoxically, their own long-term welfare. How is it that people can adhere to policies that by nearly all projections look suicidal?

Such behavior stems from individuals' not seeing beyond their short-term welfare and from their perceiving their interests to be different from the interests of humanity as a whole. For most people an immediate personal fulfillment is more attractive than some distant long-term benefit, and so they naturally go for the former. Education and social controls may help curb the pull of immediate gratification, but the pull is so strong that these are unlikely to be sufficient. But what is it that makes us want to satisfy our short-term needs to the detriment of our long-term welfare? The answer appears to lie deep within our psyche.

In the more developed nations—and it is these nations that are responsible for the major environmental issues of today—the basic needs for food, clothing, shelter, and health care are fairly well attended to. What emerges then is the need for psychological welfare, in particular the need to be liked. For many of us the major source of our personal identity lies in our interactions with other people. We need people to recognize and reaffirm our worth, and we spend considerable time and effort fulfilling this need. Much of our activity is really a search for personal reinforcement (what are often termed "positive psychological strokes"). Some psychologists estimate that as much as 80% of all our actions may be motivated by this search. And when people stand back and listen to themselves, they often find that as much as 90% of their casual conversation is prompted by this need for approval. The need to be liked has become one of our most powerful drives.

One of the most common ways we try to win approval and prestige is through material possessions. We collect many of the various accoutrements of modern living—new cars, fashionable clothes, expensive furniture, gourmet (and gourmand) diets—not because we need them physically but because we need them psychologically. It is then but a short step to translating the need for inner security into the need for financial security.

This might not be so bad if our various possessions satiated our psychological needs; but they don't. Our insecurity is rooted far deeper in our psyche than that. Instead of spotting the obvious flaw, we search for yet more things in the outer world that we hope might fill the inner gap.

Some implications of this for the way we treat the environment are obvious. We gobble up irreplaceable resources, with little regard for the long-term future, partly because the various products they are transformed into may briefly satisfy our search for identity. Thus, the consumers are as much exploiters of the environment as are the corporations who reflect the market needs.

Yet there is more to it than that. We do have choices in how we satisfy our misguided search for material well-being. We might even be able to do so in ecologically sane ways. Ultimately there are people somewhere making decisions to exploit this or that particular resource, initiate industrial processes with various environmental effects, and set in motion other activities that in one way or another upset the ecological balance. And such people are usually motivated by similar needs for approval and recognition from their peers, by the need to play the game they have chosen without losing face, and by the mistaken belief that financial security brings inner security. They are caught in the same trap as everyone else. The only difference is that they are more visible.

Another profound consequence of our inner insecurity is a lack of true caring and compassion, either for others or for the environment. Each of us, at our core, is a compassionate being capable of deep empathy and caring. If we can get back in contact with this deeper self, we can begin to experience compassion not only for other people but also for the rest of the world.

One way we block compassion is through arrogance, and one of the most dominant forms of arrogance in the Western world is scientific. The very rapid growth of a diversity of sciences has resulted in the belief that we now know how the world works and can therefore apply our considerable

manipulative might with safety. Yet in most cases we have foreseen only a tiny proportion of the long-term effects of our actions. There is probably no way we as individual human beings can fully understand the complex workings and intricate balances of all the living systems on this planet. Letting go of our self-gratifying patterns of behavior, we find not only compassion but humility. We rediscover respect for the unfathomable complexity of life on earth and for all its many species.

To summarize, the environmental sciences, laudable as they are, will remain incomplete until they take account of the human psychology that gives rise to their necessity. We need to consider not just the totality of all the systems constituting the biosphere but also the larger system that includes the human psyche and its current shortcomings. The only approach that will be successful in the long term is one that attends both to the external environment and to the internal environment, the system we call "I."

---

when several young Chinese chestnut trees were brought to the New York Zoological Park. The Chinese chestnut is immune to the fungus. However, the American chestnut, once a valuable commercial tree found in much of the eastern United States, had no resistance to the fungus and was virtually eliminated from this country between 1910 and 1940 (Figure 5-11). Now chestnut wood is found only in antiques, and the once-abundant chestnut, a tasty seed commonly roasted in embers, is only a memory of our grandparents.

Altering Abiotic Factors

Humans also tamper with many abiotic factors by polluting air, water, and land and by depleting resources, such as water, needed by species.

Creating Pollution   Water pollution and air pollution create an unfavorable environment for many organisms. For example, chlorinated compounds released from wastewater treatment plants virtually eliminate fish in rivers where the treated wastes are dumped. Oil spills on lakes, rivers, and oceans destroy fish, reptiles, and birds. Toxic pesticides eliminate birds that feed on contaminated insects and fish. Thermal pollution from plants kills

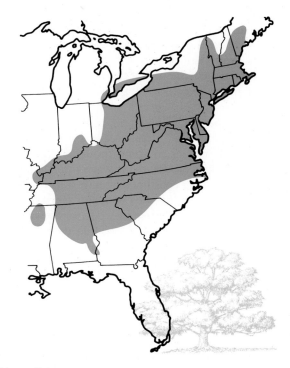

Figure 5-11

Former range of the American chestnut, a species nearly wiped out by the accidental introduction of a harmful fungus.

Figure 5-12
Parts of Miami are built on costal areas that were once marshland.

fish and many aquatic organisms on which fish feed. Possible global changes in temperature brought about by increasing atmospheric carbon dioxide could alter the climate in many regions of the world, possibly eliminating thousands of species of plants and animals. In these and many other examples, human activities create an unfavorable abiotic environment that can reduce or eliminate species and upset the ecological balance.

Depleting Resources   Human populations may deplete or destroy resources used by other species. For instance, the diversion of streams in some mountain regions to supply growing cities has left many waterways dry. Housing development along coastlines often results in the filling in of estuaries and marshes with dirt (Figure 5-12). Full-scale oil shale development may destroy the valuable wintering grounds of thousands of mule deer in Colorado, possibly resulting in the severe reduction of deer populations in the western part of the state.

Simplifying Ecosystems

Tampering with abiotic and biotic factors in the ecosystems tends to simplify them, because it reduces species diversity. Reduction in species diversity may cause ecosystem imbalance and eventual collapse.

Ecosystem simplification is best seen when natural ecosystems are converted into farmland. Grasslands, containing numerous species of plants, are greatly simplified when they are plowed under and planted with a single cash crop such as corn or wheat. Crops with only one species are called **monocultures**. Having little diversity, they are quite susceptible to damage, especially from insects and disease organisms. The reason is that monocultures provide a virtually unlimited food source for insects and plant pathogens, especially viruses and fungi. As the crops develop, the biotic growth factor of food supply suddenly shifts in favor of rapid population growth (Figure 5-13). Viruses, fungi, and insects proliferate, becoming major pests (as discussed in Chapters 8 and 9). There is little or no environmental resistance in monocultures. To control such outbreaks, humans have long relied on chemical pesticides (the subject of Chapter Supplement 9-1).

Chemical pesticides used to control fungi, viruses, and insects may be carried in the air or water to other natural ecosystems, where they may poison beneficial organisms. For instance, the widespread use of DDT in the United States has contaminated many terrestrial and aquatic ecosystems. Passed through the food chain, DDT reaches higher level consumers, including ospreys and peregrine falcons (Figure 5-14). This poison does not kill mature falcons and ospreys but interferes with the deposition of calcium in their eggshells, making the shells thinner. The fragile eggs are easily broken, so few embryos can survive.

The peregrine falcon, which nests on rocky ledges

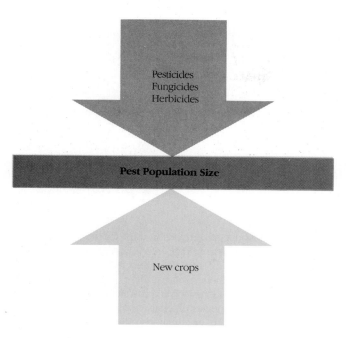

Figure 5-13
Biotic growth factors shift when crops grow in the spring and summer. The abundance of food can result in large populations of harmful insects, fungi, or viruses, which infect crops. Farmers attempt to counteract the growth factors with pesticides fungicides, and other chemicals.

throughout the world, was nearly destroyed by DDT. By the time scientists had linked the lack of reproduction to eggshell thinning caused by DDT, none of the 200 known pairs east of the Mississippi River were successfully producing young. Fortunately for the peregrine falcon, DDT was banned in the United States (but still manufactured here until 1984), and a determined program was mounted that may well save these birds. By 1982, more than 1000 peregrines had been raised in captivity and released into the wild by ornithologists from Cornell University and Colorado State University. By 1987 the release program in the eastern United States may be ended, because the population is expected to be reestablished and stable. By the early 1990s recovery should be complete in the Rockies, too. Now that DDT is no longer used in this country, eggshells of wild birds are returning to their normal thickness.

This example shows how fragile simplified ecosystems such as agricultural land are, how our arduous efforts to protect these vulnerable ecosystems damage other animals, and how costly the efforts needed to repair the damage are. Further examples will be presented in Chapter 10. Suggestions for ways to reduce the destruction of ecosystem diversity are presented throughout the book.

Figure 5-14
Peregrine falcon and her chick. The peregrine, once a nearly extinct species in the United States, has made a remarkable comeback with the assistance of researchers who have incubated eggs in captivity and released birds in the wild. DDT used to protect human crops caused eggshell thinning in peregrines and other species, nearly eliminating the natural populations of these birds.

> *For the first time in the whole history of evolution, responsibility for the continued unfolding of evolution has been placed upon the evolutionary material itself. . . . Whether we like it or not, we are now the custodians of the evolutionary process on earth. Within our own hands—or rather, within our own minds—lies the evolutionary future of the planet.*
>
> PETER RUSSELL

Summary

Mature ecosystems change with time but remain more or less the same from one year to the next. They are said to be in a *dynamic equilibrium,* or *dynamic steady state.* Ecosystem stability is the ability of an ecosystem to resist change *(inertia)* or return to its original condition when disturbed *(resilience).*

Biotic and abiotic components of the ecosystem cause populations to increase and decrease and ultimately determine ecosystem balance. Those that stimulate population are called *growth factors;* those that depress it are called *reduction factors* (the sum of them is *environmental resistance*).

Species diversity is considered to be one of the more important factors determining ecosystem stability. Species diversity is a measure of the number of different species in a community. It is generally believed that the greater the species diversity, the greater the stability. Some ecologists, however, believe that the link between stability and diversity has not been firmly established. Diverse ecosystems such as tropical rain forests may be stable because of a uniform climate. In other words, diversity may simply be the result of stable climatic conditions and not the cause of ecosystem stability. Although we are not certain whether diversity leads to ecosystem stability, we do know that simplifying ecosystems, or reducing species diversity, tends to make them more vulnerable to insects, adverse weather, and disease-producing organisms.

Small shifts in the biotic and abiotic growth and reduction factors may temporarily tip an ecosystem's balance, but appropriate responses within the biological community can return the system to normal. Larger shifts may result in a dramatic destabilization of the ecosystem, resulting in its collapse. A biological community destroyed by such large shifts recovers during a process known as *secondary succession,* in which new communities develop sequentially until a mature, or climax, community is formed. *Primary succession* is the sequential development of communities where none previously existed. (For example, when glaciers melt, exposing rock, lichens will populate the rocks and eventually be replaced by mosses and, later, ferns and other vegetation.) The first community to become established in a once-barren region during primary succession is called the *pioneer community.* In both primary and secondary succession, each biotic community alters its habitat so much that its members can no longer survive there.

The early stages of succession are characterized by high levels of productivity, low species diversity, and rapidly growing populations. The final stage, or climax community, is characterized by high species diversity, stable populations, intricate food webs, and relatively low net productivity.

Humans cause ecosystem imbalance by altering the biotic components of the ecosystem. Introducing or eliminating competitors, predators, and pathogenic organisms, for example, can permanently disrupt ecosystem balance. Imbalance may be caused by altering the abiotic components as well. Pollution and resource depletion are two major examples of ways we alter abiotic components. Tampering with abiotic and biotic factors in the ecosystem tends to reduce species diversity, or simplify ecosystems. *Monocultures,* huge single-crop plantings, represent extreme ecosystem simplifications that are vulnerable to insects, disease, and adverse weather.

Discussion Questions

1. Describe ecosystem stability. Give an example of an ecosystem you are familiar with. Is it stable? Why or why not?

2. If you were to examine a mature ecosystem over the course of 30 years at the same time each year, would you expect the number of species in the ecosystem and the population size of each of these species to be the same from year to year? Why or why not?

3. What is inertia? What is resilience?

4. Describe the model shown in Figure 5-1.

5. What is meant by environmental resistance? What role does it play in population balance? What role does it play in ecosystem balance?

6. Define the term *species diversity*. Give evidence that species diversity affects ecosystem stability. Is there any evidence to contradict this idea?

7. What is a mature ecosystem? What are the major features of a mature ecosystem?

8. Describe temporary imbalances caused in ecosystems you are familiar with and how the ecosystem returns to normal.

9. What is succession? Why is one biotic community eventually replaced by another during succession?

10. What is the difference between primary and secondary succession? Give examples of both.

11. What is a pioneer community?

12. Discuss why environmental resistance changes during succession as one community is gradually replaced by another. In what ways do human populations change environmental resistance, and how does that affect our population?

13. Describe the ecosystem impacts of human activities after studying Table 5-2. Give examples of damage that you are familiar with at the organism, population, and ecosystem level.

14. Describe how introducing and removing competitors into an ecosystem can affect ecosystem stability. Give some examples.

15. How do humans tamper with abiotic ecosystem components? Give some examples with which you are familiar, and trace the effect on plants and animals.

16. Humans are like all other organisms in many respects, except that they greatly simplify their ecosystems. Why is it necessary for them to do so? How can it be avoided? Give some examples.

17. From an evolutionary standpoint, discuss why simplified ecosystems (monocultures) are highly susceptible to fungi, viruses, and insects.

Suggested Readings

Colinvaux, P. (1973). *Introduction to Ecology*. New York: Wiley. An excellent textbook of basic ecology; good treatment of history of ecological concepts.

Curtis, H. (1979). *Biology*. New York: Worth. A must for students who want to supplement their knowledge of ecology without having to read an entire ecology text.

Dasmann, R. F. (1975). *The Conservation Alternative*. New York: Wiley. A good general work on ecology.

———. (1976). *Environmental Conservation* (4th ed.). New York: Wiley. Contains a particularly good discussion of ecological principles.

Ehrlich, P. A.; Ehrlich, A. H.; and Holdren, J. P. (1977). *Ecoscience: Population, Resources, Environment*. San Francisco: Freeman. A higher level text that covers ecology in detail. A superb reference book.

Gould, S. J. (1977). *Ever Since Darwin*. New York: Norton. Brilliant collection of essays on evolution and natural history.

———. (1980). *The Panda's Thumb*. New York: Norton. Brilliant and witty collection of essays on evolution.

Hitching, F. (1982). *The Neck of the Giraffe: Where Darwin Went Wrong*. New York: Ticknor and Fields. Popular account criticizing Darwinian theory of evolution.

Keeton, W. T. (1980). *Biological Science*. New York: Norton. A carefully written and well-illustrated book for students who want to expand their knowledge of ecology without tackling an ecology text.

Rifkin, J. (1983). *Algeny*. New York: Norton. Critique of Darwinian evolutionary theory. Contains controversial discussion on origin of theory of natural selection.

Rodgers, C. L., and Kerstetter, R. E. (1974). *The Ecosphere: Organisms, Habitats, and Disturbances*. New York: Harper and Row. A nicely written account on biomes and human disturbance of natural ecosystems.

Rosenzweig, M. L. (1974). *And Replenish the Earth*. New York: Harper and Row. A detailed and carefully written account of evolution and population ecology.

Smith, R. L. (1976). *The Ecology of Man: An Ecosystem Approach* (2nd ed.). New York: Harper and Row. Advanced readings on ecology and environmental problems.

———. (1980). *Ecology and Field Biology* (3rd ed.). New York: Harper and Row. A comprehensive textbook for students wishing to delve into this subject in more detail.

POPULATION

6

Population Growth and Its Impact

One generation passeth away, and another generation cometh, but the earth abideth forever.

ECCLESIASTES 1:4

In the 30 seconds it took you to find this book on your bookshelf and turn to this page, 128 live babies were born worldwide. During that same 30 seconds, 50 people died; the world population increased by 78 people, a rate of 2.6 people every second!

At this rate of growth, about 1.6 million people join the human population every week, approximately the number of people in Detroit. Overall, the world's population increases by 82 million people each year. In 1984, the total world population was about 4.8 billion. By the year 2000, it may exceed 6 billion.

Many scientists believe that the large world population and its rapid growth are the leading causes of problems involving food and resource supplies, housing, wildlife extinction, and environmental quality. Some scientists assert that this growth threatens the long-term survival of human society. This chapter will discuss population growth, paying special attention to measurements that give scientists clues about our future.

The Population Explosion

Until quite recently in human history, our population was quite small (Figure 6-1). During the time of Christ, for example, there were probably only about 200 million to 300 million people in the world. By 1850, though, world population had reached the 1 billion mark, after which it began to grow much more rapidly (Table 6-1). Between 1850 and 1930, the world population doubled, reaching 2 billion; 45 years later it had doubled again, reaching 4 billion in 1975.

What caused the rapid upsurge in population growth starting in the 1800s? To understand the increase, we must first understand why the human population remained relatively small and stable until the 1800s.

Natural Checks on Human Populations

Throughout most of human history, population was kept small by disease, famine, and war. These checks on population growth are the reduction factors that collectively form environmental resistance (see Chapter 5).

Disease has played a leading role in maintaining population balance throughout human history. In ancient Rome, Greece, and Egypt most adults lived only to about age 30, mainly because of poor health care and the frequent occurrence of infectious disease, illnesses caused by pathogenic bacteria and viruses that spread from individual

Table 6-1 World Population Growth and Doubling Time		
Population Size	**Year**	**Time Required to Double**
1 billion	1850	All of human history
2 billion	1930	80 years
4 billion	1975	45 years
8 billion (projected)	2017	42 years

to individual. Throughout the world, cholera, yellow fever, bubonic plague, typhus, malaria, and smallpox killed thousands of people, often sweeping across continents in devastating epidemics. For example, bubonic plague, once known as the black death, killed about 25% of the adult population in Europe in a series of epidemics in the 1300s. In the worst incident, between 1348 and 1379, half of all European adults died.

Famine was also a significant population check. Many people starved to death or were weakened and made more susceptible to disease by food shortages resulting from adverse weather (especially drought) and blight. The Irish famine of 1846–1851, which was caused by a potato blight, killed an estimated one of every ten adults. A famine in China in 1877 and 1888 caused the deaths of an estimated 9.5 million people.

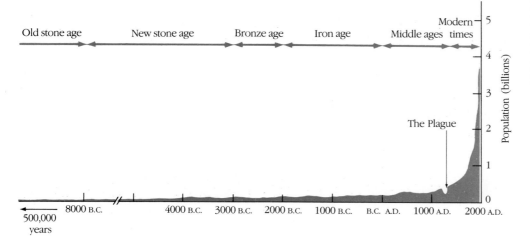

Figure 6-1
Exponential growth curve depicting world population. Note the rapid upturn in world population in the last 2000 years.

Wars have also kept populations in balance. Not only did soldiers and civilians die in battles, but wars also brought about famine and disease. Destruction of crops, for example, caused malnutrition, which made people more susceptible to disease.

Improving the Prospects for Survival

Wars, famine, and disease together kept world population small for many thousands of years. In the course of human history, though, several important changes have improved the prospect for human survival and reproduction and thus negated the population checks. These include the development of tools, the agricultural revolution, the Industrial Revolution, the opening of the New World for settlement, and the advent of modern medicine.

In Chapter 1 we saw how tools and agriculture enhanced human survival. It was not until the Industrial Revolution, however, that population began the rapid upward surge that we are still witnessing. Modern medicine and improvements in sanitation were two of the major advances of the Industrial Revolution. Better health care and sanitation both limited infectious diseases and increased the chances of survival. New drugs, such as penicillin, lowered the death rate throughout the world. The pesticide DDT was used in the tropics to combat malaria-carrying mosquitoes. As a result of these developments, death rates in many countries dropped precipitously (see the example of Ceylon in Figure 6-2). Life expectancy rose sharply, because more infants lived past the first year and because more adults survived previously fatal diseases. In 1841, for example, the life expectancy for males in England was about 40 years, but by 1971 it was 78 years. While life expectancy increased and death rates dropped, birth rates continued at high levels in many countries (Figure 6-2), fueling the rapid population growth that began in the 1800s.

Carrying Capacity

Each of the advances cited above—tools, agriculture, medicine, and technological developments—increased the earth's **carrying capacity**—the number of organisms (in this case, humans) the biosphere can support.

All ecosystems have a specific carrying capacity for each population. A hectare of grassland, for instance, may support two coyotes, ten deer, and hundreds of thousands of mice. Carrying capacity may fluctuate naturally from year to year, but most organisms do little to change it. Humans are an exception to that rule. Advances in toolmaking, agriculture, industry, and medicine all allow us to live beyond the limits set by nature.

This increase in the carrying capacity has been won

Figure 6-2
Birth rates (solid lines) and death rates (dashed lines) for two countries. In Ceylon, a continued high birth rate and a drastic drop in the death rate resulted in rapid population growth. In Sweden, the birth rate declined faster than the death rate, resulting in much slower population growth.

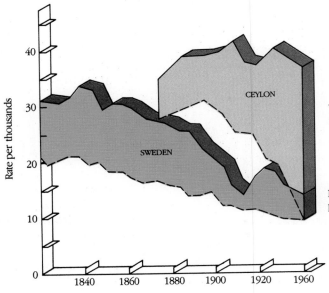

Wide difference results in rapid population growth

Birth rate and death rate nearly equal; population growth slow

partly at the expense of the rest of the biosphere and for the price of depleted resources, increased pollution, and the strains that accompany rapid growth.

To increase carrying capacity, we tend to maximize single variables such as energy, agricultural, or water production. As renowned environmentalist Garrett Hardin notes, "Maximizing one [variable] is almost sure to alter the balance in an unfavorable way." Natural systems are so complex that ecological backlash is almost certain.

Ultimately, population growth results from expanding our carrying capacity through maximization. The ecosystem effects of such actions are the subject of much of this book. In effect, removing population checks has made us a pioneer species in the world ecosystem. The growth in population of a pioneer species follows an exponential curve until it is stopped by environmental resistance.

Exponential Growth

Figure 6-1, which shows population growth over time, is an example of an **exponential, or J, curve**. **Exponential growth** takes place when something increases by a fixed percentage every year. For example, a savings account with 5.5% compounded interest grows exponentially.

The remarkable characteristic of exponential growth is that it begins slowly. Once it rounds the bend, however, it increases more and more rapidly. For example, suppose that your parents had opened a $1000 savings account in your name on the day you were born. This account earned 10% interest, and all the interest earned was applied to the balance. When you were 7, your account would have been worth $2000. By age 14, it would have increased to $4000. By age 42, you'd have $64,000 (Figure 6-3). If you left the money in a little longer, you'd find it growing faster and faster. At age 49, the account would be worth $128,000; at age 56, you'd have a quarter of a million dollars. Seven more years and you'd have a half a million dollars, but if you waited until you were 70, your account would be worth over $1 million. Looking back over your account records, you'd find that during the first 49 years, it grew from $1000 to $128,000, but during the last 21 years it increased by nearly $900,000. The rate of growth was constant over the entire period, and the account doubled every seven years, but it was not until it rounded the bend of the growth curve that things began to happen quickly.

Worldwide, the population is growing at a rate of 1.76% per year. This may seem slow, but at this rate world pop-

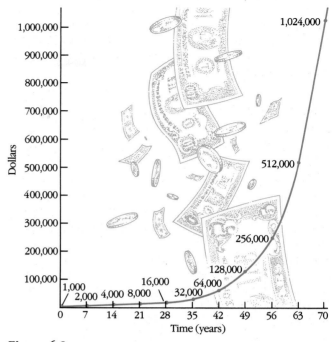

Figure 6-3
Exponential growth curve of a savings account with an initial deposit of $1000 that earns 10%.

ulation doubles every 42 years. Making our situation worse, we have already rounded the bend of the growth curve, so each doubling brings with it an extraordinarily large increase in the number of people.

As the Population, Resource, and Pollution model of Chapter 2 shows, populations acquire and use resources, thus creating pollution. Both resource demands and pollution grow exponentially along with population growth, putting a strain on ecosystems and important resources (Figure 6-4).

The environmental crisis is largely a result of our rounding the bend of the population curve, although many other factors come into play, as we saw in the Multiple Cause and Effect model. So fast has the population begun to double that civilization is hard pressed to keep up with it. As we will see in Part III of this book, the limits of many resources are in sight. As Part IV shows, the atmosphere and oceans and rivers cannot assimilate all the wastes we produce.

Too many people, rapid growth, high population density, and maldistribution of people are at the heart of the population dilemma.

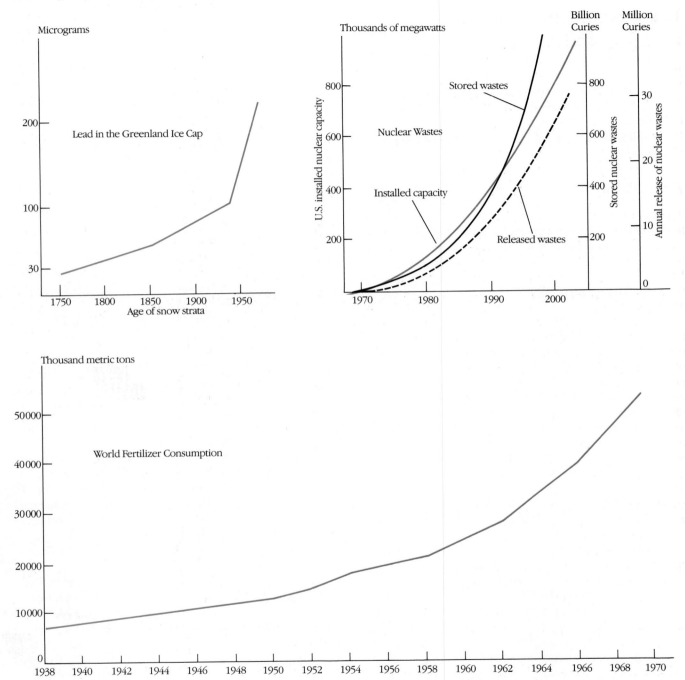

Figure 6-4
Exponential growth rate of population is mirrored by exponential growth curves for energy and other resources. Rapid growth in resource use brings about an exponential increase in pollution.

Understanding Populations and Population Growth

Before looking at the dimensions of the population problem, you should understand some terms and measurements used by *demographers,* the scientists who study population. These will help you analyze the dynamics of population growth and understand the factors affecting the future.

Population Histograms

A **population histogram**, shown in Figure 6-5, is a bar graph that displays the age and sex composition of a population. Each horizontal bar on the histogram represents the size of a certain age and sex group. For example, in Figure 6-5, the 20- to 24-year-olds represented about 10% of the total U.S. population in 1980. The number of males and females is approximately equal.

Population histograms tell us the history and a little bit about the future of populations. Let's look at some examples to see how. Figure 6-6 shows three general profiles of age–sex composition: expansive, constrictive, and stationary. Mexico, a country that is expanding, has a large number of young people. If these children produce more offspring than their parents did, the population will continue to expand at the base. If, on the other hand, family size decreases, the base of the histogram will begin to constrict. This is what has happened to the U.S. population (Figure 6-6). Sweden presents an entirely different picture. For many years adults have been having the same number of children as their parents; so its population is stationary.

Population histograms can change over time and, therefore, are not always reliable for making long-term predictions of future growth. Expansive populations can become constrictive, constrictive populations can become expansive, and so on. As shown in Figure 6-7, the U.S. population in 1910 was slightly expansive, but by 1940 women were having fewer children than their mothers did, and the population became constrictive. By 1960, though, the "baby boom" that followed World War II changed us back to an expansive population. In the 1970s, the number of offspring began to drop as a result of increased awareness of the population explosion, inflation, a larger percentage of women in the work force (they often put off having children), and delayed marriage. Thus, in 1980 the population profile was once again constrictive. Where it will go from there is hard to know. If we continue to have small families, population could stabilize, or become stationary.

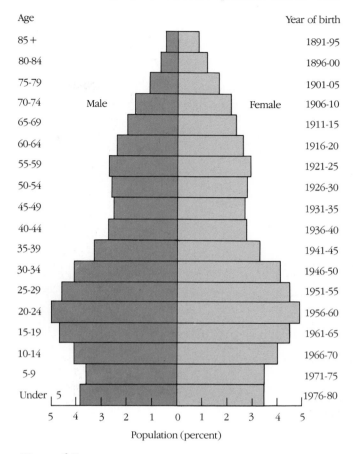

Figure 6-5
Population histogram of the United States in 1980, showing the percentage of males and females in various age groups.

Measuring Population Growth

One of the most important measurements used by demographers is the **population growth rate**. For world population, the growth rate is calculated by a simple formula:

$$\text{Growth rate (in percent)} = (\text{Crude birth rate} - \text{Crude death rate}) \times 100$$

Figure 6-6
Three general types of population histogram. Expansive populations have a large percentage of young people and are expanding at the base. Constrictive populations have a tapering base, resulting from lower total fertility. Stationary or near stationary populations show no expansion or constriction. This results from couples having only the number of children that will replace them.

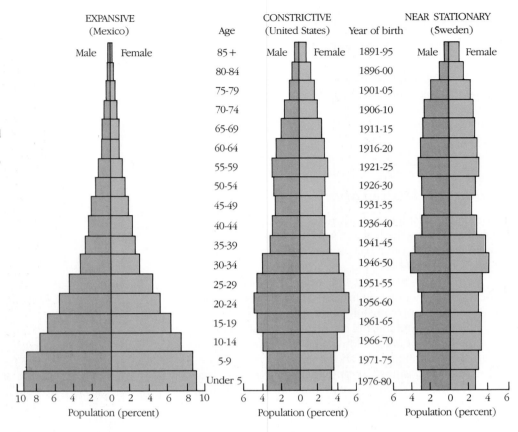

Crude birth rate is the number of births per 1000 people in a population. **Crude death rate** is the number of deaths per 1000 people in a population.

World Population Growth In mid-1984 the crude birth rate in the world was 28, and the crude death rate was 11. Thus, there were 17 new people added to the world for each 1000 people alive in 1984. In other words, world population was growing at a rate of 1.7% per year. Population growth rates, shown in Table 6-2, vary from region to region, with the less developed (developing) countries growing 3.5 times faster than more developed ones.

The **developed countries** are those that enjoy a high standard of living; their people are well fed and well educated (Table 6-3). The United States, Canada, Great Britain, and West Germany are examples. The **developing countries** are those whose standard of living and personal income are low, resulting in a population that is often

underfed and poorly educated, housed, and clothed. Ethiopia and Chad are examples. Three-quarters of the world's people (nearly 3.6 billion in 1984!) live in the developing countries. Only a quarter, or about 1.2 billion, live in the developed countries. Table 6.3 summarizes additional differences between these countries.

Table 6-2 also lists the **doubling times**—how long it would take various populations to double if crude birth and death rates continued unchanged. Slow-growing countries such as those of Europe will double in population in 175 years, whereas poor countries such as those of Africa and Asia, which are the least well-equipped to educate, feed, clothe, and shelter new people, are doubling every 24 to 37 years. Thus, by the time 1000 Europeans doubled their number, the same number of Africans would become a quarter of a million! Doubling time is calculated by dividing 70 by the growth rate. The world population doubling time is about 40 years.

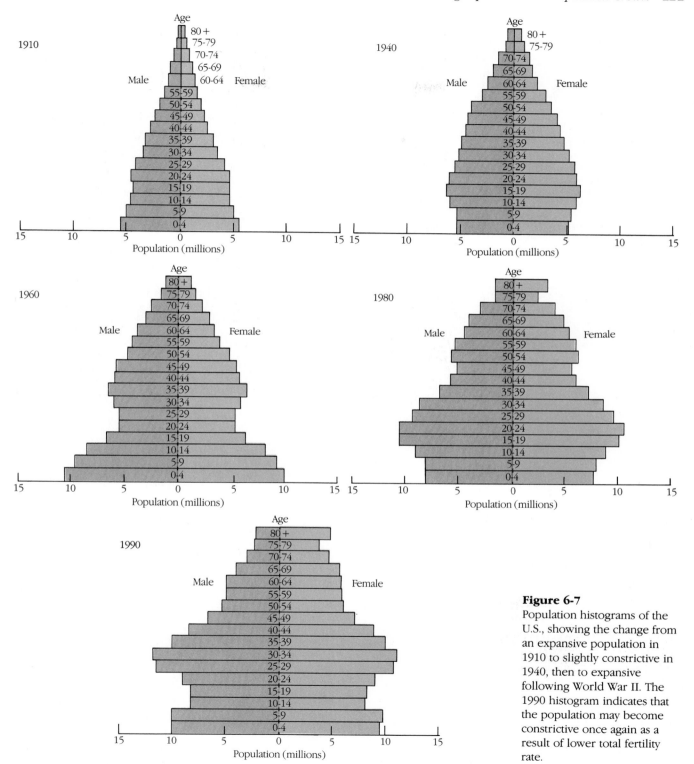

Figure 6-7
Population histograms of the U.S., showing the change from an expansive population in 1910 to slightly constrictive in 1940, then to expansive following World War II. The 1990 histogram indicates that the population may become constrictive once again as a result of lower total fertility rate.

Table 6-2 Growth Rate and Doubling Time in 1984

Region	Growth Rate (%)	Doubling Time (years)
World	1.7	40
Developed countries	0.6	112
Developing countries	2.1	33
Africa	2.9	24
Asia	1.9	38
North America	0.7	99
Latin America	2.3	30
Europe	0.4	208
U.S.S.R	1.0	68
Oceania	1.3	55

Source: Population Reference Bureau, *World Population Data Sheet, 1984.*

As discussed above, the growth rate of the developing countries far exceeds that of the much richer developed countries. Signs of a slowdown in growth in the developing countries have made many observers optimistic about their fate. Even though population growth has slightly decreased in recent years, however, the economic gap between the rich and poor nations is widening. In 1960 the gap in average per capita income between the developing and developed nations was $1240. In 1980 it had increased to $5700, and by 2000 it is projected to be nearly $8000. Many scientists believe that population control, discussed in the next chapter, is the only sure way of reversing this trend.

Table 6-3 Comparison of Developed and Developing Countries

Feature	Developed	Developing
Standard of living	High	Low
Per capita food intake	High (3100–3500 cal/day)	Low (1500–2700 cal/day)
Crude birth rate	Low (15/1000 population)	High (33/1000 population)
Crude death rate	Lower (10/1000 population)	Higher (12/1000 population
Growth rate	Low (0.6%)	High (2.1%)
Doubling time	High (116 years)	Low (33 years)
Infant mortality	Low (20/1000 births)	High (96/1000 births)
Total fertility rate	Replacement level (2.0)	High (4.6)
Life expectancy at birth	High (72 years)	Lower (57 years)
Urban population	High (69%)	Low (26%)
Wealth (per capita income) (U.S. dollars)	High ($8,130)	Low ($680)
Industrialization	High	Low
Energy use per capita	High	Low
Illiteracy rate	Low (1%–4%)	High (25%–75%)

Source: Population Reference Bureau.

Population Growth in Countries To calculate the growth of individual countries or regions, we must take into account migration, the movement of people in and out of countries. The population growth rate for a country is equal to the crude birth rate minus the crude death rate plus net migration. **Net migration** is the sum of the efflux (**emigration**) and the influx of people (**immigration**). Table 6-4, a summary of population growth statistics in the United States, shows the contribution from legal and illegal immigration. (Migration is discussed in greater detail later in this chapter.)

Fertility

One of the most common measures of population is **fertility**, or the reproductive performance of individuals in a population. We will consider three measures of fertility here.

The first measure is the **general fertility rate**, the number of babies born to 1000 women of reproductive age, 15–44. A better measure is the **age-specific fertility rate**. This is the number of live births per 1000 women of a specific age group. Figure 6-8 shows the age-specific fer-

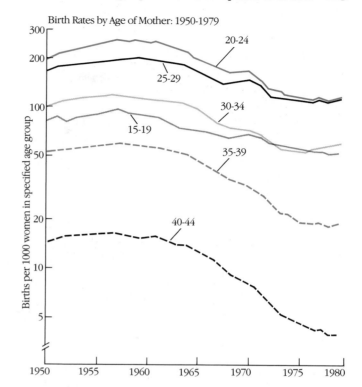

Figure 6-8
U.S. birth rate by age of mother, also known as the age-specific fertility rate.

tility rates of women in the United States from 1950 to 1979. From this graph we see that women age 20–29 produce the largest number of offspring and that women today are having fewer children than their mothers did in the 1950s and 1960s.

The most useful measure of fertility is the **total fertility rate** (TFR), the average number of children that would be born alive to a woman during her lifetime if she were to pass through all her childbearing years conforming to the age-specific fertility rates of a given year. In the United States the TFR has varied considerably over the past 100 years (Figure 6-9). After the end of World War II, for instance, the TFR exceeded 3.7. In 1972 the total fertility rate dipped below 2.1, which is **replacement-level fertility,** the number of children a couple must have to replace themselves. (The reason 2.1 children must be born to replace their parents is that not all children born will survive to reproductive age.)

Since 1972 the TFR of the United States has remained below replacement level, which is why our population

Table 6-4 Population Growth in the United States

1981 total births	3,646,000
1981 total deaths	1,987,000
1981 natural increase (approximate)	1,700,000
1981 immigrants (legal immigrants and refugees)	697,000
Emigrants	100,000
Net migration (approximate)	600,000
Total population growth	2,300,000
Population growth rate (natural increase and net migration)	1.0%
Illegal immigrants (estimated)	500,000
Total U.S. population growth (including illegal immigrants)	2,800,000
Population growth rate (including illegal immigrants)	1.2%

Source: United States Census Bureau.

Figure 6-9

Total fertility rate is a predictive measure, telling us the number of children women will have during their lifetime, based on the current age-specific fertility rates. The total fertility rate in the United States has fluctuated widely with economic conditions. In the decade of the Great Depression women had a low total fertility rate.

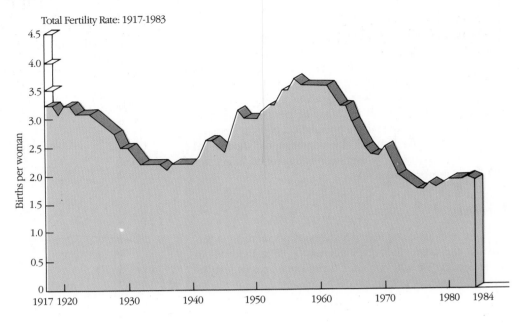

Total Fertility Rate: 1917-1983

histogram is constrictive (see Figure 6-7). This drop has also led many to believe that U.S. population growth is under control. But since the TFR can change, it is a useful predictive measure only if the age-specific fertility rates remain constant over a long period of time.

The TFR varies from continent to continent, as shown in Table 6-5. Those regions with the highest TFR are the developing countries of Africa, Asia, and Latin America. Low rates are found in developed countries. More than two dozen countries have reached replacement-level fertility, and ten more are approaching this level (Table 6-6). Just a decade ago only a handful of countries—East and West Germany, Luxembourg, and Austria—were at replacement level.

Overall, the outlook for population is still dark. The developed countries, with total fertility rates of 2.0, have only about 25% of the world's people, whereas the developing countries, with the remaining 75%, have an average total fertility rate of 4.4 and a doubling time of 33 years.

Many people equate replacement-level fertility with **zero population growth** (ZPG). ZPG occurs when the crude birth rate and crude death rate are equal and there is no net migration. The size of the population remains constant. Replacement-level fertility is one of the first steps toward zero population growth, but the two are not the same. A population can have a TFR of 2.1 but still be

growing. For example, even though the United States dropped below replacement-level fertility in 1972, the population will continue to grow for at least 50 years. Why? Because the number of women entering childbearing age is still rising (see Figure 6-7). For example, between 1975 and 1980 the number of women in the crucial age group 15–44 increased from 47 million to 51 million. Even if each of these women has 2.1 children, the population will still grow.

According to the U.S. Census Bureau in 1982, the natural increase in U.S. population will stop by the year 2035, when the birth rate and death rate are expected to be equal. Because of immigration, however, the population may continue to grow indefinitely.

Age at Marriage

One of the most telling statistics is the age of women being married, the **median age of first marriage** (MAFM). The median is a value in a set of values below and above which there is an equal number of values. For example, if the ages of women getting married for the first time in a small town are 17, 19, 21, 23, and 24, the median age is 21. Half the people getting married are older than 21, and half are younger. The median is more reliable than the average if a few extreme values would make the average

Table 6-5 Total Fertility Rate in 1984

Region		Total Fertility Rate	Population Size (Billions)
World		3.8	4.762
Developed countries		2.0	1.166
Developing countries		4.4	3.596
Africa		6.4	
Northern	5.9		
Western	6.8		
Eastern	6.6		
Middle	6.2		
Southern	5.2		
Asia		4.0	
Southwestern	5.5		
Mid-southern	5.3		
Southeastern	4.5		
Eastern (incl. China, Japan)	2.6		
North America		1.8	
U.S.	1.8		
Canada	1.8		
Latin America		4.2	
Middle	4.9		
Caribbean	3.4		
Tropical	4.3		
Temperate	2.7		
Europe		1.8	
Northern	1.8		
Western	1.6		
Eastern	2.1		
Southern	1.9		
U.S.S.R.		2.5	
Oceania		2.5	

Source: Population Reference Bureau.

Table 6-6 Countries at, Below, or Approaching Replacement-Level Fertility

Country	Total Fertility Rate
Iceland	2.5
Hong Kong	2.4
Cyprus	2.3
Poland	2.3
Romania	2.3
U.S.S.R.	2.3
Barbados	2.2
Bulgaria	2.2
Portugal	2.2
Spain	2.2
Czechoslovakia	2.1
New Zealand	2.1
France	2.0
Malta	2.0
Yugoslavia	2.0
Cuba	1.9
East Germany	1.9
Hungary	1.9
United Kingdom	1.9
United States	1.9
Canada	1.8
Japan	1.8
Singapore	1.8
Australia	1.7
Belgium	1.7
Italy	1.7
Norway	1.7
Sweden	1.7
Finland	1.6
Netherlands	1.6
Denmark	1.5
Luxembourg	1.5
Switzerland	1.5
West Germany	1.5

Source: Population Reference Bureau, *World Population Data Sheet, 1983.*

unrealistic—for example, if the town had a 70-year-old bride.

The United States and other developed countries have witnessed a small increase in the MAFM. In 1960 the MAFM was 20.3 years for females, but it had risen to 22.1 by 1980. The same pattern holds true for men: in 1960 the MAFM was 22.8, but by 1980 it was 24.6. The advancing MAFM results in a decrease in the length of time women can have children, causing a decrease in birth rate.

Death Rate

Death is measured in a variety of ways. **Crude death rate** (CDR), one of the most commonly used measures, is the number of deaths per 1000 total population. The CDR depends on a number of factors, including age, sex, race, occupation, social class, living standard, and health care. The age structure of a population is one of the leading determinants of the CDR.

The Population Debate

The Case for More People

Julian Simon

The author is a professor of economics and business administration at the University of Illinois at Champaign-Urbana. He has written several important books on population and economics, including The Economics of Population Growth *and* The Ultimate Resource.

Many technological advances come from people who are neither well educated nor well paid—the dispatcher who develops a slightly better way of deploying taxis in his ten-cab fleet, the shipper who discovers that garbage cans make excellent, cheap containers for many items, the retailer who discovers a faster way to stock merchandise, and so on. Even in science one need not be a genius to make a valuable contribution.

In the past century there have been more discoveries and a faster rate of growth of productivity than in previous centuries, when fewer people were alive. Whereas we develop new materials almost every day, it was centuries between the discovery and use of, say, copper and iron. If there had been a larger population, the pace of increase in technological practice might have been faster.

Classical economic theory has concluded that population growth must reduce the standard of living: the more people, the lower the per capita income, all else being equal. However, many statistical studies conclude that population growth does not have a negative effect on economic growth. The most plausible explanation is the positive effect additional people have on productivity by creating and applying new knowledge.

Because technological improvements come from people, it seems reasonable to assume that the amount of improvement depends in large measure on the number of people available. Data for developed countries show clearly that the bigger the population, the greater the number of scientists and the larger the amount of scientific knowledge produced.

There is other evidence of the relationship between population increase and long-term economic growth: an industry, or the economy of an entire country, can grow because population is growing, because per capita income is growing, or both. Some industries in some countries grow faster than the same industries in other countries or than other industries in the same country. Comparisons show that in the faster growing industries the rate of increase of technological practice is higher. This suggests that faster population growth, which causes faster growing industries, leads to faster growth of productivity.

The phenomenon economists call "economy of scale"—greater efficiency of larger-scale production where the market is larger—is inextricably intertwined with the creation of knowledge and technological change, along with the ability to use larger and more efficient machinery and greater division of labor. A large population implies a bigger market. A bigger market is likely to bring bigger manufacturing plants, which may be more efficient than smaller ones and may produce less expensive goods.

A bigger population also makes profitable many major social investments that would not otherwise be profitable—railroads, irrigation systems, and ports. For instance, if an Australian farmer were to clear a piece of land far from neighboring farms, he might have no way to ship his produce to market. He might also have trouble finding workers and supplies. When more farms are established nearby, however, roads will be built that link him with markets in which to buy and sell.

We often hear that if additional people have a positive effect on per capita income and output, it is offset by negative impacts such as pollution, resource shortages, and other problems. These trends are myths. The only meaningful measure of scarcity is the economic cost of goods. In almost every case the cost of natural resources has declined throughout human history relative to our income.

Conventional wisdom has it that resources are finite. But there is no support for this view. There is little doubt in my mind that we will continue to find new ore deposits, invent better production methods, and discover new substitutes, bounded only by our imagination and the exercise of educated skills. The only constraint upon our capacity to enjoy unlimited raw materials at acceptable prices is knowledge. People generate that knowledge. The more there are, the better off the world will be.

Is More Always Better?

Garrett Hardin

The author is a renowned environmentalist, writer, and lecturer. He has taught at several universities, and in 1980 he served as chairman of the board and chief executive officer of the Environmental Fund. He has written numerous books and articles on environmental ethics and is best known for his article "The Tragedy of the Commons."

To get at the heart of the "population problem," you should make careful measurements of the daily flow of water over Niagara Falls. You will discover that twice as much water flows over the falls during each daylight hour as during each nighttime hour. There in a nutshell you have the population problem.

Puzzled? You should be. The connection between Niagara Falls and population is not obvious. Before we can understand it we need to review a little biology.

For every nonhuman species there is an upper limit to the size of a population. Near the maximum, individuals are not so well off as they are at lower densities. Starvation appears. Crowded animals often fight among themselves and kill their offspring. Game managers and wildlife advocates agree that the maximum is not the optimum. If animals could talk, we suspect they would agree.

What about humans? Will we be happiest if our population is the absolute maximum the earth can support? Few people say so explicitly, but some argue that "more is better!"

Admittedly, we need quite a few people to maintain our complex civilization. A population the size of Monaco's, with about 25,000 people, could never have enough workers for an automobile assembly line. But Sweden, with some 8 million people, turns out two excellent automobiles. Eight million is a long way from nearly 5 billion, the approximate population of the world today.

Some say, "More people—more geniuses." But is the number of practicing geniuses directly proportional to population size? England today is 11 times as populous as it was in Shakespeare's day, but does it now boast 11 Shakespeares? For that matter does it have even one?

Consider Athens in classical times. A city of only 40,000 free inhabitants produced what many regard as the most brilliant roster of intellectuals ever: Solon, Socrates, Plato, Aristotle, Euripides, Sophocles—the list goes on and on. What city of 40,000 in our time produces even a tenth as much brilliance?

Of course, the free populace of Athens was served by ten times as many slaves and other nonfree classes. Forty thousand people free to apply themselves to intellectual and artistic matters is evidently quite enough to produce a first-rate civilization. Slaves gave 40,000 Athenians freedom to create. We are given creative freedom by labor-saving machines, certainly a more desirable form of slavery. But where are our geniuses?

Business economists are keenly aware of "economies of scale," which reduce costs as the number of units manufactured goes up. Communication and transportation, however, suffer from diseconomies of scale. The larger the city, the higher the monthly phone bill. More automobiles mean more signal lights per auto. More researchers mean more time spent in the library finding out what other investigators have done. Crimes per capita increase with city size. So do the costs of crime control. All these suggest that more may not be better.

Democracy requires effective communication between citizens and legislators. In 1790 each U.S. senator represented 120,000 people; in 1980 the figure was 2.3 million. At which time was representation closer to the ideal of democracy? To communicate with his or her constituents each senator now has an average of 60 paid assistants (versus zero in 1790). As for the president, Franklin D. Roosevelt had a staff of 37 in 1933, when the population was 125 million, whereas Ronald Reagan had a staff of 1700 in 1981, when the population was 230 million. We have to ask whether democracy can survive infinite population growth.

Let's look at another aspect of the more-is-better argument. An animal population is limited by the resources available to it. With humans, a complication arises. Though the quantities of minerals on earth are fixed, improved technology periodically increases the quantity of resources available to us. In the beginning we had to have copper ores that tested out at 20%; now we are using ores with less than 1%. Available copper has increased, but not the total amount of copper on earth.

Yet it is a mistake to speak of "running out" of mineral resources. When we use copper, we don't "use it up." Abrasion of our copper artifacts ultimately disperses the metal in tiny fragments over the face of the earth, but none of the copper is destroyed. It can all be gathered together again, *but* reconcentrating it uses energy. All resource scarcity finally translates into a problem of energy. Is energy limited?

This is not an easy question to answer. The rate of energy input from the sun is strictly limited, but atomic energy is something else. In principle, atomic energy seems almost unlimited. The key question is this: can we get this energy at an acceptable environmental cost? Can we dispose of the lethal waste products safely? Can we prevent nuclear sabotage and blackmail? These questions are less scientific than trans-scientific—beyond science.

Let's return to Niagara Falls. Less water flows over the falls at night because more water is diverted to generate electricity when people aren't looking at the falls. It would be possible to use all the water to generate electricity, but then there would be no falls for us to look at. As a compromise, the volume of water "wasted" falling over the falls is reduced only at night. Therefore, the turbines and generators are not fully used 24 hours of the day, which means that local electricity costs are just a bit higher.

If the population continues to grow, the day may come when electricity is so scarce and expensive that the public will demand that Niagara Falls be shut down so that all the water can be used to generate electricity. Similar dangers face every aesthetic resource. Wild rivers can be dammed to produce more electricity, and estuaries can be filled in to make more building sites for homes and factories.

The maximum is never the optimum. With human populations, *quantity* (of people) and *quality* (of life) are tradeoffs. Which should we choose—the maximum or the optimum? This is a trans-scientific question.

Is our population now below or above the optimum? In trying to answer this I suggest that you make two lists. On one list write down all the things that you would expect to be *better* if the population doubled; on the other, all the things that would be *worse*. On which list would you put the availability of wilderness? Of theatres and museums? What about the noise level? Amount of democracy? Amount of pollution? Per capita cost of pollution control? Availability of parking spaces? Personal freedom?

When you are through, compare your list with your friends'. What value judgments account for the differences? Can these differences be reconciled? How?

In general, older populations have a higher crude death rate than younger populations. For example, in 1982, Sweden, where 16 of every 100 people are over 65, had a CDR of 11 per 1000. Mexico, where only 3 persons in 100 are over 65, had a CDR of 6.

The **age-specific death rate** is a better measure of the death rate by age. It permits a better comparison of the health and economic status of countries than the crude death rate. As shown in Figure 6-10, the death rate in the United States varies considerably, being highest at ages 1–4 and above 45. This graph also shows that death rate varies by sex and race: Women, in general, have a lower death rate than males. Whites generally have a lower death rate than nonwhites.

Life Expectancy and Infant Mortality

One of the best measures of the health of a nation is the average life expectancy of its people. Life expectancy is the number of years an average individual should live having reached a certain age. **Life expectancy at birth** is one of the most commonly used measures (Figure 6-11). The average American white female born in 1900 had a life expectancy of 50 years; by 1980, however, her average life expectancy at birth had increased to 78.1. Life expectancy in males born in 1900 was about 47 years, but by 1980 it had increased to 70.5.

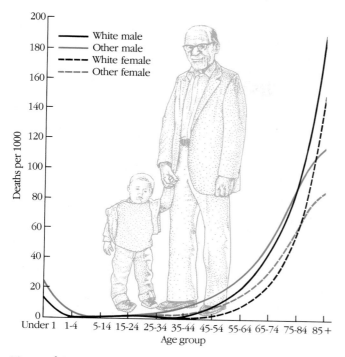

Figure 6-10
Age-specific death rates in the U.S. for 1976.

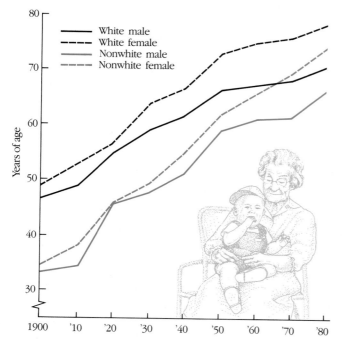

Figure 6-11
Life expectancy at birth in the U.S. from 1900 to 1980.

Table 6-7 Life Expectancy at Birth

Region	Years
World	60
Developed countries	72
Developing countries	53
Africa	49
Asia	58
North America	74
Latin America	63
Europe	72
U.S.S.R.	69
Oceania	69

Source: Population Reference Bureau, *Population Data Sheet.*

Increased life expectancy is a result of better health care, sanitation, and living conditions; thus, people in developed nations have a higher life expectancy than those in the developing nations (Table 6-7).

The reasons males have a shorter average life expectancy than females in the United States are believed to be higher stress, pollutants associated with their occupations, and smoking. With the current increases in the number of women working and smoking, the gap between male and female life expectancy is narrowing.

The **infant mortality rate** is a major determinant of life expectancy. For example, in Egypt the average life expectancy at birth is 53 years, but infants who survive their first year can expect to live to age 58. This situation also exists in other countries. Americans live longer on average than their ancestors mostly because more of them survive past the first year of life. Between 1900 and 1978 the life expectancy for an infant increased 26 years, whereas the life expectancy of a 60-year-old increased 5.2 years.

Infant mortality in the United States has dropped because of better health care and control over infectious diseases (Figure 6-12). In 1900 approximately 100 babies died in their first year for every 1000 live births. By 1984 infant mortality had fallen to 10.9 per 1000 live births.

Migration

Migration is the movement of people across boundaries to set up a new residence. Along with fertility and mortality, migration is a key component of population growth in countries.

Figure 6-12

U.S. infant mortality rate, 1915–1981.

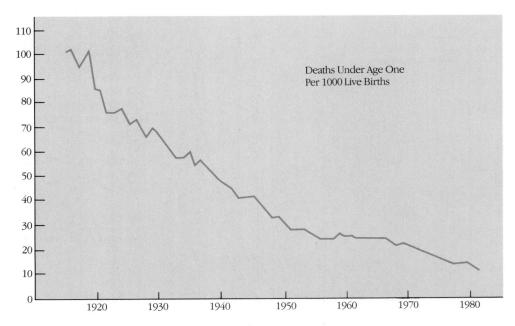

Deaths Under Age One Per 1000 Live Births

The terms *immigration* and *emigration* refer to movements into and out of countries, or international migration. *In-migration* and *out-migration* refer to movement within a country, or internal migration.

International Migration The immigration rate, the number of people entering a country per 1000 people in the population, usually takes into account only the legal immigrants, because of the difficulty in counting illegal entries. Figure 6-13 illustrates how immigration has varied in the United States. The top panel shows the number of legal immigrants in ten-year periods starting in 1880. The bottom panel shows what part immigration has played in total population growth. As shown, immigration was high in the period between 1880 and 1929 but dropped off in the 1930s during the Great Depression.

The emigration rate is the rate of outflow per 1000 people. Although no hard data are available, the U.S. emigration rate is believed to be about 1 person per 5000.

As we learned earlier, the net migration rate partly determines whether a country's population grows or shrinks. This rate rarely includes illegal immigration. In the United States illegal immigrants enter at a rate of about 500,000 to 1.5 million a year, although this flow is partly offset by return migration, which may be substantial. Added to the 700,000 legal immigrants (including legal refu-

gees), the illegal immigrants push the United States' net migration to more than a million people per year. Inasmuch as the natural increase in population is only about 1.7 million per year, nearly two-fifths of the population growth results from immigration. For a debate on immigration see Point/Counterpoint "Illegal Aliens and Population Growth" in Chapter 7.

Internal Migration People also move within the boundaries of a country, often in large numbers. Such migrations can dramatically alter local economies. Figure 6-14 shows the net migration flow in the United States. The primary flow is from the northeastern and north-central regions to the South (mostly Florida) and West (Arizona, Wyoming, Utah, Idaho, Colorado, New Mexico, Texas, and Alaska). The migration has been so dramatic in recent years that for the first time in U.S. history more than half the population lives in the West and South. This movement, called the "sunning of America," is caused by (1) expanding (sunrise) industries in the West and Southwest, especially in the fields of electronics and energy production; (2) declining (sunset) industries of the northeastern and north-central states, especially automobile and steel manufacturing; (3) a desire for a warmer climate; (4) a desire for a lower cost of living; (5) a preference for abundant recreation; (6) an aspiration for a less hectic,

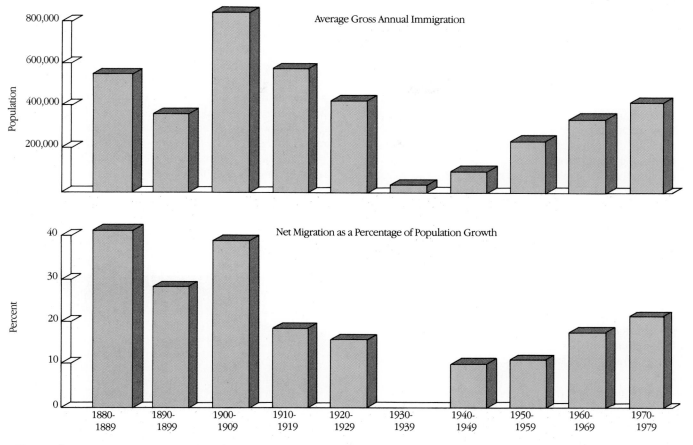

Average Gross Annual Immigration

Net Migration as a Percentage of Population Growth

Figure 6-13
Legal immigration in the U.S., 1880–1979.

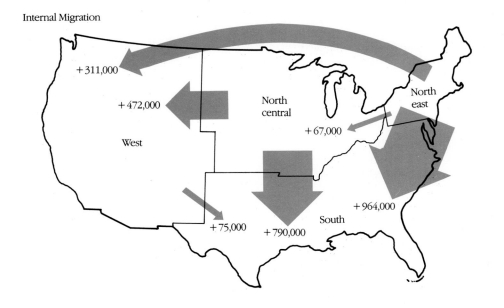

Internal Migration

Figure 6-14
Internal migration in the U.S., 1970–1975.

+311,000

+472,000

North central

North east

+67,000

West

+75,000

+790,000

South

+964,000

less crowded life-style; and (7) the growth of retirement communities.

The heavy migration to the South and West has, paradoxically, helped destroy many of the values the migrants were seeking. With growth rates in the range of 3% to 5% a year, many western cities and states have been swamped. Many national parks, such as Yosemite, require reservations for campsites. Air pollution has worsened with the increasing population; the clean air that many came for has disappeared. Traffic has become unbearable. In Houston about 2000 cars were added each week between 1975 and 1978. The 90-minute "rush hour" became a 2½-hour bumper-to-bumper nightmare. The rapid rise in demand for housing has sent the price of homes skyward, making the cost of living inordinately high.

Political changes have also occurred. For the first time in our history, the southern and western states collectively hold half the seats in the House of Representatives. The breakneck speed of growth has made it difficult for local governments to provide water, schools, sewage treatment facilities, and the like. Spreading cities engulf smaller outlying communities and change the tempo and quality of life.

Internal migrants affect the places they come from, as well. Since many of the out-migrants are young, educated, and skilled workers, they have created a significant drain on human resources in the northeastern and north-central United States.

The influx of people into the Sun Belt has had important economic impacts, too. For example, in the South the per capita income rose from 79% of the national average in 1960 to 86% by 1976. The growing prosperity of the Sun Belt has also laid the foundation for expansion in the industrial sector. The rapid growth means economic opportunity for builders and the service sector of the economy.

Demographic Transition

The population problem underlies many of today's economic, social, political, and environmental problems; but a number of countries are gaining control over their population growth. These are generally developed countries. Reduced population growth, however, is only a recent phenomenon. For many countries it has taken years to achieve.

The change from fast growth to zero growth is called a **demographic transition**. The most widely accepted

explanation of the movement toward the equalization of birth and death rates is that a population's crude birth and death rates decline when economic conditions improve as a result of industrialization.

The decline in the death rate occurs first as a result of improvements in medicine and sanitation. This decline is then followed by a more gradual decrease in the birth rate (Table 6-8). During this period of rapidly falling death rate and slowly falling birth rate, population growth is high. In time, though, the two become more or less equal.

The demographic transition consists of four recognizable stages. These are shown in Table 6-8, along with data from Finland, where the stages are well documented.

Table 6-8 The Stages of the Demographic Transition

Stage 1—	Preindustrial
	High birth rate and high death rate
	Little or no increase in population
	Example: Finland 1785–1790
	Crude birth rate = 38/1000
	Crude death rate = 32/1000
	Natural increase = 0.6%
Stage 2—	Transitional
	High birth rate and falling death rate
	High population growth rate
	Example: Finland 1825–1830
	Crude birth rate = 38/1000
	Crude death rate = 24/1000
	Natural increase = 1.4%
Stage 3—	Industrial
	Falling birth rate and low death rate
	Slower growth
	Example: Finland 1910–1915
	Crude birth rate = 29/1000
	Crude death rate = 17/1000
	Natural increase = 1.2%
Stage 4—	Postindustrial
	Low birth rate and low death rate
	Slow population growth
	Example: Finland 1970–1976
	Crude birth rate = 13/1000
	Crude death rate = 10/1000
	Natural increase = 0.3%

Source: Haupt, A., and Kane, T. (1978). *Population Handbook*. Population Reference Bureau.

Some Demographic Surprises of the Seventies

The demand for projections is insatiable. What will the population of the world be in 1990? How many children will be born? What percentage of the population will be over 65? Will the U.S. population stabilize? When? The list goes on, and for good reason: we need to project to help make the transition into the future smoothly and efficiently.

But if we look at the forecasts of the U.S. Census Bureau, whose experts spend their days studying the present and predicting the future of our population, we may be surprised to find that the experts are often quite wrong. For example, the Bureau once projected that during the 1970s, 40 million to 49.3 million children would be born in the U.S. The actual number of births was far below this—33.3 million, a sign that U.S. population growth is slowing.

The second missed guess had to do with deaths and life expectancy. The Census Bureau projected that 21 million people would die in the 1970s, but the number dying was a little lower than expected—19.3 million. The average life expectancy at birth was expected to increase in the 1970s, but only by about a half a year. Instead, it rose 3.4 years, because of success in reducing deaths from heart disease and stroke.

The Census Bureau also projected a slight decrease in the number of people per household. Its estimates showed that by 1980 the average household would contain 3.08 to 3.19 people. The actual value, however, was 2.76, considerably lower than estimated.

A fourth area of speculation was that of internal migration in the United States. The U.S. Bureau of Economic Analysis made projections for regional growth in a seven-volume report. It projected that the Northeast would grow by 7.6 million between 1970 and 1980; in fact, it grew by only 1.1 million because of a much larger than expected out-migration. The West, on the other hand, was expected to grow by 4 million during the decade of the 70s. It grew by 8.3 million. The South also fooled the "experts"—growing by 12.5 million instead of a projected 7.8 million.

Our need for projections is enormous, and it always will be. City planners want to know how big their population will be and the size of different age groups. Businesses are interested in future market size. Schools and colleges want to know the projected demand and supply of teachers. But from the examples cited above, healthy skepticism seems advisable. Perhaps Victor Hugo had the population experts in mind when he noted, "Caution is the eldest child of wisdom."

The decrease in death rate during the demographic transition is the result of better health care and sanitation, and the drop in birth rate is attributed to a shift in attitudes toward children. Preindustrial farmers view children as assets because they help with farm work and can support their parents in their old age. With industrialization and the movement of families to the city, children become an economic liability. With competition for living space, each additional child means that more money has to be devoted to family housing, and if the children do not work, they create a financial drain. As a result, smaller families become the rule.

The idea that economic development leads to zero population growth has been a controversial topic in discussions on population control in developing countries. If factories are built and jobs are created in the cities, some argue, economic development and new-found wealth will reduce population growth. They point to the United States, Finland, Denmark, and dozens of other countries that have experienced demographic transitions as a result of industrial development. If it worked for Finland, why won't it work for Ghana, China, India, or Chad?

There are four reasons why not. First, the economic resources of many of these coutries are too small to build the type of industry that ushered developed countries through their demographic transition. Second, the classic transition did not take place overnight: it took Finland more than 200 years to approach a balance between birth rate and death rate. The developing countries, doubling on the average every 33 years, haven't got that much time. Third, the rapid growth of population in these countries far exceeds their ability to raise the standard of living; just trying to keep up with the inadequate standard of living has proved a major challenge. The fourth reason is that the fossil fuel energy that was essential to the demographic transition is diminishing and is becoming ever more costly. Without the rich mines of England or the great oil deposits of Arabia and America, these people will probably never witness industrial revolutions like those of the Western world.

For these and other reasons, industrialization and improving economic wealth are unlikely. Demographic transition must come about in other ways, especially through population control, as discussed in the next chapter.

Young and Old Populations

As governing bodies plan for the needs of future generations, they must forecast the need for schools, hospitals, and Social Security benefits for the "dependent" generations—the young and the old. To aid in such planning, demographers determine the **age-dependency ratio,** the ratio of those in the dependent ages (under 15 and over 65) to those between 15 and 65, who are considered economically productive. This measurement is an indicator of the economic burden that children and older, non-working adults put on the productive population.

Shifts in the age-dependency ratio have important repercussions. In the United States, for example, the post-war baby boom dramatically increased the number of school-age children in the 1950s and 1960s, causing a rising demand for new schools and teachers. Housing later became a serious problem as members of this age group married and searched for homes. Still larger problems loom ahead in the early 21st century when those people reach retirement age. By 2030 people 65 and older will make up about 20% of the U.S. population, compared with 11% today. Health costs are almost certain to rise, because people over 65 today account for nearly one-third of the nation's health bill. Gerontologists, new hospital facilities for the aged, retirement homes, and other facilities will be needed to accommodate the elderly. Making matters worse, a smaller proportion of the population—including those in college today—will be supporting this large elderly group.

The aging of the population also means an aging of the work force, a development that has positive aspects. It means that competition for entry-level positions will lessen, and that the labor force will, on the whole, be more experienced and will require less training. This could increase overall labor productivity—the amount of output per unit of labor.

Good or bad, the effects of shifts in the age-dependency ratio are crucial in the understanding of a population. They affect a society in many fundamental and far-reaching ways.

Dimensions of the Population Crisis

The dimensions of the population crisis are shown in Figure 6-15. The problems include pollution and resource depletion as well as housing shortages, malnutrition, inadequate health care, and many others, which we will study throughout this book.

Meeting the Needs of Growing Populations

One of the most perplexing problems facing the world is meeting the needs of the new people who are added every day. In Africa, for instance, the population is growing at about 2.9% per year and doubling every 24 years. As the ecologist Paul Ehrlich points out in his book *The Population Bomb,* the standard of living in such regions is already inadequate. "In order to just keep the standard of living at the present inadequate level, the food available for the people must be doubled every 24 years. Every structure and road must be duplicated. The amount of power must be doubled. The capacity of the transport system must be doubled. The number of trained doctors, nurses, teachers, and administrators must be doubled." All of this would be necessary just to maintain what is clearly inadequate. Ehrlich continues: "This would be a fantastically difficult job in the United States—a rich country with a fine agricultural system, immense industries, and access to abundant resources. Think of what it means to a country with none of these."

Many ecologists agree that when we consider the global picture, it is clear that we cannot provide a quality life or maintain a quality environment for the majority of the world's people, let alone provide for the 1.6 million people added each week. This bind of increasing numbers and diminishing quality of life has several basic solutions. We can increase supplies to meet need, substantially reduce population growth, or do a combination of the two. To achieve a sustainable future, some observers argue, reducing population growth is a necessity.

(a)

(b)

(c)

Figure 6-15
Dimensions of the population
crisis. *(a)* Urban litter at a rural
lakeside dump. *(b)*
Overcrowding in cities; shown
here in Jakarta, Indonesia. *(c)*
Resource depletion at Mono
Lake. Note mud and toxic
alkali ring caused by diverting
water to Los Angeles for
domestic use.

Crowding

As populations grow, the concentration of the people in urban centers creates special problems such as resource depletion, social problems, and pollution.

In Mexico City, the largest city in Latin America, there are over 17 million people. Growing at a rate of 8% per year, the population will double in approximately nine years, reaching 28 million by the year 2000. Water will have to be pumped from rivers more than 350 kilometers (220 miles) away; this will consume about 20% of the country's electrical power.

Crowding has been implicated in a variety of social, mental, and physical diseases. But crowding is subjective, as Simeon Strunsky noted when he wrote, "The thing which in the subway is called congestion is highly esteemed in the night spots as intimacy." As difficult as it is to define "crowding," however, it is even more difficult to define its effects with great certainty.

Many social psychologists note that crowded inner cities are characterized by social instability, high divorce rates, mental illness, drug and alcohol abuse, prenatal death, and high crime rates. These symptoms of "inner city syndrome" may be due to stress from overcrowding, a conclusion supported by studies of human and animal populations. The most notable study was performed by the psychologist John Calhoun. In his research rats were confined to a specially built room and allowed to breed freely. As population skyrocketed, he witnessed increased violence and aggression, abnormal sexual behavior, cannibalism of young, and disruption of normal nesting and maternal behavior. The physiologist Hans Selye performed similar animal experiments, in which he noted hormonal imbalances brought about by stress. These imbalances can create ulcers, hypertension, kidney disease, hardening of the arteries, and increased susceptibility to disease.

Some studies of human populations have supported the animal studies, indicating that stress from crowding upsets the social structure and mental balance of a city's inhabitants. However, it is difficult to sort out the many factors in the equation such as education, socioeconomic level, nutrition, and housing, all of which may contribute to stress and stress-related maladies.

Although it is still unclear whether crowding in cities affects human populations, it is certain that high-density living threatens the environment. As we will see in later chapters, large population centers tend to be major polluters of the air and water. High-density populations exceed the capacity of the environment to assimilate wastes. In 1977, 39% of the world's people lived in cities; by 2000,

Figure 6-16
This street scene represents a small part of America's worst urban disaster area, the South Bronx in New York City.

it is estimated, this figure will jump to 50%. Crowding and the problems it creates will probably rise unless adequate steps are taken now to prevent them (Figure 6-16).

In sum, population-related problems vary from one country to the next. As resource needs are much greater in developed countries, so are environmental problems such as pollution, a generalization supported by the fact that 97% of all sulfur dioxide pollution in the world is located in the Northern Hemisphere, where the most developed countries are located. In the richer countries economic instability, diminishing resource supplies, and pollution seem to be the most pressing population-related issues. In the poorer countries food, water, shelter, health care, and education are the major concerns of the people and their governments.

Overpopulation and the Future of World Population

Perhaps the questions most often asked of demographers are, "What is the future of the world's population? How big will it get? Will it really double in the next 42 years?"

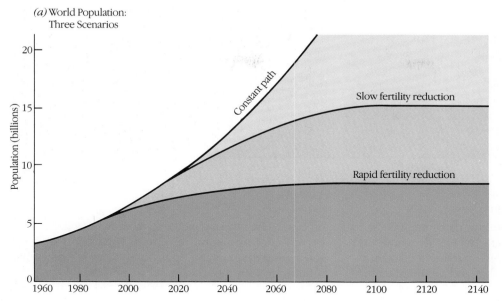

(a) World Population: Three Scenarios

Constant path

Slow fertility reduction

Rapid fertility reduction

Figure 6-17
(*a*) Future of world population. Constant path indicates population growth continuing at the current rate. The middle line indicates the future of world population if fertility drops off at a slow rate, the bottom line shows what might happen with a rapid decrease in fertility. As discussed in the text, the future may lie somewhere between the lower two lines. (*b*) The future of U.S. population depends on future total fertility rate and annual net migration.

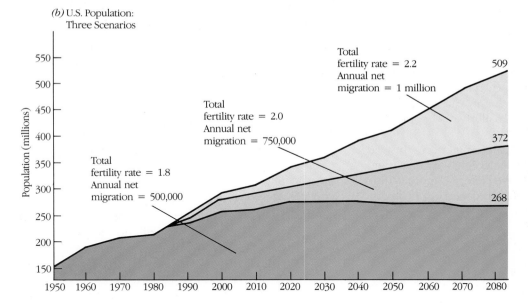

(b) U.S. Population: Three Scenarios

Total fertility rate = 2.2
Annual net migration = 1 million   509

Total fertility rate = 2.0
Annual net migration = 750,000

372

Total fertility rate = 1.8
Annual net migration = 500,000

268

The answer is that we don't and can't know, for it is impossible to predict the future. The factors that affect future population growth such as birth rates, fertility, and death rates can change dramatically and remain volatile indefinitely.

Regardless of the uncertainties involved in making estimates of future growth, many scientists have forecast future growth. (See Essay 6-1 for a look at missed guesses.) The world population growth rate, as we have seen, is now 1.76%. If this rate continues, the world's population will reach 1 trillion (1,000,000,000,000) around the year 2300.

Long before then, many demographers believe, the population growth curve will level off as a result of birth rates dropping, death rates rising, or a combination. Figure 6-17 plots this and several other possibilities for the world and the United States. A slow reduction in fertility would result in a gradual decrease in population growth and a stable population by the year 2100. The population size would be about 15 billion, more than three times what it is today. Still another projection, based on a rapid

Figure 6-18
Patterns of population growth.
(*a*) Stabilization of population
growth with a smooth
transition to a stable
population size. (*b*) Gradual
dropoff caused by population
exceeding the carrying
capacity. (*c*) Population crash
caused by irreparable damage
to the ecosystem. No doubt all
three patterns will be seen in
individual countries.

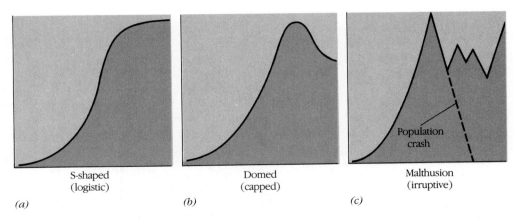

S-shaped
(logistic)

(a)

Domed
(capped)

(b)

Malthusion
(irruptive)

Population
crash

(c)

decline in fertility, shows stabilization around 2060 at 8 billion, almost twice as large as today. Exactly where the curve levels off will depend on the persistence and success of efforts toward development and family planning in the developing world, discussed in the next chapter.

Some demographers predict that the demands of the population and the accompanying pollution will eventually create so much damage that the human population begins to decrease in size, producing a **dome-shaped population graph** instead of the **sigmoidal (S-shaped) curve** shown in Figure 6-18a. The decrease in population size results from our exceeding the carrying capacity of the environment. Reduced carrying capacity caused by human intervention would result in a smaller world population (Figure 6-18b).

Still another, more ominous pattern may occur. Instead of leveling off smoothly, population may increase and decrease over time in an **irruptive** pattern (Figure 6-18c). Finally, population may be sharply reduced in a huge die-off caused by severe damage to the environment and the depletion of its natural resources. The crash may be so severe that the human population becomes extinct or is reduced to only a fraction of its present size.

No one knows what will happen to world population. The only opinion on which there is anything approaching unanimous agreement is that world population cannot grow indefinitely. Some countries will inevitably make a smooth transition to a stable state; others may experience periodic crashes (irruptive population) due to epidemics in crowded urban populations; others may die back to low population levels because of continued starvation and disease.

H. G. Wells once wrote that "human history becomes more and more a race between education and catastrophe." The population–resource–pollution bind we're in clearly illustrates this fact. What we decide today will have far-reaching effects that determine the kind of life our children and theirs will have.

*The doors we open and close each day decide the lives
we live.*

Flora Whittemore

Summary

The rapid growth of world population is a recent phenomenon. Throughout most of human history our population was small, controlled by war, disease, and famine. But advances in agriculture and industry allowed us to expand the *carrying capacity*, the number of people the earth could support.

Exponential growth, or fixed-percentage growth, follows a *J curve*. Initially, growth is slow, but once the bend of the curve is rounded, the item measured increases at a remarkable rate. The environmental crisis is largely the result of our rounding the bend of the population curve, although many other factors come into play.

Population histograms are an important tool for studying populations because they show the proportion of males and females in a population in various age groups. The shape of the histogram suggests whether populations will grow, shrink, or remain stable.

World population growth is determined by subtracting the *crude death rate* from the *crude birth rate*. These are the number of deaths and births per 1000 people, respectively. *Doubling time*, the time it takes a population to double in size, is also used to indicate population growth. The *developing countries*, those countries with low per capita income, inadequate education, and poor nutrition, contain three-fourths of the world's population and double about every 33 years. *Developed countries*, the rich, well-fed, and well-educated nations, double on the average every 116 years. Population growth in individual countries is determined by figuring in births, deaths, and the *net migration*—the sum of *emigration* and *immigration*.

The most important measure of reproductive performance, or *fertility*, is the *total fertility rate* (TFR), the number of children a woman will have during her lifetime. When TFR is equal to 2.1, or *replacement-level fertility*, a couple produces enough offspring to replace themselves when they die. Replacement-level fertility is one of the first steps toward achieving *zero population growth*.

Life expectancy at birth is the average number of years a newborn can be expected to live. Increased life expectancy is largely the result of decreased *infant mortality*.

As a nation develops wealth through industrialization, its population undergoes a *demographic transition* characterized by a rapidly falling death rate and more gradually declining birth rate until the two rates are equal. The idea that industrialization and resultant economic growth will lead to zero population growth in developing nations has been popular, although there are many reasons why this may not happen. Most important, many developing nations simply do not have the economic or resource base required for industrialization.

Population growth is at the root of virtually all environmental problems, including pollution, resource depletion, housing shortages, malnutrition, and inadequate health care. Rapid growth in population creates difficulties in meeting the basic needs of people. Crowding may lead to mental illness, drug abuse, and various forms of antisocial behavior.

The future of world population is difficult to determine, because many factors such as total fertility rate can change. Many demographers believe that world population will stabilize somewhere between 8 billion and 15 billion and that the exponential growth curve will be converted into a *sigmoidal curve*. However, other possibilities are also likely. The exponential growth curve may be transformed into a *dome-shaped curve* as population levels fall due to overextension of the carrying capacity. Or the pattern may become *irruptive*, with a series of peaks and crashes. Finally, severe damage to the carrying capacity could result in a massive crash, virtually eliminating humans from the face of the earth. The pattern growth takes is largely dependent on our efforts to control population, especially in the developing nations.

Discussion Questions

1. What is the population of the world? the United States?

2. Is the rapid growth in world population of concern to you? Why or why not? In particular, how does it affect your life?

3. How many years did it take the world to reach a population of 1 billion people? How quickly did we reach the second, third, and fourth billion?

4. What factors kept world population in check for so many years? Give some specific examples. What factors have caused the world population growth rate to increase so quickly in the past two centuries?

5. Define the term *exponential growth*.

6. What is a population histogram? Describe the three general profiles. What information do population histograms give us?

7. How is the world population growth rate calculated?

8. Define the following terms: *crude birth rate*, *crude death rate*, *net migration*, *immigration*, *emigration*, *in-migration* and *out-migration*.

9. Define *replacement-level fertility* and *zero population growth*.

10. Discuss the statement: "Our life expectancy has increased primarily because of medical advances that have decreased infant mortality."

11. Describe trends in infant mortality in the United States. How do infant mortality rates in the developing countries compare with the rates in developed countries?

12. Describe internal migration patterns in the United States. What factors account for these movements? What are the impacts of massive internal movements of this nature?

13. Define the term *demographic transition*. Why do death rates generally fall faster than birth rates?

14. You are appointed special envoy to India. Your task is to help the country reduce population growth. Your boss suggests that all India needs to do is to develop a modern industrial base, and a decline in population growth will result. How would you respond to this suggestion?

15. Debate the statement, "Population is the cause of all the world's problems."

16. Compare and contrast developed and developing countries in terms of wealth, population growth rate, literacy, and infant mortality.

17. Draw various graphs for projected world population, and describe each one.

Suggested Readings

Bouvier, L. F. (1984). Planet Earth 1984-2034: A Demographic Vision. *Population Bulletin* 39(1). Washington, D.C.: Population Reference Bureau. Excellent projection of population trends.

Brown, L. R., McGrath, P. L., and Stokes, B. (1976). *Twenty-Two Dimensions of the Population Problem* (Worldwatch Paper 5.) Washington, D.C.: Worldwatch Institute. A superb review of the impacts of population.

Ehrlich, P. R. (1971) *The Population Bomb*. New York: Ballantine. A book that startled the world, telling of the hidden dangers of overpopulation. Dated but worth reading.

Fowler, K. M. (1977) *Population: The Human Dilemma*. Washington, D.C.: National Science Teachers Association. An excellent list of readings on population and population control.

Grant, L. (1983). The Cornucopian Fallacies: The Myth of Perpetual Growth. *The Futurist* 17(4): 18–22. Important article rebutting the optimists who hold that there are no limits to growth in population and resource acquisition.

Hardin, G. (1981). An Ecolate View of the Human Predicament. *Alternatives* 7: 241–262. Superb paper on overpopulation and carrying capacity. Exceptional insights.

Haupt, A., and Kane, T. T. (1982). *Population Handbook*. Washington, D.C.: Population Reference Bureau. A superb primer on population.

Huss, J. D., and Wirken, M. J. (1977). Illegal Immigration: The Hidden Population Bomb. *The Futurist* 11(2): 114–120. An excellent article.

Population Reference Bureau (1982). U.S. Population: Where We Are; Where We're Going. *Population Bulletin* 37(2): 1–51. A fact-filled treatise on U.S. population, past, present, and future.

Population Reference Bureau (1984). *1984 World Population Data Sheet* and *The United States Population Data Sheet*. Washington, D.C.: Population Reference Bureau. Published annually with current statistics on U.S. and world population.

Short, R. V. (1972). Reproduction and Human Society. In *Reproduction in Mammals 5: Artificial Control of Reproduction*, C. R. Austin and R. V. Short, Eds. London: Cambridge University Press. An older account of world population, but extremely well-written and insightful.

Simon, J. L. (1981). World Population Growth: An Anti-Doomsday View. *Atlantic Monthly*, August, pp.70–76. A more detailed account of the benefits of population from Simon's perspective.

Simon, J. L. (1983). Life on Earth Is Getting Better, Not Worse. *The Futurist* 17(4)–14. Recommended reading, along with Grant's rebuttal.

Webb, M., and Jacobsen, J. (1982). U.S. Carrying Capacity: An Introduction. Washington, D.C.: Carrying Capacity.

7

Population Control

> *To rebuild our civilization we must first rebuild ourselves according to the pattern laid down by life.*
>
> ALEX CARREL

The human species, as we saw in Chapter 6, has gained some control over the outside, or **extrinsic, factors** that have kept populations low for millions of years. But the extrinsic factors are not gone entirely. The specters of widespread starvation and environmental upset may not appear in this century, but they may return in the next if our population does not stop rising.

In nature, the **reproductive, or biotic, potential** of a species is held in check by environmental resistance, including predation, disease, competition from other species, shortage of food, lack of suitable habitat, adverse climatic conditions, and so on. In a sense, environmental resistance is a form of natural population control. Examples of this control are plentiful; the predation of wolves on caribou in far northern Canada and Alaska is a striking one. Wolves trim the herd size, helping keep the caribou population from exceeding the carrying capacity of the tundra. Thus, the wolf population is dependent on the caribou population. When caribou are plentiful, so are the wolves; when the caribou population declines (perhaps as a result of excess predation), so does the wolf population. The caribou and wolf are halves of one whole.

Population growth in the wild is countered by extrinsic factors, as the example above illustrates. However, some species have their own social and behavioral means of controlling population, called **intrinsic factors**. For instance, in wolf packs only the dominant male and female breed and produce offspring. Their monopoly on reproduction

141

is maintained by disrupting the courting and mating attempts of subordinate pack members. This helps hold population growth to a minimum. Wolves and other animals also set up territories, which limit the number of animals within any given region to assure adequate food for the occupants.

Lions have a unique form of behavioral population control. During times of plenty, the young feed on the abundance of prey that the females kill for the pride. When prey are scarce, however, the young must compete with the adults for a share of the meat. They often go hungry and may become weak and die.

Many human societies once practiced deliberate population control by infanticide, the selective killing of newborns. Anthropologists believe that the early hunters and gatherers, for instance, may have abandoned one in every two or three children. This practice is also mentioned in European folktales and myths. In the South Pacific islands, when food from the sea was scarce, newborns were often allowed to die. Infanticide was not outlawed in Japan until 1868.

Today, humans control population on a global scale, and their efforts have the potential to be as effective as the extrinsic factors of disease, famine, and war that once held populations in check. Despite these efforts, success in many regions such as Africa, Asia, and Latin America has been limited. Food shortages, pollution, and environmental damage still remain pressing problems, reminding us of what Don Marquis once noted: "The chief obstacle to the progress of the human race is the human race."

Inevitably, starvation and disease will reduce a population that has stepped beyond the carrying capacity of the environment. The loss of 5 million to 20 million people who die directly or indirectly each year from starvation suggests that the threat is not exaggerated. See Essay 7-1 for a discussion of the consequences of overpopulation.

Limits to Growth

Although experts disagree about the impacts of increasing population, most are convinced that unlimited growth is not possible. This conclusion gained wide acceptance after the extensive computer study of the human future sponsored by the Club of Rome and published in *The Limits to Growth*. The authors of the study found from their computer analysis of population growth, resources, food per capita, pollution, and industrial output that the world society would exceed the carrying capacity of the planet within the century if exponential growth continued (Figure 7-1). Food, industrial output, and population would grow exponentially until rapidly diminishing resource supplies put a halt to industrial growth. Population would later begin to fall as a result of the rising death rate caused by decreased food supply.

In that study the authors tested other possibilities but found similar results in each situation. For instance, they doubled the presumed available supply of resources, assuming that we might be able to expand our supply through discoveries and new technologies that improve mining efficiency (Chapter 16). But they found that we would still overshoot the carrying capacity and crash—only a couple of decades later (Figure 7-2). The rise in the death rate would be due in part to rising pollution from expanded industrial output. In still another scenario the authors assumed that world resources were unlimited, a false condition that might give us unlimited growth potential. In that study population growth was halted by rising levels of pollution.

Several computer models in the study showed that a stable world system could be reached if we immediately

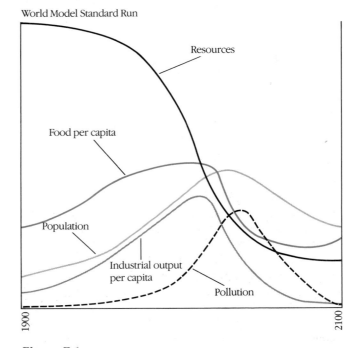

World Model Standard Run

Figure 7-1

Computer analysis of world trends. Because of natural delays in the system, both population and pollution continue to increase for some time after the peak of industrialization.

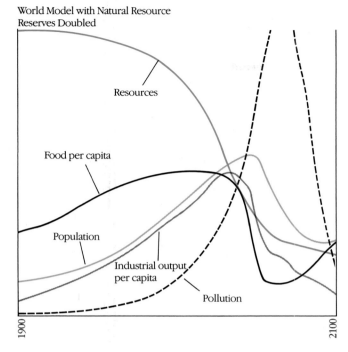

World Model with Natural Resource Reserves Doubled

Resources

Food per capita

Population

Industrial output per capita

Pollution

1900 2100

Figure 7-2
The same computer analysis as Figure 7-1, except the resource base is doubled.

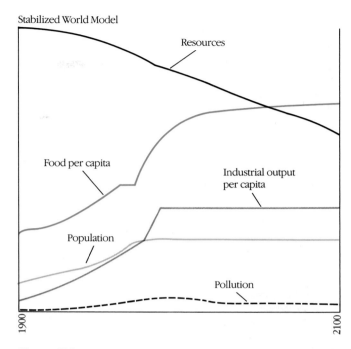

Stabilized World Model

Resources

Food per capita

Industrial output per capita

Population

Pollution

1900 2100

Figure 7-3
The same computer analysis as Figure 7-1 when global ZPG, recycling, pollution control, soil management, and farming are emphasized.

achieve zero population growth (ZPG), recycle products, control pollution and soil erosion, replenish the soil, and emphasize food production and services rather than industrial production. (Figure 7-3).

The Limits to Growth was widely criticized. In fact, a subsequent Club of Rome report developed by another group of computer scientists came to the opposite conclusions. These authors argued that industrialization of developing countries was the only way to avoid widespread starvation. Still a third report called for more economic growth throughout the world to narrow the gap between the developed and developing nations and to avoid the population crisis.

The rebuttals to the first report were not widely circulated and have been criticized by scientists. Thus, most scientists remain convinced that exponential population growth and industrial growth are undesirable in the long run. According to Professor Donella Meadows and her colleagues, who collaborated on *The Limits to Growth*: "Every day of continued exponential growth brings the world system closer to the ultimate limits of . . . growth. A decision to do nothing is a decision to increase the risk of collapse." The longer we allow exponential growth to

continue, the smaller the chance of achieving a stable, sustainable future.

The exact ways of bringing about zero population growth are still in dispute. But environmental scientists generally put this goal at the top of the list of human needs. It is the first and probably the hardest step toward a sustainable society.

How Do We Control Population Growth?

Many experts agree that we should avoid overshooting the earth's carrying capacity and prevent a population crash primarily by controlling population growth. But what should our goals be—simply to reach a stable population size, to allow continued "managed" growth, or to actually reduce the population size?

The answers to these questions differ depending on who is asked, because experts disagree on just how many people the world can support—that is, the earth's carry-

Nobody Ever Dies of Overpopulation

Those of us who are deeply concerned about population and the environment—"econuts," we're called—are accused of seeing herbicides in trees, pollution in running brooks, radiation in rocks, and overpopulation everywhere. There is merit in the accusation.

I was in Calcutta when the cyclone struck East Bengal in November 1970. Early dispatches spoke of 15,000 dead, but the estimates rapidly escalated to 2,000,000 and then dropped back to 500,000. A nice round number: it will do as well as any, for we will never know. The nameless ones who died, "unimportant" people far beyond the fringes of the social power structure, left no trace of their existence. Pakistani parents repaired the population loss in just 40 days, and the world turned its attention to other matters.

What killed those unfortunate people? The cyclone, newspapers said. But one can just as logically say that overpopulation killed them. The Gangetic delta is barely above sea level. Every year several thousand people are killed in quite ordinary storms. If Pakistan were not overcrowded, no sane man would bring his family to such a place. Ecologically speaking, a delta belongs to the river and the sea; man obtrudes there at his peril.

In the web of life every event has many antecedents. Only by an arbitrary decision can we designate a single antecedent as "cause." Our choice is biased—biased to protect our egos against the onslaught of unwelcome truths. As T. S. Eliot put it in *Burnt Norton:*

> Go, go, go, said the bird: human kind
> Cannot bear very much reality.

Were we to identify overpopulation as the cause of a half-million deaths, we would threaten ourselves with a question to which we do not know the answer: *How can we control population without recourse to repugnant measures?* Fearfully we close our minds to an inventory of possibilities. Instead, we say that a cyclone caused the deaths, thus relieving ourselves of responsibility for this and future catastrophes. "Fate" is *so* comforting.

Every year we list tuberculosis, leprosy, enteric diseases, or animal parasites as the "cause of death" of millions of people. It is well known that malnutrition is an important antecedent of death in all these categories; and that malnutrition is connected with overpopulation. But overpopulation is not called the cause of death. We cannot bear the thought.

People are dying now of respiratory diseases in Tokyo, Birmingham, and Gary, because of the "need" for more industry. The "need" for more food justifies overfertilization of the land, leading to eutrophication of the waters, and lessened fish production—which leads to more "need" for food.

What will we say when the power shuts down some fine summer on our eastern seaboard and several thousand people die of heat prostration? Will we blame the weather? Or the power companies for not building enough generators? Or the econuts for insisting on pollution controls?

One thing is certain: we won't blame the deaths on overpopulation. No one ever dies of overpopulation. It is unthinkable.

ing capacity. Have we exceeded it already, or do we have a long way to go?

Many estimates of world carrying capacity have been published, ranging from 500,000 people to over 100 billion. This range is wide for three main reasons. First, the amount of resources available to future generations is in dispute, because little is known about potential supplies of fuels and minerals and because of disagreement on many key issues regarding supply. Second, there is no consensus on the world's desired standard of living. The world cannot support many industrialized countries such as ours, but if we all chose to live in huts and grow our own food, the world's carrying capacity would be quite large. Third, no one knows what future technological advances will bring: Will new high-productivity crops feed everybody? Will genetic engineering enable us to make bacteria that can extract minerals from low-grade ores or even from seawater? Will minerals be mined from asteroids in outer space? For these reasons, the planet's carrying capacity for humans is an open question.

But do we really need an answer? Today, about one-fifth of the world's population, or about 900 million people, lives in a state of extreme poverty without adequate food and shelter. Two billion more people live with barely adequate food and shelter and with few amenities. Half a billion children receive an inadequate diet, and many of them succumb to starvation and disease. It is clear that the biosphere does not support the people already here. From this conclusion some argue that whatever else is done, our top priority must be to stop world population growth now so that many of the world's citizens can lift themselves out of poverty. Once population is under control, human needs can be planned for and met.

Others do not see catastrophe in the immediate future and consider a population freeze undesirable. Their hope is that if we increase food production and industrialization, the poor will be able to improve their life. Further, their populations will eventually stabilize through the demographic transition (Chapter 6). As mentioned earlier, economists such as Julian Simon view population growth as a necessary prerequisite for economic growth and thus see any stabilization in population size as an invitation for economic disaster. (See Point/Counterpoint, "The Population Debate," page 126.) In short, they believe that growth is the only way to reduce poverty. Other economists have begun to point out that conventional economic wisdom, both Marxist and capitalist, does not yet include important ecological realities such as the limits of resources.

Opposing Views on Population Control Policy

Setting aside the debate for now, we can address another vital question: how do we go about controlling population to achieve a sustainable society? On this particular question there is little agreement. One scholar in the field of population ethics, Arthur J. Dyck, divides the views on population control roughly into three areas.

First, there are the views of the **crisis environmentalists**, who believe that rapid population growth has already produced a serious crisis for the human species and the earth. To them population has already overtaxed the world carrying capacity. These people often favor governmental action, including restraint and coercion, to control population growth and perhaps even reduce population size.

The second group, the **family planners**, are concerned with overpopulation but focus their attention mostly on rapid growth or unwanted fertility. They hold that most parents throughout the world have children they didn't plan for. They believe that people generally favor birth control and that if governments make it available to everyone, people would have fewer children. Family planners generally do not recommend coercion but rather favor government clinics to offer advice and contraception that might otherwise be unaffordable.

The third group, the **developmental distributivists**, relies on the demographic transition as a means of improving socioeconomic conditions and halting population growth. Its answer to the population control issue is the extensive distribution of economic benefits such as foreign aid and industries to the developing nations.

Unfortunately, there is little scientific evidence to indicate which, if any, of the groups has the answer to the population control problem. Future population control strategies will undoubtedly incorporate all of these ideas. In this way regional plans can be devised to suit the needs and resources of each country.

In the United States, where individual freedom is held in high esteem, family planning may be the most appropriate measure. In countries with more autocratic control, coercion may be more likely and more severe. China has made a successful attempt to control population by a host of official coercive actions, including pressure applied on people to delay marriage and heavy penalties for having more than the allotted number of children. Economic development plans may also work, but they must be strategies that spread wealth and a higher standard of living through the society and do not concentrate it at the top.

Population control is a highly personal matter. All solutions have an ethical component, and they cannot be devised in a vacuum without knowledge of the culture, religion, values, goals, and resources of the people.

Population Control Strategies

Population control can be a relatively passive process, an active one, or something in between. The following section will discuss some of the approaches to control.

Demographic Transition Many of the world's populations have entered stage 2 of the demographic transition, in which birth rates are high but death rates have dropped swiftly because of disease control and improved sanitation. Sri Lanka is a perfect example. An intensive campaign against malaria begun in 1946 decreased the mortality rate from 22 to 13 per 1000 in only six years, but even today the birth rate remains at about 30 per 1000.

Relying on the demographic transition as a means of population control was discussed and criticized in Chapter 6. The consensus among scientists is that the transition cannot proceed much further for many countries, because economic development either is not possible or will be too limited. This leaves only two choices: an increased death rate from disease and famine or the control of birth rates through extensive family planning efforts.

Family Planning   Family planning, to many the preferred method of population control, allows couples to determine the number and spacing of their offspring. For countries stuck in stage 2 of the demographic transition, it can speed up the necessary decline in the birth rate (Figure 7-4).

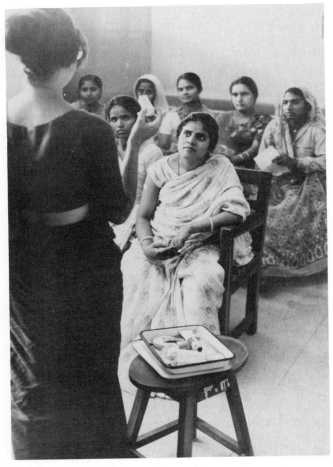

Figure 7-4
Family planning in India. A woman doctor lectures to a group of Indian wives on various methods of birth control at a family planning clinic in New Delhi.

Family planning relies on (1) the availability of information on birth control, (2) the availability of a wide variety of birth-control measures, and (3) the desire of people to practice birth control. For our purposes, a contraceptive is any chemical, device, or method which prevents fertilization (Table 7-1). Birth control includes any methods designed to reduce births, including contraception and induced abortion, the intentional interruption of pregnancy through surgical means or through drug treatments. Family planning programs may be voluntary, extended voluntary, or forced.

Voluntary family planning programs, which may be sponsored by governments, rely on the individual's desires. The goal of these programs is to help parents have the number of children they want when they want them by providing birth-control information, contraceptives, and, in many cases, abortions at reduced rates. The United States has such a program, sponsored by Planned Parenthood.

Extended voluntary programs are government sponsored. Free access to information on birth control and sterilization is provided by governmental agencies. Contraception, sterilization, and abortions may be encouraged through government payments or propaganda. Mass communications such as newspapers, television, and radio can be used to convince people of the merits of birth control and, ultimately, small family size. Informational campaigns may also attempt to change stereotypical sex roles, persuading men that masculinity and self-importance are not related to the number of their children and convincing women that the childbearing role is not the only one that makes them socially valuable.

Forced family planning programs are strict governmental programs that put limitations on family size and punish those who exceed quotas. Such programs may call for compulsory sterilization after reaching the allotted family size, limited food rations for "excess" children, or taxes on couples who exceed the allowed number of children. China and India have initiated forced family programs, which will be discussed later.

Programs may not fit these three categories neatly. The government of Singapore, for instance, uses radio, billboards, and school curricula promoting two children per family. This extended voluntary program is complemented by several coercive measures: The first two children of any family are allowed to attend local schools, but additional children must often be bused elsewhere. Furthermore, hospital costs increase for surplus children, and government employees who are not sterilized are given a low priority for public housing.

Table 7-1 Methods of Birth Control

Contraceptive Method	How It Works	Advantages	Disadvantages and Side Effects	Effectiveness
Oral medication				
The Pill—combinations of estrogen and progestin (synthetic progesteronelike hormone). Estrogen doses range from 0 to 150 micrograms; progestin from 0.35 to 10 milligrams.	Suppresses ovulation by acting on pituitary gland. Conception not possible if no egg matures. If dosage is inadequate or pill is not taken as directed, ovulation and conception may occur.	More than 99% effective. Easy to use for those motivated to remember to take pill as directed. Dissociated from sex act. Bleeding cycles are predictable.	Discomforts simulating those of pregnancy: nausea, breast tenderness, weight gain, depression, fatigue. Hazards include thrombus (clot) formation, thrombophlebitis, pulmonary embolus, and hypertension (smoking greatly increases risk). Should not be used if woman has hypertension, sickle cell disease, diabetes, or migraine headaches.	Above 99%. If one pill is missed, it should be taken when remembered; next pill should be taken as scheduled. If two or more pills are missed, follow directions above; in addition, a second form of contraceptive should be used for rest of that month.
Mini pill—progestin only (norethindrone or norgestrel 0.35 mg daily).	Antifertility effect. Makes cervical mucus impervious to sperm and/or alters endometrium, interfering with implantation. Ovulation occurs sporadically.	Reduces side effects found with other oral preparations.	Bleeding irregularity and spotting are common. Less effective than combination pills.	97% to 98%
Intrauterine devices (IUD) The following are made of flexible molded plastic: Lippes Loop, Saf-T-Coil, Cu-7, and Tatum T (which release minute amounts of copper, which has an antifertility effect); Progestasert (which releases progestin into the uterus).	Interferes with fertilization. Alters rate of egg's passage through the fallopian tube. Discourages implantation by altering endometrium.	No interference with hormonal regulation of menstrual cycle. No need to remember to take a pill each day or engage in other manipulation prior to coitus. Can be removed by physician when pregnancy is desired. Fewer complications reported with Cu-7 and Progestasert.	Expulsion may go unnoticed. Hazards—uterine perforation with intra-abdominal trauma and/or intrauterine or fallopian infection (perforation may occur during insertion). Side effects—heavy flow, spotting between periods, and cramping, especially during early months of use.	

Table 7-1   Methods of Birth Control (continued)

Contraceptive Method	How It Works	Advantages	Disadvantages and Side Effects	Effectiveness
Intrauterine Devices (IUD) continued			25% of women fitted each year have to abandon use; expulsion rate 3% to 15%; rate of medical removal because of complications 5% to 20%.	
			Ectopic pregnancy might still occur, especially with "bio-active" IUDs.	97% to 98% effective during first year; later, 98% or higher.
			Increased risk of infection of fallopian tubes, with possibility of permanent scarring and loss of fertility.	User must check for presence of IUD after each menstrual period.
Mechanical barriers Diaphragm—rubber device that fits over the cervix; should be used with spermicide.	Barrier prevents sperm from entering cervix if it is correct size and correctly placed; refitted for size after each baby, weight gain or loss, or every 2 years. Diaphragm holds spermicide in place over cervix.	Safety—no side effects. Can be inserted several hours before intercourse and is left in place at least 6 to 8 hours afterwards.	Some women find insertion and removal objectionable. Required washing with warm water and soap; careful drying; storage away from heat; and checking for tears.	Effectiveness usually given as 75% to 90% but can be 97% or more if spermicide is used consistently and extra spermicide added before repeated coitus.
Cervical cap—rubber device that fits snugly around cervix.	Barrier prevents sperm from entering cervix.	Can be inserted for a period of several days.	Still experimental, and available at only a few medical centers in U.S. Unproven safety. Possibility of cervical abrasion.	Considered as effective as diaphragm (97%), but no large-scale American studies to provide proof.
Condom—thin stretchable rubber sheath to cover the penis.	Barrier prevents sperm from entering the vagina. Is applied over the erect penis.	Safety—no side effects. Protective measure against venereal disease. No prescription needed.	Some couples object to taking time to apply sheath on erect penis. Pre-ejaculatory drops also contain sperm; conception possible even if drops fall around *external* vaginal opening. Some users feel it decreases sensation.	Effectiveness usually given as 80% to 85% but can be up to 97% if carefully used (sheath held in place as penis withdrawn), even higher if used with spermicide.

Table 7-1 Methods of Birth Control (continued)

Contraceptive Method	How It Works	Advantages	Disadvantages and Side Effects	Effectiveness
Chemical barriers Spermicide (e.g., Nonoxynol 9)—foam, jelly, cream, or vaginal suppository.	Kills sperm. Decreases sperm motility. Sperm cannot pass through chemical barrier.	Safety—no systemic side effects. Increases effectiveness of mechanical barriers. Easy to use. Aids lubrication of vagina. No prescription needed.	Described as "messy" by some. Each coitus should be preceded by a fresh application. Some products irritate user and partner.	Actual effectiveness may be only 70% to 80% when used without diaphragm or condom.
Rhythm (fertility awareness) methods Temperature method—rectal or oral temperature taken with basal thermometer each morning before any physical activity.	Body temperature varies with stage in ovulatory cycle. Conception is avoided by sexual abstinence during woman's fertile period; no sperm may be present while egg is present.	Physically safe to use—no drugs or appliances are used. Meets requirements of some religions.	Effectiveness depends on the following: high level of motivation and high diligence, daily temperature taking and record keeping for duration of childbearing years, and willingness to abstain. Requires fairly predictable menstrual cycle. Irregular cycles require long periods of abstinence. Ovulation may occur at atypical times.	60% to 85% Temperature varies with tension, infection, lack of sleep, or any prior activity. Effectiveness may be increased by checking changes in cervical mucus.
Mucus method—sample of cervical mucus is examined each day for viscosity and color.	Identifies fertile period by recognizing changes in cervical mucus. Sexual abstinence during fertile period.	Physically safe. Acceptable to certain religions.	Requires couple to recognize cervical mucus changes and engage in the manipulation necessary to sample mucus.	95% effectiveness claimed for highly motivated couples.
Sterilization Vasectomy (males) Surgically cutting vas deferens and tying off ends.	Prevents sperm from entering ejaculate.	Easy to perform. Essentially permanent.	Irreversible. Sometimes creates psychological problems in men.	100%
Tubal ligation (females) Surgically cutting and tying off fallopian tubes.	Prevents fertilizations by blocking ova and sperm.	Easy to perform. Essentially permanent.	Irreversible.	100%

Table 7-1 (continued)				
Contraceptive Method	How It Works	Advantages	Disadvantages and Side Effects	Effectiveness
Abortion Surgically remove conceptus prior to second trimester of pregnancy by vacuum aspiration of uterine contents.	Prevents pregnancy from continuing.	Fairly easy to perform. Safe, effective.	Requires minor surgery, which places woman in some jeopardy.	100%

Source: Combs, Hales, Williams, *An Invitation to Health,* 2nd ed. (1983). Benjamin-Cummings Publishing Company, Menlo Park, CA.

Developed Countries—What Can They Do?

We tend to think that population control pertains only to the poor countries of the world, because many of the developed countries have achieved replacement-level fertility. But many ecologists and demographers point out that the high per capita consumption of the developed countries, which was discussed with the Multiple Cause and Effect model in Chapter 2, must be considered in the population equation.

According to some estimates, a single American is equivalent to 25 to 38 residents of India in terms of resource use and environmental impact. Each person in the United States uses about 18,000 kilograms (40,000 pounds) of minerals, including stone, sand, gravel, salt, aluminum, iron, coal, petroleum, natural gas, and steel. Third World residents use only a small fraction of this amount. Grain consumption in the United States is nearly four times greater than that in Africa and the Middle East or Asia and Oceania (Figure 7-5).

The developed countries' disproportionate use of resources means that control of their population is as necessary for world stability as is control in poor countries. By using less, many people argue, developed countries could make possible a more equitable sharing of the earth's resources. This could help reduce world tensions. But sharing resources is controversial, being supported by developing nations but opposed by the wealthier, developed nations. (See Chapter 16 for a discussion of mining the seafloor and proposals for sharing the wealth.)

Developed countries can also help the developing nations by sharing their knowledge of birth control, agriculture, health care, and appropriate technology. Financial assistance to help achieve a moderate rate of industrialization, using appropriate technologies, can also help. Table 7-2 summarizes some suggestions for developed countries.

William and Paul Paddock, authors of the controversial book *Famine—1975, America's Decision: Who Will Survive?* proposed a triage system, similar to that used in wartime to categorize the wounded prior to treatment. According to the Paddocks, countries could be categorized in three groups: (1) those that have an adequate resource base and could survive hard times without aid, (2) those impoverished nations that would probably not survive droughts and food shortages even with aid, and (3) those that can be helped. Group 1 needs no assistance. Group 2 must be given up for hopeless, because no amount of aid will help them. Group 3, if aided, could pull through droughts or other difficult periods. Therefore, the Paddocks suggest that we maximize our aid by concentrating our efforts on group 3. To some, this seems like an unethical approach to world assistance. Others see it as the only answer to apportion the available aid.

Developing Countries—What Can They Do?

The less developed countries recognize the need for population control. Today 93% of the world's population lives in countries with population control policies. The International Planned Parenthood Federation, established in

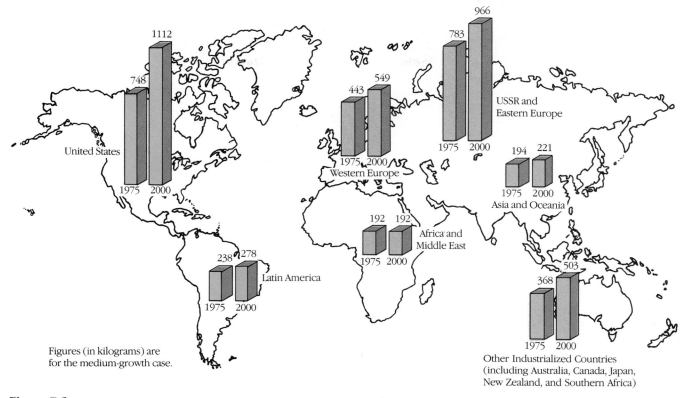

Figure 7-5
Current and projected per capita grain consumption in the world (including grain used for livestock).

the 1950s, has assisted by disseminating information on birth control and providing assistance to many countries. Since the 1960s the World Bank has provided financial aid to developing countries with population control policies.

Unfortunately, having a population control policy and funding that policy are entirely different matters. Few governments spend more than 1% of their national budget on family planning services. In addition to this monetary problem, illiteracy, rural isolation, lack of funds, and local taboos have made success difficult to achieve in many programs. For these and other reasons, population control in developing nations has been limited. Results have been especially poor in India, Mexico, Brazil, Pakistan, and Indonesia.

Table 7-3 lists population control strategies for developing countries. Accompanied by appropriate development, these suggestions could improve the life of many people.

Making Strategies Work

To effectively carry out population control programs, governments must consider three cultural factors: (1) the psychology of procreation, (2) the ways that education affects reproduction, and (3) the influence of religion.

Psychology Large families are an asset in undeveloped countries, because children help with the chores and also care for their parents when they become old. Given the high mortality rates in these countries, having many children ensures that some will survive. Despite the fact that death rates have fallen swiftly throughout the world, and that more children are now surviving, the traditional value placed on children has not been abandoned. Birth rates remain high.

Having children is a self-fulfilling activity for males and females in developing nations. Sociologists report that men and women are admired in many societies for the

Table 7-2 Population Control Strategies for Developed Countries

Strategy	Rationale	Benefits
Stabilize population growth by restricting immigration, and by spending more money and time on sex education and population awareness in public schools.	High use of resources taxes the environment. Immigrants create serious strain on the economy and create social tension in conditions of high unemployment. Education helps citizens realize the importance of population control.	Limiting resource use leaves more for future generations and developing countries.
Provide financial assistance to developing countries for agriculture and appropriate industry. Aid should come from government and private sources.	Economic growth in developing countries will raise their standard of living and aid in population control.	The rich-poor gap would narrow. A decrease in sociopolitical tension and resource shortage would result.
Provide assistance to population control programs.	Better funded population programs can afford the increased technical assistance and community outreach programs necessary to provide information to the public.	Could result in faster decrease in population growth.
Make trade with less developed countries equitable and freer.	Freer trade will increase per capita income and raise standards of living with little effect on home economy.	A higher standard of living and increased job opportunities could result.
Concentrate research on social, cultural, and psychological aspects of reproduction.	Techniques available today are effective and reliable. What is needed is more motivation for population control, especially among poor countries.	Money will be better spent; research of this nature may help facilitate family planning in less developed countries.

number of children they have, a view that is present in some developed nations as well.

Unfortunately, these psychological factors result in the birth of many children who will never have adequate food, clothing, shelter, and education. In the face of such possibilities, how can people continue to have large families? Citizens of developed countries tend to view children as an economic drain that detracts from their life-style. Recent studies show that it costs low-income families in the United States about $60,000 to raise a child, including education through a publicly subsidized college. Middle-income families spend about $90,000 per child. In the poor countries, a child deprives the family of virtually nothing. In fact, because children represent a form of material wealth (free labor and support in old age) and satisfaction, they probably represent a net gain.

Education   U.S. Department of Commerce figures show that the higher the educational level, the lower the total fertility rate (TFR) (Figure 7-6). Educated women often pursue careers that necessitate postponing marriage and childbearing. Since the childbearing years are from 15 to 44, a woman who graduates from college at age 21, marries, but postpones having children until she is 30 has decreased the number of years available for childbearing by half.

A lack of education in developing countries has several consequences. Men and women generally marry young and do not pursue careers that interfere with families. Thus, the period of childbearing is much longer than it is for couples in developed countries. A lack of education also makes it harder for people to learn about alternatives to childbearing and the proper use of contraceptives. It

Table 7-3 Population Control Strategies for Developing Countries

Strategy	Rationale	Benefits
Develop effective national plan to ensure better dissemination of information and availability of contraception, and other methods of population control. Do not rely on one type of control.	Each country better understands its people and thus can design better programs to spread population control information and devices.	More effective dissemination of information and, probably, a higher rate of success.
Finance education in rural regions, emphasizing population control and benefits of reduced population growth.	Education can help make population control a reality.	Slower population growth, more effective use of contraceptives, and more incentive.
Seek to change cultural taboos against birth control and cultural incentives for large families	Changes in culture and psychology may be needed to make population control programs effective.	Such changes will help programs succeed.
Develop appropriate industry and agriculture, especially in rural areas to reduce or eliminate the movement of people from the country to the city.	Appropriate agriculture and industry will create jobs and better economic conditions for families. A higher standard of living could translate into better health care and greater survival of young, thus destroying need for large families.	This will result in higher standard of living, better health care, and impetus for control of family size.
Seek programs of development that attain a maximum spread of wealth among the people.	Development must not help just a select few, because benefits may not trickle down to needy.	Plans of this nature yield good distribution of income and help the needy rather than select few.
Integrate population policy with economic, resource, food, and land-use policy to achieve a stable state.	Finite resources require wise allocation and use; success in the long run depends on attempts to achieve a sustainable future.	Longevity and permanence are attainable if policies are integrated and take into account the requirements of a sustainable society.
Seek funding from the United Nations and developed countries.	Developed countries have a stake in stabilizing world population growth.	Developed countries could provide significant financial support.

Figure 7-6
Total fertility rates of U.S. women in 1977, by level of education.

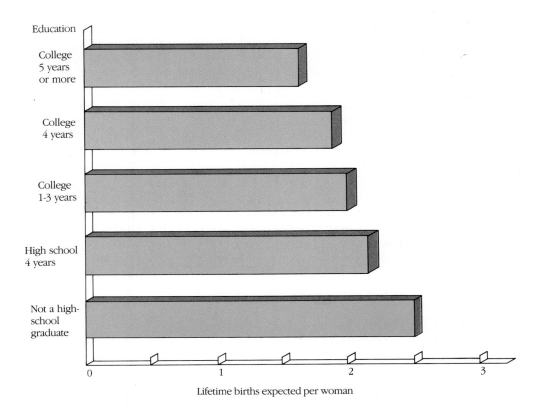

is no wonder, then, that the birth rate is still high in rural India, where 80% to 90% of the women are illiterate.

Religion Religion may also be a powerful force in reproduction. In the West, the Roman Catholic church has been cited as a prime cause of overpopulation. Strictly forbidding all "unnatural" methods of birth control, it takes a dim view of birth control pills, condoms, diaphragms, and abortion, although this has not always been so. In 1968 Pope Paul VI's encyclical *Humanae Vitae* condemned the use of contraceptives, except the rhythm method, the least effective of all measures. Theoretically, the Catholic church provides the guidelines for the sexual practices of approximately 600 million people. However, recent surveys show that the use of contraceptives by Catholic women, especially in western nations, is nearly as high as that among non-Catholics. The Church of Jesus Christ of Latter-day Saints (Mormon) likewise opposes all birth control, and Mormons commonly have large families.

Birth control is generally an undiscussed subject among other religions. And because many of the eastern and near eastern religions compete with one another for followers, birth control is not advocated.

For a family planning program to work, its workers must understand the culture, education, and religion of a people. Help must be given out of this understanding. Programs should be tailored to meet the needs of each group. People must have access to socially acceptable birth control, and in poor countries these must be available free of charge and must be easy to understand and simple to use. Trained workers must be available to counsel those seeking contraceptives, abortion, and sterilization. Most important, attitudes toward family size must be changed if programs are to be effective.

Ethics of Population Control

Perhaps no other issue in environmental science is so laden with ethical problems as that of population control. To deny the right to reproduce is to deny one of the most basic and important of all human activities. To some, population control is a violation of deep religious beliefs. To others, it is an intrusion into a private matter. And for minorities, population control has overtones of genocide.

The very phrases *excessive population growth* and *population problem* used here are value-laden. To imply that excessive growth creates problems indicates that there is some other state of population growth (perhaps no growth or negative growth) that is better. This book takes the position that we live in a finite biosphere and that exceeding the limits will inevitably create severe ecological repercussions.

This said, there are nevertheless many important ethical questions. Should the right to reproduce be left up to the individual? Can we have as many children as we want? Conversely, is it ethical *not* to control population growth? What are our goals in population control, and are these ethical? One final question, discussed in a Point/Counterpoint by Robert Mellert and Thomas Schwartz in Chapter 23, is "Do we owe anything to future generations?"

Is Reproduction a Personal Right?

Many people argue that the right to reproduce at will should be curtailed when the rights of the individual interfere with the welfare of society, the collective rights of all the people. For example, India's government under Prime Minister Indira Gandhi began a program of forced sterilization in 1975. Changes in India's constitution placed "directive principles," the rights of the whole of society, above the rights of the individual. This short-lived and extreme program illustrates that a laudable end—the welfare of an overpopulated nation's people—can prompt governments to adopt tyrannical means to achieve that end.

The other point of view was well stated in 1965 by Pope Paul in a speech to the United Nations: "You must strive to multiply bread so that it suffices for the tables of mankind, and not, rather, favor an artificial control of birth, which would be irrational, in order to diminish the number of guests at the banquet of life." To interfere with the creation of new life offends deep-seated beliefs about God's role.

Others who support the right to reproduce freely argue that denying such rights takes away personal freedom. In contrast, Paul Ehrlich argues that we "must take the side of the hungry *billions* of living human beings today and tomorrow, not the side of potential human beings. . . . If those potential human beings are born, they will at best lead miserable lives and die young." He argues that we cannot let humanity be destroyed by a doctrine of individual freedoms conceived in isolation from the biological facts of life.

Is It Ethically Proper Not to Control Population?

What if we do not control population, and let it run its own course? How does that decision affect future generations? Will uncontrolled population growth improve or worsen their world? If our actions rob from the future, can they be considered ethical?

To know how our actions will affect the future, we can use the computer to forecast major trends in population, resources, and pollution. Such exercises, as we've seen in earlier examples, may be subject to error, but they nonetheless help us predict the conditions of tomorrow based on today's actions and help us arrive at ethical decisions based on scientific information.

To make an ethical decision first requires us to consider whether the things we value are benefited or harmed by our actions. Ethical decisions require us to consider the ways we achieve our goals and our goals themselves. Will the ends and the means to these ends ultimately harm us or help us? Are they scientifically and ecologically sound? Do they destroy the hope of those who follow us, or do they enhance it? Do they make life intolerable for nonhuman species, or do they improve it?

Humans need food, shelter, clothing, and water to survive. Once these needs are satisfied, our next most important values are pleasure, happiness, knowledge, freedom, self-expression, and justice. Decisions we make in the future must provide for both sets of values.

Population Trends

As we learned in Chapter 6, the world population growth rate has slowed in recent years, and population may stabilize between 8 billion and 15 billion people. Stabilization may come from stepping up control programs in areas of especially fast growth (See Table 7-3). In this section we will look at some encouraging news and some discouraging news about population growth. Case studies help us determine which strategies have been successful and areas where more work is needed.

Encouraging Trends

In the early to mid-1970s, many countries updated their laws and policies governing family planning. Overall, four general areas witnessed significant improvement: national population control programs, contraceptive distribution,

Illegal Aliens and Population Growth

Undocumented Workers: A Solution

Tom Barry

The author has written about undocumented workers, refugees from Central America, and economic issues for more than ten years. He helped establish the Resource Center, a nonprofit organization in Albuquerque, New Mexico, which writes and produces educational materials, including Dollars and Dictators: A Guide to Central America *and* The Other Side of Paradise: Foreign Control in the Caribbean.

Workers from other countries, particularly from Mexico, have helped build America. In the last centuries, they laid the track of railroads, dug out the silver and copper mines, and formed the backbone of agriculture in the western United States. During the world wars, Mexican workers alleviated the American labor shortage. However, recession and labor surplus, as in the Great Depression, resulted in tougher immigration laws and the mass deportation of Mexican and Asian workers.

The U.S. Immigration and Naturalization Service (INS) calls foreign workers "illegal aliens." The term *undocumented workers,* a less dehumanizing label, comes from the fact that they work without required documents. A combination of push and pull factors causes the continuing flow of undocumented workers across U.S. borders.

The "pull" factors include the higher pay scale in this country and the constant need by U.S. companies for hardworking foreigners. Millions of undocumented laborers do the work that most American citizens won't do. They pick fruit, wash dishes, tar roofs, sew garments, and dig ditches at wages unacceptably low for U.S. citizens. At the same time these workers are being pulled into the United States, however, they are forever being pushed out by INS and Border Patrol agents. This situation often results in the severe exploitation of undocumented workers. Employers and landlords can underpay and overcharge them, knowing that they won't protest for fear of deportation.

The political conditions of other countries are also important factors in illegal immigration into the United States. Washington takes two different views toward political refugees. On one hand, it opens its doors to refugees escaping communist nations. On the other hand, it tries to keep out refugees who are fleeing from repressive governments that are our allies, such as Haiti and El Salvador. The U.S. government has turned its back on these refugees even though they often face arrest or death if they are deported.

Illegal immigration is a complex problem with no easy answer. Harsher immigration laws won't work, nor will increasing the number of border police. Neither can we simply open up all our borders. We need laws and solutions that protect both the rights of U.S. citizens to maintain their jobs and the rights of undocumented workers to be treated as decent human beings. Our government also needs to guarantee the rights of refugees from all countries to receive at least temporary sanctuary here while repression and wars continue back home.

Part of the solution to the immigration problem must include an international approach. U.S. workers who worry about undocumented workers' taking their jobs don't realize that the jobs are more threatened by corporations' leaving the United States to find cheaper labor and fewer environmental controls in places like Mexico and Central America. Politicians concerned about ensuring jobs for American workers should try to prevent U.S. industry from leaving.

Rather than building higher border fences and increasing surveillance, we should help improve economic and political conditions in countries south of the border. Generally, Mexicans and Central Americans don't want to leave home but must because of harsh conditions. Economic aid programs that help the poor would ease the illegal immigration problem.

Measures that could be started immediately include amnesty for all undocumented workers now working here and a temporary visa program allowing foreign workers into the United States six months a year for farm work with the proviso that they return home afterwards.

Any new law regulating immigrants must take three things into account: the United States' need for immigrant workers; the rights of these workers; and the economic and political conditions that result in illegal immigration to the United States.

Stopping the Flow of Illegal Immigrants

Richard Lamm

The author is in his third term as governor of Colorado. He was a member of the Colorado House of Representatives from 1966 to 1974. He is author of a number of articles on the future and recently published The Angry West *with Michael McCarthy.*

History plays strange tricks on civilizations. Yesterday's solutions often become today's problems. Arnold Toynbee observed that the same elements that build up an institution eventually lead to its downfall. I fear that this will hold true with immigration in the United States.

Few issues facing the United States are as important as immigration, and in no other issue are we so blinded by our past myths. The experiences of our immigrant parents and grandparents have become such a large part of our memory that we are reticent to put limits on what we feel to be the very historical fabric of our nation. But the United States is no longer a nation of frontiers. Long gone are the vast empty spaces where immigrant families drove wagons across barren plains to start new lives. Our frontier legacy has been replaced by an America of 7.6% unemployment and serious resource dilemmas. But the myth of the open border lingers on.

In today's world a country without a border is like a house without walls. Neither can function for very long in that predicament. National integrity demands that we be able to decide who can enter the country and who must leave. This is a basic tenet of sovereignty, and it is to this tenet we refer when we say that "America has lost control of its borders."

The sad truth is that our national boundaries have more holes than Swiss cheese. In 1983 the U.S. Border Patrol apprehended 1.2 million illegal aliens—the largest number in history. But veteran Border Patrol officers say that for every one apprehended, at least two others succeed in entering.

We know that anywhere from 4 million to 12 million illegal aliens are living in the United States, and we know that the nature of illegal immigration is changing. Whereas the average illegal immigrant used to be a single male who eventually returned to his homeland, today he often brings his family and stays for good.

There is a common misconception that illegal aliens take jobs that American workers don't want. That is simply not the case. In 1979 Secretary of Labor Ray Marshall estimated that illegal immigration to the United States had increased U.S. unemployment by at least 2%. Under-secretary of Labor Malcolm Lovell recently reported that 40 million Americans compete directly with illegal aliens for jobs. And whereas 20 years ago most illegal aliens were farm-workers, today they are mostly urban factory and service workers earning well above the minimum wage. The average wage earned by an illegal alien apprehended in Denver in the last two years was $6 an hour. Half of all illegals arrested in New York, Los Angeles, and San Francisco worked in manufacturing, and in 1982, 85% of those arrested were making more than the minimum wage.

Severe unemployment problems in the United States are compounded by competition for jobs from illegal immigrants. More than 30% of all minority youth are unemployed, and it is hard to see where we're going to get enough capital to create the jobs they need. In the 1970s, before the recession, our economy created an average of 2 million new jobs a year, but their potential benefits were in part negated by the 1 million legal and illegal immigrants who entered the United States to take the jobs away.

It is estimated that more than 10% of all El Salvadorans have migrated to the United States within the last few years. One out of ten persons in Los Angeles is an illegal alien, and 60% of all babies born last year in three Los Angeles County public hospitals were born to illegal-alien mothers. Without question, illegal immigrants are having a tremendous impact on our country.

By no means do all illegal immigrants come from Mexico or South or Central America. Although an estimated 50% of illegal immigrants come from Mexico, the rest are likely to come from almost any country in the world. The most recent wave of illegals to reach Miami were Bangladeshis who traveled halfway around the world to be smuggled into south Florida from the island of Bimini. In recent years, 800,000 more people arrived annually in the United States on scheduled airlines than departed. We can assume that a large number of these people came here in violation of our immigration laws.

The per capita income in Mexico is slightly more than $1000. In the United States it is slightly less than $9000. That difference creates an incredible magnet that attracts illegal immigrants from nearby Mexico. The same magnet also attracts people from all the rest of the world.

In the next 11 years the world population will increase by 1 billion, and 88% of all new births will be in three continents: Asia, South America, and Africa. More than 1 billion people today have an annual per capita income of $150—less than what an average American earns in a week. This powerful combination of factors will result in incredible pressures on our borders.

The cost of refusing to control our borders is staggering. It is estimated that, if there are 6 million illegal aliens in the United States, U.S. taxpayers will shell out $13.5 billion annually in services to these unwanted guests. This includes:

Job displacement	$ 9.0 billion
Education	$ 1.6 billion
Unemployment payments	$ 1.1 billion
Welfare	$ 690 million
Health care	$ 557 million
Crime	$ 550 million

We can no longer ignore this issue. Immigration is an idea that has served us well in times past but will hurt us in the future.

We are a country beset with serious unemployment problems and serious resource shortages. We no longer have the empty land that we had during the first 200 years of our history to absorb the flow of immigrants.

Politicians, like generals, tend to fight the last war. It is deceptively simple to treat the future as we have treated the past. But the genius of public policy is in being able to anticipate the future. As Abraham Lincoln said so well, "As our case is new, so must we think and act anew. We must disenthrall ourselves."

We must come to grips with the new realities facing us. There must be limits to immigration if this nation is to exist and prosper. There is currently an anomaly in U.S. law that makes it illegal to *be* an illegal alien but not illegal to hire one. The most effective thing we can do to solve this problem is to make it against the law to hire an illegal alien. Such a proposal was originally propounded by the Reverend Theodore Hesburgh, president of the University of Notre Dame, and has been endorsed by the National Association for the Advancement of Colored People, the Urban League, the U.S. Senate, and many church groups.

We know that we cannot accept all the people who want to come to the United States. Our immigration policy must be designed in the interests of the American people. The hope that we can hold out to all the world's people is that it is possible to have a free, decent, and caring society that intelligently plans a sound future for its children. If we want to preserve our liberty, and if we want to preserve this country's abundance, we must limit immigration now. These limits are not for us; they are for our children.

voluntary sterilization, and the use of economic incentives and disincentives. As a result of these and other factors, population growth in many developed countries has been dramatically reduced.

In the United States, abortion laws were liberalized nationwide, access to birth control was increased, a growing number of women entered the work force, educational opportunity for women increased, the feminist movement promoted a way of life in which motherhood was but one option, and many couples decided to remain childless. In addition, inflation and recession in the 1970s and early 1980s and soaring hospital costs no doubt helped reduce birth rates. The total fertility rate in the United States dropped to slightly below 2.1 in 1972, and it has remained below replacement level for over a decade. Other developed countries have experienced similar trends.

Progress in population control has been phenomenal in some developing countries. (Figure 7-7). The largest reductions in growth rate have been witnessed in China, Taiwan, Tunisia, Barbados, Hong Kong, Singapore, Costa Rica, and Egypt.

China The apparent decline in the Chinese birth rate in the 1970s is the most rapid of any country on record. China's 2.5% annual growth rate in the 1960s (doubling time 28 years) had dropped to 1.4% by 1983 (doubling time 48 years). By 2000, it is hoped, population growth will reach 1%.

What accounts for this dramatic drop in the growth rate? The Chinese began a national campaign to control growth in the late 1950s, although early efforts were unsuccessful. After a severe famine from 1959 to 1962, a new campaign was begun in the early 1960s in which couples were

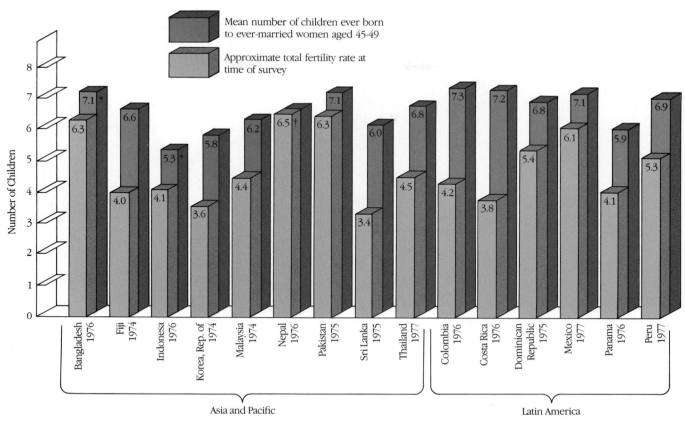

*Figure for women aged 45-49 lower than for women aged 40-44; latter shown.

†Figure for mean number of children corrected after publication of country report. Marital fertility rate shown; total fertility rate not available.

Figure 7-7
Fertility rate in 15 developing countries, past and current.

encouraged to marry in their mid- to late twenties. Later, couples were urged to have only one child. Posters on clinic walls and in public places stressed the desirability of one-child families.

The government also created disincentives to large family size. For example, ration tickets for basic supplies such as cotton are granted only for the first two children in a family. Further disincentives include wage and pension reductions for families with more than two children.

In addition to the forced family planning created by economic disincentives, extended voluntary programs were begun. Educational campaigns were launched to teach people about birth control. Free family planning was made available in rural communities. Vasectomies, the pill, and IUDs were offered at no cost. Abortions were also performed free for working women or at a small fee for others. The government compensated for time lost from work when sterilization or an abortion had been performed.

The success of the Chinese campaign was largely due to the "barefoot doctors." Trained for six months in elementary medical and contraceptive techniques, the barefoot doctors journey into the country, handing out contraceptives and teaching people about family planning. The success of China is encouraging, but the Chinese government is able to exert more control over its people than are those of many other countries. Still, some important lessons can be learned from the Chinese experience. Most notable is the need to disseminate information and trained personnel throughout the country in an effort to reach the inhabitants of rural villages. This might be especially effective in India, Indonesia, and other countries with rapid population growth in rural areas.

Figure 7-8
A large Indian family gathers
together for wedding.

Discouraging Trends

Unfortunately, the world population dilemma is far from solved; there remain some rather discouraging trends. During the 1970s there was an upturn in death rates in many poorer countries, primarily due to hunger and nutritional stress. Added to this, food demand has now outstripped production, and world food reserves are at an all-time low, dropping from 90 days in 1970 to 30 days in 1974, and remaining at this low level ever since. (For more on this topic see Chapter 8.) Making matters worse, over one-third of the world's population is under age 15 and has not reached reproductive age. They will provide a great momentum for further growth.

Discouraging trends are also visible in respect to the availability of contraceptives. Studies suggest that many women of reproductive age throughout the world do not want more children, but about half of them are not using effective methods of birth control. Furthermore, more than 80% of all married women in most countries studied in the World Fertility Survey have heard of contraceptives, but in some places such as Pakistan only one in ten women has ever used them. Another discouraging sign is the decline in nonmilitary, developmental foreign aid to poor countries, which has steadily fallen since 1960.

India One of the most visible signs of failure in population control is to be found in India, even though a national population control strategy has been in effect since 1951 (Figure 7-8).

India's family planning program was the first of its kind in the world. It all began when the census commissioner of India became alarmed at the large number of people counted in the 1951 census. Concerned by the potential impact of continued growth, he argued the necessity of a national program to reduce the birth rate. Believing that all births after the third child must be stopped, he recommended mass sterilization. Although his program was not initiated, the government did begin a small family planning program that year, but with little money and virtually no political support. The government began by promoting the rhythm method, which proved ineffective. Fifteen years later, the program was not much further ahead than it was in 1951.

In 1966 the first serious efforts at fertility control began. The Lippes loop, a type of intrauterine device (IUD), was chosen as an appropriate birth-control method to be inserted voluntarily in women. Condoms were distributed to men, and vasectomies were encouraged by the government.

Between 1969 and 1974 the government spent 2½ times as much money as was spent in the previous 18 years, but the program was still unsuccessful. The IUD insertion rate dropped, supposedly because of rumors that the IUD would swim in the bloodstream to the brain, that it stuck couples

Figure 7-9
Indira Ghandi, as Prime Minister of India, speaks to a crowd in Calcutta about her governmental policies.

together, and that it gave men a shock during intercourse. Counteracting the rumors was difficult.

The voluntary vasectomy program also failed, because Indian men were uncertain about the difference between sterilization and castration. One crew of medical personnel serving 49,000 people in more than 100 villages and actively campaigning for voluntary sterilization and IUD insertion performed only 47 vasectomies and 27 loop insertions in a ten-month period.

After years of failures and the threat of food shortages from overpopulation, India's government took a drastic step. On June 26, 1975, Prime Minister Gandhi declared a state of emergency (Figure 7-9). The previously mentioned "directive principles," overriding some personal rights, were added to the constitution and thus paved the way for compulsory sterilization. Two of India's eight states passed ordinances denying subsidized housing, maternity leave, and medical care to government employees who had refused to be sterilized after the second child. In Maharashtra, a bill calling for compulsory sterilization of all men with three living children was passed. Failure to comply would result in arrest. If for medical reasons a male could not be sterilized, his wife would have to be. The bill called for forced termination of any pregnancy that would result in the birth of a fourth child. The bill even allowed for payments of informers as well as economic incentives to those undergoing sterilization. Compulsory sterilization was unpopular and was eventually scrapped, although economic incentives are still offered to persons undergoing sterilization and to health workers recruiting and performing the operations.

Recently, India raised the minimum age for marriage from 18 to 21 years for males and from 15 to 18 for females, thus decreasing the number of childbearing years. The rate of growth has slowed from 2.6% in 1969 to 2.0%, but the population has risen to over 730 million (1984).

Why has India failed in its attempts to control population? India consists of eight states, so it is often said that it is not one country but many. Because India has 14 major languages, communication is poor. Illiteracy and poverty are prevalent and, no doubt, contribute to the failure. But so does the Indian culture, which places a high value on childbearing. In rural villages a young wife receives favored treatment only when she is pregnant. As in Asian societies, marriage in India occurs early among the majority of women, leading to early childbearing. Furthermore, because half the women who live to 59 are widowed, children, and especially sons, are a form of security for old age. Because nearly four-fifths of India's population lives in remote villages—of which there are about 560,000—reaching these people is difficult, time consuming, and costly. Thus, after years of government propaganda promoting fewer children, most couples in Indian villages are still convinced that children are economic assets.

The controversy over "solving" the world population growth problem remains. At present, we can attack population growth on several fronts, taking the best ideas of all. These include (1) increased foreign aid and the transfer of information to help develop appropriate technologies, (2) governmental programs to help stem the tide of population growth, and (3) agricultural development that is suitable to the climate, soil, energy resources, and economics of the various regions. (For more on agriculture, see Chapters 8 and 9.) Actions such as these may lead us to stabilized populations throughout the world, an essential step in achieving a sustainable society.

I cannot believe that the principal objective of humanity is to establish experimentally how many human beings the planet can just barely sustain. But I can imagine a remarkable world in which a limited population can live in abundance, free to explore the full extent of man's imagination and spirit.

PHILIP HANDLER

Summary

In nature, the *reproduction potential* of a species is held in check by a variety of *extrinsic* and *intrinsic factors*. Modern-day human societies employ special intrinsic factors to control population, including laws, governmental programs, and birth control.

Many experts believe that the growth of population and of resource use cannot continue indefinitely without overtaxing the earth's carrying capacity. This belief is supported by elaborate computer modeling studies, which suggest that the only route to a stable, sustainable society is achieving global zero population growth, recycling, controlling pollution, controlling soil erosion, replenishing soil, and emphasizing food production and services rather than industrial production.

Estimates of the world's carrying capacity range from 500,000 to over 100 billion. This range is wide primarily because of uncertainty regarding the potential supply of resources, lack of agreement over the desired standard of living, and uncertainty regarding the effects of technology on resource availability. Inasmuch as about one-fifth of the world's population lives in a state of extreme poverty without adequate food and shelter, some population experts believe that we have already exceeded the carrying capacity.

Three major views on population control have emerged in recent years. The *crisis environmentalists*, who believe that rapid population growth has already created an ecological crisis, support strict governmental action. The *family planners* are concerned with overpopulation but hold that most parents throughout the world have children they didn't plan for. They generally favor voluntary family planning promoted by governments as a means of controlling population. *Developmental distributivists* suggest that population growth will be brought under control by increasing wealth resulting from foreign aid and industrial development.

Family planning includes programs that allow couples to determine the number and spacing of offspring. Programs may be voluntary, extended voluntary, or forced.

Because the impact of each person in a developed country equals that of 25 to 38 persons in a developing country, many experts believe that the rich nations also have a moral obligation to control population growth. Developed nations can also assist the less fortunate with population control, agriculture, health care, and appropriate technology through financial aid and the sharing of information.

Many developing nations have instituted population control programs, although funds are often inadequate. Increasing expenditures on such programs could have many long-range benefits. To be effective, programs in such countries must take into account the effects of religious beliefs, psychological factors, and educational level.

No other issue in environmental science carries with it so many ethical components. To some, population control implies denial of one of the most basic and important of all human freedoms, the right to bear young. To others, it violates deep-seated religious beliefs. Still others believe that the right to reproduce should be curtailed when the rights of the individual interfere with the welfare of society. These individuals ask whether it is ethical *not* to control population.

Many encouraging signs of our increasing control over population have been visible in recent years. The world's growth rate has dropped, and population is expected eventually to stabilize somewhere between 8 billion and 15 billion. Progress in population control has been remarkable in many countries, especially China, Taiwan, Tunisia, Barbados, Hong Kong, Singapore, Costa Rica, and Egypt. Unfortunately, the population dilemma is far from being solved. In 1983, 35% of the world's population was under five years of age; this group will provide a great deal of momentum for further growth as it enters reproductive age. Per capita food consumption barely keeps pace with food production. In many countries only a small portion of the women practice birth control. One of the most frustrating situations has occurred in India, which after more than three decades of population control has failed to bring its population growth below 2%.

Discussion Questions

1. Debate the statement "We should actively seek to control population growth in order to avoid catastrophe."

2. Discuss the statement "The world cannot support the people it currently has at a decent standard of living."

3. Give reasons why countries that have experienced a rapid decline in the death rate may not be able to rely on increased economic development to bring their birth rate down.

4. Define family planning. Make a list of the three major types of family planning program. Give some specific examples of each.

5. The United Nations appoints you as head of population control programs. Your first assignment is to devise a population control plan for a developing country with rapid population growth rate, high illiteracy, widespread poverty, and a predominantly rural population. Outline your program in detail, justifying each major feature of the program. What problems might you expect to encounter?

6. Do you agree with the statement that even though developing countries such as India have more people than the developed countries, the latter pose a more significant threat to resources and the environment?

7. Describe ways that developed countries might aid developing countries in "solving" the population crisis.

8. Discuss the "value" of children in less developed countries. How do these views differ from those of the developed countries? Are they similar to or different from your views?

9. Describe the psychology of procreation.

10. Discuss reasons why the total fertility rate tends to be lower among more educated women.

11. Discuss general ways to ensure a high rate of success in population control programs.

12. Discuss the ethical questions "Do we have the right to have as many children as we want?" "Should that right be curtailed?"

13. What are the important human values described in this chapter? What is the collective good? Give examples of laws that restrict your personal freedom to benefit the whole of society.

14. Discuss the statement "If our actions rob the future, they cannot be viewed as ethical." Do you agree with this statement? Why or why not?

15. Discuss some of the encouraging and discouraging news regarding world population growth. What progress has been made? Where do we need to concentrate our efforts in the near future?

16. List the measures taken by India and China to control population growth. Why has India been unsuccessful and China successful?

Suggested Readings

Brown, L. R. (1983). *Population Policies for a New Economic Era* (Worldwatch Paper 53). Washington, D.C.: Worldwatch Institute. Informative reference.

Cole, H. S. D., Freeman, C., Jahoda, M., and Pavitt, K. L. R. (1973). *Models of Doom: A Critique of the Limits to Growth.* New York: Universe Books. Detailed rebuttal of *The Limits to Growth.*

Combs, B. J., Hales, D. R., and Williams, B. K. (1983). *An Invitation to Health: Your Personal Responsibility* (2nd ed.). Menlo Park, Calif.: Benjamin/Cummings. Excellent coverage of contraception.

Crooks, R., and Baur, K. (1983). *Our Sexuality.* Menlo Park, Calif.: Benjamin/Cummings. Excellent coverage of birth control.

Green, C. (1978). Voluntary Sterilization: World's Leading Contraception Method. *Population Reports* 2(March): 37–71. A detailed study of sterilization. Excellent reference material.

Hardin, G. (1972). *Exploring New Ethics for Survival: The Voyage of the Spaceship Beagle.* New York: Viking Press. A beautifully written exploration of ethics.

Hardin, G. (1982). Some Biological Insights into Abortion. *BioScience* 32(9): 720–727. Important reading.

Hatcher, R. A., Stewart, G. K., Stewart, F., Guest, F., Stratton, P., and Wright, A. H. (1978). *Contraceptive Technology 1978–1979* (9th ed.). New York: Halsted Press. A superb technical treatise on contraception.

Jacobsen, J. (1983). *Promoting Population Stabilization: Incentives for Small Families* (Worldwatch Paper 54). Washington, D.C.: Worldwatch Institute. Excellent paper.

Kendall, M. (1979). The World Fertility Survey: Current Status and Findings. *Population Reports* Series M(3): 73–103. An important survey of world fertility trends.

Kols, A., Rinehart, W., Piotrow, P., Doucette, L., and Quillin, W. F. (1982). Oral Contraceptives in the 1980s. *Population Reports* 10(6): 190–222. Thorough analysis.

Liskin, L., and Fox, G. (1982). IUDs: An Appropriate Contraceptive for Many Women. *Population Reports* 4(July): 101–135. Detailed analysis.

Meadows, D. H., Meadows, D. L., Randers, J., and Behrens, W. W. (1974). *The Limits to Growth* (2nd ed.). New York: Universe Books. Excellent study of population, resources, and pollution.

Mumford, S. D. (1982). Abortion: A National Security Issue. *The Humanist* 42(5): 12–42. Some interesting and controversial insights.

RESOURCES

Problems Facing World Agriculture

It is not in the stars to hold our destiny but in ourselves.
WILLIAM SHAKESPEARE

Thomas Jefferson once wrote that "civilization itself rests upon the soil." The first towns, early empires, and powerful nations can trace their origins to the deliberate use of the soil for agriculture. Today, the value of the soil remains high; whether you attend college, drive a cab, or work in a factory you are intimately linked to the soil, for it provides a variety of essential products from food to live on to wood to build homes. But as Neil Sampson once wrote, " [in most places on earth] we stand only six inches from desolation, for that is the thickness of the topsoil layer upon which the entire life of the planet depends."

This chapter discusses hunger, malnutrition, and many of the problems facing agriculture, which sets the stage for solutions to help us develop a sustainable world agricultural system that would preserve the vital link between civilization and the soil.

Worldwide Hunger and World Food Supply

In the developed countries, most people spend 10% to 25% of their incomes on food. But in the poor nations of Asia, Africa, and Latin America, many people spend up to

70% of their incomes on food. Even then, they often go hungry; and with so much money budgeted for food, there is little left for other necessities. By various estimates, hunger afflicts between 17% and 40% of the world's people. These people suffer from an inadequate food supply that may lead to **undernourishment** (lack of calories) or **malnourishment** (a lack of the proper nutrients and vitamins). About 15% of American people suffer from hunger, which is discussed in the Point/Counterpoint, "Hunger in America," in this chapter.

Malnutrition and Undernourishment

Throughout the world, tens of millions of people each year die of starvation and diseases linked to malnutrition. Many of them are children. About 10 million children under age 5 suffer from extreme malnutrition; most of them will die. Another 90 million children in this age group suffer from moderate malnutrition, which often worsens if a child develops an infectious disease or becomes infested with a parasite. It is not surprising to learn that between one-half and three-quarters of all deaths in children in developing countries result from malnutrition and infectious disease.

Many more children suffer from undernourishment. It is estimated that more than 230 million children under the age of 15 simply do not get enough to eat.

Many nutritional diseases are found throughout the world, but **protein–calorie malnutrition** in young children is the most widespread. The two main syndromes are **kwashiorkor** (resulting primarily from a lack of protein) and **marasmus** (resulting from an insufficient intake of protein and calories). Kwashiorkor and marasmus are two extremes of protein–calorie malnutrition. Most victims have symptoms of both diseases.

Kwashiorkor This condition is common in children one to three years of age and is prevalent in Latin America, Asia, and Africa. It is also found in areas of extreme poverty in developed countries. It generally sets in after children are weaned. No longer supplied with their mother's protein-rich breast milk and often fed a low-protein, starchy diet, the children show many signs of protein deficiency. These symptoms include retardation of growth; wasting of muscles in the arms and legs; accumulation of fluids in the body (edema), especially in the feet, legs, hands, and face; apathy and irritability; loss of hair and changes in hair texture and color; skin changes, especially a loss of facial pigment; and diarrhea (Figure 8-1). Irritable and lethargic, these children have no appetite and show little interest in their surroundings.

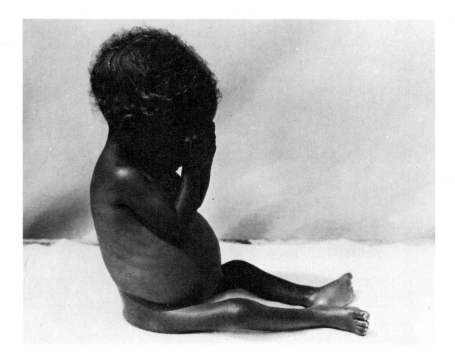

Figure 8-1
Kwashiorkor can lead to swelling of the arms, legs, and abdomen. Children are stunted, apathetic, and anemic.

Figure 8-2
Victims of marasamus await medical attention at a hospital in Angola. Survivors of malnutrition may be left with stunted bodies and minds.

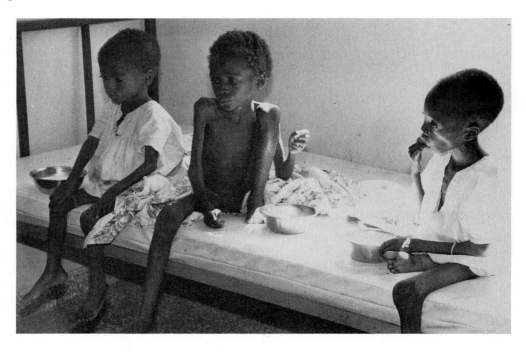

Marasmus   Occurring primarily in infants under the age of one, marasmus usually strikes children who are separated from their mother while breast feeding because of maternal death, a failure of milk production (lactation), or some other factor. Women in developing countries were often persuaded to switch from breast feeding to bottle feeding. Unable to afford enough formula, they diluted it with unsanitary water. If sterile practices are not followed, babies may contract infectious diseases that impair uptake of food, leading to marasmus. At least one producer of artificial milk has agreed to halt its promotional campaign and sale of formula.

Children with marasmus exhibit many of the symptoms of kwashiorkor, including growth failure, wasting of the limbs, anemia, and diarrhea. However, they remain mentally alert, do not develop edema, and are constantly hungry, often sucking on their hands or clothing (Figure 8-2).

For every case of marasmus and kwashiorkor there are hundreds of children with mild to moderate malnutrition, a condition much more difficult to detect. Like more severely malnourished children, they are prone to infectious disease.

Effects of Severe Malnutrition   There is growing evidence that malnutrition early in life leads to permanent retardation of physical growth. The more severe the deficiency, the more severe the stunting. A number of studies also indicate that childhood malnutrition may impair intellectual and psychological development, perhaps permanently, because 80% of the brain's growth occurs before the age of two. Early malnutrition may result in a lack of coordination and loss of intellectual ability, including language development and IQ.

Malnourished children who survive to adulthood may then be permanently impaired mentally. They become the working citizens of many poor countries. Perhaps plagued by malnutrition their whole lives, they provide little hope for improving agriculture, the literacy rate, and their economic level. Malnourished adults also remain prone to infectious diseases.

Vitamin A Deficiency   Rare in developed countries, vitamin A deficiency is a common cause of blindness in the developing world. About 100,000 children in developing countries develop symptoms of vitamin A deficiency each year.

The first noticeable symptom is a drying of the inner surface of the eyelids and the cornea. Untreated, persistent dryness leads to ulceration of the cornea. The ulcer may rupture, resulting in the loss of fluid from within the eye and infection. At this stage, blindness is inevitable.

Long-Term Challenges

More and more countries are losing the ability to feed their people. Many of the poor countries have become dependent on the wealthy nations such as Canada, Australia, and the United States with petroleum-based, mechanized agriculture. Food imports of the developing countries amounted to only a few million tons in 1950 but by 1981 had risen to more than 100 million tons. As the cost of energy rises, food may become too expensive for many of the world's poor. This chapter will explain why.

Many food and agricultural experts believe that unless decisive, far-reaching steps are taken, widespread starvation is inevitable; millions will perish in the poor countries. It would be foolish, they think, for the rich nations to think they would be immune to the upheaval that resulted.

How do we feed the world's people? Can't we simply grow more food? To answer these questions, let us first look at world food supply and demand.

From 1950 until 1970 improvements in agricultural production and expansion of the land area under cultivation had made significant inroads into world hunger. In this period, world per capita grain consumption increased by approximately 30%, resulting in a substantial improvement in the diet of many of the world's people. Since 1971, however, world food production has barely kept up with population growth. Because world population growth is not expected to stop in the near future, many experts predict that food supply will fall behind demand, creating even more widespread hunger and disease.

Four interrelated challenges face us: feeding the world's mal- and undernourished people, increasing food production to meet the needs of future generations, preventing deterioration of the soil and water, and developing a sustainable worldwide agricultural system. We will look at these solutions in detail in the next chapter. For now, let us examine the major problems facing world agriculture.

World Agricultural Problems

Climate Changes

Local and global climate may change naturally or as a result of human activities. Both types of change can profoundly affect agricultural production.

Between 1940 and 1980, the average global temperature declined 0.4° C (0.7° F). This has shortened the growing season in North America an average of nine days and has resulted in a slight decline in agricultural yield. The ways in which humans may have contributed to this temperature drop are discussed in Chapter 19.

Local climate is also subject to changes resulting from human activities. As described in Chapter 1, destruction of forests in the ancient Middle East reduced local rainfall. This reduction combined with a global shift toward aridity to foster the formation and spread of deserts (desertification) in poorly managed and overgrazed lands.

Beginning in 1968 a long-term drought in the Sahel region of Africa, coupled with poor agricultural practices and overpopulation, resulted in the rapid spread of desert southward in Mauritania, Mali, Niger, Chad, and Sudan (Figure 8-3). Approximately 250,000 people and millions of cattle died in six years. The Sahara is now spreading northward too, squeezing the people of North Africa against the Mediterranean. An estimated 100,000 hectares (250,000 acres) of rangeland and cropland are being lost in this region each year.

In Iran, Afghanistan, Pakistan, northwestern India, the United States, Australia, and Brazil, **desertification** destroys once-productive grassland and farmland (see Figure 8-3). According to the United Nations, approximately one-fifth of the world's cropland is experiencing desertification that will lead to long-term destruction.

Desertification is the result of many factors: the inherent fragility of the ecosystem in arid and semiarid (and even subhumid) regions, overgrazing, overcropping (planting too many crops per year), and plowing marginal lands. Overuse, in turn, stems from overpopulation and the failure of existing governments and land users to properly manage susceptible lands.

Soil Erosion

Soil erosion is a more critical problem than desertification. **Erosion** is the process by which rock and soil particles are detached from their original site by wind or water, transported away, and eventually deposited in another location. *Natural erosion* generally occurs at a slow rate, and new soil is usually generated fast enough to compensate.

This chapter primarily concerns itself with *accelerated erosion* resulting from human activities such as agriculture, mining, and rangeland misuse. In the short term, accelerated erosion decreases soil fertility, but in the long term it can destroy land outright.

Hunger in America

George Graham

George Graham is a doctor and a member of the White House Task Force on Food Assistance.

This interview with George Graham (GG) and Nancy Amidei (NA) was originally heard on "All Things Considered," a National Public Radio (NPR) program.

NPR: A White House Committee Task Force study released in January 1984 reported that hunger is not a massive problem in the United States. News of the study's findings have already caused controversy, and other recent reports, including one by the United States Conference of Mayors and another called the 1983 Massachusetts Nutrition Survey, have come to completely different conclusions. They say hunger in America is widespread, and because of federal spending cuts, is getting worse. But Dr. George Graham, a pediatrician and the only doctor on the White House Task Force on Food Assistance, says he stands behind the panel's findings. He told National Public Radio's Susan Stamberg the other reports have misread the facts.

DR. GEORGE GRAHAM: I think some of the studies claiming childhood malnutrition are honest distortions or misinterpretations of the data.

NPR: What do you mean, "misinterpretations," Dr. Graham?

G. G.: Do you know what we mean by percentiles? If you arrange a set of figures, like height of children at the age of seven, in rank order and there are 100 of them, the fifth percentile is the last five. In other words, the shortest five are below the fifth percentile. Now, some people are claiming that children

Nancy Amidei

Nancy Amidei is Director of the Food Research and Action Center.

who are under the fifth percentile in height for age are stunted due to chronic malnutrition, when in fact, the vast majority of those are just short children. Therefore, these are fanciful or totally erroneous interpretations.

NPR: But now these short children: do they come from any particular racial or ethnic background?

G. G.: Yes. If you load your sample with Hispanic Americans and Orientals particularly, you are going to get an excess of short children. There are racial differences and there are genetic differences; within the same race there's a wide range of the normal.

NPR: I've heard of something, Dr. Graham, called the Massachusetts Nutrition Survey. What about that?

G. G.: I've seen that data and looked at it very carefully. It's no different from the data from the National Nutrition Surveillance System. It's quite characteristic of the current U.S. population, and it does not show any excess of undernutrition. In fact, the introduction to that same document states that being under the fifth percentile does not make you, by itself, be classified as undernourished. There has to be clinical evidence of undernutrition. People have gone ahead and interpreted the data as if being under the fifth percentile meant malnutrition. Sure there are malnourished children; the abused, the neglected, the sick—and there may be some malnourished because of poverty—but there are precious few.

NPR: It sounds as if we're almost splitting hairs here. President Reagan the other week said something about "as long as one person is hungry in the United States, that's one too many." So why are we talking about racial groups, heights, weights all of this?

G. G.: I agree with the president. I think we all agree that it would be a disgrace for anybody to go hungry involuntarily. But there are thousands who do, voluntarily. But I think when you classify people as hungry or malnourished just because they are shorter than the average—and only on that basis— you're guilty of a very serious distortion of the facts.

NPR: You do feel, though, that there is hunger in the United States?

G. G.: Again, depending on how you define hunger. Hunger with undernutrition or malnutrition, yes, there is—particularly among street people and some of the elderly who are isolated. There are some children who are hungry and undernourished because of neglect or abuse, but this picture of massive hunger and malnutrition in the United States is a travesty!

NPR: A differing view now from Nancy Amidei, the director of Food Research and Action Center. She says it's Dr. Graham and his panel, not the authors of the disagreeing reports, who got the facts wrong.

NANCY AMIDEI: It's important to keep two things in mind: First, the studies are showing three times the expected number of growth-stunted children. Second, the people who have been doing the studies are professionals, trained in this area. They know the pitfalls, and they know what to look out for. They compare heights with weights. In other words, if you have children who are coming from a household full of short people, by having the weight compared with the height, you can take [the hereditary factor] into account. And they also, for example in the case of the State Department of Health Study that was carried out in Massachusetts, were very careful to check with the World Health Organization standards to make sure that they were using the appropriate standards for Southeast Asian children or for other children who might have come from immigrant families. They took all of that into account.

NPR: You're sure of that?

N.A.: Yes, I read the study myself just yesterday afternoon to make sure I hadn't missed something the first time through. They cite in their report the fact that they checked with the WHO standards and that these were the appropriate standards under the circumstances.

NPR: The study in Massachusetts said, I think, that there are more than 17,000 malnourished children in that state.

N.A.: They really said something a little bit different. They studied about 1400 children who come from low-income families and who are under the age of six. And based on that, they found that about 10% were chronically malnourished and about 3% were acutely malnourished. Now if you apply those findings from their study to the entire population of Massachusetts, then the number of children with problems related to malnutrition would be on the order of 10,000 to 17,000. That's where that number comes from.

NPR: When Dr. Graham was asked about the problem of hunger in America, he said that there are "precious few" people who are hungry in this country. How would you state that?

N.A.: Entirely differently! But then I have a lot more experience with it than Dr. Graham. It's worth keeping in mind that Dr. Graham as a member of this task force only attended two of the public hearings—and one of the two was the one in Houston where they did not allow members of the general public to testify. The only people who testified in Houston were handpicked witnesses—picked by Dr. Graham. So he didn't even go across the country listening to testimony! By contrast, I have spent a good part of the last two and a half years traveling across the country, and I can tell you from firsthand experience, as well as from a review of the studies and reports that are piling up in my office, that hunger is a problem that is national in scope and that has been growing with every passing month. The evidence is now voluminous. People like me who deal with emergency food providers on a regular basis ask the kind of questions that Dr. Graham ought to have been asking. I ask people, "Who's your typical client now? Can you describe him for me?" I asked that in a food pantry in Dallas not long ago, and the woman I was talking to said, "First I want to tell you who my typical clients were about a year and a half ago: elderly alcoholics and disoriented street people. Typical now is more likely to be a lifelong worker, now unemployed, with young children." Everywhere I go the answer is the same.

NPR: Dr. Graham was also quoted in another telephone interview (not on National Public Radio) as saying, "Don't tell me you are going to correct complex social problems by throwing food at them."

N.A.: Of course you aren't going to correct complex social problems, but you are going to correct the problem of hunger! It is self-evident that if you've got people without a source of food and you give them a source of food, they are going to be less hungry! It doesn't take a pediatrician to figure that out.

Extremely arid
Semiarid
High risk of desertification
Very high risk of desertification

Figure 8-3
Worldwide spread of deserts. Each year deserts claim about 70,000 square kilometers (27,000 square miles) of land. Over 37 million square kilometers (14 million square miles) are now threatened.

Sheet erosion results when water moves across the surface of the land, carrying soil with it. *Gully erosion* occurs when water cuts channels into the soil, forming gullies that deepen and widen at a remarkable rate. Both types of erosion decrease soil productivity, but gullies also impair the use of farm machinery.

Several factors affect the soil erosion rate, including (1) the amount of rain and snow, (2) the pattern of precipitation, (3) the terrain, (4) the type and amount of vegetation, (5) the condition of the soil, (6) the type and level of human activity, and (7) erosion-prevention measures. Figure 8-4 shows the effect of various types of vegetation on the soil erosion rate.

Wind also creates a major erosion problem, especially in the plains states. Especially vulnerable are soils of flat, open fields that are devoid of plant cover. Wind sweeping across cropless land can lift topsoil and transport it dozens, even hundreds, of kilometers.

In the United States about 2.7 billion metric tons (3 billion tons) of topsoil is lost from cropland and range-

land each year by water erosion alone. If this soil were loaded into freight cars, it would fill a train more than half a million kilometers (300,000 miles) long! Agricultural experts maintain that if crop production is to be sustained, soil loss must be cut by at least half.

Approximately 60 million hectares (150 million acres) of U.S. farmland have been seriously damaged by soil erosion in the United States. Each year 500,000 hectares (1.25 million acres) are destroyed. The average soil erosion rate from water on U.S. cropland is about 1.8 metric tons per hectare (5 tons per acre) but can reach 3.3 to 4.4 metric tons per hectare (9 to 12 tons per acre) in some areas (Table 8-1). Most good soils cannot sustain losses of more than 1.8 metric tons per hectare per year, equal to the average rate of soil formation. The tolerable rate of erosion is called the *T factor,* or the tolerance factor. Under natural conditions, a single inch of topsoil may require 300 to 1000 years to form. In agricultural land where crop residues are annually plowed under, an inch of topsoil forms in about 30 years.

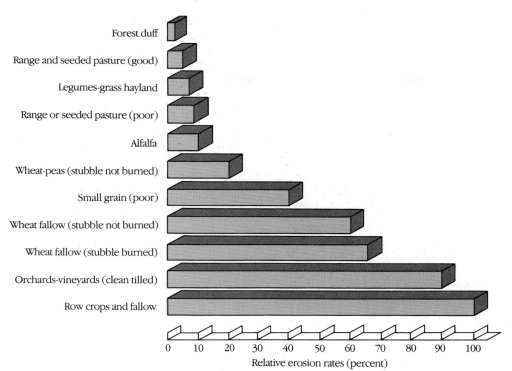

Figure 8-4
Relative soil erosion rate and
vegetative cover. Note that the
rate increases dramatically as
the amount of cover decreases.

Table 8-1 Soil Erosion from U.S. Cropland, 1977

Region	Sheet and Rill Erosion* (Metric Tons/Hectare)	Wind Erosion (Metric Tons/Hectare)
Northeast	2.42	NA**
North Central		
Lake States	0.8	NA
Corn Belt	2.94	NA
Northern Plains	1.32	0.8
South		
Appalachia	3.8	NA
Southeast	3.6	NA
Delta States	2.8	NA
Southern Plains	1.3	4.3
West		
Mountain***	0.7	2.2
Pacific****	0.6	NA
Average total	1.9	NA

Source: Scoville, O. (1980). Changes in Farmland: Policy Implications. *Population Bulletin* 36(5), p. 5.
*These values do not include streambank erosion.
**Not available.
***Does not include Arizona, Nevada, and Utah.
****Does not include Alaska and Hawaii.

So vital is the control of erosion that the U.S. Department of Agriculture wrote in a pamphlet, "The nation that destroys its soil destroys itself." It stands to reason that if soil destruction destroys nations, then soil conservation is a form of national defense (Figure 8-5).

Soil erosion is present in virtually all agricultural countries. Those with the least money for soil conservation usually have the worst problems.

Depletion of Soil Nutrients

In our study of ecology we learned that in mature ecosystems soil nutrients are cycled through food chains back into the soil for reuse. But humans can remove nutrients faster than they are replenished. In agriculture, soil nutrients such as nitrogen, calcium, sulfur, and potassium make up 10% of the plant biomass. Crop harvesting thus mines the soil of these nutrients and can gradually decrease cropland yield, especially on lands planted two or three times a year. To counteract this, nutrients can be replaced by adding manure, human waste, artificial fertilizers, or plant matter.

Soil erosion also depletes the soil of nutrients. The U.S. Department of Agriculture estimates that the annual cost of replacing nutrients lost from soil erosion alone in the United States is about $18 billion (in 1979 dollars).

Pesticides affect the productivity of soil, because they can destroy nitrogen-fixing bacteria that dwell in the soil. Studies show that persistent organochlorine pesticides such as DDT and endrin remain in sandy loam soil for 14 years or more, poisoning bacteria, blue-green algae, worms, insects, and the hundreds of other species that live there.

High Energy Cost and Diminishing Supplies

The availability of fossil fuels heavily affects the world food equation and will continue to do so as reserves shrink (Chapter 13). In the 1970s petroleum prices increased fivefold. This rise drastically increased food prices, since fuel costs affect many aspects of agricultural production, including fertilizer production, manufacturing of farm equipment, planting and cultivating, and the shipment and storage of farm products.

Figure 8-5
This hillside, which was cut to accommodate a road, has severely eroded.

Over half of the world's supply of natural gas and oil will have been consumed by 2000. Population and food demand are expected to be 50% above current levels, resulting in more costly agricultural products, and people will pay a much greater proportion of their income for food. More people will be unable to afford food and will become undernourished and malnourished unless solutions are found. See Model Application 8-1.

Water Mismanagement

Much of the world's agricultural output is dependent on irrigation from surface water and groundwater. Irrigation has been used for centuries to increase crop yields and allow farming in arid regions. In the United States, for instance, the amount of irrigated cropland has doubled since 1950. Today, one-eighth of all cropland is irrigated; this area produces approximately one-third of the country's entire agricultural output.

Several problems face irrigated agriculture worldwide: (1) depletion of groundwater, (2) competition for water supplies, (3) salinization, and (4) waterlogging of soil. Chapter 12, on water resources, discusses these problems in a wider context.

Agricultural Groundwater Depletion In parts of the American West, irrigation is indispensable for crop production. In Colorado, for instance, almost half of the cropland is irrigated. In many places, however, the rate of water withdrawal exceeds the inflow of water into underground reservoirs, or **aquifers**—zones of porous material (such as sandstone) which are saturated with water. Aquifers are naturally replenished by water from rain and snow, which percolate through the soil and rock from the surface of the earth in **aquifer recharge** zones.

Several regions in the United States are withdrawing groundwater faster than it can be recharged (Figure 8-6). This is called **groundwater overdraft**. The most notable

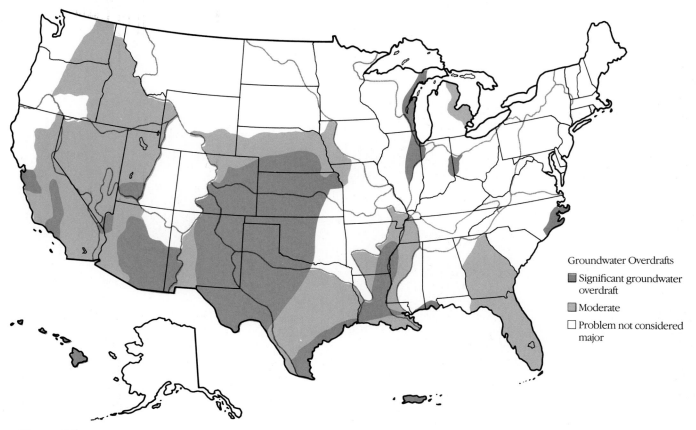

Groundwater Overdrafts

■ Significant groundwater overdraft

▨ Moderate

☐ Problem not considered major

Figure 8-6
Groundwater overdraft. Areas in color indicate regions where groundwater is being removed from aquifers by farmers, industries, and cities faster than it can be replenished.

>>> *Model Application 8-1*

Cross-Impact Analysis

In the poor nations of Asia, Africa, and Latin America, many people spend up to 70% of their income on food, leaving little money for any other necessities. Worldwide, tens of millions of people die of starvation each year. More alarming, about 10 million children under the age of five suffer from extreme malnutrition. Another 90 million are moderately malnourished. Evidence shows that malnutrition early in life leads to physical and mental retardation. Many experts suspect that mental retardation may be permanent, because 80% of the brain's growth occurs before the age of two.

Malnourished children may make it to adulthood. As adults, they may be plagued throughout the rest of their life by hunger. They offer little hope of improving agriculture, literacy, and economic wealth. Retardation from childhood and the lack of food in adulthood literally drain a society of its brainpower.

Illiteracy is very closely tied to poverty and hunger. Illiterates are the poorest, least well-fed, and least well-cared-for people in the world. Although many countries, such as Cuba and Nicaragua, have successfully reduced illiteracy, by 1990, 884 million people worldwide will still be unable to read and write. They cannot benefit from new machinery to increase productivity because many are unable to read the instructions to operate it. Many of the world's illiterates are women, a group in which the proportion of illiterates is growing larger year by year. Such women may never know how to properly nourish and educate their children. Birth control may be permanently out of their grasp.

Illiterates are trapped in a vicious circle. As long as millions live without adequate food, there is little hope of improving education, birth control, nutrition, and economic conditions. The lack of money in such regions translates into inadequate schools, teaching aids, and teachers. The schools that do exist may be miles from the rural villages, so few people can benefit from them. Making matters worse, many families keep their children at home to work in the fields to help earn money to pay for food and other necessities.

Poverty, hunger, illiteracy, and rapid population growth are all part of a cycle. To further understand the interactions between these factors, we can use cross-impact analysis, introduced in Chapter 2, which allows us to see how one set of factors affects another. This approach lets us dissect a problem to find all the underlying cause-and-effect relationships so we can better understand how to solve it.

Cross-impact analysis	Poverty	Hunger	Illiteracy	Rapid population growth
Poverty	X			
Hunger		X		
Illiteracy			X	
Rapid population growth				X

Step 1

Using cross-impact analysis, describe how rapid population growth, declining food supplies, illiteracy, and economic development are related in Third World nations. Some effects may be positive and others negative. Make two columns, one horizontal and the other vertical. Each should contain the four factors listed above. Then describe one by one how they interact. Be thorough, and study other references to expand your knowledge.

Step 2

Once you have finished your analysis, discuss ways to "solve" the problems. Specifically, what changes in population growth rate, illiteracy, food supply, and economic development are needed for Third World nations? What are the probable outcomes of each change you propose? How can these countries help themselves? In what ways can the developed nations lend assistance in this important task?

is the Ogallala aquifer underlying parts of Nebraska, Kansas, Colorado, Oklahoma, Texas, and New Mexico. To date, more than 150,000 wells have been drilled into this aquifer, mostly for agricultural irrigation. Some parts of the aquifer, which took approximately 25,000 years to fill, have been depleted in only a few decades; many wells have already been abandoned. By the end of this century many parts of the aquifer will have been drained, putting a stop to irrigated agriculture and causing enormous economic losses.

Competition for Water Groundwater used in homes and industries also depletes aquifers and thus affects irrigated agriculture. In Maricopa County, Arizona, between the late 1950s and the early 1970s, the amount of irrigated land fell by 20% partly as a result of increased water demand from Phoenix. The *water table,* which is the uppermost level of the groundwater, continues to drop 3 to 7 meters (10 to 20 feet) per year. Similar problems are prevalent in California but on a much larger scale, as water-hungry cities such as Los Angeles place a growing demand on limited groundwater supplies.

In many western states agriculture competes with energy companies for water. Neal Jensen of Cornell University predicts that water demand by the energy industry in the West will gradually eliminate irrigated agriculture there. Cities and industry generally can pay more for water than farmers; thus, demands created by population growth and economic development, if unchecked, will drive many farmers off some of our most productive land.

Depletion of groundwater will result in a steady decline in irrigated agriculture. Marginal irrigated land will be taken out of production first, forcing farmers to rely more heavily on rain-fed agriculture. In the long run the result will be a decrease in U.S. food production and food exports. To prevent this, more land could be farmed, at the cost of increased erosion, depletion of soil fertility, and loss of wildlife habitat. Good soil management, discussed in Chapter Supplement 9-2, could help maintain production and minimize land damage.

Waterlogging and Salinization Irrigating poorly drained fields often raises the water table, with two important consequences (Figure 8-7). First, if the water table rises too near the surface, roots of plants may drown as water fills the air spaces in the soil. This is called **waterlogging.** Second, water may evaporate from the soil, leaving behind salts such as calcium and magnesium sulfate

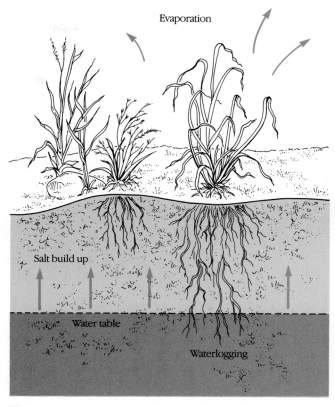

Figure 8-7
Salinization and waterlogging. Salts and other minerals accumulate in the upper layers of poorly drained soil (salinization). The rising water table saturates the soil and kills plant roots (waterlogging).

and calcium carbonate. The accumulation of these materials, called **salinization,** impairs plant growth.

Worldwide, one-tenth of all irrigated land suffers from waterlogging. As a result, productivity has fallen approximately 20% on this 21 million hectares (50 million acres) of cropland. Salinization is also common in many countries, including Pakistan, India, Iraq, Mexico, Argentina, and the southwestern United States. In Argentina alone, about 2 million hectares (5 million acres) of irrigated land has declined in productivity because of salinization.

Conversion to Nonagricultural Uses

Farmland throughout the world is being taken out of production by urbanization, energy production, transportation, and other nonfarm uses. In this **agricultural land**

Figure 8-8
Urban sprawl, as shown here in Des Moines, Iowa, swallows up farmland at an alarming rate.

conversion, roads, strip mines, shopping centers, housing developments, military installations, and airports remove land currently in production as well as potential farmland (Figure 8-8).

Every hour about 90 hectares (220 acres) of actual or potential farmland in the United States is converted to nonfarm uses. This is equivalent to about 2000 hectares (5000 acres) per day—or a strip one mile wide extending from New York City to San Francisco every year! In addition, about 600 hectares (1500 acres) of pastureland and rangeland is lost daily. The yearly loss of all forms of agricultural land thus amounts to about 950,000 hectares (2.3 million acres).

Some analysts assert that the annual loss of cropland in the United States to nonagricultural uses is not a threat to food production. They argue that current losses represent only a small portion of the 220 million hectares (540 million acres) of arable land. This view ignores two important considerations. First, farmland conversion is only one of many factors that destroy agricultural land. Every little bit hurts. Second, regional losses can be great. The 500,000 hectares (1.3 million acres) lost in two recent years in Colorado represents a 5% loss in arable farmland. Thirty states lost more land than Colorado.

Farmland conversion is a worldwide phenomenon. West Germany loses about 1% of its agricultural land by conversion every four years, and France and the United Kingdom lose about 1% every five years. Little is known about agricultural land conversion in the developing world, where the rate of urbanization and population growth is most rapid. Lester Brown of the Worldwatch Institute estimates that 25 million hectares (62 million acres) will be lost to urbanization between 1975 and 2000, enough land to feed 84 million people.

Conversion to Cropland "Fuel Farms" As the supplies of fossil fuels shrink, more people are turning to **fuel crops** such as corn and sugar cane, which can be converted to ethanol (ethyl alcohol) and burned in cars and other machinery. In the United States one part ethanol is mixed with nine parts gasoline making *gasohol.* In countries such as Brazil, cars and trucks now burn 100% ethanol.

Widespread adoption of ethanol threatens world agriculture (Figure 8-9). Brazil hopes to achieve complete self-sufficiency in automotive fuel with domestic ethanol production, which would require that half of its farmland be converted to fuel crops.

Some analysts project that the United States could eventually produce over 7.6 billion liters (2 billion gallons) of ethanol annually, but this would require 18 million metric tons (20 million tons) of corn or its equivalent—roughly one-fifth of the current exportable grain surplus. Production of this magnitude would require either the use of food destined for foreign markets or a marked increase in domestic production.

A reduction in grain exports would increase the trade deficit in the United States (the difference between imports and exports) worsening our economy. Reduced exports would probably also contribute to world food shortages,

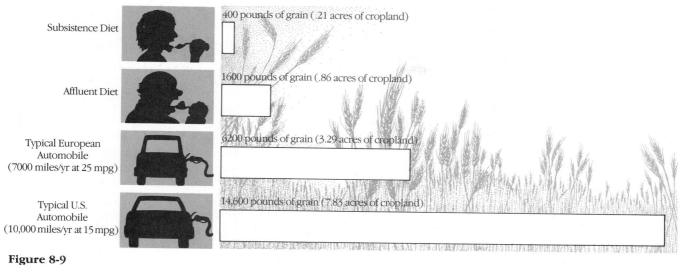

Subsistence Diet — 400 pounds of grain (.21 acres of cropland)

Affluent Diet — 1600 pounds of grain (.86 acres of cropland)

Typical European Automobile (7000 miles/yr at 25 mpg) — 6200 pounds of grain (3.29 acres of cropland)

Typical U.S. Automobile (10,000 miles/yr at 15 mpg) — 14,600 pounds of grain (7.83 acres of cropland)

Figure 8-9

Grain appetites: people versus cars. Competition for "food" is about to begin, with the wealthy car owners in a better position to pay.

because countries dependent on U.S. grain would be forced to turn to other suppliers, which might not have enough to go around. Most countries import grain today, and close to a dozen countries import more than half of the grain they consume each year. A shortage of grain for food could lead to increasing competition for existing grain supplies, which would undoubtedly raise the cost.

Another consideration is that grains would flow to sectors of the economy capable of paying the highest prices, such as the automotive fuel industry. Unless governments step in, the world's hungry will be competing for food with the automobile users of the world.

Brazilian officials argue that the increase in energy crop production will not be at the expense of current cropland but will be brought about by recruiting land currently out of cultivation. However, many agricultural experts believe that fuel crop production will compete for land, water, investment capital, fertilizers, farm managers, workers, roads, and other resources. Any significant fuel crop production program will affect food production.

Politics and World Hunger

Many of the world's food problems are political. A number of agricultural experts contend that there is plenty of food produced each year but that about half of the agricultural production in the less developed countries never reaches the tables. One reason is that well-intending gov-

ernments often become involved in the food production and distribution system. Such actions can actually reduce food supply or, in the case of the developed countries, make agriculture unprofitable.

How could this happen? Two ways are through price fixing and subsidies to farmers for production. The effects of such policies may often be difficult to discern. In Thailand, for example, the government charges a heavy tax on rice leaving the country. The money is then used to offset the cost of domestic rice, making it cheaper for city residents. The tax discourages farmers from increasing rice production for export. Their rice simply can't compete well in the world market. Experts who have studied the issue believe that Thailand's rice crop could eventually quintuple if the export tax were removed.

In the Soviet Union farmers are allowed to grow food on their own plots for private sale. Private production takes place on about 1% of the total agricultural land, yet it accounts for about one-fourth of that country's annual production. This suggests that government-managed collective farms are failing at the task of food production.

Government policies also have many subtle long-range impacts on agricultural production. For instance, in the United States a federal program called Payment in Kind (PIK) encourages farmers not to produce crops on land to reduce grain gluts that tend to drive prices down. The program works like this: Farmers who have cultivated land for more than two years can take that land out of production; to offset possible losses, the government gives them a grain payment from federal stockpiles amounting to 80% to 95% of their expected production. The farmer is then free to sell the grain on the market.

The most profitable strategy is to plow and plant marginal land for a few years and then take it out of production to collect grain payments. Some speculators purchase land strictly for this purpose. However, much of this land is former rangeland that is highly erodible if not managed properly. Through payment in kind, critics argue, the government may be encouraging soil erosion on lands that might be farmed or used as rangeland sometime in the future in conjunction with soil conservation.

Loss of Agricultural Diversity

In recent times farmers have eliminated many different breeds of animals and varieties of plants (cultivars) from their farms. In addition, the wild relatives of cultivated plants are being destroyed by expanding human settlements. These two trends represent a loss of *genetic diversity,* which may have a significant effect on world agricultural production.

Before the advent of modern agriculture, rice, wheat, corn, soybeans, sorghum, barley, potatoes, cassava (a tropical plant with an edible root rich in starch), and other vegetables existed in thousands of varieties. Now, only a few of these varieties are used; many have been lost forever. In India, for instance, more than 5500 varieties of rice were once cultivated, but today only a few dwarf varieties are in use. These were adopted during the mid-1960s because of their increased yield when artificially fertilized. Similar reductions have occurred worldwide, especially in the United States (Table 8-2).

Numerous breeds of livestock are also being lost as ranchers throughout the world adopt breeds developed for maximum yield in American-style feedlots. This trend is especially notable in Europe and the Mediterranean region, where the Food and Agricultural Organization of the United Nations estimates that 115 breeds of cattle face eventual replacement by a few new breeds. In England many of the local strains of sheep, swine, and beef cattle either have disappeared or are so rare that they are no longer available for commercial breeding. In the United States the Holstein cow accounts for 70% of the entire dairy herd.

There are many reasons for this loss of variety. The new types often have higher yield on mechanized farms. Between 1930 and 1976 American wheat farmers doubled their yields this way; corn growers increased their yields by four times. Dwarf wheat and rice varieties developed in the 1960s are better suited for machine harvesting, because their stalks are less likely to topple during harvesting. They also respond to irrigation and fertilizer by producing more grain, whereas many older varieties simply grow taller.

There are also purely economic reasons for the popularity of new high-yield varieties. One of the primary reasons is that it is easier and more profitable for large seed companies to produce and sell a few major varieties. Restricting production and sales to a few varieties greatly reduces cost and increases profit.

The Green Revolution   The development of high-yield varieties in the 1960s is part of a worldwide agricultural movement often called the **Green Revolution**. It began in 1944 when the Rockefeller Foundation and the Mexican

Table 8-2   Limited Diversity in American Agriculture

Crop	Varieties Available	Major Varieties in Use	Percentage of Total Production
Corn	197	6	71
Wheat	269	10	55
Soybeans	62	6	56
Rice	14	4	65
Potatoes	82	4	72
Peanuts	15	9	95
Peas	50	2	96

Source: Reichart, W. (1982), Agriculture's Diminishing Diversity, *Environment* 24(9): 6–11, 39–44.

Figure 8-10
Comparison of an old variety of wheat (sides) with a new short-stemmed variety (middle). The first of the short-stemmed varieties was developed under the direction of Norman Borlaug.

government established a plant-breeding station in northwestern Mexico. The program was headed by Norman Borlaug, a University of Minnesota plant geneticist, who concentrated this station's efforts on developing a high-yield wheat plant (Figure 8-10). Before the program began, Mexico was importing half of the wheat it consumed each year, but by 1956 Mexico was self-sufficient in wheat production. In 1964 it exported half a million tons.

The success in Mexico led to the establishment of another plant-breeding center in the Philippines. High-yielding rice strains developed there were introduced into India in the mid-1960s. Again, the results were spectacular. India more than doubled its wheat and rice production in less than a decade and has become self-sufficient in wheat production.

The threat of decreasing agricultural diversity often overshadows such successes. One of the most important concerns is the loss of genetic resistance to disease. Local varieties of plants are acclimated to their environment; natural selection has ensured this. New varieties, in contrast, often have little resistance to insects and disease. Moreover, the planting of monocultures facilitates the growth and spread of disease and insects. The potato famine in Ireland in the 1840s is one famous example. Only a few varieties of potatoes imported from South America were planted in Ireland. When a fungus *(Phytophthora infestans)* began to spread among the plants, there was little to stop it and no backup supply of resistant seed potatoes. Within a few years, 2 million Irish perished from hunger and disease. An additional 2 million emigrated. In the United States southern corn-leaf blight destroyed one-quarter of the corn crop in 1970. In 1980 the American peanut crop, consisting of two varieties, was almost entirely destroyed by drought and disease. High-yield hybrids are also generally less resistant to drought and flood. For example, farmers in regions of Pakistan that are prone to flooding have found that the older, tall varieties withstand occasional high water better than the new, short, high-yield varieties.

Limiting genetic variety in agriculture has its advantages and disadvantages. The future will require plants and animals that can survive climatic changes, drought, disease, and insects. However, within 5 to 15 years after the development of a new disease-resistant plant, disease organisms themselves evolve to make that resistance ineffective. This necessitates the continual development of new disease-resistant plants, partly through **genetic engineering** and plant breeding. Scientists will need to draw on numerous crop and livestock varieties that are now quickly diminishing to create high-yield, resistant plants and animals. The need for these varieties will never end (see Essay 8-1).

New Hope from Old Corn

In a forest in southwestern Mexico in 1979, four scientists discovered a few tiny patches of a wild, weedy-looking grass that could have enormous impact on corn production throughout the world. *Zea diploperennis,* a primitive near-relative of modern corn numbering only a few thousand stalks, sets itself apart from all modern corns because it is a perennial, rather than an annual, plant. To you or me that may not seem very impressive, but to geneticists, the engineers of new corn breeds, it's the discovery of the century.

How do geneticists affect corn production? The difference between the harvests of 1930 and 1980 gives us that answer. Harvests more than quadrupled in those 50 years—from 20 bushels per hectare to 100 to 250 bushels—because of successful crossbreeding.

Corn, like any other crop, is only as good as the genetic "boosts" it receives—that is, the genetic infusions of fresh germ plasm (genes) that give it its genetic resistance to disease, drought, insects, and so on. Genetic vigor results in large har-vests, and because corn accounts for one-fourth of the world's cereal grains, a large harvest is always crucial.

Geneticists get new germ plasm from wild, grassy plants and from peasant-cultivated varieties, called primitive cultivars. These wild strains aid them in developing disease-resistant, versatile breeds that grow as well in Mexico as they do in Alaska. But sometimes disaster strikes. In 1970 it came in the form of a leaf fungus that threatened much of North America's corn crop that year. It wasn't until 15% of the crop had been destroyed that geneticists were able to come up with a blight-resistant germ plasm from Mexico to halt the disease. Hence, breeders are always on the lookout for the very rare, new corn plasms that could help produce hardier, more resistant plants.

Thus, it should be easier to understand why the wild corn discovery in Mexico was met with such excitement. The primitive corn is special not only because it is a perennial but also because it is highly resistant to several diseases. Because it is genetically similar to annuals, it can be crossbred with conventional corn. The result: a very resistant perennial hybrid corn plant that grows like grass—a crop that comes up on its own each year—saving farmers annual costs of plowing and sowing. The potential savings can be enormous, projected up to $155 per hectare ($60 an acre), saving billions of dollars a year worldwide.

Though all of this is good news, some contend that perennial crops tend to produce less than annuals and will produce even smaller quantities after a few years because they grow on the same patch of land. In the United States, where large harvests are required, this could create problems, but in some Third World countries, where harvests are not as much the issue as are cutting costs, this perennial could be the answer. Farmers and economists will continue to debate this issue, but in the meantime geneticists will persist in their search for new germ plasm from the lost plasm of modern crops.

Flood Damage, Pesticides, and Air Pollution

Floods may deposit sediment on farmland and destroy crops. In the United States, flooding costs farmers about $1.3 billion a year. Floods are natural phenomena, but human intervention in the ecosystem may contribute significantly to their occurrence and severity. (For more on flooding, see Chapter 12.)

Pesticides affect agriculture in a variety of ways, as discussed in Chapter Supplement 9-1.

Air pollution also takes its toll on agriculture, either indirectly by damaging soil or directly by damaging plants, especially leafy crops and seedlings. At least 36 crops grown commercially are adversely affected by air pollution. Especially harmful are ozone, sulfur dioxide, and acid precipitation (see Chapter 19).

The agricultural expert R. Neil Sampson once noted that "the progress of civilization has been marked by a trail of wind-blown or water-washed soils." Poor land management still exists today, contributing to an ever-widening destruction of the renewable soils that civilization rests upon. In the next chapter we will look at ways to stop this trend and develop a sustainable agricultural system that provides food for all the world's people, now and in the future.

The harvest is past, the summer is ended, and we are not saved.

Jeremiah 8:20

Summary

Throughout the world, tens of millions of people die each year of starvation and diseases worsened by malnutrition. *Protein–calorie malnutrition* in children, the major nutritional disease worldwide, takes two main forms. *Kwashiorkor* results from a lack of protein and is common in children one to three years of age, generally occurring after children are taken off their mother's milk. *Marasmus,* resulting from an inadequate protein and calorie intake, occurs in children under the age of one and usually develops when they are separated from their mother while breast feeding. Many children suffer symptoms of both disorders.

There is growing evidence that malnutrition early in life leads to a permanent retardation of mental and physical growth. Unless widespread and far-reaching steps are taken, many people in the poor nations will starve or succumb to disease.

Satisfying future food demand and feeding those people alive today are two of the major challenges facing farmers and government officials. But many problems stand in the way. Climate changes resulting from deforestation and pollution may severely disrupt global agriculture. The spread of deserts, *desertification,* is occurring in many parts of the world as a result of natural climatic shift and poor land management. Millions of acres of rangeland and farmland become desert each year.

Soil erosion, which accounts for the loss of 2.7 billion metric tons of soil in the United States each year, impairs long-term agricultural productivity and lessens our chances of meeting long-term food needs. Erosion is one of the factors contributing to depletion of soil nutrients, which may also result from the extended use of artificial fertilizers, intensive farming, and pesticides. Depletion also threatens long-term productivity. Dwindling supplies of fossil fuels, which are needed for all phases of agricultural production, are another major concern. Falling supplies will inevitably result in rising prices, making grain unaffordable to many poorer nations.

Groundwater overdraft now threatens agriculture throughout the world. In many regions where the rate of water withdrawal exceeds *aquifer recharge,* the long-term prospects for agriculture are dim. Competition for irrigation water has also intensified in recent years. Energy companies and expanding cities now compete with farmers for scarce water. Who wins this competition will profoundly affect our future. Irrigation of poorly drained land results in *waterlogging*—the saturation of air spaces in the soil, which suffocates plants—and *salinization*—the buildup of salts in soils.

Agricultural land is also being taken out of production by urbanization, energy production, and road construction. Added to many other problems, such *agricultural land conversion* becomes a significant factor to control if we are to meet future food demands. The cultivation of crops to make ethanol to run cars, trucks, and other machinery will increase in the United States and other countries such as South Africa, Brazil, and Australia. Production of *fuel crops* is viewed by many experts as a potential threat to agricultural output.

Many of the world's food problems are political. Experts maintain that there is plenty of food produced each year, but about half of the agricultural production in developing nations never reaches the tables of the hungry, in part because of government meddling. Certain governmental policies may affect food production and exports in subtle ways. Government subsidies and export taxes have noticeably adverse effects on output.

Mechanized agriculture has been built on a foundation of machinery, energy, fertilizers, pesticides, and a limited number of crops. The loss of species diversity concerns many food experts, who believe that it may result in a system of agriculture more vulnerable to insects, disease, drought, and other natural calamities than one based on higher diversity. The *Green Revolution,* the development of high-yield varieties, was largely responsible for limiting the number of commercially valuable varieties of plants. Special breeding programs resulted in the development of high-yield rice, wheat, and other crops, which greatly increased agricultural output worldwide. However, the new varieties proved unsuccessful if irrigation water and fertilizer were not available. Today, new research in plant genetics and *genetic engineering,* the artificial manipulation of genes aimed at improving plants (and other organisms) for human use (discussed in the next chapter), is directed toward developing species that have high yield and resistance to insects, disease, drought, and other natural factors that might decrease yield.

Although the problems presented in this chapter may seem overwhelming, it is heartening to know that many solutions can be found to help us feed the world's people now and in the future. These are discussed at length in the next chapter.

Discussion Questions

1. What percentage of the world's population is malnourished? What are the short- and long-range effects of malnutrition?

2. Describe the symptoms of kwashiorkor and marasmus.

3. Describe trends in world population between now and the year 2000. How will these affect food demand?

4. What has happened to world per capita food supply in the past two decades? Is it increasing fast enough to keep up with the population growth?

5. How do local and global climate changes affect agricultural production? In what ways do we affect climate?

6. Where is desertification most prominent? What factors contribute to desert formation?

7. Describe the magnitude of the soil erosion problem in the United States. How much soil is lost each year? What problems does this create? How does soil erosion affect our long-range agricultural productivity?

8. What is a tolerance, or T, factor? What determines the T factor?

9. What are some factors that contribute to soil erosion and soil nutrient depletion?

10. How do the supply and demand for energy, especially oil and natural gas, affect world agriculture in developed and less developed countries?

11. Is it inevitable that the United States will lose valuable irrigation land? Why or why not? What impact would the loss of this land have on U.S. agricultural production?

12. Describe waterlogging and salinization of soils. How widespread are these problems?

13. Agricultural land conversion to nonfarm uses has created a significant amount of concern. Is this concern justified? Why? Support your answer.

14. Describe what might happen to U.S. agricultural exports if ethanol production increased to the point that it became a major source of automotive fuel. What effect would this have on food supply, especially in developing countries?

15. In what ways do government price supports for farmers, export taxes, and import taxes affect world agricultural production?

16. Describe the trend of decreasing agricultural diversity. How could this affect world agriculture? Give some examples to back up your arguments.

Suggested Readings

Brown, L. R. (1978). *The Worldwide Loss of Cropland* (Worldwatch Paper 24). Washington, D.C.: Worldwatch Institute. A comprehensive analysis of the loss of agricultural lands.

—.(1980). Fuel Farms: Croplands of the Future? *The Futurist* 14(3): 16–28. A well-written paper on one of the many threats to agricultural productivity.

—.(1982). The Food Connection: Transforming the U.S.–Soviet Relationship. *The Futurist* 16(6): 9–16. Insightful and well-documented view of the role of food in the power play between two superpowers.

Dudal, R. (1982). Land Degradation in a World Perspective. *Journal of Soil and Water Conservation* 37(5): 245–249. Excellent review of land requirements for expanding agriculture.

George, S. (1977). *How the Other Half Dies*. Montclair, N.J.: Allenheld and Osmun. A superb book on world hunger.

Gore, R., and Gerster, G. (1979). An Age-Old Challenge Grows. *National Geographic* 156(5): 594–639. A vivid view of worldwide desertification.

Jackson, W. (1980). *New Roots for Agriculture*. San Francisco: Friends of the Earth. Good discussion of fuel crops, sustainable agriculture, and other issues.

Latham, M. C., McGandy, R. B., McCann, M. B., and Stare, F. J. (1972). *Scope Manual on Nutrition*. Kalamazoo, Mich.: Upjohn. An excellent treatment of malnutrition.

McHale, M. C., McHale, J., and Streatfield, G. F. (1979). *Children in the World*. Washington, D.C.: Population Reference Bureau. Filled with important statistics on nutrition, sanitation, health, and the like.

Reichert, W. (1982). Agriculture's Diminishing Diversity. *Environment* 24(9): 6–11; 39–44. A superb discussion of the loss of diversity among crops and domestic livestock and the potential problems.

Richardson, N., and Stubbs, T. (1978). *Plants, Agriculture, and Human Society*. Menlo Park, Calif.: Benjamin/Cummings. Contains many suggestions for alternative agricultural practices.

Sampson, R. N. (1981). *Farmland or Wasteland: A Time to Choose*. Emmaus, Pa.: Rodale Press. Well-written book on world agriculture.

Scoville, O. J. (1982). Changes in Farmland: Policy Implications. *Population Bulletin* 36(5): 1–13. A thorough analysis of the threats to U.S. agricultural production.

Sheridan, D. (1981). Western Rangelands: Overgrazed and Undermanaged. *Environment* 23(4): 14–20; 29–37. An in-depth look at rangeland abuse in the U.S.

9

Feeding the World's People

You cannot escape the responsibility of tomorrow by evading it today.

ABRAHAM LINCOLN

According to a French proverb, it is in the knowledge of our follies that we show superior wisdom. In the last chapter we saw how a lack of rational conduct in soil and water management—our agricultural follies—have contributed to the decay of world agriculture. Contrary to the proverb, though, we do not show wisdom simply by knowing our errors; we must also act on our knowledge. As James Mabbe once wrote, "A wise man altereth his purpose, but a foole persevereth in his folly."

This chapter explores some of the solutions to the problem of world hunger. First in importance is population control (Chapter 7). Beyond that, we can find more agricultural land; grow more on it; develop alternative foods; reduce food losses in production, storage, and distribution; and increase agricultural self-sufficiency in developing nations.

Increasing Amount of Agricultural Land

Increasing the cropland and rangeland can be achieved by (1) exploiting farmland reserves, (2) preventing desertification, and (3) preventing soil erosion.

185

Exploiting Farmland Reserves

Food production in the United States, the world's leading agricultural nation, will probably increase in the next few decades to meet growing domestic demands. By the year 2000, there will be 50 million to 60 million more Americans. If per capita food consumption remains the same, food demand will increase about 20%.

U.S. food production also serves many foreign countries. American grain exports amounted to more than 120 million metric tons (133 millon tons) in 1983. Two-thirds of U.S. wheat and rice and about half of the cotton, soybeans, and dry edible beans are shipped abroad. U.S. grain exports represent about one-tenth of all the grain consumed by the rest of the world.

How fast will the foreign markets grow? Estimates of increases in demand vary from 2.3% to 6.5% per year between 1980 and 2000. Can the United States meet the future demands? How much land will it take? What will the consequences be?

The United States has 167 million hectares (417 million acres) of arable land and an additional 51 million hectares (127 million acres) in privately owned pasture, forest, and other land with high to medium potential for agriculture. Projected increases in foreign demand would require the land under cultivation to increase by 9 million to 47 million hectares (22 million to 117 million acres), depending on who does the estimating. Additional domestic demand could require another 15 million to 32 million hectares (37 million to 80 million acres). Taking into account increased domestic demand, many analysts believe, the United States can meet foreign demands up to the year 2000 even with losses from conversion of land to nonagricultural uses.

On the surface the immediate prospects seem good. However, these estimates do not include factors that may reduce the supply of farmland, such as the development of fuel crops, the gradual deterioration of the soil, the impacts of widespread air pollution, and depletion of groundwater (Chapter 8). Nor do they look beyond 2000.

Increasing the amount of agricultural land in the United States beyond 2000 will be difficult. Thus, it's necessary to look outside the United States for more arable land to help meet the rising demand for food.

According to the Food and Agriculture Organization, 1.4 billion hectares (3.4 billion acres) of land is available for production in less developed countries, most of it in Africa and South America. In Africa, for example, only 21% of the potentially cultivable land is in use, and in South America only 15% is being farmed. In contrast, 92% of the potential agricultural land is being farmed in Southeast Asia. In southwestern Asia, more land is currently being used than is considered suitable for rain-fed agriculture. Using untapped agricultural land can help solve the impending food crisis, but it will be at the cost of wildlife and its habitat.

Reducing the Spread of Deserts

Throughout the world, people are working to stop the spread of deserts that are destroying potential farmland and rangeland. Their efforts include proper rangeland management (Chapter 11), revegetation, wind erosion control (Figure 9-1), avoiding the use of marginal lands, and irrigating. In Australia, for example, huge semicircular banks of earth are created in the windswept plains to catch seeds and encourage regrowth in areas denuded by cattle and sheep. In Iran migrating sand dunes are sprayed with an oily residue left over from oil production. The liquid dries on the surface and forms a gray mulch that retains soil moisture and facilitates the growth of drought-resistant plants. Within six years oil-mulched sand dunes seeded with drought-resistant plants are green with vegetation. These efforts have increased the supply of valuable wood and have helped slow the spread of blowing sand. Similar measures are needed on almost every continent.

In 1977 the U.N. Conference on Desertification, held in Nairobi, Kenya, developed a world plan of action. It called for (1) long-term efforts to reduce desertification, halting it by 2000; (2) reclamation of land already lost to deserts; and (3) financial support in the form of international aid.

Conserving the Soil

Worldwide soil conservation could also help us reduce the loss of farmland and meet future food demands. The rich nations as well as the poor would benefit from it. To date, however, farmers in both the developed and developing countries have done little to reduce soil erosion. In the developing world farmers struggle to meet their most basic needs and have neither the time nor the means to care properly for the land. Furthermore, few can see the benefits of soil conservation, because the gains tend to materialize slowly and usually take the form of a decrease in losses rather than an increase in actual food output, a result that is difficult to see.

Economic factors impair soil-erosion control in the developed nations (a problem discussed in detail in Chapter 24). Caught between high production costs and low

Figure 9-1
Amongst the vegetation to the left are 7-year old trees, which in time will protect the land from such severe erosion, as shown on the right.

prices for grains, farmers may ignore the long-term effects of soil erosion while using synthetic fertilizers to maintain yield in the short term.

There are a number of important principles for long-term soil management. First, we must work to ensure a sustainable agricultural system. Second, farmers should play an integral role in developing and executing soil conservation measures. Third, new management strategies should be introduced only after they have proved successful. Fourth, strategies should be affordable for the farmer, and the most cost-effective strategies should be used whenever possible. Adherence to these principles will not necessarily result in success but will go a long way toward reducing the problem.

Increasing Yield

Another major approach to feeding the world's people is to increase the yield of agricultural lands. This can be done by developing new varieties of plants and animals, by soil enrichment programs, and by increasing the efficiency of irrigation.

New Plant and Animal Varieties

As discussed in Chapter 8, new high-yield varieties of rice and wheat developed during the Green Revolution were widely thought to represent our greatest hope of raising crop output. Under proper growing conditions, these new strains produce three to five times as much grain as their predecessors. The new varieties of plants are **hybrids**, the offspring of two closely related plants bred to combine the best features of the parents.

As the hybrids were introduced into many poor nations, the hopes of the Green Revolution dimmed, for the new varieties require large amounts of water and fertilizer, unavailable in many areas. Without these, yields are not much greater than those of local varieties. In some cases yields are even lower. In India new rice and wheat hybrids replaced high-protein legumes such as chickpeas, needed for proper nutrition. Finally, the new varieties have contributed to the loss of genetic diversity. New plants are often more susceptible to insects and disease.

The Green Revolution, now written off by its critics as a failure, is the first step in a long, tedious process of plant breeding aimed at improving yield. Today, plant breeders are developing crops with a higher nutritional value and resistance to drought, insects, disease, and wind. Plants with a higher photosynthetic efficiency are in the offing. Efforts are even under way to incorporate the nitrogen-fixing capability of legumes in cereal plants such as wheat, a change that would decrease the need for fertilizers and reduce soil nitrogen depletion.

Some researchers are exploring the use of perennial crops for agriculture. **Perennials** are those plants that produce flowers, fruit, or seeds year after year from the same root system. Today, most agricultural crops are annuals, which must grow anew from seeds each year. Preliminary research suggests that productivity from perennials may be equal to or slightly lower than conventional annuals such as wheat, but the benefits from soil conservation,

Breaking New Ground

Robert Rodale

The author is chairman of the board of Rodale Press and editor of Organic Gardening and Farming, Prevention, The New Farm, *and* Rodale's New Shelter. *He is a devoted environmentalist, an advocate of self-sufficient living, and president of the Soil and Health Society. He has also written several books.*

The United States has sufficient resources to produce more than enough food and fiber to meets its needs, with a large amount left over for export. We have more good land in favorable climatic regions than any other nation. We have ample water in many areas and large numbers of skilled, hard-working people. Plus we have a large research establishment, and our farmers use many forms of advanced agricultural technology.

Given all those blessings, we have every right to expect agriculture to be free of problems. Yet despite a level of production that is the envy of the world, our farm sector is deeply troubled. One of our most serious short-term economic problems is surplus production. But those unneeded piles of corn and other crops are not merely temporary signs that the weather has been good; they are a sign of a basic fault in the farming system.

The fault that surpluses signal is this: farmers are using methods that do not allow flexibility in the amount they produce. Conventional American agriculture works only when the throttle governing flows of energy, fertilizers, and pesticides is pulled all the way out. Farmers lack the option of switching easily to an alternate system that works well with low levels of such exterior aids yet still provides reasonable levels of production permanently without erosion.

Farm structure is an important factor. "Get big or get out," farmers are told. That advice means buy more land, borrow if necessary, buy bigger machines, build more productive capacity in all ways, and then look for the payoff in higher production. On the surface that strategy looks good to the farmer, but if the economy declines, if farm prices fall, the farmer is in big trouble. There is no way to put the system in reverse.

Our need for food is so great that we have great difficulty dealing with ideas ·of food production that don't make high yields the first priority. It is almost as if there is something morally wrong about planning a food system that produces less while giving strong consideration to other important values.

To increase production, farmers try to dominate nature. This approach to agriculture leads farmers toward self-destruction, both economically and biologically. To dominate nature, farmers turn to excessive amounts of nonrenewable resources, which are continually increasing in price.

Fortunately, alternatives to dominance exist. Organic farming is one. By avoiding synthetic fertilizers and pesticides, a farmer can give up the tools of dominance for more natural fertilizers and a totally biological approach to insect control. Eventually, the role of organic farmers should extend toward a much broader and more valuable concept I call *regenerative agriculture,* a system depending on a high degree of free goods that nature provides. We can add regenerative components to the present system bit by bit.

One component would be perennial crops. When people began to cultivate grass plants such as wheat and rye many thousands of years ago, they selected the annuals. Raising annuals meant digging the soil every year, weeding, and finding a way to store the seed for next year's planting. Common perennial grasses that produce seed of good nutritional value were ignored. Because of those decisions centuries ago, annuals like wheat, rice, oats, and barley are still the primary grains people eat.

Even today, farmers have ignored the vast range of perennial grasses that could be adapted for seed production. By using the modern breeding methods, many could be domesticated and put to use. Imagine how much easier and more efficient a regenerative system based on perennial crops would be. There would be much less need for tillage. Weed control would be simplified. Water management would be easier, because perennial grasses would store more moisture in their sod. Soil would gradually increase in fertility. At the very least erosion would be stopped.

Conceptually, the road to a regenerative agriculture is simple. All we need to do is look at problems in a different way. When a problem arises, the regenerative farmer would look for the solution within the strength of nature. The farmer would ask, "How can I insert myself and my interests within nature's plan and get a better deal for myself?"

soil nutrient retention, and energy savings may overwhelmingly favor such a system. Further benefits are discussed by Robert Rodale in his Viewpoint, "Breaking New Ground."

Just as new varieties of plants help increase yield, so do fast-growing varieties of fowl and livestock. For example, the introduction of a new crossbred broiler chicken has been a remarkable success. The new breed reaches marketable size in eight to ten weeks on 2 kilograms (4.5 pounds) of grain. Conventional breeds require twice as much food and time to reach marketable size.

Genetic Engineering Efforts are being made to improve plants by **genetic engineering**. This is a complex process involving several steps. Scientists first identify genes that give plants resistance and other important properties that might increase yield. Next, they isolate the genes and chemically analyze them so they can be chemically synthesized in the laboratory. Finally, the genes are inserted into seeds and transferred to the plant's offspring. In this process genes from one species can be transferred to the same or a completely different species, offering scientists unparalleled opportunities to create life forms, a process called *algeny*.

Genetic engineering can be used in other ways, too. For example, a new strain of bacteria was developed by scientists at the University of California. Applied to crops, these bacteria inhibit the formation of frost on plants, thus potentially offering farmers a way of reducing crop damage and increasing yield. Animal geneticists may also use genetic engineering to improve livestock, combining genes from one species with another to improve efficiency of digestion, weight gain, and resistance to disease.

Genetic engineering is a much quicker way to produce new varieties than conventional plant breeding. However, it has generated a lot of public criticism. Much fear has been raised over the potential to create hazardous life forms such as viruses, bacteria, and insects that could escape into the environment—or even be used in war—and cause widespread ecosystem disruption and death before they could be stopped. Early work with genetic engineering indicates that these fears are exaggerated. New genetic combinations are often much less hardy than the organisms they are derived from, so their chances of survival are greatly diminished.

Clearly, there is much hope in the new developments of plant and animal geneticists. No doubt there will be many disappointments in future years, but each failure yields knowledge that brings us closer to realizing our goals.

Soil Enrichment

Soil fertility can be maintained through the use of artificial fertilizer or organic fertilizer and through crop rotation. These methods are covered more thoroughly in Chapter Supplement 9-2, on soil management.

Artificial fertilizer is widely used in the United States and abroad to replace nitrogen, phosphorus, and potassium that has been removed from the soil by plants. The use of such fertilizers creates a number of problems. First, artificial fertilizer is made from natural gas (methane). The increasing cost of natural gas in the past decade has made fertilizer expensive, especially for many poor nations, and has contributed to rising food prices. Second, artificial fertilizers do not replace all of the nutrients taken by plants and do not add organic material to the soil. Thus, the addition of artificial fertilizer may help maintain crop yield over the short term but eventually results in the breakdown of soil structure. Third, artificial fertilizers create water pollution when the excess is washed from the land during rainstorms. Nitrogen and phosphorus in streams and lakes upset the natural nutrient balance and cause major changes in aquatic ecosystems (more fully described in Chapter 20).

Agricultural scientists have proposed the use of organic fertilizers from sewage treatment plants, cattle feedlots, and the like. These would (1) add valuable inorganic as well as organic nutrients to the soil, (2) reduce the flow of pollutants into lakes and streams, and (3) reduce the volume of waste material in disposal sites. A number of cities in the United States and Europe make use of human waste for cropland and rangeland enrichment. When the waste is free of toxic elements and pathogenic organisms and when farmland is nearby, the use of organic fertilizer is an excellent strategy.

Another method of reducing the loss of organic matter is by rotating crops. This ancient technique reduces erosion and maintains the nitrogen and organic content of the soil.

Irrigation

As groundwater supplies are depleted and as competition for irrigation water increases, more and more irrigated land will be abandoned. However, more efficient irrigation could reverse this trend. Lining irrigation ditches with cement saves a lot of water, as does the use of pipes rather than dirt ditches to convey water to fields (Figure 9-2a). Farmers are also beginning to use drip irrigation systems, in which water is delivered directly to the roots of the

(a)

(b)

Figure 9-2
Increasing the efficiency of irrigation. (*a*) Elevated pipes reduce water loss.
(*b*) Trickle systems that deliver water to roots cut evaporation losses.

plants (Figure 9-2b). Some systems are controlled by computers that monitor soil moisture content. These and other techniques are replacing earlier methods that waste enormous amounts of water. For hands-on experience in solving water–agriculture problems, see Model Application 9-1, page 194.

New Foods and Food Supplements

In many countries scientists have been working to develop food supplements, often rich in protein and other essential nutrients, to increase food supplies. New food sources such as fish and native animals are also being considered, because they add protein to the diet and are easily raised.

Protein Supplements and Substitutes

Fish protein concentrate (FPC) can be produced from all types of fish, even "trash" fish that are often thrown back into the sea. Added to food, FPC is an excellent protein supplement. Because it is difficult to remove the fishy taste from the powder and because of the relatively high cost, FPC has largely been abandoned.

Two well-known food supplements are incaparina and laubina, both developed from plant products. Incaparina is 25% protein and contains cottonseed flour, ground corn, yeast, calcium, and vitamin A. Laubina consists of wheat, chickpeas, bone ash, sugar, and vitamins A and D. Both supplements have been carefully blended with familiar foods to increase acceptance, but since they are not tasteless, the level of acceptance has been low.

A soybean beverage has been successful in Hong Kong for over 30 years. Called Vitasoy, the drink now captures one-quarter of Hong Kong's soft drink market. Soybean beverages have also been produced in Asia and Latin America, but the success of these products has not been overwhelming.

Concern for the effects of excessive fat in meat has led to the production of spun vegetable protein fibers (SVP). SVP is made by treating soybeans with mild alkali. The protein is then concentrated and formed into thin fibers. Made primarily from soybean concentrate and wheat gluten, SVP has been used in a variety of simulated meat

Can Genetic Engineering Spark a Second Green Revolution?

The stalk of celery you eat next year may have gotten its start in a test tube. Biotechnologists at Plant Genetics, Inc., in Davis, California, have recently developed synthetic seeds using gene splicing. Gene splicing, which promises higher agricultural yields, hardier plants, even tastier foods, is the wave of the future for agriculturalists everywhere. It could also be the solution to the world hunger problem—at least that's what optimists say.

Swelling world populations coupled with ever-dwindling food supplies make the development of better plants especially crucial; farmers must find ways of getting more out of the land. Genetic engineering looks like a fast track to the promised land.

This is how gene splicing works: scientists locate a donor plant with desirable characteristics—say, a strain of especially meaty tomato. The gene responsible for the tomato's meatiness is located, extracted, and then inserted into plant cells. The end product is a cell with a new gene.

Of course, it's easier to write about than it is to do; the failure rate is high. For one, breaking the genetic code and actually locating the specific gene that controls a certain function is no easy task. Second, when the gene is inserted into the cell, it doesn't always "take." Third, the task of producing large quantities of these engineered plants that do "take" is difficult. Cloning (the production of identical plants from a single cell) is the obvious answer, but with it comes an unobvious problem: it doesn't work with all plant types—at least not yet. Fourth, how does the engineer deliver a product to the farmer if the new plant itself is incapable of producing conventional seeds with the newly acquired traits?

A researcher named Keith Redenburg at Plant Genetics solved this problem. He created synthetic celery seeds by developing "somatic embryos" (exact replicas of the original plant in seedlike form) from cultured celery stem tissue. The seeds were then coated with an organic material much like the jelly on a fish egg and further boosted with nitrogen-fixing bacteria to encourage rapid growth. The end result was a disease-resistant hybrid seed, capable of producing seedlings in one to two days rather than the normal ten. These hybrid synthetic seeds are expected to be ready for sale soon.

Because genetic engineering's potential is so enormous, it comes as no surprise that many universities and private firms are devoting much time and money to this research. It may seem that the next Green Revolution is just around the corner, but most biotechnologists are cautious. The delicate process of gene splicing and cloning still remains very much a mystery.

---

products, including bacon, beef, sausage, and chicken. SVP is low in cholesterol and keeps indefinitely. To make it look and taste like meat, however, a variety of substances must be added, including dyes and texturizers. Another problem is that SVP is more costly than meat and not well liked by meat eaters.

Food scientists have succeeded in making protein by growing yeast, fungi, or bacteria on organic matter such as sewage, animal waste, crude oil, waste paper, and plant material. These organisms are dried and processed into a powder called single-cell protein (SCP) containing 50% to 80% protein. One enthusiastic estimate is that 3% of the world's annual crude oil production could produce the equivalent of the total worldwide animal protein consumed each year. However, there are many problems associated with SCP. First, many people develop diarrhea and nausea after eating it. Second, the high RNA (ribonucleic acid) content may promote the formation of kidney stones. Third, the cost is relatively high. Fourth, crude oil could be put to better use, as could organic waste. Because of these problems, plans to develop SCP commercially have been largely abandoned.

Algae have also been considered as a source of world food. Because algae account for most of the primary production in aquatic ecosystems, surface waters could potentially provide an abundance of food. Consuming a food so low on the food chain would also be more advantageous than upper-level feeding. But harvesting algae is difficult and costly, and converting algae to a palatable food has proven difficult. Some scientists have suggested that algae be grown commercially in tanks or ponds, but pilot production has never done as well as anticipated.

Indonesian natives make a soybean cake called tempeh. This popular and inexpensive food is high in protein and can be deep-fat fried. It is a desirable protein supplement and could be introduced into other regions, although problems of acceptability might arise. Tofu, the Japanese and Chinese version of soy cake, is gaining acceptance in this country.

Several powdered food supplements have been developed in the last few decades. These can be added to food or mixed with water to make nutritious beverages. Few have been successful.

Unexploited Species

Of the hundreds of thousands of plants and animals in the biosphere, human society relies on only a few dozen for food. Thus, we have an untapped biological reservoir of plants and animals, many of which may have a higher yield and better nutritional value than those we currently use. These facts have stimulated interest in discovering new species that we can use for food. The tropical winged bean, for example, could be a particularly valuable source of food, because the entire plant is edible. Its pods are similar to green beans, its leaves taste like spinach, its roots are much like potatoes, and its flowers taste like mushrooms. Amaranth, a staple grain of many ancient civilizations, is beginning a revival in certain areas.

Another source of food is native grazers, which in Africa have proved far superior to breeds introduced from Europe and America. Imported cattle have little resistance to disease and often overgraze the land because their movements are restricted. Native species are resistant to indigenous disease and better adapted to local climate. Because they move into new territories when food becomes scarce, they do less damage to vegetation. Native grazers also generally convert a higher percentage of the plant biomass into meat. They may also be cheaper than introduced cattle.

Fishing and Aquatic Agriculture

More Fish from the Sea? Fish provide about 5% of the total animal protein consumed by the world's population. Although three-quarters of the fish is consumed in the developed nations, fish protein is also important to the diets of many poorer countries, in many cases supplying 40% of the total animal protein consumption.

Until 1971 increasing the fish catch was viewed as an important way to increase the world's food supply. Between 1950 and 1970 the world's fish catch tripled, reaching approximately 70 million metric tons (78 million tons) per year. Since the early 1970s, though, the world catch has stabilized between 66 and 74 million metric tons per year, despite intensive efforts to increase yield. Measured on a per capita basis, the fish catch declined in the 1970s by about 15% and will probably continue to fall. Any increases in the world's fish catch might lead to widespread overfishing and a collapse of ocean fisheries.

Overfishing results when the number of fish taken exceeds the number produced. Although little is known about the dynamics of fish populations, many biologists agree that about 40% of a fish population can be taken in a given year. This leaves enough members of reproductive age to replenish the population. Currently, however, quotas for many fish species are set by trial and error. Miscalculation could have serious impacts on future fish populations.

International competition for fish creates an enormous resource management challenge. Many countries have extended their territorial waters from 19 kilometers to 320 kilometers (12 miles to 200 miles) in an effort to prevent overfishing by foreign interests. The United States, for example, now limits fishing by foreign companies to protect fish populations and its own fishing industry.

One method of increasing fish supplies is to reduce spoilage and loss through improvements in refrigeration in the entire production–consumption cycle. Preventing such losses could increase the supply of fish by 40%.

Commercial Fish Farms Commercial fish farms might also help increase fish protein supplies. Fish farms are forms of aquatic agriculture, which is called **aquaculture** in fresh water and **mariculture** in salt or brackish water.

There are two basic strategies in fish farming. In the first, fish are grown in ponds; population density is high and is maintained by intensive feeding. Catfish farms in the southeastern United States and trout farms in the West are examples of this type (Figure 9-3). In these ponds, fish are intensively fed like cattle in feedlots. Like cattle, however, they convert only a small fraction of their food into biomass. Therefore, intensive fish farming is not well suited to the developing countries.

In the second form of fish farming, fish or shellfish are maintained in enclosures or ponds but feed on natural components of the aquatic ecosystem (Figure 9-4). This system requires little external food or energy and is suitable for poorer countries. In the Philippines, wetlands have been dammed to create ponds that are stocked with

Figure 9-3
Commercial catfish farm near Monticello, Arkansas. These feeders release food pellets when a catfish nuzzles an extended rod.

Figure 9-4
Aquaculture. Fish raised in irrigation ditches and ponds in China and other countries throughout the world supply needed protein.

milkfish. Feeding largely on blue-green algae, the milkfish thrive, often yielding 2.5 metric tons per hectare per year. Similar programs have existed in freshwater canals in China and Thailand for centuries.

In Japan, New Zealand, and the United States, fish and shellfish are raised in cages immersed in estuaries and coastal waters, where they feed on plankton and other aquatic organisms. Oysters and mussels have been raised this way for hundreds of years.

Worldwide, fish farms produce about 4 million metric tons a year (4.4 million tons). Intensified efforts could double or triple this amount. Mussels, lobsters, and crabs could be produced in the coastal waters of developed countries. Poor countries, too, could depend more heavily on low-cost aquaculture and mariculture.

Another possibility for increasing fish production is the use of species often considered less desirable, such as carp, dogfish, and skate. At present, trash or rough fish are either discarded or ground into fish meal, which is fed to hogs and chickens or pets. From an annual catch of about 20 million tons of rough fish that are fed to livestock as fish meal, 1 million tons of edible meat is produced. Eaten directly, the trash fish could be a more valuable source of protein.

Reducing Pest Damage and Spoilage

Rats, insects, and birds attack crops and produce in the field, in transit, and in storage. The extent of the problem and ways to control it are the subject of Chapter Supplement 9-1. Conservatively, about 30% of all agricultural output is destroyed by pests, spoilage, and diseases. In the less developed countries this figure may be much higher, especially in humid climates where crops are grown year-round. Rats in India may consume 10% of the total grain production, and in warm climates rats may outnumber people three to one. Ratproof storage could easily prevent this problem. But rats are not the only grain-consuming pests. Birds, too, take a huge toll on world food supply. In Africa during the 1960s birds caused crop losses of $7 million a year.

Inefficient transportation can result in delays in getting grain and vegetables to market. Meanwhile, they may be consumed by rats, insects, or birds or destroyed by spoilage. Spoilage in storage and transportation can be prevented by refrigeration and by other improvements in the way people store food. For example, grain should be stored in dry silos or sheds to prevent the growth of mold, mildew, and bacteria. Safe chemical fumigants can also be used to help reduce mold and mildew. In developing nations such basic steps could be undertaken with the technical and financial assistance of the more developed nations or the United Nations. Reduction of spoilage could increase our food supply by 10% to 20%.

>>> *Model Application 9-1*

Agriculture and Water—A Cost-Benefit Analysis

In Chapter 9 you learned that agricultural irrigation water is being depleted from the Ogallala aquifer faster than it is being replenished. Annually, the net water loss is about 14 million acre-feet (1 acre-foot covers 1 acre to a depth of 1 foot). One of the proposed solutions to this problem is to divert water from the Missouri River at St. Joseph, Missouri, 850 feet (255 meters) above sea level, and pump it in a canal and pipeline to agricultural areas in western Kansas (elevation 2480 feet), eastern Colorado (3000 to 4000 feet), and Texas (3000 to 3500 feet).

Question

Do a cost–benefit analysis of this agricultural problem.

Step 1: Costs and Benefits

To balance costs and benefits, first make a list of all possible costs and benefits involved in this project. What are the major economic and environmental costs? What are the major benefits? How would you assign a numerical value to costs and benefits?

Step 2: Calculating Annual Pumping Costs

As you might have guessed, one of the chief economic costs would be incurred by pumping water uphill from St. Joseph, Missouri, to farms in Colorado, Kansas, and Texas. Let's assume that the water is going to be pumped to an average elevation of 3000 feet to make calculations easier. The electricity to pump one acre-foot of water up 188 feet costs about $25 (in 1979 dollars). How much will it cost to to pump 14 million acre-feet from St. Joseph to 3000 feet?

Unfortunately, the cost of electricity is probably only about half the total annual cost. Repayment of loans, interest, maintenance, and personnel make up the other half. With this in mind, what is the total annual cost for pumping this water?

Step 3: Gross Returns on Corn Sales

Now that you've approximated the annual pumping costs, let's look at the approximate economic benefits. First, 14 million acre-feet of water will irrigate 8.38 million acres of land yielding 754 million bushels of corn. If corn sells for $3 per bushel (1979 dollars), what would the gross return from corn sales be? Remember, the $3 selling price does not take into account any production costs. To be accurate, you'd have to subtract the cost of seed, fertilizer, herbicides, pesticides, labor, farm equipment, land rental or mortgage, and others. You might call some farmers in your area or contact an agricultural specialist at your school and find out how much profit a farmer makes per bushel of corn so you can calculate the net return.

From an economic standpoint, how feasible does this project look? What alternatives might you suggest to meeting the demand for irrigation water?

Answers

Step 1: Costs and Benefits

Costs

Pumping cost
Canal and pipeline construction costs
Canal and pipeline maintenance
Environmental costs
  Reduced water flow in Missouri River
  Effects on fish and wildlife
  Effects on pollution concentrations
  Effects on water supply for cities and farms

Benefits

Continuance of irrigated agriculture
Economic benefits
  Profit
  Jobs for farm laborers
  Spinoff economic benefits—community services such as stores and farm equipment sales

Step 2: Calculating Annual Pumping Costs

2150 feet = total elevation water must be pumped
        Cost to pump one acre-foot 2150 feet:

$$2150 \text{ feet} \times \frac{\$25}{188 \text{ feet}} = \$286/\text{acre-foot}$$

Annual cost to pump 14 million acre-feet
$286/acre-foot × 14 million acre-feet = $4 billion

Total cost for pumping, assuming pumping costs are only one half of annual costs:

$8 billion

Step 3: Gross Returns on Corn Sales

754 million bushels × $3/bushel = $2.3 billion

Increasing Self-Sufficiency

In a world of growing international trade and interdependence, increased self-sufficiency in agriculture among poorer nations may seem undesirable. Given the pressures on farmland in the leading agricultural nations, however, the developing countries may soon be unable to afford imported food. It might be better for all of us if they could grow their own food.

Self-sufficiency could be achieved by developmental aid, aimed at finding an agricultural system that (1) uses a minimum of nonrenewable energy, (2) relies heavily on human labor, (3) conserves soil and soil nutrients, (4) uses a minimum amount of water, (5) minimizes water pollution, (6) relies on a high level of species diversity, (7) reduces soil disruption from plowing and cultivating, and (8) uses perennial rather than annual crops. Such a system of appropriate agriculture can be sustained with a minimum of the external requirements common in mechanized agriculture.

Not all observers believe that a sustainable agricultural system is needed. For example, Merritt Kastens believes that multinational corporations could develop efficient but highly mechanized agricultural systems in developing nations. Such systems would be highly dependent on farm machinery, fossil fuels, fertilizers, and pesticides. To maximize profit they would improve harvesting, processing, storage, and distribution systems. Kastens argues that multinational corporations could be the savior of these countries, for they have the know-how to create efficient systems of production and distribution, can acquire the necessary capital, and are quite imaginative when it comes to making a profit. On the other hand, these giants have been criticized for concentrating wealth in the hands of a few and accused of exploiting poor people.

An Integrated Approach to World Hunger

It should be clear that there are many ways to solve the world hunger problem. But which one is the right one? The answer is that not one but many of these ideas must be adopted and integrated into a policy that strives to build a sustainable agricultural system. No single solution will suffice.

We need a concerted effort by the world's nations aimed at increasing the food supply by population control; by

increasing the amount of arable land, especially through soil management and erosion control; by increasing yield; by developing new foods; by minimizing losses; and by increasing self-sufficiency. The rich as well as the poor must contribute. The poor must become more self-sufficient; the rich can help them.

The rich might also begin to feed lower on the food chain by reducing meat protein in their diets and consuming more grains, vegetables, and fruits. The advantages of eating lower on the food chain are clear. Beef cattle produce about 7.5 kilograms of protein per hectare per year (42 pounds per acre), whereas soybeans produce 10 times as much protein on the same land, and alfalfa produces 14 times as much.

Further gains can be made by carefully selecting the vegetables we eat. For example, wheat produces about 1.8 million calories per hectare per year, whereas potatoes and sugar beets produce two and three times more, respectively. The reason for this is that we consume only about 30% of the wheat plant (the grain), whereas we consume 50% to 65% of the sugar beet and potato. Among animals, chickens and turkeys are considerably more efficient in converting grain to protein than are beef cattle, sheep, and pigs. Thus, by concentrating on more efficient food species, we could dramatically increase the world food supply. A 10% decrease in meat consumption in the United States could provide enough grain to feed 60 million people. Of course, it isn't all that simple: such actions are difficult to bring about. Even if citizens in the United States decreased meat consumption, could the poor afford the grain that was made available?

Personal Solutions to World Hunger

We are all a part of the solution to world hunger, even if our part is only a small one. But how can you help?

You can begin by becoming more knowledgeable about world hunger. Read the articles and books suggested at the end of this chapter, and find new ones. Try to learn: Who is hungry and why? What are the effects of malnourishment? What are the solutions? How can these be carried out?

Second, you can examine your own life-style to see where you can conserve food, energy, and other valuable resources. You can eat more selectively and more carefully. You can plant a garden to supplement your food purchases or join your neighbors in growing a community garden. You can avoid precooked and overly packaged foods, known as convenience foods. This will save energy and increase the nutritional value of your diet.

Third, you can take political actions. You might challenge current policies that place military demands above agricultural and economic development. Emphasize the need for agricultural self-sufficiency among poor countries, and support groups that seek this goal. Support politicians and leaders who take a strong and sensible stand on world hunger. Write the newspapers with your informed opinions. Start or join discussion groups emphasizing the need for personal as well as widespread political changes. Join groups now actively involved in combating world hunger.

Through these and other personal efforts you can help reduce world hunger, a goal necessary to create a sustainable society. Each of us can be a small part of the solution with very little effort. The choice is ours.

To a man with an empty stomach, food is God.

MOHANDAS K. GANDHI

Summary

Numerous strategies must be employed to meet current and future food demands. Population control is first in importance. Beyond that, we can increase the amount of agricultural land in production by exploiting unused farmland, reducing erosion, and controlling the spread of deserts. The United States has enough potential farmland to meet domestic and foreign demands until 2000, but not much beyond that. Most continents have little farmland reserve. Two notable exceptions are Africa and South America, where less than 20% of the land capable of supporting agriculture is being used.

Soil conservation and the control of desertification can increase farmland by reducing the rate at which it is destroyed and by reducing the decline in productivity that takes place as land slowly deteriorates under poor management. Controlling desertification can be achieved by proper rangeland management, replanting, wind erosion control, avoiding the use of marginal lands, and irrigating.

In conjunction with these efforts, food production can be increased by development of new plant and animal varieties, soil enrichment, and irrigation. New plant and animal varieties can be developed through artificial selection of *hybrids* or by *genetic engineering*. But in order for these efforts to be successful new varieties must not lose their resistance to disease, insects, and other natural factors. Some agricultural researchers are exploring the use of *perennial* crops. Such a system would reduce soil tillage, energy demands, and soil erosion. Careful soil enrichment programs, in which natural organic wastes are used to replenish lost nutrients, can be successful in maintaining productivity. Finally, because much of our agricultural production comes from irrigated land and because many supplies of irrigation water are now threatened, more efficient use of water could extend production on land that otherwise might have to be abandoned.

For the most part, new foods and manufactured food supplements have proved unacceptable to people. Traditional foods, such as tempeh, have more potential. Ecologists have suggested raising native grazers in regions such as Africa, because they are resistant to disease, are less likely to overgraze, and are often more efficient in converting plant biomass into edible meat.

Fish provide about 5% of the total animal protein consumed by the world's people. In many poor nations, fish provide 40% of the animal protein consumed each year. Increasing the fish catch, however, is unlikely and could probably be carried out only on a short-term basis before populations were depleted. A better strategy would be to improve transportation. Refrigeration could increase the amount of fish available to consumers in poor nations by 40%. Commercial fish farms, using either fresh water *aquaculture* or saltwater *mariculture,* might make it possible for rich and poor nations to double or triple their fish production. The most cost-effective systems are those in which fish or shellfish are raised in artificial enclosures and allowed to feed on natural components of the aquatic ecosystem.

Each year a large amount of food is destroyed by insects, bacteria, fungi, and rodents during production, transportation, and storage. Simple, cost-effective measures could be devised to reduce this loss and increase annual food production. Spoilage in storage and transportation could be prevented by refrigerating vegetables and meats and storing grains in airtight, rat-proof silos.

Trends in the world petroleum supply suggest the need for more agricultural self-sufficiency among the poor as well as the rich. Such systems can be developed by employing many of the strategies outlined in this chapter. Most important, rich and poor nations need to develop a sustainable agricultural system that uses a minimum amount of nonrenewable energy, relies on human labor, conserves soil and soil nutrients, uses water efficiently, minimizes water pollution, relies on a high level of species diversity, reduces soil tillage, and uses perennial rather than annual crops.

Discussion Questions

1. List the major strategies for solving world food shortages.

2. Discuss the possibility of increasing the amount of arable land by drawing on farmland reserves. What impacts might this have on wildlife habitat?

3. Debate the statement "Simply by practicing better soil conservation and replenishing soil nutrients we can reduce the need for developing new farmland."

4. Describe the Green Revolution, its successes and failures. What improvements might be made to circumvent the problems?

5. Compare the advantages and disadvantages of artificial and organic fertilizers in terms of energy use and soil nutrient replenishment.

6. List the new foods and food supplements discussed in this chapter and describe each one. Then, describe the benefits and problems associated with each.

7. Describe trends in the world fish catch. What happened to the per capita world fish catch in the 1970s? Is it likely that the annual fish catch will increase in the coming years? Why or why not?

8. Should the developing countries become more self-sufficient in agricultural production? What are the advantages of self-sufficiency for less developed countries? What are the disadvantages?

9. You have been appointed head of a U.N. task force. Your project is to develop an agricultural system in a poor African nation that imports more than 50% of its grain and still suffers from widespread hunger. Outline your plan, giving general principles you would follow and specific recommendations for achieving self-sufficiency.

Suggested Readings

Brown, L. R. (1978). *The Worldwide Loss of Cropland* (Worldwatch Paper 24). Washington, D.C.: Worldwatch Institute. A comprehensive analysis of the loss of agricultural lands.

—(1980). Fuel Farms: Croplands of the Future? *The Futurist* 14(3): 16–28. A well-written paper on one of the many threats to agricultural productivity.

—(1982). The Food Connection: Transforming the U.S.–Soviet Relationship. *The Futurist* 16(6): 9–16. Insightful and well-documented view of the role of food in the power play between two superpowers.

Dudal, R. (1982). Land Degradation in a World Perspective. *Journal of Soil and Water Conservation* 37(5): 245–249. Excellent review of land requirements for expanding agriculture.

George, S. (1977). *How the Other Half Dies*. Montclair, N.J.: Allenheld and Osmun. A superb book on world hunger.

Gore, R., and Gerster, G. (1979). An Age-Old Challenge Grows. *National Geographic* 156(5): 594–639. A vivid view of worldwide desertification.

Jackson, W. (1980). *New Roots for Agriculture*. San Francisco: Friends of the Earth. Good discussion of fuel crops, sustainable agriculture, and other issues.

Latham, M. C., McGandy, R. B., McCann, M. B., and Stare, F. J. (1972). *Scope Manual on Nutrition*. Kalamazoo, Mich.: Upjohn. An excellent treatment of malnutrition.

McHale, M. C., McHale, J., and Streatfield, G. F. (1979). *Children in the World*. Washington, D.C.: Population Reference Bureau. Filled with important statistics on nutrition, sanitation, health, and the like.

Reichert, W. (1982). Agriculture's Diminishing Diversity. *Environment* 24(9): 6–11, 39–44. A superb discussion of the loss of diversity among crops and domestic livestock and the potential problems.

Richardson, N., and Stubbs, T. (1978). *Plants, Agriculture, and Human Society*. Menlo Park, Calif.: Benjamin/Cummings. Contains many suggestions for alternative agricultural practices.

Sampson, R. N. (1981). *Farmland or Wasteland: A Time to Choose*. Emmaus, Pa.: Rodale Press. Well-written book on world agriculture.

Scoville, O. J. (1982). Changes in Farmland: Policy Implications. *Population Bulletin* 36(5): 1–13. A thorough analysis of the threats to U.S. agricultural production.

Sheridan, D. (1981). Western Rangelands: Overgrazed and Undermanaged. *Environment* 23(4): 14–20; 29–37. An in-depth look at rangeland abuse in the U.S.

Pests and Pest Control

What is a weed? A plant whose virtues have not yet been discovered.

RALPH WALDO EMERSON

Each year insects, weeds, bacteria, fungi, viruses, parasites, birds, rodents, and mammals consume or destroy approximately 48% of the world's food production. The highest rate of destruction is in the tropics and subtropics, where three crops are grown each year on the same field. But pest destruction is high even in the developed nations despite elaborate pest control strategies costing several billion dollars a year. In the United States, for instance, preharvest losses are estimated to be about 34%, and postharvest losses amount to 9% of what is left (Figure S9-1). Together, about two-fifths of the total annual production is lost to various pests, or about $9 billion worth of food for humans and livestock. Control costs approximately $2.5 billion a year.

Similar losses are reported in other developed countries. For example, in Canada's largest onion-growing region, Holland Marsh, losses in plots not protected against onion maggots have exceeded 90%. Wheat production in Saskatchewan has been reduced in some years by three-fourths as a result of wireworm infestation.

In a world where 17% to 40% of the people are hungry, such losses are tragic. Reducing losses through pest control represents an enormous opportunity to increase world food supply.

A Historical Overview

Pest control measures have been used throughout the centuries. For example, in China more than 3000 years ago, farmers controlled locusts by burning infested fields. Arsenic poisons were used as pesticides in A.D. 900, and in 1182 Chinese citizens were required to collect and kill locusts in an effort to control an outbreak. Similar techniques have been in use since the beginning of agriculture in many other parts of the world.

Development of Chemical Pesticides

In recent years chemical pesticides (biocides) have come to form the cornerstone of pest management. **Pesticides** are chemicals used to kill troublesome pests, including weeds, rodents, and insects. The first pesticides, or **first-generation pesticides**, were simple preparations made of ashes, sulfur, arsenic compounds, ground tobacco, or hydrogen cyanide. Before 1940 there were only a few dozen first-generation pesticides on the market; the major ones were poisons containing heavy metals (lead and mercury), arsenic, petroleum-based oils, and natural plant toxins. Today, few of these remain in use because of their toxicity or relatively low effectiveness.

In 1939 the Swiss chemist Paul Müller introduced a new synthetic organic insecticide called DDT (*d*ichloro*d*iphenyl *t*richloroethane). This was the first in a long line of **second-generation pesticides**, synthetic organic compounds that kill a variety of pests.

For the 25 years following its development, DDT was viewed by many as the savior of humankind. It quickly removed insects and increased crop yield. And being relatively inexpensive to produce, it spread to all corners of the world. In 1944 Müller was awarded a Nobel Prize for his contribution.

Over the years, thousands of new chemicals have been synthesized and tested. Today, about 1500 different pesticides in over 33,000 commercial preparations are being used as herbicides, insecticides, fungicides, miticides, and rodenticides, with one goal in mind: to reduce pests to tolerable levels. Some pesticides, like DDT, are **broad-spectrum biocides**, which attack a wide variety of organisms; others are **narrow-spectrum pesticides**, used in controlling one or a few particular pests.

Chemical pesticides fall into one of three chemical families: chlorinated hydrocarbons (organochlorines), organic phos-

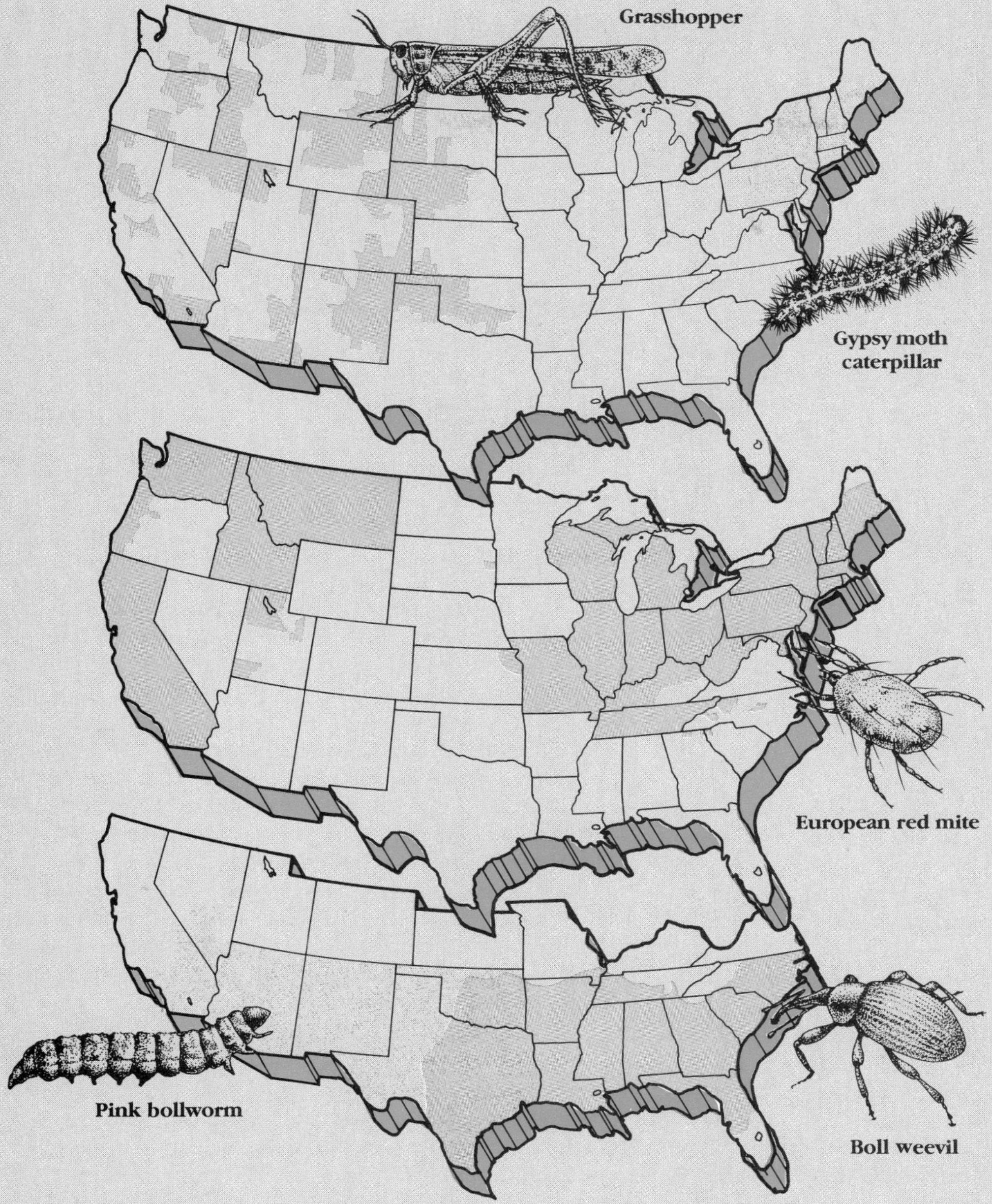

Figure S9-1
Pest damage and pest control in the United States.

Grasshopper

Gypsy moth caterpillar

European red mite

Boll weevil

Pink bollworm

phates, and carbamates. The **chlorinated hydrocarbons** are a high-risk group, including DDT, aldrin, kepone, dieldrin, chlordane, heptachlor, endrin, mirex, toxaphene, and lindane. All of these have been banned or drastically restricted or are being considered for such actions, because of their ability to cause cancer, birth defects, neurological disorders, and because of their damage to wildlife and the environment. Generally, the chlorinated hydrocarbons are extremely resistant to breakdown, persist in the environment, are passed up the food chain, and reside for long periods of time in body fat.

The second group, the **organic phosphates**, consists of chemicals such as malathion and parathion. They break down more rapidly than chlorinated hydrocarbon pesticides and therefore are less likely to pass through the food chain. However, most

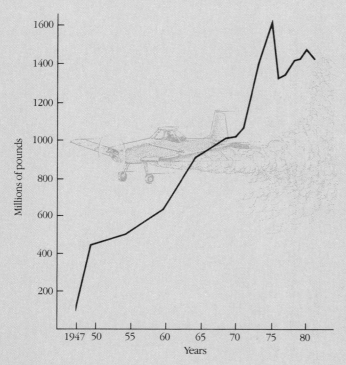

Figure S9-2
Increasing pesticide production in the United States.

are highly toxic. Humans exposed to even low levels may suffer from drowsiness, confusion, cramps, diarrhea, vomiting, headaches, and difficulty in breathing. Higher levels cause severe convulsions, paralysis, tremors, coma, and death.

The **carbamates**, the third family, are widely used as insecticides, herbicides, and fungicides. One of the most common is carbaryl (commonly known as Sevin). As a group the carbamates are less persistent than the organic phosphates, remaining a few days to two weeks after application. But like the organochlorines and organophosphates, they are nerve poisons that have been shown to cause birth defects and genetic damage in humans.

Together, approximately 2.3 million metric tons (2.5 million tons) of chemical pesticides are used annually throughout the world—approximately 34% in North America, 45% percent in Europe, and the remaining 21% primarily in developing countries (Figure S9-2).

About one-fifth of all pesticides are applied to U.S. fields each year. Of the pesticides used in agriculture, 35% are for insect control, 51% are herbicides for weed control, and the rest are fungicides, used to reduce fungal growth. Surprisingly, about one-third of all chemical pesticides (including herbicides, insecticides, and fungicides) are applied for nonagricultural uses in the United States, including home gardens, lawns, and trees. A survey taken by the Environmental Protection Agency showed

that 92% of all homeowners used pesticides, and they applied them at a higher amount per acre than farmers.

Pesticides constitute only about 3% of the commercial chemicals commonly used in the United States each year. Nonetheless, because they are released into the environment in large quantity and have the potential to alter ecosystem balance and threaten human health, their use has created widespread and often heated controversy.

Exploration, Exploitation, and Reflection

Pesticide use has progressed through three developmental stages: (1) exploratory, (2) exploitive, and (3) reflective. These periods illustrate a common progression of human behavior and attitude that follows the introduction of many new chemicals and technologies.

Exploration   During the exploratory stage, starting in the 1940s, DDT and other new pesticides were applied to a variety of crops with astonishing results. DDT was even used to delouse soldiers during World War II.

The success of these pesticides was impressive and widely publicized. They proved to be fast and efficient at controlling insects, weeds, and other pests. In India, for example, there were more than 100 million cases of malaria in the 1950s, before the use of DDT to control malaria-carrying mosquitoes. By 1961 the annual incidence had been reduced to 50,000. Pesticides allowed farmers to respond quickly to outbreaks; thus, they were often able to avoid economic disaster. Second-generation pesticides were also cheap and relatively easy to apply, and their use resulted in substantial financial gains as yields increased. Some insecticides, such as DDT and dieldrin, persisted long after application, giving extended protection and relieving farmers of the need to apply pesticides at the correct time.

Exploitation   The successes of the exploratory phase led to the exploitive phase, during which pesticide production and use expanded considerably. The development of many new pesticides followed: recommendations were drafted, and other steps were taken to protect farm workers from exposure and consumers from toxic residues remaining on vegetables and grains. Still, misuse abounded, out of ignorance and apathy.

In the rush to expand pesticide use, problems arose. First, many pesticides, especially broad-spectrum chemicals, often killed predatory and parasitic insects that were a natural population control mechanism in the ecosystem, holding in check many pests and potential pests. Thus, insects that had not been pests suddenly increased in number, creating a need for additional pesticides. The agronomist calls this population explosion of new pests an **upset**.

A classic example of such an upset took place in California.

Figure S9-3
Pesticide resistance. A tobacco budworm crawls through deadly DDT unaffected.

Spider mites, once only minor crop pests, have become a major pest because pesticides have killed off many natural enemies. Today, the spider mites cause twice as much damage as any other insect pest and cost farmers (in damage and control) five times what they cost 15 years ago.

Pesticides also destroy beneficial insects such as honeybees that play an important role in pollination. Honeybees pollinate crops that provide one-third of our food, crops annually worth over $1 billion. Apple orchards are particularly hard hit. Nationwide, more than 400,000 bee colonies are destroyed or severely damaged each year by pesticides.

Second, and worse, a small portion of the insect pests (roughly 5%) was genetically resistant to the pesticides and was not killed by a normal application (Figure S9-3). Although pesticides worked in the short term by reducing pests to a level at which they did little damage, the surviving, pesticide-resistant insects reproduced and eventually formed a new population that could be killed only by large doses or new pesticides.

Genetic resistance to DDT was first reported in 1947 by Italian researchers. By 1960 scientists had discovered 137 insect species that had become genetically resistant to DDT, a clear example of natural selection leading to increased survivability. Today, more than 400 insect pests are resistant to DDT and other pesticides.

This unexpected development called for new strategies. The first was to increase the amount of pesticide. When DDT and other insecticides were first introduced in Central America, cotton fields were sprayed with insecticide eight times each growing season; today, 30 to 40 applications are necessary. The second strategy was the development of new pesticides. However, scientists found that insects developed genetic resistance to these new chemicals. Even weeds and plant diseases can develop a resistance to pesticides, although not so quickly as insects.

The third problem was that many of the second-generation pesticides proved to be hazardous environmental contaminants. These synthetic pesticides persisted in the ecosystem because microconsumers (bacteria) lacked the enzyme to degrade them. Increased spraying resulted in widespread contamination of the ecosystem (Figure S9-4). Trout in upstate New York showed elevated levels of DDT because of spraying in nearby forests. DDT did not affect the adults but reduced survival among newly hatched fry. Insect- and worm-eating birds also perished in areas where aerial spraying was done. As a result of widespread pesticide use, the populations of many birds plummeted.

The manufacturers of pesticides argued that the chemicals were found in only minute concentrations in the environment and could not be the cause of declining populations of fish and wildlife. But numerous experimental studies showed that certain persistent pesticides—even when present in small amounts in the environment—could drastically affect reproduction and survival in birds and other animals.

One of the most important findings was that although DDT levels in aquatic ecosystems were quite low, concentrations were higher in producers and still higher in consumers. Moreover, the consumers on the highest trophic level had the highest concentrations of DDT which, though not lethal, still had a severe impact on reproduction. In fish-eating birds throughout the world—such as peregrine falcons, brown pelicans, cormorants, bald eagles, gulls, and osprey—DDT and similar chlorinated chemicals (PCBs, polychlorinated biphenyls) reduced the deposition of calcium in eggshells. This results in thin and fragile eggshells that crack easily during incubation. Many populations

Rain 0.1-0.3 ppb

Tradewinds 0.1-0.3 ppb

Soil 2-10 ppb

Rivers and lakes
0.001-0.2 ppb

Groundwater
0.001-0.2 ppb

Fat of man
6-12 ppm

Fat of cows 0.5 ppm

Figure S9-4
Pesticide sprayed from planes contaminates the ecosystem, because much of the pesticide drifts away. Various avenues for the dispersal of pesticides are shown. Average values for DDT concentrations are indicated in parts per million and billion.

were nearly wiped out. (For a more detailed discussion see Chapter 18.)

Other work soon showed the presence of DDT in fish, beef, and other foods. DDT also appeared in the fatty tissues of seals and Eskimos in the Arctic, far from their point of use, indicating that it was traveling in the atmosphere to remote parts of the globe, being washed from the sky by rain, and passing through the food chain. DDT has also been detected in human breast milk, a discovery that caused considerable alarm, although the long-term effects of low levels on humans remain unknown.

Farm and chemical workers also suffered from direct exposure to pesticides on the job. In 1981 improper use and handling of pesticides resulted in 111 deaths in the United States. Workers pick up pesticide on their clothing and skin through accidents, negligence, or entering sprayed fields too soon after spraying. Symptoms of poisoning include insomnia, loss of sex drive, reduced powers of concentration, irritability, nervous disorders, and, in severe cases, death. Nationwide, at least 100,000 workers are seriously poisoned each year, but many experts believe that this figure grossly underestimates the number of serious poi-

sonings. Surveys in California, for instance, show that three-fourths of all serious poisonings go unreported. Each year 200 to 1000 people die from pesticide poisoning in the United States. Worldwide, there are at least 500,000 pesticide poisonings. According to some experts these result in at least 5000 immediate deaths and numerous long-term illnesses that later end in death.

Although farm and chemical workers are the most heavily exposed to pesticides, residents of rural and even suburban areas are often exposed to high levels if they live near agricultural lands. Families living near fields sprayed with herbicides outside Scottsdale, Arizona, for example, suffered from persistent headaches, cramps, skin rashes, dizziness, high blood pressure, chest pains, persistent coughs, internal bleeding, and leukemia. People living near sprayed fields are heavily exposed because one-half to three-fourths of the sprayed material never reaches the ground but is carried away by light winds or simply drifts away (Figure S9-5).

Herbicides have also drawn a considerable amount of attention in recent years. Researchers have linked the spraying of the

Figure S9-5
Crop duster spraying potato fields.

herbicide 2,4,5-T (2,4,5-trichlorophenoxyacetic acid) to the abnormally high rate of spontaneous abortion in women near Alsea, Oregon. This herbicide is contaminated during its production by a highly toxic chemical known as **dioxin**. Another harmful herbicide is **Agent Orange**, a defoliant used in the Vietnam War to destroy crops and trees in forests and mangrove swamps from which guerillas often launched their attacks. Containing dioxin, it too is believed to be the cause of numerous medical problems in Vietnamese women and soldiers.

In addition to the ecological and health concerns discussed above, the efficacy of pesticide use has also begun to be questioned. Despite increased use of chemical pesticides, annual losses due to pests have remained the same or have increased. In the first 30 years after the introduction of second-generation insecticides, use increased tenfold, and insect damage doubled. The search is now on for other ways to deal with pests.

Reflection As a result of growing concern for the biological and ecological effects of pesticides and growing skepticism regarding their effectiveness, we have gradually entered the reflective stage, a period of growing caution and skepticism. The transition to the reflective stage is not easy, but momentum has gained since the publication of the late Rachel Carson's book *Silent Spring*, considered one of the most important environmental books of the century.

Pesticides are still indispensable for agriculture, but their use must be reduced and integrated with a variety of control measures that are less harmful to the environment. The integration of techniques that pose a minimum risk to the environmental and human health is called **integrated pest management** (IPM).

Integrated Pest Management

Integrated pest management calls for the combined use of four basic means of pest control: environmental, genetic, chemical, and cultural. Together, these form a more effective, long-lasting, and environmentally sound way of controlling pest damage.

Environmental Control

Environmental control methods are designed to alter the biotic and abiotic environment, making it inhospitable to the pest. Because they generally rely on knowledge more than technology, these practices are especially suitable for poor nations. Still, they can be equally as effective if used properly in modern agricultural societies.

Increasing Crop Diversity In Chapter 8, we learned that monocultures generally promote the proliferation of insects and disease organisms. Crop diversity, on the other hand, reduces the amount of food available to any one pest and helps prevent such rapid population growth. Two basic techniques increase crop diversity: heteroculture (intercropping) and crop rotation.

The planting of several crops side by side in the same field, called **heteroculture**, works because it provides environmental resistance so the biotic potential of pests cannot be reached. In heterocultures, pest populations are often much smaller than in monocultures. For example, intercropping corn and peanuts can reduce corn borers by as much as 80%. Part of the reason for this is that peanuts harbor predatory insects that feed on the corn borer.

Crop rotation provides for better soil fertility and helps reduce erosion (this is discussed in Chapter Supplement 9-2) but also helps hold down pest populations. For instance, wireworms feed on potatoes, but not alfalfa. If potatoes are grown year after year in the same field, wireworms have an ample supply of food. But if crops are rotated, food becomes a limiting factor holding the wireworm population in check.

Altering the Time of Planting   Some plants naturally escape insect pests by sprouting early or late in the growing season. A good example of this adaptation is the wild radish, which sprouts early in the season before the emergence of the troublesome cabbage maggot fly.

Agriculturalists can use their knowledge of the insect's life cycle to their advantage by coordinating plantings with the expected date of hatching. For example, delayed planting of wheat helps protect this crop against the destructive Hessian fly, which emerges early in the spring. Without food the pest will perish. If the pest emerges late in the growing season, an early planting may prove effective.

Altering Plant and Soil Nutrients   The levels of certain nutrients in soil and plants can also affect pest population size. Thus, by regulating soil nutrients a farmer may be able to control pests.

Nitrogen is one of the important nutrients that insects and parasites derive from plants. Too much or too little of this key element can affect the population size of various pests. For example, grain aphids reproduce better on grain high in nitrogen. Other insects, such as the greenhouse thrip and mites, do poorly on high-nitrogen spinach and tomatoes, respectively. Therefore, knowledge of pest nutrient requirements, soil nutrient levels, and plant nutrient levels can be helpful in controlling pests. Plants rich or poor in nitrogen can be selected to control pests as long as the level of nitrogen is adequate for human consumption.

Controlling Adjacent Crops and Weeds   Adjacent crops and weeds may provide food and habitat for pests, especially insects. In some cases plants adjacent to valuable food crops may harbor viruses that can infest pest species and can later be transmitted to crops. Thus, elimination of adjacent crops and weeds may prove helpful in the control of insects and other pests.

Sometimes adjacent low-value crops (trap crops) attract pests away from more valuable crops. Alfalfa is a good example. When planted adjacent to cotton, it draws the harmful lygus bug away and thus prevents serious damage.

Introducing Predators, Parasites, and Disease Organisms   In nature thousands of potential insect pests never become real pests because of natural controls exerted by predators, diseases, and parasites (that is, biotic components of envi-

ronmental resistance). Farmers can capitalize on this knowledge through **biological control**, or **food chain control**, to manage weeds, insects, rodents, and other pests.

There are hundreds of examples of the successful use of natural controls to manage pests. For example, the prickly pear cactus was introduced in Australia from its native Mexico, and by 1925 more than 24 million hectares (60 million acres) of land was badly infested. Half of this land was abandoned because of the thick carpet of cactus. Farmers introduced a cactus-eating insect to Australia to eradicate the pest, and seven years later much of the land had been cleared and could once again be used.

In China four species of tiny parasitic wasps are used extensively to control various crop-eating moths. The wasps are mass-produced and released into the wild, where they lay their eggs in the eggs of moths. When the wasp eggs hatch, the larvae consume the egg of the host, preventing hatching and effectively controlling the pest. Wasps are often called "living insecticides."

Entomologists in the United States are experimenting with a new method of controlling mosquitoes using a large, nonbiting mosquito whose larvae feed on the larvae of other mosquitoes. Bred in captivity, this predatory mosquito will be released in infested regions to control biting mosquitoes.

Insect pests may also be controlled by birds, a natural control organism whose potential has been overlooked. Brown thrashers can eat over 6000 insects in one day. A swallow consumes 1000 leafhoppers in 12 hours, and a pair of flickers can snack on 5000 ants and go away hungry. In China thousands of ducklings are driven through rice fields; in some places they reduce the populations of insects by 60% to 75%, allowing farmers to cut back insecticide use considerably.

Bacteria and other microorganisms can be brought to bear on pests. One common example is the bacterium *Bacillus thuringiensis* (BT), used to control many leaf-eating caterpillars. Cultivated in the lab and sold commercially as a dry powder, it can be applied as a powder or mixed with water and then sprayed on plants. Caterpillars that eat it become sick and then die.

BT is used by organic gardeners with considerable success. It has been sprayed in China to control pine caterpillars and cabbage army worms. In California it has been used for more than 20 years to control various troublesome caterpillars, and it is currently applied in the northeastern United States to help control gypsy moths, which devastate forests (Figure S9-6). BT has also been employed in the battle against mosquitoes. Although it is more expensive than chemicals, it has reduced insecticide use in California from 270,000 kilograms (600,000 pounds) in 1970 to about 23,000 kilograms (50,000 pounds) in 1983.

Viruses and fungi are similarly used. In Australia, after years of fruitless efforts to control rabbits, scientists introduced a pathogenic *myxoma* virus that eliminated almost all of the rabbits within one year. Half a gram of an experimentally produced virus applied to a hectare of cropland infested with cabbage loopers can control this pest. Other viruses are being used to control pests such as the pink bollworm, which damages cotton,

Figure S9-6
Gypsy moths kill large sections of trees by eating leaves near
their hatching site.

and the gypsy moth. U.S. scientists are now testing a fungus
(*Tolypocladium cylindrosporum*) to control mosquitoes. Special traps are set out to attract adult females. The insects enter
the traps and are contaminated with spores but are allowed to
escape, thus carrying the fungal spores back into the environment, where they infect eggs and larvae.

These biological control agents must be developed with caution to ensure that they are not harmful to humans, livestock,
and other members of the ecosystem. Pest control agents must
not become pests themselves.

Organisms can develop genetic resistance to biological controls; for example, rabbits in Australia are developing a resistance to *myxoma* virus. In such cases new controls can be introduced, but in some instances biological control agents themselves
undergo genetic changes that offset the newly acquired resistance of the pest. This process is called **co-evolution.**

Genetic Control

We will consider two major genetic control strategies: releasing
sterile males and breeding genetically resistant plants and animals. Both are important components of integrated pest

Releasing Sterile Males The **sterile male technique** has
been effective against several species of insect pests, including
the screwworm fly in Mexico and the United States, the melon
fly on the island of Rota near Guam, and the Oriental fruit fly in
Guam.

In this technique males of the pest species are raised in captivity and sterilized by irradiation or special chemicals. Then
they are released in large numbers in infested areas, where they
mate with wild females (Figure S9-7). Because many insect species mate only once, eggs produced in such a mating are infertile. If the population of sterilized males greatly exceeds that of

the wild males, most of the matings will be with sterile males.
Populations can be brought under control swiftly.

In the United States screwworms have been controlled by this
method, saving millions of dollars each year. The screwworm
fly lays eggs in open wounds of cattle and other warm-blooded
animals. The eggs hatch within a few hours, and the larvae feed
off blood and tissue fluid. This keeps the wound open, allowing
a bacterial infection to set in, which eventually kills the host.

In 1976 there were over 29,000 cases of screwworm infestation in the United States. The following year, because of inclem-
ent weather and an extensive release of sterile males, costing
$6 million, there were only 457 reported cases. The screwworm
has practically been eliminated from the southeastern United
States, but it remains in the Southwest, where new flies migrate
in from Mexico. With continued cooperation between Mexico
and the United States, though, the future of the screwworm may
be a short one. Even if the fly is never eradicated, controlling it
provides substantial economic benefits for a relatively low cost.
The program saves the cattle industry about $120 million annually.

Sterile males have been introduced in other instances with
much less success. For example, California imported sterilized
Mediterranean fruit flies (medflies) from Hawaii to control this
pest. The medfly lays its eggs in 235 different fruits, nuts, and
vegetables; its larvae develop in the ripening fruits and eventually destroy them. Agricultural interests argued that if the medfly
proliferated, it would cause $2.6 billion in damage per year in
California alone.

At first, the state opted for a combined approach to pest control, using both baited traps laced with malathion and sterile
males. This approach avoided widespread aerial spraying, which
scientists at Stanford University had argued would cause an undue

Figure S9-7
The USDA prevents buildup of screwworms by rearing and
releasing sterile male flies.

health risk. Combined programs had worked well in two areas in the state. However, in the 1980–1981 incident, poorly funded control efforts were inadequate, and fertile medflies kept appearing both inside and outside of areas believed to be infested. Farmers became nervous, and the U.S. Department of Agriculture threatened to quarantine all California produce, forcing the governor to order a massive aerial spraying program, which eradicated the medfly.

Efforts to control mosquitoes with the sterile male technique have also proved unsuccessful. Scientists believe that the chief reason for these failures is the lower sexual activity of sterilized males compared with wild males. Other reasons may include a lack of an adequate number of sterile males, a lack of knowledge about the mosquito's breeding cycle, and the in-migration of additional pests. Some researchers also suggest that wild females of insect populations could evolve a genetic resistance to sterile males. Perhaps through natural selection a new race of screwworm flies will evolve that somehow recognizes and avoids sterile males.

Despite these problems, the sterile male technique is an important tool in pest control. It is species-specific, can be used with environmental controls, and can be effective in eliminating pests in low-density infestations.

Breeding Resistant Crops and Animals Genetically resistant plants and animals can be developed through genetic engineering and artificial selection. Genetic engineering can be especially useful in this regard, because it allows for a much more rapid development of new strains than artificial selection.

As a recent example, scientists have found that certain oils in the skin of oranges, grapefruit, and lemons are highly toxic to the eggs and larvae of the Caribbean fruit fly, which lays its eggs in the skin of these fruits. The fly's larvae destroy the fruit, but scientists may now be able to selectively breed citrus fruit to increase the amount of toxic oils in their peels.

Cornell University scientists are developing a new type of insect-resistant potato plant. Its leaves, stems, and sprouts are covered with tiny, sticky hairs that trap insects and immobilize their feet and mouthparts. Field tests show that this plant can reduce green peach aphids by half. The new variety was developed by crossing cultivated potatoes with a wild species that grows as a weed in Bolivia.

British scientists have found that the leaves and stems of certain wild potatoes produce a chemical substance that repels aphids. Making plants capable of producing these natural repellents, called **allomones**, through genetic selection might prove useful in reducing annual crop loss.

Other genetic research has led to Hessian fly–resistant wheat and leafhopper-resistant soybeans, alfalfa, cotton, and potatoes. Work on chemical factors that attract insects to plants may help scientists selectively remove them to make plants unappealing.

Inbred genetic resistance is a necessary element of effective pest management. The major problem is the time, money, and labor needed to produce resistant varieties. Furthermore, genetic resistance may be overcome by adaptation of pests. In this case scientists must be waiting in the wings with new varieties.

Chemical Control

Chemical pesticides will continue to play an important role in pest management. Today, however, two new types of chemical agent have been developed—pheromones and insect hormones. These are **third-generation pesticides**.

Pheromones Pheromones are externally released chemicals produced by insects and other animals. One well-known group of pheromones is the **sex attractants**, which are emitted by female insects to attract males at the time of breeding. Effective in extraordinarily small concentrations, pheromones draw males to females, an evolutionary adaptation that ensures a high rate of reproductive success.

Now many sex attractants, synthesized in the laboratory, are commercially available for use in pest control. They are used in three ways. First, **pheromone traps** are used to lure males. Traps may contain a pesticide-laden bait or a sticky substance that immobilizes insects (Figure S9-8). Second, pheromones may be

Figure S9-8
Pheromone trap, containing a sticky substance to immobilize male gypsy moths in search of mates.

sprayed widely around the time of breeding. This is known as the **confusion technique**, because the males are drawn by the pheromone from all directions and may never find a partner. One modification of this technique involves the release of wood chips treated with sex attractants. Males are drawn to the wood chips and may attempt to breed with them. Third, pheromone traps may be used to pinpoint the time when insect eggs hatch, so that pesticides can be applied to coincide with hatching. This helps reduce the amounts of pesticide required.

Pheromone traps of various sorts have been used to control at least 25 different insect species. Early work on clearwing moths, cotton bollworms, and other species has been quite successful. Pheromones offer many advantages: they can be used with other methods, they are nontoxic and biodegradable, they can be used at low concentrations, they are highly species-specific, and they are not expected to present any environmental hazards. The major disadvantage is the high cost of developing new pheromones.

Insect Hormones   The life cycle of many insects is shown in Figure S9-9. As illustrated, insects pass through the larval and pupal stages before reaching adulthood. The entire life cycle is regulated by two hormones, the **juvenile hormone** and the **molting hormone**. **Hormones** are chemical substances that are produced by cells in the body and travel through the bloodstream to distant sites, where they exert some effect. Altering the levels of juvenile and molting hormones disrupts an insect's life cycle, resulting in death. For example, larvae treated with juvenile hormones are prevented from maturing and eventually die. If given molting hormone, they will enter the pupal stage too early

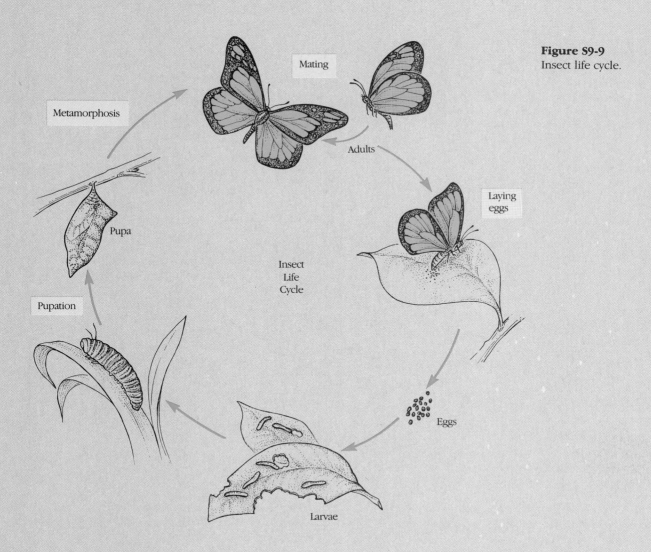

Figure S9-9
Insect life cycle.

and die. Experiments are currently under way to assess the effectiveness of spraying crops with insect hormones.

Insect hormones offer many of the same advantages that pheromones do, including biodegradability, lack of toxicity, and low persistence in the environment. Also like pheromones, they are costly and time consuming to produce. In addition, insect hormones act rather slowly, sometimes taking a week or two to eliminate a pest, which by then may have done extensive damage. Insect hormones are not as species-specific as pheromones and therefore may affect natural predators and other nonpest species. The timing of application is also critical, for hormones are effective only at certain times in an insect's life cycle.

Second-Generation Pesticides Although many environmentalists support the banning of pesticides, this action is impracticable for political and economic reasons. Pesticides will remain a part of our pest-control strategy. However, several principles should guide their use: (1) they should be applied sparingly; (2) they should be applied at the most effective time, to reduce the number of applications; (3) they should destroy as few natural predators, nonpest species, and biological control agents as possible; (4) they should not be applied near supplies of drinking water; (5) they should be carefully tested for toxic effects; (6) persistent pesticides and pesticides that accumulate in the ecosystem should be avoided; (7) exposure to workers should be minimized; and (8) pesticides should be used to decrease populations to low levels, and once this is achieved, environmental, genetic, and cultural control measures should be used to keep populations low.

Cultural Control

Cultural control refers to many other simple techniques to limit pest populations. These methods include cultivation to control weeds, noisemakers to frighten birds, lights that draw insects to electrocution devices, manual removal of insects from crops, destruction of insect breeding grounds, improved sanitation, forecasting of insect emergence, quarantines to regulate the spread of pests, and water and fertilizer management to ensure optimum crop health and resistance to pests.

Economics, Risk, and Pest Control

The central goal of pest control is to reduce populations to levels that do not cause economic damage. The costs of pest control—economic, environmental, and health—should not exceed the economic benefits of increased yield (Chapter 24). To be certain that this does not happen, thorough and fair studies must be made comparing each of the pest control strategies.

Today, most of the money for pest control research goes for conventional chemical methods. Many critics agree that we must be willing to spend money today on newer pest control strategies, such as natural predators, that can be part of a long-term, sustainable pest management strategy. Though costs may be high initially, they may become insignificant over the long term.

Society might also rethink some of its needs for unblemished fruits and vegetables. The use of pesticides to prevent harmless blemishes is probably a waste of energy, time, and money. A few more spots on our oranges could mean a few more birds overhead, cleaner waterways, and improved health for workers and the general public.

As for poor nations, pest management programs can (1) make use of people to destroy insects and weeds by hand; (2) employ environmentally sound measures, such as crop rotation, heteroculture (mixed crops), timed plantings, natural predators, and genetically resistant plants and animals; and (3) minimize the use of first- and second-generation pesticides. Developed nations must keep companies from exporting pesticides that have been banned at home. (For more on banned chemicals see Lewis Regenstein's Viewpoint, "The Myth of Banned Chemicals," in Chapter 18.) The rich can also help the poor develop a sustainable pest management program through technical and financial assistance.

Herbicides in Peace and War

Before World War II few herbicides were used in the United States. Today, however, the herbicide industry is large and prosperous, with sales of over $1.3 billion a year. In 1981 alone 284 million kilograms (630 million pounds) of herbicide was sold in this country.

In the United States herbicides account for over 50% of the chemical pesticides applied each year. Although there are over 180 different types of synthetic herbicides on the market, the leading ones are atrazine and alachlor, which collectively account for half of the total sales. In addition, butylate and 2,4-D (2,4-dichlorophenoxyacetic acid) are used in large quantity.

Despite the number of herbicides in use, two particular chemicals have received most of the attention; these are 2,4-D and 2,4,5-T, nonpersistent synthetic organic compounds similar in function to plant hormones, called **auxins**. When sprayed on plants, 2,4-D and 2,4,5-T increase the metabolic rate of cells so much that plants cannot keep up with increased nutrient demands, and literally "grow to death."

Peacetime Uses: Pros and Cons

In peacetime, 2,4-D and 2,4,5-T have been sprayed on brush and plants along roadways, powerlines, and pipelines and have been used to control poison ivy and ragweed, to eliminate unwanted trees in commercial tree farms and in national forests, to control aquatic weeds, and to rid rangelands of brush and poisonous plants. Overall, three-fourths of these chemicals have been used for weed control on farms.

The benefits of such herbicides are many:

1. They decrease the amount of mechanical cultivation needed to control weeds and thus reduce fossil fuel consumption and soil erosion (Chapter Supplement 9-2).

2. They reduce human labor and thus cut costs.

3. They reduce losses to weeds when soils are too wet to cultivate with tractors since planes can spray crops.

4. They help farmers reduce water usage, because water escapes more rapidly from tilled ground.

However beneficial their use may be, herbicides have many drawbacks:

1. Farmers have found that some weeds that are not normally pests are resistant to herbicides and tend to proliferate after spraying, thus becoming a greater pest than the ones killed by the herbicide. Elimination of the new pest may require the use of an additional herbicide.

2. Weeds can become resistant to herbicides. Many agronomists believe that the problem of plant resistance to herbicides has been underestimated.

3. Herbicide use may increase the need for insecticides. The reason for this is that when herbicides are used, farmers often reduce tillage; weeds killed by herbicides remain on the ground and provide food and habitat for insect pests. In addition, herbicides that are used to control weeds around the periphery of fields may destroy the habitat of valuable predatory insects. Herbicides may also decrease the farmer's incentive to rotate crops, an effective way to reduce insect pests.

4. Herbicides may make some crops more susceptible to disease. For example, some herbicides reduce the waxy coating on plants, change their metabolic rates, and retard or stimulate plant growth; all of these may make plants more susceptible to disease.

5. Herbicides reduce farm employment. Although this may save farmers money, it may hurt the national economy.

6. There is great concern that some herbicides are toxic and may cause birth defects, cancer, and other illnesses.

Critics of herbicide use argue that integrated weed management is needed to reduce the application of these potentially toxic chemicals. **Integrated weed management** involves the limited application of herbicides with special equipment designed to reduce loss. Special wick applicators, for example, apply herbicide only on weeds between rows and thus use much less herbicide than aerial applications and create less environmental damage. The reasonable use of herbicides would be complemented by mechanical cultivation, proper spacing of rows for healthy crops, biological weed controls, and crop rotation.

Wartime Uses: Controversy over Defoliants

Herbicides were used extensively in the Vietnam War as defoliants to prevent guerilla ambushes along roads and waterways, to discourage the movement of soldiers through demilitarized zones and across the border of Laos, to destroy crops that might feed the enemy, and to clear areas around camps. Three herbicide preparations were sprayed from planes, helicopters, boats, trucks, and portable units from 1962 to 1970: Agent Orange (58%), Agent White (31%), and Agent Blue (11%).

The most effective and the most controversial of the herbicides was Agent Orange, half 2,4-D and half 2,4,5-T. During the war more than 42 million kilograms (93 million pounds) of Agent Orange was sprayed on the swamps and forests of Vietnam, resulting in the destruction of 1.8 million hectares (4.5 million acres) of countryside and at least 190,000 hectares (475,000 acres) of farmland. Over half of the mangrove vegetation of South Vietnam—1934 square kilometers (744 square miles)—and about 5% of the hardwood forests were destroyed. The forests alone represent about $500 million worth of wood, a supply that would have lasted the country about 30 years.

The prospect for these forests sems dim, especially since hardy weeds such as cogon grass and bamboo have invaded the deforested zones. Ecologists fear that these species may greatly delay recovery or prevent it altogether. Spraying of defoliants—and numerous insecticides, as well—created an unprecedented ecological disaster in Vietnam, resulting in the death of numerous fish and animals. The total impact of such actions will never be known.

Health Effects of Agent Orange Agent Orange may have been the cause of serious medical problems suffered by soldiers and villagers throughout Vietnam. The first indication of its health effects came in 1969 from Saigon newspapers, which reported an increase in miscarriages and birth defects in babies born in local hospitals. Critics argued that this was merely a propaganda campaign aimed at the United States. But Agent Orange sprayed in Vietnam was contaminated with dioxin, a chemical that causes birth defects and cancer in mice and rats. Dioxin, discussed in more detail in Chapter 22, is believed to be 100,000 times more potent than the tranquilizer thalidomide, which has caused many birth defects in the United States.

U.S. and Australian soldiers fighting in herbicide-defoliated areas drank water and bathed in bomb craters believed to have been contaminated by Agent Orange, ate sweet potatoes and other vegetables from contaminated fields, and in some instances were doused with herbicides while in the field. Often unable to wash or change their clothes after such frequent exposures, soldiers developed severe headaches, nausea, diarrhea, internal bleeding, chloracne (a severe skin rash similar to acne), and depression.

In 1970, as a result of the public outcry in the United States over reported birth defects and miscarriages in the Vietnamese population, the federal government banned the use of Agent Orange in Vietnam. In addition, in 1970 the secretaries of health, education, and welfare and agriculture suspended the use of 2,4,5-T in U.S. lakes and ponds, where it was used to control aquatic plants; on ditch banks, where it was used to control weeds; around homes and recreation sites; and on all crops except rice. Shortly after the bans, the use of 2,4-D and 2,4,5-T was stepped up in U.S. forests, supposedly to increase growth of commercial softwood timber by reducing competition from hardwood trees. To this day, the use of 2,4-D is virtually unrestricted. Studies have shown that 2,4,5-T probably does not cause birth defects itself. This has led some people to suggest that the herbicide be reauthorized if levels of dioxin are greatly reduced. Other studies, however, indicate that 2,4,5-T causes an increase in hydrogen peroxide in cells, which, in turn, alters the DNA and may lead to cancer.

Starting in the late 1970s, some Vietnam veterans began to suffer an unusual number of medical disorders. Once-healthy people experienced bouts of dizziness, nausea, insomnia, and diarrhea. Many developed chloracne over large parts of their body, had blurred vision, and suffered from fits of uncontrollable rage and depression. A high proportion of the men fathered infants that were born dead, aborted prior to term, or had multiple birth defects. Experts estimate that over 2000 defective babies will be fathered by Vietnam veterans. Still others have developed cancers such as lymphoma, leukemia, and testicular cancer, a rare disease normally found only in 6 of 100,000 young persons. (Similar symptoms have been observed in people living near forested areas in Oregon and northern California that were sprayed with herbicide to eliminate deciduous trees and brush.)

The Australian government sponsored a study of the health effects of 2,4-D and 2,4,5-T that was contaminated with dioxin at levels at least 20 to 50 times lower than the Agent Orange used in Vietnam. This survey showed no adverse effects. In addition, health statistics from a poorly run survey of an industrial accident in Italy where dioxin had been released also showed no effects. Based on these studies, both of which had numerous faults, the Veterans Administration argued that the U.S. veterans' claims were unfounded. However, a study of pilots and their crews who were involved in the spraying of Agent Orange is now under way in the United States to determine whether defoliants were the cause of the symptoms shown by many veterans. This study will not be completed until the 1990s. The Veterans Administration has also begun a long-term study of health effects on veterans, but results are not expected until 1987 at the earliest.

To date, more than 1200 disability claims have been filed with the Veterans Administration by U.S. soldiers, arguing that Agent Orange caused a myriad of disabilities. Of these, the agency has settled three claims, granting 10% disability for chloracne, which provides the veterans each with $48 per month. The agency and chemical manufacturers continue to deny any connection between Agent Orange and these defects and have labeled the symptoms a manifestation of stress, or "post-Vietnam syndrome."

In spite of a lack of a comprehensive medical study of Vietnam veterans, however, mounting evidence from the United States and abroad strongly supports the contention that Agent Orange and dioxin are responsible for much of the illness described above. Results from studies of workers at herbicide factories in Sweden; experiments with monkeys, rats, and mice; dioxin analyses of fatty tissues in Vietnam veterans; liver function tests in veterans; and studies of birth defects among offspring of Vietnamese soldiers all support the veterans' claims that Agent Orange produced the broad spectrum of symptoms described above. The most recent evidence implicates dioxin as the cause of soft-tissue sarcomas (cancers); veterans exposed to dioxin had a rate of soft-tissue sarcomas seven times higher than expected. Such findings may shift the Veterans Administration's position on Agent Orange.

Treatment of Vietnam veterans suffering from chronic debilitation may soon be possible with a drug called cholestyramine. Used to purge victims poisoned with the insecticide kepone, this drug may prove successful in flushing dioxin from the afflicted veterans' fatty tissues, where it is stored. Such a cure, if possible, could reverse the slow and painful deterioration that as many as 40,000 veterans are now experiencing. Whether it will prevent birth defects in yet unborn children remains to be seen.

Suggested Readings

Barrons, K. C. (1981). *Are Pesticides Really Necessary?* Chicago: Regnery (Gateway). A balanced view of pesticides.

Boraiko, A. A. and Ward, F. (1980) The Pesticide Dilemma. *National Geographic* 157(2): 145–183. A general account of pesticides and pest management.

Carson, R. (1962). *Silent Spring.* Boston: Houghton Mifflin. The book that raised worldwide alarm over the use of pesticides.

Clark, D. R., and Krynitsky, A. J. (1983). DDT: Recent Contamination in New Mexico and Arizona? *Environment* 25(5): 27–32. Information on continued use of banned DDT.

Davis, D. E. (1979). Herbicides in Peace and War. *BioScience* 29(2): 84–94. An account of the controversy over Agent Orange.

Galston, A. W. (1979). Herbicides: A Mixed Blessing. *BioScience* 29(2): 85–90. An interesting view of herbicides and their effects on humans and other organisms.

Heckman, C. W. (1982). Pesticide effects on aquatic habitats. *Environ. Sci. and Technol.* 16(1): 48A–57A. Detailed analysis on the effects of pesticides on aquatic systems.

Hileman, B. (1982). Herbicides in Agriculture. *Environ. Sci. and Technol.* 16(12): 645A–650A. A thoughtful analysis of the benefits and costs of herbicides.

Josephson, J. (1983). Pesticides of the Future. *Environ. Sci. and Technol.* 17(10): 464A–468A. Overview of chemical pesticides.

McEwen, F. L. (1978). Food Production—The Challenge for Pesticides. *BioScience* 28(12): 773–776. An excellent presentation on the history of pesticide use.

Mellanby, K., and Perring, F. H. (1977). *Ecological Effects of Pesticides.* New York: Academic Press. A more technical account of pesticides' effects.

Metcalf, R. L., and Kelman, A. (1981). Integrated Pest Management in China. *Environment* 23(4): 6–13. Superb account of pesticide problems and solutions in China.

Pimentel, D., and Goodman, N. (1978). Ecological Basis for the Management of Insect Populations. *Oikos* 30: 442–437. An excellent study of pesticides and pest management.

Regenstein, L. (1982). *America the Poisoned.* Washington, D.C.: Acropolis. Detailed account of pesticides and their effects.

van der Bosch, R. (1978). *The Pesticide Conspiracy.* New York: Doubleday. A study of the influence of pesticide manufacturers on integrated pest management.

Wilcox, F. A. (1983). *Waiting for an Army to Die: The Tragedy of Agent Orange.* New York: Vintage Books. Moving account of Agent Orange's effects on Vietnam veterans.

Soil and Soil Management

To build may have to be the slow and laborious task of years. To destroy can be the thoughtless act of a single day.

WINSTON CHURCHILL

All nations depend on their soil. But throughout the world rich and poor nations alike have plowed their soil indiscriminately to grow food for expanding populations, in the process destroying the roots of plants that have held the soil in place for centuries. Through mismanagement they let wind and water carry valuable topsoil into their streams, where it kills aquatic life and fills in reservoirs. In short, nations treat soil as if it were an inexhaustible resource and as if their people could continue without it.

In the United States 500,000 hectares (1.25 million acres) of farmland is retired from use each year as a result of soil erosion. In some places erosion is so great that two bushels of soil are lost for every bushel of corn produced. (Figure S9-1 shows areas of critical sheet and gully erosion in the United States.) Soil erosion may increase by 50% to 80% in the future if marginal land is brought into production to meet increased foreign demand for American-grown grains.

If agriculture is to remain productive indefinitely in the United States and abroad, erosion control must be implemented on a wide scale. This supplement presents some cost-effective ways to reduce erosion and create a sustainable agricultural system. But first let us turn our attention to soil and its formation.

What Is Soil?

Soil is a complex mixture of inorganic and organic materials with variable amounts of air and moisture. The inorganic components of soil may be clay, sand, silt, gravel, or stones. The organic components are detritus, organic wastes, and a multitude of living organisms. Soils are described according to six

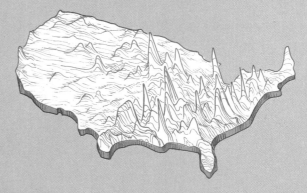

Figure S9-1
Regions of critical sheet and gully erosion in the United States. Peaks represent areas of high erosion.

general features: texture, structure, acidity, gas content, water content, and biotic composition.

Soil Formation

Soil formation is a complex and slow process, even under the best of conditions. The time it takes soil to develop depends partly on the type of **parent material**, the underlying substrate from which soil is formed. The formation of 2.5 centimeters (1 inch) of topsoil from hard rock may take 200 to 1200 years, depending on the climate. Softer parent materials such as shale, volcanic ash, sandstone, sand dunes, and gravel beds are converted to soil at a faster rate (20 years or so) if biogeochemical conditions are favorable.

A number of physical processes contribute to soil formation. Daily heating and cooling may cause the parent rock material to split and fragment, especially in climates where daily temperatures vary widely. Water entering cracks in rocks expands upon freezing, causing the rock to fragment further. Rock fragments formed by heating and cooling and by freezing are slowly pulverized into smaller particles by streams or landslides, hooves of animals, or wind and rain.

Soil formation is facilitated by a wide range of biological organisms. In Chapter 5, you learned how lichens "gnaw" away at rock surfaces by secreting carbonic acid. Lichens also capture dust, seeds, excrement, and dead plant matter, which help form soil. The roots of trees and large plants reach into small cracks and fracture the rock. Roots also serve as nutrient pumps, bringing up inorganic nutrients from deeper soil layers. These chemicals are first used to make leaves and branches, but after they fall and decay, they become part of the soil.

Grazing animals pulverize rock and gravel under their hooves and drop excrement on the ground, adding to the soil's organic matter. The white rhinoceros, for example, produces about 30 tons of manure each year, which is deposited in its territory. Finally, a variety of insects and other creatures participate in soil formation.

The Soil Profile

Holes dug in the ground at construction sites or in your own backyard show that the soil is often arranged in layers of different color and composition. These layers are called **horizons**, and they form the soil profile.

Agronomists recognize five major horizons (Figure S9-2). The uppermost **O horizon**, a thin layer of organic waste from animals and detritus, is a zone of organic decomposition, characterized by a dark, rich color. It is not present in fields that have been plowed, as it is mixed in with the next layer.

The **A horizon**, or **topsoil**, varies in thickness from 2.5 centimeters (1 inch) in some regions to 60 centimeters (2 feet) in the rich farmland of Iowa. This horizon is generally rich in inorganic and organic nutrients, and it is economically important because it supports agricultural crops. The A horizon is darker and looser than the deeper layers. It holds moisture because of its organic content and is quite porous. The A horizon is also known as the "zone of leaching," because nutrients are leached out of it as water percolates through it from the surface.

The **B horizon**, or **subsoil**, is also known as the "zone of accumulation," because it receives and collects minerals and nutrients from above. This layer is lightly colored and much denser than the topsoil since it lacks organic matter. The **C horizon** is a transition zone between the parent material below and the layers of soil above. The **D horizon** is the parent material from which soils are derived. Not all horizons are present in all soils; in some, the layering may be missing altogether.

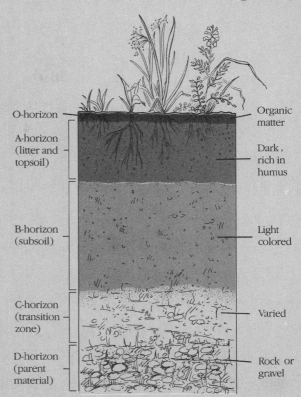

Figure S9-2
Soil profile, showing the five horizons. Not all are found in all locations.

The soil profile is determined by the climate (especially rainfall and temperature), type of vegetation, parent material, age of the soil, and the biological organisms. Soil profiles tell soil scientists whether land is best for agriculture, wildlife habitat, forestry, pasture, rangeland, or recreation. They also tell us how suitable soil might be for various other uses, such as home building and highway construction.

Soil Management

Soil management has two primary goals: to prevent erosion and to prevent nutrient depletion. These goals go hand in hand.

Erosion Control

Control of soil erosion can be achieved by a number of methods. Many of these can be used together on the same land, decreasing erosion by a substantial margin. Although implementing these measures will raise prices in the short term, they will surely save money in the long run.

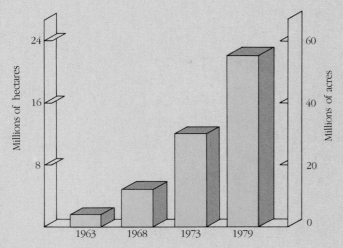

Figure S9-3
Growth in minimum (conservation) tillage in the United States.

Figure S9-4
Minimum tillage planter, designed to dig furrows in crop residue.

Soil conservation is a continuing process, not something applied once and then forgotten. It is necessary if we are to maintain worldwide agricultural productivity.

Minimum Tillage A highly effective measure for controlling soil erosion, **minimum tillage** is now practiced on over 27 million hectares (67 million acres) of land in the United States (Figure S9-3). The principal goal of this practice is to reduce the amount of mechanical disruption of the soil by not plowing a field after the crop is harvested or by not cultivating row crops such as corn to remove weeds. After a field of wheat is harvested, for example, the stubble (remaining stalks) may be left in place rather than plowed under. As a result, the field is not left barren between growing seasons, and erosion can be decreased by up to 90% for some crops. When new crops are planted, the seeds are sowed with a planter that cuts through the residue left on the surface (Figure S9-4).

Minimum tillage also reduces energy consumption by as much as 80% and conserves soil moisture by reducing evaporation. Crop residues may increase habitat for predatory insects that exert a natural control over pests.

Minimum tillage has several drawbacks. Herbicides are often used to replace mechanical cultivation to control weeds. Crop residues may harbor harmful insects. Finally, many minimum-tillage operations require new farm equipment. To reduce costs, soil conservation districts may purchase the equipment and lease it to farmers.

Contour Farming **Contour farming** involves the planting of crops along level lines that follow the contours of the land, rather than up and down slopes. As illustrated in Figure S9-5, rows are planted across the direction of water flow on hilly or

Figure S9-5
This land is farmed along the contour lines to reduce soil erosion and surface runoff, thus saving soil and moisture alike. The farmer has used strip cropping as an additional erosion control measure.

sloped land. This reduces the flow of water across the land, resulting in a tremendous reduction of erosion and a marked increase in water retention. In a Texas experiment water runoff from a contoured field was only 4 centimeters (1.6 inches) per year, compared with 11.6 centimeters (4.6 inches) per year for uncontoured fields. Soil erosion can be reduced by 60% to 80%. Practiced successfully by Thomas Jefferson in 1813, contour farming is a proven technique that could be more widely used.

Figure S9-6
Strips of corn protect small grain plants from the effects of wind.

Figure S9-7
This Iowa corn is grown on sloping land with the aid of terraces, small earth embankments that reduce water flow across the surface. The corn is planted in the stubble of last year's crop.

Strip Cropping   As illustrated in Figure S9-6, **strip cropping** is the planting of alternate crops in huge strips in fields that are subject to soil erosion by wind or water. Strip cropping can be combined with contour farming so that alternating crops are planted along the contour to further decrease erosion. As an example, farmers may alternate row crops such as corn with cover crops such as alfalfa. Water flows more easily through row crops and begins to gain momentum, but when it meets the cover crop, its flow is virtually stopped.

Terracing   For thousands of years many people have grown crops on terraces in mountainous terrain. **Terracing** has also been used in the United States for over 40 years on land with less pronounced slope (Figure S9-7).

Terracing today involves the construction of small earthen embankments on sloped cropland. These are placed across the slope to check water flow and minimize erosion. Terraces are expensive to construct and often interfere with the operation of large farm equipment; thus, farmers may prefer other, cheaper forms of soil conservation.

Figure S9-8
Shelterbelts used to protect farmland from the erosive effects of wind in Michigan.

Gully Reclamation   Gullies are a danger sign of rapid soil erosion. Some gullies work their way up hills at a rate of 4.5 meters (15 feet) per year. The dangers of gully erosion are many: it robs the land of soil; it makes it difficult to use modern farm machinery; and soil eroded from gullies can wash into streams and onto lower fields, destroying crops.

If detected early, such erosion can be stopped by seeding barren soils with rapidly growing plants, ground cover, and trees. Small earthen dams can be built across the gully to reduce water flow, retain moisture for plant growth, and capture sediment. This sediment will eventually support vegetation as erosion is reduced. Too often land with severe gullies is abandoned or haphazardly reclaimed, and erosion only worsens in time.

Shelterbelts   In 1935 the U.S. government mounted a wide campaign to prevent the recurrence of the disastrous dust bowl days. One part of this program involved planting long rows of trees as windbreaks, or **shelterbelts,** in a north/south orientation along the margins of farms in the Great Plains states (Figure S9-8). Today, thousands of kilometers of shelterbelts have been planted from Texas to North Dakota.

Shelterbelts block the wind and, therefore, decrease soil erosion and damage to crops caused by windblown dirt particles. In the winter they reduce the amount of blowing snow, thus allowing snow to build up in fields. This insulates the soil and also increases soil moisture and groundwater supplies. Shelterbelts can also improve irrigation efficiency by reducing the amount of water carried away from sprinklers. In addition, they provide habitat for animals, pest-eating insects, and pollinators. Shelterbelts protect citrus groves from wind that blows fruit from trees. They have the added benefit of saving energy by reducing heat loss from homes and farm buildings.

Few people question the effectiveness of the soil conservation methods described above. A University of Nebraska study showed that terracing or contour farming alone reduces erosion by half. Combined, they can reduce soil loss by 75%. Minimum tillage is even more effective. By itself, it can reduce erosion rates by 90%, and when it is combined with terracing and contour farming, soil erosion can be reduced by 98%.

In a sustainable agricultural system, control of soil erosion assumes a position of great importance. Inexpensive techniques that are available now can slow down the rate of erosion and help us ensure food for future generations. Despite the availability of soil conservation techniques, many farmers worldwide are reluctant to invest in such practices. An economic explanation of this phenomenon is given in Chapter 24.

Preventing the Depletion of Soil Nutrients

Preventing soil erosion saves topsoil and also preserves soil nutrients needed to maintain food output. Several ways to prevent the depletion of soil nutrients, mentioned in Chapter 9, are discussed in more detail below.

Use of Organic Fertilizers   Organic fertilizers such as cow, chicken, and hog manure and human sewage are excellent soil supplements. They replenish organic matter and important soil nutrients such as nitrogen and phosphorus. Other organic materials can be used to build soil; especially helpful are leguminous plants such as alfalfa that are grown during the off-season and plowed under before planting crops. Referred to as "green manure," they not only add organic matter to the soil and retain moisture but also reduce soil erosion during fallow periods.

Soil enrichment with organic fertilizers (1) improves soil structure, (2) increases water retention, (3) increases fertility and crop yield, (4) provides good environment for bacterial growth necessary for nitrogen fixation, (5) helps prevent shifts in the acidity of the soil, and (6) tends to prevent the leaching of minerals from the soil by rain and snowmelt. In addition, the use of human wastes on farmland could significantly reduce water pollution by waste treatment plants.

Organic wastes have been successfully applied in a number of regions. In Michigan, for instance, cow manure applied to farmland at a rate of 2 metric tons per hectare (0.7 tons per acre) increases yield by 31%. The city of Milwaukee markets human wastes in a dry sludge called Milorganite. Chicago exports sludge from sewage treatment plants to fertilize farmlands in the vicinity. In the Northeast farmers sow winter vetch between rows of corn in late August. The vetch remains on the ground in the winter, protecting the soil. In the spring the vetch is plowed under, adding about 135 kilograms of nitrogen per hectare (720 pounds per acre).

Organic fertilizers, especially human wastes, are not without their problems. One of the leading problems is transporting waste to farms, which can require extensive trucking or pipelines. Another problem is that waste from municipal sewage treatment plants may be contaminated with pathogenic organisms such as bacteria, viruses, and parasites. Theoretically, some of these could be incorporated by plants and reenter the human food chain. Toxic heavy metals such as mercury, cadmium, and lead are also present in municipal wastes.

Use of Synthetic Fertilizers   In the United States synthetic fertilizer is the greatest source of nitrogen used by farmers. It is made by chemically combining nitrogen and hydrogen to form ammonia and ammonium salts. Some nitrates and urea are also made. These compounds can be applied directly to the soil as a liquid, or they can be mixed with phosphorus and potassium to make a granular fertilizer that most of us are familiar with.

Synthetic fertilizers containing nitrogen, phosphorus, and potassium can restore soil fertility, but they do not replenish organic matter and generally do not add soil micronutrients essential for proper plant growth and human nutrition. Crop yields may be increased or be kept high by treating land with artificial fertilizer, but the soil is slowly degraded in the process. In addition, excess fertilizer may be washed from the land by rains and end up in streams, causing a number of problems. (These are addressed in Chapter 20, on water pollution.)

To preserve long-term productivity and develop a sustainable agricultural system, synthetic fertilizers must be supplemented by organic fertilizers. Synthetic fertilizers should probably be replaced entirely where feasible, especially in developing nations and on small farms that are near sources of organic fertilizer. Combined with soil-conservation and organic-enrichment programs, synthetic fertilizers will inevitably play a role in feeding the world's people. As fossil fuels become scarcer, though (Chapter 13), synthetic fertilizers may become increasingly costly.

Crop Rotation   In modern agriculture, synthetic fertilizers have allowed farmers to grow the same crop year after year. This way farmers can concentrate their efforts on one crop that they know and understand well. However profitable this might be, the practice is ecologically unsound, for it gradually depletes the soil of nutrients, increases soil erosion, and worsens problems with pests and pathogens. Crop rotation, once a common practice among farmers in the United States, can return us to a more ecologically sound and sustainable agricultural system.

Using the age-old practice of rotating crops, a farmer may plant a soil-depleting crop (corn) for one to two years, then follow it with a cover crop, such as grasses or various legumes. The cover crop reduces soil erosion and may replenish soil nitrogen. Often, cover crops are not harvested but simply are plowed under as green manure.

Putting It All Together: Organic Farming   Today, thousands of farmers are running profitable farms either without the use of synthetic chemical fertilizers and pesticides or with only small amounts of them. This system of agriculture, called **organic farming**, avoids or largely excludes synthetic fertilizers, pesticides, growth regulators, and livestock food additives, relying instead on crop rotation, green manure, animal wastes, off-farm organic wastes, mechanical cultivation, and biological pest control to the maximum extent possible. Believing that a sustainable and productive agricultural system is more important than high yields alone, organic farmers concentrate on keeping their soil in top condition.

Evidence is growing regarding the success of organic farming. The noted ecologist Barry Commoner found that organic farms produced nearly as well as their conventional counterparts of similar size. Further research has supported this conclusion: organic farms produce about 11% fewer vegetables, but the net income per hectare is about the same because of the lower costs. Organic farms require 60% less fossil fuel energy to produce corn crops with only about 3% lower yield than those grown on conventional farms.

There are some limits to organic farming: (1) organic fertilizers may not replace all of the phosphorus and potassium drained from the soil by plants; (2) nitrogen replacement by legumes may not always be enough to give high yields of crops such as corn that have a high nitrogen requirement; (3) total production may be lower than on a conventional farm because of land devoted to soil conservation; and (4) there is a three- to five-year transition period from conventional to organic farming during which yields may be low and losses to insects and weeds may be high.

Given these drawbacks, wholesale adoption of organic farming methods in developing countries seems unlikely. What is more probable, though, is the adoption of many of the techniques by traditional farmers. In developing nations, opportunities to develop organic farming are numerous. Considering the high cost of fossil fuels and fertilizers and the abundance of labor, organic farming may be well suited to such nations.

Achieving Cost-Effective Conservation

Control of soil erosion and soil infertility are economic problems as much as resource conservation problems. However, progress in soil erosion control has been slow. Today, because of rising production costs, short-term profits often preempt long-range matters of fertility and erosion control. What is most urgent to the farmer is the profit needed to keep up payments on land, fertilizer, machinery, pesticides, and seed, not the long-term stability of world agriculture.

Soil conservation is not practiced on a broader scale for several reasons. In general, many farmers do not view soil erosion as a major problem because fertilizers and new high-yield seeds have increased crop yields and masked the effects of excessive erosion. In taking the shortest path between the top and bottom line on their balance sheet, farmers ignore practices that preserve the soil at its maximum productivity.

How can we achieve cost-effective soil conservation?

1. We must target areas where erosion is the most severe (see Figure S9-1). Currently, one-half of all cropland erosion in the United States comes from about 10% of the total farmland. Concentrated efforts on this land could be highly cost effective in reducing soil erosion.

2. Governmental agencies, such as the Soil Conservation Service, should promote the most cost-effective ways of controlling erosion to decrease cost and increase benefit.

3. Agricultural zoning regulations could be enacted to prohibit highly erodible land from being used.

4. The federal government could pay farmers to abandon highly erodible and marginally productive land. Farmers could use some of the money to rent or buy land more suitable for agriculture and could plant the highly erodible land in dense cover crop to prevent further erosion.

5. Special investment tax credits or income tax deductions could be given to farmers to help defray the cost of soil conservation measures.

6. Taxes on farmland, farm machinery, and supplies could be levied, and the revenues from such taxes could go into publicly funded soil conservation programs. Taxes on food could also be levied and used for conservation. This would place part of the financial burden for good soil management on the consumers.

7. Farmers applying for government loans, crop insurance, or aid could be required to have an approved soil conservation program already in operation before money would be given to them.

8. Farmers could be given money to attend special soil conservation programs sponsored by the government but taught by other farmers with hands-on experience.

9. Some unemployed workers could be trained as government soil conservation specialists and field workers who would work with farmers, helping them implement soil conservation. Follow-up testing could be done to measure the success of erosion control and fertility enhancement programs.

10. The U.S. Department of Agriculture could strengthen the Soil Conservation Service (SCS) and increase advisors and literature available to farmers.

11. States could strengthen their role in soil conservation. Cooperation could be encouraged between state, local, and federal agencies involved in soil conservation.

12. Farmers throughout the world could be taught that conservation is a lifelong job, as much a part of farming as sowing the seed.

13. Nations could adopt national soil conservation programs that reduce erosion to tolerable levels. They could be urged to spend money now, even though returns may be decades away.

14. Rich nations could be encouraged to improve their own soil management programs and then help the poorer nations.

Whatsoever a man soweth, that shall he also reap.

GALATIANS 6:7

Suggested Readings

Brock, B. G. (1982). Weed Control versus Soil Erosion Control. *Journal of Soil and Water Conservation* (March/April): 73–76. A thorough study of weed control by tillage and herbicides.

Clayton, W. O., Johnson, J. D., and Clayton, K. C. (1982). A Policy Option for Targeting Soil Conservation Expenditures. *Journal of Soil and Water Conservation* (March/April): 68–72. A worthwhile article.

Crites, R. W. (1984). Land Use of Wastewater and Sludge. *Environmental Science and Technology* 18(5): 140A–147A. Excellent review article.

Jeffords, J. M. (1982). Soil Conservation Policy for the Future. *Journal of Soil and Water Conservation* (January/February): 10–13. A view of the needs of soil conservation policy in the United States.

Owen, O. S. (1980). *Natural Resource Conservation.* New York: Macmillan. Excellent sections on agriculture, soils, and land management.

Sampson, R. N. (1981). *Farmland or Wasteland: A Time to Choose.* Emmaus, Pa.: Rodale Press. Well-written book on agriculture and soil conservation.

U.S. Department of Agriculture (no date). *Conserving Soil.* Washington, D.C.: U.S. Government Printing Office. An elementary account of soil and soil conservation, but an excellent resource for teachers.

— (1969). *Windbreaks for Conservation* (Agriculture Information Bulletin 339). Washington, D.C.: U.S. Government Printing Office. A detailed document on shelterbelts.

— (1980). *America's Soil and Water: Condition and Trends.* Washington, D.C.: U.S. Government Printing Office. Valuable reference.

— (1980). *Soil, Water, and Related Resources in the United States* (vols. 1 and 2). Washington, D.C.: U.S. Government Printing Office. Detailed references on nonfederal soil and water resources.

— (1981). *Assistance Available from the Soil Conservation Service* (Agriculture Information Bulletin 345). Washington, D.C.: U.S. Government Printing Office. Covers the types of services offered.

— (1982). *A National Program for Soil and Water Conservation* (summary of the 1982 Final Program Report and Environmental Impact Statement for the Soil and Water Resources Conservation Act of 1977). Washington, D.C.: U.S. Government Printing Office. Outline of possible federal policy for soil conservation.

10

Plants and Wildlife: Imperiled Resources

The worst sin toward our fellow creatures is not to hate them, but to be indifferent to them; that's the essence of inhumanity.

GEORGE BERNARD SHAW

The bald eagle is a strong, majestic bird that soars with ease among the clouds. A creature that commands respect and instills a sense of awe, it seemed an appropriate symbol for a fiercely independent new nation. It was certainly better than Benjamin Franklin's candidate, the wild turkey.

Today, the bald eagle is teetering close to extinction in the continental United States. By some estimates, there may be only 1300 nesting pairs left in the lower 48 states. Though the bald eagle has been fully protected since 1940, it has fallen victim to the encroachment of human society: DDT applied to control insects; hunters in helicopters out for "sport," trophies, or profit; ranchers who have littered their land with toxic bait set out for coyotes; and housing developers who have destroyed its nesting grounds.

In 43 of the lower 48 states the bald eagle is considered endangered, and in the remaining 5 it is classified as threatened (Table 10-1). But the eagle is not alone. Hundreds of plants and animals now face extinction. Each of these species is a part of the biosphere, that living skin of this fragile planet, and each fits nicely into a cohesive whole upon which all life depends.

This chapter will examine the issue of extinction—what causes it, how we can save endangered species, and why we should.

History of Plant and Animal Extinction

As many as 500 million kinds of plant, animal, and micro-organism have made this planet home since life began over 3.5 billion years ago. Today, there are only 5 million to 10 million species alive—we do not know exactly how many, because there are many biologically uncharted areas such as the tropical rain forests, where some estimate that over 90% of the living organisms remain unclassified. Thus, since life began, about 490 million species have become **extinct**.

A study of the history of life from an evolutionary per-spective teaches us that biological extinction is a fact of

Table 10-1 · Categories of Animals at Risk

Classification	Meaning
Critically endangered	Will not survive without human assistance (example: California condor, Florida panther)
Endangered	In immediate danger of extinction (examples: whooping crane, red wolf, key deer, blue whale)
Threatened	Abundant in parts of its range, but severely depleted in others (examples: grizzly bear, sandhill crane)
Rare	Not endangered at present, but at risk because of low numbers (includes many island species)

Source: These classifications have been developed by the International Union for the Conservation of Nature and Natural Resources. The group's *Red Book* lists animals according to their proximity to ultimate extinction. The *Black Book,* also published by the organization, lists species that have become extinct since 1600.

Figure 10-1
Stages in the evolutionary history of the horse.

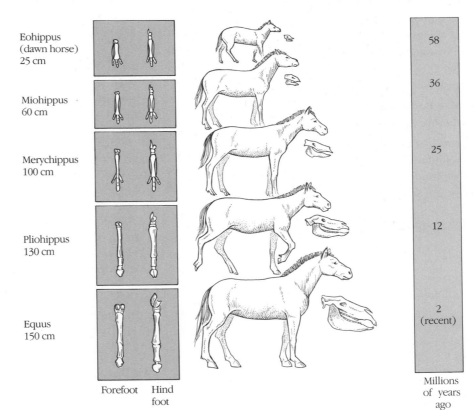

Eohippus
(dawn horse)
25 cm

Miohippus
60 cm

Merychippus
100 cm

Pliohippus
130 cm

Equus
150 cm

Forefoot   Hind foot

58

36

25

12

2
(recent)

Millions
of years
ago

life. As species evolve, the old give way to the new (Figure 10-1). Many of the so-called extinct species are represented today by their descendants. Thus, many species did not die off as such but were simply altered during evolution.

Other species vanished completely as a result of drastic climatic changes or increasing environmental resistance created by excess predation or disease. The dinosaurs, for example, perished rather abruptly all over the world 65 million years ago, possibly as a result of global cooling.

Much more recently, at the end of the Pleistocene epoch 10,000 years ago, many large mammals such as the saber-toothed tiger and giant tree sloth vanished from North America. Their extinction resulted either from climatic changes at the end of the Ice Age or possibly from over-hunting by humans entering North America from Siberia. As these people moved south and east, they hunted the large mammals such as the woolly mammoth, woolly rhinoceros, giant deer, ground sloth, mastodons, giant beavers, sabertoothed tigers, bison, and elk. They undoubtedly also competed for the same food resources.

From the end of the Pleistocene until now, the earth's climate has been fairly constant, and relatively few plants and animals have become extinct. As shown in Figure 10-2, however, species extinction has begun to rise. In the 1800s, 84 animal species and subspecies are known to have vanished. By 1984 the number had risen to 184, and if trends continue, many scientists believe, 170 more species will disappear by 2000, bringing the total to more than 350. If conditions turn considerably worse, more than 700 additional species might be destroyed before the end of the century.

One vertebrate species is becoming extinct every nine months, compared with a natural rate of one species every thousand years (Table 10-2). When plants, insects, and microbes are added, the rate may be as high as one species per day. Ecologists argue that plant extinctions will have much more profound impacts on the ecosystem than the extinction of animals, because plants form the base of the food web.

Some authors assert that if the world's population continues to grow and nations continue to destroy wildlife habitat by expanding agriculture and other activities at the current pace, the extinction rate could reach 20,000 species a year. At this rate 400,000 species of plants and animals could be wiped out in 20 years (Table 10-3). World

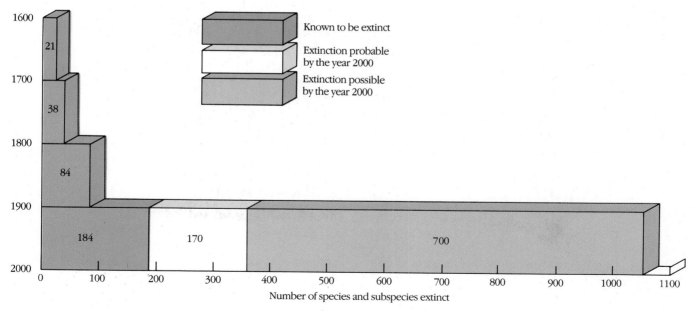

Figure 10-2
Extinction rate of animal species past and projected. Notice the rapid increase in the 20th century.

Table 10-2 Some Extinct Animal Species

Species	Location	Year or Century of Extinction
Arabian ostrich	Saudi Arabia	20th
Spectacled cormorant	Bering Island	1852
Bonin night heron	Bonin Islands	1889
Labrador duck	Eastern N. America	1875
Red-billed rail	Tahiti	19th
Hawaiian rail	Hawaii	19th
Great auk	North Atlantic	1884
Passenger pigeon	Eastern N. America	1914
Cuba red macaw	Cuba	19th
Carolina parakeet	Southeastern U.S.	20th
North Island laughing owl	New Zealand	19th
Puerto Rican nighthawk	Puerto Rico	20th
Stephen Island wren	New Zealand	20th
Oahu thrush	Oahu Island	20th
Eastern barred bandicoot	Australia	20th
Tasmanian wolf	Tasmania	20th
Stellar's sea cow	Bering Sea	1768
Sea mink	Northeastern U.S.	19th
Grizzly bear	North America	19th–20th
Long-eared kit fox	Southeastern U.S.	19th
Japanese wolf	Japan	20th
Florida wolf	Florida	20th
Cape lion	South Africa	1865
Syrian wild ass	Syria, Persia	1927
Arizona wapiti (elk)	Arizona	1906
Badlands bighorn sheep	American Midwest	20th
Rufous gazelle	Algeria	20th
Oregon bison	Oregon	19th

Source: Cousteau, J. Y. (1981), *The Cousteau Almanac. An Inventory of Life on Our Water Planet,* New York, Doubleday, pp. 140–145.

wildlife expert Norman Myers argues that we could lose 1 million species by 2000. Although such high rates of extinction are probably exaggerated, extinction will undoubtedly increase unless we make conscious efforts to curb population growth and properly manage our renewable and nonrenewable resources.

What Causes Extinction?

Chapter 2 discussed species extinction using the Multiple Cause and Effect model. This brief study showed that plant and animal extinction results from many underlying forces such as economics, politics, and psychology. Figure 10-3 shows the specific activities that cause extinction and the relative importance of each. Some of these, such as hunting, have a direct impact on species; others, such as the introduction of foreign species, have an indirect effect. In the real world, though, two or more of these factors usually act in concert, making solutions more difficult to achieve. Let's examine each of these in more detail.

Alteration of Habitat

The most visible road to extinction is habitat alteration. If an animal's habitat is destroyed or tampered with, it must either adapt to the changes, move elsewhere or die. When forced out of its territory, it often finds that suitable habitat is already in use. Consequently, either it must compete with existing animals of the same species or animals in similar niches, or it must migrate into a marginal habitat, where it may succumb to predation, starvation, or disease.

Habitat is destroyed by deforestation, drainage or filling of wetlands, overgrazing, expanding agriculture, urban and suburban development, highway construction, dam building, strip mining, and others. Some alterations may not be deliberate. For example, the control of forest fires has been a goal of U.S. society since about the turn of the century. Fires destroy wildlife habitat, valuable timber, watersheds, and homes. But fire is a natural component of the ecosystem that helps many species in unexpected ways. For example, Kirtland's warblers winter each year in the forested islands in the northern Bahamas, and they return in the spring to central Michigan to their breeding grounds. Here, the birds nest on the ground, protected from view by the dense lower branches of young jack pines. Occasional fires destroy the pines and allow new seedlings to grow, giving the warbler a renewed supply of nesting sites. Well-intentioned fire-prevention programs now protect the forests, permitting the jack pines to grow tall, but as they grow, the lower branches begin to die. This reduces the number of protected sites for nesting and has contributed to a marked decline in the warbler population. Today, there are only about 200 pairs left.

Other human activities have affected the Kirtland's warbler. For example, the clearing of the dense Michigan forests has allowed the cowbird to penetrate the warbler's breeding range. The cowbird lays its eggs in the warbler's nest, and its fast-growing chicks consume much of the food intended for warbler young, resulting in a lower survival rate among warbler offspring. Furthermore, commercial forestry in the Bahamas has destroyed much of the bird's wintering ground. Together, these unrelated actions have nearly wiped out this tiny population of birds.

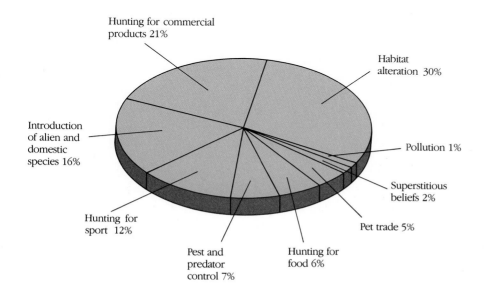

Hunting for commercial products 21%

Habitat alteration 30%

Introduction of alien and domestic species 16%

Pollution 1%

Superstitious beliefs 2%

Hunting for sport 12%

Pet trade 5%

Pest and predator control 7%

Hunting for food 6%

Figure 10-3
An approximate breakdown of the human activities that lead to extinction. More than one activity is often involved, however.

Table 10-3   Species Endangered or Threatened in the United States

Species	Status	Estimated Population	Year	Habitat	Causes for Decline, Comments
Mammals					
Florida panther *Felis concolor coryi*	E	100–300 10–15	1940s/1960s 1978	Florida's Big Cypress Swamp	Overhunting
Eastern timber wolf *Canis lycaon*	E/T	832–1332 + 22 in captivity 1000–1200	1969/1970 1978	Primarily Minnesota	Hunting and trapping, modification of habitat. Stable population in Minnesota
Red wolf *Canis rufus*	E	16 in captivity	c. 1969	Formerly Texas and Louisiana coasts	Trapping, hunting, disease
San Joaquin kit fox *Vulpes macrotis mutica*	E	1000–3000	1970	Foothills below 2000 feet, western San Joaquin Valley, California, areas of native vegetation	Destruction of habitat; illegal shooting, trapping
Black-footed ferret *Mustela nigripes*	E	31–32 + 3 in captivity	1950s/1960s	Western North Dakota, South Dakota, northern Montana; Alberta, Canada; central New Mexico	Destruction of habitat
Grizzly bear *Ursus arctos*	T	850 695–1020	1960s 1970	Colorado, Idaho, Montana, Washington, Wyoming	Expanding human activity
Utah prairie dog *Cyonmys parvidens*	E	5715	1972	South central Utah	Disease, damage to habitat
Delmarva Peninsula (Bryant) fox squirrel *Sciurus niger cinereus*	E	468 100–200	1960s 1979	Southeastern Maryland, Chincoteague National Wildlife Refuge	Destruction of habitat
Key deer *Odocoileus virginianus clavium*	E	30 300 600	1949 1964 1972	Florida Keys	Destruction of habitat, hurricanes, fires, overhunting. Slowly increasing over a small range
West Indian manatee (Florida) *Trichechus manatus*	E	1000	1978	Florida coastal waters	Excessive killing, habitat loss, boat accidents

Birds

Species	Status	Year	Range	Population	Cause
Eastern brown pelican *Pelecanus occidentalis carolinensis*	E	1977	Southeastern Atlantic coast, Texas coast	16,000	Reproduction impairment (thin egg shells), primarily from pesticides (DDT and dieldrin) in food
California brown pelican *Pelecanus occidentalis californicus*	E	1972	Pacific coastal islands	100,000 including Mexico	Reproduction impairment (thin egg shells), primarily from pesticides (DDT and dieldrin) in food
Aleutian Canada goose *Branta canadensis leucopareia*	E	1977	Breeds in western Aleutians; winters in California's central valley	1600	Reduction of secure breeding range caused by predation by arctic foxes (*Alopex lagopus*)
California condor *Gymnogyps californianus*	E	1940s / early 1960s / late 1960s / 1979	Mountains north of Los Angeles	60 / 40 / 51–53 / 25–30	Land development, decreasing food supply, pesticides, pollution
Whooping crane *Grus americana*	E	Pre-settlement / mid 1800s / 1941 / 1948 / 1950–1952 / late 1960s / 1972 / 1976 / 1979	Breeds in Wood Buffalo National Park, Mackenzie, Canada; winters on Texas coast, occasionally in Mexico	2000–4000 / 1300 / 21 / 16 / 25 / 60 / 80 / 96 / 120–125, including 29 in captivity	Shooting, reduction of breeding habitat prior to 1940s
Mississippi sandhill crane *Grus canadensis pulla*	E	1970 / 1978	Jackson County, Mississippi	39–40, including 9 in captivity / 45–48	Modification of habitat
Puerto Rico parrot *Amazon vittata*	E	1975 / 1976 / 1977 / 1978 / 1979	Luquillo Mountains, Puerto Rico	19 / 22 / 18 / 26–28 + 15 in captivity / 25 + 15 in captivity	Destruction of habitat, competition for nesting sites; taking as pets; disease; shooting

Table 10-3 (continued) Species Endangered or Threatened in the United States

Species	Status	Estimated Population	Year	Habitat	Causes for Decline, Comments
Birds (continued)					
Bald eagle *Haliaeetus leucocephalus*	E/T	More than 1300 nesting pairs; 119 nesting pairs; 118 nesting pairs	1979; 1968; 1979	Primarily Chesapeake, Northwest, Great Lakes estuarine areas. Population includes only 48 states. In National Forests of Michigan, Wisconsin, and Minnesota	Destruction of habitat, pesticides in food
American peregrine falcon *Falco peregrinus anatum*	E	120–150 + 200 in captivity	1979	Breeds from nonarctic Alaska, south to Baja California, to eastern Rocky Mountains. Population includes only 48 states	Reproduction impairment (thin egg shells), primarily from pesticides (DDT and dieldrin) in food
Arctic peregrine falcon *Falco peregrinus tundrius*	E	2000–6000 breeding pairs	1960s	Treeless tundra of arctic Alaska, Canada, western Greenland	Reproduction impairment (thin egg shells), primarily from pesticides (DDT and dieldrin) in food
Attwater's greater prairie chicken *Tympanuchus cupido attwateri*	E	2200	1971	Texas coastal prairie	Destruction of habitat
Red-cockaded woodpecker *Dendrocopos borealis*	E	3000–10,000 fewer than 1000	1970; 1979	Open, old pinewoods from southeastern Oklahoma, Texas, western Kentucky, southeastern Virginia to southern Florida	Reduction of habitat
Reptiles/ Amphibians					
Houston toad *Bufo houstonensis*	E	1000–1500	1978	Southeastern Texas	Destruction of habitat, hybridization
Green turtle *Chelonia mydas*	E	Fewer than 100 mature adults	1978	Southeastern Florida coast, Mexico (threatened worldwide)	Commercial exploitation, beach development

Species	Status	Population	Year	Location	Cause
Kemp's ridley sea turtle *Lepidochelys kempi*	E	40,000 nesting females / 500–1000 nesting females	1947 / 1979	Nesting habitat: Rancho Nuevo, Mexico; Padre Island National Seashore, Texas	Predation, poaching
American alligator *Alligator mississippiensis*	E/T	52,165 / 1 million + several thousand in captivity	1970 / 1979	North Carolina, Texas, Mississippi, Arkansas, southeastern California	Commercial exploitation, destruction of habitat prior to 1970; great population increase in 1970s
American crocodile *Crocodylus acutus*	E	1000–2000 / 100–400	1900 / 1979	Southern Florida	Urbanization, destruction of habitat
Fishes					
Snail darter *Percina tanasi*	E	3000	late 1970s	Originally in Little Tennessee River, late 1970s, stocked in Hiwassee River, Holston River, Tennessee	Loss of habitat
Plants					
Harperocallis flava	E	Fewer than 100*	1979	Apalachicola National Forest, Florida	Changes in land management, vandalism, harvest by collectors
Kokia cookei	E	1 in cultivation	1979	Formerly western Molokai, Hawaiian Islands	Destruction of habitat; grazing by cattle, goats
Ancistrocactus tobuschii	E	Less than 200*	1979	Stream banks and loose gravel bars, central Texas	Harvest by collectors, natural flooding
Echinocereus kuenzleri	E	Fewer than 200*	1979	Central New Mexico highlands	Highway construction, harvest by collectors
Sclerocactus glaucus	T	15,000*	1979	Western Colorado and eastern Utah plateaus	Harvest by collectors, recreational use of high desert
Arctostaphylos bookeri ssp. *ravenii*	E	1*	1979	San Francisco Presidio	Human trampling, competition from nonnative species
Stenogyne angustifolia var. *angustifolia*	E	Fewer than 100*	1979	Hawaiian Islands	Grazing; browsing; human trampling; exotic weeds, plants

*Excludes specimens in cultivation

E—Endangered; T—Threatened; E/T—Endangered or threatened, depending on location

Source: Council on Environmental Quality (1981). *Environmental Trends.* Washington, D.C.: U.S. Government Printing Office, pp. 169–171.

Figure 10-4
The California condor is on the verge of extinction. With only about 30 condors remaining, its future is doubtful. Because of hunting, habitat destruction and a low reproductive rate, the condor has been unable to live side-by-side with its California neighbors.

The California condor is another species imperiled by habitat alteration (Figure 10-4). The condor is a large vulture that lives in the San Gabriel Mountains north of Los Angeles. Its habitat has been destroyed by farms and homes and, ironically, by fire control. With a 3-meter (10-foot) wing span, this bird needs relatively large open spaces to take off. The control of fire has resulted in the overgrowth of chaparral and elimination of openings needed for take-off. The species is on the brink of extinction. Only about 30 California condors remain.

In the United States, habitat alteration (with other factors) has eliminated the grizzly bear from most of the lower 48 states (see Essay 10-1) Elk, which once grazed the Great Plains, were forced into the mountains by cattle and sheep ranches and farms. Bison also roamed the vast grasslands of North America in herds so large it took men on horseback three or four days to pass through them.

But since the grasslands have been taken over by humans, only a few remaining populations survive in protected habitat in Yellowstone National Park and on private land.

The story is the same throughout the world. In Asia the Bengal tiger faces extinction as its jungles are torn down to supply timber and farmland. Elephants of Africa and Asia, after years of overhunting, are now being pushed from their land by farmers attempting to feed a rapidly growing population.

In recent years the destruction of tropical rain forests and wetlands has raised serious concern among environmentalists. Tropical rain forest deforestation is debated in the Point/Counterpoint in Chapter 11. **Wetlands**, regions that are perpetually flooded or wet, such as swamps and bogs, are rapidly diminishing in the United States. (These are discussed in Chapter Supplement 12-1).

Commercial, Sport, and Subsistence Hunting

Animals are hunted for commercial profit, for sport, and for food. Collectively, these activities play a major role in species extinction.

Commercially, animals are hunted for their fur, hides, tusks, meat, antlers, and various other body parts. In Rwanda and Zaire the male gorilla is speared by tribes seeking parts of its body believed to possess magical properties. The hands and head are sold to tourists.

In Brazil the blue morpho butterfly with its iridescent wings was once a prized catch and was sold to local businesses to adorn trays and other objects for tourists. Today, the butterfly is protected by law. In the United States the elegant snowy egret was killed in large numbers by commercial hunters when its white plumes were fashionable in ladies' hats.

One of the most widely publicized commercial hunts is that of the whale. The whaling industry has generally concentrated its efforts on the large, profitable baleen whales, which were slaughtered for their blubber and baleen, the bony sieves they filter seawater with. From the blubber a high-grade oil was made for lamps and for lubricating machines. The baleen, or "whalebone," was used to make corset stays, combs, and similar products.

The history of whaling is one of overexploitation followed by abandonment. Whalers harvested a species until it approached extinction and then moved on to another profitable one, repeating the pattern many times. Commercial whalers concentrated their early efforts on the large whales of the North Atlantic, North Pacific, and Arctic

Landsat III: Keeping People and Grizzlies Apart

In the time it takes you to read this essay, the Landsat III satellite will have traveled about 1500 miles around the earth, scanning the surface with a rotating solar-powered mirror, picking up data on light-sensitive detectors. Every 18th day the satellite passes over Glacier National Park in Montana. The data it picks up there are relayed to NASA's Goddard Space Flight Center in Maryland, where they are converted into colored vegetation maps. The maps are sent to a biological technician at Glacier Park Headquarters, who, after studying them carefully, decides which trails to close in the park. The Landsat III has been looking for cow parsnips.

Cow parsnips? That's right. In early summer three things happen simultane-ously: cow parsnips bloom, grizzly bears eat them, and backpackers arrive in droves. Put a backpacker between a grizzly and cow parsnips, and there could be trouble. Says Cliff Matinka, supervisory biologist for the park. "Obviously we try very hard to keep people and grizzlies apart. We could do a pretty good job of this if we knew exactly where cow parsnips were."

Enter Landsat III. The NASA program, although still in an early stage, has been successful in helping rangers decide when and where to temporarily close camp-grounds and trails. Thus, the program helps prevent grizzly attacks on people, simply by keeping the humans out of the griz-zlies' feeding area.

The odds of a grizzly attack, more than a million to one, are narrowed only if a grizzly has somehow made a connection between humans and food. This connec-tion is usually the result of improperly stowed food and garbage, rather than an innate desire to feed on humans. There-fore, Glacier Park offers lectures and demonstrations on such things as how to pack food and garbage so bears can't smell it; how to identify the cow parsnip; and what to do if you run into a grizzly. But keeping people out of grizzly areas to begin with is actually the ideal. And to this end, Landsat offers a space-age solution to a very old problem.
Source: Adapted from Gustkey, E. (1982), *The Los Angeles Times.*

---

oceans, but when these became scarce, they moved to the smaller species in the Southern Hemisphere (Table 10-4). As an example, the California gray whale—one of the smallest of the baleen whales—was on the verge of extinction three times in the past 200 years. Now, thanks to protection, it thrives off the western coast of North America, where it annually migrates 19,000 kilometers (12,000 miles) each year from breeding grounds in the Arctic to its winter home off Baja California. The gray whale population, which had been reduced to 250 in 1947, is now believed to number 15,000, roughly the size of its prewhaling population. Every year thousands of people from all over the world travel to the coast of Cali-fornia or Baja California to catch a glimpse of these magnificent animals. Today, the whale-watching industry is as lucrative as the whaling industry of years past (Figure 10-5).

Not all commercially hunted whales have fared as well as the gray whale. The blue whale, the largest animal that has ever lived, once numbered almost 200,000, but by the

Table 10-4 Whale Populations—Then and Now

Species	Number Before Commercial Whaling	Current Estimate
Blue	196,000	2,000–20,000
Bowhead	20,000–30,000	2,300
Fin	448,000	111,900
Gray	15,000	15,000
Humpback	100,000	6,750
Minke	250,000	130,000–150,000
Right	50,000	3,250
Sei (includes Bryde's)	198,000	31,800
Sperm	950,000	628,700

Source: From Center for Environmental Education, (1982).

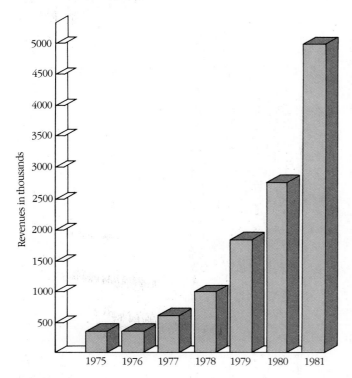

Figure 10-5
Growth in revenues from whale-watching cruises, 1975–1981.

mid-1950s it had been reduced to about 1000. Many scientists believe that the blue whale population, although now protected, may not recover.

Almost all species of large whales are protected by law and by international voluntary quotas established by the

International Whaling Commission (IWC). The IWC consists of members from whaling and former whaling nations who meet once a year to discuss populations and set quotas for the harvest. If it were not for the IWC, many whale species might well be extinct today. For many years Japan, the Soviet Union, and Norway defied the bans and quotas of the IWC. In 1983 the IWC agreed on a moratorium on commercial whaling that would begin in 1986. In 1990 the commission will undertake a comprehensive assessment of the effects of the moratorium and consider reinstituting commercial whaling. Whether such a ban will be honored by all the whaling nations remains to be seen.

One of the most controversial and widely publicized commercial hunting ventures is the annual harp seal harvest off the coast of Labrador and in the Gulf of Saint Lawrence. Once thought to have been as high as 10 million, the population of Western Atlantic harp seals has been greatly reduced by human predation (Figure 10-6). Today, there are an estimated 1.5 to 2 million harp seals (so named because of the harp-shaped pattern on the backs of adults).

What makes the harp seal so attractive to commercial interests is the beautiful white pelt of the newborn. This pelt is used to make slippers, coin purses, novelty furs, wallets, fur coats, and—ironically—stuffed toy seals. Within a few weeks of their birth, about half of the seal pups are killed with clubs and skinned. This annual harvest created a furor in the United States, Canada, and Europe. In 1971 the United States banned the importation of harp seal products, but the Canadian- and Norwegian-sponsored killing continued. Canadian officials argue that the seal is an "economic necessity" that provides winter income to

Figure 10-6
A harp seal pup sprayed with green dye by Greenpeace workers. The permanent dye makes the fur useless to hunters. Despite these and other efforts the species has an uncertain future.

Figure 10-7
Sport hunting can endanger wildlife populations that are not carefully managed.

people in sparsely populated areas badly in need of employment. They also argue that it is a threat to commercial fishing, although noted fisheries biologists assert that commercial overfishing is the real threat.

In response to criticism from environmentalists Canada took several steps to regulate the killing of the harp seal pups, including the use of special clubs to ensure that the pups were dead before they were skinned and the appointment of government inspectors to oversee the hunt. In response to further pressure, the hunt was canceled in 1983 but was reinstated in 1984, with the provision that only the older, nonwhite animals are killed.

Stuffed iguanas are sold in Mexico's streets. Ashtrays are made of elephant feet. By some estimates 30,000 elephants are illegally killed each year in Africa for ivory. Poachers kill alligators to make boots for the expensive taste of urban cowboys. All these practices, and thousands of others, have driven many species to the brink of extinction. But who is to blame, the sellers or the buyers? A French proverb gives this answer: "Whoever profits by the crime is guilty of it."

Hunting for sport is also a factor in wildlife extinction (Figure 10-7). However, the hunting of properly managed, nonendangered species frequently benefits populations by reducing population growth. It is another kind of hunting that threatens rare and endangered wildlife: poaching and sport hunting of endangered species. Trophy hunting today threatens such animals as the jaguar, cheetah, tiger, rhinoceros, and oryx. In northern British Columbia, for instance, hundreds of American and European trophy hunters visit the 700,000-hectare (1.7-million-acre) Spatsizi Park to hunt mountain goats and bighorn sheep. In a matter of a few years they have destroyed many herds, and now threaten the wildlife population of the entire region.

Poaching of wildlife for sport and profit is widespread in Ethiopia, Kenya, Uganda, and Tanzania (Figure 10-8). Much illegal hunting takes place in wildlife parks. Many poachers have been apprehended in the famed Serengeti Park.

People also hunt endangered species for food. For example, Eskimos annually kill a number of endangered bowhead whales, despite scientific evidence that the population (about 2300) cannot support any further harvesting. The continuation of subsistence hunting has pitted the environmentalists against the Eskimos. Environmentalists assert that the population cannot support further hunting, and the Eskimos argue that their survival depends on the bowhead whale. Thus, each year villagers harvest some of the whales for meat and blubber. In 1980 the IWC agreed to allow continuation of the annual subsistent hunt and set a strict limit on bowheads, despite widespread sentiment calling for the complete banning of the harvest. The hunters have agreed to the new quotas. The fate of the whale is precariously balanced between the conflicting desires of conservationists and Eskimos.

(a)

(b)

Figure 10-8
In East Africa, the elephant is hunted illegally and often on preserves for its ivory tusks, which are subsequently exported to the Orient.

Introduction of Foreign Species

The introduction of **foreign**, or **alien**, **species** into new territories can often lead to ecological and economic disaster. An introduced species' niche may overlap that of a native species; the newcomer may outcompete the native species, resulting in its extinction. Foreign species may also be predators or pathogens for which indigenous species have no defense.

Islands are particularly susceptible to introduced species. The Hawaiian Islands provide one of the most vivid examples of the effect of introduced species. More species have become extinct there than on the entire North American continent.

One of the classic examples of an unintentional introduction was that of the sea lamprey, a parasite that attaches to various fish (Figure 10-9). The lamprey eel migrates into Lake Ontario each year from the Atlantic Ocean, but for years could go no further upstream than Niagara Falls. After the completion of a barge canal, ships and lampreys could bypass the falls and travel throughout the Great Lakes. A few years after completion of the canal, the lamprey had decimated the lake trout population of Lakes Huron and Michigan, virtually eliminating a once-profitable fishing industry. Now, however, after the development of specific chemicals toxic to lamprey eggs and larvae, the eel has been effectively controlled, and commercially important fish have recovered.

Species are often intentionally introduced to improve fishing and hunting. Many such introductions have been fraught with problems. For example, in a remote lake in the mountains of Guatemala, the giant grebe hangs on to life by a thin thread. Found nowhere else in the world, this bird is endangered primarily by habitat destruction. Recent earthquakes that opened underground cracks in the lake bottom caused a sudden drop in the water level, destroying its breeding grounds along the shore. Contributing to the bird's plight, however, is the introduction of sport fish such as the bass, which compete with the grebes for food.

Figure 10-9
Sea lampreys accidentally introduced into the upper Great Lakes by a canal connecting Ontario to Erie. The lamprey attaches to the skin of fish such as lake trout and brook trout.

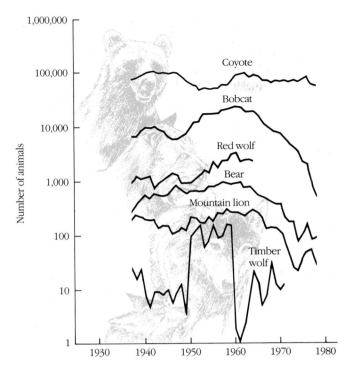

Figure 10-10
Number of predators killed by federal control programs.

Control of Pests and Predators

For many years humans have indiscriminately hunted, trapped, and poisoned predators and pests such as bears, coyotes, wolves, mountain lions, eagles, and hawks to protect livestock (Figure 10-10). In the United States, wolves, mountain lions, and grizzly bears have been eliminated from most of their original territory in the name of pest control.

In general, predator and pest control measures have two major impacts: (1) they kill natural predators that are a part of the balanced ecosystem, and (2) they can indiscriminately poison nontarget species, having a ripple effect on organisms higher in the food chain.

Predator control has been an integral part of wildlife management programs around the world. The common approach has been to eliminate predators of game such as deer and elk. Population control is then left up to hunters. Hunting of deer, elk, and other large herbivores is justified, because the natural balance has been severely altered by human management. No doubt hunting will be necessary in the future, too. Nevertheless, we should be aware of the important difference between ecosystem bal-

ance under human management and balance under more natural conditions.

Natural predators cull prey populations by removing the aged, sick, and injured members. In truth, predators are reluctant to attack a healthy deer or elk even when hunting in packs, unless hard times make it necessary. By removing the weak, predators reduce the herd size, thus decreasing intraspecific (within the species) competition that can result in overgrazing and, eventually, food shortages.

In contrast, humans generally remove the strongest specimens from the population, often preferring dominant males with the largest antlers. Such predation will diminish the genetic vigor of a population. Hunting is an example of artificial selection that unwittingly degrades a population.

In sum, humans and natural predators have opposing effects on populations of prey. Natural predators make the prey population stronger; humans make it weaker. For this reason some wildlife managers now support **integrated species management**, which allows predators a place in the ecosystem. It may be difficult for hunters and ranchers to recognize the long-term benefits of predators, but such recognition could help us comply with the laws of ecology, necessary for a sustainable society.

Pest control by environmental measures, discussed in Chapter Supplement 9-1, can have a devastating effect on native species. In Hawaii the cattle egret was introduced to control flies that swarmed around cattle. But the egrets proliferated and now compete with native birds such as the red-footed booby for food and nesting sites. Numerous other examples could be cited, all of which would remind us of the need for caution when tampering with the biotic components of the ecosystem.

Collection for Zoos, Private Collections, and Research

Animals and plants are gathered throughout the world for zoos, private collectors, pet shops, and researchers in biology and medicine. In 1983 more than 250 million fish and about 4 million reptiles were imported into the United States. Each year millions of birds are also brought into the United States and Great Britain from tropical nations, but for each bird that makes it into someone's home, 10 to 50 die along the way.

Among this influx of legally imported animals come countless members of endangered, threatened, and rare species. Smuggled in, many of these animals go to zoos and private collectors. Today, rare Madagascar boas are shipped to zoos in the United States and Western Europe. Zoos still sponsor the capture of gorillas, which number only 10,000 in the wild.

Why do so many illegal species make it into the United States when the Endangered Species Act strictly forbids such actions? In some cases animal traffickers simply mislabel tags, leading airport inspectors to believe that they are actually importing legal animals. Traffickers may also use falsified permits or bribe government inspectors to look the other way; there are often too few inspectors to police all shipments.

Animal suppliers are frequently peasants who hunt and trap native species for small fees. Regulations in the developing countries, from which most of the animals come, are usually inadequate or poorly enforced. The hunters often know little about effective live capture; deaths and injuries during capture are common. Snakes may be caught with wire snares that cut into their flesh. The pangolin, an African mammal that feeds on ants and termites, is often prevented from escaping by nailing its tail to the floor of its cage. Mothers are frequently killed to obtain their young. Three or four females may be killed to get one uninjured baby. To acquire a baby gorilla, the dominant male must be killed, or hunters cannot get to the young. Villagers may round up monkeys by encircling large areas; but having no cages to hold their captives, they simply tie the monkeys down until they can be sold. Once captured, animals are usually held in inadequate cages until the middlemen pick them up for export.

The middlemen, the ones who often make the most profit from this trade, sell the animals to dealers abroad. This may require some touching up. Snakes with fungal infections on their skin are cleaned and sold as healthy specimens. Dull-colored birds are often dyed. These animals pass through the airports aided by bribery. Ignorance among enforcement agents prevents many violations from being noticed.

Eventually, these animals make their way into the homes of people who often find they are unable to care for them properly. The big cats prove to be unmanageable pets, especially in apartments. For some people their smell becomes unbearable. Others find that veterinarians cannot treat the peculiar diseases that crop up. Still others find that their new pets carry disease and parasites that can be transmitted to humans. As a result, many animals are given to zoos, many die, and some may even be released in the alien surroundings of another land.

Animals are only one side of this story; plants such as cacti and orchids are also in high demand and support a growing industry. For example, over 7 million cacti are imported each year into the United States from more than 50 countries. At home, collectors pillage Texas and Arizona deserts in search of salable cacti to adorn the front lawns of their eager customers. In one area of Texas near Big Bend National Park, 25,000 to 50,000 cacti were uprooted in a single month for sale elsewhere. In the late 1970s about 10 million cacti were shipped out of Texas annually.

To reduce the ravaging impact of commercial cactus rustlers, Arizona has listed 222 protected plants that are illegal to remove. With penalties up to $1000 and jail sentences up to one year, Arizona has made a small step to protect its native plants. Still, with a surface area of about 260,000 square kilometers (100,000 square miles) and only seven "cactus cops" to patrol, little can be done.

Researchers throughout the world use a variety of animals for their studies, many of which come from the wild. Demand is especially great for monkeys and the great apes such as chimpanzees. Taken from their homeland in Africa, as many as five chimpanzees die for every one that enters the laboratory. Some biologists believe that the species will be extinct in the wild by the end of the decade.

Primates are desired because of their anatomical, genetic, and physiological similarity to humans (Figure 10-11). Primates have played an important part in biomedical research. The chimpanzee, for example, has been used in work on human reproduction and cancer detection. A vaccine to treat the sometimes fatal disease viral hepatitis has now been developed by testing with chimpanzees.

Annual primate imports into the United States have dropped steadily, from over 100,000 in the mid-1960s to under 25,000 in the early 1980s (Figure 10-12). In 1973, for instance, over 20,000 rhesus monkeys were imported into this country for research. In 1980, the number was down to 120. Despite this drop, some rare and endangered species are still captured and sent to the United States. According to some sources, about 200 great apes are imported each year, further diminishing the chances of survival for many wild populations of orangutans and chimpanzees. In Colombia and Venezuela, some monkey populations once used in research have been destroyed.

In 1975 the United States banned the importation of all primates for pets, but it allowed their continued importation for zoos and research facilities. Because research animals often do not breed in captivity and because they have a high mortality, continual replenishment from wild populations is likely to continue.

Today, 60 primate species are on the endangered list. Many of these have been exploited by researchers with

Figure 10-11
One of the many monkeys imported into the United States each year for biomedical research. This monkey was kept in captivity for 7 years; much of this time was spent in a restraining chair to keep her from self-mutilation. Abnormal body functions due to such treatment may invalidate research.

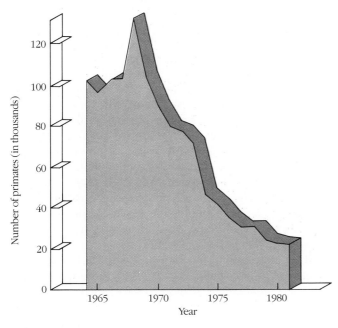

Figure 10-12
Decline in primates imported by the United States.

little concern for their declining population or ultimate demise in the wild. Most people agree that research must continue under humane conditions but that it should not be carried out at the cost of extinction. Captive-breeding programs which supply zoos and researchers can be extended in countries where primates are used. This should stop the flow of these animals from their natural habitat. Action now could prevent the extinction of many primates.

Pollution

Pollution alters the habitat of plants and animals and plays a significant role in extinction. Water pollution is especially harmful to organisms living in estuaries (mouths of rivers) and coastal zones, where many economically important marine fish breed and spend their early years. Toxic wastes entering the food chain can have devastating effects, especially on the young, which are almost always more sensitive than adults to pollution (Chapter 18).

A leading problem is the sale of pesticides banned in the United States to foreign countries (see Viewpoint, "The Myth of the Banned Pesticide," in Chapter 18). Harmful insecticides such as DDT, which was banned here in 1972, are still used in Central America. Migratory birds passing through or wintering in sprayed regions can ingest significant amounts of the harmful insecticides, making efforts to save them here much less effective. Protection of wildlife requires global cooperation.

Ecological Factors That Contribute to Extinction

At one time, the passenger pigeon inhabited the eastern half of our country and the southeastern quarter of Canada. Probably the most abundant bird species ever to live, the passenger pigeon is now extinct. In 1810, ornithologist Alexander Wilson calculated that a single flock of these magnificent birds was 380 kilometers (240 miles) long and 1.6 km (1 mile) wide and contained 2.2 billion birds! In 1871, a nesting colony of passenger pigeons in Wisconsin was found to be about 24 km (15 miles) wide and 120 km (75 miles) long and contained an estimated 136 million birds.

Early accounts describe how flocks of passenger pigeons blocked out the sun for two days at a time. Limbs broke off trees from the weight of the birds. But humans began to destroy the forests to make room for agriculture. Between 1860 and 1880, countless passenger pigeons were clubbed to death, netted, or shot by commercial hunters and shipped to the cities. In 1878, the last nesting site near Petoskey,

Michigan was invaded by hunters. When the guns were silenced, over 1.1 billion birds had perished. By this time, the passenger pigeon was nearly extinct; only about 2000 remained. Broken into small flocks, too small to hunt economically, the bird was finally left alone. The number of pigeons dwindled year after year, until in 1914 the last living specimen died in the Cincinnati zoo.

This tragic and oft-told story has a lesson, which is that some species have a **critical population size** below which survival may be impossible. The passenger pigeon's population had dropped below the critical level. It needed large colonies for successful social interaction and propagation of the species. Two thousand were simply not enough. This is the same problem that faces the blue whale today.

Scientists know very little about the critical population size for various species, a fact that concerns many wildlife advocates. Overhunting, habitat destruction, and other activities discussed in this chapter can do irreparable damage before we even realize it.

Other ecological factors contribute to species extinction. First is the degree of specialization. As discussed in Chapter 5, the more specialized an animal or plant is, the more vulnerable it is to extinction. Second is the location of the organism in the food chain. In general, the higher the animal is, the more susceptible it becomes. Mountain lions, bears, and eagles, for example, require large amounts of food and land. Destruction of their habitat and food sources can have devastating effects on them. Larger animals are also more profitable to hunt, and having fewer natural predators, they are less fearful of humans. This makes them easier targets.

Third, the size of the range also affects extinction: the smaller the range, the greater the threat of extinction. As mentioned above, populations on islands are particularly susceptible. Ecologists recognize another kind of island, the **ecological island**. This is a term used to describe any isolated habitat—for example, a lake or a small raised grove of trees (hammock) in the Everglades. Species inhabiting ecological islands are susceptible to extinction.

Fourth is the reproductive rate. Large organisms tend to produce a few offspring at widely spaced intervals. Their offspring also tend to reach reproductive age late. For example, the California condor lays a single egg every other year. Young condors remain dependent on their parents for about a year but are not sexually mature until age six or seven. Combined, these factors give the condor little resiliency to bounce back from pressures from human populations or natural disasters. Biologists have begun a

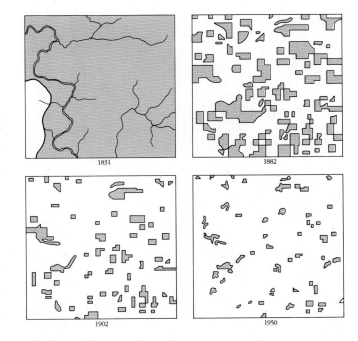

Figure 10-13
The reduction and fragmentation of wooded areas (shaded) in the Cadiz Township, Wisconsin, from 1831 to 1950. the piecemeal destruction of habitat results in a piecemeal extinction of many species.

program to take eggs from condor nests and incubate them in captivity. Under these conditions the condor produces an egg every year, potentially allowing the doubling of its normal rate of reproduction.

Fifth is an animal's tolerance of human presence or specific behavioral patterns. The grizzly, for example, is largely intolerant of human intrusion into its habitat. When humans move in, grizzlies often move out. Some species of birds nest in large, highly visible colonies that attract human predators. For example, some colonies of white-crowned pigeons may contain tens of thousands of birds, which are easy picking for people who gather up their young (squabs) for sale. Hunters may shoot a hundred pigeons in a single day. Thus, in parts of its habitat the pigeon is likely to become extinct.

Many people think of a species as extinct when all of its members have vanished. In truth, a species goes extinct in a piecemeal fashion (Figure 10-13). When an animal is eliminated from a part of its habitat, we say that it is locally or regionally extinct. Regional extinction can continue until the species is eliminated entirely or reduced to a few remnants. The grizzly bear is a good example. Once, the lower 48 states contained an estimated 1.5 million grizzlies west of the Mississippi River. Slowly, the bear was eliminated from its western range, one state at a time. Today, a total of 800 bears remain in Montana, Wyoming, Idaho, and possibly Washington. Although there are plenty of grizzlies in Alaska, they too may undergo a piecemeal extinction as one region after the next is developed for oil, timber, or water resources.

Why Save Endangered Species?

Wildlife expert Norman Myers once wrote: "We can marvel at the colors of a butterfly, the grace of a giraffe, the power of an elephant, the delicate structure of a diatom. . . . Every time a species goes extinct, we are irreversibly impoverished." Aesthetics in itself is a good argument for saving species. As we preserve art collections for future generations, so we should preserve this living art form that painters and sculptors only dream of re-creating (Figure 10-14).

A second reason for protecting species is that other organisms have a right to live. Can we not guarantee them the right to exist, something that we ourselves doggedly strive for?

The third reason for preserving other organisms is a matter of ethical responsibility. As a species capable of destroying the world, some ecologists and philosophers feel, we have a moral obligation to preserve organisms with lesser powers.

The fourth reason for protection is that it makes good economic sense to do so. As Myers wrote: "From morning coffee to evening nightcap we benefit in our daily lifestyles from the fellow species that share our One Earth home. Without knowing it, we utilize hundreds of products each day that owe their origin to wild animals and plants. Indeed our welfare is intimately tied up with the welfare of wildlife. Well may conservationists proclaim that by saving the lives of wild species, we may be saving our own."

From the biosphere we reap countless benefits: fish from the sea, medicines and other products from plants, important plant and animal genes needed to improve domestic crops and livestock, something for hunters to shoot at, something for anglers to hook and reel in, something for bird-watchers to peer at, and research animals

Figure 10-14
The North American mountain lion is threatened by hunting and dwindling habitat.

that help provide valuable insights into human physiology and behavior.

The economic benefits of these "activities" can be enormous. In 1983 alone trout and salmon anglers spent an estimated $5 billion on equipment, transportation, food, and lodging, and hunters and bird-watchers spent billions on tennis shoes, supplies, books, gasoline, food, and lodging. Billions of dollars pour into companies that cut timber or extract valuable medicines from plants.

Each time we take a prescription drug, the chances are one in two that its origin was a wild plant. The commercial value of such drugs is around $15 billion per year in the United States and about $40 billion worldwide.

The U.S. Department of Agriculture estimates that each year genes bred into commercial crops yield over $1 billion worth of food. Similar gains can be documented for Canada, Great Britain, the Soviet Union, Australia, and other agricultural nations. About half of the increased productivity in corn over the past 50 years has resulted from "genetic transfusions" from wild relatives of corn or primitive cultivars in use only in isolated regions. Some biologists argue that the current high-yielding corn, which produces 250 bushels per hectare (650 bushels per acre), could be increased fivefold with further genetic transfusions from its ancestors.

New developments are on the horizon that may offer financial gains and a more healthful life for us. For example, the adhesive that barnacles use to adhere to the bottoms of ships may provide us with a substance to cement tooth fillings in place. A chemical derived from the skeletons of shrimps, crabs, and lobsters (chitosanase) may serve as a preventive medicine against fungal infections. A new drug that kills viruses may be developed from a Caribbean sponge; till now physicians have been virtually helpless in the battle against viruses.

The future of the biological world is one of grave economic concern. The loss of fish from acid rain and overfishing results in a loss of income to owners of fishing lodges and sporting goods stores. Ecological impoverishment will keep more of us at home, diminishing income to the recreation and tourism industry.

Plants and animals lost before they are explored for possible benefits will diminish our opportunities to fight disease and increase productivity. A dozen genetic reservoirs (so-called centers of diversity) located in the tropics and subtropics are the source of virtually all commercially valuable plants and animals. And they provide genetic material needed in the continual battle to improve plant and animal resistance. Loss of these centers would have a global impact on food supplies.

The final reason for preserving species is to protect ecosystem stability. All living organisms are an integral part of the biosphere and provide invaluable services. These include the control of pests, the recycling of nutrients, the replenishment of atmospheric oxygen, the maintenance of local climate, the control of groundwater levels, the regulation of atmospheric carbon dioxide and global climate, and the control of flooding. It is no exaggeration to say that civilization depends on the survival of the biological world. Perhaps in the short term a species lost here and there may be of little consequence for overall ecosystem stability, but in the long term the cumulative effect of such losses may someday threaten our existence.

Critics of the animal protection movement argue that

Figure 10-15
Measuring only 8 centimeters (3 inches), the snail darter created a big stir between environmentalists and industry. The destruction of the snail darter by the TVAs Tellico Dam brought the multimillion dollar project to a standstill. After years of debate, Congress ordered the dam to be completed.

too much effort is directed to the saving of endangered species. Why was there so much fuss over the tiny snail darter (Figure 10-15), a fish imperiled by the Tellico Dam built by the Tennessee Valley Authority (TVA)? Surely this one species can have no great significance to us. Although the world might never miss the snail darter, and although no irreparable ecosystem damage would result from its extinction, the question that arises is where to draw the line. Wildlife advocates argue that if we take the attitude that each species by itself is dispensable, bit by bit we will destroy the rich biological world we live in. Somewhere the line has to be drawn: each endangered species is worth saving because it stops the momentum toward widespread destruction. In growth-oriented societies this momentum may be difficult to stop, much less slow down. Therefore, each hurdle put in its way becomes an important force in saving the living creatures that make up our web of life. In the words of the naturalist William Beebe, "When the last individual of a race of living things breathes no more, another heaven and earth must pass before such a one can be again."

How Can We Save Endangered Species?

Preserving species is not a simple matter; there is much work on three overlapping levels—technical, legal and personal. Let us take them in this order.

Technical Solutions: Integrated Species Management

The fate of many of the world's plants and animals is in our hands. Many experts believe that an integrated species management program is our best bet for protecting them. This approach is a diversified attack on the causes of extinction. Here are some general suggestions: (1) reduce habitat destruction by careful selection of urban and other development; (2) establish preserves to protect nesting grounds and other critical habitats; (3) reduce commercial and trophy hunting when evidence shows that the hunted species is rare, threatened, or endangered and when synthetic products can replace those acquired from these animals and plants; (4) improve wildlife management, including programs to protect and manage non-game species; (5) control the introduction of alien species, especially on islands; (6) design careful predator and pest control management programs so as not to indiscriminately eliminate nontarget species; (7) reduce pollution; (8) increase public awareness of the value of wildlife and what factors cause extinction; (9) fund captive-breeding programs to raise endangered species for release; (10) establish breeding programs to generate research animals; (11) toughen penalties, and increase the policing of animal and plant trade and poaching; (12) promote international cooperation to curb the trade of endangered species; (13) increase expenditures for all protective measures, possibly through new taxes; and (14) intensify research efforts to learn more about ecosystem stability and to identify critical plant and animal habitats.

A Case Study in Improving Predator Control
The coyote is at the center of a bitter battle between environmentalists and ranchers. Ranchers assert that coyotes kill thousands of sheep every year, costing the industry $100 million annually. Environmentalists put the damage at about one-tenth of that and argue that the environmental and economic costs of control, which exceed $18 million a year, far exceed the benefits.

Today, coyotes are controlled by shooting, aerial hunting, spring-activated guns loaded with cyanide, trapping, guard dogs, and denning—burning or gassing them in their dens. Until 1972 ranchers and federal predator control agents also used a poison called Compound 1080. Compound 1080 (sodium monofluoroacetate) is a "supertoxin." A single teaspoon of 1080 is enough to kill 100 average men. Simply handling meat containing the toxin can make a healthy adult sick. A child who has handled poisoned meat could die from licking his or her fingers.

Ranchers and government predator control agents laced meat and animal carcasses with 1080 and often dropped it from airplanes. Although it was intended primarily for coyotes that preyed on sheep, nontarget species such as badgers, eagles, dogs, foxes, and raccoons also fed on bait and died.

In 1972 President Richard Nixon banned the use of 1080 for predator control on federal lands and in federally sponsored predator control programs. That same year the Environmental Protection Agency (EPA) banned the chemical, citing evidence of 13 human fatalities, 5 suspected deaths, and 6 nonfatal poisonings.

In February 1982, President Ronald Reagan rescinded Nixon's ban, leaving it up to the EPA to determine its fate. The EPA administrator has authorized the use of 1080 in sheep collars, which contain small packets of liquid 1080 and are worn around the sheep's neck, where the coyote typically strikes. When the coyote bites the collar, it receives a lethal dose. Supporters of 1080 argue that this technique is more selective than other baiting techniques, eliminating only the troublesome coyotes. Critics argue that scavengers will feed on 1080-poisoned coyotes and the tainted meat of fallen sheep. Thus, nontarget species will continue to be killed. Critics also point out that unscrupulous ranchers could extract 1080 from the collars and continue to use it in the old dangerous ways.

There are options to coyote control other than Compound 1080. In Kansas, for example, only coyotes that raid sheep herds are shot. Kansas supports a large population of coyotes and a healthy sheep population, and the costs of control are held to a reasonable level. In many states sheep are released onto pastures and mountain meadows (many in national forests) and left unattended throughout much of the grazing season. It is argued that better management of flocks by the use of guard dogs could reduce coyote predation. These dogs, bred for this work centuries ago, live with the herds and have been successfully used in many areas (Figure 10-16). The New England Farm Center in Amherst, Massachusetts, for example, has placed over 400 of its dogs in 31 states since 1978. Guard dogs are one of the most economical and effective ways to control coyotes. A dog can be leased for $50 a year, but a good ewe may be worth much more. Guard dogs are a selective way of controlling coyote predation, but many ranchers are unwilling to try a new idea, and are used to poisons and other control methods.

Figure 10-16
Guard dogs have been used for centruies by sheep herders in Europe to watch over their sheep. This maremma is on duty in Colorado.

Other control measures include the use of coyote-proof fences, noisemakers, and taste aversion. The last is an interesting idea. The rancher laces a dead ewe or lamb with lithium chloride and places it in a field. The chemical does not kill coyotes but makes them sick. It is hoped that they will then associate the taste of mutton with illness and will not prey on sheep.

Without question, coyotes kill sheep. Many believe that the problem is worse when the coyotes are raising their young. Studies show that coyotes usually feed on small rodents, insects, birds, and other animals throughout most of the year. When there are young in the den, they prefer larger prey; that means less time hunting away from the den. At this time in the coyote's life cycle sheep predation rises, for sheep are easy to kill. Control efforts should be intensified at these times.

Coyotes have a great deal of resiliency. Following a heavy coyote "harvest," coyote populations double and quadruple in the next season. The average litter of three pups can increase to seven to nine pups that year, thus negating control efforts. Because of this, many traditional methods have proved ineffective in controlling coyote populations. An integrated approach that minimizes the use of poisons and relies on guard dogs and selective killing of troublesome coyotes may be the best solution.

Germ Plasm Repositories and Preserving of Plant Habitat Efforts to reduce plant extinction and preserve genetic material are now under way on an international scale. One solution is the establishment of genetic repositories, where cells from seed-bearing plants can be held for future study and use. The U.S. Department of Agriculture supports the National Germ Plasm System, which has 450,000 plants in "stock" and plans to add 7,500 per year for many years to come.

However important this strategy may be, it has some drawbacks. Despite storage at low temperature and humidity, many seeds rot and must be replaced. Others undergo genetic mutation when stored for long periods and are no longer useful. Finally, storage systems will not work for potatoes, fruit trees, and a variety of other plants. The problems faced in germ plasm storage suggest the need for protection of land containing wild relatives of our most important crops—corn, wheat, rice, sorghum, and potatoes. Such efforts will help ensure that geneticists have a continual supply of new genetic material.

Legal Solutions

Integrated species management requires laws that protect rare, endangered, and threatened organisms and their habitat. Today, however, poor economic conditions throughout the world caused partly by overpopulation and resource shortages have made many people unwilling to expend the necessary money.

In 1973, in response to the plight of wildlife and plants in the United States and abroad, the U.S. Congress passed the *Endangered Species Act* (ESA). This act (1) requires the U.S. Fish and Wildlife Service to list endangered and threatened species in the country, (2) creates federal protection of the habitat of listed species, (3) provides money to purchase this habitat, and (4) enables the United States to help other nations protect their endangered and threatened species, by banning U.S. importation of these species and by giving technical assistance.

Protection begins with the listing of an endangered or threatened species. Since the enactment of the ESA, 226 animals and 61 plants have been designated threatened or endangered in the United States. Next, all federal agencies and departments can cooperate in protecting listed species on land they control or regulate. This is done by requiring land development plans submitted to the Fish and Wildlife Service or the National Marine Fisheries Service before such projects can be started. Thus, no projects that these agencies fund, permit, or sponsor can be carried out without prior review. The agency responds within 90 days, either approving the proposal, denying approval, or making suggestions to modify it to protect endangered species that might be affected. In this way all development on federal land, whether it be oil drilling, digging a sewer line, or building a ski area, is scrutinized to ensure minimum impact on endangered and threatened species.

Since the ESA went into effect, hundreds of projects have been through this process, and in most cases differences have been worked out amicably. In a few widely publicized cases, however, this review and modification process came under attack. The most renowned was the battle between environmentalists and the TVA over the snail darter. Problems began in 1975 when an order came from a federal court to stop construction of the multimillion-dollar Tellico Dam, already 90% completed. The order resulted from a lawsuit filed by environmentalists contending that the dam's construction violated the ESA, because the reservoir would flood the snail darter's only breeding habitat.

The ruling was upheld in the U.S. Supreme Court. Congress soon established a committee to review requests for exemptions to the ESA. In 1979 the special committee refused to give the TVA an exemption, saying that the project was of questionable merit. Even though $100 million had been spent, the TVA was blocked from finishing construction. But the TVA continued to press Congress, and later that year Congress authorized the completion of the dam. The snail darter was transplanted to several neighboring streams, where biologists believe it can live. Another population was also discovered in a nearby stream.

Could the ESA be abused? By hiring specialists to search the land that might be affected by highways, dams, airports, and other projects, environmentalists have been able to find new candidates for the list of endangered species. According to William Tucker, an outspoken critic of the environmental movement, endangered species can be found almost everywhere because of the loose definition of the word *species*. Small populations of insects and fish may become isolated from their ancestors and evolve in their new environment. These are considered a new species. Tucker argues that we should not assume that "we are chopping the evolutionary tree from under ourselves, or destroying one of God's irreplaceable handiworks, whenever we confront (and destroy) one of these small populations." Tucker's argument is valid up to a point. Environmentalists have gone to extremes to find isolated populations of species to halt projects that they had no other way of stopping. The ESA has become a legal tool against unnecessary and costly projects; however, discovering an endangered species only rarely halts a project. In most cases slight modifications can be made to the project.

Laws such as the ESA are needed worldwide, especially in the less developed nations of Africa, where population growth is excessive and many species are quickly vanishing. Only with tough, enforceable laws backed by a willing and informed public can the erosion of the earth's rich biological diversity be stopped.

Personal Solutions

Despite the constant finger pointing that goes on as people try to fix blame for extinction, the enemy is really all of us. Through excessive consumerism, apathy, unchecked population growth, and a lack of involvement, we are all a part of the problem. But how can you help?

First, you can reduce your consumption of energy by shutting off lights, obeying the speed limit, and keeping the thermostat in your room or apartment low in the winter. You can conserve other natural resources, especially products that might come from the tropical rain forests. If each of us decreased consumption by 20% to 30%, we'd collectively have a huge impact on habitat loss.

Second, you can help others learn to change their wasteful ways. You can begin with your own family and then explain to friends and relatives our role in extinction. You can join with others to spread the word through educational campaigns, lobbying, television ads, posters, books, pamphlets, and the like. You can support citizen action groups and politicians that fight against pollution, habitat destruction, commercial and trophy hunting, indiscriminate pest and predator control, and collection of animals and plants for research and home use.

Joining wildlife groups is one of the best ways to learn from dedicated experts with well-developed plans for wildlife protection (see Appendix C for a list of organizations and their addresses). Organizations such as the Nature Conservancy, the Trust for Public Lands, and the World Environmental Fund purchase habitat for rare and endangered species. Others such as the National Wildlife Federation, the Sierra Club, the Audubon Society, and the Wilderness Society concentrate much of their effort in the legislative arena to promote sound environmental policy.

Progress and Setbacks

There is much to be encouraged about in the battle to save endangered species. More than a decade after the banning of DDT, evidence shows that many species are making a comeback. Most notable is the bald eagle, now numbering over 2500 in the lower 48, and rising. Brown pelicans, osprey, and peregrine falcons are also increasing as DDT residues in the environment drop (Figure 10-17). Studies by the New York State Department of Environmental Conservation showed that levels of persistent pesticides have dropped dramatically in many sport fish.

In 1982 the Endangered Species Act was substantially strengthened. The law was extended for three years, and measures were added to ensure that the listing of species would follow scientific, not economic, criteria. Congress also added tougher regulations on wetland development, requiring that all proposed development be reviewed prior to approval.

Many species have made a dramatic comeback as a result of special breeding programs. Most notable are the

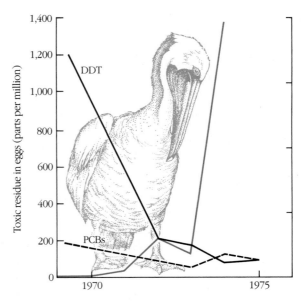

Figure 10-17
Banning of DDT resulted in a dramatic decrease in brown pelican eggs and an equally dramatic increase in the number of eggs hatched.

Hawaiian goose (nene), peregrine falcon, and whooping crane. Protection of the sea otter in Pacific waters, afforded by the Marine Mammal Protection Act, has resulted in the comeback of this intriguing species. Careful management of the pronghorn antelope of the western plains brought its population from a 1952 low of 30,000 to over 375,000 in 1983.

Special preserves and gardens are being established worldwide to protect endangered plants. Twenty-one states have enacted a voluntary tax check-off, like the one for presidential campaign contributions, that gives them money for nongame species protection. In 1982 Colorado's voluntary check-off system created $750,000 to protect nongame species. Missouri now levies a small sales tax that brings in over $20 million a year to be used for conservation projects, mostly habitat purchase.

Despite these encouraging signs, there is bad news to report, too. The world's population continues to grow. In many parts of Africa, moreover, modern medicine has not yet begun to lower death rates. When that happens, the annual growth rate could increase by one full percentage point. In addition, many nations are undergoing economic development, which will inevitably result in increasing resource consumption. China, with 1 billion people, is a classic example. Significant economic development could have devastating effects on the ecosystem, because pollution and habitat destruction are sure to rise.

Despite efforts to save it, the California condor seems doomed. The population, as we have seen, now numbers only about 30 birds. In 1982 the U.S. Department of the Interior chose not to spend funds allocated for the purchase of critical wetlands. Failure to purchase this land, as stipulated by the Endangered Species Act, could result in the loss of much valuable habitat.

Lead poisoning among waterfowl continues to be a major problem. Each year 2 million to 3 million ducks and geese perish after eating lead shot from the bottom of rivers and lakes. Almost half the states have established programs to use nontoxic steel shot in shotgun shells to reduce the severity of this problem. More need to cooperate.

Poaching of rare and endangered animals continues throughout the world. Elephants are still killed for ivory in Africa. Cactus rustling still goes on. And animal traffickers continue to deal in rare and endangered reptiles, amphibians, birds, and mammals destined for private collections—and almost certain death. The fight is far from over.

What is civilized in us is not opera or literature, but a compassion for all living things and a willingness to do more than simply care.

DANIEL D. CHIRAS

Summary

Species extinction is a natural phenomenon that occurs both during evolution, as one species transforms into an entirely new one, and also as a result of catastrophic climatic changes. Extinction has greatly accelerated in recent times as a result of many human activities.

Alteration of habitat is the most significant factor leading to extinction of plants and animals. Habitat is destroyed by deforestation, draining and filling in wetlands, overgrazing, expanding agriculture, urban and suburban development, highway construction, dam building, strip mining, and other activities.

Animals are hunted today for commercial profit, for food, and for sport. Collectively, these activities play a major role in species extinction. New laws now protect many endangered species from such activities, although poaching and illegal hunting continue.

Foreign, or *alien, species* introduced into new territories can often lead to the extinction of native species. Islands are especially vulnerable. Alien species may be introduced intentionally or unintentionally. A lack of environmental resistance (predators or diseases) in the new habitat may result in widespread destruction of existing plants and wildlife.

Control of pests and predators also influences wild populations of plants and animals. Predator control, for example, has been a cornerstone of wildlife management in the United States and many other countries for decades. Elimination of predators has endangered or wiped out populations of wolves, bears, and other animals and has unbalanced prey populations, such as deer. This necessitates human control through hunting.

The capture of species for zoos, private collections, and research contributes to wildlife and plant extinction on a worldwide scale. Although current laws now prohibit the importation and exportation of endangered species, the illegal trafficking in such species continues. Especially hard hit in recent years have been the deserts of Mexico and the United States. Rare cacti and other succulents have been harvested in the thousands to meet the demand for homes and gardens.

Pollution alters the habitat of plants and animals and thus contributes to extinction. Water pollution is especially harmful to organisms living in estuaries and along coasts. Pesticides poison birds and mammals; especially harmful to migratory birds are persistent pesticides that have been banned in the United States but are still produced here and sold to Latin American countries.

Numerous ecological factors also play a part in extinction. The *critical population size,* which is the number of organisms needed to ensure survival, varies from one species to the next. If a population is reduced below this level, survival may be impossible. Additional factors include the degree of specialization, location of an organism in the food chain, size of an organism's range, reproductive rate, and tolerance to human presence.

There are many reasons for protecting endangered species. Aesthetic consideration, animal rights, ethical responsibility, economic benefits, and ecosystem stability are all compelling ones.

We can reduce the loss of plants, animals, and microbes through *integrated species management.* Some general suggestions are to reduce habitat destruction, establish preserves, crack down on poaching and plant rustling, control the introduction of alien species, reduce pollution, finance captive-breeding programs, educate the public on the value of wild plants and animals, promote international cooperation, intensify research to learn more about ecosystem stability, and establish germ plasm centers to store seeds from wild plants that might be useful in improving the genetic stock of commercial crops.

One of the the most effective tools for reducing the loss of endangered species has been the U.S. Endangered Species Act (1973). It prohibits the importation of endangered species and sets out guidelines to protect endangered species. All federally funded projects that might have an impact on endangered species must be submitted to the Fish and Wildlife Service or the National Marine Fisheries Service. The discovery of an endangered species only rarely results in the halting of a project; in most cases slight modifications are made, and the project is undertaken.

In addition to the many technical and legal solutions, numerous personal measures can be added, including resource conservation, working with others to reduce waste, becoming active in the political process, and joining wildlife groups.

Discussion Questions

1. Debate the statement "Extinction is a natural process. Animals and plants become extinct whether or not humans are present. Therefore, we have little to be concerned about."

2. Using the Multiple Cause and Effect model described in Chapter 2, discuss the underlying reasons for extinction.

3. Give some examples of habitat destruction or alteration and how these have affected plant and animal species. Give some examples you are familiar with in your own community.

4. Describe several examples of commercial hunting that endanger animal populations. Are these operations necessary? Why or why not? What suggestions do you have for eliminating them?

5. List several examples of introduced species that have adversely affected plant and animal populations. Under what circumstances are introduced species beneficial? What precautions would you recommend before introducing a new species into a new territory?

6. Why are islands particularly susceptible to introduced species?

7. Debate the statement "It is ecologically unsound to indiscriminately kill predators in the wild."

8. How do trophy hunting and natural predation affect populations of prey species? Do both have the same effect?

9. Summarize major factors that contribute to plant and animal extinction. Describe each one in brief, and detail the efforts that can be made to curb them.

10. Discuss the ecological factors that contribute to species extinction.

11. Debate the argument "We must save endangered species of plants and animals." Do we have a responsibility to preserve all living forms? Why or why not?

12. You are placed in a high government position and must convince your fellow executives of the importance of preserving other organisms. How would you do this? Outline a general plan for preserving species diversity.

Suggested Readings

Amory, C. (1974). *Man Kind? Our Incredible War on Wildlife.* New York: Harper and Row. A powerful book written by a leader in the wildlife protection movement.

Blonston, G. (1982). Coyote. *Science 82* 3(8): 62–71. Excellent article on coyote predation and control.

Carlquist, S. (1982). The First Arrivals. *Natural History* 91(12): 20–30. Good review on effects of alien species.

Cousteau, J.Y. (1981). *The Cousteau Almanac: An Inventory of Life on Our Water Planet.* New York: Doubleday. Superb reference.

Defenders of Wildlife (1982). *1080: The Case Against Poisoning Our Wildlife* Washington, D.C.: U.S. Government Printing Office. A well-documented study of why 1080 shouldn't be reinstated.

Domalain, J. (1977). Confessions of an Animal Trafficker. *Natural History* 87(5): 54–57. Startling account of illegal practices in the animal trade.

Ehrlich, P., and Ehrlich, A. (1981). *Extinction: The Causes and Consequences of the Disappearance of Species.* New York: Random House. Good coverage of endangered species.

Koebner, L. (1982). Surrogate Human. *Science 82* 3(6): 33–39. Interesting report on the conditions of experimental chimps and successful ways to breed chimps in captivity.

LaBastille, A. (1983). Goodbye, Giant Grebe? *Natural History* 92(2): 64–72. Superb study of the natural history of the giant grebe and the factors affecting its extinction.

Laycock, G. (1966). *The Alien Animals.* Garden City, N.J.: Natural History Press. A popular account of the troubles created by species introduction. Superb.

Mills, E. A. (1919). *The Grizzly.* Sausalito, Calif.: Comstock Editions. A wonderful book.

Morell, V. (1984). Jungle Rx. *International Wildlife* 14(3): 18–24. Superb story on the value of endangered habitat.

Mowat, F. (1963). *Never Cry Wolf.* New York: Dell. A classic popular account. Humorous and touching.

Ralph, C. J. (1982). Birds of the Forest. *Natural History* 91(12): 41–44. Excellent look at endangered birds on the Hawaiian Islands.

Regenstein, L. (1975). *The Politics of Extinction.* New York: Macmillan. A must for all concerned with species extinction.

Schneider, B. (1977). *Where the Grizzly Walks.* Missoula, Mont.: Mountain Press. Detailed, readable discussion of how humans contribute to extinction.

Time-Life Books (1976). *Vanishing Species.* New York: Time, Inc. An excellent, well-illustrated book.

11

Wilderness, Parks, and Other Nonurban Land Uses

Our duty to the whole, including the unborn generations, bids us restrain an unprincipled present-day minority from wasting the heritage of these unborn generations.

THEODORE ROOSEVELT

A Tragedy of the Commons?

All life on earth depends on the land, water, and air. These resources are akin to the English commons, communal land where cattlemen once grazed their livestock. Garrett Hardin wrote about the commons and their abuse in a classic paper "The Tragedy of the Commons." In England, he wrote, each man was free to graze his herd on the commons along with his neighbors. This system became imperiled, though, as users became caught in a blind cycle of self-fulfillment. As cattle owners sought to maximize their personal gain from the commons, they increased their herds. Because each additional cow meant a gain in income with only a little extra expenditure, the addition seemed like a smart one. Though farmers realized that such actions might lead to overgrazing and the deterioration of the pasture, they knew that the negative effects of overgrazing would be shared by all members of the community. Thus, each rational herdsman arrived at the same conclusion: he had more to gain than to lose. This thinking resulted in a spiraling decay of the commons. Over and over, each increased his herd, sharing the environmental costs with his cohorts. Hardin summarized the situation as follows: "Each man is locked into a system that compels him to increase his herd without limit in a world that is limited." As each pursued what was best for himself, the whole was pushed toward disaster. As Hardin noted, "Freedom in a commons brings ruin to all."

The logic that compels people to disregard communal holdings has always been a part of human society. Today, however, the process may have begun to catch up with us. As this chapter will show, overgrazing of public land and the misuse of public forests, wilderness, and parks contribute to the deterioration of the world commons. Subsequent chapters will describe the misuse of water and air, both truly global commons.

The idea that common resources such as public land, air, and water are the only misused resources is deceiving; private lands are no better managed and cared for. Indeed, the nearsightedness in the exploitation of the commons is also prevalent on private land. Thus, there is a tragedy of all lands and all resources. It is a tragedy of exploitation without concern for the future, which is part of the frontier mentality discussed in Chapter 23.

Short-term exploitation may have been permissible at one time, when the human population was small in relation to the earth's resources. Then insults were small and generally repairable. Today, many observers warn that such actions are no longer tolerable. Too many people share this planet, and too many people are affected by exploiters who are blind to the future.

Land Ownership and Use in the United States

The United States has about 920 million hectares (2.3 billion acres) of land in the public and private domain. The largest single landowner is the federal government. It owns and manages about 290 million hectares (716 million acres), or about one-third of all the total land. About half of the federal land is in Alaska. About 90% of the rest is in 11 western states.

The two principal federal landlords are the Department of the Interior and the Department of Agriculture. Through various agencies such as the Forest Service, the Bureau of Land Management (BLM), and the Fish and Wildlife Service, the public lands are administered for the benefit of all.

The federal lands represent an enormous storehouse of resources and recreational opportunities. Competition is intense among various factions, which advocate mining, grazing, forestry, outdoor recreation, fish and wildlife management, water supplies, or wilderness. In this chapter you will explore some of these conflicts and list some guidelines for proper use of federal land. You will also look at land within the private sector.

This chapter will be limited to rangeland, forests, wilderness, and parks and ways to improve their management to ensure a sustainable society (Figure 11-1). We will examine the heated political debate between conservationists and private commercial interests over land policy and from this get a clearer picture of the true dimensions of modern land management.

Rangelands and Range Management

Rangelands (grazing or hunting grounds) are a vital component of global food production. In the rich as well as the poor nations, production of livestock on rangeland has a number of advantages over feedlots: it reduces the amount of grain needed to feed cattle, conserves energy, and often uses land not suitable for crops.

Figure 11-1
Land use in the United States.

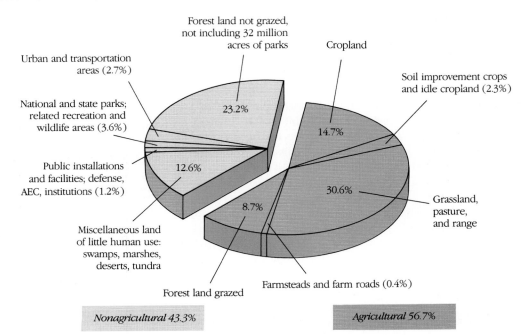

Urban and transportation areas (2.7%)

National and state parks; related recreation and wildlife areas (3.6%)

Public installations and facilities; defense, AEC, institutions (1.2%)

Forest land not grazed, not including 32 million acres of parks

Cropland

Soil improvement crops and idle cropland (2.3%)

23.2%

14.7%

30.6%

Grassland, pasture, and range

12.6%

Miscellaneous land of little human use: swamps, marshes, deserts, tundra

8.7%

Farmsteads and farm roads (0.4%)

Forest land grazed

Nonagricultural 43.3%

Agricultural 56.7%

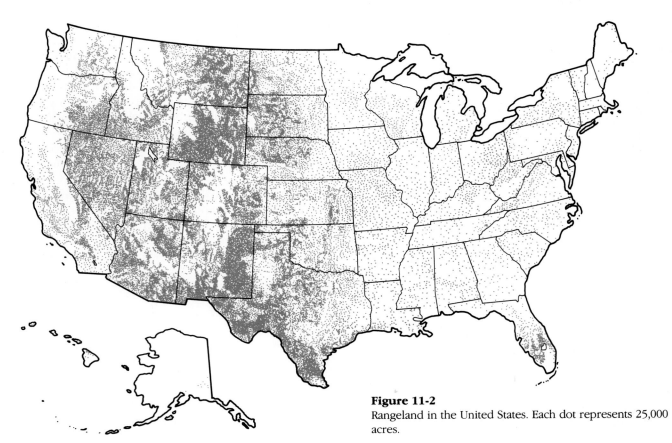

Figure 11-2
Rangeland in the United States. Each dot represents 25,000 acres.

Rangeland Use in the United States

Considering both federal and private holdings, there are about 330 million hectares (820 million acres) of rangeland in the United States. About half is federal land, administered primarily by the BLM; the remainder is held by private interests and states. Most rangeland is located in the West (Figure 11-2). Further increases in demand for beef could result in a 40% increase in rangeland used between 1977 and 2030.

A recent study found two-fifths of all federal and nonfederal rangeland to be in fair or poor condition. In general, nonfederal rangeland was in worse condition than federal rangeland. Surveys limited to nonfederal rangeland showed that 60% of it was in fair to poor condition, suffering primarily from erosion and the invasion of noxious weeds and brush. Figure 11-3 shows the lands that are most severely affected. In 1980 the Soil Conservation Service estimated that three-fourths of all rangeland and pastureland in the country needed better management.

Overgrazing is the cause of most rangeland deterioration. The browsing of too many sheep, cattle, or goats on the vegetation leads to erosion, a decrease in groundwater, desertification, the loss of wildlife species, and the invasion of weeds.

Over 90 million hectares (225 million acres) has undergone desertification in the United States as a result of overgrazing. One of the most notable examples is the Navajo Reservation in Arizona and New Mexico. Living on their 6-million-hectare (15-million-acre) reservation, the Navajos have experienced rapid population growth and a chronic lack of employment. To feed and clothe their

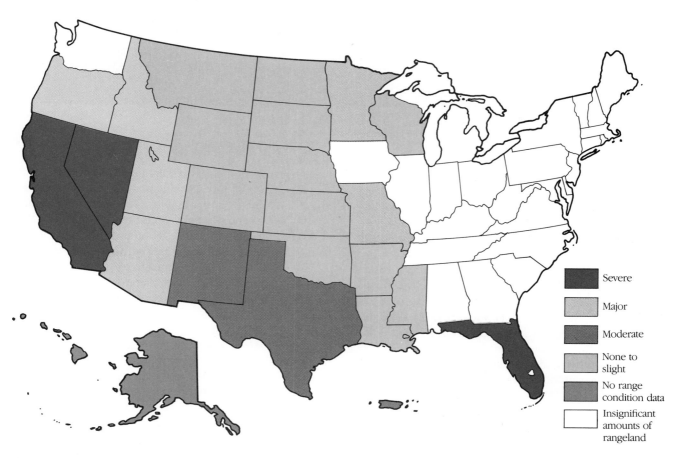

Figure 11-3
This map shows the degree of damage caused by overgrazing, erosion, and weeds on nonfederal rangeland.

Figure 11-4
Properly placed water holes help distribute cattle more evenly on the range and avoid overgrazing of select areas.

people, they have increased the number of sheep grazing this arid land. In 1937 there were about 1.3 million sheep on this land, which has an estimated carrying capacity of about 600,000. Today, despite federal efforts to reduce overgrazing, the sheep herd is about 2.2 million. Baking under the hot summer sun and swept by fierce winter winds, the overgrazed reservation is an arid dust bowl subject to wind and water erosion.

Another severely overgrazed area is the Rio Puerco basin northwest of Albuquerque, New Mexico, a land once known as the breadbasket of the state. It was grazed as far back as the late 1700s. By the late 1800s the basin showed signs of severe overgrazing. Today the land remains in a deteriorating state. Gullies have formed arroyos that widen at a rate of 15 meters (50 feet) a year. Collectively, wind and rain are eroding the soil at a rate of 2 to 4 metric tons per hectare (0.9 to 1.8 acres) per year while nature replenishes it at a rate of only .4 metric tons per hectare (0.2 acres) per year.

Range Management

Through **range management** overgrazing can be avoided. Proper range management in fact can benefit rangeland,

as cattle and other grazers help fertilize the soil and distribute seeds.

Range management generally involves two basic techniques, often employed simultaneously: grazing management and range improvement. Good **grazing management**, the first line of defense, requires the careful control of both the number of animals on a given piece of land and the duration of grazing. These two simple tasks can help reduce or eliminate damage to grasses and herbs and thus protect soil from wind and water erosion.

Range improvement involves controlling brush, revegetating barren areas, fertilizing impoverished soils, constructing fences and water holes, and similar measures (Figure 11-4). Each of these increases ecosystem productivity and minimizes damage. Collectively, they can increase the production of forage as much as tenfold.

One of the most difficult problems facing range managers is how to get livestock to graze land uniformly. Cattle and sheep naturally tend to concentrate in areas near water holes or salt licks, thus overgrazing and trampling vegetation. Ranchers may distribute salt licks and water holes throughout the range to avoid this problem (Figure 11-4). Overused water holes can be fenced off, and new water holes can be made by drilling wells, constructing basins to catch rainfall, and bulldozing ponds in areas where the water table is high. Livestock can be fenced out of unsuitable areas.

A number of other techniques can be used to deter overgrazing. Livestock can be moved (rotated) from one range to the next to give areas time to recover. Grazing can also be delayed while plants bloom and set seed; this way, they will not be eaten before they produce their annual seed crop. Rangeland damaged by overuse can be taken out of use until the vegetation recovers. Fertilization and seeding may also be necessary.

Because each range differs from the next, plans must be individually tailored to meet the rancher's needs. The key element of proper range management is to remain within the carrying capacity of the ecosystem while remaining profitable. This is often difficult, because carrying capacity varies from one year to the next depending on the weather. In dry periods the carrying capacity may be half of what it is in a normal year. In wet periods the carrying capacity may be twice normal. Thus, if a given range supports 1000 cattle in a normal year, it will support only 500 in a dry year.

Truly effective range management requires a willingness to cooperate with nature, to benefit from the good times and cut back during the bad. It also requires a knowledge of plants and their life cycles so that grazing can be timed to minimize damage. Together, range improvements and grazing management will preserve this valuable renewable resource necessary for a sustainable society.

Public policymakers in the United States have passed a number of laws to protect rangeland. One of the most important, the *Public Rangelands Improvement Act (1978)*, was designed to increase management and improve publicly owned rangeland, mostly under the control of the BLM and U.S. Forest Service.

Under the direction of this act, the BLM has called for a marked reduction of grazing on land under its control. This is an unpopular strategy among ranchers, who either cannot see the benefits of improving range conditions or dispute the claims that the land is being overgrazed. The BLM's rangeland grazing plans do not affect Indian lands in the West, where they are badly needed.

Today, rangelands seem to be gradually improving because of private and governmental efforts. As shown in Figure 11-5, the proportion of nonfederal rangeland in poor condition declined by more than half between 1963 and 1977. In the same period nonfederal rangeland in excellent, good, or fair condition increased. But that still

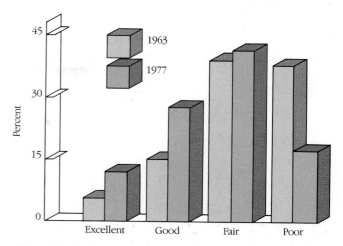

Figure 11-5
Improvement of nonfederal rangeland in 14 years indicates a growing awareness of proper range management.

leaves about 60% in only fair or poor condition, suggesting the need for continued range management.

Forests and Forest Management

Worldwide, there is about 4 billion hectares (9.8 billion acres) of forest land. Covering about one-third of the earth's land surface, forests provide us many direct and indirect benefits. The most notable direct benefits are 5000 commercial products, such as lumber, paper, turpentine, and others worth tens of billions of dollars a year. Forests also provide a refuge from hectic urban life and opportunities for many forms of recreation—bird-watching, fishing, backpacking, and cross-country skiing. In many nations forests are a source of wood for cooking and heating.

The United States has about 300 million hectares (740 million acres) of forest land (Figure 11-6). About two-thirds is commercial timberland, most of which is privately held. Each year U.S. forest products sell for over $23 billion, making them an important part of the economy. The forest products industry employs 1.4 million people and is crucial to U.S. economic well-being.

Indirectly, the forests benefit people by protecting watersheds from soil erosion, keeping the rivers and reservoirs free of silt. Forests reduce the severity of floods and facilitate the recharging of groundwater supplies. Forests also perform many important ecological functions:

Deforestation of Tropical Rain Forests

Exaggerating the Rate and Impact of Deforestation

Sandra Brown

Sandra Brown is an assistant professor of forest ecology at the University of Illinois. Her research centers on the dynamics of tropical forests and wetlands.

Ariel E. Lugo

Ariel Lugo is project leader at the U.S. Forest Service's Institute of Tropical Forestry in Rio Piedras, Puerto Rico. He has been an associate professor at the University of Florida, an assistant secretary for the Department of Natural Resources in Puerto Rico, and a staff member of the U.S. President's Council on Environmental Quality.

There is no question that the loss of tropical forests is one of the more serious problems facing the world today. But we believe that "alarming" deforestation rates and possible global impacts suggested by many popular articles are exaggerated. In this editorial we will explore the facts and fallacies of the tropical deforestation problem as well as suggesting some solutions.

Located between 23.5° N and S latitude, the tropics encompass a land area of about 4.8 billion hectares (12 billion acres) in about 80 countries. Most of these are developing nations with a high population density and rapid growth.

The tropics have more climate and soil types than any other region of the world. Rainfall varies from less than 50 centimeters (20 inches) per year to more than 1000 (400 inches). Seasonality of rainfall also varies widely. Average annual temperatures are generally hot in the lowlands but can be quite cold in the extensive mountainous regions. Using temperature, rainfall, and elevation, Holdridge classified the world into 120 life zones, of which 66 are tropical.

All ten of the soil orders are found in the tropics. It is no wonder that the tropics are reputed to have the largest number of plant and animal species in the world. The potential combinations of soil and climates are so many that an equally high number of possible ecosystems exist. For example, 32 of the 66 tropical life zones support forests, but because of the diversity in soils and topography, the actual number of unique forest types is much higher. These tropical forests are not all "rain forests." Rather, almost half of them are in arid environments.

The most up-to-date assessment (1980) of tropical forests was made by J. P. Lanly of the Food and Agriculture Organization of the United Nations. He recognized two basic forest formations: closed forests, in which the various forest stories cover a high proportion of the ground; and open tree formations, which contain a dense grass layer. The closed forest formation covers about 25% of the tropical land area, and open forest formation covers about 15% of the land.

The tropical deforestation controversy centers on the moist

Endangered Species

In 1978, the Supreme Court blocked the completion of the nearly finished Tellico Dam in Tennessee in order to save a small, ugly fish called the snail darter.

While many applauded the decision, some asked how we can allow a fish to stand in the way of progress. The answer is twofold: (1) Everytime we destroy a species, we destroy an intricate web of interdependency. The near-extinction of the Guam rail, for instance, has had a dramatic effect on both its prey and its predators. The altered ecosystem struggles to adapt or ceases to exist. (2) We can be certain that plants and animals contain some of the answers to the myriad of problems we have not yet been able to solve. Is the cure for cancer hidden in one of the thousands of yet unclassified plants that are being destroyed at the rate of 100,000 acres per day in the tropical rain forest? Can the rapidly disappearing gorilla teach us what we need to know about our own evolution? We can be sure that, as the diversity of the gene pool shrinks, so do our chances for answering some of human-kind's more serious problems.

With the *Endangered Species Act* of 1973, the government assumed legal responsibility for vanishing plants and animals, but it has done little to fulfill this obligation. For instance, during the Reagan administration, over 3800 species were nominated, but only 36 received protection.

1 The southern sea otter lives off the Pacific coast amongst the kelp beds, which are home to its favorite food—the abalone. Widespread killings by their competitors, abalone fishermen, brought the otter to the verge of extinction. Its recent comeback is a result of legal protection.

1

2 The West Indian Manatee, now numbering only 1000, makes its home in the coastal waters of Florida. Its numbers have been reduced by habitat alteration, overhunting by humans, and injuries caused by collisions with power boats.

3 The largest living primate, the mountain gorilla has been hunted to the brink of extinction. Killed for its meat, collected for zoos, and slaughtered for body parts, the population has dwindled to about 1000.

4 The Panamanian Golden Frog lives in a three-square-mile region in Panama. Attractive to tourists in search of unusual pets, the endangered frog is now protected by law.

5 Once enjoying the largest geographic distribution on this continent, the timber wolf has been reduced to a handful of small packs in Alaska, Canada, and the Soviet Union. Probably one of the most feared and misunderstood of all animals, timber wolves were victims of widespread slaughter by humans who believed they were protecting their livestock. It is now known that wolves kill only the old or infirm in the herds.

6 The nation's symbol, the bald eagle, is endangered or threatened in most of its habitats in the United States. Habitat destruction coupled with pesticide poisonings have brought the birds' numbers down to an alarming 1300 pairs in the lower 48 states.

7 A shy animal cursed with a beautiful pelt, the snow leopard was first photographed in the wilds of Nepal in 1970. Studies indicate that as few as 16 remain today.

8 A sow grizzly will charge anything that threatens her cubs. At 1000 pounds, with a 30-inch neck and a 55-inch waist, it seems unlikely that this animal could run faster than 65 kilometers (40 miles) per hour. But she can—easily catching any human or beast that might unwittingly wander between her and her cubs. Only 800 grizzlies remain in the lower 48 states today.

9 Zoos, once contributing to the decimation of wildlife populations, have come to the assistance of endangered species. Here two zoologists introduce a motherless newborn African elephant to a lactating, and hopefully cooperative, female.

4

2

3

5

6

8

7

9

10 This California condor was hatched in the San Diego Zoo in 1983. Condor eggs are taken from nests in the Los Angeles mountains, and hatched and raised in captivity. Victims of habitat alteration, it is believed that the baby condor's chance of surviving in the wild is less than 1 in 50.

11 A zooworker feeds a hatchling using a condor puppet. The use of the puppet teaches the baby to recognize its own kind and encourages it to feed normally. It's hoped that the careful avoidance of human contact will keep the birds wild, enabling them to breed once they are set free.

12 This 16-month old bird is the oldest California condor in captivity. San Diego Zoo, which has hatched 10 eggs to date, plans to free three adolescent condors in May, 1985, outside Ventura, California—the last known condor habitat. They plan to retain this condor as a breeder within the zoo. To improve the chances of chick survival, eventually the San Diego Zoo hopes to maintain six breeding pairs in captivity. Only 17 condors are left in the wild today.

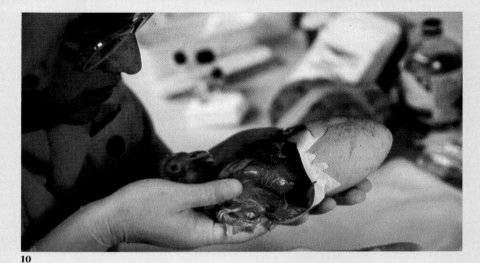

10

12

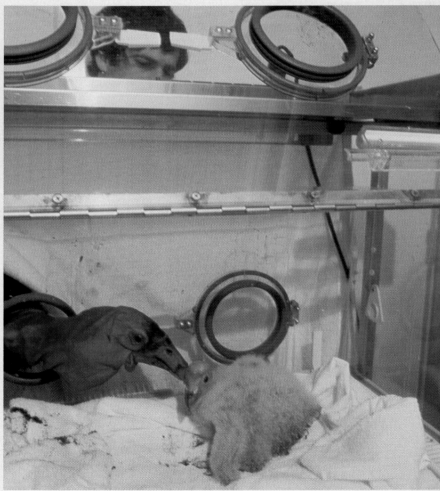

11

forest, generally the "closed" broadleaf formations (97% of the total closed forests). There is reason for concern about the fate of the open forests; they have a slower rate of recovery and are important to millions of people.

Large discrepancies exist in the reported rates of deforestation and the assessments of the implications of deforestation on the environment. A report by the U.S. National Academy of Sciences and the Global 2000 report have suggested a rate of deforestation as high as 20 million hectares (50 million acres) per year, an area nearly six times the size of Rhode Island. At the other extreme, the FAO's report suggests a loss of about 7 million hectares per year (17 million acres), or twice the size of Rhode Island. People who support the high estimate predict that, except for a few remnant patches, all tropical forests will be gone by the end of the century.

The interpretation of the word *deforestation* and of the data explains some of the disagreement. By deforestation, we generally mean completely clearing a forest; selective logging does not constitute deforestation. Proponents of the high rates of forest loss, however, consider selectively logged forests in their rates.

The quality and interpretation of the information used in the various estimates differ significantly. We have reviewed the reports by the National Academy of Sciences and Global 2000; their reported loss is an educated guess at best. The detailed country-by-country report by Lanly is the most comprehensive and objective analysis presently available. We support his low estimate of deforestation of 7.3 million hectares (18 million acres) per year.

Although the overall deforestation rate is much lower than many would have us believe, some countries have very high rates. Countries such as Costa Rica, Thailand, the Ivory Coast, and Nigeria are losing their forests at a rate of 3% to 6% a year. Unfortunately, there has been a tendency to extrapolate these rates to all countries. This is dangerous, because it ignores the fact that countries with large forest areas such as Brazil, Cameroon, and Zaire are experiencing low deforestation rates (about .2% to .4% a year). It also ignores the possibility that deforestation will decrease as the remaining forests become inaccessible or as countries undertake mitigation measures.

There is concern by many that deforestation will cause many species extinctions. Unfortunately, the relation between forest destruction and species extinction is not yet known. Whatever the relation, it follows that if deforestation is occurring more slowly, then so is species extinction.

Tropical deforestation is also blamed for increasing the global atmospheric carbon dioxide concentration and worsening the "greenhouse effect." This effect is clearly dependent on the rate of deforestation, but if the rate is lower than is often projected, there is much less to worry about. The carbon dioxide increase from deforestation each year is less than 15% of the amount produced annually by burning fossil fuels.

It has been suggested that tropical deforestation will cause extensive changes in the rainfall of some areas. Scientists estimate that half of the rain falling on the Amazon Basin originates within the basin through a process of recycling. If the forests are greatly reduced, some say, rainfall will decrease, and areas will turn into deserts. But looking at it realistically, the average annual rainfall for much of the Amazon is about 250 centimeters (100 inches), which if reduced by half will not result in a desert.

The major effects of deforestation are felt more on the local level, especially in tropical countries where water is needed for hydroelectricity and irrigation. Deforesting watershed leads to changes in the surface runoff, increased soil erosion, siltation of reservoirs, increased flooding, and reduced stream flow.

What can be done to resolve one of the most serious problems facing civilization? The first step is to look at the problem with accurate information. Research on tropical ecology and forest management is needed. Next, management must take into consideration cultural, social, and political factors. Deforestation is as much a social and political problem as it is a biological or technical one. All sectors of society must pool efforts to solve a problem that affects them all equally.

The Demise of the Tropical Rain Forest

Alwyn Gentry

The author is associate curator of botany at the Missouri Botanical Garden. He is an active botanical researcher in Peru, Columbia, and Ecuador.

A century and a half ago the world's tropical forests covered an area twice the size of Europe. Today tropical forests have been reduced to about half that area. Many scientists believe that tropical forests are being altered at such a rapid rate—an area of tropical forest the size of Great Britain is lost each year—that they will all but disappear within our lifetime. According to a recent report by the National Academy of Sciences, the only extensive areas of undisturbed tropical forest that are likely to remain at the end of this century are patches in western Brazilian Amazonia and the Congo Basin.

The destruction of large tracts of tropical forest is a tragedy. Why? Certainly the majority of people in tropical countries consider conversion of forest to farms and pastures as "progress." About half of the originally forested land area in the United States had been deforested and converted to cropland by 1920, yet relatively few extinctions occurred. Since 1920 the forested land area has remained at equilibrium, abandoned farms reverting to forest at about the same rate as forested lands are converted to new highways and urban development. Although one mourns the extinction of North American species such as the passenger pigeon and ivory-billed woodpecker, their loss is hardly one of the greatest tragedies of our time. Might one not expect tropical forests, too, to reach some state of sustainable equilibrium, just as temperate forests have?

The tragedy of the destruction of tropical forests stems from the fact that they are fundamentally different from temperate forests, a profound difference rarely appreciated by temperate-zone citizens. First, tropical forests contain a far greater number of plant and animal species than do temperate forests. One hectare of rich forest in the United States might include 20 or 30 tree species; a single hectare in Amazonian Peru can have over 250. Worldwide, at least two-thirds of all plant and animal species live in the tropics; only about one-sixth have been named. Second, unlike nutrients in temperate ecosystems, which are available in the soil, nutrients in tropical ecosystems are recycled in the living matter above the soil, which is often essentially a sterile substrate. Thus, most land, once cleared, cannot sustain agricultural production.

The first problem associated with deforestation is extinction. According to the recent Global 2000 Report to the President, between 1.5 million and 2 million species—15% to 20% of all species now on earth—are likely to be extinct by the year 2000, mostly due to clearing or degradation of tropical forests. Other estimates are even higher. This represents extinction on a scale unprecedented in history. Moreover, many species may become extinct without ever becoming known to science. The quality of life on earth will be diminished by a radically impoverished biota: a loss of the aesthetic beauty intrinsic in the diverse forms and intricate interactions of tropical life.

But the significance of the loss of diversity does not rest merely on arguments of aesthetics. More critically, we know nothing of the potential uses of the two-thirds of the world's tropical species. Loss of so many species is not only a tragic squandering of the earth's evolutionary heritage but also represents depletion of a significant part of the planet's genetic reservoir, a resource of immense potential economic value.

Fifteen years ago a person diagnosed as having leukemia had one chance in ten of surviving; today the chances of living are nine in ten, largely because of the chemicals vincristine and vinblastine, extracted from the vinca plant of tropical Madagascar. Vinca's cancer-curing chemicals were discovered because the plant is widely cultivated as an ornamental; how many undiscovered life-saving chemicals are being lost with each tropical plant species that becomes extinct?

Apologists for uncontrolled development like to point out that the relationship between the deforestation rate and the extinction rate is not linear—a 10% loss of forest cannot necessarily be equated with a 10% loss of species. Actually, the extinction picture is much worse than the overall deforestation statistics suggest. One of the problems with predicting species extinction from deforestation statistics is that most surveys of deforestation measure tree cover, without differentiating between primary and secondary forest or between natural forest and tree plantations. Equally as many species extinctions occur from conversion of virgin forest to other kinds of tree cover as from clear-cutting, but this critical difference is not recognized by many. Only the National Academy of Sciences report cited above attempts to differentiate undisturbed forest from other types of tree cover.

Coastal Ecuador provides an illustration of this problem. Between 1960 and 1970 the strip of lowland wet primary forest along the base of the Andes was deforested after the first penetration of a road. Only one small patch of this forest (.8 of a square kilometer) now survives as the Rio Palenque Field Station. About 100 plant species new to science have been discovered in this tiny area, many of them represented by a single individual plant and, thus, bound for extinction. But perhaps 200 of the 1100 plant species of Rio Palenque would have become extinct had the field station not been created.

A second reason that the destruction of tropical forests is of global importance is the potential effect on world climate. Burning extensive forests converts their biomass to carbon dioxide, significantly increasing the world's atmospheric concentration and intensifying the well-known greenhouse effect. As a result, the earth's atmosphere could become warmer, causing glaciers and polar ice caps to melt (at least in the Antarctic) and sea levels to rise, perhaps eventually inundating coastal cities. However, the contribution to atmospheric carbon dioxide of tropical forest burning is far less than the massive conversion of fossil fuels to carbon dioxide.

On a more local scale, tropical deforestation results in major changes in hydrologic balances and rainfall regimes. Clear-cutting of the forest may therefore result in a 50% decrease in rainfall in the region, converting much of the present forested area to near desert. Removing the tree cover in headwater areas also leads to rapid runoff, with increased erosion upstream and increased flooding downstream, a process that is already economically devastating in India and Pakistan and is beginning to become apparent in the Amazon and Orinoco basins.

A third problem associated with tropical deforestation is economic. In general, highly leached tropical lowland soils are incapable of supporting sustainable agricultural yields without massive infusions of costly fertilizers. Lush, high-biomass tropical forests represent the end point of a very gradual accumulation of tightly held nutrients, continually recycled through the ecosystem over millenia. Cutting and burning the forest releases sufficient nutrients for a few years of crop production before the ashes and their nutrient residue are washed away and the soil is incapable of crop production.

Small-scale slash and burn agriculture mimics the natural system of tree fall and regeneration from the surrounding forest. However, fallow periods of 50 or more years may be necessary before the process can be repeated profitably, making it impossible to maintain large populations permanently by this method. Available data suggest that when cutting and burning of trees is carried out intensively on a regional scale, tropical forests do not regenerate; instead, a permanent second-growth scrub may result when the soil fertility is exhausted and the fields are abandoned. Tremendous areas of the tropics have been converted to this sad state. A well-known example is the Zona Braganca south of Belém, Brazil, where hundreds of square kilometers of now-abandoned scrub provide mute evidence of the failure of the large-scale agricultural development undertaken in the 1960s. Increasing population pressures mean that this process will occur on such a large scale that forest regrowth may never be possible. The tragedy lies in the fact that tropical forests, utilized wisely, are almost certainly capable of producing far more revenue on a sustainable basis, but only when forest cover is maintained and resource harvests are controlled. Promising plans have been suggested for combinations of tree crops and small garden plots interspersed with areas of natural forest for hardwood lumber production.

Unfortunately, most of the world's tropical countries are engaged in a most shortsighted, Faustian bargain, postponing until too late the politically unpopular decision to control forest destruction. Meanwhile, temperate-zone countries have fallen far short in investing financial resources for research into tropical forest ecosystems and into eventually developing sustainable systems of land utilization that can support the burgeoning populations of tropical countries.

The global challenge to humankind posed by ever more people and fewer resources on a finite "spaceship earth" has been noted for some time. We are coming face to face with this problem in the tropical forests. The National Academy of Sciences report concludes that if tropical forest destruction continues at its present rate into the 21st century, it will lead to widespread human misery as well as fundamental alteration in the course of worldwide evolution. Relatively small investments now in research, population control, and land-use planning might well preserve this unique part of the world's biotic heritage indefinitely, with every citizen of the world demonstrably better off.

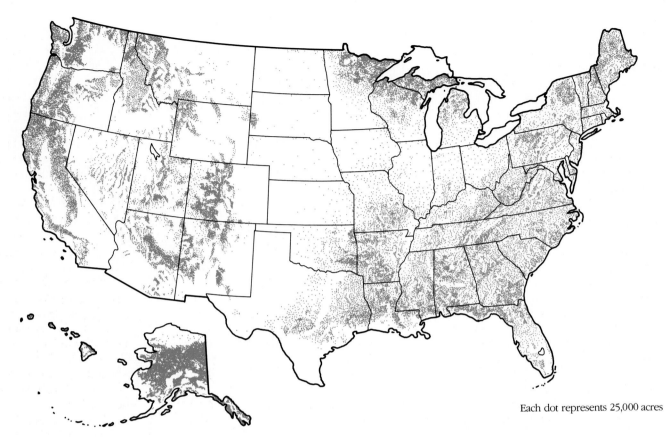

Each dot represents 25,000 acres

Figure 11-6
Map showing distribution of U.S. forest land.

they assist in the cycling of water, oxygen, nitrogen, and carbon (Chapter 4). Many plants and animals live within the world's forests. Some of these organisms are economically important; others have potential value for research, new medicines, and other commercial products.

Despite the great benefits of forests, only about 13% of the world's forest land is under any kind of management. In addition, only about 75 million hectares (190 million acres), or 2% of the world's forests, is protected in forest reserves. With populations growing and the demand for wood, fuel, and a variety of wood products rising, many scientists are greatly concerned about the forests' future.

Worldwide Deforestation

Scientists estimate that somewhere between 30% and 50% of the world's forests have been destroyed, mostly because of clearing for agriculture, firewood production, and commercial cutting. Africa has lost about 30% of its forests, and Brazil, the Philippines, and Europe have lost 40%, 50%, and over 70%, respectively. (See Point/Counterpoint, "Deforestation of Tropical Rain Forests.")

The destruction of the forests is exemplified by the American experience. When the colonists first arrived, forest covered about half the land surface. Soon, though, they began to clear land for farms and towns, to build ships and homes, to make highways, and to safeguard homes from Indian attack.

White pines were especially hard hit by commercial harvesting, which started in the early 1800s in New England. Proceeding westward as these trees became depleted, commercial harvesters reached Minnesota and Wisconsin in 1870. By the early 1900s the white pine had been reduced to the point that it was no longer commercially profitable to harvest. Lumber companies moved into the South to cut the slash, loblolly, and longleaf pines, but within a few decades most commercially profitable stands there had been felled.

Fortunately, the southern pines bounced back from heavy harvesting. The trees grow rapidly in the hot, open areas created by previous tree harvests and in abandoned cotton and tobacco fields. Today, pines support an active timber industry in the South.

Foresters also moved westward into California, Oregon, Idaho, Montana, and Washington in the early 1900s. Here, an abundance of tree species supported a profitable lumber industry that persists today under better management.

Hardwood trees such as maple, ash, and oak, in contrast, were not overharvested in the United States. The reason is that hardwood forests are a mixture of many different species and thus are not amenable to clear-cutting, in which large, uniform stands are removed in a single operation. To harvest hardwoods, foresters had to selectively cut the trees they wanted, which required a greater investment of time and money per board foot produced. Although hardwoods were not overharvested by commercial interests, American deciduous forests were cleared away to make room for farms and homesites. Thus, only about 1% of the original hardwood forests remain.

Development of United States Forest Management

Forests have been exploited for most of human history with little concern for long-term productivity. Commercial interests in the United States took an especially narrow economic view of the forests until after World War II, seeking economic gain with little concern for the future. Fortunately, however, the federal government began to see the need for forest protection. In 1891 President Benjamin Harrison established the first forest reserve, known as the Yellowstone Timberland Reserve.

President Theodore Roosevelt added more land to the Forest Reserve system. By the end of his term over 59 million hectares (148 million acres) of forest had been saved from the commercial interests. Such interests had been running roughshod over much of the public land, cutting down huge forests with the federal government's approval. Many of Roosevelt's actions were prompted by the noted conservationist and forester Gifford Pinchot. Pinchot and Roosevelt recognized that forests could be harvested without permanent damage. Carefully managed, such lands could produce valuable timber for future generations forever.

In 1905 Roosevelt established the Forest Service as part of the Department of Agriculture. Pinchot was named its director in 1908. With the establishment of the Forest Service, the Forest Reserves became known as the National Forests. Pinchot favored judicious forest development over preservation, and his ideology laid the foundation for U.S. forest management policy for decades.

Today, the U.S. Forest Service controls about 75 million hectares (187 million acres) of public land in 155 National Forests and 19 National Grasslands. Forest Service land is found in 44 states, Puerto Rico, and the Virgin Islands. About 36 million hectares (90 million acres) of Forest Service land is open for commercial harvesting.

The Forest Service manages lands that have many uses, such as commercial timber cutting, grazing of livestock, mining, and recreation. In addition, it studies numerous problems, including watershed protection, recreation enhancement, forest management, range management, pest and fire control, wildlife habitat improvement, and others—all geared to improving the National Forests. The Forest Service also cooperates with private and state foresters to promote sound forest management.

The Forest Service operates under the *Multiple Use-Sustained Yield Act of 1960*. This law requires that National Forests and Grasslands be managed to achieve the *greatest good for the greatest number of people in the long term*. But just what constitutes "greatest good" is controversial as illustrated in Essay 11-1, "The Sagebrush Rebellion."

Sustained yield means that forests and grasslands should be used so that they are not destroyed, thus allowing future generations to reap the same benefits as present generations. Multiple use ensures that National Forest land is used by the public and wildlife as well as private industry (Figure 11-7). The role of the Forest Service is to minimize conflicts and ensure multiple use with minimal environmental damage. Conflicts are inevitable, and they generally involve environmentalists on the one hand and mining interests, timber companies, or resort developers on the other.

Central to the conflict is the question of how particular parcels of land should be used. Should a region be left for backpackers, hunters, and wildlife, or should it be leased to a ski resort developer to serve urbanites? Federal law requires that an **environmental impact statement** (EIS) be prepared for all commercial projects on federal land (see Chapter Supplement 25-1). The EIS is written by the Forest Service before development can take place.

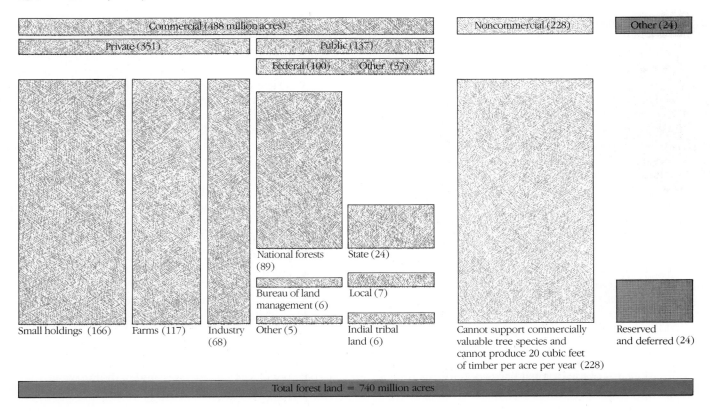

Figure 11-7
Ownership of commercial and noncommercial forests in the United States.

The agency uses this information to achieve the greatest good for the greatest number of people. Today, the Forest Service finds that purpose served most often by leasing land for timber production.

Forest Harvest and Management

Trees are commercially harvested by three basic methods: clear-cutting, selective cutting, and shelter-wood cutting.

Clear-cutting is a standard practice used primarily for softwoods (conifers), which grow in large stands with relatively few species. Commercial foresters move in and cut one tree after the next, leaving nothing but limbs and branches behind in 16- to 80-hectare (40- to 200-acre) plots (Figure 11-8).

Clear-cutting works best for evenly aged stands with limited diversity and for trees whose seedlings can tolerate sunny fields. Aspens in Michigan, Wisconsin, and Minnesota; pines in the southern states; and coniferous forests in the West are all successfully harvested by this method.

Clear-cutting is fast and economical. It creates new habitat for grazers such as deer and elk, and it can be used to increase surface runoff, thus adding to downstream water supplies. However, clear-cuts are aesthetically unappealing. Denuded areas are subject to increased soil erosion; increased runoff may cause flooding and may clog rivers and streams with debris from the clear-cut (Figure 11-9). Erosion can deplete the soil nutrient level and make reforestation more difficult. Unused limbs and branches left on the site can create a fire hazard. Finally, clear-cutting destroys climax vegetation and the habitat of organisms that are adapted to it.

Clear-cutting can be made more aesthetically and environmentally acceptable by making smaller cuts, by blending clear-cuts with the terrain to make them look more natural, by replanting with grasses and trees to control erosion and ensure rapid regrowth, and by intentionally

Figure 11-8
Clear-cuts in the South Tongass National Forest, Alaska.

Figure 11-9
Clear-cut in Kootenai National Forest, Montana.

burning waste or using it to make paper or other wood products.

Selective cutting, or selective silviculture, is used on stands of unevenly aged trees or stands with a number of different species of different commercial value. Foresters individually remove mature trees from forests, doing as little damage to the remaining trees as possible. Hemlock, maple, beech, and a variety of other hardwood trees are well suited for selective cutting, because their seedlings require shade to grow.

Selective cutting has several disadvantages, cost and time involved being the most critical. But this technique is environmentally sound, for it leaves no scar, causes little or no erosion, and does little damage to wildlife habitat.

Shelter-wood cutting is an intermediate form between clear-cutting and selective cutting. In this three-step technique, poor-quality trees are first removed to improve the growth of the remaining healthy trees. The best trees are left to reseed the forest and provide shade for seedlings. When these seedlings become established, some of the commercially valuable trees are removed, but some are left in place to continue shading the seedlings. Once the

saplings are well established, the mature trees left behind are cut down.

Shelter-wood cutting has many of the advantages of selective silviculture. It leaves no unvegetated land, minimizes erosion, and greatly increases the likelihood that the forest will regenerate. However, it causes a more drastic ecosystem shift than selective cutting, and it requires more time and money than either of the other methods.

Tree Farms

Foresters are turning more and more to private tree farms, where they grow their own trees. Using fertilizer, insecticides, and herbicides, they accelerate growth and achieve a higher yield than is possible on public lands, where such actions interfere with other public uses. There are over 34,000 tree farms in the United States, covering about 30 million hectares (75 million acres). Most of these grow timber for paper production.

Tree farms are managed like large modern farms: Plots are planted with seedlings, fertilized from airplanes, treated with herbicides to control less desirable species, and

The Sagebrush Rebellion—This Land *Was* Your Land

A mining company executive in Nevada describes the Sagebrush Rebellion as "a too-long-in-coming uprising against a bunch of federal bureaucrats who sit in the East and tell us people in the West what to do with our land." A park ranger in Utah defines it as "a fight led by land-hungry business people, eager to develop and exploit the natural resources in the West for their own financial gain."

The two sides are clearly defined. The rebels—developers, miners, and ranchers—want to manage some of the millions of acres of western land currently controlled by the federal government to take advantage of the land's natural resources: coal, oil, gas, real estate, and grazing land. On the other side are conservationists and assorted federal agencies, including the Bureau of Land Management, the Forest Service, the National Park Service, and the Fish and Wildlife Service; these people say the land should remain as is—unspoiled—to preserve wilderness and wildlife as well as provide for recreational use.

Dean Rhoads, a rancher and Nevada state legislator, was the primary instigator of the Sagebrush Rebellion, demanding during a 1979 congressional hearing that states be given the right to manage the land within their boundaries. "There are many small towns across Nevada that cannot expand, cannot attract new industry to assist a faltering economy because there is no land available," he testified. "It is all federal land. We see no reason why Nevada or Alaska or any western state should have fewer rights, privileges, and responsibilities than states admitted to the Union earlier."

The bulk of the land owned by the government is in the West—90% of all national landholdings excluding Alaska. Further, it is estimated that these lands contain 37% of the nation's undiscovered crude oil, 43% of its undiscovered natural gas, 40% of its recoverable oil shale, and more than 55% of its geothermal resources. Although many of the federal lands are being used for energy and mineral extraction as well as grazing, the laws and regulations that govern the land's use cost local industry and ranchers time and money. Rhoads and other rebels contend that they can better manage the land within their boundaries than federal agencies in Washington.

The opposing side asserts that states like Nevada want control over vast acreage so it can be sold or leased to private interests, mined for energy and minerals, and harvested by the timber industry—in other words, exploited for a quick profit. Many argue that mining and grazing will be carried out with little concern for environmental quality or reclamation. Further, some western governors and environmentalists say that the proposed enormous land transfers could create economic hardship in their states. Because they would lack federal funding, wildlife and recreation programs could not be maintained at the present level, if at all. Many states might be forced to sell the land to the highest bidder, because most western state constitutions require that land be managed to ensure maximum financial returns. The highest bidder—inevitably a huge conglomerate—would force small ranchers out of business. Once the land is sold, it becomes private: hunters, hikers, birdwatchers, and fishermen would find a no-trespassing sign denying them access to their once-favorite retreats.

The Sagebrush Rebellion rages on, although the punch of the initial uprising has waned. The reason: the rebels feel somewhat better represented by the Reagan administration. If they are not to become owners of the disputed land, at least they have second best—a sympathetic landlord. Whatever the outcome of the rebellion, it has helped focus public attention once again on an increasingly timely issue: the use and misuse of land that belongs to us all.

sprayed with insecticides and fungicides to reduce losses. When the trees have reached the desirable size, they are cut down, and the cycle begins again.

Intensive tree farming offers a fast, efficient way of producing wood for paper and other uses. It allows companies to operate on their own land outside of the scrutiny of the Forest Service and the public. Regardless, many critics argue that the simplified forest ecosystems that are created are more susceptible to insects, fungi, drought, and other potential environmental disasters. They also assert that wood produced in this manner is of lower quality, that erosion and scarring of the landscape are common, and that fertilizer and pesticides will contaminate the ecosystem, especially drinking water supplies for local residents. The same complaints are, of course, raised against ordinary agriculture.

Protecting Forests from Diseases, Insects, and Fires

Forest management involves much more than growing and harvesting trees. Forests suffer from a number of natural hazards, including diseases, insects, fires, drought, storms, and floods.

As shown in Figure 11-10, diseases, insects, and fire account for most of the damage in the United States. Diseases account for 45% of the total losses. The primary disease agent is heart-rot fungus, which attacks the hard wood in the center of the tree. Heart-rot fungus accounts for approximately a third of the total tree damage each year! Other diseases of interest are white pine blister rust, Dutch elm disease, elm-phloem necrosis, and oak wilt. These may be controlled by integrated pest management using environmental, genetic, cultural, and chemical techniques like those described in Chapter Supplement 9-1.

Insects are responsible for about 20% of the total annual destruction. Hundreds of species of insects feed on trees—some on leaves or needles, others on roots and cones, and others on the wood itself. No part of the tree is spared.

Sound management of forest land requires that foresters use an integrated plan that must, as its first requirement, maintain trees in a healthy state. This means that trees should be thinned and that soil should be protected to ensure maximum fertility and water retention. Diversity can also be encouraged, to reduce insect and disease outbreaks. Diseased trees should be removed and insect- and disease-resistant trees should be planted after harvests to minimize the future need for pesticides. Air pollution, which damages some trees and makes them susceptible to other environmental factors, is another element to be controlled. Finally, all imported trees and lumber should be carefully inspected to reduce the accidental introduction of potential pests.

Fire accounts for about 17% of the forest destruction, leveling about .8 million to 2.8 million hectares (2 million to 7 million acres) of forest each year. About 15% of forest fires are the result of lightning. The rest are started by humans. Of these, one-third are deliberately set. The remaining fires are accidental and are attributed to careless disposal of cigarettes, failure to extinguish fires, sparks created from off-road vehicles, and sparks from campfires.

The U.S. Forest Service and state governments have cooperated in attempting to reduce forest fires through public awareness and posting of fire danger signs throughout the year. Television and radio announcements help get this information to the public. The Forest Service also watches over its land from the air and from lookout towers, believing that early detection can greatly reduce fire damage.

Each year the Forest Service spends about $100 million for fire fighting and surveillance. But foresters now realize that preventing fires can be harmful to forests. Totally protected forests accumulate litter, brush, and deadwood, which are significant fire hazards if allowed to build up for long periods. Periodic minor forest fires remove this tinder without damaging much else (Figure 11-11). However, in a protected forest if a fire breaks out, the ample fuel supply permits it to burn out of control. Huge areas burn in firestorms so hot that the soil itself is burned.

The forest ecosystem is adapted to occasional fires. Some species seem to require periodic fires for optimum growth. For example, the cones of the jack pine open up during fires, facilitating the release of its seeds. Fires also return nutrients to the soil and remove brush that shades seedlings.

Today, many forest fires are allowed to burn as long as they do not threaten human settlements. The Forest Ser-

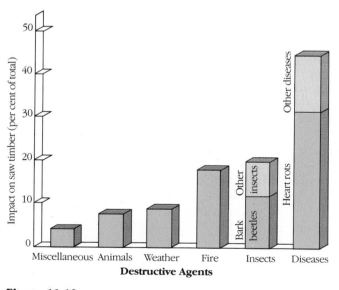

Figure 11-10
Damage to U.S. forests is expressed here as a percentage of the total annual damage.

(a)　　　　　　　　　　*(b)*　　　　　　　　　　*(c)*

Figure 11-11

Benefits of forest fires. *(a)* Dense undergrowth in an Oregon pine stand results from the control of forest fires. *(b)* Controlled burning removes the undergrowth. *(c)* Periodic burning prevents disastrous fires, returns nutrients to the soil, and increases forage for cattle and wildlife.

vice also starts hundreds of fires each year to remove underbrush and litter. These **prescribed fires** are set at times when they will burn slowly and not create intense heat. Carefully monitored to avoid uncontrolled burning, prescribed burning can improve timber production, increase livestock forage, improve wildlife habitat, and protect against disastrous fires. The practice is especially helpful for the long-term protection of Douglas fir, sequoia, redwood, longleaf pine, and ponderosa pine.

Prospects for the Future

Between 1970 and 2000 the demand for wood in the United States is expected to double. By 2020 demand is expected to exceed the supply by 280 million cubic meters (9.3 billion cubic feet); clearly, something must be done. In general, two strategies can be employed: decrease the demand for wood, and increase supply. Here are some specific suggestions.

Recycling paper and using wood products more judiciously can help reduce future demands. Each year 500 hectares (1250 acres) of Canadian forest is cut down to supply wood pulp for newsprint for the Sunday edition of *The New York Times*. Increasing the recycling of newsprint by 10% to 20% could reduce the rate of deforestation. Today, the average American consumes over 270 kilograms (600 pounds) of wood in the form of lumber and paper for packaging and advertisement. This is 4.5 times what the average European consumes and 40 times what citizens of the less developed countries use. Overall consumption could be reduced by recycling at home and at work, by using the backs of scrap paper for homework and notes, by carrying our own shopping bags to the store, and by choosing not to use a bag for small items. The constant bombardment of advertising material can be stopped by writing companies and asking them to take you off their lists. To cut lumber use, smaller homes can be built, using 20% to 30% less wood. Earth-sheltered housing, discussed in Chapter 15, can also reduce our demand for wood and can save tremendous amounts of energy and money.

Waste materials such as limbs, bark, and branches can be used whenever possible. Some companies grind these materials into chips, which are burned for energy or used for the production of paper or chipboard (particle board). This highly efficient harvest method removes debris that creates fire hazards and can increase forest yield by 200%.

Geneticists can help increase yield by developing disease- and pest-resistant and faster-growing trees. Less desirable trees can be converted into paper and other products that require lower quality wood. Wood substitutes can also be used where possible. Abandoned farmland might be planted and periodically harvested, thus increasing wood production and protecting soil from erosion.

Better forest management, too, can increase supply. Thinning of trees, soil maintenance, judicious use of fire, and erosion control can be carried out on private as well as public land. Pest control in the forest can be improved by integrated pest management.

Wilderness in the United States

Wilderness is defined by law as "an area where the earth and its community of life are untrammeled by man, where man is himself a visitor who does not remain." To some people, wilderness is much more, for it provides a deeply moving personal experience, offering a therapeutic escape from the annoyances of modern civilization (Figure 11-12). Wilderness awakens many people to the fact that they are members of an interconnected web of life.

Figure 11-12
Wilderness restores the tired and weary. It is a vital resource in our world.

Wilderness preservation is a subject of controversy between environmentalists and industry. Some environmentalists contend that wilderness should be preserved whether or not there are human benefits. Most others, however, take a less idealistic view. To them wilderness is useful because it provides solace from the hectic pace of urban life. They also argue that wilderness should be protected because it is part of the American cultural heritage. The woods that Daniel Boone walked, the great prairies where Willa Cather was raised, the vistas that Lewis and Clark recorded should not be lost, they maintain. Wilderness provides a vital glimpse into our past. Finally, the inevitable rise in population and the ever-increasing number of people who turn to outdoor sports obligate us to set aside land for future generations. (See Point/Counterpoint in Chapter 23 on obligations to future generations.)

Historically, wilderness has been viewed as something to conquer or subdue, something to exploit for short-term gain. In early colonial and postcolonial times, American lands represented wealth and an unequaled opportunity to sustain a young, growing nation. The concept of wilderness preservation—had it arisen at that time—would have seemed absurd.

But starting in the 1920s and 1930s Americans began to retreat from a long-standing cultural tradition of exploitation and growth to a mentality that promotes conservation and judicious use of resources for the survival of this and future generations. The earliest efforts at wilderness preservation began in the U.S. Forest Service, which set aside lands, designated primitive areas, that were to remain untouched. Between 1930 and 1964 the Forest Service designated over 3.7 million hectares (9.1 million acres) of primitive areas in the National Forests.

The Wilderness Act

In 1964 Congress passed the *Wilderness Act*, establishing the *National Wilderness Preservation System*. It designated the Forest Service's primitive areas as **wilderness areas** and dictated what activities could be carried out in them. Timber cutting, motorized vehicles, and other motorized equipment (for example, chainsaws) were all forbidden except to control fire, insects, and diseases or in areas where their use was already established.

The Wilderness Act sought to create an "enduring wilderness," but at the same time it allowed the continuation of livestock grazing and mining for metals and energy fuels, provisions that seem to contradict its purpose. No new mineral claims could be filed in wilderness areas after 1983; however, all claims before that time can be mined. Therefore, many mining companies filed extensive claims in wilderness areas so that they could move into these areas if they wanted to in the future.

The Wilderness Act also directed the Forest Service, the Fish and Wildlife Service, and the National Park Service to consider land within their jurisdictions for wilderness designation. This opened the door for additional land to be included in the Wilderness Preservation System including land in National Forests, National Wildlife Refuges, and National Parks.

The role of the BLM was not spelled out in the Wilderness Act; inasmuch as this agency manages 70 million hectares (175 million acres) in 10 western states and 110 million hectares (275 million acres) in Alaska, this was a serious omission. As a result, Congress passed the *Federal Land Policy and Management Act* (1976), which requires the secretary of the interior to submit recommendations on the wilderness suitability of land under BLM jurisdiction.

As of 1980 only 4000 hectares (10,000 acres) of its 132 million hectares (328 million acres) has been designated as wilderness. The reasons for this are several. First, the BLM allows commercial grazing on much of its land, and ranchers have lobbied against wilderness designation, fearing that they will lose their inexpensive rangeland. Second, BLM lands are often scattered parcels in arid and rugged terrain. This has led many to contend that these lands would not be suitable for wilderness, because they are inaccessible or undesirable for public use. This view ignores other needs for wilderness, both for its own sake and for the survival of wild animals and plants. It also passes on a misconception that forested land is the only legitimate wilderness.

Several additional laws have added considerable amounts of wilderness reserve to our holdings. *The Endangered American Wilderness Act* of 1978 set aside 500,000 hectares (1.3 million acres) in ten western states. In 1980 the *Alaska Lands Act* added about 23 million hectares (56 million acres) to the American wilderness and quadrupled the amount of land in the wilderness system. As of 1983 there was over 32 million hectares (79 million acres) of officially designated wilderness, and as large as that seems, it is only about 3.5% of the total land in the country (Figure 11-13).

Controversy over Wilderness Designation

Preservation of wilderness has been a topic of heated debate since the passage of the Wilderness Act (see Model 11-1). Environmentalists want more land set aside; the

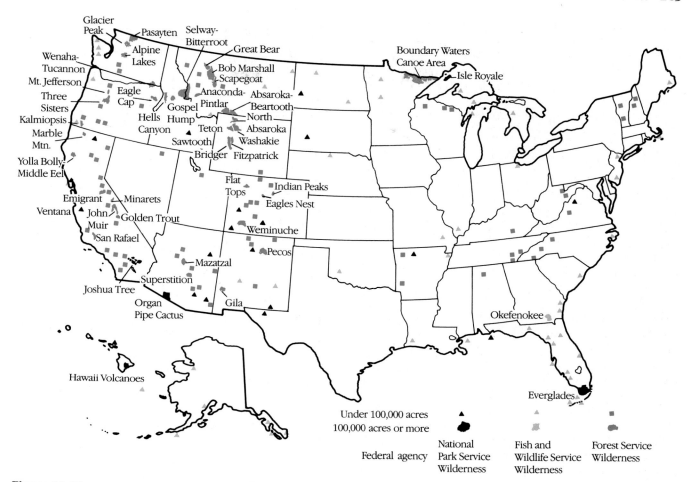

Figure 11-13
Wilderness areas in the United States.

mining and timber industries accuse the conservationists of locking up valuable resources and preventing progress so that only a few can enjoy and, conceivably, profit from this land. These industries assert that wilderness protection costs jobs, even though evidence shows that environmental protection generally creates far more jobs than it destroys. (See Point/Counterpoint in Chapter 24 for a debate on this topic.)

The value of wilderness is not easily translated into economic terms. It is difficult to compare the benefits of a wilderness camping trip with the value of mining and timber production. Nevertheless, the wilderness experience is important in a society that values recreation and the pursuit of happiness. The importance of wilderness preservation will grow in years to come as the population increases.

The timber industry is one of the strongest opponents of wilderness protection. Because only about 8% of U.S. National Forest land has been given wilderness protection, its assertion that such designations are damaging to timber cutting seems unfounded.

Mining interests complain that minerals are being locked up by the Wilderness Preservation System. If anything, many environmentalists argue, the mining interests have been catered to in excess; by allowing mining in wilderness areas, Congress has acted against the best interests of preservation, because mining conflicts with wilderness as much as any human activity could.

Should we set aside more wildlands for future generations even if they contain oil, natural gas, and minerals? Wilderness advocates think that wild, untouched land is more valuable than these resources, because there are no

Model Application 11-1

Wilderness Designation—An Ethical Analysis

Environmentalists have proposed setting aside 16,000 hectares (40,000 acres) of National Forest land in your state as wilderness. This is not a large tract, but it is a popular one that is used for camping, fishing, and hiking. However, it also is commercially valuable because of its timber. Wilderness designation, as you know, effectively closes off land to commercial development such as timber harvesting.

To date, there are about 32 million hectares (80 million acres) of wilderness in the United States, and in spite of increasing use the expansion of the wilderness system nearly stopped after 1980. The use of such areas is so high in some regions that backpackers must acquire permits, a form of advance registration, to reserve a spot in the wilderness for a weekend. Continuing population growth and rising demand for outdoor recreation in wilderness areas suggest the need to expand the wilderness system.

Question

Do an ethical analysis of the question of wilderness expansion.

Step 1

Look at the wilderness proposal from the standpoint of an unemployed lumberjack or an executive of a major wood products manufacturer who had planned to harvest the timber. Make a list of objections you would have to wilderness designation. In other words, what might you lose if wilderness designation were given? How would you calculate a dollar value for your potential losses?

Step 2

Now make a list of all the benefits that wilderness provides to backpackers, anglers, hikers, and wildlife enthusiasts. Are there benefits to the people of your state as well?

Step 3

Which position—the backpacker's or the wood products executive's—do you personally agree with? Why? (This may require you to list your priorities and to think about how you came to value wilderness, money, and so on.) In thinking about your desire to protect or not protect this area, ask yourself these questions:

- Is my decision based mostly on how I might benefit or lose?
- Is my decision based mostly on concern for others who are alive now?
- Is my decision based mostly on concern for future generations?

Step 4

Most decisions in government require a balancing of the needs of different groups. But we often forget that the needs of opposing groups overlap. What is good for one may also be good for the other. Look back over your answers to questions 1 and 2. If you have done a conscientious job, you should find that there are broad community benefits and costs to wilderness protection; for example, watershed protection must be counted as a hidden but important benefit to every one.

Step 5

Now comes the final part. Assume that you are reporting to the president on whether or not this land should be given wilderness status. What recommendations would you make? Knowing the needs of this and future generations for income and recreation and the need to protect watersheds and wild lands, how would you justify your decision? In a written report discuss the pros and cons of wilderness designation.

---

substitutes for it once it has been destroyed. In contrast, there are many alternatives to energy and mineral resources, options explored in Chapters 14–16.

Maintaining Wilderness

Human use, even the trampling of backpackers and other hikers, can significantly affect wilderness. This can be seen in many parts of the West, where trails are dug deep by the hooves of horses and the feet of backpackers and create routes for water runoff, leading to severe erosion. Some wilderness areas attract more people than the land can handle. Lured by the thought of quiet and solitude, many a backpacker is dismayed by the crowds around high mountain lakes and by special camping restrictions enforced by the Forest Service to protect lakes and streams from pollution. To many, this overcrowding is a sign of the need for more wilderness, especially if U.S. population is to grow by another 70 million to 100 million people before it stabilizes, as demographers have recently predicted.

Other ways for eliminating crowding and environmental degradation in the wilderness include the following: (1) educating campers on ways to reduce their impact, (2) restricting access to overused areas, (3) issuing permits to control the number of users, (4) designating where backpackers can and cannot camp to avoid overuse of other areas, (5) increasing the number of wilderness rangers patrolling areas to pick up garbage and monitor use, (6) disseminating information regarding infrequently used areas to divert campers from overused areas, and (7) improving trails to encourage use of currently underutilized areas.

The Plight of U.S. Parks

Park Problems

There are a variety of parks in the United States, ranging from the corner playground to medium-sized state parks to the mammoth federal parks maintained by the National Park Service. Less wild than wilderness areas, parks support numerous activities. Increasingly, though, these parks, which collectively receive about 2.5 billion visitors a year, are being threatened by overuse, air pollution, crowding, lack of funds for maintenance, proliferation of businesses within their boundaries, and mineral and energy development both within and around their borders.

Especially endangered are the National Parks. The first national park was Yellowstone, which was founded in 1872. Since its creation, the National Park System has increased to encompass 333 holdings, including 48 National Parks, 78 National Monuments, and 62 National Historic Sites. All told, the National Park System encompassed 32 million hectares (79 million acres) in 1981 and received approximately 330 million visitors. Including seashores, rivers, trails, lakes, historic sites, deserts, grasslands, and mountains, the National Park System is a showcase to the rest of the world. So popular has the idea been that now approximately 100 countries worldwide have begun similar systems.

When the National Park Service was established in 1916, its mandate specified that National Parks would be (1) protected so that they could be passed on to future generations and (2) set aside for the use, observation, health,

and pleasure of the people. All decisions regarding private or public enterprise in the parks were to be made in the best interest of the public.

Today, many National Parks are severely overcrowded and plagued by deteriorating trails, noise, air pollution, vandalism, litter, and traffic congestion. But the Park Service is helpless to control many of the problems because of budget reductions. Many of the problems also originate outside park boundaries. The most notable of these problems is air pollution created by neighboring power plants, mines, industrial development, and motor vehicles (Table 11-1). Air pollution is getting worse, creating an unsightly haze and obscuring scenic vistas, especially in the West, where many of our parks are located. Because unobstructed vistas are essential to the allure of these areas, deterioration can only diminish the value of our parks.

Perhaps the most renowned U.S. park is the Grand Canyon National Park in Arizona. It is the seventh most popular park in the country, visited by about 3 million people each year. But the canyon is sometimes blanketed with air pollution from the nearby Navajo Power Plant in Page, Arizona. At times, visitors cannot see the opposite rim of the canyon. Visibility in other western parks has also been decreasing because of rampant population growth and the burning of coal to generate electricity for new homes and businesses. Air pollution, especially acid precipitation, also threatens fish and other organisms within National Parks in the East (Chapter Supplement 19-2).

Increasingly, mineral and energy companies have pressured the U.S. government to allow mining on private land within or near park boundaries as well as on parkland itself. For example, the Glen Canyon National Recreation Area in southern Utah and northern Arizona covers some 500,000 hectares (1.2 million acres) and receives 1.6 million recreation visits each year. But because of the large deposits of minerals and energy resources thought to be in the park, developers have pressed the federal government to open this land to strip mining. Increased truck traffic associated with mining, dust escaping from mine sites, and visual disruption of the land could severely diminish the aesthetic value of this majestic land. Since 1974, visibility in the region has decreased by 25% to 50% because of air pollution. Mineral and energy development inside the park could be the last straw. Mines outside park boundaries could also add to pollution and diminish the aesthetic value of our parks. For example strip mines proposed near Utah's Bryce Canyon could create an unsightly scar. Furthermore, new homes and businesses cropping up in the vicinity of parks light up the sky and detract from the quality of the camping experience.

Table 11-1   Western National Parks: A Survey of Their Problems

Areas of Existing Development			
Sampling of Parks Threatened	Hazard	Impacts	Status
Petrified Forest National Park, Arizona	• Cholla Power Plant, 965 megawatts (mw) • Coronado Power Plant, 1050 mw	Loss of Class I air quality; socio-economic impacts—"Boom Towns."	Plants completed and on-line
Arches and Canyonlands National Parks, Utah	• Huntington Canyon Project, 845 mw • Emery Project, 860 mw	As above	Emery Project to be doubled in size by 1982
Capitol Reef National Park, Utah	• Inter-Mountain Power Project (IPP), 3000 mw, Lynndyl, Utah	• IPP plant was proposed at a site 10 miles from park. • Damage to lichens, air pollution indicator species, has already occurred.	Plant relocated due to environmental objections (1981)
Glen Canyon National Park, Utah	• Navajo Power Plant, 2310 mw • Proposed 1976 Kaiparowits power plant has been reconsidered by DOE, 3000 mw.	800-foot power plant smokestacks have had an adverse impact on park visibility, and summer winds diffuse pollutants toward Navajo Mountain and Kaiparowits Plateau. Winter inversions have reduced the visibility from 70 miles to 15 miles. Boom town development and increased demand on NPS sewage/water facilities.	Power plant burns coal strip-mined from Hopi-Mesa Indian Reservation and hauled by unit train to plant
Areas of Most Imminent Development			
Bryce Canyon and Zion National Parks, Utah	• Allen/Warner Valley System: 2 power plants, 1 strip mine. Mine would require daily blasting to remove overburden 160 feet deep. A coal slurry line would be located 15 miles from park.	• 8300-acre strip mine is 4 miles from Bryce Canyon Yovimpa visitor scenic overlook. • Strip mine would require removal of a forest and bulldozing. • Emissions would reduce visibility by 60%. • Dust from coal-haul roads would limit visual range to less than 3 miles at times. • Water used for coal slurry, up to 10,000 acre-feet, would damage wildlife habitat, limit domestic consumption of water, and reduce agricultural productivity of Utah.	On May 1, 1981, 2 California utilities withdrew from the project. Project is now dead for time being due to protests from NPS and public outcry from the National Parks and Conservation Association

Table 11-1 Western National Parks: A Survey of Their Problems

	Areas of Existing Development		
Sampling of Parks Threatened	Hazard	Impacts	Status
Kaiparowits Plateau, Utah Forest Service, BLM Land	• A proposed 50-mile complex of 20+ large, deep mines along the backbone of Kaiparow-its Plateau.	• Proposed 250-mile railroad line to haul coal to Cedar City and other power plant areas in Utah • Socioeconomic impacts due to boom towns	As above
Zion National Park, Utah	• Harry Allen Plant, 2000 mw; plant would be required to have best available control tech-nology (BACT) • Warner Valley Plant, 500 mw	• Allen plant is to be 25 miles from park, 25 miles NE of Las Vegas. • Prevailing winds would flush emissions directly northward over park. • All coal plants would divert water from Virgin River, Nevada-Utah, and fill it with wastewater, which will damage endangered fish species. • Warner plant is to be 22 miles upwind from park and would reduce area from a Class I Air Standard to a Class III Air Standard. • All electric power from these plants will go to southern Cali-fornia. Pollution stays in Ari-zona, Utah, and Nevada.	Status pending. Environ-mental Impact Statement review and review by secretary of interior. States object to electricity going to southern California.

Source: Rudzitis, G., and Schwartz, J. (1982), The Plight of Parklands, *Environment* 24(8).

Water depletion and water pollution can also affect the nation's parklands. Drainage projects in southern Florida lower the water table, making land suitable for agricul-tural development and the construction of homes. Nor-mally, this groundwater would flow to the southern tip of Florida to nourish the vast array of life in Everglades National Park. Now, much of this water is shunted into canals that lace the state and is diverted to the ocean, never reaching the park (Figure 11-14). The decreased water supply in the park has reduced its carrying capacity by half.

Commercial development—lodges, restaurants, gift shops—within some parks, such as Yellowstone, are an annoyance to many environmentalists, who assert that such development tends to turn the parks into miniature cities. Catering to the expensive tastes of the recreational vehicle crowd, parks lose much of their rustic appeal and become an extension of the urban environment, unpalatable to those who come for a respite from city life.

Possible Solutions

Solving this growing tangle of internal problems will require money to improve park management. With pop-ulation and park use on the rise, the American public may have to pay a much higher entrance fee or be willing to support increased taxes to improve, maintain, and expand

Figure 11-14
Extensive canals in
southeastern Florida cause the
water table to drop so the land
can be farmed or used for
homes. The water is then
diverted to the ocean.

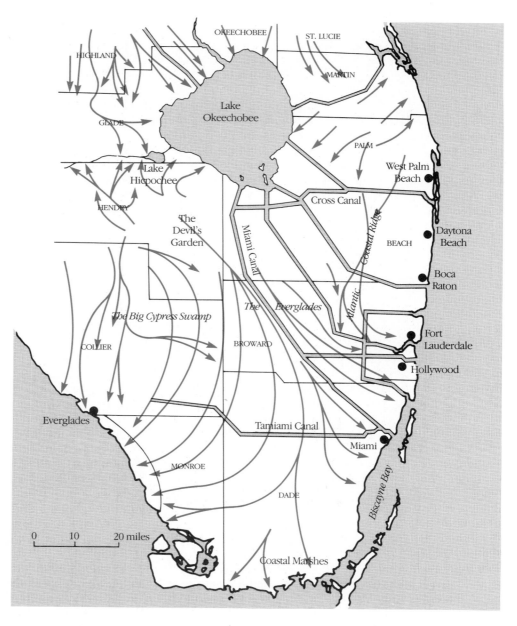

parks (Figure 11-15). Crowding could be alleviated by requiring advance reservations, as in Yosemite; traffic congestion could be reduced by making visitors leave their vehicle in a campground or at a central location, from where they could be shuttled by bus or travel by bicycle or on foot to view the scenery. Furthermore, development of lodges, restaurants, stores, and other commercial facilities within park boundaries might be held to a minimum. Such facilities could use solar energy and be built to blend as much as possible with the envi-

ronment. Development could be restricted to areas where the least damage to wildlife habitat and impairment of scenic beauty would occur.

Finally, many people advocate the expansion of the National Park System (Figure 11-16). Population growth will create a need for more parkland. Foreseeing this demand, Congress passed the *Land and Water Conservation Fund Act* in 1964. This law and a 1968 amendment provided money for the purchase of recreational land by the states as well as the federal government. Money came

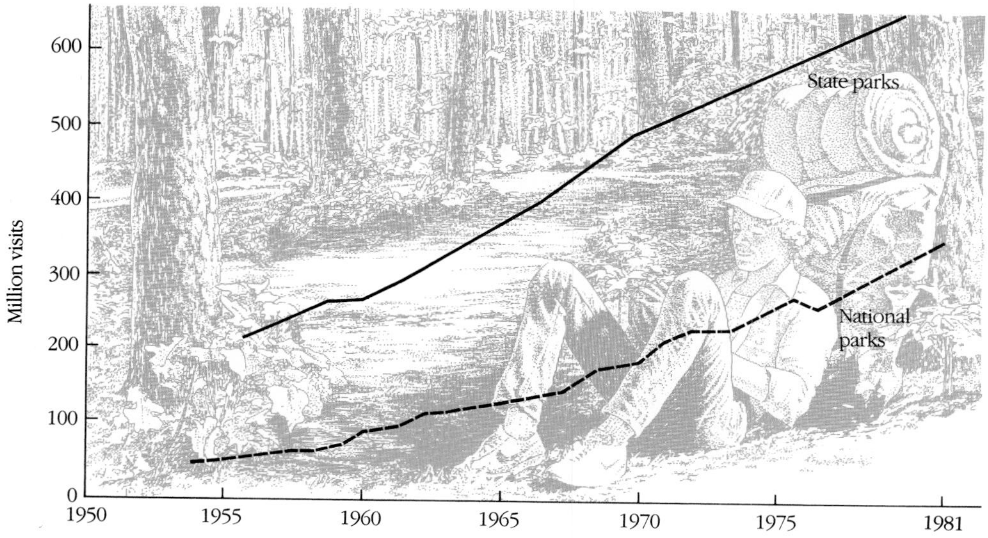

Figure 11-15
State and national park visits in the United States have dramatically increased since 1955.

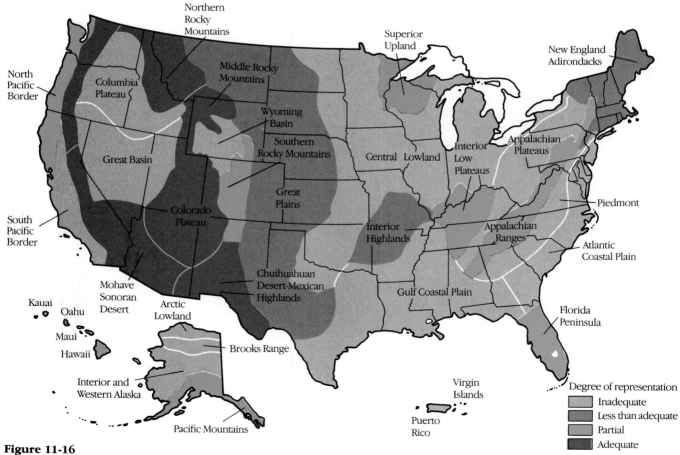

Figure 11-16
Distribution of National Parks by region. Many areas could benefit from more National Parks.

from taxes on certain items, such as motorboat fuel sold on federal land and from the sale of federal land; in addition, Congress agreed to appropriate $200 million a year for the fund. However, Secretary of the Interior James Watt eliminated the fund to help reduce federal spending, arguing that the National Park Service should concentrate its efforts on upgrading and maintaining existing parks, not expanding the system.

The parklands are a priceless treasure in a world where wilderness, peace, quiet, and clean air are rapidly deteriorating. But the National Park System is in danger. As in so many other issues, hard economic times created in part by an expanding population, runaway consumption, and disregard for resources have diverted public and governmental attention from the responsibilities of developing a sustainable society and passing on to future generations the amenities we now enjoy. We cannot let this trend continue.

The art of progress is to preserve order amid change.

A. N. WHITEHEAD

Summary

All life on earth depends on the land, water, and air. These resources are akin to the commons—tracts of land where English cattlemen once grazed their livestock. The commons deteriorated as each farmer increased his herd beyond the carrying capacity of the pasture. Such actions, compelled by individual gain, brought ruin to the English commons and may have the same result for the global commons. The misuse of biosphere resources is not limited to those held in common. Private land is, in many cases, treated with similar disregard.

Rangelands are a vital component of global food production in rich as well as poor nations. A history of overgrazing has resulted in the deterioration of both private and public rangelands, resulting in permanent loss of vegetation, erosion, desertification, wildlife extinction, invasion of weeds, and a drop in groundwater. *Range management* aims to avoid these problems by following two major strategies: *grazing management,* or control of the number of animals on a piece of land and the duration of grazing, and *range improvement,* such as fertilizing, reseeding, and the use of techniques to encourage uniform grazing.

Forests benefit society directly by providing numerous commercially valuable products, such as wood and paper, and also by providing opportunities for recreation. Indirectly, forests benefit us by protecting watersheds from soil erosion, thus keeping rivers and reservoirs free of silt; by reducing surface runoff, which decreases flooding and recharges groundwater, and by recycling water, oxygen, nitrogen, carbon, and other important nutrients.

Worldwide, many millions of hectares of forest have been cut down to provide products and to make room for farms and homes. In the United States, forest protection began in the late 1800s, starting with President Harrison, who established the first forest reserve. Theodore Roosevelt added more land to the Forest Reserve System, and in 1905 he established the Forest Service, which was soon headed by Gifford Pinchot. Pinchot promoted judicious use of forests over strict preservation, and his notions of multiple and sustained use persist today. The Forest Service manages lands for such uses as commercial timber cutting, grazing of livestock, mining, and recreation.

Many privately owned forests are now cultivated like farm fields and suffer the same problems as conventional mechanized agriculture.

Forests can be better managed by intentionally setting fire to parts of them or permitting small fires to burn. This periodically reduces the buildup of brush and dead limbs. Integrated pest management can also be used to control insects and disease.

The rising demand for wood and wood products can be met by better management aimed at reducing unnecessary losses and by efforts to increase paper recycling and reduce wasteful paper use.

Wilderness is defined by law as "an area where the earth and its community of life are untrammeled by man, where man is himself a visitor who does not remain." For some people wilderness provides an escape from hectic urban life and a chance to watch animals, exercise, or relax. To others, it is an untapped resource with valuable minerals and timber. Because of such divergent views, much controversy surrounds efforts to set wilderness aside.

In 1964 Congress passed the Wilderness Act, which established *wilderness areas* within land owned by the National Park Service, the Fish and Wildlife Service, and the Forest Service. The law prohibits timber cutting and motorized vehicles and equipment except in certain instances. Mining can take place in designated wilderness areas as long as claims were filed before 1983. The Federal Land Policy and Management Act (1976) also strengthened wilderness preservation by requiring the Interior Department to study its lands and recommend areas for wilderness designation.

Although many commercial interests continue to fight wilderness preservation, conservationists note that rising population and the fact that more people are turning to outdoor recreation every day will necessitate more wilderness to avoid overcrowding and damage. Other ways to solve this problem are educating campers on ways to camp without an impact, restricting access to overused areas, controlling the number of users, increasing the number of wilderness rangers patrolling areas and picking up garbage, disseminating information regarding infrequently used areas, and improving trails to encourage the use of underutilized regions.

U.S. National Parks, the envy of the world, are facing a number of problems: overuse, air pollution, crowding, lack of funds for maintenance, proliferation of businesses within their boundaries, and mining and energy development both within and around their borders. Solving these problems will require money to improve park management. With population and park use on the rise, the American public may have to pay a much higher entrance fee or be willing to support increased taxes to improve, maintain, and expand parks. Development on lands around National Parks should be carefully regulated to preserve air quality and scenic beauty.

Discussion Questions

1. Discuss the tragedy of the commons. Give some specific examples of "commons," as used by Garrett Hardin, and how they are mistreated.

2. What are the major problems on federally owned and private rangeland? Give some examples. What suggestions would you make to improve the condition of American rangeland and better manage it for future generations?

3. Describe reasons for the loss of American forest lands. How could better timber management have helped reduce the destruction of our early forests? Or could it have helped it?

4. Define the following terms as they relate forest to management: *sustained yield, multiple use, clear-cutting, selective cutting,* and *shelter-wood cutting.*

5. Discuss the pros and cons of clear-cutting and selective cutting. Why is clear-cutting not recommended for hardwood stands but considered to be the most desirable form of harvesting many conifers?

6. Why are many foresters intentionally burning forests or letting some forest fires burn?

7. List and discuss ways to satisfy the growing need for wood and wood products in the coming years. Which of your ideas are the most ecologically sound? How would you go about carrying out your ideas if you were an elected official?

8. What can you do to personally reduce paper and wood waste and increase recycling?

9. Discuss the controversies over wilderness preservation. What are the major arguments for wilderness preservation and wilderness exploitation for minerals and other resources?

10. Debate the statement "Wilderness areas should be opened up for timber and energy development, because we need these resources."

11. Debate the statement "More land should be designated wilderness for this and future generations."

12. Discuss problems facing U.S. National Parks. How can Americans alleviate these problems?

13. Debate these statements: "To ensure that future generations will have adequate parkland, we should set aside more parkland now." "Future generations can establish their own parks; right now we need oil and minerals."

Suggested Readings

Alexander, D. (1984). Saving the Trees, Saving Ourselves. *International Wildlife* 14(1): 18–22. Good account of efforts to curb deforestation in India.

Bell, H. M. (1973). *Rangeland Management for Livestock Production.* Norman: University of Oklahoma Press. In-depth coverage.

Caras, R. (1979). *The Forest.* New York: Holt, Rinehart and Winston. A delightful and general account of forest ecology.

Clawson, M. (1983). Reassessing Public Lands Policy. *Environment* 25(8): 6–17. Thoughtful look at managing public lands.

Eckholm, E. (1979). *Planning for the Future: Forestry for Human Needs.* Washington, D.C.: Worldwatch Institute. Superb paper.

Eckholm, E. (1982). *Down to Earth: Environment and Human Needs.* New York: Norton. Contains a thoughtful essay on forests.

Edlin, H. L. (1976). *Trees and Man.* New York: Columbia University Press. Superb coverage.

Garrett, W. E. (1978). Grand Canyon: Are We Loving It to Death? *National Geographic* 154(1): 16–51. Excellent article on the Grand Canyon and management problems. Also see the July 1979 issue of *National Geographic,* which is devoted to National Parks.

Hales, L. (1983). Who Is the Best Steward of America's Public Lands? *National Wildlife* 21(3): 5–11. Excellent reading.

Hardin, G. (1968). The Tragedy of the Commons. *Science* 162: 1243–1248. A classic paper.

Heady, H. F. (1975). *Rangeland Management.* New York: McGraw-Hill. Excellent review.

Madson, J. (1982). *Where the Sky Began: Land of the Tallgrass Prairie.* New York: Houghton Mifflin. A moving treatise.

Postel, S. (1984). *Air Pollution, Acid Rain, and the Future of Forests.* Worldwatch Paper 58. Washington, D.C.: Worldwatch Institute. Interesting but detailed look at forest protection.

Rudzitis, G., and Schwartz, J. (1982). The Plight of Parklands. *Environment* 24(8): 6–11; 33–38. Superb article on the controversy over park deterioration.

Sheridan, D. (1981). Western Rangelands: Overgrazed and Undermanaged. *Environment* 23(4): 14–20; 37–39. Superb account.

Spurr, S. H., and Barnes, B. V. (1980). *Forest Ecology* (3rd ed.). New York: Ronald Press. Excellent text.

Stoddart, L. A., Smith, A. D., and Box, T. W. (1975). *Range Management* (3rd ed.). New York: McGraw-Hill. Authoritative review of range management.

Off-Road Vehicles—
Conflicts Among Land Users

In 1947, in the bomb-shattered city of Hamamatsu, Japan, a 41-year-old mechanic named Soichiro was rummaging through the debris when he found a surplus field generator. He strapped it to his bicycle and, with some tinkering, made himself a motorized bike. Soon after this small feat, Soichiro was designing motorbikes and motorcycles that bore his last name, Honda. By 1960 he was selling his motorcycles in the United States for about one-fifth the price of most American and European models. By 1976 Honda had captured half of the U.S. market, selling hundreds of thousands each year.

Honda's success was twofold. For one, the company sold well-built machines that were dependable and easy to repair. It also mounted a wide advertising campaign to clean up the image of the motorcycle user. Ads featured well-dressed, respectable-looking actors to convey the notion that decent, law-abiding Americans could enjoy a motorcycle as transportation and a source of recreation.

The motorcycle movement grew at an enormous rate in the United States. In the early 1960s there were only 400,000 registered motorcycles in the country, but by 1976 the number had grown to 8.3 million. About two-thirds of the registered motorcycles were used off the road (usually on dirt trails) at some time, thus giving rise to the term **off-road vehicle.**

Snowmobiles had a similar history: the first commercially available snowmobiles arrived in 1959; recent figures show that there are over 2.2 million in the United States and over 1 million in Canada. The army of off-road vehicles is completed by dune buggies and four-wheel-drive vehicles. Today, there are an estimated 250,000 dune buggies and over 3 million four-wheel-drive vehicles, half of which are used off the road at some time in their life.

The off-road vehicle (ORV) craze struck without warning. Advertisements promoted the use of motorcycles, trucks, jeeps, and other vehicles on rugged terrain, showing them scrambling up steep slopes, splashing through streams, and charging through mud. One ad even showed a driver in pursuit of bighorn sheep. Managers of public lands were surprised by the sudden rise of off-road vehicles, and private landowners were irate when their property was inundated by these often noisy and potentially destructive machines.

As the popularity of ORVs rises, so do the conflicts. Private landowners, public land managers, conservationists, and scientists complained that the use of ORVs damaged plants and soils, conflicted with other forms of recreation, and adversely affected wildlife.

Snowmobiles

Snowmobiles do less damage to the environment than most other off-road vehicles, but their impact can nevertheless be significant. One of the most noticeable impacts is noise, which disturbs wildlife, homeowners, and other recreationists, especially snowshoers and cross-country skiers.

Snowmobiles compact the snow they travel on. In popular snowmobiling areas in Minnesota, scientists have noted that compacted snow is turned to ice, and this ice melts one week later than unpacked snow in the vicinity. Compacted snow is a poorer insulator than natural snow; thus, in areas frequented by snowmobiles the soil freezes to a greater depth. This deep freezing may harm the roots of small plants and trees.

Tree seedlings are easily damaged by snowmobiles. Commercial tree growers report that snowmobilers break off the tops of trees, which may not kill them but often causes them to grow crooked, thus reducing their value for timber.

Compaction of snow also affects rodents that burrow at the interface between the snow and the ground (subnivean space) during the winter. Packing of the snow can impede their movement to food sources. One study showed a doubling of mortality among rodents in an area used by snowmobiles. Snow compaction on lakes may decrease the transmission of light through the ice by making the ice more opaque. This could reduce what little photosynthesis occurs during the winter.

Snowmobiles offer hunters and anglers access to remote areas, where they may overfish and overhunt certain species. For example, one group of 150 snowmobilers recently invaded a back-country lake in Minnesota and in one day removed 250 kilograms (560 pounds) of fish, nearly the entire population of the 30-hectare (80-acre) lake.

Finally, a small minority of snowmobilers harass wild animals. Chasing these cold-stressed animals can deplete their marginal energy supplies and exhaust them. In a weakened state they can fall prey to predators, disease, and cold.

Snowmobile damage can be reduced in a number of ways. First, users can exercise self-restraint and avoid areas that could be adversely affected, especially alpine tundra, private land, stands of new trees, and critical wildlife habitat. Second, special trails can be developed where snowmobile use will not affect other recreationists and wildlife. In Rocky Mountain National Park, for instance, snowmobilers are allowed to use the main highways, which are closed to other vehicles. Third, snowmobile clubs can educate their members not to harass wildlife and to act reasonably around other recreationists. Members should be discouraged from driving when there is less than 15 centimeters (6 inches) of snow on the ground. Fourth, quieter snowmobiles can be developed. Everyone, including the users, will benefit

from this (see Chapter Supplement 21–1, on noise pollution). Fifth, land managers can do a better job of regulating hunting and fishing in remote areas that are accessible to snowmobilers.

Other Off-Road Vehicles

Four-wheel-drive vehicles, dune buggies, motorcycles, and all-terrain vehicles do considerably more damage than snowmobiles, because there are more of them and because they are used at a time when there is no protective layer over the soil and vegetation (Figure S11–1).

ORVs have damaged land from Florida to Maine and from New York to California. No ecosystem has been spared. The alpine tundra of the Rocky Mountains and the Sierra Nevadas and the arctic tundra of Alaska bear their imprints. Wooded areas in Florida, Indiana, Missouri, and Colorado have been scarred by inconsiderate ORV users. The grasslands of Kansas and Montana show the signs of damage. In some places the damage will be repaired naturally; in others, where damage is severe, repair may never occur.

Especially hard hit are the wild and semiwild areas around many western cities such as Phoenix, Denver, Las Vegas, and Los Angeles. The major problem with ORV use is that the terrain that most challenges the users and is, therefore, the most attractive to them is also most sensitive. ORV use scars land, destroys

Figure S11-1
Off-road vehicles adversely affect soil, vegetation, and wildlife.

plants, facilitates soil erosion, alters the physical and chemical characteristics of soil, impairs revegetation, damages wildlife habitat, destroys wildlife, and conflicts with other recreationists.

Large areas of the American desert, coastal sand dunes, barrier islands, forests, grasslands, and tundra are rutted by ORVs. In the tire-torn deserts of the West, archeological resources are being badly damaged. In particular, large human and animal figures called intaglios, carved into the earth by ancient people, are being badly scarred by tire tracks. Today, citizens working with the BLM are fencing off these areas to prevent further damage to these rare remnants of past cultures.

Vegetation is particularly hard hit by ORVs. Roots, seedlings, and foliage of small plants are crushed by tires. Other plants are uprooted by churning tires. The frames of ORVs tear limbs off larger plants. The destruction of vegetation has a ripple effect: It reduces the organic content of the soils, which decreases water retention and plant growth. In addition, destruction of vegetation reduces ground cover and habitat for animals, increases soil erosion, and changes soil temperature.

Of the impacts of ORVs, soil erosion is generally the most severe. Trails used by ORVs for six years near Santa Cruz, California, are now gullies 3 meters (9 feet) deep. In other areas of California, land used for less than ten years has been so severely eroded that the bedrock has been exposed. Erosion on trails removes topsoil and uproots trees and shrubs that border them. The sediment washed away by running water is deposited downstream in riverbeds and on vegetation.

ORVs also compact the soil, forming a zone that may extend 1 to 3 meters (3 to 9 feet) below the surface on popular trails. This impairs root growth and impedes the penetration of water, thus diminishing plant growth and the recharging of underground water supplies. The loss of shade-providing vegetation and the compaction of soil both contribute to a decrease in soil moisture in many areas; moisture may be decreased by 43% as deep as 3 meters below the surface on silty and clayey soils.

In hilly terrain the loss of vegetation increases water erosion, often with devastating effects. On flat areas wind erosion may be increased by vegetative destruction. ORVs destabilize sand dunes by destroying plants that help hold the sand in place. Moreover, once soils have begun to erode, reestablishment of plants and regeneration of the topsoil may become impossible. Costs for revegetation range from $8000 to $24,000 per hectare ($3200 to $9600 per acre).

ORVs destroy the habitat of ground-dwelling reptiles and mammals. Birds such as the California quail that nest on the ground can also be adversely affected. Large races with hundreds of motorcycles tearing across the deserts of the West are the most environmentally damaging of all such activities.

ORV Damage Control

Recognizing the impact of ORVs, President Richard Nixon signed an executive order designed to limit the use of ORVs on public land. President Jimmy Carter amended this order with one of his own in 1977. Carter mandated closure of public lands to ORVs where they were causing or could cause damage to soil, vegetation, wildlife, and other values.

In response to the executive orders the Forest Service developed 150 ORV management plans for its lands. The BLM also developed regulations, providing land managers with a mechanism to designate areas as either open, restricted, or closed to ORVs, but the bureau was slow to carry out its plans. Both BLM and Forest Service regulations have made inroads into the problem of ORV damage. In addition, ORV users have banded together and made considerable strides in educating their members and reducing the damage they cause.

But ORV damage still occurs. There are not enough people to patrol the vast federal lands, and individuals still continue to act carelessly. Some suggestions for reducing that damage are as follows: (1) increased enforcement; (2) enlisting the aid of ORV clubs to help watch over the lands they use; (3) raising penalties for violations of ORV regulations; (4) separating ORVs and other recreationists, especially hikers and cross-country skiers; (5) prohibiting ORV use in all areas where it will adversely affect wildlife, homeowners, nonmotorized recreationists, archeological resources, vegetation, and soil; (6) developing special areas for ORVs, used on a rotating system to minimize damage and ensure recovery; (7) educating ORV users about their impact and ways to minimize it; (8) teaching schoolchildren the value of preserving the wild areas and maintaining ecological stability; (9) strengthening cooperation between the government and ORV clubs; and (10) reclaiming damaged land with money donated from ORV clubs and taxes from the sale of ORVs and supplies.

Water Resources

A river is more than an amenity—it is a treasure.

OLIVER WENDELL HOLMES

Not all of us own land; not all of us spend time in the great outdoors. But every human being uses water. We drink it, wash with it, and play in—or on or underneath—it. In our jobs we find thousands of uses for it. Water is essential to the production of food, the processing of raw materials, and the construction of many of the products we use. The water supply often determines where we live and how well off we will be.

Despite its importance to human survival and prosperity, water remains one of the most poorly managed resources on earth. Squandered and polluted by industry, agriculture, sewage treatment plants, feedlots, and many other abusers, water is treated as if it came from an inexhaustible supply.

This chapter will explore the global and American water supply and pertinent environmental issues. Water pollution is discussed in Chapter 20.

The Hydrological Cycle

The **hydrological cycle**, or **water cycle**, is a natural system for collecting, purifying and distributing water (Figure 12-1). At its heart are two processes that are driven by energy from the sun: evaporation and precipitation.

Water evaporates from bodies of water, land areas, and vegetation (Figure 12-1). In plants it evaporates from the leaves. The resulting deficit helps draw the sap up the stem. The loss of water from leaves is called **transpiration**.

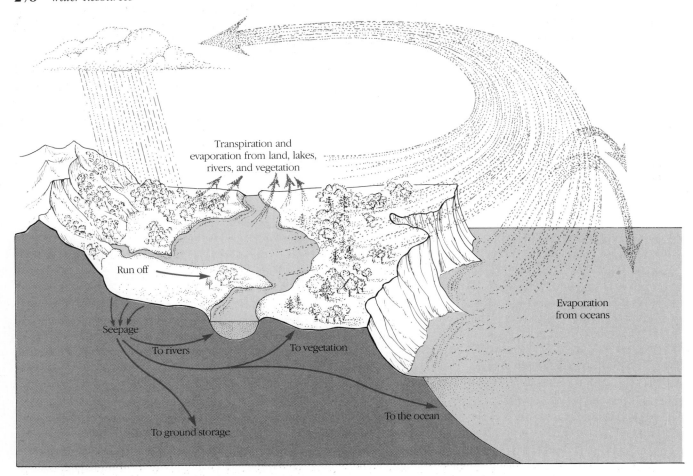

Figure 12-1
The hydrological cycle.

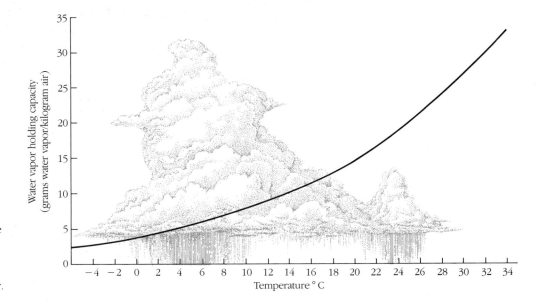

Figure 12-2
Relative humidity for a given parcel of moisture-laden air varies with temperature. If the air is cooled, the relative humidity increases. When the relative humidity exceeds 100%, precipitation will occur.

Loss from the soil and leaves is called **evapotranspiration.** When water molecules evaporate from the soil or a lake or stream, they leave behind any impurities; in this way, water entering the atmosphere is purified.

In the atmosphere water is suspended as fine droplets (water vapor) about half the thickness of a human hair. The amount of moisture the air can hold depends on the air temperature (Figure 12-2). Atmospheric moisture content can be expressed as **absolute humidity**—the number of grams of water in a kilogram of dry air—or as **relative humidity,** the more common measurement. Relative humidity measures how much moisture is present in air compared with how much the air could hold at a particular air temperature. At a relative humidity of 65%, for example, air has 65% of the water vapor it can hold at that temperature. If the relative humidity is 100%, the air is said to be saturated.

When moisture exceeds saturation, clouds, mist, and fog form. Clouds form when moist air is raised by mountain ranges, when cold air masses come in contact with moisture-laden air masses, or as warm air rises to cooler levels (Figure 12-3). For rain to form, air must contain

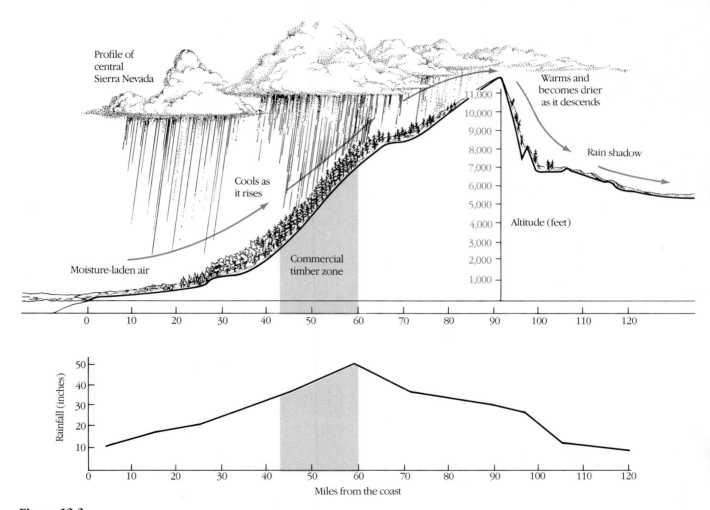

Figure 12-3

Mountain ranges thrust air upward, causing it to cool down. This increases the relative humidity of the air, forming clouds and precipitation. Most of the precipitation falls on the windward side. As the air descends on the leeward side, it warms, and the relative humidity decreases. Leeward sides of mountain ranges are often arid.

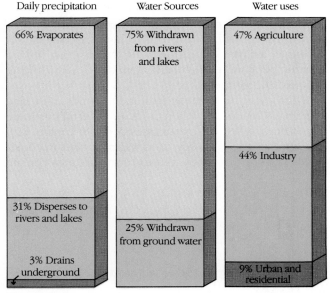

Daily precipitation | Water Sources | Water uses

66% Evaporates

31% Disperses to rivers and lakes

3% Drains underground

75% Withdrawn from rivers and lakes

25% Withdrawn from ground water

47% Agriculture

44% Industry

9% Urban and residential

Figure 12-4
Fate of precipitation, water sources, and water use in the United States.

small particles, known as **condensation nuclei**, on which the water vapor collects. Condensation nuclei may be salts from the sea, dusts, or particulates from factories, power plants, and vehicles. Over a million fine water droplets must come together to make a single drop of rain. If the air temperature is below freezing, the water droplets may form small ice crystals that coalesce and form snowflakes.

Clouds move about on the winds, which are generated by solar energy, and deposit their moisture throughout the globe as rain, drizzle, snow, hail, or sleet. Precipitation returns water to the lakes, rivers, oceans, and land from which it came, thus completing the hydrological cycle. Water that falls on the land may evaporate again, or it may flow into lakes, rivers, streams, or groundwater, eventually returning to the ocean.

On the average, over 15 trillion liters (4 trillion gallons) of precipitation falls on the United States every day. This moisture is unevenly distributed. Two-thirds of all precipitation (10.5 trillion liters) evaporates. Thirty-one percent (4.9 trillion liters) finds its way to streams, lakes, and rivers, and only 3% recharges the groundwater (Figure 12-4).

At any single moment 94% of the earth's water is found in the oceans, 4% is in inaccessible aquifers, and 1.5% is locked up in polar ice and glaciers. This leaves about .5% of the earth's water available for human use, but much of this water is hard to reach and therefore too costly to tap.

U.S. Water Use

Each day, an average of 1.3 trillion liters (340 billion gallons) of water is withdrawn in the United States. Three-fourths of this water comes from lakes, rivers, and streams—collectively called **surface waters**. The remainder comes from groundwater (Figure 12-4). The major water users are agriculture (47%) and industry (44%); urban and residential users account for the remaining 9%.

Two-thirds of the water withdrawn each day is returned to surface waters and groundwater. The remaining one-third is "consumed"; that is, it either evaporates or becomes part of the living matter of plants and animals.

Agriculture is the biggest water *user* in the United States. There can be little wonder why, inasmuch as it takes 57,000 liters (15,000 gallons) of water to grow a bushel of wheat and make bread from it. Food for a family of four requires 12,000 liters (3,200 gallons) a day to produce, process, and ship. Agriculture is also the biggest water *consumer;* 83% of the water it uses evaporates.

Water is also used to make many products. The rayon in an average home carpet, for example, requires 190,000 liters (50,000 gallons), and the steel in a washing machine requires 17,000 liters (4,500 gallons) to produce. Adding all these uses together, the per capita water use in the United States is about 5,700 liters (1,500 gallons) per day.

The average American uses about 340 liters (90 gallons) of water each day for drinking, cooking, bathing, washing clothes and dishes, and watering lawns and gardens.

Water Problems in the U.S.

Water resource problems enumerated by the National Water Resources Council are shown in Table 12-1. In this chapter we will be concerned with water shortages and flooding. The drainage of wetlands and the destruction of estuaries and coastal waters are discussed in Chapter Supplement 12-1. Water pollution and drinking water quality are discussed in Chapter 20.

Water Shortages

Water shortage is no stranger to most Americans. Whether you live in New York, San Francisco, Denver, Key West, or Bird City, Kansas, you have probably felt the impacts of a shortage at least once in your lifetime.

Drought, overuse, waste, and overpopulation all contribute to shortages of water. A *drought* technically exists

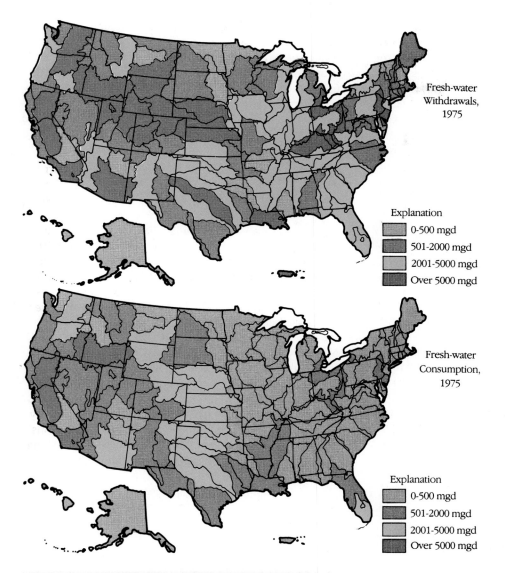

Figure 12-5
(*a*) Freshwater withdrawals in the United States by region. (*b*) Freshwater consumption by region.

Fresh-water Withdrawals, 1975

Explanation
- 0-500 mgd
- 501-2000 mgd
- 2001-5000 mgd
- Over 5000 mgd

Fresh-water Consumption, 1975

Explanation
- 0-500 mgd
- 501-2000 mgd
- 2001-5000 mgd
- Over 5000 mgd

Table 12-1 Common Water Resource Problems

Inadequate surface water supply

Overdraft of groundwater

Pollution of surface water and groundwater

Quality of drinking water

Flooding

Erosion and sedimentation

Dredging and disposal of dredged materials

Drainage of wetlands and wet soils

Degradation of bays, estuaries, and coastal waters

when rainfall is 70% below average for 21 days or longer. A severe drought results in a decrease in stream flow; a drop in the water table; a loss of agricultural crops; a loss of wildlife, especially aquatic organisms; a drop in the levels of lakes, streams, and reservoirs; a reduction in range production and stress on livestock; an increasing number of forest fires; and considerable human discomfort.

Overexploitation—taking too much—of existing water supplies can also cause water shortages. As shown in Figure 12-5, freshwater use and consumption are high in many parts of the country. A natural lack of water, combined with unrestrained industrial and population growth and agricultural expansion, creates tremendous conflicts among water users. Kayakers, rafters, and anglers battle with municipal water departments that dam recreational rivers. Developers and energy companies wrangle with farmers. Now, even states and countries are battling in the courts over water.

Overexploitation of existing water supplies can create severe limitations to growth. For example, the city of Wichita, Kansas, gets most of its water from deep aquifers, called the Equus Beds, which are recharged at a rate of 148 billion liters (39 billion gallons) a year, exactly equal to the rate of water withdrawal. With water demand expected to double in the next 20 years, Wichita will need to develop new sources, conserve or ration water, curtail its growth, or use a combination of these.

Overexploitation of groundwater in coastal zones may lead to **saltwater intrusion** into freshwater aquifers (Figure 12-6). Taking too much water from rivers and streams may allow salt water to intrude into their estuaries, upsetting the ecological balance in these important zones.

Ponds, bogs, and streams are sites where groundwater intersects the land surface and are therefore "exposed groundwater." Because of this connection, overdrawing of groundwater can lower the level of surface waters or dry them up completely, with serious impacts on wildlife and recreation.

Overexploitation of groundwater and surface waters commonly occurs as cities expand. To meet the growing water demand, water departments expand their operations and change the natural hydrological cycle. Denver,

for example, has placed a number of dams throughout Colorado to capture snowmelt for summertime lawn watering. Dams and reservoirs destroy the habitat of black bear, bighorn sheep, and many other animals. One dam, in Waterton Canyon close to Denver, is expected to destroy 50% of the bighorn sheep population. In the first few months of construction, wildlife biologists found nine bighorn sheep dead, possibly because of stress from the operation of machinery within the canyon. Dams and reservoirs also destroy recreational rivers. In some places stream water is diverted from dams through tunnels for urban consumption, leaving streambeds dry and killing organisms dependent on the stream environment.

Agricultural overexploitation of groundwater was discussed in Chapter 8, where it was noted that groundwater overdraft threatens the long-term prospects for irrigated agriculture in the West. In Nebraska, Kansas, Colorado, Oklahoma, and Texas, for example, 80,000 hectares (200,000 acres) of land used to produce corn was taken out of use between 1977 and 1980 because of water shortages. In the same period potato production in Idaho, which is heavily supported by irrigation, dropped by 10%.

Groundwater overdraft also creates **subsidence**, sinking of the land. Groundwater fills pores in the soil and thus supports the soil above the aquifer; when the water is withdrawn, the soil compacts and subsides. The most dramatic examples of subsidence in recent years have occurred in Florida and other southern states, where groundwater depletion has created huge sinkholes that may measure 100 meters (330 feet) across and 50 meters (165 feet) deep (Figure 12-7). These are created when an underground water-filled cavern collapses after the water table drops below its roof. The weight of the soil causes the collapse; the sink hole gobbles up whatever is on the surface.

Subsidence has occurred over large areas in the San Joaquin Valley in California, damaging pipelines, railroads, highways, homes, factories, and canals (Figure 12-8). Southeast of Phoenix, over 300 square kilometers (120 square miles) of land has subsided more than 2 meters (6.5 feet) because of groundwater overdraft. Huge cracks have formed, some 3 meters wide, 3 meters deep, and 300 meters long.

Between 1950 and 1982 groundwater use increased in the United States from 45 trillion liters (12 trillion gallons) to 90 trillion liters (24 trillion gallons) per year. Depletion of aquifers cannot continue without serious ecological and economic consequences.

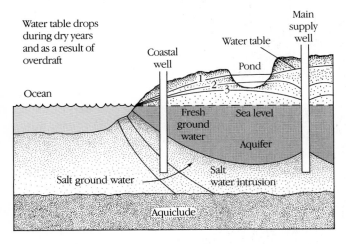

Figure 12-6
Saltwater intrusion into groundwater. Reduction of groundwater flow causes freshwater aquifer to retreat, allowing saltwater to penetrate deeper inland underground.

Figure 12-7
This large sinkhole developed quickly, swallowing part of a community swimming pool, parts of two businesses, a house, and several automobiles. It happened in Winter Park, Florida, on May 8, 1981.

Figure 12-8
Subsidence caused by groundwater overdraft damaged this building in Contra Costa, California.

Figure 12-9
Property damage from U.S. floods is in a definite upward trend.

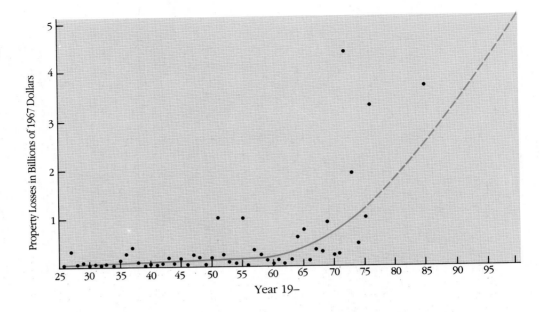

Flooding

Another major water problem is flooding. Despite years of flood control work by the Bureau of Reclamation, the Soil Conservation Service, and the Army Corps of Engineers, costing in excess of $8 billion, property damage is continuing to rise (Figure 12-9). Today, floods cause more than $3 billion a year in damage.

Floods result from a variety of factors, the most obvious being heavy rainfall and snowfall. As illustrated in Figure

Figure 12-10
Percolation–runoff ratio. When 75% of the water flows over the surface, the rest percolates into the soil (ignoring evaporation).

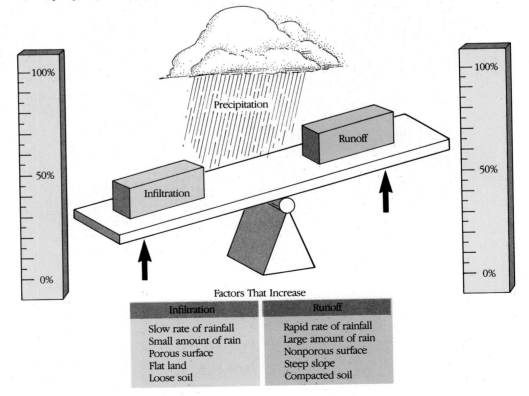

Factors That Increase	
Infiltration	**Runoff**
Slow rate of rainfall	Rapid rate of rainfall
Small amount of rain	Large amount of rain
Porous surface	Nonporous surface
Flat land	Steep slope
Loose soil	Compacted soil

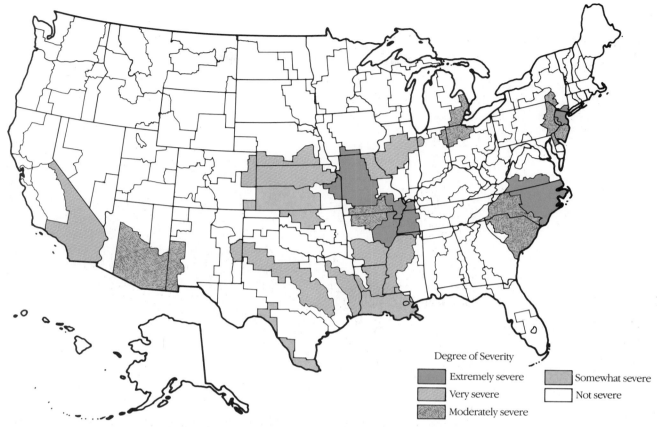

Figure 12-11
Flood-prone areas in the United States.

12-10, precipitation must either run off or percolate into the soil. Several factors determine the fate of rainwater, including the type and amount of vegetation, the physical characteristics of the soil, the steepness of the terrain, and the rate and the amount of precipitation. Because human activities affect some of these variables, humans may be a major causal element in what appear to be natural floods.

Stripping land of its vegetative cover by farming, ranching, mining, off-road-vehicle use, construction, and clear-cutting has a significant effect on runoff. Vegetation tends to reduce the velocity of water flowing over the surface and thus promotes infiltration. Heavily vegetated watersheds act as sponges. When vegetation is removed, water flows rapidly over the surface into streams, causing flooding. Devegetation also increases soil erosion. Eroded sediment fills water bodies and reduces their holding capacity. This makes flooding more likely, even after moderate rainfall.

Construction of highways, parking lots, airports, shopping centers, tennis courts, office buildings, homes, and numerous other structures decreases the amount of surface area that can absorb water. The devastating 1980 flood in Kansas City was the direct result of a heavy rainstorm falling on thousands of acres of city streets, tennis courts, rooftops and the like.

As illustrated in Figure 12-11, certain parts of the United States are naturally susceptible to flooding. Many of these areas are located along the Mississippi River and its tributaries. One of the most spectacular floods in U.S history occurred in the upper Mississippi valley in the spring of 1965. Because of late rains in 1964, the soil became saturated with water. The ground froze early in the fall, and there was a record snowfall that winter. Making matters worse, the snowmelt in April 1965 was accompanied by heavy rainfall. Consequently, the Mississippi River spilled over its banks in the spring, from Minneapolis to southern

Missouri. Thousands of acres of wheat were destroyed by the floodwaters, and thousands of people fled their homes. When the flood receded, over $140 million worth of property damage had been done, 16 people had drowned, and over 300 had been injured.

Flooding is a major problem in the United States and abroad. But much of the damage is our own fault because of our tendency to build homes and cities in **floodplains**, the flat areas along rivers that are subject to natural flooding. Continued habitation along river banks seems fairly likely; therefore, people must either learn to live with periodic flooding or learn to control it better.

Control embraces a combination of efforts. Here are a few general solutions: (1) protect watersheds better to reduce devegetation, control soil erosion, and reduce surface runoff; (2) build more dams to hold back the floodwaters coming from properly managed watersheds; (3) build levees to help hold back floodwaters (however, levees can worsen flooding downstream); and (4) design cities and towns to retain more moisture and release it more slowly following rainfall. This can be done by constructing holding ponds in parks and other locations. Rainwater diverted to ponds during storms can then be released slowly to rivers. Storm sewers can also divert water to special tanks that supply factories. Individual homeowners can install rooftop catchment systems to divert rainwater to underground holding tanks to be used later for watering lawns and gardens and washing cars.

Some water resource managers have used **streambed channelization** to reduce flooding and subsequent damage to cropland and other property. In such projects the vegetation on both sides of the stream is first removed; then bulldozers deepen and straighten the channel, creating a ditch that may be lined with concrete or rock.

Streambed channelization generally eases flooding in the immediate vicinity, but it destroys wildlife habitat, increases the rate of stream bank erosion, diminishes recreational opportunities, and significantly alters the aquatic environment. In some cases channelization may increase flooding in downstream areas.

This practice was begun seriously in 1954 after the *Watershed Protection and Flood Prevention Act* authorized the Soil Conservation Service to drain wetlands along rivers to make more farmland and to reduce flooding. To date, 13,000 kilometers (8000 miles) of U.S. streams has been channelized, and another 13,000 is targeted for "improvements." Critics argue that many projects are of dubious merit and should not be undertaken, especially when they destroy wetlands (see Chapter Supplement 12-1).

The Global Picture

Water shortages face virtually every nation in the world. Despite the abundance of sparkling blue water around the Caribbean Sea, for example, the islands are plagued with freshwater supply problems. For cooking, bathing, and drinking, water is captured on rooftops and used sparingly. In many of the less developed countries people spend a good part of their waking hours fetching water, frequently walking 15 to 25 kilometers (10 to 15 miles) a day to get water, often from polluted streams and rivers.

Three out of every five people in the developing nations do not have access to clean, disease-free drinking water. According to the World Health Organization, 80% of all disease in these countries results from the contaminated water they drink and bathe in. The U.N. General Assembly has proclaimed the 1980s as the International Drinking Water Supply and Sanitation Decade. The goal is to provide the world population with clean drinking water and adequate sanitation by 1990. The cost of this ten-year project is $300 billion.

Many countries are engaged in bitter rivalries over this precious resource. Argentina and Brazil, for instance, dispute each other's claims to the La Plata River; India and Pakistan fight over the rights to water from the Indus; Mexico and the United States have come in conflict over the Colorado River; and Iraq and Iran contest water from the Shatt-al-Arab River. All told, there are over 150 river basins shared by two or more countries.

Most of the European countries have enough surface water to go around, but many other nations currently suffer from water shortages. Thus, water shortages are a way of life today throughout the world. But what does the future hold?

Severe water shortages could be encountered soon in much of the world: Irrigated land is expected to double between 1975 and 2000. Domestic and commercial use is expected to increase fivefold, and industry's use is expected to increase twentyfold. Water demand by 2000 is expected to exceed water supply in at least 30 countries. By 2000, water use could reach 16% to 25% of the total water runoff. Of course, population growth and water demand might not grow as fast as expected, and water conservation measures may be implemented to cut losses. If not, water could become a limiting factor in population growth.

In 1982 the world population withdrew only 9% of the potentially available freshwater runoff. Eighty-five percent of this water was used for the production of crops and

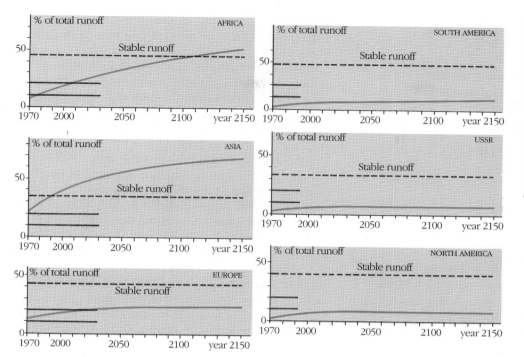

Figure 12-12

Graphic representation of water demand by continent. The bars on the left indicate 10% to 20% of the total runoff, which most countries can capture without major problems. When a country's demand exceeds these levels, it may suffer severe shortages in dry years. These graphs hide local and even regional shortages.

livestock. Industrial use (mining, manufacturing, and cooling) accounted for 7%, and domestic use made up the rest. As a general rule it is economically feasible for most nations to withdraw up to 20% of the annual stream runoff, although some wealthy countries now withdraw almost 30%. By the year 2000, global water use could reach 16% to 25% of runoff.

Figure 12-12 shows the projected water withdrawals throughout the world in terms of total annual runoff. The horizontal bars on the left mark 10% and 20% of the runoff, which is economically feasible for most countries to withdraw. As these graphs show, Africa and Asia will require large withdrawals to meet their projected needs, far in excess of the **stable runoff**, the amount of the total runoff that can be counted on from year to year. In most countries stable runoff is about 30% to 40% of the total average runoff. If a country's water demand exceeds the stable runoff, extreme water shortages can occur in dry or even moderately dry years (Figure 12-13).

According to Figure 12-12, most continents should be in fairly good shape. For now, none exceeds the stable runoff. However, continental averages can be misleading. The graph for North America, for instance, leads us to believe that all is well. However, many parts of the United States already tax their water supplies and suffer in dry

years. The graph hides these local supply problems, because it includes massive untapped water resources in Canada and Alaska.

The world is heading for huge water shortages within the next 20 to 30 years unless we act now. But what can we do?

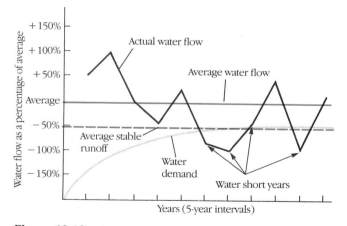

Figure 12-13

This hypothetical graph shows normal fluctuations in surface runoff and the effects of increasing water use of humans beyond the reliable supply.

Solutions to Water Shortages

Solutions to our current and impending water crises are many. One of the most important is the control of population growth, particularly in Africa, Asia, and Latin America. Measures to control population growth in water-short regions of more developed countries can also reduce water supply problems.

Beyond population control, there are numerous technological solutions and cultural controls to combat water shortages.

Technological Solutions: Some Costs and Benefits

Dams and Reservoirs Dams and reservoirs retain snowmelt and rainwater to increase our supply of water, control floods, generate electricity, and increase certain forms of recreation. They also allow people to live where they might not be able to live; that is, they increase the local carrying capacity.

Dams are no panacea, however. They are often costly, and their reservoirs may inundate towns, villages, good arable land, and wildlife habitat. Pakistan's recently completed Tarbela Dam alone displaced 85,000 people. Dams and reservoirs also destroy opportunities for certain forms of river recreation, including kayaking, rafting, canoeing,

and trout fishing (Figure 12-14). Exceptional floods can exceed the capacity of reservoirs or can cause dams to break.

Dams and reservoirs may not actually increase the amount of water available to some communities because of high rates of evaporation. On Egypt's Lake Nasser, formed by the Aswan Dam, 10% of the total water supply evaporates each year. Other problems created by the Aswan Dam are discussed in Essay 12-1.

Dams reduce stream flow into the ocean, resulting in changes in the salt concentration of estuaries, bays, and tidal waters. Reduced stream flow also reduces the nutrient inflow to coastal waters, with devastating effects on the producer organisms in the aquatic food web. Because of a reduction in algal growth at the mouth of the Nile, Egypt's annual sardine catch plummeted from 16,000 metric tons to 450 per year (18,000 tons to 500 tons).

Dams interrupt the natural flow of nutrient-rich sediment to the surrounding land, river deltas, and coastal waters. Instead of taking their natural course, the sediments are collected in reservoirs, slowly filling them. In the United States there are well over 2000 reservoirs clogged with sediment. The $1.3-billion Tarbela Dam on the Indus River in Pakistan took 9 years to build, but because of upstream soil erosion it could be filled in by sediment in 20 years.

Dams also interfere with the migration of fish to spawning grounds. In addition, they generally release the cold-

Figure 12-14
Kayaker paddles through turbulent white water. This is just one of many forms of recreation that competes for water use.

The Aswan Dam: Ecological Backlash from Blind Cost–Benefit Analysis

The Nile River flows from its headwaters in Sudan and Ethiopia through an arid region of Egypt and eventually spills into the Mediterranean Sea. For centuries this great river carried 50 million to 100 million tons of silt each year to the land stretching along its banks and the Mediterranean Sea. In the sea this nutrient-rich silt nourished a variety of microorganisms that, in turn, were food for thriving fish populations. On the land, the silty water flooded nutrient-impoverished soil as the river spilled over its banks, enriching the soil. The nutrients robbed by agriculture were replaced by the natural floods that occurred each year in late summer and early fall, floods caused by the monsoon rains along the river's headwaters.

In the early 1960s, however, Egypt built the Aswan Dam along the Nile to provide electricity for the growing city of Cairo and to provide irrigation water for the lower Nile basin. The government, of course, had studied the proposal to build the dam, but it had looked primarily at the benefits that would result from the dam versus the economic cost of construction. Little attention was given to possible ecological backlashes.

Not long after the dam was completed and Lake Nasser began to fill, the people of Egypt and the world grew alarmed. Numerous problems began to make themselves painfully evident. First, the periodic flooding that had provided an annual fertilization of the land ceased. As a result, farmers along the Nile had to import fertilizer for their land at an exorbitant cost. Second, the sardine fishery in the eastern Mediterranean collapsed. Nutrient-rich silt that had once poured into the sea almost stopped. The sardine catch, plummeted from 18,000 tons per year to 500 tons in only a few years. Third, the rising waters of Lake Nasser threatened the Ramses Temple at Abu Simbel, built over 3000 years ago. Engineers and construction workers sponsored by the United States, Egypt, and the United Nations dismantled the huge temple piece by piece and moved it to a site 60 meters (200 feet) above its original level, where it would be safe from the rising waters. The cost of this project was astronomical. Fourth, the incidence of schistosomiasis (a debilitating, sometimes fatal disease) in humans increased in Egypt as a result of the dam. The organism that causes this disease is carried by snails. Snails require a constant supply of water, which the lake and the irrigation channels provided. The spread of this disease, for which there is no known cure, is almost certain.

If a cost–benefit analysis had been done before construction of the dam began, chances are that it might not have been built. See Chapter 17 for an example of an approach you might take to making a cost–benefit analysis of the Aswan Dam.

est water from the bottom of the reservoir, making stream water exceedingly cold year-round and hampering spawning.

Because the economic and environmental costs of dams and reservoirs are so high, construction must be preceded by a thorough cost–benefit analysis. Wherever possible, nondestructive, less costly measures should be used.

Water Diversion Projects Denver, Los Angeles, Phoenix, and New York, among other cities, rely on water diversion projects to redirect water for municipal consumption. In many cases urban water departments build small diversion dams on distant streams and then pipe the water to neighboring reservoirs, where it can flow to water treatment plants.

Because up to 80% of the annual runoff of some streams can be taken, wildlife habitat and good recreational sites may be destroyed by diversion projects. In addition, these projects often transfer water from rural areas of low population density, often agricultural regions, to cities, creating bitter conflict between urban and rural residents. Because the urban water users have a larger say in state policies, they usually win in state legislative battles, leaving irrigated agriculture high and dry.

Diversion of clean high-mountain water in the tributaries of the Colorado River ultimately diminishes the flow of water and water quality of the Colorado, a source of water for over 17 million people. The Colorado carries a heavy burden of sediment and dissolved salts. By taking clean water from the spring snowmelt, upstream diversions indirectly increase the concentration of salts down-river. By the time the Colorado reaches Mexico, its salt concentration is over 800 parts per million (ppm) compared with 40 ppm at its headwaters in the Rockies.

Salts harm agricultural users as well as people who drink the water. Water with a salt concentration over 700 ppm cannot be used for agriculture unless it is desalinated or diluted. Drinking water must have a salt concentration of 500 ppm or less. A bill passed by Congress in 1973 authorized the construction of three desalination plants along the Colorado River to remove over 400,000 tons of salt each year. Costing an estimated $350 million, these projects will help purify water to be used in California and Mexico.

Diversion projects allow widespread irrigation of agricultural land. For example, over 2000 square kilometers (500,000 acres) of land was brought under cultivation in the Imperial Valley of southern California with water diverted from points north and east. In central California's San Joaquin Valley, 3.2 million hectares (8 million acres) of land is now irrigated with water from northern California. Much of this land is subject to salinization and waterlogging (see Chapter 8). By 1990 one-fourth of the San Joaquin's irrigated soils could become unproductive because of salt buildup. Salinization and waterlogging could reduce production on half of all irrigated cropland in the western United States.

Solutions to salinization are costly and time consuming. For example, soil can be taken out of production and flushed with pure water to rinse out the excess salts and minerals. In addition, porous pipes can be installed to drain off water into ditches and streams (Figure 12-15). These prevent waterlogging and evaporation, which leads to salt buildup. But the cost is astronomical. The U.S. Interior Department is involved in one project in California that will cost more than $300 million.

Water diversion projects will continue to be built to meet the needs of industry, agriculture, and the cities. The costs and benefits of proposed projects must be thoroughly analyzed.

Desalination The expense and ecological impact of dams and diversion projects often lead community planners to other approaches aimed at increasing water supply. One of these is **desalination**, the removal of salts from seawater and brackish (slightly salty) water. The two main methods are evaporation and reverse osmosis. In **evaporation**, or distillation, the salt water is heated and evap-

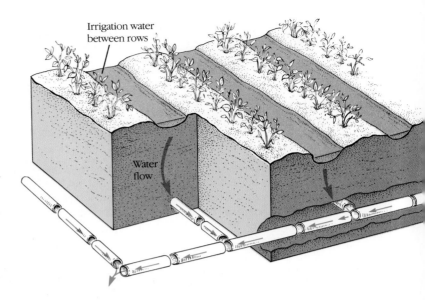

Figure 12-15
Porous pipes can be laid to drain irrigated soils to prevent waterlogging and salinization, but the costs can be prohibitive.

orated, leaving behind the salts and minerals. The steam produced is then cooled, and pure water condenses out. In **reverse osmosis**, water is forced through thin membranes, whose pores allow the passage of water molecules but not the salts and minerals.

By either of these methods, seawater with a salt content of 35,000 ppm can be converted to drinking water or irrigation water. Inasmuch as 94% of the water on earth is located in the oceans, desalination might seem like the best answer to water shortages. Unfortunately, water produced by desalination is four times more expensive than water from conventional sources.

Since 1977 the world's desalination capacity has tripled, increasing from 3.8 billion liters (1 billion gallons) a year to over 9.5 billion liters (2.5 billion gallons). But this still represents only a minute fraction (.002%) of the annual water use. In the United States over 100 desalination plants now produce over 1250 million liters (330 million gallons) per day, which is about .01% of the total freshwater requirement. Most desalination facilities are located in California, Texas, Florida, and the Northeast. Plants are also in operation in Saudi Arabia, Israel, Malta, and a few other countries.

Even though the costs of desalination plants have come down in recent years, the energy requirements and construction costs may remain prohibitively high. For agriculture, desalination seems an even more unlikely source, because water-short farming areas are usually located far from the sea.

Desalination plants permit a further extension of the carrying capacity, with potentially serious ecological impacts. For example, population growth in the Florida Keys, in part due to a new desalination plant that produces 11 million liters (3 million gallons) of water a day, threatens native wildlife, habitat for endangered crocodiles, and the precious coral reefs. Construction of homes and condominiums causes erosion that pollutes coastal waters. New residents produce an increasing amount of sewage and other pollutants that can affect water quality. In addition to increasing carrying capacity, disposal of large quantities of salt and minerals from desalination plants could pollute coastal waters.

Groundwater Management

Another technological solution to water shortages is tapping unused groundwater and regulating withdrawal so that it will not exceed recharge. In some areas groundwater can be replenished by disposing of wastewater in aquifer recharge zones. This water will be cleansed as it percolates through the soil. Irrigation water running off fields, storm runoff, cooling water from industry, and treated effluent from sewage treatment plants could also be used.

Although aquifer recharge can help replenish groundwater supplies, it can also present some problems. The most significant is the cost of disposal, because many cities are far from aquifer recharge zones.

Cloud Seeding

Another avenue is **cloud seeding**, a process in which nucleating agents such as dry ice pellets or silver iodide dust are injected into clouds to cause rain or snow. Like many of the other more novel ways of increasing water supply, cloud seeding has its disadvantages. First, after 40 years of use no one is actually certain how much extra precipitation it produces. Proponents assert that it increases precipitation by 20%. In some cases it has, but in others it may have had no effect whatsoever. Second, cloud seeding is viewed by some as a form of water rustling. When ski resorts in Colorado or farmers in Idaho sponsor cloud-seeding operations, they may be stealing moisture needed by wheat growers in the plains states. Third, cloud seeding may intensify violent and damaging thunderstorms and hailstorms in downwind states. Finally, it may adversely affect human health and ecosystem stability, because the deposition of silver iodide in rain and snow from seeded clouds may prove biologically harmful.

Icebergs

The social critic Malcolm Muggeridge once said, "The dreams of materialists are the most fantastic and absurd of all dreams." Perhaps he was referring to those who propose to solve regional water shortages by towing icebergs from Antarctica to water-needy regions such as the Arab states, Australia, and southern California. Anchored offshore, the icebergs would slowly melt, providing enormous amounts of fresh water.

Although seemingly simple, these proposals present many technical problems. The icebergs needed for such projects would be many times larger than any ever towed in the past. The energy needed to tow them would be enormous. No one knows how to tow large icebergs safely for long distances, and no one knows how to prevent them from melting en route. Icebergs lost at sea in shipping lanes could create a substantial risk to ships, especially huge oil supertankers. If we could get the icebergs to port, no one knows how to extract the water and get it ashore. No one knows the impact these icy leviathans might have on climate and coastal ecology. Political conflicts could arise over ownership of the ice, since Antarctica is not owned by any nation. Finally, no one knows if the entire operation—if engineered and carried out safely—would be cost-effective. Nevertheless, such proposals are seriously entertained in some countries, especially in the oil-rich but water-poor Arab countries.

Conservation and Recycling

Two of the most direct approaches to the problem of water shortages are conservation and recycling. Because agriculture and industry are the biggest water users, efforts to recycle and conserve water in these sectors could do much to alleviate water shortages.

Agricultural water conservation could be easily achieved. Open, dirt-lined ditches that deliver water to crops are only about 50% to 60% efficient and could be replaced by cement- or plastic-lined ditches or, better yet, by closed pipes. Sprinklers, which often waste up to half of their water, can be replaced by drip irrigation systems, which lose only 5% to 10%. With these and other measures, water losses in agriculture could be cut sharply.

In industry, water conservation results from redesigning many processes and facilities. The use of water by steam-operated electric power plants could be cut one-

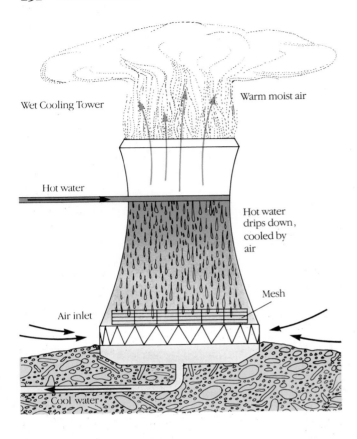

Wet Cooling Tower

Warm moist air

Hot water

Hot water drips down, cooled by air

Mesh

Air inlet

Cool water

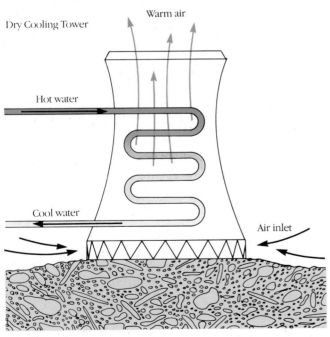

Dry Cooling Tower

Warm air

Hot water

Cool water

Air inlet

fourth by using dry cooling towers (Figure 12-16), although these require more energy and are more expensive to operate than wet ones.

Water recycling methods can also be used by industry. Wastewater from various industrial processes can be purified and reused over and over. Municipal sewage treatment plants are a common type of water purification system, though effluents are hardly drinkable. Further additions, though, could make this water pure enough to drink. A commercially available wastewater recyling system used for homes and apartment buildings can do the job (Figure 12-17). In Tokyo, for example, Mitsubishi's 60-story office building has a fully automated recycling system that purifies all of the building's wastewater.

As water shortages worsen and public and governmental awareness increases, recycling plants will become more popular. Such plants reduce water demand and cut water pollution. Although the cost of building and maintaining large-scale recycling plants for large cities can be considerable, they still may be cheaper than new water diversion projects and dams and have added ecological benefits.

Cultural and Legal Controls

The cultural and legal approaches to increasing water supply go hand in hand with technological approaches. Cultural approaches are the things you and I can do personally to reduce water use, recycle water, and promote laws to stimulate water conservation.

We can reduce water use in a number of ways. In arid climates most of the water used around the house is for watering lawns and gardens. Therefore, the most effective way to cut water losses is to reduce lawn and garden water; water at night or early in the day, when evaporation is low; use drip-irrigation systems instead of sprinklers for gardens; use drought-tolerant shrubs, trees, and grasses; replace lawns with rock gardens; plant trees that shade and reduce evaporation from lawns; use root-level watering for shrubs and grass, if possible; enrich the soil with organic matter before planting; mow lawns less frequently (tall grass holds moisture better than short grass); and mulch gardens with grass clippings, leaves, straw, or wood chips to hold in moisture. Employing these simple

Figure 12-16
Wet and dry cooling towers. Water from electric power plants is cooled in them before being reused. Dry towers cost more to operate, but conserve water.

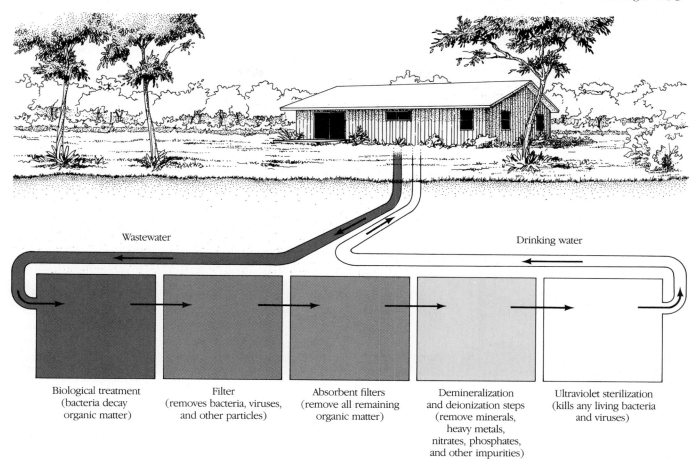

Wastewater

Drinking water

Biological treatment
(bacteria decay
organic matter)

Filter
(removes bacteria, viruses,
and other particles)

Absorbent filters
(remove all remaining
organic matter)

Demineralization
and deionization steps
(remove minerals,
heavy metals,
nitrates, phosphates,
and other impurities)

Ultraviolet sterilization
(kills any living bacteria
and viruses)

Figure 12-17
Water recycling system. Wastewater is filtered and treated in a number of steps,
producing drinkable water.

measures can cut water consumption by hundreds of liters a day in the summer months.

In regions where lawn watering is unnecessary, the toilet is the major household water user. Each flush takes about 27 liters (7 gallons) of water. By placing bricks or bottles in the water tanks and by not flushing after each use, you can cut water use by more than half. In addition, special toilets can be installed that use half the water of a conventional toilet. To save even more water, waterless toilets can be installed where local codes permit. These odorless toilets collect human wastes and kitchen wastes, which are degraded by bacteria to form a rich soil supplement for gardens (Figure 12-18). They cut total household water use by 25% or more, help reduce the need for sewage treatment, and reduce water pollution as well.

The next major use is laundry, personal cleaning, and the like. Many people leave the water running while brushing their teeth, washing dishes, and washing their hands. As shown in Table 12-2, these actions are quite wasteful.

Each of us can examine daily water use and decide where it is sensible to reduce it. Together with millions of conservation-minded neighbors we can reduce water demand now and in the future.

New laws and building codes can also help reduce household water consumption. In all areas, water-short or not, new homes could be required to use 25% to 50% less water than existing homes. This can be achieved by installing waterless or low-water toilets as well as flow restrictors on showers and faucets. Smaller lawns could

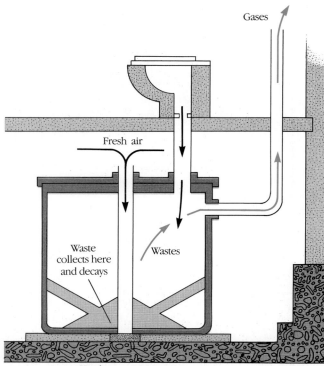

Gases

Fresh air

Waste collects here and decays

Wastes

Hard center support

Figure 12-18
Low-water toilets reduce water consumtion by 50%. Waterless toilets reduce toilet water use by 100%. Human and kitchen wastes are degraded naturally in these odorless, safe-to-operate toilets and can be used to supplement soils as they form a rich organic matter after six months to a year.

be encouraged, and they could be planted with low-water grasses. Drip and root-zone irrigation systems could be required. Systems that retain rainfall and gray water (used water from showers and faucets) could be installed. Gray water is suitable for lawn and garden irrigation. Finally, municipal water agencies could charge more in the summer for water used during the daytime, when evaporation is greatest, and less for water used early in the morning or at night.

Half the battle to ensure an adequate water supply can be won by education. Children should learn the value of water and the growing demands upon it. Learning to respect and conserve water may be as important as math or history lessons. Schools can help youngsters become resource-conscious citizens.

Laws to protect public and private watersheds from abuse can be strengthened. Overgrazing and deforestation can be controlled to reduce runoff. The Soil Conservation Service is charged with the management of 13,000 small watersheds in the United States, 61% of which have erosion and flooding problems. Protection of larger watersheds is the primary concern of the Bureau of Reclamation, the U.S. Army Corps of Engineers, and the Tennessee Valley Authority. These agencies function primarily to reduce flooding but also handle problems of erosion, wildlife management, water supply, and recreation when they are related to flooding. More emphasis must be placed on water management to ensure adequate supplies and to reduce flooding.

Perhaps the most serious deficiency in the regulation of water resources is poor coordination between water management and economic development. In many cases the two are discussed exclusively of each other. Builders put up tracts of new homes and then ask where the water will come from. City planners then scramble to build a new dam or diversion project.

Water development plans must be as environmentally sound as they are economically sound. We cannot afford to assume that adequate water supplies will always be available no matter where we go and no matter what we do. In addition, we cannot blindly continue our extension of the earth's carrying capacity. Though we can make the deserts bloom, we must ask, "Should we?" Though we can pump water uphill and through tunnels under mountian ranges, we must ask about the consequences of these actions and whether there are other, ecologically sound options. In some cases a proper analysis will cause us to abandon our plans. In others it may give us some additional time to pursue options that make more sense from an ecological perspective.

Let him who would enjoy a good future waste none of his present.

ROGER BABSON

Table 12-2 Household Water Use and Savings from Conservation

Water Use	Typical Consumption		Conservative Use	
	Liters	Gallons	Liters	Gallons
Shower	77	20	15	4
	With water running		Wet down, soap up, rinse off	
Brushing teeth	19–39	5–10	2	½
	With faucets running		Brief rinse	
Tub bath	96–116	25–30	38	10
	Full		Minimal water level	
Shaving	39–58	10–15	4	1
	With faucets running		Fill basin	
Dishwashing	77	20	20	5
	With faucets running		Wash and rinse in dishpans or sink	
Automatic dishwasher	58	15	27	7
	Full cycle		Short cycle	
Washing hands	4–8	1–2	4	1
	With faucets running		Fill basin once	
Toilet flushing	19–27	5–7	15–23	4–6
	Depending on tank size		Using tank displacement bottles or bricks	
Washing machine	116–119	30–50	104	27
	Full cycle, top water level		Short cycle, lowest water level	
Outdoor watering	40	10	—	—
	Per minute		Nighttime watering cuts use in half	

Source: Adapted from Miller, G. T., *Living in the Environment,* 1982. Wadsworth, Belmont, CA.

Summary

The *hydrological cycle* is a natural system for collecting, purifying, and distributing water driven by energy from the sun. At any single moment, only .5% of the earth's water is available for human use.

Three-fourths of the water used in agriculture, industry, and homes comes from *surface waters,* the rest from groundwater. Two-thirds of the water withdrawn each day is returned to its sources, but the remaining portion is consumed; that is, it either evaporates or becomes incorporated in living matter.

Two major water-supply problems are shortages, including overexploitation of groundwater and surface water supplies, and flooding. Water shortages are brought about by a complex set of factors including drought, overuse, waste, and overpopulation. Overexploitation occurs in many parts of the world, cre-

ating conflict among water users and severe economic impacts, especially among farmers. Groundwater depletion may also cause *saltwater intrusion* in coastal zones or in regions where freshwater aquifers lie near saltwater aquifers. In some regions groundwater overdraft has caused severe *subsidence,* or sinking of the land, which results in the collapse of highways, homes, factories, pipelines, and canals.

Flooding is also a major problem in the world. Because of natural factors and poor land management, billions of dollars worth of damage is caused by floods each year. Any human activities that increase the surface runoff and decrease infiltration can potentially increase flooding. Much of the damage from flooding is our own fault, for we tend to inhabit *floodplains,* the bottoms of river valleys. To prevent flooding, *streambed channelization* is often carried out. This involves the removal of vegetation along streams and rivers and the deepening and straightening of channels. Such actions destroy wildlife habitat, increase the rate of stream bank erosion, diminish recreational opportunities, alter the aquatic environment, and may actually increase flooding in downstream sites.

Water problems face virtually every nation in the world. Especially hard hit are some of the less developed nations, where water is far from villages and is often polluted. Polluted water supplies are responsible for 80% of all illness in these countries.

The long-term prospects for meeting water needs for industry, agriculture, and individuals are dim for many parts of the world. Africa and Asia may find adequate water supplies difficult to come by, as may many smaller regions, even in the developed world.

There are many solutions to meeting future water demands and curbing flooding. Measures to control population growth, especially in water-short regions, are most important. In addition, numerous technological solutions may be used. The environmental impacts of each of these must be carefully considered, along with long-term benefits.

Dams and reservoirs retain snowmelt and rainwater, help control floods, generate electricity, and increase certain forms of recreation. However, they are costly and often inundate towns, wildlife habitat, and farmland. Dams also reduce stream flow into the ocean, resulting in changes in the salt concentration of estuaries, bays, and tidal waters. Dams also interrupt the natural flow of nutrient-rich sediment to coastal waters with devastating effects on the aquatic food web. Replenishment of beach sand by river sediment is also impaired by dam construction, as is fish migration.

Water diversion projects increase supplies in water-short regions. But they are often costly, reduce stream flow, destroy aquatic ecosystems, affect downstream salt concentrations, and create bitter conflicts among water users.

Desalination of salt water is feasible in some places, but it is four times more expensive than conventional freshwater development projects. Desalination plants produce salts that must be disposed of and encourage home and resort construction and population growth in some regions, resulting in ecosystem destruction.

In some areas it may be prudent to replenish groundwater by disposing of wastewater, industrial cooling water, storm water runoff, and water from agricultural fields in aquifer recharge zones or in special water disposal wells. Such water is purified as it percolates through the soil, but projects of this nature are feasible only if water supplies are near recharge zones.

Cloud seeding, the dispersion of *condensation nuclei* into the air to promote cloud formation and rain, may or may not increase precipitation in desired locations. Cloud seeding is also viewed by some as a form of water theft. Such operations may also intensify thunderstorms, causing damage to crops and homes.

Some people have suggested towing icebergs from Antarctica to water-short areas, but the technique and environmental effects are yet to be worked out.

Recycling and conservation could make important contributions to increasing water supplies in the near future. Because agriculture uses a large percentage of our water, devices to reduce irrigation losses are needed. These are inexpensive and easy to install.

New laws and building codes can help reduce water consumption in and around our homes. New homes can be fitted with water-conserving toilets and shower heads, special systems in which gray water is reused to water lawns and gardens, or recycling systems that actually purify water from all domestic uses for reuse. Individuals can assist by personally reducing home water consumption.

Discussion Questions

1. What is the hydrological cycle? Draw a diagram showing how the water moves through the cycle.

2. Define *transpiration, evaporation, relative humidity, absolute humidity, saturation,* and *condensation nuclei.*

3. How much water is used daily in the United States? In general, how much is drawn from surface waters, and how much is drawn from groundwater? Who are the major water users?

4. What is the difference between water consumption and water use? Which segment of society consumes the most water?

5. Define the term *drought.* What are the effects of long-term drought? How do humans contribute to drought?

6. Define the following terms: *groundwater, water table, saltwater intrusion,* and *subsidence.*

7. Discuss the problems caused by overexploitation of groundwater and surface water.

8. You are newly appointed to a high post in city government. Your job is to provide safe drinking water to your community and provide water for a thriving agricultural business. You are facing water shortages in dry years, and farmers are starting to use their groundwater supplies faster than they they can be replenished. Your community's population will increase by about 30% over the next 20 years. Most of the domestic water used each year is for lawn watering. There are streams in a mountain range 100 miles away that could be used, but these are favorite recreation sites for the citizens of your community. Outline a plan to make certain that agricultural interests and your new residents will have adequate water. Make certain your plans do a minimal amount of ecological damage and are economically sound.

9. You are appointed by the governor of the state you live in to study floods and flood control projects. Make a list of reasons why flooding is so bad now and ways to correct your problems.

10. Discuss the benefits and costs (environmental, economic, and so on) of dams and diversion projects.

11. In what ways can desalination of seawater help solve water shortages? What are the limitations of and the problems created by this method?

12. In what ways can we artificially recharge groundwater supplies?

13. What is cloud seeding? Discuss how it works and the problems it can create.

14. Support or refute this statement: "Icebergs towed from the poles are a good source of fresh water for water-short regions of the world."

15. Draw up a list of ways in which your university or college could save water.

16. Describe the ways you and your family can help conserve water. Calculate how much water your efforts will save each day. How much will they save in a year?

Suggested Readings

Alexander, G. (1984). Making Do with Less. *National Wildlife* 22(2): 11–13. One of four articles on water resource. All well worth reading.

Ashworth, W. (1982). *Nor Any Drop to Drink.* New York: Summit Books. Delightful account of water issues.

Council on Environmental Quality (1979). *Environmental Quality: The Tenth Annual Report.* Washington, D.C.: U.S. Government Printing Office. See Chapters 7 and 8.

Falkenmark, M., and Lindh, G. (1976). *Water for a Starving World.* Boulder, Colo.: Westview Press. Thoughtful analysis of global water problems.

Ferguson, B. K. (1983). Whither Water? The Fragile Future of the World's Most Important Resource. *Futurist* 17(2): 29–36. General overview of water supply problems and solutions.

Foster, R. J. (1982). *Earth Science.* Menlo Park, Calif.: Benjamin/Cummings. Excellent introductory-level coverage.

Johnson, P. (1984). The Dam Builder Is at It Again. *National Wildlife* 22(4): 8–15. Delightful account of ecological water management.

Kierans, T. W. (1980). Thinking Big in North America: The Grand Canal Concept. *Futurist* 14(6): 29–32. Good view of the heights of technological optimism.

Lichtenstein, G. (1977). The Battle over the Mighty Colorado. *New York Times Magazine,* July 31. General review of conflicts over Colorado River water.

Stokes, B. (1983). Water Shortages. The Next Energy Crisis. *Futurist* 17(2): 37–47. Excellent survey of world water shortages.

Strahler, A. N., and Strahler, A. H. (1973). *Environmental Geoscience: Interaction between Natural Systems and Man.* Santa Barbara, Calif.: Hamilton. Excellent for background information.

U.S. Department of Agriculture (1980). *America's Soil and Water: Conditions and Trends.* Washington, D.C.: U.S. Government Printing Office. Water use and water-related problems graphically illustrated.

U.S. Department of Agriculture (1981). *Soil, Water, and Related Resources in the United States: Status, Condition, and Trends* (1980 Appraisal, Part I). Washington, D.C.: U.S. Government Printing Office. Detailed analysis of water rsources.

U.S. Geological Survey (1984). *National Water Summary 1983–Hydrologic Events and Issues.* Washington, D.C.: U.S. Government Printing Office. Excellent overview.

U.S. Water Resources Council. (1978). *The Nation's Water Resources 1975–2000* (Vol. 1: Summary; Vol. 2: Water Quantity, Quality, and Related Land Considerations). Washington, D.C.: U.S. Government Printing Office. Comprehensive sources on water.

Wetlands, Estuaries, Coastlines, and Rivers

Water management involves much more than protecting humans from floods and supplying water. It embraces protection of wetlands, estuaries, coastlines, and rivers. This supplement examines the threats to these special resources and ways to better manage them.

Wetlands

Wetlands, perpetually or periodically flooded lands, are in grave danger in the United States. Two types of wetlands are recognized. **Inland wetlands** are found along freshwater streams, lakes, rivers, and ponds (Figure S12-1). Included in this group are bogs, marshes, swamps, and river overflow lands that are wet at least part of the year. **Coastal wetlands** are wet or flooded regions along coastlines, including mangrove swamps, salt marshes, bays, and lagoons.

Wetlands are extremely valuable and productive fish and wildlife habitat. Waterfowl such as ducks, cranes, and sandpipers depend on them for food, nesting sites, protective cover, and areas to rest and feed during their annual migrations. But many other animal and plant species also make the wetlands their home. Deer, muskrats, bobcats, mink, beaver, and otter are a few of the many species that live in or around wetlands. In addition, shellfish, amphibians, reptiles, birds, and fish also call these endangered places their homes.

Wetlands also play an important role in regulating stream flow. A study in Wisconsin showed that in watersheds where 40% of the land surface was wetland, flood flows were 80% less than in areas without them. Sediment in streams was reduced by 90%, because wetlands trap sediment and reduce surface flow. Wetlands also act as nitrogen and phosphorus traps, absorbing these nutrients in plant growth and preventing water pollution downstream.

Wetlands hold water and allow an increased infiltration, thus helping recharge groundwater supplies. Wetlands are used to grow certain cash crops, including wild rice, cranberries, peat moss, and blueberries. But because their usefulness is not always apparent, they are often filled in or dredged to make way for agriculture, housing, recreation, industry, and garbage dumps.

Some authorities estimate that there were once 68 million hectares (170 million acres) of wetlands in the United States. By 1977 only 28 million hectares (70.5 million acres) of wetland remained. Today, wetlands are being destroyed at a rate of about 120,000 hectares (300,000 acres) per year.

Most wetlands in the United States are in the Southeast and the northern parts of Michigan, Minnesota, and Wisconson (Figure S12-1). Florida contains about one-fifth of all U.S. wetlands. About one-quarter of southern Florida's wetlands have been destroyed in recent years as land is drained for residential and agricultural use (mostly pastureland). Arkansas has lost half of its wetlands. Coastal wetlands in Louisiana, Texas, and Mississippi are disappearing at a rapid rate. One-tenth of Missouri's wetlands have vanished, as have most of California's. Coastal wetlands in the East have also been nearly destroyed.

Coastal wetlands are destroyed primarily by dredging streams and bays to make them navigable. Dredging has an added effect of draining adjoining swamps. Urban development such as housing, recreation, transportation, industry, and dumping also contributes to their destruction.

Concern for the loss of wetlands has stirred state governments. Florida, for example, passed legislation in 1972 to regulate all wetland development. Strict controls in Nassau County, New York, have also slowed destruction. The federal government has assumed an increasing role in wetland protection through executive orders that prohibit all U.S. agencies from supporting construction in wetlands when a practical alternative is available. The *Coastal Zone Management Act* (1972) provides inducements for states to protect coastal wetlands. Many states now regulate their wetlands to some extent.

Figure S12-1
Map of wetlands in the United States.

The federal government also purchases wetlands and adds them to the National Wildlife Refuge System, which today contains 12 million hectares (30 million acres), one-third of it wetlands. The Fish and Wildlife Service has purchased 650,000 hectares (1.6 million acres) of wetlands. The Department of Agriculture has wetland protection contracts with private landowners that stipulate payment if the lands are not filled. Such contracts protect 190,000 hectares (480,000 acres). States own another 2 million hectares (5.1 million acres), bringing the total state and federal wetland protection to 7.6 million hectares (19 million acres), a little over one-fourth of the total U.S. wetlands.

Wetland protection laws and regulations, unfortunately, are like toothless watchdogs. Little is done to enforce them in many instances. Each of us can write our representatives and find out what laws exist and how they are being enforced. Local action groups can help stimulate stronger enforcement when necessary. On an international scale, nations can cooperate to preserve wetlands. Representatives of a number of nations met in 1971 in Ramsa, Iran, to discuss the plight of wetlands. They agreed to protect lands within their jurisdiction. As of 1984 the United States had not ratified the agreement.

Estuaries

Estuaries are important coastal regions where freshwater streams mix with salt water. Like wetlands, estuaries are critical for fish and shellfish reproduction. Together, coastal wetlands and estuaries make up the **estuarine zone**. Two-thirds of all commercial and noncommercial fish and shellfish depend on this zone during some part of their life cycle.

The estuarine zone has a high ecological productivity because of the organic material and nutrients that are washed from the land and deposited there. These nutrients support an abundance of aquatic organisms, especially algae, the base of a large and productive aquatic food web.

Estuarine zones, like wetlands, absorb water pollutants that flow from sewage treatment plants, industries, cropland, and other sources. It is said that one acre of coastal wetland is the equivalent of a $75,000 sewage treatment plant.

Human Effects

Humans damage the estuarine zone in many ways. Pollutants from upstream or nearby sewage treatment plants and industries can damage these fragile, productive zones. Erosion occurring thousands of miles upstream can cause silt buildup, which destroys plants and other organisms. Oil slicks can penetrate the zone with disastrous effects. Nutrient supplies can be cut off by upstream dams that hold back sediment.

Urban and industrial users may withdraw so much fresh water upstream that rivers run dry. In Texas, for example, drought and heavy water demands in past years have critically reduced water flow into estuaries. The Mexican delta of the Colorado River is a remnant of its former self. Freshwater inflows are critical to maintaining the proper salt concentration in the brackish water of lagoons and coastal wetlands, where mollusks (clams, oysters, mussels) and other organisms dwell. Salinity may be one of the most important factors determining shellfish productivity. For instance, for hardshell clams, spawning and larval survival are best when the salinity is 20 to 24 parts per thousand (ppt). Starfish, which feed on clams, do poorly in these concentrations

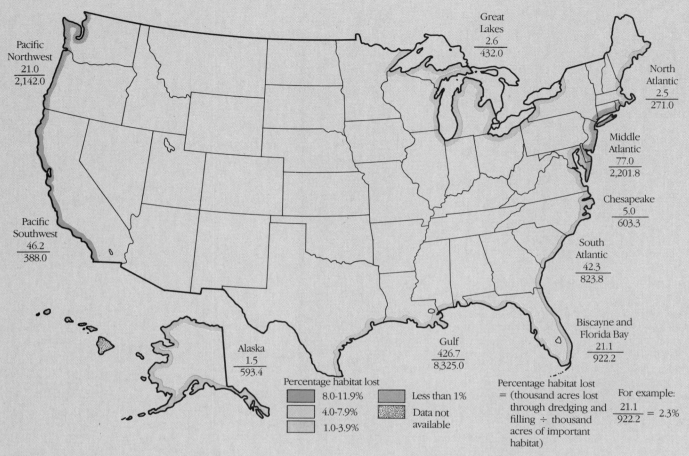

Figure S12-2

This map shows destruction of the estuarine zone (estuarine zone (estuaries and coastal wetlands)
from dredging and filling.

but thrive at higher levels. In the Great South Bay of Long Island, salinity averages 22 to 26 ppt. If these levels were to rise any further, shellfish would be stressed, and starfish predation would rise. The effects on hardshell clams could be devastating.

Among the variety of organisms inhabiting the estuarine zone, mollusks are one of the more sensitive. Pollution is generally thought to be one of the major factors responsible for the decline in mollusk harvests in the past 20 years. Mollusks can concentrate toxic heavy metals, chlorinated hydrocarbons, and many pathogenic organisms, including those that cause typhus and hepatitis. These pathogens may not affect the mollusks' survival, but they make them unsafe for human consumption.

The estuarine zones are also subject to dredging and filling operations that alter or destroy plant and animal habitat. Houses, factories, power plants, pipelines, oil refineries, condominiums,

hotels, warehouses, airports, marinas, and highways now occupy millions of acres of former estuarine zone.

Added to pollution, habitat loss, and changes in the water chemistry is the problem of overharvesting. It is generally agreed that the decline in U.S. oyster production after 1950 was largely the result of overharvesting. Clams in the Northeast have likewise been severely overharvested.

To date over 40% of the U.S. estuarine zone has been destroyed. The most severe damage has occurred in California, along the Atlantic coast from North Carolina to Florida, and along the entire Gulf of Mexico (Figure S12-2).

Despite state and federal laws to protect this zone, destruction continues. Between 1950 and 1969 estuarine habitat was destroyed at a rate of about 14,000 hectares (34,000 acres) per year. These irreversible losses continue today.

Protecting the Estuarine Zone

The preservation of the estuarine zone depends on many factors: (1) control of coastal and upstream pollution by proper land management and pollution control devices, (2) protection of water flow to maintain proper salt concentrations, (3) restrictions on dredging and filling of estuaries and coastal wetlands, and (4) laws and regulations to control fish and shellfish harvest. Protection may be difficult to achieve, however, because 90% of the coastal land in the 48 coterminous states is privately owned.

Congress passed the *Coastal Zone Management Act* in 1972 to help protect estuaries. This act set up a fund to help the 35 coastal and Great Lakes states develop their own laws and programs and provide grants to acquire estuarine and estuarylike areas in the Great Lakes states. These regions are to be set aside for scientific study; as of 1981, 12 National Estuarine Sanctuaries had been established.

Half of the U.S. population lives in counties that are at least partly within an hour's drive of the coast, and seven of the nine largest cities are located on the coast. Discoveries of offshore oil, gas, and minerals pose new problems that must be addressed. An abundant supply of cooling water makes the coastal zones prime candidates for new power plants and oil refineries. Thus, the Coastal Zone Management Act is an important step in preserving the coasts.

Still, according to critics, the act leaves too much discretion to the states. Some states, in fact, either have not adopted programs or enforce their programs poorly, leaving their coastal waters open to misuse.

Fifteen additional federal laws contribute to coastal zone management, but they are only as good as their enforcement. Without more serious efforts to improve coastal zone management, Americans will lose more of this critical habitat.

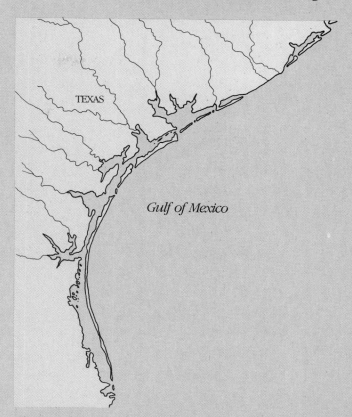

Figure S12-3
The Texas Gulf Coast has numerous barrier islands that are formed by sediment from strains and beach erosion.

Coastlines and Barrier Islands

The eastern coast of the United States and Mexico is skirted by a chain of barrier islands. These narrow, sandy islands are interrupted by small inlets and are separated from the mainland by lagoons and bays (Figure S12-3). Along the Atlantic and Gulf coasts there are an estimated 250 barrier islands, many of which are popular sites for recreation. Some have been purchased by the federal government and are used for recreation (as National Seashores) and wildlife habitat, but most barrier islands are under private ownership.

In the past 35 to 40 years many of these islands have been developed to accommodate summer vacationers. Homes, roads, stores, and other structures have been erected on them. According to estimates of the National Park Service, in 1950 only 36,000 hectares (90,000 acres) of barrier islands had been developed, but by 1980 the total had risen to 112,000 hectares (280,000 acres). Moreover, if the current rate of development continues, the Park Service estimates, by 1995 all of the remaining undeveloped barrier islands will have been developed.

Barrier islands and their beaches are quite unstable. The islands grow and shrink from season to season and year to year in response to two main forces. First, waves, which tend to arrive at an angle to the beach, erode the beaches, as illustrated in Figure S12-4a. These waves create **beach drift**, a gradual movement of sand along the beach. In addition, the wind creates a **longshore current** parallel to the beach, which also moves sand along the beach (Figure S12-4b). Combined, beach drift and **longshore drift** are called **littoral drift**. Littoral drift causes the barrier islands to move parallel to the main shoreline. They shorten on one side and become longer on the other. Homes built on the upcurrent side of the island may collapse into the sea. Second, winter storms tend to wash over the low barrier islands and move the sand closer to the land, destroying houses, roadways, and other structures.

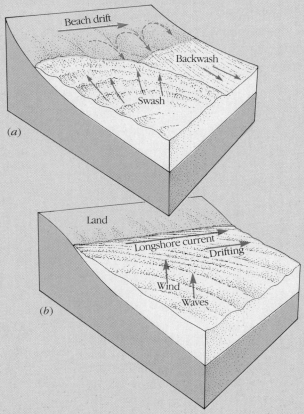

Figure S12-4
(a) Beach drift is caused by waves approaching obliquely. *(b)*
Longshore currents are formed by offshore oblique winds and
waves.

Home construction, attempts to stabilize the beaches and sand
dunes, and road construction all lead to disaster. Federal actions
and various relief programs have, in the past, encouraged development on barrier islands. When erosion and storm damage
occurred, the government stepped in with money for disaster
relief. Federal flood insurance paid for the damage, and federally subsidized construction projects helped rebuild roads and
stabilize the islands. A few years later other storms devastated
the islands, starting the rebuilding cycle all over again at considerable expense. Recognizing this fact, Congress passed legislation in 1982 to prohibit the expenditure of federal money
for highway construction and other development on barrier
islands. The *Coastal Barrier Resources Act* may put a stop to the
destruction of barrier islands.

Coastal beaches are also endangered by human activities. To
understand these dangers we must look at the natural processes
that affect these beaches. Coastal beaches, like barrier islands,
are eroded by longshore currents. Thus, American beaches have
been likened to rivers of sand constantly moving with the major
coastal currents. Sand is constantly replaced, though, by sediment carried to the sea by rivers. Consequently, dams that trap
sediment may halt the replenishment of coastal beaches.

Some communities erect barriers to prevent erosion by longshore currents, but these only slow down the process and do
not stop it. To protect the shoreline, the delicate balance between
sediment flow and erosion must be maintained. Dams that retain
sediment should be avoided if valuable coastal land is to be
preserved.

Wild and Scenic Rivers

Foreseeing the need for unspoiled places for recreation, Congress passed the *Wild and Scenic Rivers Act* in 1968 to prevent
the construction of dams, water diversion projects, and other
forms of undesirable development along the banks of some of
the country's remaining free-flowing rivers.

The designation of wild and scenic rivers often involves heated
debate between various interests. In this battle, compromises
are inevitable, and commercial interests might focus more on
water conservation as a first step in meeting water needs. Smaller
dams that flood only a small portion of the river could
be built whenever possible. Conservationists could work with
developers to minimize environmental damage. Environmentally acceptable options could be drawn up that satisfy water
demands or flood-control needs.

A river is a vital resource, but dammed and diverted to water-
hungry consumers, it becomes a tragic symbol of poor planning
and disregard for the life forms that depend on its waters. Our
goal should be to use each river wisely and efficiently, minimizing waste and damage.

Congress declared that rivers with outstanding scenery, recreational value, fish and wildlife populations, geological features, and historical significance should be preserved for posterity. Accordingly, it designated three river classes for inclusion
in the Wild and Scenic River System: **wild rivers**, which are
relatively inaccessible and "untamed"; **scenic rivers**, which are
largely undeveloped but of great scenic value; and **recreational
rivers**, which offer important recreational opportunities despite
some development. By 1981, 54 rivers had been included in the
system, totaling 11,064 kilometers (6,915 miles).

Today's Energy: Fossil Fuels

Our entire economic structure is built from and propelled by fossil fuels. We have invaded the long-silent burial grounds of the Carboniferous Age, appropriating the dead remains of yesteryear for the use of the living today.

JEREMY RIFKIN

Energy is essential to all human societies, especially industrialized countries with high standards of living. Important as it is, energy has been taken for granted—and used wastefully. The prevailing mood has been that there is always more, and it will always be cheap.

The days of energy nonchalance came to an abrupt halt in the early 1970s as a result of the 1973 oil embargo imposed by the Organization for Petroleum Exporting Countries (OPEC). As the flow of oil stopped, prices for fuel and consumer products whose production and distribution depend on petroleum shot upward. Inflation began a long climb that crippled the American and world economies. Long lines formed at gas stations. People became used to colder houses. All in all it was a rude awakening for the American public. Although this was not our first energy shortage, it was one of the most far-reaching.

The oil shortage of 1973 marks a critical turning point in our history: a time when we became more aware of our dependence on fossil fuels, especially oil, and willing

Figure 13-1
(*a*) Energy consumption in the United Stated by fuel type from 1850 to 1982. (*b*) Energy consumption from 1950 to present.

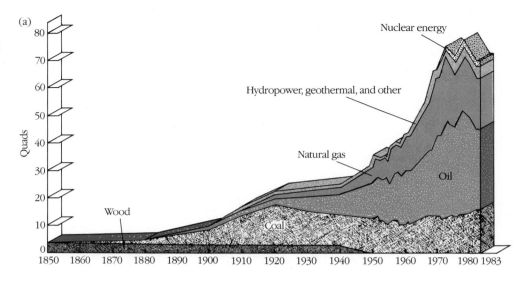

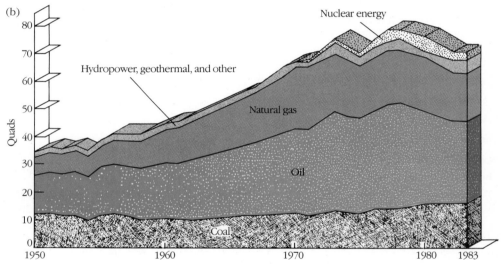

to do something other than simply find new sources. With energy use rising much more rapidly than population growth, it became apparent to many that our energy-intensive life-style was a big part of the problem.

Energy Use—Then and Now

The history of energy use has been one of shifting dependency from one source to another, a pattern that will inevitably continue in the future as today's energy sources run out and new ones are developed.

As shown in Figure 13-1, the United States was once solely dependent on wood. The early 1900s saw an increasing shift to coal, but most people found that fuel to be dirty and bulky and expensive to mine and transport. So when oil and natural gas were made available, the use of coal began to decline. Its replacements were much easier and cheaper to transport and burned cleaner. As a result, the use of oil and natural gas rose dramatically starting in the 1930s and 1940s.

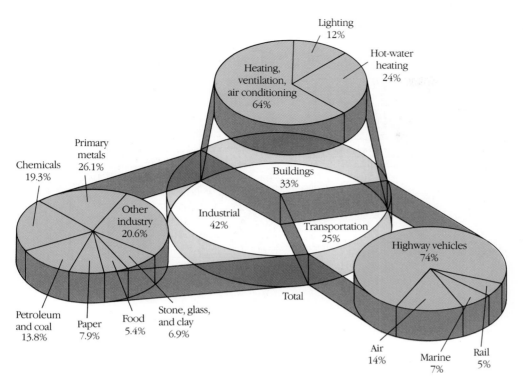

Figure 13-2
Breakdown of energy consumption in the United States.

Today, the United States depends primarily on oil, natural gas, and coal for its energy needs. In 1983 oil accounted for 42.5% of the total energy consumption; natural gas provided 25%, and coal provided 22.5%. The remaining 10% came from hydroelectric power, nuclear fission, solar generation, and geothermal energy. Although it does not show up in the energy calculus, conservation indirectly provides us with a great deal of energy, too.

Residential and commercial users consume the largest share of energy in the United States. They are followed closely by industry and transportation. Figure 13-2 breaks down energy consumption by end use. This shows us that one-third of the energy in the United States is used for heating and cooling buildings, heating water, and lighting. Transportation consumes one-fourth of the energy, most of this by highway vehicles. Finally, two-fifths of the energy is used for industrial processes; of these, mining and extraction of metals and chemical production are the largest consumers.

The United States, with only 6% of the world's population, uses about 30% of its energy. Between 1965 and 1971 U.S. energy consumption grew at an astounding rate of 4.8% per year, but since then it has slowed consider-

ably. In fact, between 1979 and 1983 total annual energy consumption dropped by 10% from 78.9 quads (quadrillion British thermal units) to 70.5 quads. This remarkable development resulted from higher prices, a poor economy, technological advances, and conservation. Home consumption of energy dropped 17% between 1980 and 1982, and energy consumption by automobiles dropped about 14%. With economic recovery, energy consumption may once again rise, but it may never grow as rapidly as it did in earlier years.

Energy waste in the United States is a troubling, but highly curable, ill. The use of energy is shown in an elaborate "spaghetti", or energy flow, diagram, which traces energy from production through consumption (Figure 13-3). This figure shows that a large quantity of the energy used in the United States is lost as waste heat.

Bruce Hannon once wrote that "a country that runs on energy cannot afford to waste it." Most experts agree, and they further believe that energy waste could be cut substantially through relatively inexpensive improvements in efficiency and conservation. Such measures would not detract from the current standard of living but would actually increase it.

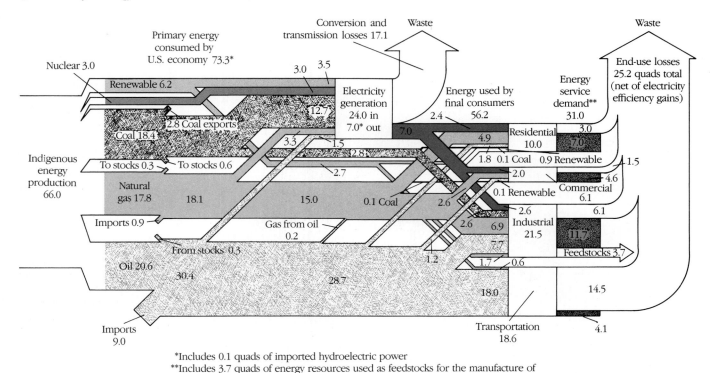

Figure 13-3
U.S. energy sources and uses in 1982 (quadrillion Btus).

*Includes 0.1 quads of imported hydroelectric power
**Includes 3.7 quads of energy resources used as feedstocks for the manufacture of non-energy materials. Based on end-use efficiencies from 1980 Brookhaven data.

Impacts of Energy Production and Consumption

Energy does not come cheap. In addition to the economic costs, society pays a price in the form of deteriorated health and environmental destruction, effects that differ with the energy source. These external costs are not often taken into account when considering the total cost of an energy project. This section will briefly review the major impacts of the three dominant U.S. energy resources, coal, oil, and natural gas.

To describe the impacts of an energy resource, we must understand each **energy system** or **energy fuel cycle**. An energy system is composed of many parts, as illustrated in Figure 13-4. To produce marketable fuel, a fossil energy source must first be extracted, transported, and often processed to remove impurities or to improve its useful-

ness. Fuels are then distributed, stored, and consumed in a variety of ways. At each step along the way, environmental damage and other impacts may occur; the most notable of these impacts occur at the extraction phase and the consumption phase.

Coal

Coal is a sedimentary rock composed mostly of carbon. It occurs in rocks of all ages, but the largest deposits mined today were formed from plant material near freshwater lakes and marshes during the hot, muggy Paleozoic era 225 million to 350 million years ago. During this period of luxuriant plant growth, plant debris fell into the water and was buried by newly fallen materials and sediments. Cut off from oxygen, it accumulated instead of decaying. Over millions of years the accumulated material was converted into coal by pressure and underground heat.

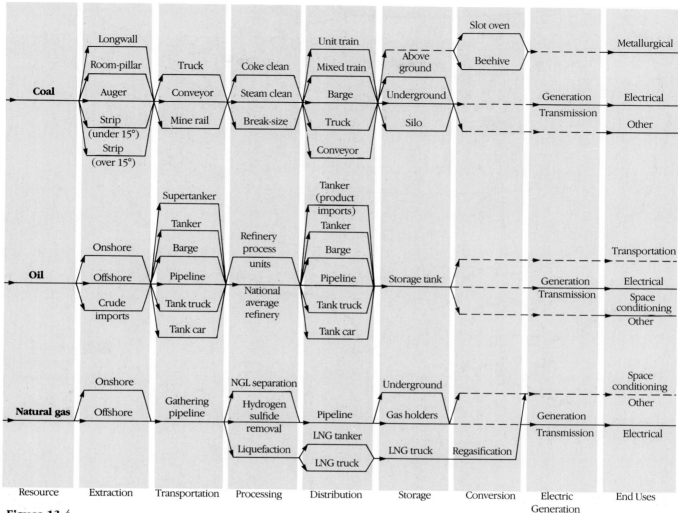

Figure 13-4
Energy system or energy fuel cycles.

There are three basic grades of coal: lignite (brown coal), bituminous (soft coal), and anthracite (hard coal). Geologists distinguish 13 subtypes differing in density, moisture content, heat value, levels of impurities, and other features.

Since the late 1800s coal has been in wide use in the United States. In 1983, 702 million metric tons (785 million tons) of coal was mined in the country, mostly for domestic markets. By 2000, coal use could reach 1.6 billion metric tons.

In 1982 coal provided 22% of U.S. domestic energy needs, up from 17% in 1977. By 2000 coal is expected to supply 34% of the country's total energy needs. As shown in Figure 13-5, the United States has huge coal reserves in the East and West. These deposits represent 30% of the global coal reserves! Coal is our most abundant domestic fossil fuel and will become increasingly important in the years to come. There are about 225 billion metric tons of minable coal within U.S. borders; this could last 150 years at the rate of consumption projected for 2000. But what

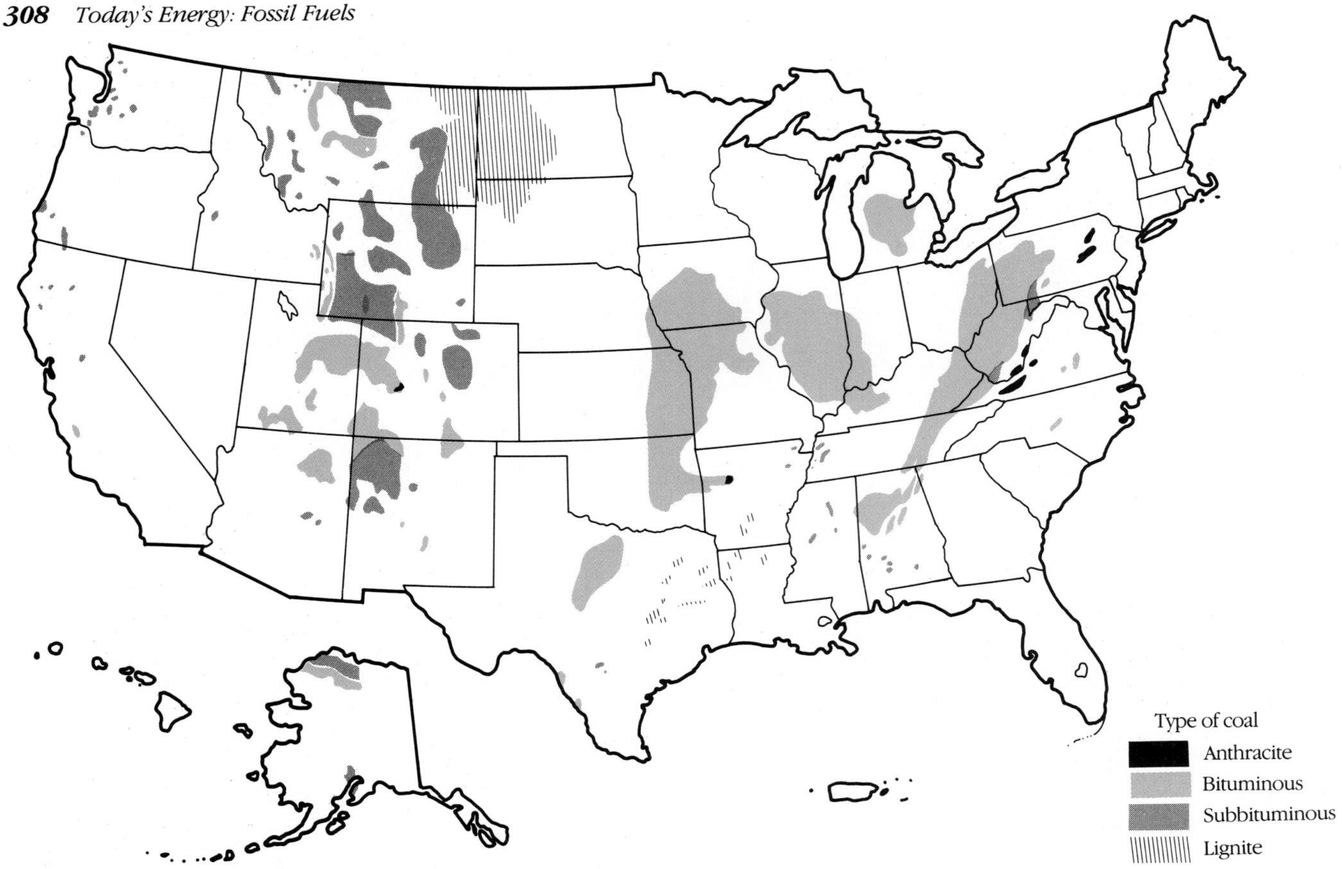

Figure 13-5
Coal deposits in the United States.

are the impacts of the coal fuel cycle, and how will they affect us in the coming years?

Exploration In general, exploration is fairly environmentally benign. In flat and rolling terrain, exploration crews drill holes into the ground and extract the core samples to locate coal deposits and determine how thick they are. With repeated sampling over a wide area, they can also determine the extent of the coal field.

Mining Coal is mined in both underground and surface mines. As shown in Figure 13-6, underground mining was the only method employed until the 1930s. After that, surface mining increased dramatically while the amount of coal produced in underground mines remained about the same. In 1979, 60% of all coal produced in the United States was from surface mines, and by 1985 it is expected to reach 67%.

The upsurge in surface mining results from simple economics. Surface mines allow a higher recovery of coal—about 80% to 90%, compared with 40% to 50% for underground mines. Surface mines are safer, cost less to start up and operate, and can be brought into production faster than underground mines. In addition the labor productivity, or amount of coal produced per worker-hour, is three times higher in surface mines.

Surface mining varies from one region to the next. In the East, where the terrain is mountainous, coal is extracted by **contour strip mining**, also called rim stripping (Figure 13-7). In this technique the rock and dirt lying over the coal, called overburden, are removed. Until 1977 the overburden was discarded on the downslope. Because of new federal legislation, the overburden must now be put back where it came from.

In the Midwest and West, where the terrain is relatively flat or gently rolling, coal is extracted by **area strip mines**. The topsoil is first removed by scrapers and is set aside

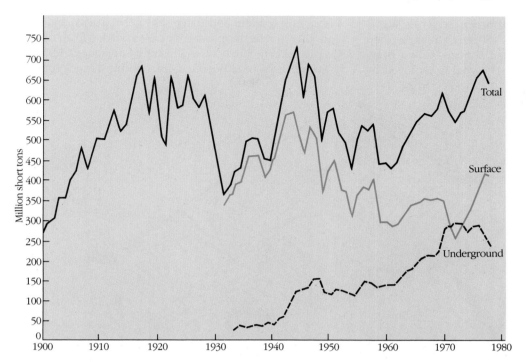

Figure 13-6
Total coal production and production by surface and underground mines in the United States.

Figure 13-7
Contour strip mining is common in the hilly terrain of eastern United States coal fields.

for later reapplication. The overburden, which is some-times 30 to 45 meters, (100 to 150 feet) thick, is then dynamited and removed by huge shovels, called drag-lines, to expose the coal seam. The coal is removed by front-end loaders and hauled away by trucks, and then another parallel strip is cut. The overburden from this cut is placed in the first cut, as illustrated in Figure 13-8. After several strips have been cut, the overburden is regraded

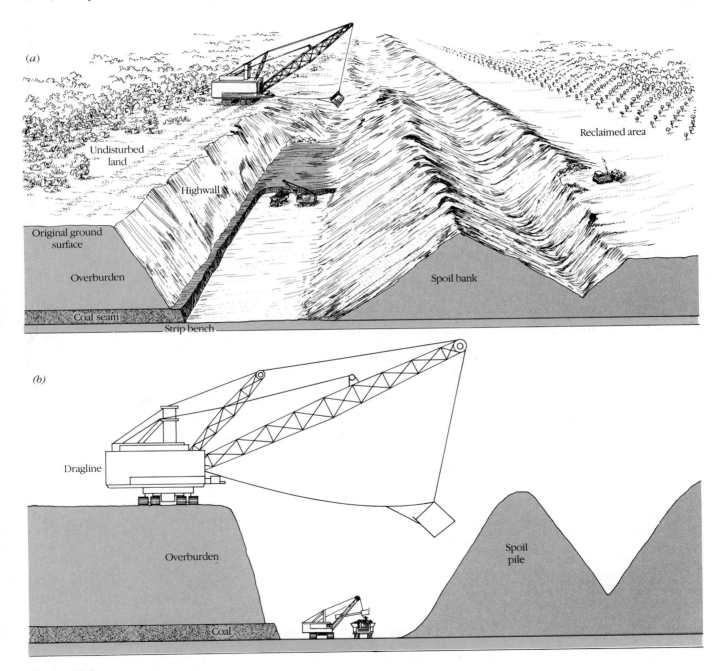

Figure 13-8
Area strip mining. Draglines remove the overburden, creating huge, parallel spoil banks. Exposed coal is then removed. Later the spoil piles are recontoured.

to the approximate original contour, the topsoil is replaced, and seeds are sown, increasing the likelihood that the area will revegetate.

Surface mining destroys the natural vegetation and the habitat of many species, some of which may already be endangered. Winter grazing grounds of other western species such as mule deer, pronghorn antelope, and elk and the nesting sites of rare predatory birds will also be affected by future surface mining. In the Yellowstone River basin, an area richly endowed with coal, 35,000 hectares (88,600 acres) will be disturbed by surface coal mining between 1977 and 2000. The impacts to wildlife from mining, road construction, and the expansion of towns to accommodate miners and their families will be severe. In an area where outdoor recreation is popular, this loss of wildlife will have aesthetic as well as economic impacts.

Destruction of the natural vegetation and stockpiling of overburden in spoil piles, especially in contour mines, leads to increased soil erosion. In Kentucky, studies show, surface mining has increased erosion from .4 metric ton per hectare to 2.4 to 145 metric tons per hectare.

Eroded sediment is eventually deposited in stream bottoms. One eastern study showed that streams in mined watersheds had 100 times as much bottom sediment as streams in unmined areas. Sediment deposition kills the bottom-dwelling (benthic) organisms such as insects and crustaceans, essential for fish and other organisms higher on the food chain. Sediment can bury and kill fish eggs, decrease a stream's water-carrying capacity, which may lead to flooding, and also fill reservoirs and lakes.

Studies in both the East and West have shown that surface mines cause **salt loading**, the discharge of salts and minerals into streams. This occurs when rainwater and snowmelt percolate through the disturbed overburden and leach out minerals and salts. High salt concentrations affect aquatic organisms, as well as agricultural and domestic water users, as described in Chapters 8 and 12. As surface mining of coal increases, salt loading will also rise, especially if efforts to reclaim mined land are abandoned or slackened.

Surface mines disrupt and pollute groundwater in the West, because many aquifers are located near or associated with coal seams. The extraction of coal from a seam of coal that served as an aquifer near Decker, Montana, resulted in a drop in the water table of 3 meters (10 feet) or more within a 3-kilometer (2-mile) radius of the mine. Residents who depended on the aquifer were forced to find new water supplies.

Coal is also removed by underground mines. Underground mines may collapse during or after mining, caus-

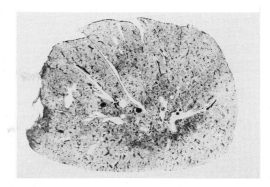

(a)

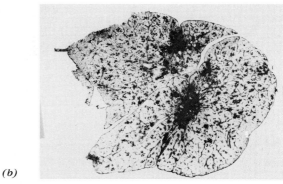

(b)

Figure 13-9
(*a*) A cross-section of a normal lung. (*b*) Cross section of a lung from a retired coal miner with black lung disease.

ing subsidence of the ground above them. Over 800,000 hectares (2 million acres) of land has already subsided in the United States from underground coal mining. For every hectare of coal mined in central Appalachia, over 5 hectares (12.5 acres) of surface is made vulnerable to subsidence.

Since 1900 more than 100,000 Americans have been killed in underground mines, and 1 million miners have been permanently disabled. Despite improved working conditions, underground coal mining has the highest rate of injury of all major occupations. Over the past 50 years, the number of deaths has dropped substantially. Underground coal mining also causes **black lung disease**, or **pneumoconiosis**, a progressive, debilitating disease caused by breathing coal dust and other particulates. Victims have difficulty getting enough oxygen because the tiny air sacs (alveoli) in the lungs break down. Exercise is difficult, and death is slow and painful. Despite improvements in mining safety, one-third of all underground coal mines still have conditions conducive to black lung disease, a problem that costs taxpayers over $1 billion a year in federal worker disability benefits (Figure 13-9).

Figure 13-10
Streams affected by acid mine drainage in the United States.

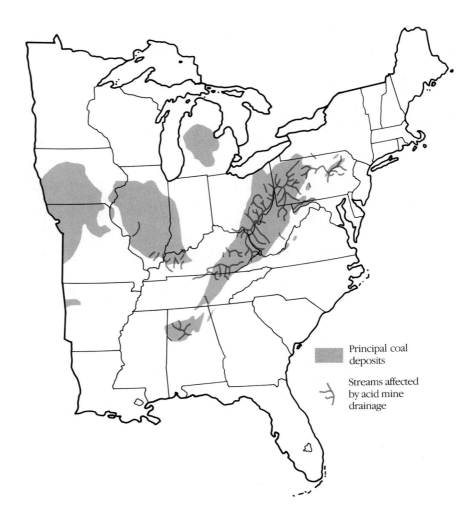

Principal coal deposits

Streams affected by acid mine drainage

Over 11,000 kilometers (7000 miles) of U.S. streams, 90% of which are in Appalachia, are badly contaminated by acid mine drainage from underground coal mines (Figure 13-10). The annual acid production is estimated at 2.7 million metric tons (3 million tons). Further increases in coal production could increase the acid pollution, although awareness of the problem has brought about many efforts to reduce the problem. Regardless, cleanup of the abandoned mines where most of the acid comes from could take decades and billions of dollars.

Cleaning After coal is mined, impurities such as slate, shale, calcite, gypsum, clay, and pyrite are sometimes removed. Cleaning reduces the coal's weight and transport costs and improves the burning efficiency—the heat output per ton. Impurities are removed by crushing, sift-

Acid mine drainage is formed when rock or soil containing various sulfide minerals (commonly iron pyrite) is exposed to air and water in mines. Sulfides are converted to sulfuric acid, which can drain into streams and lakes. Acid kills plants and animals and inhibits bacterial decay of organic matter in water, thus allowing large quantities of organic matter to build up in streams. Sulfuric acid also leaches toxic elements such as aluminum, copper, zinc, and magnesium from the soil and carries them to streams.

Acids can render water unfit for drinking and lakes unsuitable for swimming. Municipal and industrial water must be chemically neutralized before use. Acid also corrodes iron and steel pumps, bridges, locks, barges, and ships, causing damage estimated in the millions of dollars each year.

ing, and washing. By-products of coal cleaning are stored in refuse piles, which are sometimes used to build dams, or impoundments, for settling ponds used to purify water used in this stage of the coal fuel cycle.

Refuse piles and impoundments contain small particles of coal which ignite and burn when exposed to oxygen and water. This problem is mostly confined to the eastern United States.

Coal refuse piles may erode away or be leached of toxic materials, forming acidic or highly mineralized drainage that pollutes nearby streams. An estimated 4800 kilometers (3000 miles) of streams in Appalachia are contaminated from coal refuse piles.

Transportation After cleaning, coal is transported by truck, train, barge, or ship. The impacts from these activities, however, are generally quite small compared with those created by mining and combustion.

Approximately 70% of all U.S. coal travels by rail. Trains will continue to play a major role in coal transportation, and more and more coal will be carried by unit trains, 100-car trains that carry only coal. Today, about one-fourth of U.S. coal is transported this way. With expanding coal production, authorities estimate, 2700 more unit trains will be needed between 1977 and 2000. The U.S. Department of Transportation estimates that it will cost about $10 billion to upgrade existing rail systems and acquire new trains during this period. Trains create air and noise pollution and are especially bothersome in urban areas, where they often tie up local traffic.

Coal is also moved by **slurry pipelines**, which transport crushed coal suspended in water. The Consolidated Coal Company built the first pipeline in 1957. Today, there is only one functional coal slurry pipeline in the United States, the Black Mesa pipeline, which began operation in 1970. It annually carries 4.3 million metric tons of coal 435 kilometers (273 miles) from coal fields in northeastern Arizona to the Mohave Power Plant in southern Nevada.

Most experts agree that pipelines will never become a major part of the U.S. coal transportation system. A major reason is that to move 1 million metric tons of coal, 800 million liters (210 million gallons) of water is needed. In the arid West, water used for coal pipelines could be put to other uses such as supporting wildlife, recreation, and agriculture.

Combustion About two-thirds of U.S. coal is burned to generate electricity. The remainder is burned in a vari-

ety of industrial processes to create heat or produce steel and other metals. Numerous environmental pollutants are produced during coal combustion. The most notable are waste heat (Chapter 20), particulates, sulfur oxides, nitrogen oxides, and oxides of carbon (carbon dioxide and carbon monoxide). The formation and effects of the air pollutants are discussed in Chapter 19. Therefore, I will only highlight a few important facts here.

A 1000-megawatt coal-fired power plant, which produces electricity for about 1 million people, burns about 2.7 million metric tons of coal each year. In the process it produces about 5 million metric tons of carbon dioxide, about 18,000 metric tons of nitrogen oxides, 11,000 to 110,000 metric tons of sulfur oxides, and 1500 to 30,000 metric tons of particulates.

Annually, U.S. coal-fired power plants produce about 18 million metric tons of sulfur oxides and about 4.5 million metric tons of nitrogen oxides. In the atmosphere these are converted into sulfuric acid and nitric acid, respectively. These acids fall from the sky in **acid precipitation**, affecting surface waters, statues, buildings, vegetation, and soils (Chapter Supplement 19-2). They cause an estimated $5 billion worth of damage each year. The total annual damage from *all* air pollutants is projected at $12 billion to $16 billion.

Coal will undoubtedly play a major role in meeting future U.S. energy needs. By 2000 there may be 1000 industries and utilities burning coal, as compared with 594 in 1976. This inevitable increase in coal consumption will probably degrade air quality, even if pollution control devices are installed on new coal-burning facilities. Some scientists project that nitrogen oxide emissions will increase by about 2.2 million metric tons per year in the next decade because pollution control devices now in use cannot remove these gases. Carbon dioxide is also an uncontrollable pollutant. The Federal Energy Research and Development Administration reported that the most stringent existing control technologies could hold down sulfur dioxide emissions so that they did not exceed current levels, but more recent projections indicate that sulfur oxide emissions will continue to rise as energy consumption increases. By 2000 they could be 12% to 20% higher than today.

Waste Disposal Coal combustion produces large quantities of waste. A fine dust known as **fly ash** is formed during combustion. Fly ash comes from mineral matter that makes up 10% to 30% of the weight of coal that has not been cleaned. Fly ash is carried up the smokestack with the escaping gases and may be captured by some pollution control devices. It then becomes a solid waste that must be disposed of. Sulfur dioxide is also emitted in the stack gas but can be removed by **smokestack scrubbers** (special pollution control devices described in Chapter 19). Scrubbers produce a toxic sludge, containing fly ash and sulfur compounds, that must be disposed of. Some mineral matter, too heavy to form fly ash, remains at the bottom of the coal burning furnace as **bottom ash**.

A 1000-megawatt power plant may produce 180,000 to 680,000 metric tons of solid waste each year, including fly ash, bottom ash, and sludge from scrubbers. By 1990 U.S. coal-fired power plants may be producing 110 million metric tons of solid waste, almost equal to the amount of municipal trash produced in the country each year.

Solid waste disposal will require immense sites. One utility in Pennsylvania plans to dispose of its wastes in a nearby valley. In 25 years the utility expects to fill the valley with solid waste, creating an 8-kilometer-long (5-miles) 120-meter-deep (400-foot) mass of sludge and ash. Such sites will contain many toxic chemicals that could possibly leach from dumps into groundwater and surface water.

Demographic Changes The sudden upsurge in coal mining brings about often unfavorable demographic changes in both the East and West. Regions once sparsely populated become inundated as miners and their families move in. This is particularly noticeable in the West, where many of the existing coal seams can be surface mined. Towns spring up overnight to accommodate the new residents, putting a heavy strain on the existing **infrastructure**, community services, schools, highways, wastewater treatment facilities, and so on. Small towns are forced to invest heavily to meet the needs of the new workers, but county coffers are often inadequate. Thus, state governments often contribute. **Severance taxes** may be imposed to help pay the cost of such developments. These are state taxes levied against each ton of coal removed from the ground and used to pay for necessary infrastructure, shifting the financial burden to the coal company and energy consumer.

Many communities suffering extreme growing pains undergo sudden increases in the crime rate as well as in drug and alcohol abuse. This tragedy is hard felt by residents who have lived in the community for many years.

Then, if the demand for coal drops, towns are often abandoned, unemployment rises, and social problems increase further.

Even though the demographic changes bring many undesirable effects, local businesses often benefit from the sudden influx of miners and their families. In some cases, however, local businesses may be displaced by fast-food restaurants and discount stores, businesses with no roots in the community. Thus, population growth may actually work against those businesses that have survived for decades in small towns.

This review of the impacts of coal indicates the full price society pays and the price it will be expected to pay in the future. These impacts should make society aware of the hazards of a coal-powered future, help it plan ways to minimize them, and even make it reconsider its energy options.

Petroleum and Natural Gas

Petroleum is a black, viscous mixture of hydrocarbons that is refined and converted into a host of useful products, such as gasoline, propane, kerosene, tar, diesel fuel, lubricating oils, jet fuel, asphalt, and numerous chemicals used for making plastics, drugs, and synthetic fabrics. Natural gas is a mixture of low-molecular-weight hydrocarbons, primarily methane; it is burned in homes, factories, and electric utilities and is often described as an ideal fuel because it contains few contaminants and burns cleanly.

Petroleum and natural gas deposits are shown in Figure 13-11. Many of these are located offshore. To find oil and natural gas, energy companies use sophisticated electronic and seismic testing methods. When geologists determine where the potential deposits are, test wells are drilled.

Oil and gas are extracted from wells that run as deep as 10 kilometers (6 miles). On land, oil rigs generally have minimal impact, unless they are located in wilderness where roads and noise from heavy machinery and construction camps can disturb wildlife. Oil and natural gas extraction may cause subsidence. One notable example occurred in the Los Angeles–Long Beach Harbor area. Extensive oil extraction, beginning in 1928, caused severe subsidence. Over well sites, the ground dropped 9 meters (30 feet). Extensive subsidence created a need for flood control measures along the coastline. Damage to build-

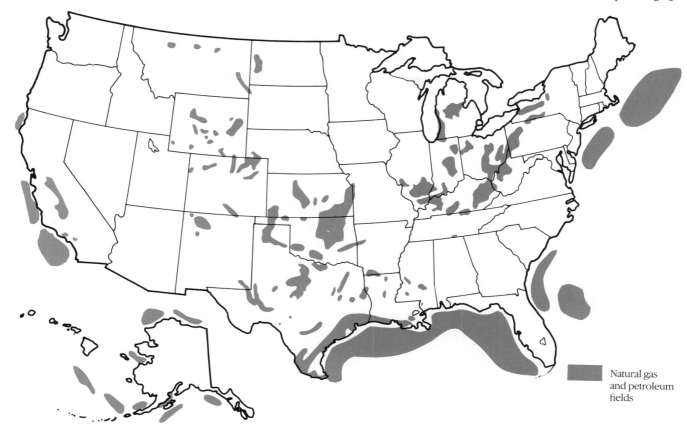

Figure 13-11
Oil and natural gas deposits in the United States.

ings, roads, and other structures was estimated at $100 million.

Another major problem with onshore oil wells in the past has been brine (salt water). Typically, for every barrel of oil produced, ten barrels of brine are also extracted. In early days the brine was simply discarded into nearby streams or on the soil. Today, most brine is reinjected into the well. But brine can contaminate freshwater aquifers if the casing that lines the well is missing or corroded.

Many oil and gas fields are offshore. Conventional offshore oil wells operate from huge platforms in waters 260 meters (850 feet) deep or less. Newer wells, like the Mississippi Canyon in the Gulf of Mexico, operate in water 300 meters (1000 feet) deep. With improvements in technology, rigs may someday operate in water much deeper. For example, a submerged production system now being tested in the Gulf of Mexico may someday be able to operate in water up to 1500 meters (5000 feet) deep.

Oil Spills About half of the oil that contaminates the ocean comes from natural seepage from offshore deposits. (Annually about 600,000 metric tons of oil seeps into the ocean from natural sources; 40% of this seepage occurs in the Pacific.) Twenty percent of the oil contaminating the ocean comes from oil well blowouts, pipeline breaks, and tanker spills. The rest comes from oil disposed of inland and carried to the ocean in rivers.

Leakage from offshore wells occurs during the transfer of oil to shore and also during normal operations. This leakage of oil has not captured public attention. Still, the constant escape can harm marine life and birds. Oil-soaked birds are commonly found along the coast of California.

Figure 13-12
The anatomy of an oil spill from an improperly drilled hole.

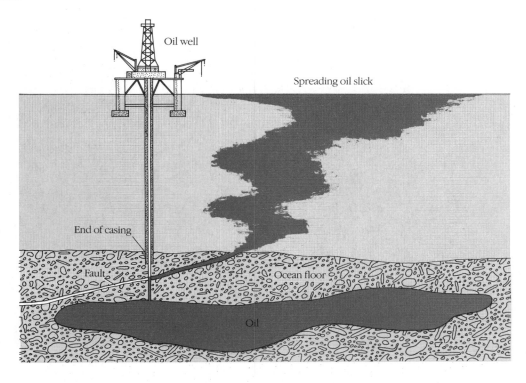

Oil well

Spreading oil slick

End of casing

Fault

Ocean floor

Oil

One major spill occurred in January 1979 off the coast of Santa Barbara, California. As shown in Figure 13-12, oil leaked out of the borehole into a natural fissure in the floor of the ocean, because the casing was not complete. From there it escaped to the surface. Normally, leakage of this nature is prevented by lining the hole with a metal casing, but in this instance, the casing extended only 12 meters (40 feet) below the ocean floor. It took 11 days for workers to plug the leak. An estimated 175,000 to 190,000 liters of oil (20,000 to 50,000 gallons) seeped out daily until the hole could be plugged, producing a 2000-square-kilometer (800-square-mile) slick. Another incident occurred in the Gulf of Mexico in 1979, when a Mexican oil well exploded, sending millions of gallons of oil into the ocean and creating the largest leak in history (Figure 13-13).

Most of us equate oil spills with tanker accidents, and there is little reason to wonder why. Such spills are spectacular in their size and devastation. On March 16, 1978, the *Amoco Cadiz* ran aground off the coast of France. This is the largest oil spill in maritime history. High winds and rough seas made it impossible to transfer the oil to

Figure 13-13
Operation Sombrero was a major effort to stop the continuous leak from the Ixtoc I oil well in the Gulf of Mexico, June 3, 1979.

other tankers, and consequently the entire 216,000-ton cargo was spilled, destroying 200 kilometers (125 miles) of France's coastline. Every conceivable cleanup measure was used, and the resulting bill exceeded $50 million.

With offshore oil wells being sunk in the North Sea, the Gulf of Mexico, and the Arctic Ocean and off the Pacific coast, pollution is likely to rise significantly. Spills from tankers are also likely to add to the problem. From 1973 to 1980 there were 88,800 spills in U.S. waters, an average of about 11,000 incidents each year. During that period 450 million liters (120 million gallons) of oil spilled into the Atlantic, the Pacific, the Gulf of Mexico, the Great Lakes, and inland rivers. These figures include all spills from vessels, land vehicles, pipelines, oil wells (both onshore and offshore), and storage facilities.

In the early 1980s the number of spills and the amount of oil spilled into U.S. waters declined, a trend caused by better safety measures as well as a drop in oil use resulting from conservation and poor economic conditions.

Tougher governmental standards for new oil tankers went into effect in 1979, and new safety standards on older tankers were phased in between 1981 and 1985. These regulations called for dual radar systems, backup steering controls on new and existing tankers, recommendations for automatic collision avoidance aids, and improvements in inspection and certification standards. Under the new regulations crude oil must be cleaned to eliminate sludge buildup in tanks. This sludge was once rinsed out at sea. New regulations also require tankers to have separate ballast tanks, which are filled with salt water for stability when ships return after unloading. In older ships, emptied oil tanks were filled with water for ballast, and when the ship arrived at port, the oil-contaminated water was dumped into the sea.

The importance of oil washing and segregated ballast is not to be underestimated. According to the Council on Environmental Quality, about 200,000 metric tons of oil enters the ocean each year from tanker spills, but 1.3 million metric tons of oil is released during tank purging and ballast tank discharge.

The harmful effects of oil spills are felt in both freshwater and marine environments. Oil kills plants and animals in the estuarine zone, especially barnacles, mussels, crabs, and rock weeds. After a major spill, it may take two to ten years for organisms to recover. Oil settles on the beaches and kills organisms that live there. It also settles to the ocean floor and kills benthic (bottom-dwelling) organisms such as shellfish and crabs. Those that survive may accumulate oil in their living tissue, making them

Figure 13-14
This bird is beyond the help of volunteers, who, after the 1981 oil spill in San Francisco, are attempting to save the oil-covered animals.

inedible. Oil poisons microscopic organisms such as algae and therefore may disrupt major food chains and decrease the yield of edible fish. It also coats the feathers of birds, impairing flight, or worse. (Figure 13-14). Because oil reduces the insulative properties of feathers, birds become more vulnerable to the cold.

Certain chlorinated hydrocarbons found in water in low concentrations, such as the pesticides DDT or dieldrin, are soluble in oil and can become concentrated in oil slicks. Such poisons can seriously affect algae and fish larvae. Finally, extremely low concentrations of some chemicals from oil spills can block the smell and taste receptors of aquatic organisms, interfering with their ability to locate food, select habitat, or escape predators. Lobsters, for example, are attracted to some crude oil compounds, which may draw them away from their normal food sources.

About 25% of the crude oil in a spill is volatile and evaporates within three months. Other compounds, relatively nonvolatile and lighter than water, float on the surface, where they are broken down by bacteria over the next few months. Still others are heavier than water and sink to the bottom. Thus, approximately 15% of the original quantity remains as an insoluble **asphaltic residue**. In cold polar waters oil is slower to degrade and persists longer than in warmer waters; some may become incorporated in sea ice and be released for years afterward.

The amount of damage caused by oil pollution depends partly on the direction it is carried by the wind and currents. If slicks reach land, they will damage beaches and shorelines, recreational areas, and marine organisms. Oil may be driven over a portion of the continental shelf, a highly productive marine zone, and there it could poison clams, scallops, cod, flounder, haddock, and other important food species. Oil driven out to sea has fewer environmental consequences, because there is little life in the deep ocean.

Combustion Natural gas and oil, like coal, produce air pollutants when burned. Natural gas is much cleaner than oil and produces only carbon dioxide, small amounts of carbon monoxide, nitrogen oxides, and water. Both fuels are burned directly for home heating and in industry and electric power plants. Nitrogen oxide and sulfur oxide emissions from oil are about one-tenth the amount emitted from an equivalent amount of coal. Oil-fired power plants also produce lesser amounts of hydrocarbons, carbon monoxide, and particulates (airborne solid particles).

Oil is refined into fuels such as jet fuel, diesel, kerosene, and gasoline. These too produce a wide variety of air pollutants, whose effects are more widely discussed in Chapter 19.

Projected Energy Needs

The energy question that most plagues us is whether there will be enough energy in the coming years to meet our needs. The answer is not easy, because it is difficult to project future demands and equally difficult to determine accurately how much oil and other fossil fuels remain. Forecasts of future energy demand are frequently wrong; for example, in early 1970s many "experts" asserted that energy consumption in the United States in 1980 would be between 95 and 110 quads. In truth, 1980 consumption was 75.9 quads. What is more, in 1982 energy consumption actually fell to 70.9 quads.

Why were the forecasters so far off? The answer is that in 1970 they could not predict the 1973 and 1979 oil embargoes. Nor could anyone predict the period of high inflation in the late 1970s and the drastic slowdown of the American economy from 1980 to 1982, which caused energy consumption in all sectors to plummet. If this experience teaches us anything, it is to beware of forecasts.

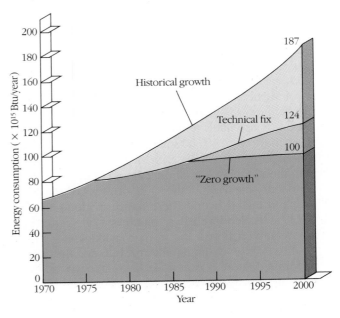

Figure 13-15
Three projections of future energy demands in the United States.

U.S. Energy Demands

As shown in Figure 13-15, U.S. energy consumption may take entirely different routes, depending on future economic conditions, governmental policies, labor costs, pricing, conservation, and other factors. The top line of this graph shows how energy demand would grow if the 1975 rates of growth continued. By 2000 energy consumption would be 187 quads. The middle line shows the projected energy consumption with a "technical fix"—that is, a concerted national effort to conserve energy in homes, industries, and transportation. By 2000 total energy consumption would be 124 quads. The third line is called a zero growth projection, with energy consumption in 2000 of 100 quads, 46% lower than the exponential growth rate.

Interestingly, energy consumption in the years 1975 to 1983 fell *below* the lowest projection. But will energy consumption continue to fall, level off, or increase? Barring economic catastrophe, energy demands are likely to begin to rise again over the next 20 years. Thus, total energy consumption by the year 2000 may be around 85 to 100 quads, but if strict conservation and energy efficiency are dramatically increased, energy usage in 2000 could be lower than current levels. Unfortunately, no one knows for certain.

U.S. Energy Supplies

What energy sources will meet future demands? Table 13-1 indicates that coal, oil, nuclear power, and natural gas will be the major energy resources in the United States. Oil is expected to be the largest fuel source, whereas solar and other renewable resources are expected to play minor roles. However, continually rising energy prices and concentrated efforts to develop solar and other renewable resources could alter this picture, as discussed in Chapter 15.

Will supplies meet demands in 2000? The answer is not easy, for energy supplies depend on a number of variables, including (1) the amount of oil, coal, natural gas, and uranium in the United States and abroad; (2) how actively new supplies are sought; (3) the price of energy; (4) how much is available from foreign suppliers; and (5) what alternative energy sources will be in production and how much energy they will yield.

If the demand in 2000 reached 109 to 143 quads, domestic supplies of oil and natural gas would probably not be adequate. Americans would have to conserve more energy, switch to other sources, increase their dependence on foreign imports, or a combination of all three. The long-

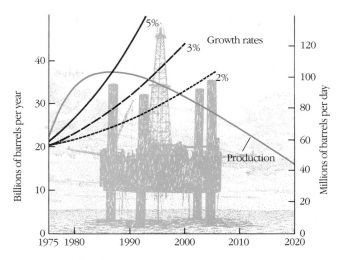

Figure 13-16
Curve of expected world oil production and oil demand at three growth rates.

term forecasts suggest that world oil production will begin to decline in the late 1980s or early 1990s, so world oil reserves will probably not be useful in meeting U.S. demand in 2000 (Figure 13-16). Moreover, most Americans agree that increasing dependence would be dangerous. See See Viewpoint, "Coping with the Next Oil Cutoff" in this chapter.

Between 1977 and 1983 U.S. imports of oil dropped from 18 quads to approximately 6.7 quads. This decrease combined with declines in domestic production will put the country in a bind: domestic oil and natural gas supplies will not meet U.S. needs in the year 2000, nor will foreign supplies. As a result, new energy resources are essential. These are the subject of the next two chapters.

Other technological solutions may also arise. The most notable of these is conservation. Energy saved in the home, in transportation, and in business represents an enormous cost-efficient resource that is only just beginning to be tapped. To illustrate the economic value of conservation, let us compare capital costs of energy from coal, nuclear power, and conservation. The production of 1 quadrillion Btus of energy from a coal-fired power plant requires about $45 billion in capital investment; this is money needed to open and operate mines and to build transportation networks and power plants. To generate 1 quad of energy with nuclear power, the capital investment is $90 billion. In contrast, 1 quad of energy produced by conservation costs only about $4 billion to $10 billion,

Table 13-1 Some Projections of the Role of Various U.S. Energy Resources in 2000[1]	
Type	**Energy Contribution (Quads)**
Hydroelectric	3.6–3.8
Geothermal	1.2–3.0
Solar/biomass	1.7–3.9
Nuclear	23.0–35.2
Domestic oil	12.7–23.5
Imported oil	14.9–32.2
Shale oil	0.2– 4.2
Domestic gas	11.5–20.1
Imported gas	1.3–5.0
Coal	19.0–43.8
Total Energy Demand	109–143[2]

[1]See Chapter 15 for different projections based on a solar-powered future.
[2]These estimates may be considerably higher than energy consumption in 2000. Some current estimates project consumption at around 65 quads, considerably lower than usage today. The columns don't add up because the values given are ranges.

Coping with the Next Oil Cutoff

James T. Bruce

The author is minority counsel of the U.S. Senate Committee on Energy and Natural Resources.

A decade after the question was first posed, there is still remarkably little consensus on an answer: what course of action or policies should the U.S. government pursue if a major portion of the world's oil supply is again cut off? The world has a dangerous vulnerability to an oil supply disruption, and this threat is likely to persist for decades. More than half of the world's estimated proved reserves of crude oil lie in countries bordering the politically unstable Persian Gulf.

Nearly all observers agree that extensive government regulation in the market is a hazardous policy, as illustrated in the last two oil cutoffs in 1973 and 1979. The dynamics of the market are too complicated for governmental regulations to anticipate or control precisely. But everyone, including free-market advocates, agrees that there will be intense political pressure from the public for heavy government involvement, especially if the crisis becomes a matter of life or death—in the figurative sense for businesses and in the literal sense for the poor. I believe that, as in any other crisis involving public health and welfare, selected government intervention to mitigate or prevent tragedy is a governmental obligation.

The chief federal program designed to cope with an oil shortage is the Strategic Petroleum Reserve (SPR). The SPR stored over 375 million barrels in salt caverns in Louisiana and Texas at the end of 1983. If there is any unanimity of opinion on emergency preparedness it is on the need for a large SPR, but there is debate over when and to whom this oil ought to be sold.

There are several reasons why government intervention in the market in a severe oil shortage will be unavoidable. First, even if the federal government refuses to address the crisis, the state and local governments are certain to intervene, probably creating a web of conflicting laws that could make the situation worse. As of April 15, 1982, 41 states had provided their governors with statutory powers to intervene in an energy supply emergency. In the same year, however, President Ronald Reagan pointed out that the courts would strike down any local laws regarding petroleum regulation that were unconstitutional.

Second, the United States is a signatory to the International Energy Agreement (IEA), in which it pledges to share its oil with 20 other nations in the free world and achieve a specified amount of reduction in U.S. consumption of oil in a severe energy supply disruption. A test exercise in the summer of 1983 simulated what would happen if Persian Gulf oil shipments were halted. In this test the Reagan administration attempted to fulfill its IEA obligations by sharing oil with its allies and reducing U.S. consumption of oil by relying exclusively on voluntary cooperation between oil companies and high oil prices to curb petroleum demand. The result was a failure. Consequently, not only do U.S. allies now question the sincerity of the U.S. commitment to the IEA, but it appears doubtful whether the country can credibly affirm those commitments without intervening in the domestic market.

Third, Department of Energy Officials acknowledge that in a dire oil shortage some form of federal aid for the poor is probably inevitable. Unless this financial assistance is planned in advance of the shortage, it may come too late, encouraging Congress to respond with price controls.

Fourth, the oil market in a severe oil crisis is not a "free market," even in the absence of government controls. When oil companies don't have sufficient product to meet their contractual obligations, they shun new customers and allocate what they have, offering each distributor (based on historical purchases) a pro rata share of what is available. This is a contractual if not a legal obligation. Thus, in a severe oil shortage, an allocation system run by the oil companies will be imposed across the country. Additionally, in a severe disruption prices may not rise to keep demand in balance with supply. There is ample evidence from past oil shortages that some large oil companies actually underpriced their products—particularly in frigid areas—probably for fear of provoking governmental reaction. The result is

> ### **Viewpoint**

that in a severe petroleum disruption the "free market" will involve a multitude of allocation systems and lag times in moving petroleum products to customers dependent on the oil suppliers hardest hit by the shortage. Amid the suspicions that inevitably arise in a severe energy supply disruption, the public may perceive little advantage in the "free market" that evolves early in the shortage as compared with a market subject to government control.

For the reasons cited above, a noninterventionist policy will probably be unworkable in the next major oil crisis. The real issue is whether the government will seek intervention in the market and contain the powerful political pressures that will arise or will instead adopt a laissez-faire approach that will be inevitably overwhelmed by these political forces and replaced by congressionally imposed federal regulatory programs, hastily fashioned in the heat of the crisis. The tragedy is this: without new legislation and new preparedness initiatives, the only option is the latter.

making conservation the best energy buy of the future. Some experts believe that the United States could probably cut energy consumption by 40% to 50% through conservation without sacrificing its high standard of living.

Other technologies may become economical by the year 2000. These include enhanced oil recovery, geothermal electric production, active solar heating, synthetic fuels (gas and oil) from coal, and new types of nuclear reactors. Others, such as solar cooling, solar voltaics, and electric automobiles, could also become economically feasible with further increases in energy prices.

Still, some insist that there is plenty of oil and natural gas left. They note that the estimated *world* reserve of fossil fuel energy is 160,000 quads, enough energy to get us through the 21st century. The noted geologist Vincent E. McKelvey calculated how long these resources would last at varying rates of consumption. If we assume that these fossil fuel reserves are our only energy resource, they will last 645 years if the world continues to use them at the present rate. But if there is a modest growth rate in energy use of 2%, they will last only 133 years. At a 5% growth rate they will last only about 70 years. Even though this exercise is a bit artificial, it points out how increasing energy use would accelerate oil depletion. It suggests that we should not be carried away with optimism because the world fossil fuel supply seems so large. Nor should we be paralyzed with pessimism. Instead, we must work together to bridge the gap between the present and the future by developing energy alternatives.

This section began with the question of whether there will be enough energy in the coming years. On the one hand, most projections indicate that there won't be enough natural gas or oil to meet all U.S. energy needs from conventional sources by the year 2000. Production levels will not keep pace with demands (see Chapter Supplement 13-1). Uranium supplies may also be inadequate. On the other hand, domestic coal supplies are eight times greater than those of oil and natural gas. So coal will undoubtedly usher the United States into the 21st century.

Our Energy Future: Guidelines for Wise Decisions

The next two chapters examine energy options to find a suitable strategy for a sustainable future. Before going on to them, let us look at some guidelines for developing our energy future.

Matching Energy Use with Energy Quality

Energy comes in a variety of forms, each with different qualities, or different amounts of available work (Table 13-2). Oil and coal are highly concentrated and are said to be high-quality energy resources. Sunlight is said to be a low-quality energy form. Judicious energy use dictates that whenever possible, low-quality energy be used for tasks that require it. Heating a home with electricity, for example, is highly inefficient. Solar heat is a more efficient

Table 13-2 Energy Quality of Different Forms of Energy

Form of Energy	Energy Quality	
	Relative Value	Average Energy Content (Kilocalories per Kilogram)
Electricity	Very high	—
Very high-temperature heat (greater than 2500°C)	Very high	—
Nuclear fission (uranium)	Very high	139,000,000[1]
Nuclear fusion (deuterium)	Very high	24,000,000[2]
Concentrated sunlight	Very high	—
Concentrated wind (high-velocity flow)	Very high	—
High-temperature heat (1000°C–2500°C)	High	—
Hydrogen gas (as a fuel)	High	30,000
Natural gas (mostly methane)	High	13,000
Synthetic natural gas made from coal	High	13,000
Gasoline (refined crude oil)	High	10,500
Crude oil	High	10,300
Liquefied natural gas	High	10,300
Coal (bituminous and anthracite)	High	7,000
Synthetic oil (made from coal)	High	8,900
Sunlight (normal)	High	—
Concentrated geothermal	Moderate	—
Water (high-velocity flow)	Moderate	—
Moderate-temperature heat (100°C–1000°C)	Moderate	—
Manure	Moderate	4,000
Wood and crop wastes	Moderate	3,300
Assorted garbage and trash	Moderate	2,900
Oil shale	Moderate	1,100
Tar sands	Moderate	1,100
Peat	Moderate	950
Dispersed geothermal	Low	—
Low-temperature heat (air temperature of 100°C or lower)	Low	—

[1]Per kilogram of uranium metal containing 0.72% fissionable uranium-235.
[2]Per kilogram of hydrogen containing 0.015% deuterium.
Source: Miller, G.T., *Living in the Environment,* Belmont, CA.: Wadsworth, (1982).

way of heating homes and water, for it closely matches the required energy quality. Electricity is best used in electric motors, lighting, and electronic equipment.

It is important to note that low-quality energy can be converted to a higher-quality form by concentration. For example, solar collectors can concentrate the light of the sun and increase the temperature, much as a magnifying lens concentrates sunlight. Concentrating diffuse energy is an economically sound way of getting energy, because the fuel is free, and our only cost is for the concentrating devices. We can also convert highly concentrated forms of energy into low-quality energy: electric stoves do it every day. But why degrade energy unnecessarily?

Minimizing Energy Transportation

The second principle of wise energy use is to minimize energy transportation. Transporting energy in any form requires energy and money, and the longer the distance, the more it takes. Energy sources close to the end user make sense from an economic standpoint.

Converting Energy Efficiently

The third rule is to convert energy into work as efficiently as possible. **Conversion efficiency** is often called **first law energy efficiency**. (See Chapter 4 for a discussion of the laws of thermodynamics.) The first law of thermodynamics states that energy is neither created nor destroyed, merely transformed from one form to another. Thus, when natural gas is burned, it is converted into light and heat energy that dissipate into the environment. To measure the conversion efficiency, simply divide the total amount of work (useful energy) obtained by the total energy input and multiply by 100 to convert it into a percentage. For example, suppose we burned 10 Btus of natural gas to make a motor work and got 2 Btus of actual work out of this fuel. The conversion, or first law, efficiency is 20%. As a practical example, conventional incandescent lightbulbs have a conversion efficiency of about 5%; thus, only 5% of the electricity it takes to run the bulb is converted into light, and the rest is converted into heat. Fluorescent bulbs, in contrast, are about 22% efficient.

First law energy efficiencies can be determined for all of our machines. By increasing machine efficiency, we can cut energy use and reduce environmental impacts.

The second law of thermodynamics tells us that when energy is converted, it is degraded; a certain amount of loss is inevitable. First law efficiency calculations do not take this into account. To determine energy efficiency taking into account the unavoidable loss, we can make a **second law efficiency calculation**. To do this, divide the minimum amount of work or useful energy needed to perform a task the most efficiently by the actual amount used. This is a more precise measurement, showing how wasteful energy systems are. If we knew, for example, that a certain task could be performed with 10 units of useful energy but that it takes 20, then our system is only 50% efficient, and we could theoretically cut energy losses by half, improving second law energy efficiency to about 100%.

Assuring Positive Net Energy Production

The fourth guideline is that the energy output from a system must not be exceeded by the energy input. Although it is self-evident, this simple principle is often overlooked.

The energy output of an energy fuel cycle is the **net useful energy production**. For example, the coal fuel cycle involves many steps, each of which requires energy. The net useful energy production from the fuel cycle, then, is the amount of electrical energy minus the total energy investment.

Net energy production may be either positive, meaning that we get more energy out of the system than we put in, or negative, meaning that we put in more energy than we get out.

The fourth rule, restated, says that the net energy balance must be positive and that the greater the net energy production, the better the option. Some examples of high net useful energy production are conservation, passive solar heating, solar hot-water heating, active solar space heating, wind, hydroelectric systems, and conventional geothermal resources. Lower net useful energy production occurs in coal gasification and liquefaction, nuclear power, extraction of oil from shale, ocean thermal energy conversion, and large centralized solar electrical generation facilities.

Few people would disagree with the four principles outlined above. For other suggestions, there is less consensus. First, energy systems should produce a minimal amount of pollution and should have minimal environmental impact. Second, society must be willing to accept the risk a system poses. Third, the energy resource must be abundantly available. Fourth, energy resources should be renewable.

Our energy future is the subject of great debate. The debate is often polarized between those who propose to concentrate on the present system and those preferring a renewable, energy-conservation strategy.

The **hard path**, a term popularized by Amory Lovins, describes the large, centralized energy plants like those in operation today. Hard-path advocates would rely on oil and natural gas for now and on coal and synthetic fuels produced from coal and oil in the future. Nuclear power in the form of fission reactors and fusion reactors would also play a major role. Extensive distribution systems would be necessary, and environmental impacts from the fuel cycle would be considerable.

The **soft path** describes a strategy based on conservation and renewable energy resources, especially the sun, biomass, and wind. These choices have the advantage of being relatively pollution free and decentralized, which reduces transportation, creates more jobs, and reduces the risk of large-scale breakdowns or hostile actions such as wars or terrorism.

The soft path includes better matching of energy quality with end-use needs and a phase-out of nuclear power. Oil, natural gas, and coal would play smaller and smaller parts in the energy future, acting as transitional fuels. (See the Point/Counterpoint in Chapter 14 for the opposing views on hard and soft paths.)

To create an energy system that is economically and environmentally sound now and in the future is an enormously complicated task, made more difficult by current controversies. As a society, the United States should abandon old allegiances and make its decisions based on what is economically viable in the long term, environmentally benign, and socially acceptable. The goal is to design an energy system that makes sense given the world's limited resources and the need for a clean environment and biological diversity.

The trouble with our times is that the future is not what it used to be.

PAUL VALERY

Summary

The history of energy use has been one of shifting dependency, a trend likely to continue in the future as conventional energy resources run out. Today, the United States depends primarily on oil, natural gas, and coal. Residential and commercial users consume the largest share of energy in this country, followed closely by industry and transportation. The United States is the leading energy consumer in the world. With only 6% of the population, it uses about 30% of the world's energy. Much of it is wasted.

Energy does not come cheap. In addition to the economic costs, society pays a price in the form of health and environmental destruction, effects that differ with each energy source.

Coal mining takes place in surface or underground mines. Surface mines in hilly or mountainous terrain are called *contour strip mines*. Rock and dirt overlying the coal are removed to expose the coal seam. In flat or gently rolling terrain *area strip mines* are common. Coal is removed in parallel strips. All surface mines destroy vegetation and wildlife habitat and increase soil erosion. Area strip mines can disrupt and pollute aquifers. Underground mines can collapse during and after mining, causing the death of workers and subsidence. Inhalation of dust in mines leads to *black lung disease,* or *pneumoconiosis. Acid mine drainage* forms when water and air come in contact with sulfide minerals in coal mines, especially underground mines. Sulfuric acid is formed and can leak from the mine, leaching toxic metals from rocks and soils and poisoning aquatic ecosystems. Acids may also contaminate drinking water and corrode steel bridges and barges.

Combustion of coal is also a major source of air pollution, including sulfur oxides and nitrogen oxides, which are converted in the atmosphere into sulfuric and nitric acids, respectively. Combustion also produces much solid waste, including sludge, fly ash, and bottom ash. An expansion of coal production will greatly increase the production of such wastes, which are disposed of in landfills, potentially becoming a source of groundwater pollution.

Coal development results in marked demographic changes in sparsely populated regions. Towns spring up overnight, increasing the need for sewage plants, water lines, hospitals, schools, and other services, called the *infrastructure*. Crime and drug and alcohol abuse may rise in such towns.

Oil and gas deposits are found both on shore and offshore. Extraction of these resources on shore may result in widespread subsidence. Brine from wells may contaminate aquifers. Today, about half the oil contaminating the ocean comes from natural seepage from offshore deposits: 20% comes from oil well blowouts, pipeline breaks, and tanker spills: the rest is from oil disposed of inland and carried to the ocean in rivers.

Damage caused by the accidental release of oil in fresh- and saltwater ecosystems can be immense. After a major spill, sea life may take years to recover. In an oil spill about one-fourth of the crude oil is volatile and evaporates within three months; much of the rest floats on the surface and is slowly degraded by bacteria. However, about 15% of the spill is insoluble and sinks to the bottom as an *asphaltic residue*. The amount of damage from a spill depends on how close it is to shore and the direction of wind and currents.

The combustion of oil and gas is generally much cleaner than that of coal. Fewer wastes are produced.

One of the most perplexing problems facing society is whether there will be enough energy in the future. To answer this question first requires a look at future energy demands, on which there is little agreement. Forecasts of energy demand for the United States in the year 2000 vary from 100 to 187 quadrillion Btus. If annual demand reaches 100 quads, supplies of domestic oil and natural gas will probably not be adequate, forcing the country to conserve, switch to other sources, increase its dependence on foreign supplies, or a combination of the three. Because world production is expected to decline in the early 1990s and because increased foreign dependence is unpopular for many reasons, it is likely that the United States will be forced to conserve more and develop alternative sources. Although not sufficient by itself, conservation is one of the most cost-effective options. Tremendous gains in energy supply can be achieved by simply designing machines and other energy-consuming devices more efficiently.

To develop a sensible energy future requires society to consider some basic guidelines. Suggestions include matching energy quality with end use, minimizing transportation, improving the efficiency of conversion, using sources with high social acceptance and minimal environmental damage, and developing sources that are abundant and, preferably, renewable. These guidelines can help us achieve a sustainable energy system that minimally disrupts the environment.

Discussion Questions

1. What is energy? Describe the first and second laws of thermodynamics and the implications they have on your life.

2. Describe the pattern of shifting energy dependency in the United States. What are the country's major energy fuels today?

3. Describe energy use by end use (consumer) in the United States.

4. Debate the statement "Increasing energy use in society increases the standard of living."

5. Describe the theory of supply and demand. Define supply and demand elasticity. What factors affect supply and demand? How does the second law of thermodynamics affect the supply of energy fuels?

6. Define the term *energy fuel cycle,* or *energy system.* Why is it important to consider the complete energy system when making an environmental impact assessment?

7. Describe the coal system. How is coal mined? How is it transported? How and where is it burned? What wastes are produced, and why? Describe the major impacts of coal production and consumption.

8. Debate the statement "Coal is our energy savior. We must rely very heavily on coal to achieve a stable future."

9. What demographic changes are brought about by the coal fuel cycle? What is the infrastructure and how is it affected?

10. Where does the oil that contaminates the ocean come from? How many oil spills occur each year? Where are the hardest hit areas?

11. Describe ways to reduce the incidence of oil spills from tankers.

12. Briefly summarize the effects of oil spills. What happens to oil spilled in the ocean?

13. You are studying future energy demands for your state. List and discuss the factors that affect how much energy you will be using in the year 2000.

14. Describe the energy demand projections discussed in this chapter. If these hold true, will there be enough coal, oil, and natural gas to meet demands?

15. Why can we consider conservation a *source* of energy? Why is conservation the best energy buy?

Suggested Readings

Atwood, G. (1975). The Strip-Mining of Western Coal. *Scientific American* 233(6): 23–29. Good background paper.

Branson, B. A. (1976). Ecological Impact of Strip Mining. In *The Ecology of Man: An Ecosystem Approach,* R. L. Smith, Ed. New York: Harper & Row. Good overview.

Chalekode, P.K., and Blackwood, T.R. (1978). *Source Assessment: Coal Refuse Piles, Abandoned Mines and Outcrops. State of the Art.* (EPA Report 600/2-78-004v). Washington, D.C.: Environmental Protection Agency. Excellent study.

Council on Environmental Quality. (1980). *The Global 2000 Report to the President.* New York: Penguin. Superb analysis of energy demands and supply.

Council on Environmental Quality. (1981). *Environmental Trends.* Washington, D.C.: U.S. Government Printing Office. Well-illustrated resource on energy and other environmental issues.

Dorf, R. C. (1981). *The Energy Factbook.* New York: McGraw-Hill. Excellent source of facts on energy.

——(1982). *The Energy Answer: 1982–2000.* Andover, Mass.: Brick House. Concise and readable.

Gilbert, B., and Kaufman, E. (1978). The Second Reign of Old King Coal. *Audubon* 80(6): 51–74. Superb review.

Glass, N. R. (1978). *Environmental Effects of Increased Coal Utilization: Ecological Effects of Gaseous Emissions from Coal Combustion* (EPA Report 600/7-78-108). Washington, D.C.: Environmental Protection Agency. Good background report.

Hayes, E. T. (1979). Energy Resources Available to the United States, 1985 to 2000. *Science* 203(4377): 233–239. Detailed review.

Letterman, R. D., and Mitsch, W. J. (1978). Impact of Mine Drainage on a Mountain Stream in Pennsylvania. *Environmental Pollution* 17: 53–73. An excellent case study of acid drainage.

Minear, R. A., and Tschantz, B. A. (1976). The Effect of Coal Surface Mining on the Water Quality of Mountain Drainage Basin Streams. *Journal of the Water Pollution Control Federation* 48(11): 2549–2569. Excellent study of watershed disturbance.

Ridgeway, J. (1982). *Powering Civilization.* New York: Pantheon. A collection of essays on energy.

The Global Outlook for Oil, Natural Gas, and Coal

The energy problem, like many other environmental issues, is international in scale because of the interdependence of energy producers and consumers. The global economy, firmly based on international trade, is nourished by energy; as energy supply and demand go, so goes the economy. This look at the global picture will focus on energy consumption and energy supplies.

Global Energy Consumption

Since 1860 growth in the use of energy has increased worldwide at a rate of 5% per year, except for a brief respite in the Great Depression years 1930–1935 and in the recent worldwide economic recession that began in 1980. In 1970 global consumption was 202 quads, but by 1980 it had grown to 250 quads. Assuming a growth rate in energy use of 4% to 5% a year, world energy consumption could be 550 to 600 quads by 2000, over twice what it was in 1980.

Projections of global energy demand are subject to change, depending on population growth, economic conditions, conservation, and many other factors. Regardless, projections give us a rough idea of the future need and allow us to determine whether supplies will meet demands.

World Energy Resources

World energy resources are also difficult to determine, and experts often disagree on how much fossil-fuel and nuclear energy are available. Before we examine their estimates, let's first look at some resource terminology.

Two key terms are used to describe energy resources—*reserves* and *resources*. Both of these refer to the amount of energy resources in the earth. They differ, though, in the degree of economic feasibility and geological surety. **Reserves** are deposits of energy fuels that are economically and geologically feasible to remove with current and foreseeable technology. There are three types of reserves: (1) **measured reserves**, whose quality, quantity, and location are known from geological studies; (2) **indicated reserves**, which are thought to exist based on a limited geological sampling; and (3) **inferred reserves**, which are thought to exist based on general knowledge of geological field studies.

Resources refer to the total quantity of an energy fuel or mineral. Resources include a wide range of deposits, from those that are identified and quantified to those that are as yet undiscovered. Obviously, our total energy resources are quite large, but when the cost of recovery is taken into account, there comes a point when resources will be left where they are: extraction would be technologically and economically out of the question. For example, thin strips of coal 2000 meters (6700 feet) below the surface of the ground are part of our total resources but will never be recovered because of the expense involved.

A word of caution at this point: Estimates of our reserves do not have the exactitude we might like; some may err by plus or minus 10% to 25%. The assessment of resources is even more imprecise; it is more speculative and is often based on incomplete data. According to Vincent E. McKelvey, former head of the U.S. Geological Survey, "Even the most conscientious estimate may be grossly in error."

Our discussion of reserves and resources should teach us an important lesson: beware of estimates of resources. Total resources should not be used to make projections of how long energy supplies will last. Such estimates grossly exaggerate energy availability (Table S13-1).

Petroleum

There are numerous estimates of global petroleum reserves. Many authorities use a figure called the ultimate production of

Table S13-1 Estimates of World Resources of Fossil Fuels

Fuel	Total Resources	Known Recoverable (Measured) Reserves
Coal (billion tons)	12,682	786
Petroleum (billion barrels)	2,000	556
Natural gas (trillion cubic feet)	12,000	2100
Shale oil (billion barrels)	2,000	?
Uranium ore (thousand tons)	4,000	1085

Source: Global 2000.

crude oil, the amount that may be produced from existing resources. Most experts agree that when the last drop of oil is burned we will have produced about 2000 billion barrels of oil. To date, approximately 460 billion barrels have been produced, leaving us with 1540 billion barrels of remaining resources. Of this, 550 billion barrels are proven (measured) reserves and, so, about 1000 billion barrels are yet to be discovered.

If production continues at the current rate of about 21 billion barrels per year, the proven reserves will last 20 years. The undiscovered resources will last an additional 48 years. But more rapid growth in consumption could cut the lifespan of oil considerably.

Petroleum production in the United States and world production are both expected to follow a bell-shaped curve. (Figure S13-1). This curve shows that production of oil will begin to decline after a peak. As proven reserves are tapped, it will become harder and harder to find new oil. Companies will search in remote areas to discover and extract it, and production will decline despite intensified efforts.

Figure S13-1(a) estimates the ultimate oil production in the United States to be about 200 billion barrels. By 1975 half of that oil had been extracted and consumed, and the United States has since begun a long downward trend in production. In 1982, for instance, the country produced about 10 million barrels of oil per day, down from 11 million barrels per day in 1973. But in 1973 only 9900 exploratory wells were drilled, whereas in 1982 over 40,000 wells were drilled. Production is likely to fall further despite increased efforts.

Globally, oil production is expected to peak in the early 1990s. If this is true, production will fall over the next 50 years, and oil will be essentially exhausted by the year 2075 (Figure S13-1(b)).

What does all this mean to us? Basically, it means that conventional oil supplies will be exhausted during our lifetime and that within the next decade new sources (oil shale and coal liquefaction) must be developed if consumption of oil is to remain at current rates or increase. Conservation could help stall the day of reckoning, providing us more time to plan and develop alternative strategies.

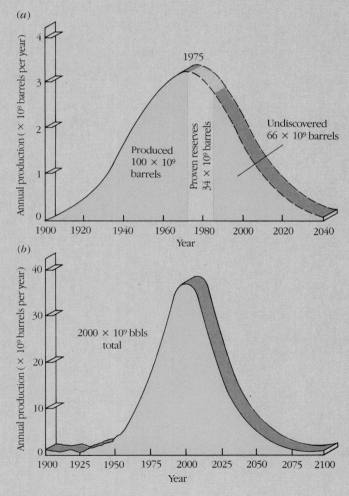

Figure S13-1
Petroleum production curves for the United States (*a*) and the world (*b*).

Some authorities suggest that because many areas of the world have not yet been explored extensively, the ultimate oil production might be considerably higher than 2000 billion barrels. If this is true, there may be more time to make the energy transition. But others argue that we would be wiser and better off in the long run to make the switch to renewable energy resources now.

Natural Gas

No consensus has developed regarding natural gas resources. The energy analyst M. King Hubbert has estimated ultimate natural gas production at about 10,000 trillion cubic feet (tcf). Others' estimates range from 5000 to 12,000 tcf. Taking the 10,000 tcf figure, let's examine our prospects. About 1900 tcf of natural gas has been produced and consumed, leaving about 8100 tcf. Of this, 2100 tcf is reserves and 6000 tcf is yet to be found.

How long will the global supply of natural gas last? At the current rate of usage of approximately 50 tcf per year, world reserves will last about 40 years. The 6000 tcf yet to be discovered will last an additonal 120 years, but increased consumption would cut the lifespan of natural gas considerably, perhaps by as much as half. As with oil, the lack of exploration in many continents may have led to a gross underestimation of natural gas reserves. If this is true, global production may last a bit longer than anticipated.

In the United States the total known reserves of natural gas are about 210 tcf, which will last about 40 more years. Production peaked in 1973 at 21.7 tcf; by 1982, it had fallen to 17.7 tcf. This drop in production occurred despite an increase in drilling from 6400 wells in 1973 to 19,000 wells in 1982. As production continues to drop, we will experience a rapid rise in prices and begin to turn to synthetic natural gas from coal or other energy resources (Chapters 14 and 15).

Coal

Coal is the most abundant nonrenewable fossil fuel remaining. World reserves are estimated to be 786 billion tons, and total resources are estimated at 12,682 billion tons. Of the total resources, half is believed to be recoverable. However, some energy analysts are skeptical of the latter figure, thinking that it exaggerates the reserves by five or six times.

By any measure, coal is still an abundant resource. At the 1976 consumption rate of 3.7 billion tons per year, global reserves will last 212 years. The recoverable resources (6300 billion tons) would last 1700 years. However, growth rates of 4% to 5% would greatly reduce the lifespan of coal. Nevertheless, coal will probably play a large part in the next two or three decades as we shift to other energy resources. We have the technology to burn coal, though not without considerable production of waste. Coal can be used to make liquid fuels to power our transportation systems, and can be converted into a synthetic natural gas for home heating.

The United States has about 30% of the world's coal reserves, or about 225 billion metric tons that can be recovered. This could last the country 100 to 200 years even at increased rates of consumption. The total coal resources in the United States are almost 3600 billion metric tons; even if only 10% were recoverable, the country would have another 360 billion metric tons.

Do we want a coal-powered future? Can we burn coal cleanly enough to prevent widespread ecosystem damage? Or will we simply accept the air pollution and solid wastes from coal use and ignore other technologies because using coal is easier for us now?

14

Future Energy: Nonrenewable Resources

I cannot say whether things will get better if we change; what I can say is they must change if they are to get better.

G. C. LICHTENBERG

Most of you will live to see the end of conventional oil and gas, and a drastic shift in our energy resource dependence. But what sources should we turn to? Which ones will be economical, socially and politically acceptable, and ecologically wise? To answer these questions requires an objective look at all possible sources.

This chapter discusses several sources that are nonrenewable—that is, ones we can exploit only once, and for a limited time, although in the case of nuclear fusion that time may be very long.

These energy sources may be useful because they can buy us time while a truly permanent energy system is emplaced. The first two to be disscussed, nuclear fission and fusion, are well suited for electrical generation and would save fossil fuel sources for their best uses, transportation and chemical production. The various nonconventional fossil fuels covered in this chapter—oil shale, tar sands, and gasified coal—hold promise for providing liquid and gaseous fuels to keep the wheels of civilization turning after petroleum supplies run out.

329

Figure 14-1
(a) Fission raction, Uranium-235-struck by a neutron is split into two smaller nuclei. Neutrons and enormous amounts of energy are also released, *(b)* Chain reaction, brought on by placing fissile uranium-235 in a nuclear reactor. Neutrons liberated during the fission of one nucleus stimulate fission in neighboring nuclei.

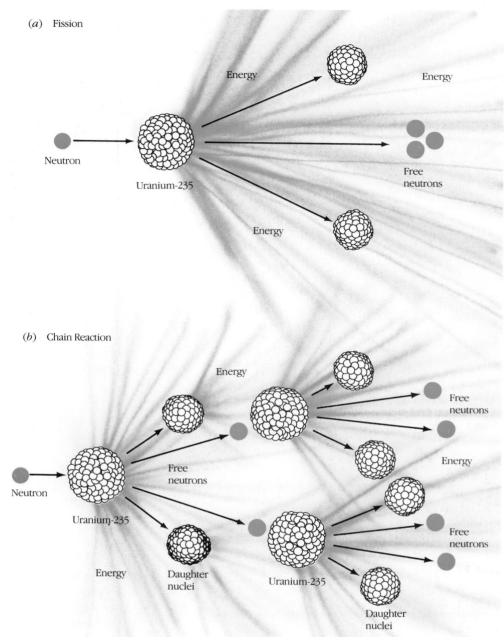

(a) Fission

(b) Chain Reaction

Nuclear Fission

The nuclear reactors in use today in the United States and most of the rest of the world are fueled by naturally occurring uranium-235. This is a form of uranium (an isotope) whose nuclei split, or fission, easily when they are struck by neutrons of the right energy. The fission of U-235 releases an enormous amount of heat energy (Figure 14-1a). In fact, one kilogram (2.2 pounds) of this material, completely fissioned, could yield as much energy as 2000 metric tons (2200 tons) of coal!

Fission reactors basically provide an environment in which uranium-235 can be bombarded with neutrons and the subsequent fission reactions carefully controlled. The energy released from the fission reactors heats water that bathes the **reactor core** where the uranium-containing

(a)

Figure 14-2
(*a*) A light water reactor at Diablo Canyon, California. (*b*) Cross-section of the light water fission reactor, showing reactor vessel and containment building seen as huge dome in (*a*). The nuclear fission reaction occurs in the reactor vessel. Heat produced here is carried away by water coolant and transferred by way of heat exchanger to the water in a steam-generating unit.

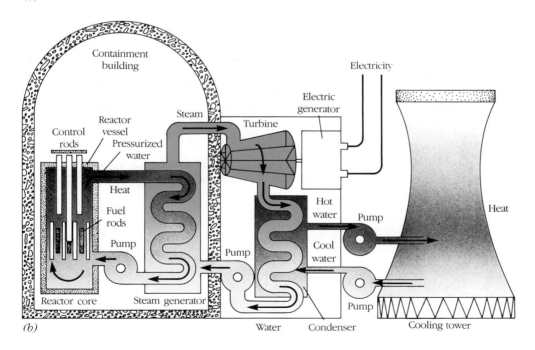

(b)

fuel rods are located (Figure 14-2). This heated water is converted to steam, which drives a turbine and generates electricity. Reactors cooled by water are called **light water reactors**. Other reactors use coolants such as liquid metal (sodium) but operate on the same principle.

The process of fission in a light water reactor is begun by neutrons naturally given off by uranium-235 in the fuel rods. When one of these neutrons strikes another U-235 nucleus, it may cause it to undergo fission, producing two smaller nuclei, **daughter nuclei**, and heat. Each fissioned

U-235 nucleus releases an average of 2.4 neutrons, which strike other nuclei and thus initiate a **chain reaction** (Figure 14-1b). The reaction is carefully controlled, not only to regulate heat production but also to prevent it from getting out of control. Runaway chain reactions could produce enough heat to melt the reactor core (**core meltdown**).

Fission is controlled by water flowing between the fuel rods. To shut down a fission reactor, the control rods are inserted between the fuel rods, and to bring it into operation the control rods are lifted out.

The entire assemblage of fuel and control rods is housed in a 20-centimeter-thick (8-inch) steel container called the **reactor vessel**. The reactor vessel is surrounded by a huge shield, and the entire unit is contained in a 1.2-meter-thick (4-foot) cement shell, the **reactor containment building**.

Production, Transportation, and Disposal of Nuclear Fuels

Nuclear fuels, like fossil fuels, pass through a complex cycle involving production, processing, shipping, storage, consumption, and disposal. At each stage of the cycle radioactive materials can escape, as a result of accidents or during normal operation, creating environmental and health hazards.

Uranium ore is mined mostly in surface mines. The ore is transported to a mill, where the uranium is extracted from the raw ore. Uranium at this stage contains .7% U-235, which is fissionable, and 97.3% U-238, which is not. The uranium is enriched to raise the concentration of U-235 from 3% to 4%. The refined fuel, in an oxide form called yellow cake, is then transported to a fuel processing plant to be packed in small pellets and loaded in fuel rods, which are delivered to reactors. The fuel in a nuclear reactor is slowly used up and must be replaced periodically. However, spent fuels contain highly radioactive materials created when U-235 undergoes fission. One of the most hazardous is plutonium-239 (Pu-239), which is formed by the capture of neutrons by U-238.

Low-level radioactive wastes from nuclear power plants (things like workers' clothes) are sealed in metal containers and discarded in landfills, but the highly radioactive wastes (high-level wastes) are now stored at the power plants, usually underwater in reactor vessels. Meanwhile, the federal government, states, scientists, and citizens are searching for the best ways to dispose of them. (See Chapter 22 for a discussion of radioactive waste disposal.)

High-level wastes must be stored for *tens of thousands or even hundreds of thousands of years,* because many of them remain dangerously radioactive this long. The common way of measuring the lifespan of a radioactive substance is by its **half-life**, the time it takes for half of the material to decay. The half-life of Pu-239 is 24,000 years; one kilogram of this compound is reduced by half after 24,000 years, and after 48,000 years a quarter of a kilogram remains. It takes about eight or nine half-lives for a material to be reduced to .1% of its original mass, which may be a safe level. For Pu-239, this is about 200,000 years!

The problem with long-lived radioactive wastes is how to store them safely for such long periods. What containers will not leak or corrode, and more importantly, what government could last that long to protect the wastes from accidental release?

High-level radioactive wastes could be reprocessed for reuse in nuclear reactors. Reprocessing involves the extraction of usable Pu-239 and U-235 from spent fuel. This would cut down on the amount of waste over the short term, but no commercial reprocessing facilities are in operation in the United States today, and even if they were, reprocessing would not eliminate the wastes altogether.

Nuclear Power: Pros and Cons

Perhaps the most convincing argument for using nuclear power as opposed to coal and oil is that it produces very little air pollution. Years of experience show that the release of radioactive materials into the atmosphere from nuclear power plants is insignificant under normal operating conditions. In fact, coal-fired power plants may emit more radioactivity from natural radionuclides in the coal than a nuclear plant.

Another advantage of nuclear power is that it requires less strip mining, because the fuel is a concentrated form of energy. The cost of transporting nuclear fuels is lower than that for an equivalent amount of coal.

Heavier use of nuclear power could reduce the amount of coal now burned to make electricity, so that the coal could be used to generate synthetic liquid and gaseous fuels, described later in this chapter. Nuclear power could also allow us to stretch the oil and gas supply.

The major problems of nuclear power are disposal of wastes, contamination of the environment with long-lasting radioactive materials, thermal pollution, the health effects of low-level radiation (detailed in Chapter Supplement 21-2), limited supplies of uranium ore, low social acceptability, high construction costs, lack of support from insurance companies and the financial community, questionable reactor safety, human error that could contribute to accidents at reactors, unforeseen technical problems that could also lead to major accidents, lack of experience with the technology, vulnerability to sabotage, proliferation of nuclear weaponry from high-level reactor wastes, questions about what to do with a nuclear plant once its useful life of 30 to 40 years is up, and the loss of individual freedom as security is tightened to protect citizens from sabotage and the theft of nuclear materials.

Mill Tailings   One of the most notable sources of contamination are uranium mills, which produce an enormous amount of radioactive waste in the form of **mill tailings**. About 24,000 metric tons of mill tailings are produced each day in the United States (Figure 14-3).

Until the late 1970s tailings were indiscriminately dumped near mills and along rivers and were even used for home and building construction. In Durango, Colorado, for example, tailings were piled on the edge of town alongside the Animas River. In Grand Junction, Colorado, several hundred thousand tons of radioactive sand from a uranium mill was placed under the foundations of 4000 new homes. Residents of these homes are exposed to radiation equivalent to ten chest X-rays per week, and the leukemia rate in Grand Junction is two times higher than it is elsewhere in the state. Today, workers are digging the tailings out from under the homes.

Twenty-two million metric tons of mill tailings have been abandoned in the West, about half of these along the banks of the Colorado River and its tributaries. To date approximately 125 million metric tons of mill tailings have been produced in the United States; most of them were discarded on or near the mill sites. Many have been buried and covered with topsoil and revegetated.

Transportation   A truck carrying 18,000 kilograms (40,000 pounds) of yellow cake in steel drums went off the road in southern Colorado late one night in 1971. About 4500 kilograms of highly radioactive fuel spilled on the ground. In some places around the truck the powder was almost knee keep. The driver was trapped in the cab, and during the night about 60 people stopped to lend assistance, walking unaware through the highly radioactive fuel. Cleanup was delayed for a full 24 hours after the spill, because neither the state nor the corporation, which owned the fuel, wanted to accept the responsibility.

Trucks carrying radioactive wastes or fuels are involved in 35 accidents in the United States each year, although very few are as serious as this one. Such accidents raise questions of grave importance. For example, what if an accident occurs near a major metropolitan area or near a reservoir on a windy day? What would the eventual health effects be? To help prevent releases, the federal government now requires crash-resistant containers for transporting of nuclear materials.

Reactor Leaks   Industry experts for years asserted that nuclear power plants were too well engineered for a major accident. Numerous backup systems were believed capable of preventing any significant release of radiation. The accident at the Three Mile Island nuclear power plant near Harrisburg, Pennsylvania, in March 1979 changed this view dramatically.

Figure 14-3
Uranium tailings.

A malfunctioning valve in the cooling system triggered a series of events that led to the worst commercial reactor accident in U.S. history. When this valve closed, water flow to the reactor core was stopped. A secondary backup cooling system also failed to activate, causing water temperature and pressure in the reactor vessel to rise. The pressure was released by a relief valve that vented radioactive steam into the containment building. When the pressure had fallen, the valve was supposed to close, but it didn't. Next, pipes in the system burst, and more radioactively contaminated water was released into the building and subsequently into a storage tank in another building. The tank overfilled and spilled onto the floor, where it began to evaporate, sending radioactive materials into the air. Radiation monitors across the Susquehanna River from the plant recorded the levels. The radiation levels at the onset of the accident were five times the average monthly exposure!

The accident then took a turn for the worse; hydrogen gas began to build up inside the reactor vessel, threatening to expose the core and cause a meltdown. The gas bubble was slowly eliminated, but thousands of the area's residents had been evacuated.

This accident at Three Mile Island had many long-term effects. It cost millions of dollars for the utility (and its customers) to replace the electricity the plant would have generated. Even more money was needed to clean up the mess (over $1 billion). Utility officials and nuclear advocates applauded the manner in which the accident was handled and pointed to the success in preventing a major catastrophe as proof of the safety of nuclear reactors. As far as health is concerned, utility authorities said the accident might cause a few cancers, but not many. Many health experts, however, disagreed. They maintained that the low-level radiation exposure the residents received over a period of 100 hours or longer would cause at least 300, and possibly as many as 900, fatal cases of cancer or leukemia. (For more on the health effects of low-level radiation, see Chapter Supplement 21-2).

Disposal of Radioactive Materials   About 2.9 million cubic meters (97 million cubic feet) of low-level radioactive waste from reactors and other facilities (hospitals, laboratories) has been buried in metal or cement containers. Three-quarters was buried on federal land; the rest was buried at privately owned disposal sites (Figure 14-4). Improper disposal has been commonplace. Drums stored underground can rust and leak radioactive materials into groundwater and surface waters.

In the past, low- and medium-level radioactive wastes were sometimes mixed with concrete, poured into barrels, and dumped at sea. Thousands of barrels of waste were dumped in Massachusetts Bay near Boston, some in the harbor itself. Forty-eight kilometers (30 miles) off the coast of San Francisco, near the Farallon Islands, approximately 47,000 barrels of radioactive wastes were dumped. Another major nuclear dumping area was 350 kilometers (220 miles) southeast of New York City. Although this activity has been banned in U.S. waters since 1970, it still occurs in the Irish Sea, where England annually dumps radioactive wastes without even containing them in barrels.

One of the worst cases of radioactive leakage occurred near the city of Richland, Washington, at the Hanford Reservation, an "Atomic City" built during World War II to make plutonium for nuclear weapons. During its first 25 years of operation the plant turned out 270 million liters (70 million gallons) of highly radioactive liquid waste, which was placed in huge underground steel tanks. Gradually, though, the tanks deteriorated. Between 1958 and 1973 an estimated 2 million liters (537,000 gallons) of these wastes leaked out of 15 tanks and into the soil and, possibly, the groundwater. Approximately 150 million liters (40 million gallons) of waste are still in storage tanks that could leak.

Thermal Pollution   Nuclear reactors produce about 50% more hot water than conventional coal-fired power plants. Released into rivers, this water drastically alters plant and animal life far downstream. Fortunately, few reactors release hot water directly into natural water bodies today. For more on thermal pollution, see Chapter 20.

Social Acceptability and Cost   One of the most important factors controlling the future of nuclear energy is its lack of widespread social acceptability. The accident at Three Mile Island raised the public consciousness and may have sealed the fate of this economically troubled industry.

Cost plays a critical role in the future of nuclear power (see Model Application 14-1: Impact Analysis: Nuclear Power). The price of uranium increased from $6 a pound in 1973 to $50 in 1976. Currently, the construction of a new nuclear reactor costs $4 billion to $6 billion, compared with $500 to $1000 million for an equivalent coal-fired power plant. Costs are high because of strict building standards, expensive labor, and special materials needed to ensure that nuclear plants will operate safely. U.S. banks are reluctant to lend money for nuclear power plants;

Figure 14-4
Location of low-level radioactive waste dumps in the United States.

capital is short, and the risks are too high. Therefore, high-interest financing must come from other countries such as Saudi Arabia. Repair costs are high, too. Saltwater corrosion of the cooling system in a reactor owned by the Florida Power and Light Company, for example, cost over $100 million to repair (see Essay 14-1). While the reactor was shut down, the utility was forced to buy replacement electricity at a cost of $800,000 per day.

Reactor Safety Uncertainties regarding safety add to the growing list of problems. A 1975 study on reactor safety, called the Rasmussen Report for its principal author, Norman Rasmussen, indicated that the probability of a major accident at a nuclear power plant, such as a core meltdown, was not more than one in 10,000 reactor-years. Therefore, if there were 5000 reactors operating worldwide, as some advocates propose for the year 2050, we could expect a major core meltdown every other year! *Each accident* might cause between 825 and 13,000 immediate deaths, depending on the location of the plant. In addition, 7500 to 180,000 cancer deaths would follow in the years after the accident. Radiation sickness would afflict 122,000 to 198,000 people, and 5000 to 170,000 genetic defects would occur in newborn infants. Property damage could range from $2.8 billion to $28 billion. The Rasmussen study did not include such possibilities as sabotage or health risks involved in the nuclear fuel cycle. Furthermore, the report was heavily criticized after its release, and in 1979 it was repudiated by the Nuclear Regulatory Commission. Its conclusions were viewed as underestimates of the real risk.

Even if nuclear power can be made safer through technological improvements, the severity of the accidents that do happen make it unacceptable to many people. Fur-

>>> **Model Application 14-1**

Nuclear Power—A Risk Assessment

You are appointed head of an environmental study group. Your goal is to determine whether the Diablo Canyon Nuclear Power Plant in California should be licensed to begin operation. The plant was built by the Pacific Gas and Electric Company and to date has cost more than $4.4 billion. The site for the plant, 130 kilometers (80 miles) north of Santa Barbara, was chosen because it is unpopulated and was thought to be a safe distance from fault lines. In 1971, though, two scientists discovered a major fault line only 4 kilometers (2.5 miles) from the plant. The U.S. Geological Survey reported that the Hosgri Fault may have been the site of a 1927 earthquake that measured 7.3 on the Richter scale. It noted that another quake of similiar magnitude was possible.

Environmentalists argue that the plant should not be licensed for the following reasons:

- The demand for electrical power has not risen as anticipated, making the plant unnecessary.
- The pressure created by a major earthquake would destroy the facility, causing widespread environmental contamination.
- Overall structural stability of the plant is questionable. A number of errors in design and construction have been discovered, leading critics to wonder what other overlooked problems might arise if the plant began full operation.

The utility argues that:

- Its investment is too large to abandon the plant.
- The pressures created by a large earthquake would be far less than environmentalists and some geologists maintain and that the reactor could withstand a quake measuring 7.5 on the Richter scale without major structural damage.
- All errors in design have been corrected.

Questions

1. Using the Impact Analysis model, presented in Chapter 2, first describe the potential positive and negative impacts of a major accident. (Use a map to indicate areas that would be contaminated.)
2. Once you have completed your analysis, use Figure 2-8 to determine the probability of each effect.
3. After careful study, should the plant be scrapped? If so, what should be done with it? Also, what energy resources should be developed to replace the electrical energy?
4. Do the risks outweigh the benefits? How likely is an accident at a plant that is so close to a major fault line?

Note: You may want to read several articles presenting both sides of the argument to fully assess the risk the plant poses.

thermore, misjudgment and performance errors among nuclear plant personnel could negate the best technological safety systems. Human errors and oversight may occur during construction. Who is to ensure that all the welds are properly done? Will a potentially fatal mistake slip by human inspectors? Will inspectors take bribes to look the other way to expedite construction?

One of the most notable performance errors occurred at the Browns Ferry nuclear power plant in Alabama in 1975. Two workers were checking for air leaks in a room where the electrical cables that controlled the reactor were located. They were using a candle (human error 1) to detect leaks. However, the candle ignited the foam insulation that the men were installing (human error 2). They also failed to report the fire immediately (human error 3). The fire spread quickly and caused most of the reactor

control system to shut down or malfunction. Control rods had to be mechanically inserted to shut the reactor down and prevent a meltdown.

Concern for safety also centers on unforeseen technical difficulties. Problems can arise for which backup safety measures and human operators are unprepared. A prime example is the hydrogen bubble at the Three Mile Island plant. No one had anticipated such an occurrence; fortunately, though, workers were able to find ways to release the pressure before a catastrophe occurred.

Terrorism   The question of terrorism is important in a world in which such activities are rising. Nuclear power plants throughout the world are vulnerable to individual or group acts that might cause a shutdown or, at worst, a core meltdown. Two French reactors were bombed by

Figure 14-5
A nuclear explosion unleashes enormous destructive power. The bomb that destroyed Hiroshima killed a total of 130,000 people.

terrorists in 1975. In November 1972 three armed men hijacked a Southern Airlines jet and threatened to crash it into a nuclear reactor at the Oak Ridge National Laboratory in Tennessee, a government-supported research facility. Protection from ground and air assaults may be impossible to provide. Even though improved security measures have been implemented, the threat of well-planned terrorist actions cannot be ignored.

Proliferation of Nuclear Weapons At least 21 countries have the necessary materials and the technical competence to build nuclear bombs (Figure 14-5). Many of these countries are politically unstable or in politically volatile regions where war could easily erupt. Six countries—the United States, China, the Soviet Union, Britain, France, and India—have already test-fired nuclear weapons. The plutonium used in these bombs comes from special reactors designed to make it and from conventional nuclear reactors. The spread of nuclear power throughout the world will make fissionable materials more widely available.

Nuclear fuels could be stolen by terrorist groups. According to the energy analyst Denis Hayes, with careful planning an armed group could steal plutonium from any

number of nuclear facilities. "No wizardry is required to build an atom bomb that would fit comfortably in the trunk of an automobile," he notes. Planted near the Pentagon, the White House, or Congress, such a bomb could prove disastrous.

Erosion of Civil Liberties Robert Jungk, author of *The New Tyranny,* argues that new and tighter security will be needed to protect power plants, fuel-reprocessing facilities, and waste-storage sites. Ironically, citizens will be subjected to more and more surveillance as governments attempt to make nuclear power safer for them. The threat of terrorist actions may well create a greater impetus to infiltrate groups that oppose nuclear weapons and nuclear power. Citizens and workers in the nuclear field will be the subject of intense surveillance. Restrictions may be placed on activities within sensitive areas, and as more and more nuclear power plants are built, the net of restrictions will catch more and more of us.

Breeder Reactors

Supporters of nuclear power have proposed a new type of fission reactor, the breeder reactor. The **breeder reac-**

Hazards to Nuclear Workers

One of the critical problems facing electric utilities is how to repair highly radioactive areas in nuclear power plants without endangering the lives of workers. In some cases radiation levels are so high that workers in protective clothing and masks receive their annual allowable dose of radiation in 15 minutes. Because major repair jobs may take hundreds of hours of labor, nuclear power plants can use up their labor force very quickly.

To solve the problem, utilities hire transient workers for short-term jobs in high-radiation zones. Workers as young as 18 have been hired to provide cheap labor. When they have received their maximum allowable dose, they are replaced.

The impact of working in highly radioactive zones may be great. Many studies indicate that even low levels of radiation—much lower than the 3 rems (a unit of radiation described in Chapter Supplement 21-2) the transient workers are allowed to receive—may cause cancer and birth defects.

Take the case of Consolidated Edison's Indian Point I nuclear reactor near New York City. Several years ago, six hot-water pipes were in need of welding repair and insulation. What would have been a routine repair in a coal-fired power plant took eight weeks and 100 workers and cost $2 million. Welders could work only 15 minutes before receiving their maximum

allowable dose of radiation. Almost every skilled welder in the New York–Westchester County area was employed by the power plant. The same job in an uncontaminated site would have taken only a few welders and a week of time.

Some health experts argue that the standard for worker safety should be lowered to .5 rem, because evidence links chromosomal damage and cancer to radiation exposure of 2 rems per year. Transient and permanent workers exposed to 3 to 5 rems per year may someday regret the day they hired on at nuclear facilities.

---

tor is like the light water reactor, but besides producing electricity it makes fissionable material that can be used to fuel other reactors. This fissionable material is produced from uranium-238 or thorium-232, both abundant. Neutrons from the breeder reactor core strike the nonfissionable U-238 placed around the core and convert it into fissionable Pu-239 (Figure 14-6). Nonfissionable thorium-232 is converted into fissionable U-233. For every 100 atoms of Pu-239 consumed in the fuel rods of a breeder reactor, 130 atoms of Pu-239 are produced from U-238.

The conversion of nonfissile materials into fissionable fuel is the key advantage of breeder reactors. Breeder reactors could in theory convert 60% to 80% of the recoverable uranium resources into fissionable plutonium fuel. Breeder reactors could use uranium-238 wastes from the enrichment process or from light water reactors' spent fuel.

Uranium waste currently stockpiled in the United States contains the energy equivalent of all the electricity needed at current rates of consumption for about 100 years. A

breeder reactor could unleash much of this energy for use. Furthermore, the nation's remaining high-grade uranium ore could suffice for several hundred years if used in breeder reactors, according to some advocates of this technology.

Besides providing abundant electrical energy, breeder reactors could reduce the need for mining, processing, and milling uranium ore. Fuel prices might remain stable because of the abundance of uranium-238. Breeder reactors themselves also do not create much air pollution (if we ignore problems from mining and milling).

Breeder reactors have been under intensive development in the United States for over 30 years. Of the different types of breeder reactors, the **liquid metal fast breeder reactor** has received most of the attention (Figure 14-7). It uses liquid sodium as a coolant and produces Pu-239. Heat produced by nuclear fission in the reactor core is transferred to the coolant, which transfers this heat to water. The water is converted to steam and then used to generate electricity.

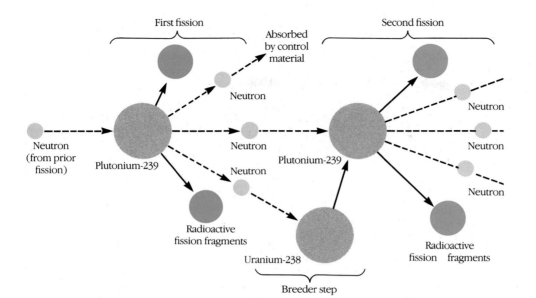

Figure 14-6
Nuclear reactions in a breeder reactor. Neutrons produced during fission strike nonfissionable "fertile" materials such as uranium-238. U-238 is then converted into fissionable plutonium-239, which can be used in the reactor as fuel.

The liquid metal breeder has numerous problems, which may thwart its development. First, it takes about 30 years for the reactor to produce as much Pu-239 as it consumes; thus, the breeding cycle is quite slow. Current work is aimed at reducing this lag. Costs also plague this technology. It would not be unreasonable to expect such reactors to cost well over $8 billion. In addition, all the problems of light water reactors are applicable.

Perhaps the most significant problem would be the large inventories of plutonium. Plutonium is long-lived and extremely toxic if inhaled. The liquid sodium coolant also can be dangerous, because it burns spontaneously in air and explodes when it contacts water. Leaks in the coolant system could trigger a catastrophic accident at a breeder.

The U.S. breeder reactor program was dealt a severe setback in 1983 when Congress voted not to continue

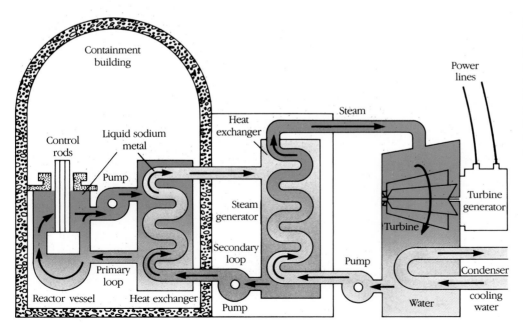

Figure 14-7
Cross-section of a liquid metal fast breeder reactor. This system uses liquid sodium as a coolant but is dangerous because of the tight packing of nuclear fuels in the core. An accident could produce a small explosion, releasing large amounts of radiation.

funding the Clinch River project in Tennessee, the country's first experimental breeder. Because of high costs the prospects of the breeder reactor are diminishing worldwide, even in France, which has long been dedicated to this technology.

The Prospects for Nuclear Power

The problems summarized here illustrate the social, economic, political, and environmental perils of conventional nuclear power. Can we overcome them, or is this technology simply too risky? Should we abandon plans for nuclear power plants or continue to build them? These are the questions society must answer when developing an energy strategy. See the Point/Counterpoint, "Hard Paths versus Soft Paths," at the end of this chapter.

In 1984 nuclear power provided the United States about 13% of its electrical needs. Energy production, which grew rapidly in the 1960s and early 1970s, had leveled off at about 250 to 276 billion kilowatt-hours a year. In 1984 there were 82 operational nuclear power plants in the United States, mostly east of the Mississippi River. Seventy-eight reactors were under construction, and 11 were in the planning stages. Between 1978 and 1980, 36 nuclear power plants in the planning stage were dropped, and 9 that were under construction were abandoned (Figure 14-8). No new domestic plants were ordered between 1978 and 1983.

Nuclear power is popular in some countries, especially with political leaders. France spends $8 billion a year building nuclear power plants. The Soviet Union has also shown a strong commitment to this energy source and currently has 40 reactors in operation. In the United States, though, nuclear power is plagued by rising uranium prices, issues of security and reactor safety, economic troubles, and many other factors. This gargantuan industry is crippled. U.S. companies, however, still design and manufacture plants for other countries.

Nuclear Fusion

Another proposed energy system is fusion power. In contrast to nuclear fission, **fusion** involves the uniting of two

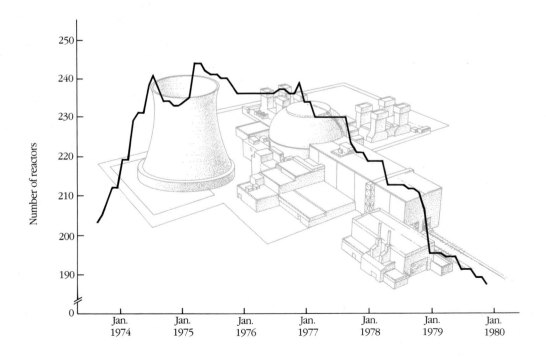

Figure 14-8
Number of nuclear power plants being built or planned in the United States.

small atoms to form a larger one (Figure 14-9). In the process, an enormous amount of energy is liberated. Fusion of 1 gram of hydrogen into helium produces 4 times more energy than the fission of 1 gram of uranium and about 10 million times as much energy as the combustion of 1 gram of coal.

The sun and other stars are prime examples of fusion power. The fusion of two hydrogen atoms in stars is caused when two atoms are forced close together (by high temperature and pressure), overcoming their mutual electrostatic repulsion. Hydrogen atoms unite to form helium, releasing heat and light.

Three fusion reactions are of special interest today. The fusion of two atoms of deuterium (heavy hydrogen, or a hydrogen nucleus with a neutron) is popular in experimental reactors. So is the fusion of deuterium and tritium (a hydrogen nucleus with two neutrons) (Figure 14-9). Both reactions produce highly energetic neutrons that render the reactor vessel radioactive. The fusion of protons and boron-11 is also considered a good choice, because it would not produce neutrons.

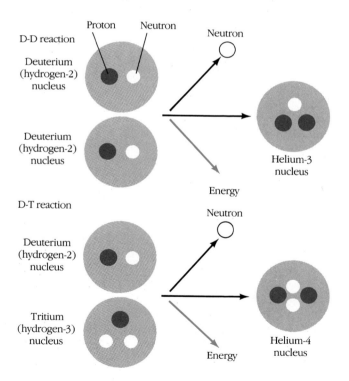

Figure 14-9
Two potentially useful fusion reactions.

Controlled fusion would offer many advantages; first and foremost, deuterium is an abundant resource found in seawater. The deuterium of the world's oceans could sustain our current world energy consumption for 30 billion years! Tritium, on the other hand, does not exist naturally and must be made from lithium, but lithium supplies will not constrain energy production. Boron, like deuterium, is also abundant. The energy analyst John Holdren estimates that 200,000 quads of energy is available from deuterium–tritium fusion supplies. At current rates of energy consumption in the United States, fusion would produce enough energy to meet the country's needs for up to 10 million years.

Before getting carried away with these claims, let us look at some problems facing fusion. First, fusion reactions take place at extremely high temperatures, measured in hundreds of millions of degrees, hot enough to vaporize metal. Thus, the main problem is how to contain the reaction.

Two containment methods are being developed. The first is **magnetic confinement,** in which the reacting plasma is suspended in a magnetic field (Figure 14-10a). Experimental fusion reactors of this type have been developed and operated in the United States, Europe, the Soviet Union, and Japan, but so far their net energy production has been negative. A recently completed $300-million experimental reactor at Princeton University is expected to reach the break-even point. From the experimental stage to commerical development, however, will be a long, expensive battle.

The second method is **inertial confinement,** in which a frozen pellet of deuterium and tritium is dropped into a reaction vessel and bombarded by lasers or particle beams (Figure 14-10b). The lasers stimulate a fusion reaction within the pellet. The problem with this technique is developing lasers powerful enough to produce a positive net energy yield.

These proposed fusion reactors would consist of reaction chambers surrounded by a liquid lithium blanket that would capture neutrons and be converted into tritium for use in the reaction (Figure 14-10). The lithium would also be used to draw off heat to boil water, producing steam to run electric generating turbines.

Scientists estimate that a prototype fusion reactor could be running by the year 2000, but commercial-scale plants would not emerge until 2020 or 2030 at the earliest. Supporters of fusion argue, however, that commercialization could come faster.

Figure 14-10

Two proposed fusion reactor vessels. Because of the high temperatures involved, the fusion reaction must be carried out either (*a*) suspended by a magnetic field (magnetic containment) or (*b*) in a special chamber where the fuel is dropped into the reactor and struck by high-power lasers to stimulate the reaction. In both vessels, heat is carried away by liquid lithium and transferred to a steam-generating system to produce electricity.

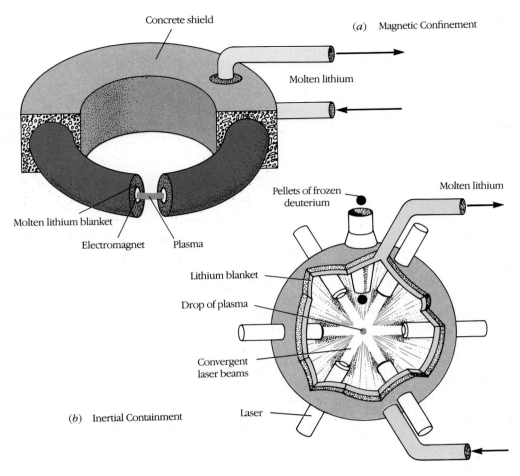

The costs of fusion are astronomical. For example, it would cost $10 billion to construct a prototype 10-megawatt fusion reactor (enough electricity for about 10,000 people). The cost of a commercial fusion reactor cannot be accurately assessed at this time, but it could be three to five times more than that of a comparable breeder reactor, or about $24 billion.

The deuterium–tritium fusion reactor is the most feasible of the three methods outlined here, but tritium is radioactive and is difficult to contain. Because of the high temperatures in fusion reactors, tritium can penetrate metals and escape into the environment. There are also other problems. Fusion reactors would produce enormous amounts of waste heat. The emission of highly energetic neutrons from the fusion reaction would weaken metals and necessitate replacement every two to ten years. Metal fatigue might lead to the rupture of the vessel and

the release of tritium and molten lithium, which burns spontaneously when it comes in contact with air. A spill might destroy the reaction vessel and the containment facilities. Neutrons emitted from the fusion reaction would also convert metals in the reactor into radioactive materials. Periodic maintenance and repair of reactor vessels would be a health hazard to workers, and radioactive components removed from the reactor would have to be disposed of properly.

Even if the problems of containment can be worked out, economics may stifle the commercial success of fusion power. In 1980 Congress passed the Magnetic Fusion Energy Engineering Act, which allocated $20 billion for fusion research and development between 1980 and 2000. The act also called for the construction of a prototype fusion reactor by the year 2000 to test the feasibility of this high-tech solution to declining fossil-fuel supplies.

Synthetic Fuels

Natural gas and oil provide much of the United States' energy, but both are quickly being depleted. Substitutes for these energy resources could come from oil shale, tar sands, and coal, all of which can be converted into liquid and gaseous fuels, collectively known as **synfuels**. The development of synfuels could minimize the social and economic disruption as oil and natural gas supplies drop, helping to keep the wheels of industry turning smoothly.

Oil Shale

Oil shale is a fine-grained sedimentary rock that contains a solid, insoluble organic material known as **kerogen**. When heated to high temperatures (460°C, or 860°F), kerogen is driven from the rock and forms a thick, heavy oil, called **shale oil**, that can be refined like conventional crude oil. Shale oil currently cannot be converted to gasoline because of the abundant nitrogen compounds that cause car engines to knock; it also contains paraffinic waxes that foul pistons and carburetors. It would have to be purified to remove these substances, adding substantially to the cost.

Oil shale is not a new discovery. As early as the 1850s U.S. companies contemplated developing a shale oil industry. But in 1859 crude oil was produced in quantity in Pennsylvania. It was cheaper and easier to handle, so shale was abandoned. Interest in oil shale has risen several other times since then, but shale oil has never been able to compete with petroleum.

Industry has for years argued that oil shale's emergence is just around the corner, waiting for the price of crude oil to increase. But with each increase in crude oil prices, oil shale seems to get shoved around another corner, never quite able to hold its own in the free market. The reason is that rising oil prices cause inflation, which adds to production costs. In addition, one-third to one barrel of oil (or an energy equivalent) is needed to mine, extract and purify a barrel of shale oil. Net energy analysis shows that shale oil production creates only about one-eighth as much energy as conventional crude oil production for the same energy investment.

Oil shale deposits lie under much of the continental United States, with rich deposits in Colorado, Utah, and Wyoming. The richest is located in Colorado's Piceance Creek Basin, the wintering ground of tens of thousands of mule deer. The basin holds an estimated 300 billion barrels of extractable shale oil. Large deposits of oil shale are also found in Canada, the Soviet Union, and China.

The U.S. Geological Survey estimates that U.S. oil-shale deposits contain more than 2 trillion barrels of oil, not all of which would be recoverable. So far as we have seen, *none* of it is considered economically recoverable. However, 418 billion barrels borders on economic recoverability or is considered producible because of government subsidies. Some is being produced in pilot plants.

Oil shale is usually mined the way coal is and then crushed and heated. The heating process, called **retorting**, drives the kerogen out of the rock. Carried out in vessels on the surface, it's called surface retorting (Figure 14-11).

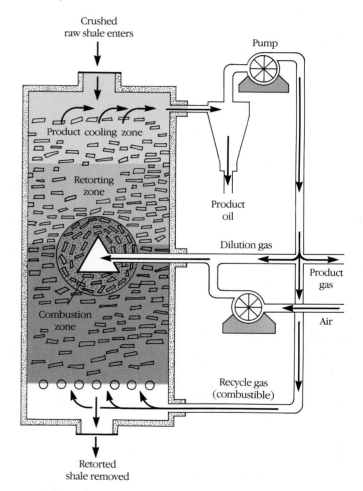

Figure 14-11
A surface retort used to extract the kerogen from oil shale. Raw shale is introduced at the top of the retort vessel. Retorted shale is removed at the bottom after being burned. Oil is driven off as a vapor in the hot gas at the top of the retort.

Figure 14-12

Modified *in situ* retorting. Oil shale is fractured in the ground and ignited. The kerogen is driven off and collected in wells drilled into the formation.

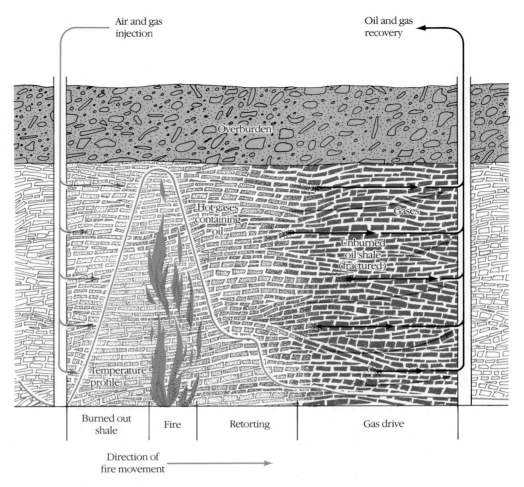

In a surface retort producing 50,000 barrels of shale oil per day, approximately 67,000 metric tons of oil shale must be mined, crushed, and retorted each day. In a year a plant of this size would require 24 million metric tons of oil shale. The surface mining necessary to produce this shale would require an enormous amount of energy and would destroy thousands of acres of land every year.

Heating shale drives off most of the kerogen, leaving behind a product called spent shale, which must then be disposed of. In a 50,000-barrel-a-day operation, approximately 53,000 metric tons of spent shale is produced each day, or about 19 million metric tons a year. Crushing and processing increase the shale's volume about 12%, so not all of it can be disposed of in the mine. Dumped elsewhere, the spent shale may be leached by water, produc-ing minerals, salts, and organic compounds that can pollute groundwater and surface waters.

A 50,000-barrel-a-day operation, which is relatively small, would require 19 million to 30 million liters (5 million to 9 million gallons) of water a day for cooling and removing impurities. This water is often polluted with salts and organic chemicals during the process and must be purified before being released into rivers and streams. Oil shale retorts would also produce significant amounts of sulfur dioxide.

Because of the huge waste-disposal problem created by surface retorting, oil shale companies have explored new ways of processing shale. One of the most promising is a process called modified *in situ* (in-place) retorting (Figure 14-12). First, part of the oil shale is removed and shipped to a surface retort. The remaining shale is then fractured with explosives. A fire is started underground and forced through the shale. The fire is sustained by burning oil shale. The heat drives off the remaining oil, which is collected and then pumped out of the ground.

Several years of experience with *in situ* retorts has proved disappointing. Groundwater seeps into the retort and extinguishes the fire; and it has proved quite difficult to fracture the shale evenly, which is necessary for uniform combustion. Finally, *in situ* retorts produce more sulfur emissions than surface retorts. Consequently, many companies have turned back to the surface retort.

What is the fate of the oil shale industry? Will it prosper, or will it falter and die? A 1980 study by the federal Office of Technology Assessment predicted that by 1990 the oil shale industry would be able to produce only about 1% of projected U.S. oil needs. The government would have to underwrite the venture at a cost of about $3 to $7 per barrel. The capital investment by the energy companies would be approximately $35 billion to $45 billion for this small amount of oil. Critics argue that the costs and environmental impacts of oil shale are too great and that the technology should be scrapped for more environmentally benign choices.

Tar Sands

Tar sands (or oil sands, or bituminous sands) are sand deposits impregnated with a dense, viscous, petroleum-like substance called bitumen. Found throughout the world, with a distribution similar to that of crude oil, tar sands are another source of liquid fuels.

Tar sands can be surface-mined and then treated with hot water, hot gases, steam, or chemical solvents to remove the bitumen. Hot-water processing is the only method used commercially. *In situ* methods similar to those used in oil shale extraction are also being tested.

The largest deposits of tar sand are in Canada in the northeastern part of Alberta. They contain an estimated 900 billion barrels of bitumen. Venezuela has tar sand deposits almost equal to those of Canada. The Soviet Union may also have sizable deposits. In the United States six states have commercially attractive deposits, collectively containing 27 billion barrels of bitumen. Ninety-three percent of all U.S. tar sands are in Utah.

Only about 4% of the bitumen in the United States and Canada can be recovered. Furthermore, each barrel of bitumen produced requires about one-third of a barrel's worth of oil for extraction. After extraction, the oil must be upgraded and purified to increase its heat content, at which stage it is called **synthetic crude oil**, or **syncrude**. A huge amount of energy is lost in this step. Therefore, to produce 1 barrel of synthetic crude oil, at least .6 barrel of energy must be used.

Even though two plants now operating in Canada produce about 175,000 barrels of synthetic crude oil each day, the long-term potential of tar sand is not great, because the deposits are not large and because low recovery rates are expected. The 900 billion barrels of Canadian tar sand will yield only about 38 billion barrels of oil—a drop in the barrel compared with the annual global oil demand, which in 1982 was about 20 billion barrels. U.S. tar sands would produce only about 1 billion barrels of oil.

Tar sands are costly and difficult to mine, too. Gigantic bucket scrapers are used in surface mines, but the tar sand is so abrasive that the teeth wear out every four to eight hours. The sand sticks to machinery, gums up moving parts, and eats away at tires and conveyor belts. Tar sand expands by 30% after processing, and as with oil shale, its production requires large amounts of water, which is badly polluted with oil in the process. Safe disposal is difficult and costly.

Coal Gasification and Liquefaction

The abundance of coal in the United States and our need for oil and natural gas substitutes have stirred interest in **coal gasification** and **liquefaction**. The two processes have many similarities. In both technologies the carbon in coal is combined with hydrogen to form hydrogen-rich organic synfuels.

Coal gasification produces high-, medium-, and low-Btu gases, which can be used in a variety of ways. The high-Btu gases are rich in methane and can replace the natural gas used in homes and factories. The medium- and low-Btu gases contain less methane and larger amounts of carbon monoxide and hydrogen. They yield less energy than methane but still can be used by industry for a variety of processes. Because of their lower heat values, though, the medium- and low-Btu gases cannot be transported economically for great distances.

To make synthetic natural gas, coal is treated with heat, oxygen, and hydrogen in large vessels. This produces methane and other gases. For each ton of coal gasified, about 50 to 75 cubic meters (1700 to 2500 cubic feet) of synthetic gas is produced.

There are three main problems with gasification. First, numerous pollutants are generated. Gasification also

Hard Paths Versus Soft Paths—Opposing Views

The Best Energy Buys

Amory B. Lovins and   *L. Hunter Lovins*

Amory Lovins is a consulting physicist; his wife and colleague, Hunter, is a lawyer, sociologist, and political scientist. They have worked as a team on energy policy in over fifteen countries, are Policy Advisors to Friends of the Earth; and are principals of the nonprofit Rocky Mountain Institute, which explores the links between energy, water, agriculture, security, and economics. Their most recent academic appointment was as Luce visiting professors of environmental studies at Dartmouth College.

Raw kilowatt-hours, lumps of coal, and barrels of sticky black goo are more messy than useful. Energy is only a means of providing services: comfort, light, mobility, the ability to make steel or bake bread. We don't necessarily want or need more energy of any kind at any price; we just want the amount, type, and source of energy that will do each desired task at least cost.

In the United States about 58% of all delivered energy is needed as heat; 34%, as liquid fuels for vehicles; and 8%, as electricity (for motors, lights, electronics, smelters, etc.). Electricity is a premium form of energy. It is able to do difficult kinds of work but is extremely expensive—far too costly to provide economical heat or mobility. Yet over the next 20 years utilities want to build another trillion dollars' worth of plants—causing spiraling rates, bankrupt utilities, and unaffordable energy.

What's the alternative? First, we ought to use energy just as efficiently as is worthwhile. We're starting to do this. Making a

dollar of gross national product (GNP) takes a quarter less energy now than it did ten years ago. Since 1979 the United States has gotten more than a hundred times as much new energy from savings (conservation and improving efficiency) as from all the new oil and gas wells, power plants, and coal mines opened in the same period. Yet it's worth saving even more. With our current technology we could double the energy efficiency of industrial motors or jet aircraft, triple that of steel mills, quadruple that of household appliances, quintuple that of cars, and improve that of buildings by tenfold to a hundredfold. Such increased "energy productivity" gives us the same services as now just as conveniently and reliably but at less cost to ourselves and the earth.

Electricity, being expensive, is especially worth saving. We are writing this under a new kind of lightbulb that gives better light than the old kind, lasts ten times as long, uses a quarter as much electricity, and repays its $20 cost in a year or two. Better motors and drive trains in factories could save more electricity than all nuclear plants produce. The best refrigerator we can make uses 1/27th as much electricity as the one in use today. If Americans used all the best technologies now on the market, they could be using less than a quarter as much electricity as they use now. And they could be paying, for each kilowatt-hour saved, less than it would cost just to run a nuclear plant to generate that kilowatt-hour. Thus, even if a new nuclear plant cost nothing to build, was perfectly safe, and didn't produce radioactive wastes or bomb materials, it would still save the country money to write it off, never run it, and buy efficiency instead.

Indeed, neither new fossil-fueled nor nuclear power plants would be necessary nor economically feasible if we used electricity efficiently. Existing and small hydroelectric plants plus a bit of wind power (or, optionally, solar cells or industrial cogeneration—the use of waste hot water to generate electricity or for heat) would be enough. A government study showed that even if by the year 2000 the United States' GNP had increased by 66%, by buying the cheapest energy options, Americans would use a quarter less energy and electricity than now and nearly 50% less nonrenewable fuel. The net saving: several trillion dollars and about a million jobs.

After efficiency, the next best energy buys are, as a Harvard Business School study found, the appropriate renewable sources. Such "soft technologies" include passive and active solar heating, passive cooling, high-temperature solar heat for industry, converting farm and forestry wastes to liquid fuel for efficient vehicles, present and small hydroelectric power, and wind power. Solar cells, too, will soon be generally cost-effective and join the list. Soft technologies tend to be smaller than huge power plants, so they can provide the cheapest energy where it's needed. Small isn't necessarily beautiful, but it usually saves money by matching the relatively small scale of most energy uses.

Careful studies in 15 countries show that the best soft technologies now available and cheaper than new power plants are enough to meet essentially all our long-term global energy needs.

Already, efficiency and renewables are sweeping the market, not because we say they should, but because millions of people are choosing them as the best buys. The United States since 1979:

- has gotten more new energy from renewable sources than from any or all of the nonrenewables
- has ordered more new electric generating capacity from small hydroelectric plants and wind power than from coal or nuclear plants or both
- is now getting about twice as much delivered energy from wood as from nuclear power, which had a 30-year head start and direct subsidies officially calculated at over $40 billion.

Wood burning, solar heat, and the like aren't always done well. People need much better information and quality control to choose and use the cheapest, most effective opportunities. But it is faster to build many small, simple technologies that anybody can use than a few huge, complex projects that take

ten years and cost billions of dollars each. And that's what Americans are doing, to the tune of $15 billion worth in 1980 alone.

Every time you buy weather stripping instead of electricity—because you can get comfort cheaper that way—you're part of the transition. And your part matters. The United States could eliminate oil imports in the 1980s, before a power plant ordered now can provide any energy whatever and at a tenth of its cost, just by making buildings and cars more efficient. Conversely, each dollar spent on reactors can't be spent on faster, cheaper ways to save oil, and hence it delays energy independence. Power plants also provide fewer jobs per dollar than any other investment. Thus, every big plant built loses the economy, directly and indirectly, about 4000 net jobs, by starving all other sectors for capital.

In the United States, 64% of the capital charge for new reactors is subsidized via taxes. The taxpayer also picks up much of the tab for nuclear fuel, decommissioning the worn-out plants, developing and regulating them, exporting them, coping with their hazards, and trying to fend off the nuclear bombs they spread. Despite the enormous government intervention, nuclear power is dying of an incurable attack of market forces throughout the world's market economies (and is in deep trouble even in the centrally planned economies, notably, France and the Soviet Union). Wall Street won't pay for more reactors; over a hundred have been canceled; and most of the industry's best people have already left.

Fortunately, the same best energy buys that are vital to a healthy economy are also keys to national security. Centralized, complex, computer-controlled nuclear plants are sitting ducks for terrorists, accidents, or natural disasters. In contrast, a more efficient, diverse, dispersed, renewable energy system could be resilient. Major failures of energy supply simply couldn't happen. Hooking together decentralized electrical sources via the existing power grid, so that they could back one another just as giant power stations do now, would actually make electrical supplies more reliable, move supplies nearer users, and reduce dependence on fragile transmission lines.

People and communities are starting to solve their own energy problems. They've discovered that the problem isn't where to get 70 quadrillion Btus a year, but how to seal the cracks around their windows. People are finding more to trust in local weatherization programs, community greenhouses, and municipal solar utilities. The energy transition is happening from the bottom up, not from the top down: Washington will be the last to know.

It's not for "the experts" to choose whether you need caulk or electricity. Pick your own best buys. The energy future is your choice.

If Energy Sources Are Thrown Away

A. David Rossin

The author is director of the Nuclear Safety Analysis Center of the Electric Power Research Institute in Palo Alto, California. He spent 16 years studying nuclear power safety at Argonne National Laboratory.

Society continually makes choices among energy alternatives. It often counts on these choices to function effectively for 20, 30, or even 40 years or more and makes large commitments of resources to them. Once commitments are made, the cost of changing them is large, and in fact it may be so large that society is unable to try alternative energy methods. As examples, consider the 50-cycle electric system in Japan's southern half and the 60-cycle system in the northern. The two force large extra costs and inconveniences on everyone, but the cost of converting either half at this time is so great that the Japanese can't do it. Or take Chicago. Its combined storm and sanitary sewer system is out of date, inefficient, and dangerous when heavy storms hit, but it is too costly to rebuild it differently.

Electric utility companies are expected to supply reliable power to all segments of society. Naturally, they prefer to build large plants that will operate for a long time. Of course, an isolated farm may get by with cylinders of propane gas for heat and windmills for electricity until a power line is built to reach it, offering a new choice. But the important thing to society at large is that choices be available and that they be rational, economically affordable, and environmentally acceptable, freeing the citizens from constant worry about the availability (and, if possible, the cost) of energy. (One need look back no further than the 1960s in the United States for an example of such an era.)

Some energy activists propose an alternative called the "soft path." By contrast, the "hard path" entails building coal and nuclear power plants linked to the electric transmission grid. The hard path is characterized by large, expensive facilities requiring much engineering to design, build, and operate. In the early days, soft-path advocates called for a stop to the building of new nuclear and coal-burning power plants and the phasing out of existing ones. Later, the theme changed. Soft-path proponents said existing electric plants could survive, and a few new coal plants would be tolerated. (Why? There was a dilemma about tidal, ocean-thermal, and large solar plants: they fit the "renewable" definition but needed the grid anyway.) The soft-path promoters had begun to recognize the obvious: the dispersed, individual, and small-is-beautiful energy sources could exist only for the very hardy and the wealthy elite. Even more important, to make any meaningful contribution to our energy supply problem, these alternative energy sources needed to be complementary to a strong electrical infrastructure.

In other words, there really is no such thing as the soft path. Ironically, it turns out to be only a strategy for closing off alternatives and eliminating some that might be preferable—the right tools for the right tasks. In fact, rather than being the cheapest, alternatives such as solar, wind, and small hydroelectric power are expensive, capital-intensive, and require money up front. These alternatives would force the consumer to pay higher electric bills or require subsidies in the form of taxes to meet their costs. (Contrary to popular belief, nuclear power plants are not subsidized. The government does support research, and thus far the greatest return to the taxpayer per energy research dollar has come from nuclear power.) Shamefully, delays have made most new nuclear power plants horribly expensive. Yet some approach half the cost of solar power.

Electric power systems with big power plants are actually efficient, resilient, and decentralized. But there must be enough power plants to generate all the electricity needed at any given time, especially at the time of peak demand. Except for a few special storage facilities (called pumped hydro dams) all electricity is generated at the instant it is used. Our well-planned systems utilize the most economical mix of plants to meet demand. Interestingly, if solar electric plants are built, they will be natural partners with nuclear plants. Solar electricity is only generated during the day, but that is when the load peaks.

The transmission and distribution systems provide diverse pathways for electricity to reach all but the most isolated neighborhoods. In the event of storms (or even sabotage) trained crews are dispatched to repair the damage. Outages occur, but repairs are made within hours or, at most, days. On the other hand, imagine finding enough plumbers and electricians to put a community of individualized energy sources back into operation after a severe storm!

Everything about our energy supply is big. Loss of only 1.5% of the total U.S. energy supply during the OPEC embargo in 1973 was enough to almost cripple the economy of the country. The United States started thinking and talking about energy, and although it has reduced its dependence on Middle East oil somewhat, it cannot rest easy for the future. The country has to replace about 3% of its power plants every year as old plants become obsolete. This allows nothing for growth or to replace oil- and gas-fired plants with coal or nuclear.

There is public concern about nuclear power. Even with the Three Mile Island accident the industry's public safety record is perfect—no other energy source can approach it. For a source that produces more than one-eighth of all the electricity in the country (more than gas or hydro), this is very important. There is no shortage of information available on nuclear safety. Every plant licensing requires extensive public hearings with full public documentation.

Safety risks are a serious matter and need to be understood. But part of the perspective needed involves understanding the risks of not having enough energy. Some are obvious: jobs, production, health care, living standards, schools, and recreation. But failure to prepare because alternatives are closed off or because there is not enough money to build anything means frightening risks for society.

We need not look far to find examples. Many nations have not been able to develop their own natural or human resources, because their electric generating base is too small. Some that were only recently building up their industry were dependent on oil imports. When prices quadrupled, development ground to a halt. Inflation depleted those nations' money, and none was left to build alternative energy sources.

Ohio faced a chronic gas shortage in the 1970s. During a severe winter, industries were forced to shut down. Businesses canceled plans for expansion in Ohio and moved elsewhere. The jobs went with them. New homes were not built in Cleveland for three years because the gas company could not guarantee supplies. Builders and laborers were out of work. The problem arose because stringent state regulation had prevented the gas companies from building the pipelines and tanks to support growth in the region. No soft-path alternatives could help.

In a number of nations today new factories or commercial establishments cannot be built without an energy permit from the government. This gives the government complete control over the economy; it can make or break business. There is a real risk of a society's falling into this mode.

The risks from energy shortages are real indeed. Prudent investment in long-term energy supply capacity may be vital in reducing international tensions. The threat of war over the Middle East continues, and oil remains the critical commodity.

In a democracy, good energy policy depends on the public's willingness to accept long-term investment in energy supply—even in technologies given unattractive names such as the "hard path."

---

requires large quantities of water. Combustion of the synthetic natural gas will result in little additional pollution (except for carbon dioxide), but the pollutants produced in gasification plants make the process a dirty alternative to natural gas and renewable energy options.

Coal can also be gasified underground *in situ*. This process offers many advantages over mining and surface gasification. Mining and all its environmental destruction, accidents, worker health problems, and costly land reclamation are eliminated. The costs for extraction are less. However, the yield of gas per ton of coal is lower than with surface gasification. There are serious difficulties in controlling the underground burning of coal. Groundwater can seep into the operation and extinguish the fire. Aquifers can be polluted by combustion products.

A second problem with synthetic natural gas is the expense. The cost of a plant may be as high as $1.3 billion to $2 billion.

A third problem is low net energy production. Coal is 1.5 times more efficient at producing electricity than is the synthetic natural gas made from coal. Furthermore, synthetic gas produced from surface mines is about 1.5 times more expensive than natural gas, and coal gas from underground mines is 3.5 times more expensive.

Coal gasification is in the experimental stage in the United States. Several pilot plants are now operating to test its feasibility and economics. The Soviet Union has been creating synthetic gas from coal for over 50 years. Several *in situ* plants now provide gas for electric power plants.

Coal liquefaction is similar in principle to coal gasification. There are four major ways of making a synthetic oil from coal, but each involves the same general process—adding hydrogen to the coal. This may be done with special solvents or suitable catalysts or by heating coal with steam. In each of these processes a thick, viscous oil is formed. It must be purified to remove ash and coal particles that remain suspended in solution.

Coal liquefaction could provide us with liquid fuels, but the process would be costly. It produces air and water pollutants and requires large amounts of energy. Like coal gasification, it might be preempted by other energy sources that make more sense from an environmental viewpoint.

There are many ways of going forward, but only one way of standing still.

FRANKLIN D. ROOSEVELT

Summary

Development of energy resources to meet future needs requires us to look at all sources. Some nonrenewable sources may have a place in the immediate future as we develop a truly permanent energy system.

Nuclear reactors are fueled by uranium-235, whose nuclei split, or *fission,* when struck by neutrons. This process releases an enormous amount of heat. Nuclear fuels pass through a complex cycle, from mining to waste disposal; at each stage radioactive materials can escape, either in accidents or through normal operations.

Nuclear power offers many advantages over coal and oil power. Reactors produce very little air pollution. Because uranium is a more concentrated form of energy than coal, less strip mining is required; consequently, less land is disturbed. The cost of transporting nuclear fuels is also lower than that for an equivalent amount of coal. The use of nuclear fuels to generate electricity frees coal for the production of synthetic oil and gas to replace waning supplies of petroleum and natural gas.

The major problems with nuclear power are disposing of radioactive wastes, contamination of the environment, thermal pollution, health impacts from radiation, limited supplies of uranium ore, low social acceptability, high construction costs, questionable reactor safety, lack of experience with the technology, vulnerability to sabotage, proliferation of nuclear weapons made from high-level wastes, and loss of individual freedom as security is tightened to protect citizens from sabotage and the theft of nuclear materials.

Supporters of nuclear power have proposed the introduction of the *breeder reactor* to get around the problem of limited fuel supply. Besides producing electricity, the breeder reactor makes fissionable material from uranium-238 and thorium-232. Both abundant, these fertile materials are placed around the reactor core and are bombarded with neutrons from fission reactions.

Breeder reactors could theoretically convert 60% to 80% of recoverable uranium resources into fissionable plutonium, and they could also use uranium-238 from waste piles or from spent fuel rods.

Liquid metal breeder reactors have been under development for more than three decades in the United States, using liquid sodium as a coolant. Such reactors have many problems. First, the rate of conversion of U-238 to plutonium-239 is quite slow, requiring about 30 years for fuel production to equal consumption. Liquid metal fast breeder reactors could cost over $8 billion each. According to some sources, the presence of large quantities of fissionable materials packed in the core could lead to meltdowns or nuclear explosions of very low magnitude. In addition, all the problems of light water reactors are applicable. Given the costs and other problems, breeder reactors will probably not be developed in the United States.

The prospects for nuclear power seem dim, at least in the United States. Electrical production from nuclear power grew rapidly in the 1960s and 1970s, but it has leveled off since then. Between 1978 and 1980, 36 nuclear power plants in the planning stages and 9 under construction were abandoned. Despite the decline in the United States, several countries still seem committed to nuclear power, notably France and the Soviet Union.

Another proposed energy system is fusion power. *Fusion,* the uniting of two small atoms to form a larger one, is accompanied by the release of energy. After three decades of research, fusion is a long way from being commercially available. But optimism still prevails, because the materials to fuel the fusion reactor are abundant and could provide energy for millions of years.

On the opposite side of the coin, fusion reactions occur at extremely high temperatures. Safely containing such reactions is a major challenge. The cost of a commercial fusion reactor could reach $24 billion, many times higher than that of conventional fission reactors, which themselves are facing financial difficulties. The emission of highly energetic neutrons from the fusion reaction would weaken metals and necessitate replacement every two to ten years. Metal fatigue might lead to the rupture of the vessel and the release of radioactive materials or lithium, which is used to capture heat.

Substitutes for natural gas and oil could come from oil shale, tar sand, and coal, which can be converted into liquid and gaseous fuels known as *synfuels. Oil shale* is fine-grained rock that contains an organic material known as *kerogen,* which can be extracted by heating the shale. The U.S. Geological Survey estimates that the United States has billions of barrels of recoverable shale oil. Widespread development of this resource would require mining of extensive regions, large energy inputs, the production of numerous air pollutants, and the production of large quantities of solid waste that must be disposed of safely to prevent groundwater and surface water contamination. The costs of shale oil compared with those of crude oil impede the development of this industry. Costs will always be high because of the low net energy yield.

Tar sands are sand deposits impregnated with a petroleum-like substance called *bitumen.* Found throughout the world, tar sands can be mined and treated with heat or chemical solvents to remove the bitumen. Despite the enormous deposits of tar sands, only about 4% of the bitumen in the Untied States and Canada can be recovered. In addition, a low net energy yield plagues this industry.

Coal can be converted to gaseous and liquid fuels. To make synthetic natural gas, coal is treated with heat, oxygen, and hydrogen, either *in situ* or in vessels. *Coal gasification* produces large quantities of air pollution and solid waste. Natural gas produced in such operations is expensive because of the low net energy yield. Surface mining destroys vegetation and habitat. *Coal liquefaction,* the production of liquid fuels, is similar in principle, and it has many of the same problems.

Discussion Questions

1. Describe how a light water fission reactor works. What is the fuel, and how is the chain reaction controlled?

2. Describe the parts of the nuclear fuel cycle.

3. What are the advantages and disadvantages of nuclear power? Comment on safety, pollution, costs, terrorism, nuclear proliferation, waste disposal, civil liberties, and social acceptability.

4. What is a breeder reactor? How is it similar to a conventional fission reactor? How is it different? Discuss its advantages and disadvantages.

5. What is nuclear fusion? Discuss ways proposed to capture energy from fusion.

6. List and discuss the advantages and disadvantages of fusion energy.

7. What is oil shale? Where is it found? How could it help us meet future energy needs?

8. Discuss the benefits and risks of oil shale development. In your opinion, do the risks outweigh the benefits, or vice versa?

9. Discuss the potential of tar sands in meeting future energy demands.

10. Define coal gasification and liquefaction. Are these technologies wise choices for the future? Why or why not?

Suggested Readings

Baughman, G. L. (1978). *Synthetic Fuels Data Handbook.* Denver: Cameron Engineers. Comprehensive technical review.

Beckmann, P. (1976). *The Health Hazards of Not Going Nuclear.* Boulder, Colo.: Golem Press. A pronuclear book worth reading.

Duderstadt, J. J., and Chihiro, K. (1979). *Nuclear Power: Technology on Trial.* Ann Arbor, Michigan: University of Michigan Press. A thoughtful analysis of nuclear power.

Gofman, J. W., and Tamplin, A. R. (1979). *Poisoned Power: The Case against Nuclear Power Plants before and after Three Mile Island.* Emmaus, Penn.: Rodale Press. Well-written analysis.

Hayes, D. (1976). *Nuclear Power: The Fifth Horseman* (Worldwatch Press 6). Washington, D.C.: Worldwatch Institute. Superb study.

Jungk, R. (1979). *The New Tyranny.* New York: Warner Books. A monumental book on nuclear power. One of the most important books of the '70s.

Kaku, M., and Trainer, J., eds. (1982). *Nuclear Power: Both Sides.* New York: Norton. Excellent, balanced coverage.

Kendall, H. W., and Nadis, S. J., eds. (1980). *Energy Strategies: Toward a Solar Future.* Cambridge, Mass.: Ballinger. Detailed survey of energy sources and their prospects for the future. Superb!

Lovins, A. B., and Price, J. H. (1975). *Nonnuclear Futures: The Case for an Ethical Energy Strategy.* Cambridge, Mass.: Friends of the Earth/Ballinger. Technical survey of nuclear energy.

Nader, R., and Abbotts, J. (1977). *The Menace of Atomic Energy.* New York: Norton. A decidedly antinuclear book.

Ross, M. H., and Williams, R. H. (1981). *Our Energy: Regaining Control.* New York: McGraw-Hill. Excellent coverage.

U.S. Environmental Protection Agency. (1980). *Environmental Perspective on the Emerging Oil Shale Industry* (EPA-600/2-80-205a). Washington, D.C.: U.S. Government Printing Office. Superb overview of the environmental impacts of oil shale development.

Weaver, K. F. (1979). The Promise and Peril of Nuclear Energy. *National Geographic* 155(4): 459–493. Graphically illustrated study of nuclear power for the layperson.

15

Future Energy: Renewable Resources

The science of today is the technology of tomorrow.

EDWARD TELLER

A permanent energy supply must be renewable. Few people would disagree. In the long run, then, society will rely on two major sources of energy, the sun and the earth's internal heat. These two sources can take many forms. The sun, for instance, creates heat that warms us but also makes the wind blow, the rain fall, and the plants grow. Each of these can be tapped for energy.

This chapter confines itself to the major forms of renewable energy. Many minor power sources, such as machines that generate electricity from ocean waves, will be ignored here to make the topic more manageable. This chapter will also cover conservation, a practice that will always be important but is especially so today. By saving energy, we can stretch out the fossil fuels and buy time to develop renewable energy systems.

Solar Energy

Oliver Wendell Holmes wrote that "the great end of living is to harmonize man with the order of things." No better example of harmony exists than solar energy. All life in the ecosystem depends on the sun and the plants that capture its energy. We are indirectly dependent on the sun's energy as we burn the fossil fuel remains of ancient plants and animals. But there is a big difference between burning fossil fuels and using the sun's daily energy radiation. Fossil fuels are stored energy laid down millions of years ago. Some day they will be gone. In contrast, the sun will last for several billion years.

Today solar energy provides only a fraction of our energy needs. But an area the size of Connecticut annually receives as much solar radiation as the United States actually uses in a year. Contrary to popular misconception, significant sources of solar radiation are available across the nation. For instance, Portland, Maine, receives 70% as much sunlight as Tucson, Arizona, which is located in the heart of America's Sun Belt (Figure 15-1).

Solar energy breaks down into two major categories: direct and indirect. **Direct solar energy** is captured from sunlight and used for heating, generating electricity, and cooling. **Indirect solar energy** is derived from natural processes driven by the sun—for example, wind, biomass, waves, and hydroelectric power. This section will cover the major types of direct solar energy.

Pros and Cons of Solar Energy

The most notable advantage of solar energy is that the fuel is free. All we pay for are devices to capture and store it. Solar energy is a nondepletable energy resource that will be available as long as the sun survives. It is also an environmentally benign form of energy: it does not pollute, produce solid waste, or make noise.

Although energy and other resources must be used to construct solar energy systems, over their lifetime these systems produce much more energy than they consume. Some systems are so efficient that the energy payback comes within the first four months of operation. Production also creates some pollution, but years of pollution-free operation offset that. Most solar systems can be mounted on rooftops or integrated with building designs and therefore do not take up valuable land.

Solar energy offers the advantage of great flexibility. Current systems provide energy for remote weather-sensing stations, single-family dwellings, and commercial

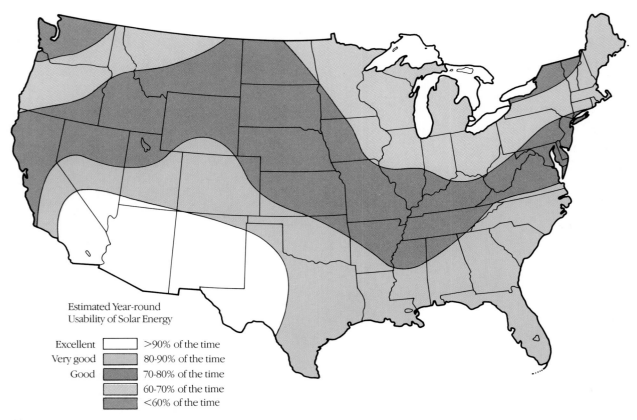

Estimated Year-round
Usability of Solar Energy

Excellent	>90% of the time
Very good	80-90% of the time
Good	70-80% of the time
	60-70% of the time
	<60% of the time

Figure 15-1
Map showing availability of solar energy across the United States.

operations. Solar energy can be collected to meet the low-temperature heat demands of homes or the intermediate- or high-temperature demands of factories. Some systems provide electricity to power radios, lights, and space satellites.

No major technical breakthroughs are required before we can use many existing solar systems such as active solar hot water heating and passive solar space heating. Some improvements in design and costs could enhance the economic appeal of certain solar systems, such as active solar space heating and cooling.

Because rising prices of natural gas and oil will take a larger and larger chunk out of family and corporate budgets in the near future, those who invest in solar now will enjoy an advantage over those who continue using costly fossil fuels. Solar homes may have utility bills of several hundred dollars a year, compared with several thousand in conventional oil- and gas-heated homes. Over a lifetime, solar can save a homeowner $50,000 or more. Banks now consider the future energy costs of homes when deciding whether a loan applicant will qualify for a loan, because they believe that monthly energy costs will soon exceed monthly mortgage payments. Solar homes may be the only affordable homes of the future.

The major limitation of solar energy is that the source is intermittent: it goes away at night and is blocked on cloudy days. Consequently, solar energy must be collected and stored, but current storage technologies are limited. As a result, many solar users must have a backup system to provide heat during cloudy periods.

There are three major types of direct solar energy systems: passive, active, and photovoltaics.

Passive Solar Systems

Passive solar heating is the simplest and most cost-effective solar system available. Often described as a system with only one moving part, the sun, it is designed to capture sunlight energy within a structure such as a house, office building, or warehouse (Figure 15-2). The simplest

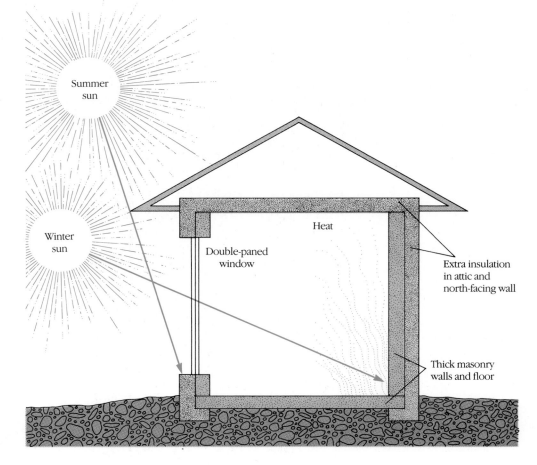

Figure 15-2
Schematic representation of a passive solar house.

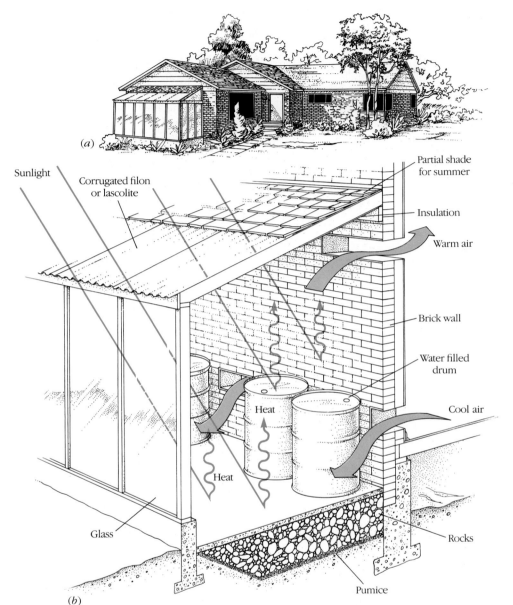

Figure 15-3
(a) Existing homes can add solar greenhouses and other passive solar ideas. *(b)* Sunlight penetrates the greenhouse glass and is stored in the floor or in water-filled drums. Warm air passes into the house.

Sunlight

Corrugated filon or lascolite

Partial shade for summer

Insulation

Warm air

Brick wall

Water filled drum

Heat

Cool air

Heat

Glass

Rocks

Pumice

(a)

(b)

passive solar system is the greenhouse. Sunlight penetrates the glass, strikes soil and objects within the greenhouse, and is converted into heat. Passive solar homes capitalize on this principle. Sunlight streams through south-facing windows and heats walls and floors of brick, tiles or cement. The heat radiates from this **thermal mass** and heats the air day and night.

Passive solar design requires good insulation, internal heat storage, south-facing windows, and, usually, shutters or heavy curtains to block the outflow of heat at night. Overhangs block out the summer sun (Figure 15-2).

Passive solar, unlike other forms of direct solar energy, may be difficult to install in existing homes without major modifications (Figure 15-3). It is best suited for new homes.

Well-designed passive systems can provide up to 100% of the building's space heating. One passive solar home in Canada built by the mechanical engineering department of the University of Saskatchewan had an annual fuel bill of $40 compared with $1400 for an average American home. The house was so airtight and well insulated that the heat from sunlight, room lights, appliances, and occupants provided enough energy to keep it warm. This house cost a little more than a tract home and the same as a custom-built home.

Passive solar can be used on office buildings, too. Sunlight, heat from office machines, workers, and lights can provide the heat.

Active Solar Systems

Active solar heating and cooling systems rely on solar collectors, which are generally mounted on roofs. Most collectors are insulated boxes with a double layer of glass on one side (Figure 15-4). These are called flat plate collectors. The inside of the box is lined with a dark absorbent material. Sunlight is absorbed by the black material and converted into heat. The heat is carried away by water (or some other fluid) that flows through pipes in the collector or by air blown in by a fan. The heated water or air is then carried to some storage medium, usually water in a basement tank. The heat is transferred to the storage medium, and the water or air is returned to the collectors.

Solar panels are becoming more elaborate and more efficient all the time. Some track the sun across the sky, collecting heat from sunrise to sunset (Figure 15-5). Tracking systems use concentrating collectors that focus sunlight on a black pipe running through the panel. These systems are 30% to 40% more efficient than the best flat plate collector. In most parts of the country, active solar hot water and space heating are competitive with electricity; by 1985 they will compete favorably with natural gas.

Solar collectors can also be used for cooling. In these systems energy from sunlight powers a small heat engine similar to the electric motor in a refrigerator. The heat engine drives a piston that compresses a special vapor

Figure 15-4

Two active solar systems for hot-water heat. *(a)* Thermosiphon system. The collector is situated lower than the water tank. When the water heats up in the collector, it flows by natural convection into the tank, forcing cool water to take its place in the panel. This water is then heated, creating a self-sustaining system that requires no pumps. *(b)* Direct pump system. A small pump moves the heat collecting water, air, or other fluid through the collector and into the storage tank.

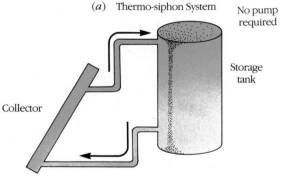

(*a*)   Thermo-siphon System

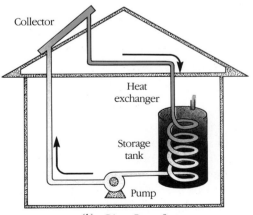

(*b*)   Direct Pump System

Figure 15-5
Solar panels use computerized tracking systems to follow the sun across the sky.

into a liquid; the liquid then revaporizes and draws heat out of the surrounding air (just as a spray can draws heat away from your hand).

Active solar cooling is not competitive with conventional cooling, but with rising fuel prices it may begin to find its way into the marketplace. Happily, the demand for cooling coincides with the sunniest days, so these systems could be reliable methods of summertime cooling.

Active solar heating is becoming popular worldwide. In Israel over one-tenth of the homes heat their water with the sun. In the United States officials estimated that there would be at least 1.6 million solar collectors by 1985, but this may underestimate the growth in solar energy, because California alone expects to have 1.5 million by 1985.

In Japan 1.6 million buildings had active solar systems in 1980; by 1990 the government plans to have 7.8 million systems installed. By 1995 one-third of all buildings will have active solar systems, bringing the grand total to about 12 million.

Photovoltaics

Photovoltaics (PVs), or **solar cells**, provide a way of generating electricity from sunlight. Solar cells consist of thin wafers of silicon or other materials (cadmium sulfide or gallium arsenide) that emit electrons when struck by sunlight (Figure 15-6).

The first photovoltaics were developed in 1954 by scientists at Bell Laboratories, and in 1958 PV cells were boosted into space aboard Vanguard I, the second U.S. satellite. Since then, they have powered virtually every American satellite launched into space.

PV production has grown at a rate of 50% per year since the early 1970s. PV cells produced worldwide in 1982 could generate about 10 megawatts, enough electricity for 10,000 people. Annual production is likely to increase to 200 to 300 megawatts by 1990 and to more than 1000 megawatts by 2000 (equivalent to one nuclear plant per year).

During this period of rapid growth, the cost has fallen rapidly. Between 1954 and 1980, it fell from $600 per watt to below $7. To make PV cells competitive with conventional electrical production, costs must drop to about 50 cents per watt, which may happen when automated production begins. New developments in production may make photovoltaics competitive with conventional electricity by 1990 or so. Governmental support of the industry could help it become competitive much sooner, but in the United States such support is rapidly declining.

Photovoltaics may have their first significant market in the less developed countries. Many lack fossil fuel resources and can't afford to import them or to build centralized plants to burn them. In addition, the needs of these countries are generally small and are concentrated regionally. Large plants that transmit energy to many small regions of low use would be prohibitively expensive. Even though

Figure 15-6

(a) Photovoltaic cells made of silicon (and other materials). When sunlight strikes the silicon atoms it causes electrons to be ejected. Electrons can flow out of the photovoltaic cell through electrical wires where they can do useful work. Electron vacancies are filled as electrons complete circuit.

(b) Array of solar voltaic cells. These cells are being used to power a railroad switching station in Alaska.

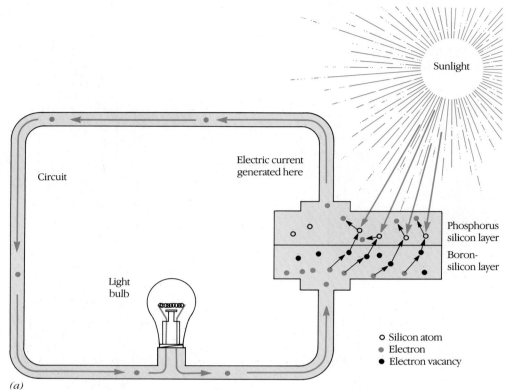

(a)

(b)

they now cost more than conventional electric-generating plants, photovoltaics can be installed in a village without costly transmission lines. Thus, the price of the PVs may be about the same as or cheaper than a conventional centralized power plant and transmission network.

Solar Thermal Electric Generation

Several large-scale projects have been constructed in the United States and France to generate electricity from solar-heated water (Figure 15-7). In such systems huge arrays of mirrors focus sunlight on a tower where the concentrated sunlight makes steam to run electrical turbines. These systems are costly and require large amounts of land to produce relatively small amounts of electricity. In addition, large centralized systems require electric transmission lines, which drive the costs up further. Mirrors are subject to wind damage and require frequent cleaning. Critics argue that centralized systems resemble the current energy system, in which a few control the price of energy, and that they create fewer jobs than decentralized systems. Taking into account the economic and social problems of large electric facilities, many observers believe that their future is dim.

Solar Satellites

One of the most futuristic of all solar energy schemes is the solar satellite. The proposed satellites would consist of elaborate arrays of solar panels with photovoltaic cells and would beam energy to earth as microwaves. Earth stations would pick up the microwaves and convert them into electricity.

This scheme is attractive, because the orbiting satellite could be in sunlight virtually all the time. Energy would be produced day and night and beamed to earth. To produce approximately 60% of the electricity needed by New York City at peak usage, however, a satellite weighing about 20,000 to 40,000 metric tons (22,000 to 44,000 tons) would have to be launched. Occupying 52 to 104 square kilometers (20 to 40 square miles), this satellite would be constructed in a low-orbit space station (not yet built), and boosted to its final orbit in outer space. The station would be virtually impossible to repair and maintain, and it could be damaged by asteroids. To construct the solar satellite, workers and many tons of materials would have to be launched into space at an exorbitant cost. At least 360 space shuttle flights would be necessary to construct

Figure 15-7
Solar One is a solar-thermal electric generalizing system in Daggett, California. In this operation sunlight, focused on a power tower, boils water, creating steam, which is used to generate electricity.

a 5000-megawatt satellite. A full-scale demonstration project could cost between $50 billion and $85 billion. The energy and resources needed to build such a leviathan might be better invested in earthbound passive and active solar systems and conservation.

Wind and Biomass

Renaissance of Wind Power

About 2% of the sunlight striking the earth is converted into the kinetic energy of wind. Winds form in two major ways. First, because sunlight falls unevenly on the earth and its atmosphere, some parts of the earth are heated more than others. The warm air rises, and cooler air flows in from adjacent areas. The earth's most important circulation pattern develops as warm air near the equator rises, drawing cooler polar air toward the tropics. The earth's rotation then causes air to circulate clockwise in the Northern Hemisphere and counterclockwise south of the equator. The second major wind-flow pattern results from the differential heating of land and water. Air over the oceans is not heated as much as air over the land. Therefore, cool oceanic air often flows landward to replace warm, rising air.

Worldwide exploitation of wind could produce 13 times the electricity currently produced on a global basis. The United States could acquire 10 to 40 quads of electricity per year from wind (the total U.S. annual consumption of all energy in 1983 was 70 quads). With aggressive governmental and industrial efforts, wind could provide up to 20% of U.S. electricity by 2000, although most estimates project that it will supply only 2% to 4% by that time.

Wind can be tapped to generate electricity and heat, pump water, provide mechanical work (grinding grain, for example), and compress air. In the United States, windmills played an important part in opening the West to cattle ranching. In the early 1900s there were over 6 million windmills in the country to pump water and produce electricity. Most have been replaced by centralized power plants and pumps running on fossil fuel or electricity.

Many regions are being considered for wind energy development, including the coast of Sweden, the northern coast of the United Kingdom (especially the North Sea region), the southern and western coasts of Australia, the Arctic coast of the Soviet Union, and many developing nations located along the trade winds. In the United States the Great Plains, especially western Kansas, western Oklahoma, and Texas, are best suited for wind generation. In addition to these generally windy areas, mountain passes, lakeside property, and coastal areas are often ideal for wind power generation.

Between 1973 and 1980 the U.S. Department of Energy spent $200 million on research and development of large wind turbine generators and smaller wind generators for home use. The world's first wind farm, built in New Hampshire, has 20 wind generators each capable of producing 30 kilowatts, collectively producing enough electricity for 240 typical homes.

Some of the most spectacular developments are occurring in California (Figure 15-8). By 2000 California hopes to get 10% of its electricity from the wind. One California company has agreed to build a 350-megawatt wind-powered electric power plant. A 120-megawatt wind farm may also be in the offing. Meanwhile, an 80-mega-watt wind farm is planned for Hawaii. It will contain 32 2.5-megawatt wind turbines located on 1000 hectares (2500 acres).

Small-scale generators in backyards and farms produce 1 to 15 kilowatts. They are easier to mass-produce than large systems and have small blades that are less subject to the stress which makes the larger ones more expensive. Small generators produce more electricity in light winds and, therefore, operate more efficiently. Small wind generators can be located close to the end use. A breakdown jeopardizes only the individual, whereas breakdowns in large-scale operations can affect a whole community. On the negative side, small generators create a wider visual impact than wind farms. Individual units require a fairly substantial investment, and many homeowners may not have enough knowledge of local wind patterns to make intelligent decisions about the economics of a proposed system.

Wind energy offers many of the advantages of direct solar energy: It is clean and renewable, uses only a small amount of land, and is safe to operate. Many experts estimate that wind energy systems can pay for their production (including mining, manufacturing, and installation) in eight months to five years. Moreover, wind technologies do not preclude other land uses; wind farms, for example, can be grazed and planted. The technology is well developed, and the fuel is free. Costs are rapidly dropping and are currently less than those of nuclear power. Mass production of wind generators in the future may bring the prices down further.

Like photovoltaics, wind may become a sustainable, small-scale power source for developing countries. The United Nations and the Colombian government constructed a medium-sized factory to produce 1400 windmills a year, which will be placed in villages to pump water. Programs like this provide jobs and energy to pump water for agriculture. Local residents could be trained to repair and maintain the windmills, making this an excellent example of an appropriate technology.

There are, of course, disadvantages to wind systems. Winds do not blow all of the time, so backup systems and storage are needed. Storage technologies seem to be one of the major weaknesses of the wind energy system, but new approaches are lessening this problem. The *Public Utilities Regulatory Policies Act* of 1978 requires power companies to buy excess electricity from customers with windmills or other electric generators. Thus, homeowners divert excess electricity produced at night and at other times into the electrical grid, where it is used by other

Figure 15-8
Windmill generators near Livermore, California.

customers. When the wind is not blowing, homeowners with windmills simply buy electricity from the power company. In essence, the utility serves as a storage site.

Large batteries can also store electricity for later use. Finally, a flywheel attached to the shaft of the wind generator may also store the wind's energy. A lightweight, low-friction flywheel turns as the blades of the wind machine rotate, but when the wind dies down, it keeps turning, slowly losing speed but generating electricity for several days on its own.

A second problem is that many states haven't extensively surveyed their winds. Until a few years ago most experts thought California was a poor prospect for wind power, because data from airports showed that the wind was undependable and weak. However, airports are usually built where the wind is minimal. More complete surveys show that California has a wealth of wind power, mainly in mountain passes that are close enough to major urban areas to be attractive.

A third problem is that wind generators may have a visual impact; this can be mitigated by proper siting. Fourth, wind systems may produce an annoying, low-frequency noise, although many designs now have eliminated it. Fifth, large wind generators may impair TV reception near a facility; however, fiberglass blades will reduce the inter-ference by half. Some also may impair microwave communications used by phone companies.

Sixth, costs are still relatively high. Oil-fired electric power plants produce electricity for 6 to 10 cents per kilowatt-hour. Large-scale wind generators produce electricity for 8 to 10 cents per kilowatt-hour; the next generation of large wind machines should bring the cost down and make wind competitive with most other power sources.

Among solar-related electrical generating options, wind is the closest to being ready for widespread adoption. Needed are time, money, a few improvements in technology, and most of all, mass production to bring costs down. Governments can help stimulate production with industry tax credits, research and development support, and purchases for governmental facilities. Wind machines may be one of the most promising and most important products the United States could offer Third World countries.

Biomass

Biomass is the organic matter contained in plants, animals, and microorganisms. Because all biomass is ultimately produced by photosynthesis, it is a form of indirect solar energy.

Table 15-1 Estimate of Available Biomass in the U.S.

Type	Total Resources (Million Tons)	Total Energy Potential (Quads)	Recoverable Energy (Quads)
Crop residues	340	5.1	1.0–4.6[1]
Forestry residues	300	4.5	0.9–4.0
Urban refuse	135	1.2	0.3–1.1
Manure	45	0.7	0.1–0.6
Total	820	11.5	2.3–10.3

[1]Recoverable energy probably lies in the middle to lower part of the range given here.
Source: Kendall, H.W., and Nadis, S.J. (1980), *Energy Strategies: Toward Solar Future*, Cambridge, Mass.: Ballinger, p. 170.

Potential for Biomass Humans already use biomass to generate energy for heating, electrical production, transportation, and other purposes. In 1980 biomass supplied about 19% of the energy worldwide; in the United States, the figure was only about 3%.

Useful biomass includes wood, crops, manure, urban waste, industrial wastes, and municipal sewage. Some of these may be burned directly and others are converted to methane or ethanol.

The simplest way of getting energy from biomass is to burn it, but it may make more sense to convert it to gaseous and liquid fuels and chemical feedstocks (raw materials for the chemical industry) to replace natural gas and oil.

The U.S. Office of Technology Assessment recently projected that biomass could supply 15% to 18% of the country's total energy needs by 2000 with aggressive research and development, government sponsorship, tax breaks, and other incentives.

A survey of the biomass produced in the United States indicates that the potential of this energy source is over-rated. Table 15-1 shows that the total biomass is only about 800 million tons, equivalent to 11.5 quads of energy if all of it could be collected and all of its energy extracted. Because much of this biomass is inaccessible, and because it takes energy to get energy, the net energy gain would be much less.

Although the potential for biomass may be lower than many projections indicate, it can still play a significant role in the future in a sustainable energy system. Biomass will help us reduce our dependence on nonrenewable energy resources, and it offers many other advantages, to be discussed below.

Combustion of Wood Wood is the major source of energy in most developing nations. In India, for example, over half of the domestic fuel used in rural villages is wood; the remainder is dried cattle dung. In the arid Sahel region of Africa wood supplies 94% of the rural energy needs. Most people in these nations, however, are finding it ever more difficult to find firewood. It is common for women and children to travel 50 kilometers (30 miles) a day to collect what they need for cooking. Some villagers in Africa have been forced to do without fuel, eating raw millet flour mixed with water. Because the flour is not cooked, fewer nutrients are absorbed. Unable to boil their water, villagers are more prone to water-borne diseases.

There are severe wood shortages in India, central Africa, and the Andes mountains of South America. Trees and underbrush may be stripped for miles in wide areas surrounding villages and towns. In the Sahel wood is being removed two times faster than it is replaced with new growth. Wood scavenging ultimately reduces wildlife habitat, increases erosion, worsens flooding, destroys farmland, and speeds up desertification.

Population growth and the rising demand for wood in developing countries start the endless cycle of inflation. In some areas laborers spend one-quarter of their salaries on firewood. Most of the rest of their money goes for food.

The firewood crisis has been recognized by many world leaders, but so far projects to slow down the destruction of forests have been largely unsuccessful. Developing nations lack the funds to develop alternative energy resources. Population growth is so rapid that there may be little hope of solving the problem before widespread destruction occurs.

Even in the developed nations, wood provides a surprising amount of energy. In the United States, wood wastes supplied half the energy used by the pulp and paper industry in 1980. In that year Congress appropriated over $400 million to encourage the wood-products industry to use more of its wasted wood—limbs, branches, and bark. Other industries in Minnesota and Wisconsin are also converting to wood fuel.

Wood has become a popular fuel for home heating since the first Arab oil embargo in 1973. Approximately one of every ten Americans burns wood as either a primary or secondary heat source. In New England one-fifth of the homes use wood as a primary heat source, and almost all of the rest use it as a secondary source. Other wooded areas such as the Northwest, Appalachia, the Great Lakes states, and the Rocky Mountain states have also witnessed a dramatic increase in wood heating.

Wood stoves produce at least ten times more particulates and carbon monoxide than oil or gas furnaces. In January 1978 wood stoves in the Portland–Seattle–Vancouver region produced an estimated 920 tons of respirable particulate matter, also known as **fine particulates**. This was 70 tons more than all other sources combined! Some cities are considering emissions standards that would require wood-stove users to install pollution control devices. Wood stoves have been banned in London and in South Korean cities.

Carl Reidel, former president of the American Forestry Association, has warned that the country's woodlands are being indiscriminately cut. Homeowners and commercial loggers are removing the wrong species, overcutting, and cutting young trees. Some experts predict that widespread domestic use of wood threatens the future of the United States' forests.

Even though wood is a renewable resource, forests can be destroyed by overharvesting. Proper forest management is needed to ensure sustained yield (Chapter 11). Ecosystem stability, wildlife habitat, and watershed protection must be considered in drafting strategies to meet energy needs.

Burning Municipal Garbage Many nations are burning refuse or garbage to make electricity and steam heat for home and industries. (Essay 15-1 gives some examples of unconventional energy strategies.) Faced with growing urban waste, land shortages, and difficulties finding suitable disposal sites, many European countries began exploring this option in the 1960s. Today at least 260 plants worldwide burn municipal garbage to generate electricity and, in some cases, steam heat. Most of these plants are in Europe; only a handful are in the United States.

Munich, Germany, gets 12% of its electricity from the combustion of garbage and other wastes. In Paris 1.7 million tons of garbage is burned each year to provide heat and electricity. This saves Paris over 480,000 barrels of oil a year. The world's largest refuse combustion facility is located in Rotterdam, where a 55-megawatt plant is powered entirely by refuse.

In the United States 50% to 60% of all urban waste is combustible. Although the heat content varies depending on the nature of the waste, 2 metric tons of waste has the same heat content as 1 metric ton of coal.

Refuse incinerators reduce our dependency on nonrenewable fuel, and help reduce the amount of waste we throw away. Moreover, these systems offer opportunities for communities to recover discarded metals such as aluminum, steel, copper (Chapter Supplement 22-1). On the other hand, refuse contains a wide assortment of nonburnable wastes, which must be removed before burning. This adds to the cost of operation. To burn successfully, wastes must contain less than 50% water. Wet refuse may require supplemental fuel such as natural gas or oil to maintain the constant temperature necessary for proper operation of electric- and steam-generating systems. Without pollution controls, waste-burning incinerators can generate a considerable amount of air pollution.

Synthetic Fuels from Biomass Biomass in the form of urban wastes, manure, crop residues, and specially grown crops can be converted into a variety of synthetic fuels. There are several ways this can be done, but the most promising is bioconversion. Two types of bioconversion are popular. In **anaerobic fermention**, organic matter is decayed by bacteria in the absence of oxygen. The bacteria's metabolic processes convert organic matter to methane (70%) and carbon dioxide (30%), a mixture known as **biogas**. In **alcoholic fermentation**, the second type of bioconversion, organic materials are degraded by yeast in the presence of oxygen. The yeast produces ethanol (grain alcohol), which can be burned by itself or mixed with gasoline to form gasohol. Ethanol is also a useful feedstock for the chemical industry.

To make biogas, organic waste such as manure is mixed with water and heated in a closed container, where anaerobic bacteria digest the material. The airtight containers used today are called **anaerobic digesters**, or **methane**

Figure 15-9
A methane digester.

digesters (Figure 15-9). They are simple to build and operate and inexpensive to make. When the digestion process is complete, a nutrient-rich sludge remains that can be used to fertilize cropland and pastures.

China has been a pioneer in methane digesters. In 1978 over 7 million were in operation throughout rural China. Ambitious government plans called for the number to increase to 70 million by 1985. Each digester produces about 1 cubic meter (33 cubic feet) of methane per day over an eight-month period (after which it requires refilling). Seventy million digesters would produce the energy equivalent of about 20 million metric tons of coal and provide fuel for cooking and other purposes.

Methane digesters are an appropriate technology for rural China, providing energy where it is needed and where there is ample fuel from animals and agricultural fields. The success of the Chinese has led many scientists and political leaders to believe that this technology could be successfully applied elsewhere.

Biogas generation is an economically feasible and environmentally sound method of producing energy in the developed countries as well. Municipal landfills are prime candidates for biogas production. In the United States over 20,000 landfills with millions of tons of rotting wastes could be tapped simply by installing vents that draw off biogas.

Dairy farmers can generate biogas from cattle manure to run electric generators that power milking machines and lights. Well-planned farms can be almost entirely energy self-sufficient. Moreover, the organic residue can be sold as fertilizer or applied to fields.

Biogas technology offers many advantages: It allows us to tap a renewable energy resource that is being wasted. It is nonpolluting. And it can produce fertilizer that reduces the use of fossil-fuel-based fertilizers. In less developed nations it could help improve public health, because human wastes properly treated in digesters can be rid of pathogenic bacteria and parasites. The technology is simple and well-developed enough that it could create small-scale industries, jobs, and income for the poor. Money saved by using this technology in developing nations could be used for other purposes.

Crops, crop residues, forest residues, kelp, and algae can be converted to ethyl alcohol to be burned in cars and other vehicles. Today, the net energy yield of ethanol production is close to zero. But the Office of Technology Assessment has indicated that ethanol could be produced with a favorable energy balance by using solar energy to run the distillery and by feeding the residual plant matter, which is rich in protein, to livestock. The manure produced by the livestock, then, could be used to produce

Novel Approaches to Energy Production

Rising energy prices have inspired many people to come up with their own solutions to creating energy.

• In Miami, the Florida Power & Light Company burns confiscated bales of marijuana, courtesy of the U.S. Customs Department, for power. The marijuana provides enough energy to produce electricity for one of their plants. "But the supply is too unreliable," says a utility spokesman.

• "There's a future in sludge" says James E. Alleman, Associate Professor of Civil Engineering at Purdue University. Alleman says that sludge, the solid material left over after sewage treatment, can replace 30% of the clay needed to make bricks. Sludge has also been tested in other products, including fences and telephone poles. It is cheap, easy to come by, and helps reduce outside energy use because it releases heat as it burns.

• In Midlothian, Virginia, Stephen Harris found a way to turn paper waste into an inexpensive fuel source for a magazine printing plant. He devised a system to shred and burn the plant's excess paper, produc-

ing enough steam and heat to generate power for both machinery and lighting. He says the system should pay for itself in about ten years.

• At the Knouse Foods Coop in Peach Glen, Pennsylvania, a food-processing plant is partially run on the sticky, fibrous pulp left over from fruits after juicing. The pulp, which has long created a problem in landfills because of its slow decomposition, is now dried and then burned, generating 60% of the plant's energy needs. The steam is also used to pasteurize apple juice. Company spokesmen report that their new system actually nets a profit of $474 per day.

• A thermal blanket helps prevent ice from melting in an indoor skating rink in Johnstown, Pennsylvania. When the rink is not being used, the blanket covers the ice, saving 54% on electric bills and 24% on heating bills. This is quite a bit when a typical electric bill for such a rink usually runs up to $12,000 per month.

• The Prudential Insurance Company uses an "ice pond" to help cut air conditioning costs by about $12,000 a year. Theodore Taylor, the inventor, created the .2-hec-

tare (half-acre) pond by using a snow-making machine. The mountain of ice was then covered with a thermal blanket. As the ice slowly melted throughout the summer, the cold water was pumped into the building air ducts to help cool circulating air.

• Bill Schultz of Grants Pass, Oregon, used rabbit power for 18 months to heat his greenhouse. Because a bunny's average temperature is about 40° C (102.6° F) about 400 rabbits were able to match the heat produced by one commercial greenhouse heater—180,000 Btus per hour. When it was 0° C (32° F) outside, it was 13° C (56° F) inside the greenhouse. Schultz saved about $25 a day in heating costs thanks to his rabbits. Adding to his profits, he sold $300 to $400 worth of rabbits each week to food outlets. His experiment ended when the stores were finally inundated with rabbit fryers.

Source: Adapted from *International Wildlife*, 1983, by Phyllis Lehmann.

---

methane. Such a closely coordinated scheme could prove cost-effective.

Another major limitation to ethanol production is land availability. Fuel farms could be started on marginal land, but at the expense of wildlife and watersheds. Timber and forest wastes could also be used to produce ethanol, but the available biomass is not large. For instance, if the *total* annual forest growth could be converted to ethanol, it would yield only 2 to 4 quads of energy. Kelp and algae farms might be used, but to produce ethanol equivalent to 1 quad would require 68,000 square kilometers (26,000

square miles) of ocean, a region about the size of West Virginia. The cost of harvesting and processing might prove too great.

Some Alternative Strategies Certain plants not grown for food can produce oils. For example, a desert shrub (*Euphorbia lathyris*) found in Mexico and the southwestern United States could become a profitable oil producer. In arid climates the shrub could yield 16 barrels per hectare (40 barrels per acre) on a sustainable basis. The copaiba tree of the Amazon region yields a liquid that can be

Figure 15-10
This view of Mono Dam shows how the reservoir was filling with silt. In succeeding years the dam filled completely and gradually was reclaimed by the surrounding forest.

substituted for diesel fuel without processing. Sunflower seed oil can also be used in place of diesel. Farmers could convert 10% of their cropland to sunflowers to produce all the diesel fuel needed to run their machinery. By 1985 the Brazilian government hopes to replace 16% of its diesel fuel with oils derived from peanuts, soybeans, sunflowers, rapeseed, and African palm.

Many of these schemes are likely to find a place in a sustainable society. The renewable liquid fuels industry may someday consist of many small facilities, each contributing to our total energy production. If marked increases are achieved in the energy efficiency of autos, trucks, buses, jets, and trains, renewable fuels could provide most, if not all, of the fuel we need in the future.

Hydroelectric Power, Tides, and Ocean Thermal Energy

Hydroelectric Power

Humans have tapped the power of flowing rivers and streams for thousands of years. For centuries, the kinetic energy of water has been trapped by water wheels used to grind grain, saw wood, and manufacture textiles; but it was not until the 1800s that this energy was converted to electricity.

Pros and Cons of Water Power As an energy source, water power offers many advantages. It is generally considered renewable, it creates no air pollution or thermal pollution, and it is relatively inexpensive. Furthermore, the technology is well developed

On the opposite side of the coin are numerous problems. Sediment fills in reservoirs, giving them a typical lifespan of 50 to 100 years (although large projects may last 200 to 300 years). Thus, even though hydroelectric power is renewable, the dams and reservoirs needed to capture this energy have a limited lifetime; and once a good site is destroyed by sediment, it is gone forever (Figure 15-10). Dams and reservoirs create many additional problems, as discussed in Chapter 12.

Potential for Hydroelectric Power Brazil, Nepal, China, and many African and South American countries have a large untapped hydroelectric potential. The potential electric generating capacity of South America is estimated to be 600,000 megawatts, and that of Africa, 780,000

megawatts. By comparison, the United States, the world's leader in hydroelectric production, has a present capacity of about 70,000 megawatts and an additional potential capacity of about 160,000 megawatts.

These figures are deceptive. For example, estimates include all possible sites whether or not dams are technically, economically, or environmentally sound. For example, half of of the U.S. potential is in Alaska, far from the places that need power.

The potential for more large projects in the United States is small, since the most favorable sites have already been developed. In addition, rising construction costs have increased the price of energy produced by large hydroelectric projects by 3 to 20 times since the early 1970s.

For the United States the most sensible strategy may be to increase the capacity of existing hydroelectric facilities and install turbines on the more than 50,000 dams already built for flood control, recreation, and water supply. Conservative estimates show that about 1 quad of electrical energy could be generated by this means. In appropriate locations small dams could provide energy needed by farms, small businesses, and small communities. In 1981 and 1982 the government reviewed nearly 4000 proposals for small dams and hydroelectric generators. On the negative side, the development of such projects could have a marked effect on stream flow and wildlife in some areas.

In the developing nations small-scale hydroelectric generation may fit in well with the demand. In China over 90,000 small hydroelectric generators account for about one-third of the country's electrical output.

Tides and Waves

The oceans represent an immense source of energy. Major strategies have been drafted to capture three aspects of it: tidal energy, wave energy, and ocean thermal energy.

Tidal Energy Tidal power projects attempt to harness the energy of the tides as they flow in and out. A dam is built across an estuary or bay, permitting the incoming and outgoing waters to flow through small openings fitted with propellers that run electric turbines (Figure 15-11).

To date, only two small tidal electric plants have been built, one in France and the other in the Soviet Union. In fact, there are only about two dozen locations in the world where tidal power could be harnessed. If every site were developed, the total electrical production would only be 5% of the annual electrical production in the United States.

Wave Power Like the tides, waves could theoretically be tapped to provide energy. **Wave power** projects would use a rocker mechanism to turn a generator. Numerous schemes have been designed to harness wave energy, but none has proven very successful.

Preliminary estimates show that the potential of wave power for the United States may be small. Other nations

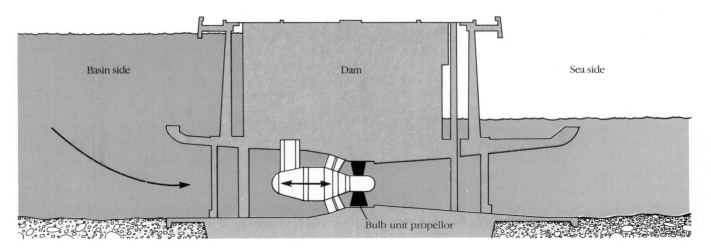

Basin side   Dam   Sea side

Bulb unit propellor

Figure 15-11
In a tidal power plant, water flows through small openings in the dam, spinning a propellor that generates electricity.

such as Great Britain and Japan may have a much larger potential.

The benefits of wave power are its renewability and lack of pollution. However, interference with ship movement, difficulties transporting the electricity ashore, corrosion by seawater, high costs, and low net energy yields may outweigh these benefits. The future of wave power depends on technological breakthroughs and economic considerations.

Ocean Thermal Energy Conversion

The oceans are an enormous solar energy storage system. The sun heats the surface water and creates a temperature difference between it and the water 600 to 900 meters (2000 to 3000 feet) below. **Ocean thermal energy conversion** (OTEC) systems exploit this temperature differential. Warm surface waters heat ammonia in a closed system (Figure 15-12). Ammonia vaporizes and then drives an electrical turbine. Cooler water is pumped up from below to recondense the ammonia vapor, thus starting the cycle over again.

OTEC seems a promising technology, because the ocean collects and stores the solar energy, eliminating the need for separate storage. Plants could operate day and night, making electricity year round. However, the technical difficulties may be insurmountable. The chief problem is that a plant would need to move huge volumes of water to create a small amount of electrical energy. A 100-megawatt plant would requires a flow rate higher than the Colorado River at peak of spring runoff in normal years. Energy for pumping cuts into the net energy yield. For instance, a 50-kilowatt experimental OTEC plant operated off the coast of Hawaii in 1979 consumed 80% of the energy it produced.

Suitable sites for OTEC plants are very limited. Potential regions must be relatively storm free, must have high temperature gradients and minimal ocean currents, and must be close to energy centers. Thus, only two good sites exist in the United States—the east coast of Florida in the Gulf Stream and the Gulf of Mexico.

Environmental problems might result from pumping cool waters to the surface. Changes in ocean temperatures could affect regional and, some suggest, even global climate. For example, northern Europe is warmer than other areas located at the same latitude because of the warming effect of the Gulf Stream. OTEC plants in the United States could steal enough warm water from the Gulf Stream to affect many "downstream" nations. OTEC plants might also cause an upwelling of nutrient- and carbon-enriched water, which could stimulate ocean plankton and other marine organisms, upsetting the natural ecosystem balance in the vicinity of these plants. Some researchers estimate that OTEC plants would also produce one-third more carbon dioxide than coal- and oil-powered plants producing the same amount of energy. Carbon dioxide is dissolved in ocean water, and when the water is warmed it escapes into the atmosphere.

Geothermal Energy

The earth harbors an enormous amount of heat, or **geothermal energy**, which comes from the decay of naturally occurring radioactive materials in the earth's crust and from **magma**, molten rock near the earth's surface. Geothermal energy is constantly being regenerated, but because the rate of renewal is slow, overexploitation could deplete this resource on a regional basis.

Geothermal resources fall into three major categories: hydrothermal convection zones, geopressurized zones, and hot-rock zones. **Hydrothermal convection zones** are common in the western United States, where magma penetrates into the earth's crust and heats rock containing large amounts of groundwater (Figure 15-13). The heat pressurizes the groundwater and drives it to the earth's surface through cracks or fissures, where it may emerge as steam (geyser), or as a liquid (hot spring).

Geopressurized zones are aquifers trapped by impermeable rock strata and heated by underlying magma. This superheated, pressurized water can be tapped by deep wells. Some geopressurized zones also contain methane gas. In the United States, geopressurized zones are located off the coasts of Texas and Louisiana.

Hot-rock zones, the most widespread geothermal resource, are regions where bedrock is heated by magma. To reap the vast amounts of heat, wells are drilled, and the bedrock is fractured with explosives. Water is pumped into fractured bedrock, heated, and then pumped out.

Geothermal energy is heavily concentrated in the so-called ring of fire encircling the Pacific Ocean and in the great mountain belt stretching from the Alps to China. Hydrothermal convection systems are the most widely used methods of capturing geothermal energy, because these zones are the easiest and least expensive to tap. Hot water or steam from them can heat homes, factories, and greenhouses. Steam can also be used to run turbines to produce electricity.

(a)

Figure 15-12
(a) Ocean thermal energy conversion plants, like the model shown in the artist's rendition, would produce 100 megawatts (net) of electricity (12.4 million kilowatt hours a day) at sea by drawing upon the virtually inexhaustable solar energy in the world's tropical oceans. *(b)* In typical operation warm surface water is drawn over an evaporator. The vapor drives a turbine to make electricity. Cold water drawn from the depths is used to condense the vapor exhausting from the turbines.

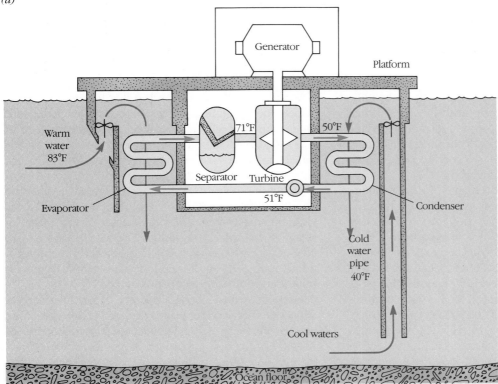

(b)

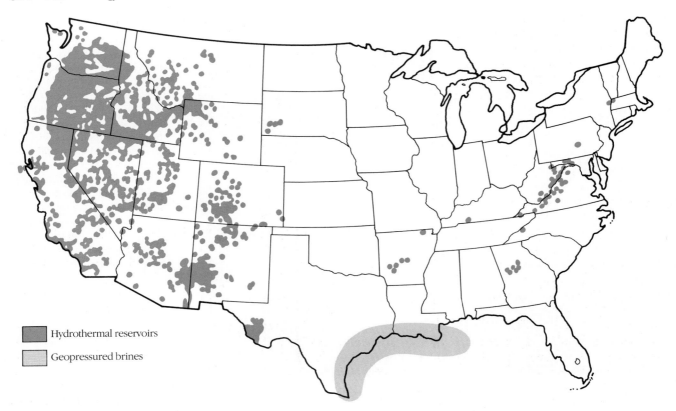

Figure 15-13
Geothermal resources in the United States.

Several countries use geothermal energy for heating. In Iceland 65% of the homes are heated by geothermal steam and hot water. Iceland's greenhouses produce nearly all of its fresh tomatoes, lettuce, and cucumbers. Hungary and the Soviet Union also have large geothermally heated greenhouses for vegetable production.

Although it is still in its early stages of development, geothermal electric production is growing quickly in the United States, Italy, New Zealand, and Japan. In 1983 U.S. geothermal energy production was approximately 1800 megawatts, or about the same as two large nuclear power plants. Nevada, California, Hawaii, and Utah are leaders in this field; by 2000 California could produce 25% of its electricity from geothermal energy. By the same year the United States could produce 27,000 megawatts of electricity per year from geothermal energy. The Philippines hopes to make geothermal its second-ranking source of electricity by 1985, because it costs one-fifth as much as electricity from oil.

Hydrothermal convection systems have several drawbacks. The steam and hot water they produce are often laden with minerals, salts, toxic metals, and hydrogen sulfide gas. Many of these chemicals corrode pipes and other metal components of the system. Steam systems may emit an ear-shattering hiss and large amounts of heat into the air. Pollution-control devices are necessary to cut down on air and water pollutants. To cut down on emissions, engineers have proposed closed systems that pump the steam or hot water out and then inject it back into the ground to be reheated. Finally, because heat cannot be transported long distances, industries might have to be built at the source of energy.

Geopressurized zones are not currently being used, although work is under way to determine if the net energy balance will be favorable. Exploitation of these zones could cause subsidence in coastal regions. Extensive offshore drilling and other problems make it unlikely that geopressurized zones will ever play much of a role.

Hot-rock zones are a potentially large energy resource, but the costs of drilling and fracturing the hot rock, the need for water, and the cost of pumping water into and out of the earth make this technique of little future value.

The U.S. Council on Environmental Quality has predicted that in the next 30 years, the country could recover 70,000 megawatts from identified geothermal reserves with existing technologies, mostly hydrothermal convection zones. Their fate depends on government and private investment and the success of pollution control efforts.

Hydrogen Fuel

Enthusiasm for hydrogen stems from the fact that it is derived from the breakdown of water, a renewable and abundant resource. Furthermore, hydrogen gas burns cleanly, producing only water and a little nitrogen oxide gas. Hydrogen gas could replace gaseous and liquid fuels; it is easy to transport; and it could be generated from intermittent renewable energy sources such as solar, geothermal, and wind energy that lack storage.

Hydrogen fuel is generated by heating or passing electricity through water in the presence of **catalysts**, chemicals that facilitate the breakdown of water into oxygen and hydrogen. Alternatively, sunlight can be the energy source, in the process called **photolysis**.

The most notable problems with hydrogen production are the negative net energy yield and the high cost. Hydrogen is more explosive than gasoline, and gaseous hydrogen contains only one-third as much energy as an equivalent volume of gasoline. To be useful as a fuel for vehicles, it must be condensed into a liquid form by cooling it to around $-253°C$ ($-423°F$). This requires more energy, which further lowers the net energy yield.

New methods of storing hydrogen hold some promise. Recent work on metal hydrides indicates that they may be a good solution. Metal hydrides are formed when hydrogen gas is pumped into containers filled with certain metallic compounds. They have a volumetric energy content approximately two-thirds that of gasoline and are much safer than liquid or gaseous hydrogen.

Hydroelectric power, wind, solar, and other renewable energy resources could be used to generate the electricity needed to make hydrogen. They are "free" energy sources and have unlimited supplies. Proponents argue that when power demand is low, renewables could generate electricity to make hydrogen, making this a more sensible strategy.

Conservation

Conservation must be at the heart of all energy strategies. Nations that rely on energy cannot afford to squander it. In Chapter 13 you learned that energy in the United States is used primarily for heating and cooling buildings, for transportation, and for industry. Energy conservation in each of these areas could substantially cut the total energy demand. This section reviews some of the most important ways to reduce energy waste.

Heating and Cooling Buildings

Cutting Heat Losses Over half of the energy used in a typical American house goes into space heating. Heat is lost from a house by moving directly through the walls, floors, ceilings, and windows. This is called **conduction**. Insulation of walls, floors, and ceilings can reduce the conduction loss. Because 70% of the heat loss in a house is through the ceiling, insulation here can pay off rather quickly (Table 15-2). Utility companies and energy consultants can help homeowners make the right choice of insulation for local conditions.

Heat is also lost by **infiltration**—escape through cracks around doors and windows and areas where ducts, pipes, and wires enter the house. In the places where two different building materials meet (cement foundation and wood frame), additional energy leaks may occur. Lost heat is replaced by cold air that creates drafts. This problem is easily treated by applying weather stripping and caulking cracks. Such efforts are cheap, take little time, save lots of energy, and make the home immediately more comfortable.

Windows are a major avenue of heat loss, but storm windows and heavy curtains can prevent this. As shown in Table 15-2, these improvements cost more than insulation and weather stripping and have a longer payback period.

Changes in Habits Life-styles and habits make a big difference in energy consumption. Years ago, American homes were typically heated to 18° C (65°F) in the winter. To stay warm, occupants simply dressed warmly, but with improvements in heating systems and cheap energy, residents shed their clothes and turned up their thermostats. Now, as the prices of fuel rise and people become more aware of the need to save energy, thermostats are being turned down, and the sweaters are coming out of storage.

Another way to save energy is to heat only rooms that

Table 15-2   Costs and Savings of Home Conservation Measures in Three States

Conservation Measures	Cost		Savings	Will Pay for Itself in[1]		Possible Tax Credit	
	Do It Yourself	Contractor	1st Year	Do It Yourself	Contractor	Do It Yourself	Contractor
CONNECTICUT Increase attic insulation from R-15 to R-30	$155	$365	$28	5.5 years	13.1 years	Yes $23	Yes $55
Increase wall insulation from R-4 to R-12	Not advised	2158	346	—	6.2 years	—	Yes $300 max.
Caulk, weatherstrip doors & windows	101	268	88	1.1 years	3.5 years	Yes $15	Yes $40
Add storm windows & doors	790	1620	155	5.1 years	10.5 years	Yes $118	Yes $243
Install automatic[2] thermostat timer	50	80	250	0.2 year	0.3 year	Yes $7	Yes $12
Insulate basement walls	621	1191	360	1.7 years	3.3 years	Yes $93	Yes $179
Have furnace burner tuned up	Not advised	45	129	—	0.3 year	Not eligible	Not eligible
Buy new boiler or furnace	—	1800	225	—	8 years	Not eligible	Not eligible
TEXAS Increase attic insulation from R-8 to R-22	$260	$315	$98	2.6 years	3.2 years	Yes $39	Yes $47
Caulk around windows	41	61	18	2.3 years	3.4 years	Yes $6	Yes $9
Add storm window (on north side only)	23	57	2	11.5 years	28.5 years	Yes $3	Yes $9
Insulate water heater	16	40	43	0.3 year	0.9 year	Yes $2	Yes $6
Install automatic[2] thermostat timer	50	110	148	0.3 year	0.7 year	Yes $7	Yes $16
Install solar reflective screens	—	221	86	—	2.6 years	Not eligible	Not eligible

are occupied or frequently used; close bedrooms until bedtime and close off unused rooms completely. Turning the thermostat down when away at school or work or on vacation can also help cut energy usage. Fans can help circulate the air in a house and keep the heat uniformly dispersed. Fans behind wood stoves are especially helpful in distributing heat. Another idea is to do baking and use other heat-producing appliances at night to supplement your furnace. Humidity also helps people feel a little warmer in winter.

Summertime Energy Conservation   Making homes warmer for winter months also helps keep them cooler in the summer. Insulation in the walls and attic, for example, will help hold out summer heat in air-conditioned homes. If a house isn't air conditioned, opening windows

Table 15-2 Costs and Savings of Home Conservation Measures in Three States (continued)

Conservation Measures	Cost		Savings	Will Pay for Itself in[1]		Possible Tax Credit	
	Do It Yourself	Contractor	1st Year	Do It Yourself	Contractor	Do It Yourself	Contractor
OREGON Increase attic insulation from R-13 to R-30	$225	$417	$32	6.9 years	12.9 years	Yes $34	Yes $63
Insulate walls to R-11	Not advised	475	168	—	2.8 years	—	Yes $71
Caulk, weatherstrip windows & doors	70	225	137	0.5 year	1.6 years	Yes $10	Yes $34
Add storm windows & doors	615	1230	90	6.8 years	13.7 years	Yes $92	Yes $185
Insulate water heater	27	35	22	1.2 years	1.6 years	Yes $4	Yes $5
Install automatic[2] thermostat timer	60	125	40	1.5 years	3.1 years	Yes $9	Yes $19
Insulate floors to R-19	315	753	92	3.4 years	8.2 years	Yes $47	Yes $113
Insulate ducts	150	330	213	0.7 year	1.5 years	Yes $23	Yes $50

[1]Tax credits can help speed up the payback.
[2]To reduce heat from 70° to 55° for two eight-hour periods each day.
Source: Mergens, E. (1981). *The Conservation Payback Book,* Shell Oil Company.

during the night will let cold air in; closing windows and doors and drawing curtains during the day will hold in the cool air. Curtains alone cut heat gain by one-third.

Turning the thermostat up in the summer will also help save energy. A small increase in the air-conditioner setting can cut the fuel bill substantially. Fans are an excellent substitute for air conditioning and much cheaper to operate. Ceiling fans are especially good at moving air in a house and increasing comfort. At night, if the humidity isn't too high, you can open windows, turn on fans, and leave the air conditioner off. Changing daily activity can also reduce cooling costs and energy consumption. Energy can be saved by drying clothes on a line.

Cutting Hot Water Heating Bills About 15% of the energy used in U.S. homes is for heating water, but half of the energy involved is wasted. Without spending a dime, you can cut down on energy waste simply by lowering the thermostat from the typical 160° F to 130° (72° C to 55°C) (if you own a dishwasher) or 120° F (49° C) (if you don't). This simple adjustment can cut energy demand for water heating by one-quarter.

Additional savings can be realized by timing hot water use. Some people save energy by turning on water heaters for a few hours each day, during which time the family showers, does the dishes, and washes clothes. This is more economical than spreading these activities throughout the day. It also helps to take shorter showers and to use less water when washing dishes. Automatic dishwashers should be operated only with full loads and should be shut off before they get to the drying cycle.

Routine maintenance can increase the efficiency of domestic water heaters; for example, sediment that accumulates on the bottom of the tank can be removed by draining 10 to 15 liters (3 or 4 gallons) of water every month or so through the faucet on the bottom. Insulation on hot-water pipes and insulation blankets on water heaters will reduce heat loss. These measures can cut energy use by 30% to 60% and most are fairly inexpensive, too. Table 15-3 shows a number of inexpensive ways to reduce energy use in the home.

Building an Energy-Efficient House Changing an existing house to save energy is called **retrofitting**. Many of these steps can be avoided if homes are built correctly from the start. For example, simply orienting an ordinary house to the south and reducing the number of north-facing windows reduces annual heating bills by one-tenth. Using double- and triple-pane windows, installing curtains or other devices to block heat loss during the night, and insulating the walls, ceiling, and floors properly can cut lifetime heating and cooling bills by 50% to 100%, all for a modest initial investment. Over a 40-year period, conservation measures that added $5000 to $10,000 to the cost of a house can save $50,000 to $80,000. Passive solar is an especially good investment. By designing a house to make use of the sun, properly insulating walls and ceilings, and installing a few other low-cost features, a homeowner may avoid ever paying another heating bill.

Many people are now building their homes partly or almost completely underground. These **earth-sheltered houses**, which are often built into a hillside, make use of the earth's insulating capacity and cut heating and cooling bills substantially. Partially earth-sheltered houses may simply back up against the hill. Earth-sheltered houses can make use of passive solar heat and backup heat from a wood stove. They are specially built to hold out moisture and permit as much sunlight to enter as possible. Good designs allow as much light to enter as in conventional homes.

Careful selection of appliances can also save hundreds of dollars over their lifetime. Natural gas appliances such as furnaces, stoves, and water heaters should have an electronic ignition, not a pilot light. Some appliances save little time or no time at all and do work that might be done as well by hand.

Legal Solutions Finally, legal approaches can contribute to energy conservation in buildings. Building codes could be updated so that all newly built houses used 80% less energy than conventional houses of the same size. Codes could require builders to install energy-efficient

Table 15-3 Energy Conservation Suggestions

1. Hot Water Heating
   Turn down thermostat on water heater.
   Use less hot water (dishwashing, laundry, showers).
   Install flow reducers on faucets.
   Coordinate and concentrate time hot water is used.
   Do full loads of laundry, and use cooler water.
   Hang clothes outside to dry.
   Periodically drain 3 to 4 gallons from water heater.
   Repair leaky faucets.

2. Space Heating
   Lower thermostat setting.
   Insulate ceilings and walls.
   Install storm window, curtains, or window quilts.
   Caulk cracks and use weatherstripping.
   Use fans to distribute heat.
   Dress more warmly.
   Heat only used areas.
   Humidify the air.
   Install an electronic ignition system in furnace.
   Replace or clean air filters in furnace.
   Have furnace adjusted periodically.

3. Cooling and Air Conditioning
   Increase thermostat setting.
   Use fans.
   Cook at night or outside.
   Dehumidify air.
   Close drapes during the day.
   Open windows at night.

4. Cooking
   Cover pots, and cook one-pot meals.
   Turn off the pilot lights on stove.
   Don't overcook, and don't open oven unnecessarily.
   Double up pots (use one as a lid for the other).
   Boil less water (only the amount you need).
   Use energy-efficient appliances (crock pots).

5. Lighting
   Cut the wattage of bulbs.
   Turn off lights when not in use.
   Use fluorescent bulbs wherever possible.
   Use natural lighting whenever possible.

6. Transportation
   Car-pool, walk, ride a bike, or take the bus to work.
   Use your car only when necessary.
   Group your trips with the car.
   Keep car tuned and tire pressure at recommended level.
   Buy energy-efficient cars.
   Recycle gas guzzlers.
   On long trips take the train or bus (not a jet).

appliances, double- and triple-paned windows, and adequate insulation in walls, floors, and basements. All new homes could have solar panels for hot water and passive solar for heating or at least be oriented to the south for solar retrofitting.

Uniform statewide building codes could be developed, establishing performance standards that stipulate the amount of energy a home should save rather than the amount of insulation or other specific features. State and federal legislators could extend tax credits for renewable energy resources and conservation.

Transportation

Trains and ships carry goods more efficiently than other vehicles, and though there will always be a need for trucks and air freight, a greater emphasis on rail and water transport would save considerable fuel.

As for transporting people, the automobile is not always the ideal means. The bicycle is the most efficient form of transportation yet devised. Good bus and rail service can make a car unnecessary for urban residents. As the U.S. population grows and as cities become denser, mass transit systems will make sense (Figure 15-14).

How can you save energy in transportation? If you own a car, keep it tuned up and operating efficiently. Check the tire pressure regularly. Car-pool to work, or take the bus. Walk or ride a bike to perform most of your errands. Consolidate your car trips.

When you drive, accelerate and brake gently, and observe the speed limits. Driving 50 miles per hour rather than 55 can cut your gas consumption by 13%. Don't race the engine or let it warm up for more than a minute. Turn off the engine if you're going to be stopped for one minute or more. Replace worn tires with good steel-belted radials, which reduce friction and improve gas mileage. Use the car air conditioner only when you really need it. For long-distance trips, trains or buses are far more energy efficient than cars and jets.

You can insist that standards for energy conservation be extended. The Japanese have a car that gets 80 miles per gallon on the highway and 55 mpg in the city, although it isn't exported to the United States. Honda recently introduced a model that gets 67 mpg on the highway and 51 mpg in the city. You can write your congressional representatives and the president and urge them to adopt legislation mandating even better gas mileage. Tax credits could be offered to people and businesses buying cars that average over 45 mpg on the highway. A gas-guzzler

Figure 15-14
BART Mass transit in San Francisco bay area.

tax could be imposed on vehicles that get fewer than 25 mpg on the highway. Proceeds from the taxes could be used to pay the tax credits or to support research on improving gas mileage and making lighter, safer cars.

Industry

Industry has great potential for energy conservation. Some suggestions include better insulation of factories and office buildings; improvements in industrial processes to reduce waste heat; **cogeneration** systems, in which waste heat from one process is captured and used for other purposes; more recycling (Chapter 16); reduction of unnecessary lighting and heating; proper maintenance of all equipment, and improvements in the efficiency of motors and other equipment.

Tax credits for energy-conservation measures could be allowed. The use of renewable resources could be encouraged. Changes in electric rates could be immediately effective in curbing waste. Currently, big users are charged a cheaper rate per kilowatt-hour than smaller users. Reversing this pricing scale would encourage conservation.

Conservation is the key to a sustainable energy future. Indisputable evidence shows that Americans can reduce their energy consumption by perhaps 50% or more and maintain, or most likely improve, their standard of living.

A Solar-Powered Future?

Experts disagree on the amount of energy the United States will be using in the year 2000 and beyond. Most estimates of future energy demand range from 100 to 140 quads, but a few mavericks have predicted that the country will actually be using less energy in the year 2000 than it is now! Estimates as low as 15 quads have been suggested.

Many observers see coal and nuclear power as the mainstay of the American energy diet in 2000. But others see a solar transition in the making. They predict that solar energy in its many forms will supply the bulk of U.S. energy demands, in conjunction with conservation.

Supporters of a sustainable future powered by the sun envision a smooth transition into the future (Figure 15-15). One major change, though, is that energy production will become a more personal matter. Photovoltaics, active and passive solar systems, and windmills will replace huge centralized nuclear- and coal-powered electric plants. This might be a good thing; knowing where their energy comes from may help people respect its importance and use it more efficiently. Mass-produced solar systems would be relatively inexpensive. After a brief period of use they would generate as much energy as was needed to produce them. They would also pay back the owner's investment by supplying free energy.

Critics of a solar-powered future primarily ask how Americans would continue their current way of life. Where would they get the fuel to power the transportation system? Increasing efficiency is the first step. Cars that routinely get 80 mpg could double or triple the existing oil supply. Hydrogen and ethanol could help stretch it further. Electricity generated from inexpensive photovoltaics could power cars and mass-transit systems (trains and buses) that move people more efficiently than cars.

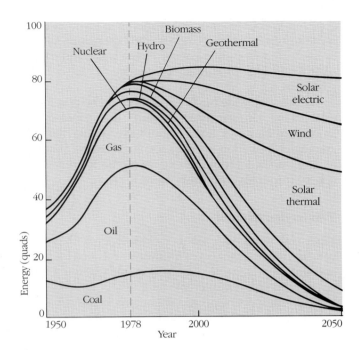

Figure 15-15
One projection of possible energy resources in the United States. These figures are based on full commitment to renewable resources.

According to solar advocates, low to intermediate thermal energy could come from direct solar energy. It could be used for home space heating, hot water, and many industrial processes. Electricity would come from the sun and wind; liquid fuels would come from biomass. Table 15-4 shows a further breakdown of energy demand by end use, showing what kind of energy is needed and how it would be used. A wise energy strategy is economically, ecologically, and socially acceptable. But society's decision should also take into account future generations.

A smooth transition to a solar-powered economy, beginning now, would ensure that future generations will not have to spend their lives cleaning up a polluted planet littered with nuclear waste dumps and scarred by surface mines. Decisive actions now would ensure that they won't have to struggle in the face of shortages to do what we could have been doing all along—tapping the generous supply of clean, renewable energy that the earth and sun offer free of charge.

As our case is new so must we think and act anew.

ABRAHAM LINCOLN

Table 15-4 Meeting Energy Needs of a Solar-Powered Society

Demand Sector	End Use Energy Form	Application	Percentage of Total Energy Use	Appropriate Energy Supply Technology
Residential and Commercial	Low-temperature thermal energy (<212°F)	Space heating, water heating, air conditioning	20–25	Passive and active solar systems, district heating systems
	Intermediate-temperature thermal energy (212–572°F)			Active solar heating with concentrating solar collectors
	Hydrogen	Cooking and drying	~5	Solar thermal, thermo-chemical, or electrolytic generation
	Methane			Biomass
	Electricity	Lighting, appliances, refrigeration	~10	Photovoltaic, wind, solar, thermal, total energy systems
			Subtotal ~35	
Industrial	Intermediate-temperature thermal energy (<572°F)	Industrial and agricultural process heat and steam	~7.5	Active solar heating with flat plate collectors, and tracking solar concentrators
	High temperature (>572°F)	Industrial process heat and steam	~17.5	Tracking, concentrating solar collector systems
	Hydrogen			Solar thermal, thermo-chemical, or electrolytic generation
	Electricity	Cogeneration, electric, drive, electrolytic, and electrochemical processes	~10	Solar thermal, photovoltaic, cogeneration, wind systems
	Feedstocks	Supply carbon sources to chemical industries	~5	Biomass residues and wastes
			Subtotal ~40	
Transportation	Electricity	Electric vehicles, electric rail	10–20	Photovoltaic, wind and solar, thermal-electric
	Hydrogen	Aircraft fuel, land and water transportation vehicles		Solar thermal, thermo-chemical, or electrolytic generation
Transportation	Liquid fuels—methanol, ethanol, gasoline	Long-distance land and water transportation vehicles	5–15	Biomass residues and wastes
			Subtotal ~ 25	
			100	

Source: Kendall, H. W., and Nadis, S. J. (1980), *Energy Strategies: Toward a Solar Future*, Cambridge, Mass.: Ballinger, p. 262.

Summary

The earth is endowed with abundant solar energy, but this source is providing only a fraction of our energy needs. *Direct solar energy* is captured from sunlight and used for heating, generating electricity, and cooling. *Indirect solar energy* is derived from natural processes such as wind, waves, flowing water, and biomass that are driven by the sun.

Passive solar systems are the simplest and most cost-effective. Buildings are designed to capture sunlight and store the energy within *thermal mass,* walls, and floors; the stored heat is gradually released into the structure. *Active solar* systems rely on collectors that absorb sunlight and convert it into heat, which is then transferred to water or air flowing through them. Pumps generally move water or air to a storage unit, where heat can be drawn off as needed. *Photovoltaics* are made of silicon or other materials that emit electrons when struck by sunlight, thus producing electricity.

The systems described offer many advantages over conventional power sources such as coal and oil. The fuel is free, nondepletable, and clean. When operating, systems produce no pollution, pay back the energy invested in their production, and offer great flexibility. The major limitations of solar energy are that the source is intermittent, making it necessary to store energy overnight or during cloudy days. Current storage technologies are fairly limited, and backup heating or electrical production systems must be available.

Winds can be tapped to generate electricity and heat, pump water, and provide mechanical work. Many proposals for using the wind have been advanced. Wind energy offers many of the advantages and disadvantages of solar energy.

Biomass, a form of indirect solar energy, has a small potential, but materials now being wasted (such as forest and crop wastes) could be used to supplement other forms. Useful biomass includes wood, crops, industrial wastes, manure, and urban waste. The simplest way of getting energy from biomass is to burn it, but many believe that a more sensible strategy would be to convert it to gaseous and liquid fuels and chemicals needed by the chemical industry.

Hydroelectric power, another indirect form of solar energy, offers many advantages: it is renewable, creates no air pollution or thermal pollution, and is relatively inexpensive. However, sediment fills in reservoirs, giving them an average lifespan of 50 to 100 years. The potential for hydroelectric power in developed countries is much less than many experts have asserted, because the best sites have already been developed. In the developing nations sites capable of producing large amounts of energy are available, but high construction costs may hinder their development.

Tidal power is another renewable energy resource, but suitable sites for capturing tidal energy are limited. *Wave power* attempts to capture energy from waves, but the potential is also probably small.

Ocean thermal energy conversion capitalizes on the heat gradient between surface and deep waters. Warm waters from the surface vaporize ammonia in a closed system; the ammonia vapor drives an electrical turbine. To recondense the ammonia, cool water is drawn up from below. A continuous cycle is maintained, allowing for the production of electricity year round. This technology eliminates the need for storage and collection because of the constant thermal gradient. But a commercial plant would have to move large volumes of water to create a small amount of electricity; this would reduce the net energy yield substantially. OTEC plants may change regional climate, alter the aquatic environment around them, and increase atmospheric carbon dioxide.

The earth harbors a great deal of energy from the decay of naturally occurring radioactive materials in the earth's crust and from *magma,* molten rock. Geothermal resources fall into three major categories. *Hydrothermal convection zones* are sites where magma penetrates into the earth's crust and heats rock containing large amounts of groundwater. The heat pressurizes the groundwater and drives it to the surface through fissures. *Geopressurized zones* are heated aquifers that can be tapped by drilling wells. *Hot-rock zones* are regions where bedrock is heated by magma. To tap the heat, wells are drilled, and the bedrock is fractured with explosives. Water is pumped into the area, heated, and then pumped out.

Hydrothermal convection zones are being used to produce space heat and electricity. Such systems produce steam and hot water laden with toxic minerals, salts, metals, and hydrogen sulfide. Noise pollution is also a problem.

Hydrogen fuel is produced by heating or passing electricity through water in the presence of a *catalyst.* Water breaks down into hydrogen and oxygen. Hydrogen is a clean-burning fuel that could replace gaseous and liquid fuels. It is easy to transport but is explosive. Electricity needed to make hydrogen could be generated from solar energy, wind energy, or hydroelectric facilities. The prospects for hydrogen are questionable today because of the negative net energy yield.

Conservation is one of the key untapped energy resources for tomorrow. By reducing energy waste in homes, factories, and transportation, the United States could inexpensively unleash an enormous supply of energy. The largest gains can be had when new homes and offices are built with passive and active solar systems, insulation, and earth sheltering.

Energy experts have shown that we can substitute renewable energy resources such as solar energy for nonrenewable resources such as oil, natural gas, coal, and nuclear power without drastically changing society. A smooth transition can be made into a sustainable future, but it will require an investment in renewable energy resources by governments and individuals.

Discussion Questions

1. Describe direct and indirect solar energy. In what ways do solar technologies pollute the environment and consume nonrenewable resources? Are these impacts justified? Why or why not?

2. Discuss the advantages and disadvantages of solar energy.

3. Describe the difference between passive and active solar systems. What features are needed in a home to make passive solar energy work well?

4. What are photovoltaic cells? What factors will bring their price down? Should we develop photovoltaic cells in preference to nuclear energy? Why or why not?

5. Discuss the advantages and disadvantages of wind-generated electricity. Wind energy is close to being competitive with conventional electricity. Should we develop this energy resource in preference to nuclear power, coal, or oil shale? Why or why not?

6. What is biomass? How can useful energy be gained from it?

7. You are a city planner in a major urban center. Design a waste recovery system to recycle valuable materials and generate energy from urban refuse. What problems would you expect to be the most significant, and how would you tackle them?

8. Why could methane digesters, solar voltaics, and wind generation prove to be valuable resources in developing nations? Would coal- or nuclear-powered plants serve people better? Discuss ways you as a head of an international development program might incorporate solar technologies in the developing nations.

9. How is geothermal energy formed? How can it be tapped? Describe its benefits and risks.

10. Debate this statement "Hydroelectric power is an immensely untapped resource in the United States and could provide an enormous amount of energy."

11. Why is this statement false: "Hydroelectricity is a renewable resource"?

12. How could existing dams (not currently producing electricity) be used in the United States to generate electricity? Would this be preferable to developing new dam sites?

13. Are tidal energy and wave energy sensible energy strategies? Defend your answer.

14. List the benefits and costs of ocean thermal energy conversion. Should more money be spent on OTEC, or should it be abandoned?

15. What are the major problems facing hydrogen power? How could these be solved?

16. Debate the statement "Conservation is our best and cheapest energy resource."

17. Discuss ways you could conserve more energy at home, at work, and in transit. Draw up a reasonable energy conservation plan for your family.

18. Make a list of criteria (cost, pollution, and the like) to judge energy resources, and list them in decreasing importance. Which energy technologies discussed in this chapter would be most suitable, according to your criteria?

Suggested Readings

Brown, L. R. (1981). *Building A Sustainable Society*. New York: Norton. General, optimistic survey of sustainable energy technologies.

Bungay, H. R. (1983). Commercializing Biomass Conversion. *Environ. Sci. and Technol.* 17(1): 24A–31A. Technical overview of biomass conversion.

Deudney, D., and Flavin, C. (1983). *Renewable Energy: The Power to Choose*. New York: Norton. Fact-filled, highly readable book on renewables.

Elridge, F. R. (1980). *Wind Machines*. New York: Van Nostrand Reinhold. Excellent overview of wind energy.

Flavin, C. (1981). A Renaissance for Wind Power. *Environment* 23(8): 31–41. Interesting look at wind energy.

—(1983). Photovoltaics: International Competition for the Sun. *Environment* 25(3): 7–11; 39–43. Good survey of economics and history of solar voltaics.

Hempel, L. C. (1982). The Original Blueprint for a Solar America. *Environment* 24(2): 25–32. A superb highlighting of solar history.

Hira, A. U., Mulloney, J. A., and D'Alessio, G. J. (1983). Alcohol Fuels from Biomass. *Environ. Sci. and Technol.* 17(5): 202A–213A. Technical review of alcohol production.

Kendall, H. W., and Nadis, S. J., eds. (1980). *Energy Strategies: Toward a Solar Future*. Cambridge, Mass.: Ballinger. Detailed survey of energy sources and their prospects for the future. Superb!

Medsker, L. (1982). *Side Effects of Renewable Energy Sources*. New York: National Audubon Society. Detailed report on negative impacts of renewables. Excellent reference.

Park, J. (1981). *Wind Power*. Palo Alto, Calif.: Cheshire Books. Good overview of wind energy.

Rosenbaum, W. A. (1981). *Energy, Politics and Public Policy*. Washington, D.C.: Congressional Quarterly Press. Political dimensions of energy planning.

Rothchild, J., and Tenney, F. (1978). *The Home Energy Guide: How to Cut Your Utility Bills*. New York: Ballantine. A practical guide to energy conservation in the home.

Tucker, J. B. (1982). Biogas Systems in India: Is the Technology Appropriate? *Environment* 24(8): 12–20; 39. Excellent study of appropriate technology and problems facing its adoption.

U.S. Department of Energy. (1980). *Final Environmental Impact Statement, Geothermal Demonstration Program* (DOE/EIS-0049). Washington, D.C.: U.S. Government Printing Office. Detailed coverage of environmental impacts.

16

Mineral Resources

*There is no medicine like hope, no incentive so great,
and no tonic so powerful as expectation of something
better tomorrow.*

O. S. MARDEN

Look around you. Whether you're sitting in your room, a library, or a cafeteria, you're surrounded by minerals: the metal pen by your hand, the gold frames of your glasses, your brass watchband, the stone walls around you, or the steel chair you're sitting on. These nonrenewable resources come from all parts of the globe, and they contribute significantly to our standard of living.

Mineral Resources and Society

Today more than 100 nonfuel minerals are traded in the world market. Worth billions of dollars to the world economy, these materials are vital to modern industry and agriculture. The major nonfuel minerals used in the United States are shown in Table 16-1. Several dozen minerals are so important that if any one of them were suddenly no longer available at a reasonable price, industry and agriculture would be brought to a standstill.

In 1982 unrefined minerals in the United States were valued at approximately $24 billion; refining raised their

Landsat Imagery

Twenty-four hours a day, 365 days a year, the Landsat satellite orbits the earth, sending back a million separate pieces of information *every second.* Flying at a height of 570 miles, the solar-powered satellite passes over the same area every 18 days around 9:30 A.M., recording earth's most subtle and sensitive changes. Because of it, we are able to predict changing weather patterns with more accuracy, determine long-term effects of agriculture, locate mineral and oil deposits, study the impact of too-large populations, monitor waste and pollution problems—and even count the grizzlies in Yellowstone National Park. The following pages illustrate a few of Landsat's many applications.

1 Uranium in the San Rafael Swell, Utah—September 1974. False color imaging creates a spectacular view of the San Rafael Swell. Color and pattern interpretation is especially tricky; each color and its subsequent variation shows the subtle differences between surface rock types. Uranium is the coveted mineral here, depicted in the central golden region. The large blue band (shale) lies intertwined with layers of sandstone (golden brown). The light pink areas are arable, fed by the waters from the magenta mountains, west. The orange-yellow San Rafael desert (east) is divided from the Swell by the blue/white San Rafael reef. Several thousand tons of uranium have been mined here in the last 12 years.

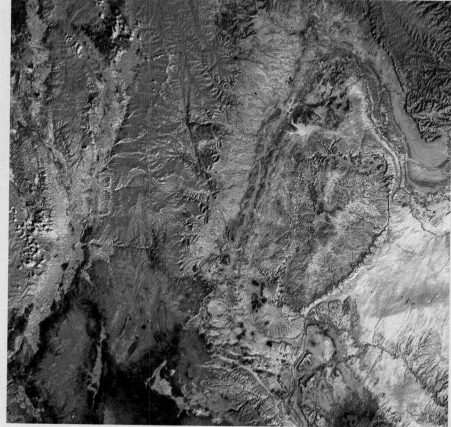

2 Buenos Aires, Argentina—December 1981. Buenos Aires, a teeming city of 9 million, exemplifies rapid development. The city, shown in blue on the west bank of the Rio de la Plata estuary, was home to a mere 1000 residents only three centuries ago. The city of La Plata, the smaller blue area to the east, grapples with a population of ½ million. Cattle and dairy industries (bright red) provide agricultural support for the area. The delta, upper left, is unusable wetland. Vivid whorls of sediment color the estuary.

2

3 The Everglades and Southern Florida—March 1978. The Everglades, a subtropical region spanning 13,000 square kilometers (5000 square miles) is one of the most delicate ecosystems existing in the world today. The extensive drainage system in the north has provided Florida with tremendously fertile farmland (recently reclaimed areas are white). Everglades National Park encompasses the southern portion. The bright red patches represent hardwood tree stands, which are firmly rooted in the southerly flowing swamp. Miami, to the east, supports a population of 1.5 million.

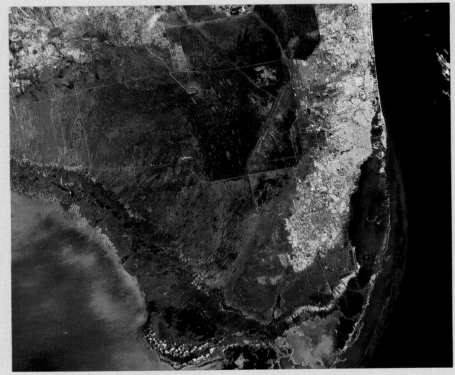

3

4 Athabasca Tar Sands, Alberta—August 1981. When OPEC prices soar and lines get long at the local gas station, thoughts turn to alternative energy sources, including bitumens, heavy oils, and tars. The Athabasca Tar Sands, an area covering over 13,000 square miles, boasts the world's largest tar deposits. Extraction facilities (blue) lie west of the Athabasca River. Impossible to pump because of its viscosity, the tar is actually mined. The facility produces well over 150,000 barrels of crude oil a day, but some 750,000 tons of earth are moved to do so. Some believe the area could produce as much as 900,000 millions barrels in its lifetime.

4

5 Clear-cutting in Western Alberta—July 1979. The forests of Alberta supply one of Canada's major exports—timber. Clearcutting, a questionable logging practice that denudes entire hillsides and leads to erosion and habitat destruction, shows up clearly from outer space in the form of patchwork patterns. The land shown here is irreparably damaged.

5

6 Alamogordo, New Mexico—November 1972. Alamogordo, New Mexico, site of the first atomic bomb test, today serves as an alternative landing site for the space shuttle. The large white area is White Sands, a gypsum deposit extending about 20 miles across. To the north lava beds cut through the image. The San Andres Mountains (parallel west) extend upward to Jornada del Muerto (Journey of the Dead Man). It was here on July 16, 1945, that the bomb was exploded from the top of a 160 foot water tower, producing an explosion equal to 20,000 tons of TNT.

6

7 Sudan Irrigation Scheme—December 1979. The country of Sudan is one of the driest regions of the world, receiving an average of only 12 inches of rainfall annually. Yet the area of El Gezira, shown here in red and gray patches, is highly productive farmland, thanks to a complicated irrigation scheme begun in 1925 when a dam was built on the Blue Nile (east). The dam allowed periodic flooding of the plains in order to irrigate croplands. By 1962, about 16,000 kilometers (10,000 miles) of canals had been built (field boundaries mark canal lines). The Nile River, some 4000 miles in length, lies to the west. The yellow areas are deserts—dry reminders of what the whole of El Geriza used to be.

All photographs © GEOPIC, Earth Satellite Corporation.

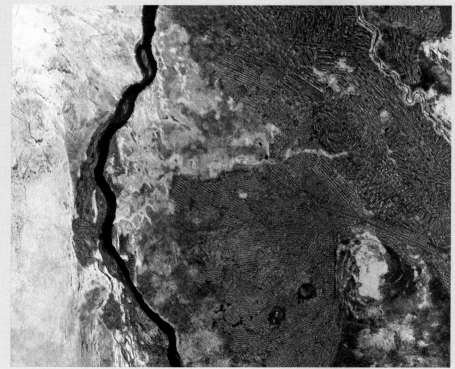

7

Table 16-1 Major Metals and Mineral Consumption in the U.S.[1]

Metal/Mineral	1978	1982
Aluminum	6,045,000	4,740,000
Antimony	40,536	33,200
Chromium	590,000	330,000
Cobalt	10,182	5,500
Copper	2,553,100	1,980,000
Gold	5,100,000 troy ounces[2]	3,800,000 troy ounces
Iron ore	115,000,000	54,000,000
Lead	1,477,300	1,171,500
Magnesium	131,000	114,000
Manganese	1,363,000	700,000
Mercury	76,547 flasks[3]	50,700 flasks
Molybdenum	33,862	16,500
Nickel	273,000	174,000
Platinum	2,635,000 troy ounces	2,200,000 troy ounces
Silver	148,000,000 troy ounces	144,000,000 troy ounces
Tin	76,904	50,600
Vanadium	8,164	6,500
Zinc	1,230,900	891,000

[1]Measured in short tons (2000 pounds) unless indicated otherwise.
[2]1 troy ounce = 31.1 grams.
[3]1 flask = 76 pounds.
Source: U.S. Bureau of Mines.

value to over $200 billion. Assembled into salable goods, they were worth over $3000 billion!

Who Consumes the World's Minerals?

The developed countries are the major consumers of minerals. With one-fourth of the world's population, they consume at least three-fourths of the world's nonfuel mineral resources. These resources come both from their own mines and from many developing countries. The United States, with only about 6% of the world's population, consumes about 20% of the world's nonfuel mineral resources. Per capita consumption is about 8 metric tons (7 tons) a year.

The developing nations use the remaining nonfuel mineral resources. Latin America, Africa, and Asia have nearly three-fourths of the world's people but use only 7% of the aluminum, 9% of the copper, and 12% of the iron ore. Continued slow economic growth will probably not change these figures much by the year 2000, although

there are notable exceptions, such as South Korea and Taiwan, which are quickly becoming industrialized.

Growing Interdependence and Global Tensions

As shown in Figure 16-1, the United States, Japan, and Europe are highly dependent on imports. This dependency has grown rapidly in recent years as high-grade ore deposits in many developed countries are depleted. The vast majority of the United States' mineral resources come from reliable sources, mostly developed countries. However, some minerals such as cobalt, chromium, and platinum are currently imported from less reliable sources (Figure 16-2).

Developing countries have been growing more and more discontented with the prices they receive for their exported raw minerals. Many argue that these prices do not reflect the real value of the minerals and are not in line with the prices of the finished products the developing nations buy from the developed countries.

Figure 16-1

Percentage of mineral consumption supplied by imports and by domestic sources from the United States, Japan, the European Economic Community, U.S.S.R., and Eastern Europe.

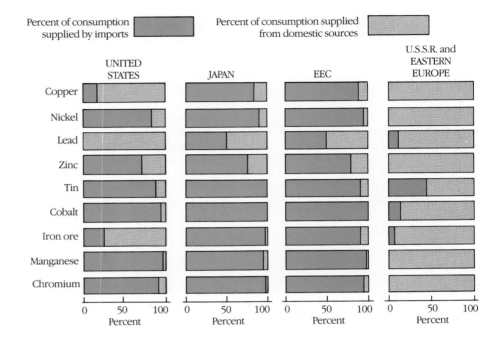

Figure 16-2

U.S. imports of some major minerals as a percentage of consumption, categorized as coming from relatively secure or relatively insecure sources.

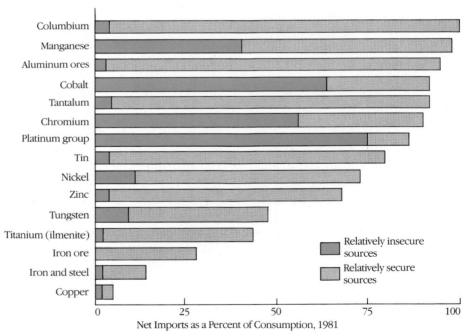

In the wake of the oil shortages in the 1970s, many observers fear that mineral-exporting countries may unite to form cartels to control the price of minerals. Fifty-six percent of the copper reserves, 87% of the tin, and 73% of the aluminum are in developing nations. Cartels could form around these commodities as demand from developing nations increases and if discontent over prices worsens. If cartels emerge, developed nations will be forced to pay higher prices for imported minerals. Worldwide inflation and depression could follow as they did after the

Organization of Petroleum Exporting Countries began its pricing policies.

One certain trend is that the developing countries will export less raw ore and more refined minerals (metals) and finished products in the coming years, gaining a larger share of the profits from their resources.

Will There Be Enough?

Estimates of future mineral resources vary considerably. Some say that there is an abundance of nonfuel mineral resources, and others say that supplies are running out.

Future Demand

Projections of future supplies are difficult to make because of many uncertainties, the most important being demand. But what controls demand? Some of the most important controlling factors are future mineral prices, energy prices, population growth, economic growth, as well as political actions.

Recent projections for 18 of the most important nonfuel minerals indicate that demand will grow at a rate of about 3% per year, doubling in 23 years. If this holds true, consumption of iron ore in the United States will increase from 960 million tons per year to 1.9 billion tons between 1978 and 2000. Demand for bauxite (used to make aluminum) will increase from 90 million to 180 million tons per year. Between 1980 and 2000 the worldwide consumption of nonfuel minerals will be three to four times greater than the total consumption in all of human history. But can supplies meet this demand?

Projections of supply are as difficult to make as projections of demand. Some people see our supplies as finite and argue that we will soon exhaust our mineral resources, which will bring on economic disaster. These "limitists" propose measures to prevent depletion.

More optimistic observers, or "cornucopians," as they are called, may agree that mineral resources are limited, but they argue that the supply is so large compared with the demand that there will be plenty to go around for a long time.

Two fundamental notions guide the thinking of the optimists. The first is the classical economic law of supply and demand, discussed in Chapter 24. According to the optimists, as minerals become scarcer, prices will rise. Rising prices will increase the supply in two ways: by reducing demand and by stimulating the search for new supplies. In other words, mining companies will search for more high-grade ores, or, if none can be found, they

may begin to extract and process domestic and foreign lower-grade ores (or even mine wastes) that had previously been too costly to develop. The second fundamental belief is that scientists will find substitutes for scarce resources, just as fiber optics made of the most abundant mineral, silica, have replaced copper in phone cables.

Meeting Future Needs

We can meet demand by expanding reserves, finding substitutes, recycling, and conservation. This section looks critically at each of these options.

Can We Expand Our Reserves?

Cornucopians assert that reserves will expand as the prices of nonfuel minerals increase. Mining companies will locate new mineral deposits. If these deposits are economically and technologically feasible to mine, they will be moved into the reserve category. Increases in the prices of minerals will also move marginal resources into the economic reserve category. (For a discussion of research terminology see Chapter Supplement 13-1.)

Advances in technology can do the same thing. Over the years, improvements in mining and extraction have increased our reserves of numerous minerals without changing the *real price* (the cost in fixed dollars). In fact, between 1950 and 1974 the reserves of five of our most economically important nonfuel minerals nearly tripled. Iron ore, bauxite, copper, lead, and platinum reserves increased by four times. Figure 16-3 shows the expansion of our reserves since 1950. This trend is the foundation of the cornucopians' argument of unending supplies.

It is important to note that reserves can shrink if production costs escalate. Several factors can raise production costs, causing a decline in reserves. Energy and labor costs, for example, can increase faster than the cost of minerals. Thus, reserves that were once economically attractive may become uneconomical to mine. Increasing environmental protection can also shrink reserves, because reclamation and pollution control add to the cost of production.

Exploration, mining, and production are influenced by interest rates and tax policies. High interest rates on capital may slow down exploration. Many economists predict that competition for capital will escalate in the coming years, driving up interest rates and slowing the expansion of our reserves.

In sum, reserves expand and contract in response to market conditions, technological development, environ-

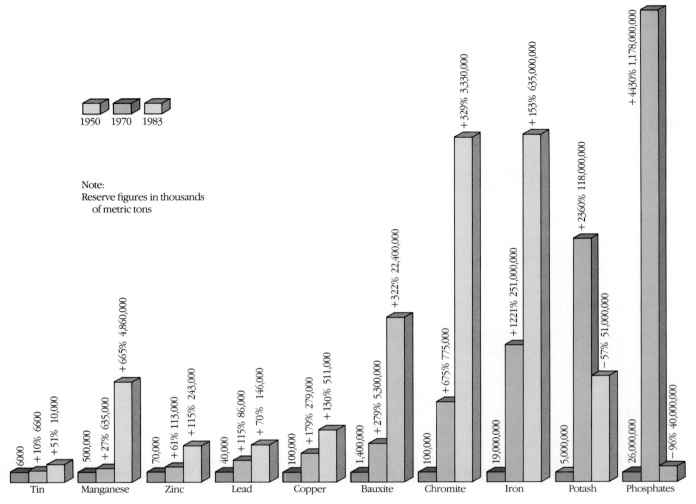

1950 1970 1983

Note:
Reserve figures in thousands
of metric tons

Figure 16-3
Expansion of world reserves of selected minerals and metals between 1950 and 1970.

mental laws, and interest rates. As technologies improve and as the real costs fall, reserves can expand considerably, as they have in the past. But increased fuel prices, labor costs, and depletion of resources can have the opposite effect. What happens to reserves in the short term depends largely on economic factors.

Rising Energy Costs: A Key Factor In the long run, it seems inevitable that the limited nature of nonfuel mineral resources will result in their **economic depletion**, the exhaustion of economically feasible resources. Even though the real prices of minerals have remained constant or have declined for many years, this trend is changing,

mostly because of rising energy costs. As energy costs rise, the real cost of minerals will probably increase.

But won't the rise in prices help us increase our reserves? As shown in Figure 16-4, as ores of progressively lower grade are mined, the amount of energy needed to mine and refine them is fairly constant up to a certain point, beyond which it increases dramatically. At that point these resources become uneconomical to mine; their costs will exceed what the market will bear. For all intents and purposes, they will be economically depleted.

According to the U.S. Department of the Interior, the real costs of nonfuel minerals will remain constant until the year 2000, despite near-term increases in energy costs.

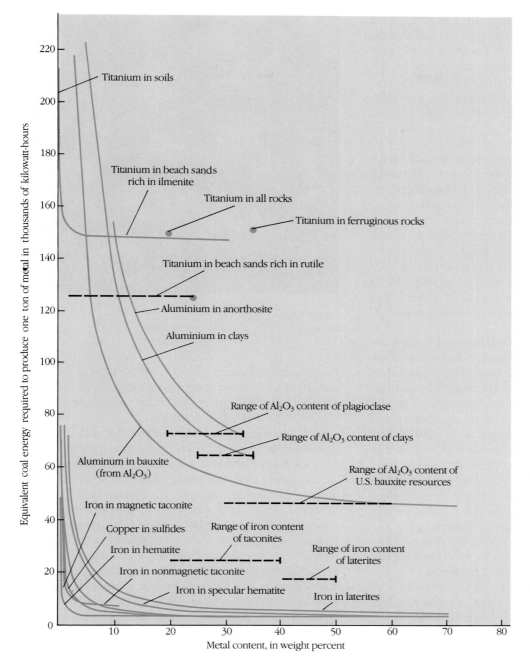

Figure 16-4
Energy investment for recovery of minerals related to the concentration of ore.

The reason is that improvements in mining and processing technologies will offset the increased energy costs as they have in the past. After 2000, though, the real cost of minerals is expected to increase at a rate of 5% per year, the same rate as energy cost increases. To mine lower-grade ores past that time, we will have to pay the higher production costs.

Resource Availability Another argument supporting projections of depletion centers on estimates of resource availability. Generally, most optimists argue that the total amount of ore increases as the grade decreases. Although this may be true for some nonfuel minerals (iron and aluminum), it cannot be applied broadly to all of them (nickel, copper, manganese). Let's take copper as an example. Copper follows this general rule to a point; there is more 1% ore than 2% ore, so reserves can still expand as this lower-grade ore is used. But below 1%, the generalization is no longer true: there is only one-fourth the amount of .3% ore as 1% ore. When this point is reached, reserves begin to shrink. With demand rising exponentially, the sudden drop in reserves of some minerals could prove economically disastrous.

Net Yield When considering the long-term outlook for minerals, it's important to look at the concept of net yield. Just as it takes energy to get energy, it takes minerals to mine and process minerals. For example, tungsten is used in cutting edges used in mining many ores. The companies that mine tungsten also use it in their mining equipment. As the cutting edges wear down, they must be replaced. Thus, in the same sense that an oil shale plant must have a positive net energy yield to be profitable, a mine must have a positive net mineral yield. When its net yield drops, a resource may become economically depleted.

Environmental Costs A final argument supporting the view of the limitists concerns the environmental costs. Environmental protection costs money. These costs affect production and the real cost of the mineral. Although increases in the real cost could increase supply, mining progressively lower-grade ores will produce more and more environmental damage: larger surface mines will be needed, more material will have to be transported to smelters for processing, more waste will be produced at the mines and smelters, and more air and water pollution will result. This, in turn, limitists argue, will necessitate greater environmental controls, which will add to the real costs and hasten the day of economic depletion.

Are the long-term prospects really this gloomy? The optimists say no, arguing that the oceans and outer space can provide us with needed mineral resources.

Minerals from the Sea The ocean is a vast resource of minerals, many of which are dissolved in the water itself. Several companies in Texas, Florida, Mississippi, Alabama, California, and New Jersey extract manganese directly from seawater, but the concentrations of most minerals are generally too low to be of economic importance. More important are mineral deposits on the ocean floor.

Most noteworthy of these minerals are the small **manganese nodules** that lie along the bottom of deep ocean waters (Figure 16-5). Abundant in the Pacific Ocean, these

Figure 16-5
Manganese nodules on the ocean floor.

nodules range from the size of a BB to the size of a cantaloupe. They contain several vital minerals, mostly manganese (24%) and iron (14%) with smaller amounts of copper (1%) and cobalt (.25%).

Most scientists believe that nodules form as dissolved minerals, washed to the sea by rivers, precipitate on small rock fragments or fossils on the ocean floor. The minerals are deposited in thin layers on these nuclei by accretion at a rate of a few millimeters per million years.

Several major mining companies have formed consortia to explore the possibility of mining these nodules. The French and Japanese are experimenting with a bucket system, to scoop the nodules up, that works something like a fishing net strung between two ships. Other more sophisticated, and energy-intensive, methods such as hydraulic lift systems have also been proposed.

The economics, environmental impacts, and legal status of seabed mining are yet to be worked out. Mining does appear to be technically feasible and possibly profitable. However, widespread dredging of the seafloor could stir up sediment and muddy the deep waters for decades, with unknown effects.

There is no international agreement on who owns the seabed. So far, exploitation of this resource has been delayed by the developing countries. Unable to afford the ships, equipment, and preliminary research, they have argued that some of the profits from this global resource should come to them to assist in economic development.

At the United Nations Conference on the Law of the Sea, the developing countries proposed an international tax on seabed minerals that could provide them $200 million to $600 million a year for agricultural and economic development. A comprehensive Law of the Sea Treaty, worked out with U.S. negotiators during the Carter administration, would have included this plan, but the succeeding Reagan administration demanded that the whole treaty be rewritten to be more favorable to mining companies.

Many people believe that proposals such as this represent a rational and fair way of helping the developing nations. Others, with a direct economic stake, see it as an unfair way of cutting into their profits. In any event, the exploitation of seabed minerals hinges largely on economic concerns. Will it be profitable given the diminishing reserves on land and the huge amounts of energy needed for mining, transportation, and processing? Only time will tell.

Substitution

The substitution of a resource for an economically depleted one has been a useful strategy in technological societies. For example, shortages of cotton, wool, and natural rubber have been eased by synthetic materials derived from oil. Synthetic fibers have found their way into American clothes. Synthetic rubber has replaced most natural rubber from trees. Substitution will unquestionably play an important role in the future, too. But is substitution a crutch we can lean on forever?

Critics argue that substitutions have created unreasonable faith among the public in the scientists' ability to come up with new resources to replace those that are being depleted. They also note that many substitutes themselves have limits. For example, plastics have replaced metals, but the oil from which plastics are made is a limited resource.

When searching for substitutes, we have to keep environmental considerations in mind. For example, wood is a substitute for fossil fuels, but overharvesting it can lead to erosion and destruction of wildlife habitat. Therefore, even though wood is a renewable resource, the costs of environmental protection should be factored into the complex economic calculus to determine if it represents a wise choice.

Substitutions are necessary but are not a cure-all to pending mineral shortages. There are physical limitations that economists often fail to take into account when arguing for substitution. For example, it may be impossible to find substitutes for the manganese in desulfurized steel, the nickel and chromium in stainless steel, the tin in solder, the helium in low-temperature refrigeration, the tungsten in high-speed tools, or the silver in photographic papers and films. We cannot expect scientists to find substitutes for every declining mineral.

As a final note, time must be considered. The technical breakthroughs trumpeted in the newspapers are generally the outcome of research that has been in progress for years, even decades. Once we round the elbow of the J-curve of demand and have depleted our high- and medium-grade ores, the time to economic depletion may be rapid, much more rapid than predicted. Unless scientists have been actively searching for substitutes for years in advance, there may well be no substitutes to replace vanishing mineral resources.

A wise political strategy would be to identify those resources that are nearest to economic depletion, then support intense research to find substitutes. Materials experts should be enlisted in this task; they should also identify minerals that have no replacements or are unlikely to have replacements. For these, recycling and conservation programs should be started.

Recycling

Recycling of materials can alleviate future resource shortages and cut energy demand at the same time. To date, however, recycling in the United States has been limited (Figure 16-6). There are several exceptions, however, one of the most notable being the automobile. Approximately 90 percent of all junked autos in the country are recycled.

Recycling is a useful way of increasing our mineral reserves in the future. Instead of being discarded in dumps, valuable minerals could be returned to key points in the mineral cycle, where they would be mixed with virgin minerals.

Economic Factors The level of mineral and metal recycling in the United States is primarily determined by economic factors. Of numerous economic variables, the relative cost of virgin and recycled materials is one of the most important. In general, high-grade ore deposits are economical to mine and refine, but the lower the grade, the more costly it becomes.

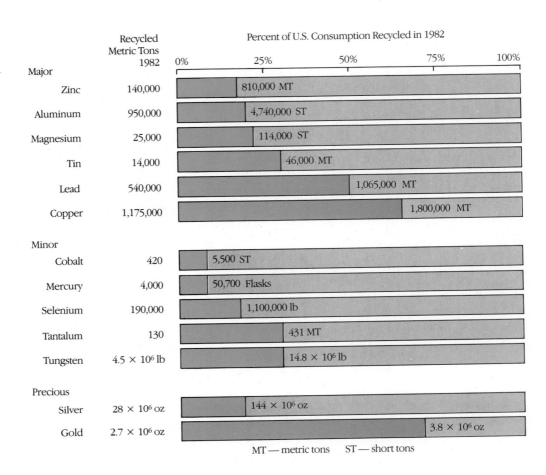

Figure 16-6
Amount of certain metals recycled in the United States.

	Recycled Metric Tons 1982	Percent of U.S. Consumption Recycled in 1982
Major		
Zinc	140,000	810,000 MT
Aluminum	950,000	4,740,000 ST
Magnesium	25,000	114,000 ST
Tin	14,000	46,000 MT
Lead	540,000	1,065,000 MT
Copper	1,175,000	1,800,000 MT
Minor		
Cobalt	420	5,500 ST
Mercury	4,000	50,700 Flasks
Selenium	190,000	1,100,000 lb
Tantalum	130	431 MT
Tungsten	4.5×10^6 lb	14.8×10^6 lb
Precious		
Silver	28×10^6 oz	144×10^6 oz
Gold	2.7×10^6 oz	3.8×10^6 oz

MT — metric tons   ST — short tons

But why is it generally cheaper to mine metals in foreign countries and transport the ore halfway around the world than to recycle the same materials we've thrown away? The reasons are many. Discarded materials are highly dispersed; as a resource, they are present in concentrations too low to be recycled profitably.

Scientists use the term **entropy** to denote disorder. All systems tend to go to maximum disorder (think of your own room) unless energy (cleaning the room) is applied to reverse this natural physical trend. Products distributed through the world and dumped in the tens of thousands of garbage dumps are said to be high-entropy (dispersed, or low-concentration) resources, and high-grade ore deposits are low-entropy (concentrated) resources. Recycling becomes profitable in an economic sense when the low-entropy ores are depleted.

One of the chief problems in recycling today originates during the design of products. Consider the typical orange-juice can, which is made of paper and is lined on the inside by foil and the outside by a layer of plastic. The top and bottom lids are often made of two different alloys (mixtures of metals). To separate all these components for effective recycling is impractical economically and technologically. At the opposite end of the spectrum, some products such as aluminum beverage cans or newsprint are easily recycled (Figure 16-7).

Awareness of the difficulty some products create for recycling could lead manufacturers and designers to redesign them. Eliminating the diverse mixture of materials is the best method, but not the only one. Other strategies may also work. For example, manufacturers of airplane parts often indicate the metals and alloys by marking the parts. This makes it easier to recycle them

Our Personal Role Personal values also play an important role in recycling. Many Americans simply refuse to recycle newspapers, aluminum cans, scrap steel and

Figure 16-7
Recycling of aluminum is catching on in the United States. New automated recycling machines like this one in a grocery store parking lot encourage people to exchange their aluminum cans for cash.

iron, tin-coated steel beverage cans, and glass bottles. This lack of personal commitment is translated into a lack of public interest, which is then communicated to the government.

Governmental policies in the past have either not promoted recycling or have worked against it. For example, until recently government regulations allowed higher freight rates for recycled materials than for virgin materials. Tax policies also favored the use of virgin materials over recycled goods, thus giving raw materials an unfair economic advantage over recycled goods. One of the key tax policies that favors virgin materials is the **depletion allowance**. This is a tax break given to mining companies as they deplete their reserves. The tax saving is supposed to be used to find more resources. What it does, in effect, is support the mining of lower-grade ores when recycling might be a better choice.

Recycling: Only a Partial Answer   Recycling helps increase the time a mineral or metal remains in use, or its **residence time**. It also helps save an enormous amount of energy. For example, manufacturing an aluminum can

Table 16-2 Energy Saved by Recycling Rather Than Processing Virgin Materials

Resource	Energy Reduction (Percentage)
Aluminum	95
Magnesium	8
Plastics	25
Steel	25
Rubber	47
Paper	97
Glass	98

from recycled aluminum uses 5% of the energy required to make it from aluminum ore (bauxite) (Table 16-2). Recycling is only one of several important steps needed to ensure that mineral resources have a longer residence time in the production–consumption cycle. Although recycling will save us a great deal of energy, it will not permit our current exponential growth in mineral use to continue indefinitely. Why is this so?

First, during the mineral production–consumption cycle some minerals and metals enter into long-term uses—for example, aluminum used for wiring or bronze for statuary. Also, some materials are lost through processing inefficiencies, are lost accidentally, or are thrown away on purpose. Because of these reasons, it is impossible to recycle 100% of a given material. A more practical, but still difficult, goal would be 60% to 80% recycling of the short-lived goods, such as cans. Thus, recycling can slow down the depletion of a mineral resource but cannot stop it. In theory, recycling can double our mineral resource base, but continually rising demand and inevitable losses will eventually deplete that reserve.

State Recycling Programs   Many people support statewide and even nationwide recycling programs, but movement in this direction has proceeded slowly. One of the first important breakthroughs was the passage of a law in Oregon in 1972 that requires a deposit on beverage containers. Vermont, Michigan, Maine, Connecticut, Iowa, Massachusetts, and New York followed suit. Other states have failed repeatedly to pass such a law because of heavily financed advertising campaigns supported by steel and aluminum companies, bottlers, supermarket chains, and retail liquor store owners.

Figure 16-8
A recycling station in Santa
Cruz, California, handles
bottles, aluminum cans, and
newspapers.

Deposit laws help reduce litter, greatly increase recycling, and reduce energy consumption by manufacturers
of cans and bottles (Figure 16-8). Nationwide recycling of
beverage containers could save the equivalent of 70,000
to 140,000 barrels of oil per day. Deposit laws also reduce
solid waste by about 6%, assuming 100% return.

Opponents of deposit laws contend that solid waste
reduction would be minimal and that mandatory recycling would cost jobs, raise the price of beverages, decrease
retail sales, and reduce tax revenues. It can be difficult to
sort through the controversy to see who's right and who's
wrong. A study by the Maryland Governor's Council of
Economic Advisers indicated that most of these arguments are invalid. This study predicted that a deposit law
that eliminated throwaway bottles and cans in Maryland
would create 1500 jobs (at pickup and recycling plants),
increase personal income in the state, and add $1.5 mil-
lion in income taxes to state and local governments. In
addition, the law would save local governments $7 million
by reducing litter pickup.

Proponents of recycling believe that a uniform national
law would help the states draw up uniform policies. If a
few major states such as California and Texas enacted
"bottle bills," the momentum created could bring about
a national program in short order. The 1983 bottle bill in
New York state was a significant step in this direction.

Conservation

Conservation is highly favored by many environmentalists
as a sensible strategy for stretching our mineral resources.
In the long term, per capita consumption of nonrenewable mineral resources will probably fall as prices begin
to rise, but limitists argue that prudent world citizens should
anticipate the inevitable resource scarcities now and cut
back on their demand.

Limitists argue that conservation must begin with individuals and spread through society to the high levels, where
it will be reflected in national policies. Combined with
recycling, conservation measures can greatly extend the
lifetime of many valuable mineral resources. As shown in
Figure 16-9, continued exponential growth is the fastest

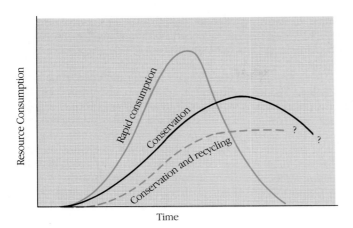

Figure 16-9
Three paths: Which one will we take?

route to depletion; recycling will slow but not stop this depletion. Recycling and conservation measures combined will give us more time to develop new mining technologies and find substitutes.

Tolstoy once wrote that "everyone thinks of changing the world, but no one thinks of changing himself." Personal changes to conserve resources are badly needed today. You can eliminate the unnecessary appliances and other goods from your wish list. If you're getting married, you can ask (politely) that your friends not shower you with energy-guzzling gadgets for the home; better still, you can make a list of energy-saving gifts (blankets, sweaters, pressure cookers, and crock pots) you need.

Careful selection of the materials you buy can also reduce unnecessary waste. Whenever possible, buy food in paper rather than metal containers. Paper can be burned to generate heat or be recycled, in some cases. If you must buy food in metal containers, you can see that they are delivered to a local recycling center rather than discarded.

When you buy soft drinks and other beverages, you can choose returnable bottles rather than recyclable aluminum cans and aluminum rather than steel cans. Returnable bottles can be reused with a minor expenditure for transportation and washing; recyclable ones have to be transported, melted down, and then reformed, requiring more energy.

As for transportation, you can buy a smaller car and use mass transit so your family can get by with only one car. Saving energy also reduces your overall mineral consumption because of a lower need for mining equipment, trucks, trains, and power plants in the energy cycle.

When buying something, you can look for quality; a well-made product, by outlasting its inexpensive imitations, will be well worth the extra labor and material that was put into it. You can write letters supporting products that last and complain to manufacturers whose junk falls apart on you soon after you get it home. Remember that consumers are to economics what voters are to government.

You can also help by supporting various legal solutions, for example, recycling programs on a local, state, or national level. Recycling bins in neighborhoods could be encouraged: volunteer groups such as church groups or youth organizations could pick up the materials regularly and sell them for profit. (The city might even assist by providing trucks.) Waste recovery systems at local dumps might also be helpful. Palo Alto, California, gives city residents a free dump pass if they bring materials to the recycling center just outside the dump gates.

Conservation seems to go against the grain of modern Americans. Blessed with cheap energy resources and abundant food sources, they have proved to be the most wasteful people in the world. Used to the no-deposit, no-return appeal of modern products, we may be unnecessarily throwing away our future.

Conservation could prevent the depletion of resources. It is not a roadblock to progress but instead a milestone of progress for a society that has heretofore viewed uncontrolled, ever-escalating production and consumption as a sign that it is getting ahead.

Tomorrow's growth depends on the use we make of today's materials and experiences.

ELMER WHEELER

Summary

Minerals are worth billions of dollars in the world market. Some are so important that industry and agriculture in developed nations would come to a standstill if they were suddenly unavailable. The developed countries are the major consumers of minerals. With one-fourth of the world's population, they consume three-fourths of the world's minerals. Most of them import large quantities from developing countries.

The developing countries have become increasingly unhappy with the low prices they receive for their raw minerals, and many have agreed to refine more of them and make more finished products to increase their profits. This could result in an upward trend in the cost of metals in developing nations.

One of the key issues regarding minerals is whether there will be enough to meet future needs. Recent projections for 18 of the most important nonfuel minerals indicate that demand will grow at a rate of about 3% a year, doubling in 23 years. Will supplies be able to meet these demands?

Limitists believe that we will soon exhaust some of our most important mineral resources. Cornucopians argue just the opposite. They believe that rising prices will stimulate exploration and new technologies that will increase our reserves. They also argue that substitutes for economically depleted mineral resources will be made available through advances in science and technology.

So far, the limitists' projections of shortages have proven wrong. But as mineral resources of decreasingly lower concentration are exploited, energy investments in mining and processing will become higher and higher. After 2000 the real cost of minerals may begin to rise by 5% a year, making many minerals uneconomical to mine and process. Competition for capital may raise interest rates, which also makes it economically unprofitable to mine and process lower-grade ores.

Minerals from the sea may help expand our mineral reserves, but economic, environmental, and legal questions have yet to be worked out. One of the most promising resources is *manganese nodules,* which are found on the seabed. They contain manganese, iron, copper, cobalt, and other minerals.

Substitution of one resource for another that is *economically depleted* has been a useful strategy in the past, but it will be of limited value in the future. Substitutes for scarce minerals may have unacceptable environmental impacts, may be depletable themselves, and may have excessive energy demands that cannot be met economically. Some minerals have no adequate substitutes. Finally, once we round the elbow of the curve of demand and have depleted our high- and medium-grade ores, economic depletion may be so rapid that substitutes cannot be developed in time.

Recycling can alleviate future resource shortages, cut energy demand, reduce environmental pollution, and create jobs, but it is not a panacea. Many materials are put into permanent use. For short-term goods, such as cans and bottles, recycling recovers only 60% to 80% of total production. In short, recycling can slow down the depletion but cannot stop it. Recycling can double our mineral resource base, but continually rising demand and inevitable losses will eventually deplete reserves.

Conservation is an approach highly favored by limitists. Combined with recycling, conservation can greatly extend the lifetime of many valuable mineral resources and give scientists and engineers more time to develop substitutes and new mining strategies.

Discussion Questions

1. Define nonrenewable and renewable resources and give examples of each. How are they different, and how are they similar?

2. Discuss why it's difficult to determine the level of future mineral demand. How would you go about calculating the demand for minerals in the year 2000?

3. Summarize the views of the limitists and optimists regarding the future availability of mineral resources. Which ones do you agree with, and which ones do you take exception to?

4. Debate the statement "Economic forces will ensure us a continual supply of mineral resources. As prices rise, we'll find new resources, develop new technologies, and find substitutes for minerals currently used."

5. What are reserves? Explain various ways that mineral reserves can expand.

6. Over the past few decades mineral reserves have increased. Why has this process occurred? Will it continue? Why or why not?

7. Outline a plan to meet the future needs of your society. Describe your plan. What are its most important components?

8. What factors can cause the reserves of a given mineral to shrink?

9. Comment on the statement "Even though we're depleting our high-grade ores, there's nothing to worry about, because the lower-grade ores generally contain a larger amount of mineral."

10. Draw a graph of the energy required to mine an ore as the grade decreases. What are the long-term implications of this graph?

11. Describe the concept *net mineral yield*.

12. Debate the statement "There's no need to worry about running out of minerals, because we'll find substitutes for them."

13. Define the term *entropy*. How can it be applied to mineral resources? Why is municipal trash considered a high-entropy mineral resource?

14. Comment on the statement "We must begin recycling now even if it's not as profitable as mining and processing virgin minerals."

15. List the advantages of recycling and resource conservation.

16. Debate the statement "Recycling will extend the lifespan of our minerals indefinitely."

17. Discuss the pros and cons of a nationwide recycling bill requiring a returnable deposit on all beverage cans.

18. Make a list of ways you can cut down your resource consumption by 20%.

Suggested Readings

Barnet, R. J. (1980). *The Lean Years: Politics in an Age of Scarcity.* New York: Simon and Schuster. Excellent book.

Kahn, H., Brown, W., and Martel, L. (1976). *The Next 200 Years.* New York: Morrow. Cornucopian view of future mineral resources.

Marsden, R. W., ed. (1975). *Politics, Minerals and Survival.* Madison: University of Wisconsin Press. Contains numerous interesting suggestions on meeting future mineral needs through government actions.

Ridker, R. G., and Watson, W. D. (1980). *To Choose a Future: Resources and Environmental Consequences of Alternative Growth Paths.* Baltimore: Johns Hopkins University Press. Interesting book; worth reading.

Simon, J. L. (1981). *The Ultimate Resource.* Princeton, N.J.: Princeton University Press. A controversial view of resources that relies heavily on assumptions from past trends in predicting the future.

U.S. Bureau of Mines (1980). *Mineral Facts and Problems,* 1980 ed. Washington, D.C.: U.S. Government Printing Office. Superb reference; published every five years.

U.S. Bureau of Mines (1983). *Mineral Commodity Summaries, 1983.* Washington, D.C.: U.S. Government Printing Office. Excellent source of information on minerals; published every year.

U.S. Bureau of Mines (1983). *The Domestic Supply of Critical Minerals.* Washington, D.C.: U.S. Government Printing Office. Full of useful information.

U.S. Council on Environmental Quality (1980). *The Global 2000 Report to the President.* New York: Penguin Books. Chapter 12 provides an excellent survey of nonfuel mineral resources.

POLLUTION

17

Environmental Decision Making: Risk Assessment and Ethical Analysis

I cannot undertake to be impartial as between the fire brigade and the fire.

WINSTON CHURCHILL

The models in Chapter 2 expand our understanding of environmental problems. The value of these models is best summarized by the saying: a problem well understood is a problem half solved. The other half of problem solving is some form of action such as new laws, governmental regulations, bans on harmful products, and personal actions.

Decisions such as these are based on considerations of risk and ethics. This chapter takes a look at these critical concepts and presents some simplified models to help us arrive at fair and cost-effective solutions.

Risk and Risk Assessment

Ralph Waldo Emerson once wrote, "As soon as there is life there is danger." Every day of our lives we face many hidden and overt dangers. In short, hazards and risks are unavoidable, especially in technological societies. Where do risks arise?

Risks and Hazards

Two types of hazard are broadly defined by risk assessors: anthropogenic and natural. **Anthropogenic hazards** are

Table 17-1 Hazards and Their Effects

Society	Natural Hazards		Anthropogenic Hazards	
	Social Cost (Percent of GNP)	Mortality (Percent of Total)	Social Costs (Percent of GNP)	Mortality (Percent of Total)
Nontechnological	15–40	10–15	Not available	Not available
Technological	2–4	3–5	5–15	15–25

Source: Harriss, R. C., Hohenemsen, C., and Kates, R. W. (1978), Our Hazardous Environment, *Environment* 20(7): 6.

those created by human beings. **Natural hazards** include events such as tornadoes, hurricanes, floods, drought, volcanoes, and landslides. We generally think of these hazards as the result of natural events, but human factors may be involved. For instance, mining may disrupt normal vegetation and cause landslides.

Natural and anthropogenic hazards may impair our health; damage our economic, social, and mental well-being; destroy the environment; and endanger other living organisms.

To measure the impact of hazards, two common measures are used: social cost and mortality rate (Table 17-1). **Social cost** can be expressed as a percentage of the gross national product (GNP, the total market value of all goods and services produced by a country). The **mortality rate** measures the deaths caused by a certain hazard. A variety of other measures can also be used, including morbidity (disease) rate, property damage, and work days lost.

Table 17-1 shows some approximations of the cost of natural and anthropogenic hazards in technological and nontechnological societies. This table indicates that the social cost and mortality from natural hazards in developed (technological) countries is rather small, but the impact of technological hazards is high. Just the opposite appears to be true for nontechnological societies.

Thus, it appears that technology "frees" us from the effects of natural hazards but exacts a price possibly equal to that of natural hazards. For example, we now have modern power plants that provide heat and reduce the risk that we'll freeze to death in winter (natural hazard). But power plants produce harmful pollutants (anthropogenic hazard) that contribute to lung cancer, emphysema, and bronchitis. Table 17-1 suggests that as many people die of these diseases as might freeze to death in the absence of power plants.

Today, people are more aware of the hazards they are

exposed to than ever before. This increase in risk awareness results from a variety of factors. First, we are more aware of risks because of television and advanced communication systems, which bring news of the hazards to our homes from all over the world. Second, our increased material wealth has given us more free time to consider the hazards around us. In poor societies people tend to ignore risks in the workplace in favor of a living wage. Third, we are more aware of hazards today because we are exposed to more hazards. As technology grows, more and more hazards are created.

Risk Assessment

Today, government officials are beginning to consider risk when they formulate public policy. Scientists are grappling with ways to measure risk. In the past ten years, a new and rather imprecise science, called **risk assessment**, has been developed to help policymakers understand and quantify risks posed by technology, our lifestyles, and our habits (smoking, drinking, and diet). Risk assessment is an important addition to environmental science. It allows us to use our scientific knowledge to formulate public policy to achieve cost-effective, socially acceptable protection from all hazards.

Risk assessment involves two interlocked steps: hazard identification and estimation of risk. **Hazard identification** involves recognizing hazards that exist and predicting hazards that might arise in the future. Identifying hazards is usually quite simple when we're dealing with existing technologies, but in the case of new technologies it must be based on speculation, guesswork, and extrapolation from similar existing technologies.

Estimation of risk generally involves two separate processes. The first is the determination of the *probability* that an event such as an accident will occur. This process answers the question "How likely is the event?" The second stage is the determination of the *severity* of an event, answering the question "How much damage is caused?" Determining probability and severity is not as easy as it may seem. Some technologies are new. Having no experience with them, we can only estimate probability and severity. These estimates may be far from the actual values, but they are all we have to rely on in these instances.

Once risks have been identified and the severity and probability have been determined (or estimated), the level of the risk can be stated. This is not as easy as it may seem, either. The reason is that hazards are characterized by two *qualitatively* different variables, probability and severity. Thus, it may be hard to formulate a single risk value. In addition to this problem, the probability and severity may indicate two very different levels of risk. Let's take nuclear power as an example to illustrate this.

The probability of a nuclear core meltdown is thought to be quite small. (Nuclear power advocates tell us that the probability is one chance in a billion years of reactor operation. Critics argue that this estimate is too optimistic. See Chapter 14 for more information on accidents at nuclear power plants.) Even though the probability of a meltdown may be small, the severity of such an event would be high. Thousands of lives might be lost, and billions of dollars in property damage would result. Thus, the probability and severity factors are not only qualitatively different but also indicate distinctly different levels of risk. What level of risk should we assign to nuclear power? To answer this and similar questions, risk scales are being designed to account for the qualitative differences in risk probability and severity. These may allow scientists to assign single risk values to potential hazards.

Risk management is left in the hands of policymakers, although in recent years citizens and scientists (especially social scientists) have taken a much more active role in defining risks that are acceptable and risks that are not.

Risk Management: Decisions about Risk Acceptability

Safety versus Relative Risk
Decisions regarding hazards are made difficult because people view hazards differently. For example, many people insist that new and existing technologies be entirely safe. Others are more concerned merely that the hazard have a low enough risk to be acceptable. The first view implies that a technology can be safe or "entirely free from harm." In actuality, nothing is free from harm; risk is inherent in all human endeavors from finance to romance. The second view is

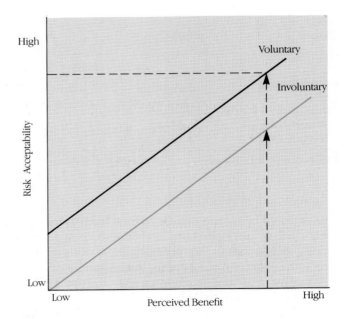

Figure 17-1
Risk acceptability rises as perceived benefit rises. Whether the risk is voluntary or involuntary affects risk acceptability.

more realistic and useful. It recognizes that a technology has inherent risks and that we must decide whether it is worth taking the risk.

Rather than thinking in terms of safety, which is absolute, we should think in terms of *risk,* which is relative, ranging from high to low. Activities we normally consider "safe" should be labeled "low-risk activities"; "unsafe" activities should be labeled "high-risk."

However, what we think is "safe" may not always be low-risk. The opposite is also true. For example, we tend to think of the automobile as a "safe" form of transportation and commercial air travel as "unsafe." The truth is quite the opposite.

Risk Acceptability
Knowing the relative risk of a technology is important for good policymaking and risk management, but it is more important to know how acceptable a given hazard is to us, or its **risk acceptability.**

The acceptability of a certain risk is determined by a number of factors. One of the most significant is the **perceived benefit,** or how much benefit people think will come from accepting the risk. In general, the higher the perceived benefit, the higher the risk acceptability (Figure 17-1). As an example, the environmental and health risks

Figure 17-2
People in Greenham Common, Great Britain, protest the deployment of U.S. "Cruise" missiles in Europe.

of a steel mill that produces pollution will probably be viewed as acceptable by citizens who will be employed by it because they will benefit from it.

Perceived harm, the damage people think will occur, also influences risk acceptability. In general, the more harmful a technology is perceived to be, the less acceptable it is to society. Efforts to find a home for the MX nuclear missiles in the early 1980s clearly illustrate this point. Law-abiding, patriotic citizens banded together to block the installation of the missile system, viewing it as harmful to the environment and possibly their lives (Figure 17-2).

Another important factor in determining risk acceptability is whether the risk is voluntary or involuntary. Generally, at any level of perceived benefit a risk is more acceptable if it is voluntary than if it is involuntary (Figure 17-1).

In determining whether a risk is acceptable, one can choose any or all of the strategies summarized in Figure 17-3. The **cost–benefit technique** is commonly used. Benefits are generally measured in financial gain, business opportunities, jobs, and other tangible items. Costs are also measured: How many jobs will be lost? How much

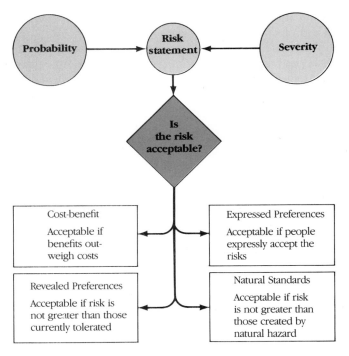

Figure 17-3
Determining the acceptability of a risk.

money will the project cost? But some costs, such as the **external costs** discussed in Chapters 1 and 24, are difficult to identify and quantify. These include environmental damage, health effects, aesthetic damage, and loss of recreational opportunity. When cost-benefit analysis encounters these costs, the technique becomes less than satisfactory. The problem is that many important costs are poorly documented, spread out, and unquantifiable, whereas the benefits are clear and quantifiable.

Recent efforts by economists to assign a dollar value to environmental and health costs may help make decisions of cost and benefit more useful. In addition, the efforts of ecologists and environmental scientists to measure the impacts of technologies and their byproducts on wildlife, the environment, recreation, health, and society in general may also help in weighing benefits against costs.

Actual versus Perceived Risk   The main purpose of risk assessment is to help us create cost-effective laws and regulations that protect human health, the environment, and other organisms. Ideally, good lawmaking requires that the **actual risk**, or the amount of risk a hazard really poses, should be equal to the risk perceived by the public. In other words, the risk we think exists should match the risk that actually is there. When they do match, a public policy can be formulated that yields the most cost-effective protection (Figure 17-4).

When the perceived risk is much larger than the actual risk, costly *overprotection* may occur. For example, laws and federal rules regulating air pollution are believed by many, especially those in industry, to be too strict. These people argue that the damage caused by air pollution (actual risk) is less than the public thinks it is (perceived risk). Therefore, they assert that the cost of air pollution control far outweighs the saving to human health and the environment.

Others argue that the perceived risk of air pollution is far smaller than the actual risk, and that current policies do not adequately protect the public. In their eyes, *underprotection* places a burden on society, affecting health, welfare, economics, and environmental quality.

Only through arduous efforts to accurately identify and quantify risk can we match perceived and actual risks. Accordingly, risk assessment will become increasingly more important as the world's population grows and our technological capabilities expand.

More and more, sound environmental decision making requires a thorough understanding of our problems and thoughtful considerations of risk. Fortunately, risk assessment allows us to analyze current issues in an objective manner. People who understand the key concepts of risk will be better prepared to deal with issues and more successful in achieving effective solutions (see Essay 17-1).

Ethical Analysis

Ultimately, environmental decisions are based on our **ethics**—that is, the values we hold, or, simply, what we view as right or wrong. Values that affect our decisions come

Figure 17-4
Matching the actual risk and the risk that a society perceives is essential to the formulation of good public policy. But perceived risk and actual risk do not always match, as shown.

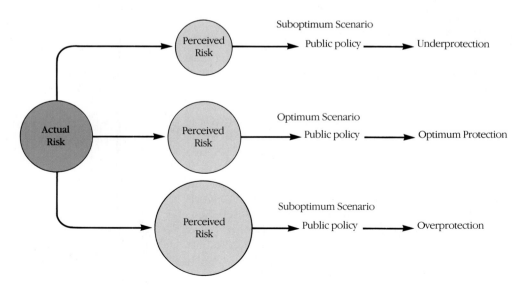

EPA Asks Tacoma: Jobs or Lives?

In Tacoma, Washington, a copper-smelting plant owned by Asarco, Incorporated, contributes up to $30 million to the local economy annually. Unfortunately, it also pours up to 765 kilograms (1700 pounds) of arsenic emissions into the air daily. In what appears to be a landmark case, the Environmental Protection Agency has essentially asked Tacoma residents to choose between the loss of 575 jobs provided by the plant or an increased risk of cancer due to the arsenic emissions.

Arsenic, which has been linked with both lung and skin cancers and neurological disease, has been found in alarmingly high quantities in the blood of smelter workers and of children at a nearby school. Despite the absence of any visible negative health effects thus far, residents know that arsenic cancers have a 13- to 50-year latency period. But Larry Lindquist, manager of the smelter, asserts, "There's been no proof that these emissions cause health problems." This belief, coupled with the fact that the smelter provides its workers with a large payroll—$22 million— means that many may vote, as Professor Ruth Weiner of Western Washington State University says, "for jobs and cancer."

William Ruckelshaus, head of the EPA, proposed that the residents hold town meetings to discuss this new method of determining risk assessment. The proposal has angered many environmental-

Asarco parents in town meeting, Tacoma, Washington. The sign reads, "Don't risk our children."

ists, who say that residents are being asked to rate the cost-effectiveness of their lives. Others counter that the environmentalists are exaggerating the problem, pointing out that the plant has taken measures to clean up, first in 1970 after the passage of the

Clean Air Act and later with the installation of new hoods that promise to reduce emissions by about 40%. Asarco officials maintain that the cost of further mandatory cleanup regulations would force them to shut down.

from our parents, relatives, peers, teachers, religious leaders, and politicians. These values shift over the years— sometimes subtly, sometimes drastically—as we become older and as our priorities change. Although our ethics are quite often not stated explicitly, they play an important role in our lives. They determine how we vote, what friends we associate with, how we treat one another, how we

carry on business affairs, and, finally, how we act with regard to the environment.

Values play an important part in decisions about risk acceptability. In virtually all of our decisions, benefits and costs will be incurred, and we must always weigh them against each other. This balancing of costs and benefits requires us to put our values in order of priority. For

Figure 17-5
Various people's spatial and temporal interests are indicated by points on this graph. Most individuals tend toward the lower end of the scales, being concerned primarily with self and the present.

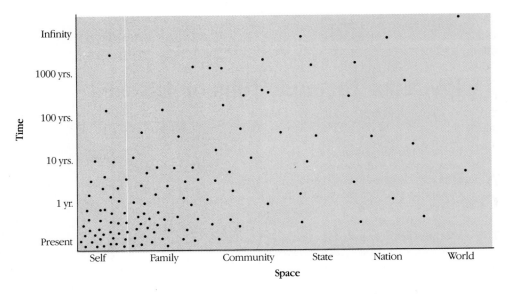

instance, if a coal strip mine were to be placed outside of your community, certain advantages might be realized—more jobs and a stronger economy. However, certain costs such as air pollution might be incurred. The decision to open the mine would be influenced by the priority of values.

Putting priorities on values requires us to ask what we value the most. What is more important to us in environmental decision making—economics? health? wildlife? A new reservoir will bring much-needed water to an area, thus allowing it to grow and prosper, but it will destroy valuable wildlife habitat and a recreation area. How do we choose? Do we save recreation areas and wildlife habitat and find other solutions to the water shortage, or do we dam the river, destroying the wildlife and the recreation area?

Even though ranking our values helps us make decisions, it is important to look a little further into what we might call **space–time values**. These are simply the concerns we have for other people and other living organisms in time (present and the future) and space (you, your family, community, state, nation, world).

Sound decision making in a sustainable society requires us to ask three important space–time questions: (1) Is our decision based primarily on self-interest? In other words, are we looking at the issue solely in terms of how we might benefit or be harmed? (2) Is our decision based primarily on concern for others who are alive now who might benefit or be harmed? And how far does our con-

cern go? Are we concerned with the well-being of stockholders or citizens of the community, state, nation, or the world? (In some cases, local actions can have global impact.) (3) Finally, is our decision based on the good of future generations? Will our decisions today benefit or harm those who follow us?

As illustrated in Figure 17-5, individual interest can be identified by a single point that denotes one's space and time concerns. Most people's interest lies toward the lower ends of the scales, tending toward self-interest and immediate concerns. This tendency to be concerned with the self and the present is very much a biological characteristic. In evolution we see that awareness of the needs of other organisms of the same kind is found in social animals such as monkeys and lions; however, concerns for the upper ends of the time and space scales are found in only the most social of all animals, *Homo sapiens.*

This capacity to consider the consequences of our actions, notably, how they will affect others and what impact they will have on the future, is a fortunate feature of our kind. It is fortunate because humans have reached a position of unprecedented power as molders of the world's environment. Our power to fashion the world to our liking has never been greater, nor has our power to destroy ever attained such heights.

René Dubos once wrote, "We cannot escape from the past, but neither can we avoid inventing the future." But how do we as a society invent a future that future residents will be happy with? This is one of the most difficult questions facing humankind. To answer it, we must first know what they will need. Many philosophers believe that it is safe to assume that their needs will not be much different from ours today. Clothing, food, shelter, warmth, a sense of belonging, meaningful employment, and a clean environment will all be required. How can we ensure that they will be able to meet these needs? The answer is, by taking their concerns into account during decision making, discussed in Chapter 25.

A Global View—Ethics for a Crowded World

Two facts are clear: (1) There will always be differing values. Some individuals will always care more about economics than the environment; others will feel just the opposite. (2) There will always be differing levels of space–time interest in any decision; some people will care more for their own rights than the rights of others. Some will care more about the present than the future. Some may lobby for the interests of the state but disregard those of neighboring countries.

What is equally clear is that we are all interdependent neighbors on a finite planet. This suggests the need for a global view that looks beyond immediate self-interest and seeks to establish a sustainable society that lives within the limits of the environment. This does not mean going back to primitive hunting-and-gathering societies. It means conserving resources by reducing consumption and by recycling and reuse. And it means using renewable resources whenever possible.

A sustainable society might develop a policy of maximum benefit–minimum cost for all environmental decisions. In other words, when decisions are made, economic benefit would be maximized, and environmental harm would be minimized.

Ethically, the sustainable society protects the rights of present generations as well as the rights of future generations. Moreover, it strives to protect the rights of other organisms that share this planet with us.

Such a policy will require sacrifice, some degree of restraint and compromise, but in the long run it will provide the maximum benefit to all the world's occupants, present and future.

Chance fights ever on the side of the prudent.

EURIPIDES

Summary

Scientists recognize two general types of hazard: natural and anthropogenic. *Natural hazards* are those posed by nature, such as tornadoes, hurricanes, and earthquakes. *Anthropogenic hazards* are those posed directly or indirectly by humans.

Risk assessment is the science dedicated to understanding risk. Risk assessors first identify actual and potential hazards and then determine the probability and severity of the hazard. Once these are determined, a statement regarding risk can be made. It is then up to *risk managers,* usually public officials, to determine how best to deal with the risk.

To better regulate hazards, risk managers must determine the *acceptability of risk.* Risk acceptability is determined by many factors, but the most important are the *perceived benefit* (the benefit people think they will gain) and the *perceived harm* (the harm they think they will suffer). Hazards that are voluntary (introduced with the consent of the people) generally have a higher perceived benefit than those that are involuntary (introduced without consent).

Risk assessment is ultimately designed to manage risks in the most cost-effective manner. To do so, the *perceived risk* (the amount of risk people think is posed) must be equal or very close to the *actual risk* (the level of risk that really exists). The actual risk may be difficult to determine, especially in the case of new technologies with which society has had little experience.

Ethics is the science of human duty. An ethical system is a code of what is right and wrong, something we develop through experiences at home, school, church, and daily life. All decision making requires ethical considerations, but ethics are not often clearly understood by individuals. Thus, it is helpful to put priorities on our values—list what means the most to us under different circumstances. Such a listing can help us think about our decisions in terms of what is right and wrong.

Our concerns can be placed on a space–time continuum starting with immediate self-interest and extending to infinity and the interests for all future generations. Most people tend to be concerned with immediate gain and their own interests. The interests of future generations are, therefore, often neglected.

Decision making requires a better understanding of the *space–time values*. Through education, more people can be made aware of the needs of future generations and the effects that current actions have on them. A value system that seeks to optimize the future by acting in the present is critically needed to build a sustainable society.

Discussion Questions

1. What are the two major types of risk? Give examples.

2. What is risk assessment? Describe the major steps in determining the level of risk posed by technology.

3. Give some examples of measurements used to express risk probability and risk severity.

4. What is risk acceptability? What factors determine whether a risk is acceptable to a population?

5. Many more people die in Montana and Wyoming from falling while hiking than are killed by grizzly bears. Why, then, are people so much more concerned about being killed by a bear?

6. Describe four ways in which decisions are made regarding the acceptance or rejection of risk. What are the strengths and weaknesses of each?

7. What is the main purpose of risk assessment? What happens when the actual risk of a given technology is much greater than the perceived risk in terms of public policy? What happens when the actual risk is smaller than the perceived risk? Why is it so important to be certain that the actual and perceived risks for a given technology match?

8. What are space–time values? Where does your own concern lie in space and time?

9. Discuss some ways to encourage people to think about the future when making decisions in government and their everyday life.

Suggested Readings

Center for Ethics and Social Policy. (1977). *Ethics for a Crowded World.* Berkeley, Calif.: Graduate Theological Union. A concise, readable book that raises ethical consciousness regarding environmental issues.

Chiras, D. (1982). Risk and Risk Assessment in Environmental Education. *Amer. Biol. Teacher* 44(4): 460–465. A more technical presentation of risk and risk assessment.

Fischhoff, B., Slovic, P., and Lichtensten, S. (1979). Weighing the Risks. *Environment* 21(4): 17. An excellent article on risk assessment.

Harriss, R. C., Hohenemsen, C., and Kates, R. W. (1978). Our Hazardous Environment. *Environment* 20(7): 6. Another fine article on risk.

Kates, R. W. (1978). *Risk Assessment of Environmental Hazards.* New York: Wiley. A good source on risk, but fairly technical.

Kieffer, G. H. (1979). Can Bioethics Be Taught? *Amer. Biol. Teacher* 41(3): 176. A superb article on the teaching of environmental ethics in the classroom.

Lowrance, W. W. (1976). *Of Acceptable Risk: Science and the Determination of Safety.* Los Altos, Calif.: Kaufmann. A fine book on risk that covers many important issues.

Toxic Substances and Environmental Health

Life is a perpetual instruction in cause and effect.

RALPH WALDO EMERSON

Citizens of developed countries rely on a vast number of chemical preparations: cosmetics, shampoos, preservatives, plastics, solvents, detergents, insecticides, petroleum fuels, inks, fertilizers, and many more. Although life is improved by chemicals, some of them can harm human health, poison fish and wildlife, and pollute rivers, air, and land (Table 18-1).

Today, 50,000 chemical substances are sold commercially in the United States. Chemical usage has grown dramatically since 1940 (Figure 18-1). The chemical industry has become an industrial giant. In 1980 it reported total sales of $162 billion and employed 1.1 million people at 11,500 plants across the country.

Of these commercially important chemicals, only a small number—perhaps 2%—are harmful. The remaining 98% are relatively harmless, either because they are not poisonous or because people are not exposed to them during the production–consumption cycle. Still, that small percentage amounts to hundreds of potentially dangerous chemicals.

Table 18-1 Some Toxic Chemicals and Their Effects

Category	Original Source	Past, Present Uses	Human Health Effects	Environmental Effects
Pesticides				
Aldrin/dieldrin	Chemically manufactured	Insecticide	Tremors, convulsions, damage to kidneys, suspected carcinogen	Reproductive failure of birds and fish
DDT	Chemically manufactured	Insecticide	Tremors, degradation of central nervous system (CNS), suspected carcinogen	Reproductive failure of fish, eggshell thinning in birds
Parathion	Chemically manufactured	Insecticide	Acute toxicity	Kills wildlife
Toxaphene	Chemically manufactured	Insecticide	Chromosome change in female workers, suspected carcinogen	Accumulation in fish, inhibition of growth, damage to liver of fish
2, 4-D	Chemically manufactured	Herbicide	Forms nitrosamines in intestinal tract	Reduces natural habitat
Industrial Chemicals				
Acrylonitrile	Chemically manufactured	Plastic resin in pipes, textiles, appliances, until 1977 in plastic beverage bottles	Suspected carcinogen	Releases toxic chemical, hydrogen cyanide, when burned
Asbestos	Mining, milling	Brake linings, fireproofing, insulation, cement pipes, consumer products	Lung damage, lung cancer, stomach cancer	
Benzene	Petroleum refining	Gas additive, insecticides, arts and crafts supplies, detergents, moldings, fibers	Anemia, bone marrow damage, leukemia	
Phthalates	Chemically manufactured	Plasticizer (added to plastics, resins)	CNS damage	Accumulation in birds, eggshell thinning in birds, toxic to fish

Table 18-1   Some Toxic Chemicals and Their Effects

Category	Original Source	Past, Present Uses	Human Health Effects	Environmental Effects
Polychlorinated biphenyls (PCBs)	Chemically manufactured	Industrial fluids, capacitors, transformers, heat transfer fluids, plasticizers	Fatigue, vomiting, skin blemishes, abdominal pain, temporary blindness, stillbirths, suspected carcinogen	Liver damage in mammals, kidney damage, eggshell thinning in birds, suspected reproductive failure in fish
Vinyl chloride	Chemically manufactured	Plastics, polyvinyl chloride	Liver damage, birth anomalies, liver, respiratory, brain, lymph cancers; circulatory, bone damages	
Metals				
Arsenic	Mining, ore smelting	Glass, pesticides, hardening agent for copper, lead, and alloys	Vomiting; poisoning; degeneration of liver and kidneys; lung, liver, lymph, skin cancers	Persists in soil, toxic to legume crops
Cadmium	Mining, zinc smelting, sewage sludge	Electroplating, batteries, pigments, pesticides, stabilizer in plastics, tires	Headache, vomiting, chest pains, hypertension, emphysema, heart disease, suspected carcinogen and mutagen, kidney and liver disease	Toxic to fish in low concentrations
Lead	Mining, leaching	Batteries, gas additives, paint, tank linings, pipings	Anemia, kidney damage, CNS damage	Poisoning in domestic animals, birds, and fish
Mercury	Mining, leaching, volcanic action	Chlorine production (Chlor-alkali), scientific and industrial instruments, pesticides, batteries, contraceptive jellies and creams	Irritability, nervousness, depression, hallucinations, kidney damage, liver damage, CNS damage, fetus abnormalities	Reproductive failure, death of fish

Source: Council on Environmental Quality.

Annual Production of Synthetic Organic Chemicals, 1920-80

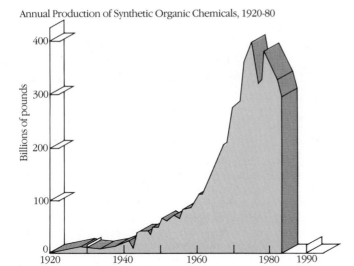

Figure 18-1
Growth in the production of synthetic organic chemicals in the United States.

The task of testing potentially harmful substances is enormous, and it is made more difficult by the 700 to 1000 new chemicals entering the marketplace each year. For many of these there is little or no information on toxic effects.

This chapter looks at the effects of toxic substances and how they can be controlled to minimize the risk to humans and the environment. Additional information on toxic substances can be found in Chapters 19–22, and Chapter Supplement 18-1, "Global Lead Pollution."

Principles of Toxicology

Toxic substances, or **toxins**, are those chemicals that cause any of a wide number of adverse effects in living organisms. **Toxicology** is the study of these effects.

In many cases our exposure to toxic substances is unintentional—for example, breathing polluted air from a nearby highway or power plant. But in other cases exposure is intentional—for example, smoking.

The possible range of harmful effects from chemicals is wide. Some effects may be subtle, such as a slight cough or headache caused by air pollution, but others can be quite pronounced, such as the violent convulsions brought on by exposure to certain insecticides. How do toxicologists classify effects?

Chemical Effects

There are two basic classes of toxic effect: acute and chronic. **Acute effects** are manifested immediately after exposure. For example, a headache that comes on while you are riding home in rush-hour traffic is an acute effect, which may have been caused by carbon monoxide from automobile exhaust. Acute effects are often short-lived, disappearing shortly after the exposure ends, and are generally caused by fairly high concentrations of chemicals during short-term (acute) exposures (Figure 18-2).

Chronic effects are delayed but long-lasting responses to toxic agents. They may occur months to years after exposure and usually persist for years, as in the case of emphysema caused by cigarette smoke or pollution. A chronic effect is generally the result of low-level exposure over a long period (chronic exposure). It is important to note, though, that short-term exposures may also have delayed effects.

Chronic and acute effects include changes in the normal anatomy and physiology of an organism: changes in the liver, kidneys, lungs, heart, lymph glands, and other tissues and organs. Cancer, mutations, birth defects, and reproductive impairment may also result from chemical exposures.

Figure 18-2
Billowing auto exhaust.

Cancer Cancer annually kills 400,000 people in the United States. A **cancer** is an uncontrolled proliferation of cells. Many cells in the body divide naturally to replenish cells that are lost in the normal functioning of the organism or from disease. But this cellular replacement is a controlled process: once the lost cells are replenished, cell division stops. In cancer, though, the mechanisms that stop cellular division do not seem to operate; cells keep on proliferating, forming a mass, or **primary tumor**. Cells may break off from the tumor and travel in the blood and other body fluids. For example, most lung cancers, if not detected early, spread to the brain. The spread of cancerous cells is called **metastasis**. In distant sites, the cancerous cells form **secondary tumors**. Widespread dissemination of cells and the establishment of numerous secondary tumors eventually kill the patient.

Every cancer starts as a single cell gone haywire. The conversion of normal cells into cancerous ones frequently occurs in tissues that undergo rapid cellular division—for example, bone marrow, lungs, lining of the intestine, ovaries, testes, and skin. Cells that do not typi-

cally divide, such as nerve cells and muscle cells, rarely become cancerous.

The causes of cancer are not completely understood despite years of intensive research. But we have many reasons to believe that changes in the genetic material, DNA, are involved. Ninety percent of all chemicals known to cause cancer also cause mutations in bacterial test systems. A **mutation** is a structural change in the genetic material. Thus, many experts believe that cancer is caused by genetic changes brought on by certain viruses, chemical substances, and physical agents such as X rays and ultraviolet light. Chromosomes in cancer cells are typically abnormal in structure or number. But a number of carcinogens such as asbestos, plastics, and hormones apparently do not alter the DNA or cause mutations. Thus, other mechanisms may be involved.

As shown in Figure 18-3, most cancers increased between 1930 and 1950 but have leveled off since then. What caused this initial rise? Part of the reason was improvement in diagnosing and reporting cancers. Health departments in almost every state now gather cancer data; 30 to 50 years

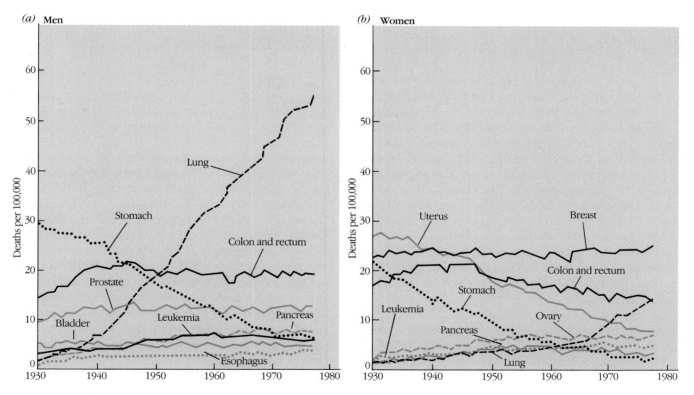

Figure 18-3

Cancer rates in men and women in the United States.

ago few of them were concerned with the problem. Thus, the upsurge in cancer in recent years is partially related to centralized reporting and also better diagnosis by physicians.

Until recently, many scientists believed that about 90% of all cancers resulted from environmental pollutants and other agents such as X rays, ultraviolet light, and viruses. The popular view held that chemicals from automobiles, power plants, factories, and other sources were resulting in an epidemic of cancers. But more careful research has shown that only 20% to 40% of all cancers are caused by work-place and other environmental pollutants. The rest are the result of natural cellular changes.

Mutations Agents that cause mutations are called **mutagens**. In general, three types of genetic alteration are seen: (1) changes in the DNA itself, (2) alterations of the chromosomal structure that are visible with a microscope (deletion or rearrangement of parts of the chromosome), and (3) missing or extra chromosomes. For our purposes the term *mutation* loosely encompasses all three.

Mutations may be caused by chemical substances, such as caffeine (Chapter 21), or physical agents such as ultraviolet light or radiation (see Chapter Supplement 21-2). Occurring at a rapid rate, they are usually repaired by cellular enzymes.

In humans, mutations can occur in normal body cells, or **somatic cells**, such as skin or muscle. Mutations in these cells, if not repaired, may lead to cancer years later.

The reproductive cells, or **germ cells**, in the male and female gonads are also susceptible to mutagens. Germ-cell mutations, if not repaired, may be passed on to offspring. If a genetically damaged ovum, for example, were fertilized by a normal sperm, the mutation would be passed on to every cell in the offspring. The defective gene may cause the fetus to die or may manifest itself as a birth defect or a metabolic disease. Germ-cell mutations may not be evident in the first generation but may be expressed in the second and third generations. This delayed effect makes it difficult for scientists to pinpoint the causes of various diseases.

Genetic mutations are present in about 2 of every 100 newborns. In fetuses, mutations are more prevalent. About 6% of all fetuses have some form of genetic mutation.

The causes of mutations in humans are not well understood. Abnormal chromosome numbers responsible for diseases such as Down's syndrome have been related to maternal age (Figure 18-4), and so have chromosome

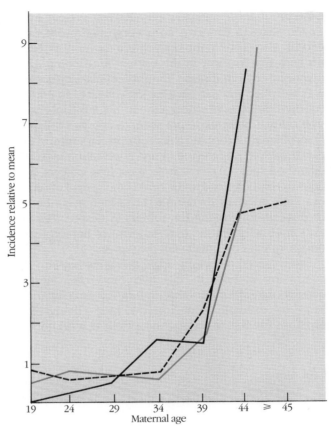

Figure 18-4
Incidence of three chromosomal abnormalities in newborns, involving the wrong number of chromosomes, related to mother's age.

defects (breaks and rearrangements). As women enter their 30s, the chances of having a baby with an abnormal number of chromosomes increase; after age 40 the chances skyrocket. No such relationship has been found for fathers. Geneticists suggest that mutagenic agents may affect the woman's germ cells; the older she is, the greater the chance that she has been exposed to mutagens, hence the greater the likelihood that her child will have a genetic mutation.

Other diseases associated with actual structural defects in the DNA molecule itself seem to increase in incidence as the father gets older but are not related to the mother's age (Figure 18-5). These defects may be caused by physical mutagens such as radiation and may result in birth defects, cancer, and other diseases.

Birth Defects Seven percent of all children born in the United States have a **birth defect**—a physical (structural),

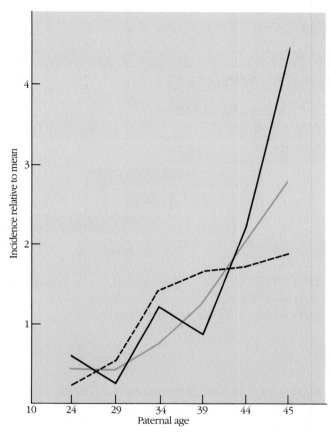

Figure 18-5
Incidence of three diseases due to DNA damage in newborn children, related to father's age.

Table 18-2 Some Known and Suspected Teratogens in Humans	
Known Agents	**Possible or Suspected Agents**
Progesterone	Aspirin
Thalidomide	Certain antibiotics
Rubella	Insulin
(German measles)	Antitubercular drugs
Alcohol	Antihistamines
Irradiation	Barbiturates
	Iron
	Tobacco
	Antacids
	Excess vitamins A and D
	Certain antitumor drugs
	Certain insecticides
	Certain fungicides
	Certain herbicides
	Dioxin
	Cortisone
	Lead

biochemical, or functional abnormality. The most obvious ones are the physical defects, such as cleft palate, lack of limbs, or spina bifida.

According to many scientists, the incidence of birth defects is greater than 7% because many minor defects escape detection at birth. For example, mental retardation, defects of the sensory organs, abnormal sexual development, and certain enzyme deficiencies are commonly missed by physicians. In addition, a large number of embryos and fetuses die in the uterus because of defects in development; some are born dead (stillbirths), and others are aborted naturally. Each year in the United States, spontaneous abortions, stillbirths, and early infant deaths claim the lives of over 500,000 defective embryos, fetuses, and children.

Agents that cause birth defects are called **teratogens**; the study of birth defects is **teratology** (from the Greek *teratos,* monster). In humans, teratogenic agents may be drugs, physical agents such as radiation, or biological agents such as the rubella (German measles) virus and several other viruses (Table 18-2). Estimates indicate that 1% to 5% of all human birth defects (congenital defects) are caused by drugs or chemicals in the environment, but no one is certain how valid these estimates are.

Embryonic development is divided into three parts: (1) a period of early development right after fertilization, (2) a period when the organs are developing (organogenesis), and (3) a period during which the organs have formed and the fetus mainly increases in size. Chemical substances can damage embryonic cells during the first period of development, but they do not generally cause abnormalities. During organogenesis, however, teratogenic agents have a pronounced effect on development (Figure 18-6).

The effect of a teratogenic agent is related to the time of exposure and also to the type of chemical. Certain chemicals only affect certain systems; for example, methyl mercury damages the developing brain of an embryo. Other chemicals, such as ethyl alcohol, can affect numerous developing systems; for instance, children born to alcoholic mothers exhibit growth failure, facial disfigurement, heart defects, and skeletal defects.

Figure 18-6
Schematic representation of human development, showing when some organ systems develop. Sensitive periods are indicated by cross-hatching. Exposure to teratogens during these times will almost certainly cause birth defects.

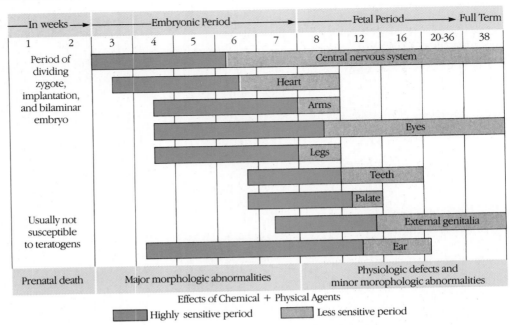

The list of proven human teratogens is rather small (Table 18-2); however, many agents are suspected of causing birth defects. Most of these are chemicals intentionally ingested for treatment of illness.

Reproductive Toxicology   Reproduction is a complex process involving many steps. Ova and sperm must be formed and successfully united. The zygote, the product of this union, must divide by mitosis and become implanted in the wall of the uterus, where it acquires nutrients from the mother's blood. Tissues develop from the ball of cells, and then organs develop from these tissues. During all of this the mother undergoes metabolic and hormonal changes. At the end of the developmental period birth takes place, requiring hormones that contract the uterus and expand the cervix (the end of the uterus where it opens into the vagina). Next, the breasts begin to produce milk, a hormonally regulated process called lactation. Chemical and physical agents may interrupt any of these complex processes, interfering with reproduction. The field of study that examines the effects of physical and chemical agents on reproduction is called **reproductive toxicology**.

The effects of drugs and environmental chemicals on reproduction have become a major health concern in recent years. Studies have shown, for example, that male factory workers become sterile when exposed on the job to DBCP (1,2-dibromo-3-chloropropane). Men who routinely handle various organic solvents often have abnormal sperm cells, unusually low sperm counts, and varying levels of infertility. A wide number of chemicals such as diethylstilbestrol (DES), borax, cadmium, methyl mercury, and many cancer drugs are toxic to the reproductive systems of males and females.

Some examples will help illustrate the effect of chemical toxins on reproduction. Jacqueline Fabia and Truong Thuy of Laval University in Quebec examined the records of 386 children who died of cancer before the age of five. Their study showed that many of the fathers of these children had been working at the time their children were conceived in occupations in which they were exposed to high levels of hydrocarbons (for example, painters exposed to paint thinners and mechanics exposed to car exhaust). This study suggests that hydrocarbons had entered the bloodstream, traveled to the testes, and there damaged the germ cells. The resulting genetic defect (mutation) was passed to the offspring and showed up during the first few years of life as cancer.

In the 1950s and 1960s diethylstilbestrol (DES) was given to pregnant women. It was prescribed for women who either had a history of miscarriages or had begun to bleed during pregnancy, an early symptom of miscarriage. DES had a profound but delayed effect on the female offspring of DES-treated women. Uterine and cervical cancers began to appear in high frequency in the daughters of these women. Research is uncovering reproductive damage in their sons, too.

The range of possible effects of physical and chemical agents on reproduction is immense. We have only scratched the surface here.

How Do Toxins Work?

Toxic substances exert their effects at the cellular level in three major ways: First, they can affect **enzymes**, the cellular proteins that regulate many important chemical reactions. A disturbance of enzymatic activity can seriously alter the functioning of an organ or tissue. For example, mercury and arsenic both bind to certain enzymes, blocking their activity. Second, toxins may bind directly to cells or molecules within the cell, thereby upsetting the chemical balance within the body. Carbon monoxide, for example, binds to hemoglobin in the blood; this interferes with the transport of oxygen and can lead to death if levels are high enough (see Chapter 19). Third, toxins may cause the release of other naturally occurring substances that have an adverse effect. The toxin carbon tetrachloride, for example, stimulates certain nerve cells to release large quantities of epinephrine (adrenaline), believed to cause liver damage. Toluene diisocyanate released during the production of plastics may cause the release of histamine, serotonin, and similar internal substances that have harmful effects on the organism.

Factors That Affect the Toxicity of Chemicals

Numerous factors determine the effects of toxic agents on organisms. Because of this, it is not always easy to predict the exact effects of various toxins. To illustrate this, consider the family of six living near a Canadian lead and zinc smelter that released large quantities of lead. Each member was exposed to high levels of lead, but the health effects were varied: The father and a four-year-old boy suffered from colic and pancreatitis. The mother developed a neural disorder. Two other children experienced convulsions, and the last developed diabetes.

Dose Three of the most important factors that influence the effects of a given chemical are the dose received, the length of exposure, and the biological reactivity of the chemical in question. In general, the higher the dose and the longer the exposure, the greater the effect. To demonstrate the effect of dose, toxicologists frequently plot **dose–response curves** using various laboratory animals such as rats and mice (Figure 18-7).

As shown in Figure 18-7, the dose that kills half of the test animals is called the LD_{50}, or the lethal dose for 50% of the test animals. By comparing LD_{50} values, scientists can judge the relative toxicity of two chemicals. For example, a toxin with an LD_{50} of 200 milligrams per kilogram of body weight is half as toxic as one with an LD_{50} of 100 milligrams per kilogram. The lower the LD_{50}, the more toxic a chemical is.

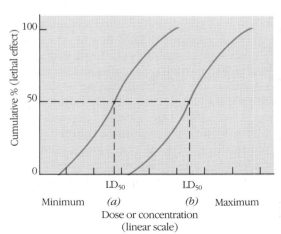

AGENT	LD50 (mg/kg)
Ethyl alcohol	10,000
Sodium chloride	4,000
Ferrous sulfate	1,500
Morphine sulfate	900
Phenobarbital sodium	150
DDT	100
Picrotoxin	5
Strychnine sulfate	2
Nicotine	1
d-Tubocurarine	0.5
Hemicholinium-3	0.2
Tetrodotoxin	0.10
Dioxin (TCDD)	0.001
Botulinus toxin	0.00001

APPROXIMATE ACUTE LD50s OF A VARIETY OF CHEMICAL AGENTS

Figure 18-7

Dose-response graph for two chemicals (*a* and *b*). The LD_{50} is the amount of chemical that kills one-half of the experimental animals within a given time. The higher the LD_{50} value, the less toxic the chemical is.

Biological Activity The LD$_{50}$ measures the toxicity of different chemicals, but what determines how toxic a chemical is? Basically, the toxicity of a chemical is a function of its biological activity—how it reacts with enzymes or other cellular components. The more reactive it is in biological organisms, the more effect it has. Inert substances, those that do not chemically react with cellular components, generally are not toxic, although there are notable exceptions such as asbestos.

Route of Entry Generally, toxins enter through the skin, the intestinal tract, or the lungs. Inhalation is usually more dangerous than other routes, because chemicals readily enter the bloodstream and are quickly transported throughout the body. Thus, many cells can be exposed to the harmful toxin in a brief span of time. Toxins consumed in food or in drinking water or beverages pass into the blood after being absorbed through the wall of the small intestine, but blood from the small intestine immediately flows through the liver, which destroys or detoxifies many chemical agents, thus minimizing exposure to other organs. The skin prevents most substances from penetrating the body, so dermal (skin) exposure is usually the least harmful of all.

Age Young, growing organisms are generally more susceptible to toxic chemicals than are mature adults. For example, two common air pollutants, ozone and sulfur dioxide, affect young laboratory animals two to three times more severely than they affect adults. Among humans, infants and children are more susceptible to lead and mercury poisoning than adults.

Health Status Poor nutrition, stress, bad eating habits, heart and lung disease, and smoking all contribute to poor health and make individuals more susceptible to certain toxins. Genetic factors may also determine one's response to toxic substances. Some individuals are genetically prone to heart disease, lung cancer, and other disorders brought on by environmental factors.

Synergy and Antagonism The presence of two or more toxic substances can alter the expected response. Different chemical substances can act together to produce a **synergistic response** that is stronger than simply combining the two responses. Probably the most familiar example of toxic synergy is the combination of barbiturate tranquilizers and alcohol; although neither taken alone is highly dangerous, the combination can be deadly.

Chemicals can also negate the effects of each other, a phenomenon called **antagonism**. In these cases a harmful effect is reduced by certain combinations of potentially toxic chemicals. For example, when mice are exposed to nitrous oxide gas, mortality is substantially reduced when particulates are also present.

Biological Concentration and Magnification

Two factors not mentioned in the previous discussion but profoundly influencing toxicity are biological concentration and biological magnification.

Biological concentration refers to an organism's ability to selectively accumulate certain chemicals within its body or within certain tissues. For example, the human thyroid gland concentrates iodide, which is needed to make the thyroid hormone thyroxin. Levels of iodide in the thyroid are thousands of times higher than in the blood. Scallops selectively take up certain elements from seawater, such as zinc, copper, cadmium, and chromium. The level of cadmium in scallops, for example, is 2.3 million times that of seawater. Harmful chemicals may become concentrated in the same way. For example, certain fat-soluble organic molecules such as the PCBs (polychlorinated biphenyls) and pesticides such as DDT can concentrate in body fat.

When organisms higher on the food chain eat DDT-contaminated prey, DDT is eventually deposited in the predators' fat, accumulating again in high concentrations. The higher one goes in the food chain, the greater the level of DDT. This phenomenon is called **biological magnification**. The concentration of DDT may be several million times greater in fish-eating water birds than it is in the water itself (Figure 18-8). For humans, the magnification that occurs in our food chain may be on the order of 75,000 to 150,000.

In general, biological magnification depends on a chemical's fat solubility, an organism's capacity to concentrate, and finally a chemical's persistence. The more resistant a chemical is to breakdown by bacteria, fungi, heat, sunlight, and other environmental factors, the longer it will remain in the environment; hence, the chances of its coming in contact with an organism are greater.

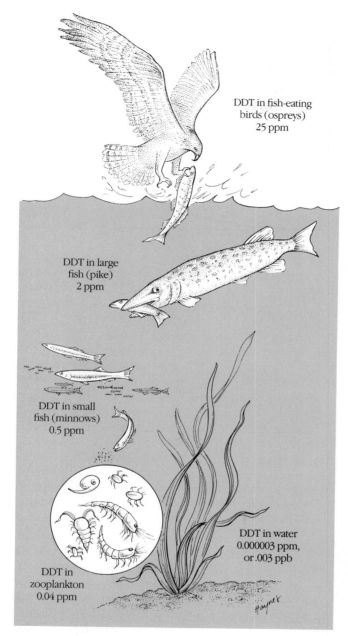

Figure 18-8
The biological magnification of DDT increases as you go higher in a food chain.

Controversy Over Toxic Chemical Effects

Despite much effort, we are still ignorant regarding the effects of various chemicals on human health. The reasons for our lack of knowledge are many, one of the most important ones being that it is neither practical nor ethical to perform experiments on humans. The results of experiments on laboratory animals cannot always be extrapolated to humans. Animals frequently react differently to chemicals than humans; they may be able to break them down better, or they may not be able to break them down as well. In any event, such physiological differences make it difficult to predict whether a chemical harmful to an animal will be injurious to us.

Another reason for our ignorance is that whereas humans are frequently exposed to low levels of many potentially harmful chemicals over long periods of time, most toxicity tests are performed on one substance at a time. Because of synergy and antagonism, extrapolating the results from single-chemical tests to the real world can be misleading.

Another problem is that most tests of toxicity, especially those for mutations and cancer, are performed at high exposure levels rarely if ever experienced by the average citizen and most workers. Thus, the fact that high levels of a certain chemical induce cancer in a lab animal does not necessarily mean that the chemical will cause cancer in humans (Figure 18-9).

Figure 18-9
Laboratory rats being fed carcinogenic items.

Scientists use such high doses because it speeds up their experiments. The time required to develop a noticeable cancer is quite long. Human cancers develop 5 to 30 years after exposure. As a general rule, the entire process from induction to manifestation takes about one-eighth of the lifespan of an animal. Thus, anything that speeds up the induction of cancer, such as high doses, helps cut costs. To test for low-level effects, scientists would need very large numbers of experimental animals to generate statistically valid results.

Toxicologists note that the incidence of cancers in lab animals is a function of dose: the higher the dose, the greater the incidence of cancer. The same relationship is known to be true of some human cancers; for instance, the incidence of lung cancer clearly increases with the number of cigarettes smoked. Some workers assume that if a chemical is harmful at high levels, it will also be harmful at the lowest levels. Others argue that there is a dose level—the **threshold level**—below which no harmful effect occurs (Figure 18-10); in other words, extremely low levels of certain chemicals are held to be completely safe. As yet, this controversy is unresolved.

Control of Toxic Substances

The United States produces over 136 million metric tons (150 million tons) of synthetic chemicals each year and creates over 36 million metric tons of toxic wastes each year. Congress has established a number of laws to regulate the production, consumption, and disposal of these and other potentially harmful substances, protecting workers, the public, and the environment (Table 18-3). (See Essay 18-1.)

Toxic Substances Control Act

Traditionally, U.S. laws and regulations (from various governmental agencies such as the Environmental Protection Agency) have dealt with hazardous chemicals already in use. These laws are considered *retrospective,* because they address the issue of toxicity after the fact. In 1976, however, Congress passed the *Toxic Substances Control Act,* which deals with hazardous substances before they are manufactured and sold. This is a prospective **law,** aimed at screening new chemicals and banning or limiting the use of those that present an unreasonable risk.

The act has three major parts: (1) a requirement that all chemical manufacturers and importers notify the EPA of new chemicals they want to introduce into the market,

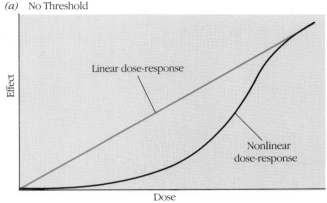

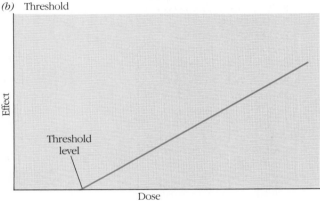

Figure 18-10
(a) A hypothetical dose–response curve indicating the absence of a threshold level, a level below which no effect occurs. *(b)* A hypothetical dose–response curve showing a threshold level.

(2) requirements for testing new or existing chemicals believed to present a risk to the public and the environment, and (3) stipulations for the control of several existing hazardous chemicals.

Premanufacture Notification Companies are required to notify the EPA 90 days before they import or manufacture chemical substances not in commercial use. The EPA then has 90 days to decide whether the chemical can be introduced and whether any restrictions are necessary to minimize risk during its production, distribution, and disposal.

Scientists at the EPA review all existing toxicity data on the chemical and decide whether to approve it. Most new substances have not been tested for toxicity, carcinogenicity, and other adverse effects, however, and manufac-

Table 18-3 Federal Laws and Agencies Regulating Toxic Chemicals

Statute	Year Enacted	Responsible Agency	Sources Covered
Toxic Substances Control Act	1976	EPA	All new chemicals (other than food additives, drugs, pesticides, alcohol, tobacco); existing chemical hazards not covered by other laws
Clean Air Act	1970, amended 1977	EPA	Hazardous air pollutants
Federal Water Pollution Control Act	1972, amended 1977	EPA	Toxic water pollutants
Safe Drinking Water Act	1974, amended 1977	EPA	Drinking water contaminants
Federal Insecticide, Fungicide, and Rodenticide Act	1948, amended 1972, 1973	EPA	Pesticides
Act of July 22, 1954 (codified as § 346(a) of the Food, Drug and Cosmetic Act)	1954, amended 1972	EPA	Tolerances for pesticide residues in food
Resource Conservation and Recovery Act	1976	EPA	Hazardous wastes
Marine Protection, Research and Sanctuaries Act	1972	EPA	Ocean dumping
Food, Drug and Cosmetic Act	1938	FDA	Basic coverage of food, drugs, and cosmetics
Food additives amendment	1958	FDA	Food additives
Color additive amendments	1960	FDA	Color additives
New drug amendments	1962	FDA	Drugs
New animal drug amendments	1968	FDA	Animal drugs and feed additives
Medical device amendments	1976	FDA	Medical devices
Wholesome Meat Act	1967	USDA	Food, feed, and color additives; pesticide residues in meat, poultry
Wholesome Poultry Products Act	1968		
Occupational Safety and Health Act	1970	OSHA	Work-place toxic chemicals
Federal Hazardous Substances Act	1966	CPSC	Household products
Consumer Product Safety Act	1972	CPSC	Dangerous consumer products
Poison Prevention Packaging Act	1970	CPSC	Packaging of dangerous children's products
Lead Based Paint Poison Prevention Act	1973, amended 1976	CPSC	Use of lead paint in federally assisted housing
Hazardous Materials Transportation Act	1970	DOT (Materials Transportation Bureau)	Transportation of toxic substances generally
Federal Railroad Safety Act	1970	DOT (Federal Railroad Administration)	Railroad safety
Ports and Waterways Safety Act	1972	DOT (Coast Guard)	Shipment of toxic materials by water
Dangerous Cargo Act	1952		

CPSC = Consumer Product Safety Commission
DOT = U.S. Department of Transportation
EPA = U.S. Environmental Protection Agency
FDA = Food and Drug Administration
OSHA = Occupational Safety and Health Administration
USDA = U.S. Department of Agriculture

Source: Council on Environmental Quality

Acrylonitrile: What Cost for Protection?

Acrylonitrile (AN) was one of many new chemicals that ushered in the age of plastics following World War II. Used in clothing, rugs, and numerous other home furnishings, AN and the host of other synthetic polymers created a new and prosperous industry. But in 1977 Du Pont, the maker of AN, linked it with lung and colon cancer in textile workers at its plant in Camden, South Carolina. The company and the government were forced into a precarious bind: how to balance the health of the workers with the cost of reducing their exposure to the hazardous chemical.

Acrylonitrile is big business. Its annual production and sale bring in over $1.5 billion in the United States each year. However, at least 10,000 workers are exposed to AN concentrations believed to cause cancer, and the cost of eliminating the cancer threat could run from $3.5 million to over $100 million *per life saved*.

In 1978, the Occupational Safety and Health Administration's safety standard for AN was 20 parts per million over an eight-hour workday. OSHA proposed to drop that standard to 2 ppm and considered a further reduction to .2 ppm. Economists at Du Pont, however, calculated that reductions to 2 ppm would cost millions of dollars. According to the company, reducing the level to 2 ppm would prevent seven cancer deaths among workers per year at a cost of about $3.5 million per life saved. Further reductions to .2 ppm would prevent one additional cancer death per year but would cost $126.2 million!

From a purely economic viewpoint, the investment in pollution controls makes little sense. Can we expect industry to spend billions of dollars to reduce all risks to insignificant levels? As industry officials remind us, there would be no industry if that were the case. By the same token, industry cannot be given a free license to kill people for the sake of profit.

The only principle on which there seems to be universal agreement is that a balance must be struck between the costs of doing business and the costs a business creates among the public and workers. Even this is not so easy as it may sound, however, because no universally accepted formula has been derived to balance the economic good with the health and welfare of the people.

Source: Adapted from: Behr, P. (1978). Controlling Chemical Hazards. *Environment* 20(6): 25–29.

turers generally do little toxicity research because of the cost. Thus, the EPA must rely on toxicity data from similar chemicals. In many cases, new chemicals belong to classes of compounds that have been adequately tested, so the EPA can make a sound decision on that information.

If the new chemical is believed to represent little risk because of low toxicity, low exposure, and low production, it is approved. If it is potentially hazardous (because of a high toxicity or large potential exposure), however, the EPA may ask the manufacturer to conduct studies of its toxicity to generate more data for a sound decision. As of 1981 over 1000 new chemicals had been reviewed, but only 15 were believed to pose enough risk to warrant a more thorough review; in most cases, the manufacturer withdrew them from consideration.

Chemical Testing The Toxic Substances Control Act also requires the EPA to make recommendations for toxicity research on chemicals already in use. A systematic review of the existing chemicals was carried out by the Interagency Testing Committee, a group of scientists from several key governmental agencies. The committee surveyed the list of chemicals in use and recommended research on those that might present an unacceptable risk. Included were those chemicals produced in high volumes and those to which a large number of people were exposed.

In response, the EPA proposed testing of several potentially harmful chemicals but also recommended against testing many more chemicals that the committee felt should be studied. The EPA argued that industry was testing some of these voluntarily, that the government was already testing others, and that some were not worth testing because of low exposure.

One area in which the EPA has performed admirably is the establishment of uniform testing methods. Advisory guidelines for testing drawn up by the EPA yield reliable and consistent results that can be compared with results

The Myth of the "Banned" Pesticides

Lewis Regenstein

The author wrote America the Poisoned, *published by Acropolis Books. He is vice president of the Fund for Animals and is past president of the Monitor Consortium, a coalition of 35 national environmental and animal protection groups. He is also the author of* The Politics of Extinction: The Story of the World's Endangered Wildlife *(Macmillan, 1975).*

As of 1977 there were 33,000 to 35,000 registered pesticide products on the market, using 1500 active ingredients combined with 2000 other possibly toxic substances. Over 100 of the pesticides in general use today are thought to cause cancer. The EPA estimates that about one-third of the active ingredients used in pesticides are toxic and that one-fourth are carcinogenic.

Since its beginning the EPA has effectively banned the domestic use of only about a dozen of these by canceling their registration. (In addition, an unknown number of pesticides have either not been granted registration or been withdrawn voluntarily by the manufacturer.)

One often comes across erroneous references to certain highly toxic pesticides, such as DDT, as having been "banned." Ronald Reagan has even complained that "the world is experiencing a resurgence of deadly diseases spread by insects because pesticides like DDT have been prematurely outlawed." The sad fact, however, is that after many years of efforts by scientists, conservationists, and some government officials, very few restrictions have been placed on pesticides. Despite the overwhelming evidence that many pesticides cause cancer and are extremely damaging to humans and the environment, almost none of these

chemicals has ever been "banned" by the government in the true sense of that word. In the very few cases where pesticides have been the subject of suspensions, cancellation proceedings, or court actions, the results have usually been restrictions or bans placed on some or most uses while other applications are allowed to continue.

Even in the handful of cases where all domestic use has been prohibited (such as with kepone), manufacture for export can still be (and often is) legally undertaken. When production for export continues, it inevitably results in exposure of workers and the public through pollution, dumping of wastes, and other accidental and intentional releases of the substance, as well as through foodstuffs imported from foreign countries to which the chemical is exported.

The way the EPA has carried out its policy on "banning" toxic pesticides is contradictory and nonsensical. In numerous instances the agency has proclaimed a chemical hazardous to humans and the environment and prohibited major uses of the compound. At the same time, it has allowed other uses to continue as before, often depending on label instructions to ensure adherence to the prohibitions. Several cancer-causing chemicals that have been restricted but not banned are aldrin, dieldrin, chlordane, heptachlor, DDT, 2,4,5-T, mirex, and DBCP. In these and other instances, the EPA action has often been presented to the public by the news media as another pesticide "ban."

In canceling the registrations for major uses of these most obviously dangerous pesticides, the EPA in many cases allowed them to be slowly phased out or permitted the sale and distribution of existing stocks. This made it possible for large quantities to continue to be sold and used long after they were "banned" and even for users to stockpile them for future use.

The implications of this EPA policy should be obvious. It is impossible to know what use will be made of these products. Indeed, EPA end-use restrictions are considered a joke within the agricultural community, and many farmers use certain chemicals as they always have, regardless of whether such applications have been banned.

Moreover, there is no way to determine how and where such carefully restricted and regulated chemicals are being disposed of. Common sense would dictate that if a chemical is so dangerous that it has been declared a threat to humans and the environment, it should simply be banned—its manufacture, sale, transport, use, or possession prohibited.

Pesticides that have been restricted are listed in the EPA publication "Suspended and Cancelled Pesticides," which gives the conditions, if any, under which these substances may be used. The rules and regulations outlined in this largely incomprehensible document are so complex and unfathomable that their only real use and value are to lawyers and bureaucrats interested in the byzantine world of federal regulations. It is difficult to believe that farmers and agricultural workers, particularly illiterate or Spanish-speaking migrants, could understand the meaning of these rules or the labels on pesticides.

For example, 2,4,5-T cannot be used in "ponds" or on "food crops intended for human consumption" but can be applied to rice, a food crop grown in pond-like areas. It cannot be sprayed on pastureland, where cattle graze, but can be used on rangeland, where livestock also forage. The regulations for endrin prohibit spraying within certain distances from lakes, ponds, and streams, varying from 15 to 200 meters (50 feet to one-eighth of a mile), depending on the crop being sprayed. The instructions allow spraying closer to ponds that are owned by the user but warn against its causing fish kills. The document also gives detailed instructions on what to do if fish kills do occur and how to dispose of the fish (burial), and requires the posting of a "No Fishing" sign for half a year or a year after the kill has occurred.

Under "aerial application," the regulations warn,

> Do not operate nozzle liquid pressure over 40 psi or with any fan nozzle smaller than 0.4 gpm or fan angle greater than 65 degrees such as type 6504. Do not use any can type nozzles smaller than 0.4 gpm nor whirl plate smaller than #46 such as type D-4-46.

Ground application instructions are equally bizarre. But in the final analysis these details don't really matter. What happens in real life is that a migrant worker is given a container of endrin and told to spray it on the crops, and that's that.

Label requirements for other potentially toxic chemicals, even when clearly written, are equally useless. For example, the brochure requires that metaldehyde, used to kill slugs and snails, "must have the following statement on the front panel of the product label: 'This pesticide may be fatal to children and dogs or other pets if eaten. Keep children and pets out of treated areas.'" But such a warning in no way prevents this extremely toxic chemical from being widely used throughout the nation in precisely the way the label cautions against. U.S. government agencies, including those oriented toward the environment, pay little attention to the labels. In recent years the National Park Service used metaldehyde on the White House lawn and the public grounds around and between the White House and the Capitol. In 1977, 40 kilograms (88 pounds) was used just in the President's Park, an area adjacent to the White House. Such use in these areas not only potentially endangers the president and his family but also countless thousands of tourists who flock to the Ellipse, the Mall, and other areas around the White House.

The EPA's labeling and restricted-use policies, unintelligible and contradictory as they may seem, do serve several purposes. They keep the public reassured that it is being protected from "banned" and "restricted" pesticides while allowing chemical and agribusiness interests to carry on business as usual with many of these products. It is, in fact, an ideal arrangement: it keeps the bureaucrats, the politicians, and industry happy, even if the public gets poisoned in the process.

---

of other research. Standardized test methods are a good way to build a strong base of data for making sound policies.

Controls on Hazardous Chemicals Congress also took specific actions against certain chemicals it thought were hazardous. The most radical controls were placed on PCBs, which are used for insulation in electrical transformers. Congress banned the manufacturing and distribution of uncontained PCBs because of their stability in the environment, widespread contamination, ability to biologically magnify, and toxicity. Disposal plans for PCB-contaminated liquids were to be developed by the EPA.

What Is Acceptable Risk?

The Toxic Substances Control Act and other chemical-control laws generally seek to regulate the production,

transportation, distribution, and disposal of chemicals to protect human health and the environment in a cost-effective manner. Numerous problems arise in this process, as discussed in Chapter 17. Perhaps the most difficult hurdle is determining the **actual risk** a chemical presents to society and the environment. Ideally, if the actual risk can be determined, laws and regulations can be drawn up to protect humans and the environment in a cost-effective manner.

Although there is no legal requirement for risk assessment in any U.S. laws, numerous agencies have been involved in such actions for many years. Unfortunately, regulatory agencies may do only partial or even shoddy risk assessments that are of little value. They may condemn chemicals that pose no real threat to humans or the environment, or worse, they may judge dangerous ones acceptable because the threat is too hard to quantify. (See Viewpoint, "The Myth of the 'Banned' Pesticides.")

Two improvements are needed in the risk-assessment practices carried out by the government. The first is uniform guidelines for estimating the health and environmental effects of hazardous chemicals. The second is an objective assessment of risk that draws distinct lines between the scientific assessment of risk and social judgments of risk acceptability.

Some suggest the establishment of a nonpolitical risk-assessment board composed of scientists in many disciplines, such as toxicology, medicine, public health, air pollution, and statistics. The board would employ standardized methods for assessing the probability and severity of risks. This information could be supplied to the policymakers, who balance the scientific evidence with social, ethical, economic, and political concerns. By separating risk assessment from the actual determinations of risk acceptability, we could better manage potentially hazardous chemicals and, at the same time, create laws that do not expose the public to undue risk or the chemical companies to unnecessary costs.

We must indeed all hang together or, most assuredly, we shall all hang separately.

BENJAMIN FRANKLIN

Summary

Citizens of developed countries depend on a vast number of chemical substances, some of which may be harmful to human health and the environment. Toxic substances, or *toxins,* are those chemicals that cause any of a wide number of adverse effects in organisms. *Toxicology* is the study of these effects. In many cases, exposure to toxins is unintentional; in others, we are directly responsible for it. *Acute effects* are manifest immediately after exposure, are often short-lived, and are generally caused by high levels of exposure. *Chronic effects* are delayed and long-lasting and are generally the result of low-level exposure. Toxic effects include changes in the normal anatomy and physiology of an organism. They may include cancer, mutations, birth defects, and reproductive impairment.

Cancer, an uncontrolled proliferation of cells, is often caused by an alteration of the genetic material. Indeed, 90% of all chemicals known to cause cancer also cause mutations in bacterial test systems. Other mechanisms may be involved in some cancers.

The incidence of cancer increased in the United States between 1930 and 1950 but has leveled off since then, except for lung cancer and a few other types. The rise in the incidence of cancer may have been partially due to better diagnosis and vast improvements in cancer reporting. Only a relatively small percentage of cancers are brought on by environmental and workplace pollutants.

Mutations are structural changes in the genetic material of cells caused by chemical and physical agents, called *mutagens.* Mutations occur in humans at a fairly rapid rate but are usually repaired. If not repaired, they may lead to cancer. If they occur in *germ cells,* they may be passed on to offspring, leading to birth defects, stillbirth, or spontaneous abortion.

Birth defects, structural and functional defects, are observed in 7% to 10% of all newborn American children. The study of birth defects is called *teratology.* Agents that cause them are called *teratogens.* In humans, there are few known teratogens, although many substances are suspected.

Reproductive toxicology is the study of toxic effects of chemical and physical agents during the reproductive cycle. Most studies are concerned with the effects of toxic agents on sperm and ova and their subsequent ability to fertilize and form a normal embryo. Numerous chemical agents impair reproduction in humans.

Toxins exert their effects at the cellular level by blocking enzyme activity, binding to cells or molecules within cells, and causing the release of naturally occurring substances in harmful amounts. Numerous factors affect toxic agents, making it difficult to predict the effects. Some of these include dose, age, route of entry, synergy, and antagonism. *Synergy* occurs when different substances act together to produce a response that is stronger than expected. *Antagonism* occurs when substances negate the effects of each other.

Toxicity is also profoundly influenced by *biological concentration,* the ability of an organism to selectively accumulate certain chemicals within its body in certain tissues. *Biological magnification,* the buildup of chemicals within food chains, also affects toxicity. Biological magnification occurs with chemicals that can be concentrated in certain tissues (such as fat) and are resistant to chemical breakdown.

The Toxic Substances Control Act (1976) is a powerful tool for regulating toxins in the United States. It requires premanufacture notification to the EPA of all new chemicals to be produced or imported into the country, calls for EPA-mandated testing of new and existing chemicals, and establishes specific controls on several existing hazardous chemicals.

Ultimately, all decisions on toxic chemicals require an accurate assessment of risk. Once risk is determined, cost-effective control measures can be designed that give society reasonable protection. Although there is no legal requirement for risk assessment in any U.S. laws, numerous agencies have been involved in it for many years. Unfortunately, regulatory agencies may do only partial or even shoddy assessments that are of little value. To improve the assessment of risk, uniform guidelines could be established for estimating the health and environmental effects of chemicals, and an objective risk-assessment board could be created that would be separate from the decision-making functions.

Discussion Questions

1. Define the terms *toxin, carcinogen, teratogen,* and *mutagen.*

2. Compare and contrast the terms *acute effects* and *chronic effects* in terms of time to onset of symptoms, persistence of the effect, level of the toxic agent, and duration of exposure.

3. What is cancer? Discuss how it may form. How does it spread?

4. Describe the three types of mutations that occur in cells. Describe the possible consequences of somatic and germinal cell mutations in humans.

5. What is teratology? What types of agent cause birth defects? Do teratogenic chemicals always create birth defects when given during pregnancy? Why or why not?

6. Define *environmental toxicology.*

7. Briefly discuss what effects toxins have on cells.

8. Why is it sometimes difficult to predict the effect a toxin will have on an individual? Make a list of factors that influence the toxicity of a chemical in a given person.

9. Define the terms *synergy* and *antagonism,* and give examples of each.

10. Define the terms *biological magnification* and *bioconcentration.* What factors can be used to predict whether a chemical will be magnified?

11. Why is our knowledge of the effects of toxic chemicals on humans so limited?

12. You are appointed the director of the health effects section of your state's Health Department. Your job is to determine the potential health effects of several toxic chemicals produced in your state. Describe how you would go about testing these chemicals as economically as possible.

13. Describe the major provisions of the Toxic Substances Control Act.

Suggested Readings

Doull, J., Klaassen, C. D., and Amdur, M. O. (1980). *Toxicology: The Basic Science of Poisons* (2nd ed.). New York: Macmillan. Superb reference.

Horne, R. A. (1978). *The Chemistry of Our Environment.* New York: Wiley. Excellent reference.

Loomis, T. A. (1974). *Essentials of Toxicology* (2nd ed.). Philadelphia: Lea and Febiger. Good overview of toxicology.

Mausner, J. S., and Bahn, A. K. (1974). *Epidemiology: An Introductory Text.* Philadelphia: Saunders. Excellent reference.

Waldbott, G. L. (1978). *Health Effects of Environmental Pollutants* (2nd ed.). St. Louis: Mosby. Good coverage of toxic effects of pollutants.

Willgoose, C. E. (1979). *Environmental Health: Commitment for Survival.* Philadelphia: Saunders. Good introductory text.

Global Lead Pollution

Lead is one of the most useful metals in modern industrial societies. Used by humans since 3500 B.C., it is found today in ceramic glazes, batteries, fishing sinkers, solder, pipe, and gasoline, where in the form of tetraethyl lead it enhances the combustion of gas and helps reduce engine knocking.

Lead has long been known as a highly toxic poison. No metal toxin has been studied more extensively. It affects various organs and may enter the body in many ways. High-level exposure causes a number of neurological defects. Continued high exposure may lead to coma, convulsions, and death. Scientists suggest that lead, used by fashionable circles in ancient Rome in drinking vessels and water systems, may have resulted in a fall in the birthrate and an increased incidence of psychosis in Rome's ruling class, contributing to the fall of the empire.

Today, because of controls on work-place exposure and more judicious use of lead in beverage and food processing, acute poisonings occur infrequently in the United States and other developed nations. Nonetheless, Americans are still regularly exposed to low levels of lead in the environment from a variety of sources.

Sources of Lead

Lead is found in food, water, air, and soils in both inorganic and organic forms. The highest exposures are in men and women working in lead smelters. Workers in factories that make storage batteries may also be exposed to high lead levels.

Lead enters the human body primarily through ingestion and secondarily through inhalation (Figure S18-1). For example, lead-based paints in old, neglected dwellings are a major source for young children of low-income families (Figure S18-2), who may ingest chips from their surroundings. Paint applied in the 1940s, before lead paint was banned, could contain as much as 50% lead by dry weight. Children may also ingest dirt contaminated

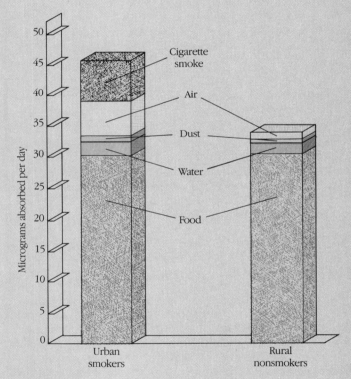

Figure S18-1
Sources of lead absorption in humans.

with lead from nearby roadways or may inhale it in the atmosphere.

According to the National Academy of Sciences, food accounts for 65% to 92% of an American adult's average lead intake. This lead may come from lead-arsenate pesticides or from automo-

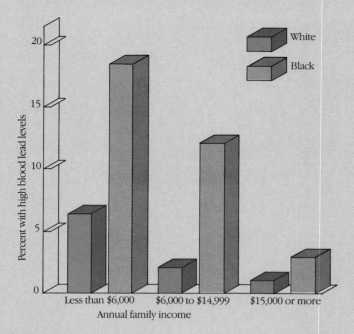

Figure S18-2
High lead levels in U.S. children from six months to five years old, according to their parents' income and race (1976–1980).

biles, power plants, smelters, and other sources. Deposited in the soil, it is taken up by food crops. Recent estimates indicate that up to 50% of the lead consumed by adults may come from foods in cans with lead solder in their seams.

The most important sources of lead in ambient air are vehicle emissions. In a recent study the Environmental Protection Agency estimated that 88% of the atmospheric lead emissions come from automobiles. In some areas, however, lead smelters and steel factories may make the most significant contribution to atmospheric lead levels. For example, studies of lead levels in rainwater near a copper smelter in Wollongong, Australia, showed that concentrations within 380 meters (1270 feet) of the smelter were four to five times higher than they were 600 meters from the plant and were about 20 times higher than they were several kilometers away. Residents living nearby may, therefore, be exposed to extremely high levels. The major natural source—volcanic dust—produces less than 1 percent of the emissions from human activities.

In unpolluted areas of the world, lead levels in the atmosphere are about 10 nanograms per cubic meter (a nanogram is one-billionth of a gram). As low as this may sound, these levels are 100 to 100,000 times higher than they were 10,000 years ago. Urban dwellers are typically exposed to much higher concentrations of lead in their ambient air—frequently 500 to 10,000

ng/m³. The U.S. federal standard set for lead in 1978 is 1500 ng/m³.

Scientists have estimated that lead concentrations in salt water from the preindustrial era were about .02 to .04 micrograms per kilogram. Samples today from deep salt waters now have concentrations ten times greater.

Effects of High-Level Exposure

High-level lead exposure may cause fatigue, headache, muscular tremor, lack of appetite, clumsiness, and loss of memory. These symptoms are a result of damage caused by inorganic lead in the brain and spinal cord (which make up the central nervous system). As we saw earlier, if the damage is severe enough, death may result. But even if the patient survives, residual damage such as epilepsy, retardation, and fluid accumulation in the brain is common. Organic lead (alkyl lead in gasoline, for example) causes a host of psychic disorders, including hallucinations, delusions, and excitement, which may lead to delirium and death.

Lead exposure may also affect the nerves that arise from the brain and spinal cord (the nerves make up the peripheral nervous system). The most common symptom in individuals exposed to high levels of lead is weakness of the extensor muscles (muscles that cause joints to open). On a cellular level, lead destroys the insulating sheath of nerve cells, perhaps causing the reduction in nerve impulse velocity commonly seen in patients who have been exposed to high levels of lead.

Lead also damages the kidneys, causing a disturbance in mechanisms that help us conserve valuable nutrients (such as glucose and amino acids) that might otherwise be lost in the urine. Prolonged high-level exposure causes a progressive buildup of connective tissue in the kidney and degeneration of the filtering mechanism that separates wastes from the bloodstream.

Finally, lead causes anemia, presumably because it damages red blood corpuscles and inhibits the synthesis of hemoglobin, the oxygen-carrying protein molecule found in red blood cells.

Effects of Low-Level Exposure

The toxic effects of large doses of lead have long been known, but only recently have we begun to understand what effects low-level exposure may have in human populations.

About 8% to 10% of the lead ingested by adults is absorbed by the intestines, but children have a much higher absorption rate—perhaps as high as 40%. In addition, children are more sensitive to the effects of lead than adults. The developing brain seems to be the most sensitive organ. Therefore, children are in an especially high-risk group. Because the toxicity of lead is increased in malnourished and iron-deficient people, urban children from poor families are particularly susceptible.

A number of epidemiological studies have been carried out on children exposed to a wide range of lead levels. Herbert Needleman and his colleagues performed a study of over 3000 children in the first and second grade in two towns near Boston. Children with high lead levels (but still below toxic levels) had significantly lower IQ scores than those with low lead levels. Attention span and classroom behavior were also significantly impaired. Several other studies showed similar results, which indicate that blood lead levels greater than 40 micrograms per 100 milliliters diminish intelligence and mental capacity in children under six years of age. A recent study in England showed that at an early age even marginally elevated blood lead levels may have lasting adverse effects on intelligence and behavior.

Lead has profound effects on reproduction in laboratory animals and humans alike. Numerous reports show that the rate of spontaneous abortion is much higher in couples if either partner is exposed to high levels of lead in the work place. More recent studies show decreased fertility and an increase in damaged sperm in male workers with high to medium levels of lead in their blood. According to one study, exposure of a pregnant woman to high levels of lead in household drinking water nearly doubles the risk of having a retarded child.

Lead contaminates livestock and wildlife as well as humans. Studies in Illinois, for example, show that lead levels in urban songbirds were significantly higher than in their rural counterparts, although the lead concentrations in urban birds did not approach toxic levels. Rodents living near major roads had significantly higher levels of lead than those living near less frequently used roads, but the elevated lead blood levels were apparently not toxic. Possible long-term effects on reproduction were also believed to be minimal.

No one is free from lead exposure today, not even the residents of rural, nonindustrialized countries. Sergio Piomelli and his colleagues estimated that blood levels in humans before lead pollution became prevalent were about 100 times lower than the normal range found today in the United States. However, even residents of Nepal had levels 10 times higher than those estimated to be present before the widespread use of lead.

Clearly, the highest exposures occur in the citizens of technological societies, whose air is polluted by automobiles, power plants, and smelters and whose food is contaminated by lead solder and atmospheric fallout. Studies in Copenhagen showed that lead levels in precipitation and soil were four to five times higher in the city center than in rural areas. A careful analysis of lead contamination during the processing of tuna showed that fresh albacore contained about 0.3 nanograms of lead per gram, whereas albacore in lead-soldered cans had a lead concentration of 1400 nanograms per gram. As a result of contemporary exposures such as these, lead levels in humans are much higher than in earlier days. Studies of lead in the skeletons of

Peruvian mummies from the preindustrial era show that bone concentrations are approximately .17% of those found in us today.

What can we make of all this evidence? Surely, high-level exposure in the work place represents a serious threat to human reproduction and the mental development of children born to lead workers. Children exposed to lead-based paint and food contaminated with lead are particularly susceptible. Among these, the malnourished, iron-deficient poor are at greatest risk. But is the general population endangered by lower levels of lead? In other words, is there a threshold below which there are no effects? Only time will tell, because no studies have been undertaken to determine the effects of widespread global lead exposure.

Control of Lead Emissions

Alarmed by the mounting evidence regarding the effects of lead on children, the EPA in 1973 began a progressive restriction of the lead content of gasoline. The use of unleaded gasoline was required in cars equipped with catalytic converters beginning in the 1975 model year. By October 1979, lead levels were not to exceed .5 gram per gallon, but because of industry lawsuits this deadline was postponed until October 1980. Between 1974 and 1980, lead consumed in gasoline dropped by 62% and ambient lead levels decreased by 54%. In 1977, 27% of the gasoline burned in the United States was unleaded; in 1980 the figure was 47%. According to a study released in 1983, average blood levels in over 27,000 Americans living in 64 areas dropped from an average of 14.6 micrograms per 100 milliliters in February 1976 to 9.4 in February 1980.

Whereas the United States has taken aggressive actions to reduce lead in gasoline, European nations had taken no action at all as of 1983; moreover, it appears that regulations may be a long way off, for several reasons. First, even though many nations favor the conversion to unleaded gasoline, a uniform policy is necessary, because Europeans make frequent border crossings. Cars that burn unleaded fuels cannot burn leaded fuels without destroying their catalytic converters. France and Italy are strongly opposed to unleaded fuels, largely based on economics. It would cost about 2 cents per gallon more to burn it and about $150 to $400 per car more to manufacture cars equipped with catalytic converters. Not until a consensus can be reached will unleaded fuels be introduced throughout Europe.

As noted above, food is Americans' major source of lead. The lead concentration in the average American diet is 100 times that of our prehistoric relatives. In 1979 the Food and Drug Administration issued an advance notice of allowable lead levels in food that was aimed at reducing the intake of lead from lead-soldered cans by one-half over a five-year period. This will go a long way in reducing lead levels in the American diet. As a personal measure, we could reduce our consumption of vegetables, beverages, meats, and other foods packed in tin cans. Fresh or frozen vegetables would be preferable in this regard.

In 1971 Congress passed the *Lead-Based Paint Poisoning Prevention Act*. This act authorized the Department of Housing and Urban Development to fund research on reducing the hazards of lead-based paints. Private groups and local governments have also made efforts to remove such paints from old apartment buildings and houses.

Suggested Readings

Doull, J., Klaassen, C. D., and Amdur, M. O. (1980). *Toxicology: The Basic Science of Poisons.* New York: Macmillan. Good, technical resource.

Needleman, H. L., and Landrigan, P. J. (1981). The Health Effects of Low Level Exposure to Lead. Annual Review. *Public Health* 2: 277–298. A critical look at the effects of lead in children.

Singhal, R., and Thomas, J. A. (1980). *Lead Toxicity.* Baltimore: Urban and Schwarzenberg. Excellent technical review.

Air Pollution

Not life, but a good life, is to be chiefly valued.

SOCRATES

Each day we breathe approximately 23,000 times, typically inhaling about 2000 liters (525 gallons) of air. With this air, we also breathe in a wide variety of pollutants from automobiles, trucks, factories, power plants, and other sources.

This chapter describes where air pollution comes from, what natural processes affect its levels, how it affects us, and how it is controlled.

The Air We Breathe

Ambient air, the air we breathe, is a mixture of gases, including nitrogen (79%), oxygen (20%), carbon dioxide (.03%), and several inert gases—argon, helium, xenon, neon, and krypton. It also holds water vapor in varying amounts. Air is a dynamic mixture, though, constantly moving across the land, picking up moisture and pollutants in one region and depositing them far away. Transparent, powerful, nurturing, air is a reusable resource, shared and abused by all the earth's inhabitants; it is, in truth, a world resource unconfined by political boundaries and essential to life.

Natural and Anthropogenic Air Pollution

Atmospheric contaminants come from a variety of natural sources, shown in Table 19-1. Despite the prevalence of

Table 19-1 Natural Air Pollutants

Source	Pollutants
Volcanoes	Sulfur oxides, particulates
Forest fires	Carbon monoxide, carbon dioxide, nitrogen oxides, particulates
Wind storms	Dust
Plants (live)	Hydrocarbons, pollen
Plants (decaying)	Methane, hydrogen sulfide
Soil	Viruses, dust
Sea	Salt particulates

natural pollutants, it is the **anthropogenic pollutants**—the products of human activities—that represent the most significant long-term threat to the environment and its inhabitants. The reasons for this are simple: Natural pollution sources generally do not raise the ambient concentration of a given pollutant very much, because they are usually widely dispersed (diffuse) or infrequent events. For example, diffuse processes such as bacterial decay of organic matter produce small amounts of pollution over large areas. In contrast, anthropogenic sources of pollution tend to be concentrated, so their contribution to local pollution levels is often quite significant.

Air Pollutants and Their Sources

There are hundreds of air pollutants; this chapter, however, will be concerned primarily with the six major pollutants: carbon monoxide, sulfur oxides, nitrogen oxides, particulates, hydrocarbons, and photochemical oxidants. (Lead, an important air pollutant, was discussed in Chapter Supplement 18-1; radiation and noise pollution are discussed in Chapter Supplements 21-1 and 21-2.)

In 1970, the United States produced about 200 million metric tons, or a little under 1 metric ton of air pollution for every man, woman, and child. By 1980, the United States had cut its production of air pollutants to about 162 million metric tons.

The six major air pollutants listed above come from five main sources in the United States: transportation (55%), power plants (17%), industry (15%), agricultural fires (7%), and the incineration of solid wastes (4%) (Figure 19-1).

Air pollutants are released from vaporization (or evaporation), attrition (or friction), and combustion. *Combustion* is by far the major source of air pollution, producing both gases and particulates. All fuels consist of organic compounds composed primarily of carbon and hydrogen atoms. When organic matter is burned, the bonds between the carbon and hydrogen atoms are broken, yielding energy. The atoms react with oxygen and form a variety of products. Complete combustion, for example, produces carbon dioxide (CO_2) and water (H_2O), two pollutants discussed later. Incomplete combustion leads to the formation of carbon monoxide (CO) gas, a potentially lethal substance. Incomplete combustion also releases unburned or partially burned organic molecules. Combustion of organic fuel is rarely complete outside the laboratory.

Most fuels except for natural gas contain some mineral contaminants. These unburnable contaminants may be carried off by the hot gases of combustion, escaping into the air as particulates. Other contaminants, such as sulfur, react with oxygen at high combustion temperatures, forming sulfur oxide gases, notably sulfur dioxide (SO_2) and sulfur trioxide (SO_3) (Figure 19-2), which escape with the smokestack gases.

In the combustion of all organic fuels, gaseous nitrogen (N_2) reacts with oxygen at high temperatures and is converted into nitric oxide (NO), which is quickly converted to nitrogen dioxide (NO_2), a brownish-orange gas.

Primary and Secondary Pollutants

Pollutants released into the environment from anthropogenic sources are called **primary pollutants**. In the atmosphere, primary pollutants may undergo chemical changes by reacting with sunlight, moisture, or even other primary pollutants. The resulting pollutants, **secondary pollutants**, may be more harmful than the chemicals from which they were derived. For example, sulfur dioxide gas is released from a variety of sources such as coal-fired power plants and oil shale retorts (Chapters 13 and 14). In the atmosphere this primary pollutant reacts with oxygen and water, producing sulfuric acid (H_2SO_4), a secondary pollutant with far-reaching effects.

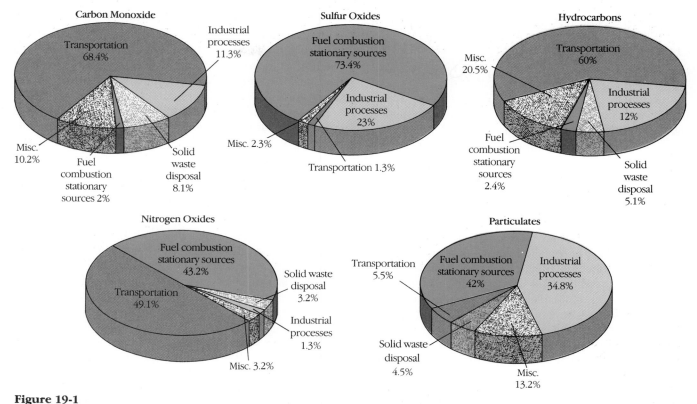

Figure 19-1

The major air pollutants and their sources. In most cases, transportation and fossil fuel combustion at stationary sources are the major sources.

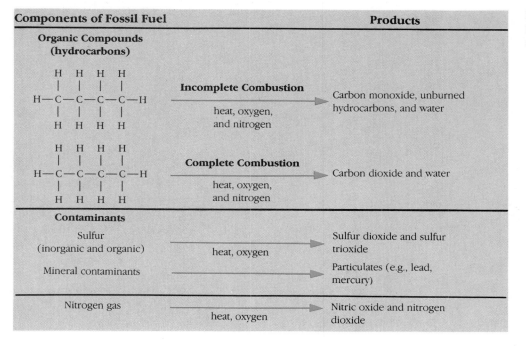

Figure 19-2

Products of fossil fuel combustion.

Effects of Climate and Topography on Air Pollution

Brown-Air and Gray-Air Cities

Cities can be placed into one of two broad classes, depending on the climate and the type of air pollution. Older industrial cities like Nashville, New York, Philadelphia, St. Louis, and Pittsburgh belong to a group of **gray-air cities** (Figure 19-3a); newer, relatively nonindustrialized cities such as Denver, Los Angeles, and Albuquerque belong to the group of **brown-air cities** (Figure 19-3b).

Gray-air cities like New York are generally located in cold, moist climates. The major pollutants, sulfur oxides and particulates, combine with atmospheric moisture to form the grayish haze called **smog**—a term coined in 1905 to describe the mixture of smoke and fog that plagued industrial England. The gray-air cities generally rely on coal and oil for electrical generation and oil for home heating, and they are usually heavily industrialized. The air in these cities is especially bad during cold, wet winters, when demand for home heating oil and electricity is high and the atmospheric moisture content is high.

Brown-air cities are typically located in warm, dry, and sunny climates, and they are generally newer cities with few polluting industries. The major sources of pollution in these cities are the automobile and electric power plants; the major primary pollutants are carbon monoxide, hydrocarbons, and nitrogen oxides.

In brown-air cities atmospheric hydrocarbons and nitrogen oxides from automobiles and power plants react in the presence of sunlight, forming a number of secondary pollutants such as ozone, formaldehyde, PAN (peroxyacylnitrate), and many others. The reactions are called **photochemical reactions**, because they involve both sunlight and chemical pollutants. The resulting brownish-orange shroud of air pollution is called **photochemical smog**. Ozone (O_3) is the major photochemical oxidant; a highly reactive chemical, it erodes rubber and irritates the respiratory system.

In brown-air cities early morning traffic provides the ingredients for photochemical smog, which reaches the highest levels in the early afternoon (Figure 19-4). Because the air laden with photochemical smog often drifts out of the city, the suburbs and surrounding rural areas may have higher levels than the city itself. Major pollution epi-

(a)

(b)

Figure 19-3
Two types of air pollution. (*a*) Gray-air smog in Detroit. (*b*) Brown-air smog in Los Angeles.

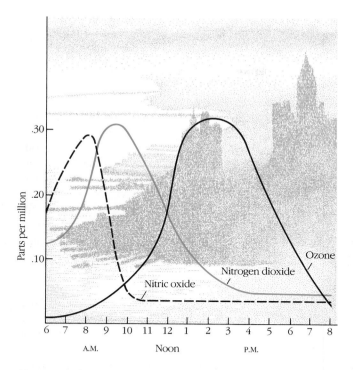

Figure 19-4
Nitrogen oxides and hydrocarbons (not shown here) react to form ozone and other photochemical oxidants. Because sunlight and time are required for the reactions to occur, maximum ozone concentration occurs in the early afternoon. Hydrocarbon levels would follow the same pattern as nitric oxide levels.

sodes in brown-air cities usually occur during the summer months, when the sun is most intense. Today, the distinction between gray- and brown-air cities is rapidly disappearing, with most cities having brown air in the summer and gray air in the winter.

Factors Affecting Air Pollution Levels

A number of factors affect regional air pollution levels, including (1) wind, (2) topography, (3) location, (4) precipitation, and (5) susceptibility to temperature inversions.

Wind Winds sweep air pollutants away from cities while bringing in fresh air. But pollutants may persist in the air, traveling hundreds or perhaps thousands of kilometers to other cities and unpolluted regions. For instance,

southern Norway and Sweden are troubled by sulfuric and nitric acids in their rain, blown in from industrial England and Europe (see Chapter Supplement 19-2).

Location and Topography To a large extent, geography determines the amount and intensity of the wind. It also determines the amount of rain and snow, which, in turn, affects pollution levels. Because rain and snow tend to cleanse the air of solid and gaseous particulates, they are air purifiers.

The topography of an area affects local wind patterns. Hills and mountains generally inhibit the flow of air and, therefore, slow the dispersion of pollutants, leading to a buildup.

Temperature Inversions Under normal atmospheric conditions (Figure 19-5a) the air temperature falls with increasing altitude. The temperature decreases at about 5.5° C (10° F) for each 300-meter (1000-foot) increase in altitude. Under normal conditions, sunlight heats the earth, and the heat is transferred to the air immediately above the ground. The warm air then rises, mixing with cooler air. As a result, pollutants located near the ground are carried upward by the warm air.

When a **temperature inversion** occurs, though, the air temperature decreases up to a point, then begins to rise, forming a warm-air lid over cooler air (Figures 19-5b, 19-6). The temperature profile is inverted. Thus, the air closest to the ground is actually cooler than the air above it and cannot rise through it. Because of this, pollutants at ground level increase in concentration, often reaching dangerous levels.

There are two types of temperature inversion. A **subsidence inversion** occurs when a mass of high-pressure air stagnates, holding a layer of warm air over a region that may extend over many thousands of square kilometers. A **radiation inversion**, in contrast, is usually local and short-lived. It starts to form one to two hours before the sun sets when the air near the ground begins to cool. Cooling faster than the air above it, the cool layer becomes trapped by a layer of warm air. The cool air is unable to rise, and thus, can accumulate pollutants. Such inversions usually break up in the morning when the sun warms the ground, beginning the vertical mixing.

Temperature inversions are more common in some regions than others, but they usually last only a few hours or a few days. Long-lasting temperature inversions may

Figure 19-5
(*a*) During normal conditions, air temperature decreases with altitude; thus, pollutants ascend and mix with atmospheric gases. (*b*) In a temperature inversion, however, warm air forms a "lid" over cooler air, thus trapping air pollution.

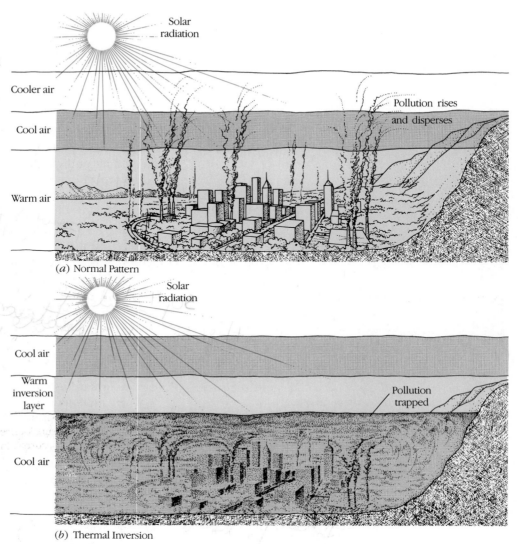

(*a*) Normal Pattern

(*b*) Thermal Inversion

extend over large areas (Figure 19-7), making it necessary to curtail industry, as well as the activities of children, old and infirm adults, and athletes—all more susceptible to pollution.

Radiation inversions on a smaller scale are common in mountainous regions, especially in the winter, when the sun is unable to break the inversion because of the mountains that shadow the valleys.

Cities also alter air temperature, with an interesting effect on air pollution. Cities are like huge islands of heat amidst a cooler suburban and rural sea. The large number of heat sources (power plants, autos, factories, and buildings) and the heat-absorbing cement and asphalt concentrated in a small area are responsible for the elevated temperature in cities relative to the surrounding areas. The lack of vegetation and water bodies also contributes to the higher city temperatures.

Because cities are warmer than surrounding areas, air tends to circulate in an unusual way. Warm air rises over the city, carrying with it particulates and other pollutants.

Figure 19-6
A temperature inversion in Phoenix, Arizona.

Figure 19-7
This large subsidence inversion occurred in August 1969.

Figure 19-8
Heat islands create convective air currents that sweep pollutants up into the air over the city, forming pollution or dust domes.

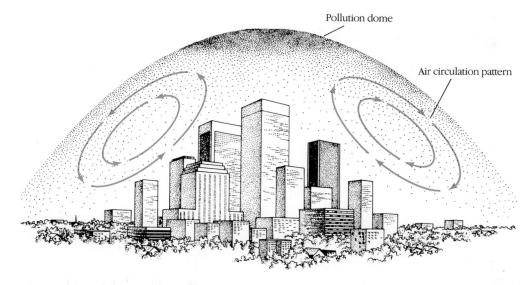

Pollution dome

Air circulation pattern

As it rises, it cools, sinks, and moves outward, creating a huge dust and pollutant dome over the city that can be seen for miles on a calm, sunny day (Figure 19-8).

Effects of Air Pollution

Debate over the impact of air pollution has been riddled with emotion, lack of information, oversimplification, speculation, and generalization. To adequately assess the risk of air pollution, we must have facts. But even today, in many instances, there is hardly enough known to make sound environmental, economic, and political decisions. This section describes some of the major effects of air pollution.

Health Effects

Knowledge of the effects of air pollution on health has accumulated slowly. In 1950 little was known despite the record of severe air pollution episodes in the past (Table 19-2) and knowledge of several occupational diseases caused by industrial air pollution.

The 1948 disaster in Donora, Pennsylvania, was one of those notable episodes that helped focus attention on the health risks of air pollution. Twenty people died and thousands became ill after a prolonged temperature inversion

Table 19-2	Major Air Pollution Episodes	
Date	**Location**	**Deaths**
February 1880	London	1000
December 1930	Meuse Valley, Belgium	63
October 1948	Donora, Pennsylvania	20
November 1950	Poca Rica, Mexico	22
December 1952	London	2500
November 1953	New York	250
January 1956	London	1000
December 1957	London	700 to 800
December 1962	London	700
January 1963	New York	200 to 400
November 1966	New York	168

increased the concentrations of pollutants from steel mills and zinc smelters to hazardous levels. The 1952 London disaster was much worse. Nearly 2500 people died in a weeklong inversion that trapped sulfuric acid, particulates, and sulfur dioxide gas.

Acute Effects In the past 30 years considerable evidence has accumulated showing that ambient air pollution can indeed affect health (Table 19-3). In a 1966 epidemiological study of 950 residents of New York City, J. R.

Table 19-3 Major Air Pollutants—Their Sources and Health Effects

Pollutant	Major Anthropogenic Sources	Health Effects
Carbon monoxide	Transportation Industry	Acute exposure: headache, dizziness, decreased physical performance, death
		Chronic exposure: stress on cardiovascular system, decreased tolerance to exercise, heart attack
Sulfur oxides	Stationary combustion sources, industry	Acute exposure: inflammation of respiratory tract, aggravation of asthma
		Chronic exposure: emphysema, bronchitis
Nitrogen oxides	Transportation, stationary combustion sources	Acute exposure: lung irritation
		Chronic exposure: bronchitis
Particulates	Stationary combustion sources, industry	Irritation of respiratory system, cancer
Hydrocarbons	Transportation	Unknown
Photochemical oxidants	Transportation, stationary combustion sources (indirectly through hydrocarbons and nitrogen oxides)	Acute exposure: respiratory irritation, eye irritation
		Chronic exposure: emphysema

McCarroll and his colleagues examined the health effects of an air pollution episode during which sulfur dioxide levels increased dramatically over a short period. They found that the incidence of colds, coughs, rhinitis (nose irritation), and other symptoms increased fivefold. Visitors to Los Angeles know the discomfort caused by photochemical smog—irritated eyes and burning throat. Commuters in heavy traffic are familiar with the headaches caused by carbon monoxide from automobile fumes. These impacts, however, are ignored or viewed as part of the price we pay for city living.

Chronic Effects Long-term exposure to air pollution may result in a number of ailments, including bronchitis, emphysema, and lung cancer.

One out of every five American men between the ages of 40 and 60 has chronic **bronchitis**, a persistent inflammation of the bronchial tubes, which carry air into the lungs. Symptoms include persistent cough, mucus buildup, and difficulty in breathing. Cigarette smoking is, without a doubt, a major cause of this disease, but urban air pollution is also a contributing factor. Sulfur dioxide, nitrogen dioxide, and ozone are believed to be the major agents responsible for this condition, which can lead to a worse disease, emphysema.

Emphysema kills more people than lung cancer and tuberculosis combined and it is the fastest growing cause of death in the United States. Over 1.5 million Americans suffer from this chronic, essentially incurable disease. For them, there is virtually no treatment. As they become older, the small air sacs, or alveoli, in the lungs gradually break down. This reduces the surface area for exchange of oxygen with the blood. Breathing becomes more and more labored, so victims suffer shortness of breath when exercising even lightly.

Health studies show that emphysema may be caused by urban air pollution. One study, for example, showed that the incidence of emphysema was higher in polluted St. Louis than in relatively unpolluted Winnipeg (Figure 19-9). Studies in Great Britain showed that mail carriers who worked in polluted urban areas had a substantially higher death rate from emphysema than those who worked in unpolluted rural areas. Ozone, nitrogen dioxide, and sulfur oxides are believed to be responsible for this disease.

A number of studies have shown that lung-cancer rates are higher for urban residents than for rural residents (even after the influence of cigarette smoking has been ruled out). However, because other factors (such as occupation) may be involved, the link between lung cancer and urban pollution is still in question.

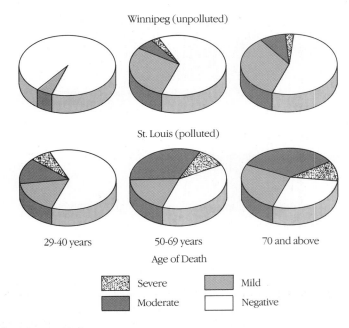

Winnipeg (unpolluted)

St. Louis (polluted)

29-40 years   50-69 years   70 and above

Age of Death

Severe   Mild

Moderate   Negative

Figure 19-9
Incidence of emphysema in St. Louis and Winnipeg. Note the increased incidence of emphysema in all three age groups in the more polluted urban environment of St. Louis.

High-Risk Populations   Not all people are affected by air pollution equally. Particularly susceptible are the old and infirm, especially individuals with lung and heart disorders. Carbon monoxide is especially dangerous to those with heart ailments, because it binds to hemoglobin in the red blood corpuscles and thus interferes with oxygen transport. For oxygen to be delivered to the body's cells, the heart must work harder. This puts a strain on the heart and may trigger a heart attack in individuals with weakened hearts. The young are more susceptible than healthy adults, because children breathe more as a result of being more active. In addition, children typically suffer from colds and nasal congestion and thus tend to breathe more through the mouth. Air then bypasses the normal filtering mechanism of the nose, and more pollutants enter the lungs.

Effects on Other Organisms

Fluoride and arsenic poisonings have occurred in cattle grazing downwind from major pollution sources. Lead from automobile exhaust has been shown to contaminate sheep grazing along major highways, though this problem should be reduced by the shift to unleaded gasoline. Acids produced from power plants, smelters, and industrial boilers have been shown to be extremely harmful to wildlife, especially fish (see Chapter Supplement 19-2).

Reports from Scandinavia suggest that forest productivity may be reduced significantly by acid precipitation. In southern California millions of ponderosa pines have been damaged by air pollution from Los Angeles.

Ozone, sulfur dioxide, and sulfuric acid are the pollutants most hazardous to plants. Farms in southern California and on the East Coast have reported significant damage to important vegetable crops. City gardeners report damage to flowers and ornamental plants.

Damage to plants may be direct or indirect. For instance, sulfur oxides discolor the leaves of plants and may stunt growth, two direct effects. Sulfuric and nitric acids, on the other hand, may deplete the soil of essential plant nutrients, thus indirectly impairing growth.

Effects on Materials

Air pollutants may severely damage metals, building materials, paint, textiles, plastics, rubber, leather, paper, and ceramics (Table 19-4). The two most caustic and harmful pollutants are sulfur dioxide and sulfuric acid.

The damage to human materials is both costly and tragic, for many of the structures attacked by air pollution are irreplaceable works of art. The stone in the Parthenon in Athens, for instance, has deteriorated more in the past 50 years from air pollution than it had in the previous 2000 years. The Statue of Liberty suffers from corrosion, presumably from sulfuric and nitric acids. The Taj Mahal in India, too, is being defaced by air pollution.

Caustic acids corrode the surfaces of metal and steel, resulting in cosmetic damage and a loss of strength. Particulates blown in the wind erode the surfaces of stone, doing significant damage. Hydrogen sulfide gases tarnish silver and blacken leaded house paints. Ozone cracks windshield wipers, tires, and other rubber products, necessitating costly antioxidant additives. Particulates sully buildings, such as the Louvre and Notre Dame in Paris, necessitating costly sandblasting, which also erodes stone surfaces.

The economic damage caused by air pollution is immense. Society pays for cleaning sooty buildings, repainting houses and automobiles pitted by air pollutants, and replacing damaged rubber products and cloth-

Table 19-4 Damage to Materials from Air Pollution

Material	Damage	Principal Pollutants
Metals	Corrosion or tarnishing of surfaces; loss of strength	Sulfur dioxide, hydrogen sulfide, particulates
Stone and concrete	Discoloration, erosion of surfaces, leaching	Sulfur dioxide, particulates
Paint	Discoloration, reduced gloss, pitting	Sulfur dioxide, hydrogen sulfide, particulates, ozone
Rubber	Weakening, cracking	Ozone, other photochemical oxidants
Leather	Weakening, deterioration of surface	Sulfur dioxide
Paper	Embrittlement	Sulfur dioxide
Textiles	Soiling, fading, deterioration of fabric	Sulfur dioxide, ozone, particulates, nitrogen dioxide
Ceramics	Altered surface appearance	Hydrogen fluoride, particulates

ing. Furthermore, the economic value of damaged statues and other works of art cannot even be calculated.

Effects on Climate

Scientists have long known that air pollution can affect the local climate, particularly the amount of rainfall. In recent years, however, there has been considerable debate over the potential impact of air pollution on global climate. Before examining how pollutants alter climate, let us first look at the global energy balance, the basis for all climates.

Global Energy Balance Each day the earth is warmed by the sun. Light strikes the earth and heats the surface; this heat is then slowly radiated back into the atmosphere. Eventually this heat, or **infrared radiation**, escapes from the earth's atmosphere and returns to space. Thus, an energy balance is set up; energy input is balanced by energy output.

This balance can be altered by changes in the gas composition of the air. Naturally occurring CO_2 absorbs infrared radiation escaping from the earth's surface and radiates it back, thus helping to maintain the earth's temperature. Any artificial increase in the concentration of CO_2 would thus slow down the escape of heat.

The Greenhouse Effect Between 1870 and 1980 global concentrations of CO_2 increased over 11%, from 290 to 335 parts per million. This rise is attributed to increasing consumption of fossil fuels throughout the world. Some

scientists fear that global CO_2 levels could increase to about 380 ppm by the year 2000 with increasing combustion of fossil fuels. A rise of this magnitude might increase the average daily temperature by .5° C (1° F). This is called the **greenhouse effect**, since CO_2 acts like the glass in a greenhouse.

A doubling of ambient CO_2 levels may occur by the year 2050, raising the average temperature by about 2° C (3.5° F). An increase of this magnitude could dramatically change global climate.

What many scientists fear most are the potential effects of a temperature rise on arctic and antarctic ice packs and the world's glaciers (Figure 19-10). Melting of the land-based antarctic ice packs and glaciers, for example, could raise the sea level 75 to 90 meters (200 to 300 feet), flooding about one-fifth of the world's land area. The consequences are easy to imagine.

Melting would be a gradual process, taking 1000 years or more. The amount of ice and snow on the earth would slowly decrease, exposing more dark surfaces and leading to further increases in global temperature. Increased oceanic temperatures could make the problem even more serious, because warmer water both expands in volume and decreases in its ability to dissolve and store CO_2. The ocean contains 60 times more carbon dioxide than the atmosphere, and a drop in dissolved CO_2 could result in a rapid rise in global carbon dioxide, creating a vicious circle.

Even a small change in average global temperature would significantly affect climate. Major shifts would occur in rain patterns and agriculture. Some regions now border-

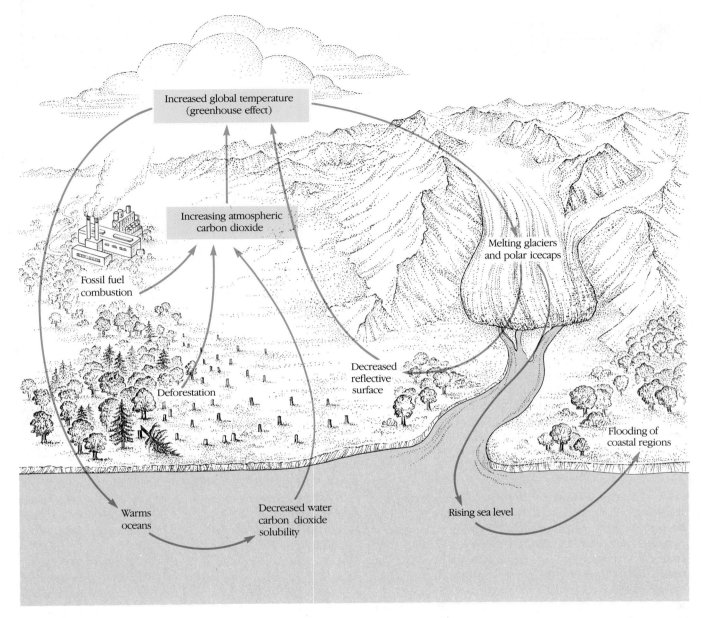

Figure 19-10
Possible elements of a global temperature increase.

ing on desert would become drier, and vegetation would die off. Major agricultural regions might be no longer useful.

Fossil fuel combustion, a major source of atmospheric CO_2, will undoubtedly continue to rise as industrial production increases and as new countries such as China enter the industrial age. Deforestation, also blamed for rising global carbon dioxide, will continue as tropical forests are stripped away to make room for agriculture, highways, and new cities. The effect of reduced forest cover is not known, although many suspect that it, too, will contribute to rising atmospheric levels of CO_2.

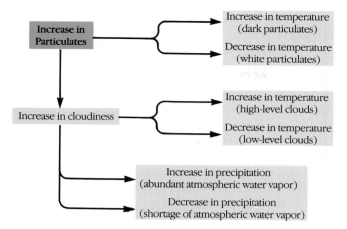

Figure 19-11
Effects of particulates on global temperature.

Effects of Particulates on Climate Many poorly understood factors determine global climate. One such factor is particulate levels. Particulates from combustion, agriculture, and many natural sources (especially volcanoes) may affect the climate by cooling, heating, or changing precipitation patterns (Figure 19-11).

Particulates may increase or decrease atmospheric temperature, according to some sources, depending on their size, their color, and their height in the atmosphere. White particulates, on the one hand, tend to reflect sunlight, decreasing the earth's temperature (Figure 19-11). Dark particulates, on the other hand, tend to absorb sunlight and radiate the heat toward the earth's surface, thus increasing the temperature. The net effect depends, in part, on the relative proportion of dark and light particulates.

Particulates may also affect cloud cover, because they serve as nuclei for cloud formation (see Chapter 12). The average daily cloud cover for the globe is approximately 31%; a 5% increase in cloudiness, some say, could decrease the global temperature enough to trigger another glacial age. Rainfall patterns could also be affected.

A classic case of increased rainfall resulting from particulate pollution is LaPorte, Indiana, lying 48 kilometers (30 miles) downwind from the steel factories of Gary, Indiana, and Chicago. Between 1951 and 1964, LaPorte had 31% more rain, 38% more thundershowers, and 245% more days of hail than neighboring towns. These increases were correlated with increases in steel production and, thus, particulate pollution. In contrast, a 25% decline in rainfall was reported in Queensland, Australia, during the

sugar cane harvesting season. Cane leaves burned in the fields created fine smoke particles that increased cloud formation, but because of the naturally low atmospheric moisture content there was not enough moisture to form larger droplets needed to cause rain. Thus, there was a decrease in precipitation (compared with similar regions not polluted by smoke).

A Greenhouse or a New Ice Age? Are we bringing on a new ice age or a major global warming trend? Global temperature increased by .6° C (1.1° F) from 1885 to 1940. But since 1940, global temperature has fallen slightly. The net effect is that global temperature has risen .4°C (.6°F) in the last century. Two of the hottest years in the past century occurred in the 1980s. Global warming trends, however, may be offset by an increase in cloudiness. It has been estimated that a 10% increase in CO_2 could offset a 1% increase in cloudiness; unfortunately, no one knows what the net effect of increasing particulates and CO_2 will be.

The Cost of Air Pollution

The cost of air pollution is difficult to assess, because so many of the costs are hidden, obscure, or unquantifiable. The U.S. Council on Environmental Quality estimates that air pollution costs Americans $16.2 billion each year: health damage and work loss came to $6.1 billion; damage to materials, $4.8 billion; reduced property values, $5.2 billion; and crop damage, $100 million. Estimates by the U.S. Environmental Protection Agency put the cost at $12.3 billion annually. But many costs cannot be calculated, including the loss of clean air, unobstructed views, and works of art. (For more detail on economics and pollution, see Chapter 24.)

Air Pollution Control

Air pollution must be controlled at two interlocking levels—the legal and the technological. This section examines major strategies for the control of this pervasive problem.

Air Pollution Legislation in the United States

The first effective federal legislation dealing with air pollution control was the *Clean Air Act* of 1963. This act included federal grants-in-aid to help finance regional, state, and local air pollution controls and a program to control air pollution from one state that travels to neighboring states.

In 1967 the *Air Quality Act* shifted more responsibility for air pollution control to the federal government. It required the government to assume responsibility for air pollution control in states that had failed to do so. It also directed the Department of Health, Education and Welfare to (1) designate **air quality control regions**, areas targeted for pollution control; (2) determine at what levels pollutants present a risk; (3) develop air pollution control techniques; and (4) supervise the establishment of air quality standards, that is, levels not to be exceeded in air quality control regions.

The 1967 act, though a significant step, still provided little effective regulation. For instance, even though the National Air Pollution Control Administration set air pollution standards, their enforcement was left entirely up to the states. If a state rejected the standard, the federal government was powerless.

1970 Air Quality Amendments In 1970 a series of amendments to the Air Quality Act gave the federal government more power in air pollution control. The EPA was given the power to shut down industries when ambient air pollution reached emergency levels—a power first exercised in November 1971, when the EPA closed down 23 companies near Birmingham, Alabama, during an air pollution episode. In addition, the amendments (1) established strict emission standards for automobiles, (2) directed the EPA to develop national ambient air quality standards, and (3) directed the EPA to establish emission standards for new industries.

Auto manufacturers were required to reduce emissions of carbon monoxide, hydrocarbons, and nitrogen oxides. The law stated that by 1975 carbon monoxide and hydrocarbon emissions from automobiles were to be 90% lower than those of 1970 models. Nitrogen oxide emissions of 1976 models were to be 90% lower than those of 1971 models.

U.S. automakers applied to the EPA for later deadlines. They were granted four separate one-year delays, pushing back the deadline for hydrocarbon and carbon monoxide to 1979 and the one for nitrogen oxides to 1980. Nevertheless, the industry met the 1975 emission standards in

cars sold in California, where controls were stricter than the federal standard. So did the Japanese Honda CVCC.

Under the new law, two types of national ambient air quality standard were required of the EPA. **Primary standards** were set to protect human health, including a margin of safety for people particularly susceptible to pollution. **Secondary standards**, often called welfare standards, were set to protect crops, visibility, and materials.

New-source performance standards were established by the EPA for all new plants and plant expansions that would produce more than 100 tons of pollution per year. Construction permits would not be given to facilities that would exceed these standards.

The 1970 amendments were successful in reducing air pollution from automobiles and industry and in getting air pollution laws on the books in most states. They also created some major problems. For instance, no new or expanded pollution sources were allowed in areas that were violating the air quality standards if those new sources (or expansions) would generate pollutants for which the areas were in violation. In effect, this stipulation prevented much business expansion in these areas. In addition, some of the wording of the 1970 amendments was vague and required clarification. Of special interest were sections dealing with the deterioration of air quality in areas that already met federal standards.

1977 Clean Air Amendments Because of these and other problems, the Air Quality Act was once again amended in 1977.

The amendments pushed back the compliance deadlines for automobile hydrocarbon emissions to 1980 and for carbon monoxide and nitrogen oxide to 1981, and they relaxed the emission standard for nitrogen oxides from .4 to 1 gram per mile.

Because many states had failed to meet the deadlines of the 1970 amendments for achieving the national ambient air quality standards, the 1977 amendments extended them and required states to submit revised plans for reaching the standards by 1982 or, at the latest, 1987. Failure to submit a plan would result in (1) a cutoff of federal highway funds and (2) a ban on the construction and operation of all new major air pollution sources.

To deal with the limits on industrial growth in areas that exceed the national ambient air quality standards, or **nonattainment areas**, the amendments presented a creative policy: new or expanded facilities would be allowed in nonattainment areas only if the new sources achieved the lowest possible emission rates and if other sources of pollution under the same ownership or control in that state complied with emission-control provisions. A newcomer could ask existing companies to reduce their emissions, thus allowing the newcomer a portion of the air resource. The last provision, the **emissions offset policy**, has been quite successful. As of 1980 the EPA had approved 650 emissions offset proposals. This policy, combined with the stipulations described above, allows industrial expansion while ensuring a net decrease in pollution. In many cases the newcomers pay the cost of air pollution control devices.

How to protect air quality in areas that already met the standards sparked considerable debate in Congress. Environmentalists felt that the ambient air quality standards, in effect, gave industries a license to destroy clean air by letting them pollute up to permitted levels.

The 1977 amendments set forth rules for the **prevention of significant deterioration** (PSD) of air quality in clean-air areas. Accordingly, areas that meet the primary and secondary ambient air quality standards are given one of three designations: Class I, where very little air quality deterioration will be allowed; Class II, where moderate deterioration will be allowed; and Class III, where more significant deterioration will be allowed, without exceeding the secondary standards. Mandatory Class I areas include International Parks, National Memorial Parks, and National Wilderness Areas that exceed 2000 hectares (5000 acres) and National Parks that exceed 2400 hectares (6000 acres).

PSD requirements currently apply only to sulfur oxides and particulates, the pollutants viewed by Congress as the two most deserving of immediate action.

The 1977 amendments also strengthened the enforcement power of the EPA. In previous years when the agency wanted to stop a polluter, it had to initiate a criminal lawsuit; violators would often engage in a legal battle, because the cost of litigation was lower than the cost of installing pollution control devices. Now, however, the EPA can initiate civil lawsuits, which do not require as heavy a burden of proof as criminal suits.

More important, the EPA can levy noncompliance penalties without going to court. These penalties are assessed on the ground that violators have an unfair business advantage over their competitors that comply with the law. Penalties equal to the estimated cost of pollution control devices eliminate the cost incentive of polluting. When a company installs pollution control devices, the EPA may return the fine to the violator if it was more than the actual cost of purchase and operation. Conversely, if the fine was less than the actual cost, an additional penalty can be imposed.

By 1977, two decades after the first Clean Air Act, U.S. policy had become refined and effective. With the severe economic troubles of the late '70s and early '80s, however, air pollution control laws came under attack. Industry and the Reagan administration claimed that the Clean Air Act was delaying new industrial construction, inflating the costs of doing business, impeding energy development, and increasing unemployment. Industry banded together to lobby for drastic weakening of the act.

These efforts to weaken the Clean Air Act were unsuccessful because of strong public support for a clean environment and strong environmental protection laws. Still, industry continued to apply pressure on Congress, questioning how the Clean Air Act could be reconciled with two other national goals: economic revitalization and energy security.

A failure to rewrite the act did not stop the Reagan administration from cutting the EPA's budget and work force, severely crippling the agency, even though its workload was expected to double in the early 1980s and again by the end of the following decade. Overriding presidential budget cuts, Congress voted in 1983 to reinstate the EPA's budget, an encouraging sign for an agency that helped reduce particulate emissions by 56% from 1970 to 1980 and, during that same period, helped reduce emissions of sulfur oxides by 15%, hydrocarbons by 20%, and carbon monoxide by 23%. (The only air pollutants that increased were the nitrogen oxide gases, which rose by 12%.)

Control Technologies

Reductions in air pollution can be brought about by such preventive measures as (1) using less energy, (2) using energy more efficiently, and (3) relying on more noncombustive sources of energy, such as solar and wind energy.

Emission Devices Decreasing air pollution is also possible by taking remedial actions such as (1) removing harmful substances from emission gases and (2) converting harmful pollutants in emission gases into harmless substances. The first strategy is the most common for stationary combustion sources, and the second is used more often for mobile sources.

Figure 19-12
Four pollution control devices used for stationary combustion sources.

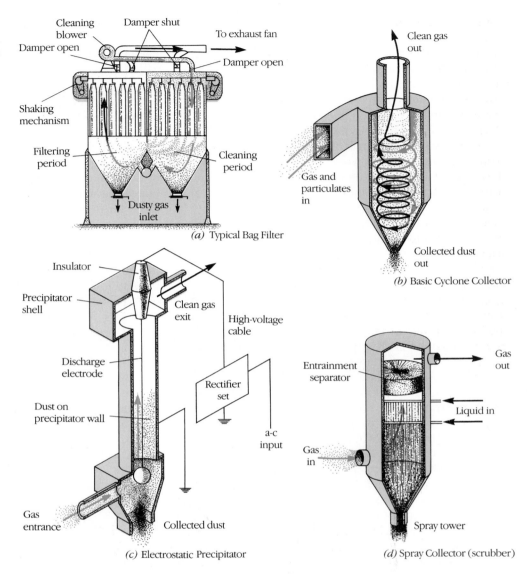

(a) Typical Bag Filter

(b) Basic Cyclone Collector

(c) Electrostatic Precipitator

(d) Spray Collector (scrubber)

In electric power plants, for example, **filters** separate particulate matter from the stack gases (Figure 19-12a). Smoke passes through a series of cloth bags, which trap the particulates; the bags are later cleaned, and the solid waste is disposed of. Although filter systems such as this remove well over 99% of all particulates, they do not rid the air of gases such as sulfur dioxide.

Cyclones are used in smaller operations and are best suited for larger particulates or as a first-stage filter (Figure 19-12b). In the cyclone, particulate-laden air is passed through a metal cylinder at high speed; the particulates strike the walls and fall to the bottom, where they can be removed. Cyclones remove 50% to 90% of the large particulates but few of the small and medium ones. Like filters, cyclones have no effect on gaseous pollutants.

Electrostatic precipitators, also used to remove particulates, are about 99% efficient; many of the major coal-burning facilities in the United States have installed them (Figure 19-12c). In electrostatic precipitators, particulates become electrically charged as they pass through. The charged particles then attach to the wall of the device, which is oppositely charged. The current is periodically turned off, allowing the particulates to fall to the bottom.

The **scrubber**, unlike the other methods, removes both particulates and sulfur dioxide gases (Figure 19-12d). In scrubbers, pollutant-laden air is passed through a fine mist of water, which traps both particulates (well over 99%) and sulfur oxide gases (approximately 80% to 95%).

The removal of air pollution from stack gases helps clean up the air but creates an additional problem—that of toxic solid and liquid wastes (see Chapter 22). Particulates from electrostatic precipitators, cyclones, and filters contain harmful trace elements and other inorganic substances that must be disposed of properly. Scrubbers produce a toxic sludge rich in sulfur compounds and mineral matter.

Reducing pollution from mobile sources such as the automobile can also be achieved by conservation. Engine design changes can also reduce emissions, but most design changes cannot reduce carbon monoxide, nitrogen oxides, and hydrocarbons to acceptable levels. This makes it necessary to pass the exhaust gases through a **catalytic con-** **verter**. This device is attached to the exhaust system and converts carbon monoxide and hydrocarbons into water and carbon dioxide and nitrogen oxides into nitrogen gas. Most cars today are equipped with converters that rid the exhaust only of carbon monoxide and hydrocarbons.

Cars with catalytic converters can meet emission standards if kept well tuned. The use of leaded gasoline in cars with catalytic converters destroys the catalytic surface.

New Ways to Burn Coal   Recent technological developments may help us use coal more efficiently while reducing air pollution. One of these is **magnetohydrodynamics** (MHD) (Figure 19-13). In a power plant, coal is first crushed and mixed with potassium carbonate or cesium, substances that are easily ionized (stripped of electrons). The mixture, burned at extremely high temperatures, produces a hot ionized gas—a **plasma**—containing electrons, which is passed through a nozzle into a magnetic field. The passage of the ionized gas through this field generates electrical current. The heat of the gas generates steam, which powers an electric turbine.

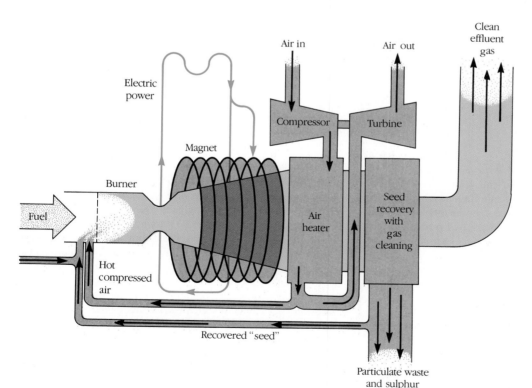

Figure 19-13
Magnetohydrodynamics. Coal is mixed with an ion-producing substance, such as potassium, and burned. A hot, ionized gas is given off and shot through a magnetic field. The movement of the ionized gas through the magnetic field creates the electrical current. Air or water is also heated and used to run an electrical generator.

MHD is about 60% efficient, whereas a conventional coal-burning power plant is only about 30% to 40% efficient. MHD systems remove 95% of the sulfur contaminants in coal, have lower nitrogen oxide emissions, and produce fewer particulates than conventional coal plants, but they release more fine particulates.

Coal can also be burned more cleanly and more efficiently by **fluidized bed combustion**. Finely powdered coal is mixed with sand and limestone and then fed into the boiler. Hot air, fed from underneath, suspends the mixture for more efficient combustion. The limestone reacts with sulfur, forming calcium sulfate, thus reducing sulfur oxide emissions.

The Cost of Control

Air pollution control costs money, but many companies are finding that it can be financially rewarding. For instance, the Long Island Lighting Company recovers vanadium from particulates collected at its power plants; in 1976 the company sold 362 tons of vanadium—about 9% of the total U.S. production—for $1.2 million. The chemical division of the Sherwin-Williams Company installed pollution control systems that recover valuable materials at a Chicago plant, saving it $60,000 a year.

The EPA estimates that an annual expenditure of $5 billion in the United States would eliminate or sharply decrease most air pollution damage, saving between $7 billion and $9 billion a year, improving the quality of life, bettering Americans' health, improving visibility, reducing damage to buildings and statues, and protecting wildlife.

Air pollution is a problem for the private citizen as well as a government and a business problem, and only through concerted personal efforts can significant progress be made against it.

The power of man has grown in every sphere, except over himself.

WINSTON CHURCHILL

Summary

Air pollutants come from a variety of *natural* and *anthropogenic sources*. Anthropogenic pollutants—the products of human activities—represent the most significant threat to the environment and its inhabitants. The six major pollutants are carbon monoxide, sulfur oxides, nitrogen oxides, hydrocarbons, particulates, and photochemical oxidants. The major sources are transportation, power plants, and industry.

Cities fall into two categories. *Brown-air cities* are new and relatively nonindustrialized. Their major pollutants are carbon monoxide, ozone, and nitrogen oxides. In these cities hydrocarbons and nitrogen oxides react in the presence of sunlight and form secondary pollutants, which make up the *photochemical smog* that hovers above them. *Gray-air cities* are older and more industrialized. Their major pollutants are particulates and sulfates. The atmospheric pollution combines with moisture to form *smog*.

Numerous factors affect regional air pollution, such as wind, topography, location, precipitation, and the frequency of temperature inversions. A *temperature inversion* occurs either when a high-pressure air mass stagnates over a region and forces a layer of warm air down over it *(subsidence inversion)* or when ground air cools faster than the air above it *(radiation inversion)*. Both inversions can result in a buildup of ground levels of air pollutants.

Air pollution affects human health in many ways. Short-term pollution episodes have numerous chronic effects, including discomfort, burning eyes and throat, colds, coughs, heart attacks, and even death. Particularly susceptible are children, patients with heart and lung diseases, and athletes. Chronic effects are also possible. *Bronchitis,* a persistent inflammation of the bronchial tubes, is characterized by a constant cough, mucus buildup, and difficulty in breathing. Cigarette smoking and air pollution are two major causes of this condition. *Emphysema,* the progressive breakdown of the air sacs in the lungs, is also caused by air pollution and smoking. Numerous studies have linked air pollution with cancer, but the evidence is contradictory.

Domestic animals are also affected by many air pollutants. But the most noticeable impacts are on materials, such as rubber, stone, and paint. Ozone, sulfur dioxide, and sulfuric acid are the most damaging pollutants. Crops and forests are also damaged by air pollutants, particularly ozone, sulfuric acid, and sulfates, although the exact magnitude of the effect is unknown.

The most potentially hazardous effects are those on climate. Carbon dioxide released from the combustion of fossil fuels acts as a heat reflector. Thus, heat that normally escapes into space is reradiated to earth, warming the atmosphere. This so-called *greenhouse effect* may gradually change global climate, melting glaciers and antarctic ice, raising the sea level, and disrupting agriculture. Particulates also affect climate, but the effect is not clear-cut. The global temperature appears to be warming, but this rise may be offset by cooling from increased cloudiness.

Air pollution is controlled at two interlocking levels—the legal and the technological. A powerful tool is the U.S. Clean Air Act, its amendments, and the resultant regulations, which collectively provide for emission standards for automobiles, national ambient air quality standards for major pollutants, emissions standards for new stationary pollution sources, ways to prevent deterioration of pristine and less polluted air, and stronger EPA enforcement.

Reductions in pollution can also be brought about by energy conservation and by using alternative energy sources such as solar energy and wind energy. Harmful pollutants can be removed from smokestacks by cyclones, filters, electrostatic precipitators, and scrubbers, but each of these produces solid wastes that must be safely disposed of.

Air pollution costs money, but many companies are finding it makes good business sense to reduce pollution by recovering waste products. The EPA estimates that an annual expenditure of $5 billion would save $7 to $9 billion annually in reduced damage to crops, forests, buildings, and health.

Discussion Questions

1. Why do anthropogenic air pollutants generally have more impact than natural pollutants?
2. What are the three processes that produce anthropogenic pollution? Describe each and give examples.
3. What are the six major air pollutants, and what are the major sources of each? What control strategies could reduce the emission of these pollutants?
4. What specific pollutants should most of our control efforts be directed toward? Why? Give specific examples of damage caused by these pollutants.
5. Describe the pollutants produced by burning fossil fuels. How is each product formed? Why is coal a "dirtier" fuel than gasoline?
6. Define the terms *primary pollutant* and *secondary pollutant.*
7. In what ways are brown-air and gray-air cities different? What are the major air pollutants in each type of city?
8. What is photochemical smog? What are its components? How is it formed? Why are suburban levels of photochemical smog often higher than urban levels?
9. Describe the factors that affect air pollution levels in a given region.
10. What are temperature inversions? How are they formed?
11. What are the acute health effects of (1) carbon monoxide, (2) sulfur oxides and particulates, and (3) photochemical oxidants?
12. What are the chronic health effects of air pollution? Which pollutants are thought to be the cause of these effects?
13. Describe the effects of air pollution on (1) aesthetics, (2) nonhuman animals, and (3) plants. How can these effects have an economic impact? Give specific examples.
14. Describe the effects of air pollution on materials. Which pollutants are the most damaging?
15. Of all the impacts of air pollution, which are of the most concern to you?
16. Describe the global energy balance and how anthropogenic (and natural) pollutants affect it.
17. Make a complete list of your ideas for controlling air pollution in your city or town, and rank them according to their effectiveness and their feasibility. Which ones are practical?
18. Coal combustion produces a large amount of sulfur oxide gas. What are the risks of this activity? Can you fill in the impact analysis chart presented in Chapter 2 to help in your analysis?
19. Discuss the air pollution control legislation enacted by the U.S. Congress, highlighting important features of the acts and amendments. Define *emissions offset policy, national ambient air quality standard,* and *prevention of significant deterioration.*
20. Discuss the control of air pollution from stationary pollution sources. In what general ways can pollution be reduced? Give specific examples of how you can help reduce air pollution.

Suggested Readings

Aynsley, E. (1969). How Air Pollution Alters Weather. *New Scientist* 44: 66–67. Good overview.

Bach, W. (1972). *Atmospheric Pollution*. New York: McGraw-Hill. Good introduction to air pollution.

Becker, W. H., Schilling, F. J., and Verma, M. P. (1968). The Effect on Health of the 1966 Eastern Seaboard Air Pollution Episode. *Arch. Environ. Health* 16: 414–419. Excellent case study on acute toxicity of air pollution.

Buell, P., and Dunn, J. E. (1967). Relative Impact of Smoking and Air Pollution on Lung Cancer. *Arch. Environ. Health* 15: 291–297. Excellent study.

Carnow, B. W., and Meier, P. (1973). Air Pollution and Pulmonary Cancer. *Arch. Environ. Health* 27: 207–218. Valuable review.

Ferris, B. G. (1978). Health Effects of Exposure to Low Levels of Regulated Air Pollutants: A Critical Review. *Jour. Air Pollution Control Assoc.* 28(5): 482–497. A technical review.

Goldsmith, J. R., and Landaw, S. A. (1968). Carbon Monoxide and Human Health. *Science* 162: 1352–1359. Superb review.

Henderson, B. E., Gordon, R. J., Menck, H., SooHoo, J., Martin, S. P., and Pike, M. C. (1975). Lung Cancer and Air Pollution in Southcentral Los Angeles County. *Am. Jour. Epidem.* 101(6): 477–488. Excellent study of air pollution and cancer.

Hileman, B. (1982). Crop Losses from Air Pollutants. *Environ. Sci. Tech.* 15(9): 495A–499A. General overview.

—— (1982). The Greenhouse Effect. *Environ. Sci. Tech.* 16(2): 90A–93A. Update on this important issue.

Kane, D. N. (1976). Bad Air for Children. *Environment* 18(9): 26–34. A look at an overlooked problem.

Kellog, W. W., Schware, R., and Friedman, E. (1980). The Earth's Climate. *Futurist* 14(5): 50–55. Excellent overview.

McCarroll, J. R., Cassell, E. J., Ingram, W. T., and Wolter, D. (1966). Health and the Urban Environment: Health Profiles versus Environmental Pollutants. *Am. Jour. Public Health* 56(2): 66–75. Eye-opening study.

Mountain, I. M., Cassell, E. J., Wolter, D. W., Mountain, J. D., Diamond, J. R., and McCarroll, J. R. (1968). Health and the Urban Environment. VII. Air Pollution and Disease Symptoms in a "Normal" Population. *Arch. Environ. Health* 17(3): 343–352. Worthwhile study.

Seidel, S., and Keyes, D. (1983). *Can We Delay a Greenhouse Warming?* Washington D.C.: U.S. Government Printing Office. Excellent study of ways to avert disaster.

Waldbott, G. L. (1978). *Health Effects of Environmental Pollutants*. St. Louis: C. V. Mosby. Good overview.

The Ozone Controversy

Encircling the earth is a thin, protective layer of ozone gas (O_3) that screens out 99% of the sun's harmful ultraviolet light. The **ozone layer** occupies the outer two-thirds of the stratosphere, 20 to 50 kilometers (12 to 30 miles) above the earth's surface (Figure S19-1). The screening effect of the ozone layer protects all organisms from the damage caused by ultraviolet light, which is known to be mutagenic and carcinogenic.

When ultraviolet light strikes ozone molecules, it causes them to split apart (Figure S19-2). But this reaction is reversible. As

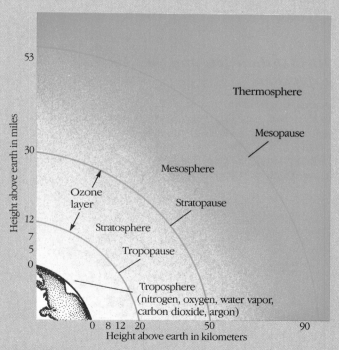

Figure S19-1
The earth's atmosphere is divided into layers. Ninety-five percent of the oxygen is found in the troposphere. The ozone layer occupies the outer two-thirds of the stratosphere.

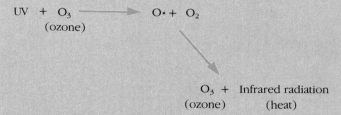

Figure S19-2
Screening effect of ozone in the stratosphere. The ozone molecule is split by ultraviolet (UV) light, but the reaction is reversible. When ozone reforms, infrared radiation or heat is given off.

ozone is regenerated, heat is given off. The ozone layer thus screens out harmful ultraviolet light and produces heat that escapes into space.

Life on earth depends on this screening mechanism; without it, bacteria and plants would die in large numbers, and animals would be seriously burned and would develop cancer and lethal mutations.

Activities That May Deplete the Ozone Layer

Many scientists and public policymakers are concerned about the fate of the ozone layer. Some human activities could destroy it, wreaking havoc on the biosphere. Three major activities have been singled out: (1) the use of spray cans and refrigerants that contain freon gas, (2) high-flying supersonic jets, and (3) the detonation of nuclear weapons.

Freons

In the United States up to the late 1970s, nearly all of the spray-can propellants and refrigerants were **freons**, also known as

447

Table S19-1 Commonly Used Freons

Generic Name	Use	Chemical Name	Chemical Formula
Freon-11	Spray-can propellant	Trichloromonofluoromethane	$\begin{array}{c} Cl \\ | \\ Cl-C-Cl \\ | \\ F \end{array}$
Freon-12	Coolant in refrigerators, freezers, and air conditioners	Dichlorodifluoromethane	$\begin{array}{c} Cl \\ | \\ F-C-Cl \\ | \\ F \end{array}$

fluorocarbons or chlorofluoromethanes. Two freons were commonly used: (1) freon-11, a spray-can propellant now banned from use here and in several other countries, and (2) freon-12, still used in refrigerators, air conditioners, and freezers (Table S19-1).

Until the early 1970s freons were generally perceived as inert (unreactive) chemicals; their release into the atmosphere, which occurs every time a spray can is used or when refrigerators, freezers, and air conditioners leak, was of little concern. It was thought that the gases simply diffused into the upper layers of the atmosphere, where they were broken down by sunlight, a reaction called *photodissociation* (Figure S19-3).

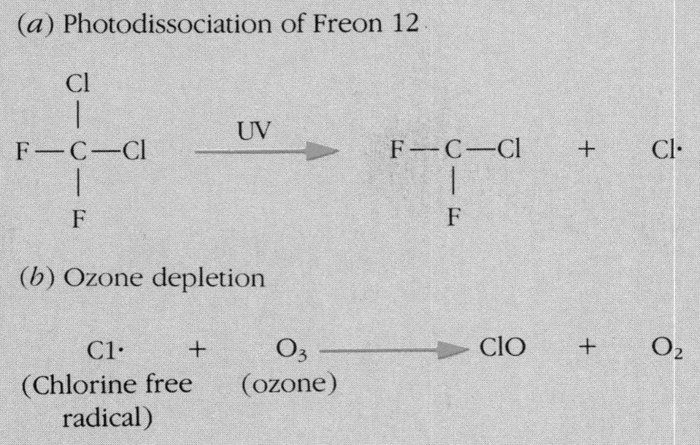

In the early 1970s two U.S. scientists reported that products of the photodissociation of freons could react with ozone in the stratosphere, as shown in Figure S19-3. This, they suggested, could eventually deplete the ozone layer. Shortly after their announcement, three groups of scientists substantiated their theory, showing that a single chlorine free radical could react with as many as 100,000 molecules of ozone and might represent a serious threat to the ozone layer. This is illustrated in Figure S19-4.

High-Altitude Jets and Nuclear Explosions

Aircraft that fly in the stratosphere, such as the supersonic transport, or SST, may also reduce stratospheric ozone through the release of nitric oxide (NO), a pollutant produced in jet engines (Figure S19-5).

In 1971 the U.S. Congress killed plans to help finance the construction of 300 to 400 SSTs. However, British and French

(*a*) Photodissociation of Freon 12

$$\begin{array}{c} Cl \\ | \\ F-C-Cl \\ | \\ F \end{array} \quad \xrightarrow{UV} \quad \begin{array}{c} \\ F-C-Cl \\ | \\ F \end{array} \quad + \quad Cl\cdot$$

(*b*) Ozone depletion

$$\underset{\substack{\text{(Chlorine free} \\ \text{radical)}}}{Cl\cdot} \quad + \quad \underset{\text{(ozone)}}{O_3} \quad \longrightarrow \quad ClO \quad + \quad O_2$$

Figure S19-3
(*a*) The freons, or fluorocarbons, are dissociated by ultraviolet light in the stratosphere. This produces a highly reactive chlorine free radical. (*b*) The free radical can react with ozone in the ozone layer, thus reducing the ozone concentration and eliminating the ultraviolet screen.

$$\underset{\substack{(a)\ \text{(Chlorine} \\ \text{oxide)}}}{ClO} \quad + \quad \underset{\substack{\text{(oxygen free} \\ \text{radical)}}}{O\cdot} \quad \longrightarrow \quad \underset{\substack{\text{(chlorine free} \\ \text{radical)}}}{Cl\cdot} \quad + \quad \underset{\substack{\text{(molecular} \\ \text{oxygen)}}}{O_2}$$

$$(b)\ ClO \quad + \quad O_3 \quad \longrightarrow \quad ClO_2 \quad + \quad O_2$$

Figure S19-4
(*a*) A single molecule of freon gas can eliminate many thousands of molecules of ozone, because the chlorine free radical is regenerated. (*b*) Chlorine oxide (formed when the chloride free radical reacts with ozone) can also react with ozone.

Supersonic ——→ NO + O$_3$ ——→ NO$_2$ + O$_2$
Transport   (nitric) (ozone)   (nitrogen) (oxygen)
Jet   oxide)   dioxide)

Figure S19-5
Supersonic and subsonic jets produce nitric oxide, which can react with ozone and reduce the ozone layer.

Concordes (an SST) are now in use on a limited scale. Because the Concorde flies lower and burns less fuel than the proposed American SST, it has less impact on the ozone layer. Ordinary commercial jets also produce nitric oxide (and other pollutants), which depletes the ozone layer to a smaller degree.

The detonation of nuclear weapons in the atmosphere also produces nitric oxide, which can react with stratospheric ozone. The active period of atmospheric nuclear weapons testing in the 1940s and 1950s caused a moderate and short-lived decrease in ozone, suggesting that nuclear war could cause a dangerous reduction.

Several other sources of nitric oxide have recently been identified. For example, nitrogen fertilizers may be converted into nitric oxide gas that could gradually diffuse into the stratosphere. Although the use of fertilizers has risen dramatically in the past decade, it is difficult to estimate what harm they may cause in the long run.

Other chemical pollutants such as methyl chloride and carbon tetrachloride may also diffuse into the ozone layer and eliminate ozone molecules. Natural pollutants such as nitrogen oxides from volcanoes and chloride ions from sea salt may also reduce the ozone layer, although these processes are presumably in balance with natural ozone replenishment.

In summary, then, it appears that the freon gases have the most significant impact on the ozone layer.

Extent and Effect of Depletion

Various authors estimate that the ozone layer has already been depleted by .5% to 1%. Because the concentration of ozone in the ozone layer naturally varies from one year to the next, however, it is difficult to know whether there has been a permanent decrease. To detect a permanent depletion in the ozone layer, the concentration would have to fall by 5% to 10%.

With usage of freons increasing at a phenomenal rate throughout the world, some scientists project a 30% depletion by 1994. More conservative estimates project a 16% depletion by 2000.

Ozone depletion will increase the amount of ultraviolet light striking the earth. In reasonable amounts, ultraviolet light tans skin and stimulates vitamin D production in the skin. But excess exposure causes serious burns and may induce skin cancer. It is also lethal to bacteria and plants.

A 1% depletion of the ozone layer could lead to a 2% increase in skin cancer. Given a conservative 16% decrease in ozone by 2000, skin cancer would rise by 32%, resulting in 100,000 to 300,000 more diagnosed cases yearly in the United States. Assuming a 4% mortality rate, about 4000 to 12,000 additional deaths would occur yearly. Worldwide, a 16% decrease in the ozone layer could result in an additional 20,000 to 60,000 deaths.

Studies of human skin cancer show that light-skinned people are much more sensitive to ultraviolet light than more heavily pigmented ones. In addition, some chemicals commonly found in drugs, soaps, cosmetics, and detergents may sensitize the skin to ultraviolet light. Thus, exposure may lead to a greater incidence of skin cancers than expected.

Plants are also affected by excess ultraviolet light. Intense ultraviolet radiation is usually lethal to plants, but smaller doses that do not kill plants (sublethal doses) damage leaves, inhibit photosynthesis, cause mutations, and may stunt growth.

Ozone depletion may also affect world climate, because heat is given off when ozone molecules are regenerated (see Figure S19-2). As a result, the upper stratosphere is almost as warm as the earth's surface. A reduction in the ozone layer would lower stratospheric temperature, which would influence the surface climate in unknown and possibly profound ways.

Preventing Ozone Depletion

Not everyone is convinced that the ozone layer is in danger. Considerable scientific debate has been stimulated by the projections discussed above. The United States, which produced 40% of the world's freons, banned the use of freon-11 used in spray cans in 1978. However, freon-12, which is used as a refrigerant and coolant and also in the production of plastic foam, was not affected by the ban. Because freon-12 accounted for half of the total U.S. production of fluorocarbons before the ban, the net effect was a 20% drop in world freon production.

Freon production was also banned in Sweden, but most of the rest of the world continues to produce it. Global fluorocarbon production peaked in 1974 at 800,000 metric tons. In 1981 production had leveled off at about 640,000 metric tons.

Unilateral actions of the sort taken by the United States and Sweden are of little value in the long run, except that they may inspire other countries to follow suit. Worldwide cooperation is essential if we are to deal with this potentially disastrous problem. Similar efforts by Japan and European nations, major producers of fluorocarbons, are needed.

Some scientists warn that further delays only lead us perilously close to disaster. By the time we are able to detect decreases in the ozone concentration, it may be too late, because millions of tons of freons will already be in the atmosphere, slowly working their way into the stratosphere.

Acid Precipitation: Roadblock or Environmental Hazard?

In the 1960s a forest ranger named Bill Marleau built the cabin of his boyhood dreams on Woods Lake in the western part of New York's Adirondack Mountains. Isolated in a dense forest of birch, hemlock, and maple, the lake offered Marleau excellent fishing and an unequaled opportunity to escape for solitude. Ten years after Marleau finished his cabin, however, something bizarre happened: Woods Lake, once a murky green suspension of microscopic algae and zooplankton, teeming with trout, began to turn clear. As the lake went through a mysterious transformation, the trout stopped biting and soon disappeared. Then the lily pads began to turn brown and die; soon afterward, the bullfrogs, otters, and loons disappeared, too.

What happened to Woods Lake? What ripped apart the web of life at this small, isolated lake, far from any sources of pollution?

Scientists from New York State's Department of Environmental Conservation say that Woods Lake is "critically acidified." As a result, virtually all forms of life in and around the lake have died or moved elsewhere. The lake became a "victim" of acids deposited by rain and snow.

Acid rain and snow, collectively known as **acid precipitation**, are becoming widespread, as are damaged lakes like Marleau's. Globally, thousands of other lakes are endangered.

Widely publicized as one of the most serious environmental threats facing us today, acid precipitation has broad economic importance. It is also, as one person in the coal industry said, "the core of the next battle between the coal industry and the environmentalists." Focusing on this battle, Ann Hughey reiterated a popular industry view when she called acid precipitation "the latest roadblock in a long series that always seems to keep coal from becoming the energy savior." Stephen Gage of the Environmental Protection Agency calls it "one of the most significant environmental problems of the coming decade."

Evidence is mounting that acid precipitation turns lakes acidic, kills fish and other aquatic organisms, damages crops, alters soil fertility, and destroys sandstone and marble structures. Moreover, scientists are finding that it is much more widespread than once thought and is taking a larger toll on our environment and pocketbooks than originally imagined.

What Is Acid Precipitation?

Acidity is measured on the pH (potential hydrogen) scale, which ranges from 0 to 14 (Figure S19-1). Substances that are acidic such as vinegar and lemon juice have low pH values, less than

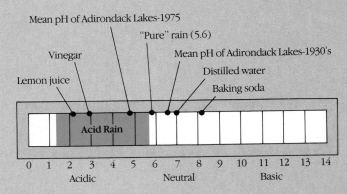

Figure S19-1
A pH scale to indicate acid–base level.

7. Basic (alkali) substances such as baking soda and lime have pH values greater than 7. Neutral substances such as pure water have a pH of 7. A change of 1 pH unit represents a tenfold change in the level of acidity; thus, rain with a pH of 4 is 10 times more acidic than rain with a pH of 5 and 100 times more acidic than rain with a pH of 6.

In an unpolluted environment, rainwater is slightly acidic, having a pH of approximately 5.7; therefore, acid precipitation is defined as rain and snow that have a pH below 5.7. The normal acidity of rainwater is created when atmospheric CO_2 is dissolved in water suspended in the atmosphere in clouds, mist, or fog and is converted into a mild acid, carbonic acid.

In a polluted environment, the sulfur oxides and nitrogen oxides in the atmosphere may combine with water to form sulfuric acid and nitric acid.

Types of Acid Precipitation

After the sulfur and nitrogen oxide gases—collectively known as **acid precursors**—are converted into acids in the atmosphere, they may fall from the sky in rain and snow, a process known as **wet deposition**.

Sulfate and nitrate particulates may also form from the acid precursors and may drift down from the sky through **dry deposition**, which is believed to be responsible for a large portion of the total acid deposition. Settling onto surfaces, these particulates can combine with water to form acids. In addition, sulfur and nitrogen oxide gases may be adsorbed (collected in concentrated form) onto the surfaces of plants or solid surfaces (rock, buildings), where they, too, combine with water.

Where Do Acids Come From?

Acid precursors come from both natural and anthropogenic sources. Natural sources include volcanoes, forest fires, and bacterial decay. Anthropogenic sources include the combustion of fossil fuel, the application of fertilizer, and many others.

There are two major sulfur oxides, sulfur dioxide (SO_2) and sulfur trioxide (SO_3). Globally, natural sources produce far more sulfur oxides than anthropogenic sources; however, natural sources are spread out over a large surface area and therefore do not generally raise the ambient level of sulfur oxides. Anthropogenic sources, in contrast, are often concentrated in urban and industrialized regions, causing local levels to be quite high.

Of the many anthropogenic sources of sulfur oxides, coal-fired plants appear to be the major one. Thus, about 70% of all human-caused sulfur dioxide emissions in the United States come from electric power plants, most of these coal-burning.

Like the sulfur oxides, the nitrogen oxides arise from a wide variety of sources. The natural sources include the bacterial decay of plant matter and the oxidation of atmospheric nitrogen by lightning; the anthropogenic sources include all forms of com-

Figure S19-2
Anthropogenic sources of nitrogen oxides.

bustion as well as agricultural fertilizers. Electric power plants are a major source in the United States, producing 50% of all anthropogenic nitrogen oxides (Figure S19-2).

In 1980 the United States produced approximately 22 million metric tons of sulfur dioxide and about 19 million metric tons of nitrogen oxides. The EPA estimated that annual sulfur dioxide emissions might increase to around 26 million metric tons by the year 2000 and that annual nitrogen oxide emissions would increase to 25 million metric tons.

The Transport of Acid Precursors

It is not uncommon for rains in the northeastern United States to have pH values of 4 to 4.21; values similar to these have been

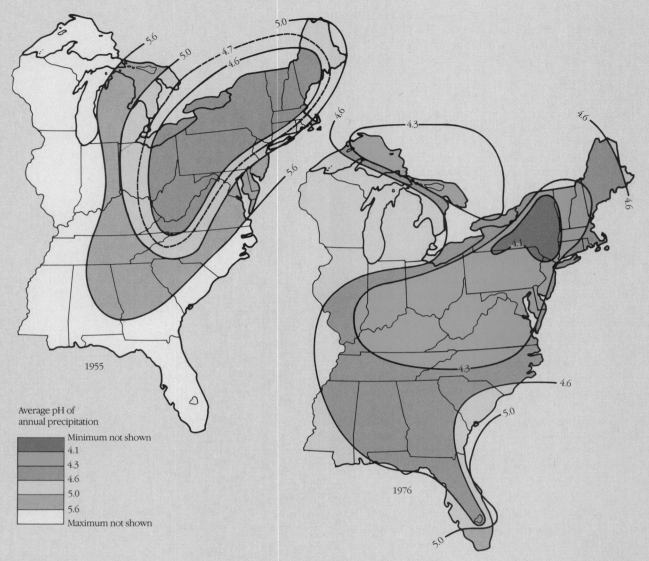

Figure S19-3
Acid precipitation in the United States, 1955 and 1976. Note the spread of acid precipitation.

reported consistently for the past two decades (Figure S19-3). The acidic substances in the rain of this region often originate many hundreds of kilometers away.

Acid precursors and acids can remain airborne for two to four days and can travel hundreds, perhaps even thousands, of kilometers before dropping out of the sky. Scientists have found that the acid rain and snow in southern Norway and Sweden origi-

nate in England and Germany. In the United States, acid precipitation falling in the Northeast originates in the industrialized Midwest, primarily the upper Mississippi and Ohio River valleys. Moving eastward, the poisonous clouds tend to converge on New York and New England.

Acid precipitation is not restricted to the northeastern United States, as was once thought. Studies in Montana, Florida, Colorado, New Jersey, California, Canada, the Amazon Basin, and Europe, to name a few areas, have all documented acid precipitation. Acid precipitation can be found downwind of most major urban or industrial centers.

The level of precipitation acidity at such locations can be quite high. In the White Mountains of New Hampshire between 1964 and 1974, the average annual pH was about 4, nearly 100 times more acidic than normal precipitation. During that decade the acid level increased 36%. In Europe, rain and snow samples frequently have pH values between 3 and 5; in Scandinavia, rain with a pH as low as 2.8 has been recorded. Rainfall samples collected in Pasadena, California, in 1976 and 1977 had an average pH of 3.9. One of the lowest recorded pH measurements was made in Kane, Pennsylvania, where a rainfall sample with a pH of 2.7 was recorded—rain as acidic as vinegar. The grand prize, however, undeniably goes to Wheeling, West Virginia, where a rainfall sample had a pH of 1.5—stronger than lemon juice.

In well-studied areas such as southern Norway and Sweden and the northeastern United States, two notable trends have been observed. First, acid precipitation is falling over a wider area than it was 10 or 20 years ago; second, the areas over which the strongest acids are falling are expanding (Figure S19-3).

Impacts of Acid Precipitation

Acidification of Lakes

Throughout the world, lakes and rivers and their fish are dying at an alarming rate. In the 1930s, for example, scientists surveyed lakes in the western Adirondacks. Sampling the pH of 320 lakes, they found that most were fairly normal, with pHs ranging from 6 to 7.5. In 1975 a survey of 216 lakes in the same area showed that a large number had pH values below 5, a level at which most aquatic life dies (Figure S19-4). Of the acidified lakes, 82% were devoid of fish life. Currently, at least 237 lakes and ponds in the western Adirondacks have passed the critical mark. Hundreds of other lakes are fast approaching it.

In the low mountains of southern Scandinavia the same story is being repeated, but on a much larger scale. Acidification of surface waters has occurred at a rapid rate for 20 to 30 years. In the Tovdal River Basin in southern Norway, 48 of 266 lakes were found to be acidified and without fish in 1950. In 1965 the total had reached 75, and by 1975, 175 lakes were devoid of fish.

In Sweden alone there are approximately 20,000 lakes without or soon to be without fish. In Norway, salmon runs have been entirely eliminated because of the impact of acid precipitation on egg development. As a result, inland commercial fishing has ended in some areas.

In southern Ontario and Quebec acid precipitation has destroyed hundreds of lakes. Because much of the acid reaching these lakes is believed to come from the United States and because 48,000 lakes are believed to be in danger, Canada has exerted considerable pressure on the United States to reduce air pollution. Some U.S. utility officials assert that Canada is conducting a misleading propaganda campaign and that there is no proof that U.S. companies are to blame. Some members of Congress hint that Canada is seeking to close down U.S. power plants to create a wider market for excess Canadian hydroelectric power.

Some parks and wilderness areas in the United States are endangered by acid precipitation because they lie downwind of major industrial centers and have thin soils and pure waters incapable of neutralizing acids. Preliminary data suggest that acid precipitation in the Great Smoky Mountains National Park

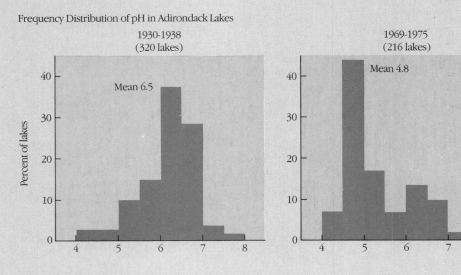

Frequency Distribution of pH in Adirondack Lakes

Figure S19-4
The pH level in Adirondack lakes.

Figure S19-5
Rainfall pH values in Florida.

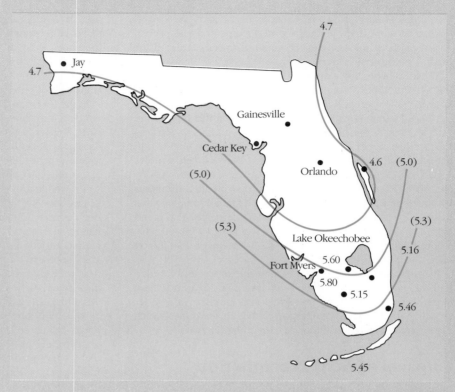

has already injured trout populations. Of particular concern is the Quetico-Superior Lake country of Canada and northern Minnesota. There are three major parks in this area: Quetico Provincial Park in Canada and Voyageurs National Park and the Boundary Waters Canoe Area Wilderness in the United States. A recent EPA report stated that one-third of the lakes in the two U.S. parks had become so acidified that fish and other life forms were in imminent danger.

Recent studies have shown that acid precipitation occurs widely over the northern and central portions of Florida, with precipitation ten times more acidic than normal (Figure S19-5). Furthermore, the pH of some lakes has decreased from 5.5 in 1957 to 4.9 in 1979. Such lakes are in serious danger because of their inability to neutralize acids falling from the sky.

Fish deaths in acidified lakes and streams, as we have seen, generally occur when the pH drops below 5 (Figure S19-6). Scientists have found that when a lake's pH falls below the critical level, the concentration of toxic trace elements such as aluminum rises. Dr. Carl Schofield has shown that aluminum affects the gills of brook trout fry, causing a buildup of mucus and ultimately death by asphyxiation. Adult and yearling brook trout similarly exposed to aluminum and acidic water exhibited irregular opercular (gill cover) movements and lassitude, and they eventually died. Autopsies showed gill damage.

High levels of toxic elements result when acidic rainwater or melted snow dissolves elements like aluminum, mercury, and lead naturally found in the soil and rocks. Normal rainwater is incapable of leaching these elements to any great extent.

Another important finding is that each spring when the snow begins to melt, the concentration of acids (and often aluminum) in lakes and streams increases rapidly. This sudden increase in acidity is lethal to fish (Figure S19-7). During the winter, snow polluted by sulfate and nitrate particulates and sulfuric and nitric acids collects on the ground. When the snow begins to melt, the surface melts first. The water drains through the unmelted snowpack and leaches out the majority of the acids. The first 30% of the snowmelt contains virtually all of the acid and typically has a pH of 3 to 3.5.

Fish are not the only organisms affected by acid precipitation. Professor Erik Nyholm of Sweden's University of Lund found that songbirds living near acid-contaminated lakes lay eggs with softer shells than birds feeding deep in the forest around unaffected lakes. He also found elevated levels of aluminum in the bones of the birds that live near acidic lakes, and he hypothesized that the aluminum built up from eating insects living in acidified waters. The aluminum interferes with normal calcium deposition, resulting in defective eggshells and, ultimately, fewer offspring.

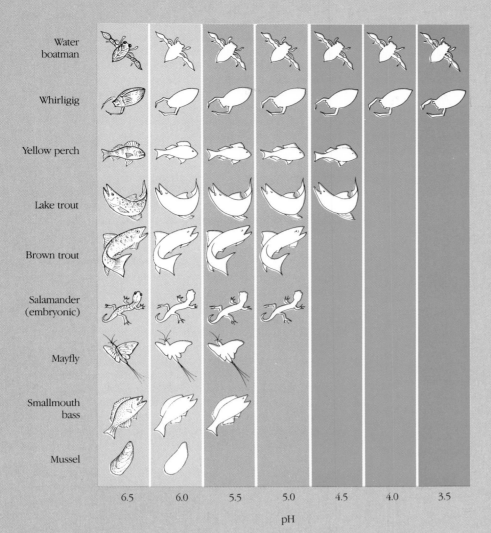

Water
boatman

Whirligig

Yellow perch

Lake trout

Brown trout

Salamander
(embryonic)

Mayfly

Smallmouth
bass

Mussel

6.5   6.0   5.5   5.0   4.5   4.0   3.5

pH

Figure S19-6
The sensitivity of fish and
other aquatic organisms to
acid levels varies.

Figure S19-7
These fish were confined to a
cage in a stream affected by
acid rain. Because of the lack
of algae and other oxygen-
producing marine plants,
which were killed by high
acid levels, these fish died
of asphyxiation.

Professor F. Harvey Pough of Cornell University studied fertilized eggs of the spotted salamander in his laboratory and found that exposure to water with a pH of 5 prevented normal embryonic development and resulted in gross deformities that were usually fatal. The mortality of fertilized eggs was 60% at pH 6 but only 1% at pH 7.

Spotted salamanders breed in temporary ponds created by melted snow. These ponds are likely to be highly acid in regions of acid precipitation; as a result, the fate of the spotted salamander is bleak. The spotted salamander is as important as birds and small mammals in the food chain. "A drastic change in its population," Pough says, "would be likely to have repercussions throughout the entire ecosystem."

Human Consequences

Acids and acid precursors affect our health and may damage crops, forests, buildings, and statues. Current estimates hold the economic costs of acid precipitation to be around $5 billion a year in the United States.

The Ohio state government contends that if something is not done quickly to control acid precipitation, 2500 lakes a year will die yearly in Ontario, Quebec, and New England throughout the remainder of the century. Predictions of this nature are alarming partly because many of the areas most susceptible to acid precipitation depend on the recreation industry. In Ontario alone there are approximately 2000 fishing lodges that contribute $150 million each year to the economy and employ 6% of the province's northern labor force. An official of the Ontario Ministry of the Environment says that even at the current rate of acid precipitation, "There could be a $64 million loss and serious survival problems for 600 lodges over the next 20 years."

The same ominous future seems probable for parts of the U.S. recreation industry. Take as an example Vilas County, Wisconsin, an area supported by the tourist industry. There are 50,000 fishing licenses issued annually in Vilas County; the net revenue from fishing and related activities is estimated to be $112 million. Approximately $2.5 million in sales tax is raised each year in the county. Because one-third of the visitors go there solely to fish, widespread destruction of lakes in the area by acid precipitation may significantly affect the regional economy. In New York, the estimated revenue loss caused by the destruction of lakes and the subsequent decrease in sport fishing is estimated at about $1 million annually.

Numerous authors have noted that acid precipitation damages forests and may cause significant decreases in productivity. Studies have shown that it causes foliar damage to birch and pines, impairs germination of spruce seeds, erodes protective waxes from oak leaves, and leaches nutrients from plant leaves. Whether this kind of damage will affect the long-term productivity of forests, however, remains to be seen. In any case, the stakes are high for countries such as Canada, where the forestry industry contributes about 15% of the gross national product.

Concern for crops has also been raised by numerous authors, but the results of many studies are not conclusive. Some research has shown that simulated acid precipitation decreases crop productivity; other studies show increases; still others show no effect. Acid precipitation below pH 3 damages leaves on bean plants. Laboratory studies of tobacco plants show that simulated acid precipitation leaches calcium from leaves. Furthermore, timothy grass treated with simulated acid rain with pHs ranging from 2.2 to 3.7 die after extended exposure.

Acid precipitation is particularly harmful to buds; therefore, acids falling on plants in the springtime might impair growth. In addition, acid precipitation appears to inhibit the dark reactions of photosynthesis, a series of chemical reactions in which plants produce carbohydrates and other important organic chemicals such as amino acids and fats.

Acid precipitation may damage plants directly, as noted above, or it may exert an effect on plants through the soil. It may leach important elements from the soil, resulting in lower yield and reduced agricultural output. Acidification of soils may also impair soil bacteria that play an important role in nutrient cycling and nitrogen fixation.

In the final analysis, it is difficult to assess damage from acid precipitation to crops and forests, because productivity depends on many factors. Concern is justified, but not all areas will be affected in the same way. Mountainous regions with poorly developed soils are more susceptible than others, because such soils are unable to neutralize acids (Figure S19-8). Areas most susceptible in the United States are the northeastern states, the Rocky Mountains, the Cascade range and the Sierra Nevada. Southern Ontario and Quebec are particularly sensitive regions in Canada.

Acid precipitation is also capable of corroding man-made structures and has taken its toll on some of special importance, such as the Statue of Liberty, the Canadian Parliament in Ottawa, Egypt's temples at Karnak, and the caryatids of the Acropolis. John Roberts, Canadian environmental minister, estimates that erosion of buildings in North America may be costing on the order of $2 billion to $3 billion a year. Acid rain may also damage house paint and etch the surfaces of automobiles and trucks.

Solutions to a Growing Problem

The first significant governmental action against acid precipitation in the United States came in 1979. President Carter proposed a ten-year program, funded at $10 million per year, to study acid precipitation and its effects. As an outgrowth of Carter's proposal, Congress passed the *Acid Precipitation Act* in 1980. The purpose was to identify the causes and sources of acid precipitation and to evaluate its environmental, social, and economic effects. Congress further declared that actions would be taken to limit or eliminate identified sources of acid precipitation and to remedy or ameliorate the harmful effects if deemed necessary. Congress established a ten-year program to carry out

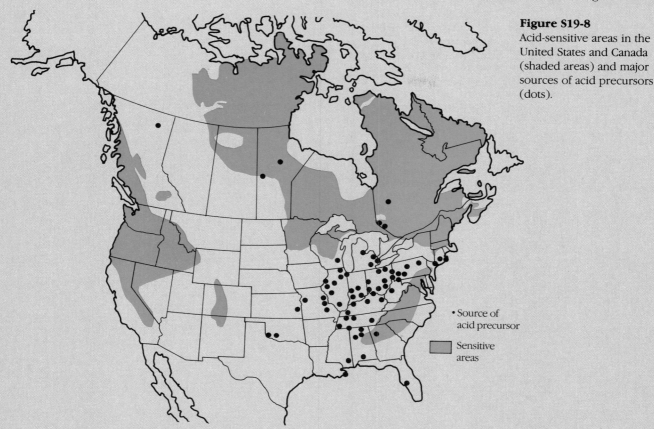

Figure S19-8
Acid-sensitive areas in the United States and Canada (shaded areas) and major sources of acid precursors (dots).

· Source of acid precursor

Sensitive areas

the necessary research, appropriating $5 million for the first year, 1981, and allowing a maximum of $45 million for the following nine years.

Efforts to measure acid precipitation have gained considerable momentum in the United States and abroad. There are 84 monitors in 32 states in the United States and 55 monitors in Canada. Data from this network will help determine levels of precipitation acidity.

Research funded by the Acid Precipitation Act is important, but many critics contend that the United States should start reducing sulfur oxide emissions now by requiring (1) scrubbers to be installed on all existing coal-fired power plants, (2) utilities to burn low-sulfur coal, and (3) coal to be cleaned before combustion, which removes about two-fifths of its sulfur.

A second major way of addressing the problem of acid rain would be to lessen or eliminate its impact. In Sweden a $9 million program has been undertaken to apply lime—a basic substance that neutralizes acid—to acidic lakes. Measures of this nature are costly and of limited value. A similar program in Canada showed the futility of such efforts. At a cost of $120 per hectare ($50 per acre), liming a single lake can cost between $4000 and $40,000 In five years, treated lakes turned acid again.

Dr. Carl Schofield has attempted to develop strains of acid-resistant brook trout. But this is also a limited answer, for even if a strain of trout that could survive at pH 4.8 were developed, what would happen when the pH dropped to 4.5?

The conversion of oil-fired plants to coal and the installation of additional coal-fired power plants will result in a significant increase in sulfur dioxide and nitrogen dioxide emissions, leading to an inevitable increase in acid precipitation. Between 1979 and 1995, the power industry projects, 350 coal-burning power plants will go on line in the United States.

Many environmentalists and congressional representatives believe that the United States and Canada should immediately begin to reduce air pollution by half. Utilities in the Northeast and Midwest have been targeted by the Senate's Environment and Public Works Committee, which has recommended a bill requiring an annual reduction in sulfur dioxide emissions of more than 8 million tons by 1995. Such important actions, however, will not reduce nitrogen oxide emissions. To reduce these, fossil fuel combustion must be cut back. Energy conservation, solar energy, and wind energy could become valuable allies in this battle. Responsible actions now will have far-reaching effects, saving hundreds of lakes from destruction by acid rain and snow.

Suggested Readings

Beamish, R. J. (1976). Acidification of Lakes in Canada from Acid Precipitation and the Resulting Effects on Fishes. *Water, Air and Soil Pollution* 6: 501–514. Technical report on toxic effects of acid rain on fish.

Environment Canada (1982). *Downwind: The Story of Acid Rain*. Ottawa: Minister of Supply and Services. Good overview.

Havas, M., Huchinson, T. C., and Likens, G. E. (1984). Red Herrings in Acid Rain Research. *Environ. Sci. and Technol.* 18(b): 176A–186A. Excellent review.

LaBastille, A. (1981). Acid Rain: How Great a Menace? *National Geographic* 160(5): 652–681. Vividly illustrated and well written.

Likens, G. E. (1976). Acid Precipitation. *Chemical and Engineering News* 54(48): 29–44. Good review.

Luoma, J. R. (1980). Troubled Skies, Troubled Waters. *Audubon* 82(6): 88–111. Exquisitely written.

Osterman, R. J. (1982). *Acid Rain: A Plague upon the Waters*. Minneapolis: Dillon. The best of several small books on the subject.

Rhodes, S. L., and Middleton, P. (1983). The Complex Challenge of Controlling Acid Rain. *Environment* 25(4): 6–9; 31–38. Good review of the politics of acid rain control.

Schofield, C. L. (1976). Acid Precipitation: Effects on Fish. *Ambio* 5(5–6): 228–230. Good overview.

Schofield, C. L. (1977). Acid Precipitation's Destructive Effects on Fish in the Adirondacks. *New York's Food and Life Sciences* 10(3): 12–15. Excellent review.

Sholle, S. R. (1983). Update: Acid Deposition and the Materials Damage Question. *Environment* 25(8): 25–32. Fairly detailed account of material damage from air pollution.

U.S. Environmental Protection Agency (1980). *Acid Rain*. Washington, D.C.: U.S. Government Printing Office. Good overview.

U.S. Senate Committee on Environment and Public Works (1981). *Hearings on Acid Rain, October 29, 1981* (Serial No. 97-H30). Washington, D.C.: U.S. Government Printing Office. Testimony by scientists doing research on acid rain. Excellent.

U.S. Senate Committee on Environment and Public Works (1982). *Acid Rain: A Technical Inquiry, May 25 and 26, 1982* (Serial No. 97-H53). Washington, D.C.: U.S. Government Printing Office. Excellent.

Vermeulen, A. J. (1978). *Acid Precipitation in the Netherlands*. Haarlem, The Netherlands: Department of Environmental Control. Interesting study.

Wetstone, G. S., and Foster, S. A. (1983). Acid Precipitation: What Is It Doing to Our Forests? *Environment* 25(4): 10–12; 38–40. Good review.

Indoor Air Pollution

Our own homes can be sources of dangerous air pollutants. These **indoor air pollutants** come from wood and kerosene stoves, natural gas appliances, tobacco smoke, plywood, paneling, furniture, rugs, and a host of other things. Even making homes highly energy-efficient, if it is not done correctly, can increase the danger.

This supplement will discuss three major types of indoor air pollution: the products of combustion, formaldehyde, and radioactive pollutants. Asbestos, a pollutant found in both homes and factories, was discussed in Chapter 18.

Products of Consumption

Cigarettes, pipes, cigars, gas stoves and ovens, gas space heaters, water heaters, kerosene stoves, and wood stoves are the major combustive sources of indoor air pollution. Water heaters and furnaces are generally vented to the outside of the house, so gaseous pollutants do not build up inside. But gas stoves and kerosene space heaters are often not vented. As the fuel burns, carbon monoxide and nitrogen dioxide enter the room air.

As shown in Figure S19-1, carbon monoxide (CO) levels in the kitchen can increase from a few parts per million to over 40 parts per million when four burners are in operation for half an hour or so. Carbon monoxide levels increase appreciably in neighboring rooms, too. Nitrogen dioxide levels often follow the same pattern.

Concentrations of indoor air pollutants decrease after combustion sources are turned off, of course, but it may take one to two hours before normal levels are reached in conventional, poorly sealed homes (Figure S19-2). In well-sealed, energy-efficient homes that haven't made allowances for ventilation, it could take much longer. If several lengthy meals are cooked during a day, the total exposure to these pollutants can be quite high.

In certain homes the nitrogen oxide levels can exceed the U.S. Clean Air Act standards of .05 part per million. Carbon monoxide levels can also exceed the standards of 9 ppm for an eight-hour exposure or 35 ppm for a one-hour exposure. Homes

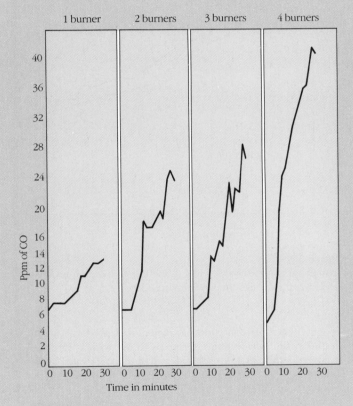

Figure S19-1
Carbon monoxide levels in the kitchen rise significantly when gas burners are used.

heated with gas or coal have been found to have CO levels of 50 ppm or more for periods of one hour or more.

Sulfur dioxide is not generally a problem in homes unless kerosene stoves are used. New kerosene space heaters introduced in the late 1970s, for example, can release significant

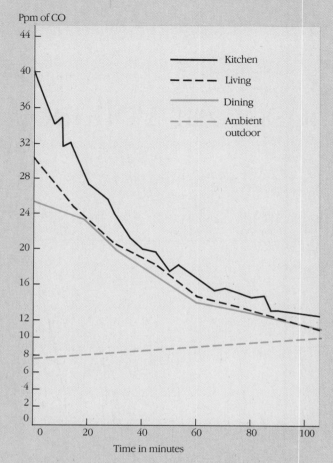

Figure S19-2
Drop in carbon monoxide level in the kitchen, dining room, and living room after the stove is turned off.

amounts of carbon monoxide, nitrogen dioxide, and sulfur dioxide if they are functioning improperly. If the wick is damaged or covered with soot, for example, or if there is water in the fuel, carbon monoxide and sulfur dioxide cause headaches, coughing, and irritation of the throat.

Particulates are generally not a problem in homes unless there are smokers present. For example, one study showed that the average particulate level was 40 μ per cubic meter ($\mu g/m^3$) in a home without smokers. Smokers raised particulate levels in some cases to 700 $\mu g/m^3$, well above the U.S. national ambient air quality standards for particulates of 60 $\mu g/m^3$ for an average annual exposure or 150 $\mu g/m^3$ for a one-hour exposure.

Carbon monoxide is especially harmful to people with heart and lung diseases. Sulfur and nitrogen oxides are lung irritants and are responsible for emphysema and chronic bronchitis. In the long term they may also cause lung cancer. Cigarette smoke contains several known carcinogens (see Chapter 21).

To reduce the buildup of these toxic chemicals, all combustion sources can be properly vented. When a gas stove is used, the overhead fan can be used. Kerosene stoves could be avoided altogether, especially in small rooms. Cigarette smoking can be prohibited, especially if young children or older adults are present.

Some scientists have suggested that gas stoves should be eliminated from homes and replaced with electric stoves, even though electric cooking is less efficient. Passive solar heating can help reduce gas space heating. In tightly sealed, energy-efficient homes, air exchange systems can be installed. These periodically replace room air with outside air; when heat exchangers are used, little heat is lost to the outside.

Formaldehyde

Formaldehyde is the familiar preservative for biological specimens, but it is also used in many other ways. For instance, adhesives in plywood, particle board, and wood paneling all contain formaldehyde. Foam insulation (urea formaldehyde, which is injected into walls) contains it, as do permanent-press clothes, paper products, carpets, toothpaste, shampoos, and some medicines (it kills bacteria, fungi, and viruses).

About 3.2 million metric tons of formaldehyde are used in the United States each year. Because it is in so many consumer products, formaldehyde may be the chemical we are most often exposed to.

The levels of formaldehyde in homes insulated with urea formaldehyde foam insulation are four times higher than those in homes with other types of insulation. Furniture containing formaldehyde in the wood and fabric, introduced into a previously unfurnished house, has been shown to increase the levels three times.

People with the greatest risk are those living in trailers or in homes with a lot of newly installed foam insulation, particle board, plywood, or paneling. The better sealed a home or trailer is, the higher the levels of formaldehyde (Table S19-1). In conventionally built homes, with their abundance of cracks and poor insulation, air exchange between the inside and the outside occurs roughly once every hour. In airtight homes, the turnover is much slower, perhaps once every five hours. Thus, the tighter the home, the greater the concentration of formaldehyde.

Formaldehyde irritates the eyes, nose, and throat, but sensitivity among people varies. Some are sensitive to levels of 1.5 to 3 ppm, but others who have been exposed for long periods become sensitized and respond to levels as low as .05 ppm.

Formaldehyde is a carcinogen in rats, and possibly mice, at high levels. Given to monkeys at levels that humans are exposed to at work and at home, formaldehyde causes cellular changes (squamous metaplasia) in the linings of the respiratory tracts; these changes are believed to represent the early stages of cancer. Formaldehyde has also been shown to cause mutations in

Table S19-1 Formaldehyde in Mobile Homes and Houses Insulated with Urea-Formaldehyde Foam (UFF)

Type	Average Level of Formaldehyde (Parts per Million)
Homes without UFF	0.03
Homes with UFF	0.12
Mobile homes with UFF	0.38
Background[1]	0.01

[1]The background level is the normal atmospheric concentration of formaldehyde.

bacteria and many other organisms; many mutagens are also carcinogens. So far there is little evidence linking formaldehyde to cancer in humans. One epidemiological study showed a possible link between formaldehyde exposure and skin cancer.

The U.S. Consumer Product Safety Commission banned urea-formaldehyde insulation in 1981 but removed the ban in 1983. So far the Environmental Protection Agency, which could regulate formaldehyde under the Toxic Substances Control Act, has declined to take any action, despite recommendations from independent health scientists as well as scientists in the agency itself.

The EPA's decision not to regulate formaldehyde reflects a new attitude. In previous regulatory decisions, the fact that a chemical caused cancer in any laboratory animal was enough to warrant controls. Under the Reagan administration, though, the EPA has taken a more conservative view, maintaining that without conclusive proof from epidemiological studies that formaldehyde is carcinogenic in humans, regulations are unwarranted.

Many experts have criticized the EPA. Norton Nelson, a highly regarded health scientist, contends: "Epidemiological studies must be regarded as a crude and insensitive tool. Only the most violent and intense carcinogens are likely to be detected by epidemiological techniques." Many critics are satisfied with the animal carcinogenicity studies. They argue that the EPA should ban the use of formaldehyde in plywood, particle board, paneling, and textiles and that states should require local building codes to provide for more frequent air exchange in homes to limit the overall exposure to all indoor pollutants.

Radioactive Pollutants

A more difficult indoor air pollutant to control is the naturally occurring inert radioactive gas radon. A daughter product of radium found naturally in rocks and soils, radon enters homes through cracks in the foundation or by diffusing up from the soil in homes without foundations. In some cases, stone, brick,

and cement contain small quantities of radium, which emits radon.

Indoor concentrations of radon may be several times the natural, or background, level. Homes built on tailings from uranium mines have levels two to five times higher than normal background, as do the more energy-efficient, airtight homes without proper ventilation.

Radon gas is inhaled by humans and their pets; within the lungs it emits radiation that can cause mutations and lung cancer. The EPA estimates that radon in U.S. homes may account for one out of every ten deaths from lung cancer.

Radon is more difficult to control than other indoor air pollutants because it is naturally occurring. But careful selection of building materials and seals on basement walls can help reduce radon levels. More frequent air exchange and special air filters may also be helpful.

Controlling Indoor Air Pollutants

No current U.S. laws directly address indoor air pollution. Some experts argue that the Clean Air Act could apply, but the EPA has never attempted to use it to regulate the indoor pollutants, except asbestos. One way to address indoor air pollutants would be to develop indoor air standards, but the technical and legal problems would undoubtedly be enormous. Standards would have to be developed for each pollutant, and ways established to monitor them in individual homes. The difficulties would be insurmountable.

One provision of the Clean Air Act that could be used authorizes the EPA to draw up standards for hazardous air pollutants. The EPA could develop emission standards for indoor pollutants as it did with asbestos. Therefore, manufacturers of plywood, particle board, and paneling could be required to eliminate or greatly reduce formaldehyde emissions from their products.

A second approach might be to use the Toxic Substances Control Act, which gives the EPA broad authority to control the production, distribution, and disposal of potentially hazardous chemicals. Bans on plywood, carpets, furniture, and other products containing formaldehyde could be applied. To date, the EPA Toxic Substances Office has been too burdened with other duties to take such actions.

A final legal weapon is the Consumer Product Safety Act, which gives the Consumer Product Safety Commission the authority to regulate consumer products that might be dangerous to the public. Products that generate indoor air pollution could certainly qualify. The commission could also develop safety standards for various products. Standards for stoves, for example, could indicate the permissible emissions of carbon monoxide, and standards for plywood, textiles, and furniture could stipulate acceptable amounts of formaldehyde. The commission can also require manufacturers to warn the public of potential dangers associated with the use of their product. Finally, if an imminent hazard is uncovered, the commission can sue the manufacturers; money recovered from lawsuits can be used to warn the public of the hazard and, if necessary, recall, repair, or replace defective products.

As straightforward as it may seem, however, it's not all that easy for the Consumer Product Safety Commission to take action against manufacturers of indoor air pollution. In particular, the commission may not have jurisdiction over building materials, because they are not generally considered consumer products.

Many people assert that there are enough laws on the books now and that amendments to the Toxic Substances Control Act, the Clean Air Act, and the Consumer Product Act would be sufficient to regulate indoor air pollutants. The EPA could also work with state governments to develop building codes that require (1) energy-efficient air exchange systems for houses to ensure proper ventilation to reduce the indoor levels of all pollutants and (2) the use of low-emission appliances and building materials. Such simple steps could help reduce exposure to potentially harmful substances in the air at home.

Suggested Readings

Hileman, B. (1984). Formaldehyde: Assessing the Risk. *Environ. Sci. and Technol.* 18(7):216A–221A. Update on formaldehyde risks.

—— (1982). Formaldehyde. *Environ. Sci. and Technol.* 16(10): 543A–547A. Superb overview.

Kirsch, L. S. (1983). Behind Closed Doors: I. The Problem of Indoor Pollutants. *Environment* 25(2): 16–20; 37–42. Good survey of the problem.

Kirsch, L. S. (1983). Behind Closed Doors: II. Indoor Air Pollution and Government Policy. *Environment* 25(3): 26–39. In-depth study of laws that might apply to the control of indoor air pollution.

Leff, H. S. (1984). Kerosene vs Electric Portable Heaters: The Question of Risk. *Environment* 26(2): 31–36. A look at risk assessment in action.

Sterling, T. D., and Sterling, E. (1979). Carbon Monoxide Levels in Kitchens and Homes with Gas Cookers. *Jour. Amer. Pollution Control Assoc.* 29(3): 238–241.

20

Water Pollution

It's a crime to catch a fish in some lakes, and a miracle in others.

EVAN ESAR

Loren Eiseley once wrote, "If there is magic in this planet, it is in water." Covering 70% of the earth's surface and making up two-thirds or more of the weight of living organisms, water is indispensable to life. Despite its pivotal role in our lives, water is one of the most badly abused resources. Chapters 8 and 12 described how overexploitation of groundwater and surface water creates regional shortages that disrupt agriculture and society. Pollution of estuaries was discussed in Chapter Supplement 12-1, and oil pollution in the world's oceans was discussed in Chapter 13. This chapter will cover water pollutants: where they come from, how they affect living organisms, and, finally, legal, technological, and personal measures to reduce pollution.

Water and Water Pollution

Water pollution is any physical or chemical change in water that can adversely affect organisms. It is a global problem, affecting both the industrialized and the developing nations. The water pollution problems in the rich and the poor nations, however, are quite different in many respects. Heat, toxic metals, acids, sediment, animal and human wastes, and synthetic organic compounds foul the waterways of developed nations. Human and animal wastes, sediment, and pathogenic organisms head the list in the

463

nonindustrialized nations. In these countries, unsanitary water and malnutrition account for most of the illness and death.

Water has many different uses, each requiring different levels of purity. For example, water from the Ohio River may be clean enough to wash steel but may be toxic to fish and wildlife; water suitable for boating or fishing may be unsuitable for swimming; water safe to swim in may be too polluted to drink.

Like air pollutants, water pollutants come from numerous natural and anthropogenic sources. Likewise, water pollutants produced in one nation may flow into others, creating complex international control problems that may take decades to solve.

Point and Nonpoint Sources

Factories, power plants, and sewage treatment plants are considered **point sources** of water pollution, because they emit pollutants at discrete locations, usually a pipe that leads to a lake or stream (Figure 20-1a). Because of this, control is fairly straightforward.

In contrast, **nonpoint sources** of water pollution are scattered or diffuse. Cropland, forests, urban and suburban lands, roadways, and parking lots are nonpoint sources of a variety of substances, including dust, sediment, pesticides, asbestos, fertilizers, heavy metals, salts, oil, grease, litter, and even air pollutants washed out of the sky by rain (Figure 20-1b). Nonpoint water pollutants are generally harder to control than point sources.

Nine major nonpoint sources, shown in Table 20-1, produce about half of the total U.S. water pollution. By weight, the major pollutant is sediment. Approximately 9,000 metric tons of sediment are released each day in the United States from human nonpoint sources, compared with about 30 metric tons from point sources. Agriculture is generally the predominant nonpoint source except in urban and suburban areas.

(a)

(b)

Figure 20-1
Water pollution. (*a*) This boat dumping waste into Cuyahoga River, Cleveland, Ohio, is an example of a *point source*. (*b*) Runoff from a feed lot is a *nonpoint source*.

Table 20-1   Major Nonpoint Pollution Sources in the U.S.

Activity	Explanation
Silviculture	Growing and harvesting trees for lumber and paper production can produce large quantities of sediment.
Agriculture	Disruption of natural vegetation leads to increased erosion; pesticide and fertilizer use, coupled with poor land management, can pollute neighboring surface water and groundwater.
Mining	Leaching from mine wastes and drainage from mines themselves can pollute surface and groundwater with metals and acids; disruption of natural vegetation accelerates sediment erosion.
Construction	Road and building construction disrupts vegetation and increases sediment erosion.
Salt use and ground-water overuse	Salt from roads and storage piles can pollute groundwater and surface water; saltwater intrusion from groundwater overdraft pollutes ground and surface water.
Drilling and waste disposal	Injection wells for waste disposal, septic tanks, hazardous waste dumps, and landfills for municipal garbage can contaminate groundwater.
Hydrological modification	Dam construction and diversion of water both can pollute surface waters.
Urban runoff	Pesticides, herbicides, and fertilizers applied to lawns and residues from roads can be washed into surface waters by rain.

Some Features of Surface Waters

This chapter is concerned primarily with surface water pollution. Therefore, it is important to pause for a while to examine some features of surface waters that affect pollution. Information on groundwater can be found in Chapters 8 and 12. Model Application 20-1, "Water Pollution: Multiple Cause and Effect," found later in this chapter will help you examine the roots of the pollution problem.

Freshwater ecosystems fall into one of two categories. **Lentic** (standing) **systems**, such as lakes and ponds, are usually more susceptible to pollution, because water is replaced at a slow rate. A complete turnover of a lake's water may take 10 to 100 years or more; thus, pollutants can build up to hazardous levels. **Lotic** (flowing) **systems**, such as rivers and streams, vary in their rate of flow. But even the slowest-flowing rivers purge their pollutants in a matter of a few weeks, unless of course the supply of pollutants is constant or spread evenly along its banks, as is common along midwestern rivers. The time or the distance of flow required for a river to recover depends on the size of the river, the flow rate, and the volume of wastes dumped into it.

As shown in Figure 20-2, lakes consist of three zones: (1) the **littoral zone**, the shallow waters along the shore where rooted vegetation (such as cattails and arrowheads) may grow; (2) the **limnetic zone**, the open water that sunlight penetrates and where phytoplankton such as algae live; and (3) the **profundal**, or deep, zone into which sunlight does not penetrate.

Lakes can also be divided into temperature zones (Figure 20-3). The upper, warm water is called the **epilimnion**. The deeper, cold water forms the **hypolimnion**, and the transition zone between the two is called the **thermocline** or **metalimnion**.

Lakes go through an annual cycle, during which surface and deeper waters are exchanged. In the fall, the air temperature begins to drop, and the surface water becomes colder than the water below. When the surface water reaches 4° C (40° F), it becomes heavier than the warmer water below and sinks to the bottom, causing the lake waters to turn over.

Figure 20-2
The three ecological zones of a lake.

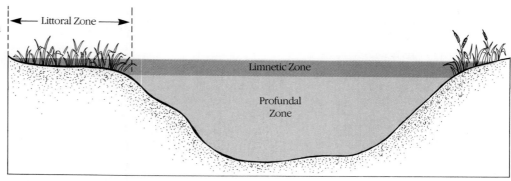

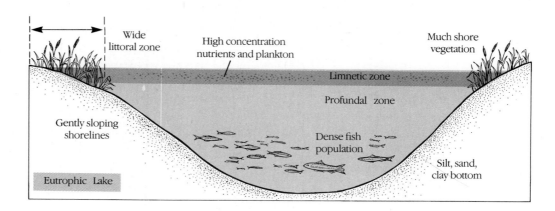

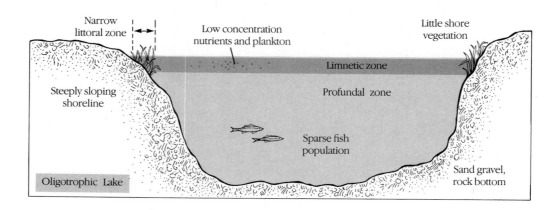

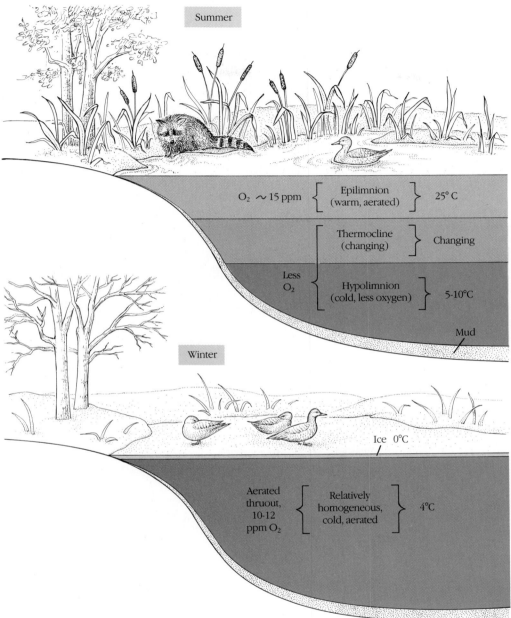

Figure 20-3
The three thermal zones of a lake.

In the spring, the lake turns over again. Water expands when it freezes, which is why it floats. As ice melts, it warms from 0° C (32° F); when the meltwater is at 4° C, it becomes denser than the water below and then sinks to the bottom, causing another turnover. The seasonal turnover of lakes provides oxygen-rich water to the lake's bottom, allowing life to survive in the profundal zone. With these few basics in mind, let's look at water pollution.

Types of Water Pollution

Nutrient Pollution and Eutrophication

Rivers, streams, and lakes contain many organic and inorganic nutrients needed by the plants and animals that live in them. In higher than normal concentrations they become pollutants.

Organic Nutrients   Organic compounds are found in unpolluted water, but generally in small quantities; these compounds are an important food source for aquatic bacteria and fungi. Feedlots, municipal sewage treatment plants, and industries such as paper mills and meat-packing plants are major producers of organic water pollutants.

Naturally occurring bacteria break down organic molecules during aerobic respiration. In unpolluted streams the small amount of organic matter limits bacterial growth. In streams polluted by organics, however, bacterial growth is accelerated. In such instances, the bacteria consume oxygen dissolved in the water and may deplete it entirely (Figure 20-4). As oxygen levels drop, fish and other aquatic

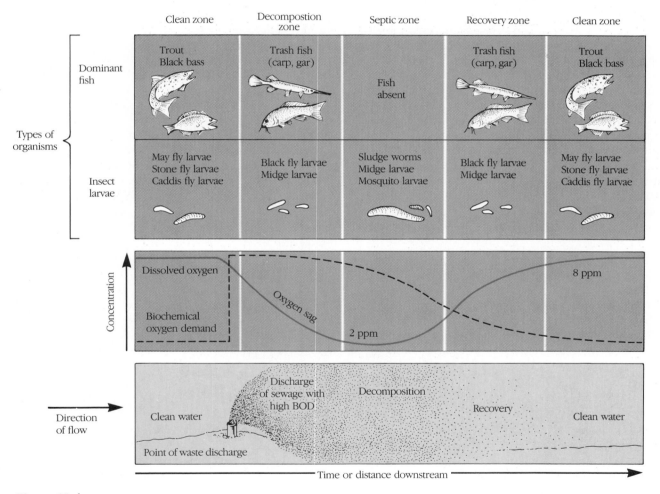

Figure 20-4
The oxygen sag curve. Oxygen levels and biochemical oxygen demand are shown below a point source of organic nutrients.

organisms perish. Trout and bass, which require high levels of oxygen, are eliminated first. Leeches, catfish, and carp can survive if dissolved oxygen levels do not fall too drastically. If oxygen levels continue to fall, only a few hardy aquatic worms can survive. Further bacterial decay of the organic pollutants, at this point, takes place by anaerobic bacteria, which produce foul-smelling and toxic methane and hydrogen sulfide gases.

As the organic matter is depleted, oxygen levels return to normal, and rivers recover, or self-purify (Figure 20-4). Several important points should be emphasized: (1) When numerous sources of organic pollutants are found along the course of a river, recovery may be impossible. (2) Dissolved oxygen levels are replenished by oxygen from the air and by photosynthesis occurring in aquatic plants. (3) Oxygen replacement is generally quite slow unless the water is turbulent. (4) Oxygen depletion in rivers and streams occurs more readily in the hot summer months than at any other time of year because stream flow in the summer is generally lower, and organic pollutant concentrations are higher. In addition, increased water temperatures speed up bacterial decay. (5) Natural organic pollution can occur during the fall when leaves fall and begin to decay in small streams, temporarily overwhelming them and seriously depleting their oxygen. (6) Lakes recover from organic pollutants, but usually much more slowly than rivers.

The organic nutrient concentration in streams is measured by determining the rate at which oxygen is depleted from a test sample. Polluted water is saturated with oxygen and kept in a closed bottle for five days; during this period bacteria degrade the organic matter and consume the oxygen. The amount of oxygen remaining after five days gives a measurement of the organic matter present: the more polluted a sample, the less oxygen is left. This standard measurement is called the **biochemical oxygen demand**, or **BOD**. Because certain chemical pollutants may also react directly with oxygen, depleting it, a measure called **chemical oxygen demand** is also used. This takes into account the total depletion of oxygen in polluted water and is used to give a complete and more accurate picture of oxygen consumption.

Immediately downriver from a sewage treatment plant or meat-packing plant, the BOD is high, but as the bacteria consume the oxygen, the BOD drops (Figure 20-4). The legal standard for dissolved oxygen, which was set to sustain most forms of aquatic life, is 5 milligrams per liter of water. In the United States, about 5% of the water samples taken in a given year violate this standard.

Inorganic Plant Nutrients Whereas organic nutrients nourish bacteria, certain inorganic nutrients stimulate the growth of aquatic plants. These include nitrogen, phosphorus, iron, sulfur, sodium, and potassium.

Nitrogen, in the form of ammonia and nitrates, and phosphorus, in the form of phosphates, are often limiting factors for populations of algae and other plants. Consequently, if levels become high, plant growth can go wild, choking lakes and rivers with thick mats of algae or dense growths of aquatic plants. In freshwater lakes and reservoirs, phosphate is usually the limiting nutrient for plant growth. Marine waters are usually nitrate-limited.

Excessive plant growth impairs fishing, swimming, navigation, and recreational boating. In the fall most of these plants die and are degraded by aerobic bacteria, which can deplete dissolved oxygen, killing aquatic organisms. As oxygen levels drop, anaerobic bacteria resume the breakdown and produce noxious products. Thus, inorganic nutrients ultimately create many of the same problems that organic nutrients do, except that the drop in dissolved oxygen is delayed until the fall.

Inorganic fertilizers from croplands are the major source of plant nutrients in fresh waters. When highly soluble fertilizers are used in excess, as much as 25% may be washed into streams and lakes by the rain. More careful use could greatly reduce this problem.

Laundry detergents are the second most important source of inorganic nutrient pollution in the United States. Many detergents contain synthetic phosphates, called tripolyphosphates (TPPs). TPPs constitute about half the weight of modern detergents (except low-phosphate ones). They soften the water and keep dirt in suspension until the water can be flushed out of the washing machine. Highly water soluble, TPPs support aquatic algae, causing sudden spurts in growth, or **blooms**.

Nearly 60% of the U.S. population lives in soft-water regions, where soap-based cleansing agents work as well as detergents. In the hard-water regions, harmless substitutes for TPPs can be used. For example, lime soap dispersing agents have been used in bar soaps for years and could easily be used for laundry detergents.

The phosphate standard to prevent the growth of nuisance plants is .1 milligram per liter of water. In 1980, 48% of all U.S. rivers and streams violated this standard,

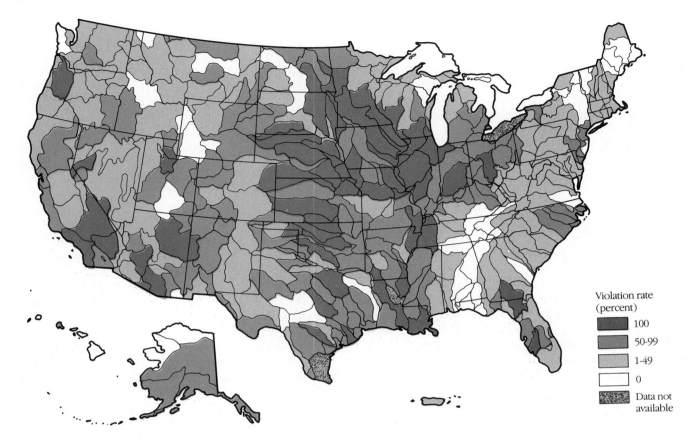

Figure 20-5
Phosphorus violation rates in United States rivers.

a rate that has remained constant since the early 1970s. Areas of most frequent violation are shown in Figure 20-5. Many rivers have shown dramatic declines in the violation rate, even though the overall violation rate remains high.

Eutrophication and Natural Succession Lakes in undisturbed watersheds receive small quantities of inorganic nutrients which are washed from the land or supplied by rainfall. The level of these nutrients becomes excessive when watersheds are disturbed by lumbering or farming or when major pollutant sources such as sewage treatment plants are built.

The natural accumulation of nutrients in lakes is called **natural eutrophication**. Eutrophication (literally, "good

nourishment") contributes to **natural succession**, the gradual conversion of a clean lake into a cloudy lake, then a swamp, and eventually dry land (Chapter 5). Under normal conditions natural succession takes hundreds of years, as sediment from natural sources is deposited in lakes. Accelerated erosion, caused by human activities, and **cultural eutrophication**, resulting from inorganic nutrients released from farms, feedlots, and sewage treatment plants, speed up the process (Figure 20-6).

Not all lakes are susceptible to eutrophication. Deep lakes that lack plant nutrients (*oligotrophic,* or poorly nourished, lakes) tend to be immune to sediment and nutrient pollution. The most vulnerable lakes are generally shallow and therefore easily fill with sediment. As nutrients accumulate in these lakes, littoral-zone plants

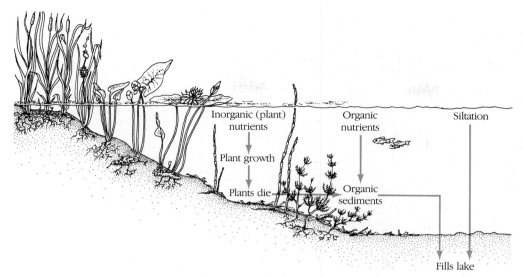

Figure 20-6
Contributions of inorganic and organic nutrients and sediment to succession of a lake.

proliferate. Heavy algal growth and frequent summer stagnation with a drop in oxygen levels are common.

The prospect for culturally eutrophic lakes is not as dim as once believed; if nutrient inflow is greatly reduced or stopped, a lake may make a slow comeback. As an example, Lake Washington near Seattle became eutrophic after decades of poor management. Millions of gallons of treated and untreated sewage were dumped into the lake, turning it into a putrid, rust-colored (due to algae) eyesore. In 1968 local communities began to divert their wastes to Puget Sound, an arm of the sea with a greater capacity to assimilate the wastes. Lake Washington began a slow recovery.

Eutrophication is the most widespread problem in U.S. lakes. Today, seven out of eight lakes are experiencing accelerated eutrophication. Nearly all receive wastes from industry and municipalities, but even if these sources were eliminated, only half of the lakes would improve because of a continued inflow of sediment and nutrients from nonpoint sources.

Infectious Agents

Water may be polluted by pathogenic (disease-causing) bacteria, viruses, protozoans, and parasites. Waterborne infectious diseases are a problem of immense proportions in the less developed countries of Africa, Asia, and Latin America. They were once the major water pollutants of developed nations before the widespread adoption of sewage treatment plants and facilities to disinfect drinking water.

The major sources of infectious agents are (1) untreated or improperly treated sewage, (2) animal wastes in fields and feedlots beside waterways, (3) meat-packing and tanning plants that release untreated animal wastes, and (4) some wildlife species that transmit waterborne diseases. The major infectious diseases include viral hepatitis, polio, typhoid fever, amebic dysentery, botulism, cholera, schistosomiasis, salmonellosis, and primary amebic meningoencephalitis.

Waterborne infectious disease is uncommon in the United States, not only because of widespread disinfection of municipal sewage but also because of vigilant monitoring of water quality. Measuring the actual level of each pathogenic organism is costly and time-consuming. Therefore, water quality control personnel routinely monitor *coliform bacteria,* naturally occurring, harmless bacteria found in the human intestine and human feces. Coliform levels in water samples give an indication of how much fecal contamination has occurred. The higher the coliform count, the more likely it is that the water contains some pathogenic agent from fecal contamination.

In 1980 one-third of all measurements taken in the 5 million kilometers (3 million miles) of U.S. rivers and

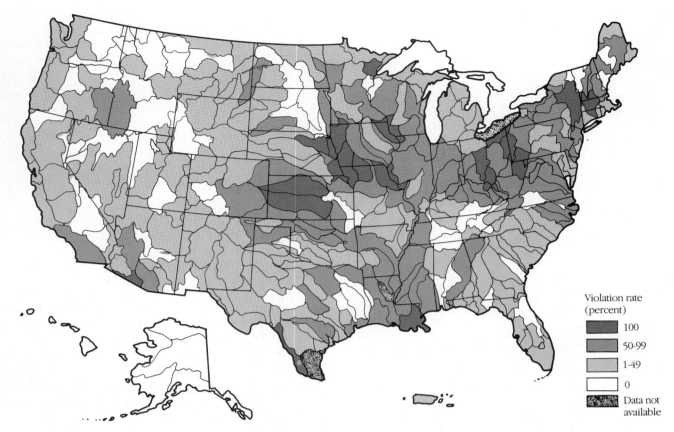

Figure 20-7
Violations of fecal coliform standards in United States rivers.

streams violated the coliform standard for safe swimming. This rate has remained more or less constant since the early 1970s. Figure 20-7 shows areas in frequent violation of the standard.

Toxic Organic Water Pollutants

About 10,000 synthetic organic compounds are in use today in the United States. Many of these find their way into the water, creating what may be the country's most important water pollution problem.

The reasons for concern over these pollutants are several: (1) Many toxic organic compounds are nonbiodegradable or are so slowly degraded that they persist in the ecosystem. (2) Some are magnified in the food web (Chapter 18). (3) Some may cause cancer in humans; others are converted into carcinogens when they react with chlorine used to disinfect water. (4) Some kill fish and other aquatic organisms. (5) Some are nuisances, giving water and fish an offensive taste or odor.

Unfortunately, our knowledge of the effects of numerous synthetic organics, which are often found in low concentrations with scores of others, is rudimentary. Reports of diseases traceable to a single chemical are few; but many experts warn that long-term effects such as cancer may be inevitable. Many American rivers have been polluted by toxic organics, but a lack of monitoring data for most of them makes it impossible to estimate how widespread the problems are or to determine whether conditions are getting better or worse.

Polychlorinated biphenyls (PCBs), used for many years as insulation in electrical capacitors and transformers, are among a multitude of newly recognized toxic organic water pollutants. Our first awareness of their effects came in 1968, when 1000 Japanese became severely ill after eating rice accidentally contaminated by PCBs. In the developed countries, millions of pounds have been released into the environment.

PCB production has been banned in Japan and sharply curtailed in the United States, but because PCBs are resistant to biological degradation, they will remain in the water and bottom sediments for decades. Making matters worse, PCBs are magnified in the food chain (see Essay 20-1).

Phenols are fairly common toxic organic water pollutants, especially in the rivers of the East and Midwest. Although phenols are produced from rotting vegetation and sewage treatment plants, industry is the major source. Iron and steel factories, coking operations, chemical plants, oil refineries, and coal and wood distillation facilities are the top producers.

Phenols are toxic compounds that kill fish and other aquatic organisms. The toxicity of phenols is increased by warm water, increased salinity, and low levels of oxygen. Chlorinated phenols are a well-known source of odor and taste problems in water and fish.

Toxic Inorganic Water Pollutants

Inorganic water pollutants encompass a wide range of chemicals, including metals, acids, and salts from a diverse array of sources.

Most states in the United States report that toxic metals, such as mercury and lead, are a major water pollution problem. Metals come from industrial discharge, urban run-off, mining, soil erosion, sewage effluents, air pollution fallout, and many natural sources. Surveys of drinking water in the United States show many samples with excessive quantities of copper, iron, zinc, manganese, and lead, coming from water pipes and from polluted ground and surface waters. Some water may be polluted by natural sources.

Mercury   One of the more common and potentially most harmful toxic metals is mercury. In the 1950s mercury was thought to be an innocuous water pollutant, although it was known to have been hazardous to miners and nineteenth-century hatmakers, who frequently developed tremors, or "hatter's shakes," and lost hair and teeth from mercury poisoning.

In the 1950s an outbreak of mercury poisoning in Japan raised awareness of the hazard. Residents who ate seafood from Minamata Bay that had been contaminated with methyl mercury developed numbness of the limbs, lips, and tongue and lost muscle control. Deafness, blurring of vision,

clumsiness, apathy, and mental derangement also occurred. Of 52 reported cases, 17 people died and 23 were permanently disabled.

Methyl mercury (organic mercury) is a potent toxin that acts primarily on the brain, affecting all age groups. (Inorganic mercury is far less dangerous.) Low levels of methyl mercury that are not toxic to adults may cause birth defects such as mental retardation and cerebral palsy.

Mercury is a byproduct of manufacturing the plastic vinyl chloride. It is also emitted in aqueous wastes of the chemical industry and incinerators, power plants, laboratories, and even hospitals. Worldwide, about 10,000 metric tons (11,000 tons) of mercury is released into the air and water each year. In 1980 over two-thirds of water samples in the United States exceeded the national standard for safe drinking water.

In streams and lakes inorganic mercury is converted into dimethyl and methyl mercury by aerobic bacteria. Dimethyl mercury evaporates from water; methyl mercury remains in the bottom sediments and is slowly released into the water, where it enters organisms in the food chain and is biologically magnified.

In 1970 the U.S. Food and Drug Administration temporarily banned canned swordfish in the United States because 80% of the samples exceeded federal mercury standards. Mercury contamination has also been a major problem in the Great Lakes.

Nitrates and Nitrites   Nitrates and nitrites are common water inorganic pollutants. **Nitrates** come from septic tanks, barnyards, heavily fertilized crops, and sewage treatment plants and are converted to toxic **nitrites** in the intestines of humans.

Nitrites combine with the hemoglobin in red blood corpuscles and form methemoglobin, which has a reduced oxygen-carrying capacity. Nitrites can be fatal to humans, especially infants younger than three months. Serious and sometimes fatal infant poisonings have been reported from drinking untreated well water with nitrates greater than 10 milligrams per liter. Over 2000 cases of infant nitrite poisoning, about 160 of which resulted in death, have been reported in Europe and North America in the last 40 years. Most poisonings occurred in rural areas, where solid wastes from septic tanks and farmyards had contaminated private wells.

Salts   Sodium and calcium chloride salts are used on winter roads to melt snow, especially in the eastern United States. Melting snow carries the salts into streams and

Essay 20-1

Mussel Watch

Mussel watching is not a new hobby for those too sedentary to watch birds; rather, it is an EPA program to monitor water quality by studying contamination in mussels and oysters along the nation's coasts. Mollusks accumulate many pollutants and are therefore an excellent indicator organisms for water pollution studies.

Each year oysters and mussels are taken by EPA scientists from over 100 locations in the United States. Tissue samples are examined for the presence of six heavy metals, two polychlorinated biphenyls, two breakdown products of DDT, hydrocarbons from the petroleum industry, and certain radioactive substances.

The study so far has shown that PCBs are found in high concentrations in many locations along the East and West coasts and that pesticides appear to be a more serious problem in sites off southern California than elsewhere. Little change has occurred in the water quality of coastal waters since the project began in 1976.

California, with over 1750 kilometers (1100 miles) of shoreline, has added its own mussel watch program with about 40 stations in estuaries and coastal waters. The state surveys show heavy contamination by metals at eight stations and high levels of oil pollution along the entire coast, especially in the south. Surveys also show that DDT byproducts and PCBs are on the decline.

---

groundwater. Uncovered storage piles of salt are another important source.

Salts in roadside soil can kill salt-sensitive plants such as New England's sugar maples. In surface waters salt can kill the salt-intolerant organisms, allowing salt-tolerant species to thrive. But the fluctuations in the flow of salt lead to varying concentrations, so that neither salt-tolerant nor salt-intolerant organisms can survive.

Other sources of salts include brine from oil-drilling operations (see Chapter 13) and certain agricultural practices such as the summer fallow system, in which fields are left unplanted to replenish soil moisture content. Here, rainwater may leach the soil of salts and deposit them in surface waters, especially ponds (Figure 20-8).

Two easily implemented solutions to salt pollution exist. The first is to use less salt, a strategy employed in many eastern states. Second, salt storage piles can be covered to prevent leaching by rainwater (and to save salt).

Acids   Acids may enter water from acid precipitation (Chapter Supplement 19-2), underground coal mines (Chapter 13), and various industrial sources. Industries use sulfuric acid to cleanse metals such as steel. The wastewater may then be discharged into streams.

Acids remain a problem in many parts of the United States and throughout northern Europe. Now that many industries have reduced their discharge of acids, controls on acid precipitation and underground coal mines are needed.

Chlorine   Chlorine is a highly reactive inorganic chemical commonly used (1) to kill bacteria in drinking water, (2) to destroy potentially harmful organisms in treated wastewater released from sewage treatment plants into streams, and (3) to kill algae, bacteria, fungi, and other organisms that grow inside and clog the pipes of the cooling system of power plants. Because such **biological fouling** can temporarily close down a power plant, operators tend to apply chlorine rather generously. Wastewater treatment plants and drinking water purification plants apply chlorine constantly.

The impact is most severe where chlorine is used to control biological fouling, because concentrations are high. Streams receiving intermittent doses of chlorine from power plants are often devoid of fish. Chlorine may reduce algal reproduction by 70% in seawater.

Chlorine released from sewage treatment plants may also have a severe impact on fish. Hypochlorite and chloramines—two major chlorine byproducts—are highly toxic and may eliminate fish from streams below the plants. Salmon and oysters are the most sensitive species.

Chlorinated organic compounds are produced during chlorination of wastewater and may show up in drinking water downstream. Many of these are known carcinogens and teratogens. Epidemiological studies indicate, however, that the rates of certain cancers (liver, intestinal tract) are only slightly elevated in populations consuming water contaminated by these compounds. Chlorinated compounds from wastewater treatment plants find their way

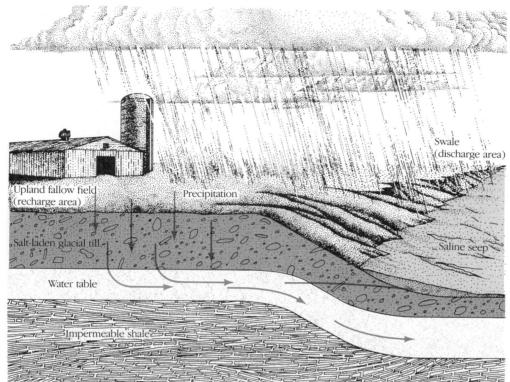

Labels in figure: Swale (discharge area); Upland fallow field (recharge area); Precipitation; Salt-laden glacial till; Saline seep; Water table; Impermeable shale

into our drinking water but apparently play an insignificant role in cancer.

Sediment

Sediment, the leading water pollutant in the United States, is a byproduct of silviculture (Chapter 11), agriculture and ranching (Chapter 8), mining (Chapters 13 and 16), and construction of roads and buildings. Agriculture increases erosion rates 4 to 8 times above normal. Poor construction and mining may increase the rate of erosion by 10 to 200 times. Sediment destroys spawning and feeding grounds for fish, reduces fish and shellfish populations, destroys deep pools in rivers used as resting spots for fish, smothers eggs and fish fry, fills in lakes and streams, and decreases light penetration, killing plants.

The deposition of sediment in lakes speeds up natural succession. Filling in of stream beds, or **streambed aggradation**, results in a gradual widening of the channel, and as streams become wider, they become shallower. Water temperature may rise, lowering the dissolved oxygen and making streams more vulnerable to organic pollutants that deplete oxygen. Streambed aggradation also makes streams more susceptible to flooding. Sediment can fill

shipping channels, which must then be dredged. In the United States, over 2000 reservoirs have been filled in by sediment. Hydroelectric equipment may be worn out by sediments. Finally, some pollutants such as pesticides, nitrogen, and phosphorus from agricultural fertilizers and pathogenic organisms are frequently bound to sediment. This extends their lifetime and their effects.

Sediment pollution can be checked, even eliminated, by good land management, as described in Chapters 9 and 12.

Thermal Pollution

Rapid or even gradual changes in water temperature brought about by human activities can change the aquatic ecosystem. For example, some dams release deep, cold waters into streams. This impairs reproduction and eliminates native warm-water fish.

When industries use water for cooling, they create thermal pollution. The electric power industry uses about 75% of all cooling water in the United States, or about 9 billion liters (2.4 billion gallons) per day (Figure 20-9). Steel mills, refineries, and paper mills also use large amounts of water for cooling.

Figure 20-9
The cooling system of an electric power plant and its effects on surface waters and organisms.

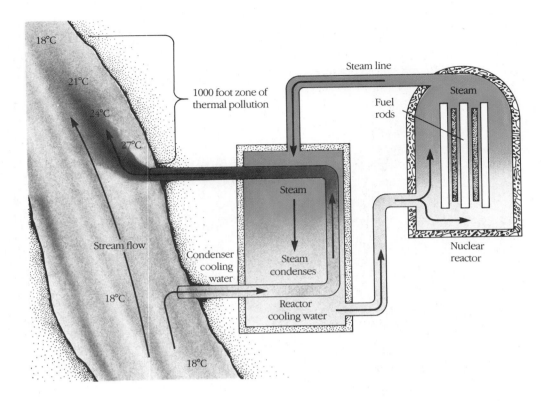

Small amounts of heat have no serious effect on the aquatic ecosystem; but large quantities can kill heat-intolerant plants and animals outright, harming animals dependent upon the aquatic food chain. Elimination of heat-intolerant species may allow heat-tolerant species to take over. These are usually less desirable species.

Thermal pollution lowers the dissolved oxygen content of water, at the same time increasing the metabolic rate of aquatic organisms. Because metabolism requires oxygen, some species may be eliminated entirely if the water temperature rises 10° C (18° F). At the Savannah River nuclear power plant in Georgia the number of rooted plant species and turtles was at least 75% lower in ponds receiving hot water than in ponds of normal temperature. The number of fish species was reduced by one-third.

Sharp changes in water temperature cause **thermal shock**, a sudden death of fish and other organisms that cannot escape the temperature change. This occurs when new plants open or when plants shut down for short periods for repair. The latter change can devastate heat-tolerant species that inhabit artifically warmed waters. Aquatic life cannot adapt to sudden, unpredictable temperature changes.

Fish spawn and migrate in response to changes in water temperature. Heated water, therefore, may interfere with spawning or with migrations. Water temperature influences the survival and early development of aquatic organisms. For instance, trout eggs may not hatch if the water is too warm. In some other species, growth may be accelerated by warm waters, as is true for bass, yellow-bellied slider turtles, and frogs. This acceleration alters the life cycle with devastating results. Frogs, for instance, may leave the water in the spring earlier than normal. If the insects they feed on have not yet emerged or if the weather is still unsuitable, they may die. Breeding seasons can also be extended in heated water, so young may be produced too late in the season for survival.

Thermal pollution can increase the susceptibility of aquatic organisms to parasites, certain toxins, and pathogens. Similarly, higher water temperatures increase the lethality of acids, salts, and some toxic chemicals.

Thermal pollution not severe enough to kill a species directly can eliminate its food source. The aquatic food web is especially hard hit by shifts in the phytoplankton.

Thermal pollution can be put to good use. One ingenious use of waste hot water is the cultivation of oysters in lagoons, as is done in Long Island Sound and in Japan. Using warm water from power plants accelerates growth and cuts the time to harvest by more than half.

Partially treated sewage from municipal treatment plants and hot water from power plants could be put into cooling ponds to create a nutrient-rich environment for raising shrimp, fish, and algae. However, shutdowns might jeopardize freshwater and saltwater cultures, and toxic metals and chlorine compounds emitted from cooling systems could accumulate in fish and shellfish.

Hot water could be used for heating buildings near the source or for desalination of brackish water or saltwater. Hot water could be used for crop irrigation or to protect fruit trees from frost. But these uses are possible for only part of the year.

Groundwater Pollution

Many pollutants are present at much higher concentrations in groundwater than they are in the most contaminated surface supplies. Many of these compounds are tasteless and odorless at concentrations believed to pose a threat to human health.

In 1979 one-third of Massachusetts' 351 communities were found to have contaminated groundwater. In North Reading, levels of trichloroethylene (TCE, a toxic degreaser) were recorded at 900 parts per billion in wells that supplied one-third of the town's people. The state's allowable level for TCE is 10 ppb.

The major groundwater contaminants are chloride, nitrates, heavy metals, and hydrocarbons. Of special interest are low-molecular-weight chlorinated hydrocarbons, because many are carcinogenic in humans or animals. Some medical experts suggest that there is no threshold level for these compounds and that many may act synergistically. Because of the great number of contaminants, budget cuts in the early 1980s, and growing responsibilities in other areas, the EPA has not issued standards for most groundwater pollutants.

About 4.5 trillion liters (1.2 trillion gallons) of contaminated water seeps into the ground in the United States every day from septic tanks, cesspools, petroleum exploration and development, municipal and industrial landfills, agriculture, and surface waste impoundments (Figure 20-10). The most significant source is the disposal of industrial wastes at industrial impoundments (evaporation ponds) and solid waste disposal sites, discussed in Chapter 22.

The rate and extent of groundwater pollution is determined by many factors. For instance, soil lying over an aquifer acts as a filter. Bacteria may contribute to this filtering by degrading some organic pollutants. But continuing disposal of hazardous chemicals may overwhelm the natural filtering mechanism.

Because groundwater generally moves slowly through an aquifer, it may take years for water polluted in one location to appear in another. Additionally, once an aquifer is contaminated, the pollutants may remain for centuries. Aquifers polluted with brine from oil wells, for example, may take 250 years to cleanse themselves.

Figure 20-10
Contaminated surface water can reach groundwater. In December 1978 U.S.D.A. officials sprayed the area of George Neary's ranch in Chico, California. The water supply and grasses in the area were contaminated. The rancher lost one-eighth of his adult cattle and 600 aborted calves. Total damage was estimated at $1.1 million.

Detection of groundwater pollution is costly and time-consuming. Numerous deep wells must be drilled for sampling. In addition, sophisticated chemical analyses need to be made, which requires the use of expensive instruments.

Groundwater supplies one-fourth of the water in the United States, and use has been growing at a rate of about 5.6% per year to meet the needs of agriculture (the biggest user), industries, and cities. Prevention, as always, is the cheapest way to protect groundwater. Better treatment of wastes, discussed in Chapter 22, is an important alternative. To reclaim polluted aquifers, it may be necessary to pump contaminated groundwater to the surface, purify it, and then return it to the aquifer. In June 1983 the Aerojet Corporation of Sacramento, California, began withdrawing 6.4 million liters (1.7 million gallons) of water a day from aquifers it had contaminated with freon-113, dichlorethylene, and tetrachlorethylene. Projects like this invariably cost millions of dollars more than prevention, but they are needed to save important groundwater supplies.

Water Pollution Control

Legal Controls

The first substantive water pollution legislation in the United States came in 1948 with the passage of the *Water Pollution Control Act*. This law provided low-interest federal loans to build sewage treatment plants and small grants to pay for planning water pollution control projects. In 1956 the *Federal Water Pollution Control Act,* commonly called the *Clean Water Act,* provided the first long-term control of water pollution. The act has been amended six times. The most important amendment, enacted in 1972, established a national goal of "zero discharge"—the complete elimination of all water pollutants from navigable waters in the United States by 1985. It also called on the EPA to establish effluent limitations for industries and made money available for building municipal sewage treatment plants.

Amendments in 1977 provided financial incentives to small communities to build innovative, alternative, less costly technologies to reduce pollution from municipal wastes. These amendments also directed the EPA to take a closer look at less common water pollutants, notably the toxic organic compounds.

From 1972 to 1981 Congress authorized the expenditure of approximately $40 billion to finance wastewater treatment plants. As of September 1981, 4000 plants had been put in operation; 6200 plants were scheduled to begin operation between 1981 and 1983.

Progress in cleaning up the country's waters has been slow because of continued population growth and expansion of agriculture and other nonpoint pollution sources. Still, the Clean Water Act and its amendments have been quite successful. About three-fourths of the major sewage treatment plants built with federal support meet the EPA's effluent guidelines. Had they not been built, U.S. waterways would be in far worse shape. The chemical and paper industries have made impressive strides in cleaning up their effluents.

To date most efforts in the United States and abroad have been aimed at point-source pollution, especially by building sewage treatment plants. However, large-capacity sewage treatment plants have often encouraged urban and suburban growth. In such cases urban and suburban runoff may offset the gains made by treatment plants. Thus, water quality may not improve in areas experiencing rapid growth. Control of nonpoint sources will be the next major step in pollution control. Agricultural and urban runoff will probably be targeted first, but the Clean Water Act does not yet give the EPA authority to regulate nonpoint sources.

A number of states have passed legislation to regulate nonpoint water pollution with federal assistance. Local governments have passed zoning ordinances to protect water quality from agricultural and urban runoff. Local soil conservation districts identify trouble spots and work with farmers. Illinois enacted a cost-sharing program to promote minimum tillage farming (Chapter 9) to reduce erosion and sediment pollution. In 1984, $20 million of federal money was earmarked for farmers to set aside and replant highly erodible land. The city of Winter Park, Florida, requires erosion control measures on all lakefront development.

New laws at all levels of government can help reduce pollution from all sources. Laws requiring terracing of steep roadbanks, revegetation, use of mulches to hold soil in place while grasses are growing, sediment ponds to collect runoff before it can reach streams, and porous pavements that soak up rain water could help. A special law for groundwater protection is probably necessary.

Each year Americans spend over $125 million to dredge sediment from harbors and riverways. Over $100 million a year is lost as hydroelectric dams and recreation sites become clogged with sediment. The annual cost of sedi-

▶▶▶ *Model Application 20-1*

Water Pollution—Multiple Cause and Effect

Despite two decades of work, water pollution remains a significant problem in the United States. Especially bothersome are sediment pollution and toxic organic pollutants.

Obviously, there is no simple answer to explain why water pollution continues to be such a large problem.

The Multiple Cause and Effect model, introduced in Chapter 2, shows us how to get at the roots of complex issues. Such an analysis not only helps us see the underlying causes but also helps us devise new, comprehensive solutions to current problems. The model shows that population, technology, politics, biology, religion, psychology, economics, and per capita consumption all contribute to environmental issues.

Question

Using the Multiple Cause and Effect approach, dissect the problem of toxic organic water pollutants and write a brief analysis of each factor. Listed below are some questions that will help you.

Step 1: Population

In what ways has the growth of population contributed to the growing problems of toxic organic water pollution? Would zero population growth reduce the problem? Is it, in your opinion, important to reduce the ultimate size of the world's population to help solve this problem?

Step 2: Per Capita Consumption

Where do the toxic organic pollutants come from? agriculture? silviculture? industrial production? Is U.S. consumption of these resources excessive compared with that of countries with a similar standard of living? In what ways could Americans cut back on resource demand to reduce toxic organic pollutants? How could such programs be implemented?

Step 3: Technology

In what ways could technological or scientific advances reduce toxic organic pollutants? In what ways do such advances make our problems worse? (Give some specific examples.)

Step 4: Politics

What laws have been passed to deal with toxic organic pollutants? In your view, are they effective? Why or why not? Who is in favor of stronger controls on toxic organic pollutants? Who is opposed to such controls? How are differences between these two groups worked out in the political arena?

Step 5: Economics

Control of toxic organic pollutants costs money. Do the benefits of control exceed these costs? What are the benefits of control, and how much are they worth?

Step 6: Psychology

The United States has spent a much larger amount of money on controlling air pollution than it has on water pollution. Are there any psychological reasons why? Today, economic concerns seem to outweigh environmental concerns such as the need for clean air and water. In what ways have the economic hard times of the 1980s contributed to this? How do the 1970s, when there was a flurry of environmental interest, compare psychologically with today?

Step 7: Biology

Look up the concept of biological imperialism in this book and discuss its role in current water pollution problems. How does biological magnification worsen the problem?

You have probably come up with a list of ideas about toxic organic pollutants that apply to many environmental problems. For instance: a large population with a high per capita consumption of food, produced with the aid of organic pesticides, is bound to have a problem with toxic organic pollutants, because spraying insecticides always results in contamination of surrounding areas. What other broad generalizations can you make?

Figure 20-11
A vast sewage treatment plant in Des Moines, Iowa.

ment damage is expected to increase to about $500 million a year in the near future, according to the U.S. Department of Agriculture, if sediment-control measures are not adopted throughout the country. Preventive technologies could save millions of dollars a year.

Control Technologies

The first sewage treatment plant in the United States was built in Memphis, Tennessee, in 1880; today, there are over 13,000 of them (Figure 20-11). Sewage entering a treatment plant contains pollutants from homes, hospitals, schools, and industry. It contains human wastes, paper, soap, detergent, dirt, cloth, food residues, microorganisms, and a variety of chemicals used for cleaning. In some cases water from storm drainage systems is mixed with municipal wastes to save the cost of building separate systems for each. Combined systems generally work well, but during storms, inflow may exceed plant capacity. Consequently, some untreated storm runoff and sewage are allowed to pass directly into waterways. Sewage treatment can take place in three stages: primary, secondary, and tertiary.

Primary Treatment Sewage arrives at the treatment plant and first passes through a series of grates and screens that remove large objects (Figure 20-12a). After filtration it enters settling chambers, where sand, organic sediment, dirt, and other solids settle out. Primary treatment removes

about 60% of the solid materials and about 30% of the oxygen-demanding organic wastes.

Secondary Treatment The secondary stage removes biodegradable organic wastes using biological methods. One common way is to pass the wastes through a **trickling filter**, where long pipes rotate slowly over a bed of stones (and sometimes bark), dripping wastes onto an artificial detritus food chain consisting of bacteria, protozoa, fungi, snails, worms, and insects (Figure 20-13). The bacteria and fungi consume the organics and, in turn, are consumed by protozoans. Snails and insects feed on the protozoans. Some inorganic nutrients are also removed.

An alternative method, the *activated sludge process* (Figure 20-12b), also relies on detritus consumers to degrade organic wastes. After primary treatment the sewage is pumped into a huge tank, where it is mixed for several hours with air bubbles and a bacteria-rich sludge. The bacteria consume the organic matter. After several hours of mixing, the mixture is pumped to a sedimentation tank, where the sludge settles out for reuse. Excess sludge is removed and disposed of.

In most municipalities liquid remaining after secondary treatment is chlorinated to kill potentially pathogenic viruses, bacteria, and protozoans.

As shown in Table 20-2, primary and secondary treatment remove 90% of the oxygen-demanding organic wastes and solids. Most of the phosphates, nitrates, salts, radioactive materials, and pesticides, however, remain in the

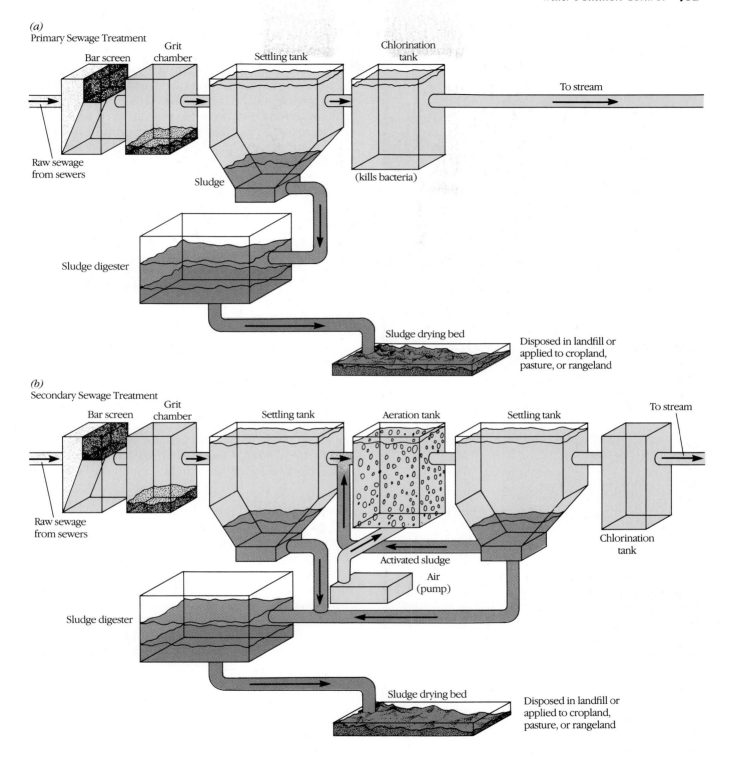

(a)
Primary Sewage Treatment

Bar screen

Grit chamber

Settling tank

Chlorination tank

To stream

Raw sewage from sewers

Sludge

(kills bacteria)

Sludge digester

Sludge drying bed

Disposed in landfill or applied to cropland, pasture, or rangeland

(b)
Secondary Sewage Treatment

Bar screen

Grit chamber

Settling tank

Aeration tank

Settling tank

To stream

Raw sewage from sewers

Activated sludge

Air (pump)

Chlorination tank

Sludge digester

Sludge drying bed

Disposed in landfill or applied to cropland, pasture, or rangeland

Figure 20-12
Primary and secondary sewage treatment facilities.

Figure 20-13
Trickle drip system. A detritus food chain consisting of bacteria and other microorganisms in the rock or bark bed of the system consumes organic matter, nitrates, and phosphates in the liquid sewage.

waste stream. Because most sewage treatment plants have only primary and secondary treatment facilities, excessive amounts of plant nutrients are continuously being added to waterways.

Table 20-2 Removal of Pollutants by Sewage Treatment Plants

| | Percentage Removed by Treatment | |
Substance	Primary	Primary and Secondary
Solids	60%	90%
Organic wastes	30	90
Phosphorus		30
Nitrate		50
Salts		5
Radioisotopes		0
Pesticides		0

Tertiary Treatment Many methods exist for removing the chemicals that remain after secondary treatment. The major tertiary methods are (1) *coagulation* and *sedimentation,* in which lime, alum, or salts of iron are added to precipitate inorganic chemicals; (2) *adsorption,* in which wastes are filtered through activated carbon, which removes chlorinated hydrocarbons; (3) *oxidation,* in which oxidizing agents (ozone and potassium permanganate) are used to oxidize and hence destroy organic contaminants; and (4) *reverse osmosis,* in which water passes through a membrane that is impermeable to dissolved ions.

Tertiary treatment plants are approximately twice as expensive to build and about four times as expensive to operate as secondary plants. Fortunately, there are cheaper options. For example, effluents can be transferred to holding ponds after secondary treatment. Algae and water hyacinths grown there consume the nitrates and phosphates. Certain aquatic plants such as duckweed can even absorb dissolved organic materials directly from the water. Algae and duckweed grown in such ponds can be harvested and converted into food for humans or livestock. In Burma, Laos, and Thailand, duckweed has been consumed by rural farmers for years. In Thailand, where the average protein yield of soybeans is about 300 kilograms per hectare, the approximate yield of protein from duckweed grown in ponds is about 2000 kilograms per hectare.

Water hyacinths and duckweed may also prove valuable in water pollution control, because they remove toxic metals from water. Consumption by humans and livestock, however, would have to be carefully monitored.

Land Disposal A final suggestion is the age-old process of **land disposal**. In ancient times land disposal of human sewage was commonplace; it is still practiced in many developing nations such as China and India. As the populations of developing countries grew and as they became more urbanized, this natural method of recycling wastes was gradually eliminated. Discussed in Chapter 12 as a means of recharging groundwater, land disposal uses the surface vegetation, soil, and soil microorganisms as a natural filter for many potentially harmful chemicals. Sewage can be piped to pastures, fields, and forests (Figure 20-14).

Organic matter in the effluent enriches the soil and improves its ability to retain water. Nitrates and phosphates are taken up by plants. The water supports plant growth and helps recharge aquifers. Crops nourished by effluents from treated sewage show a remarkable increase in yield. Hay fields sprayed with sewage are three times as productive as unsprayed fields.

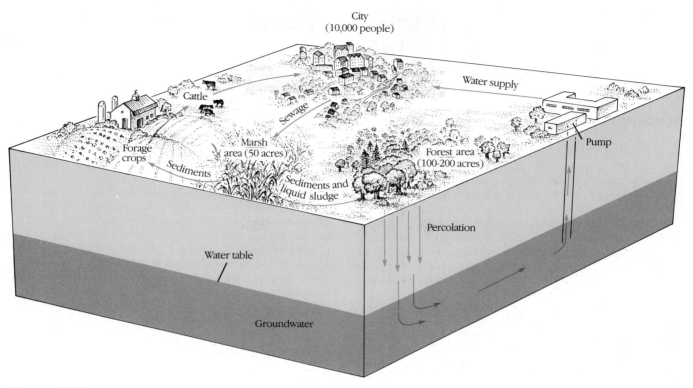

Figure 20-14

Land disposal of sewage helps fertilize farmlands and forests, reduce surface water
pollution, and replenish groundwater supplies.

This technique has some inherent problems. First, treated
sewage may still contain harmful bacteria, protozoans,
and viruses that could be incorporated in plants for human
or animal consumption or become airborne after the
effluent dries. In Switzerland and Germany sewage sludge
is heated to destroy potentially harmful organisms and
then applied to pastures and farmland. Alternatively, sewage sludge can be composted and allowed to decay before
being applied. The heat given off during composting kills
virtually all of the viruses, bacteria, and parasitic eggs.
Natural decay in compost piles also produces methane
gas, which if collected and burned provides additional
heat. Second, toxic metals (copper, cadmium, nickel, and
zinc) found in some sewage may accumulate in soils and
be taken up by plants and then by sheep or cattle. Metal-
contaminated sewage usually comes from industries. By
removing these polluters from the waste stream, the problem could be eliminated altogether. Third, transporting
the sewage to farms and forests would substantially increase
the cost of sewage treatment and eliminate some of the

incentive to treat it. Land disposal is no panacea, but it
could be a practical method in some areas, provided it is
carefully and continuously managed.

Personal Solutions

Personal efforts can improve our waterways. Reduced
population growth and reduced consumption of unnecessary goods can help cut down on water pollutants by
eliminating waste that ends up in municipal landfills as
well as the hazardous wastes generated during manufacturing. Waterless or composting toilets (Chapter 12) can
reduce the flow of human wastes to sewage treatment
plants; the composted wastes can be added safely to gardens, eliminating the need for synthetic fertilizer. Each of
us can use fewer chemicals in and around our home. The
use of synthetic fertilizers, insecticides, herbicides, bleaches,
detergents, disinfectants, and other household chmicals
can be lowered or eliminated. Finally we can use energy
more efficiently and cut energy demand.

It is astonishing with how little wisdom mankind can be governed, when that little wisdom is its own.

W. R. INGE

Summary

Water pollution is a global problem. Water pollutants come from *nonpoint* and *point* sources. The effects on aquatic systems depend, in large part, on whether polluted waters are *lentic* (standing) or *lotic* (flowing). Lentic systems (lakes and ponds) are generally more susceptible because of slow turnover.

The major water pollutants are organic nutrients, infectious agents, toxic organics, toxic inorganics, sediment, and heat. *Organic nutrients* come from feedlots, municipal sewage treatment plants, and industry. They serve as food for aerobic bacteria and cause proliferation of natural populations of aquatic bacteria, causing a drop in dissolved oxygen.

Two inorganic plant nutrients, nitrogen and phosphorus, are also major anthropogenic pollutants. Inorganic fertilizer and laundry detergents are the leading sources in the United States. Both cause excessive plant growth and clogging of navigable waterways. Bacterial decay of plants in the fall results in a drop in dissolved oxygen, which may suffocate fish and other organisms.

Water may contain pathogenic bacteria, viruses, protozoans, and parasites. Waterborne infectious diseases are a problem in developing nations. Untreated or improperly treated sewage, animal wastes, meat-packing wastes, and some wild species are the major sources. Although uncommon in developed countries, infectious agents are not altogether absent.

Toxic organic pollutants include a large number of chemicals, many of which are nonbiodegradable or only slowly degraded, are biologically magnified, and are carcinogenic in humans. Two of the major toxic organics are PCBs and phenols.

Toxic inorganic pollutants include a wide range of chemicals such as metals, acids, and salts. Most states report that toxic metals such as mercury and lead are major pollutants. Mercury can be converted into methyl and dimethyl mercury by aerobic bacteria. These forms are more toxic than inorganic mercury. Methyl mercury is magnified in the food chain.

Nitrates are common inorganic water pollutants coming from septic tanks, barnyards, heavily fertilized crops, and sewage treatment plants. They are converted to nitrites in the intestines of humans. In the blood, they combine with hemoglobin, reducing its oxygen-carrying capacity. They may be fatal, especially to children under three years old.

Salts used on roadways to melt snow and ice enters streams and lakes and can upset the ecological balance. Salt-sensitive trees along salted roads may also be killed as the salt water percolates down to the roots. Acids come from acid precipitation, underground coal mines, and various industries. Chlorine is used to kill bacteria in drinking water and treated sewage and to kill algae, fungi, bacteria, and other organisms that might clog pipes used to cool water in power plants and industry. When chlorine is used to control *biological fouling,* the buildup of organisms inside pipes, the impact is most severe, because concentrations are generally fairly high. Released into lakes and streams, chlorine may kill many aquatic organisms. Chlorine and chlorinated compounds in drinking water may cause cancer in humans, but the evidence is inconclusive at this time.

Sediment, the leading water pollutant in the United States, is a byproduct of silviculture, agriculture, ranching, mining, and construction of roads and buildings. Sediment destroys spawning and feeding grounds for fish, reduces fish and shellfish populations, destroys deep pools used for resting, smothers eggs and fish fry, fills in lakes and streams, and decreases light penetration, harming aquatic plants.

Thermal pollution refers to heating or cooling of water, both of which drastically alter the biota in a water body. Large quantities of heat can kill heat-sensitive organisms and harm others dependent on the aquatic ecosystem. Heat lowers the dissolved oxygen levels but increases the metabolic rate of organisms. Sudden changes in temperature bring about rapid death, *thermal shock.* Temperature changes can also interfere with migrations, spawning, and early development.

The concentration of pollutants in groundwater is often higher than it is in contaminated surface water supplies. Many of these chemicals are tasteless and odorless at concentrations believed to pose a threat to human health. The major groundwater pollutants are chloride, nitrates, heavy metals, and hydrocarbons. Because groundwater usually moves slowly through an aquifer, it may take years for pollution to show up in nearby locations. Additionally, once an aquifer is contaminated, the pollutants may remain for centuries.

The first major U.S. water pollution legislation was the Water Pollution Control Act (1948). It provided federal loans for the construction of sewage treatment plants. In 1956 the *Federal Water Pollution Control Act* was passed. A 1972 amendment established a national goal of zero discharge—the complete elimination of all water pollutants from navigable rivers by 1985. It also called on the EPA to establish effluent limitations for industries and provided funds for more sewage treatment plants.

Despite these advances, progress in cleaning up U.S. waters has been slow. Continued population growth, industrial growth, and agricultural expansion have negated much progress. Pollution from nonpoint sources often offsets gains at point sources, making it important that further controls be directed at them.

Discussion Questions

1. List the major types of water pollutants found in developing and developed nations.

2. Define the terms *point source* and *nonpoint source.* Give some examples of each and explain why nonpoint sources of water pollution are often more difficult to control than point sources.

3. Define the terms *lotic system* and *lentic system.* What are the three major ecological zones in lakes? Describe each one.

4. Explain why a lake "turns over" in the spring and fall and how this natural turnover benefits aquatic organisms.

5. Describe where organic nutrients come from, what effects they have on aquatic ecosystems, and how they can be controlled.

6. What are the inorganic plant nutrients, and how do they affect the aquatic environment?

7. Define the term *eutrophication.* Describe how inorganic and organic nutrients accelerate the natural succession of a lake.

8. What are the major sources of infectious agents in polluted water? How can they be controlled?

9. What dangers do synthetic organic water pollutants pose? List some of the common synthetic organic water pollutants.

10. What are some of the major inorganic water pollutants? How do they affect the aquatic environment and human populations?

11. Why is chlorine used in the treatment of human sewage and drinking water? What dangers does its use pose? How would you determine if the risks of chlorine use outweigh the benefits?

12. What are the major sources of sediment, and how can they be controlled? What are the costs and benefits of sediment control?

13. In what ways is thermal pollution good, and in what ways is it harmful? Describe ways to eliminate or reduce thermal pollution. What personal measures can you take?

14. If you were going to survey your state for groundwater pollution, how would you go about locating sources and taking measurements of groundwater?

15. What are the major sources of groundwater pollution? What factors determine whether a toxic waste disposal site or some other source will pollute groundwater? How can groundwater pollution be reduced or eliminated? What can you do?

16. Even though thousands of new wastewater treatment plants have been built in the United States, water quality in many areas has not improved. Why?

17. Be creative. List and discuss programs a state might develop to control nonpoint water pollution. Which ones might be the most cost-effective?

18. Describe primary and secondary wastewater treatment. What happens at each stage, and what pollutants are removed? Also list and discuss some tertiary treatment processes. Why aren't these used more often?

19. Debate the pros and cons of land disposal of wastewater.

20. Using the Multiple Cause and Effect model (Chapter 2), discuss reasons for worldwide water pollution. Which factors in the model seem to be the most important?

Suggested Readings

Barton, K. (1978). The Other Water Pollution. *Environment* 20(5): 12–20. Good overview of nonpoint water pollution.

Burmaster, D. E. (1982). The New Pollution: Groundwater Contamination. *Environment* 24(2): 6–13; 33–36. Good overview.

Clark, J. W., Viessman, W., and Hammer, M. J. (1977). *Water Supply and Pollution Control* (3rd ed.). New York: Harper and Row. Excellent.

Crites, R. W. (1984). Land Use of Wastewater and Sludge. *Environ. Sci. and Technol.* 18(5): 140A–147A. Technical review of land application of sewage.

Gibbons, J. W., and Sharitz, R. R. (1974). Thermal Alterations of Aquatic Ecosystems. *Amer. Scientist* 62: 660–670. Good review.

Halloway, T. (1978). Back from the Dead: The Restoration of the River Thames. *Environment* 20(5): 6–11. Interesting.

Hileman, B. (1982). The Chlorination Question. *Environ. Sci. and Technol.* 16(1): 15A–18A. Excellent overview.

Hillman, W. S., and Culley, D. D. (1978). The Uses of Duckweed. *Amer. Scientist* 66: 442–451. Excellent look at an alternative biotechnology.

Jolly, R. L., Gorchev, H., and Hamilton, D. H., Jr. (1978). *Water Chlorination. Environmental Impact and Health Effects* (Vols. 1 and 2). Ann Arbor, Mich.: Ann Arbor Science. Excellent collection of articles.

McWilliams, L. (1984). Groundwater Pollution in Wisconsin: A Bumper Crop Yields Growing Problems. *Environment* 26(4): 25–34. Excellent case study of groundwater pollution.

Pye, V. I. (1983). Groundwater contamination in the United States. *Science* 221: 713–718. Technical overview.

Regier, H. A., and Hartman, W. L. (1973). Lake Erie's Fish Community: 150 Years of Cultural Stress. *Science* 180: 1248–1255. Excellent case study.

U.S. Geological Survey (1984). National Water Summary—1983. *Hydrologic Events and Issues.* Washington, D. C.: U.S. Government Printing Office. Survey of current water quality problems.

Weaver, G. (1984). PCB Contamination in and Around New Bedford, Mass. *Environ. Sci. and Technol.* 18(1): 22A–27A. Technical review.

Wolman, A. (1977). Public Health Aspects of Land Utilization of Wastewater Effluents and Sludges. *Jour. Water Pollution Control Federation,* November: 2211–2218. Interesting article.

Zeitoun, I., and Reynolds, J. Z. (1978). Powerplant Chlorination. *Environ. Sci. and Technol.* 12(7): 780–783. Good review.

21

Personal and Occupational Pollution

It is more important to live well than it is to live long.

MANLY HALL

Air pollution, water pollution, radiation, hazardous wastes, and noise make up an impressive list of modern-day hazards. Although these hazards result from our own activities and the standard of living we have achieved, our exposure is considered more or less involuntary. Someone else controls the pollution at the nearby power plant. Someone else determines the rate at which chlorine compounds are released into streams from sewage treatment plants.

Two classes of pollutants have been ignored so far; these are the personal pollutants and the occupational pollutants. **Personal pollutants** include the harmful chemicals that we voluntarily introduce into our bodies such as cigarette smoke, alcohol, drugs, and food additives. **Occupational pollutants** are those contaminants we are exposed to at work. Of all of the various forms of pollution to which we are exposed, the combined effect of workplace and occupational pollution poses the largest threat to human health.

Smoking

Some Vital Statistics

Sir Walter Raleigh introduced tobacco to Europe. Even then, smoking met with resistance. King James I of England

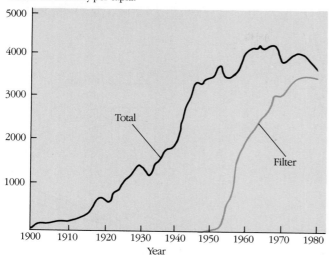

Number of cigarettes
consumed annually per capita

Figure 21-1
Per capita consumption of cigarettes by those over 18 in the United States, 1900–1980.

became incensed with his pipe-smoking subjects. "Have you not reason," he exhorted in 1603, "to be ashamed and to forbear this filthy novelty so basely grounded?"

In the United States today there are about 56 million cigarette smokers—one of every three persons over 18. In 1982 the average consumption for American adults was 187 packs, or about 3740 cigarettes a year (Figure 21-1). Total sales in 1983 were estimated to be $27 billion.

Smoking among adults appears to be on the decline in the United States. In 1965, 52.4% of the adult males and 34.1% of the adult females smoked, but in 1980, 38.3% of the males and 29.4% of the female population were smokers. The trend among teenagers is mixed. Among males 12 to 18 years old the percentage of smokers dropped from 17% to 11% from 1968 to 1979; in females of the same group it rose from 10% to 13%.

The image of smoking has changed drastically from the days of John Wayne and Humphrey Bogart (who both died of cancer). The first U.S. surgeon general's report on smoking, issued in 1964, identified it as a health hazard and stirred Congress to pass the *Federal Cigarette Labeling and Advertising Act* in 1965, which required manufacturers to print a warning label on cigarette packs. In 1970 the wording was strengthened to "Warning: The Surgeon General has determined that cigarette smoking is dangerous to your health." As a result of the act, cigarette ads were taken off radio and television. In 1983 the Senate Labor and Human Resources Committee pushed for a new, more explicit label for cigarettes. In 1984 Congress passed legislation calling for four new labels describing the effects of smoking.

Public resentment over cigarette smoking has risen in recent years. For a debate on smoking in public places see the Point/Counterpoint in this chapter.

Effects of Smoking on Health

In 1982, some 430,000 Americans died of cancer; about one-third of these cancers were caused by smoking. After several decades the evidence clearly shows that smoking causes a wide variety of illnesses beside cancer.

Lung Cancer Lung cancer is the most prevalent form of cancer among Americans. It is one of the few cancers that continues to increase (Figure 21-2). One of every four persons dying of cancer each year has lung cancer; 85% of these are caused by smoking.

The correlation between smoking and lung cancer was first made over 50 years ago. Since then, more than 40 studies on humans have substantiated the early work, showing that smokers in general are 10 times more likely to die from lung cancer than nonsmokers. Heavy smokers (more than 20 cigarettes a day) are 15 to 25 times more likely to die from lung cancer than nonsmokers. An American Cancer Society study shows that males who inhale slightly are 9 times more likely to contract lung cancer than nonsmokers, and deep inhalers are 17 times more likely. Smokers of filtered cigarettes generally have a lower lung cancer rate than smokers of unfiltered cigarettes.

Only 10% of the people found to have lung cancer are alive after five years; most die within the first year despite treatment because cancerous cells from the lung spread rapidly to the brain and lymphatic system. People who quit smoking gradually decrease their chances of getting lung cancer, but even 15 years after quitting they are twice as likely as nonsmokers to contract lung cancer.

Smoking-related lung cancer kills about 94,000 people each year in the United States, almost twice as many as are killed in auto accidents. Although no recent estimates are available, it was estimated in 1975 that lung cancer from smoking cost the nation about $3.8 billion in lost earnings and medical expenses.

Figure 21-2
Lung cancer in white males and females (*a*) and nonwhite males and females (*b*) by age group and period. Note the increase in recent times, especially in males.

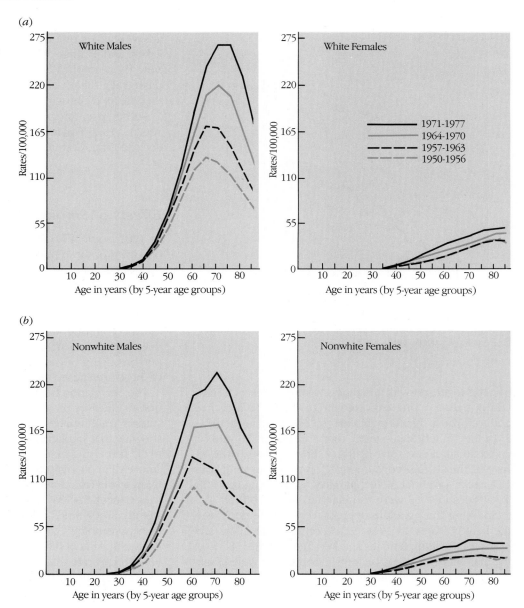

Other Cancers Cancer of the larynx, oral cavity, and esophagus have also been linked to cigarette smoking (Figure 21-3). Pipe and cigar smokers have about the same risk of contracting these cancers as cigarette smokers.

Cigarette smoking may also contribute to cancer of the urinary bladder, stomach, pancreas, and kidney, but the risk of developing these cancers is only slightly greater in smokers than in nonsmokers.

Infant Survival and Pregnancy Smoking affects pregnancies in a number of ways. For instance, babies of women who smoke are, on the average, smaller and approximately 200 grams (about half a pound) lighter than babies born to nonsmokers. Smoking also slightly increases the risk of spontaneous abortion, fetal death, and early infant death (Table 21-1). The more a woman smokes, the greater the probability of these effects. Up to

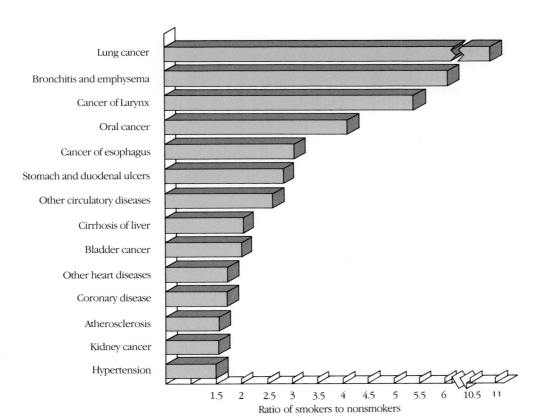

Figure 21-3
Increased ratio of smoker deaths from fourteen disorders. A smoker is 10.8 times as likely to die of lung cancer as a nonsmoker—108 smokers will die of lung cancer for every 10 nonsmokers in the general population.

Problem	Incidence among Nonsmokers	Incidence among Smokers	Unit of Measure
Spontaneous abortion	7.2	9.4	Per 100 pregnancies
Stillbirth	1.3	1.54	Per 100 births
Premature birth	33.0	65.0	Per 100 births
Early infant death Up to age 25[1]	12.1	16.1	Per 1000 live births
25–34[1]	12.6	13.2	
35 and over[1]	23.0	41.7	

Table 21-1 Smoking and Pregnancy

[1]Maternal age

14% of all premature births in the United States may be caused by maternal smoking. Some physicians maintain that smoking during pregnancy may impair physical growth, mental development, and behavior of children up to 11 years after birth.

Chronic Obstructive Lung and Cardiovascular Diseases   Smoking is a major cause of **chronic obstructive lung diseases**, which are characterized by restricted air flow. The two major types are bronchitis (irritation of the bronchi) and emphysema (breakdown of the air sacs in the lung). Patients usually have symptoms of both diseases.

Smoking greatly increases the likelihood that an individual will die from a chronic obstructive lung disease. In a 20-year study of British physicians, for example, the death rate was 3 per 100,000 for nonsmokers but from 38 to 88 per 100,000 for smokers, depending on daily tobacco consumption. Smokers also suffer more frequent colds

Table 21-2 Lung Cancer Risks of Smokers and Ex-Smokers

Study	Years since Smoking Stopped	Increased Risk as Compared with Nonsmokers
British physicians	1–4	16 times more likely
	5–9	6
	10–14	5
	Over 15	2
	Current smoker	14
Americans	1–4	18.8 times more likely
	5–9	7.7
	10–14	4.7
	15–19	4.8
	Over 20	2.1
	Current smoker	11.3

and other respiratory infections. They miss more days of work than nonsmokers.

Several studies have also shown that smoking increases the incidence of atherosclerosis (hardening of the arteries) and myocardial infarction (heart attacks).

Breaking the Habit

If the ambient air resembled the air inside a smoker's lungs, a state of national disaster would be proclaimed.

Tobacco smoke contains high concentrations of hundreds of harmful chemicals, including nitrogen oxides, sulfur dioxide, carbon monoxide, particulates, lead, tar, resins, nicotine, benzopyrene, cadmium, polonium-210, and nickel. Dozens of chemical components of cigarette smoke are carcinogenic (for example: polycyclic organic compounds such as benzopyrene, nitrosamines, nickel, cadmium, and polonium-210).

Many people attempt to give up the habit, but only about 20% to 30% succeed. The reason for the low success rate is that smoking is both addictive and enjoyable. To some, smoking may be a mild tranquilizer or a mild stimulant, depending on the amount of smoke inhaled and other factors. Smoking is also woven into the social fabric. Among teenagers and in some other circles it is taken as a sign of maturity or sophistication. Furthermore, the threat from smoking is not immediate. The distant but real risks to health are outweighed by personal gains in social acceptance. Smokers often express a distrust in official statistics. There are always 85-year-olds who have

smoked three packs a day for 50 years to support their contention that smoking isn't bad for their health.

The benefits of giving up smoking probably exceed the pleasures of smoking. Carbon monoxide levels in the blood drop within a day; symptoms of cough, mucus production, and shortness of breath disappear in a few weeks; the incidence of stillbirth and early infant death drops to normal in women who stop smoking by the fourth month of pregnancy; deterioration of lung function slows down; death rates from heart attack, bronchitis, and emphysema are lowered; and the risk of developing cancer of the lungs, larynx, and oral cavity declines (Table 21-2).

Voluntary and Involuntary Smokers

In an enclosed area tobacco smoke may increase the particulate and carbon monoxide concentrations well beyond the levels considered safe for public health. The "sidestream" smoke coming from the tip of a cigarette has a higher particulate level than the smoke inhaled through the filter. Because smokers freely mingle with nonsmokers, there is no such thing as a smoker or a nonsmoker, only voluntary (active) smokers and involuntary (passive) smokers (Figure 21-4).

Research in Greece, Japan, and the United States showed that nonsmoking wives of smokers had a significantly higher risk of lung cancer than nonsmoking wives of nonsmokers. The risk increased with the number of cigarettes their husbands smoked. In general, nonsmokers exposed for

Figure 21-4
Second-hand smoke is irritating to nonsmokers and may affect their health as well.

20 years or more had the same incidence of lung cancer as smokers of 11 cigarettes a day.

High carbon monoxide levels in smoke-filled rooms may cause one's attentiveness and cognitive function to deteriorate and may cause chest pain in a person with heart disease.

The incidence of upper respiratory disease is two times higher in children whose parents smoke than it is in children of nonsmoking parents. Their illnesses also last longer than those of children of nonsmoking parents.

Smoking is restricted in 36 of the United States, and it is increasingly viewed as a public transgression rather than a private freedom. In June 1983 the city of San Francisco passed an ordinance requiring private employers to provide reasonable accommodations for smokers and nonsmokers. Failure to comply can cost a company $500 per day in fines. In California alone at least 20 communities have restricted smoking in recent years. In Berkeley, for instance, no-smoking signs outnumber stop signs ten to one. San Diego requires restaurants that seat 20 or more people to provide no-smoking sections.

Minnesota leads the nation in controls on smoking. Its Clean Indoor Air Act bans smoking in banks, stores, offices, and virtually every public space—covering most buildings except bars and homes.

The Outlook for Smoking

The long-term prognosis for stopping smoking is probably not good. With annual cigarette sales of $27 billion, we can hardly expect the tobacco companies to stop producing cigarettes and other tobacco products. Nor can we expect the federal government, even though it has banned comparatively minor health hazards, to put a stop to smoking. The government seems to be straddling the fence on this issue. Each year it buys up surplus tobacco to support the industry. At the same time, it publishes lengthy reports on the hazards of tobacco, spends millions of dollars to learn more about smoking, bans ads from television, and requires manufacturers to print health warnings on cigarette packages. This inconsistency bodes poorly for the health of the American smoker.

Cigarette manufacturers have remained aggressive and innovative in the increasingly antismoking climate, changing to meet the times and appealing to women and young people (Figure 21-5). Low-tar cigarettes were introduced in recent years with great success, but new research suggests that they may be as harmful as the ones they've replaced, because smokers inhale deeper and longer and end up with the same dose of harmful substances. In addition, the tobacco industry spends about $1 billion per year for advertising and efforts to quell fears about the

Figure 21-5
Tobacco companies often gear their advertising to appeal to the young adult. Obviously that should not include minors: however, more and more children and adolescents smoke.

Smoking in Public Places—Whose Rights?

An Attack on Personal Freedom

Anne Browder

The author is assistant to the president of the Tobacco Institute, a trade association. Its member companies make cigarettes and other tobacco products.

Tobacco has meant many things to many people. But if it had another name, it would be "controversy," for as long as we've known about tobacco, controversy has surrounded its use. The boundaries of the controversy seem to keep widening. Today they go far beyond just the effect on the smoker or the occasional bother to the nonsmoker. We are involved in civil rights, human rights, life-styles. We are involved in the controversy of individual rights versus government regulations. We are involved in environmental, occupational, and national health policies. In the largest sense, we are involved in the fundamental questions of American life and the role of government in relation to it.

Those adults who choose to smoke as part of their heritage of free choice deserve defense. Efforts to make social outcasts of smokers reveal one of the sorrier sides of those who condemn those who do not share their convictions. They are seeking to affect smoking behavior by inconvenience and compulsion.

We believe business in general, and the tobacco business in particular, has a right and a necessity to be heard. For where free enterprise does not respond, its very existence is jeopardized. It is in recognition of this reality that the Tobacco Institute represents tobacco companies on the basis of this three-point platform:

1. The question of smoking and health is still open.
2. Tobacco smoke has not been shown to cause disease in nonsmokers.
3. The freedom of choice of our industry's customers must be preserved.

The Tobacco Institute neither encourages smoking nor discourages quitting. We regard tobacco use as an adult custom— not for children—to be decided on by mature minds.

The 1964 Report of the Surgeon General's Advisory Committee, which was a review of selected population and other studies involving smoking and health, linked smoking with several diseases. The report focused on a statistical association between smoking and increases of such maladies as lung cancer, heart disease, and emphysema. However, its authors conceded that "statistical methods cannot establish proof of a causal relationship in an association."

Although the Surgeon General's Advisory Committee reached a judgment that smoking causes certain diseases, it was just that— the committee's judgment. Other scientists did not—and do not—agree. They say the theories have not been established. Dr. Milton Rosenblatt, a former professor at New York Medical College, testified at a congressional hearing that "the smoking– lung cancer theory is fraught with inconsistencies both statistical and biological."

Twenty years ago when that first report was given to the press, per capita cigarette consumption for those 18 years of age and over was 4194. Ten years ago it was 4141, hardly any different. Since antismoking activists were unsuccessful in reducing cigarette consumption, the focus of their attention switched from the smoker to the environmental smoke issue and efforts to control the behavior of smokers. Their strategy clearly was, and has been, to make smoking socially unacceptable. They attempt to turn public opinion by telling nonsmokers that their health is endangered by tobacco smoke.

In 1983 Dr. Ragnar Rylander organized a second international symposium on environmental tobacco smoke at the University of Geneva. The medical and scientific experts gathered at that symposium concluded that many frequently heard claims concerning exposure levels and adverse health effects are unfounded and unrealistic.

No one says tobacco smoke can't be annoying or bothersome at times and under certain circumstances. In a closed, crowded, or confined room or a poorly ventilated area, smokers as well as nonsmokers are likely to be aggravated. But tobacco smoke, with its high visibility, has become an easy target for people anxious to solve our nation's health problems. Leaders of drives seeking to prohibit smoking in public places have used emotional propaganda and scare tactics in their effort to make smoking socially unacceptable.

The constituents found in environmental tobacco smoke—particularly carbon monoxide, particulates, and nicotine—are often mentioned as having a significant impact on the quality of indoor air. Quite often those studies that report high levels of these pollutants have been performed under extreme test conditions. However, scientific evidence appears to indicate that under realistic conditions environmental tobacco smoke does not have a significant effect on indoor air quality.

In fact, research shows that the main sources of carbon monoxide in the indoor environment include infiltration from traffic, industry, cooking, and heating. Evidence regarding the minimal impact of tobacco smoke on the indoor environment has recently been published.

The issue of "rights" is one that has been argued throughout the history of our court system. As it pertains to cigarette smoking, the issue is equally as prevalent. Several years ago, a federal judge dismissed a complaint that asked a ban on smoking in the New Orleans Superdome. The plaintiffs contended that several of their constitutional rights were being violated. Judge Jack Gordon's decision held that permission to smoke in the Superdome "adequately preserves the delicate balance of individual rights without yielding to the temptation to intervene in purely private affairs." Judge Gordon decided that the "Constitution does not provide judicial remedies for every social and economic ill." He held that to prohibit smoking would create a "legal avenue . . . through which an individual could attempt to regulate social habits of his neighbor."

In September 1983 the Tenth U.S. Circuit Court of Appeals in Denver dismissed a lawsuit by an Oklahoma Department of Human Services employee who contended that the state of Oklahoma had violated his constitutional rights by not prohibiting smoking in his office. The court rejected his plea, saying he had failed to prove he was being deprived of a federally protected right by the lack of a no-smoking area.

Judge William Pryor of Washington, D.C., ruled in another case that "common law does not impose upon an employer the duty or burden to conform his work place to the particular needs or sensitivities of an individual employee."

Some antismokers argue that smoking on the job leads to loss of productivity. But smoking bans impose unnecessary costs on many businesses, adversely affect employee morale and may

possibly lead to a loss in productivity and profits themselves. It must be pointed out, however, that productivity can be reduced by many things—gossiping, personal phone calls, frequent coffee breaks. Perhaps those concerned with productivity will want to regulate these, too.

Some have also asserted that absenteeism is a characteristic of smoking employees. But that, however, is a multifactorial problem faced by many employers, with reasons including family and personal problems, alcohol and drug abuse, boredom, lack of commitment, and low pay.

Some antismokers urge that employers shouldn't hire smokers. They advocate a situation no different from that which exists when women, blacks, and others are systematically excluded for reasons unrelated to job performance.

Several communities today are considering legislation similar to that enacted in 1983 in San Francisco. It leaves veto power to nonsmokers, whose preference—no smoking at all—becomes the rule if a mutually acceptable policy can't be established in the work place.

The *San Francisco Examiner* said of this ban, "This ordinance, affecting office workers but failing to include many other businesses, would introduce unnecessary conflict and expense into the work place for benefits that are vague indeed. The law would barge in where voluntary adjustments should be allowed to work . . . and are working in a great many places."

In a society where individual freedom of action is a basic right and productivity a major concern, laws that make smoking illegal in most enclosed places are ill-advised. Once the principle of legislating behavior becomes established, where does it stop?

Most people would prefer to work out social annoyances for themselves by using a little common sense rather than by official fiat. Common sense tells us not to raise our voice in a restaurant or a busy office. It tells us not to bathe in heavy perfume. Common sense tells us that cooperation and mutual understanding—respect for the preferences and sensitivities of others—are the simplest and least intrusive means by which smokers and nonsmokers continue to get along.

There is no attempt to deny the government an opportunity to advise the American public. Everyone is familiar with the health warning message appearing on the side of every pack of cigarettes, as well as in every cigarette ad in this country. How many inherent freedoms can these same people recite from the Bill of Rights? The issue becomes whether any government should attempt to force or coerce a people to follow its edict regarding personal life-styles and freedom of choice.

Abe Lincoln really summed it all up when he said, "In all that an individual can do as well for himself, the government ought not interfere."

Let's Clear the Air

Clara L Gouin

The author is the founder of GASP (Group Against Smokers' Pollution), an organization dedicated to promoting the rights of nonsmokers, which began in 1971 and now has chapters across the United States.

Everyone has the right to breathe clean air, but some people choose not to do so, and others have no choice. Smokers maintain that they have the right to choose to smoke. They say it's their business, their health and their decision. But they fail to realize that by making this choice they are often depriving someone else of the choice of breathing clean air. It would be fine if a person's tobacco smoke were contained in a plastic bubble, but smoke knows no bounds. Any nonsmoker who happens to be in the vicinity of the smoker becomes an involuntary smoker himself. He has no choice. Why should the only choice be the smoker's?

Laws and regulations to limit smoking in public places are helping to give everyone a choice. Smokers may still choose to smoke in designated smoking areas, and nonsmokers may choose to breathe clean air. Only where there are alternatives can there be choices.

But public places are not the only spaces that smokers and nonsmokers must share—the work place brings them together and presents a special set of problems. Nonsmokers are often trapped for eight hours a day, every day, in a smoke-filled atmo-sphere without any escape. Although it may impair their work performance, lower their productivity and decrease their job satisfaction, they must accept smoke as a condition of their employment. Studies show that a nonsmoker in this situation can inhale as much tobacco smoke as if he smoked several cigarettes a day!

The air pollution level in some work places has been measured at ten to one hundred times higher than the allowable limits set for outside air. Some nonsmokers work every day in conditions that would warrant designation as an air pollution emergency zone. And in these days of energy conservation, most work places have been sealed tighter to reduce energy loss, causing less fresh air to circulate. Further energy cutbacks often result in less ventilation.

The chemicals swirling around in tobacco smoke are every bit as dangerous, and more so, than the substances found in air pollution alerts. Many are known irritants, some are carcinogens and others are biologically toxic. Yet, the nonsmoker is expected to passively accept this chemist's nightmare of ingredients into his lungs.

It should not be surprising that inhaling smoke causes health problems for nonsmokers. Most severely affected are people who have medical conditions such as asthma, bronchitis, or heart disease. Others at risk are pregnant women and persons with allergies. At least ten percent of the population can be considered smoke-sensitive. But even otherwise healthy nonsmokers are affected, whether they have visible symptoms or not. A 1980 study published in the *New England Journal of Medicine* concluded that chronic exposure to smoke in the work environment significantly reduces small airways function in the lungs. This condition often precedes such crippling diseases as emphysema. To argue that smoke is merely an annoyance misses the point and ignores documented medical findings.

Tobacco smoke has been defined not only medically but also legally as an occupational health hazard. In a precedent setting case in 1975, Donna Shimp, an employee of Bell Telephone Company in New Jersey sued for her right to work in a smoke-free environment and won. The presiding judge, Philip A. Gruccio of the New Jersey Superior Court, declared: "The right of an individual to risk his or her own health does not include the right to jeopardize the health of those who must remain around him or her in order to properly perform the duties of their jobs." Since that time other nonsmokers have been successfully challenging smoky conditions on the job, and employers have begun to realize that reducing work place smoking is better for business.

Thirty percent of United States businesses limit smoking on the job to some extent (including tobacco companies that prohibit smoking in factory areas where cigarettes are manufactured, as a fire-preventive measure). Many employers have found that the work place becomes more pleasant, production improves, and there is less absenteeism. The bottom line is that reducing smoking on the job saves money.

Not only do the nonsmokers and employers benefit, but so do the smokers. Surveys show that most smokers would rather quit than smoke, but find it difficult to do in an atmosphere that is supportive of smoking. Where smoking regulations are in effect, it is often easier to smoke less or to give it up entirely. The result can be a healthier work force with fewer workers becoming prematurely disabled by chronic respiratory diseases.

But what of the addicted smoker who needs to have that cigarette? Doesn't he have any rights? Our society prides itself on considering the rights of the minority, and in this case, smokers are clearly in the minority, representing slightly more than one-fourth of the population (and their proportion continues to shrink). Certainly there can be concessions made to smokers such as special areas for smoking, private offices, or smoking breaks away from meetings. But smoking should always be superseded by the right to breathe clean air whenever the two conflict.

For too long the prevalent attitude about smoking has been that it is a socially acceptable, even desirable activity. We need to question this premise and look at smoking for what it really is—a socially unacceptable practice that pollutes the indoor air and causes health problems for everyone around.

Years ago, another undesirable practice was very much in evidence—the custom of spitting in public. At the turn of the century, spittoons were as common as ashtrays are today. And spitters were as adamant about their right to spit as smokers are now about their right to smoke! In 1905, Governor Pennypacker of Pennsylvania declared: "Spitting is a gentleman's constitutional right. To forbid it is an infringement of liberty."

However, spitting spread disease, and concerned citizens set out to protect the public health by passing laws and making spitting unpopular. One of these social reformers was an attorney named Sam Scoville who wrote in 1909 what is as applicable to smoking today as it was to spitting then:

"The object of law is the protection of the public. The great majority of our public have not yet learned to use their own rights so as not to injure the rights of their neighbors. Every man has, for example, the inalienable right to spit on his own domain. In fact, the right of expectoration seems to be as constitutional in America, judging from appearances, as the right to life, liberty, and the pursuit of happiness. If, however, by exercising this right a citizen spreads disease and death, or encourages others to do so, he should be impelled to forgo this American birthright."

If history repeats itself, perhaps one day the ashtray will be as obsolete as the spittoon.

---

numerous health impacts. The industry has 12 lobbyists active in Washington.

Without a doubt, a complete ban on smoking would be the most cost-effective way of reducing cancer of the lung, oral cavity, and esophagus in the United States, but opposition would be stiff. It would come not only from addicted smokers but from half a million farmers and 2 million workers in 23 states (especially North Carolina and Kentucky) who rely on the proceeds from tobacco both in the United States and abroad.

Alcohol and Its Effects

Alcohol is another pollutant we voluntarily ingest. About 13 million Americans are believed to be alcoholics or problem drinkers. Three million problem drinkers are teenagers age 14 to 17. Each year, alcohol kills over 200,000 Americans. More than half of the 50,000 deaths a year in auto accidents on U.S. highways are caused by alcohol consumption on the part of one or more drivers. Nationally, alcohol costs Americans an estimated $50 billion in property damage, medical expenses, lost work, rehabilitation programs, and so on. Alcoholism is also a serious problem in many European countries, including the Soviet Union, France, Sweden, and Italy.

Effects of Alcohol

Ethanol (ethyl alcohol) has a depressant effect on the central nervous system. Alcohol is believed to interfere with the normal functioning of nerve cells by inhibiting the transfer of sodium and potassium ions across the membranes. This destroys the nerve cell's ability to generate its bioelectric impulses, essentially deadening the nerve.

The immediate effect of alcohol ingestion is to depress activity of the cerebral cortex (the thin outer layer of the brain), which controls speech, thinking, movement, and other higher mental functions (Table 21-3). The result is a loss of inhibition, memory, judgment, concentration, and self-control. Coordination, speech, vision, hearing, and walking progressively deteriorate as the alcohol content of the blood increases. Wide fluctuations in mood may occur; the initial euphoria may turn into depression. If blood alcohol levels climb substantially (to .4% to .6%), regions of the brain that control respiration and heart rate are impaired, resulting in death. Alcohol is much more dangerous when used with other drugs, especially barbiturates, sleeping pills, sedatives, tranquilizers, narcotic painkillers, antihistamines, aspirin, and antidepressants.

Alcohol also adversely affects the liver, kidney, muscles, esophagus, and digestive tract. The liver converts most of the alcohol into acetaldehyde, which helps reduce the level of blood alcohol. However, acetaldehyde often causes headaches, gastritis, dizziness, and nausea. These effects are all symptoms of a hangover.

When alcohol is used for cellular energy, other foods are stored as fat, causing weight gain. In addition, although the caloric content of alcohol (7 kilocalories per gram) is higher than that of carbohydrates (4 kcal/gm), alcoholic beverages have only minuscule amounts of nutrients, so alcoholics are prone to nutritional deficiencies.

Impairment of liver function is found in three-fourths of all alcoholics. **Cirrhosis** is also common. Cirrhosis is a progressive degeneration of the liver characterized by a buildup of fat (which begins after consuming only the equivalent of two martinis a night) and a gradual replacement of normal liver cells by connective tissue. As the disease progresses, the liver progressively deteriorates. Approximately 8% of all alcoholics develop cirrhosis; the incidence is about six times higher than in nonalcoholics. Alcohol is also an irritant to the esophagus and other parts of the gastrointestinal tract. Damage to the stomach lining may lead to ulcers.

Alcohol freely crosses the placenta of pregnant women and enters the fetal bloodstream, but the fetus has no way to rid itself of alcohol. Liver enzymes have not yet developed, and kidney function is likewise not adequate. Thus, the fetal blood alcohol levels are directly proportional to the mother's.

Table 21-3 Effects of Blood Alcohol Concentrations

Number of Drinks[1]	Blood Alcohol Concentration	Psychological and Physical Effects
1	.02–.03%	No overt effects; slight feeling of muscle relaxation; slight mood elevation.
2	.05–.06%	No intoxication, but feeling of relaxation, warmth; slight increase in reaction time; slight decrease in fine muscle coordination.
3	.08–.09%	Balance, speech, vision, and hearing slightly impaired; feelings of euphoria; increased loss of motor coordination.
4	.11–.12%	Coordination and balance becoming difficult; distinct impairment of mental facilities, judgment.
5	.14–.15%	Major impairment of mental and physical control. Slurred speech, blurred vision, lack of motor skill.
7	.20%	Loss of motor control— must have assistance in moving about; mental confusion.
10	.30%	Severe intoxication; minimum conscious control of mind and body.
14	.40%	Unconscious, threshold of coma.
17	.50%	Deep coma.
20	.60%	Death from respiratory failure.

[1]The typical drink—three-fourths ounce of alcohol—is provided by:
  · a shot of spirits (1½ oz of 50-percent alcohol—100-proof whiskey or vodka);
  · a glass of fortified wine (3½ oz of 20-percent alcohol);
  · a larger glass of table wine (5 oz of 14-percent alcohol);
  · a pint of beer (16 oz of 4½-percent alcohol).
Source: Girdano, D. A., and Dusek, D. (1980), *Drug Education.* Reading, Mass.: Addison-Wesley, p. 71.

Children born to alcoholic women may have **fetal alcohol syndrome**, a physical addiction to alcohol found in 1 of every 300 to 750 live births. Treatment is needed to withdraw them from the alcohol. Infants of alcoholic

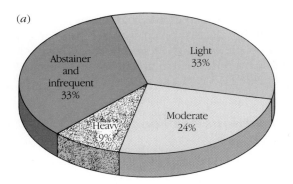

(a)

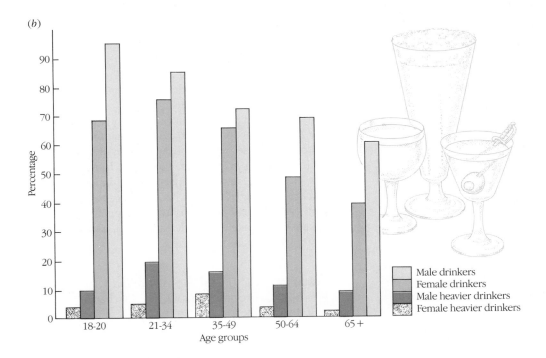

(b)

Figure 21-6
(a) A breakdown of drinkers and nondrinkers. *(b)* Percentage of male and female drinkers in the United States.

mothers or even of women who have as few as two drinks a day are often smaller than normal. Birth defects such as heart anomaly, facial disfiguration, intellectual impairment, and psychomotor retardation show up in children of alcoholic mothers. Spontaneous abortion is noticeably higher, even in women who drink only 1 ounce of alcohol twice a week.

Controlling Alcohol Consumption

As shown in Figure 21-6, a large percentage of American adults drink. In general, males are heavier drinkers than

women. On the average, each drinker in the United States consumes 15 liters (4 gallons) of pure ethyl alcohol each year, the equivalent of 20 bottles of 4% beer or 3 fifths of 12% table wine per week. As averages go, these are particularly deceptive. Few people drink that much, which means that others drink a tremendous amount; about 20% of the drinking population consumes 75% of the alcohol.

Tough new laws have been passed in states throughout the country to crack down on drinking and driving, and for good reason. Over 25,000 people die each year in automobile accidents involving alcohol. The likelihood of having an accident after drinking varies with the blood alcohol level. It is 7 times higher if the level is .05% to .10% and 20 to 50 times higher if the level is above .10%.

An alcoholic is someone who has lost control of his or her drinking; one out of ten Americans who drinks is an alcoholic. Some suggestions for reducing alcohol abuse are (1) better information on the effects of alcohol, the symptoms of alcoholism, and what each of us can do to help alcoholics (especially family members) recognize their problem and seek help; (2) more funding for research on the social, psychological, and other factors that contribute to alcoholism; (3) more funding for research on effective treatment of alcoholism; (4) government and private sponsorship of alcoholic treatment centers, which might be built with tax money levied on alcoholic beverages; and (5) controls on advertisements that promote excessive consumption.

Food Additives

Humans have been adding chemicals to their food for centuries. The first substance intentionally added to food was salt, which was used as a preservative for meat and fish and played an important part in commerce among early societies. Throughout the centuries dozens of chemicals have been used to preserve food. During the days of the Industrial Revolution food colorings developed from coal tar were used to conceal inferior products. Some of these dyes turned out to be highly toxic.

Over 2800 chemical substances are being added to foods and beverages in the United States today. These **food additives** are nonnutritive substances that improve a food's taste, appearance, texture, or shelf life.

Chemicals unintentionally added to food during production, packaging, and storage are considered **food contaminants**. These include pesticides, antibiotics, heavy metals, animal and insect wastes, parasites, growth-promoting substances (hormones), microorganisms, and solvents.

Food additives are usually classified by function. The most common categories include anticaking and emulsifying agents, preservatives, stabilizers, and synthetic flavorings; also added are nutrients and dietary supplements.

A recent survey of 5420 packaged food items from grocery stores in the United States found that 54% contained additives that may be harmful to health. Another 11% of the products contained items harmful to special groups such as people allergic to certain ingredients, including grains or milk products; women who are pregnant or lactating; or people with high blood pressure. Thus, 65% of the food items purchased in grocery stores contained items of concern (Table 21-4).

How Hazardous Are Food Additives?

Food additives are certainly prevalent, but are they hazardous? Many health experts believe that they cause only a minor fraction of the cancers reported each year. Americans ingest 2 to 5 kilograms (4.5 to 11 pounds) of food additives a year (excluding the 50 kilograms of sugar and 7 kilograms of salt), but there is a great deal of ignorance regarding the harmful effects of many of these substances. Considering that it costs from $200,000 to $1 million to test *each* one for toxicity, there can be little wonder why we know so little about their effects.

Some food additives once thought to be safe have been found to be hazardous and have been taken off the market. Cyclamates, used as an artificial sweetener in soft drinks, were banned in 1969 because they were found to be carcinogenic in laboratory animals. Red dyes No. 2 and 4 were also banned. Poisonings have been caused by nitrites, niacin, phosphates, monosodium glutamate, potassium bromate, cobalt acetate (added to beer), and an emulsifier, ME 18, used in margarine.

Saccharin In 1977 the U.S. Food and Drug Administration (FDA) proposed a ban on saccharin, the only licensed sweetener in the United States at the time. Saccharin was used as a tabletop sweetener, in prepackaged foods such as soft drinks, in toothpaste and mouthwash, and in baby food. It was important for dieters and for diabetics. Studies in the United States and Canada prompted the FDA to propose a ban on saccharin under authority invested in it by the **Delaney Amendment**, which prohibits the use of any food additive shown to cause cancer in a laboratory animal.

The proposed banning produced an enormous public outcry and a vocal debate about the validity of the Delaney Amendment. Over 100,000 letters poured into the FDA, mostly in opposition to the ban. Congress reacted immediately and imposed an 18-month moratorium on the FDA's ban. This provided time for more research and consideration of the effect of a saccharin ban—in short, time to

Table 21-4 Presence of Food Additives in Grocery and Health Food Items

Major Food Categories[1]	Grocery Stores National, Regional, and Private Brands				Health Food Stores Items Sold in These Outlets			
	Total Number of Items	Percent with A-O-C for All[2]	Percent with A-O-C for Some[3]	Percent with No A-O-C	Total Number of Items	Percent with A-O-C for All	Percent with A-O-C for Some	Percent with No A-O-C
Jellies and other sweet spreads; nut and seed butters	200	6%	1%	93%	65	*%	*%	100%
Vegetable juices and vegetables	434	17	1	82	48	*	10	90
Baking ingredients	99	20	*	80	31	3	3	94
Fruit, fruit drinks, fruit juices	336	22	1	77	82	5	7	88
Pasta; potatoes (instant); rice	118	53	3	44	35	6	23	71
Baby foods	202	44	14	42	2	*	*	*
Beverage mixes and beverages	256	53	9	38	24	4	13	83
Snack items	187	60	6	34	46	20	4	76
Bread and bread products; crackers	580	38	29	33	61	8	21	71
Fish and shellfish	139	58	10	32	12	*	*	*
Cereal, cereal bars (breakfast and snack)	110	65	5	30	27	30	11	59
Dairy products and substitutes	598	55	15	30	88	50	9	41
Gravies, sauces, and seasonings	138	65	7	28	28	7	21	71
Candy and gum	144	65	13	22	35	20	6	74
One-course dinners	179	75	7	18	44	23	9	68
Pickles, salad dressings, and other condiments	147	73	13	14	45	40	18	42
Baked sweet goods, not frozen or refrigerated	507	74	14	12	19	58	21	21
Low-calorie beverages and foods	202	84	6	10	*	*	*	*
Baking mixes, dessert toppings, gelatin, pudding	279	89	2	9	17	23	12	65
Soups	164	59	32	9	40	5	17	78
Meat and poultry and substitutes	163	85	7	8	29	62	3	35
Baked goods, frozen and refrigerated	138	83	11	6	7	*	*	*
Frozen dinners, pizza, pot pies	100	91	5	4	7	*	*	*
Total All Categories	5420	54%	11%	35%	792	20%	11%	69%

*Insufficient representation for percentages to be meaningful
[1]Arranged in descending order of absence of additives-of-concern (A-O-C) in grocery store items.
[2]A-O-C for all = food additives believed to cause health problems in all humans.
[3]A-O-C for some = food additives of concern to special groups such as pregnant women and individuals allergic to certain natural and synthetic chemicals.
Source: Freydberg, N., and Gortner, W. A. (1982), *The Food Additives Book.* New York: Bantam.

do a better risk analysis to weigh the benefits and hazards of saccharin. Congress also required labels on saccharin-containing products. The National Academy of Sciences reviewed the toxicological data and concluded in 1979 that saccharin was a weak carcinogen in rats. In 1979, 1981, and 1983 Congress extended the moratorium because of uncertainties in animal toxicology studies and because substitutes for all uses of saccharin were not yet available. Ironically, one of saccharin's replacements, aspartame, has recently come under close scrutiny, because it, too, is believed to cause adverse health effects.

Caffeine Another common food additive is caffeine. It is also found naturally in some beverages, such as coffee. Consumed in tea, coffee, chocolate, and numerous colas throughout the world for many years, caffeine was long considered safe by the FDA. Now, the FDA has limited the use of caffeine in foods and drinks and has placed strict limits on the allowable concentration in colas.

Numerous studies in humans and other animals have not answered all the questions about the potential harm of this substance. We know that three cups of coffee per day may impair speech, and higher levels may produce symptoms that are indistinguishable from anxiety neurosis. We know that caffeine is mildly addictive or at least habit-forming. It causes chromosomal damage in certain microorganisms and has similar effects on mammalian cells in culture at high concentrations. However, tests in live mice and rats have not shown it to be a mutagen.

Caffeine increases the incidence of birth defects in most rat and mouse studies at levels not much higher than those humans are exposed to. Nonetheless, a study of nearly 1300 human newborns showed no relationship between maternal caffeine ingestion and birth defects. A 1983 study in Norway, where coffee is drunk copiously, showed an 11% rise in the blood cholesterol in those who drank nine cups a day or more.

Based on a study of over 50 years of toxicologic research on caffeine, a panel of experts appointed by the Federation of American Societies for Experimental Biologists recommended that caffeine should not be kept on the list of those additives generally recognized as safe. The FDA began considering (1) requiring labels on caffeine-containing products to warn pregnant women to reduce their consumption, (2) removing caffeine from the safe list, (3) requiring warning labels on drugs (sinus medicine, aspirin compounds) that contain it, and (4) beginning consumer education programs.

Nitrites Nitrite salts have been added to meats for decades to protect against botulism and to improve appearance. These salts were not believed harmful until recently. In the mid-1960s several studies indicated that ingested nitrites might be converted to carcinogenic nitrosamines. In 1971 a study at the Massachusetts Institute of Technology showed that nitrites increased the incidence of cancer (lymphoma) in rats. A much larger study in 1978 confirmed these results.

Regulating Food Additives

As discussed in the previous paragraphs, the Food and Drug Administration is in charge of protecting the U.S. public from food poisonings and other harmful effects of food contaminants and food additives. The first federal legislation in this area was the *Food and Drug Act* (1906), which grew out of widespread public indignation caused by a flurry of reports about unsanitary conditions in meat-packing plants and the use of poisonous dyes and preservatives in foods. The Food and Drug Act prohibited the interstate transportation of adulterated foods, drinks, and drugs and permitted the government to seize unhealthy foods and prosecute violators.

The 1938 *Food, Drug and Cosmetic Act* strengthened government control on the processing and packaging of foods, cosmetics, and drugs. The law called for ceilings on substances that might be poisonous, imposed standards for food containers, required factory inspections, and authorized court injunctions to stop the flow of potentially hazardous foods, drugs, and cosmetics.

In 1958 Congress passed the *Food Additives Amendment*, commonly called the *Delaney Amendment*. In addition to directing the FDA to ban any additive shown to be carcinogenic in lab animals, the amendment required strict testing of proposed food additives. Companies were required to test the proposed substance and present their information in a petition to the FDA for approval. Data must show that the additive does what it is supposed to do and that the level for which the company is seeking approval is not higher than necessary. The petition must also show that the food additive is safe for its intended use. If FDA scientists believe that the additive is not safe, the petition will be denied. If, on the other hand, scientists at the agency view the additive as safe, the agency issues a regulation stipulating how it can be used and at what levels. The prior approval method applies to food additives, food packaging materials, and chemicals added to animal feeds that may eventually end up in foods consumed by people.

The Delaney Amendment, however, provided exemptions for chemical substances that were generally recognized as safe. Thus, over 600 food additives, some of which had been used for many years, were exempted from testing. The list was updated a few years later to include over 1100 food additives.

Substances on the safe list can be removed if testing indicates they may be harmful. In 1970 the FDA began an extensive review of compounds on the list. The review was stimulated by public outcry after scientists began to independently study the supposedly safe additives and found that some, such as cyclamates, were not as free from risk as once thought. A distinguished group of scientists began the review of safe substances and published over 135 reports covering some 400 compounds. The FDA will use these reports to determine whether an additive should be taken off the safe list.

Most nations have some laws regulating food and food additives; however, more and more foods are being shipped from one nation to another. A legal food additive in one country may be illegal in another. The World Health Organization and the Food and Agricultural Organization of the United Nations publish recommendations for the acceptable daily intake of many additives. Through these organizations, this information is available to all nations.

Making Choices

Some food additives have been found to cause cancer and birth defects in animals and have been banned by the FDA. Others simply cause illnesses, such as vomiting and diarrhea. In years to come the list of banned chemicals will grow. The decision to ban a chemical is not as easy as it may seem (see Essay 21-1).

Opinions on food additives vary widely, from a hysteria that equates these chemical substances with the downfall of civilization to an almost oblivious nonchalance. Critics assert that many food additives are unnecessary and are added only to give color or texture to foods and drinks. But many serve useful purposes, such as preserving food on its way to the market or while on the shelves of stores and consumers. Bearing in mind the importance of food additives, our challenge becomes twofold: (1) to determine which additives are the most useful and (2) to determine the level of risk for the useful additives so that we

can then select the ones that do the most good with the least harm.

Given the FDA's uncertainties about additives, we can all take an active role in protecting our own health. We can also insist that Congress, the FDA, the food manufacturers, and the food processors consider our health to be as important as profit. Some suggested solutions are (1) more testing of substances generally recognized as safe; (2) requiring labels to show the specific ingredients in foods; (3) funding research on the hazards of additives; (4) promoting public knowledge.

Pollution in the Work Place

Approximately two-thirds of all adults in the United States—over 80 million people—work. Inasmuch as most people work 40 years or more and spend about one-fourth of their adult life on the job, it's hardly a surprise to learn that occupations can profoundly influence their health. Numerous studies have shown that occupational exposure to many chemical and physical agents contributes to heart disease, hearing loss, arthritis, lung diseases, skin disorders, and cancer (Table 21-5).

The list of chemical and physical occupational hazards is large. Chemical agents include a wide variety of organic and inorganic substances, which may enter the body through ingestion, skin absorption, and inhalation. Exposure may be acute (short-term) or chronic (long-term). Physical agents include dust, noise, radiation, ultraviolet light, heat, and cold.

Work place pollutants may cause overt or acute changes in health (Chapter 18). Chemical irritants such as ammonia, for example, may cause respiratory difficulty, coughing, and headaches. High levels of other chemicals may result in death. In other cases, the effects may be subtle or may not appear for years. In still other cases—for example, noise pollution—exposure may produce both immediate effects and profound long-term effects.

Chemical and physical agents and the work atmosphere (the pace of work, expectations of the employer, interpersonal relations, and such) may lead to stress. This, in turn, may result in an elevated incidence of cardiovascular disease or nervous breakdown. However, not all work is bad for us. Studies in the late 1950s and 1960s showed that working at physically demanding jobs, such as construction, may protect workers against heart diseases.

Table 21-5   Occupational Diseases, and Agents That Contribute to Them

Disease	Contributory Agents	
	Nonoccupational	Occupational
Heart disease (cardiovascular, including coronary occlusion)	Age Heredity Sex Smoking Diet Obesity Stress Medication or drugs Climate	Various chemicals, solvents, gases Pulmonary irritants Unusual exertion Temperature
Hearing loss	Age Heredity Noise Impacted cerumen (ear wax) Foreign body in ear canal Ear infection Nasopharyngitis Medication or drugs Trauma	Noise Foreign body in ear canal Trauma Nasopharyngeal irritants
Arthritis or "rheumatism"	Age Heredity Diet Trauma Infection Obesity Stress	Repeated articular movement Trauma Cold, damp work environment Improper lifting Work-required poor posture
Pulmonary (lung) diseases	Age Heredity Sex Smoking Allergy Air pollution Infection Climate	Various dusts, gases, mists Allergens Wearing of respirators Decreased oxygen supply Temperature, humidity

Source: U.S. Department of Health, Education and Welfare, National Institute for Occupational Safety and Health, *A Guide to the Work-Relatedness of Disease,* DHEW (NIOSH) Publication No 77-123, Washington, D.C.: U.S. Government Printing Office, 1976, p. 14.

How Large a Problem?

At least one of every four workers in the United States is exposed to some substance capable of causing death or disease. The same statistics apply to other industrial nations.

In the United States about 400,000 cases of occupational illness are reported each year, most of these skin and eye conditions. About 100,000 deaths each year are attributable to occupational diseases. The most notable examples of occupational disease are (1) **black lung disease** (pneu-

EDB—Panic in the Pantry

In February 1984 cake and muffin mixes, peanuts, tortillas, and 73 other products were suddenly pulled from grocery shelves across the United States. Ethylene dibromide (EDB), a cancer-linked pesticide used to treat grain and citrus crops for 30 years, was the cause of the scare at the supermarket. State officials had recently discovered unsafe traces of the chemical in certain foods.

The nationwide alert caused the Environmental Protection Agency to immediately ban the chemical, despite claims from William Ruckelshaus, head of the EPA, as well as scientists such as Bruce Ames, a biochemist at U.C. Berkeley, that "a peanut butter sandwich is more of a risk."

Although some scientists believe that EDB poses a serious threat to human health, the real furor seemed to revolve around what many saw as the EPA's mishandling of the situation. Apparently, scientists discovered EDB's deadly link to cancer in 1974. Slow-reacting government officials, however, did not perform the regulatory testing needed to determine EDB's immediate potential harm. In 1983 anxious state officials and scientists took matters into their own hands and performed the tests, finding higher-than-normal traces of the chemical. Their information triggered a muffin-mix mania at grocery stores all over the country.

Some scientists believe EDB to be as dangerous as dioxin; others counter that eating a steak is potentially more harmful. The EPA, in an effort to allay fears, reminded consumers of three things: First, only a very small fraction of the products tested for residue actually contained levels higher than EPA standards; hence, the probability of actually purchasing a contaminated cake mix was small. Second, if the mix was contaminated, baking the cake would destroy up to 95% of the residue. Third, it would take years of cumulative exposure to EDB to produce a cancer. With EDB's recent ban, the chemical was expected to be absent from the nation's food supply as early as 1987.

moconiosis), which affects over 200,000 coal miners and costs over $1 billion a year in worker compensation; (2) **abestosis** and cancer from asbestos, which are expected to kill over 400,000 of the 1 million Americans exposed to asbestos at work (Chapter 22); (3) lung cancer among painters; and (4) lung cancer among vinyl chloride workers.

Since its establishment in 1971 the National Institute of Occupational Safety and Health (NIOSH) has amassed a list of about 23,000 chemicals that might be harmful to workers exposed to sufficient concentrations.

Not all occupational diseases have a known specific chemical cause. For example, the incidence of cancer in the nasal cavity and sinuses of furniture workers is three to four times higher than expected in the general population, but the specific agent is unknown. Shoe workers have seven times as many cancers of the nasal cavity and sinuses, but the cause is not certain (it may be dusts, dyes, or solvents). Part of the reason for uncertainty is that most workers are exposed to a mixture of chemicals, sometimes at low levels. Synergy and antagonism (Chapter 18)

may make it difficult to trace the line between cause and effect. Nonoccupational factors such as health, age, sex, smoking habits, drinking, and diet may also complicate the picture. Finally, long delays between exposure and effect make it even more difficult to trace a disease back to its cause. (Model Application 21-1 encourages you to define the risk in taking a job in a chemical factory.)

Protecting Workers

Protecting workers from hazardous physical and chemical agents is an important social task with great humanitarian and economic advantages. Strategies generally fall into several categories: (1) legal controls that require employers to reduce or eliminate hazardous exposures, (2) design modifications to reduce work place pollution, and (3) protective garb for workers (Figure 21-7).

Protection of U.S. workers from pollutants and safety hazards first came under the control of state governments.

Figure 21-7
Protection of the worker. Special vents are used to draw off potentially harmful vapors, and protective clothing or gas masks reduce worker exposure; but they can be cumbersome and uncomfortable to workers.

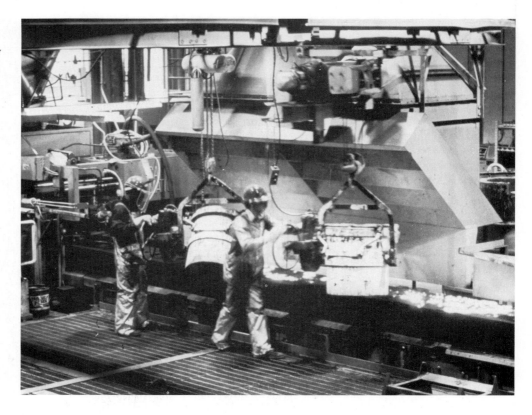

However, as in all environmental laws, control gradually shifted to the federal government.

In 1970 the *Occupational Safety and Health Act* introduced a new idea into the law: the worker has a legal right to a safe and healthful place to work. The act also established the *Occupational Safety and Health Administration (OSHA)* in the Department of Labor. The purpose of OSHA was to (1) encourage both employers and employees to reduce work place hazards and start or improve health and safety programs; (2) establish a system of reporting and record keeping to keep track of job-related illnesses and injuries; (3) develop mandatory safety standards for workers in industries involved in interstate commerce; (4) enforce safety and health standards; and (5) encourage the states' worker safety and health programs as long as they are as stringent as the federal program.

OSHA develops standards for occupational pollutants and may send inspectors to see if companies are comply-ing. Inspectors may appear at factories without notice, or workers may contact them when they believe that there is a threat to their health or safety. If a violation is discovered, a fine can be imposed.

Although OSHA may seem like a powerful worker protection agency, lack of money and personnel have plagued it since its beginning. A study of the agency concluded in 1976 that it was doing only a small part of what was needed and that it had developed a reputation for nitpicking regulation.

In 1977 OSHA redirected its policies and began emphasizing the prevention of occupational disease, concentrating on high-risk industries, and eliminating unnecessary paperwork—a remarkable turnaround. In 1979 alone 900 irrelevant safety standards were dropped, and 95% of the inspections were in industries with the most severe hazards.

During the Reagan administration OSHA made drastic

Personal Risk Assessment

You are considering a job with a company that manufactures several chemicals. You will be involved in the actual manufacture of the finished products and will thus be exposed daily to low levels of these potentially hazardous substances. Your employer tells you there are some risks, but that they are negligible. He says that people have worked at the plant for years without any major problems.

Not satisfied with this information, you do some checking and find that the pesticides you will be working with are nerve poisons that cause convulsions in people exposed to high levels. Other studies indicate that the possibility of an accident that would release enough pesticide to cause such symptoms is about 1 in 100,000. You also find that the pesticide is believed to cause one case of cancer per 100,000 people exposed and birth defects in offspring of male and female workers exposed to levels the same as those you will be exposed to in the factory.

Question

Determine for yourself whether the risks of the job outweigh the benefits.

Step 1

What other information might you look for in making your decision?

Step 2

Part of your decision whether to accept the job hinges on personal factors. Suppose, for instance, your personal situation shapes up as follows: You have been out of work for six months, have few marketable skills, are behind in house and car pay-ments, are expecting a child, and have nearly wiped out your savings. Weigh these against the following benefits offered by your employer:

- salary of $20,000 a year
- full health and dental insurance
- two-week paid vacation
- job security
- profit-sharing plan
- unlimited free use of recreational facilities owned by the company

Make a list of risks and benefits of taking the job. Would you take the job? Why? What factor swayed your decision?

Step 3

Suppose the job benefits were as follows:

- salary of $12,000 a year
- health but no dental policy
- one-week paid vacation
- no profit sharing

and that your personal situation was as follows:

- You are single.
- You've only been out of work a few weeks and are collecting unemployment, which pays all the bills and still provides money for entertainment.
- You have no car or house payments.
- You have $5000 in your savings account.

Does the risk outweigh the benefit now? Would you take the job if your new salary gave you $100 more per month? $200? $500?

---

cuts in safety and health regulations, made fewer inspections, and issued far fewer citations, taking the pressures off industry to maintain a healthy working environment.

The need to protect workers has grown as more and more hazardous substances are produced. This need has not been answered with expanded budgets for the occupational health agencies. Also lacking are support for education to inform workers of their legal rights; means to inform workers and employers about safety techniques; and streamlined litigation when citations are issued.

Exposure to pollutants in the work place costs taxpayers and workers billions of dollars a year in medical bills, lost income, and funeral expenses. But how much should we pay for protection? From this question spins a whole constellation of questions that beg for answers: Should worker protection be determined by a cost–benefit analysis? Or should we completely protect workers, regardless of the cost? Essay 18-1 looks at a case study and opens up the complex package of issues once neatly sealed up by ignorance and apathy.

Thou shouldst not decide till thou hast heard what both have to say.

ARISTOPHANES

Summary

Personal pollutants are the harmful substances we voluntarily introduce into our bodies, such as cigarette smoke, alcohol, and food additives.

After several decades the evidence overwhelmingly shows that smoking is hazardous to health. It causes 85% of the lung cancers in the United States and is associated with a number of other illnesses. Tobacco smoke contains high concentrations of hundreds of harmful chemicals such as sulfur dioxide, benzopyrene, and lead. Dozens of these substances are carcinogenic.

The conflict over smoking in public places is growing more intense. Recent evidence indicates that nonsmokers may be placed in jeopardy by breathing tobacco smoke. It is highly doubtful that we will see an end to smoking, although continuing public pressure will undoubtedly curtail smoking in public places.

Alcohol is a depressant that is addictive and harmful if ingested in large quantities over long periods. Because alcohol freely crosses the placenta, it can be especially harmful if ingested during pregnancy.

Over 2800 chemical substances are being added to foods and beverages in the United States. These *food additives* improve taste, appearance, texture, and shelf life. A recent survey of numerous packaged food items from grocery stores showed that more than half contained additives harmful to health. Another 11% contained substances harmful to some groups.

Many health experts believe that food additives cause only a minor fraction of the cancers reported each year, but there is a great deal of ignorance regarding the harmful effects of these chemicals. Some once thought to pose a low risk to humans now appear much more hazardous. Many additives serve useful purposes, so it is important to determine the risk each poses and weigh that against the benefits.

The work place is a source of pollutants for many Americans. At least one of every four workers in the United States is exposed to some substance capable of causing death or disease. About 400,000 cases of occupational illness are reported each year, and about 100,000 deaths occur from occupational diseases.

Workers can be protected by strong enforcement of existing laws, designed to reduce exposure to harmful substances.

Discussion Questions

1. What are personal pollutants? How do they differ from other pollutants discussed in earlier chapters?

2. How prevalent is smoking in the United States? Discuss the health effects of smoking. How does smoking affect pregnancy?

3. Debate the statement "smokers have a right to smoke wherever they want."

4. Define the terms *voluntary smoker* and *involuntary smoker*. Are the levels of risk to passive, or involuntary, smokers the same as those to active, or voluntary, smokers?

5. You are appointed surgeon general of the United States. What will you do about smoking? Will you push for a smoking ban in public places and at work? Will you push for the government to cease its support for the industry?

6. How prevalent is alcohol consumption in the United States? How much alcohol is consumed? Describe the effects of alcohol on the nervous system. What is cirrhosis?

7. How is alcohol removed from the body?

8. Debate the statement "There's nothing wrong with a few drinks a week while you're pregnant."

9. Define food additives. What are they? Why are they added to food? How do they differ from food contaminants?

10. Debate the statement "Synthetic chemicals in food are bad for our health."

11. Which packaged foods and drinks are the most harmful to your health?

12. Discuss the legal approaches to regulating food additives in the United States. Describe the Delaney Amendment. Should it be rewritten or eliminated?

13. You are appointed head of a special commission to study food additives and make recommendations to the FDA regarding their risk. How would you go about studying the thousands of food additives on the market today?

14. Discuss the statement "Work place pollution is one of the main forms of exposure in the United States and a significant health threat to the nation's workers."

15. Give some examples of occupational diseases and their causes.

16. You are a physician working in occupational medicine. One of the companies you work for is a major chemical manufacturer that produces several dozen potentially harmful substances. You discover several cases of liver cancer in your workers. How would you determine whether the cancer was caused by exposure at work, and then how would you go about tracking down the cause?

17. Discuss the Occupational Safety and Health Act and the Occupational Safety and Health Administration. What are their main functions?

18. You are the president of a small chemical company. You find that one of the substances you're producing, which accounts for the majority of your profit, causes cancer in one of your workers every year. However, your calculations show that it will cost $10 million a year to prevent that possible death. Your annual profit is only a few million dollars. What would you do?

Suggested Readings

Behr, P. (1978). Controlling Chemical Hazards. *Environment* 20(6): 25–29. Insightful treatise on the costs of protecting workers.

Combs, B. J., Hales, D. R., and Williams, B. K. (1983). *An Invitation to Health: Your Personal Responsibility.* Menlo Park, Calif.: Benjamin/Cummings. Contains an excellent overview of drinking and smoking.

Derr, P., Goble, R., Kasperson, R. E., and Kates, R. W. (1983). Responding to the Double Standard of Worker/Public Protection. *Environment* 25(6): 6–11; 35–36. Exemplary treatise on worker protection.

Freydberg, N., and Gortner, W. (1982). *The Food Additives Book.* New York: Bantam Books. Extensive reference of packaged foods showing additives of concern.

Girdano, D. A., and Dusek, D. (1980). *Drug Education: Content and Methods* (3rd ed.). Reading, Mass.: Addison-Wesley. Good reading on personal pollution.

Graham, J., Shakow, D. M., and Cyr, C. (1983). Risk Compensation—in Theory and Practice. *Environment* 25(1): 14–20; 39–40. Insightful essay on worker risk and compensation.

Kasperson, R. E. (1983). Worker Participation in Protection: The Swedish Alternative. *Environment* 25(4): 13–20; 40–43. Interesting article on worker protection.

Kilgore, W. W., and Li, M. (1980). Food Additives and Contaminants. In *Toxicology: The Basic Science of Poisons,* J. Doull, C. D. Klaassen, and M. O. Amdur, eds. New York: Macmillan. Good overview.

Lowrance, W. W. (1983). The Agenda for Risk Decisionmaking. *Environment* 25(10): 4–8. Interesting and relevant discussion of risk.

U.S. Department of Health and Human Services (1983). *Alcohol and Health.* Washington, D.C.: U.S. Government Printing Office. Update on alcohol research.

U.S. Surgeon General (1981). *The Health Consequences of Smoking.* Washington, D.C.: U.S. Government Printing Office.

Willgoose, C. E. (1979). *Environmental Health: Commitment for Survival.* Philadelphia: Saunders. Excellent coverage of occupational health.

Radiation Pollution

What Is Radiation?

The fundamental unit of matter, the **atom**, is composed of a **nucleus** and an **electron cloud**. The nucleus contains protons and neutrons and constitutes 99.9% of the mass of an atom. The much lighter, negatively charged **electrons** orbit in the cloud around the positively charged nucleus. For a more detailed discussion of atoms see Appendix A.

Atoms of a given element all have the same number of protons in their nuclei, but they may differ in the number of neutrons. These slightly different forms of the same atom are called **isotopes**. For example, uranium-238 and uranium-235 are isotopes. U-238 has 146 neutrons and U-235 has 143, but both have 92 protons. Some isotopes have energetically unstable nuclei (caused by too many neutrons); these may emit **radiation** to reach a more stable state. Such unstable, radioactive nuclei are called **radionuclides**. They may occur naturally or may be produced by humans. For the most part, the naturally occurring radionuclides are isotopes of heavy elements from lead (atomic number 82) to uranium (atomic number 92). There are four major types of radiation: alpha particles, beta particles, gamma rays, and X rays.

Alpha particles are positively charged and consist of two protons and two neutrons, the same as a helium nucleus (Figure S21-1). Of all the different forms of radiation, alpha particles have the largest mass. In air they travel only a few centimeters. They can be stopped by a single sheet of paper, and in living tissue they travel only 30 micrometers (about the width of three cells). Because alpha particles generally cannot penetrate skin, they are often erroneously assumed to pose little harm to humans. But if alpha emitters enter internal body tissues, such as the lung and bone, they can do irreparable damage to nearby cells and their chromosomes.

Beta particles are negatively charged particles emitted from nuclei, equivalent to ordinary electrons except for their high

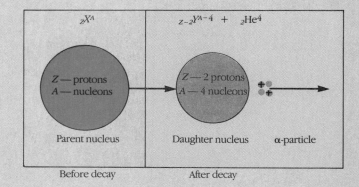

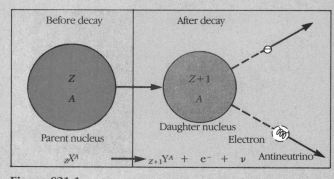

Figure S21-1
Alpha and beta emissions from the nuclei of unstable radionuclides.

energy. They arise when neutrons in the nucleus are converted into protons, making the nucleus more stable. During this process, a small amount of mass, the beta particle, and energy are lost; the energy ejects the electron out of the nucleus. The beta particle is much lighter than the alpha particle and can travel much farther. It can penetrate a 1-millimeter lead plate and can travel

Resources Misuse

Throughout much of history, humans have been able to ignore the impact of their activities on natural resources. However, in recent years, we have been forced to recognize the error of our ways; air and water pollution, unsafe disposal of toxic wastes, the near catastrophe at Three Mile Island, depletion of precious minerals, extinction of endangered species, and more. These misuses threaten the resources needed to sustain not only our civilization, but our planet as well. Today, the earth's future lies in a combined and difficult task; not only must we correct our past mistakes, we must *understand* how and why they happened, and take steps to ensure that they don't happen again.

1 There goes the neighborhood... A wet cooling tower stands in bold contrast to a farmhouse in rural northern Ohio.

2 A denuded hill in Alaska has been clear-cut to remove timber for domestic and foreign markets.

3 Controlled fires burn the grassy vegetation of cleared rain forest. Some experts feel that removal of tropical rain forests will have a direct effect on climatic conditions. The release of great amounts of carbon dioxide into the atmosphere is said to contribute to the green-house effect, a phenomenon which may produce an unfavorable warming trend in the earth's atmosphere.

4 Land in a tropical rain forest is cleared for farming or grazing. After removal of vegetation, the nutrient-poor soil is often washed away or baked into a brick-like consistency, rendering it useless.

5 Overgrazing turned a once-rich grassland into a lifeless desert. Without the plant-root network that once bound it, the soil is unable to retain moisture and is easily blown away.

6 An infrared aerial view of Love Canal, Niagara Falls, New York. The dump, home to dozens of chemicals including PCBs and dioxin, was sold to the city in the 1950s as a school and playground site. Healthy vegetation appears red; brown vegetation indicates contamination. The toxic wastes were spread throughout the neighborhood via underground streams; 237 families were evacuated from the area.

7 Toxic wastes are stored in steel drums, then buried or stored in toxic waste dumps like this one. The steel drums, which are supposed to separate the dangerous wastes from you and me, are reliably rusted to their corrosive contents, leaking deadly poisons into the soil and groundwater, producing what many call "the Love Canal Effect."

8 Workers wrapped in protective clothing prepare to bury toxic wastes. About 90% of the country's toxic and chemical wastes are dumped illegally.

9 Industrial society produces massive quantities of refuse, some of which gets buried, burned, or recycled. The rest ends up along highways, in empty lots, or, as in this case, in someone's backyard.

10 Boats at dock on the Amazon sit immersed in a sea of floating garbage.

2

3

4

5

6

7

8

9

10

11 Waste from an iron ore processing plant colors the water of this artificial pond a bright orange. Such wastes seep into the earth, contaminating groundwater supplies.

12 Nitrogen fertilizer added to irrigation water to boost crop production in the Oro Valley, Arizona, may contaminate groundwater in this area.

13 New York City lies enshrouded in a layer of filthy air.

14 In 1977, raw sewage poured into the ocean near Miami Beach, Florida. Less than 100 yards away, sunseekers enjoy a swim.

13

11

12

14

up to 8 meters in air and 1 centimeter in tissue. Beta particles from some radionuclides have enough energy to penetrate the skin, but they generally do not reach underlying tissues. They can, however, damage the skin and eyes (causing skin cancer and cataracts).

Gamma rays are a high-energy form of radiation with no mass and no charge, much like visible light but with much more energy. Gamma rays are emitted by nuclei to achieve a lower-energy, more stable state. They are often emitted after a nucleus has ejected an alpha or beta particle, because the loss of these particles may not have allowed the nucleus to reach its most stable state. Some gamma rays can travel hundreds of meters in air and can easily penetrate the body. Some have enough energy to penetrate walls of cement and plaster.

Unlike the three types previously discussed, the **X ray** does not originate from unstable nuclei. Rather, X rays are a form of radiation produced in X-ray machines when a high voltage is applied between a source of electrons and a collecting terminal in a vacuum tube (Figure S21-2). When the electrons are ejected, they strike the tungsten collecting terminal. Colliding with tungsten atoms, they are rapidly brought to rest. The energy they carry is released in the form of X rays.

All forms of radiation described above are called **ionizing radiation**, because they possess enough energy to rip electrons away from atoms, forming ions. Ions are the primary cause of damage in tissues.

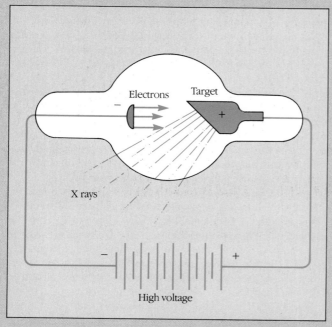

Figure S21-2
An X-ray machine.

How Is Radiation Measured?

Radioactive elements lose mass over time because of the emissions from their nuclei. Each radionuclide gives off radiation at its own rate, called the **radioactive decay rate** and measured in disintegrations per second (dps). For example, 1 gram of radium decays at a rate of 37 billion dps! The rate of radioactive decay determines the half-life of a radionuclide. The **half-life** is the time it takes for a given mass of a given radionuclide to be reduced to half by radioactive decay.

Radiation exposure in humans is expressed in several different ways. One of the most widely used measures is the rad. **Rad** is the radiation absorbed dose, or, simply, the amount of energy that is deposited in tissue (or some other medium) when it is struck by radiation. One rad is equal to 100 ergs of energy deposited in 1 gram of tissue.

As radiation travels through tissue, it loses its energy. The rate of energy loss is called the **linear energy transfer**, or LET. Put another way, LET is the amount of energy lost per unit of distance the radiation travels. Because of their mass, alpha particles travel only short distances through tissue and, therefore, lose their energy rapidly. They are said to have a high LET. The energy is transferred to the tissues. X rays, gamma rays, and beta particles travel farther through tissues and lose their energy more slowly; they have low LETs. Consequently, 10 rads of energy from beta particles would do less damage than 10 rads from an alpha particle, because the energy from an alpha particle is lost in a smaller volume.

The term **rem** takes into account the linear energy transfer and thus indirectly indicates the damage that a given amount of radiation will cause in tissue. For X rays, gamma rays, and beta particles, 1 rem is essentially equivalent to 1 rad, but for alpha particles, because of their high LET, one rad is equivalent to 10 to 20 rems.

As a point of reference, a medical X ray may be equivalent to about .1 to 1 rem, depending on the type of X ray. The safety standard for workers in the United States is 5 rems per year. Background radiation is measured in thousandths of rems, or millirems (mrem).

Sources of Radiation

Natural Sources

Natural sources of radiation include the rocks, soil, water, air, and even the distant sun and stars. Rocks and soil contain tiny amounts of radioactive substances such as carbon-14, uranium-238, radium-226, and potassium-40.

In the United States the average exposure rate from natural terrestrial sources is estimated to be about 40 mrem per year, but depending on where you live, your exposure may be as low as 15 mrem or as high as 140 mrem per year (Table S21-1). This

Table S21-1   Estimated Radiation Exposure in the U.S.

Source	Average Exposure (mrem/year)[1]
Natural	
Soil and rock	40
Cosmic radiation	28–44
Internal exposure	18–24
Total	80–100
Anthropogenic	
Medical	74
Nuclear-weapons fallout	4
Nuclear energy	.05–5
TV (1 hour/day)	5
Watch (luminous dial)	1–4
Air travel	4
Total	80–100
Total	160–200

[1]These values are averages published in several different studies.

wide variation results from differences in the natural level of radionuclides in the soil, rocks, air, and water.

The sun and stars produce high-energy **cosmic rays**, or **cosmic radiation** (much like gamma radiation) from periodic solar flare-ups. Its energy is so high that it can penetrate cement walls, exposing us day in and day out. The greatest exposure to cosmic radiation occurs at the North and South poles and at high altitudes. In fact, exposure to cosmic radiation increases by a factor of three between sea level and 3000 meters (10,000 feet) and by about 20% between the equator and the 49th parallel, the U.S.–Canadian border.

On the average, Americans receive approximately 28 to 44 mrems of cosmic radiation per year, but geographical differences in exposure are common (Table S21-1). For example, residents of Montana and Wyoming receive 75 mrem, whereas Louisiana and Florida residents receive about 38 mrem.

Some naturally occurring radioactive materials are present in water and food, and they may be deposited in bone or other tissues in the body, where they irradiate cells. Potassium-40 is the predominant internal source in humans. Annual dose rates from all internally deposited radioactive materials are estimated to be about 18 to 24 mrems for the U.S. population, but, again, this varies considerably depending on background levels (Table S21-1).

The average exposure from all naturally occurring sources of radiation is about 80 to 100 mrem per year. In some areas such as Denver and Salt Lake City, because of altitude and high background levels, the average exposure may be as high as 200 mrem per year.

Anthropogenic Sources

Anthropogenic radiation sources are many: (1) the entire nuclear fuel cycle; (2) combustion of coal; (3) accidents at nuclear power plants and weapons facilities; (4) medical therapy and diagnosis; (5) scientific research; (6) detonation of nuclear weapons in testing and war; (7) television sets; and (8) pacemakers.

Anthropogenic sources are responsible, on the average, for about half of the total annual dose to the general public (see Table S21-1). Medical diagnosis and treatment constitute about 80% of the anthropogenic exposure. Medical X rays are the largest medical source, with the U.S. average being about 74 mrem. However, averages cover up the fact that some individuals receive large doses of radiation from X rays each year, and others receive none.

Effects of Radiation

How Does Radiation Affect Cells?

All forms of radiation cause ionization and excitation of biologically important molecules in tissues. Positively charged alpha particles, for example, attract electrons from atoms in body tissues, creating positively charged ions in their path. Negatively charged beta particles in tissues may repel electrons of various atoms, causing them to be expelled from their atoms. They, too, produce positively charged ions. Gamma rays and X rays, on the other hand, are uncharged, but they possess lots of energy, which may be transferred to electrons as they pass through tissue. Excited by the new energy, the electrons may be expelled, thus forming ions. Alternatively, the energy imparted to the electrons may make chemical bonds more susceptible to breakage.

Ionization of water and other molecules in tissues is responsible for much of the damage caused by radiation. When electrons are ripped from water molecules in body tissues, these molecules are left positively charged. The electrons themselves may end up in other water molecules, making these negatively charged. Both positively and negatively charged water molecules rapidly break up into highly reactive fragments called free radicals (Figure S21-3).

Free radicals react almost instantaneously with other molecules. When they react with oxygen, for example, hydrogen peroxide is formed. This powerful oxidizing agent damages or destroys proteins and other molecules, causing cell death. If

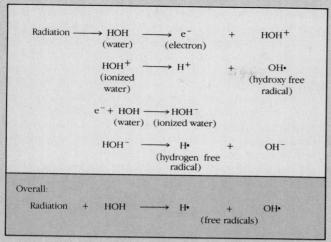

Figure S21-3
Ionization of water by radiation.

extensive enough, cellular destruction can kill the organism. In some instances, damage may be quickly repaired by the cells without any long-term effects; in other cases, the damage may not be expressed until years after the exposure, in the form of mutations and cancer (Chapter 18).

Health Effects of Radiation

The effects of radiation on human health depend on many factors, such as the amount of radiation, the length of exposure, the type of radiation, the half-life of the radionuclide, the health and age of the individual, the part of the body exposed, and whether the exposure is internal or external.

Numerous studies of radiation have revealed some interesting generalizations: (1) Fetuses are more sensitive to radiation than are children—who are, in turn, more sensitive than adults. (2) Cells undergoing rapid cellular division appear to be more sensitive to radiation than those that are not. This is especially true for cancer induction. Thus, lymphoid tissues (bone marrow, lymph nodes, and circulating lymphocytes) are the most sensitive of all the body's cells. Epithelial cells—those that line the inside and outside of body organs such as the intestine—also undergo frequent cellular division and are highly sensitive to radiation. In sharp contrast, nerve and muscle cells, which do not divide, have a very low sensitivity. (3) Most, if not all, forms of cancer can be increased by ionizing radiation.

Health experts are concerned with the effects both of high-level exposure, usually over a short duration, and of low-level exposure, often occurring over extended periods of time. Exposures below 5 to 10 rems per year are generally considered low-level.

High-Level Radiation Perhaps the most important information on high-level radiation comes from studies of the survivors of the two atomic bombs dropped on Japan at the end of World War II. Studies of these and other groups have led to several important findings. First, the lethal dose for one-half of the people within 60 days is about 300 rads. Second, a dose of 650 rads kills all people within a few hours to a few days. Third, sublethal doses, or doses that do not result in immediate death, range from 50 to 250 rads. Victims suffer from **radiation sickness** (Figure S21-4). The first symptoms, which develop immediately, are nausea and vomiting; 2 to 14 days later, diarrhea, hair loss, sore throat, reduction in blood platelets (needed for blood clotting), hemorrhaging, and bone marrow damage occur. Fourth, sublethal radiation has many serious delayed effects, including cancer, leukemia, cataracts, sterility, and decreased life span. Fifth, sublethal radiation also increases the number of spontaneous abortions, stillbirths, and early infant deaths. Sixth, the survivors of Nagasaki and Hiroshima suffer socially, too. Known as the *hibakusha* (the bombed ones), they are shunned by their people. Neither the *hibakusha* nor their descendants are viewed as desirable marriage partners.

Figure S21-4
Hiroshima survivors.

High-level radiation exposure is rare. We can anticipate such exposures to workers in badly damaged nuclear power plants or munitions factories or possibly to nearby residents. Nuclear war, even on a limited scale, would of course expose large segments of the human population to dangerously high levels of radiation (Chapter Supplement 23-1).

Low-Level Radiation Considerable controversy arises in discussions of the effects of low-level radiation. A growing body of evidence shows that low-level radiation adversely affects human health (Figure S21-5). For example, studies of individuals who years before were treated with radiation for acne, spinal disorders, and even syphilis show elevated levels of cancer and leukemia. In addition, children whose necks had been irradiated by medical X rays have an elevated rate of thyroid gland cancer. Lung cancer rates are elevated in uranium and fluorspar (calcium fluoride) miners, who are exposed to radon gas. Factory workers who painted watch dials with radium early in this century developed bone cancer and a serious disease of the bone marrow called aplastic anemia. Several studies show that the rates of leukemia, tumors of the lymphatic system, brain tumors, and other cancer are 50% higher in infants whose mothers were exposed to ordinary diagnostic X rays (2 to 3 rads). One study showed that a 1-rem exposure to a fetus causes an 80% increase

in mortality from childhood cancer. Low-level radiation from nuclear-weapons testing in the 1950s and 1960s has reportedly caused 400,000 deaths in children. Studies of atomic workers at Hanford, Washington, the U.S. government's source of radioactive materials for nuclear weapons, showed the death rate from cancer to be 7% higher than expected. Workers who died of cancer had received on the average only about 2 rems per year, well below the supposed safe level of 5 rems per year.

Low-level radiation is probably much more harmful than many scientists estimated a decade ago. One radiation biologist, Dr. Irwin Bross, estimates that low-level exposure is about ten times more harmful than previously calculated. He and others have called for major revisions of the maximum allowable doses for workers.

But is there a threshold level below which no damage occurs? No one can say for certain. Some health officials believe that no level is safe, because the effects of continued low-level exposure are cumulative.

According to two radiation experts, John Gofman and Arthur Tamplin, exposure to the current public health standard set for anthropogenic sources—.17 rad per year—will result in a 30-year exposure of 5 rads. This would cause 14 additional cases of cancer each year for every 100,000 people exposed, or about 14,000 additional cancer cases per year in adults over 30 years

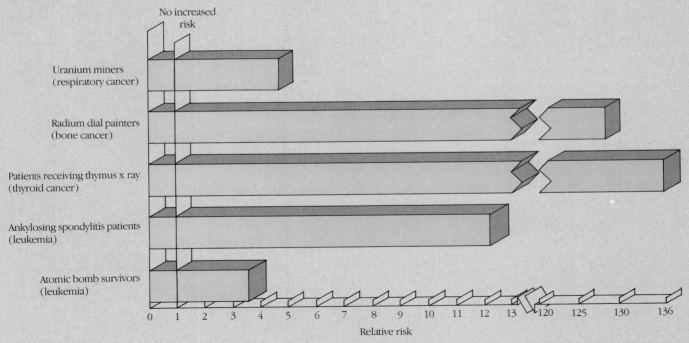

Figure S21-5
The relative risk of cancer in people exposed to various kinds of radiation. Relative risk is the number of observed cases divided by the number of expected cases.

old and at least 2000 cases of cancer in people under 30. Studies by the National Academy of Sciences and the National Research Council suggest that a .17-rad exposure to anthropogenic radiation will probably increase the rate of cancer by 2% and will increase the incidence of serious genetic diseases by about 1 birth in every 2000.

However, genetic disorders caused by radiation may be passed from generation to generation and may increase in frequency in subsequent generations. For example, if the incidence of genetic disorders and birth defects with a genetic basis were 1 in 2000 in the first generation, it might be 5 in 2000 in their offspring.

A major consideration, then, is what impact radiation exposure today will have on subsequent generations. Are current policies and radiation standards posing a danger to future generations?

Low-level effects are small and hard to detect. The long latent period between exposure and disease makes it difficult for scientists to link cause and effect. Thus, studies such as those cited above have stirred a considerable amount of controversy. Although the results and conclusions of individual studies of low-level radiation are debatable, on the whole they seem to point consistently to one conclusion: a substantial risk is created by subjecting people to low-level radiation. There are several questions involved: What level of risk is acceptable? At what point do the benefits of X rays, nuclear power, and other uses outweigh the risks?

Biological Concentration and Magnification Table S21-2 lists some radionuclides emitted from nuclear weapons and nuclear power plants. Some of these are absorbed by humans and other organisms and may become concentrated in particular tissues.

Table S21-2 Radionuclides from Nuclear Weapons and Reactors

Nuclear Weapons	Nuclear Reactors
Strontium-89	Tritium (Hydrogen-3)
Strontium-90	Cobalt-58
Zirconium-95	Cobalt-60
Rubidium-193	Krypton-95
Rubidium-106	Strontium-85
Iodine-131	Strontium-90
Cesium-137	Iodine-130
Cerium-141	Iodine-131
Cerium-144	Xenon-131
	Xenon-133
	Cesium-134
	Cesium-137
	Barium-140

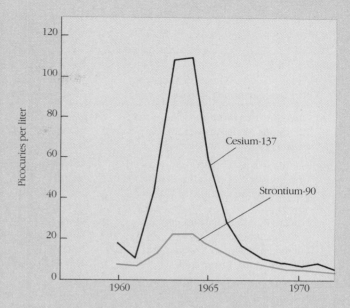

Figure S21-6
Radiactive strontium and cesium levels in pasteurized milk following nuclear testing in the Soviet Union and the United States in 1950s and early 1960s.

For example, iodine-131 is released from nuclear power plants during normal operations and during accidents. From the ground it may be incorporated in grass eaten by dairy cows. It is then selectively taken up by the human thyroid gland (biological concentration), where it irradiates cells and may produce thyroid tumors. Milk contaminated with iodine-131 is especially harmful to children.

Strontium-90 is released during atomic bomb explosions (Figure S21-5). Small amounts may also be released from reactors under normal operating conditions and in large quantities in accidents. Strontium-90 is readily absorbed by plants and may also be passed to humans through cow's milk. It seeks out bone, where it is deposited like calcium. With a half-life of 28 years, it irradiates the bone and causes leukemia and bone cancer.

Cesium-137, produced by bomb detonations (Figure S21-6) and nuclear reactors, is also picked up by cattle and transferred to humans in milk and meat. This radionuclide has a half-life of 27 years and tends to concentrate in muscle. Environmental levels of cesium-137 have dropped substantially since the banning of surface testing of nuclear weapons. Cesium is also excreted from the body within two weeks, which minimizes exposure to its high-energy gamma rays.

Accumulation of radionuclides within tissues has important implications for human health because seemingly low levels may become dangerously high in localized regions. Some radionuclides may be biologically magnified in food chains, adding further to their effects.

Table S21-3   Approximate Radiation Exposure from Various Medical X Rays

Average Effective Doses of Common X-Ray Examinations (Somatic Doses)	Average Dose to the Reproductive Organs from Common X-Ray Examinations (Genetic Doses)	High Doses to the Uterus and Fetus
A. *High-dose examinations* (more than 125 mrads or mrems per average examination) Mammography (breast examination) Upper GI Series (barium swallow) Thoracic spine (middle or dorsal spine) Lower GI Series (barium enema, colon examination) Lumbosacral spine (lower spine) Lumbar spine (lower back) B. *Medium-dose examinations* (25–125 mrads or mrems per average examination) Intravenous pyelogram, IVP (exam of kidney, ureter, and bladder) Cervical spine (upper spine) Cholecystography (gallbladder examination) KUB (kidney, ureter, or bladder examination) Skull Lumbopelvic (examination of pelvis and lower spine) C. *Low-dose examinations* (less than 25 mrads or mrems per average examination) Chest Hip or upper femur (hip or upper thigh examination) Shoulder Dental (whole mouth or bitewing examination) Extremities (feet, hands, forearm)	A. *High-dose examinations* (exposure of male gonads, more than 200 mrads per average exam) Lower GI (barium enema, colon exam) Intravenous pyelogram (IVP) (exam of kidney and ureter) Lumbar spine (lower back) Lumbopelvic (exam of pelvis and lower spine)[1] Hip or upper femur (exam of hip or thigh)[1] B. *Medium-dose examinations* (exposure of male gonads between 10 and 200 mrads per average exam) Upper GI (barium swallow) Cholecystography (gallbladder exam)[2] Thoracic spine (middle spine) Upper GI (barium swallow)[2] Abdomen KUB (kidney, ureter, and bladder) C. *Low-dose examinations* (exposure of gonads less than 10 mrads or mrems per average exam) Cervical spine (upper spine) Skull Shoulder Chest Dental Extremities	The following examinations of a pregnant woman may expose her unborn child to more than 4,000 mrads or mrems: Abdominal aortography (examination of the main arteries in the abdominal region) Lower GI series (barium enema) Celiac angiography (examination of the blood vessels in the abdominal cavity) Upper GI series (barium swallow) Hysterosalpingography (examination of the uterus and oviducts) Pelvimetry (examination to measure the size of the pelvis) Placentography (examination of the placenta) Renal arteriography (examination of the kidney) Urethrocytography (examination of the kidneys, urinary tract, bladder, and urethra) Cystogram (examination of the bladder)

[1]High category for females
[2]Medium category for females
Source: Laws, P. W (1983). *The X-Ray Information Book.* New York: Farrar, Straus, Giroux, pp. 54–56.

Minimizing the Risk

Radiation can be reduced in several ways. Because X rays are the most significant source of exposure from anthropogenic sources, prudence would dictate caution. Table S21-3 lists X-ray procedures that involve high, medium, and low doses. High-dose exposures warrant discussion with your doctor.

Certain medical practices also involve the injection of radio-opaque dyes into the body; these dyes show up on X-ray film and allow physicians to determine blood flow and other impor-

Table S21-4   High-Risk Medical X-Ray Procedures[1]

Type of Study	Method	Uses
Bronchogram	Dye injected into lung bronchi (air passages)	Outlines bronchial tree
Cerebral angiogram (arteriogram)	Dye injected into carotid and/or vertebral arteries in neck	Outlines blood vessels in neck and brain
Coronary angiogram (arteriogram)	Dye injected into chambers of heart	Outlines heart chambers, valves, and surrounding arteries and veins
Pneumoencephalogram (PEG)	Air injected (as per myelogram); air rises into brain	Outlines chambers and surface of brain
Pulmonary angiogram (arteriogram)	Dye injected into pulmonary arteries as they leave heart	Outlines blood vessels in lungs

[1]These procedures require introduction of a contrast medium into the body to highlight certain organs, creating additional risks such as stroke or nerve damage.
Source: Levin, A. (1975). *Talk Back to Your Doctor.* New York: Doubleday & Co., Inc.

tant facts about your health. Tables S21-3 and S21-4 list procedures that have the potential for harm.

Important ways to reduce radiation exposure include (1) asking the physician if previous X rays or diagnostic procedures would provide the same information; (2) reducing X-ray exposure in children; (3) informing physicians and dentists if you are pregnant; (4) if you are pregnant, avoiding unnecessary X rays of the pelvis, abdomen, and lower back; (5) avoiding mobile X-ray units, which tend to give higher than necessary doses; (6) if you are a woman under the age of 50 and have no family history of breast cancer, avoiding routine mammographs; (7) questioning the necessity of preemployment X rays; (8) if you must be X rayed, requesting that a full-time radiologist do it; (9) asking if the X-ray machine and facilities have been inspected and set to minimize excess exposure; (10) requesting that a lead apron be placed over your chest and lap for dental X rays and that a thyroid shield be placed around your neck; (12) cooperating with the X-ray technologist (do not breathe or move during the X ray); and (13) making sure the operator exposes only those parts of the body that are necessary.

Radiation exposure from medical diagnosis and treatment is by far the easiest to control on an individual level. Controls on exposures from nuclear weapons testing, possible nuclear war, and possible catastrophic accidents at nuclear power plants are out of the average citizen's hands. As a whole, society must decide whether to accept the risk of widespread biospheric contamination.

A growing body of evidence shows that the supposed safe levels of radiation for workers and the general public need revision. Some health officials believe that the current 5-rad standard for workers should be reduced to .5 rad per year. The current standard for protecting the general public—.17 rad per year above background—may also be too high. Some experts suggest lowering it to .017 rad. The costs involved would be in the billions, but so might the harm done if today's standards are truly too high.

Suggested Readings

Gofman, J. W., and Tamplin, A. R. (1970). Low Dose Radiation and Cancer. In *Global Ecology: readings Toward a Rational Strategy for Man.* J. P. Holdren and P. R. Ehrlich, eds. New York: Harcourt Brace Jovanovich. Excellent article.

Hobbs, C. H., and McClellan, R. O. (1980). Radiation and Radioactive Materials. In *Toxicology: The Basic Science of Poisons* (2nd ed.), J. Doull, C. D. Klaassen, and M. O. Amdur, eds. New York: Macmillan. More-technical review.

Johnson, C. J., Tidball, R. R., and Severson, R. C. (1976). Plutonium Hazard in Respirable Dust on the Surface of Soil. *Science* 193: 488–490. Interesting case study.

Laws, P. W., and The Public Citizen Health Research Group (1983). *The X-Ray Information Book.* New York: Farrar, Straus, and Giroux. Elementary coverage of X rays, their effects and ways to minimize exposure.

Mancuso, T. F., Stewart, A., and Kneade, G. (1977). Radiation Exposures of Hanford Workers Dying from Cancer and Other Causes. *Health Physics* 33: 369–385. Excellent study.

Solon, L. R., and Sidel, V. W. (1979). Health Implications of Nuclear Power Production. *Annals of Internal Medicine* 90(3): 424–426. Good review.

Noise Pollution

Noise Pollution

Noise is rapidly becoming the most widespread environmental pollutant. Few of us can escape it. Even the silence of a back-country camping trip is broken by the roar of jets overhead, chain saws, and off-road vehicles. Especially noisy are cities and factories, where many of us live and work (Figure S21-1). So congested are many cities that the quiet, traffic-free period has shrunk to only a few hours.

To understand noise pollution and the ways it affects us in scientific terms, let us first take a look at sound.

What Is Sound?

Sound is transmitted through the air as a series of waves of compression. For a simple example, take the bass speaker element of a loudspeaker. When the music is loud, the speaker can be seen to vibrate, and a hand placed in front of it can feel the air move. If we could slow down the speaker cone to observe what was happening, we would see that as it moves outward, it compresses the air molecules in front of it. As the speaker cone returns inward, the compressed air expands in both directions like a spring, compressing neighboring air molecules slightly farther away. A wave of expansion and compression is set up. Thus air molecules do not travel with the sound but only oscillate back and forth in the direction the sound is traveling. Sound is, therefore, a train of high-pressure regions following one another at a rate of 340 meters per second (760 miles per hour) in air.

Sound can be described in terms of its loudness and its pitch or frequency. **Loudness** is measured in decibels (dB). The decibel scale, illustrated in Table S21-1, encompasses a wide range

Figure S21-1
A new freeway or an airport can drastically change the stress and comfort levels in neighborhoods. Some people do not have the resources to relocate.

Table S21-1 A Decibel Scale

Sound Intensity Factor	Sound Level, dB	Sound Sources	Perceived Loudness	Effects — Damage to Hearing	Community Reaction to Outdoor Noise
1,000,000,000,000,000,000	180—	• Rocket engine			
100,000,000,000,000,000	170—				
10,000,000,000,000,000	160—				
1,000,000,000,000,000	150—	• Jet plane at takeoff	Painful	Traumatic injury	
100,000,000,000,000	140—			Injurious range; irreversible damage	
10,000,000,000,000	130—	• Maximum recorded rock music			
1,000,000,000,000	120—	• Thunderclap • Textile loom • Auto horn, 1 meter away	Uncomfortably loud		
100,000,000,000	110—	• Riveter • Jet flying over at 300 meters			
10,000,000,000	100—	• Newspaper press		Danger zone; progressive loss of hearing	
1,000,000,000	90—	• Motorcycle, 8 meters away • Food blender • Diesel truck, 80 km/hr, at 15 meters away	Very loud		Vigorous action
100,000,000	80—	• Garbage disposal		Damage begins after long exposure	
10,000,000	70—	• Vacuum cleaner • Ordinary conversation	Moderately loud		Threats
1,000,000	60—	• Air conditioning unit, 6 meters • Light traffic noise, 30 meters			Widespread complaints
100,000	50—	• Average living room			Occasional complaints
10,000	40—	• Bedroom	Quiet		
1000	30—	• Library • Soft whisper			No action
100	20—	• Broadcasting studio	Very quiet		
10	10—	• Rustling leaf	Barely audible		
1	0—	• Threshold of hearing			

Source: Turk et.al. (1978). *Environmental Science*. Philadelphia: Saunders, p. 523.

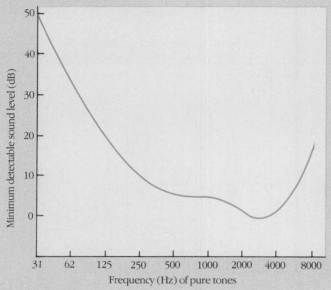

Figure S21-2
Sensitivity of the human ear to various frequencies.

of volume. The lowest sound the human ear can detect is set at 0 dB; this is the threshold of hearing. In the decibel scale, a tenfold increase in sound intensity is represented by a 10-dB increase on the scale. That is, a 10-dB sound is ten times louder than a 0-dB sound; a 20-dB sound is ten times louder than 10-dB sound.

Pitch, or **frequency**, is a measure of how high or how low a sound is. Bass notes played by a tuba have a low pitch, whereas a violin's treble notes have a high pitch. Pitch is measured in cycles (that is, waves) per second (cps). This is the number of compression waves passing a given point each second. Cycles per second is commonly called hertz (Hz), after the German physicist Heinrich Rudolf Hertz.

The human ear is sensitive to sounds in the range of 20 to 20,000 Hz, but the ear is not as sensitive to low- and high-frequency sounds as it is to medium-frequency sounds (Figure S21-2). Sounds below 20 Hz are not detected by the human ear and are described as **infrasonic**; sounds above the audible range are called **ultrasonic**.

Frequency is a function of wavelength, or the distance between two areas of compression. The greater the wavelength, the lower the frequency.

What Is Noise?

Ambrose Bierce once wrote that "noise is a stench in the ear, and the chief product of civilization." To the scientist, **noise** is any unwanted, unpleasant sound. Beyond that, it is hard to say

with any certainty what a group of people would consider noise. The rumble of construction machinery at a building site may be pleasing to the owner of the new building but insufferable to the doctor whose office is next door. The sound of a bulldozer may not bother its operator; but that same operator may find the cries of the neighbor's baby irritating.

What any individual considers noise depends on his or her background, mood, occupation, location, and hearing ability. But the time of day, the duration and volume of a sound, and other factors also contribute to our judgment. A sound may be pleasant when it is soft but noise when it is loud, or it may be acceptable when you generate it but obnoxious when someone else does. People generally agree that the louder a sound is, the more annoying it becomes and the more likely people are to describe it as noise. Table S21-1 shows some examples of sounds we encounter in everyday life.

Sources of Noise Pollution

Sources of noise fall into four categories: transportation, industrial, household, and military. As the world becomes more dependent on technology, noise pollution grows worse. Of greatest concern are noises from off-road vehicles, construction, air traffic, home appliances, and surface transportation.

Impacts of Noise

Robert A. Baron once wrote, "Air pollution kills us slowly but silently; noise makes each day a torment." Noise affects us in many ways. It damages hearing, interferes with our sleep, and is an annoyance in our everyday life. It interferes with conversation, concentration, relaxation, and leisure.

Hearing Loss

Our hearing declines from aging and exposure to noise. Hearing loss with age is called **presbycusis**, and hearing loss from anthropogenic noise is called **sociocusis**.

Natural hearing loss results from degeneration of the **organ of Corti**, a structure in the ear that translates sound into nerve impulses (Figure S21-3). This natural decline is presumably brought about by infections in the inner ear and natural aging of the sound receptors (hair cells). The natural loss of hearing is greater at some frequencies than others. The loss of hearing at 4000 Hz (which includes the "sh" and "th" sounds), for example, is greater than the loss at 2000 Hz. In 40-year-old men, there is an average hearing loss of 10 dB at 4000 Hz, but only 4 dB at 2000 Hz.

Men generally suffer a greater loss of hearing with age than women. For example, in 60-year-old men the hearing loss at 4000 Hz is about 30 dB, but it is only 20 dB in women of the

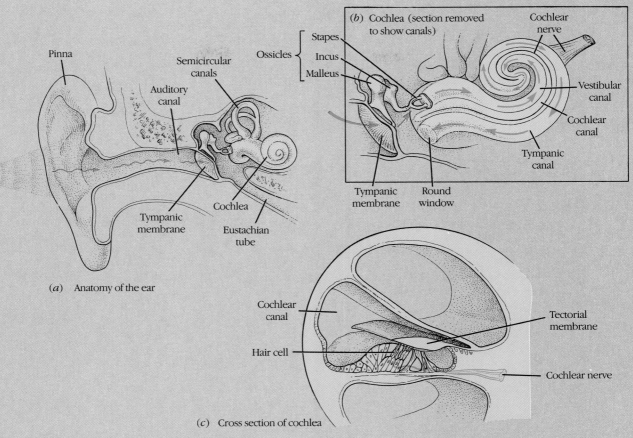

(a) Anatomy of the ear

(b) Cochlea (section removed to show canals)

(c) Cross section of cochlea

Figure S21-3

Anatomy of the ear. (*a*) Sound waves enter the auditory canal, causing the tympanic membrane (eardrum) to vibrate. The vibrations are transferred to the cochlea by the ossicles, three small bones. (*b*) Vibrations travel in the fluid of the cochlea and cause the tectorial membrane to vibrate. (*c*) Nerve impulses are generated and sent to the brain. Thus, sound waves are first converted to vibrations of the eardrum, and then converted to fluid compression waves in the cochlea. These waves stimulate the organ of Corti. The brain translates these fluid waves into sound.

same age. This difference probably results from factors other than sex, such as firing guns or exposure to noise at work. Therefore, what appears to be a natural decline may in fact be brought about by factors under our own control.

Many sounds from a variety of sources impinge upon our ears. Some of these, if loud and persistent enough, can cause premature degeneration of the organ of Corti. Studies published in the 1960s indicate that 1 of every 40 persons in the U.S. suffers from sociocusis. These studies, however, probably greatly underestimate the loss of hearing from anthropogenic sources. Most likely, 1 in every 10 to 20 persons suffers some hearing loss from anthropogenic noise.

We have all been exposed to noise so loud that we experienced a temporary decrease in our ability to hear. This is called a **temporary threshold shift**. A loud concert, a party with a loud stereo and lots of noisy friends, a drive in the car with the windows open, noisy machinery, or gunfire—all can deafen us for a little while.

A permanent loss of hearing, or a **permanent threshold shift**, occurs after continued exposure to loud noise. Recent studies suggest that continuous long-term exposure to noise levels as low as 55 dB can permanently damage hearing. Noise of this level is common in many factories and jobs, especially construction and mining. Even city traffic noise can damage the hearing of people exposed on a regular basis. A 20-year-old New York City resident hears as well as a 70-year-old inhabitant of Africa's grasslands.

As a general rule, the higher the sound level, the less time it takes to induce a permanent threshold shift. In addition, intermittent noise is generally less hazardous than continuous noise. Different frequencies produce differing amounts of damage. The lower frequencies, for example, do less damage than the higher-pitch sounds at the same loudness.

Explosions (130 dB) and other extremely loud noises can cause instantaneous damage to the organ of Corti, resulting in deafness. Noise levels over 150 dB can severely damage the organ of Corti, rupture the eardrum, and displace the tiny bones in the ear, the **ossicles**, which convey sound waves from the eardrum to the organ of Corti.

According to many sources, occupational noise is slowly deafening millions of Americans. Large numbers work at jobs where the noise levels are over 80 dB. Military personnel are victims of noise from tanks, jets, helicopters, artillery, and rifles. Studies show that about half of our soldiers who complete combat training suffer so much hearing loss that they can no longer meet the enlistment requirements for combat units. Bars, nightclubs, discotheques, and traffic noise (especially diesel trucks and buses) are also important contributors to the deafening of America.

The importance of good hearing cannot be emphasized enough. In children it is important for learning language. The loss of hearing impairs speech comprehension—our ability to understand what's being said. Communication with family, friends, and coworkers can be severely impaired, causing increased tension, not only because the sufferer can't understand what's being said but also because deafened individuals tend to talk annoyingly loud.

Because speech comprehension is so crucial, techniques have been devised to measure social impairment caused by hearing loss. Called the **social adequacy index**, this measure takes into account effects of hearing loss in pitch and loudness. Studies show that there can be a fairly large intensity loss without loss of social adequacy. However, a loss of frequencies—for example, the inability to hear sounds of 4000 Hz—greatly impairs social functioning. A classic study compared social adequacy in weavers who had been exposed to a 100-dB work environment to a control group of people not exposed to loud noises. Nearly 75% of the weavers said they had difficulties at public meetings, compared with 5% of the control group. Eighty percent of the weavers experienced difficulty talking to strangers, compared with 16% of the controls. Sixty-four percent of the weavers had difficulty understanding phone conversations, compared with 5% of the controls.

Effects on Sleep

Noise affects sleep in many ways. It may (1) prevent us from falling asleep as soon as desired, (2) keep us from sleeping at all, (3) wake us during the night, or (4) alter the quality of sleep. A number of factors are involved in sleep disturbance, both noise-related and individual. The noise-related variables are the kind of noise, its intensity, its duration, and whether it is repeated or continuous. Individual variables include age, sex, occupation, state of health, use of certain drugs, and stage of sleep when the noise occurs.

Some generalizations on the noise-related variables may be helpful. In general, each type of noise has a different threshold for awakening us: parents might be awakened by the baby crying but not by a siren. Regarding intensity, it is difficult to draw conclusions. Several studies show that 40-dB sounds awaken light sleepers and that 60-dB sounds awaken heavy sleepers. Regular and frequent sounds, such as traffic, are less likely to awaken a sleeper than intermittent sounds, such as explosions.

Noise affects the amount of time we spend in various stages of sleep. For example, noisy environments increase the time we spend in light sleep and decrease deep sleep. Because deep sleep helps recharge the body and mind, such shifts can have serious consequences. Individuals deprived of stage 5 (deepest) sleep, for example, can suffer mental confusion, withdrawal, irritability, and, in severe cases, mental derangement.

The quality of sleep becomes lighter, and awakenings become more frequent. Adults are more sensitive to noise than children; old people are the most easily disturbed.

Women are more easily awakened by noise than men. In addition, it has been shown that individuals of certain occupations may be more easily awakened than others. According to a limited number of studies, college professors seem to be deeper sleepers than manual laborers, who, in turn, seem to be deeper sleepers than female homemakers.

Certain mental and physical illnesses make people more likely to be awakened by a given noise. These include depression, psychosomatic illnesses, neuroses, and heart disease.

Finally, the use of certain drugs may affect sleep. Alcohol robs us of deep sleep and makes us irritable. Certain sleeping medicines help us to relax and fall asleep faster but decrease the time we spend in deep sleep.

Taking the individual factors into account, it appears that about a third of the U.S. population can be easily disturbed by noise. Persons deprived of sleep may function more slowly and more clumsily. Reaction times are inevitably slower. Moreover, the long-term effects of moderate sleep deprivation are unknown.

Sonic Booms and Infrasound

When jet aircraft travel faster than the speed of sound, they create a **sonic boom**. A sonic boom is much like the wake that trails behind a speedboat. As a supersonic jet moves through the air, it creates a high-energy, cone-shaped wake that trails behind the jet, as shown in Figure S21-4.

Residents in the flight paths of supersonic military jets and of the supersonic transports (SSTs) operated by France, England,

(a) 3-dimensional view

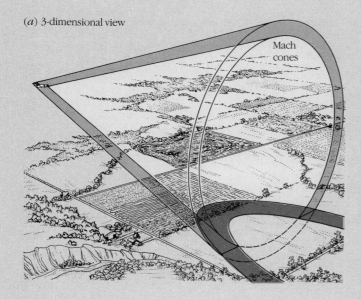

(b) Cross sectional view

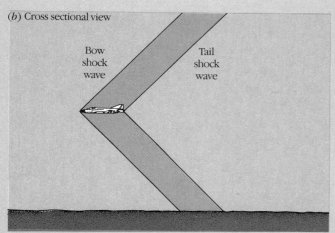

Figure S21-4
The sonic boom is created when a jet travels faster than the speed of sound. A high compression wave trails the jet much like the wave of a speeding power boat, but is a conical wave of compression that sounds like an explosion.

and the Soviet Union complain about interrupted sleep, rest, conversation, and radio and television reception caused by sonic booms. Studies in the United States and England show that most people are startled by sonic booms, even if they live in an area where they are common. Because there is no warning of its coming, the sonic boom invariably catches them off guard.

Sonic booms do minor damage to buildings, monuments, and other structures in a state of poor repair. Very little is known about their effects on animals.

Sonic booms are likely to become more frequent as the world's military capability expands and as population centers grow. Careful siting of military bases and regulation of population growth around bases and in flightways could help reduce exposure to sonic booms. Commercial supersonic transport jets designed to carry passengers and cargo have not been successful in this age of declining fossil fuel supplies, so our major exposure will continue to be military aircraft.

As we have seen, the human ear is insensitive to sound lower than 20 Hz, or infrasound. Such low-frequency sounds are created by many sources in the modern industrial world, such as airplanes, fans, trucks, and heavy machinery.

Few effects of infrasound are known, but it may cause organs within the body to vibrate or resonate at the same low frequency. A person exposed to 7-Hz sound waves, for example, may complain of a general feeling of discomfort and may lose mental concentration, becoming unable to perform even the simplest math. As the intensity (loudness) increases, dizziness may set in; this is often followed by fatigue and sickness. At even higher intensities the internal organs may vibrate so much that death results. Clearly, careful monitoring of the machines of modern society is necessary to reduce our exposure to infrasound.

Controlling Noise

Sociocusis has received little attention compared with air and water pollution. One reason is that hearing loss is generally progressive, so victims are unaware of the gradual loss in auditory acuity. Workers who are exposed to loud noises eventually become accustomed to them, partly because their hearing declines.

To control noise, we must know where it comes from and factors that influence it. In general, noise comes from mechanical vibration and air turbulence. For example, a lawn mower vibrates as it operates, producing noise. A car moving along the highway produces some mechanical vibration, and the air turbulence it generates creates a hissing noise.

Sound Transmission and Dissipation

Several natural factors determine the transmission of sound and how quickly it dissipates—distance, atmospheric conditions, and geological and biological barriers. For example, sound fades as it travels through air. Noise from a point source of sound such as a factory decreases by 6 dB for every doubling of distance. If the noise level is 100 dB at .5 kilometer, it will be 6 dB less at 1 kilometer. If noise is produced by a line source, such as a highway, it drops 3 dB for every doubling of distance. These general rules can help us determine how far homes should be built from highways or other sources of noise, but it should be noted that high-frequency noise drops off faster than low-frequency noise.

Table S21-2   Strategies to Control Noise Pollution

Design and Planning

Minimize air turbulence created by vehicles.
Minimize vibration from vehicles, machines, and home appliances.
Build railroads and highways away from densely populated areas.
Build better-insulated subways, railroad cars, trucks, and buses.
Eliminate noisy two-stroke motorcycle engines.
Install better mufflers on motorized vehicles and equipment.
Build airports away from high-density population centers.
Restrict growth in the vicinity of existing airports.
Require low-noise home appliances, tools, and office equipment.
Pass laws to eliminate or block noise.
Control traffic flow to eliminate stop-and-start driving.

Barriers and Sound Absorbers

Build embankments along noisy streets.
Use smooth road surfaces.
Build level streets to cut down on engine noise generated on steep inclines.
Plant dense rows of trees along highways and around sources of noise.
Construct artificial noise barriers along streets and around factories.
Install better insulation in houses.
Use double- and triple-paned windows.
Add sound-absorbent materials in factories, offices, and homes.
Provide earplugs for ground personnel at airports and workers in factories and construction.

Personal Solutions

Use fewer power tools and appliances.
Time activities to minimize disturbance of others.
Use mass transit.
Refuse to buy noisy vehicles, tools, office equipment, and appliances.
Maintain vehicles to eliminate noise.
Wear ear guards when engaged in noisy activities.
Work with employer to reduce noise.

Methods of Control

Noise control can be carried out on many levels (Table S21-2). In general, we can make design changes to minimize sound in all new products. Simple alterations in design can cut air turbulence and vibration. Communities can separate people from noisy activities; railroads, highways, factories, and airports should be placed away from residences and office buildings. Furthermore, legal controls on noise emissions may also be helpful. Many countries have regulations to control noise from motorized vehicles; these include Japan, Norway, the Netherlands, Sweden, Switzerland, the United Kingdom, Denmark, France, Italy, and Canada. In the United States the *Noise Control Act* (1972) gave the Environmental Protection Agency the authority to establish maximum permissible noise levels for motor vehicles and other sources. Individual cities and towns have passed noise ordinances. In 1971, for example, Chicago set noise limits on every new vehicle, to be effective in 1980. Members of the European Economic Community have coordinated their efforts to limit noise on new vehicles to provide uniform standards.

In the United States, noise in the work place is controlled by the Occupational Safety and Health Administration. It set the standard at 90 dB for an eight-hour exposure, a level many authorities believe is too high. The Occupational Safety and Health Administration can issue abatement orders for noise violations.

They require the employer to first tackle the problem through engineering and design changes in the equipment. Should these prove infeasible, workers must be provided with personal protective equipment or must be moved regularly from noisy jobs to quieter jobs to reduce their overall exposure. Protective ear guards or earplugs are less than optimal solutions, because they are uncomfortable to wear and also block out important sounds or signals necessary for worker safety.

In May 1977 the EPA released its first comprehensive national plan for reducing noise, with the chief goal of eliminating sociocusis. It called for a reduction of the average daily exposure to no more than 65 dB in the short term and 55 dB in the long term; product labeling; cooperation from states and local agencies; and federal policies to encourage buffer zones around noisy airports and the use of quieter equipment on federal construction projects. To date, however, noise control has been pushed to the back burner in favor of seemingly more pressing environmental problems, especially hazardous wastes.

Suggested Readings

Berland, T. (1970). *The Fight for Quiet.* Englewood Cliffs, N.J.: Prentice-Hall. Good general introduction.

Bugliarello, G., Alexandre, A., Barnes, J., and Wakstein, C. (1976). *The Impact of Noise: A Socio-Technological Introduction.* New York: Pergamon Press. Detailed analysis.

Milne, A. (1979). *Noise Pollution: Impact and Countermeasures.* New York: David and Charles. Well worth reading.

Hazardous Wastes

There is nothing more frightful than ignorance in action.

GOETHE

Shenandoah Stables was a large and successful quarter-horse ranch in Moscow Mills, Missouri, 65 kilometers (40 miles) northwest of St. Louis. But in the last week of May 1971, tragedy struck. The road in the area was oiled with 3800 liters (1000 gallons) of waste automobile oil applied to control dust, a routine procedure in many states.

Shortly after the oil had been applied, one of the owners noticed strong chemical odors in the air in the barn and on the grounds. The day after, she discovered dozens of dead sparrows on the floor of the barn. Soon the dogs and cats at the ranch began to lose their fur and become dehydrated and thin. By mid-June, 11 cats and 5 dogs had died, each with the same symptoms.

Of 85 horses routinely exercised in the arena, 43 died within a year. Autopsies revealed that internal organs were swollen and bloody. In 1971, 41 horses on the ranch were bred; most of the pregnancies ended in spontaneous abortion. Of the foals born alive, all but one died within a few months.

The daughters of one of the owners became ill, complaining of severe headaches. One developed sores on her hands; the other developed severe internal bleeding and was hospitalized. The owner suffered chest pains, headaches, and diarrhea.

What caused the poisonings and deaths? Tests on the oil applied to the arena showed dioxin, polychlorinated biphenyls (PCBs), and other highly toxic contaminants.

The Dangers of Asbestos

Asbestos is the generic name for several naturally occurring silicate mineral fibers. It is useful because of its resistance to heat, friction, and acid; its flexibility; and its great tensile strength. Over 3 million metric tons of asbestos is used worldwide each year for thousands of different commercial applications.

Two-thirds of all asbestos produced is added to cement, giving it a better resistance to weather. Asbestos also insulates steel girders in buildings and serves as heat insulation in factories, schools, and other buildings. In addition, it can be found in brake pads, brake linings, hair dryers, patching plaster, and a multitude of other products.

Asbestos is dangerous because fibers are easily dislodged. Floating in the air, these fine particles may be inhaled into the lungs, where they are neither broken down nor expelled but remain for life. Three disorders may result: pulmonary (lung) fibrosis, lung cancer, and mesothelioma.

Pulmonary fibrosis, or **asbestosis,** is a buildup of scar tissue in the lungs that may occur in people who inhale asbestos on the job or in buildings with exposed asbestos insulation. The disease takes 10 to 20 years to develop after the first exposure.

Exposures to asbestos at low levels even for only short periods can cause lung cancer. As shown in the figure, the death rate from lung cancer in asbestos insulation workers in the United States is four times the expected rate. The incidence of lung cancer in asbestos workers who smoke is 92 times greater than in asbestos workers who don't smoke, providing a striking example of synergism.

Asbestos is the only known cause of **mesothelioma**, a cancer that develops in the lining of the lungs (the pleura). Highly

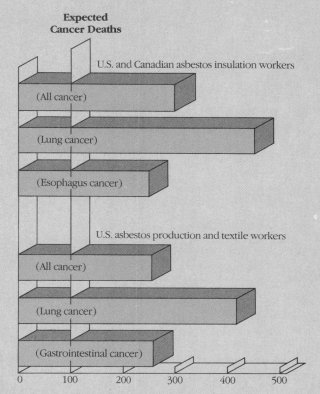

Incidence of cancer in asbestos workers in the United States and Canada. (Ratio of the number of observed to expected death times .00.)

malignant, this cancer spreads rapidly and kills its victims within a year from the time of diagnosis.

An estimated 8 million to 11 million American workers have been exposed to asbestos since World War II. Studies of the workers who have since died show that over a third had lung cancer, mesothelioma, or gastrointestinal cancer. The expected death rate in the population for these diseases is roughly 8 percent.

The use of asbestos in the United States for insulation, fireproofing, and decorative purposes was banned in 1978. In 1979 the EPA began to assist states and local school districts in identifying and removing hazardous asbestos crumbling from pipes and ceilings. Since that time, Johns Manville, a major supplier of asbestos products, has been inundated with personal damage suits amounting to over $2 billion. In 1983 the corporation filed for bankruptcy and reorganization under federal law. This move was an obvious maneuver to avoid going under.

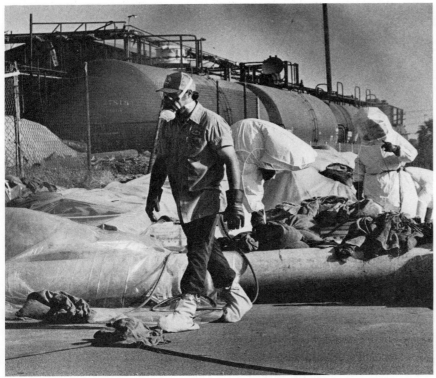

(a)

(b)

Figure 22-1
(a) In May 1984, workers from Neville Chemical Plant in Santa Fe Springs, California, began covering soil believed to be contaminated with highly toxic chemical wastes. The covering prevented the soil from blowing from the site. *(b)* Pollution Abatement Services (PAS) chemical dump at Oswego, N.Y. The dump is now inactive and awaiting cleanup.

The oil had been sold to a company that was supposed to clean it up so it could be used again. Instead, the company spread the oil on at least four sites in Missouri, leaving behind "a trail of sickness and death," in the words of a state assistant attorney general.

Hazardous Wastes: How Large a Problem?

The tragedy at Shenandoah Stables is representative of a much larger problem: illegal and irresponsible hazardous waste disposal (Figure 22-1). Each year in the United States, an estimated 54 million to 72 million metric tons (60 million to 80 million tons) of waste considered hazardous under federal standards is produced. Likewise, about 200 million metric tons of hazardous waste covered by state regulations is produced. The total is well over a ton per person per year. Two-thirds of this waste comes from ten states, listed in order of decreasing importance: Texas, Ohio, Pennsylvania, Louisiana, Michigan, Indiana, Illinois, Tennessee, West Virginia, and California.

European countries also produce millions of tons of hazardous waste each year. In Britain, for example, the figure is about 11 million metric tons a year, and in France, 2 million to 3 million tons.

The Environmental Protection Agency estimates that, until recently, only about 10% of the hazardous wastes in the United States are disposed of properly. The remainder end up in abandoned warehouses; in rivers, streams, and lakes; in leaky landfills that contaminate groundwater; in fields and forests; and along the sides of or even on the highways (see Figure 22-1). In Illinois in the late 1970s, approved chemical disposal sites received 2 million tons of hazardous waste per year, but 14 million tons was produced. The rest is unaccounted for. In California in that same period, 100,000 tons of hazardous waste was produced monthly; 92% went straight into the ground, and much of that wound up in groundwater.

The EPA estimates that there are about 1200 hazardous waste dump sites in the United States that may pose a health hazard to nearby residents or threaten the environment (Table 22-1). Only about 200 sites are actually licensed to handle such wastes. The cost of cleaning up all U.S. sites could come to $260 billion, equivalent to about one-third of the federal budget in 1984.

The major impacts of improper hazardous waste disposal are many: (1) groundwater contamination, (2) well closures, (3) habitat destruction, (4) long-term and short-term diseases, (5) soil contamination, (6) fish kills, (7) illness and death of livestock, and (8) damage to sewage treatment plants.

Table 22-1 The 20 Most Hazardous Waste Dumps in the U.S.

Site	City or County and State
FMC	Fridley, Minn.
Tybouts Corner	New Castle County, Del.
Bruin Lagoon	Bruin, Pa.
Industri-Plex	Woburn, Mass.
Lipari Landfill	Pitman, N.J.
Sinclair Refinery	Wellsville, N.Y.
Price Landfill	Pleasantville, N.J.
Pollution Abatement Services	Oswego, N.Y.
LaBounty Site	Charles City, Iowa
Helen Kramer Landfill	Mantua, N.J.
Army Creek	New Castle, Del.
CPS/Madison Industries	Old Bridge Township, N.J.
Nyanza Chemical	Ashland, Mass.
Gems Landfill	Gloucester Township, N.J.
Picillo Coventry	Coventry, R.I.
Berlin & Farro	Swartz Creek, Mich.
Tar Creek	Cherokee County, Kans.
Baird & McGuire	Holbrook, Mass.
Lone Pine Landfill	Freehold, N.J.
Somersworth Landfill	Somersworth, N.H.

Source: U.S. Environmental Protection Agency, December 1982.

The horror stories of improper hazardous waste disposal appear regularly in the nation's—and the world's—newspapers and magazines; they have created a tremendous outcry and new, tough legal controls. This chapter looks at improper and unethical waste disposal practices, the legal solutions, and some proper ways of reducing the threat posed by hazardous wastes (see also Model Application 22-1).

Improper Waste Disposal Practices

Love Canal: Rapid Awakening of the American Public

The problem of hazardous waste caught the attention of the American public in the 1970s when toxic chemicals began to ooze out of a dump, known as Love Canal, in Niagara Falls, New York. The incident has forever changed the way Americans view hazardous wastes.

The story of Love Canal began in the 1880s when William T. Love began digging a canal that would run from the Niagara River just above Niagara Falls to a point on the river below the falls, but the canal was never completed.

Only a small remnant of the canal remained in the early 1900s. Measuring 18 meters (60 feet) wide and 900 meters (3000 feet) in length, it filled with water from rains and was a favorite swimming spot for years. But in 1942 the Hooker Chemical Company signed an agreement with the canal's new owner, the Niagara Power and Development Corporation, to dump wastes in the canal. Hooker bought the site in 1946 and from 1947 to 1952 dumped over 21,000 tons of highly toxic and carcinogenic wastes, including the pesticide lindane and the deadly poisonous dioxin.

In 1952 the city of Niagara Falls began condemnation proceedings on the property to take the land from Hooker to build an elementary school and residential community. In April 1953 Hooker sold the land for $1 and a release from any liability for damage that might be caused by chemicals in the dump. Hooker insists that it warned against any construction on the dump site itself, but the company is alleged never to have disclosed the real danger of construction on the abandoned dump. The company sealed the dump with a clay cap and topsoil, a standard procedure once thought sufficient to prevent leakage.

Troubles began in January 1954, when workers constructing the 99th Street Elementary School removed the

(a)

(b)

Figure 22-2
(a) House is bulldozed in the Love Canal area of Niagara Falls,
(b) A young but concerned resident.

clay cap. In the late 1950s rusting and leaking barrels of toxic waste began to surface (Figure 22-2). Children playing near them suffered chemical burns; some became ill and died. Hooker asserts that it warned the school board not to allow children to play in chemically contaminated

>>> *Model Application 22-1*

Risk Acceptability

You are assigned the task of finding a site for a chlorine waste-water treatment plant. Your company is concerned with good community relations and asks you to visit several small towns in your area and talk with their residents about the new plant. You must find out what risks and benefits the townspeople think will accompany your facility. Wherever possible, you must point out benefits they might miss. Your goal, in essence, is to convince them that the benefits outweigh the risks.

Step 1

Before visiting prospective communities, make a list of benefits and possible costs. Some examples are listed below:

Pros:
- improved economy
- reduced unemployment (construction jobs, then maintenance personnel)

Cons:
- possibility of an accident (release of chlorine gas) causing death and sickness
- odor problems

Step 2

Analyze that list from the viewpoint of a resident in the community and from your own viewpoint.

To help you with this project you might want to do some research on the possible effects of chlorine on workers and the probability and severity of accidents at the facility. Some important facts are listed below:

- The primary risk associated with chlorine is exposure to the gaseous form.
- Long-term exposure to levels as low as 5 parts per million can result in nausea, respiratory difficulty, increased susceptibility to tuberculosis, and corrosion of the teeth.
- Long-term effects are difficult to diagnose but may include difficult and painful breathing.
- Much more visible are the acute effects of higher doses at 7 parts per million; throat irritation is seen. At higher levels, cough, eye irritation, fluid accumulation in the lungs, or death may occur.
- The rate of injury to workers in chlorine facilities is difficult to determine for many reasons. Studies by the Water Pollution Control Federation show that in wastewater treatment facilities that store large tanks of chlorine, for every 1 million person-hours there are about 560 hours of work lost due to illness from accidents. Illness or injury from the exposure to chlorine accounts for less than 4% of the total injury and illness problem, according to a study by the American Waterworks Association.

areas, but it apparently made no effort to warn local residents of the potential problems.

The problems continued for years. Chemical fumes took the bark off trees and killed grass and garden vegetables. Smelly pools of toxins formed on the surface. After a period of heavy rainfall in the early 1970s the water table rose, and basements in homes near the dump began to flood with a thick, black sludge of toxic chemicals. The chemical smells in homes immediately around the dump site became intolerable.

Tests in 1978 on water, air, and soil in the area detected 82 chemical contaminants, a dozen of which were known or suspected carcinogens. The State Health Department found in 1978 that miscarriages had occurred in 29% of the women, a rate 50% higher than expected. Birth defects were observed in 5 of 24 children born that year. Another survey, released in 1979 by Dr. Beverly Paigen of the Roswell Cancer Institute, showed that of 16 children born to fam-

ilies living in "wet areas" (where groundwater was leaching toxic chemicals from the dump) between 1974 and 1978, 9 had birth defects. The overall incidence of birth defects in the Love Canal area was 1 in 5. The miscarriage rate was 25%, compared with 8.5% in women moving into the area. Asthma was four times as prevalent in wet areas as dry areas in the region; the incidence of urinary and convulsive disorders was almost three times higher. The rate of suicide and nervous breakdown was almost four times higher than in neighboring dry areas. The incidence of ear and sinus infections, respiratory diseases, rashes, and headaches was also elevated. The study also showed that the health of most residents improved dramatically if they moved out of the area.

The school was closed down, the canal was fenced off, and several hundred families were evacuated. Thousands of others were advised to leave, and President Jimmy Carter declared the dump a disaster area. In May 1980 a new study revealed high levels of genetic damage among residents living near the canal. An additional 780 families were evacuated from outlying areas.

To date, Love Canal has cost the state of New York over $35 million and the federal government over $7 million for cleanup, research, and relocation of residents. Lawsuits amounting to over $3 million have been filed against the city of Niagara Falls.

The EPA did a comprehensive study on the canal in the summer and fall of 1980. The $5.4-million study showed that chemical contamination was pretty much limited to the canal area (the actual dump), an area immediately south of it, and two rows of houses on either side of the canal (Figure 22-3). The 780 residents evacuated from the area in 1980 were most probably evacuated unnecessarily. The EPA study also showed that the dump had contaminated shallow groundwater, but there was no evidence of contamination in deeper bedrock aquifers. The EPA concluded that further migration of toxic chemicals to surrounding residences was highly unlikely.

According to the EPA, Love Canal is only 1 of 15 dump sites in Niagara Falls alone that are considered an "imminent hazard." Moreover, there are at least 1000 hazardous waste sites in the United States similar to Love Canal.

Figure 22-3

Love Canal. Area within the dark rectangle was closed off, and citizens were evacuated. Citizens were also evacuated from the declaration area, but recent tests show that hazardous wastes have not migrated into this area.

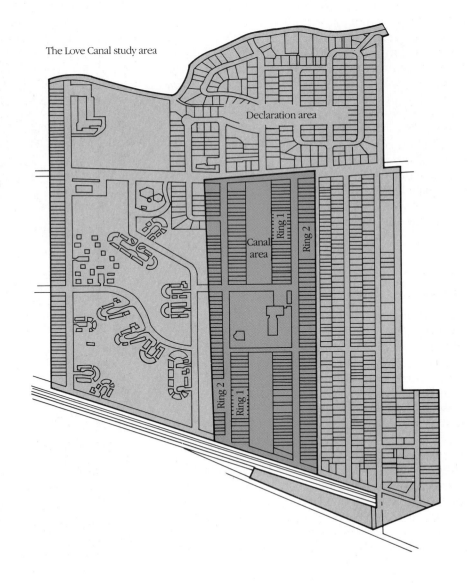

The Love Canal study area

Illegal Dumping: On-Site and Off-Site

Until recently, it was common to dump hazardous wastes in unlined landfills or even in rivers, streams, lakes, and fields. Wastes are commonly stored in barrels that soon rust and leak. The major threat from such practices is the contamination of groundwater.

Only a small fraction of the illegally and improperly disposed of wastes are ever detected, partly because many of them are discarded at the site of production. Some companies simply pipe their wastes to sandy-bottomed pits, where they gradually seep into the groundwater. Others may pump them into nearby rivers through hidden pipes. Some manufacturers hire disposal companies that truck the wastes away and dump them wherever they can. According to Paul Keough, the EPA's deputy administrator in Boston, truckers carrying hazardous liquid wastes have been known to "just drive down the Massachusetts Turnpike and open their spigots." In Tennessee, hazardous wastes have been shipped by freight to fictitious addresses.

State and local governments have difficulty policing illegal dumpers. The territory for illegal disposal is immense, and tracking down offenders is next to impossible. Abandoned, unlabeled barrels leave few clues of their previous owners. Expensive chemical analyses are needed to determine what the material is and where it might have come from.

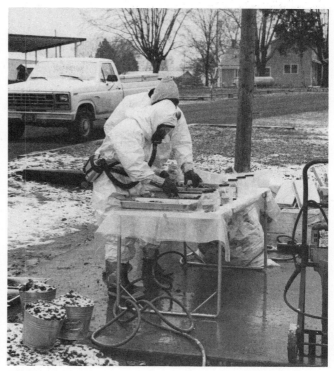

Figure 22-4
Times Beach, Missouri. Two EPA workers testing the soil for dioxin.

Disposal of Toxic Wastes and Waste Oil

Another fairly common practice is to mix hazardous wastes with oil that is later used to control road dust or is burned in apartments and office buildings. The EPA studied waste oil from nine companies and found that six were selling oil contaminated with PCBs.

In June 1983 the 2400 residents of Times Beach, Missouri, agreed to sell nearly all of their 800 homes and 30 businesses to the federal government for $35 million. Dioxin-contaminated oil had been sprayed on the roads by the same company that sprayed contaminated oil on the arena at Shenandoah Stables (Figure 22-4). Studies showed that dioxin levels in the soil were 100 to 300 times higher in places than the level considered harmful for long-term exposure. However, Times Beach is only 1 of 31 dioxin sites in the state, and Missouri is only 1 of 7 dioxin-contaminated states known to date. Because of this,

the EPA has been looking for easier ways of decontaminating towns; it has even proposed building a football stadium-sized bunker in Times Beach for storing contaminated soil from all over the state.

Warehousing of Hazardous Substances

Another unsavory and highly profitable way of "disposing" of hazardous wastes has been to warehouse them. Companies rent a warehouse and pick up hazardous wastes from their customers, sometimes at a cost of $50 to $150 a barrel, promising to dispose of them properly. The company fills the warehouse and then declares bankruptcy, leaving the building's owner or the state to dispose of the wastes. Unscrupulous operators can underbid legitimate operators and therefore command a large percentage of the business.

Deep Well Injection

In the United States about 650,000 wells are being used to inject hazardous wastes deep into the ground. Theoretically, **deep well injection** traps wastes between impermeable rock layers (Figure 22-5). This procedure, however, may be riddled with problems. In Denver in the 1960s, for example, 570 million liters (150 million gallons) of hazardous waste from the production of nerve gas at the Rocky Mountain Arsenal was pumped into a well. As a result, Denver suffered its first earthquake in 80 years; some 1500 tremors followed, because the liquids had altered underground pressure and caused geologic faults to slip. The pressure built up so much that hazardous wastes and gases shot up from abandoned wells like geysers in some places. When deep well injection stopped, so did the earthquakes. Similar problems have been encountered elsewhere.

Solutions: Proper Waste Disposal

Worldwide attention has been focused on hazardous wastes. In Europe, governments and international organizations are developing new regulations and technologies to address

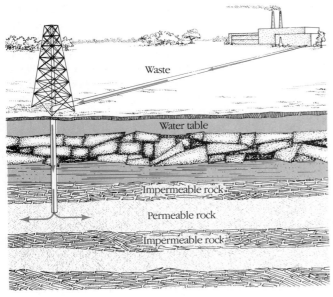

Figure 22-5
Deep well injection. Careful site analysis must be made to ensure that wastes will not migrate into groundwater.

this serious problem. In Denmark, for example, county governments have united to form a central waste disposal company. Wastes may be chemically treated to render them less harmful, incinerated at high temperatures, or permanently stored. Sweden requires disposal or treatment by a state-owned company or by one of 20 state-licensed disposal firms. Still, much more work at the legal, technical, and personal level is needed to prevent the careless disposal of hazardous wastes.

Legal Controls

The U.S. **Resource Conservation and Recovery Act** of 1976 addressed the hazardous waste problem all the way from generation to disposal. The act was amended in 1980. The act requires the EPA (1) to establish what chemicals are considered hazardous wastes; (2) to devise a system to track hazardous substances from generation through disposal; (3) to establish regulations for handling them; and (4) to set up permit requirements for waste treatment, storage, or disposal sites. The act provides stiff penalties for violators and also gives the EPA the authority to halt, through a court order, any improper handling of toxic wastes if evidence shows that an "imminent hazard" to health and the environment "may" be present. The 1976 law excludes wastes from mines and oil wells.

Implementation has been painfully slow. The 1976 act required the EPA to develop necessary regulations within 18 months of its passage, but it was not until four years later that the EPA issued its first regulations. So many loopholes existed in these regulations that about 40 million metric tons of pollutants escaped control each year! Furthermore, the regulations exempted small hazardous waste generators from any kind of controls, so companies producing less than 1000 kilograms (2200 pounds) per month could dispose of their wastes as they pleased—generally, in landfills.

Technological Controls

There are many technological options for controlling industrial wastes, but most are expensive. More stringent toxic waste control will invariably drive up the cost of the products we use. The challenge is to balance the costs of better controls and a clean environment with the risks of improper waste disposal.

Because poor practices today may create headaches for hundreds of years into the future, today's decision about

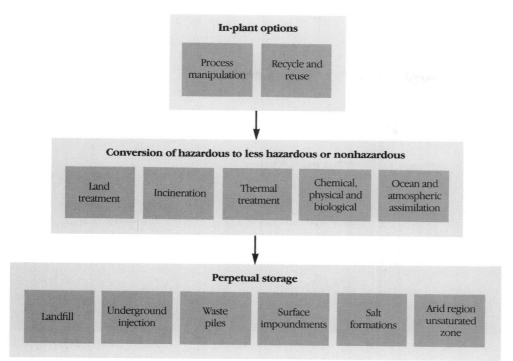

Figure 22-6
A three-tier hierarchy of options for handling hazardous wastes. The top tier reduces the hazardous waste stream; it contains the most desirable options. The middle tier converts hazardous materials into nonhazardous or less hazardous substances. Perpetual storage, the lowest tier, is the least desirable, but often the cheapest, alternative.

hazardous waste disposal must consider future generations. The following sections will cover three major ways of dealing with hazardous wastes: (1) reduction of the amount of waste disposed; (2) detoxification and stabilization, or the conversion to nonhazardous or less hazardous materials; and (3) perpetual storage.

Reduction: Process Manipulation, Recycling, and Reuse

In 1983 the National Academy of Sciences recommended a three-part hierarchy of options for handling toxic wastes (Figure 22-6). At the top of the list is **process manipulation**, which requires manufacturers to redesign manufacturing processes to eliminate or reduce hazardous wastes.

Sharing top billing is the **recycling-and-reuse option**. Ironically, many hazardous materials produced by one company are identical in chemical form and purity to raw materials that another company needs. Others can be extracted from a mixture of wastes or slightly purified to make them economically attractive. Thus, instead of dumping wastes, some companies sell or reuse them.

The recycling-and-reuse option eliminates the cost of waste disposal, cuts down on potential environmental and

health damage, and saves valuable raw materials, including energy. But not every coproduct can be used. A variety of factors determine whether it makes sense to recycle and reuse wastes: the complexity of the waste stream (how many chemicals are present and how hard it is to extract them), the technical capabilities of the plant, the distance to potential buyers, the market or demand for its coproducts, and other economic factors such as the cost of the material from other suppliers and tax rates.

Detoxification and Stabilization

Remaining unusable wastes can be converted to nonhazardous or less hazardous materials—that is, detoxified. This can be accomplished by applying wastes to land and mixing them with the top layer of soil, where they are broken down by chemical reactions, oxidation by sunlight, or bacteria or other organisms in the soil. Some nondegradable wastes are adsorbed onto soil particles and held there indefinitely. Others migrate into deeper layers, possibly entering water but not polluting it if levels are kept sufficiently low. Land treatment is an inexpensive option, but great care is necessary to avoid polluting ecosystems, poisoning

Figure 22-7
A mobile hazardous waste incinerator owned and operated by the United States EPA eliminates the problem of transporting exceptionally dangerous materials.

cattle and other grazing animals, and contaminating groundwater.

Incineration is an attractive alternative for organic wastes. High-temperature furnaces at stationary waste disposal sites, on ships that can burn their wastes at sea, and on mobile trailers are all workable alternatives (Figure 22-7). In each of these, oil or natural gas is burned, and hazardous substances are injected into the furnace or mixed with the fuel before combustion.

Incineration at sea has been used by West German companies to dispose of 1.5 million tons of toxic chemicals each year. Two ships were available in the United States in 1983, and two more were expected to be in operation shortly. One ship, the *Vulcanus,* is 100 meters (335 feet) long and is equipped with two incinerators that burn liquid wastes at temperatures from 1350° to 1500° C (2460° to 2730° F). Special monitoring systems measure air pollutants and waste flows so personnel can check combustion efficiency. The ship can burn about 38,000 liters (10,000 gallons) of waste a day.

High-temperature incineration can provide energy for plant operations, can efficiently eliminate toxic organic wastes such as dioxin and PCBs, and can reduce the need for perpetual storage. Communities often object to incin-erators, however, fearing environmental contamination. Incineration at sea may help overcome these problems. Incineration at sea is not a panacea, however, for ship personnel will inevitably be exposed to fumes from toxic wastes, and accidents may release toxic chemicals at sea, killing fish and other marine life. Illegal dumping will inevitably occur.

Thermal decomposition of cyanide and toxic organics such as pesticides also offers some promise. Wastes are mixed with air and maintained under high pressure while being heated to 450° to 600° C (840° to 1110° F); during the process, organic compounds are broken into smaller biodegradable molecules. A thermal decomposition system can treat 53,000 liters (14,000 gallons) of waste a day. Valuable materials can be extracted and recycled, and the process saves energy compared with incineration. It cannot be used for acids or heavy metals, however.

Chemical, physical, and biological agents can be used to detoxify or neutralize hazardous wastes. For example, lime neutralizes sulfuric acid. Ozone breaks up small organic molecules, nitrogen compounds, and cyanides, although the process is fairly expensive. Cyanides can also be oxidized by chlorine and other chemicals. Liquid toxic wastes can be chemically stabilized and then solidified and possibly even made into bricklike units coated with a waterproof seal. In this encapsulated form, wastes are less likely to be readily leached from properly maintained landfills and may pose a much lower risk.

Many bacteria can degrade or detoxify organic wastes and may prove helpful in the future. New strains capable of destroying a wide variety of organic wastes may be developed through genetic engineering.

Perpetual Storage The third tier, perpetual storage of hazardous wastes, should be used for remaining materials. Residual waste can be dumped in **secured landfills** lined by synthetic liners or thick, impermeable clay liners. To lower the risk, they can be placed in arid regions— neither over aquifers nor near major water supplies. Special drains can be installed to catch any liquids that leak out of storage containers.

Finding acceptable areas is often difficult because of community opposition; it seems that everyone wants the products that make waste, but no one wants the wastes dumped near them.

According to EPA regulations, secured landfills must be maintained for 30 years after dumping ceases. Wells must be drilled around each site so groundwater pollution can be monitored. Critics argue that no matter how well-constructed they are, landfills will eventually leak; therefore, secured landfills should be monitored far longer.

Secured landfills are the cheapest waste disposal practice today and are favored by industry, but present savings are inevitably at the expense of future generations. Leaks that contaminate groundwater and endanger the health of future generations raise the price significantly, as does the continued monitoring necessary to protect public health. Critics suggest that future costs be considered and that landfills be phased out or greatly reduced.

To strengthen existing regulations, the EPA might develop a list of chemicals that cannot be disposed in landfills, require more frequent monitoring of groundwater near the dump site, and require companies to test air around the site to ensure that toxic fumes are not escaping.

Other methods of perpetual storage include (1) waste piles, a dubious solution that invites many problems; (2) surface impoundments and specially built warehouses that hold wastes in ideal conditions and prevent any material from leaking into the environment; (3) deposition in geologically stable salt formations; and (4) deposition deep in the ground in arid regions where groundwater is absent.

Disposing of Radioactive Wastes

Radioactive wastes are a special problem for society. The seriousness of radioactive waste disposal is underscored by three factors: the long lifetime of many wastes, the ability of some radioactive materials to concentrate in certain tissues, and the serious damage radiation poses to human health.

Although nuclear power in the United States has floundered in recent years (Chapter 14), radioactive wastes from existing plants continue to build up in temporary storage sites. Expanded nuclear capacity (possible in the future), continued operation of the existing facilities, and construction of nuclear weapons suggest the need for long-term, low-risk storage of nuclear wastes. But progress in developing storage sites has been slow because of a lack of agreement among experts and widespread resistance to siting waste disposal sites in many proposed states.

The 1982 **Nuclear Waste Policy Act** established a strict timetable for the Department of Energy to choose sites for disposing radioactive wastes. According to the act, the first site must be in operation by 1998. The site must be chosen by 1987, but the targeted state may veto the selection. Its veto holds unless overridden by both houses of Congress. If the veto stands, a new site must be selected.

Many authorities believe that deep geological disposal is the best option for disposing of most dangerous radioactive wastes. However, little is known about the interaction between heat generated from radioactive wastes and rock and water in the surrounding rock. Still, deep rock and salt formations 600 to 1200 meters (2000 to 4000 feet) below the surface in geologically stable regions are believed to be the best option for keeping wastes from entering groundwater and contaminating the environment.

Some people have suggested transporting wastes into space. Cost, energy requirements, and material requirements would be major problems. Disposal of radioactive wastes from a single 1000-megawatt nuclear plant would cost over $1 million a year. Radioactive capsules shot into space might someday return to earth.

Others have suggested dumping radioactive wastes on uninhabited lands in the Arctic and Antarctic. Too little is known about the effects of this disposal technique.

Radioactive waste can be bombarded with neutrons in special reactors to **transmute**, or convert, some of it into less harmful substances. But existing reactors do a poor job of altering cesium-137 and strontium-90, two of the more dangerous byproducts of nuclear fission.

Seabed disposal has been used by the United States and

European countries but is now forbidden. Regardless, some scientists suggest that high-level wastes could be deposited in deep underwater valleys, in deep abyssal plains, on the seafloor in sediment, or in areas where sedimentation rates are high, so the wastes will be rapidly buried. This type of disposal is difficult to monitor. A final suggestion has been to build special above-ground tanks; individual canisters would be placed in enormous 35-ton steel casks surrounded by a thick concrete. Canisters might also be stored in cooled and guarded warehouses.

Ironically, although the United States has spent billions of dollars of private and public money on the production of nuclear reactors, very little has been spent on research into radioactive wastes.

The disposal issue is independent of the future of nuclear weapons and nuclear power; a complete ban on nuclear weapons and nuclear power will not solve the problems of accumulated waste. Therefore, it would be wise to establish a cost-effective and low-risk disposal method, keeping in mind the costs to future societies.

Who Pays for Past Mistakes?

Abandoned waste dumps litter the landscape. Their owners and operators may not be known or may have declared bankruptcy. If trouble develops—a leak into groundwater, for example—who will pay for the damage to property and health? And who will foot the bill for cleanup?

The EPA Superfund

Following the Love Canal incident, Congress passed the *Comprehensive Environmental Response, Compensation and Liability Act* of 1980. This act makes owners and operators of hazardous waste disposal sites liable for cleanup costs and property damage. Transporters and producers must also bear some of the financial burden. This legislation also established a $1.6-billion cleanup fund ("Superfund") to be developed over a five-year period, with 90% of the money coming from taxes levied on the production of oil and chemicals by U.S. industries and the rest from taxpayers. The fund is designed to clean up imminent hazards.

The act requires states to provide 10% of the cleanup costs if the dump is on private land and 50% if it is on public land. However, as of 1983 only eight states had

funds for this purpose. Without money, the other states were disqualified.

The Superfund cannot be used to reimburse or compensate victims of illegal dumping of hazardous wastes for personal injury or death. Victims must take their complaints to the courts. The Superfund provides only for the cleanup of contaminated areas and compensation for damage to property. According to Senator George Mitchell of Maine, "Under the legislation it's all right to hurt people but not trees."

The implementation of the Superfund was exceedingly slow as the EPA negotiated with owners of hazardous waste dumps to begin private cleanup, partly to eliminate the need for state money. Critics argue that the EPA has let some companies off too easily, that only superficial cleanups have been made, and that future liability has been waived in some agreements, meaning that if problems develop in the future, companies bear no responsibility. Finally, in mid-1983 evidence that EPA officials had manipulated Superfund money with political considerations in mind started a scandal that led the EPA's top leadership to resign or be fired.

Federal Victim Compensation

A committee headed by Professor Frank Grad of Columbia University Law School studied personal damage from hazardous wastes. The Grad report, issued in September 1982, made two important and controversial suggestions. First, it called for a federal program of no-fault compensation for victims of improper and illegal disposal of hazardous wastes. A victim would only have to prove that he or she had been exposed to toxic wastes, had incurred some disease or injury as a result, and had suffered compensable damage. The fund would provide immediate compensation. Similar to worker compensation, it would provide money for all medical expenses, about two-thirds of the lost wages, and death benefits for surviving dependents.

The second suggestion was that personal injury law should be altered and that ceilings on the amount one can receive in a damage suit should be lifted in exchange for tougher standards of proof. Thus, a victim could receive money from the victim compensation fund and still sue the individual or company responsible for damage. Awards from such suits would reimburse the victim compensation fund. In addition, the victim could recover punitive damages. Punitive damages are a legal punishment or an award given to the victim, meant to punish the party responsible for damage and to deter others from operating in irresponsible or illegal ways.

Solving the problems created by improper disposal of hazardous wastes and making improvements needed in waste disposal practices and legal controls is a gargantuan project. With 60,000 producers of hazardous materials and 15,000 haulers, complicated legal and technological solutions are necessary. Many contend that a massive reduction in hazardous waste disposal—through decreases in material consumption, modifications at processing plants, recycling and reuse, and conversion—is necessary for the long-term survival of the human race and ecosystem stability. A sustainable society, they say, cannot be built on a foundation that reeks of toxic chemicals haphazardly dumped into the air, water, and land.

Liberty exists in proportion to wholesome restraint.

DANIEL WEBSTER

Summary

An estimated 54 million to 72 million metric tons of waste considered hazardous by the federal government are produced in the United States each year. Until recently, only about 10% of these wastes were disposed of properly. The remainder end up in abandoned warehouses; in rivers, streams, and lakes: in leaky landfills that contaminate groundwater: in fields and forests: and on or beside highways. Improperly disposed hazardous wastes contaminate groundwater: destroy habitat, kill fish, cause many human illnesses, contaminate soil, kill livestock, and even damage sewage treatment plants.

Worldwide attention has been focused on hazardous wastes. In the United States, the 1976 *Resource Conservation and Recovery Act* protects human health and the environment from hazardous wastes. Implementation of this act has been slow, but if fully enforced, the law should go a long way toward reducing the country's hazardous waste problem.

There are many technological options for controlling hazardous wastes, but most are expensive. The first line of defense is to reduce hazardous waste production through *process manipulation, recycling,* and *reuse* of waste products. *Detoxification* and *stabilization* are the second line of attack. Detoxification takes place through land treatment, in which wastes are broken down by chemical reactions, bacteria, or even sunlight. *Incineration* is also an attractive alternative for organic wastes. High-temperature furnaces at stationary waste disposal sites, on ships, or on mobile trailers are all workable options.

Hazardous wastes that cannot be broken down can be stored permanently in *secured landfills* lined by synthetic liners or thick, impermeable layers of clay. Although landfills are the cheapest option, they have many disadvantages, the most noteworthy being that leaks are inevitable. Other methods of perpetual storage include (1) storage in waste piles, (2) surface impoundment storage, (3) warehousing in specially built structures that prevent wastes from leaking out, (4) deposition in geologically stable salt formations, and (5) deposition deep in the ground in arid regions in groundwater-free zones.

Disposal of radioactive wastes creates a special problem for society. The 1982 *Nuclear Waste Policy Act* establishes a strict timetable for the Department of Energy to choose appropriate sites for disposal.

Many experts believe that deep geological disposal is the best technical option for getting rid of most dangerous radioactive wastes. Other options include catapulting wastes into space, disposal in the Arctic and Antarctic, *transmutation* (bombardment with neutrons to change them into less harmful substances), seabed disposal, and special above-ground tanks and storage facilities.

The U.S. *Comprehensive Environmental Response, Compensation and Liability Act* of 1980 makes owners and operators of hazardous waste disposal sites liable for cleanup costs and property damage. This legislation also established a $1.6-billion fund, called the Superfund, to be used to clean up imminent hazards. The Superfund has major drawbacks; the most notable is that it requires states to pay 10% of the money for cleanup costs on private land and 50% for state-owned land. Few states have funds for this purpose. One of the most critical weaknesses in the Superfund legislation is that it fails to address damage to human health. New legislation may help eliminate this problem by providing compensation for victims.

Discussion Questions

1. Summarize the major events occurring at Love Canal. Who was to blame for this problem? What might have been done to avoid it?

2. Discuss illegal and improper waste disposal techniques and hazards they can create. Also discuss reasons why waste disposers have resorted to illegal and improper methods.

3. You are appointed to head a state agency on hazardous waste disposal. You and your staff are to make recommendations for a statewide plan to handle hazardous wastes. Draw up a plan for eliminating dumping. Which techniques would have the highest priority? How would you bring your plan into effect?

4. Discuss the major provisions of the Resource Conservation and Recovery Act (1976) and the Comprehensive Environmental Response and Liability Act (1980), or the so-called "Superfund Law." What are the weaknesses of each?

5. Describe the pros and cons of the major technological controls on hazardous wastes, including process modification, recycling and reuse, conversion to nonhazardous or less hazardous materials, and perpetual disposal.

6. Debate the statement "All hazardous wastes should be recycled and reused to eliminate disposal."

7. A hazardous waste disposal site is going to be placed in your community. What information would you want to know about the site? Would you oppose it? Why or why not?

8. List personal ways we can each contribute to lessening the hazardous waste problem.

9. Debate the statement "Victims of improper hazardous waste disposal practices should be compensated by a victim compensation fund developed by taxing the producers of toxic wastes."

10. Discuss some of the options we have for getting rid of radioactive wastes. Which ones seem the most intelligent to you? Why?

Suggested Readings

Belliveau, M. (1983). Toxics on Tap—Poisoned Water in L.A. *CBE Environmental Review* (May/June): 8–11. Good case study.

Bond, D. (1984). At-Sea Incineration of Hazardous Wastes. *Environ. Sci. and Technol.* 18(5): 148A–152A. Technical review of this controversial disposal technique.

Durso-Hughes, K., and Lewis, J. (1982). Recycling Hazardous Wastes. *Environment* 24(2): 14–20. Excellent article.

Epstein, S. S., Brown, L. O., and Pope, C. (1982). *Hazardous Waste in America*. San Francisco: Sierra Club Books. Thorough and dramatic coverage of hazardous wastes.

Haarhoff, F. E. (1983). Managing Hazardous Waste: The Search for New Approaches. *Chemical Business,* May 2: 25–30. Informative overview of waste disposal options.

Hileman, B. (1983). Hazardous Waste Control. *Environ. Sci. and Technol.* 17(7): 281A–285A. Good overview.

Hinga, K. R., Heath, C. R., Anderson, D. R., and Hollister, C. D. (1982). Disposal of High-Level Radioactive Wastes by Burial in the Sea Floor. *Environ. Sci. and Technol.* 16(1): 28A–37A. Comprehensive article.

Regenstein, L. (1982). *America the Poisoned*. Washington, D.C.: Acropolis Books. Chapter 3 is a good overview of the hazardous waste problem.

Solid Waste

A society in which consumption has to be artificially stimulated to keep production going is a society founded on trash and waste.

DOROTHY L. SAYERS

All organisms produce wastes, but none produce so much or of such diverse composition as humans. The wastes of human societies are solids, liquids, and gases, and they arise from many different activities such as manufacturing, agriculture, mining, and day-to-day living. This section will concentrate on **municipal solid wastes**—materials discarded in solid form from schools, stores, and homes (Figure S22-1).

Municipal solid wastes make up only about 4% of the total solid waste discarded in the United States each year. But municipal waste production is increasing at a rate of 2% to 4% a year. This growth and the sheer volume of waste create major problems in cities, where land for disposal is in short supply (Figure S22-2).

Each year, over 135 million metric tons of solid waste is generated in the United States. About 11 million metric tons is recycled. A city of 1 million people produces enough solid waste each year to fill a large football stadium. Each of us produces about a half a ton a year.

Arthur C. Clarke once wrote, "Solid wastes are only raw materials we're too stupid to use." The paper, glass, metals, tires, and plastics that daily flow from our cities to disposal sites represent a waste of valuable materials. The cost to municipalities of discarding these wastes is often exceeded only by the cost of education and highway construction and maintenance. Waste disposal is also a potential source of water and air pollution, a waste of energy, and a consumer of large quantities of land in and around urban centers, competing with agriculture and other interests.

Like so many other problems, municipal solid waste is the

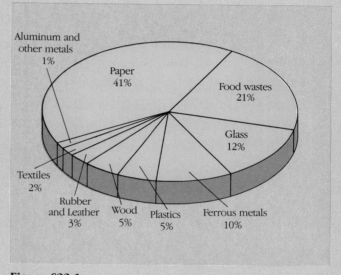

Figure S22-1
Composition of typical municipal solid waste by weight.

end product of many interacting factors: large population; high per capita consumption; low product durability; an abundance of disposable items on the market; a lack of recycling; little product reuse; a lack of personal and governmental commitment to reduce waste; widely dispersed populations, so that producers of recyclable and reusable items are separated from those willing to purchase these materials; and traditionally cheap energy and abundant land for disposal.

Reducing solid waste requires an attack on many fronts. The three general approaches are (1) the **output approach**, which involves finding better ways of dumping solid wastes and of reducing the volume of waste; (2) the **throughput approach**, which reduces solid waste production by reusing and recycling

Figure S22-2
Projected growth in municipal solid waste in the United States.

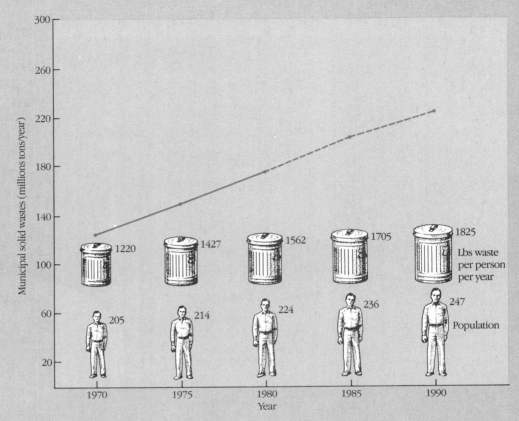

materials before they enter the solid waste stream; and (3) the **input approach**, which attempts to reduce the amount of materials traveling through the production–consumption cycle by reducing demand or by other techniques (Figure S22-3).

The Output Approach

The output approach takes a narrow look at solid wastes as something to be discarded as cheaply and as safely as possible. It answers the simple questions: "How do we get rid of municipal wastes?" "How can we reduce the volume of existing solid wastes?"

From Dumps to Sanitary Landfills

The dump was a prevalent feature of the American landscape until the 1960s, when public objection to odors and vermin as well as the new air pollution laws forced cities to phase them out. The federal Resource Conservation and Recovery Act required all open dumps to be closed or upgraded by 1983.

The open dump has largely been replaced by the **sanitary landfill**, a natural or artificial depression into which solid wastes are dumped, compressed, and daily covered with a layer of dirt.

The advantages of the landfill are many: Because the wastes are not burned, air pollution is negligible. The daily covering of wastes with dirt reduces odors, flies, insects, rodents, and potential health problems. Once a landfill is filled, the site can be reused for a park, shopping center, homes, school, office buildings, or even a football stadium. Mount Trashmore in Evanston, Illinois, is a prime example. Built from a 19-hectare, 20-meter-high (48-acre, 65-feet) mass of solid wastes, Mount Trashmore is now a recreational area with a baseball diamond, tennis court, and sledding hills. Mile High Stadium in Denver was once the site of a sanitary landfill.

Landfills have some notable problems. (1) They have large land requirements at a time when competition for urban land is increasing. The trash from 10,000 people in a year will cover 1 acre 10 feet deep. (2) They require a lot of energy for excavation, filling, and hauling trash. (3) They can pollute groundwater. (4) They produce methane gas from anaerobic decomposition of organic wastes. Methane can seep through the ground

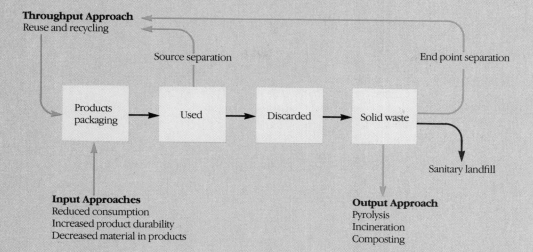

Throughput Approach
Reuse and recycling

Source separation

End point separation

Products packaging → Used → Discarded → Solid waste

Sanitary landfill

Input Approaches
Reduced consumption
Increased product durability
Decreased material in products

Output Approach
Pyrolysis
Incineration
Composting

into buildings built above and around reclaimed sites, and it is explosive at relatively low concentrations. (5) They subside as the organic trash decays, requiring additional regrading and filling. Buildings constructed on top of reclaimed landfills may suffer serious structural damage. (6) Finally, they have low social acceptability; most people don't want the noise, traffic, and blowing debris.

Fortunately, there are many solutions for reducing the energy and land requirements of landfills.

The energy used in waste disposal can be reduced by new methods of waste collection. For example, packer trucks now reduce waste volume by 60%; thus, fewer trucks are needed to haul garbage to landfills.

Vacuum collection systems can also be used to save energy. Combined with resource recovery systems, they help reduce the land requirements. Solid waste is simply dumped into pipes that carry the trash to a central collection point. Vacuum collection systems are feasible in concentrated areas, such as apartment buildings, where population density is high. One such system is in operation in Sundbyberg, Sweden. Garbage is whisked away from wall chutes to a central collection facility, where the glass and metals are removed. The burnables are incinerated, providing heat for the 1100 apartments that use the system. A similar system handles 50 tons of waste per day in Disney World, Florida. Today, over 400 systems are in operation in Europe in hospitals, apartment buildings, and housing tracts.

Water pollution problems can be reduced or eliminated by locating sanitary landfills away from streams, lakes, and wells. Test wells around the site can be used to monitor the movement of pollutants away from landfills. Drainage systems and landscaping can reduce the flow of water over the surface of a landfill and reduce the amount of water penetrating it. Impermeable clay caps and liners can reduce water infiltration and the escape of pollutants. In addition, toxic liquids that leak from a dump

site can be collected by a specially built drainage system and then detoxified.

The problems of methane production can be eliminated by proper venting of reclaimed landfills. Methane can be drawn off by vents and sold to utilities or used in neighboring buildings as a fuel supply supplementing or replacing natural gas. Subsidence damage to buildings built on reclaimed sites can be reduced by removing organic wastes before disposal and by allowing organic decay to proceed for a number of years before construction.

Ocean Dumping

At one time there were 126 dump sites off the shore of the United States: 33 in the Gulf of Mexico, 42 in the Pacific Ocean, and 51 in the Atlantic. Most of the solid waste dumped at sea was mud and sediment from dredging of harbors, estuaries, and rivers. The remaining material consisted of industrial wastes (acids, alkaline substances, PCBs, and arsenic compounds) and sewage sludge left over from treatment plants (Chapter 20).

Proposals for offshore "islands of trash" have been advanced. The islands, to be used for recreation sites and airports, would be made up of automobiles, demolished buildings, and other solid wastes. Artificial reefs made of discarded stone, cement slabs, and automobiles have also been proposed to get rid of solid wastes and improve wildlife habitat.

The concerns over ocean dumping are many. The disposal of some toxic wastes might contaminate commercially valuable fish and shellfish. Biological magnification of these chemicals might harm organisms higher on the food chain, including birds and humans (Chapter 18). The long-term effects of ocean dumping are uncertain. Will the wastes eventually be washed ashore onto beaches, or will they be carried out to sea? Finally, aesthetic

S22-4
World's largest composting facility at Wijster in the Netherlands.

concerns have been raised by people such as the explorer Thor Heyerdahl, who has witnessed oil and trash floating far out at sea and deadened areas of the ocean that have been dumping sites for New York City's sewage sludge for years.

U.S. regulation of ocean dumping began in earnest with the *Marine Protection, Research and Sanctuaries Act* (1972). This law requires companies to file for an EPA permit to transport wastes on or dump them in the ocean. It also directed the EPA and the U.S. Army Corps of Engineers to locate suitable ocean disposal sites, preferably beyond the continental shelf. The long-term goal of this act is to phase out all ocean dumping. Thus, in January 1977 the EPA isued regulations calling for an end to all dumping of industrial wastes and sewage by 1981 in the Atlantic Ocean, where 90% of the ocean waste disposal was occurring. Dredged materials can continue to be dumped at sea in appropriate locations.

Composting, Incineration, and Pyrolysis

Composting and incineration are two important output strategies. **Composting** is a process in which the organic wastes are allowed to undergo aerobic bacterial decay. Compost is used to build soil fertility, decrease soil compaction, decrease soil erosion, increase water percolation, and promote soil aeration (Chapter Supplement 9-1).

Where there is an abundance of organic matter—such as slaughterhouses and vegetable and fruit-packing plants—composting is a good strategy. Some successful composting opera-

tions can be found in the United States, but most are in Europe—in the Netherlands, Belgium, England, and Italy—and in Israel (Figure S22-4).

Composting has a few drawbacks: (1) open piles of decaying matter require large tracts of land and produce odor and breeding sites for pests, (2) sorting out the noncompostable materials such as metals and glass is costly, (3) the demand for the organic compost is often low, and (4) sites are aesthetically unappealing.

For successful municipal composting, cities might use abandoned lots or outlying plots that could be cared for by county, state, or federal prisoners; welfare recipients; the unemployed; or even 4-H groups. Citizens could be required to separate all organic garbage (paper, leaves, grass clippings, kitchen wastes) from metals, plastics, and glass before trash pickup. Source separation would eliminate the cost of separating the wastes later.

Composting can be practiced successfully at home. Gardeners can make their own compost piles of leaves, grass clippings, and vegetable wastes from the kitchen. The product can be added to vegetable gardens and flower beds. Simply burying organic wastes in gardens may also work well, reducing the need for artificial fertilizers and increasing garden productivity.

Another way of getting the most out of our garbage is the incineration of organic wastes to generate heat (discussed in Chapter 15). But incinerators are costly to build and operate, on the whole costing more than landfills. The increased expense is partly due to the fact that each incinerator must be individually designed to accommodate the particular local mixture of burnable and nonburnable refuse. Operation is made more difficult because the mixture varies from season to season. To lessen this problem, individual homeowners might be required to separate burnables from wet organic matter such as grass clippings. Incinerators emit toxic pollutants, especially when plastics are burned.

In 1977 Denmark burned 60% of its solid wastes, the Netherlands and Sweden burned about one-third, and the United States burned less than 1%. In 1980 there were numerous projects under construction or in planning to burn municipal waste for energy recovery. The total capacity of these came to 122,000 metric tons per day. This is almost one-third of our annual municipal waste production. As attractive as this strategy may seem, it is usually better to recycle paper and cardboard, because recycling saves energy, and incineration may have a negative net energy balance.

Pyrolysis is the high-temperature decomposition of organic wastes in anaerobic conditions. The pyrolysis of 1 ton of ordinary municipal garbage results in the production of 2 gallons of light oil, 5 gallons of pitch and tar, 230 pounds of organic solid (char), and 17,000 cubic feet of combustible gas. Some of these products can be sold to offset the production cost; others can be burned to generate useful energy.

Pyrolysis has a low net energy yield. The high cost of operation is also another serious drawback, making it a questionable strategy at current prices. Additional strategies for energy production from organic wastes were discussed in Chapter 15.

The Throughput Approach

In addition to those output approaches (incineration, composting) that reduce waste volume and allow us to regain a little of something we normally discard, certain throughput approaches are needed (see Figure S22-3). Throughput approaches—reuse and recycling—take out useful materials reducing the volume of the waste stream.

Reuse is simply the return of usable or repairable goods into the market system for someone to use. In most cities a variety of organizations will pick up usable discards or broken products, including clothes, furniture, books, and appliances. In other cities central collection stations are provided. The Salvation Army, Goodwill Industries, and the Disabled American Veterans all collect items throughout the United States. Garage sales also provide an outlet.

Packaging materials such as cardboard boxes, bottles, and grocery bags can be reused by consumers, saving both energy and materials. Reusable beverage containers are well worth their slight extra cost; they can be sterilized, refilled, and returned to the shelf—sometimes completing the cycle as many as 50 times (Chapter 16).

The advantages of reuse are many: (1) it saves energy; (2) it reduces the land area needed for solid waste disposal; (3) it provides jobs for teenagers, the handicapped, or the disabled; (4) it provides inexpensive products for the poor and the thrifty;

Table S22-1   Reuse and Recycling of Solid Wastes

Material	Reuse and Recycling
Paper	Repulped and made into cardboard, paper, and a number of paper products. Incinerated to generate heat. Shredded and used as mulch or insulation.
Organic matter	Composted and added to gardens and farms to enrich the soil. Incinerated to generate heat.
Clothing and textiles	Shredded and reused for new fiber products, or burned to generate energy. Donated to charities or sold at garage sales.
Glass	Returned and refilled. Crushed and used to make new glass. Crushed and mixed with asphalt. Crushed and added to bricks and cinderblocks.
Metals	Remelted and used to manufacture new metal for containers, building, and other uses.

Source: Modified from Nebel, B. J. (1981). *Environmental Science.* Englewood Cliffs, N.J.: Prentice-Hall, p. 297.

(5) it reduces litter; (6) it reduces the amount of materials consumed by producers; and (7) it thus helps reduce pollution and environmental disruption.

The benefits of reuse have not gone unnoticed by 11,200 auto salvage operations in the United States. In 1982, sales of used auto parts from the salvage industry were about $4.5 billion. Instead of hunting through greasy auto yards for parts, customers now consult with sales personnel who search through the company's computer for the parts they need. Still, only about 3% of the population buys from the used parts dealer.

Recycling can effectively reduce the volume of the municipal waste stream by returning a wide variety of materials to manufacturers, where they can be broken down and reincorporated in products. From an energy and resource standpoint, recycling is not as good an option as reuse, but it is far better than throwing materials away. Many materials commonly discarded in municipal trash can be recycled at a huge energy saving (Table S22-1). Chapter 16 discusses recycling of metals.

Recycling is not always feasible, as groups have found out over and over since the late 1960s. A steady market must always be accessible; if not, recyclers unable to sell their materials must store them until a market is opened up. Fluctuating markets for recyclables make it difficult for marginally profitable operations to survive.

Extracting recyclable goods from municipal trash can create an enormous headache. Source separation requires widespread cooperation among residents. Recycling trash may also create extra costs that cannot be offset by the money made on the recycling itself. If trash is collected two or three times a week, one pickup can be devoted to recyclables at no extra cost to the community; but in communities where trash is picked up once a week, two trucks may be necessary. This increased cost may prove too great to make the operation profitable.

The chief advantage of separating trash after collection is that it requires little citizen cooperation. Raw trash is simply shredded at a central collection facility; then, blowers separate the plastics, paper, and organic matter from heavier items such as cans and bottles (Figure S22-5), and magnets separate the steel.

According to the National Center for Resource Recovery, there were 56 resource recovery systems in operation or in construction in the United States in 1980. Most of these are designed to generate energy from trash. Fifty-four communities were considering the same approach.

However beneficial resource recovery systems may be, they have some drawbacks. End point separation is more expensive than source separation and sometimes more expensive than traditional disposal in landfills. The equipment is costly and requires maintenance and energy. Furthermore, complete separation may not be possible. The lack of complete separation decreases the value of recyclable materials.

Recycling is necessary to attain a sustainable society. Most critics of recycling realize its necessity but assert that the economics are not right yet; they prefer to wait for the day when recycling is profitable. But if declining mineral resources, nonrenewable energy supplies, and land shortages will make recycling profitable in the near future, why not start now, even if the profit is marginal or if the operation requires government support to make it work? An investment now in a nationwide recycling system may pay huge dividends in the future.

The economic system should take into account multigenerational costs and savings, but it does not. As shown in Figure S22-6, when the costs of mining and mineral processing exceed the cost of recycling, the latter will become the preferred way of supplying production. Government subsidies can make it feasible. Subsidies could pay off in future years as the supply of raw materials drops.

The EPA estimates that the United States could recycle about 25% of its urban solid waste by 1990, about twice what it does now. Increased recycling requires our personal attention. Each of us can make a commitment to recycle cans, bottles, and papers and urge that our employers do, too. Tax breaks for recycling businesses may prove helpful. New laws that require the return of bottles and cans on a nationwide basis will also help (Chapter 15). Local governments can donate unused land for recycling centers.

Recycling is more prevalent in most of the less developed countries than in the industrialized nations. The poor raid the dumps for food, clothing, and materials for shelter and also seek out discarded metals and other goods they can sell. The United States can help promote recycling as it assists developing nations in their efforts to raise their economic well-being. Information on the energy and material savings as well as technologies for recycling could be built into global industrialization at the start. To be credible, however, Americans will need to increase their own recycling efforts.

A sustainable society requires maximum recycling—on the order of 80% of the materials passing through the production–consumption cycle. Such a strategy would help reduce the economic depletion of natural resources, reduce pollution, and give us more time to control population and find alternative resources.

The Input Approach

Reductions in solid waste problems can also be achieved by an **input approach:** an attempt to reduce the amount of material entering the consumption phase of the production–consumption cycle. Three ways of doing this are (1) increasing product life span, (2) reducing the amount of materials in goods, and (3) reducing consumption (demand for goods).

Longer Life Span Durable toys, garden tools, cars, and clothing require less frequent replacement and thus decrease our overall resource use. The trouble is that, as John Ruskin once noted, "There is hardly anything in the world that some man cannot make a little worse and sell a little cheaper." In the long run, however, cheaply made goods end up costing more than well-made and more expensive goods.

Fewer Materials A great deal of resource waste and solid waste production comes from packaging. Each year, for example, packaging requires 75% of the glass consumed in the United States, 40% of the paper, 14% of the aluminum, and 8% of the steel. Thirty percent to 40% of the municipal solid waste is discarded packaging!

Of course, packaging is necessary, but much of it is superfluous and wasteful. The Campbell Soup Company realized this and redesigned its soup cans; today, they use 30% less material. Some beverage companies now package drinks in aseptic containers, boxes constructed of several thin layers of polyethylene, foil, and paper. The containers hold milk, a variety of juices, and wine, and keep them fresh for several months without refrigeration. Aseptic containers could save large amounts of energy. The reason is that canned drinks must be pasteurized for 45 minutes, whereas the contents of aseptic packages are sterilized out of the package for only 1 minute. This reduces energy demand and preserves flavors. Milk and juices contained in aseptics do not require refrigeration during transportation and storage, which also lowers the energy demand. Being lighter than cans, aseptics also help cut down on transportation costs.

Some manufacturers are experimenting with biodegradable

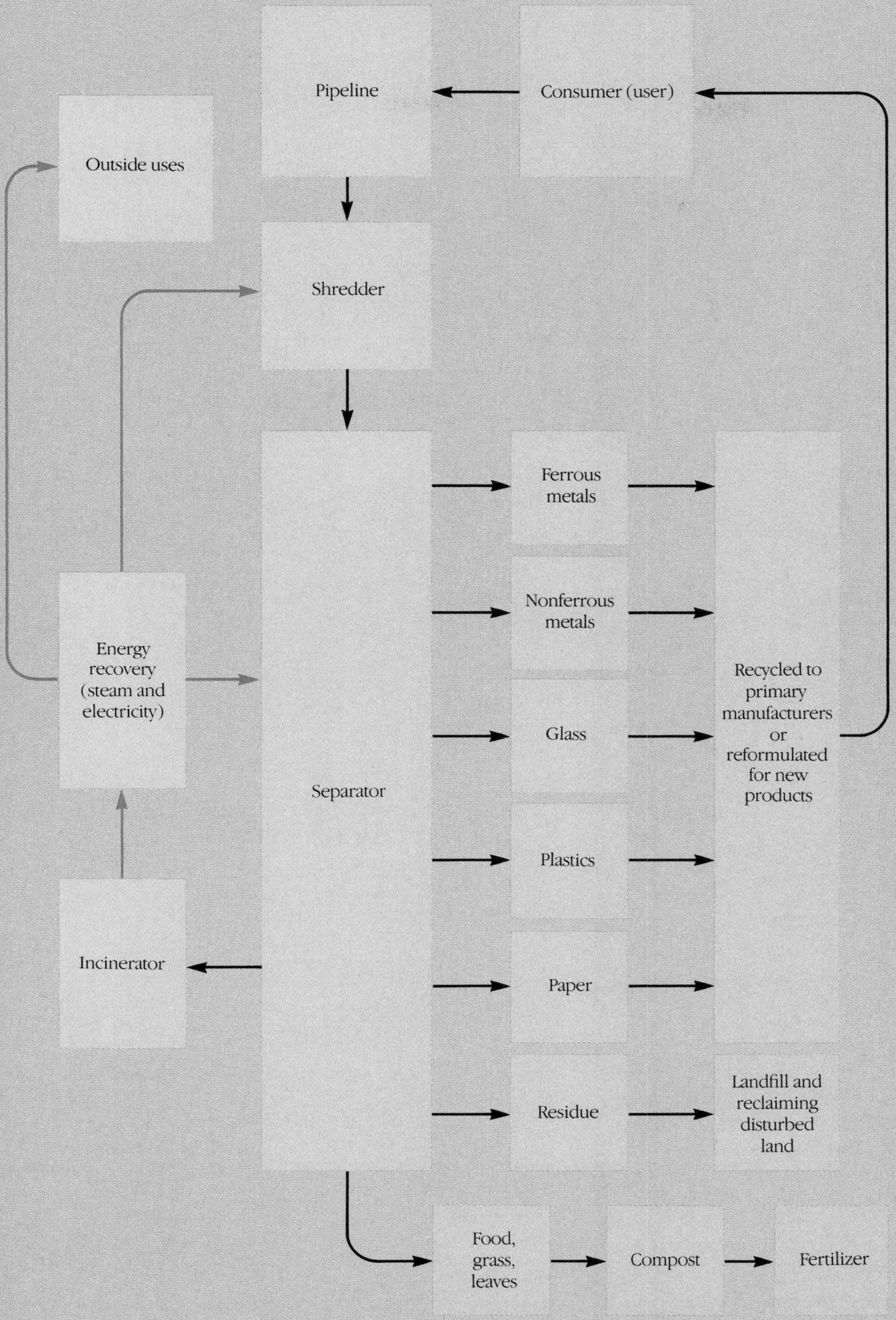

Figure S22-5
Separation of solid waste at a centralized waste recovery plant.

Figure S22-6
Theoretical relationship
between declining resources
and profitability of recycling.

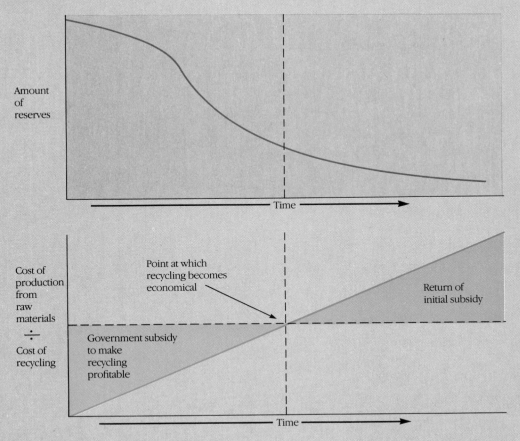

packages. Most notable are biodegradable plastics and food containers that dissolve in water when cooked, not only reducing solid waste but also adding nutrients to the food.

Packaging is not the only area in need of improvement. Virtually all products can be redesigned to reduce waste. Many large national newspapers have gone to a more economical design that has cut the use of newsprint by 5%. Smaller cars and trucks have emerged, too.

Reduced Consumption H. W. Shaw once wrote, "Our necessities are few, but our wants are endless." It is argued that our ceaseless efforts to satisfy our wants in an age of technological marvel are a big part of the solid waste problem. By reducing our endless accumulation of questionable goods, we can help the solid waste problem as well as so many others documented in this book. Added benefits may also come from a simpler life-style.

Each of us can make a personal effort to reduce consumption by 20% with little noticeable change in life-style. There are limitless possibilities for reducing consumption; all we have to do is try them.

Suggested Readings

Brown, L. R. (1984). *State of the World, 1984.* New York: Norton. Superb overview of world trends toward sustainability.

Chandler, W. U. (1983). *Materials Recycling: The Virtue of Necessity.* Worldwatch Paper 56. Washington, D.C.: Worldwatch Institute. Detailed study of recycling.

Goldstein, J. (1979). *Recycling: How to Reuse Wastes in Home, Industry and Society.* New York: Schocken Books. Informative and practical guide.

Packard, V. (1960). *The Waste Makers.* New York: Pocket Books. Dated, but good reading.

Parkinson, A. (1983). Responsible Waste Management in a Shrinking World. *Environment* 25(10): 61–67. Good overview.

Purcell, A. H. (1980). *The Waste Watchers: A Citizen's Handbook for Conserving Energy and Resources.* New York: Doubleday (Anchor). Helpful reference.

Purcell, A. H. (1981). The World's Trashiest People. Will They Clean Up Their Act or Throw Away Their Future? *Futurist* 15(1): 51–59. Excellent article.

White, P., and Psihoyos, L. (1983). The Fascinating World of Trash. *National Geographic* 163(4): 424–457. An interesting and humorous look at trash.

V

ENVIRONMENT AND SOCIETY

23

Environmental Ethics: The Foundation of a Sustainable Society

Modern man is the victim of the very instruments he values most. Every gain in power, every mastery of natural forces, every scientific addition to knowledge, has proved potentially dangerous, because it has not been accompanied by equal gains in self-understanding and self-discipline.

LEWIS MUMFORD

This book began with an outline of today's environmental crisis. Each part explored a facet of it. Part II covered the population question, Part III surveyed resource problems, and Part IV described the many faces of pollution. Each chapter had remedies for the many problems we now face, solutions that were technical, legal, and personal.

These diverse techniques and solutions amount to a hodgepodge without another ingredient: a set of informed beliefs as a framework and backbone—that is, an appropriate ethical system. The sustainable society, a concept that has cropped up throughout this book, needs sustainable ethics.

Those ethics will not spring into being and move into an ethical niche standing empty for them; instead, they will have to displace an earlier set of beliefs, some of them unspoken, that have deep roots and far-reaching effects. These make up the frontier mentality and underlie the environmental crisis in every detail.

The Frontier Mentality

Today's industrial world operates largely with a frontier mentality. The **frontier mentality**, or ethic, is a human-centered view characterized by three precepts: First, it sees the world as an unlimited supply of resources for human use with the basic premise that "there is always more." Second, it views humans as apart from nature rather than a part of it. Third, it views nature as something to overcome.

The frontier mentality has been a part of human thinking for many tens of thousands of years, perhaps all of human history. It was prevalent in both the hunting-and-gathering and agricultural societies. For example, the European settlers in North America cut down the forests and grew crops on the soil until the nutrients had been depleted or the soil had been eroded away by rain. After this, they headed into new territory and began the cycle over again.

The frontier mentality sees the natural world as a means of fulfilling human needs, showing little regard for the consequences of exploitive actions. Today, the frontier mentality is fueled by an irrational commitment to maximum material output and consumption. That commitment leaves little room for anything but a narrow look at the costs of our technologies. Indeed, frontier societies prefer to see only the most immediate and apparent costs—costs of materials, energy, and labor that go into manufacturing. Economists call these internal costs—that is, costs that are incurred during the manufacturing and distribution of goods. The frontier mentality ignores the external costs, such as environmental damage and health impacts, which are usually difficult to calculate.

The frontier mentality sees humans as separate from nature; our chief role, then, becomes one of domination of nature. This view was expressed by the 19th-century English poet Matthew Arnold: "Nature and man can never be fast friends. Fool, if thou canst not pass her, rest her slave!" Feeling apart from nature and in charge of it as well, humans have wreaked considerable damage on the earth. In many instances experience has shown that cooperation with nature would have been better (Figure 23-1).

Modern economics reinforced this tendency to dominate nature. Walter Chryst and William Pendleton, Jr., outlined the economic view of the environment in 1958. Land use, they said, should be based on the principle that each acre of land be devoted to the use that gives the highest

Figure 23-1
This Santa Cruz, California, beachside home was damaged by the big coastal storms in the winter of 1983.

economic return. Simply by allocating environmental resources according to economic returns, they maintained, we can achieve the highest efficiency in satisfying our wants. Plants and animals, for instance, are often viewed as having no value outside of what they provide to society in the form of food, research, or entertainment.

The question "Is it economic?" governs the actions of people, governments, and society in general. The late E. F. Schumacher, author of the widely acclaimed treatise on economics *Small Is Beautiful,* put this in strong terms: "In the current vocabulary of condemnation, there are few words as final and conclusive as the word 'uneconomic.' If an activity has been branded uneconomic, its right to existence is seriously denied. The religion of economics has its own code of ethics, and the First Commandment is to behave 'economically.'" When economic thinking pervades a society, things without dollar values such as beauty, health, happiness, and security rarely enter into decisions.

In a world of limits, there is no longer a place for a belief that "there is always more." The attitude that seeks fulfillment in the unrestrained pursuit of materialism simply no longer fits into this world, for it has no limiting principle, whereas the environment in which it operates is strictly limited. The ideas that we are apart from nature and here to dominate it are equally outdated.

Roots of Our Attitudes toward Nature

Where did our attitudes toward nature come from? To date, most historians who have explored that question have been interested primarily in the origin of the view that humans are "apart from and above nature" and "here to subdue it." But equally important are the roots of the attitude that "there is always more." Let's look at the first set of attitudes.

The University of California historian Lynn White argues that our attitudes toward nature are linked to the prevalent Judeo-Christian teachings that direct us to be fruitful, multiply, and subdue the earth. In a widely read paper, "The Historical Roots of Our Ecologic Crisis," he stated that this Western ethic holds that nature has only one purpose: to serve humans. Furthermore, Christians believe it to be God's will that we exploit nature for our own purposes.

The biologist René Dubos, however, asserts that exploitation of the natural world is a universal trait of all humans. Erosion of the land, destruction of animal and plant species, excessive exploitation of natural resources, and ecological disasters are not unique to the Judeo-Christian peoples. At all times and all over the world, thoughtless interventions into nature have had disastrous consequences. Two examples mentioned in Chapter 1 were the widespread extinction of many large animals by early North American hunters and gatherers and the destruction of forests and grasslands by fire used by hunters.

A critical rethinking of this debate reveals some interesting insights. First, the causes of environmental damage are not exclusively the result of the attitude that humans are above and in control of nature. As illustrated in Figure 23-2, environmental damage results in part from a biological trait: every organism seeks to convert as much of the environment as possible into itself and its offspring. Each organism is a biological imperialist; humans are no different, except that our technologies have allowed us to expand our populations beyond limits imposed on earlier societies.

Second, even though we have always damaged our environment through imperialistic exploitation, in more recent human history Judeo-Christian teachings have reinforced this tendency. To say that these teachings are responsible for our feelings of superiority and control over nature is only a half-truth; it would be more accurate to say that they are a fine veneer over a deeply rooted biological trait.

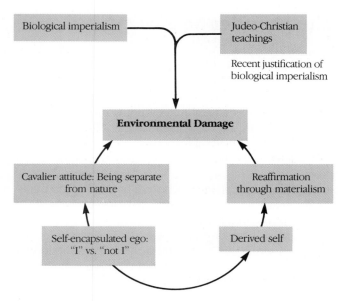

Figure 23-2
Roots of environmental damage caused by humans.

Some insights from psychology may help us learn more about the attitude that we are apart from nature. For example, psychologists assert that humans create mental models, or "sets," that determine what reality is for us and how we view the world. The psychologist Alan Watts coined the term **skin-encapsulated ego** to define the prevalent model we use: what is inside the skin is "I," and what is outside is "not I." Thus, humans operating with this simplistic model see nature as "not I," an inaccurate view considering how closely linked we are to many natural processes. Aside from this fairly obvious observation, what dangers does the self-encapsulated ego create?

According to psychologists, as we pass from infancy to adulthood, we develop a sense of the self, our own separate identities, from those things outside ourselves ("not I"). We realize we are not a great athlete or a brilliant physicist (or perhaps that we are!) by comparing ourself to those who excel in these areas. In short, our view of ourself is derived from what surrounds us. The skin-encapsulated ego, or what is "I," becomes a derived self.

Once the derived self becomes established, it also needs reaffirmation. We know who we are, but is that OK? As we all know, insecure egos need support. This need for reaffirmation affects the environment, because reaffirmation is often derived from status, which comes from material goods. For example, material goods—a fast car, the latest fashions—build status and make us who we are.

Table 23-1　Frontier and Sustainable Society Mentalities Compared

Frontier	Sustainable Society
The earth is an unlimited bank of resources.	The earth has a limited supply of resources.
When the supply runs out, move elsewhere.	Recycling and the use of renewable resources will prevent depletion.
Life will be made better if we just continue to add to our material wealth.	Life's value is not simply the sum total of our banking accounts.
The cost of any project is determined by the cost of materials, energy, and labor. Economics is all that matters.	The cost is more than the sum of the energy, labor, and materials. External costs such as damage to health and the environment must be calculated.
Nature is to be overcome.	We must understand and cooperate with nature.
New laws and technologies will solve our environmental problems.	We must all act individually to solve the pressing problems.
We are above nature, somehow separated from it and superior to it.	We are a part of nature, ruled by its rules and respectful of its components. We are not superior to nature.
Waste is to be expected in all human endeavor.	Waste is intolerable; every wasted object should have a use.

We may not be a movie star, but we do have the right clothes.

We use the world to feed the self. We exploit the water, air, wildlife, minerals, timber, and soils to serve the ego, whether it is wise or not. Materialism and environmental destruction are the price we pay for ego building. This phenomenon is not limited to the self. States and nations, like individuals, have an ego that needs support.

In summary, environmental damage is rooted in biological imperialism, Judeo-Christian thinking, the self-encapsulated ego, and the need to reaffirm the derived self by status building. But where does the current attitude that "there is always more" come from?

For most of human history, population size has been small in comparison with the earth's resource supply. We know from history that civilization has been constantly on the move in search of new resources, and it has almost always found what it wanted. In fact, there was always more, but now with an enormous worldwide and widespread exploitation of the earth's resources, we are beginning to doubt whether this attitude is valid.

Low-Synergy Society

The frontier mentality and the economic bent of modern society create a low-synergy society. **Synergy** means working together. Low-synergy societies create a system in which the individual parts work against the benefit of the whole.

Earlier societies possessed a higher level of synergy, because numbers were small and technology was simple. They fitted into the environment, and what damage they caused was often repairable. Today, however, snyergy has dropped. To build a high-synergy, or sustainable society, mentality will require changes in technology, industry, political institutions, housing, and transportation as well as a fundamental change in our ethics.

Sustainable Ethics

Sustainable ethics holds that the earth has a limited supply of resources, that humans are a part of nature, and that they are not superior to it (Table 23-1).

The main concept of the sustainable society ethic is that "there is not always more." The earth has a limited supply of nonrenewable resources such as metals and oil. Thus, citizens must learn that infinite growth of material consumption in a finite world is an impossibility and that ever-increasing production and consumption can only damage the life-giving environment. These realizations will lead to new resource-consumption strategies. The first will be conservation, or the curtailment of excessive resource use. In the words of Gandhi, "Earth provides enough to satisfy every man's need, but not any man's greed." The second strategy will be reuse of materials and recycling. Third, we will learn to use renewable resources

Figure 23-3
Short-term exploitive approach. An Australian hillside has been denuded by the emission of sulfurous acid gasses from the Mt. Lyell copper mine.

(sunlight) rather than nonrenewable resources (coal and oil).

The second basic precept of the sustainable society ethics is that "we are all one." Humans are not apart from but rather a part of nature. The British scientist James Lovelock argues that the earth is alive, not just teeming with life but an organism itself. From a scientific standpoint this new view of the earth is quite valid. For example, you maintain your body temperature and blood glucose levels at fairly constant levels. This maintenance of internal constancy is called homeostasis. Like you and other living organisms, the earth also maintains homeostasis. It maintains atmospheric oxygen at about 21%, and it maintains a fairly constant temperature.

Lovelock's idea is called the Gaia hypothesis (Chapter 1). It says that all living matter on earth and the nonliving components as well are part of a giant self-regulatory system, the earth superorganism. According to this view, then, each human being is akin to a single cell in a giant organism.

Peter Russell contends that humankind is the "nervous system" of the earth superorganism. Human societies amass information and transmit it around the superorganism by cable and microwaves. We search for knowledge and think about the future of the planet. We make decisions that affect the whole planet. We are the brain. But we are an integral part of the earth superorganism, no more important or less important than the rest.

Sustainable society ethics embrace the Gaia hypothesis. This new view of the world engenders a respect for the land, air, water, and all of the living organisms that are a part of the superorganism earth. It nurtures a reverence for life that would inevitably result in a curtailment of some of our activities, would diminish our view of self-importance, and would result in a decrease in the destructive, narrow thinking so prevalent in frontier societies. In what other ways would this view change our life?

First, we would learn to fully examine our economic and resource decisions in terms of what preserves the integrity, stability, and beauty of the world. Short-term exploitive approaches would become incompatible (Figure 23-3). We would take a critical look at economics, too, insisting that not everything has a price in dollars and cents. We would take a dim view of those activities that rob us of security, happiness, beauty, and health. To strive for a quality existence rather than a quantity existence means turning away from materialism. Realizing that conspicuous consumption only hastens the day of ecological reckoning, a sustainable society will resist the coercion of advertising.

Second, we would become more and more aware of the interconnection of all components of the earth and aware that our actions often have many unforeseen effects (ecological backlashes). Francis Thompson (1859–1907) stated this case in a poem, *The Mistress of Vision*:

All things by immortal power
Near or Far
Hiddenly
To each other linked are,
That thou canst not stir a flower
Without troubling of a star.

Our growing knowledge of the global interconnection would create a more thoughtful approach to development and engineering.

Third, as an outgrowth of our changes in view, we would exercise more restraint. In regard to technology and development, the ability to say "I can" would not inevitably be followed by "I will." Instead, new questions would be asked: Should we build this dam? Should we introduce this product? Should we build more nuclear weapons? Should I have another child?

The notion of restraint seems foreign now. As resources become scarce, however, restraint will become more natural and will not carry the negative connotations that it may have for many people today. In essence, necessity will promote restraint. As the futurist John Naisbitt once wrote, "Change occurs when there is a confluence of both changing values and economic necessity."

Restraint will cause us to focus on our responsibility to the earth, future generations, and other living organisms. Where personal actions threaten the good of another or of an entire population, we will favor the collective good. Restraint is exercised because it benefits the whole of society, future generations, and the earth. Restraint will help create a high-synergy society in which the individual parts function for the good of the whole. Restraint will help us achieve harmony with nature, a state where humans and nature benefit by their interdependence.

The shift to the sustainable society is a tall order for the frontier society. Some say that a profound shift in attitude is necessary. Thus, as people accept the doctrines of sustainable society ethics, society will make the shifts in life-style. This is the bottom-up approach. Others assert that disaster must strike before we make the necessary changes in attitude and life-style. This is the crisis approach. A third option is the transitional approach. It asserts that changes in life-style and attitude will occur in synchrony as a result of growing scarcity. As resources become scarcer and more expensive, life-styles will shift, and values will also be altered to reflect the realization that the frontier doctrine—"there is always more"—is invalid.

The bottom-up approach would cause the least hardship of the three options. But it is also the most difficult approach. It requires some unified insight into our problems and their solutions. Moreover, it requires a sense of unity among people throughout the world and a sense that they are an integral part of the earth superorganism.

The Transition to a Sustainable Society: Appropriate Technology

Ethical changes are needed to make the shift to a sustainable society, but these must be accompanied by changes in the way people interact with the environment, especially through industry. In this section we will explore the new technologies that harmonize with nature rather than destroy it.

High technology has played a major role in environmental destruction throughout the world; over the years, however, society has benefited greatly from it. Technological advances allow me to type this manuscript on a word processor, saving months of work in manuscript preparation. Technological advances have made mining and processing of ores more efficient, allowing us to use lower-grade ore deposits while keeping the cost down. Pollution control technologies such as the catalytic converter used in cars help reduce pollution in our cities. New products from the chemical industry may replace dangerous products. Although a boon to society, technology has also exacted a price. The challenge, then, is how to redirect its use to make it more energy efficient, less risky, cleaner, and more humane.

According to John Naisbitt, author of *Megatrends,* citizens in the United States began to revolt in the 1960s and 1970s against technology, especially the large, impersonal factories that spewed out air pollution, produced goods by assembly line, and reduced human labor to near meaninglessness. Citizen revolt resulted in important value changes. Naisbitt associates the discontent with drastic alterations in technology and a remaking of our machines and the whole structure of corporate business. In many respects technology and business are becoming more human. They have become better geared to human needs and resources.

This emerging technology is called **appropriate technology.** Unlike high technology, appropriate technology relies on (1) small- to medium-sized machines that are easy to use and repair and (2) production methods that use energy and materials frugally and at the same time produce little pollution. It benefits people, communities,

Figure 23-4
Even in developed countries such as the United States, human labor will remain a valuable resource for many tasks. A balance between technological advances and low unemployment must be reached.

and nations, helping them become more self-sufficient by using materials that are available locally (Table 23-2).

Appropriate technology is a concept made popular by Schumacher in *Small Is Beautiful*. He emphasizes that it works well in both developing countries and highly industrialized countries. The advantage of appropriate technology is that it puts people to work in a meaningful way. It requires less money to construct and operate, is efficient on a small scale, and is more compatible with the environment because of the low energy requirements and minimal pollution.

Appropriate technology is especially useful in developing countries that have neither the capital nor the energy resources to develop modern-day high technologies. Countries such as India and China have an abundance of people who can be employed by factories with appropriate technology but not by highly automated factories (Figure 23-4).

Appropriate technology also extends to the farm. For example, the use of heavy machinery such as mechanical reapers is an inappropriate use of technology in rural Pakistan. Although it increases production, such machinery tends to put people out of work. These people then move to already overpopulated cities in search of employment. In addition, the cost of reapers, repair, and energy

Table 23-2 Characteristics of Appropriate Technology

1. Small- to medium-sized machines maximize human input.
2. They are simple and easy to understand.
3. Meaningful work increases—employees do a variety of tasks.
4. It is less capital intensive for construction and maintenance.
5. Local resources are used; self-sufficiency is attempted.
6. Products are created for local use.
7. Decentralized production and control exist at local level.
8. It produces durable products that are unique and often handcrafted.
9. It emphasizes the use of natural materials.
10. Small amounts of energy and material input are needed.
11. It creates small amounts of pollution.
12. The use of renewable energy resources is emphasized.
13. It is efficient on a small scale.
14. It is more compatible with the environment.
15. It is more compatible with the local culture.

Source: Adapted from Miller, G. T., *Living in the Environment*, 1982. Wadsworth, Belmont, CA. P. 13.

is prohibitive in poor rural regions of developing countries.

Gandhi put it best when he said that the poor of the world cannot be helped by mass production, only by production of the masses. Therefore, India, Latin America, and Africa need slightly improved methods of agriculture that keep agricultural workers employed while using a minimum amount of energy. For example, a well-designed metal plow produced from local resources and easily repaired by farmers would utilize abundant human labor.

Appropriate technology in developed countries should not be viewed as a step backward in time but as a step forward—toward the wise use of people, resources, and energy. Some modern examples include solar panels for domestic and industrial heating; passive solar design for heating buildings; organic wastes from yard and house instead of artificial fertilizer; energy from the wind instead of from coal; bicycles for making short trips; microcomputers to control energy consumption in homes; and waterless toilets that convert human wastes into a humus-like substance good for gardening.

In developed countries the shift to appropriate technology will eliminate some jobs that have been a part of our economy for decades. Auto and steel workers and miners will be especially hard hit. But many new jobs will emerge, and some already have. There will be a need for energy auditors to help improve energy conservation in homes and factories. Demand for solar and wind energy experts will increase. The need for family planning experts and a host of other workers to help maintain a sustainable society will increase (Table 23-3).

Table 23-3 New or Expanded Employment Sources in a Sustainable Society

Energy auditors	A Princeton University study estimates that 200,000 are needed in the United States over the next few years to identify the profitable conservation potential in existing housing.
Wind prospectors	Given the enormous potential for harnessing wind power, they may become the equivalent of today's petroleum geologists.
Recycling experts	They are needed to help plan and execute community recycling of valuable resources.
Agronomists	They are necessary as agriculture expands into other areas such as the production of plant material to make alcohol fuel.
Foresters	They are needed to plan and direct reforestation (primarily in the Third World), to serve as advisors, and to manage forests to achieve maximum sustainable yields with minimal environmental damage.
Solar architects	They are needed to plan new construction and retrofitting of existing facilities.
Biogas experts	They are required throughout the world to design and build plants to convert organic waste into methane, which can be used to heat homes and small industries.
Family planning experts	They are needed in both developing and developed countries to help people decide on optimum family size and to help find options to limit family size.
Repair and service personnel	With an emphasis on durability in products, repair and service personnel will be needed to maintain existing technologies, factories, and homes.

Source: Modified from Brown, L. R. (1982), Living and Working in a Sustainable Society, *Futurist* 16(2): 66–74.

Obligations to Future Generations

What We Do Not Owe to Future Generations

Thomas Schwartz

The author is professor of government at the University of Texas at Austin. His research has been in moral and political philosophy, logic, legislative behavior, and mathematical modeling of political and economic processes.

You have heard it said that we owe certain things to posterity, remote as well as near. These things include an adequate supply of natural resources, a clean environment, a healthy and varied gene pool, a rich cultural heritage, and a limit on population size.

I disagree: We have no obligation extending indefinitely or even terribly far into the future to provide widespread, continuing benefits to our descendants. We may have some limited obligations to some of our descendants, but no obligations of the sweeping sort proclaimed by certain policy advocates. I will prove my thesis using a theoretical equation.

Let *P* be any policy that would provide widespread, continuing benefits of some sort to future generations, remote as well as near, at some cost to ourselves. My thesis is that with the possible exception of the next few generations, we do not owe it to our descendants to adopt *P*.

I begin with a premise:

If we owe it to our distant descendants to adopt *P*, but if in fact we do not adopt *P*, then there will exist at least one individual distant descendant who will have been wronged by our failure to adopt *P*.

One might conceivably try to escape my argument by denying this premise, contending that we can have an obligation that is not to any individual person but rather to some such abstraction as Society, The State, or The Human Race. This position implies that one can do wrong, and so deserve blame or punishment, without wronging even one person. It also implies that certain nonhuman abstractions can have claims to scarce resources that conflict with, and override, the claims of human beings. Given my premise, it suffices to show that if we do not adopt *P*, we will not thereby have wronged any distant descendant.

Suppose, then, that we do not adopt *P*. Let Mr. D be any one of our distant descendants. We cannot have wronged Mr. D by failing to adopt *P*, I will argue, because Mr. D would not have existed had *P* been adopted—and surely we cannot wrong someone by making it possible for him to exist.

The reason why Mr. D would not have existed had *P* been adopted is that *P* would have brought about a future world different from the (supposed) actual future world, and so the circumstances of Mr. D's life would not have been fully replicated under *P*. One or both of Mr. D's parents might not have existed under *P*. Had they both existed, they might not have met. Had they met, they might not have mated. Had they mated, they might not have procreated. Even had they procreated, their offspring, Master X, would have been conceived under conditions at least a little different from those of Mr. D's conception.

But that makes it virtually impossible for Master X to have developed from the same pair of gametes as Mr. D, hence virtually impossible for Master X to have the same genotype as Mr. D. After all, trivial circumstantial differences could easily have determined whether intercourse, ejaculation, or conception took place at any given time. And the most minute circumstantial difference—a difference of 1 degree in temperature, say, or one drop of some chemical—would have determined which particular spermatozoon fertilized the ovum and what particular pattern of meiosis was involved in its production. Let the circumstances surrounding Master X's conception be as similar to those surrounding Mr. D's conception as one can realistically suppose, given my assumption about Mr. D and Master X. Still, Master X would have been no more likely than Mr. D's non-twin sibling to have had Mr. D's genotype.

The combination of a different genotype and a different environment ensures all manner of further difference: Master X would not have been composed of the same matter as Mr. D; he would not have looked the same as Mr. D; and he would not have had the same perceptions, the same memories, the same beliefs or attitudes, the same capacities, the same character or the same personality as Mr. D. As a result, Master X would not have had the same psyche as Mr. D—by any sensible standard of sameness of psyche. Neither would Master X have fulfilled just the same social roles and relationships as Mr. D.

In sum, Master X would have differed from Mr. D in origin (different gametes), in content (different matter, different mind), and in basic "design" (different genotype), and he would have been shaped by a different environment to perform different functions. We have no more reason to identify Master X with Mr. D than we have to identify siblings reared apart with each other.

In deciding whether to adopt *P*, we do not have the options of making one and the same distant-future population better off or worse off. Our only choice is to produce one distant-future population or another distant-future population. Perhaps the distant-future population that would exist in the absence of *P* would be less happy, on the whole or on the average, than the distant future population that would exist under *P*. But no person would thereby be less happy in the absence of *P* than he or she would be under *P*, since under *P*, he or she would not be. In particular, Mr. D cannot reproach us for not having adopted *P*, since the alternative would have blocked his very existence.

Arguing that we owe it to Mr. D to adopt *P* is like arguing that I owe it to my future children to procreate with the healthiest, wealthiest, most beautiful, and most intelligent woman who will have me: if I fail to do so, my actual children will not be able to reproach me for having violated any obligation to them, because they would not have existed had I not procreated with their actual mother. My doing something cannot be an obligation to someone who would not exist were the thing done.

Let none of this suggest that it would be wrong for the present generation to bequeath certain environmental, cultural, or other benefits to posterity. It is part of human nature to seek a kind of immortality that way. My thesis is just that we have no obligation to make such a bequest. The practical import of this thesis lies in its denial of one possible justification for society's use of government or other instruments of coercion to exact from us any massive gift to our remote posterity.

Why We Should Feel Responsible for Future Generations

Robert Mellert

The author teaches philosophy and future studies at Brookdale Community College in Lincroft, New Jersey. He has published What Is Process Theology? *and numerous articles on process philosophy, ethics, and future studies.*

"Why should I feel obligated to future generations? We're inevitably separated by time and space. My presence here on earth now will have no influence on someone living 200 years from now."

You may have heard this opinion expressed by your friends—perhaps you even hold it yourself. But if you have ever explored a wilderness preserve, used a library, or visited a historical monument, you already have some reasons for being responsible. Much of what we value in our family, our society, and our world has been provided by our predecessors, sometimes at considerable cost and effort on their part.

In today's world we face a number of issues that will affect future generations even more profoundly than they affect us now. Exploding world populations, shrinking nonrenewable resources, and plant and animal organisms threatened with extinction all add up to one thing—an ailing environment.

These are not isolated problems. Each stems from a common perception of our relationship to the world and our future. This perception can be characterized by a description of people and things as unique, immediate, individual, and separate from

Point/Counterpoint (continued)

everything else. Any solutions that we might use to resolve our problems would have to start by challenging this perception.

Let me propose four basic considerations that may suggest a new paradigm for understanding our relationship to the world and our future. I believe our moral responsibility to coming generations will follow directly from these.

1. Future generations will be essentially the same as we are. They may have different wants and priorities, but they will manifest the same basic needs for food, water, air, and space. In addition, they will have the same basic physical and mental capacities with which to interact with their environment. Once born, they too, will claim a right to life and protection from life-threatening conditions, such as extreme temperatures, toxins, famine, and disease. To give them life without also providing the basic means to sustain and enhance life would be cruel. If we expect the species to continue, we are obliged to leave a hospitable environment for those still to come.

2. One is born into a given generation by historical accident. None of us chose when to be born, or to whom. Because we have no special claim to the time and place of our birth, justice would require that we have no more rights over the world and its resources than anyone else.

3. Our survival as a species is more important than our individual survival. This is confirmed in nature every day; parents, whether they be rabbits, wolves, whales, or humans, spend their energies to reproduce and care for their young before they themselves die. Many will even risk their own lives for their offspring. This is because life is not ours to keep, but to share with others.

4. Even after we die, the effects of our life continue. We will be present in the memories of others and in the habits and traditions we shared with them. Our ideas will continue to enlarge the range of options for others; and even when these memories and ideas are no longer consciously a part of the future, they will ripple onwards, actively influencing the course of future events and people. What has been can never die. We are what we have been given and what we have chosen to make of these "gifts." In short, we are the product of our ancestors—all that they died for and believed in—and we are the product of our decisions. Future generations will be the result of what we are now and how they use what we leave them.

If we accept these four simple ideas, it is easy to see why we have an obligation to future generations. Our obligation is based on the truth that we are more than unique and separate individuals, living only the immediacy of the now. We are, rather, parts of a much larger whole, one that transcends space and time.

As John Locke, the great English philosopher, once said, we owe the future "enough and as good" as we received from the past.

Progress in Achieving a Sustainable Society

Conservation

Many people in the United States are simplifying their lifestyles, either because materialism has lost its appeal or because economic forces leave them no other choice. Americans have also turned to smaller, more fuel-efficient cars and public transportation (Figure 23-5). Since 1978 per capita gasoline consumption has fallen sharply.

Americans have become more energy conscious in their cities and homes. More builders install better insulation and solar collectors for domestic hot water. By 1983, overall domestic energy consumption had dropped about 20% from its peak in the late 1970s. Portland, Oregon implemented one of the nation's toughest building codes, requiring insulation in old as well as new houses, apartments, and office buildings. By 1995, the city predicted, insulation alone will have cut energy usage by about 35%.

Environmental Protection

We have also made some dramatic improvements in the environment. For instance, there is a general awareness of environmental impacts in both rich and poor nations. Worldwide, over 3000 organizations are now involved in the critical issues of energy, population, resources, and the environment. Between 1964 and 1980, for example, United States sulfur dioxide emissions from oil and coal combustion were reduced by about 60%, and particulate emissions were reduced by an estimated 30%.

Each year more and more companies are turning from the old attitude that it pays to pollute to a new philosophy that pollution prevention pays. For example, Dow Corning invested $2.7 million to recover hydrogen and harmful chlorine gas once released into the atmosphere from its chemical plant in Hemlock, Michigan. The saving from the modifications, which also reduce operating costs, is approximately $900,000 a year.

On a broader scale, world population growth has slowed. The number of governmental environmental protection

(a)

(b)

Figure 23-5
Energy conservation in the United States (*a*) This 1962 Cadillac coupe gets 12 miles per gallon, whereas this 1984 Volkswagen GTI (*b*) gets 45 miles per gallon.

agencies in poorer nations increased tenfold between 1972 and 1984.

End of the Industrial Age

The shift from the industrial age to the information age is also encouraging. The **information society** creates,

processes, sells, and distributes information and the devices (computers) that facilitate these processes. Today, almost half of Americans work in what is broadly called the information field as lawyers, teachers, engineers, managers, accountants, architects, writers, stockbrokers, members of the clergy, librarians, computer programmers, bankers, researchers, and insurance agents (see Figure 23-6). In

Figure 23-6
The shifting labor force in the United States from 1860 to 1980. Note the drop in agriculture and industry and the increase in information and services.

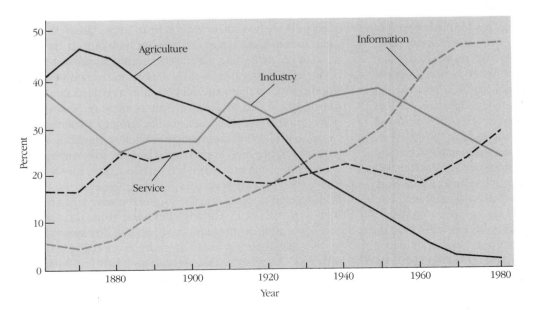

Figure 23-7
These agricultural agents in the Dominican Republic are being trained to use video equipment.

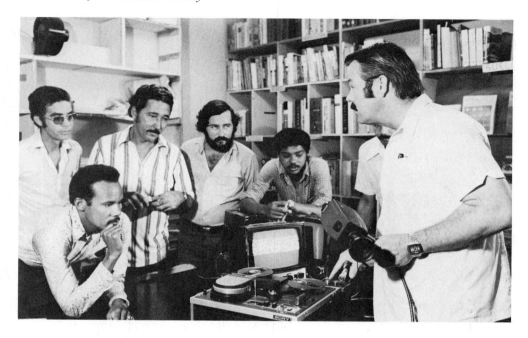

the 1970s over 80% of all new jobs created were in the information sector. Information companies have emerged as some of the world's largest corporations, replacing the giant steel and auto manufacturers that have long dominated the economic picture. The shift to the information age is happening in all industrial nations.

Why is this transition to the information age so promising? First, advanced communications networks help create a global community ("We are all one") (Figure 23-7). We have become increasingly more aware of our neighbors and their needs. We are also made more aware of environmental damage. City dwellers, for instance, may never see the damage caused by strip mines except on television. Such awareness helps foster a more responsible consumer. Second, the products of the information age such as microprocessors—small computer chips that process information—help decrease resource use and waste. Microprocessors, for example, can be used in industry to control chemical manufacturing processes, increasing efficiency and decreasing waste. They can also be used in office machines, greatly reducing their size and the amount of resources needed to make them (Figure 23-8). In some instances, they can be used to regulate energy use in homes and factories. In Crystal City, Virginia, for instance, a $110,000 computer system manages energy use in an apartment complex, saving $50,000 per year in electricity. Third, information is a unique product

that has low energy and resource demands. When we manufacture an automobile, steel and other nonrenewable resources are used. In contrast, information "manufacturing" uses a great deal of brainpower, a nondepletable and self-generating resource.

Attitudinal Changes

The frontier mentality of "doing more with more" is being replaced by a new attitude of "doing more with less" according to the futurist Kimon Valaskakis. This new attitude, thrust upon developed countries by the high cost of energy, dwindling resource supplies, and the economic turmoil that has resulted, is an important change. But the attitude that material growth is still desirable cannot be preserved in a sustainable society. As Valaskakis notes, the principal element in the strategy of achieving "more with less" is "reforming inefficient ways." We can have our large cars, extravagant homes, wasteful appliances, and much more, but we will do it with a little less energy and fewer resources.

More changes are needed to reach a true sustainable society. We must eventually shift away from the "more with less" attitude, probably in steps. The first step would be the development of an attitude of "doing the same with less." In other words, we will maintain our standard of living but reduce our resource demands.

(a)

(b)

Figure 23-8
Resource conservation using microprocessors. (*a*) In 1952 Walter Cronkite was given a tour of Sperry Corporation's UNIVAC I by its builder Dr. J. Presper Eckert. (*b*) Because of microprocessors, office computers are much smaller today as is this 1984 portable Apple IIc.

Today, there are signs that some people are adopting this attitude. What they mean is that we will still have two (small) cars per family, and huge (solar-powered) homes with twice as much living space as we need, three (energy-efficient) color TV sets, and electric or gas-powered tools to do everything from fingernail polishing to clearing the snow off our sidewalks—but we will do it with fewer resources.

The next, and perhaps final, step toward a sustainable society is the big one. We will no longer yearn for more or seek to continue our current levels of consumption; rather, we will accept decreased consumption. According to Valaskakis, we will learn to "do less with less." This requires us to examine the ways we do business and run our daily life. It means having only one small, energy-efficient car per family, using mass transit and walking; sharing tools with neighbors or renting them; digging gardens by hand and shoveling sidewalks; forgoing the latest fashion or the newest gadget designed to make life easier; taking a train home from college or for business trips; and building a small, energy-efficient, solar-powered, earth-sheltered home that is warm and comfortable instead of an oversize electric-powered home with single-paned windows, drafts, and cold spots. It means restraining our consumptive habits.

The profound shift from "doing more with less" to "doing less with less" will not come easily. It will require a radical change in our attitude. Already, there are signs that the changes may be taking place. Many people have adopted sustainable ethics and simplified their life-style. Today, for example, the United States is witnessing a dramatic shift in population to rural areas. During the 1970s small towns and rural areas grew 15.5% faster than cities. And people are becoming more and more independent. Today, over 33 million American households grow some of their own food. On the average, a home garden costing about $19 produces food worth about $325. In Boston, hundreds of vacant lots have been converted into gardens for local neighborhoods. Americans are salvaging food resources typically wasted during production and harvesting. For example, "gleaners" in Arizona, California, Michigan, Oregon, and Washington go into fields after harvest and pick food passed over by machines. Nationwide, millions of pounds of food are being "conserved."

With all the changes that we are undergoing in both attitude and life-style, there is room for optimism; but there is a lot more to be done. In 1984 the world's population reached 4.8 billion. Damage from acid precipitation is estimated to be over $5 billion a year in the United States. The California condor is on the verge of extinction. One animal species becomes extinct every nine months. Clearly, any optimism we have should be cautious optimism.

Making the Transition

Making the transition to a sustainable society is the challenge and the opportunity of a lifetime. But we must avoid numerous pitfalls many of which were first outlined by the ecologist G. Tyler Miller, Jr.

First, we must avoid the paralysis that comes with an attitude that we are doomed to perish because of overpopulation, food shortage, war, or pollution. Such paralysis will prevent us from thinking creatively and acting with determination to make necessary changes in our own life.

We must also avoid putting blind faith in technologies. Technology is not *the* answer but a part of the answer to our problems. The problems of today are caused by the conditions of today so looking back and lamenting easier times will not cure our current ills. New solutions to new problems are what the times call for.

We must avoid narrow thought and restricted imagination. All our creativity and humor will be called upon to achieve a sustainable society. Even though we don't know the exact form of the future society we're working for, we know the principles that will work. That gives us enough to start thinking now. As the social critic John Tukey once wrote, "Far better an approximate answer to the right question . . . than an exact answer to the wrong question."

We must also avoid apathy and the attitude that someone else will solve the problem. The sustainable society comes closer to being a reality with each person's effort, no matter how small or large.

Once you have achieved your personal goals, you might take a more active role in your community. You could organize recycling on your campus or in your apartment building or dormitory. You could work with your school or employer to reduce energy consumption by decreasing lighting, adding insulation, and taking other measures. As you become more informed on issues, you can write your elected representatives (see Essay 25-1, "The Right to Write").

Remember the saying "You're either part of the solution or part of the problem." We live in an age of cooperation; we succeed as we work together. We succeed as each of us makes the small changes that will eventually translate into a global revolution.

A human being is part of the whole, called by us Universe. . . . He experiences himself, his thoughts and feelings as something separated from the rest—a kind of optical delusion of his consciousness. This delusion is a kind of prison for us, restricting us to our personal desires and to affection for a few persons nearest to us. Our task must be to free ourselves from this prison by widening our circle of compassion to embrace all living creatures and the whole of nature in its beauty.

ALBERT EINSTEIN

Summary

Our attitudes toward nature determine how we damage the environment and also how we protect it. Today, many people operate with a frontier mentality based on three main ideas: (1) the world is an unlimited supply of resources for human use; (2) humans are apart from nature, not a part of nature; and (3) nature is something to overcome. This attitude toward nature stems in part from Judeo-Christian teachings and in part from biological imperialism. Technological advances increase our ability to use the earth's resources and thus increase the damage we're capable of creating.

The psychological roots of our behavior are found in the common perception of the self as "I" versus "not I." As a result, we think of ourselves as apart from nature, not a part of it. Environmental damage also results from ego reaffirmation in the form of status building. Material goods and, hence, resources are a major means of building status.

The frontier mentality creates a low-synergy society whose parts tend not to function for the benefit of the whole. A high-synergy society might be created by adopting sustainable ethics, which hold that the earth is a limited supply of resources and that humans are a part of nature and not in any way superior to it. Sustainable ethics embrace the idea that the earth is a living organism of which we are a part (the Gaia hypothesis). The new ethical system will help us learn to fully examine our economic and resource decisions in terms of what creates a sustainable society.

Adoption of the sustainable ethics and individual actions could help change society from the bottom up. This society would be based on appropriate technology, which uses small- to medium-sized machines that are easy to repair and production methods that use energy and materials frugally and produce little pollution. Appropriate technology can be used in the rich as well as the poor nations.

There are encouraging signs that we are shifting toward a sustainable society. Energy conservation in all sectors of society, new attitudes, increasing self-reliance, widespread environmental protection, and the coming of the information age—all signal the beginning of this new society. Still, we are a long way from becoming a truly sustainable society. To make the changes we must avoid the paralysis that comes with an attitude that humans are doomed. We must also avoid blind optimism in technology and the "good-old-days" trap, which seeks to answer today's problems with yesterday's answers. We must avoid narrow thought and restricted imagination. And we must avoid apathy and the attitude that someone else will solve the problem.

Discussion Questions

1. Describe the three major concepts of the frontier mentality. How does this attitude affect the way humans interact with the environment?

2. How is your personal attitude similar to, and different from, the frontier mentality?

3. What is an external cost? Who pays these costs, and in what ways are they "paid"?

4. Debate the statement "The frontier mentality comes from Judeo-Christian teachings that give humans dominion over the world."

5. Describe the terms *biological imperialism, self-encapsulated ego,* and *derived self.* How are these related to environmental damage?

6. Define *synergy.* What is a low-synergy society?

7. Discuss the tenets of sustainable ethics. Indicate which of these tenets coincide with your personal beliefs. Which ones don't? Why?

8. Describe the Gaia hypothesis. What role might human societies play in the earth superorganism?

9. In what ways would society change if it adopted sustainable ethics?

10. In what ways would a sustainable society be a high-synergy society?

11. What is appropriate technology? Give examples from both industrialized and nonindustrialized nations. What are the benefits of appropriate technology?

12. How can appropriate technology be used in your own life to reduce energy and resource consumption and waste production?

13. Debate the statement "We are a long way from achieving a sustainable society."

14. Do you agree that the United States is no longer an industrial society but is an information society?

15. In what ways might the transition to an information society help us develop a sustainable society?

16. Which of the following attitudes best fits yours? "More with more," "more with less," "the same with less," or "less with less."

17. What is the attitude of most of your friends?

Suggested Readings

Barbour, I. G. (1973). *Western Man and Environmental Ethics.* Reading, Mass.: Addison-Wesley. A collection of thought-provoking essays on environmental ethics.

Brown, L. R. (1981). *Building a Sustainable Society.* New York: Norton. Highly readable discussion of the need for and ways to build a sustainable society.

Brown, L. R., et al. (1984). *State of the World.* New York: Norton. Excellent analysis of world trends and progress toward a sustainable society.

Elder, F. (1974). The New Asceticism. In *Environment and Society,* R. T. Roelofs, J. N. Crowley, and D. L. Hardesty, eds. Englewood Cliffs, N.J.: Prentice-Hall. A delightful article on sustainable ethics.

Hardin, G. (1970). To Trouble a Star: The Cost of Intervention in Nature. *Bulletin of the Atomic Scientists,* January: 17–20. A well-written analysis of the ethics of our modern world.

Johnson, W. (1978). *Muddling Toward Frugality.* San Francisco: Sierra Club Books. An important, thoughtful book, offering a view of the transition to a more frugal society.

Lovelock, J. E. (1979). *Gaia: A New Look at Life on Earth.* Oxford, England: Oxford University Press. Detailed argument in support of the Gaia hypothesis.

Meeker, J. W. (1972). *The Comedy of Survival: In Search of an Environmental Ethic.* Los Angeles: Guild of Tutors Press. An interesting treatise on environmental ethics expressed in literature.

Naisbitt, J. (1982). *Megatrends: Ten New Directions Transforming Our Lives.* New York: Warner Books. Superb analysis of social trends.

Norman, C. (1981). The New Industrial Revolution: How Microelectronics May Change the Workplace. *Futurist* 15(1): 30–40. An important examination of the new industrial era and the role of microelectronics.

Partridge, D. (ed) (1980). *Responsibilities to Future Generations.* Buffalo, N.Y.: Prometheus Books. Superb collection of essays on ethics.

Russell, P. (1982). *The Global Brain.* Los Angeles: Tarcher. A thoughtful, visionary book on achieving a unified society. Important reading.

Schumacher, E. F. (1973). *Small Is Beautiful: Economics As If People Mattered.* New York: Harper and Row. One of the best books ever written on the subject of a sustainable society, appropriate technology, and new ethical systems necessary for survival on our limited planet.

Winn, I. J. (1972). *Basic Issues in Environment: Studies in Quiet Desperation.* Columbus, Ohio: Merrill. An important collection of essays on ethics.

Nuclear Weapons and Nuclear War

Noise pollution, air pollution, and water pollution pale in comparison with the environmental disaster that would be caused by nuclear war. A glimpse into the horror of a nuclear war is a sobering, sometimes shocking, look at the destructive potential of humankind.

Nuclear Weapons

There are two basic types of nuclear weapon: fission bombs and fusion bombs. In a fission bomb (or atomic bomb) a runaway chain reaction proceeds without interference. Several kilograms of uranium can produce an explosion of immense proportions.

The smallest amount of uranium-235 needed to generate a runaway chain reaction is called the **critical mass**. Fission bombs contain at least a critical mass of fissionable material—either U-235 or plutonium-239—divided into pieces. In a fission bomb a preliminary explosion of TNT brings the material together, creating a critical mass (Figure S23-1).

A fusion bomb (or hydrogen bomb) is a combination of two bombs. As shown in Figure S23-1, a small fission bomb, called a nuclear trigger, is first detonated. This provides the extraordinarily high heat necessary to generate a fusion reaction, with its immense release of energy. (See Chapter 14 for a discussion of the fusion reaction.) The hydrogen bomb produces nearly three times as much energy as a fission bomb of equal weight.

(*a*) **Fission Bomb.** The trigger (1) ignites TNT charge (2) propelling subcritical masses (3) into each other to form super-critical assembly of fissionable material.

(*b*) **Fusion Bomb.** This bomb works in the same way, but (4) consists of the tritium–deuterium fusion–mixture instead of being a nonreactive casing or neutron reflector.

(*c*) **Fission–Fusion–Fission Bomb.** This is also similar but the outer casing (5) consists of uranium-238 (covered by a protective skin), which fissions when triggered by the fusion explosion.

Figure S23-1
Types of nuclear weapons.

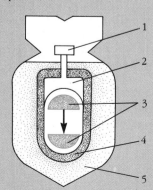

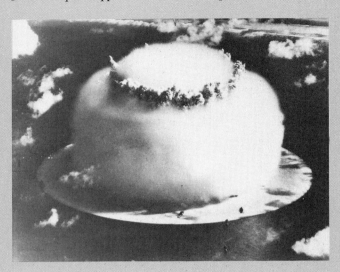

Figure S23-2
Fireball and mushroom cloud produced by a thermonuclear blast.

Nuclear bombs are rated in terms of their explosive power compared with TNT. The fission bomb dropped over Hiroshima, Japan, on August 6, 1945, had the equivalent explosive power of 12,500 tons of TNT. A thousand tons of TNT is a kiloton, so it was a 12.5-kiloton bomb. These bombs, while powerful enough to devastate large sections of cities and kill tens of thousands of people, are small in comparison with those deployed today, which have the explosive power of 1 million to 2 million tons of TNT. A million tons is called a megaton; so the new bombs equal 1 to 2 megatons.

Effects of Nuclear Detonation

Nuclear weapons can be exploded on the ground (surface burst) or in the air above the target (air burst). The point above the explosion is called **ground zero**. When the bomb explodes, it creates an immense fireball, about 1000 meters (3400 feet) high in the case of a 1-megaton explosion (Figure S23-2).

A nuclear explosion produces (1) heat and light, (2) an explosive blast and high winds, (3) a blast of nuclear radiation, (4) a pulse of electromagnetic radiation, and (5) fallout.

Heat and Light

About one-third of the energy from a nuclear explosion is dissipated in heat and light. The light flash may produce temporary blindness in victims looking in the general direction of ground zero at the time of detonation. This **flash blindness** lasts only a few minutes, and recovery is expected to be complete except in victims who were looking directly at the fireball. They may suffer serious retinal burns that may lead to partial or complete blindness.

The intense heat flash accompanying the light flash has more serious impacts. The most common injury among survivors of atomic explosions is burns. People as far away as 11 kilometers (7 miles) from a 1-megaton explosion would suffer first-degree burns (similar to sunburns) on exposed skin. Second-degree burns, characterized by blistering of the skin, would be inflicted on anyone within a 10-kilometer (6-mile) radius of the blast. More serious charring of the skin, or third-degree burns, would be common on exposed skin of people as far away as 8 kilometers (5 miles) from ground zero.

Third-degree burns over one-fourth of the body and second-degree burns over one-third of the body could produce serious shock, which would probably prove fatal unless medical treatment were immediately available—an unlikely possibility for two reasons. First, in the event of a nuclear explosion cities would crumble and with them hospitals, ambulances, and roads, making immediate health care impossible. Second, all the burn-care facilities in the United States combined have room for only about 2000 people. In a single major city, tens of thousands of people will be seriously burned.

The heat flash would also ignite buildings and any combustible material in its path. The fire zone would extend about 8 kilometers (5 miles) in all directions from a 1-megaton blast. Individual fires started by the heat flash and feeding on broken fuel lines might coalesce into one huge firestorm, destroying cities.

Explosive Blast and Winds

Several seconds after the heat and light flashes, an explosive blast sweeps out from ground zero. The blast would be felt as a sudden increase in air pressure, called a **static overpressure**, which would topple buildings and walls and crush objects. It might take several seconds for the overpressure to pass. High winds (dynamic overpressure) would follow. Six and a half kilometers (4 miles) from a 1-megaton explosion, the overpressure would be 5 pounds per square inch (psi) above the normal 14.7 psi. This pressure could rupture human eardrums and would put tremendous strain on materials. A 5-psi pressure wave exerts 180 tons of pressure on the wall of a typical two-story house, causing it to topple. The winds at that distance would exceed 290 kilometers per hour (180 miles per hour).

The damage from the blast and winds depends on the distance from ground zero, as shown in Table S23-1. The impact of a nuclear explosion also depends on the detonation height. Overpressure and winds from ground bursts generally affect a smaller area than air bursts.

Table S23-1   Blast Effects of Nuclear Explosions[1]

Distance from Explosion		1-Kiloton Weapon	150-Kiloton Weapon	1-Megaton Weapon	10-Metagon Weapon
1 mile	Overpressure: Winds:	1.4 psi 50 mph Cuts and blows from flying debris; many buildings moderately damaged	18 psi 420 mph Humans battered to death; heavy machinery dragged; reinforced concrete building severely damaged	43 psi 1700 mph Many humans killed	Above 200 psi Above 2000 mph Buried 20-centimeter-thick concrete arch destroyed
2 miles	Overpressure: Winds:	.5 psi Below 35 mph Many broken windows	6 psi 190 mph Some eardrums ruptured; bones fractured; all trees blown down; telephone lines dragged severely	17 psi 400 mph Humans battered to death; lung hemorrhage; eardrums ruptured; heavy machinery dragged severely	50 psi 1800 mph Humans fatally crushed; severe damage to buried light corrugated steel arch
5 miles	Overpressure: Winds:		1.5 psi 55 mph Cuts and blows from flying debris; many buildings moderately damaged	4 psi 130 mph Bones fractured; 90% of trees down; many buildings flattened	14 psi 330 mph Eardrums ruptured; lung hemorrhage; reinforced concrete building severely damaged
10 miles	Overpressure: Winds:	.6 psi Below 35 mph Many broken windows	1.4 psi 50 mph Cuts and blows from flying debris; many buildings moderately damaged	4.4 psi 150 mph Bones fractured; 90% of trees down; many buildings flattened	
20 miles	Overpressure: Winds:			Below 1 psi Below 35 mph many broken windows	1.5 psi 55 mph Cuts and blows from flying debris; many buildings moderately damaged
40 miles	Overpressure: Winds:				Below 1 psi Below 35 mph Many broken windows

[1]The range of effects required dictates the optimum height at which the weapon would be detonated.
Source: Goodwin, P. (1981). *Nuclear War: The Facts on Our Survival.* New York: Rutledge Press, pp. 28–29.

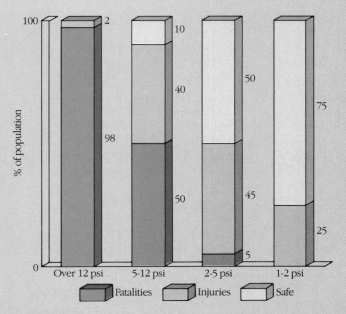

Figure S23-3
Estimated fatalities and injuries from overpressure and winds created by a nuclear bomb blast.

The main danger from overpressure is the toppling of buildings. Destruction of homes, apartments, and office buildings would crush tens of thousands of people. It is estimated that a 1-megaton blast in downtown Detroit at night would kill everyone within a 2.7-kilometer (1.7-mile) radius of the blast. Seventy thousand urbanites at work or at sleep in their downtown apartments would perish. If the bomb were dropped during the daytime, the number of casualties would be many times higher.

The high winds would send debris and shattered glass flying and throw people against hard objects. The combined effects of static overpressure and winds are shown in Figure S23-3.

Direct Nuclear Radiation

A highly intense blast of ionizing radiation also spreads out in all directions from a nuclear explosion. For large weapons in the megaton range, the range of intense nuclear radiation is smaller than that of the heat and static pressure, so radiation would not be the principal cause of death. In the case of small weapons, such as those in the kiloton category, the range of intense radiation exceeds the range of heat and blast. It would therefore be the major cause of death.

The effects of radiation depend on dose, which, in turn, depends on the distance from ground zero and the size of the weapon (Tables S23-2 and S23-3). A 1-megaton explosion would create a lethal zone 1 kilometer (1.6 miles) surrounding ground zero. Radiation levels would exceed 500 rads in this area (see Chapter Supplement 21-1). But they would decrease in time as the radionuclides disintegrated. Still, intensely radioactive zones would be unsafe for a decade or more after an explosion. Surrounding areas would also be contaminated with lesser amounts of radiation.

Electromagnetic Pulse

Nuclear detonations create a single momentary pulse of electromagnetic energy that spreads in all directions from the bomb blast. This energy is similar to the electrical signal given off by lightning, but of a much higher strength.

The **electromagnetic pulse** would cause short circuits in radio stations and electrical equipment that was not heavily shielded. Radio transmission and, possibly, telephone service would be damaged at a time when they would be badly needed to coordinate rescue operations and health care. Most computers would be rendered useless. In addition to direct physical damage, the pulse might create instabilities in the electrical grid, causing shutdowns. Service in outlying areas not destroyed by the bomb blast would be stopped, further impairing rescue and medical treatment. A single large bomb exploded in space 400 kilometers (250 miles) above Omaha could affect the United States from coast to coast.

Fallout

Ground bursts and low-altitude air bursts scoop up dirt and dust and irradiate it, making much of the material radioactive. The force of the explosion and the hot air sweep the material into the air; it returns to earth as **radioactive fallout**. Some of it may fall back immediately, landing near the site of the explosion and making the area intensely radioactive. Some fallout is carried higher, forming the top of the mushroom cloud. It will later fall back to earth, but the pattern of deposition depends on wind and rainfall.

Some fallout may be thrust into the stratosphere and may circulate there for decades, falling to earth gradually but exposing a larger area. The short-lived radionuclides decay in the stratosphere and pose no real threat, but the longer-lived radionuclides may present a more substantial hazard to humans. Some fallout from the U.S. and Soviet bomb tests performed in the 1950s and early 1960s can still be detected.

Atmospheric dust created by nuclear war could bring about a drastic reduction in global temperature by blocking out sun-

Table S23-2 Facts about Nuclear Explosions[1]

Weapon Yield	1-Kiloton	150-Kiloton	1-Megaton	10-Megaton	20-Megaton
Fireball maximum size	220 feet	1580 feet	3400 feet	8450 feet	11,350 feet
Minimum height of explosion for no local fallout	180 feet	1320 feet	2750 feet	6850 feet	9250 feet
Crater width (inner lip)[2]	126 feet	530 feet	950 feet	1800 feet	2300 feet
Crater depth[2]	28 feet	140 feet	210 feet	420 feet	530 feet
Range of lethal initial radiation (500 rads)	.5 mile	1.2 miles	1.6 miles	2.5 miles	3 miles
Range for skin reddening	.5 mile	5.5 miles	10 miles	24 miles	30 miles
Range for charred skin	.4 mile	3.5 miles	8 miles	18 miles	23 miles
Range for 2% of buildings gutted by fire (2-psi blast)	.8 mile	4.2 miles	8 miles	17 miles	22 miles
Range for 10% of buildings gutted by fire (5-psi blast)	.4 mile	2.2 miles	4.3 miles	9.3 miles	12 miles
Range for fatal wind drag (a human could be dragged along at 40 feet per second)	.2 mile	1.6 miles	3.3 miles	8 miles	10 miles
Duration of severe blast (4 psi)	.3 second	1.8 seconds	3 seconds	7 seconds	9 seconds
Arrival time of blast wave (4 psi)	2 seconds after flash	10 seconds after flash	20 seconds after flash	42 seconds after flash	53 seconds after flash
Range of devastation for above-ground buildings (12 psi)	.3 mile	1.3 miles	2.5 miles	5 miles	7 miles
Range of severe blast damage (4 psi)	.5 mile	2.6 miles	5 miles	11 miles	13 miles
Range at which all windows broken (1 psi)	1.3 mile	7 miles	13 miles	28 miles	36 miles

[1]The range of effects required dictates the explosion's optimum height. For example, when a 1-megaton weapon is exploded at 5000 feet there is a 1.2-mile range of devastation, compared with a 4.4-mile range when the height of explosion is 10,000 feet.
[2]Surface-burst only.
Source: Goodwin, P. (1981). *Nuclear War: The Facts on Our Survival.* New York: Rutledge Press, p. 31.

light. The global nuclear winter could destroy agricultural crops and endanger many wild species.

Combined Injuries

One area often ignored in reports on the effects of nuclear war are the combined injuries. For example, people might receive nonlethal doses of radiation but also be burned. Or people might be irradiated and suffer cuts or broken bones.

Death rates are generally calculated using the predominant factor, but the combined injuries would raise the already high toll. For example, laboratory studies suggest that people exposed to more than 100 rems of ionizing radiation (nonlethal) would have difficulty recovering from burns. Other evidence shows that puncture wounds, broken bones, concussions, and internal injuries are all more serious if a person is exposed to 300 rems of radiation.

Table S23-3   Effects of Radiation Exposure

Dose	Vomiting Incidence	Initial Phase[1]	Latent Phase[2] Duration	Final Phase[3] Duration
0–100 rads No illness				
100–200 rads Slight illness	100 rads: seldom 200 rads: common	Begins after 3–6 hours. Continues up to 1 day	Up to 2 weeks	Up to 2 weeks
200–600 rads[4] Survival possible	Above 300 rads: all	Begins after ½–6 hours. Continues 1–2 days	1–4 weeks	1–8 weeks
600–1000 rads Survival possible	All	Begins after ¼–½ hour. Continues up to 2 days	5–10 days	1–4 weeks
1000–5000 rads Lethal range	All	Begins after 5–30 minutes. Continues up to 1 day	0–7 days	2–10 days
Over 5000 rads	All	Almost immediately	No latent phase	1–48 hours

[1]**Initial phase**—nausea; vomiting; headache; dizziness; loss of appetite; tiredness
[2]**Latent phase**—apparent recovery, but changes continuing in blood-forming tissues; gut and nerve tissue complications develop at higher doses
[3]**Final phase**—High temperature and fever with all symptoms of final phase; bleeding and bruising affecting skin, mouth, lips and gut; blood in urine; lower resistance to infection could lead to ulceration; diarrhea; loss of hair; delirium (as temperature rises out of control); emaciation (through not eating); seizures; extreme pain

Predicting the Effects of Nuclear War

No one can predict the effects of a nuclear war. Clearly, for any single explosion, many variables determine how much destruction will occur and how many people will die. What sized weapons will be used? What time of day will the bombs be dropped? Will they fall on target or miss by several kilometers? Hills and mountains could block the effects of weapons that missed their target. What will the weather be like? If it's raining, the fallout will be close to ground zero. If the wind is blowing, it may spread farther. If it's foggy, the light and heat flash will be stunted.

Prediction is made more difficult because no one knows on what scale a war of this nature might be fought. Will only a few bombs be dropped, or will all the world's 50,000 warheads find their way to warring countries? Where will they be dropped? How many will fall on each city?

A fraction of the weapons possessed by the United States and the Soviet Union could devastate the major population centers of every country in the world, destroying all buildings, factories, roads, and people. The potential for global destruction is not exaggerated.

Of this we can be certain: Any nuclear explosion over an urban area would have catastrophic effects. Widespread nuclear war would have consequences beyond our comprehension. Health care and transportation and public sanitation would all be imperiled, making it difficult or impossible for us to recover in any reasonable time. Widespread detonation of nuclear weapons might well destroy the ultraviolet-screening ozone layer, as discussed in Chapter Supplement 19-1, creating widespread cancer and global climatic changes.

Table S23-3 Effects of Radiation Exposure

Main Organ Involved	Distinguishing Signs	Convalescence Period	Incidence of Death	Death Occurs Within
	Above 50 rads: slight changes in blood cells			
Blood forming systems: bone marrow, lymph glands	Moderate fall in white blood cell count	Several weeks		
Blood forming systems: bone marrow, lymph glands	Severe loss of white blood cells; bleeding; infection; anemia (loss of red blood cells); loss of hair (above 300 rads)	1–12 months	0–90%	2-12 weeks
Blood forming systems: bone marrow, lymph glands		Long	90–100%	2–12 weeks
Gastrointestinal tract	Diarrhea; fever; shock symptoms		100%	2–14 days
Central nervous system	Convulsions; tremor; involuntary movements; lethargy		100%	days

Source: Goodwin, P. (1981). *Nuclear War: The Facts on Our Survival.* New York: Rutledge Press, pp. 44–45.

According to Paul Warnke, former U.S. coordinator for the Strategic Arms Limitation Talks, "In this the fourth decade of the nuclear age, it is tempting to assume that a nuclear exchange won't take place and that, in any event, there is nothing the average human being can do about it. But the fact is that a nuclear war could happen and very well may happen unless we, as citizens of a threatened world, decide that we will do something."

Suggested Readings

Goodwin, P. (1981). *Nuclear War: The Facts on Our Survival.* New York: Rutledge Press. Excellent coverage.

Lifton, R. J., and Falk, R. (1982). *Indefensible Weapons.* New York: Basic Books. Eloquent analysis of the nuclear age.

Riordan, M. (ed.) (1982). *The Day After Midnight: The Effects of Nuclear War.* Palo Alto, Calif.: Cheshire Books. Detailed account worth reading.

Schell, J. (1982). *The Fate of the Earth.* New York: Avon. A stirring account.

Economics and the Environment

A penny will hide the biggest star in the Universe if you hold it close enough to your eye.

SAMUEL GRAFTON

In southern India people once made traps for monkeys by drilling holes in coconuts, filling the shells with rice, and chaining them to the ground. The success of this trap was based on a simple principle: the hole was large enough for a monkey to insert its empty hand, but too small for it to pull a handful of rice out. Monkeys were trapped by their own refusal to let go of the rice.

Some economists believe that the same plight grips humankind: we're caught in a spiraling cycle of greed, trapped by our own refusal to let go of the material goods we've lavished upon ourselves. The economist Herman Daly once wrote, "We seem to be trapped in a growth-dominated economic system that is causing growing depletion, pollution and disamenity, as well as increasing the probability of ecological catastrophe." This chapter will look at some of the flaws in our current economic system, examine how the prevalent economic philosophy creates problems in resource management and pollution control, and evaluate some new proposals for an economic system for a sustainable society.

Economics: the Science of Growth

Economics is an imprecise science concerned basically with the production, distribution, and consumption of resources, goods, and services. **Macroeconomics** deals with the economic activities of nations, and **microeconomics** takes a narrower look at particular markets.

Noted ecologist Paul Ehrlich claims that most economists impose a qualitative restriction on their science—the assumption that growth is the major goal of all economic activity. The noted economist Paul Samuelson of the Massachusetts Institute of Technology once called economics "the science of growth." Most economists, politicians, businesspersons, and citizens today agree: growth is sacred, and bigger is better. Their collective goal is to ensure that production, distribution, and consumption of resources, goods, and services always increases. Entangled in this "growth mania" is the notion that economic growth represents true progress. Society has been willing for many years to pay almost any cost for this sort of progress.

Economic growth depends on increasing consumption, which comes from a combination of greater per capita consumption and larger population. Thus, population growth has traditionally been viewed as an asset, an opportunity for economic expansion. The underlying challenge for many people is not to control population growth but to increase production to meet the people's needs. This is the **demand-satisfaction approach.**

The growth mania of the developed countries has spread to the developing nations. Many developing nations have launched concerted campaigns to westernize with generous assistance from the World Bank and developed nations, but without resources at hand the campaigns often fail. The southern African nation of Tanzania, for example, built a huge fertilizer factory with assistance from the World Bank, but it had to import raw phosphate from overseas at considerable expense. Then, the fertilizer had to be transported throughout a country as big as California, Nevada, and Oregon combined, but the rail system was decrepit, and petroleum was scarce. The lack of money for oil and raw materials often meant that fertilizer was unavailable when needed. All in all, western agriculture failed in Tanzania. For quite practical reasons, the growth-oriented philosophy could not take root there (Figure 24-1).

Figure 24-1
Young agricultural students in Upper Volta (West Africa) learn use and maintain plows—the technology is appropriate to the region's agricultural needs and capabilities.

Measuring Economic Growth

If economic growth is the religion of modern economics, the gross national product, or GNP, is its high priest. The GNP is the total national output of goods and services valued at market prices, or the sum of personal and governmental expenditures on all goods and services in a given year. It also includes the net exports (or the value of exports minus the value of all imports) and all private investment. Per capita GNP is the GNP divided by the total population. GNP and per capita GNP are widely used measurements for tracking the economy, but they have weaknesses.

First, per capita GNP is often used by economists as a measure of standard of living, which it clearly is not. The reason is quite simple: in general, the cost of equivalent goods and services varies considerably from one country to another. Imagine that Country A has a per capita GNP of $20,000 and Country B one of $2000. A home in Country A may cost $70,000, but the same home in Country B may cost only $7000. If this cost difference is true for all goods and services, for one-tenth as much money residents of Country B enjoy the same goods and services as those in Country A, even though their per capita GNPs are different.

Per capita GNP may also be irrelevant in poor countries where wealth is concentrated in the hands of a few. A few wealthy individuals may give the country a false appearance of adequate per capita GNP. Thus, per capita GNP is blind to the actual distribution of wealth.

Annual growth in the GNP is one of the most sacred of all economic indicators. Countries are often compared with one another on the basis of GNP growth. But growth in the GNP does not take into account accumulated wealth—the goods built up over the years. Growth in the GNP simply assumes that a high growth rate is preferable regardless of the accumulated wealth.

Growth in the GNP is also blind to population growth. For example, a 5% growth in GNP in a country with a 5% population growth rate results in no per capita increase. In contrast, the same growth in GNP in a country with a 1% population growth rate is a 4% increase in per capita GNP. Thus, GNP growth is meaningless unless expressed on a per capita basis.

As a measure of standard of living, GNP is blind to the quality of the air and water and the well-being of all other resources, including wildlife and wilderness. GNP is a lump sum for all goods and services and does not take into account what a country is spending its money on. For example, GNP includes all expenditures on homes, books, art shows, concerts, and food; at the same time, it includes expenditures on cancer treatment, air pollution control, hospitals and health services, and water pollution projects. Therefore, a country with filthy air and polluted water faced with epidemics of environmental disease and mental disorders caused by stress might register a high GNP. Envious politicians from other countries might see this as a high standard of living while residents decry the putrid mess they live in. Truly, GNP tells us little about the quality of life.

Several suggestions have been forwarded to improve the GNP or develop a "value-conscious" measurement of economic activity. The economist Edwin Dolan proposed

the **gross national cost,** or **GNC,** which would be divided into two parts: Type 1 GNC would measure the value of goods from renewable resources, and Type 2 GNC, the value of goods from nonrenewable resources. An important goal would be to maximize the Type 1 GNC.

A **pollution cost index** (PCI) might also be determined each year. Type 1 PCI would indicate expenditures on pollution control devices and programs. Type 2 PCI would indicate the cost of pollution in terms of health and environment. A low or declining Type 2 PCI would be optimal and would indicate an increase in the standard of living. But would we want a high or low Type 1 PCI? Obviously, if the costs of pollution control fall because of redesigned processes, conservation, and recycling, that is desirable.

An economic measure that reflects the standard of living would be the per capita **measure of economic welfare,** or **MEW.** MEW could measure accumulated wealth such as the value of homes, TV sets, and furniture per person. In essence, MEW would measure how well off we are. To make it more reflective of the economic welfare of the majority of people, economists might exclude the highest income groups from their calculations.

Supply and Demand

If GNP is the high priest of modern economics, the law of supply and demand is its chief doctrine. Supply, demand, and price are corners of the same economic triangle. As the demand for a product or resource rises, the supply shrinks. This creates competition among buyers, which results in higher prices. Higher prices, in turn, usually give the producers incentive to make more of their product or find more resources to increase supply. The net effect, at least in theory, is that increases in supply should hold down prices.

The law of supply and demand operates well in certain instances, describing most aptly the economic behavior of given markets but only poorly explaining the economic behavior of nations and declining resources. The law fails to take into account the laws of thermodynamics and the finite nature of nonrenewable resources. Economists who rely on this theory typically assume that price increases caused by excessive demand in relation to current supply will stimulate new discoveries, thus increasing supply. This failure to recognize that nonrenewable resources run out is a major weakness in the economic system's most sacred doctrine. Some critics view it as a fatal flaw.

Figure 24-2
OPEC oil refinery and storage tanks in Saudi Arabia.

The law of supply and demand also falls apart in macroeconomics, because it ignores the political element. Our experience with the Organization of Petroleum Exporting Countries drives this lesson home. OPEC nations control a large percentage of the world's oil supply. Even though demand rises in relation to their production, this is no guarantee that they will increase supply. In fact, rising prices may actually stimulate further cuts in supply.

This economic anomaly is the result of social, political, and religious factors. In 1980 OPEC nations had an annual surplus of $100 billion from oil sales; by 2000 the surplus is expected to reach $350 billion per year (Figure 24-2). The OPEC nations simply cannot absorb all of this money, so they cut down on supply. They cannot spend all the excess money partly because materialism goes against the grain of Islamic beliefs, which are held by the majority of the OPEC nations, and partly because heavy investment in Western countries gives the impression that leaders are too pro-Western and creates fears that the Western countries might seize the money. In any event, increasing demand and rising prices may only lead to further reductions in supply, creating a backward sloping supply curve.

Despite its serious flaws, the law of supply and demand still governs the thinking of most economists and politicians.

Economic Behavior, Environment, and Resources

Chapter 2 presented the Multiple Cause and Effect model, which showed the multiplicity of factors that affect environmental problems. Economics was one of those factors. But economics profoundly influences other factors including politics, government, and personal behavior. In some cases economics and these other factors are inseparable. Thus, private and governmental decisions about natural resources and pollution must be examined from an economic perspective. Essay 24-1 explores the political power of Political Action Committees (PAC).

Economics of Natural Resource Management

Most private decisions about natural resources are influenced by economic considerations. Two of the most important ones are time preference and opportunity costs.

Time preference is a measure of one's willingness to give up some current income for greater returns in the future. For example, suppose a friend offered you $100

Essay 24-1

Political Action Committees: A New Force

Political Action Committees, or PACs, are consortiums of individuals or businesses that share a common outlook on political issues and donate their money to congressional and presidential candidates in the hope of reaping some benefits if their candidate wins office. This pooling of economic resources is growing more popular in the United States, making PACs an important political entity. In 1980 PACs donated approximately $58 million to congressional candidates. By 1982, an off-year election, the donations had grown to $86 million.

PACs have been formed among teach-ers, sympathizers with Israel, businesses concerned with governmental environmental regulations, and environmentalists who want to get in on the action.

Obviously, PACs are effective because of the large sums of money that can be raised and donated. A candidate is not likely to forget a check for $100,000 from his or her "constituency." The economic influence wielded by PACs, however, has created an outcry of criticism among individuals concerned that the democratic system is becoming more a government of the money, by the money, and for the money—a government that leaves the common everyday citizen in the dust while it caters to the rich.

Businesses and labor are the predominant organizers of PACs in the United States. In 1982 business organizations collectively donated $45.5 million, and labor gave a record $20.6 million. What are the long-term political ramifications of a PAC system of government?

Political action committees clearly concentrate power into the hands of a few, but what can we do about them? Should we ban them or put limits on their contributions? Questions such as these will continue as PACs increase their power.

---

today or $108 a year from now. Your choice would be partly based on your time preference. If you needed the money right away to pay for books for school, you might take the $100 now. Your current need would outweigh the benefits of waiting a year for a slightly higher reward.

As this example shows, time preference is determined by your immediate needs. It may also be influenced by uncertainty. How certain are you that your friend will give you the $108 at the end of the year? The greater your uncertainty, the less chance you'll take. A third factor affecting time preference is the rate of return. If your friend had offered you $150 a year from now, you might be willing to wait.

This analogy applies to the management of renewable resources such as farmland, forests, rivers, and grasslands. For example, farmers have two basic choices when it comes to managing their land. They can choose a **depletion strategy** to acquire an immediate, high rate of return for a short period of time. This might involve the use of multiple cropping, artificial fertilizers, herbicides, and pesticides to maximize production (Chapters 8 and 9). It would probably avoid strip cropping, terracing, and crop rotation, because they cut into the immediate financial returns.

In the alternative approach, the **conservation strategy**, the farmers use methods to conserve topsoil and maintain or build soil fertility. These actions require immediate monetary investments that will produce a lower return in the short run. Over the long run, however, profit from the conservation strategy will be likely to exceed that from the depletion strategy.

The choice of strategy depends on the time preference which, in turn, is affected by (1) the farmer's age and income preference (immediate needs), (2) his or her uncertainty about future prices and the long-range prospects of farming, (3) the opportunity costs, (4) interest rates, and (5) the farmer's ethics.

Let's look at an example. A young farmer looking forward to a productive farming career may opt for the conservation strategy. Her immediate needs may be small. She may have no family and few debts. She can sacrifice income now for larger returns in the long run. However, an older farmer may go the other way. He may have a large family to support, excessive debt, and only a few years left to farm. His income preference is high. He may therefore want to maximize his profits through a depletion strategy.

Uncertainty also enters the picture. If the price of corn is high this year but could drop significantly in coming years, a farmer may choose to make his money now. If the bottom falls out of the market in the next few years, he will have made the most of this short-term opportunity. If interest rates are uncertain and likely to rise, short-term profit making may be the preferable choice.

Opportunity cost is the cost of lost money-making opportunities. The conservation strategy requires an investment of time and money that might be better spent elsewhere. It might cost a farmer $5000 to invest in terraces or windbreaks to stop wind erosion. That money might yield more in the stock market.

High *interest rates* on land and machinery the farmer has purchased tend to encourage an immediate time preference, leading to depletion strategies.

Ethics can be as powerful as any of the previously mentioned factors. Widespread adoption of *sustainable earth ethics* (Chapter 23), for example, can eliminate the demand for immediate monetary returns. A long-term view, seeking to maximize yield for future generations and ensure the survival and well-being of all life, should lead to a conservation strategy with benefits accruing to all of humankind now and in the future. The opposing view, the *frontier mentality,* seeks to maximize personal gain with little concern for the future; in effect, this view leaves future generations to fend for themselves.

Resource management is also affected by the cost of products and their potential profitability; prices of energy, materials, and labor; and governmental policy. The higher the margin of profit, the more likely good resource management will be carried out (but don't count on this rule). Low profit margins generally translate into poorer resource management. The price of materials, labor, and energy determines the profitability of businesses.

Government policy can encourage or discourage resource management. During the Carter presidency, for example, thermostats in all federal buildings were required to be set at 68° F (20° C) in the winter and 78° F (26° C) in the summer, to help save energy. Provisions of the Surface Mine Control and Reclamation Act improved management of surface-mined land. On the other side of the coin, national monetary policy affects interest rates and investment in pollution control and conservation. Federal loans for housing and tax deductions for interest on home mortgages make it easier for people to buy homes, and federal policy emphasizes high timber production to help hold prices down. These two factors probably discourage conservation and proper forest management.

Economics of Pollution Control

Economics also plays an important role in pollution control. This section looks at some of these factors. (Model Application 24-1 allows you to do your own impact analysis.)

Internalizing Costs Both the free market economic system in the United States and other countries and the planned economic system of socialist and communist nations treated pollution with almost uniform disregard until the late 1960s and early 1970s. Pollution was something that issued from the smokestacks and symbolized economic progress. Where it landed no one seemed to know or care.

In this context, pollution and its impacts were considered an **economic externality**, an economic value external to traditional calculations of the cost of doing business. Only the benefits and the easily observable costs of labor, energy, and materials were factored into the cost of doing business. Taxpayers and private citizens bore the brunt of industrial pollution.

To be fair, in many instances businesses were simply unaware of the external costs of pollution. Gradually, though, as citizens began suing over pollution damage and as the U.S. government began establishing pollution standards for industry, businesses began to install pollution control devices, and the economic externalities began to enter businesses' calculations. The major laws forcing this internalization of costs have been the Clean Air Act, the Water Pollution Control Act, and the Surface Mine Control and Reclamation Act. This movement toward internalization is far from complete, and it remains one of the country's foremost economic and social challenges.

Who Pays for Environmental Damage? The chief goal of pollution control is to achieve the maximum reduction of pollution, which yields the maximum benefit, at the lowest cost. This goal is evaluated by *cost–benefit analysis,* a concept introduced in Chapter 17 in our discussion of risk assessment. The cost of pollution control and the benefits of pollution control can be plotted on a graph (Figure 24-3). This graph shows that removal of pollutants from uncontrolled processes is initially quite cheap, but as pollution reduction grows, the cost increases substantially. The graph also shows how the costs of harmful effects fall as pollution control increases. The point where the two lines meet represents the optimum level of control, where the total costs are lowest.

Impact Analysis of a Uranium Mine

Suppose that you were appointed head of a task force in your community to determine the potential impacts of a uranium mine that might open on the eastern edge of town. Uranium would be surface-mined, and the ore would be transported by truck through town to a plant 50 kilometers away, where it would be processed.

Question

You are asked to study all the possible effects of this project.

Step 1

Using the Impact Analysis model, draw up a plan to organize your study. What major committees will you form to study impacts and what will each of these study? What kind of people

(scientists, ordinary citizens, and so on) will you put on each committee?

Step 2

Once you have finished your work, the mayor cuts your budget and asks you to eliminate committees studying the impacts least likely to occur. Which ones will you eliminate? Which ones will you keep?

Step 3

Study Figure 3-13 and project how a surface mine for uranium would affect air, water, land, plants, human health, and non-human animals. Take some time and do further reading on each of these impacts to determine how likely they are.

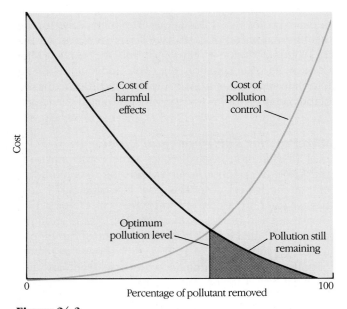

Figure 24-3
The cost of pollution control versus the benefits.

Determining the true costs of pollution is quite difficult, for two reasons. First, it is hard to assign economic values to lost wilderness, deteriorated air, lost wildlife, and obstructed views. Second, estimating the total damage to health and the environment is difficult due to hidden effects, which are not easily detectable; latent effects, which appear years after the pollution; ignorance about impacts because of insufficient scientific research; and the confounding influence of different causative agents, including many natural agents such as climate.

An accurate estimate of the cost of pollution will always elude us, for these reasons, but we can still make good estimates and revise them as our analyses improve. An estimation of cost helps us institute pollution control strategies. Once the costs have been determined, an important question is, "Who will pay them?"

This question is the focal point of much of the controversy in pollution control. In general, businesses that create pollution are reluctant to pay the economic externalities, primarily because it drives up the cost of production, making their products more expensive. This could cut demand. Therefore, businesses look to the taxpayer to pay.

Should the corporation pay for pollution control and pass the cost on to customers—the **consumer-pays option**? Or should society pay (the **taxpayer-pays option**)? Those who favor the consumer-pays option assert that the consumer who uses the products should bear the cost. Nonusers should not have to subsidize the costs of users. In addition, passing the cost directly to the consumer might lead to more frugal buying habits. Those who support the taxpayer-pays option argue that taxpayers have allowed industry to pollute for years with impunity. Now, new standards are imposed that place costly burdens on existing industries. Shouldn't society, which has suddenly changed the rules of the game, pay for the controls? Furthermore, they argue, society has elected and continues to elect officials who make deals with polluters to entice them to locate in their community. Local support has often been strong. Or elected officials have simply failed to sue violators on the public behalf for fear of reprisals. If society is responsible for its elected officials, who permitted pollution and other forms of environmental destruction, then society must bear at least some of the cost.

As in most controversies there is validity to both arguments; thus, a third view—the **everyone-pays option**—has been advanced. That is, in cases of old industries, taxpayers should probably bear much of the burden; but in new industries, starting up after the laws have been passed, pollution control costs should be borne by the corporation and consumers.

This discussion leaves one with the impression that pollution prevention always costs money: but pollution prevention can pay, because recovered pollutants become valuable resources a company can trade or sell for cash. This money may not only pay for the cost of installing and maintaining pollution control equipment but may also generate a profit.

Economic Incentives for Pollution Control

To date, pollution control by governments has been a policy of punitive action; violators were given stiff fines, sometimes without court trials. But in recent years government officials have looked at *economic incentives* as a gentler way to get companies to comply with pollution laws.

One possibility is the issuance of **marketable permits**. Companies in a given region would be issued permits by the Environmental Protection Agency to emit certain amounts of pollutants. However, a company could sell its permit to another company in the same area under certain circumstances. For example, Company A, allowed to emit 200,000 metric tons of sulfur dioxide each year, finds a way to cut its emissions to 50,000 metric tons. It can then sell its permit for 150,000 metric tons to Company B. For Company B, purchasing the permit might be cheaper than installing pollution control devices. In any event, the total emissions in the region remain the same. Chapter 19 discussed the **emissions offset policy**, which is similar to the marketable permit system.

Another similar concept is the **bubble policy**, which is being used by the EPA. The bubble policy allows a polluter to increase pollution in one part of a facility if it reduces it in another, where the cost of reduction may be less.

Following the hard economic times of the late 1970s and early 1980s, some governmental officials have begun to reconsider the strict emission standards set for new facilities (Chapter 19). The Clean Air Act required emission standards for new facilities that were much more stringent than those for older or existing facilities. In some cases, however, the new-source performance standards have made it cheaper to keep old polluting facilities in operation. Such delayed retirement avoids capital investment for new facilities with costly pollution control equipment.

To reduce delayed retirement, some have suggested relaxing the standards for new sources if they can secure equal or greater reductions from other sources in the same region. This is an example of the emissions offset policy. Such a strategy might lower the cost of bringing new, more efficient equipment on line and result in more rapid attainment of desired air quality.

Other suggestions for reducing pollution include (1) the decontrol of energy prices, allowing them to reflect the actual cost, a move that would stimulate more conservation; (2) faster depreciation for pollution control equipment, allowing businesses to recover their costs more quickly in tax returns; and (3) the use of microprocessors, advanced sensors, and controls to monitor and regulate industrial processes.

Balancing Costs and Benefits

Pollution and environmental destruction cost the United States an enormous amount; air pollution alone causes some $12 billion to $16 billion in damage each year. But pollution control and environmental protection also have an economic cost.

Table 24-1 Federal Expenditures on Environmental Programs, 1981[1]

Item	Expenditure (Billions of Dollars)
Water pollution control	7.63
Air pollution control	0.56
Land	0.15
Other	3.01
Total on all environmental programs[1]	12.85

[1]Includes pollution control projects, as well as research and other functions related to the environment.
Source: Council on Environmental Quality.

In 1981, for example, the federal government spent nearly $13 billion on environmental programs (Table 24-1), most of it on water pollution control. That same year, industry spent approximately $10 billion just on new plant and equipment to control pollution. Total expenditure including daily operating expenses came to over $30 billion. Although industry and government pick up the pollution control bills, the costs are later passed on to taxpayers and consumers.

Conventional wisdom often suggests that environmental regulations and permits delay projects, increase the cost of doing business, decrease productivity, and cost society jobs. Studies by the Conservation Foundation and other groups, however, show that delays are often the result of uncertainty and poor planning by companies and agencies, not compliance with environmental laws. Corporations may be reluctant to invite the public or the government to participate in the early planning stages of projects for fear that disclosure will hurt their projects. But early consideration of the public viewpoint can reduce delays and even lawsuits that might later arise as the public becomes aware of an objectional project.

Productivity is the dollar value of output per hour of paid employment. This figure has been used to show how healthy an economy is. Between 1948 and 1965 U.S. productivity rose an average of 2.5% per year. Between 1965 and 1975 it rose by an annual rate of 1.6%. But between 1973 and 1978 growth in productivity slowed down to an annual rate of .8%. In 1979 productivity actually fell in the United States by .9%, and it fell again in 1980.

This decline in productivity has been blamed on environmental regulations that divert workers from productive jobs (for example, mining) to nonproductive jobs (for example, mine safety inspector). Careful analysis, however, shows that many other factors play a larger role, including (1) a decline in automation (which increases productivity); (2) a rise in the number of unskilled workers entering the labor force, especially in cities; (3) higher energy prices, which encourage the use of labor over energy-intensive equipment; and (4) a shift from manufactured goods to services. On balance, environmental regulations decrease productivity by an estimated 5% to 15%. This is the price for safer working conditions and a cleaner environment.

The assertion that environmental protection costs us jobs is debated in this chapter's Point/Counterpoint.

New Vistas in Economic Thought

The previous sections take a critical look at the current growth-oriented economic system and give many ways to improve it. The changes discussed so far fall short of proposals by some prominent economists, such as Kenneth Boulding and Herman Daly, who assert that a major economic transformation is necessary for the long-term survival of the human race.

Spaceship Economics: Toward a Sustainable Society

Boulding first wrote on the needed changes in 1966. He coined the phrase **cowboy economy** to describe the present economic system, characterized by maximum flow of money, maximum production, maximum consumption, maximum resource use, and maximum profit. He suggested that the cowboy, or frontier, economy (as many now call it) be replaced by a **spaceship economy** recognizing that the earth, much like a spaceship, is a closed system wholly dependent on a fragile life-support system. Individuals within such an economy would value recycling, conservation, use of renewable resources, product durability, and a clean and healthy environment. Throwaways would be eliminated. Repair of broken-down goods would be encouraged to minimize the need for replacements. Waste would be eliminated as much as possible. People would live within the limits posed by earth.

Table 24-2 Characteristics of a Steady-State Economy

Strives for constant GNP (growth in some areas of the economy, shrinkage in others).

Emphasizes essential goods and services.

Stresses product durability.

Avoids throwaway (disposable) products.

Reduces resource use to ensure long-term supplies.

Minimizes waste and pollution.

Relies on recycling and conservation.

Maximizes use of renewable resources.

Decentralizes certain businesses.

Uses appropriate technology.

Strives for equitable distribution of wealth.

The features of an economic system of this nature are listed in Table 24-2. It can succeed, however, only with widespread population control (Chapter 7) and new political directions (Chapter 25). The spaceship economy is founded on the important concepts of getting by comfortably and living well but not wastefully. Making a comfortable living replaces getting rich quickly. The tradeoff is between more material wealth and a better environment.

The concept of the spaceship economy and the system of ethics forming the foundation of the new economic system were not widely accepted in the late 1960s and still remain out of vogue. Today, however, more and more people recognize their inevitability. Dissatisfaction with the frontier economy stems from its inadequacies in dealing with natural resources and environmental pollution. The critics recognize, as most economists and businesspersons do not, that the production and consumption of goods and services hinge on the availability of resources, which are governed by the law of conservation of matter and the first and second laws of thermodynamics (Chapter 4). They also comprehend the true nature of exponential growth and the rapid change that occurs once something—be it resource depletion or population growth—rounds the bend of the growth curve.

Common misconceptions about the steady-state economy are that it will make for dull living and that it is a no-growth system. Neither of these is true. Excitement, however, might be gauged differently. Instead of getting a thrill out of being the owner of the fastest car on the block,

we would find our excitement in physical fitness, music, games, improved interpersonal relationships, learning, peaceful coexistence, wildlife observation, camping, and other forms of recreation (Figure 24-4). The focus of society would be away from quantitative and toward qualitative enjoyment. Growth would occur in some sectors such as renewable energy, conservation, and repair. Other areas such as the production of plastic throwaways would shrink.

Achieving a Sustainable Economy   A vision of the future is one thing; a plan to get there is another (Table 24-3). How do we make the dramatic shift from the frontier system to the sustainable system of economics?

The most fundamental change is the ethical change. Such changes are hard to bring about, but concerted efforts on the part of teachers, parents, and even governmental leaders could make inroads into the outdated frontier mentality. To be convinced that such changes are needed, we need to better understand the future and the dangers implicit in the frontier mentality (for more on this, see Chapter 23). Research on the future is needed more now than ever to help guide our decisions.

Figure 24-4
Several hundred runners of all ages, sexes, and sizes, enjoy the annual Angel Island cross-country race in the middle of San Francisco Bay.

Environmental Protection—Job Maker or Job Taker?

Job Blackmail and the Environment

Richard Grossman and Richard Kazis

The authors are staff members of Environmentalists for Full Employment, a policy research organization. They are the authors of the book Fear at Work: Job Blackmail, Labor and the Environment.

About 100,000 of the Americans fortunate enough to have jobs die each year from exposure to toxins at work; additionally, some 400,000 contract occupationally caused diseases. Environmental destruction from air and water pollution and diseases caused by industrial practices and waste disposal cost the United States tens of billions of dollars annually.

Yet employers and politicians keep saying that we must put up with high levels of occupational disease and extensive environmental damage. This, they say, is the price of economic growth, jobs, and the good life. The price of progress.

When workers and communities have demanded and organized for health and environmental protections along with their jobs, employers and politicians have risen to the occasion. Now that major national health and environmental laws have been in place for over a decade, we can see overwhelming evidence that protecting the public and the natural environment from industrial and government pollution is technically possible. We can also see that sound environmental policies make economic and employment sense. We don't have to be engineers or economists to understand that in a land ravaged by toxic dumps, chemical abuse, soil erosion, poisoned wells, polluted work places and choking cities, there can't be much "life" worth living.

Then what was going on when President Ronald Reagan announced that a strong Clean Air Act was a barrier to economic recovery? Why has it seemed that his appointees were doing their best to undermine health, environmental, and consumer protection laws in the name of jobs and economic growth? Why has the nuclear power industry been countering nuclear opponents over the past decade with threats of "freezing and starving in the dark"? Why did Interior Secretary James Watt sell publicly owned coal for bargain-basement prices because he "loves jobs"? Why did the *Wall Street Journal* editorialize that increased lead in the air would create "more wealth and more jobs," which

"will most likely do more for ghetto children" than stringent health standards?

Call it job blackmail. Reagan, Watt, the nuclear industry, the *Wall Street Journal*—all of them have used jobs, the promise of new jobs or the threat of unemployment, in order to control decisions over investment, resource, and labor use, and profit. Business and government leaders hope they can use job blackmail to keep a citizens' challenge in check, to "persuade" the public to support certain investments that are often harmful to public health and the environment.

Job blackmail is not new. Employers have long used it to fight off child labor laws, worker's compensation, Social Security, and the minimum wage. Here's an example: In 1982, the fat-melting industry of New York City threatened to shut down and throw all its employees out of work if it was forced to change production processes to eliminate the stench of slaughtered animals. When the city stood firm, however, the melters developed a closed-tank process that solved the problem, saved money, and kept workers on the job.

Now, as then, environmental protection is good for public health, good for environment, good for jobs, and good for the economy. Since 1970 many pollution trends have been reversed; air is getting cleaner, and water quality is improving. More than 100,000 new jobs have been created because of clean-air laws, and more than 200,000 have resulted from clean-water regulations.

By contrast, according to the Environmental Protection Agency, fewer than 3000 workers a year since 1971—out of a work force of more than 100 million—are even alleged to have lost their jobs because of environmental regulations. The Industrial Union Department of the AFL-CIO has concluded that "environmental regulations have not been the primary cause of even one plant shutdown."

Despite evidence that sound environmentalism is sound economics, employers, polluters, and their political supporters in government can use job blackmail effectively as long as they control where and how investments are made and how many and what kinds of jobs are created. Today, they are eying trillions of taxpayer dollars and vast public resources that they say they want to use to "rebuild" the nation. But don't expect extensive public discussions on (1) the values on which investment policies will be based; (2) the kinds of jobs to be created; (3) the rights of workers and the distribution of the jobs; (4) health and environmental protection; (5) how the profits will be shared; or (6) how much control communities across the nation will have over their futures. Rather, they will try to convince us that there is no way but their way, that suggested alternatives are "impractical" or "extremist." We can anticipate that they will dangle the job claims and roll out the threats of lost jobs.

The public's fight against job blackmail is a fight for control over our lives and work. This is fundamentally a struggle for an equitable share of the nation's wealth and democratic participation in decision making.

Fortunately, there is a history of successful opposition to corporate and government job blackmail. The key has been the joining of workers, communities, environmentalists, and other constituencies to challenge "business as usual." Together, such coalitions have been able to make progress toward jobs and health, jobs and environment, jobs and civil rights, jobs and worker rights, jobs and women's rights, and jobs and democratic participation in decision making.

Today, with unemployment, pollution, and environmental mismanagement all around us, people in communities all across the United States must lead the struggle to integrate employment and environmental policies. There is no other option. If we are forced to choose between our jobs and our health, we'll end up with neither.

The Impact of Environmental Laws on Jobs

Catherine England

The author is a policy analyst at the Heritage Foundation. Previously, she was on the faculty of the economics department at American University in Washington, D.C. She specializes in regulatory issues.

Statutes as complex and far-reaching as the U.S. environmental laws certainly have an impact on the number of jobs generated by the economy. Since the major pieces of legislation were passed in the early 1970s, there has been some debate about the exact nature of that impact, however. Many have argued that the environmental statutes and their accompanying regulations have increased employment opportunities in the United States, and there are some econometric studies that would seem to support such a claim. There is certainly no doubt that job opportunities have increased in at least one industry over the past decade— the manufacturing of pollution control equipment.

However, there are strong reasons to believe that environmental laws, as currently written and administered, have done more than merely shift jobs from regulated sectors to control equipment industries. Rather, the current enforcement of environmental regulations has almost certainly reduced the employment-creating potential of the U.S. economy, thus costing a substantial number of jobs.

From the beginning it should be understood that the criticism here is not directed at the broad goals of the environmental statutes. There is a clear need to ensure that U.S. citizens enjoy clean air, safe water, and freedom from toxic substances and hazardous wastes. But the means used to achieve these ends have been needlessly inefficient, posing higher than necessary costs on society.

Let us agree that businesses, like individuals, families, or ever governments, have limited financial resources. There is only so much money a company can borrow or generate through selling its product or issuing stock. Therefore, any change that increases the costs of doing business in one area requires cutbacks, however minor, somewhere else. That is not to say that a regulation may not be worth the cost, but to ensure continued economic growth, the full costs of government regulations should be understood and minimized.

In the case of environmental regulations, it is generally argued that firms cut back on investments in new plants and equipment to make the sometimes substantial expenditures needed to meet environmental requirements. But it is exactly this investment in new plants and equipment that is necessary to maintain worker productivity at a level enabling U.S. firms to remain competitive in world markets. Growing concerns about trade deficits and the relative expense of U.S. goods in international markets must, then, be laid at least partially at the door of the EPA and Congress.

The important question is, Could we meet the fundamental goals of environmental statutes at a lower cost? Yes. This response means that corporate funds could be freed up to invest in new equipment, to lower costs to consumers, or for a myriad of other uses that would lead to more jobs in the country. But how?

First, the focus of environmental regulations should be changed. Currently, most EPA regulations are extremely detailed, describing the specific technology a firm must use to comply with environmental standards. This general policy has substantially reduced the potential payoff to independent research in pollution control technologies. One author has described this focus on specific technologies as "chok[ing] off the imagination and innovation of American industry." Redirecting attention to performance standards, that is, specifying acceptable behavior and leaving businesses to decide how to comply, should encourage the more rapid introduction of less expensive means of accomplishing stated goals.

Secondly, the centralized nature of decision making in the environmental area has needlessly raised compliance costs. The United States is a country marked by geographic diversity. Accordingly, the environmental impact of a particular plant in the Northeast may be very different from its impact in the desert Southwest. Not only does population density vary, but also climate, elevation, water tables, prevailing winds, and so on. It shouldn't be surprising, then, that a single national policy has satisfied almost no one.

State officials are in a much better position to recognize and react to the existing regional diversity. Furthermore, decisions made at the state level are closer to the citizens who are actually affected by changes in environmental quality. As a result, some states may wish to impose standards tougher than those contained in national guidelines. State experimentation with mechanisms for setting standards and achieving compliance could result in creative ways of reaching environmental goals.

Finally, and perhaps most important for the job-creation question, current environmental laws and regulations are biased against emerging industries and new technologies. Environmental standards for new plants are much more stringent than those applied to existing sources of pollution. Yet the newer technologies employed in modern factories often cause less pollution than older ways of doing things. Despite this, federal regulators are only beginning to explore market-oriented means of encouraging economic growth while reducing pollution levels. Two promising ideas are "bubbles" and emissions trading.

To summarize, existing environmental laws and the regulations they have spawned have cost the U.S. economy an unknown number of jobs by inhibiting the job-creating potential of American business. The costly way in which current environmental statutes are enforced has sapped the financial resources of affected firms, placed U.S. products at a cost disadvantage in world markets, and inhibited growth of new technologies and industries. Providing more flexibility through the use of plant-wide performance standards would encourage businesses to search for less expensive means of attaining environmental goals. Shifting more decision-making responsibilities to the state level would allow recognition of and response to regional diversity. Encouraging the trading of emissions rights would lead to economic growth without sacrifices in environmental quality.

The underlying aims of the environmental laws are important, but just as important is the nation's economic health. Luckily, the two goals need not be mutually exclusive.

Government could take important steps in making the transition to the future. New laws could be passed that encourage resource conservation, recycling, reduction in wastes, use of renewable resources, and product durability. Old laws that contradict these goals could be amended or repealed.

One important step would be the decentralization of some industries. This move is made necessary by the fact that large-scale industries often become inefficient as a result of of their overwhelming size and lack of flexibility. Communication failures and alienation of workers add to the inefficiency. Furthermore, as energy prices rise, the costs of distributing goods rises.

A decentralized economic system would rely on local materials to produce products for local consumption, within reason, of course. Small decentralized industries, or cottage industries, might be appropriate for producing soap, toothpaste, and towels but not for manufacturing ships or

Table 24-3 How to Achieve a Steady-State Economy

Education

New ethical directions can be taught in schools, with emphasis on responsibility to future generations, the value of a clean and healthy environment, preservation of wildlife and wilderness, personal growth, and peaceful coexistence.

New emphasis in economics: Big is not always better. More is not always desirable. Continued economic growth can be devastating.

Population Control

Population growth rate can be reduced to replacement level, and then population size can be reduced.

Resources

Nonrenewable resources can be rationed. Recycling of all cans, bottles, paper, and metals can be made mandatory. Widespread use of renewable resources, especially solar energy, can be encouraged. Energy conservation in homes, businesses, and all forms of transportation can be required.

cars. The primary goal would be to achieve a proper mixture of large and small industry that uses resources (especially energy) efficiently to meet basic human needs.

The economist, Herman Daly also suggests the need for a redistribution of wealth, possibly imposed by governmental limits on corporate and personal income. This would reduce resource consumption and put a halt to growth mania, which he views as unsustainable and damaging in the long run. Proponents of this view suggest that only strict rationing by the government would slow or stop the depletion of nonrenewable resources. Redistribution would yield a more equitable sharing of resources. (For a criticism of this view, see Chapter 25.)

Daly suggests that strict depletion quotas on resources be set by the government. Nationwide and regional plans would establish the amount of oil, coal, bauxite, and other resources that could be used in a given year from domestic and foreign supplies. This would reduce excessive consumption and force recycling, conservation, and product durability. The cost of products would inevitably rise, reducing consumption of all but the most essential items and reducing pollution as well.

Depletion quotas go against the current growth ethic and the high degree of freedom that has been a part of American society from its beginning. They would be hard to establish and enforce unless an economic catastrophe or severe shortage arose. They would result in a change in life-style that is undesirable to many Americans. Opportunities for the rich to become richer and for criminals to operate black markets would be plentiful. Regardless, quotas may become a palatable—indeed, a desirable—alternative if the United States is faced with widespread economic collapse and resource shortage.

Perhaps one way of setting quotas would be the allocation of nonmonetary units, called natural resource units. Under this system, each person would annually receive a given number of coupons for the purchase of food, clothing, shelter, heat, and amenities. For example, an individual might receive 25,000 natural resource units, or coupons, each year. Ten thousand would be necessary to purchase the basics—food, clothing, and energy. The additional 15,000 could be spent on a vacation or material goods such as backpacking equipment, a new calculator, or a ten-speed bicycle. To buy large items, an individual would have to save up coupons.

Coupons would be an adjunct to money, not a replacement for it. For instance, someone buying a car pays the $25,000 price and hands over 100,000 natural resource coupons he or she has been saving for the past five years. No amount of money can buy the car without the required number of resource coupons. Coupons might also be refunded when an individual returns an item for recycling. A car delivered to the recycling plant might generate enough coupons to buy another.

This proposal was first advanced by two Australian ecologists, Walter Westman and Roger Gifford. It limits resource depletion and equally distributes impact at some predetermined level. It says that you are allowed a certain amount of impact on the environment regardless of your personal wealth. Such a system would be difficult to initiate, requiring objective enforcement and honest administration.

An allotment system may become a reality if energy or other resources are severely depleted. Such programs are not as foreign as many people believe. During World War II sugar, gasoline, and other items were rationed. The system operated well because of the crisis environment. A severe resource shortage might provide a similar environment for the natural resource coupon system, but to minimize economic and social dislocation, rationing should ideally be implemented long before the crisis develops. This would require reliable information on resource availability and demand, a coordinated governmental plan, and cooperation of the people. (See Chapter 25.)

The Impetus for Change   The transition to a steady-state economy can come from a combination of economic changes (rising prices), governmental changes (stricter laws—see Chapter 25), or personal changes in attitude (Chapter 23). Prices of many resources, especially energy, are likely to increase throughout the 1980s and into the 1990s. This will undoubtedly stimulate the beginnings of a steady-state economy. So far, the needed governmental and personal changes are lacking.

Some believe, however, that the most probable stimulus for the drastic governmental and personal change required is a crisis—a sudden drop in oil production or mineral resources, for example. They note that the United States is a crisis-oriented society, often able to act only when the dangers are immediate and severe.

As we will see in the next chapter, this crisis orientation is a feature of the democratic system, but it is not the sole feature. A great deal of foresight has gone into U.S. environmental laws. New laws that help protect the air, water, land, and wildlife are all an essential part of the new governmental strategy for a sustainable society. These laws help correct some of the inadequacies of the U.S. economic system (especially by forcing us to internalize economic externalities). Still lacking, however, is a commitment to the steady-state economy that some economists believe is needed for the survival of a sustainable society.

As foreign as these ideas may seem, many economists believe that they are necessary for the long-term survival of the human race on a planet of finite resources. A long journey lies ahead in the transformation of society, but as Lao Tzu once said, "A journey of a thousand miles must begin with a single step." That step into a bold new future still awaits us.

A New Global Economic System

Obviously, a steady-state economy, to be successful, must be adopted on a worldwide scale. Table 24-4 outlines some of the major goals that the developed and developing countries would have to set to achieve a sustainable society based on a steady-state economy. The primary concerns of the developed nations would be lower pop-

Table 24-4   Goals Leading to a New Global Economic Order

Developed Nations

Population reduction is achieved through attrition.

Resource consumption is reduced.

Self-sufficiency is increased.

Recycling and conservation are increased

Knowledge is spread throughout the developing nations.

Peace and stability is striven for and ultimately achieved.

Arms sales are reduced.

Cooperation occurs on a global basis.

A new ethical system based on sustainable ethics becomes reality.

Developing Nations

Population growth rate is stabilized and population reduced.

A sustainable agricultural system is developed.

Resources meet the basic needs of the country.

Restraint is exercised in adoption of western agriculture and technology.

Widespread education is promoted.

Maximum self-sufficiency is achieved.

ulation, reduced material consumption, increased self-sufficiency, and global peace and stability.

The developing countries would have to bring their population growth rate under control and eventually strive for population reduction. They would develop sustainable agricultural systems and dedicate their energies toward education, housing, and other basic needs. In most cases, they would refrain from adopting large-scale western agriculture and industry.

A global economic system that seeks to meet basic human needs and operate within the limits posed by the earth would be a giant leap for humankind, but as Friedrich Schiller once wrote, "Who dares nothing, need hope for nothing."

Civilization is a slow process of adopting the ideas of minorities.

ANONYMOUS

Summary

Herman Daly, an economist critical of our economic system, once wrote, "We seem to be trapped in a growth-dominated economic system that is causing growing depletion, pollution, and disamenity, as well as increasing the probability of ecological catastrophe." Most economists believe that growth is desirable and that economic growth represents true progress. Because economic growth hinges on rising per capita consumption and rising population, growth-oriented societies view population growth as desirable. They ultimately seek to meet the demands of such growing populations with little concern for the long-term future of resources.

Economic growth is the foundation of most economies. The most widely used measure of growth is the gross national product, or GNP, the total output of goods and services valued at market prices. GNP does not always reflect the standard of living. GNP as a measure of standard of living also fails to take into account how money is spent and ignores accumulated wealth. New measures of wealth might be used to replace GNP, giving a clearer picture of income distribution and true wealth throughout a society.

The law of supply and demand influences most economic thinking. It describes the economic behavior of given markets but does not explain the economic behavior of nations. The law frequently fails to take into account the finite nature of some resources and political factors that can strongly influence supply, demand, and prices.

Resource management is significantly affected by economic considerations. Two of the most important ones are *time preference* and *opportunity costs*. Time preference is a measure of one's willingness to give up some current income for greater returns in the future. For example, farmers may choose *depletion strategies,* which favor immediate income, or *conservation strategies,* which favor long-term gains. The choice of a strategy hinges on time preference for accruing income. Time preference is influenced by many factors, including age and income preference, uncertainty about future prices and interest rates, opportunity costs, current interest rates, and ethics.

Opportunity costs are the costs of lost money-making opportunities. For example, soil conservation requires a monetary investment that might reap higher profits if invested elsewhere. Thus, applying soil conservation measures represents an opportunity cost.

Economics plays an important role in pollution control, one form of resource management. The chief goal of pollution control is to achieve the maximum reduction of pollution, which yields the maximum benefit, at the lowest cost. This can be done by cost–benefit analysis, but determining the true cost of pollution, including all *externalities,* can be quite difficult.

Who pays the cost of pollution control is an issue of hot debate. Some argue that consumers should bear the burden, because pollution is a coproduct of the goods they buy. Others argue that taxpayers should pay, because they have long allowed many industries to pollute and, now that the rules have changed, should bear some if not all of the responsibility for cleaning up the environment. An intermediate group suggests that there are times when consumers should pay; for example, when new plants are being built, the cost of pollution control should be incorporated into prices so the consumer pays the price of environmental protection. This group also argues that the taxpayer should at least help bear the burden of older industries facing new rules.

Historically, pollution control has been enforced by punitive measures, mostly fines. Economic incentives could also be used to get companies to abide by environmental laws and regulations.

Pollution and environmental destruction cost society billions of dollars a year, but so does pollution control. Conventional wisdom suggests that environmental regulations and laws delay projects, increase the cost of doing business, decrease productivity, and ultimately cost society jobs. Careful studies show that these beliefs are largely blown out of proportion.

Some economists suggest that a new economic system is necessary for the long-term survival of the human race. A spaceship, or sustainable economy would promote recycling, conservation, the use of renewable resources, product durability, and a clean and healthy environment. People would live within the limits posed by earth. Such a system can succeed only with widespread population control and new political directions. The most fundamental change would have to be an ethical shift, promoted by teachers, government officials, and parents. Government can take important steps by developing new laws that encourage resource conservation, recycling, reduction in wastes, use of renewable resources, and product durability, to mention a few. Some selective decentralization of industries may be required. Some redistribution of wealth and ways to ration resource use may also be important. Overall, the shift to a sustainable society can come from a combination of economic, governmental, and personal actions.

Discussion Questions

1. Debate the statement "Economics has become a dangerous preoccupation of our time, so much so that we have become singularly attached to making money and blind to the quality of environment."

2. Define your own economic goals. Would you classify them as consistent with a frontier economy or a spaceship economy?

3. Debate the statement "In a growth-oriented economy, population growth has traditionally been viewed as an asset."

4. In your view, is continued economic growth possible? If so, why and for how long?

5. Describe the gross national product and its strengths and weaknesses as an economic measure.

6. You are appointed chief economic analyst for the United Nations. What economic measurements would you use to determine how well off the world's nations are?

7. Discuss the weaknesses of the law of supply and demand.

8. Discuss in detail the economic factors that determine how people manage natural resources. Be certain to include *time preference* and *opportunity costs*.

9. Define the term *economic externality* and describe why economic externalities are increasingly becoming internalized.

10. What is the optimal level of pollution control? Why is it impractical to consider reducing pollution from factories and other sources to zero?

11. Who should pay for pollution controls—the consumer, the taxpayer, or both?

12. There are three factories in your community. A new factory wants to move in. How could it be allowed to start operation without increasing existing levels of air pollution?

13. Debate the statement "When environmental protection reduces productivity, it should be avoided."

14. Describe the steady-state economy. What are its main goals? In your view, is it a practical alternative to the current economic system? What are its strengths and weaknesses?

15. Would depletion quotas and natural resource units be a fair way of reducing consumption and ensuring a sustainable future? What are the purchases you will make in your lifetime that will have the most impact on the environment?

Suggested Readings

Brown, L. R. (1983). The Changing Global Economic Context. *Environment* 25(6): 28–34. A necessary look at deteriorating economic conditions in the world.

Brown, L. R., et al. (1984). *State of the World, 1984.* New York: Norton. Superb look at progress in developing a sustainable society.

Daly, H. E. (ed.) (1973). *Toward a Steady-State Economy.* San Francisco: Freeman. Collection of technical essays critical of current economics that also offer suggestions for changing our economic thinking.

Grant, L. (1983). The Cornucopian Fallacies: The Myth of Perpetual Growth. *Futurist* 17(4): 16–22. A rebuttal to the optimistic views of Julian Simon and Herman Kahn.

Kazis, R., and Grossman, R. L. (1982). Environmental Protection: Job-Taker or Job-Maker? *Environment* 24(9): 12–20; 43–44. Excellent study of an important question.

Simon, J. (1983). Life on Earth Is Getting Better, Not Worse. *Futurist* 17(4): 7–14. An optimistic economic projection based on past trends that many critics doubt will continue.

Politics, Government, and Environment: Toward a Sustainable Society

The loftier the building the deeper must the foundation be laid.

THOMAS À KEMPIS

We need a future we can believe in—one that is neither so hopeful as to be unrealistic nor so grim as to invite apathy and despair. In short, we need a future that is not only hopeful but attainable. But can we determine our future, or are we helpless victims of events too complex to understand and control?

Most times, events may seem beyond our personal control. Nevertheless, society as a whole does shape the future. History shows us that conscious and unconscious decisions have made a tremendous impact on the present. Consider the development of nuclear weapons or the Green Revolution.

Now, more than ever, as the human population grows and as resources become increasingly depleted, we must think about the future and take decisive actions. Some call the changes required in our thinking a revolution. What ways can government help shape the future of humankind and ensure the survival of our rich biosphere?

The U.S. Government: A Need for Change?

As Abraham Lincoln once wrote, "The legitimate object of government is to do for a community of people whatever they need to have done, but cannot do at all, in their separate and individual capacities." Thus, government among other things is concerned with distributing resources among the people.

Structurally, the national government has changed very little since its form was ratified almost 200 years ago. Three branches of government were established in the Constitution: executive, legislative, and judicial (Figure 25-1). The role of each of these is varied but complementary. Thus, each branch plays an important part in virtually all matters of governance, creating a unique and valuable balance of power among the arms of government.

The American system of government has been widely

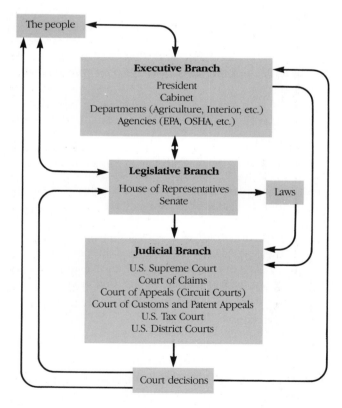

Figure 25-1
The three branches of the American government.

Table 25-1 Actions of a Sustainable Society
Recognizes that the earth has a limited supply of nonrenewable resources such as coal, oil, natural gas, and minerals.
Operates within the limits posed by natural resource supplies by recycling, conservation, reducing its superfluous needs, and using renewable resources.
Strives for a quality life, clean air, clean water, abundant recreation opportunities for all, and intellectual achievement rather than material wealth.
Recognizes that we can never do just one thing—that all actions have hidden effects that must be determined when making cost–benefit analyses.
Cooperates with nature, rather than trying to overcome it, by using natural pest control, organic farming to replace nutrients, crop rotation, and solar and wind energy.
Stresses individual responsibility and actions to cut resource use, promote recycling, reduce pollution, and achieve a sustainable future.
Recognizes that we are a part of nature, not superior to it, and that our long-term fate is intricately linked to the health of the biosphere.
Minimizes waste through resource conservation, reduction in superfluous needs, redesigning manufacturing processes, and reusing and recycling materials.

criticized by political analysts. One of the most frequent criticisms is that it is slow to change, a real detriment in an era of rapid change. Only a few major changes have been made in this system in 200 years, and few are likely to be made in the future unless a catastrophe strikes. To achieve a sustainable society, however, great changes must come about (Table 25-1). To make changes, however, many obstacles must first be overcome.

Some Obstacles to Change

Lack of Consensus The first problem in reshaping government is trying to achieve a consensus about the future. It has become increasingly obvious that the United States is an amalgamation of people with markedly different ideas and philosophies. Even within a single political party, diversity of opinion is commonplace. The ideological, religious, ethical, and political differences inherent in American society create tensions and, often, bitter conflict. As Herbert Prochnow once asked, "How can a government know what the people want when the people don't know?"

The wide differences among people present a colossal obstacle to the long-range planning needed to achieve a sustainable society. The problem of planning arises from a quite practical matter: we cannot agree on a course for the future when few agree on which future is best.

Crisis Politics A second problem is that government officials must frequently put aside critical planning and decisions that are important to the future because of the need to address more immediate issues (strikes, polluters, new technologies to regulate). This way of operating is called **crisis politics**. In government, the urgent always displaces the important. With immediate issues taking precedence over important long-term problems, government often seems to lumber along from crisis to crisis applying temporary remedies to cover up the symptoms of deeper, more complex problems.

Single-Issue Politics A third obstacle is **single-issue politics**, handling issues as if they existed in a vacuum. Energy, immigration, population, natural resources, and even military policies—to name a few—all affect one another. They are nevertheless often viewed in separate categories and dealt with separately. There is little attempt to integrate them.

Budgetary Constraints A fourth problem is created by budget deficits and inflation, which leave little money for important resource and pollution issues. Rupert Cutler, former assistant secretary of agriculture for conservation, research and education, notes that "compared to the problems addressed by many programs, . . . natural resource issues develop more slowly and it often takes a long-term commitment to resolve them." Concern for the immediate problems and budgetary constraints thus compel decision makers to put their money where the most visible good can be produced.

A related obstacle is the way the federal government budgets money for natural resource programs that will affect the future, such as soil conservation. By law, agencies must invest in projects that show a benefit-to-cost ratio greater than 1 to reduce unsound expenditures. This requirement has undoubtedly eliminated some long-term conservation measures. As the costs of conservation efforts increase, more and more projects may prove economically unfeasible in the short term. The cost–benefit method

of selecting conservation projects, furthermore, tends to identify only the easily observable benefits. It also has the effect of encouraging "structural" programs that are capital intensive. This orientation may divert attention from "nonstructural" measures such as floodplain zoning and requirements for better land management.

Limited Planning Horizon A fifth, and obvious, problem is the limited planning horizon of most politicians. Some political analysts ascribe difficulties in achieving long-range planning to the realities of political life, in which "long-term" implies the time until the next election. In this vein Winston Churchill noted, "The nation will find it very hard to look up to the leaders who are keeping their ears to the ground."

Lack of a Focal Point The sixth hindrance to change in the U.S. government is that there is no central focal point for federal environmental and resource policy; there is no uniform agreement on environmental and natural resource issues that the government should address. Existing long-range programs are split up into many smaller, often uncoordinated programs. For example, natural resource programs are administered by the Departments of Agriculture, Commerce, Interior, and Defense. In the Department of Agriculture, there are several agencies administering approximately 30 land and water conservation programs. This division of responsibility for natural resource and environmental programs creates some duplication of effort and even some contradictions.

Other problems of significance are (1) the extraordinary control of governmental decisionmaking by corporations and consortiums of business interests such as the political action committees (see Essay 24-1); (2) the all-too-common governmental deception or withholding of information that is necessary for the public to make educated decisions about long-range problems; (3) a frontier mentality among many elected officials; (4) huge, unmanageable bureaucracies that become bogged down with burdensome rules, inept management, and infighting; and (5) a blind commitment to economic growth as an indication of progress (see Chapter 24).

Some Suggested Changes

The American democratic system is viewed as the problem by many critics, but the system is also the solution. Improvements in the existing system can make it more responsive to the long-term needs of society (Figure 25-2).

The Right to Write

Congressman Morris K. Udall

The author, an Arizona Democrat, is Chairman of the House Interior Committee.

Surprisingly few people ever write to their United States senators or congressional representatives. Perhaps 90% of our citizens live and die without ever taking pen in hand and expressing a single opinion to the people who represent them in Congress. This reluctance to communicate results from the typical and understandable feeling that legislators have no time or inclination to read their mail, that a letter probably won't be answered or answered satisfactorily, that one letter won't make a difference anyway. Based on my own experience, and speaking for myself at least, I can state flatly that these notions are wrong.

I read every letter written to me by a constituent. A staff member may process it initially, but it will be answered, and I will insist on reading it and personally signing the reply. On several occasions, a single, thoughtful, factually persuasive letter did change my mind or cause me to initiate a review of a previous judgment. Nearly every day my faith is renewed by one or more informative and helpful letters giving me a better understanding of the thinking of my constituents.

Mail to modern-day members of Congress is more important than ever before. In the days of Clay, Calhoun, Webster, and Lincoln, members of Congress lived among their constituents for perhaps nine months of the year. Through daily contacts with constituencies of less than 50,000 people (I represent at least ten times that many), they could feel rather completely informed about their constituents' beliefs and feelings. Today, with the staggering problems of government and increasingly long sessions of Congress, senators and representatives must not only vote on many more issues than early-day members, but rarely get to spend more than 60 days in their districts. Thus, their mailbags are their best "hot lines" to the people back home.

Here are some fundamentals:

• Address it properly: "Hon. _____ , House Office Building, Washington, D.C. 20515," or "Senator _____, Senate Office Building, Washington, D.C. 20510." This may seem fundamental, but I once received a letter addessed like this: "Mr. Morris K. Udall, U.S. Senator, Capitol Building, Phoenix, Arizona . . . Dear Congressman Rhodes . . ."

• Identify the bill or issue. About 22,000 bills are introduced in each Congress; it's important to be specific. If you write about a bill, try to give the bill number or describe it by popular title ["BLM Organic Act," "Toxic Substances Bill," etc.].

• The letter should be timely. Sometimes a bill is out for committee, or has passed the House, before a helpful letter arrives. Inform your representative while there is still time for him or her to take effective action.

• Concentrate on your own delegation. The representative of your district and the senators of *your* state cast your votes in the Congress and want to know your views. However, some writers will undertake to contact all 435 members of the House and 100 senators, who cast votes for other districts and other states. If you happen to be acquainted personally with a member from, say, Nebraska, he or she might answer your letter, but there is a "congressional courtesy" procedure which provides that all letters written by residents of any district to other members will simply be referred to me for reply, and vice versa.

• Be reasonably brief. Every working day the mailman leaves some 150 or more pieces of mail at my office. Tomorrow brings another batch. All of this mail must be answered while I am studying legislation, attending committee meetings, and participating in debate on the House floor. I recognize that many issues are complex, but your opinions and arguments stand a better chance of being read if they are stated as concisely as the subject matter will permit. It is not necessary that letters be typed—only that they be legible; the form, phraseology, and grammar are completely unimportant.

In the course of my years in Congress, I have received every kind of mail imaginable—the tragic, the touching, the rude, the crank; insulting, persuasive, entertaining, and all the rest. I enjoy receiving mail, and I look forward to receiving it every morning; in fact, my staff people call me a "mail grabber" because I interfere with the orderly mail-opening procedures they have established. Whatever form your letter takes, I will welcome it, but to make it most helpful, I would suggest the following "do's and don'ts."

First, the do's:

• Write your own views—not someone else's. A personal letter is far better than a form letter, or signature on a petition. Many people will sign a petition without reading it just to avoid offending the circulator; form letters are readily recognizable—they usually arrive in batches and usually register the sentiments of the person or lobbying group preparing the form. Form letters often receive form replies. Anyway, I usually know what the major lobbying groups are saying, but I don't often know of *your* experiences and observations, or what the proposed bill will do to and for you. A sincere, well-thought-out letter from you can help fill this gap.

• Give your reasons for taking a stand. Statements such as "Vote against H.R. 100; I'm bitterly opposed" don't help much, but a letter which says, for example, "I'm a small hardware dealer, and H.R. 100 will put me out of business for the following reasons . . ." tells me a lot more. Maybe I didn't know all the effects of the bill, and your letter will help me understand what it means to an important segment of my constituency.

• Be constructive. If a bill deals with a problem you admit exists, but you believe the bill is the wrong approach, tell me what the *right* approach is.

• If you have expert knowledge, share it with your congressional representatives. Of all the letters pouring into a legislator's office every morning, perhaps one in a hundred comes from a constituent who is a real expert in that subject. The opinions expressed in the others are important, and will be heeded, but this one is a real gold mine for the conscientious member. After all, in the next nine or ten months, I will have to vote on farm bills, defense bills, transportation bills; space, health, education, housing and veterans' bills, and a host of others. I can't possibly be an expert in all these fields. Many of my constituents *are* experts in some of them. I welcome their advice and counsel.

• Say "well done" when it's deserved.

Members of Congress are human, too, and they appreciate an occasional "well done" from people who believe they have done the right thing. I know I do. But even if you think I went wrong on an issue, I would welcome a letter telling me you disagree. It may help me on another issue later.

Now some don'ts:

• Don't make threats or promises. Members of Congress usually want to do the popular thing, but this is not their *only* motivation; nearly all the members I know want most of all to do what is best for the country. Occasionally a letter will conclude by saying "If you vote for this monstrous bill, I'll do everything in my power to defeat you in the next election." A writer has the privilege of making such assertions, of course, but they rarely intimidate a conscientious member, and they may generate an adverse reaction. Members of Congress would rather know why you feel so strongly. The reasons may change their minds; the threat probably won't.

• Don't berate your representatives. You can't hope to persuade them of your position by calling them names. If you disagree with them, give reasons for your disagreement. Try to keep the dialogue open.

• Don't pretend to wield vast political influence. Write your senators or representatives as an individual, not as a self-appointed spokesperson for your neighborhood, community, or industry. Unsupported claims to political influence will only cast doubt upon the views you express.

• Don't become a constant "pen pal." I don't want to discourage letters, but quality, rather than quantity, is what counts. Write again and again if you feel like it, but don't try to instruct your representative on every issue that comes up. And don't nag if his or her votes do not match your precise thinking every time. Remember, a member of Congress has to

consider all of his or her constituents and all points of view. Also, keep in mind that one of the pet peeves on Capitol Hill is the "pen pal" who weights the mail down every few days with long tomes on every conceivable subject.

• Don't demand a commitment before the facts are in. If you have written a personal letter and stated your reasons for a particular stand, you have a right to know your representative's present thinking on the question. But writers who "demand to know how you will vote on H.R. 100" should bear certain legislative realities in mind: (1) On major bills there usually are two sides to be considered and you may have heard only one. (2) The bill may be 100 pages long with 20 provisions in addition to the one you wrote about, and a representative may be forced to vote on the bill as a whole, weighing the good with the bad. (3) It makes little sense to adopt a firm and unyielding position before a single witness has been heard or study made of the bill in question. (4) A bill rarely becomes law in the same form as introduced; it is possible that the bill you write about you would oppose when it reached the floor. The complexities of the legislative process and the way in which bills change their shapes in committee are revealed by a little story from my own experience. One time several years ago, I introduced a comprehensive bill dealing with a number of matters. I was proud of it, and I had great hopes for solving several perennial problems coming before Congress. However, after major confrontations in committee and numerous amendments I found myself voting *against* the "Udall Bill."

Your senators and representatives need your help in casting votes. The "ballot box" is not far away: it's painted red, white and blue and it reads "U.S. Mail."

Figure 25-2
President Reagan addresses a
Joint Session of the U.S.
Congress in the Capitol
building.

***Proactive and Reactive Government: Finding the
Proper Mix***   A government that "lives and acts for today"
is by definition a **reactive government**. Its laws and regulations are sometimes ill-conceived and ineffective, but
they satisfy a basic need of politics: they give the impression that something is being done. Thus, hurriedly passed
laws are often valuable vote getters; in the long run, though,
they can further complicate an already serious problem,
making a truly effective solution harder to reach.

The laws passed by a reactive government are generally
retrospective; that is, they attempt to regulate something
that has gotten out of hand. For example, the Clean Air
Act (Chapter 19) was passed after public outcry over air
pollution. It largely attempts to regulate an already chronic
problem. The Superfund legislation (Chapter 22) provides money to clean up toxic waste dumps. Retrospective
laws are part of a "patch-it-up-and-move-to-the-next-cri-
sis" syndrome typical of a reactive government.

Congress has begun to take a long-term outlook and to
write prospective laws that seek to prevent potentially
hazardous events from occurring. One example is the
Toxic Substances Control Act, with its provisions for
screening new chemicals before they are commercially
introduced (Chapter 18).

The government has long been making strides to plan
for the future. Some examples include:

1. The establishment in 1946 of the National Science
   Foundation to perform research.
2. Passage in 1965 of the *Water Resources Planning Act*
   to provide for comprehensive water assessment and
   planning.
3. Passage in 1969 of the *National Environmental Policy
   Act*, which requires environmental impact statements
   for all projects sponsored or supported by the federal
   government.
4. Creation in 1972 of the Office of Technology Assessment, which critically examines the costs and benefits
   of new technologies.
5. Authorization of the Congressional Research Service
   to create a Futures Research Group.
6. Passage in 1974 of the *Resources Planning Act* and in
   1977 of the *Resources Conservation Act*, both of which
   require the Department of Agriculture to make periodic assessments of the supply of and demand for wildlife, farmland, water, rangeland, and recreation.
7. Passage of the *Resource Conservation and Recovery
   Act* (Chapter 21).

Each of these is a sign of a **proactive or anticipatory
government**—one that takes action before a crisis has
arisen, one that plans for the future.

Some laws offer a mixture of prospective and retrospective measures. For example, the *Surface Mining Control and Reclamation Act* (Chapter 13) provides money for reclaiming abandoned coal surface mines and establishes a program to promote active reclamation of existing coal surface mines. Ideally, government should provide an appropriate mix of proactive and reactive measures.

As the United States moves into the last years of the 1900s, and as its population continues to grow past the bend in the exponential growth curve, anticipatory government becomes more necessary than ever before. But how can this be achieved? How can the future be made to weigh more heavily in the present workings of government?

Education and Future Planning One solution is to better educate citizens regarding the necessity of long-range planning and the obligation to future generations. As a result, long-term problems such as resource shortage, overpopulation, and animal extinction would become more immediate concerns of the people and their elected officials (see Essay 25-1). Teachers and religious leaders can contribute to a better understanding of the long-term threats posed by modern society. Young people would learn how to think about the long-range future and their responsibilities to future generations. Environmental groups now dedicated to legislative change and habitat acquisition could begin campaigns to educate children on the ecological viewpoint.

Another way of meeting the challenge of the uncertain future would be to study it more intensively. The study of the future has often been left in the hands of science fiction writers and technological optimists, who fill our heads with unrealistic, fanciful, or entertaining notions that do little to advance our understanding of what is practical, sensible, and possible. American society could, instead, promote an organized and objective scientific study of the future. A major goal of this research would be to explore alternative futures and identify the major forces that affect them. Social scientists can play a big role in this research by identifying values and studying the ways values can be changed. To support this work, more private and government money could be made available.

Government agencies could also put more emphasis on future planning. Special commissions on the future could be appointed by the president. In 1977 President Jimmy Carter directed the Council on Environmental Quality, the Department of State, and several federal agencies to study "the probable changes in the world's population, natural resources and environment through the end of the century" to serve as a "foundation for longer-term planning." The resulting study, *The Global 2000 Report to the President,* is a gold mine of information about the future upon which population, resource, and environmental decisions can be made. Rather than stopping here, the federal government can update estimates and projections periodically. Great lessons can be learned in the coming decades from these projections. Were they too pessimistic? Were the methods of projecting resource and environmental trends faulty, and how can they be improved?

Special study sections on the future in the various governmental agencies such as the Departments of Agriculture, Energy, and Interior could be better funded and better equipped to project hundreds of years into the future. Reports from futurist groups could be widely distributed to political leaders, teachers, and the public.

Some observers, such as the ecologist G. Tyler Miller, have suggested that the Constitution be amended to include a Department of Long-Range Planning, with members elected to long terms. As an adjunct to the current executive, legislative, and judiciary branches of government, the planning branch might make recommendations to Congress and the president on all contemporary issues. The planning branch would consider the broader picture behind seemingly narrow topics, encompassing the interaction of population, resources, and pollution on a gobal scale. Its main purpose would be to assess long-term trends to ensure a sustainable future.

Such a new governmental department could coordinate information on the future and help political leaders develop a long-term survival strategy for the United States. The expense of the new bureaucracy, however, might be high. Some argue that a central interagency committee might better coordinate the long-term activities of all federal agencies, be less costly, and require less expansion of the present bureaucracy.

A New Economic Order Another major task is converting the current economic system of unlimited growth to one of a steady-state economics (Chapter 24). Government can play a major role here. The *Employment Act* of 1946 explicitly declares that it is the continuing policy and responsibility of the federal government to "promote maximum employment, production and purchasing power." Realizing the limitations of fossil fuels, minerals, and other resources, Congress could pass a *Future Security and Sustainable Earth Society Act*. Such a law would state that it is the continuing policy and responsibility of the federal government to promote a society that lives within the limits posed by nature—a society that conserves resources to the maximum extent possible, protects the environment, controls population growth, and eliminates laws and policies that result in the waste of resources, contamination of the environment, and destruction of habitat for plants and animals.

New Leaders and Longer Terms Farsighted leaders would be needed to carry out these plans. They would take a more active leadership role, using information from scientific studies on the future to guide them on what might be unpopular paths in our current growth-oriented political environment.

On a personal level, Americans can support their congressional representatives when they take strong, reasonable stands on issues that will affect the future. They can become involved in the political process on many levels. They can run for the city council or present their ideas there, write their elected officials, visit them personally, and provide them with information on the future (Figure 25-3).

Many political scientists and critics of the American government have suggested that government officials be elected for longer terms. A six-year nonrenewable term for the president, they argue, would reduce the reelection pressure that leads to politically motivated decisions. Extended terms for House members, who currently serve only two-year terms, would have the same effect. Such changes would reduce the amount of time spent on campaigning and increase the time devoted to governing.

An Emerging Role of the City and Town President Ronald Reagan instituted a shift of power back to the states and local governments by cutting federal support for local projects. This "new federalism" offers several potential advantages and disadvantages. The secret of success lies in balance: Which functions and how much power are shifted back to local government? What is the optimal mix of federal and local control, especially in regard to resource and other environmental issues?

Advocates of more decentralized government see the state and local governments as a way of building a more

Figure 25-3
Voting is the first step in becoming politically active.

self-reliant and responsible society—one that lives within its limits. They argue that people will feel less alienated from government and more eager to participate in community decisions. One possible outcome of this movement is local population control measures—limiting growth to reduce congestion, pollution, and the need for new and costly services such as water, electricity, and sewers. In a sense, the city can establish an optimum population size and environment.

Forced to rely more on their own tax revenues and less on federal support, communities may turn to conservation and recycling to cut the costs of services. Methane generated from sewage treatment plants can be used to generate electricity for city buildings or nearby residents. Sewage sludge can fertilize crops fed to cattle or be sold to local markets. Fort Collins, Colorado, disposes about 30% of its sewage on 145 hectares (360 acres) of corn it sells for cattle feed. Instead of building new water projects, city governments might institute inexpensive water conservation measures (Chapter 12). Energy conservation and renewable sources nearby, such as biomass and solar, will be favored over coal-fired power plants and other centralized, polluting, and costly sources. Oceanside and Davis, California, require all new homes to install solar hot water systems. Hagerstown, Maryland, uses its sewage sludge to fertilize 500,000 poplar trees, which are sold for fuel and industrial feedstock.

A community that lives within the limits posed by its economic and natural resources is more easily sustainable than one that imports energy, natural resources, food, and goods from afar. Such a community strives for the essential goods and services within a limited environment and is called an **essential community**.

There are disadvantages to the shift away from a centralized government, too. A lack of money on the local level could lead to relaxed pollution laws and resource depletion. Local governments also rarely have the resources to sponsor feasibility studies on pollution control, recycling projects, alternative energy systems, and such. (Further disadvatages to increasing local control are discussed in Chapter Supplement 25-1.)

A proper balance between local and federal power is important in developing a sustainable society. The federal government must be ready to assist communities in finding the most cost-effective and least resource-intensive approaches to providing services. Federal demonstration programs, standards for pollution control, and research are all essential for a sustainable local government to evolve.

Electronic Voting The home computer is viewed by many as an important tool in making American government more responsive to human needs. Two experts debate teledemocracy in this chapter's Point/Counterpoint.

Value-Free Decisions and Science Courts Too often, political decisions are based less on facts and more on values that may be outmoded or counterproductive to the long-term welfare of humankind. Especially harmful are those decisions based on frontier ethics. Decisions based largely on values are called **value-dependent**. A good example might be the decision whether to reduce acid precipitation.

In sharp contrast, technical decisions can be relatively free of values—or should be. A decision on, say, how best to control acid precipitation can be made on the basis of economics and technology. For example, economists and scientists might determine that the cheapest control would be a mandatory 20% reduction in electrical consumption in homes and industry. This nonstructural approach might

be cheaper than installing smokestack scrubbers. The decision tends to be **value-free**. It is based on science, not value.

Value-free decisions are important to good government. They might be more prevalent in government if we were to delegate some of our federal decision making to **science courts**, groups of experts who can assess scientific issues without bias. First proposed in the late 1960s by Arthur Kantrowitz, an engineer and member of the National Academy of Sciences, the science court has been used to settle a number of scientific controversies.

In a sustainable society, Congress would call on objective panels of experts to make value-free decisions on important issues such as energy and pollution. An extensive value-free analysis might be made of the various energy options. A uniform set of criteria might be established to determine which options made the most sense now and in the future. These criteria would include (1) renewability, (2) pollution levels, (3) health and environmental effects, (4) cost, (5) availability or supply, and (6) possible public acceptance, based on sound sociological research. A value-free analysis could provide complete and credible information to the public, needed to make sound policy.

The changes suggested in this section should contribute to the formation of a sustainable society in the United States. Not until many of these ideas become commonplace, however, will a sustainable future be possible.

A Sustainable World

The information presented in this text leads to the inescapable conclusion that a sustainable society on a global scale is an absolute necessity if we are to survive. There are basically two ways to achieve such a new world order. The **passive approach** entails sitting back and letting things happen, stumbling from crisis to crisis. Not to plan is the plan; not to act is the way to act. The **active approach** entails concerted efforts on the part of the world's governments and people. This approach means (1) a shift away from war and the enormous expenditures that are involved; (2) more sharing of knowledge between the rich and the poor, especially in areas of population, food, and energy; (3) investments in recycling, conservation, and renewable resources; and (4) strict population control policies.

A global sustainable community can be planned for, but such planning on a global basis requires cooperation unwitnessed in the history of the human race. A stronger

Teledemocracy

Teledemocracy to the Rescue

Ted Becker

The author is professor of political science at the University of Hawaii at Manoa. He has written eight books on the American government and legal system. After cofounding Hawaii Televote (1978) and the Community Mediation Service (1980) with his wife, Christa Slaton, he spent six months at Victoria University of Wellington, where he developed and coordinated New Zealand Televote (1981).

It is hard to deny that the United States presently faces multiple environmental catastrophes. In the past few years alone, acid rain, the greenhouse effect, toxic waste, and the nuclear winter have raised ugly specters of disasters that turn dreams of the future into terrifying nightmares.

Worse yet, the American system of government seems paralyzed—incapable of remedying the situation. One reason for this is that the same people who are mainly responsible for creating this ecological mess have enormous power in the present government. Another reason is that the American public seems frozen into inaction, believing that there is little it can do and that the problem can be solved only by various technical experts.

Just as war is too important to be left to the generals and politicians, so is the future of our environment too important to be left to elected officials, scientists, and corporate executives. If there is any hope for a safe, sane, and healthy planet in the immediate future, the public must be brought into the decision-making process massively and rapidly. Fortunately, the way to

do so exists. It is called teledemocracy, the use of state-of-the-art telecommunications technology to spread the use of direct democracy and to improve representative democracy.

The sad state of today's environment is largely a result of deficiencies in our present representative process. This is a system in which big money talks. Many of the major despoilers, exploiters, and poisoners of our planet are the biggest multinational companies and conglomerates, and they have tremendous push and pull at the highest and lowest reaches of our government. Because they are among the heaviest contributors to major political campaigns, the leaders of these gigantic companies consort closely and intimately with our political leadership. These magnates and goliaths expend great sums on research to prove that the harm they do the land, sea, and air is minimal and, further, that nothing can be done about it without causing great economic harm to the American people. Our present government usually accepts these positions.

There are many who say that even if the American people had the chance to be decision makers on environmental policy, they would prove ineffective because of (1) a general ignorance of the relevant facts; (2) an unwillingness to think through the facts even with sufficient access to them; (3) a greater concern with jobs than with safety (to say nothing of ecology); and (4) an inability to organize a direct democratic system at the national level.

All these allegations are demonstrably untrue.

First, teledemocracy has the capacity to liberate the American public from its present level of ignorance and apathy because of its capacity to provide balanced, in-depth information and a wide range of solutions and trade-offs in readily understandable and entertaining ways.

Second, it has been shown in numerous experiments around the world that people at all levels of education, income, and ethnic and social background enjoy participating in teledemocratic processes.

Third, evidence shows that significant differences exist in the values and preferences between the general public and those (often wealthy) people who make major environmental decisions in the legislatures and the corporate board rooms.

Fourth, teledemocracy would involve anyone who has a television set and telephone in the household. In the United States that would include over 95% of the population. That means that the poor would have an equal say on the environment with the rich and powerful; that men and women would have an equal vote on the environment (women make up less than 4% of Congress); that all races, creeds, ideologies, and ethnic groups would have a say on the environment, equal to their proportion in the population (there are no black U.S. senators and few, if any, truly radical members of Congress).

Fifth, teledemocracy can work at any level of government and even in the largest societies because of the immense strides that have been made in the development of television, radio, telephones, communications satellites, computers, and computer conference networks. Distance and time have shrunk to the twist of knobs and the push of buttons.

Sad to say, the United States has lagged behind other modern industrial societies in allowing the public to decide major issues. In recent years general publics decided by nationwide votes whether (1) Great Britain should join the Common Market, (2) Spain should adopt a new national constitution, and (3) abortion should be legalized in Italy.

In order for the American public to help decide the future of the national (and, perhaps, global) environment, I would recommend a two-track·system of teledemocracy. The first track would consist of a network of state initiatives and referenda using teledemocracy in those 26 or more states that have them, in addition to those many localities that have official, binding town meetings (mostly in the New England area). This would provide for more widespread voter participation in state and local issues.

The second track would be a nationwide "electronic town meeting" that would utilize the resources of one or more TV networks (including cable), a major radio network, a community radio network, one or more major newspaper chains, a nationally distributed magazine, and a major polling organization. This would run for at least one year and would include regular nationwide "voting" by the citizenry through the telephone system. A computer system would tabulate the results.

Although at this time such a "vote" would not be binding to our official decision makers, it would become a source of pressure from the public on the various environmental decision-making centers. Teledemocracy would enrich the public consciousness on the issues, stimulate concern, and organize action. It would help develop novel sets of priorities and answers to the problems and make a great leap forward in saving our environment from those who have created the greatest threats to its future health.

Teledemocracy is inevitable in the United States. Not only is it futuristically consistent with what Robert Naisbitt has perceived as a "megatrend" in the 1980s, but it is morally and politically consistent with the vision of one of the greatest thinkers of the 20th century, R. Buckminster Fuller.

The time is now. The place is here. The future is in our hands—if we help teledemocracy come to its rescue.

Teledemocracy: A Bad Idea Whose Time Has Come

Victor Ferkiss

The author is a professor of government at Georgetown University and the author of Technological Man, The Future of Technological Civilization, *and* Futurology. *He teaches in the areas of political theory, technology, and politics and lectures and consults widely.*

Technology now makes possible radical changes in discovering what it is that people prefer. Television is still primarily a one-way medium—station to viewer—but it can be altered to permit viewer-to-station communication. Viewers could register their opinions simply by pressing buttons on the TV set to register agreement or disagreement when propositions or persons are presented. As a result of this possibility, some theorists advocate substituting such two-way TV sets—or computer versions of the same process—for the traditional polling places, through which democracies have ascertained the opinions of voters on candidates and issues. "Teledemocracy," as it is sometimes called, is clearly technically feasible, but whether it is desirable is an entirely different matter.

In essence, teledemocracy would represent a mechanization of the traditional public opinion poll. As any student of politics and polling is aware, what results one gets from polls largely depends on the way questions are presented. The wording of questions can largely predetermine the answers received. The order in which questions are asked can also have a tremendous impact on the answers given. Teledemocracy would give tremendous power to whoever phrased the questions. But even leaving these possibly engineered biases aside, the basic issue of who decides the subjects for questioning is also vital. Half the battle in legislative bodies is over controlling the agenda. In ordinary legislatures each member has a chance, in theory, to introduce bills. Although these bills may not make it through committees and actually get to the floor, where all legislators can make their will felt, the opportunity does exist. In a teledemocracy the agenda would necessarily be completely controlled by a small group charged with deciding which questions could be asked. Even if suggestions could be solicited from viewers—a technically more difficult and economically more costly procedure—someone would have to control the actual "screening" of questions.

Teledemocracy presents yet another problem: who would vote? In democratic societies, registered voters must be of a certain age and citizenship status; these qualifications are enforced. But who could control society's access to buttons on TV sets? Conceivably, buttons could be pushed at random by small children. Prevention of multiple voting—a relatively easy problem in current voting procedures—would present special problems if sets were used.

But even if all these difficulties could be surmounted, real questions would still remain. Even under current electoral procedures, voter participation is low and disproportionate. Some groups such as the elderly and the economically better off vote in greater numbers than others. These problems would be exacerbated by teledemocracy. Who would actually stay home and vote through their sets under such a system? Largely, the groups that already turn out disproportionately in elections. Thus, teledemocracy would necessarily make what many consider a bad situation even worse. One reason supporters often push for teledemocracy is the conviction that it would be easier to consult public opinion. Logically, this means there would be more questions posed to the population than there are now elections. But all research indicates that frequent elections are a major cause of voter apathy and nonparticipation. Even today, programs on public affairs normally find it difficult to compete for public attention with sports events and pure entertainment. What kind of people would show up at their sets regularly in order to register their opinions on public issues? Who would be prepared to register opinions off the top of their heads without having had even the nominal exposure to conflicting viewpoints that today's normal election campaigns provide? The answer is clear. Teledemocracy would become the plaything of activist minorities, usually ideologically inflamed, who would use it to present their opinions as those of the general public.

Teledemocracy may be practical in a technological sense, but it is hardly an adequate substitute for our current electoral process. It would simply aggravate the weaknesses of these processes when it comes to actually enabling us to ascertain the considered judgment of a majority of the citizenry. Those who advocate it are seduced by gimmickry. It is another example of the general tendency of many people to believe that if something is technologically possible, it must be done, all other considerations of value being shunted aside.

United Nations or a world governing body devoted to settling world disputes, building cooperation, and solving critical issues of resources, population, and pollution would be required. The main functions of a global government would be to regulate forces that can determine the destiny of humankind. It might draw up a global plan for resource use to create an orderly system of distribution that works within the limits imposed by nature. If conditions became severe enough, a world government might actually ration resources.

Many support this system of "global resource sharing," in which the wealthy countries would give up some of their riches (food, minerals, and energy) for the benefit of the poor. This is called *de-development*, a term coined by Paul Ehrlich, a leading proponent of this view.

The ecologist Garrett Hardin takes strong exception to this view, arguing that moving wealth from the rich to the poor would create universal poverty and instability. The rich would become poorer, and the poor would have no incentive for responsible action. Population growth and good resource management would be ignored if all necessities were guaranteed under a world government that sought to distribute the earth's wealth according to the Marxian principle "to each according to his need."

Hardin argues that redistribution of food and other resources creates a "zero-sum" society in which one person's gain is another's loss. Universal sharing of the earth's goods leads to a tragedy of the commons (Chapter 11). Hardin argues that rather than sharing wealth, countries should share knowledge, because that is a renewable resource not subject to the zero-sum principle (law of conservation of matter and energy). The sharing of knowledge would create a "plus-sum" society, in which one person's gain is also another's gain. For example, knowledge transferred to the poor nations may come back in a richer form, to be passed on and refined once again.

A global sustainable society and government may seem like utopia—a fanciful, unrealistic dream. But as Rolf Edberg reminds us, "The utopia of one generation may be recognized as a practical necessity by the next." He adds that such goals depend on our ability to free ourselves from "ideas and emotions that once had a function in our battle for survival but have since become useless." The universal fear of nuclear war and the starving masses may be the psychological forces that set the stage for a new world society governed by one government of all peoples.

Not too long ago, the world seemed unlimited, and our problems few. Today, though, the globe has seemed to shrink with better transportation and communication and rapid depletion of resources. Our problems now seem as unlimited as the world once seemed. To solve them, our community must be nothing less than all of humankind. No greater challenge ever faced us; none ever will.

Honest differences of view and honest debates are not disunity. They are the vital process of policymaking among free men.

HERBERT HOOVER

Summary

We need a future that is hopeful but also attainable. Now, more than ever , we must take some decisive actions to reshape society to fit within the constraints of the biosphere.

Redirecting government is one essential way to create a sustainable society. But several obstacles remain. A lack of agreement on what is the optimal future remains one of the most difficult hurdles. Second is an orientation toward solving crises while ignoring long-term needs. Third is dealing with issues in isolation from the big picture. Fourth is budget constraints that cause funds to be directed toward immediate problems rather than those projects with long-term benefits. Fifth is the limited planning horizon of most politicians, and sixth is a lack of a central focal point in governmental policy on environmental issues.

Changes are necessary to overcome these problems. Anticipatory government, concerned with the needs of future generations as well as the present, could greatly help. Education and long-range planning could apprise people of the critical nature of population, resource, and pollution issues. Revisions in the present economic system might help achieve a sustainable state. New leaders and election reforms that promoted the emergence of long-range planners willing to tackle tough issues could go a long way. More self-reliance in communities can bring resource and pollution questions to the doorstep of the average citizen.

Finally, science courts can provide value-free decisions based on sound scientific information.

A global sustainable society seems imperative if we are to survive in the long run. Planning such a society would require great cooperation through the United Nations. The main functions of a global government would be to create an orderly system of distribution for resources and to regulate forces that can affect the destiny of humankind.

Discussion Questions

1. Describe the needs of the sustainable society and the governmental system that could help meet them.

2. Discuss the weaknesses of the current U.S. government in respect to achieving sustainability, and then draw up ways in which these could be remedied.

3. Debate the statement "All public decisions should be made on the basis of sound scientific information by a science court."

4. How can we create a global sustainable society?

Suggested Readings

Becker, T. (1981). Teledemocracy. *Futurist* 15(6): 6–9. Interesting view worth considering.

Enloe, C. H. (1975). *The Politics of Pollution in a Comparative Perspective*. New York: David McKay. Good comparison of different political systems and their responses to pollution.

Ferkiss, V. (1983). The Future of the U.S. Government: Change and Continuity. *Futurist* 17(1): 53–57. Excellent, although possibly too conservative, assessment of future political change in the U.S.

Hardin, G. (1981). An Ecolate View of the Human Predicament. *Alternatives* 7: 241–262. Controversial and thought-provoking. As important as his classic paper "The Tragedy of the Commons."

Hawken, P., Ogilvy, J., and Schwartz, P. (1982). *Seven Tomorrows*. New York: Bantam Books. Interesting book promoting a thoughtful consideration of our possible futures.

Klay, W. E. (1981). Nurturing Foresight in Government. *Futurist* 15(6): 25–28. Good overview.

Little, D. L. Dils, R. E., and Gray, J., eds. (1982). *Renewable Natural Resources: Management Handbook for the 1980s*. Boulder, Colo.: Westview Press. Collection of thoughtful and thought-provoking essays.

Morris, D. (1983). City-States: Laboratories of the 1980s. *Environment* 25(6): 12–20; 36–42. A lengthy treatise on changes in local government leading to a sustainable society.

Olsen, R. L. (1981). Filling the Vacuum: New Politics for a New Age. *Futurist* 15(6): 21–23. Insightful article.

Rubens, J. (1983). Retooling American Democracy. *Futurist* 17(1): 59–64. Thought-provoking essay.

Rutter, L. (1981). Strategies for the Essential Community. *Futurist* 15(3): 19–28. Interesting insight into one possible future of the community consistent with the sustainable society.

Environmental Law

An ancient Roman legal axiom proclaims that "the people's safety is the highest law." Today, many environmental and worker protection laws in the United States embrace this principle, but it was not until the late 1960s that this idea took hold.

During the late 1960s and 1970s environmental protection became increasingly important to U.S. citizens and their congressional representatives.

Numerous acts were passed during those years, so that today the United States has the world's most comprehensive and toughest set of environmental laws and regulations. Many other nations have followed the United States, benefiting from some of the errors Americans made in their eagerness to address resource and pollution issues.

National Environmental Policy Act

One of the most significant advances in environmental protection was the *National Environmental Policy Act* (1969). NEPA, a brief, rather general statute with several major goals, calls on the federal government to "use all practicable means" to minimize environmental impact in its actions. It requires officials overseeing federally controlled or subsidized projects such as dams, highways, and airports to describe possible adverse impacts in an **environmental impact statement (EIS)**. These must detail what the project is, and why it is needed. They must also discuss the environmental impact of the project, both in the short term and long term. Finally, all EIS's must describe ways to minimize environmental impact, including alternatives to the project. Drafts of the EIS are first made available for public comment and review by various governmental agencies. Public concerns must be addressed in a final EIS.

The EIS is a political carrot (a gentle inducement) rather than a political stick (a legal punishment). The EIS increases awareness of potential impacts with the idea that enlightenment will lead to preventive measures. Available early on in the planning stage, the EIS can help decision makers determine whether they

are directing their policies, programs, and plans in compliance with the national environmental goals expressed in NEPA.

NEPA also established the *Council on Environmental Quality* in the executive branch. The Council publishes an annual report (*Environmental Quality*) on the environment and protection efforts by the federal government. It also develops and recommends to the president new environmental policies and has recently established streamlined regulations for writing environmental impact statements.

NEPA has been one of the few statutes that has significantly affected federal decision making. It has led to hundreds of lawsuits, perhaps more than any other environmental statute. In addition, several states and nations have passed laws or issued executive or administrative orders patterned after it.

Some environmentalists believe that NEPA should require agencies to select the most environmentally benign and cost-effective approach—both in the short term and in the long run. Currently, environmental groups can sue an agency that they believe should have filed an EIS or has filed an inadequate EIS, but they cannot recover attorney's fees from such suits. If they could, that would ease the costly burden of forcing governmental agencies to heed the law; it might also open the door to numerous costly lawsuits, however, which would be a burden on the taxpayer.

Although it has its critics and still stands in need of improvement, NEPA is the cornerstone of U.S. environmental policy. Numerous federal agencies have reported important environmental benefits from NEPA and economic savings from the recently revised rules. NEPA is a landmark law of fundamental importance to a sustainable society.

Environmental Protection Agency

Another major environmental accomplishment was the establishment of the *Environmental Protection Agency* in 1970. The EPA was founded by a presidential executive order calling for a major reorganization of 15 existing federal agencies working on important environmental issues.

The EPA was directed to enforce the Federal Water Pollution Control Act and the Clean Air Act. Having grown in size, it now manages many of the environmental protection laws that issue from Congress. Current responsibilities of the EPA include research on the health and environmental impacts of a wide range of pollutants, as well as the development and enforcement of health and environmental standards for pollutants outside of the work place. The EPA is concerned with a variety of areas: pesticides, hazardous wastes, toxic substances, water pollution, air pollution, radiation, and noise pollution. Table S25-1 lists the responsibilities of other federal agencies involved in environmental protection.

The EPA can provide incentives to state and local communities through grants for substantial portions of water pollution control projects (Chapter 20). Grants to universities have helped expand the research capability of the EPA. The EPA carries out much of its own research at four National Environmental Research Centers, located in Cincinnati; at the Research Triangle Park, in North Carolina; in Las Vegas, Nevada; and in Corvallis, Oregon.

The EPA is often caught in a crossfire between the public, which seeks tighter controls, and the businesses it regulates, which commonly complain that regulations are too stringent and costly.

In the late 1970s widespread interest in the environment was

Figure S25-1
James Watt, former head of the Department of the Interior, drew heavy fire from the environmental community for his seemingly anti-environmental views.

Table S25-1 Some Federal Agencies and Their Responsibilities for the Environment and Health

Agency	Responsibility
Environmental Protection Agency	Research, demonstration programs, and enforcement of most environmental laws
Occupational Safety and Health Administration	Research and enforcement of worker safety and health laws
Food and Drug Administration	Research and enforcement of laws to protect consumers from harmful foods, drugs and cosmetics
Health Services Administration	Family planning programs and community health programs
Health Resources Administration	Research, planning, and training; collection of statistics on health in the U.S.
National Institutes of Health	Study of cancer, through the National Cancer Institute, and of radiation and other environmentally related diseases, through the National Institute of Environmental Health Services
Centers for Disease Control	Epidemiological studies on disease
National Oceanic and Atmospheric Administration	Research into and monitoring of the oceans and atmosphere; ecological baseline information and models to better predict the impacts of air and water pollution

displaced by economic hardship brought on by the oil shortage and inflation. This created a powerful political movement in the early 1980s to dismantle or weaken the EPA. The most common argument from the business sector was that the cost of protection was excessive and that stiff environmental protection laws were preventing a healthy economy. (See the Point/Counterpoint in Chapter 24.) But Japan has tough laws, continues to fight pollution, and has done well economically. Furthermore, as Russell Peterson, former administrator of the EPA and president of the National Audubon Society, noted, "We cannot have a thriving economy without a thriving ecosystem."

The American people continue to express a strong concern for a healthy environment; they support maintaining existing laws or even strengthening them (Figure S25-1). New problems such as acid precipitation and hazardous wastes constantly crop up, demanding the attention of the EPA and other federal bureaucracies. A growing population and an expanding economy create an everincreasing burden on the environment and on the agencies that regulate environmental issues. Thus, many argue that the EPA and other agencies involved in environmental protection must be strengthened.

Evolution of U.S. Environmental Law

Although environmental laws and regulations are too strict for some and too lax for others, they have become an integral part of the complex American legal system. How did this happen?

State and federal environmental laws gradually evolved over the years from scattered ordinances imposed by local governments. Interested in protecting health and environmental quality, officials of cities and towns passed local ordinances limiting the activities of private citizens for the good of the whole. For example, municipal ordinances regulated trash burning within city limits to reduce air pollution.

By the end of the 1800s, however, it was clear that local control of many problems such as water pollution was inadequate in densely populated regions. Disputes arose between neighboring municipalities with different laws. Regions with strict laws were hampered in cleaning up their rivers by upstream cities with lax pollution laws. Thus, states began drafting legislation to regulate water pollution.

Soon, state laws proved inadequate, too, because air and rivers flow freely across state borders. Thus, interstate conflicts over pollution replaced the conflicts between neighboring municipalities. State programs were inadequately funded, and their officials lacked the technical expertise to set pollution standards. States also found themselves powerless against large corporate polluters, which had influence in the courts and legislatures. Because of these problems, environmental controls shifted to the federal government, gradually in the 1940s and 1950s and then more rapidly thereafter.

Initially, the federal government restricted itself to research on health and development of pollution control technologies. This approach met with little opposition from state and local governments. Next, the federal government stepped in with grants to fund pollution control projects and the formation of state pollution enforcement agencies. But with increasing pressure from environmental groups and citizens, it began to take a larger role in enforcement. Today, it sets ambient pollution standards and standards for emissions from factories, automobiles, and other sources and can take strict enforcement actions if needed.

The shift to federal control is based on at least two important principles of American federalism: (1) When it is important to maintain uniform standards, the federal government provides the best route. Uniform policies help minimize interstate conflicts and help create an economically fairer system for businesses. (2) The power of the federal government to tax is much stronger than a state's. To effectively control pollution requires much expensive research, which the federal government can more easily afford. Furthermore, it would be costly, time consuming, and redundant for each state to carry out this extensive research when it could be done once by the federal government.

These two principles have allowed the passage of more stringent laws than might be possible on the state level, partly, too, because the federal government is less influenced by big businesses, which sometimes have a stranglehold on state and local government.

The shift to the federal level has disadvantages, as well. The federal government does not know the regions it tries to regulate as well as the governing officials within the regions do. This remoteness is the price paid for fairness and objective regulation. Another criticism of federal control is that states should have the right to do as they please with their own resources; in other words, federal control diminishes self-determination and self-governance. But without central controls, states impinge on one another's quality of life. For example, poor watershed management in the Sierra Nevadas leading to erosion could have long-term adverse impacts on downstream users to the east and west.

One way of sidestepping the issue is to develop federal standards but allow the states to manage their own programs. Thus, the Clean Air Act, the Surface Mining Control and Reclamation Act, and the Resource Conservation and Recovery Act all permit the states to run their own programs as long as they are at least as stringent as the one set up by federal law. These acts also provide money to assist the states in setting up their own programs.

Principles of Environmental Law

Environmental protection in the United States is conferred by the U.S. Constitution, state constitutions, common law, federal and state statutes, local ordinances, and regulations promulgated by state and federal agencies. Statutory law and common law are the mainstays of environmental protection, and the concepts they share enter into every law and lawsuit that involves the environment.

Statutory Law

Throughout this book have appeared many examples of state and federal laws covering environmental protection and resource management. These **statutory laws** generally state broad principles, such as the protection of health and the environment by reducing air pollution or the judicious use of natural resources. Congress and the state legislatures, however, lack the time and expertise to determine specifically how these goals can be met. Thus, Congress assigns the setting of standards, pollution control requirements, and resource management programs to executive agencies such as the EPA. (See discussions of the Clean Air Act in Chapter 19, the Toxic Substances Control Act in Chapter 18, and the Occupational Safety and Health Act in Chapter 21 for examples.)

Common Law

Many environmental cases are tried on the basis of **common law**, the body of unwritten rules and principles derived from thousands of years of legal decisions dating back to ancient Rome. It is based on proper or reasonable behavior.

Common law is a rather flexible form of law that attempts to balance competing societal interests. As an example, a noisy factory may be brought to court by a nearby landowner who contends that the factory is a nuisance. The landowner may sue to have the action stopped through an injunction. In deciding the case, the court relies on common-law principles. It weighs the legitimate interests of the company in doing business (and thus making noise); the interests of society, which wants its people employed and taxes from the company; and the interests of the landowner, who is trying to protect the family's rest, health, and enjoyment of property.

The court may favor the plaintiff if the damage (loss of sleep, health effects, and inconvenience) is greater than the cost of preventing the risk (costs of noise abatement, loss of jobs, and loss of tax revenues). But the court, rather than issuing an injunction requiring the factory to shut down, may simply require the company to reduce noise levels within a certain period. This way, a balance is struck between competing interests.

Cases such as this illustrate the balance principle. But on what legal principles are cases involving common law based? There are two—nuisance and negligence.

Nuisance   Nuisance is the most common ground for action in the field of environmental law. A **nuisance** is a class of wrongs that arise from the unreasonable, unwarrantable, or unlawful use of a person's own property that obstructs or injures the right of the public or another individual, producing annoyance, inconvenience, discomfort, or hurt. What this means is that one can use one's personal property or land in any way one sees fit, but only in a reasonable manner and as long as that use of the property does not cause material injury or annoyance to the public or another individual.

Generally, two types of remedy are available in a nuisance suit: compensation and injunction. Compensation is a monetary award for damage caused. Injunctions are court orders requiring the nuisance to be stopped.

Nuisances are often characterized as either public or private. Until recently, the two were distinctly different concepts. A public nuisance is an activity that harms or interferes with the rights of the general public. Typically, public nuisance suits are brought to court by public officials. A private nuisance is one that affects only a few people. For example, the pollution of a well affecting only one or two persons is considered a private nuisance. A public nuisance would be pollution that affected hundreds, perhaps thousands, of landowners along a river's shores.

Historically, this distinction has hampered pollution abatement, because the courts have traditionally held that an individual could sue against a public nuisance only when the person had suffered a unique injury, or one different from that suffered by others. An individual would be unable to sue a company for polluting a river shared by many others. Relief was possible only through a public nuisance suit brought by an official (the local health department, for instance). Public officials might be unwilling to file suit against local businesses that provide important dollars for the community—and campaign support as well.

Increasingly, the distinction between private and public nuisance is fading; private persons can bring suit to stop a public nuisance. As a result, the private individual has more power to stop polluters.

The most common environmental nuisance is noise (Chapter Supplement 21-2). Water pollutants and air pollutants such as smoke, dust, odors, and other chemicals are other major nuisances.

Several common defenses are used to fight nuisance suits. Because most nuisance suits are decided by balancing the rights and interests of the opposing parties, good-faith efforts of the polluter may influence the decision. On the one hand, if a small company had installed pollution control devices and had attempted to keep them operating properly but was still creating a nuisance, the court would hold it liable but might be more lenient in damages or conditions of abatement. If, on the other hand, the company had made no attempt to eliminate pollution and had created a public or private nuisance, the court would generally be more severe.

The availability of pollution control also enters the equation. If a company is using up-to-date control devices and still creates a nuisance, the court may not impose damages or an injunction. In contrast, if the company has failed to keep pace with pollution control equipment, the court may order that it install such controls.

Class-action suits can be used in states that still distinguish between public and private nuisance. **Class-action** suits are brought by a group on behalf of many people. They emphasize the composite damage caused by a nuisance. In order for a class-action suit for compensation to be allowable, however, each person named in the suit must have suffered at least $10,000 in damage. If not, the suit can be dismissed. This requirement, then, provides an opportunity for a defense.

Another defense is that the plaintiff has "come to the nuisance." Coming to the nuisance occurs when an individual moves into an area where a nuisance—such as an airport, animal feedlot, or factory—already exists and then complains about the nuisance. An old common-law principle holds that if you voluntarily place yourself in a situation in which you suffer an injury, you have no legal right to sue either for damages or injunction. In most courts, however, even though you purchase property and know of the existence of a nuisance, you still have the right to file suit to abate it or recover for damages. This is based on another common-law principle that clean air and the enjoyment of property are rights that go along with owning property. Thus, if population expands toward a nuisance, it may be the responsibility of the liable party to put an end to it.

According to one environmental attorney, Thomas Sullivan, "The courts are moving to strict liability for environmental nuisances, so that practically speaking, there are no good defenses. The solution is: do not create nuisances."

Negligence   A second major principle of common law is negligence. From a legal viewpoint, a person is negligent if he or she acts in an unreasonable manner and if these actions cause personal or property damage. For example, in July 1972 the oil tanker *Tamano* spilled 100,000 gallons of oil in Casco Bay in Maine. The state of Maine filed suit against the federal government, contending that the damage caused to the state resulted from negligent action on the part of the U.S. Coast Guard. According to Maine, the Coast Guard, which was in charge of cleaning up the oil, failed to do so in a timely and proper fashion. The courts held that the Coast Guard had been negligent and that the federal government was liable for damages. Negligence provides a basis for liability, just as nuisance does, but negligence is generally more difficult to prove. What is a reasonable action in one instance may not be reasonable in another.

Statutory laws and regulations help the courts determine whether behavior is reasonable. For example, regulations drawn up by the EPA specify how certain hazardous wastes should be treated. Failure to comply with those standards may be evidence of negligence.

Negligence may be shown in instances in which a company fails to use common industry practices. For example, a company may be found negligent if it fails to transport hazardous wastes in containers like those used by other companies. Still, common practices may themselves be inadequate. Suppose that it is common for companies to transport hazardous wastes in unlined cardboard boxes; a reasonable individual would realize the inadequacy of this approach. Thus, the courts would probably find the company negligent.

In a much broader sense, the courts may decide that a company is negligent simply if it fails to do something that a reasonable person would have done. For example, negligence might be proved if a company failed to test its wastes for the presence of harmful chemicals when a reasonable person would have done so. Likewise, negligence may stem from action that a reasonable person would not have taken.

In summary, negligence can result from either inaction or action that may be deemed unreasonable considering the circumstances. The concept of knowing also plays a role. Briefly, negligence can be determined on the basis of what a defendant knew or should have known about a particular risk. The standard of comparison is what a reasonable person should have known under similar circumstances. For example, a man on trial may argue that he is not negligent because he did not know that a harmful chemical was in the materials that he dumped into a municipal waste disposal site and that subsequently polluted nearby groundwater. His argument will be valid if a reasonable person in his position could not have known about the chemical.

The standard of reasonableness applies also to past mistakes. In other words, even though the operators of a hazardous waste dump did not know of the hazards it created 20 years ago, they may be ruled negligent for failing to eliminate the risk when they learned of it or should have learned of it.

Liability for damage or harm need not be based on negligence in cases where the risk is extraordinarily large (in legal terms, an "abnormal risk"). Practically speaking, in proving liability for an activity of abnormally high risk, such as the housing of hazardous materials, one need only prove that injury or damage occurred, not that the operator was negligent or acted unreasonably.

Problems in Environmental Lawsuits

Legal actions to stop a nuisance or collect damages from a nuisance or act of negligence carry with them a burden of proof. Plaintiffs must prove that they have been harmed in some significant way and that the defendant is responsible for that harm. This is not always easy, for several reasons. First, the cause-and-effect connection between a pollutant and a disease may not be definitely established by the medical community. If doubt exists, the case is weakened. Second, diseases such as cancer may occur decades after the exposure to a pollutant, making it extremely difficult to prove causation. It is generally easier to link cause and effect with acute diseases. Third, it is often difficult or impossible to identify the party responsible for damage, especially in areas with a preponderance of industry or in cases in which illegal acts, such as midnight dumping of hazardous wastes, have occurred. Any reasonable doubt over the party responsible for personal or property damage may severely cripple a lawsuit

The statute of limitations, which sets the period of time during which a person can sue after a particular event, also creates problems in cases of delayed diseases. Statutes of limitations help reduce lawsuits in which evidence is no longer available or the memories of potential witnesses have faded and become unreliable. In latent-disease cases, though, they create a major obstacle to individuals seeking compensation. In states that measure the limitation period from the onset of exposure, it is essentially impossible for cancer victims to file suit. Other states start the judicial clock from the time the victim learns of the disease. This makes it a little easier to collect compensation for diseases such as cancer, black lung disease, and emphysema.

Out-of-court settlements have hindered environmental law. Anxious to avoid a costly settlement, companies may pay victims if they agree to relieve the company of further liability. Out-of-court settlements may also benefit plaintiffs, saving them the time, headaches, and costs of environmental litigation. Although advantageous to both parties, these settlements provide no precedents for environmental law. This may discourage attorneys and citizens from filing court cases. Without clear examples from the past, they may simply be unwilling to face costly, time-consuming legal battles.

Resolving Environmental Disputes Out of Court

An increasing number of disputes between environmentalists and businesses are being settled out of court by **dispute resolution**, or **mediation**. This innovative approach often employs a neutral party who keeps the proceedings on track, encourages rivals to work together, and tries to resolve the dispute in a way that is satisfactory to both groups.

The benefits of mediation over litigation are many. It is much less costly and time-consuming. It also tends to create better feelings among disputants, whereas court settlements create winners and losers and, often, bitter feelings. In addition, and perhaps most important of all, mediation may bring about a more satisfactory resolution. For instance, environmental lawsuits often hinge on specific points of law rather than substantive issues and thus may have little to do with what the plaintiff really wants. An environmental group might bring a suit over the adequacy of an EIS, but in reality it wants the government to ensure protection of a valuable species that might be affected by the project. In mediation, this will be the central issue.

Mediation also tends to promote a more accurate view of problems. In lawsuits, for instance, each party tends to bring up evidence that favors its goal and ignore or dismiss unfavorable information or ambiguous information that might weaken its stand. In mediation, the parties are encouraged to openly discuss the uncertainties of their position, discovering many points of agreement and building a better understanding of the opposing position.

Mediation has its drawbacks, too. First, funding is inadequate. In the past, mediation has been financed largely by foundations. Federal, state, and local governments need to develop programs to fund mediation. Second, some groups (environmentalists, for example) fear that they will lose their constituency if they enter negotiations on certain issues, because doing so gives the impression that they are failing at their stated goals and compromising with the "enemy." A third drawback is a lack of faith in the outcome of mediation. Unlike court orders, resolutions drawn up in mediation are not legally enforceable. Thus, months of discussion may do nothing but produce a piece of paper that polluters will ignore.

Effective mediation requires a truly neutral party to serve as mediator. A formally agreed upon agenda for discussion and a point of focus are also important. Resource and pollution issues should be the mainstay of discussion; disputes over values should not dominate the proceedings, because they cannot be solved by mediation. Although values will surely come out in the debate, they should not be the focal point. There must be a willingness to explore new ideas and possibilities on both sides. The disputants must deal honestly with each other. An adequate representation of all interested parties must also be achieved. If someone is not represented, a solution that is unsatisfactory may result. This could lead to a lawsuit. Finally, strict rules should be imposed regarding news releases. The media should not be employed as a lever by either group.

Dispute resolution is growing in the United States, but it will not replace litigation. Still, it can play a valuable role in the future. The first environmental mediations began in 1975, and as of 1983 approximately 70 disputes had been settled using this approach. Eight states have organizations that offer mediation services, and a growing number of private organizations have been formed to provide professional mediators with experience and knowledge in environmental issues. Thus, more and more disputes may be settled by this noncombative approach.

Suggested Readings

Arbuckle, J. G., Frick, G. W., Hall, R. M., Miller, M. L., Sullivan, T. F. P., and Vanderver, T. A. (1984). *Environmental Law Handbook*. Washington, D.C.: Government Institutes. Good overview of environmental law.

Epstein, S. S., Brown, L. O., and Pope, C. (1982). *Hazardous Waste in America*. San Francisco: Sierra Club Books. See Chapter 10 for a good overview of principles of environmental law.

Findley, R. W., and Farber, D. A. (1981). *Environmental Law: Cases and Materials*. St. Paul, Minn.: West Publishing Company. In-depth presentation of important legal cases in environmental law.

Ragsdale, J. W. (1977). Ecology and the Role of the Federal Courts. *UMKC Law Review* 46(2): 222–238. Thoughtful essay.

Wenner, L. M. (1976). *One Environment under Law: A Public-Policy Dilemma*. Pacific Palisades, Calif.: Goodyear. Superb reading.

Chemistry

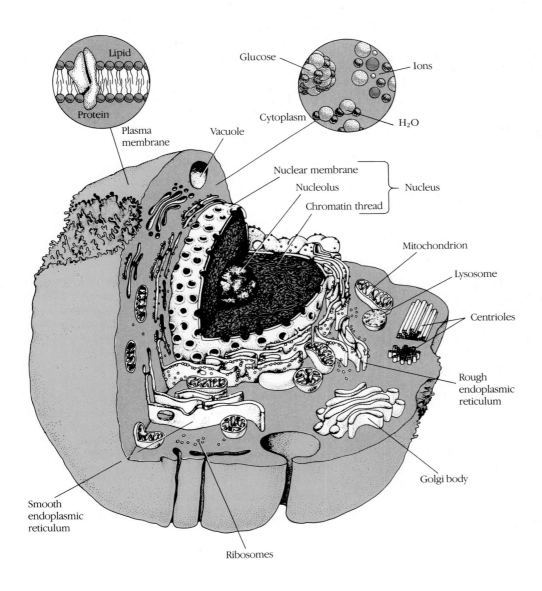

Lipid

Protein

Plasma
membrane

Vacuole

Glucose

Ions

Cytoplasm

H_2O

Nuclear membrane

Nucleolus

Chromatin thread

Nucleus

Mitochondrion

Lysosome

Centrioles

Rough
endoplasmic
reticulum

Golgi body

Smooth
endoplasmic
reticulum

Ribosomes

Figure A-1
This stylized diagram of an
animal cell shows the
molecular construction of
various cellular components.

Some Principles of Matter

The basic concepts of chemistry are essential to understanding many fundamental environmental problems and solutions presented in this book.

All living organisms are composed of cells. Cells are made up of numerous chemicals, including fats (lipids), proteins, carbohydrates, and others. In some parts of the cell these chemicals are arranged in a very specific way, as shown in Figure A-1. In the environment around us are hundreds of additional chemicals found in the water, soil, and air. Together these constitute a complex chemical environment that all living organisms depend on for survival.

The Atom

Matter is anything that occupies space and has mass. The fundamental unit of all matter is the atom. But all atoms are made up of smaller subunits called **subatomic particles**. These particles, shown in Figure A-2, include protons, neutrons, and electrons.

All atoms consist of two regions, the **nucleus** and the **electron cloud** (Figure A-2). The nucleus occupies the central region and contains positively charged particles, called **protons**, and

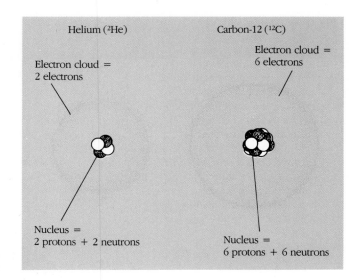

Figure A-3
Comparison of two common atoms, helium and carbon.

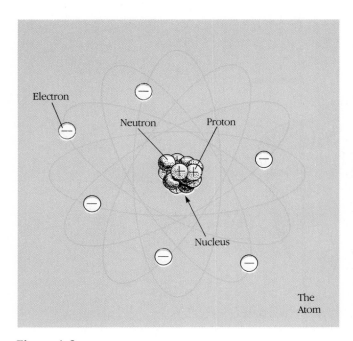

Figure A-2
Atoms consist of a dense central region, the nucleus, containing protons and neutrons. Electrons orbit around the nucleus in the electron cloud.

uncharged particles, called **neutrons**. Neutrons and protons are densely packed within the nucleus. Because they are many times heavier than electrons, over 99% of an atom's mass is concentrated in the nucleus.

Orbiting around the nucleus in the electron cloud are the **electrons**, small, negatively charged particles with almost no mass. The number of electrons in an atom is always equal to the number of protons in its nucleus; thus, the atom has no net charge.

Within the electron cloud, electrons occupy different levels (sometimes called shells), depending on the amount of energy they possess. More highly energetic electrons are generally found farther from the nucleus than lower-energy electrons. The outer-shell electrons are responsible for the formation of bonds that link atoms to form molecules.

The Elements

Elements are substances that cannot be separated by chemical means into other substances. Oxygen, carbon, lead, and mercury are all elements. Each element consists of many atoms. To date, scientists have identified 93 naturally occurring elements. Physicists have made 13 additional elements from some of the naturally occurring ones.

The elements differ from one another in the number of subatomic particles they possess. For example, the element helium contains two protons, two neutrons, and two electrons; the element carbon contains six protons, six neutrons, and six electrons (Figure A-3). The differing numbers of protons, electrons, and neutrons give the atoms different weights and different chemical features.

Each element is represented by a symbol consisting of one or two letters; these symbols are shorthand representations used by chemists. For example, F stands for fluorine, Cl stands for chlorine, As stands for arsenic, and N stands for nitrogen.

Symbols can also be written to include the atomic number and atomic weight of each element. The **atomic number** is simply the number of protons in the nucleus. For example, the atomic number of carbon is six, because it has six protons in the nucleus. The **atomic weight** is a measure of the weight of each atom. Because electrons are virtually weightless compared with protons and neutrons, the atomic weight is equal to the number of protons and neutrons. For carbon, then, the chemist might write the symbol $^{12}_{6}C$. The subscript 6 represents the

atomic number (the number of protons); the superscript 12 indicates the number of protons and neutrons and is the atomic weight.

All the elements known to science are listed on a chart called the **periodic table of elements**. A simplified version of the chart is shown in Figure A-4. As shown, the elements are listed on this chart by increasing atomic number.

Isotopes

If we had many carbon atoms together, the average weight of the group would be 12. But not all carbon atoms have the same weight, because not all have the same number of neutrons in

I	II	III	IV	V	VI	VII	VIII
1 H Hydrogen 1.0							2 He Helium 4.0
3 Li Lithium 7.0	4 Be Beryllium 9.0	5 B Boron 11.0	6 C Carbon 12.0	7 N Nitrogen 14.0	8 O Oxygen 16.0	9 F Fluorine 19.0	10 Ne Neon 20.2
11 Na Sodium 23.0	12 Mg Magnesium 24.3	13 Al Aluminum 27.0	14 Si Silicon 28.1	15 P Phosphorus 31.0	16 S Sulfur 32.1	17 Cl Chlorine 35.5	18 Ar Argon 40.0
19 K Potassium 39.1	20 Ca Calcium 40.1						

Labels on the Carbon cell: Atomic Number, Atomic Symbol, Atomic Weight

Figure A-4
A simplified periodic table showing a few of the atoms found in living and nonliving matter. Note that the atoms are listed according to their atomic number (the number of protons in the nucleus) and atomic weight (number of protons and neutrons).

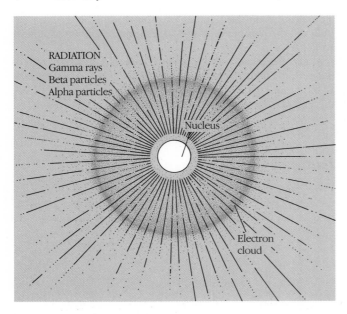

Figure A-5
Radioactive emissions from isotopes.

their nucleus. Several different forms of the carbon atom are shown here:

$$^{12}_{6}C \qquad ^{13}_{6}C \qquad ^{14}_{6}C \qquad ^{15}_{6}C$$

Each of these is called an **isotope** of carbon. Isotopes all have the same number of protons and electrons, but they have different numbers of neutrons.

Isotopes are important to us because some of them have unstable nuclei that release small energetic particles, or energy (Figure A-5). The particles released from unstable nuclei are called **radiation**, or **radioactive emissions**. The unstable isotopes are called **radioactive isotopes**, or **radionuclides**. For example, $^{14}_{6}C$ is a radionuclide of carbon that emits radiation called gamma rays. These may cause harmful changes in the genetic material of cells. This damage may alter cellular structure and function, possibly causing cancer.

Molecules

Atoms bind together by way of chemical bonds and thus form **molecules**. For example, when two oxygen atoms join, they form a molecule of oxygen with the chemical formula O_2. The subscript in this formula tells us that two atoms of oxygen are linked together by a chemical bond. Most atoms, however, do not bond to atoms of the same type; they usually form bonds with atoms

of different types. For example, two hydrogen atoms bond with one oxygen atom to form water (H_2O). Two oxygen atoms bond to one atom of carbon to form carbon dioxide (CO_2). An atom of carbon bonds with four hydrogen atoms to form methane (CH_4), a combustible gas that is produced during the degradation of plant and animal matter.

The chemist divides molecules into two major groups: organic and inorganic. The **organic molecules** are those that primarily contain carbon, hydrogen, and oxygen. Organics are an important source of food and energy. Examples of organics include methane, ethanol (grain alcohol), glucose, sucrose (table sugar), starch, protein, and amino acids. The **inorganic molecules** are often described as those molecules that do not contain carbon, such as water, nitrogen, ammonia, oxygen, and chlorine. There are a few exceptions to this rule, however. Carbon dioxide, for example, is a molecule that contains carbon and oxygen but is considered inorganic.

Chemical Bonds

Ions and Ionic Bonds

Atoms contain an equal number of protons and electrons; therefore, the positive charge of the protons is balanced by the negative charge of the electrons, and the atom is noncharged, or neutral.

In some cases, however, the number of electrons may be greater or less than the number of protons. The resulting structure is not an atom but rather an **ion**. An ion that has a negative charge due to the excess of electrons is called an **anion**. An ion with a positive charge is called a **cation**.

Negatively and positively charged ions are attracted to one another because of their opposite charges; the force of attraction holds these oppositely charged ions together and is called an **ionic bond**. Ionic bonds are not very strong bonds, and they can be easily broken.

Covalent Bonds

The covalent bond is of great importance to us in our study of environmental science. It is formed when two atoms share their electrons. To understand this concept, let us look at a simple example—the gas hydrogen (H_2). Hydrogen gas consists of two hydrogen atoms joined by a covalent bond. What happens in this case is that the two atoms come in close proximity to each other; the electrons then begin to orbit around the nuclei of both atoms (Figure A-6). Therefore, we say that the two atoms are sharing electrons. Because of this sharing of electrons, the atoms are held together as one molecule.

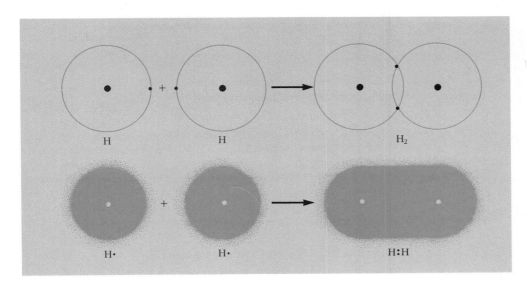

Figure A-6
Covalent bonds are formed by the sharing of electrons between one or more nuclei.

One of the important features of covalent bonds besides the fact that they hold atoms together to form molecules is that when they are broken, they can yield an enormous amount of energy. Why is this so important?

For one thing, fuels such as coal, oil, and natural gas are made of organic molecules, which we break down during combustion. During the combustion of these organic fuels, energy is produced in the form of heat; this energy comes from the breakage of the strong covalent bonds.

Covalent bonds of organic molecules are also broken apart in the cells of living organisms in an intricate series of reactions. This breakdown is important to the survival and daily activity of all organisms. The chemical reactions that are collectively involved in the breakdown of organic molecules are part of a process called **cellular respiration**. During this process, some of the energy from bond breakage is released as heat. This gives warm-blooded creatures something we call body heat. The remainder of the energy released during cellular respiration, however, is captured by the cell and used for a variety of purposes, including muscle contraction, nerve impulse transport, and chemical reactions such as protein synthesis.

In summary, the breakdown of organic matter—whether it occurs in a power plant, a fireplace, or a cell of your body—yields valuable energy that we can harness to run our industries, to heat our homes, or to power the elaborate machinery of our own bodies.

This appendix has covered the basic chemistry you need to understand how the world works. You've read about a few chemicals, but of course there are many others that have a great effect on how we live. Table A-1 lists the basic compounds, including their type and importance, to give you an insight into the chemical requirements of living things.

Suggested Readings

Curtis, H. (1979). *Biology.* New York: Worth. Contains excellent material on energy, matter, and life for students wishing to expand their general knowledge.

Horne, R. A. (1978). *The Chemistry of Our Environment.* New York: Wiley. A detailed study of the chemistry of our environment. A good book for science students wishing to greatly expand their knowledge of environmental chemistry.

Jensen, W. A., Heinrich, B., Wake, D. B., Wake, M. H., and Wolfe, S. L. (1979). *Biology.* Belmont, Calif.: Wadsworth. Contains a delightful account of matter.

Turk, J., and Turk, A. (1977). *Physical Science with Environmental and Other Applications.* Philadelphia: Saunders. A good account of matter and the physical laws important to the study of environmental science.

Table A-1 Some Important Organic and Inorganic Molecules

Chemical	Type	Importance
Water	Inorganic	Primary component of all living organisms
		High heat absorbance; used for industrial cooling
		Good solvent; used for industrial cleaning; dissolves nutrients and wastes in organisms
Oxygen	Inorganic	Necessary for cells to break down foods
		Necessary for combustion
Carbon dioxide	Inorganic	Waste product of combustion and energy production in animal cells
		Pollutant that may shift global temperature balance
		Used by plants to make organic molecules such as starch and cellulose
Amino acids	Organic	Necessary for plants and animals to build proteins that form enzymes, hormones, and important structural components of cells
Carbohydrates	Organic	Source of energy for animal cells
Nucleic acids	Organic	Genetic material that controls all cellular function and heredity

Environmental Publications

The following journals, magazines, and other publications will help you learn more about specific environmental issues and stay abreast of current changes. The address of the publication is listed so you can contact it for subscription costs.

American Forests. Monthly. American Forestry Association, 1319 18th Street NW, Washington, DC 20036. Promotes public appreciation of natural resources

Audubon. Bimonthly. National Audubon Society, 950 Third Avenue, New York, NY 10022. Conservation and environmental concerns; covers more than bird watching.

BioScience. Monthly. American Institute of Biological Sciences, 1401 Wilson Boulevard, Arlington, VA 22209. Both popular and technical; major coverage of biological aspects of the environment.

Bulletin of the Atomic Scientists. Ten times a year. Educational Foundation for Nuclear Science, 5801 South Kenwood, Chicago, IL 60637. Increasingly concerned with environmental issues in relation to nuclear power, nuclear testing, and nuclear war.

Code of Federal Regulations. Office of the Federal Register, U.S. Government Printing Office, Washington, DC 20402. Covers federal regulations in agriculture, aliens, energy, energy conservation, food and drugs, minerals, parks, national forests, environmental protection, public health, public lands, transportation, and wildlife.

The CoEvolution Quarterly. P.O. Box 428, Sausalito, CA 94965. Environment and self-sufficiency. Also publishes *The New Whole Earth Catalog.*

Conservation Foundation Letter. Monthly. Conservation Foundation, 1717 Massachusetts Avenue NW, Washington, DC 20036. Concise, solid summaries of important issues.

Demographic Yearbook. Department of International Economic and Social Affairs, Statistical Office, United Nations Publishing Service, United Nations, NY 10017. Information on populations, including growth rate, population size, and mortality.

Design and Environment. Quarterly. RC Publications, 6400 Goldsboro Road NW, Washington, DC 20034. Concerned with technology and the environment.

Earth Shelter Digest. Six times a year. 479 Fort Road, St. Paul, MN 55102. Current information on earth-sheltered housing.

The Ecologist. Ten times a year. Ecostems, Ltd., 73 Molesworth Street, Wadebridge, Cornwall PL27 7DS, United Kingdom. International viewpoint on environmental issues.

The Energy Consumer. Monthly. U.S. Department of Energy, Office of Consumer Affairs, Forrestal Building, 1000 Independence Avenue SW, Washington, DC 20858. Free. Summaries of energy developments, government programs, and related publications.

Environment. Ten times a year. 4000 Albemarle Street NW, Washington, DC 20016. In-depth articles on important issues.

Environmental Abstracts. Monthly. Environment Information Centers/Intelligence, 48 West 38th Street, New York, NY 10018. Basic bibliographic reference; in most libraries.

Environmental Action. Monthly. Environmental Action, Inc., 1346 Connecticut Avenue NW, Suite 731, Washington, DC 20036. Political, social-action orientation. Environmental issues covered from a broad spectrum of viewpoints.

Environmental Quality. Yearly. Council on Environmental Quality, 722 Jackson Place NW, Washington, DC 20006. Report of environmental problems and progress in environmental protection.

Environmental Science & Technology. Monthly. American Chemical Society, 1155 16th Street NW, Washington, DC 20036. Basic reference for current technological developments. Emphasizes air, water, and solid waste chemistry.

EPA Journal. Monthly. Environmental Protection Agency. 1961

Stout, Room 117, Washington, DC 20003. Environmental issues and EPA activity updates.

Family Planning Perspectives. Bimonthly. Planned Parenthood-World Population, Editorial Offices, 666 Fifth Avenue, New York, NY 10019. Free. Detailed information on population problems.

FDA Consumer. Ten times a year. U.S. Department of Health and Human Services. Public Health Service, 5600 Fishers Lane, Rockville, MD 20857. Excellent information on food additives and health issues.

The Futurist. Bimonthly. World Future Society, 4916 St. Elmo Avenue, Bethesda, MD 20814. Covers broad range of social problems, including some major issues.

Journal of Environmental Education. Quarterly. Haldref Publications, 4000 Albemarle Street NW, Washington, DC 20016. For educators.

Living Wilderness. Quarterly. Wilderness Society, 1901 Pennsylvania Avenue NW, Washington, DC 20006. Articles on wilderness, forestry, and related issues.

Monthly Energy Review. National Energy Information Center, EI-20, Energy Information Administration, Room 1F-048, Forrestal Building, Washington, DC 20585. Monthly updates on U.S. energy production and consumption.

National Parks and Conservation Magazine. Monthly. National Parks and Conservation Association, 1701 18th Street NW, Washington, DC 20009. Park and wildlife issues.

National Wildlife. Bimonthly. National Wildlife Federation, 1412 16th Street NW, Washington, DC 20036. Wildlife emphasis; action oriented.

Natural History. Ten times a year. American Museum of Natural History, Central Park West at 79th Street, New York, NY 10024. Popular. Regular coverage of environmental issues.

Nature. Weekly. Macmillan Journals, Ltd., Brunel Road, Basingstoke, Hants RG21 2X5, United Kingdom. British publication, similar to *Science*.

New Scientist. Weekly. 1-19 New Oxford Street, London WEI A 1 NG, United Kingdom. General science; good coverage of environmental issues and technological breakthroughs.

Not Man Apart. Monthly. Friends of the Earth, 1045 Sansome Street, San Francisco, CA 94111. National and international environmental issues.

Population and Vital Statistics Report. Quarterly. United Nations, Publications Sales Section, New York, NY 10017. Up-to-date world figures.

Population Bulletin. Bimonthly. Population Reference Bureau, Inc., 1337 Connecticut Avenue NW, Washington, DC 20036. Nontechnical coverage of human population issues.

Population Bulletin. Irregular. United Nations, Publications Sales Section, New York, NY 10017. Statistical summaries.

Population Reports. Population Information Program, Johns Hopkins University, Hampton House, 624 North Broadway, Baltimore, MD 21205. Up-to-date information on birth control and population.

Resources. Four times a year. Resources for the Future, Inc., 1755 Massachusetts Avenue NW, Washington, DC 20036. Recent research and findings on resource use and development.

Statistical Yearbook. Department of International Economic and Social Affairs. Statistical Office. United Nations Publishing Service, United Nations, NY 10017. Wide range of information, including gross domestic products, world exports, food production, housing, forestry, and energy.

Science. Weekly. American Association for the Advancement of Science, 1515 Massachusetts Avenue NW, Washington, DC 20005. Excellent but technical information on important environmental issues.

Science for Society—A Bibliography. Annually. American Association for the Advancement of Science, Education Department, 1515 Massachusetts Avenue NW, Washington, DC 20005. Environmental bibliography.

Science News. Weekly. Science Service, Inc., 1719 N Street NW, Washington, DC 20036. Popular; summarizes scientific developments.

Scientific American. Monthly. 415 Madison Avenue, New York, NY 10017. Covers all scientific issues, with many articles on the environment.

The Sierra Club Bulletin. Monthly. Sierra Club, 530 Bush Street, San Francisco, CA 94108. Citizen action viewpoint; covers a wide range of environmental issues.

Technology Review. Eight times a year. Massachusetts Institute of Technology, Room 10-140, Cambridge, MA 02139. Sophisticated. Frequent coverage of environmental material and science policy.

UNESCO Courier. Eleven issues per year. The United Nations Educational, Scientific, and Cultural Organization. United Nations, New York, NY 10017. Covers broad issues.

United States Population Data Sheet. Published annually. Population Reference Bureau, Box 35012, Washington, DC 20013. Superb source.

World Population Data Sheet. Published annually. Population Reference Bureau, Box 35012, Washington, DC 20013. Superb source.

Worldwatch Papers. Worldwatch Institute, 1776 Massachusetts Avenue NW, Washington, DC 20036. Designed to give early warning on major environmental problems.

Yearbook of World Energy Statistics. Department of International Economic and Social Affairs. Statistical Office. United Nations Publishing Service, United Nations, NY 10017. Detailed information on worldwide energy production.

Environmental and Governmental Organizations

Environmental Organizations

American Forestry Association, 1319 18th Street, NW, Washington, DC 20036. Focuses on forest and soil conservation, but concerned with air and water pollution and preserving and creating parklands.

Animal Protection Institute of America, P.O. Box 22505, Sacramento, CA 95822. Education and information on humane treatment of animals. Has concentrated on whale, porpoise, and seal slaughter, leg-hold traps, and dog and cat population problems.

Center for Environmental Education, 624 Ninth Street NW, Washington, DC 20001. Dedicated to citizen involvement in improvement of environmental quality. Special emphasis on whales and marine ecosystems. Initiated a campaign to reauthorize the Endangered Species Act.

Center for Renewable Resources, 1001 Connecticut Avenue NW, Washington, DC 20036. Educates the public and policymakers; conducts policy research.

Center for Science in the Public Interest, 1755 S Street NW, Washington, DC 20006. Public-interest scientists concerned especially with food and nutrition issues but also with the environment and the effects of science and technology on society.

Center for the Study of Responsive Law, P.O. Box 19367, Washington, DC 20036. Research and education organization working in public interest.

Citizens Energy Project, 1110 6th Street NW, Suite 300, Washington, DC 20001. Specializes in research and education in renewable energy technologies.

Clean Water Action Project, 1341 G Street NW, Suite 200, Washington, DC 20005. National citizen-action organization working for strict pollution controls and safe drinking water. Seeks to preserve national wetlands.

Common Cause, 2030 M Street NW, Washington, DC 20036. One of the most important citizen groups in the country. Over 200,000 members active in many political issues.

The Conservation Foundation, 1717 Massachusetts Avenue NW, Washington, DC 20036. Resource conservation; analysis of ecological impact of foreign aid.

Consumer Action Now, 110 West 34th Street, New York, NY 10001. Emphasizes energy and resource conservation.

The Cousteau Society, 777 Third Avenue, New York, NY 10017. Concerned with environmental matters, education, research, and evaluation. Plans to construct an evaluation center to digest scientific environmental data and to monitor the accuracy of public announcements made by industry or by the government.

Critical Mass Energy Project, P.O. Box 1538, Washington, DC 20013. Sponsors national conferences on nuclear energy and alternative energy; promotes safe and efficient energy.

Defenders of Wildlife, 1244 19th Street NW, Washington, DC 20036. Works to protect all wildlife. Education, lobbying, and research.

Ducks Unlimited, P.O. Box 66300, Chicago, IL 60666. Conservationists in the United States, Canada, Mexico, and New Zealand interested in migrators and wildlife habitat conservation. Has acquired or protected millions of acres of important waterfowl breeding habitats.

Environmental Action, 1346 Connecticut Avenue NW, Suite 731, Washington, DC 20036. Lobbies for legislative protection and reform.

Environmental Defense Fund, 444 Park Avenue South, New York, NY 10016. Lawyers, scientists, and laypeople working to link law and science together for environmental defense.

The Environmental Law Institute, 1346 Connecticut Avenue NW, Suite 600, Washington, DC 20036. Joint project of the Conservation Foundation and the Public Law Education Institute; conducts research and education in environmental law.

Environmental Policy Center, 317 Pennsylvania Avenue SE, Washington, DC 20003. Lobbies for water policy and energy development.

Foundation on Economic Trends, 1346 Connecticut Avenue NW, Washington, DC 20036. Studies energy, economic, and health issues.

Friends of the Earth, 1045 Sansome Street, San Francisco, CA 94111. Powerful lobbying group.

The Fund for Animals, 140 West 57th Street, New York, NY 10019. Preserves wildlife and promotes humane treatment of animals.

Institute for Local Self-Reliance, 1717 18th Street NW, Washington, DC 20009. Promotes appropriate technologies for communities; promotes decentralized self-reliance.

International Planned Parenthood Federation, 105 Madison Avenue, 7th Floor, New York, NY 10016. Committed to informed voluntary family planning. Seeks to persuade governments to establish family planning programs. Provides information, education, and services.

Izaak Walton League of America, 1800 North Kent Street, Suite 806, Arlington, VA 22209. Works for wise resource use and the development and protection of outdoor recreation.

John Muir Institute for Environmental Studies, 743 Wilson Street, Napa, CA 94559. Research and education on environmental issues.

Keep America Beautiful, 99 Park Avenue, New York, NY 10016. Public service organization; works to improve the physical quality of life. Sponsors community programs for the improvement of waste handling. Provides assistance, materials, and advice for community grass-roots efforts.

League of Conservation Voters, 317 Pennsylvania Avenue SE, Washington, DC 20003. Nonpartisan; part of Friends of the Earth. Promotes and supports congressional candidates who have sound environmental platforms. Notifies the public of roll-call votes on environmental issues.

League of Women Voters of the United States, 1730 M Street NW, Washington, DC 20036. Outstanding membership organization committed to political responsibility and an informed, active citizenry.

National Audubon Society, 950 Third Avenue, New York, NY 10022. Research, education, and lobbying. Operates wildlife sanctuaries across the country; conducts research to aid endangered species.

National Parks and Conservation Association, 1701 18th Street NW, Washington, DC 20009. Works to acquire and protect public parklands. Active in general environmental issues.

National Recreation and Park Association, 3101 Park Center Drive, 12th Floor, Alexandria, VA 22302. Recreation and park development and conservation.

National Resources Defense Council, Inc., 122 East 42nd Street, New York, NY 10168. Works to protect natural resources and environmental quality.

National Wildlife Federation, 1412 16th Street NW, Washington, DC 20036. Education and research. Promotes citizen and government action.

The Nature Conservancy, 1800 North Kent Street, Suite 800, Arlington, VA 22209. Membership organization. Works to preserve natural areas. Often acquires endangered property and holds it until a public agency can buy and protect it.

Population Crisis Committee, 1120 19th Street NW, Suite 550, Washington, DC 20036. Promotes public understanding and action on the world's population crisis.

Population Reference Bureau, 1337 Connecticut Avenue NW, Washington, DC 20036. Publishes current information on population.

The Public Citizen, P.O. Box 19404, Washington, DC 20036. Ralph Nader's political action organization.

Public Interest Research Group, 1346 Connecticut Avenue NW, No. 415, Washington, DC 20036. Research and education on the environment.

Resources for the Future, 1775 Massachusetts Avenue NW, Washington, DC 20036. Conducts research and education on environment and natural resources. Provides grants to other research institutions.

Scientists' Institute for Public Information, 355 Lexington Avenue, New York, NY 10017. Scientists of all disciplines; disseminate objective scientific information on social issues related to science and technology.

Sierra Club, 530 Bush Street, San Francisco, CA 94108. Educators, publishers, and lobbyists devoted to the protection of national wilderness and scenic resources.

Solar Lobby, 1001 Connecticut Avenue NW, Fifth Floor, Washington, DC 20036. Dedicated to alternative energy sources; lobbies for solar energy.

Union of Concerned Scientists, 1384 Massachusetts Avenue, Cambridge, MA 02238. Research, education, and lobbying; especially concerned with nuclear safety.

The Wilderness Society, 1901 Pennsylvania Avenue NW, Washington, DC 20006. Main goal is to promote acquisition and protection of wilderness and primitive areas by the federal government.

Wildlife Society, 5410 Grosvenor Lane, Bethesda, MD 20814. Wildlife preservation.

World Environmental Fund, 3127 South Grant, Englewood, CO 80110. Founded by the author to purchase wildlife habitat for rare and endangered species and to educate children on the feasibility and desirability of a sustainable society.

World Environment Center, 605 Third Avenue, 17th Floor, New York, NY 10158. Established by the United Nations, with support of the U.N. Environment Program. Worldwide network to foster public understanding of global environmental problems and international cooperation. Tracks down environment data anywhere in the world.

Worldwatch Institute, 1776 Massachusetts Avenue NW, Washington, DC 20036. Research, education, and early warning on important environmental problems.

World Wildlife fund, 1601 Connecticult Avenue NW, Washington, DC 20009. Research and education.

Zero Population Growth, 1346 Connecticut Avenue NW, Washington, DC 20036. Works for family planning in effort to stabilize population growth.

See also *Conservation Directory*. National Wildlife Foundation, 1412 16th Street NW, Washington, DC 20036; *World Directory of Environmental Organizations*. San Francisco: Sequoia Institute, 1976.

Governmental Agencies

Bureau of Land Management, Interior Building, Room 5660, Washington, DC 20240.

Bureau of Mines, Columbian Plaza, 2401 E Street NW, Washington, DC 20506.

Bureau of Outdoor Recreation, Interior Building, Room 4410, Washington, DC 20240.

Bureau of Reclamation, Interior Building, Room 7654, Washington, DC 20240.

Conservation and Renewable Energy Inquiry and Referral Service, P.O. Box 8900, Silver Spring, MD 20907. Call toll free for information on energy conservation and renewable energy sources: 1-800-523-2929 outside of Pennsylvania; 1-800-462-4983 in Pennsylvania.

Council on Environmental Quality, 722 Jackson Place NW, Washington, DC 20006.

Department of Agriculture, Washington, DC 20250.

Department of Energy, Forrestal Building, 1000 Independence Avenue SW, Washington, DC 20585.

Department of the Interior, Interior Building, Washington, DC 20240.

Department of Transportation, 400 7th Street SW, Washington, DC 20590.

Environmental Protection Agency, 401 M Street SW, Washington, DC 20460.

Federal Power Commission, 825 North Capitol Street NE, Washington, DC 20426.

Fish and Wildlife Service, Department of the Interior, Interior Building, Room 3256, Washington, DC 20240.

Food and Drug Administration, Department of Health and Human Services, 5600 Fishers Lane, Rockville, MD 20857.

Forest Service, South Agriculture Building, Independence Avenue between 12th and 14th Streets SW, Washington, DC 20250.

Geological Survey, U.S. Geological Survey National Center, 12201 Sunrise Valley Drive, Reston, VA 22092.

National Academy of Sciences, 2101 Constitution Avenue NW, Washington, DC 20418.

National Center for Appropriate Technology, P.O. Box 3838, Butte, MT 59701.

National Oceanic and Atmospheric Administration, Washington Science Center, Building 5, 6010 Executive Boulevard, Rockville, MD 20852.

National Park Service, Interior Building, Room 3256, Washington, DC 20240.

National Technical Information Service, Department of Commerce, Sills Building, 5285 Port Royal Road, Springfield, VA 22161.

Nuclear Regulatory Commission, 1717 H Street NW, Washington, DC 20555.

Solar Energy Research Institute, 1617 Cole Boulevard, Golden, CO 80401.

Superintendent of Documents, U.S. Government Printing Office, Washington, DC 20402.

Water Resources Council, 2120 L Street NW, Washington, DC 20423.

Glossary

Abiotic factor Nonliving components of the ecosystem including chemical and physical factors such as availability of nitrogen, temperature, and rainfall.

Acid mine drainage Sulfuric acid that drains from mines, especially abandoned underground coal mines in the East (Appalachia). Created by the chemical reaction between oxygen, water, and iron sulfides found in coal and surrounding rocks.

Acid precipitation Rain or snow that is more acidic than precipitation from unpolluted skies.

Active solar Capture and storage of solar energy through special solar collection devices (solar panels) that absorb heat and transfer it to air, water, or some other medium, which is then pumped to a storage site (usually a water tank) for later use. Contrast with *passive solar*.

Actual risk An accurate measure of risk posed by a certain technology or action.

Acute toxicity Poisoning generally caused by short-term exposures to high levels of one or more toxic agents. Symptoms appear soon after exposure.

Adaptation A genetically determined structural or functional characteristic of an organism that enhances its chances of reproducing and passing on its genes.

Aerosol Fine solid and/or liquid particles suspended in air.

Age-specific death rate Number of deaths per 1000 persons of a specific age group.

Age-specific fertility rate Number of live births per 1000 women of a specific age group.

Agricultural-based urban society A society primarily urban in nature but highly dependent on farmers and surrounding land for food, minerals, and fuel. The first large cities arose in these societies. Characterized by enormous environmental impact from overgrazing, deforestation, and poor farming practices.

Agricultural land conversion Conversion of agricultural land to other purposes, primarily cities, highways, airports, and the like.

Agricultural society People that lived in villages and, later, towns, relying on domestic animals and crops grown in nearby fields. A society characterized by specialization of work roles.

Algal bloom Algal population explosion in surface waters due to increase in inorganic nutrients, usually either nitrogen or phosphorus.

Alpha particles Positively charged particles consisting of two protons and two neutrons, emitted from radioactive nuclei.

Alveoli Small sacs in the lungs where oxygen and carbon dioxide exchange between air and blood occurs.

Ambient air quality standard Maximum permissible concentration of a pollutant in the air around us. Contrast with *emissions standard*.

Anaerobic organism An organism that does not require oxygen to survive.

Antagonism In toxicology, when two chemical or physical agents (often toxins) counteract each other to produce a lesser response than would be expected if individual effects were added together.

Anthropogenic hazard A hazard created by humans.

Appropriate technology A term coined by the late E. F. Schumacher to refer to technology that is "appropriate" for the economy, resources, and culture of a region. It is characterized by small- to medium-sized machines, maximum human labor, ease of understanding, meaningful employment, use of local resources for local use, decentralized production, production of durable products, emphasis on renewable resources, especially energy, and compatibility with the environment and culture.

Aquaculture Cultivation of fish and other aquatic organisms in freshwater ponds, lakes, irrigation ditches, and other water bodies for human consumption.

Aquifer Underground stratum of porous material (sandstone) containing water (groundwater), which may be withdrawn from wells for human use.

Area strip mining Type of surface mining especially for coal in flat or rolling terrain. Coal is exposed in long parallel strips by removal of overburden.

Asbestos One of several naturally occurring silicate fibers. Useful in society as an insulator but deadly to breathe even in small amounts. Causes mesothelioma, asbestosis, and lung cancer.

Asbestosis Lung disease characterized by buildup of scar tissue in the lungs. Caused by inhalation of asbestos.

Asthma Lung disorder characterized by constriction and excessive mucus production in the bronchioles resulting in periodic difficulty in breathing, shortness of breath, coughing. Usually caused by allergy and often aggravated by air pollution.

Atmosphere Layer of air surrounding earth.

Barrier islands Small, sandy islands off the coast, separated from the mainland by lagoons or bays.

Beach drift Wave-caused movement of sand along the beach.

Beta particles Negatively charged particles emitted from nuclei of radioactive elements when a neutron is converted to a proton.

Biochemical oxygen demand (BOD) Measure of oxygen depletion of water (largely from bacterial decay) due to presence of biodegradable organic pollutants. Gives scientists an indication of how much organic matter is in water.

Bioconcentration Ability of an organism to selectively accumulate certain chemicals, elements, or substances within its body or within certain cells.

Biofouling Buildup of organisms such as algae and bacteria in pipes and other equipment, especially in power plant cooling systems.

Biogas A gas containing methane and carbon dioxide. Produced by anaerobic decay of organic matter, especially manure and crop residues.

Biogeochemical cycle Complex cyclical transfer of nutrients from the environment to organisms and back to the environment. Examples include the carbon, nitrogen, and phosphorus cycles.

Biological control Use of naturally occurring predators, parasites, bacteria, and viruses to control pests. Also called food chain control.

Biological extinction Disappearance of a species from part or all of its range.

Biomagnification Buildup of chemical elements or substances in organisms in successively higher trophic levels. Also called biological magnification.

Biomass As measured by ecologists, the dried weight of all organic matter in the ecosystem. In the energy field, any form of organic material (from both plants and animals) from which energy can be derived by burning or bioconversion such as fermentation. Includes wood, cow dung, agricultural crop residues, forestry residues, scrap paper.

Biomass pyramid See *pyramid of biomass.*

Biome One of several immense terrestrial regions, each characterized throughout its extent by similar plants, animals, climate, and soil type.

Biosphere All the life-supporting regions (ecosystems) of the earth and all the interactions that occur between organisms and between organisms and the environment.

Biotic factor The biological component of the ecosystem, consisting of populations of plants, animals, and microorganisms arranged in complex communities.

Biotic (reproductive) potential Maximum reproductive potential of a species.

Birth control Any measure designed to reduce births, including contraception and abortion.

Birth defect An anatomical (structural) or physiological (functional) defect in a newborn.

Breeder reactor Fission reactor that produces electricity and also converts abundant but nonfissile uranium-238 into fissile plutonium-239, which can be used in other fission reactors.

Broad-spectrum pesticide (or biocide) Chemical agent effective in controlling a large number of pests.

Bronchitis Persistent inflammation of the bronchi caused by smoking and air pollutants. Symptoms include mucus buildup, chronic cough, and throat irritation.

Brown-air cities Newer, relatively nonindustrialized cities whose polluted skies contain photochemical oxidants (especially ozone) and nitrogen oxides, largely from automobiles and power plants. Tend to have dry, sunny climates. Contrast with *gray-air cities.*

Calorie Amount of energy necessary to raise the temperature of one gram of water 1° C.

Cancer Uncontrolled proliferation of cells in humans and other living organisms. In humans, includes more than 100 different types of cancer afflicting individuals of all races and ages.

Carbon cycle The cycling of carbon between organisms and the environment.

Carcinogen A chemical or physical agent that causes cancer to develop, often decades after the original exposure.

Carrying capacity Maximum population size that a given ecosystem can support for an indefinite period or on a sustainable basis.

Cation Any one of many kinds of positively charged ions.

Chlorofluoromethanes See *fluorocarbons.*

Chronic obstructive lung disease Any one of several lung diseases characterized by obstruction of breathing. Includes emphysema, bronchitis, and diseases with symptoms of both of these.

Chronic toxicity Poisoning generally caused by long-term exposures to low levels of one or more toxic agents. Symptoms appear long after exposure. Examples: emphysema and cancer.

Clear-cutting Removal of all trees from a forested area.

Climax community or ecosystem See *mature community*.

Closed system A system that can exchange energy, but does not exchange matter, with the surrounding environment. Example: the earth. Contrast with *open system*.

Cloud seeding Dispersion of condensation nuclei into the atmosphere to stimulate cloud formation and precipitation.

Coal gasification Production of combustible organic gases (mostly methane) by applying heat and steam to coal in an oxygen-enriched environment. Carried out in surface vessels or *in situ*.

Coal liquefaction Production of synthetic oil from coal.

Coastal wetlands Wet or flooded regions along coastlines including mangrove swamps, salt marshes, bays, and lagoons. Contrast with *inland wetlands*.

Cogeneration Production of two or more forms of useful energy from one process. For example, production of electricity and steam heat from combustion of coal. Increases energy efficiency.

Coitus interruptus (withdrawal) Relatively inefficient contraceptive technique. Penis is withdrawn from vagina prior to ejaculation.

Commensalism Interaction between two species that is beneficial to one but offers no benefit to the other.

Common law Body of rules and principles based on judicial precedent rather than legislative enactments, founded on an innate sense of justice, good conscience, and reason. Flexible and adaptable.

Commons Any resource used in common by many people, such as air, water, and grazing land.

Community Also called a biological community. The populations of plants, animals, and microorganisms living and interacting in a given locality.

Composting Aerobic decay of organic matter to generate a humus-like substance used to supplement soil.

Condom A thin, synthetic rubber sheath worn over the penis during sexual intercourse. Used to prevent spread of venereal diseases and prevent pregnancy.

Confusion technique (of pest control) Release of insect sex attractant pheromones identical to pheromone released by normal breeding females to attract males for mating. Release in large quantities confuses males as to the location of the females, thus minimizing the chances of males finding females and helping to control pest populations.

Conservation A strategy to reduce the use of resources, especially through increased efficiency, reuse, recycling, and decreased demand.

Conservation tillage See *minimum tillage*.

Consumer (or consumer organism) An organism in the ecosystem that feeds on autotrophs and/or heterotrophs. Synonym: heterotroph.

Contour farming Soil erosion control technique in which row crops (corn) are planted along the contour lines in sloping or hilly fields rather than up and down the hills.

Contour strip mining A surface mining technique to remove coal or other minerals in mountainous areas. Seams are exposed along the rims of hills or mountains by removing overlying dirt and rock (overburden). Also called rim stripping.

Control rods Special rods containing neutron-absorbing materials. Inserted into the reactor core to control the rate of fission or to shut down fission reactions.

Cooling tower Device used to cool water from a variety of industrial processes. See *wet* and *dry cooling towers*.

Cosmic radiation High-energy electromagnetic radiation similar to cosmic rays, but originating from periodic solar flare-ups. Possesses extraordinary ability to penetrate materials, including cement walls.

Cost–benefit analysis Way of determining the economic, social, and environmental costs and benefits of a proposed action such as construction of a dam or highway. Still a crude analytical tool because of the difficulty of measuring environmental costs.

Crop rotation Alternating crops in fields to help restore soil fertility and also control pests.

Crude birth rate Number of births per 1000 people in a population at the midpoint of the year.

Crude death rate Number of deaths per 1000 people in a population at midyear.

Crude marriage rate Number of marriages per 1000 people in a population at midyear.

Cultural control (of pests) Techniques to control pest populations not involving chemical pesticides, environmental controls, or genetic controls. Examples: cultivation to control weeds and manual removal of insects from crops.

Cultural eutrophication *Eutrophication* (see definition) due largely to human activities.

DDT An organochlorine insecticide used first to control malaria-carrying mosquitos and lice and later to control a variety of insect pests, but now banned because of its persistence in the environment and its ability to bioaccumulate. Dichlorodiphenyltrichloroethane.

Decibel (dB) A unit to measure the loudness of sound.

Decomposer Also microconsumer. An organism that breaks down nonliving organic material. Examples: bacteria and fungi.

Decomposer food chain A specific nutrient and energy pathway in an ecosystem in which decomposer organisms (bacteria and fungi) consume dead plants and animals as well as animal wastes. Essential for the return of nutrients to soil and carbon dioxide to the atmosphere. Also called detritus food chain.

Deep-well injection Disposal of hazardous wastes in deep wells. Theoretically, waste should be deposited between impermeable rock layers to prevent it from polluting aquifers.

Deforestation Destruction of forests by clear-cutting.

Demand elasticity Change in demand as prices increase or decrease.

Demographic transition A phenomenon witnessed in populations of industrializing nations. As industrialization proceeds and wealth accumulates, crude birth rate and crude death rate decline, resulting in zero or low population growth. Decline in death rate usually precedes the decline in birth rate, producing a period of rapid growth before stabilization.

Demography The study of human populations.

Desert Biome located throughout the world. Often found on the downwind side of mountain ranges. Characterized by low humidity, high summertime temperatures, plants and animals especially adapted to lack of water.

Desertification The formation of desert in arid and semiarid regions from overgrazing, deforestation, poor agricultural practices, and climate change. Found today in Africa, the Middle East, and in the southwestern United States.

Detritus Any organic waste from plants and animals.

Detritus food chain See *decomposer food chain.*

Deuterium An isotope of hydrogen whose nucleus contains one proton and one neutron (a hydrogen atom has only one proton).

Developed country A convenient term that describes industrialized nations, generally characterized by high standard of living, low population growth rate, low infant mortality, excessive material consumption, high per capita energy consumption, high per capita income, urban population, and low illiteracy.

Developing country Same as *less developed country.*

Diaphragm A soft rubber, cuplike device inserted into the vagina and placed over the cervix prior to sexual intercourse. Creates a mechanical barrier to the uterus, thus preventing pregnancy. Fairly effective when used in conjunction with spermicidal jelly.

Dioxin A large group of highly toxic, carcinogenic compounds contaminating some herbicides (2,4-D and 2,4,5-T) and Agent Orange. Once disposed of by mixing with waste crankcase oil that was spread on dirt roads to control dust.

Diversity A measure of the number of different species in an ecosystem.

Doubling time The length of time it takes some measured entity (population) to double in size at a given growth rate.

Dry cooling tower Large structure used in power plants to cool water. Operates on same principle as radiator. Hot water passes through pipes and is cooled by air blown across pipes. Contrast with *wet cooling tower.*

DNA (deoxyribonucleic acid) A long-chained organic molecule that is found in chromosomes and carries the genetic information that controls cellular function and is the basis of heredity.

Ecological equivalents Organisms that occupy similar ecological niches in different regions of the world.

Ecological niche See *niche.*

Ecological pyramid A graphic representation of energy, biomass, or population size at each trophic level in the food chain.

Ecology Study of living organisms and their relationships to one another and the environment.

Economic externality A cost (environmental damage, illness) of manufacturing, road building, or other actions that is not taken into account when determining the total cost of production or construction. A cost generally passed on to the general public and taxpayers; external cost.

Economy of scale Refers to profitmaking by mass production and marketing of items for only a small profit each.

Ecosphere See *biosphere.*

Ecosystem Short for ecological system. A community of organisms occupying a given region within a biome. Also, the physical and chemical environment of that community and all the interactions between organisms and between organisms and their environment.

Ecosystem stability Dynamic equilibrium of the ecosystem. Also a characteristic of ecosystems causing them to return to their previous state (resilience) and their resistance to change (inertia).

Ecotone Transition zone between adjacent ecosystems.

Emigration Movement of people out of a country to establish residence elsewhere.

Emissions offset policy Strategy to control air pollution in areas meeting federal ambient air quality standards, whereby new factories must secure emissions reductions in existing factories to begin operation; thus the overall pollution level does not increase.

Emissions standard The maximum amount of a pollutant permitted to be released from a *point source* (see definition).

Emphysema A progressive, debilitating lung disease caused by smoking and pollution at work and in the environment. Characterized by gradual breakdown of the *alveoli* (see definition) and difficulty in catching one's breath.

Endangered species A plant, animal, or microorganism that is in immediate danger of biological extinction. See *threatened* and *rare species.*

Energy The capacity to do work. Found in many forms, including heat, light, sound, electricity, coal, oil, and gasoline.

Energy fuel cycle Same as *energy system.*

Energy pyramid See *pyramid of energy.*

Energy quality The amount of useful work acquired from a given form of energy. High-quality energy forms are concentrated (e.g., oil and coal); low-quality energy forms are less concentrated (e.g., solar heat).

Energy system The complete production–consumption process for energy resources, including exploration, mining, refining, transportation, and waste disposal.

Entropy A measure of disorder. The second law of thermodynamics applied to matter says that all systems proceed to maximum disorder (maximum entropy).

Environment All the biological and nonbiological factors that affect an organism's life.

Environmental control (of pests) Control methods designed to alter the abiotic and biotic environment of pests, making it inhospitable or intolerable. Examples include increasing crop diversity, altering time of planting, and altering soil nutrient levels.

Environmental impact statement (EIS or ES) Document prepared primarily to outline potential impacts of projects supported in part or in their entirety by federal funds.

Environmental resistance Abiotic and biotic factors that can potentially reduce population size.

Environmental science The interdisciplinary study of the complex and interconnected issues of population, resources, and pollution.

Epilimnion Upper, warm waters of a lake. Contrast with *hypolimnion.*

Estuarine zone Coastal wetlands and estuaries.

Estuary Coastal regions such as inlets or mouths of rivers where salt and fresh water mix.

Ethanol Grain alcohol, or ethyl alcohol, produced by fermentation of organic matter. Can be used as a fuel for a variety of vehicles and as a chemical feedstock.

Eutrophication Accumulation of nutrients in a lake or pond due to human intervention (cultural eutrophication) or natural causes (natural eutrophication). Contributes to process of *succession* (see definition).

Evapotranspiration Evaporation of water from soil and transpiration of water from plants.

Evolution A long-term process of change in organisms caused by random genetic changes that favor the survival and reproduction of the organism possessing the genetic change. Through evolution, organisms become better adapted to their environment.

Exponential growth Increase in any measurable thing by a fixed percentage. When plotted on graph paper it forms a J-shaped curve.

Extinction See *biological extinction.*

Extrinsic limiting factor A factor affecting population size imposed on a population from outside, such as rainfall or temperature. Contrast with *intrinsic limiting factor.*

Family planning Process by which couples determine the number and spacing of children.

Feedlot Fenced area where cattle are raised in close confinement to minimize energy loss and maximize weight gain.

Fertility A demographic term referring to the reproductive performance of organisms. See *general fertility rate, age-specific fertility rate,* and *total fertility rate.*

First-generation pesticides Earliest known chemical pesticides such as ashes, sulfur, ground tobacco, and hydrogen cyanide. Contrast with *second-* and *third-generation pesticides.*

First-law energy efficiency A measure of the efficiency of energy use. Total amount of useful work derived from a system divided by the total amount of energy put into a system.

First law of thermodynamics Also called the law of conservation of energy. States that energy is neither created nor destroyed; it can only be transformed from one form to another.

Floodplain Low-lying region along rivers and streams, periodically subject to natural flooding. Common site for human habitation and farming.

Fluorocarbons Organic molecules consisting of chlorine and fluorine covalently bonded to carbon. CCl_3F (Freon-11) and CCl_2F_2 (Freon-12). Used as spray-can propellants and coolants. Previously thought to be inert, but now known to destroy the stratospheric ozone layer. Also called chlorofluoromethanes and freon gases.

Fly ash Mineral matter escaping with smokestack gases from combustion of coal.

Food additive Nonnutritive chemical substance intentionally added to food, generally in small quantities, to improve its taste, appearance, texture, or shelf life.

Food chain A specific nutrient and energy pathway in ecosystems proceeding from producer to consumer. Part of a bigger network called the food web. See *decomposer food chain* and *grazer food chain.*

Food web Complex intermeshing of individual food chains in an ecosystem.

Foreign (alien) species A species intentionally or accidentally introduced into an ecosystem it has not previously inhabited. Aso known as an exotic.

Fossil fuel Any one of the organic fuels (coal, natural gas, oil, tar sands, and oil shale) derived from once-living plants or animals.

Freons See *fluorocarbons.*

Frontier mentality A mind set that views humans "above" all other forms of life rather than as an integral part of nature and sees the world as an unlimited supply of resources for human use regardless of the impacts on other species. Implicit in this view are the notions that bigger is better, continued material wealth will improve life, and nature must be subdued.

Fuel rods Rods packed with small pellets of radioactive fuel (usually a mixture of fissionable uranium-235 and uranium-238) for use in fission reactors.

Gamma rays A high-energy form of radiation given off by certain radionuclides. Can easily penetrate the skin and damage cells.

Gasohol Liquid fuel for vehicles containing nine parts gasoline and one part ethanol.

General fertility rate Number of live births per 1000 women of reproductive age (15–44).

Genetic control (of pests) Development of plants and animals genetically resistant to pests through breeding programs and genetic engineering. Also, introduction of sterilized males of pest species (see *sterile-male technique*).

Genetic engineering Isolation and production of genes which are then inserted in bacteria or other organisms. Can be used to produce insulin and other hormones. May someday also be used to treat genetic diseases.

Geopressurized zone Aquifer containing superheated, pressurized water and steam trapped by impermeable rock strata and heated by underlying magma.

Geothermal energy Energy derived from the earth's heat that comes from decay of naturally occurring radioactive materials in the earth's crust, magma, and friction caused by movement of tectonic plates.

Grasslands Found in both temperate and tropical regions and characterized by periodic drought, flat or slightly rolling terrain, and large grazers that feed off the lush grasses.

Gray-air cities Older industrial cities characterized by predominantly sulfur dioxide and particulate pollution. Contrast with *brown-air cities*.

Grazer food chain A specific nutrient and energy pathway starting with plants that are consumed by grazers (herbivores).

Greenhouse effect Mechanism that explains atmospheric heating caused by increasing carbon dioxide. Carbon dioxide is believed to act like the glass in a greenhouse, permitting visible light to penetrate but impeding the escape of infrared radiation, or heat.

Green Revolution Developments in plant genetics in the late '50s and early '60s resulting in high-yield varieties producing three to five times more grain than previous plants but requiring intensive irrigation and fertilizer use.

Gross national product (GNP) Total national output of goods and services valued at market prices, including net exports and private investment.

Gross primary productivity The total amount of sunlight con-

verted into chemical-bond energy by a plant. This measure does not take into account how much energy a plant uses for normal cellular functions. See *net primary productivity*.

Groundwater Water below the earth's surface in the saturated zone.

Habitat The specific region in which an organism lives.

Half-life Time required for one-half of a given amount of radioactive material to decay, producing one-half the original mass. Can also be used to describe the length of residence of chemicals in tissues. Biological half-life refers to the time it takes for one-half of a given amount of a substance to be excreted or catabolized.

Hard path A term coined by Amory Lovins to describe large, centralized energy systems such as coal, oil, or nuclear power, characterized by extensive power distribution, central control, and lack of renewability.

Hazardous waste Any potentially harmful solid, liquid, or gaseous waste product of manufacturing or other human activities.

Heat island Pocket of relatively warm air surrounded by cooler air, often occurring in cities due to heat sources and absorption of sunlight by asphalt and buildings.

Heavy metals Metallic elements with relatively high atomic weights, such as lead and mercury.

Herbicide Chemical agent used to control weeds.

Herbivore Heterotrophic organism that feeds exclusively on plants.

Heterotroph An organism that feeds on other organisms such as plants and animals. It cannot make its own foodstuffs.

Hot-rock zones Most widespread geothermal resource. Regions where bedrock is heated by underlying magma.

Human ecology The study of the relationship between humans and all biotic and abiotic factors in the environment.

Humus Mixture of decaying organic matter and inorganic matter that increases soil fertility, aeration, and water retention.

Hunting-and-gathering society People that lived as nomads or in semipermanent sites from the beginning of human evolution until approximately 5000 B.C. Some remnant populations still survive. They gathered seeds, fruits, roots, and other plant products and hunted indigenous species for food.

Hybrid Offspring produced by cross-mating of two different strains or varieties of plants or animals.

Hydrocarbons Organic molecules containing hydrogen and carbon. Released during the incomplete combustion of organic fuels. React with nitrogen oxides and sunlight to form photochemical oxidants in photochemical smog.

Hydrological cycle Way water moves through the environment from atmosphere to earth and back again. Major events include evaporation and precipitation. Also called the water cycle.

Hydrosphere The watery portion of the planet. Contrast with *lithosphere* and *atmosphere*.

Hydrothermal convection zone Rock strata containing large amounts of water heated by underlying magma and driven to the surface through cracks and fissures in overlying rock layers. Forms hot springs and geysers.

Hypolimnion Deep, cold waters of a lake. Contrast with *epilimnion*.

Identified resource A mineral or nonmineral resource, the location and amount of which are well known.

Immature ecosystem An early successional community characterized by low species diversity and low stability. Contrast with *mature ecosystem*.

Immigration Movement of people into a country to set up residence there.

Indoor air pollution Generally refers to air pollutants in homes from internal sources such as smokers, fireplaces, woodstoves, carpets, paneling, furniture, foam insulation, and stoves.

Induced abortion Surgical procedure to interrupt pregnancy by removing the embryo or fetus from the uterus. In the first trimester, generally carried out by vacuum aspiration. Contrast with *spontaneous abortion*.

Industrial smog Air pollution from industrial cities (gray-air cities), consisting mostly of particulates and sulfur oxides. Contrast with *photochemical smog*.

Inertia Tendency of an ecosystem to resist change.

Infant mortality rate Number of infants under one year of age dying per 1000 births in any given year.

Infectious disease Generally, a disease caused by a virus, bacterium, or parasite that can be transmitted from one organism to another (example: viral hepatitis).

Infrared radiation Heat, an electromagnetic radiation of wavelength outside the red end of the visible spectrum.

Inland wetlands Wet or flooded regions along inland surface waters. Includes marshes, bogs, and river overflow lands. Contrast with *coastal wetlands*.

In-migration Movement of people into a state or region within a country to set up residence.

Inorganic fertilizer Synthetic plant nutrients added to the soil to replace lost nutrients. Major components include nitrogen, phosphorus, and potassium. Also called artificial fertilizer or synthetic fertilizer.

Insecticide One form of biocide used specifically to control insect populations.

Integrated pest management Pest control with minimum risk to humans and the environment through use of a variety of control techniques (including pesticides and biological controls).

Integrated wildlife or species management Control of populations through the use of many techniques including the reintroduction of natural predators, habitat improvement, reduction in habitat destruction, establishment of preserves, reduced pollution, and captive breeding programs.

Internal costs The costs of production, mining, or other activities that are typically paid by the manufacturer, such as labor, materials, and energy costs. Contrast with *economic externality* (external cost).

Intrauterine device A small metallic or plastic object placed in the uterus to prevent pregnancy, probably by preventing implantation of the fertilized ovum.

Intrinsic limiting factor A factor affecting population size but arising from within the population, such as competition or territoriality. Contrast with *extrinsic limiting factor*.

Isotope Atoms of the same element that differ in their atomic weight because of variations in the number of neutrons in their nuclei.

J curve A graphical representation of exponential growth. Shaped like the letter J.

Juvenile hormone Chemical substance in insects that stimulates growth through early life stages. Used with some success as an insecticide. When applied to infested fields, JH alters normal growth and development of insect pests, resulting in their death.

Kerogen Solid, insoluble organic material found in oil shale.

Kilocalorie One thousand calories. See *calorie*.

Kilowatt One thousand watts. See *watt*.

Kinetic energy The energy of objects in motion

Kwashiorkor Dietary deficiency caused by insufficient protein intake and common in children one to three years of age in less developed countries. Characterized by growth retardation, wasting of muscles in limbs, and accumulation of fluids in the body, especially in feet, legs, hands, and face.

Laterite Soil found in some tropical rain forests. Rich in iron and aluminum but generally of poor fertility. Turns bricklike if exposed to sunlight.

Lentic system Standing or nonflowing freshwater system such as a pond or lake.

Less developed country Term describing the nonindustrialized nations, generally characterized by low standard of living, high population growth rates, high infant mortality, low material consumption, low per capita energy consumption, low per capita income, rural populations, and high illiteracy.

Life expectancy Measure of the average number of years an individual can expect to live. Life expectancy at birth is the most common measure.

Light water reactor Most common fission reactor for generating electricity. Water bathes the core of the reactor and is used to generate steam, which turns the turbines that generate electricity. Contrast with *liquid metal reactor*.

Limiting factor A chemical or physical factor that determines whether an organism can survive in a given ecosystem. In most ecosystems, rainfall is the limiting factor.

Limnetic zone Open water zone of lakes through which sunlight penetrates; contains algae and other microscopic organisms that feed off dissolved nutrients.

Liquid metal reactor Fission reactor that uses liquid metals such as sodium as a coolant.

Lithosphere Crust of the earth. Contrast with *hydrosphere* and *atmosphere*.

Littoral drift Movement of beach sand parallel to the shoreline. Caused by waves and longshore currents parallel to the beach.

Littoral zone Shallow waters along a lakeshore where rooted vegetation often grows.

Lotic system A flowing freshwater system such as a river.

Macronutrient A chemical substance needed by living organisms in large quantities (for example, carbon, oxygen, hydrogen, and nitrogen). Contrast with *micronutrient*.

Malnourishment A dietary deficiency caused by lack of the right nutrients and vitamins.

Manganese nodules Nodular accumulations of manganese and other minerals such as iron and copper found on the ocean floor at depths of 300 to 6000 meters. Particularly abundant in the Pacific Ocean.

Marasmus A dietary deficiency caused by insufficient intake of protein and calories and occurring primarily in infants under the age of one, usually the result of discontinuation of breast feeding.

Mariculture Cultivation of fish and other aquatic organisms in salt water (estuaries and bays) for human consumption.

Mature community A community that remains more or less the same over a long period of time. Climax stage of succession. Also called a climax community.

Mature ecosystem An ecosystem in the climax stage of succession, characterized by high species diversity and high stability. Contrast with *immature ecosystem*.

Megawatt Measure of electrical power equal to a million watts, or 1000 kilowatts. See *watt*.

Mesothelioma A tumor of the lining of the lung (pleura). Caused by asbestos.

Metabolism A general term for all the chemical reactions that occur in cells. Includes two major types: breakdown (catabolic) reactions and synthesis (anabolic) reactions.

Metalimnion See *thermocline*.

Methyl mercury Water-soluble organic form of mercury formed by bacteria in aquatic ecosystems from inorganic (insoluble) mercury pollution. Able to undergo biomagnification.

Microconsumers Bacteria and single-celled fungi that are part of the decomposer food chain.

Micronutrient An element needed by organisms, but only in small quantities, such as copper, iron, and zinc. Contrast with *macronutrient*.

Migration Movement of people across state and national boundaries to set up new residence. See *immigration, emigration, in-migration*, and *out-migration*.

Mineral A chemical element (e.g., gold) or inorganic compound (e.g., iron ore) existing naturally.

Minimum tillage Reduced plowing and cultivating of cropland between and during growing seasons to help reduce soil erosion and save energy. Also called conservation tillage.

Monoculture Cultivation of one plant species (such as wheat) over a large area. Highly susceptible to disease and insects.

Mutagen A chemical or physical agent capable of damaging the genetic material (DNA and chromosomes) of living organisms in both germ cells and somatic cells.

Mutation In general, any damage to the DNA and chromosomes.

Mutualism Interaction between organisms that is beneficial to both organisms.

Narrow-spectrum pesticide (or biocide) A chemical agent effective in controlling a small number of pests.

Natural erosion Loss of soil occurring at a slow rate but not caused by human activities. A natural event in all terrestrial ecosystems.

Natural eutrophication See *eutrophication*.

Natural gas Gaseous fuel containing 50–90% methane and lesser amounts of other burnable organic gases such as propane and butane.

Natural hazards Hazards that result from normal meteorologic, atmospheric, oceanic, biological, and geological phenomena.

Natural resource See *resource*.

Natural selection Process in which slight variations in organisms (adaptations) are preserved if they are useful and help the organism to better respond to its environment.

Negative feedback Control mechanism present in the ecosystem and in all organisms. Information in the form of chemical, physical, and biological agents influences processes, causing them to shut down or reduce their activity.

Net energy See *net useful energy production*.

Net migration Number of immigrants (number of people entering legally and illegally) minus the number of emigrants (people leaving). Can be expressed as a rate by determining immigration and emigration rates.

Net primary productivity Gross primary productivity (the total amount of energy that plants produce) minus the energy plants use during cellular respiration.

Net useful energy production Amount of useful energy extracted from an *energy system* (see definition).

Neutralism Interaction that has no significant impact on either organism involved.

Niche Also called an ecological niche. Describes how an organism fits into the ecosystem: where it lives, what it consumes, what consumes it, and how it interacts with all biotic and abiotic factors.

Nitrate (NO_3^-) Inorganic anion containing three oxygen atoms and one nitrogen atom linked by covalent bonds.

Nitrite (NO_2^-) Inorganic anion containing two oxygen atoms and one nitrogen atom. Combines with hemoglobin and may cause serious health impairment and death in children.

Nitrogen cycle The cycling of nitrogen between organisms and the environment.

Nitrogen fixation Conversion of atmospheric nitrogen (a gas) into nitrate and ammonium ions (inorganic form), which can be used by plants.

Nitrogen oxides Nitric oxide (NO) and nitrogen dioxide (NO_2) produced during combustion when atmospheric nitrogen (N_2) combines with oxygen. Can be converted into nitric acid (HNO_3). All are harmful to humans and other living organisms.

Noise An unwanted or unpleasant sound.

Nonpoint source (of pollution) Diffuse source of pollution such as an eroding field, urban and suburban lands, and forests. Contrast with *point source.*

Nonrenewable resource Resource that is not replaced or regenerated naturally within a reasonable period (fossil fuel, minerals).

Nuclear power (or energy) Energy from the fission or fusion of atomic nuclei.

Nuclear fission Splitting of an atomic nucleus when neutrons strike the nucleus. Products are two or more smaller nuclei, neutrons (which can cause further fission reactions), and an enormous amount of heat and light energy.

Nuclear fusion Joining of two small atomic nuclei (such as hydrogen and deuterium) to form a new and larger nucleus (such as helium) accompanied by an enormous release of heat and light. Source of light and heat from the sun.

Nuptiality As a demographic term, it refers to measures related to marriage, such as marriage rate, divorce rate, and characteristics of those married (age at marriage, number of marriages).

Nutrient cycle Same as *biogeochemical cycle.*

Ocean thermal energy conversion (OTEC) Use of ocean thermal gradients to generate electricity. Warm surface waters evaporate ammonia in closed system. Ammonia vapor runs a turbine which generates electricity. Subsurface waters then are pumped up to cool the vapor so the process can be started over again. Highly experimental.

Off-road vehicle (ORV) Any vehicle used off-road, especially in a recreational capacity (four-wheel-drive vehicles, dune buggies, all-terrain vehicles, snowmobiles, and trail bikes).

Oil See *petroleum.*

Oil shale A fine-grained sedimentary rock called marlstone and containing an organic substance known as kerogen. When heated, it gives off shale oil, which is much like crude oil.

Oligotrophic lake Lake with low dissolved plant nutrient (nitrate and phosphate) content.

Omnivore An organism that eats both plants and animals.

Open dump Land disposal site for solid wastes where materials are periodically burned and eventually covered with dirt.

Open-pit mining A type of surface mining that creates huge, open pits. Overburden is removed so that desirable minerals such as copper and granite can be removed. Difficult to reclaim.

Open system Any system that freely exchanges energy and matter with the environment. Example: all living organisms. Contrast with *closed system.*

Opportunity costs Costs of lost money-making opportunities (and potentially higher income) incurred when we make a decision to invest our money in a particular way.

Oral contraceptive Any one of a number of contraceptive pills taken by women to prevent pregnancy. Most contain a mixture of synthetic female hormones, estrogen and progesterone. Highly reliable form of contraception.

Ore deposit A valuable mineral located in high concentration in a given region.

Organic fertilizer Organic material such as plant and animal wastes added to cropland and pastures to improve soil. Adds valuable soil nutrients and increases the organic content of soil (thus increasing moisture content).

Out-migration Movement of people out of a state or region within a country to set up residence elsewhere in that country.

Overgrazing Excessive consumption of producer organisms (plants) by grazers such as deer, rabbits, and domestic livestock. Indication that the ecosystem is out of balance.

Overpopulation A condition resulting when the number of organisms in an ecosystem exceeds its ability to assimilate wastes and provide resources. Creates physical and mental stress on a species as a result of competition for limited resources and deterioration of the environment.

Oxidants Oxidizing chemicals (for example, ozone) found in the atmosphere.

Oxygen-demanding wastes Organic wastes that are broken down in water by aerobic bacteria. Aerobic breakdown causes the oxygen levels to drop.

Ozone (O₃) Inorganic molecule found in the atmosphere, where it is a pollutant because of its harmful effects on living tissue and rubber. Also found in the stratosphere, where it helps screen ultraviolet light. Used in some advanced sewage treatment plants.

Ozone layer Thin layer of ozone molecules in the stratosphere that absorbs ultraviolet light and converts it to infrared radiation. Effectively screens out 99% of the ultraviolet light.

Parasitism Interaction between two organisms in which one (the parasite) attaches to the other (host) and receives nutrients from it.

Particulates Solid particles (dust, pollen, soot) or water droplets in the atmosphere.

Passive solar Capture and retention of solar energy (heat) within a building through south-facing windows and some form of heat storage in the building (brick or cement floors and walls). Contrast with *active solar*.

PCBs See *polychlorinated biphenyls*.

Permafrost Permanently frozen ground found in the tundra.

Permanent threshold shift Loss of hearing after continued exposure to noise. Contrast with *temporary threshold shift*.

Personal pollution Voluntary introduction of potentially harmful chemicals into our own bodies from smoking, drinking, drug abuse, and food additives.

Pest Organism that interferes or competes with humans in agriculture, gardening, horticulture, meat production, etc.

Pesticide A general term referring to a chemical, physical, or biological agent that kills organisms we classify as pests, such as insects and rodents. Also called biocide.

Petroleum A viscous, liquid containing numerous burnable hydrocarbons. Distilled into a variety of useful fuels (fuel oil, gasoline, and diesel) and petrochemicals (chemicals that can be used as a chemical feedstock for the production of drugs, plastics, and other substances).

pH Measure of acidity on a scale from 0 to 14, with pH 7 being neutral, numbers greater than 7 being basic, and numbers less than 7 being acidic.

Pheromone Chemical substance given off by insects and other species. Sex attractant pheromones released into the atmosphere in small quantity by female insects attract males at breeding time. Can be used in pest control. See *pheromone traps* and *confusion technique*.

Pheromone traps Traps containing pheromones to attract insect pests and pesticide to kill pests or a sticky substance to immobilize them. These traps may be used to pinpoint the emergence of insects, allowing conventional pesticides to be used in moderation.

Photochemical oxidants Ozone and a variety of oxygenated organic compounds produced when sunlight, hydrocarbons, and nitrogen oxides react in the atmosphere.

Photochemical smog A complex mixture of *photochemical oxidants* (see definition) and nitrogen oxides. Usually has a brownish-orange color.

Photosynthesis A two-part process involving (a) the capture of sunlight and its conversion into cellular energy, and (b) the production of organic molecules such as glucose and amino acids from carbon dioxide, water, and energy from the sun.

Photovoltaic cell Thin wafer of silicon or other material that emits electrons when struck by sunlight, thus generating an electrical current. Also solar cell.

Pioneer community The first community to become established in a once-lifeless environment during *primary succession* (see definition).

Pitch (or frequency) Measure of the frequency of a sound in cycles per second (hertz, Hz)—compressional sound waves passing a given point per second. The higher the cps, the higher the pitch.

Plankton Free-floating, single-celled microscopic plant and animal organisms found in surface waters.

Pneumoconiosis (black lung disease) A debilitating lung disease caused by prolonged inhalation of coal and other mineral dusts. Results in a decreased elasticity and gradual breakdown of air sacs (alveoli) in the lungs. Eventually leads to death.

Point source (of pollution) Easily discernible source of pollution such as a factory. Contrast with *nonpoint source*.

Pollution Any physical, chemical, or biological alteration of air, water, or land that is harmful to living organisms.

Polychlorinated biphenyls (PCBs) Group of at least 50 different chlorinated organic compounds, used for many years as insulation in electrical equipment. Capable of biomagnification. Disrupts reproduction in gulls and possibly other organisms high on the food chain.

Population A group of organisms of the same species living within a specified region.

Population control In human populations, refers to all methods of reducing birth rate, primarily through pregnancy prevention and abortion. In an ecological sense, it refers to a regulation of population size by a myriad of abiotic and biotic factors.

Population crash (dieback) Sudden decrease in population that results when an organism exceeds the carrying capacity of its environment.

Population density Population size divided by land area (measured in square kilometers, acres, or hectares).

Population distribution How organisms of a population are distributed or dispersed within the ecosystem. May be clumped or even.

Population growth rate Rate at which a population increases on a yearly basis, expressed as a percentage. For world population: GR = (crude birth rate − crude death rate) × 100. For a given country, population growth rate must also take into account the net migration rate.

Population histogram Graphical representation of population by age and sex.

Positive feedback Control mechanism in ecosystems and organisms in which information influences some process, causing it to increase.

Potential energy Stored energy.

Predation Feeding relationship in which one organism (predator) hunts and kills another (prey).

Predator An organism that actively hunts its prey.

Presbycusis Loss of hearing with age through natural deterioration of the organ of Corti, the sound receptor in the ear. Contrast with *sociocusis*.

Prey Organism (e.g., deer) attacked and killed by predator.

Primary air pollutant A pollutant that has not undergone any chemical transformation; emitted by either a natural or an anthropogenic source.

Primary consumer First consumer organism in a given food chain. A grazer in grazer food chains or a decomposer organism or insect in decomposer food chains. Belongs to the second trophic level.

Primary standard (for air pollution) Ambient air quality standard to protect human health, with a built-in margin of error to protect particularly susceptible individuals in a population. Compare with *secondary standard*.

Primary succession The sequential development of biotic communities where none previously existed.

Primary treatment (of sewage) First step in sewage treatment to remove large solid objects by screens (filters) and sediment and organic matter in settling chambers. See *secondary* and *tertiary treatment*.

Proactive government Government concerned with long-range problems and lasting solutions. Contrast with *reactive government*.

Producer (autotroph or producer organism) One of the organisms that produce the organic matter cycling through the ecosystem. Producers include plants and photosynthetic algae.

Productivity The rate of conversion of sunlight by plants into chemical-bond energy (covalent bonds in organic molecules). See *gross* and *net primary productivity*.

Profundal zone Deeper lake water into which sunlight does not penetrate. Below the limnetic zone.

Prospective law A law designed to address future problems and generate long-lasting solutions. Contrast with *retrospective law*.

Pyramid of biomass Graphical representation of the amount of biomass (organic matter) at each trophic level in an ecosystem.

Pyramid of numbers Graphical representation of the number of organisms of different species at each trophic level in an ecosystem.

Pyrolysis High-temperature breakdown of organic matter in anaerobic conditions. Used to generate liquid and gaseous fuels from organic wastes such as solid municipal waste.

Quad One quadrillion (10^{15}) Btus of heat.

Rad (radiation absorbed dose) Measure of the amount of energy deposited in a tissue or some other medium when struck by radiation. One rad = 100 ergs of energy deposited in one gram of tissue (or other substance).

Radioactive waste Any solid or liquid waste material containing radioactivity. Produced by research labs, hospitals, nuclear weapons production facilities, and nuclear (fission) reactors.

Radioactivity Radiation released from unstable nuclei. See *alpha, beta,* and *gamma radiation*.

Radionuclides Radioactive forms (isotopes) of elements.

Rain shadow Arid downwind (leeward) side of mountain ranges.

Rangeland Grazing land for cattle, sheep, and other domestic livestock, mostly located in the West.

Range of tolerance Range of physical and chemical factors in which an organism can survive. When the upper or lower limits of this range are exceeded, growth, reproduction, and survival are threatened.

Rare species Not endangered but, because of small population size, is at risk of becoming endangered.

Reactive government A government that lives and acts for today, addressing present-day problems as they arise. Shows little or no concern for long-term issues and solutions. Contrast with *proactive government*.

Reactor core Assemblage of fuel rods and control rods inside the reactor vessel where the fission reaction takes place. Bathed by water to help control the rate of reaction and absorb the heat from fission.

Real price (or cost) The price of a commodity or service in fixed dollars—that is, the value of a dollar at an earlier time. Helpful way to determine whether a resource has experienced a real increase in cost or whether higher costs are simply due to inflation.

Reclamation As used here, the process of returning land to its prior use. Common usage: to convert deserts and other lands into habitable, productive land.

Recycle To pass through a cycle again. A strategy to reduce resource use by returning used or waste materials from the consumption phase to the production phase of our economy.

Reduction factors Abiotic and biotic factors that tend to decrease population growth and help balance populations and ecosystems offsetting growth factors.

Relative humidity Measure of atmospheric moisture content relative to temperature; that is, the amount of moisture in a given quantity of air divided by the amount the air could hold at that temperature. Expressed as a percentage.

Rem (roentgen equivalent man) Measure of radiation that accounts for the damage done by a given type of radiation. One *rad* (see definition) = one rem for X rays, gamma rays, and beta particles, but one rad = 10 to 20 rems for alpha particles because they do more damage.

Renewable resource A resource replaced by natural ecological cycles (water, plants, animals) or natural chemical and physical processes (sunlight, wind).

Replacement-level fertility Number of children a couple must have to replace themselves in the population.

Reproductive age Age during which most women bear their offspring (ages 14–44).

Reserve Deposits of energy or minerals that are economically and geologically feasible to remove with current and foreseeable technology.

Resilience Ability of an ecosystem to return to normal after a disturbance.

Resource (in general) Anything used by organisms to meet their needs, including air, water, minerals, plants, fuels, and other animals.

Resource (as a measurement of a mineral or fuel) Total amount of a mineral or fuel on earth. Generally, only a small fraction can be recovered. Compare with *reserve*.

Retorting Process of removing kerogen from oil shale, usually by burning or heating the shale. Can be carried out in surface vessels (surface retorting) or underground in rubbleized (fractured) shale (*in situ* retorting).

Retrospective law A law that attempts to solve an existing problem without giving much attention to potential future problems. Contrast with *prospective law*.

Reverse osmosis Means of purifying water for pollution control and desalination. Water is forced through porous membranes; pores allow passage of water molecules but not impurities.

Rhythm method A fairly ineffective way of preventing pregnancy by avoiding intercourse before, during, and after ovulation.

Risk acceptability A measure of how acceptable a risk is to people.

Risk assessment The science of determining what risks a society is exposed to from natural and human causes and the probability and severity of those risks.

Risk probability The likelihood a hazardous event will occur.

Risk severity A measure of the total damage a hazardous event would cause.

Salinization Deposition of salts in irrigated soils, making soil unfit for most crops. Caused by rising water table due to inadequate drainage of irrigated soils.

Saltwater intrusion Movement of salt water from oceans or saltwater aquifers into freshwater aquifers, caused by depletion of the freshwater aquifers or low precipitation or both.

Sanitary landfill Solid waste disposal site where garbage is dumped in the ground and covered daily with a layer of dirt to reduce odors, insects, and rats.

Saprophytic organism (saprobe or saprophyte) Heterotrophic organism that feeds on dead organic matter such as leaves.

Scrubber Pollution control device that removes particulates and sulfur oxide gases from smokestacks by passing exhaust gases through fine spray of water containing lime.

Secondary consumer Second consumer in food chain. Belongs to the third trophic level.

Secondary pollutant A chemical pollutant from a natural or anthropogenic source that undergoes chemical change as a result of reacting with another pollutant, sunlight, atmospheric moisture, or some other environmental agent.

Secondary standard (for air pollution) Ambient air quality standard set to protect crops, visibility, plants, and materials.

Secondary succession The sequential development of biotic communities occurring after the complete or partial destruction of an existing community by natural or anthropogenic forces.

Secondary treatment (of sewage) After primary treatment, removal of biodegradable organic matter from sewage using bacteria and other microconsumers in activated sludge or trickle filters. Also removes some of the phosphorus (30%) and nitrate (50%). See *primary* and *tertiary treatment*.

Second-generation pesticides Synthetic organic chemicals such as DDT that replaced older pesticides such as sulfur, ground tobacco, and ashes. Generally resistant to biological breakdown.

Second-law efficiency Measure of the efficiency of energy use, taking into account the unavoidable loss (described by the second law of thermodynamcs) of energy during energy conversions. Calculated by dividing the minimum amount of energy required to perform a task by the actual amount used.

Second law of thermodynamics States that when energy is converted from one form to another, it is degraded; that is, it is converted from a concentrated to a less concentrated form. The amount of useful energy decreases during such conversions.

Secured landfill Hazardous waste disposal site lined and capped by an impermeable synthetic or clay sealer.

Sediment Soil particles, sand, and other mineral matter eroded from land and carried in surface waters.

Selective cutting Selective removal of trees. Especially useful for mixed hardwood stands. Contrast with *clear-cutting* and *shelter-wood cutting*.

Severance tax A tax applied to raw materials extracted from a state to cover the expense of highways and community infrastructure.

Sewage treatment plant Facility where human solid and liquid wastes from homes, hospitals, and industries are treated primarily to remove organic matter, nitrates, and phosphates.

Shale oil Thick, heavy oil formed when oil shale is heated (retorted). Can be refined to produce fuel oil, kerosene, diesel fuel, and other petroleum products and petrochemicals.

Shelterbelts Rows of trees and shrubs planted alongside fields to reduce wind erosion and retain snow to increase soil moisture. May also be used to reduce heat loss from wind and thus conserve energy around homes and farms.

Shelter-wood cutting Three-step process spread out over years: (1) removal of poor-quality trees to improve growth of commercially valuable trees and allow new seedlings to become established, (2) removal of commercially valuable trees once seedlings are established, and (3) cutting remaining mature trees grown from seedlings.

Simplified ecosystem Ecosystem with lowered species diversity, usually as a result of human intervention.

Sinkhole Hole created by sudden collapse of the earth's surface due to groundwater overdraft. A form of subsidence.

Slash-and-burn agriculture Agricultural practice in which small plots are cleared of vegetation by cutting and burning. Crops are grown until the soil is depleted; then the land is abandoned. This allows the natural vegetation and soil to recover. Common practice of early agricultural societies living in the tropics.

Sludge Solid organic material produced during sewage treatment.

Smelter A factory where ores are melted to separate impurities from the valuable minerals.

Smog Originally referred to a grayish haze (atmospheric moisture) found in industrial cities. Also pertains to pollution called photochemical smog found in newer cities. See *industrial smog*.

Sociocusis Hearing loss from human activities. Contrast with *presbycusis*.

Soft path A term coined by Amory Lovins to describe such practices as conservation, efficient use of energy, and renewable energy systems such as solar and wind. Characterized by high labor intensity, decentralized energy production, and small-scale technology. Contrast with *hard path*.

Soil horizons Layers found in most soils.

Solar collector Device to absorb sunlight and convert it into heat.

Solar energy Energy derived from the sun (heat) and natural phenomena driven by the sun (wind, biomass, running water).

Solid waste Waste products from agriculture, mining, forestry, and municipalities handled in solid form.

Sonic boom A high-energy wake creating an explosive boom that trails after jets traveling faster than the speed of sound.

Spaceship earth Metaphor introduced in the 1960s to foster a better appreciation of the finite nature of earth's resources and the ecological cycles that replenish oxygen and other important nutrients.

Species A group of plants, animals, or microorganisms that have a high degree of similarity and generally can interbreed only among themselves.

Species diversity Measure of the number of different species in a biological community.

Spermicidal jelly A gel that kills sperm and is introduced into the vagina prior to intercourse. Used alone or in conjunction with the diaphragm.

Spontaneous abortion Loss of an embryo or fetus from the uterus not caused by surgery. Generally the result of chromosomal abnormalities. Contrast with *induced abortion*.

SST (supersonic transport) Jets that travel faster than the speed of sound.

Stable runoff Amount of surface runoff that can be counted on from year to year.

Statutory law Laws enacted by Congress and state legislatures.

Steady-state economy Economic system characterized by relatively constant GNP, dedication to essential goods and services, maximum reliance on recycling, conservation, and use of renewable resources. Also spaceship or sustainable economy.

Sterile-male technique Pest control strategy whereby males of the pest species are grown in captivity, sterilized, then released en masse in infested areas at breeding time. Sterile males far exceed normal wild males and mate with normal females, resulting in infertile matings and control of the pest.

Sterilization A highly successful procedure in males and females to prevent pregnancy. In males the ducts (vas deferens) that carry sperm from the testicles are cut and tied (vasectomy); in females the Fallopian tubes, or oviducts, which transport ova from the ovary to the uterus, are cut and tied (tubal ligation). Sterilization is not to be confused with castration in males (complete removal of the gonads).

Stratosphere Outer region of the earth's atmosphere, found outside the troposphere, extending 7 to 25 miles above the earth's surface. Outermost layer of the stratosphere contains the ozone layer.

Streambed channelization An ecologically unsound way of reducing flooding by deepening and straightening of streams, accompanied by removal of trees and other vegetation along the banks.

Strip cropping Soil conservation technique in which alternating crop varieties are planted in huge strips across fields to reduce wind and water erosion of soil.

Strip mining See *area strip mining* and *contour strip mining*.

Subeconomic resources Mineral and energy resources not economically feasible to extract.

Subsidence Sinking of land caused by collapse of underground mines or depletion of groundwater.

Subsistence hunting Hunting for food to sustain life.

Subsistence-level farming A system of agriculture that provides only for the needs of the farmer and his family; early agricultural societies practiced slash-and-burn agriculture on the subsistence level.

Succession The natural replacement of one biotic community by another. See *primary* and *secondary succession.*

Sulfur dioxide (SO₂) Colorless gas produced during combustion of fossil fuels contaminated with organic and inorganic sulfur compounds. Can be converted into sulfuric acid in the atmosphere.

Sulfur oxides (SOₓ) Sulfur dioxide and sulfur trioxide, common air pollutants arising from combustion of coal, oil, gasoline, and diesel fuel. Also produced by natural sources such as bacterial decay and hot springs. Sulfur dioxide reacts with oxygen to form sulfur trioxide, which may react with water to form sulfuric acid.

Supply and demand theory Economic theory explaining the price of goods and services. The supply of and demand for goods and services are primary price determinants. High demand diminishes supply, creating competition for existing goods and services, thus driving up prices.

Supply elasticity Changes in supply (amount of goods and services available) as prices increase or decrease. Generally, supply is thought to increase as prices increase.

Surface mining Any of several mining techniques in which all the dirt and rock overlying a desirable mineral (coal, for example) are first removed, exposing the mineral. See *contour strip mining, open-pit mining,* and *area strip mining.*

Surface runoff Water flowing in streams and over the ground's surface during rainstorm or snowmelt.

Sustainable mentality (ethics) A mindset that views humans as a part of nature and earth as a limited supply of resources, which must be carefully managed to prevent irreparable damage. Obligations to future generations require us to exercise restraint to ensure adequate resources and a clean and healthy environment.

Sustainable society Based on sustainable ethics. A society that lives within the limits imposed by nature. Based on maximum use of renewable resources, recycling, conservation, and population control.

Sustained yield concept Use of renewable natural resources, such as forests and grassland, that will not cause their destruction and will ensure continued use.

Swidden agriculture Same as *slash-and-burn agriculture.*

Synergism When two or more agents (often toxins) act together to produce an effect larger than expected based on knowledge of the effect of each alone. (This is a superadditive effect.)

Synthetic fertilizer Same as *inorganic fertilizer.*

Synfuel See *Synthetic fuel.*

Synthetic fuel Gaseous or liquid organic fuel derived from coal, oil shale, or tar sands.

Taiga Biome found south of the tundra across North America, Europe, and Asia, characterized by coniferous forests, soil that thaws during the summer months, abundant precipitation, and high species diversity.

Tar sands Also known as oil sands or bituminous sands. Sand impregnated with viscous, petroleum-like substance, bitumen, which can be driven off by heat, producing a synthetic oil.

Technical fix See *technological fix.*

Technological fix A purely technological answer to a problem. Also called a technical fix.

Temperate deciduous forest Biome located in the eastern United States, Europe, and northeastern China below the taiga. Characterized by deciduous and nondeciduous trees, warm growing season, abundant rainfall, and a rich species diversity.

Temperature inversion Alteration in the normal atmospheric temperature profile so that air temperature increases with altitude rather than decreases as is normal.

Temporary threshold shift Temporary dulling of the sense of hearing after exposure to loud sounds. Can lead to permanent hearing loss, permanent threshold shift.

Teratogen A chemical or physical agent capable of causing birth defects.

Terracing Construction of small earthen embankments or terraces on hilly or mountainous terrain to reduce the velocity of water flowing across the soil and reduce soil erosion.

Tertiary treatment (of sewage) Removal of nitrates, phosphates, chlorinated compounds, salts, acids, metals, and toxic organics after secondary treatment.

Thermal pollution Heat added to air or water that adversely affects living organisms and may shift climate.

Thermocline Sharp transition between upper, warm waters (epilimnion) and deeper, cold waters (hypolimnion) of a lake. Also called metalimnion.

Thermodynamics The study of energy conversions. See the *first* and *second laws of thermodynamics.*

Threatened species Abundant in parts of its range but severely depleted in others.

Threshold level A level of exposure below which no effect is observed or measured.

Tidal energy Energy captured from the tides by damming river mouths and installing electrical turbines in the path of incoming and outgoing tides.

Total fertility rate Average number of children that would be born alive to a woman during her lifetime if she were to pass through all her child-bearing years conforming to the age-specific fertility rates of a given year.

Toxic agent Same as *toxin*.

Toxin A chemical, physical, or biological agent that causes disease or some alteration of the normal structure and function of an organism. Impairments may be slight or severe. Onset of effects may be immediate or delayed.

Transpiration Escape of water from plants through pores (stomata) in the leaves.

Tree farms Private forests devoted to maximum timber growth and relying heavily on herbicides, insecticides, and fertilizers.

Tritium (hydrogen-3) Radioactive isotope of hydrogen whose nucleus contains two neutrons and one proton. Can be used in fusion reactors.

Trophic level Describes the position of an organism in the food chain or the stage in the nutritive series.

Tropical rain forest Lush forests near the equator with high annual rainfall, high average temperature, and notoriously nutrient-poor soil. Possibly the richest ecosystem on earth.

Troposphere Innermost layer of the atmosphere, containing 95% of the earth's air. Extends 5 to 7 miles above the earth's surface.

Tundra (alpine) Life zone found on mountaintops. Closely resembles the arctic tundra in terms of precipitation, temperature, growing season, plants, and animals. Extraordinarily fragile.

Tundra (arctic) First major life zone or biome south of the North Pole. Vast region on far northern borders of North America, Europe, and Asia. Characterized by lack of trees, low precipitation, and cold temperatures.

Ultraviolet (UV) light or radiation Electromagnetic radiation from sun and special lamps. Causes sunburn and mutations in bacteria and other living cells.

Undernourishment A lack of calories in the diet. Contrast with *malnourishment*.

Water cycle See *hydrological cycle*.

Water diversion Transfer of water from one watershed of water abundance to another with water shortage, usually involving dams and tunnels.

Waterlogging High water table causing saturation of soils due to poor soil drainage and irrigation. Decreases soil oxygen and kills plants.

Watershed Land area drained by a given stream or river.

Water table Top of the zone of saturation.

Watt Unit of power indicating rate at which electrical work is being performed.

Wavelength Distance between the crest or trough of one wave and the crest or trough of the next. Used to measure electromagnetic radiation (light). Of sound waves, distance between the center of one compressional wave to the center of the one before or after it.

Wave power Energy derived from waves.

Wet cooling tower Device used for cooling water from power plants. Hot water flows through vertical rising air, which draws off heat. Cool water is then returned to the system.

Wetlands Land areas along fresh water (inland wetlands, such as bogs, marshes, and swamps) and salt water (coastal wetlands, such as salt marshes, tidal basins, and mangrove swamps) that are flooded all or part of the time.

Wilderness An area where the biological community is relatively undisturbed by humans. Seen by developers as an untapped supply of resources such as timber and minerals; seen by environmentalists as a haven for escape from hectic urban life, an area for reflection and solitude.

Wilderness area An area established by the U.S. Congress under the Wilderness Act (1964) where timber cutting and use of motorized vehicles are prohibited. Most are located in National Forests.

Wind energy Energy captured from the wind to generate electricity or pump water. An indirect form of solar energy.

Wind generators Windmills that produce electrical energy.

Zero population growth A condition when population is not increasing; when the population growth rate is zero.

Photo and Text Credits

Part I Opener   Ric Ergenbright

Chapter 1 Figures

1–1	NASA
1–2	Cleveland Plain Dealer
1–3	Dave Baird/Tom Stack & Associates
1–5a	Marjorie Shostak/Anthro-Photo
1-5b	Marjorie Shostak/Anthro-Photo
1–8a	Irven DeVore/Anthro-Photo
1–10	UN Photo 150858/Tomas Sennett
1–11	B. von Hoffman/Tom Stack & Associates
1–12	Jean Whitney/Atoz Images
1–13	Pittsburg Photographic Library of Carnegie
1–14	USDA—Soil Conservation Service
Essay	Anthony Bannister

Tables

1–2	Modified from LIVING IN THE
1–5	ENVIRONMENT, Third Edition, by G. Tyler Miller, Jr. © 1982 by Wadsworth, Inc. Reprinted by permission Wadsworth Publishing Company, Belmont, California 94002.

Chapter 2 Figures

2–5	Joseph S. Rychetnik/Atoz Images
2–7	U.S. Geological Survey 187
Essay	STRATEGY FOR SURVIVAL by Arthur S. Boughey, © 1976 by W.A. Benjamin: Menlo Park, California. Modified and reprinted with permission.

Chapter 3 Figures

3–1	Modified and redrawn ECOLOGY AND THE QUALITY OF OUR ENVIRONMENT by C.H. Southwick, © 1976, Van Nostrand Reinhold: New York.
3–2a,b	Courtesy H.B.D. Kettlewell
3–4a	John J. Cardomone, Jr./BPS
3–4b	J. Robert Waaland/BPS
3–5a	Carolina Biological Supply Co.
3–5b	Warren Rosenberg/BPS
3–6	J. Robert Waaland/BPS
3–7	BPS
3–9a	Dan Hardy/Anthro-Photo
3–9b	Jeff Foott/Bruce Coleman
3–9c	Frans Lanting
3–15	Gilles Peress/Magnum Photos, Inc.
3–16a	Leonard Lee Rue III/Tom Stack & Associates
3–16b	Leonard Lee Rue III/Animals Animals
3–17a	Charles G. Summers, Jr./Stock Imagery
3–17b	Charles G. Summers, Jr./Stock Imagery
3–18a	National Parks & Wildlife Service, Sydney, Australia
3–18b	W. Perry Conway
3–19a	Keith Gunner/Bruce Coleman
3–19b	Charles G. Summers, Jr./Stock Imagery
3–19c	Len Rue, Jr./Tom Stack & Associates
Essay	Modified and redrawn from THE GLOBAL BRAIN by P. Russell, © 1983, J. P. Tarcher, Inc.: Los Angeles

Chapter Supplement Figures

S 3–1	Tim Thompson/Alaska Photo
S 3–2a	USDA—Soil Conservation Service
S 3–2b	USDA—Soil Conservation Service
S 3–3	USDA

Chapter 4 Figures

4–5	Modified and redrawn from R. L. Smith (1974). ECOLOGY AND FIELD BIOLOGY. Second Edition, Harper and Row: New York.
4–8a	Tom Bean/Tom Stack & Associates
4–8b	Anthony Bannister
4–11	Modified and redrawn from B. J. Nebel, (1981). ENVIRONMENTAL SCIENCE. Prentice-Hall, Englewood Cliffs, NJ 07362.
4–14	From FUNDAMENTALS OF ECOLOGY. Third Edition by Eugene P. Odum. © by W. B. Saunders Company. Reprinted by permission of CBS College Publishing.

Table

4–1	From FUNDAMENTALS OF ECOLOGY. Third Edition by Eugene P. Odum, © 1971 by W. B. Saunders Company. Reprinted by permission of CBS College Publishing.

Chapter 10 Figures

10–4	Carl Koford/Photo Researchers, Inc.
10–5	Reprinted with permission from Kelly et al. (1981) THE GREAT WHALE BOOK. Center for Environmental Education, Washington, D.C. 20001.
10–6	Gleizes/Greenpeace
10–7	John Launoi/Black Star
10–8a	Leonard Lee Rue III/Tom Stack & Associates
10–8b	Karen Tweedy-Holmes/Animals Animals
10–9	Gary Milburn/Tom Stack & Associates
10–11	LIFEFORCE photo by Peter Hamilton
10–13	J. Curtis (1955). "The Modification of Midlatitude Grasslands and Forests by Man," in W. L. Thomas (ed), MAN'S ROLE IN CHANGING THE FACE OF THE EARTH. University of Chicago Press: Chicago.
10–14	Denise Hendershot/Tom Stack & Associates
10–15	Courtesy of Tennessee Wildlife Resources Agency
10–16	Ray Coppinger, Hampshire College

Table

10–4	Reprinted with permission of the Center for Environmental Education, Washington, D.C. 20001.

Chapter 11 Figures

11–4	USDA—Soil Conservation Service
11–8	Forest Service, USDA
11–9	Hank Lebo/Jeroboam, Inc.
11–10	From CONSERVATION OF NATURAL RESOURCES. Guy-Harold Smith, © 1965. Reprinted with permission of John Wiley and Sons, Inc.
11–11a	U.S. Forest Service
11–11b	Forest Service, USDA
11–11c	Steve Botti, National Park Service
11–12	Photography by Ansel Adams. Courtesy of the Ansel Adams Publishing Rights Trust. All rights reserved.

Table

11–1	Reprinted with permission from G. Rudzitis and J. Schwartz (1982) "The Plight of Parklands." ENVIRONMENT 24 (6): 6–11. 33–38. A publication of the Helen Dwight Reid Educational Foundation.

Chapter Supplement Figures

S 11–1	Bureau of Land Management
S 11–2	Bureau of Land Management

Chapter 12 Figures

12–6	Modified and redrawn from A. N. Strahler and A. H. Strahler (1973). ENVIRONMENTAL GEOSCIENCE. Hamilton Publishing Company: Santa Barbara, California. © 1973 by John Wiley and Sons.
12–7	U.S. Geological Survey
12–8	USDA—Soil Conservation Service
12–14	Doug Lee Photography

Tables

12–2	Modified from LIVING IN THE ENVIRONMENT, Third Edition, by G. Tyler Miller, Jr., © 1982 by Wasdworth, Inc. Reprinted by permission Wadsworth Publishing Company, Belmont, California 94002.
13–2	

Chapter 13 Figures

13–9	Dr. W. Laqueur, Veterans Administration Hospital, Beckley, WV, and NIOSH
13–13	Hoagland/Gamma–Liason
13–14	Hank Lebo/Jeroboam Inc.

Chapter 14 Figures

14–2a	G. French/The Photo File
14–3	Doug Lee Photography
14–5	U.S. Department of Energy

Chapter 15 Figures

15–5	Dan Chiras
15–6	W. Perry Conway
15–7	Nadine Orabona/Tom Stack & Associates
15–8	Emilio A. Mercado/Jeroboam Inc.
15–9	Rodale Press, Inc.
15–10	USDA Forest Service
15–12	Johns Hopkins Applied Physics Laboratory
15–14	Jeffrey Blankfort/Jeroboam Inc.

Tables

15–1	From Kendall and Nadis'
15–4	ENERGY STRATEGIES:

15–15	TOWARD A SOLAR FUTURE, © 1980, Union of Concerned Scientists. Reprinted with permission from Ballinger Publishing Company.
15–2	Courtesy of Shell Oil Company.

Chapter 16 Figures

16–6	NOAA
16–8	Golden Goat Recovery Systems
16–9	Ecology Action, Santa Cruz, CA

Part IV Opener Dan Morrill

Chapter 17 Figures

17–2	Pierre Perrin/Gamma-Liason
Essay	Bruce Larson/Tacoma News Tribune

Table

17–1	Reprinted with permission from Harriss et al. (1978). OUR HAZARDOUS ENVIRONMENT 20 (7): 6. A Publication of the Helen Dwight Reid Educational Foundation.

Chapter 18 Figures

18–1	From "Cancer and Industrial Chemical Production," D. L. Davis and B. H. Magee, SCIENCE. vol. 206, pp. 1356–1358, 21 December, 1979. © 1979 by AAAS. Modified and redrawn with permission of the American Association for the Advancement of Science and the Authors.
18–2	John Pawlowski/Tom Stack & Associates
18–4 18–5	Modified and redrawn with permission from W. G. Thilly and H. L. Liber (1980). "Genetic Toxicology," in TOXICOLOGY, Doull, Klaassen, and Amdur, eds. Macmillan: New York.
18–6	Modified and redrawn with permission from R. D. Harbison (1980). "Teratogens," in TOXICOLOGY, Doull, Klaassen, and Amdur, eds. Macmillan: New York.
18–7	C. D. Klaassen and J. Doull (1980). "Evaluation of Safety: Toxicologic Evaluation," in TOXICOLOGY, Doull, Klaassen, and Amdur, eds. Macmillan: New York.

18–9   William Thompson/Limited Horizons

Chapter 19 Figures

19–3a   J. W. Goodspeed/Freelance Photographers Guild
19–3b   Dave Baird/Tom Stack & Associates
19–6   Adrienne T. Gibson/Tom Stack & Associates

Chapter Supplement Figures

S 19–1   From T. D. Sterling and E.
S 19–2   Sterling (1979). "Carbon Monoxide Levels in Kitchens and Homes with Gas Cookers." J. AMER. POLLUTION CONTROL ASSOC. 29 (3): 238–241 Reprinted with permission.
S 19–5   From "Acid Precipitation and Sulfate Deposition in Florida," Brezoni et al., SCIENCE Vol. 208 30, May 1980, © by AAAS. Reprinted with permission of the American Association for the Advancement of Science.
S 19–8   Ted Spiegel/Black Star

Chapter 20 Figures

20–1a   Dave Baird/Tom Stack & Associates
20–1b   USDA—Soil Conservation Service
20–10   Fred Ward/Black Star
20–11   The Des Moines Register
20–13   Bureau of Reclamation

Chapter 21 Figures

21–4   Peress/Magnum Photos, Inc.
21–5   Frank Siteman/Jeroboam, Inc.
21–6   From Combs et al. AN INVITATION TO HEALTH. Benjamin/Cummings: Menlo Park, California, pp. 232–234. Modified for this edition.
21–7   R. A. Taft Labs

Table

21–3   D. A. Girdano and D. Dusek, DRUG EDUCATION. © 1980, Addison-Wesley, Reading, Massachusetts. Table 3.2. Reprinted with permission.

Chapter Supplement 1 Figure

S1 21–4   Gilles Peress/Magnum Photos, Inc.

Table

S21–3   THE X-RAY INFORMATION BOOK. (Tables 1, 2, and 3) by Priscilla W. Laws and the Public Citizen Health Reasearch Group, © 1983, Farrar, Straus, and Giroux, Reprinted with permission.

Chapter Supplement 2 Figures

S2 21–1   James T. Coit/Jeroboam, Inc.
S2 21–2   From ENVIRONMENTAL SCI-
S2 21–4   ENCE, Second Edition by Amos Turk, Jonathan Turk, Janet T. Wittes, and Robert Wittes. © 1978 by W. B. Saunders Company. Reprinted by permission of CBS College Publishing.

Tables

21–1   From ENVIRONMENTAL SCIENCE, Second Edition by Amos Turk, Jonathan Turk, Janet T. Wittes, and Robert Wittes. © 1978 by W. B. Saunders Company. Reprinted by permission of CBS College Publishing.
S22–2   From S. L. Blum, "Tapping Resources in Municipal Solid Waste." In MATERIALS: RENEWABLE AND NONRENEWABLE RESOURCES. P. H. Abelson and A. L. Hammond, eds., Vol. 191, 20 Feb. 1976, pp. 669–675, © 1976 by the American Association for the Advancement of Science.

Chapter 22 Figures

22–1a   Whittier Daily News © 1984
22–1b   fpg/David M. Doody
22–2a   Joe Traver/Gamma-Liason
22–2b   Ron Schifferle/Niagara Gazette
22–4   Richard Nichols/Gamma-Liason
22–7   Courtesy of the U.S. EPA, OHMSB-MERL, Edison, NJ.

Chapter Supplement Figure

S 22–4   © Louie Psihoyos/Contact

Part V Opener   Bruce Davidson/Magnum Photos

Chapter 23 Figures

23–1   Dennis A. Noonan
23–3   A. B. Joyce/Photo Researchers, Inc.

23–3   Charles Harbutt/Archive Pictures, Inc.
23–5a   The Bettmann Archive
23–5b   Volkswagen of America, Inc.
23–6   C. Norman (1981). "The New Industrial Revolution." THE FUTURIST 15 (1): 32. Published by the World Future Society, 4916 St. Elmo Avenue, Washington, D.C. 20014.
23–7   Kay Chernush, AID Photo
23–8a   Photo courtesy of Sperry Corporation
23–8b   Courtesy of Apple Computer, Inc.

Tables

23–2   Modified from LIVING IN THE ENVIRONMENT, Third Edition, by G. Tyler Miller, Jr., © 1982 by Wadsworth, Inc. Reprinted by permission Wadsworth Publishing Company, Belmont, California 94002
23–3   From L.R. Brown (1982). "Living and Working in a Sustainable Society." THE FUTURIST 16 (2): 72. Published by the World Future Society, 4916 St. Elmo Avenue, Washington, D.C. 20014.

Chapter Supplement Figures

S23–1   From P. Goodwin (1981). NUCLEAR WAR. THE FACTS ON OUR SURVIVAL. New York: Rutledge Press, Reprinted with permission.
S23–2   AP Wide World Photos

Tables

S23–1   From P. Goodwin (1981).
S23–2   NUCLEAR WAR. THE FACTS
S23–3   ON OUR SURVIVAL. New York: Rutledge Press, Reprinted with permission.

Chapter 24 Figures

24–1   FAO photo by J. Van Acker
24–2   Gamma-Liason Agency
24–4   B. Kliewe/Jeroboam, Inc.

Chapter 25 Figures

25–2   Illustrator's Stock Photo
25–3   Peeter Vilms/Jeroboam Inc.

Chapter Supplement Figure

S 25–1   James Pozarik/Picture Group

Color Photo Credits

Gallery 1   Biomes

1 Stock Imagery
2 Tom Till
3 Tom Till
4 G. T. Bernard/Oxford Scientific Films
5 Tom Till
6 W. Perry Conway
7 E. R. Dagginger/Earth Sciences
8 David Muench
9 W. Perry Conway
10 Tom Till
11 S. Belyavoi/Tass-Sovfoto
12 David Muench
13 C. W. Perkins/Animals Animals

Gallery 2   Endangered Species

1 Frans Lanting
2 C.C. Lockwood/Animals Animals
3 Tom McHugh/Photo Researchers, Inc.
4 Michael Fogden/Oxford Scientific Films
5 Tom Stack/Tom Stack & Associates
6 Jeff Foott/Bruce Coleman, Inc.
7 Art Wolfe/Aperture
8 W. Perry Conway
9 Zoological Society of San Diego
10 Zoological Society of San Diego
11 Zoological Society of San Diego
12 Ron Garrison/Zoological Society of San Diego

Gallery 3   Landsat Imagery

1–7 Earth Satellite Corporation

Gallery 4   Resources Misuse

1 Gary Randall/Tom Stack & Associates
2 Joel W. Rogers/Alaska Photo
3 Gesig Gerster/Photo Researchers, Inc.
4 Fiona Funquist/Tom Stack & Associates
5 Tom Stack/Tom Stack & Associates
6 New York State Department of Health Division Laboratories
7 Gary Milburn/Tom Stack & Associates
8 Gary Milburn/Tom Stack & Associates
9 Dan Merrill
10 Walt Anderson/Tom Stack & Associates
11 Russ Kinne/Photo Researchers, Inc.
12 Suzi Barnes/Tom Stack & Associates
13 Porterfield-Chickering/Photo Researchers, Inc.
14 Russ Kinne/Photo Researchers, Inc.

INDEX

NOTE: Italicized page numbers indicate figure; t following page number indicates table.